# Mexico: The Strategy to Achieve Sustained Economic Growth

**Edited by Claudio Loser and Eliot Kalter, with a staff team comprising Sharmini Coorey, Mohamed El-Erian, Saul Lizondo, Liliana Rojas-Suarez, and Philippe Szymczak**

**INTERNATIONAL MONETARY FUND**
Washington DC
September 1992

© 1992 International Monetary Fund

**Cataloging-in-Publication Data**

Mexico : the strategy to achieve sustained economic growth / edited by
    Claudio Loser and Eliot Kalter ; with a staff team comprising
    Sharmini Coorey . . . [et al.]. — Washington, D.C. : International
    Monetary Fund, 1992.
    p.  cm. — (Occasional paper ; no. 99)
    Includes bibliographical references.
    ISBN 1-55775-312-1
    1. Mexico — Economic policy — 1970– 2. Mexico — Economic
conditions — 1982–. I. Loser, Claudio. II. Kalter, Eliot.
III. Coorey, Sharmini. IV. Series: Occasional paper (International
Monetary Fund) ; no. 99.
HC135 .M48 1992

ISSN 0251-6365

Price: US$15.00
(US$12.00 to full-time faculty members and
students at universities and colleges)

Please send orders to:
International Monetary Fund, Publication Services
700 19th Street, N.W., Washington, D.C. 20431, U.S.A.
Telephone: (202) 623-7430     Telefax: (202) 623-7201

# Contents

The following symbols have been used throughout this paper:

. . .   to indicate that data are not available;

—   to indicate that the figure is zero or less than half the final digit shown, or that the item does not exist;

–   between years or months (e.g., 1991–92 or January–June) to indicate the years or months covered, including the beginning and ending years or months;

/   between years (e.g., 1991/92) to indicate a crop or fiscal (financial) year.

"Billion" means a thousand million.

Minor descrepancies between constituent figures and totals are due to rounding.

The term "country," as used in this paper, does not in all cases refer to a territorial entity that is a state as understood by international law and practice; the term also covers some territorial entities that are not states, but for which statistical data are maintained and provided internationally on a separate and independent basis.

# Preface

This Occasional Paper is based on research papers prepared during 1991, in part in connection with the 1992 Article IV consultation with Mexico. The authors are grateful to the Mexican authorities for their cooperation in this project. The authors would like to thank S. T. Beza for his encouragement and support of this project and Jean-Pierre Amselle, Eduard Brau, Ajai Chopra, John Clark, Robert Flood, Thomas Leddy, Thomas Reichmann, Brian Stuart, and Frits Van Beek for their valuable comments. Thanks are also due to Can Demir, Kellet Hannah, Anne Jansen, and Hassanin Ismeail for research assistance, and Gisela Castueil Ulmschneider, Alice Smith-Rodlauer, and Delrene Alvis for secretarial support. Juanita Roushdy of the External Relations Department edited the paper for publication and coordinated production. The views expressed here, as well as any errors, are the sole responsibility of the authors and do not necessarily reflect the opinions of the Government of Mexico, Executive Directors of the IMF, or other member of the IMf staff.

# I    Introduction

In recent years, Mexico has made a major transformation in its economic structure and a significant improvement in its financial performance. In response, inflation has fallen markedly, output and employment have risen substantially, and financial savings have soared. Furthermore, the balance of payments has become stronger. This is in response to the restructuring of public sector external debt and a sharp increase in private inflows, including capital repatriation and direct investment, which helped finance private sector activity and increase net international reserves.

Mexico's experience, which many have followed with great interest, was not the result of a rapid policy fix but the consequence of a persistent, courageous, and difficult process of adjustment that started at the beginning of the 1980s and was intensified in subsequent years. The process of adjustment and adaptation was without setbacks. Policy initiatives were taken that proved insufficient to achieve the authorities' objectives; crucial structural reforms were implemented only later in the decade; policies taken in response to changing external conditions sometimes took time to be adopted; considerable costs in terms of the required adjustment were expended to regain the credibility of government policies. In the end, the policy stance of the Mexican authorities, while involving risks, has paid off, and the country is now poised to enter a new phase of sustained economic growth and financial stability.

The observed success of Mexico has to be attributed first and foremost to the efforts of the Mexican authorities and support of the Mexican people, who, in the end, were the true protagonists in this process. Mexico was not alone in its efforts, however. Government policies were facilitated by the support of the multilateral financial institutions (including the International Monetary Fund), the governments of creditor countries and their agencies, and commercial banks. The process of cooperation was sometimes difficult, but adequate solutions were found to address the sometimes conflicting demands of Mexico and its creditors.

Central to Mexico's achievements has been the pursuit of strong financial policies, particularly in the fiscal and credit areas. Burdened by high levels of domestic and foreign debt, the authorities took measures as early as 1983 to strengthen the primary balance of the public sector. These were later reinforced by a broad-based tax reform and a process of reform and privatization of a significant number of public sector enterprises. The eventual improvement of the overall public finances helped the authorities implement a strong monetary and credit policy, based on simplified and transparent rules, and with market-based determination of interest rates.

Exchange rate policy has evolved considerably in recent years, as it sought to strike an appropriate balance between strengthening the external sector and providing an anti-inflationary nominal anchor. The authorities have been successful in this strategy in the context of prudent financial policies and the general agreements reached on prices and wages among the public sector, labor unions, and the private sector. In the process, the peso appreciated in real terms at a time when the balance of payments strengthened, helped by a process of external and internal liberalization and reform that the authorities pursued. This process of reform led to lower financing costs and major improvements in productivity and allowed for a sustained increase in non-oil exports. In the end, however, it was the tight rein on macroeconomic policy that helped reduce existing imbalances and provided a strong basis for a return of private sector confidence.

The strengtheing of the overall balance of payments in recent years has been accompanied by a dramatic change in its structure. The external current account, which initially was associated closely with the improvement of public finances, has recently reflected large movements in private capital. There are risks arising from the resulting growing current account deficit, but with the strong fiscal effort the private sector has used foreign savings—in part in the form of returning Mexican savings held abroad—to finance investment under clear rules and with no government guarantees on commercial or exchange rate risk. Furthermore, the progress made in reducing Mexico's external public debt burden has reduced these risks.

Questions may be raised about the availability to Mexico of external resources in a period of global saving scarcity; about an observed decline in measured private savings; and about possible additional required changes in Mexico's economic structure. It is clear, however, that today Mexico is much better positioned to deepen its process of integration into the world economy, helped by improved economic management, modern economic institutions, and a lean public sector. It is hoped that the material presented in this paper will be helpful in illustrating the lesson's emerging from Mexico's path toward sustained growth and lower inflation.

The IMF has been associated closely with the process of adjustment carried out in Mexico over the last decade. The association has been reflected in the extended arrangement of 1982–85, the stand-by arrangement of 1986–88, and most recently the extended arrangement that was approved in 1989 and extended through early 1993. The various papers in this volume have been prepared by staff members who participated in the process of cooperation between Mexico and the Fund over the last five years. This volume does not seek to present a complete description of policies and developments, but rather reviews in detail some central aspects of the Mexican experience of recent years. Included are discussions on macroeconomic policies; an analysis of the evolution of structural reforms in key areas, such as in the financial system, trade, and foreign investment; and the changing nature of external private market financing from concerted lending to debt reduction and the re-emergence of voluntary lending. The dynamics of inflation, the balance of payments, and certain other key variables are also discussed.

Section II deals with the main developments in the Mexican economy over the last decade. It presents an overview of policies, particularly in the last four years, and provides a setting for the discussions of other sections. In explaining Mexico's recent success, it stresses the importance in achieving sustainable economic growth of financial policies; incomes policy; structural reforms; external financial support; and measures to protect the economy from adverse shocks.

Section III reviews the interrelationship among fiscal, monetary, and exchange rate policies during the period since the late 1970s. The section explores the links between the implementation of macroeconomic policies, private sector expectations, and the performance of the economy. It notes that with the low confidence about government policies that existed during much of the 1980s, the turnaround in private sector expectations—critical to the eventual success of the Mexican program—required considerably tighter policies than otherwise would have been the case.

Section IV analyzes the process of international trade and foreign investment policy reform, as a mechanism for integration of Mexico in the world economy. It describes Mexico's policies in these areas prior to 1983 and the transformation to an open economy. It also reviews the recent trade initiatives to consolidate earlier gains, including the North American Trade Agreement and arrangements with Latin American countries.

Section V reviews the program of domestic financial liberalization and reform. These reforms, which started in the mid-1980s and had a notable effect on financial performance, involved a market-oriented approach to the determination of interest rates, as well as major structural changes, including the re-privatization of the commercial banks that had been expropriated in 1982. The section also reviews the changes in the rules governing other financial intermediaries and the importance of these changes for Mexico's competitiveness in attracting financial saving.

Section VI deals with Mexico's external debt policies. It focuses on the evolution of the authorities' approach to commercial bank debt restructuring since the 1982 debt crisis. The section discusses the key elements of the approach, their implementation, and their relationship with the "international debt strategy." It focuses in particular on the movement away from liquidity support in the form of repeated principal reschedulings and concerted new money loans, and toward comprehensive debt stock operations. Together with the sustained implementation of appropriate economic policies, these operations have contributed to Mexico's return to voluntary international capital market financing.

Section VII supplements the previous chapter by discussing Mexico's return to voluntary capital markets—a trend that started in 1989 and has intensified markedly with respect to both the magnitude of funds mobilized and the range of Mexican borrowers. The section also reviews the evolving structure of the instruments that were used to obtain foreign financing by both the private and public sectors, and some reasons behind the success in returning to voluntary financing.

Section VIII analyzes the dynamics of Mexican inflation over the period 1988–91. While the section does not seek to test any specific theory about inflation, the results show a clear response of domestic inflation to adjustments in public sector prices, to external price and exchange rate movements, as well as to credit policy, but less to wages. In turn, it is shown that nominal wages are associated with movements in minimum wages, while monetary expansion is shown to adjust endogenously in light of the existing exchange rate policy. The section concludes that no simple and unique model can explain inflation in Mexico but suggests the importance of policy imbalances in explaining prices, wages, and monetary developments.

# II The Mexican Strategy to Achieve Sustainable Economic Growth

## Eliot Kalter

In the first years following the 1982 debt crisis, the Mexican authorities adopted significant financial and structural measures to redress the situation. Particular emphasis was placed on fiscal policy, with substantial cuts made to noninterest expenditure. This policy stance was not comprehensive, however, and the fiscal effort was insufficient to bring back confidence to financial markets. In the context of high public sector debt, accelerating inflation, and rising interest rates, interest payments rose substantially in relation to gross domestic product (GDP), and the overall public sector deficit remained high. Private sector confidence in government policies remained low and economic activity was stagnant.

It became apparent that a more comprehensive effort was required to foster the conditions for sustainable economic growth. Thus, in December 1987 the authorities introduced an economic program, reinforced in late 1988, that is based on five key elements: tight financial policies; an incomes policy; significant structural reforms; innovative support from the international financial community; and, the implementation of policies aimed at protecting the economy from adverse shocks.

The results of this strategy, which was seen as risky at the time of the introduction of the economic program, have been impressive. The 12-month rate of inflation has declined from 159 percent in December 1987 to 19 percent in December 1991 while, after years of stagnation, real GDP grew in 1991 by around 4 percent for the second year in a row.[1] Further, reflecting strong private sector capital inflows, the overall balance of payments registered a surplus of over $7 billion during 1991. Underpinning this performance has been a strong fiscal adjustment with the overall public sector borrowing requirement (PSBR) declining from 16 percent of GDP in 1987 to 1.5 percent in 1991.

The first part of this section presents an historical overview of the economic policies leading to the debt crisis and the subsequent strategy of economic adjustment during 1982–87. The second discusses the strategy used by the authorities since late 1987 to foster conditions for sustained economic growth in the context of a strength-ening of the balance of payments. The third offers some concluding remarks.

## Historical Overview

Between 1955 and 1970 Mexico experienced rapid industrialization and urbanization. Widely characterized as a period of "stabilizing development," the country enjoyed high growth, low inflation, and moderate debt accumulation.[2] This was achieved through the maintenance of a tight fiscal stance, accompanied by inward-looking policies.[3] Sizable private sector investment was associated with strong economic growth, with the ratio of private sector investment relative to GDP increasing by over 8 percentage points of GDP to 20 percent, and with an average annual increase of real GDP of around 6½ percent. This allowed for an increase of real per capita consumption at an average annual rate of 3⅓ percent. At the same time, the rate of inflation was both stable and moderate (an average rate of 4 percent during the period). External debt remained below 20 percent of GDP throughout the period.

The strategy was highly successful in the beginning but not sustainable as it was framed by high protective barriers, focusing on import-substitution and rapid expansion of the domestic market. Correspondingly, economic inefficiencies became prevalent, with industrial growth mostly a result of capacity expansion with little productivity gains.[4] With expenditure growing rapidly, the external current account balance changed from a surplus equivalent to 2 percent of GDP in 1955 to a deficit of 3½ percent of GDP in 1970, with the U.S. dollar value of exports growing only at an annual rate of 3 percent during this period.

---

[1] Data for 1991 in this section are from Bank of Mexico, *Informe Anual, 1991*. Fiscal data exclude proceeds from the privatization of public enterprises.

[2] The period of "Stabilizing Development" included the presidencies of Adolfo López Mateos (1958–64) and Gustavo Díaz Ordáz (1964–70). See James Capel and Co. (1991) for a summary of political developments in Mexico.

[3] Beginning in the mid-1950s, Mexico started to increase nominal tariff levels and to impose quantitative import restrictions and domestic price controls. The "inwardness" of Mexico's industrial growth is contrasted with the "outward" policies of Korea and Taiwan Province of China in Lustig (1991).

[4] See Lustig (1991) for a description of the relative importance of the supply factors of production and productivity changes on economic growth

**Table 1. Public Sector Fiscal Balances**
(*In percent of GDP*)

| | Overall Balance [1] (Nominal) | Primary | Operational |
|---|---|---|---|
| 1965 | −0.8 | 0.0 | −0.7 |
| 1966 | −1.1 | −0.2 | −0.6 |
| 1967 | −2.1 | −0.8 | −1.7 |
| 1968 | −1.9 | −0.7 | −1.4 |
| 1969 | −2.0 | −0.7 | −1.3 |
| 1970 | −3.4 | −1.3 | −2.6 |
| 1971 | −2.3 | −0.4 | −1.3 |
| 1972 | −4.5 | −2.2 | −3.3 |
| 1973 | −6.3 | −3.5 | −2.5 |
| 1974 | −6.7 | −3.7 | −3.1 |
| 1975 | −9.3 | −6.0 | −6.8 |
| 1976 | −9.1 | −4.6 | −4.1 |
| 1977 | −6.3 | −2.2 | −3.4 |
| 1978 | 6.2 | −3.7 | −3.4 |
| 1979 | −7.1 | −4.8 | −3.8 |
| 1980 | −7.5 | −3.8 | −3.6 |
| 1981 | −14.1 | −9.4 | −10.0 |
| 1982 | −16.9 | −5.0 | −5.5 |
| 1983 | −8.6 | 4.6 | 0.4 |
| 1984 | −8.5 | 4.8 | −0.3 |
| 1985 | −9.6 | 3.4 | −0.8 |
| 1986 | −15.9 | 1.6 | −2.4 |
| 1987 | −16.0 | 4.7 | 1.8 |
| 1988 | −12.4 | 5.9 | −3.6 |
| 1989 | −5.5 | 7.9 | −1.7 |
| 1990 | −3.5 | 7.9 | 1.8 |
| 1991 | −1.5 | 5.4 | 3.3 |

Sources: Secretariat of Finance and Public Credit; and Bank of Mexico.

[1] Public sector borrowing requirement.

In the early 1970s, the policy of private sector-led growth was replaced by a policy of "shared development," with the Government adopting an active policy of public expenditure led growth.[5] The PSBR increased from 2½ percent of GDP in 1971 to over 9 percent of GDP in 1975 (Table 1).[6] At the same time, private sec-

tor savings declined and the external current account deficit increased by 1 percentage point of GDP to over 4½ percent of GDP. External debt more than tripled to almost $22 billion by the end of 1975. While the annual rate of economic growth still averaged 6½ percent, the rate of inflation rose to 12 percent during this period and the real effective exchange rate appreciated markedly.

In 1976, Mexico experienced a financial crisis, as capital flight accelerated in the face of mounting imbalances. A new government responded with economic measures, supported by a stand-by arrangement from the Fund, which included a devaluation of the peso and tighter fiscal policies.[7] Financial policies were relaxed, however, after major oil discoveries were made the following year. Public sector revenue increased markedly with rising oil proceeds but was accompanied by even larger public sector expenditure that led to a sizable rise in the PSBR. From 1975 to 1982, the level of total external debt increased threefold to $88 billion, while private sector debt rose to $18 billion. Furthermore, short-term debt rose to one third of total debt outstanding.

During 1980–82, aided by the impact of increasing oil production and, initially, increased foreign borrowing, public budgetary expenditure rose by 10 percentage points of GDP to 42 percent of GDP and real GDP rose at a rate of over 5 percent (Table 2). However, with public sector deficits increasing during this period, the rate of inflation averaged 37 percent and the real effective exchange rate appreciated markedly; together with low controlled nominal interest rates, capital flight rose. The authorities sought to arrest the existing imbalances but were unsuccessful. In the context of weakening oil prices, the balance of payments was subject to considerable pressure that was aggravated by increased reluctance in international markets to lend to Mexico.

In August 1982, the Mexican authorities announced their inability to service fully the country's external debt. Subsequently, the Government imposed strict exchange and trade controls and nationalized the banking system, while Mexico began to develop external payments arrears on private sector debt service. The combination of a large public sector deficit and the lack of foreign financing led to a rapid acceleration of inflation, from an annual rate of under 30 percent in 1981 to almost 100 percent in 1982.

---

[5] The period of "shared development" was introduced by President Luis Echeverría Alvarez.

[6] The high inflation rate that prevailed during much of the 1980s and the large outstanding stock of domestic debt complicated the assessment of fiscal policy. The Mexican authorities employed several measures of fiscal performance to deal with this problem. The traditional measure of fiscal performance is the PSBR, which measures the difference between total expenditure and revenue of the nonfinancial public sector. In an environment of high inflation, the concept of the PSBR contains a large element of debt amortization in its interest component. Thus, the concept of the operational balance is also employed,

which corrects for this component. The operational balance was derived by subtracting from the overall balance the inflationary component of interest payments on the internal public debt denominated in Mexican currency and thus measures the inflation adjusted savings-investment balance of the public sector; this measure provides the best association, in conjunction with the savings-investment balance of the private sector, with the external current account balance. The operational balance also measures movements in the real stock of public sector debt. Finally, to assess the fiscal effort resulting from measures being implemented, the concept of the primary balance is employed. The primary balance can be viewed as an intermediate fiscal target and is defined as the overall balance, excluding all interest payments.

[7] José López Portillo took over the office of the presidency from Luis Echeverría Alvarez.

**Table 2. Public Sector Budgetary Revenue and Expenditure[1]**
*(In percent of GDP)*

|                          | 1980 | 1981 | 1982 | 1983 | 1984 | 1985 | 1986 | 1987 | 1988 | 1989 | 1990 | 1991 |
|--------------------------|------|------|------|------|------|------|------|------|------|------|------|------|
| Budgetary expenditure    | 31.1 | 38.7 | 41.8 | 39.0 | 37.7 | 37.5 | 42.5 | 43.7 | 38.4 | 34.1 | 33.4 | 29.7 |
| Current                  | 22.7 | 26.8 | 32.9 | 32.7 | 32.0 | 32.3 | 37.8 | 38.8 | 34.8 | 31.0 | 29.4 | 25.5 |
| Of which: interest       |      |      |      |      |      |      |      |      |      |      |      |      |
| payments                 | 3.2  | 4.9  | 8.0  | 12.1 | 11.7 | 11.3 | 16.4 | 19.6 | 16.5 | 12.9 | 9.9  | 5.7  |
| Capital                  | 8.4  | 11.9 | 8.9  | 6.3  | 5.7  | 5.1  | 4.6  | 4.8  | 3.6  | 3.2  | 4.0  | 4.2  |
| Budgetary revenue        | 25.5 | 26.3 | 27.8 | 31.7 | 31.3 | 30.4 | 29.4 | 29.5 | 28.7 | 27.6 | 27.5 | 26.2 |
| Oil sector               | 7.8  | 8.1  | 11.1 | 16.1 | 15.1 | 13.3 | 11.4 | 11.9 | 10.0 | 8.7  | 9.0  | 7.9  |
| Exports                  | 5.2  | 5.5  | 8.3  | 10.8 | 9.4  | 8.1  | 4.9  | 6.0  | 3.4  | 3.2  | 3.7  | 3.0  |
| Domestic                 | 2.6  | 2.5  | 2.8  | 5.2  | 5.7  | 5.2  | 6.5  | 5.9  | 6.6  | 5.4  | 5.3  | 4.9  |
| Non-oil sector           | 17.7 | 18.3 | 16.7 | 15.6 | 16.2 | 17.0 | 18.0 | 17.6 | 18.7 | 18.9 | 18.5 | 18.3 |

Sources: Secretariats of Finance and Public Credit and of Programming and Budget.
[1] Excludes nonbudgetary operations and financial intermediation.

In late 1982, the new administration of President Miguel de la Madrid Hurtado adopted an adjustment program.[8] Mexico obtained financial resources and a rescheduling of its external debt from official and commercial bank sources and the program was supported by the Fund with an extended arrangement covering 1983–85. The program called for a major strengthening of financial policies and for a liberalization of exchange and trade controls; it also provided for a large initial devaluation, followed by frequent adjustments in the exchange rate based on projected inflation. The program's early achievements were considerable: internal and external imbalances were reduced greatly, inflationary pressures declined, and economic activity began to recover.

By early 1985, however, it became evident that the initial adjustment efforts were not being sustained. Moreover, the efforts of the authorities were hampered by emergency spending necessitated by the September 1985 earthquake and by the sharp drop in the price of oil (from $25 a barrel in 1985 to an average price of $12 a barrel in 1986). As a result, the fiscal and external positions weakened, with public sector revenues and export receipts plummeting by the equivalent of about 6 percent of GDP.

In mid-1986, the Mexican Government responded to the worsening economic situation by adopting a new economic program, which the Fund supported with a stand-by arrangement. Financial support was sought from all of the creditors that had financed Mexico's development in the past, with a view to restructure Mexico's external debt from official and commercial bank sources and to offset the loss in export earnings. Fiscal and monetary policies were tightened; the exchange rate was depreci-

ated sharply in real terms; and substantial efforts were made to liberalize trade and privatize public sector enterprises. These efforts, aided by a marked increase in oil prices, led to a sizable external current account and balance of payments surplus and allowed Mexico to enjoy a period of moderate economic growth in 1987.

The strong improvement in the external position of Mexico in 1986–87 was accompanied, however, by a marked deterioration in price performance, with the 12-month rate of inflation accelerating from under 65 percent in December 1985 to 159 percent in December 1987 (Chart 1). Nominal interest rates were correspondingly high, which put additional pressure on the borrowing requirement of the public sector. The inflationary spiral, which was aggravated by the increased frequency of wage and official price adjustments, together with the crash in the Mexican stock market in October 1987, resulted in significant capital outflows late in that year. In response, the Bank of Mexico withdrew its support of the exchange rate in the free market, causing the peso to depreciate sharply.

## Strategy to Achieve Sustainable Economic Growth

It became apparent that a broader-based effort, building on the authorities' previous policy stance, was required to achieve a sustainable recovery. Thus, in December 1987, the authorities introduced an economic program based on a pact with labor and business (the Pact for Economic Solidarity, or PACTO), which aimed at correcting remaining imbalances and, in particular, at bringing down the rate of inflation. Financial policies were tightened further and additional structural reforms were instituted.

---

[8] The elements of the authorities' adjustment effort following the 1982 debt crisis are reviewed in Kalter and Khor (1990).

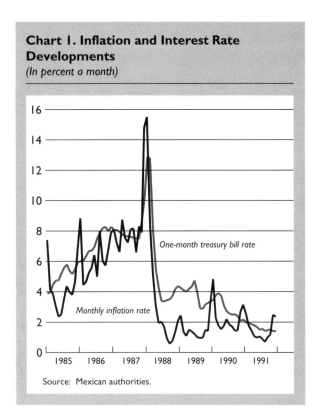

**Chart 1. Inflation and Interest Rate Developments**
*(In percent a month)*

One-month treasury bill rate

Monthly inflation rate

Source: Mexican authorities.

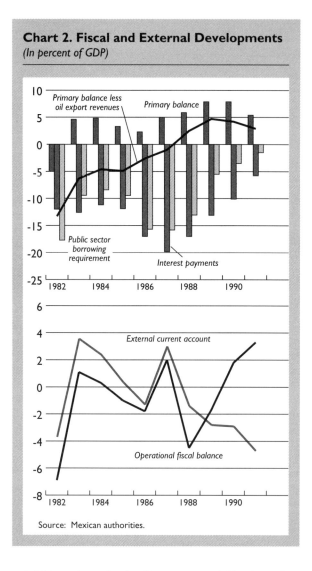

**Chart 2. Fiscal and External Developments**
*(In percent of GDP)*

Primary balance less oil export revenues

Primary balance

Public sector borrowing requirement

Interest payments

External current account

Operational fiscal balance

Source: Mexican authorities.

The measures adopted were effective in reducing the rate of inflation from 159 percent during 1987 to 52 percent during 1988, while real GDP growth remained at around 1½ percent. The program was not without risk, however, and despite an increase in the primary fiscal surplus, continued economic uncertainties resulted in a substantial rise in real interest rates and, consequently, a large fiscal operational deficit. The external current account shifted by about 4½ percentage points to a deficit of around 1 percent of GDP in 1988, while net international reserves declined by $6.8 billion (Chart 2).

In late 1988, under President Carlos Salinas de Gortari, the Mexican authorities broadened further their economic policies. While pursuing a continued reduction in the rate of inflation, more emphasis was given to fostering conditions for sustained economic growth in the context of a strengthening of the balance of payments.

The strategy was based on five key elements. First, strict financial policies, which had been in place for much of the decade and had been strengthened in late 1987, were to be maintained. Second, the incomes policy that was instituted in late 1987 was broadened. This was accomplished through a revised wage-price pact (the Pact of Economic Growth and Stability, or PECE), as well as a social welfare program (PRONASOL). Third, significant additional structural reforms were put in place. Fourth, these policies were supported by assistance from bilateral, multilateral, and commercial creditors, including debt

and debt-service reduction from commercial banks and an extended Fund arrangement approved in May 1989. Finally, emphasis was placed on implementing policies to protect the economy from any adverse shocks.

**Fiscal Policy**

Throughout 1982–87, financial policies were tight with particular emphasis on fiscal adjustment.[9] The primary fiscal balance moved from a deficit of 5 percent of GDP in 1982 to a surplus of 5 percent of GDP in 1987 (see

---

[9] Given the managed exchanged rate policy used by the Mexican authorities since 1982, monetary policy is largely ineffective in influencing prices and output; rather, for a given fiscal policy, monetary policy affects the domestic and foreign component of the total money supply. See Section III for an analysis of the respective role of fiscal, monetary, and exchange rate policy in meeting economic objectives in Mexico since 1982. It is concluded that fiscal policy was central in achieving the authorities' macroeconomic objectives.

Table 1 and Chart 2). However, this fiscal effort was off-set, mostly, by a spiral of high inflation and high interest rates with the result that the PSBR declined by only about 1 percentage point to 16 percent of GDP. Moreover, fiscal rigidities impeded the authorities' ability to adjust quickly the primary balance to exogenous shocks.[10]

The foundation of the authorities' present economic program has been a further strengthening of fiscal policy at the level of the primary balance aided by structural fiscal reforms. In combination with the other elements of the economic program, this strategy broke the inflation-interest rate spiral and allowed the fiscal effort at the level of the primary balance to be associated with significant fiscal adjustment at the level of the PSBR and operational balance.

### Impediments to Fiscal Adjustment

After the 1982 debt crisis, the authorities' ability to reduce the size of the PSBR was hampered by numerous and inefficient public sector enterprises, structural impediments to adjusting public sector revenue and expenditure, and the adverse impact of the sizable domestic debt in relation to GDP that existed at the beginning of this period.

The number of public sector enterprises had increased significantly during the 1970s and reached over 1,100 by 1982, with the overall deficit of these enterprises accounting for about one fourth of the public sector's borrowing requirements. The growing deficit of the public sector enterprises, which was financed mainly by transfers from the federal budget, reflected a sharp rise in public sector investment, non-market-related pricing policy, and increasing inefficiency. By the end of 1982, the authorities had determined that the size of the public sector affected adversely both economic productivity and efficiency; moreover, it affected the ability to adjust quickly fiscal policy to meet economic objectives.

Impediments to increasing public sector revenue hampered fiscal adjustment efforts, with additional public sector revenue contributing only 1½ percentage points to the 10 percentage points of adjustment in the primary balance during 1982–87 (see Table 2). A dominant factor behind the poor revenue performance was a large decline in revenue from oil exports, with sales falling from over 8 percent of GDP in 1982 to an average of under 5 percent of GDP in 1986–88. This deterioration was partly offset by increased proceeds from the domestic sale of petroleum, reflecting adjustments in domestic prices to international levels. Another reason for the lack-luster revenue performance was the narrow tax base, high marginal income tax rates, and, for taxes collected with a lag, the negative effects of higher inflation on revenue collections in real terms.

The inertial element of fiscal imbalances that resulted from the link between debt, inflation, and interest rates also impeded fiscal adjustment during this period. In 1982, the total stock of domestic debt was already equivalent to 25 percent of GDP, while the average annual cost of debt financing was 20 percent.[11] As a result, interest payments on domestic debt were equivalent to almost 5 percent of GDP, accounting for over one third of the borrowing requirement of the public sector. Despite the sizable fiscal effort at the level of the primary balance during 1982-87, the average overall public sector deficit during the period was equivalent to 13 percent of GDP. Reflecting a heavy reliance on the issue of money to finance the fiscal deficit during this period, total domestic debt declined to under 17 percent of GDP by the end of 1987. However, with the average cost of funds rising to over 90 percent, interest payments on domestic debt rose to over 16 percent of GDP. As a result, by 1987 a significantly larger fiscal effort at the level of the primary balance was required to maintain an unchanged borrowing requirement of the public sector.[12]

### Road to Fiscal Adjustment

During 1982–87 the reduction of public sector non-interest expenditure was equivalent to almost 10 percentage points of GDP (see Table 2). This was accomplished by equivalent sizable reductions in non-interest current and capital expenditure, with the decline in capital expenditure shared between the Federal Government and the public enterprises. However, the cuts in current expenditure hurt the Government's ability to meet certain social needs and maintain current services, while the reduced public investment caused infrastructural bottlenecks. The adverse effect of the cuts in expenditure may have been compounded by their impact on economic activity, which in turn would then have adversely affected the capacity of the Government to raise revenues.

In their efforts to reform the public sector, the authorities placed emphasis on the divestiture of public sector enterprises. The number of state-owned entities was cut from over 1,100 in 1982 to 420 by the end of 1988 through a process of mergers, liquidations, and sales. Since the end of 1988, the effort to streamline the public sector has continued with the number of state-owned entities estimated at less than 250 by the end of 1991; moreover, the recent divestitures have included some of the largest enterprises in the country, including two air-

---

[10] See Ize and Ortiz (1987).

[11] Total domestic debt including that held by the central bank was equivalent to 25 percent of GDP; while excluding that held by the central bank, it was only 4 percent of GDP.

[12] As shown by Sargent and Wallace (1981), the effect on inflation of financing a fiscal deficit by bonds, instead of money creation, can be ambiguous. More specifically, it is possible for inflation to increase in response to lower money creation today, in anticipation of higher money creation tomorrow.

lines, a truck manufacturing company, two steel companies, and the Cooper Mining Company. More recently, the large telecommunications company and the commercial banks were privatized. This policy has allowed the public sector to concentrate its limited resources on priority sectors and has allowed the private sector to participate in the development of critical areas of the economy.

On the revenue side, in 1987, the authorities implemented a major reform of the tax system to correct distortions (especially the effects of inflation) and to enhance Mexico's external competitiveness by harmonizing the domestic tax system with those abroad. The reform was accelerated in 1989–90 by widening the tax base and reducing marginal tax rates. In particular, the Government introduced a new minimum tax of 2 percent on firms' assets; abolished tax exemptions granted to certain sectors of the economy; reduced the corporate tax rate from about 40 percent to 36 percent, while changing the system of taxing corporate dividends to discourage tax evasion and encourage reinvestment of profits; and lowered the tax rate on the highest personal income bracket to 35 percent.

In response to government policies, including an increase in the fiscal primary surplus from 4.7 percent of GDP in 1987 to 7.9 percent of GDP in 1989, the rate of inflation and nominal interest rates declined in both 1988 and 1989; moreover, private sector confidence began to recover as evidenced by a decline in 1989 of real interest rates in association with a net inflow of private capital. As a result, in 1989 both the PSBR and the operational deficit declined. Domestic debt, however, rose to almost 24 percent of GDP, reflecting the authorities' determination to avoid central bank financing of the PSBR. In 1990, the improvement in the fiscal balances continued with the primary surplus remaining at 7.9 percent of GDP and the PSBR declining to 3½ percent (the lowest PSBR in ten years). In addition, the operational balance moved to surplus, resulting in a slight decline in the real level of domestic debt.

In 1991, the process was reinforced with declines in inflation, nominal and real interest rates, and the level of domestic debt. Domestic interest payments declined to 3½ percent of GDP (compared with 6.9 percent of GDP in 1990 and 13 percent of GDP in 1988), reflecting lower interest rates (an average of around 20 percent in 1991 compared with 35 percent in 1990), and a lower level of domestic debt (estimated to have declined by over 4 percentage points of GDP to 19 percent of GDP). The PSBR (excluding revenues from privatization) declined to 1.5 percent of GDP, while the operational surplus increased to over 2.3 percent of GDP. This was consistent with a decline in the fiscal effort at the level of the primary balance and allowed for some increase in public sector investment and current expenditure.[13]

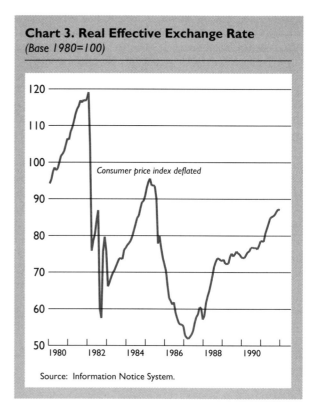

**Chart 3. Real Effective Exchange Rate**
*(Base 1980=100)*

Consumer price index deflated

Source: Information Notice System.

### Incomes Policy

A crucial part of the authorities' overall strategy to achieve economic stability and a sustainable rate of growth has been the implementation of an incomes policy, including an exchange rate policy based on a preannounced and declining path of inflation (Chart 3). The incomes policy is comprised of two distinct parts. The first is an economic solidarity pact between government, business, and labor to control prices and wages within the context of the Government's overall program aimed at economic recovery. The second is a government spending program aimed at eradicating extreme poverty and better integrating the poor into the process of economic recovery.

### Wage-Price Pact

As part of the wage-price pact of December 1987, the minimum wage, the controlled exchange rate, and public sector prices and tariffs were, after an initial adjustment, frozen throughout 1988.[14] A new pact of economic growth and stability (PECE) was announced in December 1988. Minimum wages and public sector prices and tar-

---

[13] Nevertheless, higher private sector investment has been the main source of increased economic activity.

[14] There were small adjustments to the exchange rate and wages early in the year.

iffs were adjusted while the peso was made subject to a daily preannounced schedule of depreciation against the U.S. dollar. The authorities have extended the PECE at unannounced, although fairly regular, intervals. The nominal rate of adjustments to minimum wages has declined with inflation; adjustment to public sector prices and tariffs has met microeconomic objectives; and the preannounced crawl of the peso has decreased steadily.[15]

In combination with tight financial policies, the wage-price pact has aided in reducing inflation. "A major component of inflation in many countries stems from what may be called the imposition of an external diseconomy by each firm and household acting in isolation as it seeks to protect itself against inflation."[16] Hence, even in the absence of pervasive indexation, inertial inflation may exist, which is costly to eliminate by using financial policies alone. The use of an incomes policy, in combination with tight financial policies, can reduce this inertial element and the degree of monetary and fiscal restraint needed to achieve lower inflation. In turn, the costs of adjustment are reduced.

### Program of National Solidarity

The second element of the Government's incomes policy has been the "Program of National Solidarity," or "PRONASOL." This program was initiated in 1989 with the purpose of eradicating extreme poverty and integrating the poor into the process of economic stability and recovery, with an emphasis on specific programs rather than broad and costly subsidies. PRONASOL seeks to expand and strengthen programs in education, nutrition, and health, as well as those related to the provision of drinking water, sewage, and electricity. The program is decentralized, with the Government acting closely with individual communities.

The amount of government resources targeted for programs within PRONASOL has increased significantly since its inception. Social expenditure totaled 36 percent of total noninterest expenditure in 1989, of which 2.1 percent was within PRONASOL. Social expenditure increased to 38 percent of total noninterest expenditure (2.6 percent within PRONASOL) in 1990, 46 percent of total noninterest expenditure in 1991 (3.5 percent within PRONASOL), and the 1992 budget programmed social expenditure at 51 percent of total noninterest expenditure (4 percent within PRONASOL). With noninterest expenditure increasing somewhat in real terms as interest payments declined,

social expenditure has increased in real terms by 16 percent in 1990 and an equivalent increase is estimated in 1991. This increased social expenditure, as well as its careful management, has helped improve social equity while Mexico undergoes its economic stabilization program.

## Structural Reforms

In addition to reforming the tax system and divesting public sector enterprises (described above), Mexico took measures to liberalize its external trade and investment system, to enter into free trade arrangements, to liberalize and privatize its financial system, and to deregulate specific economic activities. Overall, the program of structural reform initiated in the mid-1980s and intensified since 1989 has paved the way for a more efficient and dynamic economy based on market signals while opening it up to international capital and competition. In combination with the other elements underpinning Mexico's policy effort, these reforms have helped create the conditions for sustainable economic growth.

### International Trade and Investment Liberalization

Mexico has liberalized its international trade and investment regimes in stages. In 1985, Mexico began dismantling its tariff and nontariff trade barriers and joined the General Agreement on Tariffs and Trade (GATT) in August 1986.[17] Import substitution policies and reliance on oil exports for foreign exchange earnings were replaced with policies aimed at attracting foreign investment, lowering trade barriers, and generally making the country more competitive for non-oil exports. In 1989, foreign investment regulations were also liberalized. The new regulations simplified the procedures for authorizing investment projects, relaxed limits on foreign ownership, and reduced some barriers to entry by foreigners into the Mexican stock market.

The implications of this transformation into a highly open economy have been significant as the incentive structure has been reoriented while major distortions have been removed, leading to greater efficiency. Export growth has picked up, and exports have been diversified. Moreover, the economy's productive base is being modernized as a result of the access to imports at international prices and greater amounts of foreign direct investment. Mexico is currently involved in the negotiation of four free trade agreements, one with the United States and Canada and three with Latin American countries.

---

[15] The latest extension of the wage-price pact was announced on November 10, 1991. Actions included (1) a slower pace of depreciation of the peso with respect to the U.S. dollar, from an annual rate of 5 percent to 2½ percent; (2) an increase in minimum wages of 12 percent; (3) a lowering of the value-added tax to 10 percent from 15 percent (from 20 percent for some luxury items); (4) increases in the price of petroleum products of up to 55 percent; and (5) an increase in the price of electricity for home and industrial use of around 15 percent.

[16] See Cline (1991), p. 14.

---

[17] See Section IV. In addition to commitments to reduce tariffs and phase out quantitative restrictions, Mexico signed the GATT codes on licensing procedures, antidumping, customs valuation, and technical barriers to trade. In a number of instances, Mexico moved beyond its commitments in the context of the GATT.

Until the late 1980s, despite a period of gradual transformation and liberalization, the financial system in Mexico was characterized by interest rate restrictions, domestic credit controls, high reserve requirements, and fragmented financial markets causing inefficiencies in the intermediation between borrowers and lenders.[18] Capital markets were not well developed, and firms often had to turn to informal markets. Moreover, the shallowness of the bond market and the existence of informal credit markets hampered the conduct of monetary policy by restricting the scope for open market operations and limiting the ability of the Bank of Mexico to monitor overall credit market conditions.

In 1988, the Mexican Government accelerated the process of financial reform. The objectives were to enhance efficiency through greater reliance on market forces, to promote the growth and deepening of financial markets, and to improve the effectiveness of monetary policy. In addition, the reforms sought to improve the capitalization of Mexican financial institutions with a view to preparing them for international competition.

Key liberalization measures included the freeing of interest rates and the elimination of direct controls on credit. In November 1988, quantitative restrictions on the issuance of bankers' acceptances were lifted, and banks were allowed to invest freely from these resources. In April 1989, major reforms were introduced that eliminated controls on interest rates and maturities on all traditional bank instruments and deposits, as well as remaining restrictions on bank lending to the private sector. But the cornerstone of the institutional reform was the reprivatization of Mexico's commercial banks, announced in 1990, and subsequently successfully implemented, which was part of a wider plan to promote financial integration through a universal banking system.

### Deregulation of Economic Activities

Complementing the measures mentioned above, steps have been taken to deregulate specific sectors, particularly in the areas of transportation, communication, petrochemicals, fisheries, and most recently agriculture. These measures are enabling market forces in Mexico and abroad to take advantage of available opportunities. Most recently, an agricultural reform bill was introduced in Congress that would allow the owners of agricultural land to rent or sell their land, while putting an end to the distribution of land that has been in place since the rural reform in 1917. This change should allow for a substantial increase in agricultural productivity.

In the context of the authorities' exchange rate and incomes policy, the structure of the balance of payments has changed dramatically in recent years. During much of the 1980s, improvements in the fiscal operational balance were related directly to improvements in the external current account balance. Since 1989, the current account balance has been linked directly to movements in private capital flows, with increased net private inflows resulting in growing private sector imports of intermediate and capital goods. The strong fiscal outcome during this period has strongly influenced the willingness of the private sector to make use of foreign savings for investment in Mexico and has been associated with rising current account deficits.

### International Financial Support

The fourth element underpinning Mexico's economic recovery is the form and extent of support that Mexico received from the international financial community. Since 1982, international financial support has been a critical aspect of the adjustment strategy. During 1982–87, there was increased coordination between Mexico and its international financial creditors with a strategy of striking an appropriate balance between concerted financing, debt rescheduling, and macroeconomic adjustment. Concern about the impact of the external debt burden led in 1989 to support from the international financial community that emphasized debt and debt-service reduction.

During 1982–87, Mexico undertook repeated rescheduling of debt-service obligations to both commercial banks and official bilateral creditors, in the context of adjustment programs aimed at macroeconomic stabilization.[19] However, Mexico's external debt grew from some $75 billion (45 percent of GDP) at the end of 1981 to $101 billion (57 percent of GDP) by the end of 1988. Of this amount, public sector external debt increased from some $53 billion at the end of 1981 to $86 billion by the end of 1988. Reflecting this increase, public sector debt service, before rescheduling, reached 77 percent of exports of goods, services, and transfers (46 percent, after rescheduling) in 1988, while there was a net resource transfer abroad equivalent to 3½ percent of GDP.[20]

A crucial element in support of the present economic program is the backing of the international financial community and official donors with an emphasis on reducing Mexico's debt overhang.[21] The Fund approved a three-year extended arrangement with Mexico in May 1989

---

[18] See Section V.

[19] See Section VI for an analysis of the evolution of Mexico's approach to commercial bank debt restructuring since the 1982 debt crisis.

[20] The net resource transfer is defined as the balance of goods and nonfactor services.

[21] These features of the backing by the international financial community are discussed in Kalter and Khor (1990).

for the amount of SDR 2.8 billion (equivalent to about $3.6 billion). Some SDR 800 million of the initial access under the arrangement was set aside for support for debt and debt-service-reduction operations and the amount of the arrangement was subsequently augmented by SDR 466 million (about $600 million) for this purpose.

Shortly after the approval of the Fund arrangement, the Paris Club creditors agreed to reschedule $2.6 billion of Mexico's debt-service obligations on official debt falling due in the next three years. In June 1989, the International Bank for Reconstruction and Development (IBRD) approved sectoral loans to Mexico amounting to almost $2 billion (of which $760 million was earmarked for debt and debt-service-reduction operations) and agreed to provide additional loans averaging $2 billion during the subsequent three years. In January 1990, the IBRD approved an additional $1.3 billion for financing debt and debt-service operations.

In support of their program, the authorities also asked for a multiyear financing package with commercial banks, which would involve debt and debt-service-reduction operations sufficient to produce a substantial decline in the country's external debt. Negotiations were initiated with the commercial banks in April 1989; an agreement in principle was reached in July of that year; and the exchange of instruments under the agreement took place in March, 1990.[22]

The direct impact of the package on Mexico's balance of payments has been to reduce interest obligations. On the basis of international interest rates prevailing during 1990, the gross saving on account of the bond exchanges amounted to some $1½ billion annually. After taking into account the cost of the collateral, the annual net saving on contractual interest amounts to around $¾ billion. More broadly, this operation has contributed to a decline in total public sector external debt service (after accounting for rescheduling) to an estimated 28 percent of exports of goods, services, and transfers in 1991 from 46 percent in 1988. The net resource transfer moved from an outflow of $6 billion in 1988 to an estimated inflow of $4 billion in 1991.

During this period, Mexico's total external debt declined from 57 percent of GDP in 1988 to an estimated 39 percent of GDP in 1991, with public sector external debt declining from 49 percent of GDP to 31 percent of GDP. This decline in external debt and debt service has contributed importantly to the improved confidence in the economy and has been reflected in Mexico's return to a voluntary access to foreign capital.

### Insulating the Economy from Unexpected External Shocks

The authorities attached great importance to insulating their program from possible adverse shocks. Since the

mid-1980s, they have taken progressive actions to minimize the risk of failure in achieving sustainable economic growth. The strategy has included prearranging external assistance to compensate for unexpected events, while adjusting economic policies, saving windfall gains resulting from favorable exogenous shocks, and restructuring the economy to minimize the impact of future shocks.

The strategy of arranging contingencies for possible future events was adopted in Mexico's 1986–87 stand-by arrangement with the Fund. The program used a mechanism that linked some of the program targets and the amount of the required external financing package to the evolution of international oil prices. Under this mechanism, additional external financing was available if the price of oil dropped below a certain point; moreover, beyond a certain decline in the price of oil, adjustment in domestic policies would also help fill the emerging gap. The 1986–87 stand-by arrangement also contained a mechanism that allowed for increased external financing for public sector investment in selected projects if the Mexican economy did not grow by the targeted amount.

The strategy of insulating the economy from external shocks was further developed in Mexico's 1989–92 extended Fund arrangement. In the 1989 economic program, the contingency mechanism was broadened to include possible adverse movements in both the evolution of international oil prices and interest rates. A combination of a decline in international oil prices and an increase in international interest rates would be met by a mixture of additional economic adjustment measures and some drawdown in net international reserves. In the 1990 and 1991 economic programs under the extended arrangement, the evolution of international interest rates was excluded from the mechanism because of the reduced sensitivity of the Mexican balance of payments to these movements. In both years, a decline in the price of oil beyond a certain threshold point would trigger automatically a full adjustment in economic policies.

The concept of saving windfall gains resulting from favorable external events also was first introduced in the 1986–87 stand-by arrangement with the Fund. Through the above-mentioned link between economic targets and the evolution of international oil prices, higher-than-anticipated prices beyond a certain threshold point resulted in a larger accumulation of net international reserves and less permissible domestic financing for the public sector deficit. This strategy was continued in the 1989–92 extended Fund arrangement, with a total saving of windfall gains from oil prices (and international interest rates in the 1989 economic program) above a certain threshold point. Moreover, the 1991 economic program provided for relevant quantitative performance criteria to be adjusted for the proceeds from the sale of public sector enterprises. In effect, at least 85 percent of these proceeds would be used to increase net international reserves or reduce external or domestic debt.

---

[22] The main features and results of the financing package are discussed in El-Erian (1991a).

The authorities have placed considerable emphasis on managing the country's economic and financial structure to reduce the impact of future adverse shocks. The impact of lower international oil prices has been reduced with the diversification of the export base (nonpetroleum exports have grown from 25 percent of the total in 1982 to an estimated 75 percent of the total in 1991). More recently, the possible impact of a recession in one of Mexico's trading partners has been reduced by the diversification of the destination for Mexico's exports (the share of exports to the United States declined from 76 percent in 1990 to an estimated 70 percent in 1991). Also, the possible impact of higher international interest rates has been reduced significantly by the results of the 1990 financial package with commercial banks. Finally, the authorities have engaged actively in the use of financial options (the use of puts and calls in the options market for oil) to minimize the impact of possible fluctuations in the price of oil on the Mexican economy.

## Conclusion

Mexico introduced an economic program in December 1987, which was broadened in late 1988, to reduce inflation and foster conditions for sustained economic growth in the context of a strengthening of the balance of payments. The comprehensive strategy pursued by the authorities has been carefully planned and implemented. It is critical to the strategy's success that it includes strict control of the public finances and credit aggregates, a broad-based structural reform, an incomes policy, innovative support from the international financial community, and the allowance of sufficient margin in the application of economic policies to absorb external exogenous shocks.

In May 1989, the authorities presented the country's medium-term objectives for the period 1989–94. This plan set out to achieve a sustained economic recovery, with the growth of real GDP gradually increasing to an annual rate of close to 6 percent by the end of the period; a reduction in the rate of inflation to international levels, or close to 5 percent by the end of the period; and, equilibrium in the balance of payments. The plan projected the fiscal effort at the level of the primary balance consistent with these targets at a surplus of around 6½ percent of GDP during 1989–91 and 5 percent of GDP during 1992-94.

The authorities have made good use of this framework, adjusting economic policy as required to ensure success. These efforts have produced a significant reduction in the rate of inflation, a sustained pickup in the rate of growth of output, and the strengthening of Mexico's foreign reserve position, while modernizing the economy and improving social policies. The authorities' approach has sought to incorporate the interests of all segments of the Mexican population, reducing the costs of economic adjustment and gaining the confidence of the private sector. This strategy has turned the vicious cycle that existed during 1982-88 between large fiscal deficits and high inflation and interest rates into a virtuous cycle. Recently, this has allowed some real increase in government current and capital expenditure consistent with continued fiscal adjustment at the level of the PSBR and operational balance.

The success of Mexico's economic strategy since 1989 has led to its gradually regaining access to voluntary international capital market financing after having been virtually excluded for much of the decade. This private sector access to capital, in combination with Mexico's broad economic reform, augurs well for the achievement of sustainable economic growth in the medium term.

# Bibliography

Banco de Mexico, *Indicadores Económicos* (Mexico, various issues).

Brau, Eduard H., and Chanpen Puckahtikom, *Export Credit Cover Policies and Payments Difficulties*, IMF Occasional Paper, No. 37 (Washington: International Monetary Fund, 1985).

Buffie, Edward, "Economic Policy and Foreign Debt in Mexico," in *Developing Country Debt and Economic Performance*, ed. by Jeffrey Sachs (Chicago: University of Chicago Press, 1990), pp. 393–551.

James Capel and Co., "Mexico: Bordering on Prosperity" (London, 1991).

Cline, William R., "Mexico—Economic Reform and Development Strategy," EXIM Review, Research Institute of Overseas Investment (Fall 1991).

Criterios Generales de Política Económica, Presidencia de la República (1992).

Dooley, Michael, and others, *Debt, Reduction and Economic Activity*, IMF Occasional Paper, No. 68 (Washington: International Monetary Fund, March 1990).

El-Erian, Mohammed (1991a), "Mexico's External Debt and Return to Voluntary Capital Market Financing," IMF Working Paper, WP/91/83 (Washington: International Monetary Fund, 1991).

_____, (1991b), "The Restoration of Latin America's Access to Voluntary Capital Market Financing—Developments and Prospects," IMF Working Paper, WP/91/74 (Washington: International Monetary Fund, 1991).

International Monetary Fund, *International Capital Markets: Developments and Prospects* (Washington, various issues).

_____, *International Financial Statistics* (Washington, various issues).

_____, *Multilateral Official Debt Rescheduling—Recent Experience* (Washington, various issues).

_____, *Determinants and Systemic Consequences of International Capital Flows: A Study by the Research Department of the International Monetary Fund*, IMF Occasional Paper, No. 77 (Washington: International Monetary Fund, 1991).

Ize, Alain, and Guillermo Ortiz, "Fiscal Rigidities, Public Debt and Capital Flight," Staff Papers, International Monetary Fund (Washington), Vol. 34 (June 1987), pp. 311–32.

Kalter, E., and H.E. Khor, "Mexico's Experience with Adjustment," *Finance and Development* (Washington), Vol. 27 (September 1990), pp. 22–25.

Lessard, Donald, and John Williamson, *Capital Flight and Third World Debt* (Washington: Institute for International Economics, 1987).

Lustig, Nora, "Mexico: Background Paper," Second Global Prospects Conference, sponsored by IEC/DEC (1991).

Mundell, Robert A., *International Economics* (New York: Macmillan, 1968).

Plan Nacional de Desarrollo, Poder Ejecutivo Federal (Mexico, May 1989).

Sargent, Thomas, and Neil Wallace, "Some Unpleasant Monetarist Arithmetic," *Federal Reserve Bank of Minneapolis Quarterly Review*, Vol. 5 (1981), pp. 1–17.

Tanzi, Vito, "Inflation, Lags in Collection, and the Real Value of Tax Revenue," Staff Papers, International Monetary Fund (Washington), Vol. 24 (March 1977), pp.154–67.

# III   An Analysis of the Linkages of Macroeconomic Policies in Mexico

## Liliana Rojas-Suarez

This section examines the interrelationship between fiscal, monetary, and exchange rate policies in Mexico from the late 1970s to mid-1991. The main purpose is to evaluate critically the consistency of the macroeconomic policies that were undertaken by Mexico after the emergence of the debt crisis in 1982 and to analyze some key policy issues that arose during subsequent stabilization efforts.

The most recent Mexican stabilization program, which started at the end of 1987, has resulted in a sharp decline of inflation and in renewed growth. While Mexico's economic achievements are substantial, it is important to recognize that attempts at economic stabilization started in 1983 and that during the period 1983–88 the Mexican economy experienced the lowest rate of growth of economic activity since the early 1950s. This recognition provides the motivation for this section, which examines a key policy issue faced by the Mexican authorities in their stabilization efforts, namely, the linkages between economic policies and the authorities' objectives of price stability and sustainable economic growth. Indeed, while Mexico experienced an average surplus in the primary fiscal balance—defined as the overall cash balance of the public sector exclusive of total interest payments and exchange losses—of 4 percent during the period 1983–87, the average annual inflation rate during the same period was 89 percent. Why did the fiscal effort during the period 1983–87 not produce a substantial reduction in inflation? What was the role of domestic monetary policy and the exchange rate and of the increasing issuance of domestic public debt? What policy changes may have accounted for the reduction of inflation and the recovery of output growth since 1989?

To help answer these questions, this section analyzes the sustainability of domestic policies using a simple framework based on the government budget constraint. The purpose of the exercise is first, to provide an indicator of the long-run inflation rate consistent with the fiscal and monetary policies that were implemented and second, to provide an explanation of the divergence between the observed and the long-run inflation rates. A major finding is that since 1982 the interaction between economic policies and the perceptions of economic agents about the sustainability of those policies was at the core

of explaining the dynamics of key macroeconomic variables.

During their stabilization efforts, the authorities also confronted two additional and related issues: the persistence of high real interest rates and the volatility of capital flight. A major problem faced by the authorities since 1982 was that adverse expectations regarding the future course of economic policy or adverse exogenous shocks to the Mexican economy (such as increases in international interest rates or declines in the price of oil) resulted in substantial capital flight and loss of foreign reserves. This section explores the factors underlying the persistence of high real interest rates and identifies causes and problems associated with capital flight.

Three periods are considered: (a) the pre-debt crisis period characterized by expansionary fiscal and monetary policies that were accompanied by both an inflow of foreign loans to the public sector and a flight of private capital; (b) the period 1983–87, when serious attempts were undertaken to correct domestic economic imbalances to deal with the high inflation and a stagnant economy; and (c) the period 1988–91 that was characterized by a substantial improvement in economic conditions.

The rest of the section is organized as follows: The first part derives a proxy for the long-run rates of inflation consistent with the domestic policies that were implemented in the Mexican economy during the period 1978–90. In the second, third, and fourth parts is an analysis of the divergence of the observed inflation rates from the estimated long-run rates that corresponds to the three periods under study. An attempt is made throughout to highlight central policy issues and lessons derived from the Mexican experience. The last part summarizes major findings.

## Fiscal Deficits and Long-Run Equilibrium Rates of Inflation

A salient feature regarding fiscal policy in Mexico has been the evolution of the primary fiscal balance, which shifted from an average deficit of more than 5 percent of GDP during 1978–82 to a surplus averaging 4 percent during 1983–87 and more than 7 percent of GDP during 1988–90. In this context, a major policy issue is the extent to which the evolution of the fiscal position has influenced inflation in Mexico as well as the sustainability of the adjustment effort. This section attempts to deal with this issue using a simple framework based on the government budget constraint to provide an indicator of the inflation rate that would prevail in the long run given the observed primary fiscal balance.[1]

The exercise is based on the following definition of the government budget constraint.

$$- prim_t + i_{t-1}\, dd_{t-1} + fd_{t-1}\, i^*_{t-1} = \Delta m_t + \Delta dd_t + \Delta fd_t, \quad (1)$$

where

$prim$ = primary balance as a proportion of GDP, with the primary balance defined as public sector receipts less expenditures (exclusive of total interest payments and exchange losses).[2]

$dd_{t-1}$ = domestic government debt in period $t$-1 as a proportion of GDP in period $t$,

$fd_{t-1}$ = foreign public debt (expressed in Mexican pesos) in period $t$-1 as a proportion of GDP in period $t$,

$m$ = central bank credit to the Government as a proportion of GDP,

$i$ = the domestic interest rate on government bonds,

$i^*$ = interest rate on foreign borrowing,

and for any variable $X$, $x = X / GDP$ and $\Delta x_t = (X_t - X_{t-1}) / GDP_t$.

At every period of time, any fiscal deficit needs to be financed either by increases in the credit of the domestic financial sector to the Government or by new issues of government debt outside the domestic financial sector.

In the context of the budget constraint, the following question can be asked: ceteris paribus, what is the inflationary tax rate needed in the long run to finance the observed primary balance? A simple answer is to characterize a long-run equilibrium as one in which economic agents achieve their desired long-run holdings of money and bonds relative to GDP and are able to keep those ratios invariant over time.[3] Alternative values of the primary balance, hence, have corresponding values of the proxy for the long-run inflation rate.

Since an additional feature of long-run equilibrium is that the actual rate of inflation equals the expected inflation rate, the nominal interest rate can be approximated as: $i = r + \pi$, where $r$ is the real rate of interest and $\pi$ is the inflation rate.

Denoting $\pi$ as the rate of growth of real output, the long-run version of equation (1) is[4]

$$- prim + r\, dd + i^*\, fd = \Delta fd + m\, (\pi + \rho) + dd\, (\rho), \quad (2)$$

where

$- prim + r\, dd + i^*\, fd$ corresponds to the operational fiscal deficit, (def) that is, the overall fiscal deficit corrected for the amortization of domestic public debt owing to inflation.

Equation (2) can be solved for the rate of inflation that, ceteris paribus, would be needed in the long run to finance the fiscal deficit.[5] However, for equation (2) to be a strict representation of the long run, it would be necessary to model the markets for money and bonds in order to estimate the desired holdings of real money and bonds in the long run. In this section, a more simplified procedure is followed by using the actual ratios $dd_t$ and $m_t$ in the estimation of the long-run inflation rate. This restriction implies that the estimated long-run inflation rate derived from equation (2) should only be taken as a proxy for the long-run rate.[6]

Before proceeding with the estimation of such a proxy for the long-run inflation rate, it may be useful to note that equation (2) gives no explicit independent role to the exchange rate. Indeed, given the rate of foreign inflation, equation (2) could also be used to solve for the rate of exchange rate depreciation consistent with the fiscal deficit in the long run, if the following long-run equilibrium condition were to hold:

$$\pi = \hat{e} + \pi^*, \quad (3)$$

where

$\hat{e}$ is the rate of change of the exchange rate and $\pi^*$ is the rate of foreign inflation.

## The Real Interest Rate

A problem encountered in estimating equation (2) is deciding on the appropriate value of the real interest rate.[7]

---

[1] A similar framework is contained in Calvo and Fernandez (1982). A fiscal framework was also utilized by Guidotti and Kumar (1991) in their analysis of domestic public debt of externally indebted developing countries.

[2] Thus, $-prim$ represents the primary fiscal deficit.

[3] In this simplified characterization of the long run, the rate of growth of both money and domestic bonds is assumed to equal the rate of growth of nominal GDP. That is, the long run is identified with a steady state equilibrium where the level of real variables is kept constant.

[4] The time subscript has been deleted since equation (2) represents the fiscal budget constraint in the steady state.

[5] Gil Diaz and Tercero (1988) also uses the arithmetic of the budget constraint to answer a related question: What would be the necessary primary balance consistent with price stability in the Mexican economy?

[6] The estimated inflation rate derived from equation (2) would equal the "true" long-run rate only in those periods where the observed ratios $dd_t$ and $m_t$ do not differ significantly from their long-run values. This is, of course, highly unlikely in the high-inflation years of the Mexican economy.

[7] In the absence of evidence on the "true" rate of discount used by economic agents to estimate the present value of their assets, the ex post real interest rate, that is, the nominal interest rate minus the observed inflation rate is a concept widely used. However, agents base their decisions on portfolio allocation on the ex ante real interest rate, that is, the nominal interest rate minus the *expected* inflation rate.

## Table 3. Fiscal Deficits and Real Interest Rates

|  | Primary Balance (*prim*) | Ex Post Real Interest Rate | Ex Ante Real Interest Rate (*r*) | Primary Deficit Plus Real Interest Payments on Government Debt (*def*) [1] |
|---|---|---|---|---|
|  | (As percent of GDP) |  | (Annual Averages) |  |
| 1978 | −3.7 | −6.0 | −9.1 | 3.6 |
| 1979 | −4.8 | −4.9 | −8.5 | 4.3 |
| 1980 | −3.8 | −1.0 | −6.6 | 4.8 |
| 1981 | −9.4 | 2.6 | 0.26 | 10.9 |
| 1982 | −5.0 | −26.8 | −11.8 | 10.5 |
| 1983 | 4.6 | 4.0 | 2.96 | 3.6 |
| 1984 | 4.8 | 2.3 | 4.64 | 1.7 |
| 1985 | 3.3 | 15.2 | 18.2 | 4.2 |
| 1986 | 2.2 | 16.7 | 22.9 | 6.6 |
| 1987 | 5.0 | 0.1 | 18.8 | 3.5 |
| 1988 | 5.9 | 25.1 | 24.1 | 4.2 |
| 1989 | 7.9 | 23.8 | 22.6 | 0.9 |
| 1990 | 8.0 | 14.4 | 13.3 | −0.6 |

Sources: Appendix I, Bank of Mexico, *Indicadadores Economicos* ; and Fund staff estimates.
[1] A negative number indicates a fiscal surplus. Adjusted for the financing requirements associated with financial intermediation and statistical discrepancy.

Table 3 presents estimates of the fiscal deficit (*def*) based on the ex ante real interest rates on three-month treasury bills in Mexico during the period 1978–90. The series for the expected inflation rate used to estimate the ex ante real interest rates is presented in Appendix I.

The most important features of Table 3 are as follows: (a) The operational deficit based on an ex ante real interest rate (*def*) was negative only in 1990, while the primary balance showed a continuous surplus from 1983. (b) During 1978–81—the pre-debt crisis period—the estimated values for the expected inflation rates surpassed the actual inflation rates, resulting in ex ante real interest rates that were lower than the ex post rates. The opposite pattern is observed during 1984–87. (c) During the first two years of the recent Mexican adjustment program, 1988 and 1989, the ex ante real interest rate was lower than the ex post rate, reflecting expectations about the inflation rate greater than the observed inflation. During that period, both the ex ante and the ex post real interest rates remained very high. As the stabilization efforts were consolidated in 1990, real interest rates declined sharply.

### Rate of Inflation in Long-Run Equilibrium

Based on equation (2), Table 4 presents a proxy for the long-run inflation rate given the fiscal position and the behavior of output growth, real holdings of bonds and money, and the availability of external financing. This simple framework cannot be interpreted as a model of inflation since most of the variables involved are endoge-

nous. A detailed explanation of the derivation of the long-run inflationary tax rate as well as the underlying assumptions are contained in Appendix II.

Table 4 shows the evolution of the divergence between the actual inflation rate and the proxy for the long-run inflation rate. The salient features of these estimates, which will provide the background for the analysis in

## Table 4. Inflation Rates
*(Average of the year)*

| Year | Actual Inflation Rate | Estimated Proxy for the Long-Run Inflationary Tax Rate |
|---|---|---|
| 1978 | 17.5 | 19.5 |
| 1979 | 18.2 | 24.7 |
| 1980 | 26.3 | 28.9 |
| 1981 | 27.9 | 79.9 |
| 1982 | 58.9 | 100.2 |
| 1983 | 101.9 | 43.4 |
| 1984 | 65.5 | 21.4 |
| 1985 | 57.7 | 57.8 |
| 1986 | 86.2 | 92.6 |
| 1987 | 131.8 | 53.7 |
| 1988 | 114.2 | 82.9 |
| 1989 | 20.0 | 11.6 |
| 1990 | 26.6 | −19.7 |

Sources: Table 3; Bank of Mexico; *Indicadores Economicos*; and Fund staff estimates.

**Table 5. Public Sector Deficit and Its Financing**
*(As percentage of GDP)*

| | 1978 | 1979 | 1980 | 1981 | 1982 | 1983 | 1984 | 1985 | 1986 | 1987 | 1988 | 1989 | Prel. 1990 |
|---|---|---|---|---|---|---|---|---|---|---|---|---|---|
| Primary balance [1] | –3.7 | –4.8 | –3.8 | –9.4 | –5.0 | 4.6 | 4.8 | 3.3 | 2.2 | 5.0 | 5.9 | 7.9 | 8.0 |
| Overall public sector deficit | 5.7 | 6.8 | 7.7 | 14.8 | 17.8 | 8.0 | 6.4 | 8.7 | 14.8 | 15.0 | 11.3 | 5.4 | 3.6 |
| Financing | | | | | | | | | | | | | |
| External financing, net | 2.5 | 2.4 | 2.5 | 7.5 | 3.7 | 3.4 | 1.3 | 0.1 | –0.2 | 2.6 | –0.5 | –0.4 | 0.7 |
| Domestic financing, net | 3.2 | 4.4 | 5.2 | 7.3 | 14.1 | 4.6 | 5.1 | 8.6 | 15.0 | 12.4 | 11.8 | 5.9 | 3.0 |
| Bank of Mexico | 2.6 | 3.2 | 3.3 | 4.3 | 7.4 | 4.2 | 2.6 | 4.0 | 5.3 | 0.4 | 5.6 | 1.2 | 1.6 |
| Banks (official and commercial) | 0.4 | 1.0 | 1.1 | 2.8 | 4.7 | –0.3 | 1.4 | 3.7 | 7.9 | 7.2 | –0.5 | –0.2 | –4.5 |
| Bonds placed outside the banking system | 0.2 | 0.2 | 0.8 | 0.2 | 2.0 | 0.7 | 1.1 | 0.9 | 1.8 | 4.8 | 6.7 | 4.9 | 5.9 |

Sources: Secretariat of Finance of Public Credit; and Fund staff estimates.
[1] A positive number means a surplus.

the next sections are as follows: (1) During the period 1978–82, the estimated proxy for the long-run inflation rate exceeded the observed inflation rate; the divergence became very large in 1981–82. (2) Adjustment efforts undertaken to correct fiscal imbalances during 1983–84 resulted in a sharp decline in the proxy for the long-run inflation rate, which in fact dropped below the observed inflation rate. (3) This pattern was reversed during 1985–86, when the fiscal stance deteriorated reflecting, partly, two adverse shocks faced by the Mexican economy, namely, the earthquake that struck Mexico City in 1985 and the sharp decline in oil prices in 1986. (4) Consistent with a strong fiscal effort in 1987, the proxy for the long-run inflationary tax rate declined significantly. However, owing to factors discussed below—including rigidities in the wage salary structure—the observed rate of inflation remained very high. (5) Since the implementation of the recent economic stabilization program in 1988, which involved further adjustments in the fiscal stance combined with structural reforms and the adoption of an incomes policy, both the long-run and the observed inflation rates declined significantly. However, as will be shown below, economic agents' concerns about the permanence of the economic policies during 1988–89 may have resulted in an observed inflation rate that was higher than the one that was consistent with the fiscal stance in the long run. Moreover, the negative value obtained for the proxy for the long-run inflation tax rate during 1990 indicates that the fiscal stance not only ceased to require the inflationary tax as a source of finance, but even exerted deflationary pressures on the economy.

The next three sections analyze the three most recent subperiods and attempt to provide an explanation for the divergence between the observed inflation rate and the proxy for the long-run rate.

## Unsustainable Public Sector Deficits and Balance of Payments Crisis, 1978–82

The evolution of the public sector deficit and the sources of financing during 1978–90 are shown in Table 5. During the period 1978–82, the overall public sector deficit as a proportion of GDP tripled. While credit from the central bank was the main source of finance in 1978, foreign loans became the most important contributor to the financing of the government deficit by 1981. As shown in Table 4, the inflation rate averaged 22 percent during the period 1978–81.[8]

While the availability of external loans allowed the Government to finance the deficit without a substantial increase in the inflation rate during the period 1978–81, the situation was not sustainable. Consider equation (2) once more. An increase in the primary deficit largely financed by foreign debt produces a bigger rise in the left-hand side of equation (2) than in the right-hand side, owing to the interest payments on the increased debt. For the budget constraint to be satisfied, an additional variable

---

[8] A comprehensive analysis of the Mexican economy covering developments since the late 1950s to 1986 is contained in Buffie (1990).

in equation (2) needs to adjust.[9] In the context of this simple framework, an increased fiscal deficit would be consistent with an unchanged rate of inflation in the long run only if any of the following conditions (or a combination of them) holds: (1) there is a sustainable increase in output growth that would provide for sufficient resources to service the external debt, (2) there is a further and sustainable inflow of foreign funds, and (3) there is an increase in the desired holdings of domestic real money.

None of these conditions held in the Mexican economy. Appendix II discusses the reasons that prevented conditions (1) and (2) from holding. In essence, a large proportion of government investment—in particular, by the government-owned state enterprises—that was undertaken during the period 1978–81 did not contribute to the long-run productive capacity of the economy.[10] Finally, as evidenced by the large amounts of capital flight and the resulting balance of payments crisis of 1982 (to be discussed below), condition (3) also did not hold. Specifically, real holdings of money (as measured by currency in circulation plus demand deposits denominated in domestic money) declined by 15 percent during 1982.[11]

The discussion above serves to explain how the persistence of large fiscal deficits in the Mexican economy during the period 1978–81 exerted substantial inflationary pressures on the economy, even when they were not fully financed by monetary expansion and the economy was experiencing a short-run expansion in output. As domestic residents' perceptions about the unsustainability of the nonmonetary sources of finance increased, they moved away from domestic money in the expectation that the Government would need to rely increasingly on the inflationary tax as a source of financing the rising fiscal deficits. As a result, in every year during the period 1978–81 the estimated proxy for the inflationary tax rate needed to finance the fiscal deficit in the long run surpassed the observed inflation rate (see Table 4). The discrepancy between the two rates reached a maximum in 1981 when the largest primary deficit experienced during the period was registered (see Table 3). As the demand for real money declined, capital flight accelerated and the speed of new foreign lending to Mexico declined in 1982, the share of credit from the central bank in the

### Table 6. Depreciation of the Exchange Rate Consistent with Fiscal Deficit
*(In percent)*

|  | Actual Depreciation of Exchange Rate | Long-Run Depreciation of Exchange Rate Consistent with Fiscal Deficit | Average Premium in Forward Market for Mexican Peso[1] |
|---|---|---|---|
| 1978 | 0.1 | 11.9 | 14.4 |
| 1979 | 0.4 | 13.4 | 21.2 |
| 1980 | 2.0 | 15.4 | 41.7 |
| 1981 | 12.9 | 69.6 | 81.1 |
| 1982 | 465.7 | 93.6 | 127.7 |

Source: Table 4; International Monetary Fund, *International Financial Statistics*, various issues; Chicago Mercantile Exchange, *International Money Market Yearbook*, various issues; and Fund staff estimates.
[1]The premium is defined as the ratio of the 30-days' forward exchange rate to the spot exchange rate. Data correspond to the average premium for the year.

financing of the overall fiscal deficit (17.8 percent of GDP) increased substantially from 29 percent (in 1981) to 42 percent (in 1982). Inflation increased sharply and the economy experienced a balance of payments crisis that ended with a large depreciation of the Mexican peso.

Indeed, the same analysis can be used to show how the exchange rate policy undertaken by the authorities also was not sustainable, using equation (3) to obtain a proxy for the depreciation of the exchange rate that would have been consistent with the fiscal deficit in the long run. Table 6 shows that during 1978–81 the exchange rate policy followed by the authorities was inconsistent with the expansionary fiscal policy that was being pursued. It also shows how the discrepancy between the proxy for the long-run depreciation of the Mexican peso and the actual depreciation increased continuously during the period. The perception that the exchange rate system had to be abandoned if large fiscal deficits were to continue was also reflected in the evolution of the forward exchange rate. As shown in the third column of Table 7, the premium in the forward market for the Mexican peso also increased continuously during the period. This suggests that economic agents' perceptions about the sustainability of the exchange rate regime sharply deteriorated as inflationary pressures mounted in the Mexican economy.

It is estimated that the flight of capital increased sharply during 1981 and 1982 (Table 7).[12] This shift away from

---

[9] Once again, it is important to recall that the usefulness of this exercise lies in evaluating the long-run consistency between fiscal policies and other key macroeconomic variables, but cannot be used to explain the behavior of either inflation or economic activity. Such a task would require the specification of a complete macroeconomic model.

[10] Moreover, Appendix II shows that the net flows of foreign debt consistent with satisfying the condition that the government be solvent on a long-run basis (in the sense of being able to repay its outstanding debt) were much lower than the actual flows.

[11] The studies by Ramirez-Rojas (1985) and Ortiz (1983) show that the phenomenon of currency substitution—the substitution of foreign money for domestic money by domestic residents—was evident in Mexico during this period. Their empirical analyses show that holdings of domestic real money were inversely related to expectations about the devaluation of the Mexican peso.

[12] In addition, deposits in U.S. dollars denominated accounts also increased sharply. Perceptions of a possible devaluation were reinforced in mid-1981 when developments in the oil market indicated that the planned sales of oil by the Mexican Government could not be made without a reduction in the price of oil. (See Zedillo (1985) for a further discussion of these developments.)

**Table 7. External Debt and Resource Transfer as Financing Components of Capital Flight**

*(In billions of U.S. dollars)*

| | Change in Stock of Capital Flight | Change in Total External Debt | Resource Balance[1] | Change in Net International Reserves |
|---|---|---|---|---|
| 1978 | 0.1 | 4.1 | −1.2 | 0.5 |
| 1979 | — | 6.6 | −2.4 | 0.9 |
| 1980 | −0.2 | 11.0 | −4.7 | 0.9 |
| 1981 | 11.6 | 23.7 | −6.5 | 1.1 |
| 1982 | 6.4 | 8.0 | 5.9 | −6.2 |
| 1983 | 2.7 | 2.8 | 14.7 | 5.5 |
| 1984 | 1.6 | 3.1 | 14.3 | 3.0 |

Sources: Gurria and Fadl (1991), p. 6.
[1] Defined as net exports of goods and nonfactor services.

the Mexican peso and into foreign accounts exerted great pressure in the stock of foreign reserves, which declined by $6 billion in 1982, after recording an average increase of $1 billion a year from 1978 to 1981. During 1978–81, capital flight was more than offset by the increasingly large inflows of foreign loans. As a result, international reserves expanded and the resource balance—net exports of goods and nonfactor services—was negative. As the proceeds from exports and other external inflows were still used to finance imports, the impact of capital flight on growth was not perceived as severe. The situation changed drastically in 1982, when Mexico faced a sharp reduction in its access to external credit. Greater capital flight had to be financed through reduction in international reserves and a contraction in net imports, which impinged negatively on economic growth. Facing the pressures on international reserves exerted by the large amounts of capital flight, the authorities implemented two large devaluations of the mexican peso during 1982.[13]

## Fiscal Adjustment, Domestic Debt, and the Persistence of Inflation, 1983–87

In contrast with developments during 1978–82, there was a marked fiscal adjustment at the level of the primary balance in the period 1983–87.[14] In spite of these efforts, the inflation rate averaged 89 percent during this period and peaked during 1987 at 160 percent. In addition, with the exception of a temporary recovery in 1984,

economic activity remained weak and, on average, real GDP contracted by 0.2 percent a year during the period. This section examines the factors that may have contributed to the persistence of inflation and the extent to which the fiscal adjustment undertaken during the period was insufficient to achieve the Government's stabilization goals.

### Shift from Foreign to Domestic Debt, 1983–84

In December 1982, Mexico embarked on a stabilization program to reduce inflation and improve balance of payments conditions by reducing the public sector deficit and the monetary expansion of the central bank.

In the context of sharply reduced access to international capital markets, fiscal deficits were financed increasingly by the sale of government bonds to the banking system and the public.[15] This form of financing resulted in a sharp increase in real rates of interest. As shown in Table 3, real interest rates on treasury bills, measured on either an ex ante or an ex post basis, moved from being highly negative in 1982 to being positive in 1983–84.

It is estimated that capital flight continued during 1983, albeit at a lower rate than in 1982 (see Table 7). The continuation of capital flight in the context of severely reduced access to international capital markets implies that the buildup of international reserves that Mexico achieved during 1983–84 was only possible through substantial transfers of real resources, which imposed an important constraint on growth.

Although the stabilization efforts reduced the inflation rate during 1983 and 1984, inflation remained high and above the proxy for the estimated rate that would be sustainable if the surplus in the primary balance were to be maintained (see Table 4). Consider equation (2) once more. As Table 4 indicates, the fiscal efforts during 1983–84 led to a substantial reduction of the left-hand side of equation (2). The exercise conducted earlier suggests that the fiscal policy may have been consistent in the long run with a significant reduction of inflation even in the context of sharply reduced access to foreign financing. In the short run, however, the crowding out of private investment arising from the need to finance public deficits with domestic debt and the substantial transfer of real resources exacerbated the slowdown of economic activity and the persistence of inflation. Had the fiscal efforts continued, increased confidence in the program might have improved, which would have then translated into an increased demand for domestic real money (a further

---

[13] The perception of economic agents regarding the probability of a devaluation are examined in Blanco and Garber (1986).
[14] See Section II for a description of the fiscal effort during this period.

---

[15] The $3.4 billion of net external financing in 1983 reflects new loans amounting to $5 billion to the public sector in the context of rescheduling operations with commercial banks. Indeed, during the period 1983–90, new credit to the Mexican Government was largely accounted for by official credit and restructural arrangements with external commercial banks.

reduction in capital flight) and a decline in inflationary pressure.

Part of this convergence toward a lower rate of inflation actually occurred in 1984. As the primary surplus continued to increase during that year (relative to GDP), economic activity recovered and inflation declined. Consistent with these developments, capital flight decreased significantly in 1984.

### Adverse Shocks and Renewal of Inflationary Pressures, 1985–86

As previously described, pressures on the fiscal stance including those arising from significant fiscal rigidities, were clearly evident during 1985–86.[16] The weakening of the fiscal position renewed the inflationary pressures in the economy and caused the estimated proxy for the long-run inflationary tax rate to exceed the observed rate of inflation during 1985–86 (see Table 4). As the fiscal stance deteriorated, the Government needed to rely increasingly on the issuance of domestic debt as a source of finance. Indeed, the stock of public sector domestic debt—excluding debt held by the central bank—increased from 3 percent of GDP at the end of 1984 to 5.4 percent at the end of 1986. Higher real interest rates, crowding out of domestic private investment, and further financial disintermediation (as evidenced by a decline in real money balances), followed. Indeed, as indicated in Table 3, real interest rates (on an ex ante basis) may have exceeded 20 percent by 1986.

In examining equation (2) once more, we find that the decline in economic activity and in real money balances, as well as rising real interest rates, implies that in the steady state the inflationary tax rate would have to accelerate even further to finance the overall fiscal sector deficit. An important lesson from these developments is that increasing fiscal deficits are inflationary in the long run because there is a limit to the sales of public sector bonds to the private sector. As this limit is approached, the persistence of fiscal deficits requires the inflationary tax as a financing source.

### Wage Indexation and Persistence of Inflation, 1987

A new economic program, initiated in 1987, focused on improving the fiscal stance and maintaining monetary discipline. During 1987, the primary surplus reached 5 percent of GDP and credit from the central bank to the Government constituted only 3 percent of the financing of the public accounts. However, as in the previous attempts to achieve a sustainable reduction of inflation and a recovery in economic activity, the strong reliance of the public sector on domestic debt and its effects on real

interest rates constituted an important constraint in achieving the desired targets.

While many similarities existed between the adjustment efforts in 1983–84 and those implemented in 1987, there were two important differences. First, by 1987, the real stock of public sector domestic debt held by the private sector was significantly higher than at the end of 1984, which increased the perceived risks involved in holding domestic assets. As a result, real interest rates (on an ex ante basis) remained high in spite of the fiscal adjustment (see Table 3). Second, while minimum wages were adjusted twice a year in 1984, they were adjusted five times in 1987, introducing a de facto wage-indexation scheme that contributed to the persistence of inflation. As a result, the observed rate of inflation was significantly higher than the proxy for the long-run rate in 1987 (see Table 4). As is well known, however, wage indexation may sustain the inflationary process for a longer time than in the absence of indexation, but it can not produce a steady-state inflation rate different from the one that would result from a non-indexed process, unless an increase in monetary expansion were to validate the increases in nominal wages. In the absence of such a monetary expansion, the inflation rate would decline in the long run. In the process, a reduction in the rate of increase in wages associated with the decline in inflation constitutes an additional factor contributing to the achievement of lower inflation.

The policy response to these considerations was the introduction in December 1987 of a comprehensive program in which orthodox fiscal and monetary policies were complemented by a freeze in wages and prices, and the pegging of the exchange rate in the context of a social pact between labor, business, and the Government.

### Dynamics of a Successful Stabilization Program, 1988–91

The main features of the economic program initiated in December 1987 are discussed in detail in Section II.[17] By 1991, Mexico's achievements were impressive; inflation is estimated to have declined to 19 percent by the end of 1991; real GDP grew by an estimated 4 percent; and the overall balance of payments registered a surplus of $5 billion in the first ten months of 1991. These achievements, which some observers have called the "Mexican miracle," were not obtained, however, without difficulties. This section focuses on two crucial and related problems that the Mexican authorities faced in achieving and consolidating their stabilization efforts: (1) the initial concerns of economic agents about the maintenance of the economic program, in general, and in the announced exchange rate policy in particular, and (2) the persistence

---

[16] See also Ize and Ortiz (1987).

[17] Also, see Ortiz (1991).

of high real interest rates, which raised doubts about the sustainability of the adjustment effort.

## The Credibility Problem

The incomes policy undertaken under the December 1987 program broke the process of wage indexation, and as such the inflation rate declined from 160 percent during 1987 to 52 percent during 1988. In spite of this progress, concerns about the sustainability of the economic program remained, in particular, with respect to the Government's ability to maintain the announced fixed exchange rate policy.

An indication of such concerns with regard to the exchange rate policy can be obtained by comparing the actual depreciation of the currency with a measure of the expected depreciation of the exchange rate as represented by the interest rate differential between a peso-denominated Mexican treasury bill (CETES) and a dollar-denominated Mexican treasury bill (PAGAFES).[18] The evidence shown in Chart 4 suggests that expectations of the future spot exchange rate consistently overestimated the actual future rate, indicating lack of full credibility in the exchange rate policy. This differential was greatest during 1988 when, with the exception of a small change in February, the exchange rate was pegged to the U.S. dollar.

The most serious effect of these concerns about the sustainability of the exchange rate policy was on the external position. In the context of an acceleration of the trade reform, expectations of a future devaluation resulted in a sharp increase in private sector imports, a deterioration of the current account, and—given the lack of access to international capital markets and the amortization and interest payments on the large outstanding stock of external debt—a loss in international reserves of $6.8 billion during 1988.

An additional problem was that, in the context of the structural reforms that included the liberalization of financial markets, interest rate parity implied high domestic interest rates. To the extent that the incomes policy was successful, at least partially, in reducing inflationary expectations, the increase in nominal interest rates also involved an increase in real interest rates. As shown in Table 3, on an ex ante basis, real interest rates attained an average of 24 percent during 1988.[19]

High real interest rates impinged negatively on the fiscal deficit as shown in Table 5; issuance of domestic debt continued to be the most important source of financing of

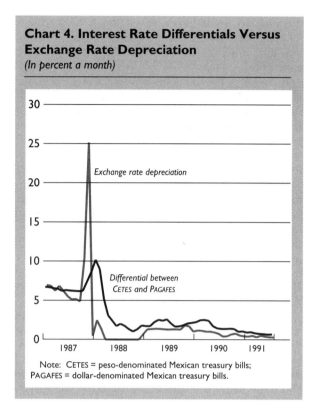

### Chart 4. Interest Rate Differentials Versus Exchange Rate Depreciation
*(In percent a month)*

Note: CETES = peso-denominated Mexican treasury bills; PAGAFES = dollar-denominated Mexican treasury bills.

the fiscal deficit. As fiscal deficits increase, further issuance of domestic public debt becomes necessary, raising real interest rates even further and depressing economic activity. The slowdown in economic growth would, in turn, increase the attractiveness of the inflationary tax relative to the issuance of government bonds as a source of financing for the fiscal deficit. Indeed, as it was evident from the behavior of the monetary aggregates, the Government at times intervened in the credit market to prevent further rises in interest rates, reinforcing expectations about a probable abandonment of the program.

## The Policy Response: Overshooting the Primary Surplus and the Depreciation of the Mexican Peso

As shown in Table 4, the high real interest rates experienced during 1988 implied that the estimated proxy for the inflation tax rate needed to finance the fiscal deficit in

---

[18] See Khor and Rojas-Suarez (1991) for a study on interest rate parity in Mexico.

[19] International perceptions of Mexico's creditworthiness also contributed to the persistence of high real domestic interest rates. As shown in Khor and Rojas-Suarez (1991), the evidence suggests that the domestic and external U.S. dollar-denominated debt issued by Mexico are linked on the basis of default risk, that is, there appears to be no perceived differences in the credit standing of domestic and external debt of Mexico, implying that both kinds of debt are subject

to the same country risk premium. Since the price in the secondary market for Mexican external debt reflects a risk premium associated with the probability of default, the paper shows that domestic interest rates of Mexican assets denominated in U.S. dollars are closely linked to the behavior of the implicit yield derived from the secondary market for Mexican debt. Perceptions of default risk on total Mexican debt (either domestic or external) would then contribute to the persistence of high real interest rates.

the long run would have reached almost 83 percent.[20] Although this was below the average inflation rate of that year, it was inconsistent with the objectives of the authorities.

In response, the authorities reinforced their economic program in 1989. The evidence indicates that these policies had the desired effect. As shown in Chart 4, the differential between the spread in the interest rates on Cetes and Pagafes and the preannounced depreciation of the exchange rate declined sharply during 1989–90 and even further during 1991, indicating that the credibility of exchange rate policy improved substantially. Moreover, real interest rates (estimated either on an ex ante or an ex post basis) declined, slowly at first during 1989 and much faster in 1990, especially after the completion of the financing package with commercial banks.[21] As a result, the overall public sector deficit declined and new issuance of government bonds as a percentage of GDP declined in 1989 for the first time since 1985, reinforcing the reduction in real interest rates (see Table 5).

An examination of Table 4 suggests that the fiscal adjustment of 1989–90 was somewhat greater than the improvement in the primary surplus needed for price stability in the long run. By 1989, the financing of the fiscal deficit would have been consistent with an estimated proxy for the inflation tax rate of slightly more than 10 percent in the long run, and, by 1990, the maintenance of the observed fiscal stance would have exerted deflationary pressures on the economy. By 1991, the primary surplus is estimated to have declined to 6 percent of GDP. In light of the previous discussion, the decline in the primary surplus appears compatible with a further reduction in the inflation rate.

In the context of the improved credibility of government policies and the associated recovery of the Mexican economy, a question remains: to what extent does the incomes policy associated with the social pact still impose a distortion on relative prices and, therefore, a constraint on growth? Chart 5 shows the ratio of controlled items and noncontrolled items. While the ratio declined sharply during 1988 and part of 1989, it started increasing again by the end of 1989 and, by mid-1990, was close to unity. This pattern indicates that the distortions in relative prices originally created by the pact have been, at least partially, reversed in recent years. Moreover, although real minimum wages have remained well below wages negotiated in the free market, it is important to recall that only about

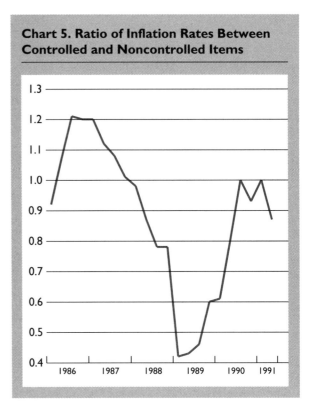

**Chart 5. Ratio of Inflation Rates Between Controlled and Noncontrolled Items**

20 percent of the labor force receive minimum wages. These developments taken together indicate that the pact has incorporated a great deal of flexibility and that, implicitly, the authorities have chosen to abandon it in a gradual form. To a large extent, it appears as if, de facto, the social pact no longer constrains the functioning of efficient resource allocation in the Mexican economy.

## Conclusion

This section has used a simple framework based on the government budget constraint to analyze the consistency of macroeconomic policies undertaken by the Mexican authorities during the period 1978–91.

An important conclusion derived from examining this experience is that the interaction between the actual implementation of economic policies and economic agents' perceptions about the sustainability of those policies can explain, to a large extent, the behavior of certain key macroeconomic variables during the three subperiods under study. For example, the persistence of large fiscal deficits during 1978–81 created substantial inflationary pressures in the economy, even when a large proportion of those deficits was financed through foreign loans and output was expanding. As concern about the unsustain-

---

[20] To the extent that the persistence of economic policies would have reduced real interest rates even in the absence of further adjustments in the fiscal deficit, the "true" long-run inflation tax rate would have been lower.

[21] An examination of the real interest rate on a quarterly basis (presented in Appendix I) indicates that ex ante real interest rates declined sharply during the third and fourth quarter of 1989 following the announcement of an agreement with commercial banks to reduce Mexico's external debt and debt-service obligations. See also El-Erian (1991).

ability of fiscal policy increased, domestic economic agents moved away from domestic money in the expectation that the Government would increasingly need to rely on the inflationary tax as a source of finance and on a devaluation of the Mexican peso. Inflationary expectations were validated in 1982. As capital flight accelerated and new foreign loans to Mexico were severely curtailed, the Government increased its reliance on monetary financing; inflation increased sharply and the economy experienced a balance of payments crisis that ended with a large depreciation of the Mexican peso.

Concern about the sustainability of the fiscal and monetary efforts was also a major factor limiting the success of adjustment programs in the period 1983–87. After a partial reduction of inflation during 1983–84 resulting from a substantial improvement in the fiscal stance, existing rigidities in the fiscal structure and adverse shocks resulted in a reduction of the fiscal primary surplus. As the fiscal stance deteriorated, the Government relied increasingly on the issuance of domestic debt. Fiscal deficits exerted inflationary pressures, even when domestic bond issuance rather than money was mostly used as a financing instrument, as the resulting rise in real interest rates increased the probability that the Government would resort to the inflationary tax and to an acceleration of the rate of depreciation of the peso.

The analysis of the Mexican experience from 1978 to 1987 led to an important lesson: Although tight fiscal and monetary policies were essential tools in achieving a sustainable reduction in inflation in the long run, rigidities in the public and financial sectors, as well as lack of access to foreign credit markets, made economic programs vulnerable and highly sensitive to adverse shocks. Moreover, it was evident that economic agents' concerns about the maintenance of the announced policies could jeopardize the adjustment efforts by inducing capital flight and balance of payments problems. These considerations were at the core of the design of the comprehensive program launched by the Government in December 1987. Incomes policy was implemented as a complement to tight fiscal and monetary policies to control inflationary expectations.

# Appendix I   Real Interest Rates in Mexico

## Real Interest Rates in Mexico

| Year | Ex Post Real Interest Rates [1] | Expected Inflation Rates [2] | Ex Ante Real Interest Rates [3] | Year | Ex Post Real Interest Rates [1] | Expected Inflation Rates [2] | Ex Ante Real Interest Rates [3] |
|---|---|---|---|---|---|---|---|
| 1978 = Q1 | -4.5 | | | 1985 = Q1 | 19.4 | 43.4 | -4.1 |
| Q2 | -5.9 | | -11.1 | Q2 | 25.7 | 60.6 | 24.8 |
| Q3 | -1.5 | 21.6 | -11.4 | Q3 | 16.7 | 41.0 | 25.1 |
| Q4 | -12.8 | 22.8 | -6.9 | Q4 | -0.8 | 43.6 | 20.4 |
| 1979 = Q1 | -0.3 | 20.1 | -16.1 | 1986 = Q1 | 17.3 | 53.7 | 5.3 |
| Q2 | -0.6 | 31.2 | -6.7 | Q2 | 12.3 | 73.2 | 22.5 |
| Q3 | -2.3 | 21.6 | -6.4 | Q3 | 18.8 | 61.5 | 24.0 |
| Q4 | -16.5 | 22.3 | -6.4 | Q4 | 18.4 | 70.4 | 31.8 |
| 1980 = Q1 | -0.82 | 24.7 | -15.8 | 1987 = Q1 | 13.1 | 73.8 | 18.2 |
| Q2 | -3.9 | 38.7 | -6.4 | Q2 | 9.4 | 83.6 | 13.5 |
| Q3 | 3.7 | 28.4 | -7.1 | Q3 | -3.5 | 84.9 | 10.4 |
| Q4 | -3.5 | 31.1 | 1.4 | Q4 | -18.5 | 85.1 | 33.0 |
| 1981 = Q1 | 5.0 | 26.2 | -6.9 | 1988 = Q1 | 35.4 | 80.0 | 39.6 |
| Q2 | 7.6 | 36.1 | -1.1 | Q2 | 15.3 | 39.2 | 18.2 |
| Q3 | 8.8 | 29.5 | 6.4 | Q3 | 20.3 | 14.8 | 10.8 |
| Q4 | -11.0 | 27.1 | 2.3 | Q4 | 29.5 | 21.2 | 27.8 |
| 1982 = Q1 | -21.8 | 30.7 | -10.7 | 1989 = Q1 | 32.9 | 23.2 | 33.9 |
| Q2 | -24.4 | 47.1 | -5.7 | Q2 | 42.2 | 14.8 | 38.2 |
| Q3 | -25.1 | 57.9 | -20.4 | Q3 | 17.8 | 16.8 | 11.3 |
| Q4 | -36.2 | 73.8 | -13.2 | Q4 | 2.5 | 24.4 | 7.1 |
| 1983 = Q1 | 2.7 | 73.1 | -20.4 | 1990 = Q1 | 24.5 | 33.2 | 26.1 |
| Q2 | 13.3 | 89.1 | 0.6 | Q2 | 15.8 | 19.6 | 18.3 |
| Q3 | 9.0 | 61.7 | 4.5 | Q3 | 8.7 | 19.2 | 2.5 |
| Q4 | -8.9 | 51.2 | 3.7 | Q4 | 8.5 | 29.2 | 6.0 |
| 1984 = Q1 | -2.1 | 49.6 | -16.6 | 1991 = Q1 | 10.5 | 24.4 | |
| Q2 | 12.7 | 62.8 | 0.2 | | | | |
| Q3 | 9.6 | 50.5 | 7.6 | | | | |
| Q4 | -10.9 | 41.9 | 5.7 | | | | |

Note: CETES = peso-denominated Mexican treasury bill.

[1] Three-month CETES minus the inflation rate observed in the subsequent quarter.

[2] For the period 1978:1–1988:2, data correspond to estimations using an autoregressive process of the following form: $\Delta pt = 0.0238 + 0.8497 \Delta p_{t-1} + u_t$ where $\Delta p_t$ is the inflation rate in period $t$ and $u_t$ is a white noise disturbance. For the period 1988:3–1991:1, data are taken from Section VIII of this report.

[3] Three-month CETES minus the inflation rate expected to prevail in the subsequent quarter.

# Appendix II    Derivation of the Steady-State Requirement for Inflationary Finance

From equation (2) in the main text, the derivation of the proxy for the steady-state rate of inflation consistent with the fiscal deficit requires estimating the value of *def, m, dd,* $\Delta fd$ and $\rho$. The estimation of *def* has already been discussed and presented in Table 3. While the series for *m* (the stock of domestic money—defined here as M1—as a proportion of GDP) and *dd* (the stock of public sector domestic debt—excluding debt held by the Central Bank—as a proportion of GDP) have been obtained from the Banco de México, it is necessary to introduce some assumptions regarding the steady-state rate of output growth ($\rho$) and the sustainability of foreign finance for each subperiod under study.

With respect to the steady-state rate of growth of output, the following considerations were taken into account:

(a) Although actual real GDP grew at an average rate of about 8 percent during the period 1978–81 fueled by a rapid rise in government expenditures, it is widely agreed that such real growth could not be sustainable. Since the addition of foreign resources had little impact on productive capacity, it is assumed here that the sustainable rate of growth during the period 1978–81 did not differ substantially from the average rate of about 4 percent experienced in the previous four-year period—1974–77.

(b) In the context of a sharply reduced access to international capital markets during the period 1982–87, Mexico experienced an average rate of growth of –2 percent. While part of such negative growth was due to exogenous adverse factors, it is assumed here that the debt-overhang problem (i.e., the effects of a large outstanding external debt on domestic private investment) and the associated lack of investors' confidence in the Mexican economy imposed a zero rate of growth constraint in the economy during that period.

(c) On the basis of the comprehensive adjustment and structural program that has been undertaken by the authorities since 1988 and the significant debt-reduction operations conducted under the Brady plan, a sustainable rate of growth of 1 percent was assumed for 1988 and a rate of 3.5 percent was assumed for the period 1989–90. A higher rate of growth for 1989–90 relative to 1988 reflects the assumption of a positive effect on output growth of the reduction in the stock of debt.

Next, it is necessary to specify assumptions regarding the sustainable flow of public sector external debt. The issue of the sustainability of external debt inflows, as discussed earlier, arose in Mexico during the period 1978–81.[22] Two elements were considered here:

(a) Large amounts of capital flight accompanied the increase in external debt during this period. Since, by definition, capital flight constitutes resources that are not used to increase the productive capacity in the economy, it is necessary to subtract capital flight flows from total foreign inflows in order to obtain an approximate magnitude of the funds available to finance the government budget deficit. Therefore, estimates of the stock of capital flight were subtracted from the recorded stock of public sector debt to obtain an estimate of the adjusted stock of foreign debt available for financing the activities of the public sector.

(b) The condition that the government be solvent on a long-run basis in the sense of being able to repay its outstanding debt was assumed here.[23] This solvency condition, which requires that the present value of foreign debt be nonnegative, was imposed on the estimated adjusted stock of foreign debt to obtain an estimation of the inflow of foreign debt that could have been repaid without rescheduling operations. The estimations yielded the following approximation for the sustainable inflow of foreign debt as proportion of GDP ($\Delta f$):

|      | Actual $\Delta f$ | Sustainable $\Delta f$ |
|------|------|------|
| 1978 | 2.5  | 1.1  |
| 1979 | 2.4  | 1.2  |
| 1980 | 2.6  | 1.3  |
| 1981 | 7.4  | 2.8  |

As shown above, the actual net inflow of foreign capital during the period 1978–81 was much greater than the net flow of foreign debt that would have been consistent with the solvency condition.

---

[22] The issue of sustainability of foreign inflows did not arise during the period 1983–89, since external creditors largely ceased to extend loans to Mexican residents during that period. In this section, sustainable private foreign flows were then assumed to equal zero during that period. Since the signature of the agreement on the financing package with commercial banks in early 1990, Mexico has started its return to voluntary capital market financing. It is in this context that, for 1990, actual foreign flows are assumed to be consistent with the long-run solvency requirement of the Mexican Government.

[23] The solvency condition implies that the rate of growth of foreign debt to GDP should be lower than the foreign interest rate minus the rate of output growth. See Blanchard (1990) and Horne (1991).

# References

Blanchard, Olivier Jean, "Suggestions for a New Set of Fiscal Indicators" (Paris: OECD, Economics and Statistics Department, Working Papers, 1990).

Blanco, Herminio, and Peter Garber, "Recurrent Devaluation and Speculative Attacks on the Mexican Peso," *Journal of Political Economy,* Vol. 94 (February 1986), pp. 148–66.

Buffie, Edward F., "Economic Policy and Foreign Debt in Mexico," in *Developing Country Debt and Economic Performance*, Vol. 2, ed. by Jeffrey D. Sachs (Chicago: University of Chicago Press, 1990), pp. 393–551.

Calvo, Guillermo, and Roque Fernandez, "Pauta Cambiaria y Deficit Fiscal" in *Inflacion y Estabilidad*, ed. by Roque Fernandez and Carlos A. Rodrigues (Buenos Aires: Ediciones Maachi, 1982), pp. 175–79.

Chicago Mercantile Exchange, *International Money Market Yearbook*, various issues.

El-Erian, Mohamed, "Mexico's External Debt and the Return to Voluntary Capital Market Financing," IMF Working Paper, WP/91/83 (Washington: International Monetary Fund, August 1991).

Gil Diaz, Francisco, and Paul Ramos Tercero, "Lessons from Mexico," in *Inflation Stabilization: The Experience of Israel, Argentina, Brazil, Bolivia, and Mexico*, ed. by Michael Bruno and others (Cambridge, Massachusetts: MIT Press, 1988), pp. 361–90.

Guidotti, Pablo E., and Manmohan S. Kumar, *Domestic Public Debt of Externally Indebted Countries*, IMF Occasional Paper, No. 80 (Washington: International Monetary Fund, 1991).

Gurria, J., and R. Fadl, "Estimacion de la Fuga de Capitales en México, 1970–1990," serie de monografia, no. 4 (Washington: Banco Interamericano de Desarrollo, 1991).

International Monetary Fund, *International Financial Statistics* (Washington, various issues).

Ize, Alain, and Guillermo Ortiz, "Fiscal Rigidities, Public Debt and Capital Flight," *Staff Papers*, International Monetary Fund (Washington), Vol. 34 (June 1987), pp. 311–32.

Horne, Jocelyn, "Indicators of Fiscal Sustainability," IMF Working Paper, WP/91/5 (Washington: International Monetary Fund, January 1991).

Khor, Hoe E., and Liliana Rojas-Suarez, "Interest Rates in Mexico: The Role of Exchange Rate Expectations and International Creditworthiness," *Staff Papers*, International Monetary Fund (Washington), Vol. 38 (December 1991), pp. 850–71.

Ortiz, Guillermo, "Currency Substitution in Mexico: The Dollarization Problem," *Journal of Money, Credit and Banking*, Vol. 15 (May 1983), pp. 174–85.

_____,"Mexico Beyond the Debt Crisis: Toward Sustainable Growth with Price Stability" in *Lessons of Economic Stabilization and Its Aftermath,* ed. by Michael Bruno and others (London: MIT Press, 1991), pp. 283–313.

Ramirez-Rojas, C.L., "Currency Substitution in Argentina, Mexico, and Uruguay," *Staff Papers*, International Monetary Fund (Washington), Vol. 32 (1985), pp. 629–67.

Rojas-Suarez, Liliana, "Risk and Capital Flight in Developing Countries" in *Determinants and Systemic Consequences of International Capital Flows*, IMF Occasional Paper, No. 77 (Washington: International Monetary Fund, 1991), pp. 83–92.

Zedillo, Ernesto, "The Mexican External Debt: The Last Decade," in *Politics and Economics of External Debt Crisis: The Latin American Experience,* ed. by Miguel S. Wionczek, in collaboration with Luciano Tomassini (Boulder and London: Westview Press, 1985), pp. 294–324.

# IV International Trade and Investment Liberalization: Mexico's Experience and Prospects

## Philippe Szymczak

In the wake of the debt crisis, Mexico embarked on a comprehensive reform of its international trade and investment policies. The reform aimed at a more complete integration of the Mexican economy into the world economy. This effort reflected the realization that an open trading environment and a liberalized foreign investment regime were essential to promote an efficient allocation of resources and enhance the external competitiveness of the economy.

In 1985, Mexico began liberalizing its international trade and investment regimes and dismantling unilaterally its tariff and nontariff trade barriers. In August 1986, it joined the General Agreement on Tariffs and Trade (GATT).[1] Import substitution policies and reliance on oil exports for foreign exchange earnings were replaced with policies aimed at attracting foreign investment, lowering trade barriers, and generally making the country more competitive in non-oil exports.

In the event, Mexico's external trade regime has been substantially liberalized; it has been transformed from an inward-looking economy into an open one, in a relatively short time. The incentive structure has been reoriented and major distortions have been removed, leading to major improvements in efficiency. Export growth has picked up and the export base has been diversified. The economy's productive base is being modernized as a result of the renewed access to imports at international prices. This has enabled Mexico to participate in the proposed North American Free Trade Area (NAFTA).

This section describes Mexico's international trade and investment policies prior to 1983; discusses the various stages of Mexico's trade and investment liberalization strategy since 1983; and assesses the impact of these reforms on the country's economic structure and performance. It then reviews the most recent trade liberalization initiatives, including the NAFTA and the recent initiatives with Chile, Colombia, and Venezuela, and the five Central American countries.

## International Trade and Investment Policies Prior to 1983

### A Historical Overview

In Mexico, import substitution policies and restrictions on foreign investment were a major part of the postwar development strategy. High tariffs and a wide-ranging import-licensing system on competing imports were put in place to encourage import substitution and a high degree of self-sufficiency. The 1982 balance of payments crisis initially led to a further tightening of Mexico's trade regime. Reliance on quantitative import controls reached the maximum degree of restrictiveness in 1982, and duties on selected items were increased further (the maximum tariff was 100 percent). Duties were particularly high on consumer goods and agricultural items. At this time, import-licensing requirements, or "prior import permits" (PIPs), were the primary policy tool used to control imports. In late 1982, virtually all imports required a prior permit. Finally, exchange restrictions reinforced trade restrictions.

As a result of the protective system, the overall incentive structure favored production for the domestic market. The average rate of effective protection for the home market was high, and the range of effective protection rates wide. Although some direct incentives for exports were provided, there was a distinct bias against exports. In the 1970s and early 1980s, the external competitiveness of most tradable goods industries deteriorated and non-oil exports were slowed by the combination of an appreciating exchange rate and severe import restrictions.[2]

Policies with respect to foreign direct investment were based on Article 27 of Mexico's Constitution, which specifically forbids foreign control of natural resources and other parts of the "national patrimony" and on the 1973 "Law to Promote Mexican Investment and Regulate Foreign Investment" (LFI). The LFI specifically reserves certain economic activities for the Government and oth-

---

[1] In addition to commitments to reduce tariffs and phase out quantitative restrictions (QRs), Mexico signed the GATT codes on licensing procedures, antidumping, customs valuation, and technical barriers to trade.

[2] Traditionally, export taxes played a relatively minor role and were applied mainly to petroleum products and agricultural exports. Similarly, export controls or prohibitions applied to a limited number of items.

ers for Mexican nationals. The first category includes petroleum and other hydrocarbons, basic petrochemicals, development of radioactive minerals and the generation of nuclear energy, mining in specified cases, electricity, railroads, telegraphic and wireless communications, and other specified activities. The second category includes radio and television, automotive transportation and transportation on federal highways, domestic air and maritime transportation, development of forestry resources, gas distribution, and other specified activities.

As a result of the implementation of restrictive investment policies, foreign direct investment played a relatively small and declining role in Mexico prior to the mid-1980s. The only form of foreign direct investment favored by the authorities was under the *maquiladora* (in-bond industry) program.[3] *Maquiladora* establishments were allowed to be 100 percent foreign owned, whereas other ventures were restricted to minority foreign ownership.

### Implications of Traditional Trade and Investment Policies

By the early 1980s, the long-term implications of the extensive protection of the domestic economy became apparent. Trade and exchange restrictions limited trade flows and severely distorted the relationship between international and domestic prices. The import substitution policy promoted and protected an industrial sector that was generally inefficient and therefore unable to compete in international markets. The wide disparities in effective protection across industries meant that resource allocation remained significantly distorted.

The restrictive legal and regulatory environment for foreign direct investment had deterred non-debt-creating capital inflows and instilled a structural bias in favor of foreign debt accumulation. As a result of its long-standing restrictive foreign investment policy, Mexico had, in 1985, the lowest share of foreign investment of any large nonsocialist country (about 5 percent of total gross fixed investment).[4]

Together with the marked recovery of domestic demand in 1984 and an appreciation of the peso in real effective terms, this trade policy stance contributed first to a deceleration of non-oil export growth, and then to a decline in 1985; at the same time, voluntary non-debt-creating capital flows dropped. Faced with such developments, the authorities adopted a far-reaching program of unilateral

trade and investment liberalization. Trade and investment policies were revised in stages to replace prior import permits by tariffs, ensure greater transparency of the effective protection structure, and reduce tariff dispersion.

## Policy Changes Since 1983

### Changes Prior to July 1985

During the first stage of trade liberalization, from early 1983 to July 1985, Mexican markets were only selectively opened to foreign participation, by relaxing the prior import permit requirement; at the same time, tariffs were raised and the tariff structure was rationalized, including through reducing tariff dispersion. The process began with a simplification of the import tariff schedule,[5] moderate reductions in import-licensing requirements, and some reductions in the number of items covered by official import reference prices. During this stage, import-licensing requirements for intermediate and capital goods that were not manufactured in the country were eliminated.[6] Overall, these liberalization measures remained limited in scope and by the middle of 1985 quantitative restrictions (import licenses and official reference price) still applied to about 75 percent of total imports. Moreover, restrictions continued to apply for nearly all items that could be produced domestically.

Regarding foreign direct investment, the authorities began to liberalize Mexico's foreign investment regime in the mid-1980s, moving away from a restrictive interpretation of the LFI in a series of successive regulations. The effects of such liberalization were manifest in an upward trend of foreign investment.

### Trade Reform Policies During 1985–90

The trade liberalization process was accelerated in July 1985 with a major liberalization of Mexico's trade and investment regimes. In stages, Mexico's trade reforms

---

[3] Under the *maquiladora* program introduced in 1965, component and raw materials needed for *maquiladora* operations are imported duty free. The finished products are then exported (mainly to the United States) with the manufacturer paying U.S. tariffs on the value added in Mexico only.

[4] See United States International Trade Commission (1985), p. 185 and (1990).

[5] The number of tariff categories was reduced from 13 to 10, but tariffs remained in the 0–100 percent range.

[6] This included the provision of unrestricted authorization for certain essential items, such as pharmaceuticals; the exemption from prior authorization for some 1,703 tariff items; the shift of certain raw materials and intermediate goods not produced locally to the free exchange market; the automatic approval of permits for 275 essential inputs for small and medium enterprises; the permission for unrestricted imports of machinery up to $100,000, subject to certain requirements; and selective authorizations to address problems associated with the scarcity of some items or oligopolistic practices in certain sectors. Concurrently, however, imports of 1,850 items were prohibited for protective reasons and to discourage the consumption of luxuries, and import quotas were set for a number of items; import authorizations for most of the items subject to prohibition or quota had not been granted since late 1981.

have reduced the coverage of quantitative restrictions, as well as the level and dispersion of tariffs. Import licensing was phased out gradually, while the use of official import prices was discontinued. To a lesser extent, the number of products subject to export taxation and control also has been reduced.

### The Phasing Out of Quantitative Restrictions

In order to foster a broadly neutral system of incentives, nontariff trade barriers were phased out in stages. Effective protection was lowered by shifting from QRs to tariffs and, subsequently, by reducing tariffs. In the process, the transparency of Mexico's structure of protection was enhanced.

As part of the reform of the import regime announced on July 25, 1985, the requirement of import permits for 3,604 tariff items (representing some 36 percent of the value of 1984 imports) was eliminated, reducing the ratio of controlled imports to total import value from 75 percent to 39 percent. Additional licensing requirements were eliminated in October 1986 and in April, July, and October 1987. These measures brought Mexico into compliance with its GATT accession commitment to eliminate import-licensing requirements to the fullest extent possible. By the end of 1987, only 329 tariff categories (out of more than 8,300 and representing about 23 percent of imports) were subject to prior licensing requirements.

The subsequent changes in the trade system have been relatively minor. In December 1989, changes affecting imports of new automobiles were announced.[7] The coverage of licensing requirements continued to be narrowed, and by the end of 1990 only 210 items, representing less than 15 percent of total imports, were subject to import licenses. The weighted average tariff rate of controlled items was 4.1 percent in 1990. The remaining QRs cover essentially agricultural (including exportable products, subject to support price controls and international marketing agreements), agro-industrial, and petroleum and derivative products. In the industrial sector, QRs apply mainly to sectors where sectoral programs continue to be implemented; they include pharmaceuticals, automobiles and auto parts, and microcomputers. Action plans for elimination of some of the remaining import controls have been prepared and have started to be implemented.

### Tariffs

The import tariff schedule introduced on July 25, 1985 reduced the highest Mexican tariff from 100 percent to 50 percent. In general, tariff rates under the new schedule increased with the degree of processing of the product, with goods produced domestically tending to have higher rates. As a result of the changes in tariff rates and other steps taken in the first half of 1985, the dispersion of the tariff schedule was reduced but the weighted tariff was raised somewhat, from 23.4 percent to 25.4 percent (on the basis of 1984 imports). During the initial phase of the liberalization program, the number of tariff categories was increased temporarily but reduced in April 1986.

Also, the envisaged sequence of tariff reform over the next 30 months was preannounced, which helped remove uncertainties concerning the direction and timing of future trade reforms and convince economic agents of the irreversibility of the reform process.[8] Thus, the authorities made it clear from the outset that the lifting of quantitative restrictions would be accompanied by a general reduction in tariffs and import-related taxes.

Tariffs were used increasingly to offset, but only in part, the impact of the phaseout of QRs. The April 1986 and February 1987 tariff cuts were implemented as planned, and the program of tariff cuts was accelerated when on December 15, 1987, as part of the Pact of Economic Solidarity and Economic Strategy, all tariff rates were reduced. The maximum tariff rate (i.e., that applied to imports of consumer goods also produced in Mexico) was lowered to 20 percent from 40 percent, and new tariff categories of 5 percent, 10 percent, and 15 percent were established. In addition, the 5 percent general import tax was abolished. The 5 percent tariff was applied to goods not produced in Mexico, while priority goods not produced in Mexico were exempted from tariffs.[9]

Subsequently, only a few adjustments have been made to the tariff structure. The minimum tariff (with few exceptions) was raised to 10 percent (from 5 percent) in January 1989, to reduce further the dispersion of tariff rates.[10] Overall, the number of tariff categories was reduced from ten in 1985 to three in 1990, while the average tariff rate was reduced from over 25 percent in 1985 to less than 13 percent in 1990; the average rate fell from 13 percent to 10 percent during this period.

### Official Import Prices

Official import prices, which applied to about 25 percent of the value of domestic production of tradables in 1985, were phased out progressively in 1986 and 1987.

---

[7] Starting January 1, 1991, imports of new automobiles were allowed up to a limit equivalent to 15 percent of domestic sales while the liberalization of regulations affecting imports of light trucks will enter into effect in 1993 and those for heavy trucks in 1994.

[8] It was announced that by October 1988 tariff rates would be in the range of 0–30 percent, with not more than five tariff levels.

[9] The terms of Mexico's accession to the GATT allowed for maximum tariff barriers of 50 percent ad valorem until the end of 1994. Given the significant reduction in tariffs that has been achieved, Mexico has moved beyond its commitments in the context of the GATT.

[10] Some basic food items and medicines continued to be exempt from duties or subject to lower tariff rates.

In 1986, the number of import categories subject to official import prices declined from 1,191 (equivalent to 9.1 percent of total categories of imports) to 960 (equivalent to 7.6 percent of total categories of imports). In 1987, the remaining official import prices were eliminated in several steps.

### Exports

Export regulation in Mexico traditionally had been less binding than import restrictions, and export taxes and controls have become even less restrictive in recent years. The number of goods subject to export taxes and export controls has been reduced significantly. Also, with the collapse of the International Coffee Agreement, QRs, reference prices, and taxes on coffee exports were lifted. More generally, the overall production coverage of export controls has been reduced by about one fourth since mid-1988. At present, most controls or prohibitions on exports are imposed on agricultural commodities. Exports of steel and textile products and certain other industrial items are also subject to control to ensure compliance with international export restraint agreements.

Since 1985, a number of initiatives have been taken to promote nonpetroleum exports, including the introduction of a drawback system for import duty payments under the Export Promotion Program (PROFIEX), measures streamlining administrative procedures, the easing of requirements for admission of imported intermediate inputs, the greater access of credit for exporters, and reduction of restrictions on the use of export earnings. Also, on July 28, 1989 a joint commission for the promotion of non-oil exports was established with the participation of the public and private sectors. Finally, understandings were reached with the United States on subsidies and countervailing duties.

### Liberalization of Foreign Investment

The liberalization of regulations concerning international trade was complemented by a liberalization of foreign investment regulation. The Government aims at increasing foreign investment inflows to $5 billion a year during the early 1990s, as compared with an average of less than $2 billion in the 1980s. Consequently, efforts to attract foreign direct investment have been intensified in general by a more lenient interpretation of the 1973 LFI and, in 1989, by the revision of the regulations regarding foreign investment in Mexico.

Approval and licensing procedures for foreign investment have been streamlined since 1983. Initially, the Mexican authorities conducted a selective policy of promoting foreign investment, with special emphasis in areas related to non-oil exports and the transfer of technology, within the legal framework defined by the 1973 LFI. Steps were taken to simplify the administrative procedures for initiating and approving foreign investment

projects to increase the flow of foreign capital into selected sectors. During the period 1983–85, more than 150 projects with 100 percent foreign-owned capital were approved.

In May 1989, significant regulatory changes were enacted.[11] These "Regulations of the Law to Promote Mexican Investment and Regulate Foreign Investment" were designed to increase the inflow of investment capital by providing legal certainty and by clarifying investment rules. The regulations simplified the procedures for authorizing investment projects, relaxed limitations on foreign ownership by widening the range of activities open to foreign investors, and lengthened the duration of permits for certain activities.[12] Also, foreign investors were allowed to own 100 percent of enterprises valued up to $100 million without need of approval from the National Foreign Investment Commission, provided that certain conditions were met.[13] Finally, the new regulations on foreign investment reduced some of the barriers to entry by foreigners into the Mexican stock market. Under the new regulations, foreigners may hold certificate of participation in neutral investment trusts, which provide holders with pecuniary rights but no voting rights. As a result of the adoption of these regulations, almost 73 percent of the economy is now open to 100 percent foreign ownership without prior approval by the Mexican Government.

## Implications of the Reforms

The trade and investment liberalization measures that have been implemented since 1985 have helped transform an inward-looking economy characterized by high tariffs and heavy reliance on quantitative import controls into an open economy. They have increased international competition in the domestic market, improved resource allocation, and increased productive efficiency. They have allowed Mexican companies to import capital and inter-

---

[11] See Pastor (1989) for a discussion of these changes.

[12] In particular, the May 1989 regulations liberalized investment in telecommunications services (up to 49 percent of foreign equity was allowed), secondary and tertiary petrochemical products, tourism-related businesses, and financial services. To that extent, the liberalization of foreign investment has facilitated the privatization process since several state-owned companies that were or are being sold have been opened to foreign equity investment, including companies in the telecommunications and banking industries.

[13] The regulations provide for automatic approval upon registration of investment projects that meet six criteria: (1) the project is funded by foreign resources; (2) it is expected to provide permanent jobs and enhance workers' training facilities; (3) it is deemed to involve "adequate technology" and to satisfy environmental requirements; (4) the investment in fixed assets before beginning operations amounts to the Mexican peso equivalent of $100 million or less; (5) cumulative net foreign exchange receipts are expected to balance within the first three years; and (6) industrial projects are located outside Mexico City, Guadalajara, and Monterrey. Projects that do not meet these six criteria are subject to authorization by the Foreign Investment Commission on a 45-day lapse-of-time basis.

mediate goods at international prices, thus strengthening their productivity. More generally, they have contributed to the establishment of a predictable and rational incentive structure for the private sector.

## Contribution to Macroeconomic Performance

The comprehensive liberalization of Mexico's international trade and investment regimes has helped reorient the system of incentives, and restructure the country's productive base, resulting in a shift in the base of Mexico's growth from domestic to external markets. The replacement of import quotas by tariffs improved the fairness of the trade regime and may have allowed an increase in capacity utilization in the tradable goods sector.[14] Also, confronted with stronger foreign competition, companies have increased their efficiency. The manufacturing sector in particular has experienced a marked increase in productivity. Because Mexico's trade liberalization has implied a major restructuring of domestic industry, it made Mexico's participation in a North American Free Trade Area a realistic objective.

Also, trade liberalization measures have helped moderate pressures on consumer prices through greater external competition and have permitted access by Mexican producers to inputs at international prices, which has helped export performance and the recent acceleration of economic growth.[15] Finally, success in controlling inflation and in attracting foreign capital has helped lower nominal and real interest rates, which has reduced significantly producers' costs. This in turn has dampened further inflationary pressures and helped sustain Mexico's external cost competitiveness.

## Balance of Payments Structure

Partly as a result of the major changes in incentives, the structure of Mexico's balance of payments has changed significantly since 1985. Non-oil exports have performed well, and automotive products, other machinery and equipment, chemicals, iron and steel products, electrical and electronic goods, and textile and clothing have become major export items.[16] The value of non-oil exports (excluding proceeds from the *maquiladora* industry) increased by 275 percent between 1985 and 1991, while the share of non-oil exports in total export receipts rose from 32 percent in 1985 to 70 percent in 1991. More

specifically, the share of manufactured exports in total export receipts increased from less than 30 percent in 1984–85 to 56 percent in 1990–91. In the event, manufactures have replaced petroleum as Mexico's main source of foreign exchange proceeds. Also, the aggregate index of concentration of Mexico's export base has improved significantly.[17]

The diversification of Mexico's export base has reduced the vulnerability of the balance of payments to changes in oil prices. The economy may be somewhat more vulnerable to recessionary conditions in the economies of Mexico's main trading partners, but Mexican exports have withstood reasonably well the recent recession in the United States.

Throughout the liberalization process, the *maquiladora* industry has continued to be one of the most dynamic sectors in the economy. Domestic value added by in-bond industries increased by 326 percent between 1985 and 1991 to reach $4.1 billion, while employment in this sector rose from 212,000 workers in 1985 to 472,000 workers in 1990. As a result, net proceeds from these operations have represented an increasing proportion of Mexico's foreign exchange earnings, rising from 3.5 percent of total earnings in 1984 to 8.1 percent in 1990.

As expected, trade liberalization has been associated with a surge in merchandise imports. However, as a result of the more appropriate incentive structure prevailing in the economy, these imports have helped modernize Mexico's production and export bases, enhancing the country's medium-term external prospects. Imports of consumer goods registered the strongest percentage increase during the period under review. The value of consumer goods imports has registered a 660 percent increase since 1984 and doubled its share of total imports, to represent 15 percent of total merchandise imports in 1991. In absolute terms, however, the growth of imports has been concentrated in capital and intermediate goods. Capital goods imports, boosted by efforts to rebuild an aging capital stock, increased in value by 335 percent during the period 1984–91, while the value of intermediate goods imports increased by close to 310 percent.[18]

While both export and import indicators reflect the increasing outward-orientation of the Mexican economy, the growth of exports has not kept pace with that of

---

[14] For an analytical discussion of the impact of a replacement of quotas by tariffs on capacity utilization and the fairness of the trade regime, see Sahay (1990).

[15] Ize (1990) concluded that trade liberalization in Mexico may have played an important role in stimulating exports and investments but the author found no evidence that it had contributed to price stabilization.

[16] An increase in nontraditional exports during the initial stages of liberalization has been observed in a number of countries, see, for example, Krueger (1978).

[17] The Gini-Hirschman concentration index, which is a standard indicator of the degree of diversification of a country's export base, dropped from 68 in 1985 to 45 in 1990. The higher the value of the index (i.e., the closer it is to 100), the more concentrated the country's export base. The Gini-Hirschman index is defined as:

$$C = 100\left(\sum \left(\frac{X_i}{X}\right)^2\right)^{1/2} \quad i = 1, \ldots, n$$

where $X_i$ is the value of the $i$th export good, and $X$ is the total value of exports.

[18] In 1991, intermediate inputs represented 63 percent of total imports and capital goods represented 23 percent of Mexico's imports.

imports. As a result, the merchandise trade account (excluding net proceeds from the *maquiladora* industry) has shifted to a deficit position since 1989. However, beyond the liberalization of Mexico's trade system, the shift to a merchandise trade deficit and the widening of the current account deficit since 1989 reflect the greater availability of foreign financing related to a large extent to Mexico's renewed access to voluntary foreign financing.[19]

Another implication of Mexico's liberalization efforts has been the marked growth registered in foreign direct investment and portfolio investment. Foreign direct investment increased from an annual average of $750 million in 1982–85 to $4.8 billion in 1991. Also, portfolio investment rose from $0.5 billion in 1989 to $7.5 billion in 1991. These trends, associated in large part with a repatriation of flight capital, have contributed to the emergence of large surpluses in the capital account of the balance of payments.

## Consolidating the Gains from Trade Liberalization Through a Series of Trade Initiatives

Mexico is currently involved in four regional free trade initiatives, one with the United States and Canada and three with Latin American countries. The unilateral liberalization of Mexico's international trade and investment regimes since 1985 made feasible the NAFTA with the United States and Canada. In turn, these are expected to consolidate the economic gains from liberalization.

### The Proposed North American Free Trade Area

In June 1990, the Presidents of Mexico and the United States announced their intention to pursue the establishment of a free trade area between the two countries. During the 12 months that followed, informal discussions were held on a free trade agreement, first on a bilateral basis, then on a trilateral basis when Canada announced in February 1991 that it would join in the negotiation of a North American Free Trade Agreement.

Formal negotiations with the United States and Canada for the establishment of the NAFTA began in June 1991, after the U.S. Congress granted the U.S. Administration "fast-track" negotiating authority. After 14 months of negotiations, agreement was announced on August 12, 1992. The treaty is scheduled to come into force on January 1, 1994, after approval by the legislatures of the three signatory states.

---

[19] This aspect of Mexico's recent experience is discussed in Section VII.

The objectives of the agreement are to eliminate barriers to trade, promote conditions of fair competition, increase investment opportunities, establish effective procedures for the resolution of disputes, and promote further trilateral, regional, and multilateral cooperation (see Box 1 for the main provisions of the NAFTA).

The NAFTA provides for the gradual elimination of tariff and nontariff barriers to the movement of goods, services, and capital in the zone over a 10–15 year period. In sensitive sectors, the NAFTA provides special transitional safeguard mechanisms. Regarding agriculture, Mexico would convert its nontariff barriers into tariffs and phase them out over a 10–15 year period. After 15 years, the agreement will guarantee total market access in agriculture. The agreement would totally eliminate quotas on textiles among its parties. It would also create free trade in services, opening Mexico's telecommunications market and its insurance market. Finally, the NAFTA breaks new ground for trade pacts by including provisions on the environment.

To ensure that NAFTA benefits are accorded only to goods produced in North America, strict rules of origin are specified, which would vary by sector. For instance, in the automotive sector, 62.5 percent of parts, labor, and other costs must be added in North America for a car or truck to qualify for lower duties. For computers, only 20 to 40 percent of a computer's value need to be North American to qualify.

The negotiating parties expect that, through stimulating trade among the three countries and expanding investment opportunities, the NAFTA will spur economic growth, generate employment, and enhance the competitiveness of North American producers. The Mexican authorities in particular expect that Mexico's expanded access to the North American market will open new opportunities for Mexican companies, help generate employment in Mexico, and increase wages. The NAFTA would reduce Mexico's vulnerability to unilateral actions by its trading partners and would thereby reduce the uncertainty faced by Mexican producers, both through the rules being negotiated and the envisaged dispute settlement mechanism. Improved prospects for gaining access to foreign markets would help generate economies of scale, and hence efficiency gains in a number of sectors.

Also, the NAFTA is expected to improve Mexico's position in the current international competition for capital. Secure access to the North American market would be an added incentive to investors willing to exploit Mexico's comparative advantages. The corresponding financing flows and imports of modern technology through foreign direct investment would be an important element of Mexico's modernization strategy and would strengthen the country's production base and external competitiveness. Greater access to goods from Canada and the United States would give Mexicans a wider choice of products at lower prices. Finally, Mexico's prospective participation in the NAFTA has been seen as a sign of the irreversibility of the recent structural reforms, including trade liberalization, and has already contributed to heightened interest on the part of potential investors.[20]

The North American Free Trade Agreement will contain an accession clause that would facilitate the subsequent entry of other Latin American countries into the NAFTA. In that sense, NAFTA can be seen as a first step toward a wider trading region encompassing all the Americas.

### Contributing to a More Open Trade System Within Latin America

In the context of a broader process of regional economic integration in Latin America, Mexico is involved in three separate trade initiatives: one with Chile, one with Colombia and Venezuela, and one with the five Central American countries. The free trade agreement between Mexico and Chile has been signed already.

After nine months of formal negotiations, Chile and Mexico signed on September 22, 1991 an Agreement of Economic Complementarity. The agreement was facilitated by the fact that both countries already had implemented comprehensive liberalization of their international trade regimes and had been implementing macroeconomic and financial policies that had helped them improve their medium-term external viability. Also, consensus in both countries exists on the potential benefits to be expected from free trade.

The agreement involves a program of reciprocal trade liberalization that eliminated nontariff barriers for most goods on January 1, 1992 and will reduce tariffs in a four-year period. Beginning in 1992, a maximum tariff of 10 percent will be applied to 95 percent of the tariff categories. The treaty also provides for the liberalization of maritime and air transport. Regarding investment, the

two nations pledged to grant favorable treatment to the other partner. Finally, the treaty envisages an arbitration structure to settle trade disputes. It is expected that the agreement would help raise trade flows between the two countries to $500 million by 1996.

On January 11, 1991, the Governments of Mexico, Costa Rica, El Salvador, Guatemala, Honduras, and Nicaragua signed an Agreement of Economic Complementarity, providing for the gradual establishment of a Free Trade Area between the six countries by the end of 1996. It is envisaged that the agreement will be implemented through a series of bilateral treaties, partly because of the economic heterogeneity of the six countries.

Finally, in April 1991, Mexico, Colombia, and Venezuela announced a plan to establish a free trade zone by July 1994. The nature of the agreement would be basically the same as in the agreement with Chile. A Memorandum of Understanding defining the rules of the negotiations has been agreed upon.

## Conclusion

Since 1985, Mexico has made significant progress in liberalizing its international trade and investment regimes. This has resulted in the restructuring of international trade and a sharp increase in foreign investment in Mexico.

This successful experience highlights the favorable impact of liberalizing international trade and investment regimes in the context of a comprehensive macroeconomic adjustment program. Throughout Mexico's experience with trade liberalization, cautious financial policies, improved macroeconomic conditions, and a competitive exchange rate have proven to be essential in sustaining structural reforms, including through bolstering the credibility of the preannounced trade liberalization program.

With the various trade initiatives now under way with the United States, Canada, and eight Latin American countries, Mexico has entered a new phase in its efforts to reform its trade regime leading to an even greater integration in the world economy. Such regional integration could contribute to improved economic performance in Mexico and help the country achieve external viability through the implied higher level of exports and the inflows of foreign capital.

---

[20] In that regard, the U.S. administration has stated that a NAFTA would lock in the process of trade liberalization in Mexico and assure even greater access for U.S. exports in the future. A free trade agreement would secure U.S. access to Mexican markets by preventing possible future movement toward more protectionist policies. By providing a guarantee against future protectionist trade policies, a free trade agreement would improve confidence in the Mexican economy, boosting Mexican growth and demand for imports, particularly from the United States. See Office of the U.S. President (1991).

## Box 1. Main Provisions of the NAFTA

### General Provision on Trade in Goods

The North American Free Trade Agreement (NAFTA) provides for the progressive elimination of all tariffs on goods qualifying as North American under its rules of origin. For most goods, existing customs duties would either be eliminated upon the agreement taking effect or phased out in five or ten years. Tariffs would be phased out from rates applied in effect on July 1, 1991.

All three countries are to eliminate prohibitions and quantitative restrictions applied at the border, such as quotas and import licenses. Each country, however, maintains the right to impose border restrictions in limited circumstances, and special rules would apply to trade in agriculture, automotive goods, energy, and textiles.

### Rules of Origin

The rules of origin specify that goods originate in North America if they are wholly North American, or if the nonregional materials are sufficiently transformed in the NAFTA region so as to undergo a specified change in tariff classification. In some cases, goods must include a specified percentage of North American content in addition to meeting the tariff classification requirement.

### Agriculture

When the agreement goes into effect, Mexico and the United States will eliminate immediately all nontariff barriers to their agricultural trade, generally through their conversion to either "tariff-rate quotas" (TRQs) or ordinary tariffs.[1] Tariffs would be eliminated immediately on a broad range of agricultural products. All tariff barriers between Mexico and the United States will be eliminated not later than ten years after the agreement takes effect, with the exception of duties on certain highly sensitive products. Tariff phase-out on these few remaining products will be completed after five more years. Canada and Mexico will eliminate gradually all tariff and nontariff barriers on their agricultural trade, with a few exceptions.

### Automotive Goods

The NAFTA would eliminate gradually barriers to trade in North American automobiles, trucks, buses, and parts within the free-trade area, and eliminate investment restrictions in this sector, over a ten-year transition period. Each NAFTA country would phase out all duties on its imports of North American automotive goods during the transition period.

In order to qualify for preferential tariff treatment, automotive goods must contain a specified percentage of North American content (62.5 percent for passenger automobiles and light trucks as well as engines and transmissions for vehicles, and 60 percent for other vehicles and automotive parts) based on the net-cost formula.[2]

### Energy and Basic Petrochemicals

In the NAFTA, the Mexican state retains full control of the Mexican oil, gas, refining, basic petrochemicals, nuclear and electricity sectors. The NAFTA opens new private investment opportunities in Mexico in nonbasic petrochemical goods and in electricity-generating facilities. To promote cross-border trade in natural gas and basic petrochemicals, NAFTA provides that state enterprises, end users, and suppliers have the right to negotiate supply contracts.

### Textiles and Apparel

The three countries would eliminate either immediately or over a maximum period of ten years their customs duties on textile and apparel goods manufactured in North America that meet the NAFTA rules of origin. The rules of origin generally stipulate that apparel must be manufactured in North America from the yard-spinning stage forward. The United States will immediately remove import quotas on such goods produced in Mexico.

### Government Procurement

The NAFTA would open gradually a significant portion of the government procurement market in each signatory country on a nondiscriminatory basis to suppliers for the other NAFTA countries for goods, services, and construction services.

### Cross-Border Trade in Services

The provisions for the cross-border trade in services establish a set of basic rules and obligations to facilitate trade in services between the three countries.[3] The agreement extends the national treatment rule to services. Under this rule, each NAFTA country would have to treat service providers of other NAFTA countries no less favorably than it treats its own service providers in like circumstances. Also, a NAFTA country could not require a service provider of another NAFTA country to establish or maintain a residence, representative office, branch, or any form of enterprise in its territory as a condition for the provision of a service.

The NAFTA provides for the gradual phaseout of restrictions on cross-border land transportation services among the three countries.

### Financial Services

Under the agreement, financial service providers of a NAFTA country may establish in any other NAFTA country banking, insurance, and securities operations, as well as other types of financial services. Each country must permit its residents to purchase financial services in the territory of another NAFTA country. Each country would provide both national treatment and most-favored-nation treatment to other NAFTA financial service providers operations in its territory.

Under the agreement, Mexico would apply market share limits during a transitional period ending by the year 2000. Thereafter, temporary safeguard provisions may be applicable in the banking and securities sectors.

### Investment

The NAFTA removes investment barriers, ensures basic protection for NAFTA investors, and provides a mechanism for the settlement of disputes between such investors and a NAFTA country. Each country would have to treat NAFTA investors no less favorably than its own investors.

### Intellectual Property

NAFTA sets out specific commitments for the protection of intellectual property. Each country is to provide adequate and effective protection of intellectual property rights on the basis of national treatment and would provide effective enforcement of these rights against infringement.

### Institutional Arrangements and Dispute Settlement Procedures

The NAFTA provides for the creation of a Trade Commission that would use good offices, mediation, conciliation, or other means of alternative dispute resolution to find a solution to disputes. If the Commission fails to hammer out an agreement, the NAFTA provides that a bilateral arbitral panel would be set up. Each stage of dispute will be subject to a strict time limit, ensuring a speedy resolution process.

### Environment

The signatory governments have committed to implementing the agreement in a manner consistent with environmental protection and to promoting sustainable development. The agreement affirms the right of each country to choose the level of protection it considers appropriate and provides that no NAFTA country should lower its health, safety, or environmental standards for the purpose of attracting investment. Disputes regarding a country's standards can be submitted to NAFTA dispute settlement procedures.

Source: "Description of the Proposed North American Free Trade Agreement" prepared by the Governments of Canada, the United Mexican States, and the United States of America, August 12, 1992.

[1] Under TRQs, no tariff would be imposed on imports within the quota amount. The quantity eligible to enter duty free under the TRQ will be based on recent trade levels and will grow generally at 3 percent a year. The over-quota duty—initially established at a level designed to equal the existing tariff value of each nontariff barrier—will progressively decline to zero during either a 10- or 15-year transition period, depending on the product.

[2] The net-cost method is based on the total cost of the good less the cost of royalties, sales promotion, and packing and shipping. It also sets a limitation on allowable interest.

[3] Excludes government procurement, financial services and energy-related services, air services, basic telecommunications, social services, and maritime industries.

# Bibliography

Banamex, "Inversión Extranjera Directa" (Mexico, 1990).

Banco de México, *The Mexican Economy* (Mexico, various issues).

Bond, Martan, and Elizabeth Milne, "Export Diversification in Developing Countries: Recent Trends and Policy Impact," *Staff Studies for the World Economic Outlook*, World Economic and Financial Surveys (Washington: International Monetary Fund, August 1987).

Calvo, Guillermo, "Costly Trade Liberalizations: Durable Goods and Capital Mobility," Staff Papers, International Monetary Fund (Washington), Vol. 35 (September 1988), pp. 461–73.

Camil, Jorge, "Mexico's 1989 Foreign Investment Regulations: The Cornerstone of a New Economic Model," *Houston Journal of International Law* (U.S.), Vol. 12 (Fall 1989).

Coorey, Sharmini, "Effects of Canada–U.S. Free Trade Agreement Likely to be Positive," *IMF Survey* (Washington), Vol. 18 (May 15, 1989), pp. 147–51.

Corden, W. Max, *Protection and Liberalization: A Review of Analytical Issues*, IMF Occasional Paper, No. 54 (Washington: International Monetary Fund, August 1987).

Edwards, Sebastian, "Stabilization with Liberalization: An Evaluation of Ten Years of Chile's Experience with Free Market Policies, 1973–83," in *Economic Liberalization in Developing Countries*, by A.M. Choksi and D. Papageorgiou (London: Basil Blackwell, 1986), pp. 241–71.

Gurria, Jose Angel, "What Eastern Europe Can Learn from Mexico," *The International Economy* (May/June 1991), pp. 28–32.

International Finance Corporation, "Emerging Stock Markets Factbook" (Washington: International Finance Corporation, 1991).

Ize, Alain, "Trade Liberalization, Stabilization, and Growth: Some Notes on the Mexican Experience," IMF Working Paper, WP/90/15 (Washington: International Monetary Fund, March 1990).

Michaely, M., "The Timing and Sequencing of Trade Liberalization Policy," in *Economic Liberalization in Developing Countries*, by A.M. Choksi and D. Papageorgiou (London: Basil Blackwell, 1986), pp. 41–59.

Office of the U.S. President, "Response of the Administration to Issues Raised in Connection with the Negotiation of a North American Free Trade Agreement," transmitted to the Congress by the President on May 1, 1991.

Petricioli, Gustavo, "U.S.-Mexican Free Trade Pact Would Be a Boon to Both Countries," *IMF Survey* (Washington) Vol. 19 (July 30, 1990), p. 230.

Sahay, Ratna, "Trade Policy and Excess Capacity in Developing Countries," Staff Papers, International Monetary Fund (Washington), Vol. 37 (September 1990), pp. 486–508.

Schott, Jeffrey J., "More Free Trade Areas?" *Policy Analysis in International Economics, No. 27* (Washington: Institute for International Economics, May 1989).

SECOFI, Mexico's International Trade Relations: Challenges and Opportunities (Mexico, 1990).

Serra Puche, Jaime, "Principios para Negociar el Tratado de Libre Comercio de América del Norte," *Comercio Exterior* (Mexico), Vol. 41 (July 1991), pp. 653–60.

United States International Trade Commission (USITC), "Operation of the Trade Agreements Program," 37th Report, USITC Publications 1871 (Washington, 1985).

—————, "Review of Trade and Investment Liberalization Measures by Mexico and Prospects for Future United States–Mexican Relations," Investigation No. 332–282, USITC Publications 2326 (Washington, October 1990).

World Bank, *World Development Report* (Washington, 1987).

# V  Financial Liberalization and Reform in Mexico

## Sharmini Coorey

Until the late 1980s, despite a period of gradual transformation and liberalization, the financial system in Mexico was characterized by interest rate restrictions, domestic credit controls, high reserve requirements, fragmented financial markets, and other elements causing inefficiencies in the intermediation between borrowers and lenders. Capital markets were not well developed and firms often had to turn to informal markets for their long-term financing needs. The lack of an established bond market and the existence of an informal credit market impeded the conduct of monetary policy by restricting the scope for open market operations and limiting the ability of the Bank of Mexico to monitor overall credit market conditions.

In late 1988, the Government substantially accelerated the process of financial reform in the context of its overall economic program. The objectives were to enhance efficiency through greater reliance on market forces, to promote the growth and deepening of financial markets, and to improve the effectiveness of monetary policy. In addition, recognizing the increasing globalization of capital markets, the Government sought to improve the capitalization and integration of Mexican financial institutions with a view to preparing them to be competitive internationally. The approach was based on the two complementary processes of liberalization and institutional reform. Key measures included the liberalization of interest rates, the elimination of direct controls on credit, the re-privatization of the commercial banks, and the promotion of a universal banking system.[1]

This section reviews the program of financial liberalization and reform undertaken by Mexico since the late 1980s and the issues that have arisen in this regard. The first part outlines some important reforms that preceded this liberalization as well as financial market conditions before 1988, while the second reviews liberalization measures undertaken since the end of 1988. The privatization of the commercial banks is discussed in the third part and the impact of the liberalization on financial aggregates and interest rates is analyzed in the fourth part. The conclusion identifies some factors that have contributed to the success so far of Mexico's financial liberalization and areas in which the reforms could be taken further.

## Background and Developments, 1974–88

The foundation for the financial liberalization that took place after late 1988 was laid by institutional reforms undertaken since the mid-1970s, the most significant of which were the move from specialized banking to full-service banking, the modernization of the securities market, and the formation of a domestic public debt market. By the early 1970s, restrictions on the scope of the financial services credit institutions could offer had led to a proliferation of banks specializing in different types of services: commercial banks, mortgage banks, and *financieras*, which mostly financed trade and commerce. In 1974, the Government sanctioned the merger of these separate institutions into full-service banks that could benefit from economies of scale and the diversification of risk. In 1975, the Securities Market Law was enacted modernizing the structure of the securities market, institutionalizing brokerage houses, and substantially strengthening the regulatory role of the National Securities Commission (CNV).[2] Mexican treasury bills (CETES) were created in 1978 to provide the Government with a tradable instrument to issue domestic debt and to conduct open market operations. Within a short period, the yield on these instruments became the most representative quotation in the money market.

Until the mid-1970s, the banking sector had been highly regulated, and featured ceilings on deposit rates and

---

[1] Universal banking is a system that permits banks to accept deposits as well as engage in securities market activities. In Mexico, universal banking signifies the horizontal integration of financial institutions, such as commercial banks, brokerage houses, and insurance companies, subject to certain restrictions on cross ownership; commercial banks are permitted to invest in equities.

[2] Individual brokers were given strong incentives to incorporate through the offer of specific operating advantages. The Law has been updated several times since, including in 1978 to establish INDEVAL, a centralized depository institution, which features a computerized settlement and custodial system.

requirements to channel credit to a specified range of activities within given limits on lending interest rates. This system became unmanageable in 1974 when deposit rates had to be increased sharply to reflect the acceleration of inflation. In response, a weighted average deposit rate (CPP) was introduced to provide a more flexible basis for determining loan rates; subsequently, loan rate restrictions were gradually removed. Deposit rates, however, remained regulated, and banks continued to be required to allocate credit to certain sectors, including the Government. While these policies favored borrowers with access to bank credit, they also discouraged financial savings in formal markets and hindered the intermediation function of the formal banking sector. For much of the 1980s, reserve requirements of over 50 percent and required lending to the public sector crowded out credit to the private sector. In addition, monetary control was based mainly on quantitative credit controls rather than on market mechanisms, such as open market operations.

The commercial banks were nationalized in September 1982 at the height of Mexico's debt crisis. The years from 1982 to 1988 were a period of financial disintermediation. The high implicit tax that reserve requirements and credit controls imposed on banks increased the cost of intermediation to such an extent that a parallel informal market for credit developed rapidly, particularly in 1987–88 when inflation picked up. By the end of this period, the growth and expansion of intermediaries outside the control of monetary authorities had eroded considerably the competitiveness of the commercial banks and weakened the effectiveness of monetary policy.

## Liberalization and Reform, 1989–91

Faced with disintermediation in financial markets and in the context of a new adjustment program the authorities, in late 1988, embarked on a major reform of the financial system. This section reviews the major deregulation measures undertaken, including the legislative groundwork that was laid to privatize commercial banks and to foster the development of universal banking.

### Interest Rate Deregulation and Changes in Reserve Requirement System

In November 1988, the Government eliminated quantitative restrictions on the issuance of bankers' acceptances.[3] Banks were allowed to invest freely from these resources, subject to the restriction of maintaining a liquidity ratio of 30 percent in the form of certain govern-

ment debt instruments (CETES and BONDES) and interest-bearing deposits at the Bank of Mexico.[4]

In April 1989, the Government introduced several major reforms to allow banks to carry out their intermediation function more efficiently:

(1) controls on interest rates and maturities on all traditional bank instruments and deposits were eliminated;

(2) the reserve requirements on bank deposits were replaced by a 30 percent liquidity ratio similar to that applicable to bankers' acceptances.[5] Government paper held to satisfy the liquidity ratio would earn market interest rates and would be fully tradable;

(3) restrictions on bank lending to the private sector were removed; and

(4) mandatory lending at below-market interest rates to the public sector by commercial banks was discontinued.

In addition, banks were given a greater degree of managerial flexibility and the autonomy of bank boards was expanded. The role of providing preferential credit was limited to the development banks and trust funds; NAFINSA, the largest of such institutions, ceased its commercial banking activities in early 1989.

While deposit and lending rates previously had been set to ensure the profitability of the nationalized banks, these reforms allowed banks to set their own terms on deposit and credit operations, and increased the competitiveness of the formal banking sector. The decision to finance the public sector from the sale of bonds in the open market rather than through mandatory subsidized lending from commercial banks helped reduce distortions in interest rates and enhanced the effectiveness of open market operations. Although the abolition of forced lending schemes and the lowering of reserve requirements strengthened the liquidity of the banking system and freed a considerable amount of resources for the private sector, the 30 percent liquidity ratio still appeared higher than what banks would have determined voluntarily. The requirement to hold government paper had a negative impact on the yields of these instruments and constituted an implicit tax on the financial system.

In August 1991, in response to a rapid increase in foreign short-term borrowing by commercial banks, the authorities imposed liquidity coefficients on foreign currency deposits of up to 50 percent (depending on deposit maturities).[6] At the same time, the public sector was reducing its domestic debt sharply, aided by revenue from privatization and a reduction in nominal and real interest rates. In these circumstances, faced with a strong growth in the demand for private credit, commercial

---

[3] At the time, there was a 100 percent reserve requirement against bankers' acceptances issued beyond an authorized limit.

[4] CETES are treasury bills with a maturity of mostly 28 or 90 days, while BONDES are government bonds with a maturity of one to two years; both kinds of bonds are denominated in pesos.

[5] At the time, banks were required to channel at least 50 percent of these deposits to the public sector (inclusive of reserve requirements).

[6] This ratio could be satisfied by holding U.S. Treasury bills or other specified high quality foreign currency instruments.

banks encountered increasing problems trying to fulfill their liquidity requirements. As a result, CETES rates fell to about 16 percent while deposit rates rose sharply to between 50–60 percent at the end of August. In September, the authorities acted to reduce the liquidity coefficient on domestic currency deposits from 30 percent to 25 percent applicable to the total stock of deposits outstanding at the end of August 1991 and to eliminate the liquidity ratio for deposits in excess of that level.[7] This move to a zero marginal requirement was expected to reduce the spread between interest rates and channel additional resources.

## Changes in Structure of Government Debt

An important aspect of the financial system in Mexico in recent years has been the rapid growth and diversification of the market for government debt. The development of this market aided the process of liberalization by providing the public sector with an alternative to forced lending from the banking system. It also has expanded the range of financial assets available to private investors; over 90 percent of the volume of trading in the Mexican securities market (Bolsa de Valores) is accounted for by public debt instruments.[8]

During the early and mid-1980s, CETES, which yield market-determined interest rates, constituted 80–90 percent of domestic public debt (excluding *Bonos de la Deuda Pública* which are bonds held exclusively by the Bank of Mexico). Starting in 1988, the Government began to change the composition of its domestic debt in order to lengthen the maturity structure and increase the variety of options offered to the public. The share of the shorter-term CETES in domestic public debt was gradually lowered while the share of the longer-term BONDES, which had been introduced in late 1987, was increased. In addition to PETROBONOS (three-year bonds with a capital gain or loss linked to the price of oil), in 1986 the Government introduced indexed instruments in the form of PAGAFES (28- to 364-day dollar-denominated treasury bills payable in pesos at a fixed interest rate), and in 1989 AJUSTABONOS (three- to five-year bonds with returns indexed to the consumer price index) and TESOBONOS (one- to three-month bonds with returns indexed to the free exchange rate).

## Institutional Reforms

In December 1989, in order to further the process of liberalization and strengthen banks and other financial institutions involved in credit and stock market operations, Congress approved additional wide-ranging institutional reforms.[9] The measures were intended to increase competition and reduce market segmentation by expanding the scope of permissible activities for different types of financial institutions and by allowing a greater degree of integration in the provision of financial services. In addition, the reforms eliminated government regulation of insurance premiums and policies, deregulated and simplified the operations of mutual fund societies, strengthened the supervision and regulation of bank and nonbank financial institutions, and relaxed restrictions against the participation of foreign investors in the capital of some nonbank financial institutions.

In 1990, the Government launched two major interrelated initiatives to allow the privatization of commercial banks and to establish the framework for the formation of financial groups (the latter were envisaged as the main organizational structure of financial markets). On May 2, 1990, a bill was submitted to Congress to amend Articles 28 and 123 of the Constitution, permitting full private ownership of the commercial banks.[10]

The new Credit Institutions Law, enacted in July 1990, allows commercial banks to be majority owned and controlled by the private sector (with private foreign ownership restricted to 30 percent of capital), regulates banking, and establishes the terms under which the state exercises supervision and control over the banking system. The provisions regarding bank regulation are intended to limit the concentration of credit risk in the banking sector, to ensure the separation of interests between banking and other activities, and to avoid conflicts of interest in the management of banks.[11]

The Law Regulating Financial Groups regulates and permits the formation, under a common structure, of groups of companies performing different financial functions. It thus ends the traditional separation of banking from other types of financial activities, and in particular, allows banks and brokerage houses to come under the control of a single holding company. In order to limit the concentration of risk, ensure the adequacy of capital, and prevent the pyramiding of the capital base, the legislation restricts the participation of more than one kind of intermediary within a single financial group, exempts

---

[7] However, banks were required to keep all reserves held in excess of the 30 percent liquidity ratio as of August 1991. Government debt instruments corresponding to these excess reserves and to the new 25 percent liquidity ratio were to be held until maturity when they would be exchanged for interest-bearing three- or ten-year bonds (respectively) at the Bank of Mexico. These new bonds would be negotiable only with the Bank of Mexico or with other commercial banks.

[8] Although, on average, stocks accounted for only about 1.5 percent of the total trading in the Bolsa from 1988–90, the Mexican stock market is the largest in Latin America in terms of capitalization.

[9] The reforms included amendments to five laws governing financial institutions.

[10] Article 28 of the Constitution establishes certain areas of activity as the exclusive functions of the state; during the debt crisis in 1982, this Article was amended to include banking. Since 1987, up to 34 percent of bank stock could be held by the private sector.

[11] A more detailed description of these reforms is given in the Appendix to this section.

members of a group (but not the holding company) from liabilities stemming from losses of any other member, and prohibits members from investing in each other's or the holding company's stock.

The new law was the result of close cooperation between government officials and private sector financial experts; it was based on the recognition that the expansion of services offered by Mexican intermediaries was rapidly making the distinction between traditional banking and other financial activities more and more tenuous. According to the authorities, the legislation "opens the possibility of establishing financial holding companies, which would be the hub for the shaping of a universal banking system providing all financial services by a financial group."[12]

## Privatizing Commercial Banks

A gradual process of consolidation since the nationalization of the commercial banks had reduced the number of institutions from 60 in 1982 to 18 by 1988. Except for the chief executive officers, the management of these banks remained for the most part unchanged after nationalization. At the time of the privatization, 15 banks had up to 34 percent of shares held by the private sector and traded in the stock market, while 3 were fully owned by the Government.

The experience of commercial banks during the period of nationalization varied considerably. Money market activities and the market for government debt were important sources of profits for most banks, which at the same time also had profitable subsidiaries in areas such as foreign exchange dealing, investment banking, and leasing. These profits mostly were reinvested in new technology and product expansion.[13] Following deregulation in early 1989, competition between banks and the privately owned brokerage houses intensified significantly, particularly in the management of money market and other relatively liquid funds.

The guidelines for the divestiture of the banks were established in the presidential decree of September 5, 1990. According to government statements, "the privatization process does not only seek to obtain a fair price for the banks, but also to shape a more efficient and competitive financial system and to foster sound financial practices. A diversified participation in the capital stock of banks is deemed desirable. The formation of a controlling group with a distinct identity which is accountable to the authorities is considered necessary. This controlling group should be balanced by a broad number of minority interests."[14]

Controlling 51 percent blocks of shares are sold by auction to groups of individuals with Mexican citizenship who pass through an approval process (discussed below); the remaining 49 percent is floated in secondary offerings to institutional investors, companies, funds, and foreign investors subject to certain ceilings. In July 1991, the Mexican Government restructured some $1.2 billion of interbank credit lines belonging to the six largest Mexican banks.[15] The restructuring enhanced the market value of these banks and facilitated their privatization by reducing the outstanding value of such debts by about 30 percent on average. By mid-1992, all the commercial banks were privatized, selling at considerably higher prices than initially expected by government officials.

The process of privatization raised a number of challenges. In order to retain public confidence, the Government has taken precautions to ensure the transparency of the process of privatization and its consistency with general principles followed in other divestitures. A Committee for the Divestiture of Commercial Banks was established to oversee the registration and approval of potential bidders, the valuation of the institutions, and the sale of the Federal Government's equity.[16] The approval process was designed to be open while ensuring that interested parties are able to accept the responsibilities involved.

Upon registering, groups or financial holding companies submitted a business plan, including the possible incorporation of the bank into the financial group, the areas of market concentration, and plans for capitalization. Approval by the Committee was required for these groups to participate in public auctions of controlling shares. In evaluating an application, the Committee took into consideration the overall strength and expertise of the partners, as well as their ability to commit fresh capital, since the growing lending market, technological developments, and the higher capital adequacy requirements demand substantial additional investments from the holding company. Approval was granted only to groups seeking to acquire the entire package that is being auctioned. The Committee was required to inform the public periodically regarding the progress at each stage of the privatization process.

The actual bids were received from approved parties after the Committee published the notice for the auction, which also specifies the conditions of payment. The auc-

---

[12] Bank of Mexico (1991), p. 90.

[13] Mexico's commercial banks remained outside the public sector budget and were allowed to retain and reinvest their profits.

[14] Bank of Mexico (1991), p. 93.

---

[15] These debts, which had been rolled over since 1982, arose from short-term deposits made by foreign banks before the nationalization of the Mexican banks. The restructuring involved an auction that exchanged some of the credit lines for negotiable ten-year floating rate government bonds that could be redeemed at par for equity in Mexican banks.

[16] The Committee is chaired by the Under Secretary of Finance and Public Credit and is composed of the representatives of the Secretariat of Finance and Public Credit, the Bank of Mexico, the National Banking Commission, the National Securities Commission, and the Divestiture Unit, as well as individuals recognized for their expertise in the field.

tion was carried out under a closed bid system, and the bid price is the most important element at this stage of the process. After analyzing the offers, the Committee proposed the decisions necessary to implement the divestiture to an Intersecretarial Expenditure-Finance Commission.

Another issue that had to be addressed in the privatization process is the valuation of the banks. Under the procedures, each bank established the book value of its assets and liabilities based on the standards set by the Committee for Bank Divestiture; this valuation is verified by external consultants hired by the National Banking Commission. The economic valuation is determined by the Committee, which takes into consideration pertinent elements not included in the book value, such as the value of intangible assets and the bank's potential for generating profits.

The order in which the banks are sold off is also an important issue, since, once sold, they are likely to put competitive pressure on those banks remaining under state ownership. The Government addressed this problem by first setting up an orderly procedure (discussed above) and then proceeding with the divestitures quite quickly. Some two thirds of total commercial banking assets, including the two largest banks, were sold within the first 12 months of the process. In addition, several small regional banks were sold first, allowing the Government to streamline the process before selling the larger banks.

A distinctive feature of financial liberalization in Mexico has been its emphasis on horizontal integration in the form of financial groups. Since the end of 1989, the private sector has been active in forming financial groups, including gaining access to a large amount of capital to purchase the banks. The private financial sector is likely to undergo a further restructuring as the newly formed financial groups strive to achieve integration within each group with a view to eliminating duplication and reducing costs.[17] The regional distribution capabilities of these groups are likely to be an important determinant of their relative success. Moreover, competition may intensify in the future in light of recent indications that the Government may authorize new banking licenses (possibly to foreign banks). While a new supervisory and regulatory structure has been put in place, it is too early to assess how well this system will perform in the new, more competitive environment and how it will deal with marginal financial institutions that remain or become insolvent.

## Effects of Financial Liberalization

The 1989–91 period when most of the significant financial reforms took place coincided with the implementation of a successful economic adjustment program. It is, therefore, difficult to distinguish between the effects of financial liberalization and those of the economic adjustment program on the gradual return of private sector confidence. Moreover, some of the important financial reforms have been introduced only recently and it is too early to evaluate their effects. Subject to these caveats, this section analyzes some quantitative evidence on the effects of deregulation and liberalization on financial variables.

As noted earlier, the deregulation of interest rates and the lifting of credit ceilings in early 1989 allowed banks to compete effectively in financial markets and encouraged private savings in financial assets. At the same time, beginning in the first quarter of 1989, the behavior of financial savings underwent a marked turnaround. Chart 6 shows that the ratio of broad money (M2) to GDP, which had declined from 1982 to 1988, rose markedly from the first quarter of 1989 to the second quarter of 1991.[18] The relationship between currency and GDP remained relatively stable throughout the entire period, indicating that the expansion of bank deposits was mainly responsible for the growth in monetary aggregates after 1988. The ratio of money and bonds (M4) to GDP, which had been relatively flat in 1982–88 (except for a brief period in 1986–87), also increased strongly during the 1989–91 period.

Further evidence of the contrast in financial intermediation between the periods 1982–88 and 1989–91 is provided in Chart 7. Following a sharp dip during the debt crisis in 1982–83, the growth rate of M2 in real terms remained consistently negative from mid-1985 to late 1988. The intensification of financial disintermediation is evident in the sharp fall in the ratio of M2 to currency in 1987–88. The ratio of M1 to currency remained relatively stable throughout this period as disintermediation was strongest in certain instruments, such as bankers' acceptances. The financial reintermediation that occurred after 1988 is evident in the sustained pickup in the real rates of growth of the monetary aggregates. As shown in Table 8, in contrast to the declines in real terms observed in 1982–88, M2 grew at an average annual rate of almost 14 percent in real terms and M4 grew at an average annual rate of about 19 percent in real terms during the period from the begining of 1989 to the second quarter of 1991. This expansion coincided with an increase in the ratio of M2 to currency reflecting the relatively stronger growth of short-term bank deposits.

---

[17] For example, banks, as well as brokerage houses, manage their own money market funds, while banks also invest in fixed income funds and equity funds; portfolio management activities of insurance companies also duplicate some of these activities. In addition, while the loan portfolios of banks are generally thought to be free of major problems, the weaker, particularly medium-sized, banks may not survive the more competitive environment following privatization.

---

[18] M1 = currency held by public + checking accounts;
M2 = M1 + other short-term bank deposits and bankers' acceptances;
M4 = M2 + long-term bank deposits and government bonds held by public.

## Chart 6. Behavior of Financial Aggregates

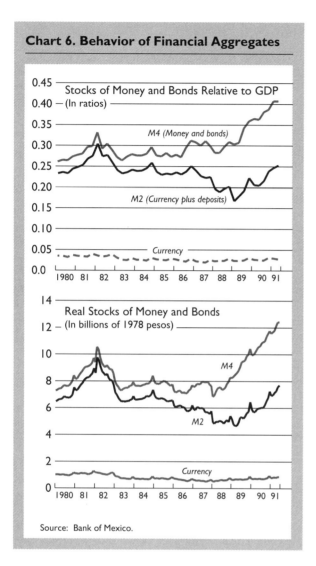

Source: Bank of Mexico.

## Table 8. Real Growth of Financial Aggregates
*(Average annual growth rates in percent)[1]*

|          | 1982:IV– 1985:II | 1985:III– 1988:IV | 1989:I– 1991:II |
|----------|-------------------|-------------------|-----------------|
| M4       | −5.7              | −1.3              | 19.2            |
| M2       | −7.7              | −8.5              | 13.8            |
| Currency | −12.4             | −4.1              | 10.9            |

[1]Quarterly averages of 12-month changes.

The effects of the financial liberalization are also evident in the behavior of the money multiplier.[19] The replacement of the high reserve requirement with a lower liquidity ratio and the removal of credit restrictions in early 1989 raised the money multiplier and permitted a greater supply response as the demand for Mexican financial assets rose with the return of confidence. Chart 8 illustrates the marked increase in the money multiplier, particularly for M2, after the first quarter of 1989.

In some contexts, interest rate deregulation has led to sharply higher real interest rates. In the case of Mexico, real interest rates remained mostly negative during the period of financial disintermediation, particularly in

1986–87 (Chart 9).[20] They appear to have risen sharply to high levels before the financial liberalization, and then to have increased again immediately after interest rate deregulation in early 1989, before reaching a peak in the middle of that year.[21] Thereafter they declined steadily from 36 percent in mid-1989 to about 6 percent by mid-1991 as financial intermediation improved and the economic adjustment program gained credibility. Hence, there is little evidence that financial liberalization increased real interest rates, other than temporarily.

Another aspect of financial developments in Mexico has been the evolution of the market for domestic public debt and the declining significance of monetary assets in relation to other financial assets. Chart 10 shows the sharp, but gradual, decline of the monetary aggregate M2 as a share of M4 from over 90 percent before 1982 to between 50 percent and 60 percent after 1989. The bottom panel illustrates the change in the composition of public debt, particularly since 1988. The share of CETES as a proportion of the total value of outstanding government bonds declined from 88 percent in December 1987 to 47 percent in June 1991, while the share of the longer-term BONDES increased from 1 percent to 31 percent during the same period. The average maturity of public domestic debt increased from under four months in 1988 to almost one year in June 1991. The chart also shows the increasing significance of AJUSTABONOS; the returns of which are linked to the consumer price index; although introduced only in July 1989, they constituted 18 percent of public debt by June 1991.

---

[19] The money multiplier is measured as the ratio of the monetary base to M2 or M1; the monetary base is defined as currency held by the public and the deposits of the banking system with the Bank of Mexico.

[20] Real interest rates are estimated on an ex post basis as one plus the nominal yield on one-month treasury bills divided by one plus the actual one-month rate of increase of the consumer price index. This assumes that the expected rate of inflation over the month can be approximated by the actual rate of inflation during the previous month.

[21] Measured real interest rates appear to have increased in the first half of 1988 mostly because there was a sharp deceleration of inflation during this period (see Chart 10). To the extent that the turnaround in inflation was largely unanticipated and expectations took some time to adjust, the measured real rate is likely to overstate the true real rate in 1988.

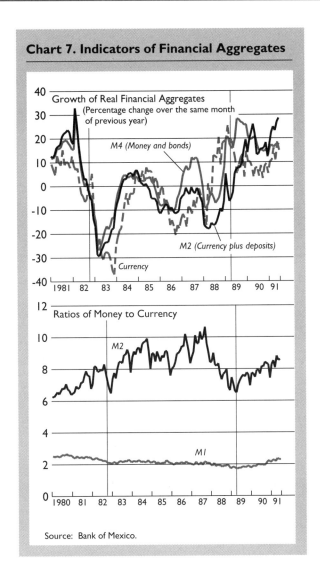

**Chart 7. Indicators of Financial Aggregates**

Growth of Real Financial Aggregates
(Percentage change over the same month of previous year)

M4 (Money and bonds)

M2 (Currency plus deposits)

Currency

Ratios of Money to Currency

M2

M1

Source: Bank of Mexico.

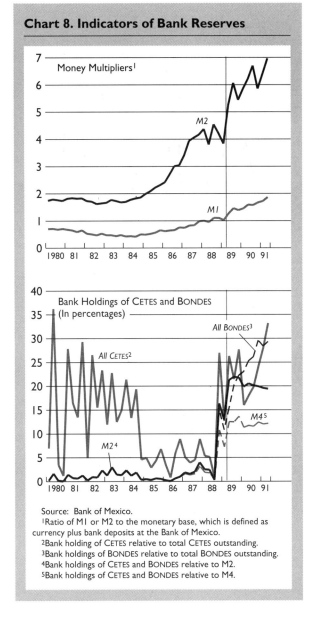

**Chart 8. Indicators of Bank Reserves**

Money Multipliers[1]

M2

M1

Bank Holdings of CETES and BONDES
(In percentages)

All BONDES[3]

All CETES[2]

M4[5]

M2[4]

Source: Bank of Mexico.
[1]Ratio of M1 or M2 to the monetary base, which is defined as currency plus bank deposits at the Bank of Mexico.
[2]Bank holding of CETES relative to total CETES outstanding.
[3]Bank holdings of BONDES relative to total BONDES outstanding.
[4]Bank holdings of CETES and BONDES relative to M2.
[5]Bank holdings of CETES and BONDES relative to M4.

## Conclusion

A salient feature of the financial liberalization in Mexico has been the implementation of a clearly defined strategy in gradual, well-ordered stages. The deregulation of interest rates and the liberalization of direct controls preceded the privatization of the banks by almost two years, affording banks an opportunity to adapt to the more competitive environment and increase their market value. Nonbank financial institutions were first allowed to form financial groups on a limited basis before the more general relaxation of restrictions against universal banking. In addition, the legislation permitting the formation of financial groups was in place in advance of the privatization of the commercial banks, enabling the domestic financial sector to put together the necessary

capital and expertise. Moreover, the liberalization was comprehensive and placed the domestic financial system on a competitive basis.

Another important feature of the Mexican financial liberalization is that it took place in the context of a successful adjustment effort. The 1989–91 period when most of the important financial reforms took place was also a period of tight government budgets and strict financial discipline. The mutually reinforcing effects of these policies and the financial liberalization are likely to have con-

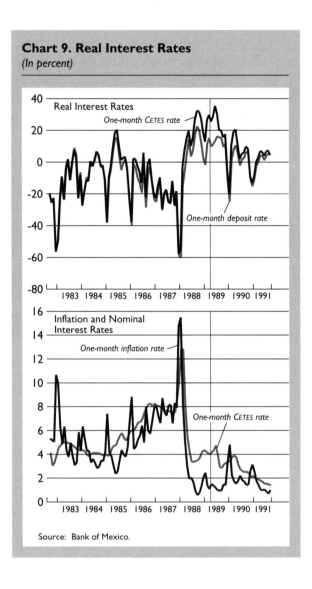

**Chart 9. Real Interest Rates**
*(In percent)*

Source: Bank of Mexico.

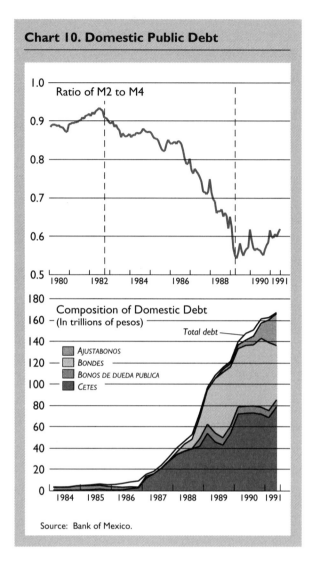

**Chart 10. Domestic Public Debt**

Source: Bank of Mexico.

tributed to the reintermediation in financial markets, the return of flight capital, and the gradual and marked decline in real interest rates.

As noted above, a great deal of the institutional foundation that made the post-1988 financial liberalization effective had been laid gradually over about a 15-year period. At the time of the liberalization, Mexico had a fairly active stock market, an array of private nonbank financial institutions and a significant government securities market. Moreover, except for some limited periods, the balance of payments had been relatively free of capital controls. These factors formed an adequate institutional context in which further liberalization and reform could take place.

Although the Government has actively promoted the integration of financial services, it has restricted the for-

mation of links based on ownership and control between financial institutions and industrial concerns. The nationalization of the banks in 1982 broke up the traditional industrial-financial groups that had developed around the banks since World War II. An important consideration underlying financial reform, including the privatization of the commercial banks, has been the need to preserve the independence and objectivity of credit decisions and to limit the concentration of banking risk in specific industries. The separation of ownership and control between banks and financial groups on the one hand, and industrial and commercial concerns on the other, has been a basic characteristic of financial reform in Mexico.

While Mexico has made significant gains in liberalizing its financial markets, the reforms can be taken further in some areas. Foreign participation in Mexican financial markets is heavily restricted. Apart from one or two minor exceptions, foreign banks, insurance companies, brokerage houses, and other financial concerns are not permitted to operate in Mexico; foreign investors can own only nonvoting shares in Mexican financial institutions and that participation is limited to 30 percent of total stock. The authorities have indicated that an objective of financial liberalization is to allow Mexican financial institutions to be competitive internationally, and the opening up of trade in financial services is an issue that is being examined in the context of the Uruguay Round, as well as in the ongoing discussions on the free trade agreement with the United States and Canada.

# Appendix I   Legislation Introduced in 1990

## The Credit Institutions Act

The new Credit Institutions Law, which abrogated the Law Regulating the Public Service of Banking and Credit, was enacted in July 1990. Under the terms of this act, the following apply.

(1) While development banks remained national credit institutions under public administration, commercial banks were transformed once again into business corporations from the July 1990 effective date. The incorporation of a new bank now requires an "authorization" from the Government rather than a "concession."

(2) Commercial banks may now be majority-owned and controlled by the private sector. Up to 30 percent of the stock of a bank may be held by foreign investors with the exception of foreign governments and government-owned entities. Corporate rights of foreigners would be similar to those of national investors. Any one individual may own up to a maximum of 5 percent of the equity of a bank; this maximum may be increased to 10 percent with the prior authorization of the Government. Institutional investors may hold up to 15 percent of bank shares; financial holding companies are exempted from this maximum.

(3) Provisions are made to limit the concentration of credit risk and stock investments by banks and to ensure the separation of interests between banking and other activities. Lending to managers or partners of a bank is restricted.

(4) To ensure the professional management of banks, the National Banking Commission must authorize the appointment of a bank's chief executive officer, members of its Board of Directors, statutory auditors, and other senior executives. The Commission is authorized to remove or suspend these officers in certain circumstances. The Board of Directors will be elected by shareholders and its composition will correspond to the type of share issued by the bank.

(5) The functions of the Fund for the Protection of Savings will be expanded. In addition to its traditional preventive role, it would provide "express and direct protection to depositors."[22]

## The Act Regulating Financial Groups

According to this new law, the following applies.

(1) Groups can now be formed with a wider range of institutions. There would be two different types of groups: those headed by a holding company and those headed by a bank or brokerage firm. The creation of a financial group requires the prior authorization of the Government. Groups headed by a holding company would offer the widest range of services and could comprise the holding company and at least three other financial institutions including banks, brokerage houses, insurance and bonding companies, investment companies, and auxiliary credit organizations.[23] Groups headed by a commercial bank may acquire, with government authorization, controlling interests in financial institutions other than brokerage houses and insurance or bonding companies. Similarly, groups headed by a brokerage house may not hold an interest in commercial banks or insurance or bonding companies.

(2) With the purpose of diversifying the activities of these groups, two or more intermediaries of the same kind would not be permitted to form part of a group, except for investment or insurance companies, provided that they engage in different risks or activities.

(3) The holding company would be fully responsible for liabilities and losses of any of the financial entities of the group, while each of the entities would not be held responsible for the holding company's losses nor for those of any other member of the group. According to the Mexican authorities, this provision "retains one of the main advantages of specialized financial intermediation, while providing for the benefits of a system of integrated financial services."[24]

(4) Apart from some limited exceptions, the holding company may not contract any direct or contingent liabilities nor pledge its assets. Financial group members cannot invest in the holding company's or in the other members' capital stock. The purpose of this measure is to avoid the pyramiding of the capital base and to ensure

---

[22] Bank of Mexico (1991), p. 89. All banks contribute a premium to this fund; although there is no formal deposit insurance in Mexico, this fund provides some safety net in emergencies.

[23] Auxiliary credit organizations encompass credit unions, warehouse companies, leasing firms, financial factoring firms, and exchange houses.
[24] Bank of Mexico (1991), p. 91.

the adequacy of capital requirements for the operations undertaken.

## The Securities Market Act

This law, which had been originally introduced in 1975, was amended to (1) permit the formation of financial groups headed by brokerage firms, and (2) allow foreign investment of up to 30 percent of capital in brokerage houses and to set a limit of 10 percent on individual shareholdings.

# Bibliography

Bank of Mexico, *The Mexican Economy* (Mexico, 1989, 1990, 1991).

Baring Securities, *Mexico: Emerging from the Lost Decade* (March 1991).

Barnes, Guillermo, "Liberalization and Regulation of the Securities Market: the Mexican Case," a paper prepared for the seminar on Financial Sector Liberalization and Regulation, organized by the World Bank and the Harvard Law School Program on International Financial Systems, May 1990.

———, "Modernizacion del Sistema Financiero Mexicano," Seminario Sobre Financiamiento y Promocion Industrial, NAFIN (August 1990).

Berdeja, Augustin, "Mexico's New Financial Laws: A Peaceful Revolution," *International Financial Law Review* (November 1990), pp. 34–36.

Laurie, Samantha, "Oxygen of Recovery," *The Banker* (April 1990), pp. 49–53.

———, "Aperture of Opportunity," *The Banker* (April 1990), pp. 53–54.

Mancera, Miguel, "Reformas de los Sistemas Financieros: Desregulacion y Supervision en la Experiencia Mexicana," *Boletin Cemla* (November–December 1990), pp. 310–14.

Marray, Michael, "Privatization Can Be a Complicated Process" *Euromoney* (September 1990), pp. 163–66.

Ortiz, Guillermo, "La Reforma Financiera" (mimeograph, December 1989).

———, "Discurso en La Sexta Reunion Nacional de la Banca" (Ixtapa: August 1990).

# VI  Mexico's External Debt Policies, 1982–90

## Mohamed A. El-Erian

Since the outbreak of the 1982 "debt crisis," external debt-management policies have played a critical role in the Mexican authorities' efforts to restore sustained economic growth in the context of internal and external financial stability.[*] The authorities, recognizing the heightened awareness of the adverse impact of growing public sector indebtedness on private sector confidence and economic growth, placed increased emphasis on the need to lower debt-servicing obligations by reducing contractual claims rather than rescheduling of payments falling due. The primary focus was on reaching agreements with bank creditors to restore access to voluntary international capital market financing. This reflected the importance of bank debt in Mexico's total indebtedness and the greater preparedness of Mexico's official creditors to provide new financing. The authorities' efforts toward a comprehensive bank debt restructuring included the signing on February 4, 1990 of a far-reaching financing agreement affecting some $48 billion of Mexico's estimated total indebtedness of $95 billion at the end of 1989. The agreement incorporated an innovative "menu" of financing options featuring principal reduction, interest rate reduction, and a new money option. It also included waivers for future market-based debt-reduction operations, as well as a "value recovery facility," linking incremental debt-servicing payments to better-than-anticipated developments in Mexico's oil export prices.

Appropriate debt restructuring has had a dramatic impact on Mexico's economy, together with the sustained implementation of a comprehensive medium-term economic adjustment and reform program. In addition to reduced debt-servicing obligations, the package contributed to a sharp improvement in private sector perceptions of Mexican transfer risk. Diminished concerns about Mexico's external indebtedness were reflected in a sudden and substantial fall in real domestic interest rates, a surge in domestic share prices, a recovery in secondary market prices for Mexican external bank claims, and a reduction in interest rates on foreign bond issues. These developments were associated with large private capital inflows—in the form of foreign direct investment and the repatriation of flight capital—and the restoration of Mexico's access to voluntary international capital market financing.

This section analyzes the evolution of Mexico's debt-restructuring approach from the outbreak of the 1982 debt-servicing problems up to the recent restoration of access to voluntary financing. It discusses the key elements of the approach, the manner in which they were implemented, and how they developed into comprehensive debt and debt-service reduction operations. This provides the basis for an analysis of the country's return to voluntary capital market financing—an issue addressed in greater detail in the next section. This section is organized as follows: The first part outlines the background to the 1982 crisis and the authorities' initial approach, including an analysis of the elements that led to the growing consensus, both at home and abroad, on the need to address the debt problem through debt-reduction operations rather than repeated rescheduling and new money exercises. The second describes the authorities' debt-reduction approach, focusing in particular on the structure of the bank debt-reduction package finalized in 1990 and the associated debt-equity program. The last part analyzes the 1990 package's direct and indirect impact on the Mexican economy. It also outlines some of the implications for debt-management policies in what has been labeled by some as the era of "life after debt."

Developments in Mexican debt issues have had effects that go even beyond their contribution to the restoration of the country's medium-term viability and the rationalization of creditors' balance sheets. In effect, Mexico's bank packages are often viewed as having created precedents for more generalized adaptations in debt-restructuring terms. At the same time, Mexico has been among the first developing countries to benefit from international initiatives concerning commercial bank debt restructurings, such as the Baker Plan and Brady Initiative. Moreover, it was among the first countries with recent debt-servicing problems to restore access to voluntary financing from international loan, equity, and bond markets. For these reasons, the present analysis of Mexico's

---

[*] An earlier version of this section was published as part of "Mexico's External Debt and the Return to Voluntary Capital Market Financing," IMF Working Paper, WP/91/83 (Washington: International Monetary Fund, 1991).

debt-management policies is conducted within a broader framework emphasizing the two-way interactions between developments in Mexico and the evolution of the "international debt strategy."

## Debt-Management Policies in 1982–87—Liquidity Support

### Emergence of Debt-Servicing Problems

In August 1982, Mexico announced to its commercial bank creditors that it was unable to meet fully its scheduled debt-service payments. It requested a three-month moratorium on principal payments and the formation of a bank "advisory group" to negotiate the restructuring of its bank claims. The action is often regarded as marking the outbreak of the "international debt crisis," since it was followed by similar developments in many other developing countries. This, in turn, was reflected in a sharp increase in debt-rescheduling agreements, with the average number of agreements a year increasing from 4 in 1978–81 to 18 in 1983–84 for bank debt, and from 4 to 15 in the case of Paris Club debt.[1]

Although the debt problems of Mexico and several other developing countries came to prominence in 1982, their causes reflected developments over a number of years. The emergence of severe debt-servicing difficulties was due to the implementation of inappropriate domestic policies (particularly overexpansionary fiscal and monetary stances and maintenance of an overvalued exchange rate), unfavorable exogenous developments (including adverse terms of trade and international interest rate developments, sluggish demand in industrial country trading partners, and growing protectionist tendencies abroad) and a sharp cutback in the availability of private external financing. The combined effect of these factors was a reduction in debtor countries' debt-servicing capacity at a time of increasing debt-service payments obligations.

In Mexico's case, pursuing overly expansionary domestic demand-management policies resulted in a sharp deterioration in the fiscal balance. This was accompanied by a sharp appreciation of the real effective exchange rate, an acceleration in inflation, and a marked deterioration in the current account deficit in 1981, despite the sevenfold increase in petroleum receipts.[2]

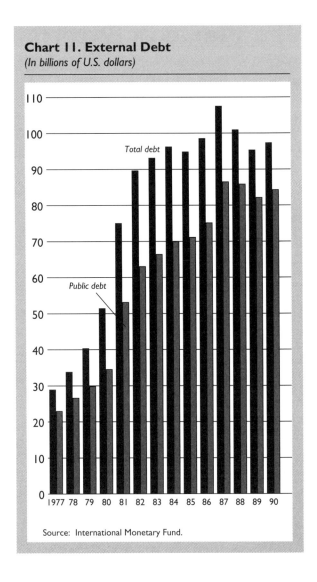

**Chart 11. External Debt**
*(In billions of U.S. dollars)*

Source: International Monetary Fund.

---

[1] Details on commercial bank and Paris Club debt restructurings are contained in the International Monetary Fund's annual reviews of international capital markets and multilateral official debt reschedulings, respectively.

[2] The current account deficit increased from $2.3 billion (equivalent to 3.1 percent of GDP) in 1978 to $13.9 billion (5.8 percent) in 1981. The deficit had averaged $2.1 billion in the 1970–77 period (3.0 percent of GDP). Discussions on economic developments during this period are contained in Cumby and Obstfeld (1983), Solis and Zedillo (1984), and Zedillo (1985a and 1985b).

The country's worsening current account position was financed in large part through increased external borrowing, especially by the public sector. As a result, external debt grew from under $30 billion at the end of 1977 to $75 billion at the end of 1981; in 1981 alone, the country's external indebtedness grew by almost 50 percent (Chart 11). The situation was aggravated by the deterioration in the structure of debt, with the share of short-term claims (with maturity of less than one year) in total debt increasing from 13 percent at the end of 1978 to 30 percent at the end of 1981. Accordingly, the Mexican economy was extremely vulnerable to the major adverse exogenous developments that occurred in 1981–82, including the sharp increase in international interest rates.

Mobilizing nonconcerted external financing sufficient to cover the balance of payments requirements became more difficult during 1982 as concern mounted in financial markets regarding Mexico's deteriorating economic situation. The arrangement in midyear of what turned out to be the final voluntary bank syndication of $2.5 billion proved protracted—with only 75 banks accepting out of the 650 invited—despite the attractive pricing of the loan.[3] Analysts have observed that by July 1982, "it became clear that the only debt-management expedient left was to continue rolling over short-term credits—at any price and at any maturity."[4] New bond issues fell to $1.6 billion from $2.3 billion in 1981, while access to new short-term commercial bank credit lines was significantly curtailed.[5]

Yields on existing international bond issues rose sharply reflecting heightened risk perceptions among international investors.[6] At the same time, domestic residents' loss of confidence in peso-denominated assets caused a sharp growth in currency substitution (with the share of dollar deposits in total deposits increasing from less than 20 percent in the late 1970s to over 40 percent in 1981–82)[7] and substantial private capital outflows (with capital flight estimated in the $17–23 billion range for 1980–82).[8] Thus, despite a sharp contraction of imports and an improvement in the current account balance (by 2 percentage points of GDP), Mexico resorted to a substantial drawdown in reserves during 1982; by the end of the year, reserves stood at the historically low level of 2.9 months of imports.

Mexico's debt-servicing problems were recognized to have adverse implications not only for the country's growth and development prospects but also for the financial integrity of the international banking system. For example, by 1982, the capital of U.S. banks covered only 50 percent of external claims on developing countries, with Mexico accounting for a significant portion of these claims. The nine largest U.S. money center banks had an exposure to Mexico (i.e., claims adjusted for guarantees and other risk transfers) of $13 billion at the end of December 1982; this was equivalent to 45 percent of their total capital and accounted for 15 percent of their exposure to all developing countries.[9]

The systemic implications of developing countries' debt difficulties led to a recognition of the need to approach the problem within a comparably systemic "international debt strategy." Based on increased coor-

dination among debtors, creditors, and international financial institutions, the strategy sought to strike an appropriate balance between financing and adjustment, while ensuring equitable burden sharing among creditors. Under the strategy, which was applied on a case-by-case basis, debtors were urged to adopt adjustment programs that would restore financial viability, and official bilateral and commercial bank creditors were urged to provide liquidity support through principal reschedulings and new money facilities. The Fund and the World Bank were given a central role in assisting in the formulation and implementation of debtors' adjustment policies and mobilizing external assistance in support of these policies.[10]

## Period of Repeated Debt Reschedulings

After intense negotiations,[11] the Mexican authorities succeeded in rescheduling debt-servicing obligations to commercial banks, in the context of an adjustment program aimed at macroeconomic stabilization. The bank agreement, which was made effective in March 1983, included (1) the rescheduling over eight years (including four-year grace periods) of $19 billion of obligations (reflecting 100 percent of eligible principal falling due over the period August 23, 1982–December 1984); (2) the concerted rollover through the end of 1986 of $5 billion of short-term interbank obligations; and (3) $5 billion in new money through a medium-term (six years, including three years' grace period) international syndicated credit.[12] Thus, in total, the package was to provide Mexico gross cash flow relief of some $30 billion over the period 1983–86. In an attempt to introduce a degree of "fairness" among the 500-plus participating banks, an individual bank's new money contribution was based on its outstanding exposure to Mexico as of August 1982. Moreover, the inclusion of short-term obligations ensured that several late lenders were not "bailed out."[13]

Pending the satisfactory conclusion of the bank financing package, Mexico received substantial bridge financing from official sources. These included advance payments for sales of petroleum and $4 billion of official bridge loans, of which $925 million each from the Bank for International Settlement (BIS) and the U.S. authorities (Treasury and Federal Reserve Board) and swaps with Spain and France for $450 million. In addition, Mexico signed a rescheduling with the Paris Club in June 1983 covering $1 billion of obligations to 15 industrial country creditors.

---

[3] See Castro (1983).

[4] Solis and Zedillo (1984), pp. 44–45.

[5] After growing by $9 billion during 1981 to $28 billion, short-term claims on Mexico of BIS (Bank for International Settlements) reporting banks remained broadly unchanged in 1982.

[6] A discussion of developments in bond yields during this period is contained in Edwards (1986).

[7] A discussion of currency substitution in Mexico is contained in Ortiz (1983).

[8] Estimates reported in Lessard and Williamson (1987).

[9] Estimates based on data contained in Federal Financial Intitutions Examination Council (1985).

[10] The role of the Fund in the debt strategy is discussed in the institution's annual reports, in Coats (1989) and in Guitián (1992).

[11] Accounts of the negotiations are contained in Kraft (1984) and Leeds and Thompson (1987).

[12] The new money facility carried spreads of 2⅛–2¼ percentage points over the London interbank offered rate (LIBOR), while the spreads on the rescheduled debt amounted to 1¾–1⅞ percentage points.

[13] The rescheduling of Mexican private sector debt is not addressed in this paper.

The terms of the Mexican financing package (coverage, interest rate, and maturity structure) created precedents for subsequent debt reschedulings for other heavily indebted developing countries. It also established procedures for mobilizing concerted financing from various creditors; for example, in the approach taken by the international financial institutions as they sought to ensure the effectiveness of their role as catalysts for financial assistance from official bilateral and commercial bank creditors. The December 4, 1982 telex sent by the Mexican Secretary of Finance to bank creditors stated that the Managing Director of the International Monetary Fund would not recommend to the Executive Board approval of an arrangement in support of the Mexican program "without assurances from both official sources and commercial banks that adequate external financing was in place . . . and the principles of a realistic restructuring scheme would be favorably considered by the community."[14] This approach was formalized through the subsequent implementation of the "critical mass" procedure. Under this procedure, the entry into effect of a Fund arrangement was made conditional on sufficient formal commitments for bank support (usually for at least 90 percent of the programmed new money). In addition to providing assurances that the program would be adequately financed, the procedure assisted in limiting free-rider problems—the latter associated with withdrawals of banks that would place an "undue" financing burden on the remaining participating banks.

Despite the implementation, although with some slippages, of substantial corrective measures, Mexico faced recurrent problems in meeting contractual debt-service obligations. Accordingly, the 1983 commercial bank rescheduling was followed by similar but more comprehensive agreements in 1984 and 1985.[15] Throughout this period, as well as in later years, Mexico remained current on its interest obligations to banks. As in 1983, the 1984–85 agreements centered on the reduction of payments to banks through principal reschedulings and on de facto interest refinancing through concerted new money facilities. Thus, in April 1984, Mexico secured a new money facility of $4 billion;[16] this was followed by the March 1985 multiyear rescheduling covering some $30 billion of principal obligations corresponding to previously rescheduled debt, payments falling due in 1987–90, and obligations on the 1983 syndicated credit. The agreement also committed Mexico to introducing a debt-equity conversion program. This package foreshadowed several of the elements of later restructurings, including the gradual move toward stock-of-debt operations and allowance for

banks to "exit" at a discount through debt-equity swaps.

The debt-equity program was initiated in April 1986, allowing the exchange of eligible credits for capital stock.[17] New authorizations under the program were suspended in November 1987 in response to, inter alia, concerns about the program's inflationary pressures,[18] doubts about the additionality of the related foreign investments, and public perceptions that Mexican capital was being sold at "unduly low prices." During 1986–90, external bank claims of some $3.8 billion were exchanged under the program for equity valued at $3.2 billion, involving a weighted average discount of 17 percent (Chart 12).

Mexico's external accounts improved as a result of the implementation of adjustment efforts.[19] By 1985, the current account had moved into surplus (amounting to $1.3 billion, equivalent to 0.7 percent of GDP, mainly due to a 45 percent reduction in nominal import values since 1981) and gross international reserves (excluding gold and balances under payments agreements) had recovered to 4.3 months of imports. The sustainability of this improvement, however, was increasingly questioned. Given the extent and nature of the initial economic and financial imbalances, the adjustment efforts were accompanied by an initial deceleration of economic growth. Despite the repeated debt restructurings, debt-service payments averaged around 35 percent of receipts from exports of goods and services, with the bulk of payments representing interest obligations. Moreover, the economy remained vulnerable to adverse exogenous shocks at a time when access to concerted bank loan facilities became increasingly difficult as a result of weakening creditor cohesion and associated free-rider problems. This compounded the impact of the near total absence of voluntary external bond financing.[20]

These types of concerns were instrumental in the decision to strengthen the international debt strategy through a plan put forward in October 1985 by U.S. Treasury Secretary Baker (the "Baker Plan"). The plan maintained a case-by-case approach and called for (1) the implementation by debtor countries of strong growth-oriented adjustment policies; (2) increased structural adjustment-

---

[14] Solis and Zedillo (1984), p. 49.

[15] These dates correspond to the finalization of agreements with all banks, rather than the initial agreements with the steering committee of bank creditors.

[16] The 1984 new money facility carried better terms than that of 1983, including a 10-year maturity, 5½ years' grace period, and spreads of 1⅛–1½ percentage points over LIBOR.

[17] The modalities of the program were set out in Comisión Nacional de Inversiones Extranjeras (1986).

[18] In its 1986 Annual Report, the Bank of Mexico warned that "This scheme can have inflationary effects in that it has recourse to the issuance of currency to finance the repurchase of foreign debt. To avoid these effects it is necessary for the Government to finance its reacquisition of its debt through the placement of securities [which has] the disadvantage of exerting upward pressure on the internal cost of credit and displacing private users of capital." Some of the costs and benefits of debt-equity swaps in general are discussed in United Nations Center on Transnational Corporations (1990).

[19] The tightening of economic and financial policies is discussed in Gil Diaz (1987) and Dornbusch (1988).

[20] After declining to $1.6 billion in 1982, Mexican international bond issues averaged only $72 million a year in the next five years, with three of these years characterized by no new issues.

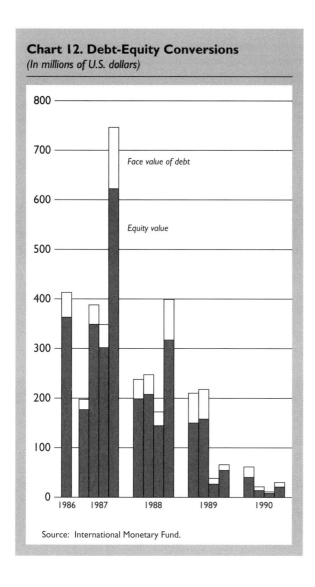

**Chart 12. Debt-Equity Conversions**
*(In millions of U.S. dollars)*

*Face value of debt*

*Equity value*

Source: International Monetary Fund.

type lending by multilateral institutions (more specifically a 50 percent increase in net disbursements); and (3) additional net lending by commercial banks (amounting to 2.5–3 percent of exposure a year for the period 1986–88). These actions were to be supported by a growing world economy and open industrial country markets for developing country exports. While the strategy still focused predominately on the liquidity problems of heavily indebted developing countries, the Baker Plan reflected greater recognition of the deep-rooted nature of the debt problems facing these countries.

After protracted discussions during the course of 1986—which took place in the context of a strengthening of adjustment policies in response to, inter alia, a sharp decline in international oil prices—the authorities finalized in April 1987 an innovative and comprehensive agreement, consistent with the emphasis of the Baker Plan.[21] The agreement contained the traditional new money and principal rescheduling elements, as well as growth and investment contingency financing facilities. Specifically, it included (1) a new money facility of $5 billion; (2) $1 billion in cofinancing with the World Bank; (3) $2 billion in growth contingency and contingent investment support facilities; and (4) the rescheduling of $45 billion of principal claims. The agreement also carried significantly more favorable terms, including maturities of up to 20 years (including seven-year grace periods) on the rescheduled portion and a uniform spread of $13/16$ of 1 percentage point over LIBOR.[22] As regards official bilateral debt, Paris Club creditors granted a multiyear rescheduling agreement in September 1986 covering $2 billion of non-previously rescheduled obligations falling due between September 1986 and March 1988. Mexico had also received exceptional support in the form of a $1.6 billion bridge financing from industrial country governments and other Latin American countries.[23]

**Secondary Market for Bank Claims**

The protracted nature of bank restructuring exercises and the introduction of officially sanctioned debt-equity conversions contributed to a marked growth in the importance of the secondary market for bank claims on developing countries. Although there are no comprehensive data on the size of the market in its early stages, partial indicators point to a steady growth throughout the second half of the 1980s. Annual turnover is estimated to have increased from less than $5 billion in 1985–86 to $30–40 billion in 1987–88, with Mexican paper accounting for a significant proportion of this trading. The bulk of the transactions reflected banks swapping assets as a means of reallocating their loan portfolios, purchases of claims for use in debt conversions, and retirement by the corporate sector of own-debt at a discount.

Secondary market prices exhibited considerable volatility during these years around a declining trend. As illustrated in Chart 13, the secondary market price for bank claims on Mexico declined from 63 cents on the dollar (discount of 37 percent) in early 1986 to around 40 cents on the dollar (60 percent discount) at the end of 1988. This decline reflected Mexico-specific factors (including the suspension of the debt-equity program) and, perhaps more important in this period, general market influences. Most significant among the latter was the announcement

---

[21] Agreement on the "critical mass" for the new money facility was reached in late 1986.

[22] Additional information on the package is contained in Wertman (1986) and Gardner (1986).

[23] Disbursements from the facility included $545 million from the United States, $400 million from 12 European countries, and $155 million from Argentina, Brazil, Colombia, and Uruguay.

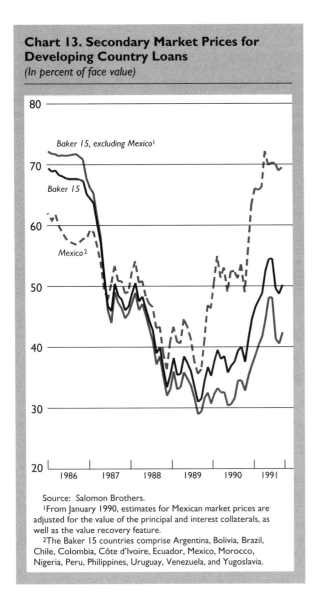

**Chart 13. Secondary Market Prices for Developing Country Loans**
*(In percent of face value)*

Source: Salomon Brothers.
[1]From January 1990, estimates for Mexican market prices are adjusted for the value of the principal and interest collaterals, as well as the value recovery feature.
[2]The Baker 15 countries comprise Argentina, Bolivia, Brazil, Chile, Colombia, Côte d'Ivoire, Ecuador, Mexico, Morocco, Nigeria, Peru, Philippines, Uruguay, Venezuela, and Yugoslavia.

by major U.S. and U.K. banks during 1987 of significant provisioning measures on exposure to highly indebted developing countries. Such actions increased the immediate costs to banks of carrying these claims on their books. Moreover, the actions were perceived by the market to imply a greater willingness among banks to dispose of their claims on debtor countries.

## Concerns About Excessive Indebtedness

As noted earlier, the main objective of the financing packages during the 1982–87 period was to provide developing countries with the short-term cash flow support needed to facilitate the restoration of balance of payments viability. The objective of liquidity support was broadly met, despite generally more protracted negotiations and uncertainties about their outcome, especially in the area of new money mobilization. Questions increased, however, both in Mexico and in other highly indebted countries, as to the prospects for medium-term external viability. The relaxation in short-term liquidity constraints was accompanied by a growth in contractual debt obligations, contributing to a further deterioration in market sentiments regarding the creditworthiness of borrowing countries and the eventual restoration of access to voluntary foreign financing.

There were thus growing concerns regarding the impact of new money and principal reschedulings on highly indebted countries' growth potential—that is, the so-called debt overhang concerns. Although these were expressed in various ways, the fundamental issue involved the implications of growing indebtedness for private sector investment activities.[24] Specifically, as the stock of contractual debt surpasses agents' perceptions of the debtor country's capacity to service it, foreign and domestic assessments of country risk deteriorate significantly.[25] Thus, even in the context of sustained domestic adjustment efforts, questions arise about the authorities' ability to meet debt-service payments without, inter alia, further increases in effective taxation. The latter lowers the expected return on domestic investment activities, thereby discouraging inflows of foreign direct investment resources and encouraging capital flight and diversion of resources to consumption. In an attempt to counter the associated credit rationing, domestic borrowers are forced to offer relatively high rates of return to foreign and domestic savers to compensate for the increased risk premiums. In some cases, such rates may impose costs that are in excess of the expected return on the debt-financed activities or prove insufficient to relax the credit rationing.[26] These adverse effects cannot be addressed through rescheduling of debt-service payments but, rather, require dealing with the overall stock of indebtedness through operations to reduce debt and debt service.

The increasing emphasis on operations to reduce debt and debt-service was accompanied by growing evidence of banks' willingness to dispose of developing country claims, often at substantial discounts. This reflected banks' growing ability to "exit"—partly owing to the gradual

---

[24] A fuller exposition of the debt overhang concept is contained in Dooley and others (1990).

[25] The linkages between domestic and foreign indicators of country risk are discussed in Khor and Rojas-Suarez (1991).

[26] In the presence of imperfect information, borrowers may be denied access to credit even if they are willing to pay more than the market interest rate. This reflects essentially the difficulties faced by lenders in adequately pricing the riskiness of loans, taking into account also that this price may affect the subsequent behavior of the borrower or attract more risky borrowers, or both (i.e., moral hazard and adverse selection risks). A discussion of these issues is contained in Stiglitz and Weiss (1981).

strengthening of their capital base[27]—as well as greater incentives to do so as a result of more stringent regulatory provisioning requirements on developing country exposure and prospects of seemingly endless episodes of concerted new money packages based on existing bank exposure. The erosion of cohesion within the banking community intensified, and seriously impeded the coordination needed to formulate and implement concerted new money packages. These developments were part of a larger phenomenon of portfolio rationalization and reconsideration of asset structures by international commercial banks. In these circumstances, increased attention was directed to the use of a "menu" that includes a range of several financing options to reconcile banks' differing circumstances.[28]

## Operations to Reduce Debt and Debt Service

Mexico appeared to meet many of the "stylized facts" associated with the above-cited concerns about a high stock of external debt. The economy's external indebtedness had grown from some $75 billion (45 percent of GDP) at the end of 1981 to $108 billion (76 percent of GDP) by the end of 1987. As a result, and despite a sustained growth in nonpetroleum exports, the debt service ratio (before rescheduling) rose in the mid-1980s, fluctuating in the 60–80 percent rate in 1985–87; interest obligations amounted to around one fourth of receipts from exports of goods and services during this period (Chart 14). This compared to debt-service and interest-service ratios of around 16 percent and 6 percent, respectively, for developing countries without recent debt-servicing problems.[29] Moreover, as shown in Chart 15, Mexico's debt-service ratio after restructuring during this period remained above the average for the group of developing countries with recent debt-servicing problems, with the margin increasing through the mid-1980s.

The continued deterioration in Mexico's debt situation was accompanied by increasing uncertainties about timely and adequate new financing from banks. A growing number of bank creditors (particularly smaller ones) resisted further increases in exposure associated with concerted new money exercises.[30] The associated concerns about the country's financial prospects contributed

**Chart 14. Debt-Service Ratios Before Rescheduling**
(In percent)

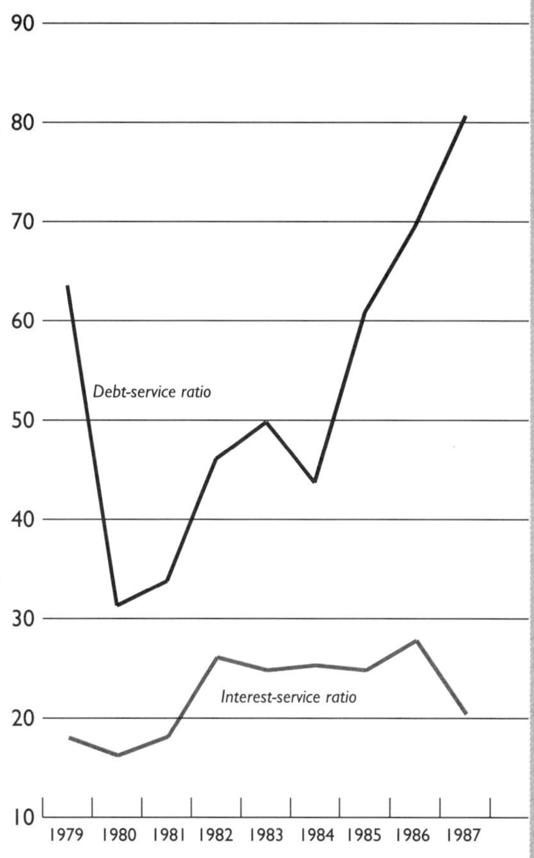

Source: International Monetary Fund.

to capital flight, including in the form of a sharp rise in deposits held outside Mexico by Mexican residents.[31]

In these circumstances, the authorities sought ways of gaining debt relief through a reduction of claims at discounts from face value. Although the international climate was not conducive to a comprehensive debt-reduction package, there was scope for some partial operations. In the context of a voluntary market-based approach, this required a bank agreement to waive clauses governing the prepayment of principal and the sharing of payments among creditors grouped together through syndications

---

[27] In the case of U.S. banks, for example, the ratio of capital to external claims on developing countries increased from 49 percent at the end of 1982 to 119 percent at the end of 1987.

[28] See Devlin (1990).

[29] IMF (1991).

[30] The 1987 new money package, for example, was delayed substantially by reluctance on the part of U.S. regional banks to participate.

---

[31] For example, the Fund's *International Financial Statistics (IFS)* reported stock of Mexican residents' deposits in U.S. banks increased from $7.2 billion at the end of 1981 to $14.5 billion at the end of 1986 (IMF (1988)).

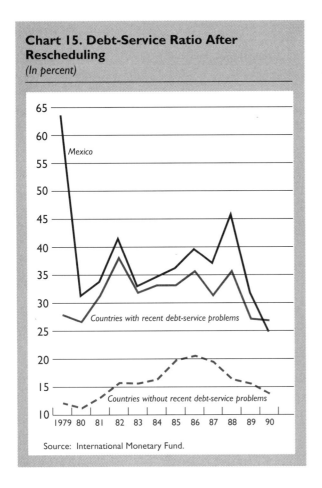

**Chart 15. Debt-Service Ratio After Rescheduling**
*(In percent)*

Source: International Monetary Fund.

and rescheduling agreements. Moreover, to the extent that debt reduction involved collateralized debt exchanges, it was also necessary to obtain a waiver of the negative pledge clause.[32]

## Aztec Debt Exchange

In late December 1987, the Mexican authorities and Morgan Guaranty announced a debt-conversion operation involving the voluntary exchange of bank claims for newly issued 20-year bullet repayment bonds; the principal on these bonds was fully guaranteed by U.S. Treasury zero-coupon bonds. The new Aztec bonds (also

---

[32] The sharing clause commits creditors that are party to an agreement to share on a proportional basis any payments received from the debtor. The negative pledge clause commits the debtor not to create for new debt a lien on any present or future assets or revenues without offering to share that security with existing creditors on an equal basis.

referred to in the literature as the Mexico-Morgan bonds) carried a spread of 1⅜ over LIBOR, twice that on the rescheduled debt.[33]

The bonds were allocated through an auction completed in February 1988, with 139 banks tendering 320 bids for a total value of $6.7 billion of bank claims. The authorities accepted bids from 95 banks for a total face value of $3.7 billion in claims—substantially below their goal of $10 billion. The claims were exchanged for $2.6 billion in new bonds. The new bonds—which were reportedly acquired primarily by Japanese banks, followed by U.S. (mainly regional) and Canadian banks—were collateralized through the Mexican purchase of $0.5 billion of U.S. Treasury zero-coupon bonds.

While welcoming the results of the debt exchange, the Mexican authorities emphasized the need to expand the scope of debt and debt-service reduction beyond the small-scale operations that had been undertaken to date. For example, in setting out the economic objectives for his administration, President Salinas emphasized a reduction in the "historical" stock of debt, lowering the net external resource transfer, and securing multiyear agreements with creditors in order to reduce the uncertainty caused by recurrent debt negotiations.[34] Similarly, in a 1988 presentation to other Mexican officials, Angel Gurria, Mexico's debt negotiator, noted that "every step would be taken to explore market-based, voluntary debt alternatives. If they should fail, the international community must offer a solution or else face unilateral action."[35]

## Comprehensive Debt-Reduction Operations

The Aztec debt exchange had an impact that went well beyond its modest net debt-reduction effects. It represented the first officially sanctioned, market-based, bank debt-reduction exercise for a large middle-income developing country debtor.[36] It confirmed the gradual movement toward debt- and debt-service reduction operations based on a voluntary market-based approach, and the associated recognition that some write-down of contractual debt to banks was inevitable in some cases. After a number of proposals for official initiatives—emanating from academic, banking, and official circles[37]—indus-

---

[33] Additional information on the exchange is contained in Folkerts-Landau and Rodriguez (1989).

[34] Aspe Armella (1990).

[35] Hacienda's "Politica de Deuda y Financiamiento Externo," quoted in Dornbusch (1988).

[36] In November 1987, Bolivia finalized waivers from its commercial bank creditors to buy back its debt at a discount. During the first quarter of 1988, banks tendered about half of the outstanding principal claims, the bulk of which were bought back at a discount of 89 percent. The buy-back was financed by official grants to Bolivia administered and disbursed through a "voluntary contribution account" held at the IMF.

[37] Some of which are discussed in Prasad and Vasudevan (1990).

trial country support for comprehensive commercial bank debt-reduction operations in highly indebted developing countries coalesced around the proposals put forward in March 1989 by U.S. Treasury Secretary Brady.[38]

The Brady proposals stressed four key elements: (1) the adoption of medium-term reform programs in debtor countries, with special emphasis on measures to encourage investment and capital repatriation; (2) a stronger emphasis on instruments that reduce debt and debt service as a complement to new lending; (3) the use of international financial institution resources to facilitate debt- and debt-service reduction operations; and (4) continued creditor government support through Paris Club reschedulings, support of international financial institutions, ongoing export finance, and a review of constraints to debt operations imposed by the regulatory, tax, and accounting regimes.[39]

### The Bank Package to Reduce Debt and Debt Service

The above-mentioned proposals established the framework for the July 1989 preliminary agreement on the restructuring of $48 billion of Mexico's bank debt through a menu incorporating principal and interest reduction instruments. In April of that year, Mexico initiated discussions with its bank creditors on a comprehensive package to reduce debt and debt service. Such a package was to support the implementation of the authorities' medium-term economic program, including important structural reform efforts (in the areas of production, trade, investment, and financial services) and prudent fiscal, monetary, and pricing policies.[40] Preliminary agreement on the broad elements of the package was reached with the advisory committee of banks on July 23 and the "term sheet" for the agreement was finalized on September 13 and subsequently marketed to over 500 banks. With positive responses from almost all bank creditors, the financing package was signed on February 4, 1990. The exchange of instruments under the agreement took place on March 29, 1990, or almost one year after the initiation of the negotiations.

In dealing with the bulk of Mexico's medium- and long-term indebtedness to banks, the financing package offered creditors a menu with three options.[41] The first involved the exchange of claims for 30-year bullet discount bonds (at 65 percent of face value) carrying a "market interest rate" (spread of $^{13}/_{16}$ over LIBOR) and collateralization of all principal obligations and 18 months of interest (on a rolling basis). The second involved the exchange of claims for 30-year bullet reduced interest par bonds (fixed interest rate of 6¼ percent), with the same collateralization structure. Taking account of the residual Mexican risk in these new instruments, their implicit pricing was broadly consistent with secondary market prices for bank claims prevailing at the time of the initial agreement on the package. The third option involved a net increase in bank exposure through a new money facility for 1989–92 amounting to 25 percent of eligible exposure, carrying a spread of $^{13}/_{16}$ of 1 percentage point over LIBOR and repayable over 15 years (including 7 years' grace). The financing package also granted Mexico the necessary waivers to conduct additional market-based debt- and debt-service reduction operations in the future.

A total of $4.4 billion of claims was allocated to the new money option, implying bank loan disbursements of $1.1 billion over the three-year period, well below initial expectations. By contrast, the banks' response to the debt and debt-service reduction instruments was larger than expected. Banks accounting for $20.6 billion chose the discount bond option, while $22.5 billion of claims was allocated to the reduced interest par bonds. These bond instruments involved setting up collateral for a total of $7.1 billion, based on the net present value of the associated guarantees. The collaterals took the form of U.S. Treasury zero-coupon bonds (at a yield of 7.925 percent) for the principal guarantee and the establishment of an interest guarantee account at the Federal Reserve Bank of New York. The collateral was financed through loans from the IMF (total of SDR 1.3 billion— $1.7 billion at the end of January 1990 exchange rate— available over three years), the World Bank ($2.0 billion disbursed up front), and Mexico's own resources ($1.3 billion). In addition, the Japanese Export-Import Bank provided an incremental $2.1 billion of import financing over three years, thereby freeing an equal amount for funding the debt and debt-service reduction operations. Since not all of these resources were disbursed to Mexico up front, the authorities arranged for bridge financing from the banks of $1.2 billion.

---

[38] See remarks by Secretary Brady to the Brookings Institution and the Bretton Woods Committee Conference on Third World Debt, reproduced in Department of Treasury (1990). The move on commercial indebtedness was preceded by adaptations in Paris Club rescheduling practices for low-income countries (known as the "Toronto Initiative") involving, inter alia, options to reduce debt and debt service for maturities falling due.

[39] As summarized in U.S. Under-Secretary of the Treasury Mulford's 1990 statement to the House of Representatives' Subcommittee on International Development, Finance, Trade, and Monetary Policy, House Committee on Banking, Finance and Urban Affairs. See also Mulford (1989).

[40] The main elements of the 1989–92 program, supported by a three-year Fund arrangement under the extended Fund facility and World Bank financing, are described in Kalter and Khor (1990).

[41] Main features of the financing package are discussed in El-Erian (1990).

The new debt and debt-service reduction bonds (also commonly referred to as "Brady" bonds) carry a "value recovery" facility providing for incremental payments to banks should the real price for Mexican oil exports exceed $14 a barrel. These payments would start in 1996 and amount to 30 percent of the "windfall" oil revenue, subject to an annual limit of 3 percent of the banks' eligible claims at the time of the agreement. In establishing the terms for this recapture clause, a delicate balance had to be struck between providing a more direct linkage between Mexico's debt- servicing capacity and its obligations (thereby allowing for a reduction in contractual noncontingent payments obligations) and avoiding excessive marginal taxation of incremental export receipts.

The Mexican authorities sought to introduce symmetrical downside financing contingencies in the event of unanticipated adverse exogenous events. This attempt did not succeed, however, reflecting banks' general reluctance at that time to agree to increases in their exposure. (Banks also refused to include downside contingency financing in the subsequent financing agreements with Venezuela and Uruguay.)

### Debt-Equity Program

Under the terms of the financing package, Mexico committed itself to resume the debt-equity program for a minimum amount of conversions of $3.5 billion (face value of debt) over a three-year period. The modalities for this program, announced in March 1990, specified, inter alia, (1) the range of eligible debt (that restructured under the 1990 package plus new money commitments); (2) modalities for conversion (auction mechanism, with successful bidders required to deposit, within ten days of the auction, claims in an amount of 5 percent of the swap rights awarded and having 18 months to acquire the remaining rights);[42] and (3) the sectoral distribution of the allowable equity participation (infrastructure projects and privatization purchases—the latter subject to a ceiling of 50 percent of sales).

In formulating these modalities, the authorities sought to limit the negative consequences perceived to have been associated with the earlier debt-equity program. As noted earlier, these included potential adverse domestic liquidity implications, the scope for hidden subsidies, and unfavorable effects on future investment flows. To this end, the aggregate limit on conversions was derived consistent with the potential under the financing program for sterilization through issuance of domestic debt or for reduced total budgetary outlays, or for both. Moreover,

the associated domestic liquidity creation was spread over a number of years. The announcement of strict adherence to the aggregate limit (and the relatively rapid allocation of swap rights within this limit—see below) reflected concerns among officials that an open-ended program would delay future untied private foreign direct investment inflows. At the same time, the authorities sought to ensure the additionality of the external resources and the positive externalities associated with the debt-equity operations through the specification of the allowable sectoral allocation. Finally, the adoption of an auction system with relatively few barriers to entry reflected the authorities' desire for transparent and competitive pricing.

## Impact of Debt Reduction

### Magnitude of Debt Reduction

The discount bond option extinguished $7.1 billion of Mexican bank debt. At the same time, the par bond option reduced the contractual interest rate on $22.5 billion of claims, equivalent to an additional reduction of $7.9 billion in principal (based on then-prevailing interest rate conditions). Thus, in total, the bond instruments involved a gross effective principal reduction of $15.0 billion, representing some 16 percent of Mexico's outstanding debt at the end of 1989.[43]

As regards the debt-equity program, auctions were held in July and October 1990. In the July auction, the authorities offered to convert $1 billion of claims (original face value) using a "marginal pricing" system. They accepted 27 of the 359 offers tendered, with the lowest successful discount amounting to 52.05 percent. In the second auction, the authorities reserved the right to increase the offered amount above the initially-specified limit of $1.5 billion. This limit was reached at a marginal discount of 53.15 percent. In view of the favorable offers, and to avoid the direct and indirect costs of holding an additional auction, the authorities proceeded to accept bids up to the global limit of $2.5 billion. This was achieved at a discount of 52.0 percent.

In total therefore, the authorities accepted to convert $3.5 billion of claims into equity at an average discount of 52.01 percent. The overwhelming majority of the successful bids involved par and discount bonds (as opposed to new money claims). If successful bids are fully exercised, the book value reduction in the post-package debt stock (i.e., after taking account of the discount bond

---

[42] Swap rights not exercised under the program may be eventually converted back at par into new debt instruments carrying no enhancements.

[43] As noted earlier, the reduction in contractual claims required Mexico to provide partial collateralization (present value of $7.1 billion) for the debt and debt-service reduction bonds. This was associated with the acquisition of a "contingent foreign asset" (in the form of the zero-coupon bonds and cash balances at the Federal Reserve Bank of New York) that may be used in meeting final interest and principal payments on the bonds, provided Mexico remains current until then.

adjustments) would amount to $2.6 billion. As a result, the total gross effective debt reduction associated with the package would amount to some $17½ billion (some 19 percent of external debt at the end of 1989).

Since the operations were market based (i.e., priced consistent with conditions on the secondary market for bank claims), they involved, on average, no change in banks' expected stream of receipts even though the contractual value of their obligations was reduced. Should Mexico meet fully its debt-service payments—and abstracting from the additional costs/benefits associated with provisioning requirements, tax allowances, and other institutional factors—the stream of receipts (measured in ex post net present value terms) would be larger, ceteris paribus, for holders of the debt and debt-service-reduction bonds as compared with creditors who exited fully through the debt equity route.[44] At the same time, however, the total yield for the bond holders would be below that for creditors who opted for larger Mexican risk exposure through the new money option. Finally, the relative yield ranking within the debt and debt-service reduction bonds will depend, ceteris paribus, on developments in international interest rates. Thus, given that the bonds were broadly equivalent in net present value terms at the time of the initial agreement, LIBOR rates well below 9½ percent would involve higher relative yields for holders of the par bonds.[45]

### Cash Flow Impact of Debt Reduction

The direct impact of the package on Mexico's balance of payments will be felt through the savings in interest obligations. On the basis of international interest rates prevailing in 1990—which were much higher than at present—the gross saving amounts to some $1½ billion annually on account of the bond exchanges and some $¼ billion on account of the debt-equity conversions. After taking into account the financing costs of the collateral (including forgone interest receipts due to the use of Mexico's own reserves), the total annual net savings in contractual interest obligations amount to about $1 billion, equivalent to 0.6 percent of GDP (of which $¾ billion (0.5 percent) on account of the bond exchanges).[46] The beneficial cash flow impact of the package will increase over time as a result of the lower interest payments that Mexico will have to make as external financing requirements are met through the continued

impact of the debt and debt-service reduction elements rather than new money. The package also reduced Mexico's vulnerability to unfavorable movements in international interest rates. Specifically, in excess of one fourth of Mexico's remaining debt is now subject to a fixed interest rate.

The financing package also involved the effective rescheduling of amortization obligations falling due, thus significantly changing the contractual maturity profile of bank indebtedness. Under the debt and debt-service reduction bonds, principal payments of $43 billion were deferred to a single payment due in 2020. Principal repayments on the remaining eligible claims were rescheduled over 15 years, including 7 years' grace. Unlike the reduction in interest payments, however, it may be assumed that the refinancing of principal obligations would have been granted under the previous rescheduling approach—albeit involving a series of debt negotiations.

## Addressing Concerns About Excessive Indebtedness

More important than the direct cash flow impact is the change in the private sector's perceptions of Mexico's creditworthiness and economic prospects, brought about by the package. In the context of sustained implementation of sound economic and financial policies, the fall in Mexico's contractual debt obligations and the associated reduction in uncertainties about the need and outcome of periodic debt renegotiations contributed to a turnaround in private sector sentiment. This, in turn, facilitated the country's restoration of access to voluntary financing from international capital markets and enhanced its ability to attract foreign direct investment and repatriated flight capital.

A number of financial indicators illustrate the turnaround in private sector perceptions of Mexican risk. Domestic real interest rates declined by 20 percentage points (to around 10 percent a year, measured in ex post terms) immediately after the announcement of the preliminary agreement on the bank package—a decline was subsequently sustained. Domestic share prices rose sharply and the secondary market price for Mexican bank claims generally improved. By the end of November 1991, the ratio of the secondary market price of Mexican bank claims (calculated on the basis of the stripped yield for Mexican risk)[47] to the weighted average of the other countries constituting the "Baker 15" group of heavily indebted developing countries had risen by around 40

---

[44] A comprehensive discussion of the distribution of the benefits of the package between Mexico and its commercial bank creditors is contained in van Wijnbergen (1990).

[45] This factor has been reflected in secondary market price developments since the issuance of the bonds, with the par bonds appreciating at a faster rate than the discount bonds.

[46] These calculations do not take into account profit and dividend transfers associated with the new participation obtained through debt-equity swaps.

[47] The derivation of the Mexican price is based, inter alia, on adjusting (or "stripping") the reported discount and par bond market prices for the value of the principal and interest collateral, as well as a notional estimate of the value recovery feature.

percent as compared with its level before the announcement of the package (see Chart 13).[48]

Perhaps the most dramatic manifestation of the change in perceptions of Mexican risk is provided by the extent and speed with which the country has been able to restore access to voluntary capital market financing—an issue that is documented in more detail in the following section. The implementation by Mexico of appropriate economic policies and the comprehensive debt restructurings consistent with medium-term viability were preconditions for access to such financing. The process was also facilitated by the use of techniques addressing investors' concern about transfer and credit risks—including the use of credit enhancements in the initial phases of market re-entry.[49]

Mexican international bond issues rose from an estimated $0.6 billion in 1989 to over $2 billion in 1990. Preliminary data for the first three quarters of 1991 indicate that a somewhat larger amount was raised during this period. This greater volume of bond issues was placed among a widening group of investors in industrial countries (primarily the United States, Germany, Spain, and Switzerland), as well as reportedly mobilizing Mexican resident capital held abroad—the latter appears to have been particularly important in the initial phases of the market re-entry process.

The relaxation in credit rationing on international bond markets was accompanied by a sharp improvement in terms. By the second half of 1991, average yield spread at issue fell to around half the level prevailing in 1990.[50] Similar developments occurred with regard to secondary market yields for Mexican bonds. Moreover, maturity terms lengthened substantially. Finally, as documented in the following section, the market re-entry process was not limited to international bonds. Mexico also mobilized voluntary financing through, inter alia, placements of equities, Euro-commercial paper, and Euro-certificates of deposit.

**Policy Implications**

Mexico's return to more normal capital market financing has been a difficult and protracted process. It is generally believed that the attainment of the authorities' objectives of sustained economic growth and financial stability will require the maintenance and strengthening of normal financial relations with domestic and external

creditors. As recognized by the authorities, it is therefore critical that the country consolidate the progress achieved so far.[51] Two important elements may be identified in this regard: (1) the maintenance of sound economic and financial policies; and (2) responsive adaptations in debt-management policies, including in the use of credit enhancements, hedging, and other financial risk-management instruments.

The following are selected aspects of debt-management policies.

*Credit Enhancements*

The use of collateralization and other credit enhancement techniques in the initial re-entry issues strengthened Mexican entities' ability to overcome high levels of market risk aversion. Thus, through appropriate design of debt instruments, Mexican borrowers have been able to minimize investors' exposure to credit and transfer risks.[52] At the same time, however, as recognized by the authorities, the continued use of such techniques may involve potentially significant costs and should be carefully monitored.

Collateralization techniques should be used only by entities that have already strengthened their underlying financial position. In effect, unless the borrowers' fundamentals are sound—with respect to both actual and prospective creditworthiness and the transfer risk associated with the country's economic and financial conditions—credit enhancements will not lastingly improve market perceptions of risk. Even in circumstances where fundamentals are sound, the benefits of credit enhancements should be assessed in terms of their overall impact on liquidity management. By pledging existing assets or future receipts, borrowers may lose financial flexibility in

---

[48] If Chile and Venezuela are excluded from the denominator on the basis that they have also major appropriate restructuring operations, the relative increase in the Mexican price is more pronounced.

[49] An analysis of these issues is contained in El-Erian (1991). An overview discussion of the restoration of some Latin American countries' access to voluntary capital market financing is provided in El-Erian (1992).

[50] Calculated relative to "risk-free" industrial country sovereign issue of same currency and maturities.

[51] It may be noted that Mexico's recent return to voluntary financing is not an unprecedented phenomenon. After defaulting in the early part of the twentieth century, Mexico's entire debt was renegotiated in 1942–46, including through a reduction in contractual principal. By 1960, Mexico had redeemed the affected obligations (see Green (1976)). This was followed by a restoration of access to voluntary international markets leading the *New York Times* to observe: "Mexico is closing a checkered page in financial history, a story of default and rebirth that goes to the misty era of international promise that preceded World War I . . . The 46 years between the defaulting of the external bonds in 1914 and the granting of the [new voluntary $100 million] loan will go down as marking the financial coming-of-age of the Latin republic . . . . With most of the old bonds sucked out of the market by the redemption last week, most of this lingering public evidence of Mexico's long struggle to live down the old debt default has been wiped out for good" (*New York Times*, July 2, 1960, quoted in Dornbusch (1988)).

[52] For example, some of the early bond placements by TELMEX provided the investor with protection in the form of a claim on future payments from AT&T on account of international communications. Accordingly, investors' exposure to TELMEX credit risk and Mexican country transfer risk was effectively transformed into an exposure to AT&T credit risk and U.S. transfer risk. Other forms of collateral have included bank deposits, electricity accounts, and credit card receivables.

the future, with potentially adverse implications in the event of short-term liquidity problems. Accordingly, it is important that the use of credit enhancements be based on an intertemporal maximization process. This would need to take account of, inter alia, the immediate gains in terms of lower financing costs, the correlation between the borrowers' expected stream of receipts and expenditures, and possible costs owing to the deterioration in the relative status of creditors with unsecured claims. Indeed, under certain circumstances, wide-scale resort to credit enhancements could impair rather than improve certain borrowers' prospects for sustaining their return to voluntary capital market financing. Moreover, this could have contagion effects for other entities accessing the market, thereby increasing their borrowing costs and raising public policy issues.

An application of the above considerations to Mexico would suggest that, with the authorities' sustained implementation of economic and financial policies to reduce market perceptions of transfer risk, the recent significant reduction in the use of collateralization by established Mexican entities should continue. The immediate costs in terms of borrowers accepting less favorable interest rate and fee structures is offset by the gains accruing from avoiding the potentially escalating costs of credit enhancements. At the same time, care should be taken to ensure that the uses of credit enhancements are not generalized to include firms that are yet to strengthen their financial positions. Given potential adverse externality effects for other Mexican borrowers and possible market information failures, a case could be made for continued government involvement, particularly in the initial stages of market re-entry. This could include the monitoring of borrowing amounts and terms and the provision of information to actual and prospective borrowers to assist in evaluating the potential net costs of credit enhancements.

### Risk-Management Techniques

In the earlier discussion of the origins of Mexico's debt problems, the section alluded to the impact of adverse developments in international oil prices and interest rates. As demonstrated by conventional standard deviation-based volatility measures, the Mexican economy has also been exposed to considerable fluctuations in these key exogenous variables since the emergence of the debt crisis.[53] The maintenance of relatively "open positions" in such circumstances allows for the volatility in exogenous variables to be quickly translated into the country's international obligations and receipts. Moreover, estimations of simple correlation coefficients for this period indicate that adverse developments in one of the vari-

ables were not offset, on average, by favorable developments in the other.[54]

In recognition of the above, Mexico has taken steps recently to reduce its vulnerability to exogenous shocks. As noted earlier, the 1990 bank package has enabled the central government to lower its interest rate risk through agreement on a fixed below-market rate on an important portion of its outstanding indebtedness. The authorities have also reduced the country's exposure to international oil price movements through sustained export diversification.[55] Nevertheless, adverse exogenous developments would have a significant impact on the country's prospects.[56] Accordingly, as recognized by the authorities, further steps in these areas would be beneficial and would contribute to an improvement in country transfer risk.

It may be noted that between December 1990 and the end of February 1991, the Mexican authorities sold futures contracts in the oil market covering about three months of crude oil exports. The pricing of these operations is reported to have been above the central budget assumption of $17 a barrel, leading a Finance Ministry official to state that "it is extremely important for us that investors know that, no matter what happens to the price of oil, the economic program is on for 1991. Regardless of what happens, we've got $17 a barrel."[57]

The reduction in country transfer risk has also facilitated nongovernment borrowers' access to market-based risk management instruments.[58] This should allow, inter alia, for Mexican corporate issuers of variable interest rate notes to improve their management of interest rate risk through the use of forward, swap, or contingent contracts.[59] For certain borrowers, such activities could be complemented by commodity hedging operations, particularly through future market transactions. This would be particularly relevant for exporters of commodities

---

[53] See El-Erian (1991).

[54] Specifically, the correlation coefficient for changes in monthly U.S. dollar-denominated international oil prices and LIBOR interest rates amounts to 0.02; it falls to minus 0.2 when account is taken of the average lag between LIBOR interest rate changes and actual interest payments.

[55] The share of oil receipts in total exports (including in-bond transactions) has declined from an average of over 70 percent in 1980–82 to an estimated 30 percent in 1988–90.

[56] For example, computed on the basis of 1990 oil exports, a 10 percent decline in oil prices would be associated with a $1 billion loss in export receipts on an annual basis. On the same basis, a 1 percentage point rise in LIBOR would involve incremental interest obligations of some $0.7 billion.

[57] Moffett and Truell (1991). At the same time, the authorities have set up a contingency fund in which the windfall oil and privatization receipts are deposited.

[58] Several of these instruments involve the borrower making future payments under certain conditions (e.g., in the case of a swap where the borrower agrees with its counterparty to exchange a string of certain types of payments obligations for other types of payments obligations).

[59] Additional information is contained in Mathieson and others (1989).

(e.g., the copper companies) or manufacturing enterprises that rely heavily on imports of certain commodities (e.g., glass producers). Increased commodity price and interest rate hedging is an appropriate goal within a framework that takes account of their market costs and their administrative requirements.

## Conclusion

The section has examined the evolution of Mexico's bank debt restructurings since the outbreak of debt-servicing problems in 1982. It analyzed the development of the approach to debt away from one based on liquidity/cash flow concerns toward one placing greater emphasis on the need to address the adverse impact of a growing stock of indebtedness on private sector investment and growth. When implemented in the context of a comprehensive economic adjustment program, the adaptations in debt policies played a critical role in facilitating Mexico's return to voluntary capital market financing—the latter constituting a fundamental component of the economy's progress toward medium-term viability.

Mexico's 1990 financing package with commercial banks was important in improving market perceptions of Mexico's country transfer risk. Thus, although its direct, immediate financial impact was relatively limited, indications show that, together with the sustained implementation of sound policies, it reduced concerns about Mexico's indebtedness. This was reflected, inter alia, in a sharp reduction in domestic real interest rates and a fall in secondary market yields on external loan and bond claims on Mexico. The associated restoration of access to voluntary capital market financing was accompanied by a steady improvement in market terms, including a sharp fall in the risk premiums paid by Mexican borrowers. Large repatriation of flight capital and increased foreign direct investment inflows reinforced the beneficial impact on the economy's private investment and growth performance.

As recognized by the authorities, the consolidation of Mexico's return to voluntary credit markets requires, inter alia, the maintenance of sound economic and financial policies and responsive debt-management polices. As regards the latter, this section has noted the importance of careful monitoring of the risks inherent in re-entrants' reliance on credit enhancements. The section also noted the merit of Mexican borrowers making greater use of financial risk-management techniques to reduce further their exposure to adverse exogenous price developments. As was the case for Mexico's debt-management policies in the past, these actions are likely to have effects that go well beyond the country's economic and financial prospects. Thus, it is probable that Mexico will continue to influence the approach of other developing countries to debt management, particularly through "demonstration effects."

# Bibliography

Aspe Armella, Pedro, "The Renegotiation of Mexico's External Debt," *IDS Bulletin*, Vol. 21 (April 1990), pp. 22–32.

_____, Rudiger Dornbusch, and M. Obstfeld, eds., *Financial Policies and the World Capital Market: The Problems of Latin American Countries* (Chicago: University of Chicago Press, 1983).

Banco de México, *Indicatores Económicos* (Mexico, various issues).

_____, *Informe Anual* (Mexico, various issues).

Besanko, David, and Anjan V. Thakor, "Rationing and Rationing: Sorting Equilibria in Monopolistic and Competitive Credit Markets," *International Economic Review*, Vol. 28 (October 1987), pp. 671–89.

Bank for International Settlements (BIS), *The Maturity Distribution of International Bank Lending* (Basle, various issues).

Bruno, M., and others, *Stopping High Inflation* (Massachusetts: MIT Press, 1987).

Castro, E., "Algunas Consideraciones sobre el Financiamiento Externo de México en los años de 1980–82" (mimeograph, 1983).

Citibank, "Latin America Accesses the International Capital Markets: Debt Financing Alternatives," International Capital Markets (New York: Citibank, 1991).

Coats Jr., Warren L., "LDC Debt: The Role of the International Monetary Fund," *Contemporary Policy Issues*, Vol. VII (April 1989), pp. 41–49.

Comisión Nacional de Inversiones Extranjeras, *Manual Operativas para la Capitalización de Pasivos y Substitución de Deuda por Inversión* (México, 1986).

Committee on Banking, Finance and Urban Affairs, House of Representatives, *Hearing on the Mexican Bank Agreement* (Washington, February 7, 1990).

Cumby, Robert E., and Maurice Obstfeld, "Capital Mobility and the Scope for Sterilization: Mexico in the 1970s," *Financial Policies and the World Capital Market: The Problem of Latin American Countries,* ed. by Aspe Armella, P. R. Dornbusch, and M. Obstfeld (Chicago: University of Chicago Press, 1983), pp. 245–69.

Department of the Treasury, *Treasury News* (Washington) March 10 Bulletin (1990).

Devlin, R., "The Menu Approach," *IDS Bulletin*, Vol. 21, No. 2 (April 1990), pp. 11–16.

Dooley, Michael, and others, *Debt Reduction and Economic Activity*, IMF Occasional Paper, No. 68 (Washington: International Monetary Fund, 1990).

Dornbusch, R., "México: Estabilización, Deuda y Crecimiento," *El Trimestre Económico*, Vol. 55 (October–December 1988), pp. 899–937; also printed as "Mexico: Stabilization, Debt and Growth: A European Forum," Economic Policy, Vol. 7 (October 1988), pp. 231–83.

Edwards, S., "The Pricing of Bonds and Bank Loans in International Markets," *European Economic Review*, Vol. 30 (June 1986), pp. 565–89.

El-Erian, M.A., "Mexico's Commercial Bank Financing Package," *Finance and Development* (Washington), Vol. 27, No. 3 (September 1990), pp. 26–27.

_____ "Mexico's External Debt and the Return to Voluntary Capital Market Financing," IMF Working Paper, WP/91/83 (Washington: International Monetary Fund, August 1991).

_____ " Restoration of Access to Voluntary Capital Market Financing—The Recent Latin American Experience," *Staff Papers*, International Monetary Fund (Washington), Vol. 39 (March 1992), pp. 175–94.

Federal Financial Institutions Examination Council, *Statistical Release: Country Exposure Lending Survey* (Washington, 1985).

Folkerts-Landau, David, and Carlos A. Rodriguez, "Mexican Debt Exchange: Lessons and Issues," in *Analytical Issues in Debt*, ed. by Jacob A. Frenkel, Michael P. Dooley, and Peter Wickham (Washington: International Monetary Fund, 1989), pp. 359–71.

Frenkel, Jacob A., Michael P. Dooley, and Peter Wickham, eds., *Analytical Issues in Debt* (Washington: International Monetary Fund, 1989).

Gardner, David, "Package Offers a Breathing Space on Debt," *Financial Times*, October 2, 1986.

Gil Diaz, F., and Paul Ramos Tercero, "Inflation Stabilization: Lessons from Mexico," in M. Bruno and others (1987).

Green, R., *El Endeudamiento Público Externo de México, 1940–73* (Mexico: El Colegio de México, 1976).

Griffith-Jones, Stephany, ed., *Third World Debt: Managing the Consequences* (London: IFR Publishing Ltd., 1989).

Guitián, Manuel, *Rules and Discretion in International Economic Policy* (Washington; International Monetary Fund, 1992).

Hernández-Estrada, Julio, Manuel R. Villa-Issa, and A.Q. Loya, "Mexican External Debt and Its Effects on U.S.-Mexico Agricultural Trade," *American Journal of Agricultural Economics*, Vol. 71, No. 5 (December 1989), pp. 1117–22.

International Monetary Fund, *Annual Report of the Executive Board for the Financial Year Ended April 30, 19—* (Washington: International Monetary Fund, various issues).

_____, *International Capital Markets—Developments and Prospects* (Washington: International Monetary Fund, various issues).

_____, *International Financial Statistics* (Washington: International Monetary Fund, various issues).

_____, *International Financial Statistics—Supplement on Economic Indicators*, No. 10 (Washington: International Monetary Fund, 1985).

_____, *Multilateral Official Debt Rescheduling—Recent Experience* (Washington: International Monetary Fund, various issues).

_____, *World Economic Outlook,* World Economic and Financial Surveys (Washington: International Monetary Fund, 1991).

Kalter, E., and H.E. Khor, "Mexico's Experience with Adjustment," *Finance and Development* (Washington), Vol. 27, No. 3 (September 1990), pp. 22–25.

Khor, Hoe E., and Liliana Rojas-Suarez, "Interest Rates in Mexico: The Role of Exchange Rate Expectations and International Creditworthiness," IMF Working Paper, WP/91/12 (Washington: International Monetary Fund, 1991).

Kraft, Joseph, *The Mexican Rescue* (New York: Group of Thirty, 1984).

Leeds, Roger S., and Gale Thompson, *The 1982 Mexican Debt Negotiations: Response to a Financial Crisis*, FPI Case Study No. 4 (Washington: Johns Hopkins University, 1987).

Lessard, Donald, and J. Williamson, *Capital Flight and Third World Debt* (Washington: Institute for International Economics, 1987).

Mathieson, D., and others, *Managing Financial Risks in Indebted Developing Countries*, IMF Occasional Paper, No. 65 (Washington: International Monetary Fund, 1989).

Mattesini, Fabrizio, "Screening in the Credit Market: The Role of Collateral," *European Journal of Political Economy*, Vol. 6, No. 1 (1990), pp. 1–22.

Moffett, M., and P. Truell, "Mexico Moves to Lock-in Oil Prices in Gulf Crisis," *Wall Street Journal*, March 11, 1991, p. C12.

Mulford, David C., "The Brady Plan: Strengthening the Current International Debt Strategy," in *Third World Debt: Managing the Consequences*, ed. by Stephany Griffith-Jones (London: IFR Publishing Ltd., 1989).

_____, Statement to the House of Representatives' Subcommittee on International Development, Finance, Trade, and Monetary Policy, Committee on Banking, Finance and Urban Affairs, House of Representatives, Hearing on the Mexican Bank Agreement, Serial No. 101–73, February 7, 1990.

Organization for Economic Cooperation and Development, *Financial Statistics Monthly* (Paris: OECD, 1991).

Ortiz, Guillermo, "Currency Substitution in Mexico: The Dollarization Problem," *Journal of Money, Credit and Banking*, Vol. 15 (May 1983), pp. 174-85.

Prasad, A., and A. Vasudevan, "International Debt: A Survey of Major Reform Proposals," *Journal of Foreign Exchange and International Finance*, Vol. 4 (April–June 1990), pp. 135–49.

Ruíz-Suárez, A., "La Deuda Externa como factor Limitante del Crecimiento Económico: Los Casos de Costa Rica, Ecuador, México y Venezuela," Serie Cuadernos de Investigacion (Mexico: Centro de Estudios Monetarios Latinomericanos, 1987).

Salomon Brothers, *Indicative Prices for Developing Country Claims*, various issues.

Solis, L., and E. Zedillo, "A Few Considerations on the Foreign Debt of Mexico" (mimeograph, 1984).

Spar, Raymond D., Debora Spar, and G. Tobin, *Iron Triangles and Revolving Doors: Cases in U.S. Foreign Economic Policymaking* (New York: Praeger Press, 1991).

Stiglitz, Joseph E., and Andrew Weiss, "Credit Rationing in Markets with Imperfect Information," *American Economic Review*, Vol. 71 (June 1981), pp. 393–410.

Thompson, Gary D., and Jimmye S. Hillman, "Agricultural Trade between the United States and Mexico: The Impacts of Mexico's Foreign Debt," *American Journal of Agricultural Economics*, Vol. 71 (December 1989), pp. 1123–34.

United Nations Center on Transnational Corporations, *Debt Equity Conversions: Guide for Decision Makers* (New York: United Nations (1990).

van Wijnbergen, Sweder, "Mexico's External Debt Restructuring in 1989–90," PRE Working Paper, No. 424 (Washington: The World Bank, 1990).

Vazquez Pando, F.A., "The Mexican Debt Crisis in Perspective: Faulty Legal Structures and Aftershocks," *Texas International Law Journal*, Vol. 23 (Spring 1988), pp. 171–231.

Wertman, Patricia, "The Mexican Debt Accords and their Financial Implications: An Overview," *Congressional Research Service*, Report No. 86–179 E (1986).

Wionczek, Miguel, ed., *Politics and Economics of the External Debt Crisis* (Boulder: Westview Press, 1985).

World Bank, *World Debt Tables* (Washington, various issues).

Zedillo, E. (1985a), "The Mexican External Debt: The Last Decade," in *Politics and Economics of the External Debt Crisis*, ed. by Miguel S. Wionczek (Boulder: Westview Press, 1985).

_____(1985b), "Mexico's Recent Balance of Payments Experience and Prospects for Growth," Report to the Group of Twenty-Four, UNDP/UNCTAD, INT/84/021.

# VII    Mexico's Return to Voluntary International Capital Market Financing

## Philippe Szymczak

Since mid-1989, Mexico has gradually regained access to voluntary international capital market financing after having been virtually excluded for much of the decade. The renewed acceptability of Mexican securities among international investors has been accompanied by a notable improvement in interest rates and maturities. In the event, Mexico has been at the forefront of the process of re-entry by developing countries into the international capital markets.

Mexico's return to capital market financing followed the sustained implementation of a far-reaching program of macroeconomic adjustment and structural reforms, accompanied by a comprehensive restructuring of existing indebtedness, which served to address "debt-over-hang" concerns. This process is of considerable significance both for Mexico and for other potential market re-entrants in their attempt to overcome the credit rationing that characterized most of the 1980s.

This section focuses on private sector portfolio flows, which have been the main vehicle of re-entry. The first part presents the various instruments used by Mexican entities in their efforts to raise capital abroad. The second analyzes the factors that facilitated re-entry. The concluding part discusses the macroeconomic implications of this process and highlights some of the policy implications.

## Instruments and Markets Used in the Re-Entry Process

Mexico's re-entry process has been characterized by a marked shift in the range of financing instruments used by Mexican entities to raise funds abroad. In contrast with the late 1970s and early 1980s, when the bulk of foreign financing was in the form of syndicated bank loans, Mexican borrowers, since mid-1989, have raised capital abroad in significant amounts using a progressively broader range of negotiable instruments, including bonds, Euro-certificates of deposit (Euro-CDs), Euro-commercial paper (Euro-CPs), and equities. This has helped Mexico broaden its financing base, adopt more flexible financing strategies, and avoid saturating individual markets.

## Bond Issues

So far, spontaneous market financing for Mexico has taken predominantly the form of bond issues. Since the placement of the landmark June 1989 BANCOMEXT issue (see below), a large number of bond issues has been placed on progressively better terms. Between June 1989 and December 1991, Mexican borrowers raised the equivalent of $6.2 billion in international bond markets through 50 issues; of this amount, the public sector (including the Government) issued the equivalent of $4.1 billion while private entities raised about $2.1 billion.

Mexican bond issues rose from $100 million during the first semester of 1989 to the equivalent of $1.7 billion a semester in 1991. As both the value and the number of issues increased, the range of markets and investor pools tapped by Mexican borrowers was also diversified. While the U.S. dollar segment of the market (both Euro-markets and the U.S domestic private placement market, including under Rule 144A)[1] remained the main source of funds, Mexican public sector entities have successfully raised funds in the deutsche mark, Austrian schilling, ECU, peseta, Canadian dollar, and pound sterling segments of the market.

Financing costs have declined over time, with a lower yield premium above "risk-free" paper reflecting the increased acceptance of Mexican securities by international investors. When the re-entry process began in June 1989 with a $100 million five-year note issue by Bancomext—the first unsecured voluntary public sector issue by a Mexican borrower since 1982—the combination of a 10.25 percent coupon and a steep launch discount pushed the initial yield-to-maturity to 17 percent, some 820 basis points over the yield on comparable maturity U.S. Treasury bonds.

Subsequently, yields on Mexican bond issues, both by public and private sector entities, have fallen sharply. Yield spreads over risk-free paper have narrowed in the primary market from an average of 800 basis points on unenhanced paper (i.e., unsecured or without convertibility options) during the second half of 1989 to 329

---

[1] See pp. 68–69 for a discussion of Rule 144A.

**Table 9. Characteristics of Bonds Issued by Mexican Entities, June 1989–December 1991**

| | 1989 Semester | | 1990 Semester | | 1991 Semester | |
|---|---|---|---|---|---|---|
| | 1st | 2nd | 1st | 2nd | 1st | 2nd |
| Yield spread (in basis points) | 820 | 483 | 448 | 401 | 281 | 298 |
| Of which: unenhanced issues[1] | 820 | 800 | 602 | 377 | 345 | 329 |
| Maturity (in years) | 2.5 | 3.5 | 3.5 | 4.3 | 4.3 | 5.2 |
| Of which: unenhanced issues[1] | 2.5 | 2.0 | 5.0 | 4.2 | 4.0 | 5.4 |
| Public sector | | | | | | |
| Yield spread (in basis points) | 820 | 165 | 306 | 322 | 261 | 232 |
| Of which: unenhanced issues[1] | 820 | ... | 348 | 349 | 261 | 261 |
| Maturity (in years) | 2.5 | 5.0 | 4.7 | 4.4 | 3.6 | 5.7 |
| Of which: unenhanced issues[1] | 2.5 | ... | 5.0 | 4.4 | 3.6 | 6.1 |
| Private sector | | | | | | |
| Yield spread (in basis points) | ... | 800 | 660 | 560 | 305 | 429 |
| Of which: unenhanced issues[1] | ... | 800 | 760 | 570 | 555 | 482 |
| Maturity (in years) | ... | 2.0 | 1.6 | 4.0 | 5.3 | 4.0 |
| Of which: unenhanced issues[1] | ... | 2.0 | 2.0 | 3.0 | 5.0 | 3.8 |

Source: IMF staff estimates, based on *International Financing Review, Euroweek, Latin Finance*, and the *Financial Times*.
[1] Bond issues not involving collateralization or convertibility options.

basis points during the second half of 1991. The yield spread on unenhanced public sector paper narrowed from 820 basis points in 1989 to 261 basis points during the second half of 1991, while for private sector borrowers it declined from 800 basis points in 1989 to 482 basis points during the second half of 1991 (Table 9). In line with the improvement observed in the primary markets, the yield spread over U.S. Treasury bonds implied by reported movements in secondary market prices of publicly traded bonds has declined to less than 250 basis points for several issues by public sector borrowers (Chart 16).

A gradual lengthening in the average maturity of bonds has also been observed, although maturities on issues by Mexican borrowers remained in the short-term range (five years or less) during most of the 1989–91 period. The landmark BANCOMEXT issue, which marked the initiation of the re-entry process in June 1989, had an effective average maturity of two and a half years. In contrast, in successive issues since September 1991, Mexican borrowers have set benchmarks for the longest dated deal from Latin American issuers since 1982. In September 1991, PEMEX, the state-owned oil company, successfully tapped the U.S. dollar segment of the market with a seven-year bond; this was followed by the placement of ten-year bonds by NAFINSA in October and by PEMEX in November. These issues by NAFINSA and PEMEX were particularly important in that they established a complete yield curve for Mexican credit, which constitutes an important benchmark for future bond issues for borrowers from the region. More generally, the average maturity

lengthened from about 3 years in 1989 to 5.2 years during the second half of 1991 (see Table 9).

The bond issues to date have been mainly on behalf of entities with established international reputations and, in general, a strong export base. Their placement was facilitated in the initial re-entry phase by the use of enhancements, including collateralization techniques, bond-equity conversion facilities, and early redemption options ("puts").[2] Various kinds of assets have been pledged as collateral, including foreign exchange receivables generated abroad, assets located abroad, and Mexican mortgages.[3] During June 1989–December 1991, public sector borrowers used collateralization techniques in 7 out of 32 issues, while private sector companies enhanced their debt instruments in 9 out of 18 issues. From June 1989 through December 1990, collateral backed offerings accounted for about 58 percent of total Mexican bond placements. In contrast, Mexican borrowers—particu-

---

[2] Put options allow the holder to resell (put), at his discretion, the bond to the borrower at specified times for a prespecified price. Conversion rights provide for conversion into equity in the borrowing enterprise at a prespecified price. For further details on these enhancement techniques, see International Monetary Fund (1991). The rationale for using enhancements and their costs and benefits are discussed below.

[3] More specifically, these deals involved the collateralization of future long distance receivables on AT&T by TELMEX, credit card receivables by commercial banks, deposits with commercial banks abroad, and the future energy sales to Californian utilities by the Comisión Federal de Electricidad.

## Chart 16. Yield Spreads on Selected Debt Instruments[1]
*(In percent)*

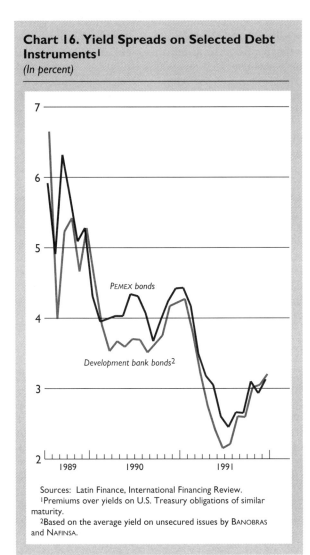

Sources: Latin Finance, International Financing Review.
[1]Premiums over yields on U.S. Treasury obligations of similar maturity.
[2]Based on the average yield on unsecured issues by BANOBRAS and NAFINSA.

to be establishing EMTN programs for significant amounts, which would give Mexico increased flexibility in approaching the markets, including with respect to the currency denomination and the maturity of the notes that may be issued.

Finally, Mexican borrowers have made increasing use of equity-linked debt instruments. During the second quarter of 1991, CEMEX launched the first ever convertible issue by a Mexican entity in the Euro-markets and opened a potentially promising segment of the market for Mexican private companies.[4] Also, TAMSA (Tubos de Acero de México) successfully placed a $50 million convertible, and Apasco (Mexico's second largest cement company) issued convertible subordinated debentures for $50 million. In December 1991, NAFINSA placed an innovative five-year bond with detachable warrants linked to the Mexican Stock Exchange index. This was the first index-linked debt transaction for a Latin American borrower.

### Short-Term Debt Instruments

Mexican borrowers have also been at the forefront of the entry of Latin American entities into the markets for short-term notes. These instruments have consisted of Euro-certificates of deposit (Euro-CDs) since April 1990 and Euro-commercial paper (Euro-CPs) since April 1991.

Since Banca Serfin made its first public Euro-CDs issue in April 1990, Mexican commercial banks have raised large amounts of capital through the placement of U.S. dollar-denominated short-term instruments through their London and, to a lesser extent, New York and Cayman Island branches.[5] These resources have accounted for a significant proportion of the net private capital inflows received by Mexican banks in 1990 and 1991. At mid-April 1992, an estimated $12 billion of Mexican Euro-CDs was outstanding. In a departure from earlier issuance patterns, reflecting growing acceptance worldwide of Mexican issues, the recently privatized BANCOMEX issued Euro-yen CDs through its London branch in November 1991.

In line with the developments observed in the Eurobond markets, the yield to maturity on Euro-CDs issued by Mexican commercial banks has declined substantially. In the initial phase (early 1990), six-month Euro-CDs were sold at yields of between 15 percent and 16.5 percent; however, by the end of 1991, yields for newly issued six-month Euro-CDs had fallen to an average of 8.6 per-

larly public sector entities—reduced significantly their reliance on such techniques in 1991.

In their effort to diversify the range of borrowing options, Mexican entities have also established several Euro-medium-term note (EMTN) programs. BANCOMEXT set up the first EMTN facility for a Latin American borrower in April 1991, and CEMEX, a large cement producer, became the first private Latin American company to tap the EMTN market in September 1991, in the context of a $250 million program. In December 1991, Banca Serfin became the third Mexican issuer in the EMTN market with a $250 million program featuring multicurrency options and allowing for paper maturities from one year to five years. Several other institutions are reported

---

[4] Investors in the CEMEX convertibles will have the option to convert part of the semi-annual coupon and principal payments into shares of the CEMEX-controlled TOLMEX common stock represented by American depository receipts (ADRs).

[5] These interest-bearing CDs are negotiable instruments in bearer form, cleared through Euroclear.

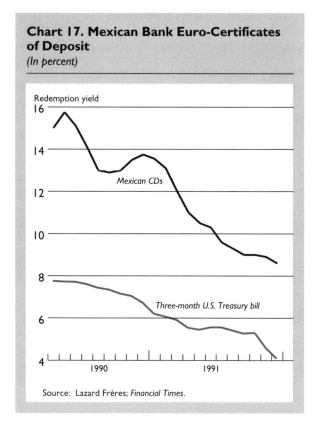

**Chart 17. Mexican Bank Euro-Certificates of Deposit**
*(In percent)*

Source: Lazard Frères; *Financial Times.*

cent (Chart 17).[6] The investor base for such short-term instruments has widened steadily through the period and by mid-1991 reportedly embraced a number of European investment houses, London branches of U.S. banks, private banking units of commercial banks, fixed income funds, and European and Latin American money managers.

For its sheer magnitude and the risks assumed by Mexican commercial banks in the process, the surge in issuance of Euro-CDs has been a cause of concern. In August 1991, the Mexican authorities imposed liquidity requirements against funds raised in foreign currencies, including through Euro-CD offerings. Commercial banks were also requested to match the currencies and the maturity of their foreign currency-denominated short-term assets and liabilities to limit their risk exposure. These measures are expected to reduce the profitability of rais-ing funds abroad through issuance of Euro-CDs, curtailing sharply additional commercial bank short-term indebtedness abroad. Market observers consider that the measures may lead to a wider use of Euro-commercial paper by Mexican corporations, which would reinforce the trend toward disintermediation of the banks already evident since April 1991.

Mexican companies began raising capital directly through the issuance of Euro-commercial paper prior to the imposition of the new liquidity requirements.[7] After Hylsa, a private sector steel company, had arranged the first Euro-CP program for a Mexican company in April 1991, five other companies (Aeroméxico, CEMEX, Grupo DESC, TAMSA, and TMM) established Euro-CP programs with financial intermediaries in 1991, raising some $400 million. Other established Mexican corporations are expected to tap the Euro-CP market in the period ahead since interest rates on Mexican peso-denominated CPs are still higher than those on Euro-CPs with a similar maturity, after taking into account the preannounced devaluation of the peso against the U.S. dollar.

### Equity and Equity Derivatives

Renewed access to the international equity markets is another important feature of Mexico's return to international capital markets. International share offerings, and more generally equity financing, have surged during the last two years and have accounted for a significant share of voluntary financial flows to Mexico. Also, as equity prices have continued to increase and investment is on the rise, in part as a result of the envisaged Free Trade Agreement with the United States and Canada, Mexican companies are expected to make greater use of equity markets as a source of financing and to launch a steady stream of international equity issues in the near term.

Equity financing in Mexico has taken several forms, including the foreign purchase of shares in Mexican corporations either directly in the Mexican stock market and through Mexican corporate equity issues in industrial country stock markets (including through ADRs), or indirectly through country funds that specialize in investing in the Mexican stock market.

The value of foreign equity holdings has risen from under $1 billion at the end of 1989 to $18.5 billion by the end of December 1991—reflecting both new inflows and

---

[6] This compares with a 4.1 percent level on LIBOR U.S. dollar rates in December 1991; in the second quarter of 1990, LIBOR on six-month U.S. dollar deposits averaged 8.6 percent. The issuance of Euro-CDs was profitable even in early 1990 owing to the large spread between U.S. dollar and peso interest rates, given the credibility of the preannounced devaluation rate. Mexican banks used the proceeds to buy peso instruments or to on-lend the funds to corporate customers.

[7] These Euro-CPs are typically issued and paid through a commercial bank in London. Available information suggests that these short-term notes are structured as zero-coupon bonds (i.e., are issued at a discount), are denominated in U.S. dollars, have a maturity of between one day and one year, and have been placed both in the Euromarkets and on a private placement basis. Mexican Euro-CPs are registered with the Special Section of the Mexican National Registry of Securities and Brokers. The interest is normally subject to a 15 percent Mexican withholding tax, but the Euro-CPs are sold to investors free of any withholding taxes.

the strong appreciation of share prices in the Mexican Stock Exchange. Also, 17 equity offerings that featured an international tranche have allowed Mexican corporations, including TELMEX, to raise abroad the equivalent of some $3.6 billion between April and December 1991. While Vitro's offering was the first Mexican international equity deal done under Rule 144A (see below), TELMEX represents a landmark as it was one of the largest international equity offerings ever ($2.2 billion), the first global equity offering for a Latin American corporation since the early 1980s, and the first time a developing country sold equity in a public utility through the international capital markets.[8] The TELMEX offering is seen to have opened new market segments and to have facilitated subsequent equity and bond placements by Mexican companies.

Most equity offerings have involved the use of ADRs, highlighting the important role these instruments can play in facilitating the placement of shares abroad by companies in developing countries. In 1990, the number of Mexican companies with ADRs in circulation increased from 3 (TELMEX, TAMSA, and Cifra B) to 8 with new issues by Interceramica, San Luis, Sidek, EPN, and Tolmex (a subsidiary of CEMEX). Several additional ADR placements occurred during 1991, most of which were marketed through private placements in the United States under Rule 144A. In addition, in July, Grupo Gigante, Mexico's second largest supermarket chain, became the first Mexican company to make an initial public offering with an international tranche. At the end of December 1991, balances invested in ADRs amounted to $13.7 billion (74 percent of total foreign equity portfolio investment in Mexico), up from $2.1 billion at the end of 1990.[9]

## Factors Facilitating Re-Entry

A number of interrelated factors have contributed to the process of re-entry to voluntary capital market financing described above. Besides structural features, such as Mexico's political stability and the fact that Mexico has a number of well-known high quality companies with potential for productive investments, the restoration of Mexico's creditworthiness through the sustained imple-

mentation of adjustment policies and the removal of "debt overhang" concerns through the comprehensive restructuring package with commercial banks have been the key to regaining access to voluntary financing. In addition, the re-entry strategy adopted by the authorities has facilitated the re-entry process, while several "favorable" external factors have helped in gaining access to voluntary financing through the issuance of negotiable instruments.

### Macroeconomic Stabilization and Comprehensive Debt Restructuring

Mexico's recent re-entry experience has shown that re-establishing credibility with foreign investors hinges critically on the sustained implementation of appropriate adjustment policies and the ensuing macroeconomic stabilization (see Section II). Fiscal consolidation, a strengthened international reserves position, market-oriented structural reforms (including trade reform and the prospective North American Free Trade Area), and a credible exchange rate policy have contributed to re-establish confidence in the country's macroeconomic environment.

Mexico's renewed access to voluntary market financing is also associated with the removal of "debt-overhang" concerns that was achieved through the innovative debt- and debt-service reduction package with commercial banks. This helped to alleviate private sector concerns about country transfer risk and improved the prospects for non-debt-creating inflows. The comprehensiveness of the 1989 debt package convinced international investors that the operation was a once-and-for-all deal, and that thereafter the country would be in a position to meet all scheduled debt-service obligations on newly contracted debt. The debt- and debt-service reduction package was followed very rapidly by a sharp reduction in risk premiums and by significant inflows of foreign direct and portfolio investment, including repatriation of flight capital.

Mexico's re-entry has been facilitated by the fact that the country has generally been perceived to have acted responsibly concerning the servicing of its external debt and by the realization that Mexico had kept an excellent record in the securities market for interest and principal payments throughout the debt crisis. This has contributed to the significant shift in financing instruments observed during the last three years, as bonds, rather than syndicated bank loans, have been the avenue for regaining access to international capital markets.

### Re-Entry Strategy

Re-entry has also been facilitated by the authorities' management of the process. Since its initial stages, the process of re-entry and broadening of Mexico's foreign financing base has been monitored carefully. In order to avoid saturating the market with Mexican paper, the authorities carefully phased the successive bond issues by

---

[8] A simultaneous offering of TELMEX was carried out in the United States, the United Kingdom, Japan, France, Switzerland, Germany, Canada, and other countries.

[9] In addition to owning stocks through ADRs and country funds (which account for some $0.5–0.6 billion), foreign investors also hold a significant portion of Mexican equities directly, normally through the purchase of nonvoting shares. Foreign purchase of voting shares are permitted in cases where there are no nonvoting shares, but they must be held in trust in the Neutral Fund administered by NAFINSA, the state-owned development bank. Since the creation of the Neutral Fund in late 1989, shares held in trust form rose to $1.3 billion at the end of December 1991.

the public sector and limited the amounts placed, even in the face of reported oversubscriptions in a number of cases. The strategy was essentially to avoid forcing the re-entry, and instead to exploit perceived opportunities.[10]

The public sector played a leading role in lowering the benchmark borrowing terms for Mexican borrowers, including private sector entities, and it is accepted generally that the private sector has benefited from the leadership of the public sector in this regard. In the aftermath of the debt crisis, the public sector generously priced its first bond issues to attract investors' attention and overcome the image Mexico had within the investor community. As discussed above, the launch yield of the June 1989 BANCOMEXT bonds was close to 17 percent, implying a yield spread of some 820 basis points. This issue was launched during the negotiations with commercial banks, without collateral, and with no benchmark. In addition to the high yield spread, the bonds were of short maturity (2.5 years) and modest in size. The first four unenhanced issues by the public sector were for an average of $83 million only.

Subsequently, public sector bond issues were priced at progressively lower yield spreads over "risk-free" paper rates, while the investor base being tapped was broadened. Also, as discussed above, the maturity of the bond issues has been increased gradually with a view to establishing a complete yield curve (i.e., from one to ten years) for Mexican debt instruments. This was achieved with the issuance of two ten-year bonds in October and November 1991 by NAFINSA and PEMEX, respectively.

The public sector also played a leading role in opening new markets, and tapping new investor pools.[11] As noted above, the deutsche mark, Austrian schilling, ECU, peseta, Canadian dollar, and pound sterling segments of the market were successfully tapped at progressively better terms. In particular, the three issues by the UMS were seen as important benchmarks and helped other Mexican borrowers to regain access to capital markets on more favorable terms. Finally, the authorities have also authorized placement of foreign currency-denominated bonds with Mexican investors. The April 1991 issue by BANCOMEXT was simultaneously placed in Mexico and in the international capital market.

Part of the re-entry strategy was the acceptance by the authorities that enhancement of debt instruments by the public sector may be required in the initial stages of the re-entry process. Enhancements such as collaterals, put options, and equity conversion rights (in the case of private sector entities) were seen as means to improve the marketability of debt instruments and to reduce risk premiums through overcoming extreme initial perceptions of counterparty credit and transfer risks. The use of collateral relaxed the rationing facing Mexican borrowers and in some cases may have paved the way for future access by promoting familiarity with new borrowers under conditions of reduced risks. It is estimated that the use of collateralization techniques has lowered borrowing costs by between 100 to 200 basis points.

Collateralization techniques, if used indiscriminately and for an unduly long period, have the potential, however, of fundamentally impairing rather than improving a country's ability to borrow on an unsecured basis over the medium term. Mindful of such risks, Mexican public sector borrowers have reduced the frequency of collateralized borrowing. As discussed above, public sector borrowers used collateralization techniques in two instances only in 1991.

## Other Developments

A number of favorable external factors have helped Mexico's renewed access to voluntary financing through the international capital markets. Among these are changing strategies by international investors (including Latin American investors), regulatory changes abroad, and the rating of Mexico by a credit rating agency.

The gradual widening of the investor pool has resulted from several developments. Investors went through an "education process" and became more familiar with Mexican instruments. The investor pool (mainly flight capital) initially was composed largely of private investors attracted by high yields.[12] More recently, U.S. and European retail and institutional investors have been increasingly involved, with strong institutional participation being reported for most recent issues. This reflects institutional investors' demand for cross-border diversification of risks, the ratcheting down of U.S. Treasury yields, which has inclined international investors to seek higher yield quality paper, and the weakness of the U.S. market for high-yielding corporate debt ("junk bonds"), which has led to U.S. funds being diverted abroad. Also,

---

[10] In the context of this gradualist move, the three landmark issues by the United Mexican States (UMS) in the deutsche mark, the peseta, and the pound sterling markets were for a limited amount (equivalent to some $270 million). On each occasion, the authorities made it clear that the UMS had returned to the market essentially to establish a benchmark for the Mexican private sector.

[11] The three recent UMS issues were placed at tight yield spreads over risk-free paper in three different sectors of the Euromarket. The February 1991 UMS issue in deutsche mark carried a yield spread of 190 basis points over German Government securities of comparable maturity. The second issue, denominated in pesetas and placed in July 1991 in the Matador market with a five-year maturity carried an initial yield of 175 basis points over the yield on corresponding Spanish Government bonds. Finally, the UMS tapped the pound sterling sector with a seven-year issue at 227 basis points over the comparable gilt.

[12] Indications are that initial demand for Mexican debt and equity instruments placed internationally came, to a large extent, from Latin American, including Mexican, investors who had invested offshore. Since mid-1989, international capital markets have played an important role in the flight capital repatriation process that has helped improve Mexico's capital account.

investors have been more receptive to Mexican paper as secondary market activity has been developed to enhance the liquidity of the instruments.

Regulatory changes abroad also have played a positive role in helping Mexico regain access to certain segments of the international capital market. The attractiveness of bond and equity issues as a vehicle for Mexican borrowers has been enhanced by recent regulatory changes designed to reduce transaction costs and improve liquidity. First, the approval of "Regulation S" and "Rule 144A" by the U.S. authorities in April 1990[13] has created significant new opportunities in the U.S. capital markets for Mexican issuers that may have been unwilling to meet the disclosure and other requirements of the federal securities laws applicable to offerings in the United States. Second, recent developments in Spain and Japan may facilitate Mexican borrowers' access to the domestic bond markets of those countries. Already, the decision by the Spanish authorities to permit the United Mexican States to issue bonds in the Matador market in July 1991 allowed the first issue of noninvestment grade paper in that market. In June 1991, the Japanese authorities lowered the minimum bond rating required for an issuer to make a placement on the Samurai market from A to BBB in the case of sovereign (or sovereign-guaranteed) borrowers. This opens new possibilities for a number of developing countries, including Mexican borrowers.

In June 1990, the Mexican stock market (BMV) was granted the status of an "Offshore Designated Securities Market" by the Japanese financial authorities. This allows Japanese brokerage houses to deal with securities listed in the BMV. A similar agreement was reached in February 1991 when the British International Stock Exchange permitted operations in Mexican securities in the London market, while the U.S. Securities and Exchange Commission (SEC) granted the BMV the status of "Offshore Designated Securities Market" for the purpose of Regulation S.[14] Indeval, the centralized depository institution, has been recognized by the U.S. Securities and Exchange Commission and the office of the Comptroller of the Currency as a qualified foreign custodian. Furthermore, Mexican brokerage firms have been allowed to open foreign subsidiaries, trade eligible Mexican securities abroad, and participate in international arbitrage operations.

Finally, the establishment of a formal rating by a credit rating agency may have reinforced interest among international investors. In December 1990, Moody's Investors Service assigned Mexico a sovereign ceiling rating of Ba2—a below-investment-grade rating—and rated the bonds issued in the context of the debt- and debt-service reduction package (also known as the "Brady" bonds) Ba3. Since then, the agency has rated several Mexican Eurobonds Ba2.[15] Continued pursuit of appropriate macroeconomic and structural policies opens the way to eventual attainment of investment grade status. Although the market seems to have disregarded the rating assigned by Moody's and allowed Mexican borrowers to raise resources at terms more favorable than would be implied by the Ba2 rating, attainment of a formal investment grade rating would, ceteris paribus, open to Mexican borrowers new segments of the market and would reduce Mexico's borrowing costs.

## Conclusion

Mexico's re-entry into the international capital market demonstrates the feasibility of a debt strategy aimed at restoring access to spontaneous capital flows in the context of a strong economic program supported by the international financial community. Moreover, this process has set an important precedent for other developing countries.

Together with the reduction in debt-service obligations implied by the comprehensive restructuring of the commercial bank debt, this has been reflected in a sharp improvement in the capital account of the balance of payments and has allowed a positive net resource transfer. Correspondingly, access to international financial flows on improving terms has helped fund investment projects in Mexico that would bolster Mexico's international competitiveness and external viability over the medium term.

---

[13] Regulation S facilitates the marketing of Euro-securities in the United States by clarifying registration requirements; Rule 144A relaxes the waiting period requirement for secondary market trading in privately placed securities.

[14] As a result of this regulatory action, the securities of Mexican companies registered in the BMV may now be placed in the U.S. market without prior registration with U.S. authorities and may be resold in the BMV by the U.S. investors who purchased them.

[15] For developing countries, Moody's Investors Service issues ratings in accordance with a "sovereign ceiling rule," whereby no bond issuer can be rated above the sovereign rating given to the country in which it operates.

# Bibliography

Banamex, "Inversión Extranjera Directa" (Mexico, 1990).

Banco de México, *The Mexican Economy* (Mexico, various issues).

El-Erian, M.A., "The Restoration of Latin America's Access to Voluntary Capital Market Financing—Developments and Prospects," IMF Working Paper, WP/91/74 (Washington: International Monetary Fund, August 1991).

————, "Mexico's External Debt and the Return to Voluntary Capital Market Financing," IMF Working Paper, WP/91/83 (Washington: International Monetary Fund, August 1991).

*Euroweek* (London, various issues).

Fadl Kuri, S., "Evolución Reciente de los Mercados Internacionales de Capital," *El Mercado de Valores* (Mexico), No. 6 (March 15, 1991), p. 13.

Fedder, Marcus J.J., and M. Mukherjee, "The Reemergence of Less Developed Countries in the International Bond Markets" (Washington: The World Bank, 1991).

Gurria, Jose Angel, "What Eastern Europe Can Learn from Mexico," *The International Economy* (May/June 1991), pp. 28–32.

*International Financing Review* (London, various issues).

International Monetary Fund, *Private Market Financing for Developing Countries*, World Economic and Financial Surveys (Washington: International Monetary Fund, December 1991).

Leipold, Alessandro, and others, *International Capital Markets: Developments and Prospects*, World Economic and Financial Surveys (Washington: International Monetary Fund, May 1991).

Perez, V., "A Silent Explosion," *Latin Finance*, No. 27 (1991).

Purcell, J.F.H., and others, "Developing Countries Sovereign Bonds: Recent Developments in a New Asset Class" (Salomon Brothers, September 1991).

# VIII    The Dynamics of Inflation, 1988–91

## Saul Lizondo

This section examines the relationship between the rate of inflation and other macroeconomic variables in Mexico over the period 1988–91, using a vector autoregressions model.

During this period, the sustained implementation of comprehensive adjustment policies reduced sharply the rate of inflation in Mexico. Those policies have included fiscal and monetary restraint, trade reforms, and the determination of certain key prices in the framework of an agreement among the Government, labor, and business firms, namely the PACTO (Pacto de Solidaridad Económica), and its successor, the PECE (Pacto para la Estabilidad y el Crecimiento Económico). Within this framework, a social consensus has been formed on the target path for the exchange rate, the minimum wage, public sector prices, and some private sector prices. These targets have been revised periodically in light of the evolution of the economy.

This section examines to what extent the rate of inflation was associated with the evolution of other macroeconomic variables, such as the rate of change of the exchange rate, foreign inflation, wage developments, and monetary expansion, during this period of reduced inflation. The vector autoregression methodology used here is based on the estimation of reduced form equations and does not require being explicit about the specific channels of transmission of shocks in the economy. Therefore, the results presented do not constitute a test of any specific theory about inflation. Instead, they summarize key stylized facts about inflation dynamics and describe the statistical association between a number of related macroeconomic variables. They are also useful for testing some selected hypotheses about the determinants of inflation and for forecasting.[1]

The estimation results indicate that, during the period under study, the rate of inflation responded significantly to adjustments in public sector prices, foreign inflation,

exchange rate changes, and monetary expansion, and to a lesser extent to wage changes. The results also reveal some puzzling aspects of the behavior of wages.

The remainder of the section is organized as follows. The first part describes briefly the methodology. The second presents the variables included in the model, the estimation results, some exercises regarding the dynamic response of inflation to various shocks, and some forecasting exercises. The third part contains a summary of the results and some concluding remarks. An appendix contains a more formal presentation of the methodology.

## Methodology

The vector autoregression (VAR) methodology consists of estimating a system of equations in which each endogenous variable is regressed on lagged values of all endogenous variables and on current (and sometimes also lagged) values of the exogenous variables. The resulting system can be interpreted as the reduced form equations of some underlying system of structural equations.

These reduced form equations capture the effects of the exogenous variables and the intertemporal relationship between the endogenous variables in the model. The contemporaneous relationship between the endogenous variables, on the other hand, is estimated from the residuals of the regressions, under a suitable set of assumptions regarding which endogenous variables are more likely to adjust to changes in other endogenous variables within the same period. This permits the identification of the exogenous shocks, or innovations, that affect the endogenous variables in the structural system. In the interpretation of this type of model, the dynamics of the endogenous variables are driven by the realization of the innovations and the evolution of the exogenous variables. The innovations represent shocks that are not captured by the exogenous variables explicitly incorporated into the model.

This methodology is useful for tracing the effects of the various innovations on the endogenous variables. The procedure to follow is (a) estimate the reduced form system; (b) use the estimated reduced form errors together with some additional assumptions to identify the innovations; and (c) use those results to derive the dynamic

---

[1] For a discussion about divergent views regarding the valid uses of vector autoregressions, see Cooley and LeRoy (1985), Leamer (1985), and Sims (1986). Vector autoregressions have been used to analyze Mexican inflation for periods prior to the one examined in this section. See, for example, the papers included in Ize and Vera (1984), Leiderman (1984), Puente (1989), Guerrero and Arias (1990), and Kaminsky (1991).

effect of the innovations on the path of the endogenous variables. The model also generates forecasts for the endogenous variables, for a given path of the exogenous variables, by assuming that there are no innovations during the forecasting period. The variance of the forecast error can be decomposed into the parts stemming from the uncertainty regarding the evolution of each type of innovation. The model can also be used to examine the role played by the various innovations in a particular period, within the estimation period, by means of a historical decomposition of the forecast error. For this, the model is used to forecast within sample, and the actual forecast error is decomposed into the parts due to the accumulated effects of the various innovations.

## A Model for Mexican Inflation

### Variables Included in the Model

The rate of inflation in Mexico is postulated to depend on a number of factors representing cost and demand pressures. (1) One factor is imported inflation, defined as the nominal effective rate of depreciation of the Mexican peso plus the rate of foreign inflation. Imported inflation may affect the domestic price level directly through its effect on the prices of traded consumer goods, and indirectly through its effect on the costs of producing non-traded goods that use traded inputs. (2) Another factor affecting domestic inflation is the behavior of wages, through its effect on costs of production. (3) The evolution of minimum wages may also affect inflation to the extent that prices react immediately to anticipated wage increases that may be influenced by the level of the minimum wage. (4) Domestic inflation is also likely to be affected by the rate of monetary expansion, under the assumption that higher monetary expansion will be associated with higher demand pressures. (5) Another variable that needs to be included is the adjustment of public sector prices. Since detailed information on those adjustments is not available, and since most of the important revisions of public sector prices took place in the months of December and January, an attempt is made to capture their effect by using dummy variables for those two months.

The variables included in the model (described more fully below) are denoted by:

$p$    rate of domestic inflation
$ii$   rate of imported inflation
$w$    rate of wage increase
$z$    rate of minimum wage increase
$m$    rate of monetary expansion
$s1$   dummy variable for January
$s12$  dummy variable for December.

The exogenous variables in the system include policy variables and external factors. Thus, they include the dummies for January and December, the rate of change of minimum wages, and the rate of imported inflation. Imported inflation is exogenous because the foreign rate of inflation is exogenous, and the nominal rate of crawl of the Mexican peso with respect to the U.S. dollar was predetermined during the period under consideration.[2]

In addition to the rate of inflation, the other endogenous variables in the system are the rate of increase in nominal wages and the rate of monetary expansion. Nominal wages are endogenous because they are likely to respond to changes in inflation, and to the external and policy factors mentioned above. Unless money is represented by the monetary base, monetary expansion is endogenous to the extent that the multiplier responds to other endogenous variables in the system. Under a regime of a predetermined exchange rate, the monetary base also becomes endogenous since changes in domestic credit can be partially or totally offset by endogenous changes in international reserves. Furthermore, monetary expansion may also become endogenous because the authorities adjust domestic credit in response to the evolution of other endogenous variables in the economy.

The estimation of the system thus described would include one regression for each of the endogenous variables: the rate of inflation ($p$), the rate of growth of nominal wages ($w$), and the rate of monetary expansion ($m$). The regressors would include lagged values of all endogenous variables, and current (and maybe also lagged) values of the rate of growth of minimum wages ($z$), the dummy variables for January and December ($s1$ and $s12$), and the rate of imported inflation ($ii$). In order to consider explicitly the dynamics of imported inflation as one of the sources of errors in forecasting domestic inflation, the model was modified, however. An additional equation was estimated for imported inflation as a function of its own lagged values, and the errors from this regression were considered as innovations in imported inflation. In addition, the current value of imported inflation was excluded from the estimated equations for the endogenous variables.

With this modification, the estimated model consists of four equations: $ii$ is regressed on its own lagged values; and $p$, $w$, and $m$ are regressed on lagged values of $p$, $w$, $m$, and $ii$, and on $z$, $s1$, and $s12$. In the interpretation of this model, the evolution of imported inflation depends only on innovations in $ii$, while the evolution of domestic inflation, money expansion, and wage increases depend on innovations in $ii$, $p$, $m$, $w$, and on the values of $z$, $s1$, and $s12$.

---

[2] Although it could be argued that policy variables were really endogenous because they were adjusted according to the evolution of other variables in the economy, those adjustments were very infrequent in terms of monthly observations. Modeling the timing and size of those adjustments as endogenous would require a substantial effort in relation to the benefits to be obtained, and is not attempted here.

## Data and Estimation Period

The model was estimated with monthly data for the period June 1988–March 1991. The beginning of the period was chosen so as to exclude the initial few months with the new policy regime in which the structure of the system was in transition from a period of high inflation to a period of low inflation. The end of the period was determined by the availability of data on wages.

Data on prices, wages, and money were obtained from *Indicadores Económicos* (Banco de México). The rate of inflation ($p$) was measured by the monthly rate of increase of the national consumer price index.[3] The rate of monetary expansion ($m$) was measured by the monthly rate of growth of M2.[4] As explained below, this variable was seasonally adjusted before the estimation. The monthly rate of growth of wages ($w$) was derived from the series on average hourly salaries and benefits in the manufacturing sector. Since this series includes the payment of a large annual bonus in December of each year, the rate of growth of wages presents a sharp increase every December and a sharp decline every January. In order to correct for this factor, and in the absence of accurate information about the size of the annual bonus, the value of wages for December was estimated by taking the average values of the two adjacent months. Imported inflation ($ii$) was calculated as the sum of the nominal effective rate of depreciation of the Mexican peso with respect to the currencies of a group of countries plus the weighted average of the rates of inflation of those countries, with data from *International Financial Statistics*.[5] The rate of increase of minimum wages ($z$) was measured on the basis of the national average minimum wage as reported by the Comisión Nacional de los Salarios Mínimos.

Some characteristics of the variables included in the analysis are presented in Table 10 and Chart 18. The means of the monthly growth rates of wages and money are substantially higher than the mean of domestic inflation, reflecting the increase in real wages and the process of monetization of the economy in this period of reduced inflation. Minimum wages, on the other hand, increased by less than domestic prices. The mean of imported inflation is lower than the mean of domestic inflation, reflecting the process of real appreciation of the Mexican peso during the period.

---

[3] For any variable $x(t)$, its rate of growth is measured as $\log(x(t)/x(t-1))$.

[4] M2 is defined as private sector holdings of currency, demand deposits, and short-term banking instruments. It is not clear which is the most appropriate monetary aggregate to include in the estimation. M2 was preferred over M1 because M1 showed some large increases during part of 1990, owing to changes in regulations that are not necessarily associated with changes in the rate of inflation or other variables included in the model.

[5] The countries included in the group and their respective weights are United States (0.638), Japan (0.109), Germany (0.079), France (0.038), Canada (0.037), United Kingdom (0.035), Italy (0.033), and Spain (0.030).

## Table 10. Vector Autoregression Analysis of Inflation Sample Statistics, June 1988–March 1991
*(Monthly rates of change)*

| Variables | Mean | Standard Error | Minimum | Maximum |
|---|---|---|---|---|
| $p$ | 1.74 | 0.82 | 0.60 | 4.71 |
| $ii$ | 1.18 | 1.12 | −1.70 | 2.96 |
| $w$ | 2.32 | 3.07 | −3.29 | 7.61 |
| $z$ | 1.17 | 2.81 | 0.00 | 8.67 |
| $m$ | 2.77 | 4.48 | −6.78 | 15.65 |
| $m$ (seasonally adjusted) | 2.91 | 1.41 | −1.05 | 5.19 |

The rate of monetary expansion is the variable with the largest fluctuations. It shows the highest standard error, as well as the widest range of variation in the sample. In Chart 18, it is also possible to observe its strong seasonal pattern. In order to isolate the seasonal component, which does not necessarily affect inflation, the series was seasonally adjusted,[6] which significantly reduced the variability of the series. The adjusted series was used in the estimation of the model.

The rate of growth of wages also shows a much higher variability than the rate of domestic inflation. In addition, the rate of growth of wages exhibits a zigzag pattern, with high values usually followed by low values and vice versa. The rate of domestic inflation shows peaks in December and January, which are likely to be captured by the dummy variables in the regressions.

## Estimation Results

The system of four equations was estimated by the method of seemingly unrelated regressions.[7] There is a

---

[6] The series was seasonally adjusted by the exponential smoothing technique included in the RATS computer package, using a model with an additive seasonal term and no trend.

[7] In order to test for stationarity of the data, an augmented Dickey-Fuller test was applied to each series. Nonstationarity could be rejected at the 5 percent level of significance for the series on domestic inflation, and wage increases. For the series on money growth and foreign inflation, nonstationarity could only be rejected at the 25 percent and 30 percent levels of significance, respectively. Although these results indicate that the rejection of nonstationarity is not definite for money growth and foreign inflation, these series were not differenced before estimation due to strong priors about the relationship between these variables and domestic inflation. In order to determine the number of lags to include in the estimation, four different criteria were applied to the data for a range from zero to six lags. Two criteria, Hannan-Quinn and Schwarz, indicated that the appropriate lag length was one. The FPE criterion indicated a lag length of two, while the Akaike criterion indicated a lag length of six, thereby using up almost all the degrees of freedom. Based on these results, two lags were included in the estimation. For a comparison of the various criteria see Lütkepohl (1985).

**Chart 18. Domestic Inflation, Imported Inflation, Wages, and Money, June 1988–March 1991[1]**
*(Monthly rates of change, in percent)*

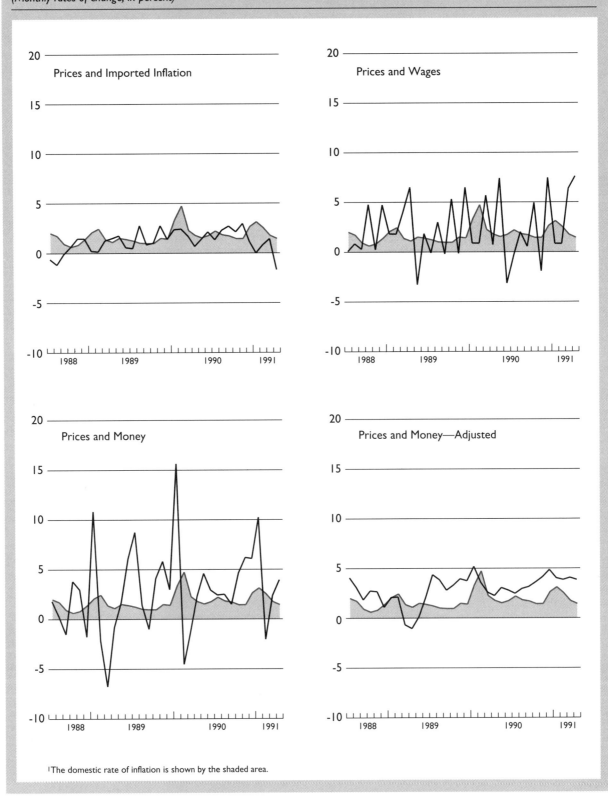

[1]The domestic rate of inflation is shown by the shaded area.

**Table 11. Vector Autoregression Analysis of Inflation Estimation Results, June 1988–March 1991**

| | Equations | | | |
|---|---|---|---|---|
| | p | ii | w | m |
| constant | 0.25 | 0.58 | 1.41 | 1.31 |
| | (0.23) | (0.29) | (1.57) | (0.45) |
| s1 | 1.00 | | −2.55 | 0.88 |
| | (0.33) | | (2.26) | (0.66) |
| s12 | 1.21 | | −1.50 | 1.21 |
| | (0.36) | | (2.47) | (0.72) |
| z | 0.03 | | 0.39 | −0.04 |
| | (0.03) | | (0.21) | (0.06) |
| $ii(t-1)$ | 0.17 | 0.47 | 0.54 | 0.05 |
| | (0.08) | (0.20) | (0.55) | (0.16) |
| $ii(t-2)$ | 0.03 | 0.02 | −0.49 | 0.42 |
| | (0.08) | (0.20) | (0.59) | (0.17) |
| $p(t-1)$ | 0.33 | | 0.42 | −0.79 |
| | (0.13) | | (0.89) | (0.26) |
| $p(t-2)$ | 0.03 | | 0.13 | 0.44 |
| | (0.12) | | (0.84) | (0.24) |
| $w(t-1)$ | 0.01 | | −0.34 | −0.13 |
| | (0.03) | | (0.21) | (0.06) |
| $w(t-2)$ | 0.05 | | 0.08 | −0.09 |
| | (0.03) | | (0.22) | (0.06) |
| $m(t-1)$ | 0.15 | | −0.80 | 0.96 |
| | (0.08) | | (0.54) | (0.16) |
| $m(t-2)$ | −0.06 | | 0.90 | −0.30 |
| | (0.08) | | (0.55) | (0.16) |
| $R^2$ | 0.81 | 0.19 | 0.34 | 0.74 |
| $R^2$ | 0.71 | 0.14 | 0.00 | 0.61 |
| SSE | 0.44 | 1.04 | 3.06 | 0.88 |
| DW | 1.79 | 1.77 | 1.68 | 1.90 |
| Q(15) | 17.05 | 8.53 | 10.40 | 5.64 |
| Sig. level | 0.32 | 0.90 | 0.79 | 0.99 |

Note: Numbers in parentheses indicate standard errors.

**Table 12. Vector Autoregression Analysis of Inflation Exclusion Restrictions**

| Variables | Equations | | | |
|---|---|---|---|---|
| | p | ii | w | m |
| p | 12.64 | | 0.57 | 9.34 |
| | (—) | | (0.75) | (0.01) |
| ii | 7.09 | 7.89 | 1.08 | 9.92 |
| | (0.03) | (0.02) | (0.58) | (0.01) |
| w | 3.18 | | 4.29 | 5.01 |
| | (0.20) | | (0.12) | (0.08) |
| m | 4.83 | | 2.80 | 61.30 |
| | (0.09) | | (0.25) | (—) |

Note: This is a chi-square test with 2 degrees of freedom. The numbers in parentheses indicate the level of significance at which it is possible to reject the hypothesis that the lagged values of the variable shown in each row can be excluded from the equation indicated in each column.

gain in efficiency from using this method instead of ordinary least squares when the set of explanatory variables is not the same for all the equations in the system, and the errors are correlated across equations. As mentioned above, the set of explanatory variables in the equation for imported inflation differs from the one used in the other three equations, and the errors are likely to be correlated across equations.

The results of the estimation are presented in Table 11. Although these coefficients cannot be given a structural interpretation, they are useful for determining to what extent changes in one variable are associated with changes in other variables. The equation for inflation shows significant positive coefficients for the two dummy variables, presumably capturing the effect of adjustments in public sector prices. Changes in minimum wages, on the

other hand, have little effect on domestic inflation, but have a significant effect on the rate of increase of nominal wages.

The significance of the lagged values of the various endogenous variables in accounting for the evolution of each endogenous variable can be seen in Table 12, which presents the results of exclusion restriction tests for each of the regressions. The current level of domestic inflation is affected significantly by lagged values of domestic inflation, imported inflation, and money expansion. The effect of lagged values of wage changes, on the other hand, is weaker. These results indicate that the empirical evidence would not support a structural model of inflation that emphasizes past changes in wages as the main source of current inflation.

Lagged levels of imported inflation have a substantial effect on the current level of imported inflation. The current rate of wage increase is affected significantly only by lagged wage increases. This implies that a model that stresses the role of past inflation as the main determinant of current wage changes, owing for example to lags in adjusting real wages or to expectations about future inflation, would be inconsistent with the data. The current level of monetary expansion, on the other hand, is affected significantly by lagged values of all the endogenous variables. This is consistent with the presumption that monetary expansion should be considered an endogenous variable.

The ability of the model to account for the behavior of the endogenous variables during the estimation period can be assessed from the goodness-of-fit measures presented in Table 11, and from Chart 19. Estimated values for domestic inflation and monetary expansion follow actual values closely. This, however, is not the case for imported inflation and for wage changes.

**Chart 19. VAR Analysis of Inflation:  Actual and Estimated Values, June 1988–March 1991[1]**
*(Monthly rates of change, in percent)*

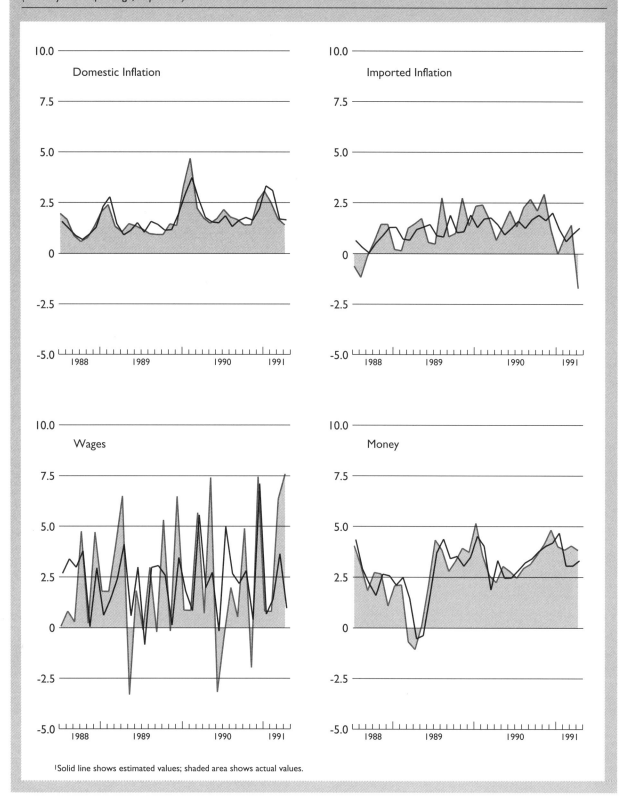

[1]Solid line shows estimated values; shaded area shows actual values.

In the case of imported inflation, the poor fit is not surprising, because it is mainly due to the difficulty found in modeling monthly changes in exchange rates between countries with floating or managed exchange rates. Imported inflation in Mexico is composed of the nominal effective depreciation of the Mexican peso with respect to the currency of a group of countries, plus the weighted average inflation of those countries. Since inflation in those countries behaves smoothly, most of the variation in imported inflation is due to changes in the nominal effective exchange rate. Given the crawling peg policy for the Mexican peso with respect to the U.S. dollar, sharp changes in the nominal effective exchange rate reflect exchange rate changes between the U.S. dollar and the other currencies in the basket, which are difficult to model.

The poor fit of the equation for wage changes is surprising, however. Both past inflation and past wage changes were expected to be important influences on the behavior of current wage changes. Past inflation would be important if there were some formal or informal backward-looking wage-indexation mechanism. Even in the presence of forward-looking indexation, past inflation would be relevant if it helped to predict future inflation. Past wage changes would be important if there were some inertia in wage determination. However, in the case of inertia lagged wage changes would have a positive effect on current wage changes, in contrast to the one-lag negative effect in the estimation results.

These unexpected results regarding the equation for wage changes may reflect the way in which the information on wages is collected, and the coverage of this series. Wage data are obtained monthly from a group of firms. In a given month, however, only about half the firms in the group are sampled, and the rest is sampled the following month. This alternation of sample sets may introduce some bias that produces the zigzag pattern shown by wage changes. Furthermore, the series on wages also includes some benefits that are paid during the year. To the extent that those benefits are not distributed uniformly throughout the year, this may introduce an additional bias in the estimation.

## Dynamic Response to Innovations

VAR models may be used to derive the dynamic response of the endogenous variables to the various innovations. As indicated above, the first step is to recover the innovations from the residuals of the estimation of the reduced form equations, under a suitable set of additional assumptions. Explaining this procedure, however, requires that we refer to some of the concepts presented in the Appendix.

In terms of equations (1) and (2) in the Appendix, we want to derive the dynamic response of $y(t)$ to the innovations $e(t)$, having estimated (1). To do this, it is necessary to model the relationship between the errors in equation (1) and the innovations in equation (2). In other words, it is necessary to estimate $(I-B_0)$ in equation (5). The elements in the matrix $(I-B_0)$ indicate to what extent the various shocks have an immediate effect on the various endogenous variables.

The usual way of modeling the relationship between the reduced form errors $u(t)$ and the innovations $e(t)$ has been to use a Cholesky factorization, which assumes that $(I-B_0)$ is a lower triangular matrix, thereby implying a recursive structure for the immediate effect of the various innovations.[8] Thus, the first variable is affected immediately only by the first innovation, the second variable by the first and the second innovation, and so on. However, Bernanke has suggested that the assumption of a recursive structure is rather restrictive and proposed a method for estimating more general relationships between $u(t)$ and $e(t)$.[9] This method can be used either with an exactly identified system, or with an overidentified system and then tested for the overidentification restrictions.[10]

An overidentified system was estimated for the residuals from the model above. In this system, domestic inflation was assumed to be affected immediately by all the innovations, while wage changes and monetary expansion were assumed to be affected within the same month only by their own innovations.[11] The results from the estimation are

$$u_p = 0.03\, u_{ii} - 0.04\, u_w + 0.03\, u_m + e_p, \quad (1)$$
$$\phantom{u_p = }(0.06) \quad\;\; (0.02) \quad\;\; (0.08)$$

with $u_{ii} = e_{ii}$, $u_w = e_w$, and $u_m = e_m$, where $u_j$ and $e_j$ denote the reduced form residual and the structural form innovation, respectively, for variable $j$, and the numbers in parentheses indicate standard errors. The coefficients for innovations in imported inflation and monetary expansion have the expected positive sign, but they are not statistically significant. The coefficient on wage innovations, on the other hand, is significant, but it has a negative sign, which is difficult to account for. It implies that a positive innovation in wages causes domestic inflation in the same month to be lower than otherwise. This may be just another consequence of the peculiar behavior

---

[8] This method is applied, for example, by Leiderman (1984), Puente (1989), and Guerrero and Arias (1990).

[9] See Bernanke (1986). This method is applied, for example, by Kaminsky (1992).

[10] Since there are four types of innovations, the covariance matrix of the reduced-form contains ten independent moments. Since identification is achieved here by assuming that some innovations have no contemporaneous effect on some endogenous variables, whether the model is exactly identified or overidentified depends on whether six or more off-diagonal elements of the $(I-B_0)$ matrix are assumed to be equal to zero. If the model is overidentified, the decomposition will not be able to replicate exactly the correlation matrix of the residuals. The test for overidentification checks to what extent this departure is significant.

[11] Thus, nine elements of $(I-B_0)$ were assumed to be zero.

shown by the series on wages, as mentioned before.[12] A chi-square test indicates that the overidentification restrictions cannot be rejected at the usual levels of significance. With three degrees of freedom the chi-square statistic was 1.35, implying a significance level of 0.72.[13]

The dynamic effect of innovations in domestic inflation, imported inflation, wage increases, and monetary expansion are presented in Charts 20–23. In each case, the graphs show the dynamic response over a year to an initial shock of the size of one standard deviation of the innovation under consideration.[14]

The magnitude of the innovation in domestic inflation is relatively small when compared with the other innovations. Its effect on domestic inflation declines quickly, practically disappearing after two months. It has a negative effect on monetary expansion for about five months, and no effect on imported inflation, because imported inflation is exogenous. It has a positive effect on wage increases in the two months following the shock, and a smaller negative effect afterward.

The innovation in imported inflation has a larger and more persistent effect on all the variables. Domestic inflation increases for about nine months, while monetary expansion increases for about seven months and then declines somewhat. It also has a persistent effect on wage increases, with a zigzag pattern for the first few months following the shock.

The magnitude of the innovation in wages is the largest one, but its effect on domestic inflation is relatively small. It has no effect on imported inflation, and a negative effect on money growth that lasts for about six months and is followed by a smaller positive effect. It produces a marked zigzag pattern for wage increases that lasts for several months after the shock. Given the relative small

**Table 13. Vector Autoregression Analysis of Inflation: Decomposition of Variance**

| Series | Horizon (months) | Standard Error | Innovations | | | |
|--------|-----------------|----------------|-------|-------|-------|-------|
| | | | $e_p$ | $e_{ii}$ | $e_w$ | $e_m$ |
| Domestic inflation | 1 | 0.35 | 90 | 1 | 9 | 0 |
| | 3 | 0.47 | 56 | 27 | 8 | 9 |
| | 6 | 0.53 | 45 | 40 | 7 | 8 |
| | 9 | 0.53 | 44 | 41 | 7 | 8 |
| | 12 | 0.53 | 44 | 41 | 7 | 8 |
| Imported inflation | 1 | 0.99 | 0 | 100 | 0 | 0 |
| | 3 | 1.12 | 0 | 100 | 0 | 0 |
| | 6 | 1.13 | 0 | 100 | 0 | 0 |
| | 9 | 1.13 | 0 | 100 | 0 | 0 |
| | 12 | 1.13 | 0 | 100 | 0 | 0 |
| Wages | 1 | 2.46 | 0 | 0 | 100 | 0 |
| | 3 | 2.87 | 1 | 5 | 89 | 5 |
| | 6 | 2.90 | 1 | 5 | 88 | 6 |
| | 9 | 2.91 | 1 | 6 | 87 | 6 |
| | 12 | 2.92 | 1 | 6 | 87 | 6 |
| Money | 1 | 0.70 | 0 | 0 | 0 | 100 |
| | 3 | 1.23 | 8 | 5 | 13 | 74 |
| | 6 | 1.48 | 6 | 22 | 18 | 54 |
| | 9 | 1.50 | 6 | 23 | 18 | 53 |
| | 12 | 1.51 | 6 | 23 | 18 | 53 |

effect on domestic inflation, changes in real wages follow changes in nominal wages.

The innovation in monetary expansion has a relatively small effect on domestic inflation that lasts for about five months, and no effect on foreign inflation. It has a persistent effect on wage increases, with a zigzag pattern during the first few months following the shock. Monetary expansion increases for about four months, and then declines somewhat for the next six months.

## Decomposition of Variance of Forecast Error

One way of assessing the relative importance of each innovation in causing movements in a given endogenous variable is to calculate the proportion of the variance of the forecast error for that variable that can be attributed to each of the innovations. Innovations with large fluctuations and with large effects on the endogenous variable will account for a large proportion of the variance of the forecast error. These calculations are presented in Table 13 for several forecast horizons.

For all the variables, the forecast standard error tends to some upper bound as the forecast horizon lengthens. From the magnitude of the standard errors, it is clear that

---

[12] A possible explanation for this result could be based on productivity shocks. A positive productivity shock, for example, would lead to an increase in wages, while simultaneously increasing output and thus reducing inflationary pressures. This explanation, however, would require a rather curious process generating productivity shocks to account for the magnitude and behavior of observed monthly wage changes.

[13] Alternative systems were estimated for the residuals, where monetary expansion was also assumed to be affected immediately by other innovations, but the results were unsatisfactory. For an exactly identified system, the likelihood function was ill-behaved. For overidentified systems, the overidentification restrictions were rejected at the 10 percent level of significance, with one exception. The restriction was not rejected when only imported inflation innovations were assumed to affect monetary expansion in the same period. However, in this case the estimated coefficient is small and statistically nonsignificant, so that the results are essentially the same as those presented in this section.

[14] All the graphs, except one, are drawn using the same vertical scale so as to facilitate a visual comparison of the size of the various shocks and the magnitude of the response of the various variables. The one exception is the graph on the behavior of wages upon an innovation in wages, in Chart 22. In this case, the vertical scale was reduced by half because changes in wages show very large fluctuations when compared with other cases and other variables.

**Chart 20. Impulse Response to Innovation in Domestic Inflation**
*(Monthly rates of change, in percent)*

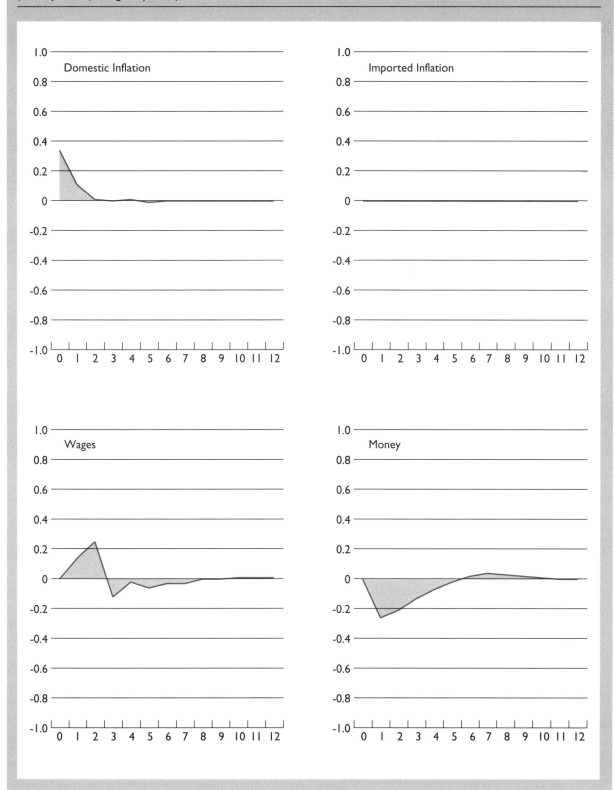

**Chart 21. Impulse Response to Innovation in Imported Inflation**
*(Monthly rates of change, in percent)*

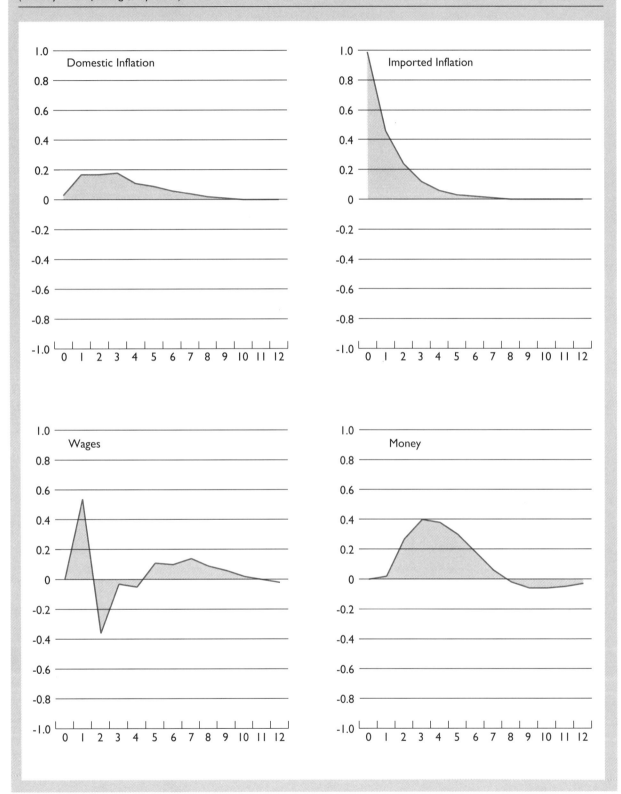

**Chart 22. Impulse Response to Innovation in Wages**
*(Monthly rates of change, in percent)*

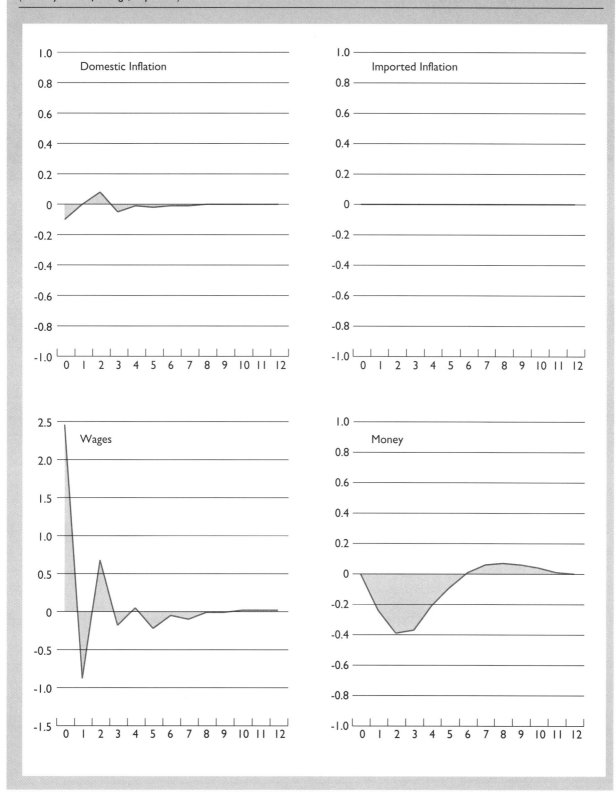

**Chart 23. Impulse Response to Innovation in Money**
*(Monthly rates of change, in percent)*

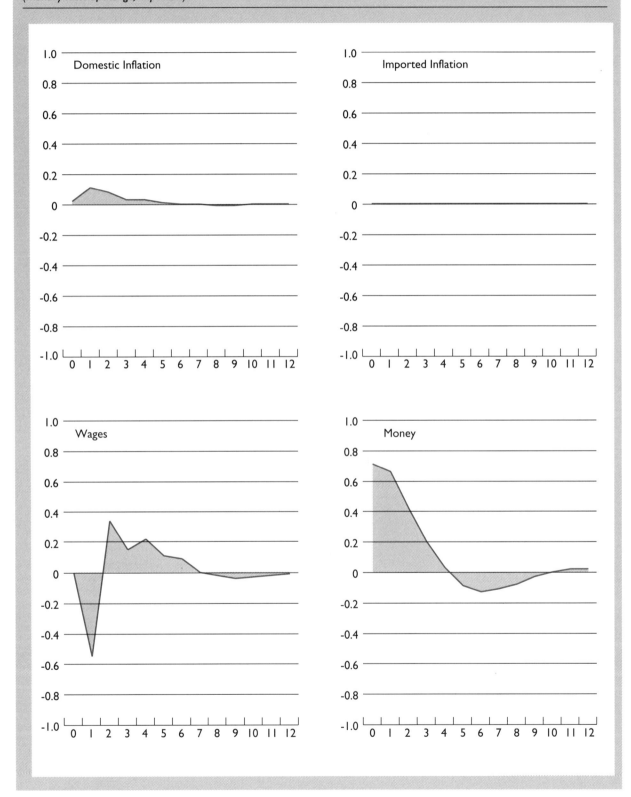

this model would generate more precise forecasts for domestic inflation, and less precise forecasts for wage changes, than for the other variables in the system.

The variance of the forecast error for domestic inflation is almost entirely explained by innovations in domestic inflation and in imported inflation. Innovations in wages and in monetary expansion combined account for only about 15 percent of total variance. While innovations in domestic inflation are the most important factor for all horizons, innovations in imported inflation are almost as important for six-month and longer horizons.

The only important component in the decomposition of the forecast error for wage increases is wage innovations. All the other innovations taken together account for only 13 percent of the variance of the forecast error. This is consistent with the results of the exclusion restriction tests presented in Table 12, where only past wage increases have a significant effect on current wage changes, and with our assumption that innovations in other variables do not have an immediate effect on wage changes.

The variance of the forecast error for monetary expansion is explained by its own innovation, and by innovations in imported inflation and in wages, with virtually no contribution from innovations in domestic inflation. While monetary expansion innovations dominate for short horizons, imported inflation and wage innovations taken together also become important for six-month and longer horizons.

### Decomposition of the Forecast Error for 1990–91

The model can also be used to assess the contribution of each of the innovations in producing the actual forecast error for a given period within the estimation sample. Charts 24 and 25 present such decomposition for the period January 1990–March 1991. Chart 24 shows the actual inflation rate during that period, and the inflation rate that would have been forecast using the estimated model and information on $p$, $ii$, $w$, and $m$ up to December 1989.[15] The vertical difference between the two lines represents the forecast error. This error is attributed to the various innovations in Chart 25, where the vertical sum of the various lines adds up to the forecast error.

From Chart 24, it is clear that actual inflation was higher than forecasted inflation for most of this period. The forecast error is positive and particularly large for June, July, and November 1990, and negative and significant for January 1991. According to Chart 25, the June 1990 error was mostly due to wage innovations, while the July 1990 error was due to domestic inflation innovations. The

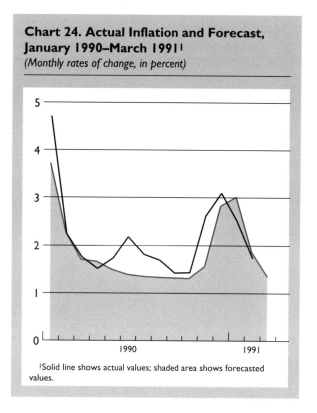

**Chart 24. Actual Inflation and Forecast, January 1990–March 1991[1]**
*(Monthly rates of change, in percent)*

[1]Solid line shows actual values; shaded area shows forecasted values.

November 1990 error was due to both imported inflation and domestic inflation innovations. Imported inflation was higher than forecasted for most of the period, which is reflected in its positive contribution to the forecast error. The positive contribution of domestic inflation innovations in November 1990, and their negative contribution in January 1991, may be due to a modification in the calendar for announcing new measures under the PECE with respect to past experience. While in previous years adjustments in public sector prices and wages were announced in December, in 1990 these adjustments were announced in November. Therefore, the main impact of the new measures may have taken place in November and December 1990, rather than in December 1990 and January 1991, as predicted by the dummies used in the forecasting exercise.

As a final exercise, the model was used to forecast beyond the estimation period. With the model estimated with information up to March 1991, and with the values of the endogenous variables observed up to that month, the forecasted cumulative inflation for the next eight months was 9.0 percent, while the actual cumulative inflation was 9.3 percent.[16]

---

[15] Since the model was estimated using data up to March 1991, and the value of the increase in minimum wages up to March 1991 was assumed to be known, this forecast exercise uses some information from the forecasting period that was not available in December 1989.

[16] Minimum wages were assumed to be increased by 12 percent in November 1991.

**Chart 25. Historical Decomposition of Forecast Error, January 1990–March 1991**

*(Monthly rates of change, in percent)*

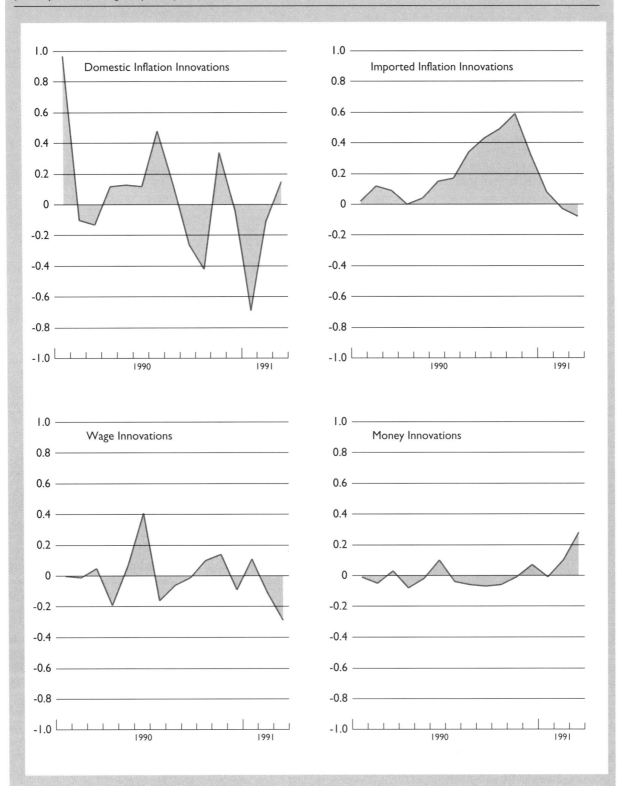

## Conclusions

During the period June 1988–March 1991, the monthly rate of inflation in Mexico responded significantly to adjustments in public sector prices and to lagged values of domestic inflation, imported inflation, and monetary expansion, but showed little reaction to lagged values of wage changes. Regarding contemporaneous effects, the response to imported inflation and monetary expansion was weak, while the reaction to wage changes was significant but negative, which is difficult to explain.

The evolution of nominal wages during this period responded primarily to changes in the minimum wage rate, and to lagged changes in wages, but showed relatively small reaction to lagged values of domestic inflation, imported inflation, and monetary expansion. Monetary expansion, on the other hand, responded to lagged values of all the other variables.

The dynamic effects of the various innovations were derived under the assumption that domestic inflation adjusts within the same month to all types of innovations, while wage increases and monetary expansion adjust with a one-month lag to innovations in other variables. The results indicate that innovations in imported inflation have a significant and persistent effect on domestic inflation, while innovations in domestic inflation have a significant but less persistent effect. The effects of innovations in monetary expansion and wage changes are considerably smaller.

These results have a number of implications regarding the appropriate modeling of transmission channels in a structural model for inflation. Inflation should not be modeled as being determined primarily by a markup over wages, since inflation is associated with other variables, and the contemporaneous effect of wage changes seems to be negative rather than positive. In addition, modeling wage adjustments as responding predominantly to past changes in prices would fail to account for a large fraction of the variability in wage changes. Also, monetary expansion should not be considered an exogenous variable, since it responds to the other endogenous variables in the system.

Clearly, these results depend on the particular identifying restrictions regarding the contemporaneous effects of the various innovations, and on the particular set of variables included in the model. While modifying the identifying restrictions would not affect significantly many of the results, modifying the set of variables might do so.

Regardless of the particular model used, attempts to identify the various forces that determine inflation in Mexico on a monthly basis must, however, confront two problems. One is the peculiar behavior of the data on wages, for which a satisfactory explanation is not readily available. There is the possibility that the quality of the data is poor, and thus the conclusions could be based on erroneous data. The other problem is that many exogenous shocks in Mexico take place simultaneously. Usually, minimum wages and public sector prices are adjusted, and a new path for the exchange rate is announced at the end of the year. This problem of simultaneous shocks at the end of the year is compounded by the adjustments that must be made to the series on monetary expansion, because of seasonality, and to the series on wage changes, because of the December bonus. To the extent that these adjustments are not perfect, they may introduce additional biases in the estimation.

# Appendix I    Description of Model

Denoting the endogenous variables by $y_1, \ldots, y_n$, and the exogenous variables by $x_1, \ldots, x_m$, the system to estimate is

$$
\begin{aligned}
y(t) = C_0\, x(t) + \ldots + C_q\, x(t{-}q) + D_1\, y(t{-}1) \\
+ \ldots + D_p\, y(t{-}p) + u(t),
\end{aligned} \tag{1}
$$

where $y(t)$ is an $nxl$ vector of endogenous variables at time $t$, $x(t)$ is an $mxl$ vector of exogenous variables at time $t$, $C_j$ is an $nxm$ matrix of coefficients associated with the exogenous variables' lagged $j$ periods, $D_j$ is an $nxn$ matrix of coefficients associated with the endogenous variables, lagged $j$ periods, and $u(t)$ is an $nxl$ vector representing the reduced form errors.

The system described by equation (1) can be interpreted as resulting from a structural model such as

$$
\begin{aligned}
y(t) = A_0\, x(t) + \ldots + A_q\, x(t{-}q) + B_0\, y(t) \\
+ B_1\, y(t{-}1) + \ldots + B_p\, y(t{-}p) + e(t),
\end{aligned} \tag{2}
$$

where $A_j$ is an $nxm$ matrix, $B_0$ is an $nxn$ matrix with diagonal elements equal to zero, $B_j$ (for $j > 0$) is an $nxn$ matrix, and $e(t)$ is an $nxl$ vector of structural innovations, which are assumed to have zero cross-correlation. The relationship between the reduced form system in equation (1) and the structural system in equation (2) is given by

$$
\begin{aligned}
(I{-}B_0)\, C_j &= A_j \tag{3} \\
(I{-}B_0)\, D_j &= B_j \tag{4} \\
(I{-}B_0)\, u(t) &= e(t), \tag{5}
\end{aligned}
$$

where $I$ is the $nxn$ identity matrix.

According to equation (2), the dynamics of the endogenous variables are driven by the realization of the innovations $e(t)$, and the evolution of the exogenous variables $x(t)$. The innovations $e(t)$ represent exogenous shocks to the variables $y(t)$, which are not captured by the exogenous variables $x(t)$.

From the estimated reduced form errors (the estimated $u(t)$), it is possible to recover the innovations (the $e(t)$) by estimating $(I{-}B_0)$ in equation (5) under certain additional assumptions. These assumptions refer to the contemporaneous response of the endogenous variables to the various innovations. To the extent that the $i$th variable does not respond to the $j$th innovation within the same period, the $(i, j)$ element of the $(I{-}B_0)$ matrix is equal to zero. The structural errors can be recovered from the reduced form errors by choosing a sufficient number of off-diagonal elements in the $(I{-}B_0)$ matrix to be zero.

# Bibliography

Bernanke, Ben S., "Alternative Explanations of the Money-Income Correlation," *Carnegie-Rochester Conference Series on Public Policy*, Vol. 25 (1986), pp. 49–100.

Cooley, Thomas F., and Stephen F. LeRoy, "A Theoretical Macroeconometrics: A Critique," *Journal of Monetary Economics*, Vol. 16 (1985), pp. 283–308.

Guerrero, Victor M., and Luis G. Arias, "Analisis de la Inflacion en Mexico de 1970 a 1987 Mediante Vectores Autorregresivos," *El Trimestre Economico*, Vol. 57 (1990), pp. 379–401.

Ize, Alain, and Gabriel Vera, eds., *La Inflacion en Mexico* (Mexico: El Colegio de Mexico, 1984).

Kaminsky, Graciela, "Dual Exchange Rates: The Mexican Experience 1982–1987," a paper presented at an IMF Seminar on April 2, 1992.

Leamer, Edward E., "Vector Autoregression for Causal Inference?," *Carnegie-Rochester Conference Series on Public Policy*, Vol. 22 (1985), pp. 255–304.

Leiderman, Leonardo, "On the Monetary-Macro Dynamics of Colombia and Mexico," *Journal of Development Economics*, Vol. 14 (1984), pp. 183–201.

Lütkepohl, Helmut, "Comparison of Criteria for Estimating the Order of Vector Autoregressive Process," *Journal of Time Series Analysis*, Vol. 6 (1985), pp. 35–52.

Puente, Francisco, "Resultados Preliminares del Uso de un Modelo "VAR" para Analizar el Proceso de Inflacion en Mexico," *Boletin de Economia Internacional* (Banco de México), Vol. 15 (1989), pp. 23–35.

Sims, Christopher A., "Are Forecasting Models Usable for Policy Analysis?" *Quarterly Review*, Federal Reserve Bank of Minneapolis, Vol. 10 (Winter 1986), pp. 2–16.

## Recent Occasional Papers of the International Monetary Fund

99. Mexico: The Strategy to Achieve Sustained Economic Growth, edited by Claudio Loser and Eliot Kalter. 1992.

98. Albania: From Isolation Toward Reform, by Mario I. Blejer, Mauro Mecagni, Ratna Sahay, Richard Hides, Barry Johnston, Piroska Nagy, and Roy Pepper. 1992.

97. Rules and Discretion in International Economic Policy, by Manuel Guitián. 1992.

96. Policy Issues in the Evolving International Monetary System, by Morris Goldstein, Peter Isard, Paul R. Masson, and Mark P. Taylor. 1992.

95. The Fiscal Dimensions of Adjustment in Low-Income Countries, by Karim Nashashibi, Sanjeev Gupta, Claire Liuksila, Henri Lorie, and Walter Mahler. 1992.

94. Tax Harmonization in the European Community: Policy Issues and Analysis, edited by George Kopits. 1992.

93. Regional Trade Arrangements, by Augusto de la Torre and Margaret R. Kelly. 1992.

92. Stabilization and Structural Reform in the Czech and Slovak Federal Republic: First Stage, by Bijan B. Aghevli, Eduardo Borensztein, and Tessa van der Willigen. 1992.

91. Economic Policies for a New South Africa, edited by Desmond Lachman and Kenneth Bercuson with a staff team comprising Daudi Ballali, Robert Corker, Charalambos Christofides, and James Wein. 1992.

90. The Internationalization of Currencies: An Appraisal of the Japanese Yen, by George S. Tavlas and Yuzuru Ozeki. 1992.

89. The Romanian Economic Reform Program, by Dimitri G. Demekas and Mohsin S. Khan. 1991.

88. Value-Added Tax: Administrative and Policy Issues, edited by Alan A. Tait. 1991.

87. Financial Assistance from Arab Countries and Arab Regional Institutions, by Pierre van den Boogaerde. 1991.

86. Ghana: Adjustment and Growth, 1983–91, by Ishan Kapur, Michael T. Hadjimichael, Paul Hilbers, Jerald Schiff, and Philippe Szymczak. 1991.

85. Thailand: Adjusting to Success—Current Policy Issues, by David Robinson, Yangho Byeon, and Ranjit Teja with Wanda Tseng. 1991.

84. Financial Liberalization, Money Demand, and Monetary Policy in Asian Countries, by Wanda Tseng and Robert Corker. 1991.

83. Economic Reform in Hungary Since 1968, by Anthony R. Boote and Janos Somogyi. 1991.

82. Characteristics of a Successful Exchange Rate System, by Jacob A. Frenkel, Morris Goldstein, and Paul R. Masson. 1991.

81. Currency Convertibility and the Transformation of Centrally Planned Economies, by Joshua E. Greene and Peter Isard. 1991.

80. Domestic Public Debt of Externally Indebted Countries, by Pablo E. Guidotti and Manmohan S. Kumar. 1991.

79. The Mongolian People's Republic: Toward a Market Economy, by Elizabeth Milne, John Leimone, Franek Rozwadowski, and Padej Sukachevin. 1991.

78. Exchange Rate Policy in Developing Countries: Some Analytical Issues, by Bijan B. Aghevli, Mohsin S. Khan, and Peter J. Montiel. 1991.

77. Determinants and Systemic Consequences of International Capital Flows, by Morris Goldstein, Donald J. Mathieson, David Folkerts-Landau, Timothy Lane, J. Saúl Lizondo, and Liliana Rojas-Suárez. 1991.

76. China: Economic Reform and Macroeconomic Management, by Mario Blejer, David Burton, Steven Dunaway, and Gyorgy Szapary. 1991.

75. German Unification: Economic Issues, edited by Leslie Lipschitz and Donogh McDonald. 1990.

74. The Impact of the European Community's Internal Market on the EFTA, by Richard K. Abrams, Peter K. Cornelius, Per L. Hedfors, and Gunnar Tersman. 1990.

73. The European Monetary System: Developments and Perspectives, by Horst Ungerer, Jouko J. Hauvonen, Augusto Lopez-Claros, and Thomas Mayer. 1990.

72. The Czech and Slovak Federal Republic: An Economy in Transition, by Jim Prust and an IMF Staff Team. 1990.

71. MULTIMOD Mark II: A Revised and Extended Model, by Paul Masson, Steven Symansky, and Guy Meredith. 1990.

70. The Conduct of Monetary Policy in the Major Industrial Countries: Instruments and Operating Procedures, by Dallas S. Batten, Michael P. Blackwell, In-Su Kim, Simon E. Nocera, and Yuzuru Ozeki. 1990.

69. International Comparisons of Government Expenditure Revisited: The Developing Countries, 1975–86, by Peter S. Heller and Jack Diamond. 1990.

68. Debt Reduction and Economic Activity, by Michael P. Dooley, David Folkerts-Landau, Richard D. Haas, Steven A. Symansky, and Ralph W. Tryon. 1990.

67. The Role of National Saving in the World Economy: Recent Trends and Prospects, by Bijan B. Aghevli, James M. Boughton, Peter J. Montiel, Delano Villanueva, and Geoffrey Woglom. 1990.

66. The European Monetary System in the Context of the Integration of European Financial Markets, by David Folkerts-Landau and Donald J. Mathieson. 1989.

65. Managing Financial Risks in Indebted Developing Countries, by Donald J. Mathieson, David Folkerts-Landau, Timothy Lane, and Iqbal Zaidi. 1989.

64. The Federal Republic of Germany: Adjustment in a Surplus Country, by Leslie Lipschitz, Jeroen Kremers, Thomas Mayer, and Donogh McDonald. 1989.

63. Issues and Developments in International Trade Policy, by Margaret Kelly, Naheed Kirmani, Miranda Xafa, Clemens Boonekamp, and Peter Winglee. 1988.

62. The Common Agricultural Policy of the European Community: Principles and Consequences, by Julius Rosenblatt, Thomas Mayer, Kasper Bartholdy, Dimitrios Demekas, Sanjeev Gupta, and Leslie Lipschitz. 1988.

61. Policy Coordination in the European Monetary System. Part I: The European Monetary System: A Balance Between Rules and Discretion, by Manuel Guitián. Part II: Monetary Coordination Within the European Monetary System: Is There a Rule? by Massimo Russo and Giuseppe Tullio. 1988.

60. Policies for Developing Forward Foreign Exchange Markets, by Peter J. Quirk, Graham Hacche, Viktor Schoofs, and Lothar Weniger. 1988.

59. Measurement of Fiscal Impact: Methodological Issues, edited by Mario I. Blejer and Ke-Young Chu. 1988.

58. The Implications of Fund-Supported Adjustment Programs for Poverty: Experiences in Selected Countries, by Peter S. Heller, A. Lans Bovenberg, Thanos Catsambas, Ke-Young Chu, and Parthasarathi Shome. 1988.

57. The Search for Efficiency in the Adjustment Process: Spain in the 1980s, by Augusto Lopez-Claros. 1988.

56. Privatization and Public Enterprises, by Richard Hemming and Ali M. Mansoor. 1988.

55. Theoretical Aspects of the Design of Fund-Supported Adjustment Programs: A Study by the Research Department of the International Monetary Fund. 1987.

54. Protection and Liberalization: A Review of Analytical Issues, by W. Max Corden. 1987.

**Note:** For information on the title and availability of Occasional Papers not listed, please consult the IMF *Publications Catalog* or contact IMF Publication Services.

# THE WEST

## Encounters & Transformations

### Second Edition, Atlas Edition

This Atlas Edition is designed to help students with geography, one of the most difficult parts of the course for many students. Questions provided with outline and four-color maps call for identifying important geographical areas and think critically about the importance of geography thoughout history. The maps are on perforated pages and are organized by book chapter so they can be easily assigned.

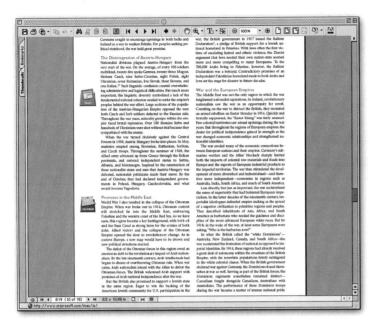

## Would your life be easier if you had an electronic version of your textbook?

MyHistoryLab contains the complete text with icons that link to selected sources. You can print sections of the text to read anytime, anywhere.

## Are you overwhelmed by the time it takes to find primary source documents, images, and maps for your research papers?

MyHistoryLab contains over 1,100 documents, images, maps, and video clips—all in one place —to help make writing your research paper easier and more effective and to help you better understand the course material.

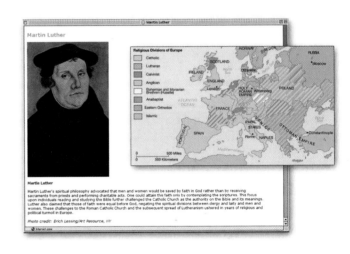

## Are you sometimes overwhelmed when you study for exams?

MyHistoryLab provides an integrated quizzing and testing program that includes chapter pre-tests, post-tests, and exams. A customized study plan, generated from the chapter pre-tests and post-tests, shows what you've mastered as well as where you need more work. Look for these icons in MyHistoryLab.

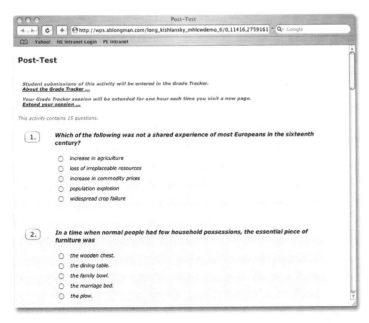

## Need extra help during evening hours?

Get help from The Tutor Center when your instructor is often unavailable—5 pm to midnight, Sunday through Thursday, spring and fall terms (Sunday through Wednesday, summer term). Tutors can help you navigate MyHistoryLab or review your paper for organization, grammar, and mechanics.

The Tutor Center
Addison-Wesley • Allyn & Bacon • Benjamin Cummings • Longman

## Did your professor assign other books to read?

MyHistoryLab allows you to read, download, or print over fifty of the most commonly assigned works for this course—all at no additional cost! The following titles are all available on History Bookshelf.

1. *Aesop's Fables* (c. 500 BCE)
2. *Histories*, Herodotus (c. 450 BCE)
3. *Lysistrata*, Aristophanes (c. 448 BCE)
4. *The Oedipus Trilogy*, Sophocles (c. 425 BCE)
5. *The Republic*, Plato (360 BCE)
6. *The Ethics of Aristotle* (c. 350 BCE)
7. *The Bhagavad-Gita* (c. 100 CE)
8. *The Iliad*, Homer (c. 800 BCE)
9. *The Upanishads* (c. 600 BCE)
10. *Letters of Marcus Tullius Cicero* (c. 45 CE)
11. *De Agricultura*, Marcus Cato (141 CE)
12. *The Lives of Plutarch* (c. 200 CE)
13. *The Confessions of St. Augustine* (401 CE)
14. *The Secret History of the Court of Justinian*, Procopius (558 CE)
15. *The Arabian Nights* (c. 800 CE)
16. *Beowulf* (c. 1000 CE)
17. *Four Arthurian Romances*, De Troyes, (c. 1170)

18. *The Song of Roland* (c. 1200 CE)
19. *The Prince*, Machiavelli *(1505)*
20. *95 Theses,* Martin Luther (1517)
21. *Romeo and Juliet*, Shakespeare (c. 1590)
22. *The Essays of Francis Bacon* (1601)
23. *Leviathan*, Thomas Hobbes (1651)
24. *When London Burned*, G.A. Henty (1665)
25. *Captivity and Restoration*, Mary Rowlandson (1682)
26. *Treatise on Government*, John Locke (1690)
27. *Gulliver's Travels*, Jonathan Swift (1726)
28. *Three Sermons*, Jonathan Swift (1750)
29. *An Inquiry into the Slave Trade*, Anthony Benezet (1771)
30. *Wealth of Nations*, Adam Smith (1776)
31. *Pilgrim's Progress*, John Bunyan (1794)
32. *Sense and Sensibility*, Jane Austen (1811)
33. *The Napoleon of the People*, Honore Balzac (1812)
34. *The Afghan Wars*, Forbes (1839)
35. *The Communist Manifesto*, Karl Marx (1848)

36. *Origin of Species*, Charles Darwin (1859)
37. *Narrative of the Overland Expedition to Northern Queensland*, Fredrick Byerley (1867)
38. *Japanese Manners and Customs*, J. Silver (1867)
39. *20,000 Leagues Under the Sea*, Jules Verne (1870)
40. *To the Gold Coast for Gold*, Sir Richard Burton (1883)
41. *The Jungle Book*, Rudyard Kipling (1894)
42. *Heart of Darkness*, Joseph Conrad (1899)
43. *Moorish Literature*, Rene Basset (1901)
44. *River Wars of the Sudan*, Winston Churchill (1902)
45. *The Woman Who Toils*, Vorst (1903)
46. *Congo Free State*, Marcus Dorman (1905)
47. *The Beginnings of Israeli History*, Kent & Jenks (1912)
48. *Clairvoyance*, Swami Panchadasi (1916)
49. *The Psychology of Dreams*, Sigmund Freud (1920)
50. *A Biography of Simon Bolivar*, Sherwell, (1921)

Now, flip through *The West: Encounters & Transformations*. You will find the icons shown on the next page. Each icon will direct you to a place in MyHistoryLab to help you better understand the material. For example, when reading about 19th-century European politics, you may find an icon that links you to an original source document by Martin Luther or Karl Marx.

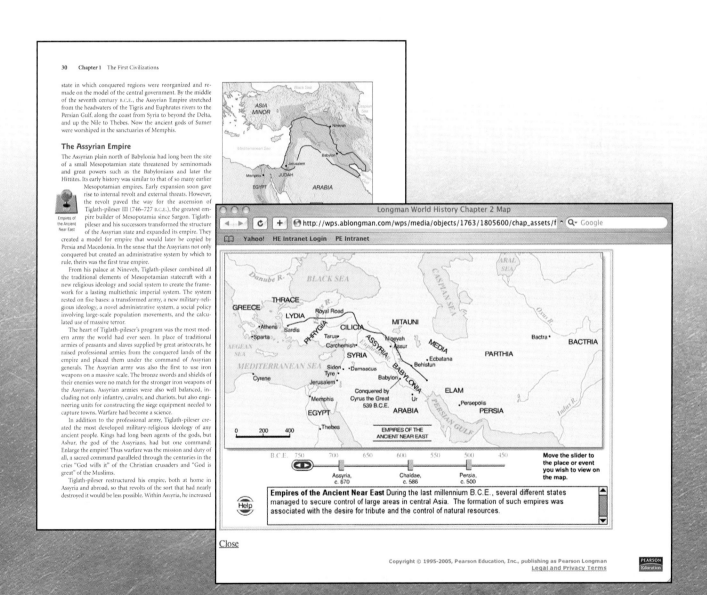

## DOCUMENT

This icon directs students to primary source documents that support the material they are reading. In addition, the documents offer headnotes and analysis questions to focus students' reading.

## IMAGE

Photos, cartoons, and artwork offer students opportunities to learn the course content in a more visual way. Each image includes a headnote and analysis questions.

## MAP

Interactive maps with headnotes and questions help students visualize the material they are studying. Atlas maps and printable map activities from a Longman workbook give students hands-on experience.

## VIDEO CLIP

Historical video clips are included, along with headnotes and thoughtful questions.

# myhistorylab™

### Where it's a good time to connect to the past!

If your professor has not ordered MyHistoryLab, you can still purchase access to all of these resources.

Go to
www.MyHistoryLab.com
and click the STUDENTS button for FIRST TIME USERS and follow the instructions to purchase online access.

PEARSON
Longman

## Connecting to the past has never been easier.

# MyHistoryLab.com

# Key Eras in the Transformation of the West

## Map 1 Roman Empire at Its Greatest Extent, ca. 117 C.E.

Western civilization has undergone many transformations throughout its history. When the Roman Empire was at its greatest extent, the basic intellectual, religious, political, and geographic outlines of what we call the West today were drawn.

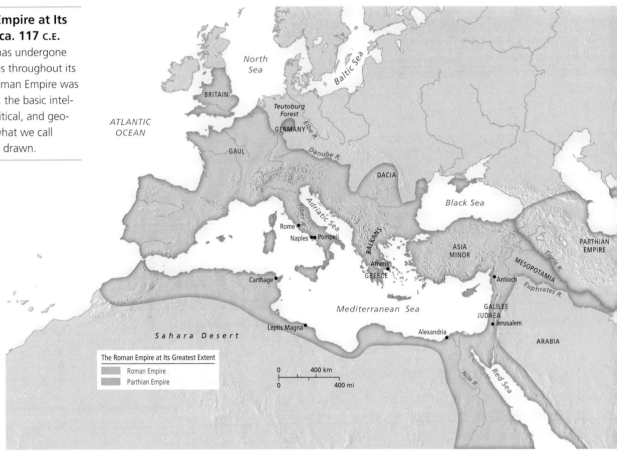

## Map 2 Carolingian Empire

During the Carolingian Empire, Europe experienced greater political cohesion, as the Carolingian armies successfully reunified most of the western European territories of the ancient Roman Empire, distinguishing it from the Byzantine Empire in the east.

## Map 3 Europe After the Congress of Vienna, 1815

The major European powers re-drew the map of Europe with the Congress of Vienna in 1815 after the defeat of Napoleon. This map shows the dismantlement of the massive empire France had acquired under his leadership.

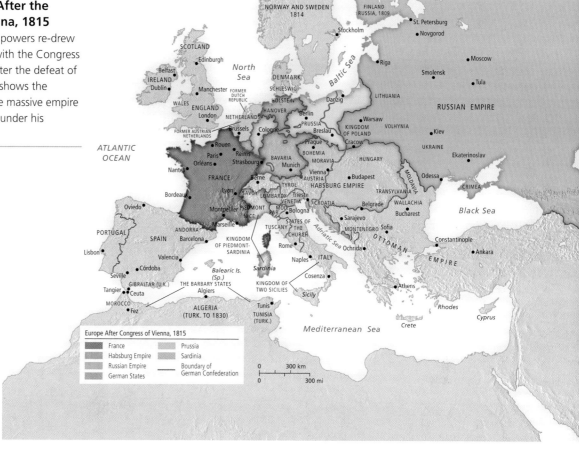

Europe After Congress of Vienna, 1815

- France
- Habsburg Empire
- Russian Empire
- German States
- Prussia
- Sardinia
- Boundary of German Confederation

## Map 4 Europe After World War I

The map of Europe changed dramatically after World War I with the collapse of the old authoritarian empires and the creation of independent nation-states in eastern Europe. What neither Map 3 nor Map 4 can show, however, is the expansion of "the West" beyond European borders to embrace cultures on other continents, including Australia, Africa, and North America.

Europe and the Middle East After World War I

- To Great Britain
- To France
- To Italy
- To Rumania
- To Denmark
- To Yugoslavia (Serbia and Montenegro)
- To Belgium
- To Greece
- Became independent
- 1914 boundaries
- New boundaries

# ATLAS EDITION

# THE WEST

## Encounters & Transformations

### Second Edition

### VOLUME II: SINCE 1550

**Brian Levack**
*University of Texas at Austin*

**Edward Muir**
*Northwestern University*

**Meredith Veldman**
*Louisiana State University*

**Michael Maas**
*Rice University*

PEARSON

Longman

New York   San Francisco   Boston
London   Toronto   Sydney   Tokyo   Singapore   Madrid
Mexico City   Munich   Paris   Cape Town   Hong Kong   Montreal

Senior Acquisitions Editor: Janet Lanphier
Assistant Director of Development: David B. Kear
Executive Marketing Manager: Sue Westmoreland
Supplements Editor: Brian Belardi
Media Editor: Melissa Edwards
Production Manager: Donna DeBenedictis
Project Coordination, Text Design, and Electronic Page Makeup:
    Elm Street Publishing Services, Inc.
Cover Designer/Manager: John Callahan
Cover and Frontispiece Art: *The Indoor Wedding Dance* by Pieter Brueghel the Younger
    ca. 1585–1638. © Christie's Images/CORBIS. All Rights Reserved.
Cartography: Maps.com
Photo Researcher: Photosearch, Inc.
Manufacturing Buyer: Roy L. Pickering, Jr.
Printer and Binder: Quebecor World Versailles
Cover Printer: Coral Graphic Services, Inc.

For permission to use copyrighted material, grateful acknowledgment is made to the copyright holders on pp. C-1–C-2, which are hereby made part of this copyright page.

Please visit us at http://www.ablongman.com/levack2e

ISBN-13: 978-0-205-55697-7    ISBN-10: 0-205-55697-3 (single-volume edition)
ISBN-13: 978-0-205-55811-7    ISBN-10: 0-205-55811-9 (volume I)
ISBN-13: 978-0-205-55698-4    ISBN-10: 0-205-55698-1 (volume II)

1 2 3 4 5 6 7 8 9 10—QWV—10 09 08 07

# Brief Contents

# Detailed Contents

# 26 World War II 848

# 27 Redefining the West After World War II 884

# Documents

# Maps

# Features

# Chronologies

# Preface

We wrote this textbook to answer questions about the identity of the civilization in which we live. Journalists, politicians, and scholars often refer to our civilization, its political ideologies, its economic systems, and its cultures as "Western" without fully considering what that label means and why it might be appropriate. The classification of our civilization as Western has become particularly problematic in the age of globalization. The creation of international markets, the rapid dissemination of ideas on a global scale, and the transmission of popular culture from one country to another often make it difficult to distinguish what is Western from what is not. *The West: Encounters & Transformations* offers students a history of Western civilization in which these issues of Western identity are given prominence. Our goal is neither to idealize nor to indict that civilization but to describe its main characteristics in different historical periods.

*The West: Encounters & Transformations* gives careful consideration to two basic questions. The first is, how did the definition of the West change over time? In what ways did its boundaries shift and how did the distinguishing characteristics of its cultures change? The second question is, by what means did the West—and the idea of the West—develop? We argue that the West is the product of a series of cultural encounters that occurred both outside and within its geographical boundaries. We explore these encounters and the transformations they produced by detailing the political, social, religious, and cultural history of the regions that have been, at one time or another, a part of the West.

## Defining the West

What is the West? How did it come into being? How has it developed throughout history? Many textbooks take for granted which regions or peoples of the globe constitute the West. They treat the history of the West as a somewhat expanded version of European history. While not disputing the centrality of Europe to any definition of the West, we contend that the West is not only a geographical realm with ever-shifting boundaries but also a cultural realm, an area of cultural influence extending beyond the geographical and political boundaries of Europe. We so strongly believe in this notion that we have written the essay "What Is the West?" to encourage students to think about their understanding of Western civilization and to guide their understanding of each chapter. Many of the features of what we call Western civilization originated in regions that are not geographically part of Europe (such as northern Africa and the Middle East), while ever since the fifteenth century various social, ethnic, and political groups from non-European regions (such as North and South America, eastern Russia, Australia, New Zealand, and South Africa) have identified themselves, in one way or another, with the West. Throughout the text, we devote considerable attention to the boundaries of the West and show how borderlines between cultures have been created, especially in eastern and southeastern Europe.

Considered as a geographical and cultural realm, "the West" is a term of recent origin, and the civilization to which it refers did not become clearly defined until the eleventh century, especially during the Crusades, when western European Christians developed a distinct cultural identity. Before that time we can only talk about the powerful forces that created the West, especially the dynamic interaction of the civilizations of western Europe, the Byzantine Empire, and the Muslim world.

Over the centuries Western civilization has acquired many salient characteristics. These include two of the world's great legal systems (civil law and common law), three of the world's monotheistic religions (Judaism, Christianity, and Islam), certain political and social philosophies, forms of political organization (such as the modern bureaucratic state and democracy), methods of scientific inquiry, systems of economic organization (such as industrial capitalism), and distinctive styles of art, architecture, and music. At times one or more of these characteristics has served as a primary source of Western identity: Christianity in the Middle Ages, science and rationalism during the Enlightenment, industrialization in the nineteenth and twentieth centuries, and a defense of individual liberty and democracy in the late twentieth century. These sources of Western identity, however, have always been challenged and contested, both when they were coming into prominence and when they appeared to be most triumphant. Western culture has never been monolithic, and even today references to the West imply a wide range of meanings.

# Cultural Encounters

The definition of the West is closely related to the central theme of our book, which is the process of cultural encounters. Throughout *The West: Encounters & Transformations,* we examine the West as a product of a series of cultural encounters both outside the West and within it. We show that the West originated and developed through a continuous process of inclusion and exclusion resulting from a series of encounters among and within different groups. These encounters can be described in a general sense as external, internal, or ideological.

## External Encounters

External encounters took place between peoples of different civilizations. Before the emergence of the West as a clearly defined entity, external encounters occurred between such diverse peoples as Greeks and Phoenicians, Macedonians and Egyptians, and Romans and Celts. After the eleventh century, external encounters between Western and non-Western peoples occurred mainly during periods of European exploration, expansion, and imperialism. In the sixteenth and seventeenth centuries, for example, a series of external encounters took place between Europeans on the one hand and Africans, Asians, and the indigenous people of the Americas on the other. Two chapters of *The West: Encounters & Transformations* (Chapters 12 and 17) and a large section of a third (Chapter 23) explore these external encounters in depth and discuss how they affected Western and non-Western civilizations alike.

## Internal Encounters

Our discussion of encounters also includes similar interactions between different social groups *within* Western countries. These internal encounters often took place between dominant and subordinate groups, such as between lords and peasants, rulers and subjects, men and women, factory owners and workers, masters and slaves. Encounters between those who were educated and those who were illiterate, which recur frequently throughout Western history, also fall into this category. Encounters just as often took place between different religious and political groups, such as between Christians and Jews, Catholics and Protestants, and royal absolutists and republicans.

## Ideological Encounters

Ideological encounters involve interaction between comprehensive systems of thought, most notably religious doctrines, political philosophies, and scientific theories about the nature of the world. These ideological conflicts usually arose out of internal encounters, when various groups within Western societies subscribed to different theories of government or rival religious faiths. The encounters between Christianity and polytheism in the early Middle Ages, between liberalism and conservatism in the nineteenth century, and between fascism and communism in the twentieth century were ideological encounters. Some ideological encounters had an external dimension, such as when the forces of Islam and Christianity came into conflict during the Crusades and when the Cold War developed between Soviet communism and Western democracy in the second half of the twentieth century.

*  *  *

*The West: Encounters & Transformations* illuminates the variety of these encounters and clarifies their effects. By their very nature encounters are interactive, but they have taken different forms: they have been violent or peaceful, coercive or cooperative. Some have resulted in the imposition of Western ideas on areas outside the geographical boundaries of the West or the perpetuation of the dominant culture within Western societies. More often than not, however, encounters have resulted in a more reciprocal process of exchange in which both Western and non-Western cultures or the values of both dominant and subordinate groups have undergone significant transformation. Our book not only identifies these encounters but also discusses their significance by returning periodically to the issue of Western identity.

# Coverage

The *West: Encounters & Transformations* offers both balanced coverage of political, social, and culture history and a broader coverage of the West and the world.

## Balanced Coverage

Our goal throughout the text has been to provide balanced coverage of political, social, and cultural history and to include significant coverage of religious and military history as well. Political history defines the basic structure of the book, and some chapters, such as those on the Hellenistic world, the age of confessional divisions, absolutism and state building, the French Revolution, and the coming of mass politics, include sustained political narratives. Because we understand the West to be a cultural as well as a geographical realm, we give a prominent position to cultural history. Thus we include rich sections on Hellenistic philosophy and literature, the cultural environment of the Italian Renaissance, the creation of a new political culture at the time of the French Revolution, and the atmosphere of cultural despair and desire that prevailed in Europe after World War I. We also devote special attention to religious history, including the history of Islam as well as that of Christianity and Judaism. Unlike many other textbooks, our coverage of religion continues into the modern period.

*The West: Encounters & Transformations* also provides extensive coverage of the history of women and gender. Wherever possible the history of women is integrated into the broader social, cultural, and political history of the period. But there are also separate sections on women in our chapters on classical Greece, the Renaissance, the Reformation, the Enlightenment, the Industrial Revolution, World War I, World War II, and the postwar era.

## The West and the World

Our book provides broad geographical coverage. Because the West is the product of a series of encounters, the external areas with which the West interacted are of major importance. Three chapters deal specifically with the West and the world.

- Chapter 12, "The West and the World: The Significance of Global Encounters, 1450–1650"
- Chapter 17, "The West and the World: Empire, Trade, and War, 1650–1815"
- Chapter 23, "The West and the World: Cultural Crisis and the New Imperialism, 1870–1914"

These chapters present substantial material on sub-Saharan Africa, Latin America, the Middle East, India, and East Asia. Our text is also distinctive in its coverage of eastern Europe and the Muslim world, areas that have often been considered outside the boundaries of the West. These regions were arenas within which significant cultural encounters took place. Finally we include material on the United States and Australia, both of which have become part of the West. We recognize that most American college and university students have the opportunity to study American history as a separate subject, but treatment of the United States as a Western nation provides a different perspective from that usually given in courses on American history. For example, this book treats America's revolution as one of four Atlantic revolutions, its national unification in the nineteenth century as part of a broader western European development, its pattern of industrialization as related to that of Britain, and its central role in the Cold War as part of an ideological encounter that was global in scope.

# Organization

The chronological and thematic organization of our book conforms in its broad outline to the way in which Western civilization courses are generally taught. We have limited the number of chapters to twenty-eight, in an effort to make the book more compatible with the traditional American semester calendar and to solve the frequent complaint that there is not enough time to cover all the material in the course. However, our organization differs from other books in some significant ways:

- Chapter 2, which covers the period from ca. 1600 to 550 B.C.E., is the first in a Western civilization textbook to examine the International Bronze Age and its aftermath as a period important in its own right because it saw the creation of expansionist, multi-ethnic empires linked by trade and diplomacy.
- In Chapter 4 the Roman Republic, in keeping with contemporary scholarship, has been incorporated into a discussion of the Hellenistic world, dethroned slightly to emphasize how it was one of many competing Mediterranean civilizations.
- Chapter 12 covers the first period of European expansion, from 1450 to 1650. It examines the new European encounters with the civilizations of sub-Saharan Africa, the Americas, and East Asia. By paying careful attention to the characteristics of these civilizations before the arrival of the Europeans, we show how this encounter affected indigenous peoples as well as Europeans.
- Chapter 16 is devoted entirely to the Scientific Revolution of the seventeenth century in order to emphasize the central importance of this development in the creation of Western identity.
- Chapter 17, which covers the second period of European expansion, from 1650 to 1815, studies the growth of European empires, the beginning of global warfare, and encounters between Europeans and the peoples of Asia and Africa. It treats the Atlantic revolutions of the late eighteenth and early nineteenth centuries, including

the American Revolution, as episodes in the history of European empires rather than as revolts inspired mainly by national sentiment.

- Chapter 26 not only offers a comprehensive examination of World War II, but also explores the moral fissure in the history of the West created, in very different ways, by the Holocaust and the aerial bombings of civilian centers that culminated in the use of the atomic bomb in August 1945.
- Chapter 28, "The West in the Contemporary Era: New Encounters and Transformations," includes an extended discussion of the emergence of European Islamic communities and the resulting transformations in both European and Islamic identities.

## What's New in this Edition?

In preparing the second edition of *The West: Encounters & Transformations* we have focused on two goals: to make the textbook more teachable and to strengthen our emphasis on the encounters that have transformed the West.

### Organization

We have reduced the number of chapters from twenty-nine to twenty-eight, in order to make the book even more compatible with the typical fifteen-week semester. In a number of chapters, moreover, we have made significant rearrangements of material:

- In Chapter 3, we have discussed the Persian Empire before beginning our study of Hebrew and Greek civilizations to emphasize the argument that the latter two civilizations emerged in a political world dominated by Persia.
- Chapters 6 through 9, which deal with the period from about 300 to 1300 C.E., have been rearranged along more thematic, less chronological lines. We have adopted this strategy to emphasize the importance of the interactions among different religious communities during a period that was crucial to the development of Christianity and Islam.
- Chapter 17, "The West and the World: Empire, Trade, and War, 1650–1815," which appeared as Chapter 19 in the first edition, has been placed earlier in the book because it is concerned mainly with eighteenth-century developments. It now precedes the discussion of eighteenth-century society and culture.
- In Chapter 22, "The Coming of Mass Politics: Industrialization, Emancipation, and Instability, 1870–1914," we have replaced the "nation-by-nation" narrative with a thematic approach that more effectively conveys the processes by which European elites sought both to capitalize on and control the new forces of popular nationalism.
- Our treatment of both the Holocaust and the decision to use atomic bombs against Japan, which appeared as a separate chapter in the first edition, is now embedded in Chapter 26, "World War II." This volume still includes a far more extensive and in-depth exploration of these developments than any other Western civilization textbook.
- New sections on "Postwar Nationalism, Westernization, and the Islamic Challenge" in Chapter 25, and "Islam, Terrorism, and European Identity" in Chapter 28 are the most striking examples of our decision to give more coverage to Islam throughout the book.

### New Feature: "Encounters & Transformations"

We have introduced a new feature, "Encounters & Transformations," in about half the chapters. These essays reinforce the main theme of the book by giving specific examples of the ways in which cultural encounters changed the perception and identity of the West.

# Features and Pedagogical Aids

In writing this textbook we have endeavored to keep both the student reader and the classroom instructor in mind at all times. The text includes the following features and pedagogical aids, all of which are intended to support the themes of the book.

## What Is the West?

MANY OF THE PEOPLE WHO INFLUENCE PUBLIC OPINION—POLITI-cians, teachers, clergy, journalists, and television commenta-tors—refer to "Western values," "the West," and "Western civilization." They often use these terms as if they do not re-quire explanation. But what *do* these terms mean? The West has always been an arena within which different cultures, religions, values, and philosophies have interacted, and any definition of the West will inevitably arouse controversy.

The most basic definition of the West is of a place. Western civilization is now typically thought to comprise the regions of Europe, the Americas, Australia, and New Zealand. However, this is a contemporary definition of the West. The inclusion of these places in the West is the result of a long history of European expansion through colonization. In addition to being a place, Western civilization also encompasses a cultural history—a tradition stretching back thousands of years to the ancient world. Over this long period the civilization we now identify as Western gradually took shape. The

## "What Is the West?"

*The West: Encounters & Transformations* begins with an essay to engage students in the task of defining the West and to introduce them to the notion of cultural encounters. "What Is the West?" guides students through the text by providing a framework for understanding how the West was shaped. Structured around the six questions of What? When? Where? Who? How? and Why?, this framework encourages students to think about their understanding of Western civilization. The essay serves as a blueprint for using this textbook.

## NEW! "Encounters & Transformations"

These features, which appear in about half the chapters, illustrate the main theme of the book by identifying specific encounters and showing how they led to significant transformations in the culture of the West. These features show, for example, how encounters among nomadic tribes of Arabia led to the rapid spread of Islam; how the Mayas' interpretation of Christian symbols transformed European Christianity into a hybrid religion; how the importation of chocolate from the New World to Europe changed Western consumption patterns and the rhythms of the Atlantic economy; and how Picasso's encounter with African art led to the transformation of modernism. Each of these essays concludes with a question for discussion.

## Focus Questions

The introduction to each chapter includes a statement of the main question that the entire chapter addresses. It also includes a set of questions that the individual sections of the chapter seek to answer. Each of these questions is then repeated at the beginning of the relevant section of the chapter. The reason for this strategy is to remind the student that the purpose of studying history is not only to learn what happened in the past but also to explain and interpret the course of events. This pedagogical strategy reinforces the approach that the essay, "What is the West?," introduces at the beginning of the book.

## Encounters & Transformations

### Ships of the Desert: Camels from Morocco to Central Asia

A remarkable thing happened when the Arab followers of the dynamic new religion of Islam encountered the humble beast of burden the camel. The camel helped make Arab armies lethal in battle, which meant that the message of Islam spread rapidly through conquest. In addition the caravan trade that transported goods on the backs of camels brought the Arabs into contact with a vast stretch of the world from Spain to China. In the exchanges that took place along the caravan routes, Islamic religious ideas were widely disseminated, and Arab merchants gained access to a lucrative trade that enriched Muslim cities. The success of the caravan trade changed the very appearance of large parts of the West by making obsolete the old Roman roads and the shipping lanes that had unified the Mediterranean, Europe, and North Africa in the ancient world. Narrow camel tracks replaced roads, oases and cities along the caravan routes supplanted ports in economic significance.

Before Muhammad began to recite, the camel had already transformed the life of Arabia. Camels were highly efficient beasts of burden, especially in arid regions, because of their bodies' capacity to conserve water. Able to drink as much as twenty-eight gallons at a time, camels can last four to nine days without water and travel great distances in this period. The fat in their humps allows camels to survive for even longer without food. As pack animals, camels are more efficient than carts pulled by animals because they can traverse roadless rough terrain and cross

rivers without bridges. They require fewer people to manage them on a journey than do wheeled vehicles.

Arab fighters were especially menacing because they developed the "North Arabian saddle" that let them ride the one-humped Arabian camel with comfort in battle. The new saddle required only one rider who could grasp the camel's reins with one hand while slashing downward at enemy troops with a sword in his other hand. Warriors on camels could attack infantry with speed and crushing force. By 300 C.E., camel-breeding Arab tribesmen, empowered by their new military technology, inaugurated the "Caravan Age." The Arabs seized control of the lucrative spice trade routes and became an economic, military, and political force by exploiting and guarding the wealth of the caravans.

After Muhammad established his community in Mecca, Islam literally "took off" on camelback. Tribesmen on camels proved an unstoppable force as they spread Islam first throughout Arabia and the Middle East, and then with lightning speed across North Africa into Spain and Central Asia. Camels played a significant role in the expanding Islamic economy because they made long-distance trade extremely profitable. The transformations the camel brought were most evident in the former

Roman provinces wh mous Roman roads h primary conduit of la Thousands of miles c nected the provinces Empire and let troops from one front to an ever, camels changed Because these "ships do not need paved r routes did not have t Roman road systems. chants bypassed ther New trade routes acr and other harsh terra to camels quickly de Morocco to Central astonishing consequ 700 paved roads star pear. Because camels walk on narrow path streets and wide mar carts and wagons tha Greek and Roman cit use. Bazaars with nar lanes appropriate to sprung up to replace peared in these land just roads and the sh that changed. There consequences as wel caravan traffic reach China, bringing Chine Chinese ideas to the

**Question for I**
How might the history have differed had not c replaced the system of

**The Camel Caravan**
This modern photograph shows a string of camels cross-

## "Justice in History"

Found in every chapter, this feature presents a historically significant trial or episode in which different notions of justice (or injustice) were debated and resolved. The "Justice in History" features illustrate cultural encounters within communities as they try to determine the fate of individuals from all walks of life. Many famous trials dealt with conflicts over basic religious, philosophical, or political values, such as those of Socrates, Jesus, Joan of Arc, Charles I, Galileo, and Adolf Eichmann. Other "Justice in History" features show how judicial institutions, such as the ordeal, the Inquisition, and revolutionary tribunals, handled adversarial situations in different societies. These essays, therefore, illustrate the way in which the basic values of the West have evolved through attempts to resolve disputes, contention, and conflict.

Each "Justice in History" feature includes two pedagogical aids. "Questions of Justice" helps students explore the historical significance of the episode just examined. These questions can also be used in classroom discussion or as student essay topics. "Taking It Further" provides the student with a few references that can be consulted in connection with a research project.

## "The Human Body in History"

Found in about half of the chapters, these features show that the human body, which many people tend to understand solely as a product of biology, also has a history. These essays reveal that the ways in which various religious and political groups have represented the body in art and literature, clothed it, treated it medically, and abused it tell a great deal about the history of Western culture. These features include essays on the classical nude male body, the signs of disease during the Black Death, bathing the body in the East and the West, and the contraceptive pill. Concluding each essay is a single question for discussion that directs students back to the broader issues with which the chapter deals.

## Primary Source Documents

In each chapter we have presented a number of excerpts from primary source documents—from "Tales of the Flood" to "Darwin's 'Descent of Man'"—in order to reinforce or expand upon the points made in the text and to introduce students to the basic materials of historical research.

## Maps and Illustrations

Artwork is a key component of our book. We recognize that many students often lack a strong familiarity with geography, and so we have taken great care to develop maps that help sharpen their geographic skills. Complementing the book's standard map program,

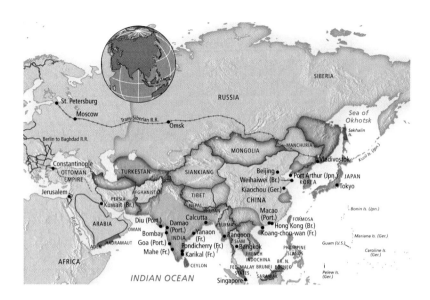

we include maps focusing on areas outside the borders of Western civilization. These maps include a small thumbnail globe that highlights the geographic area under discussion in the context of the larger world. Fine art and photos also tell the story of Western civilization, and we have included more than 350 images to help students visualize the past: the way people lived, the events that shaped their lives, and how they viewed the world around them.

## Chronologies and Suggested Readings

Each chapter includes chronological charts and suggested readings. Chronologies outline significant events, such as "The End of World War II," and serve as convenient references for students. Each chapter concludes with an annotated list of suggested readings. These are not scholarly bibliographies aimed at the professor, but suggestions for students who wish to explore a topic in greater depth or to write a research paper. A comprehensive list of suggested readings is available on our book-specific website, www.ablongman.com/levack2e.

## Glossary

We have sought to create a work that is accessible to students with little prior knowledge of the basic facts of Western history or geography. Throughout the book we have explained difficult concepts at length. For example, we present in-depth explanations of the concepts of Zoroastrianism, Neoplatonism, Renaissance humanism, the various Protestant denominations of the sixteenth century, capitalism, seventeenth-century absolutism, nineteenth-century liberalism and nationalism, fascism, and modernism. Key concepts such as these are identified in the chapters with a degree symbol (°) and defined as well in the end-of-text Glossary.

## MyHistoryLab Icons

Throughout the text, you will see icons that will lead students to additional resources found on MyHistoryLab.com. These resources fall into four categories:

The **document** icon directs students to primary source documents that support the material they are reading in the textbook. In addition, most documents offer headnotes and analysis questions that focus students' reading.

The **image** icon leads students to photos, cartoons, and artwork that relate to the topic they are reading. Most images include a descriptive, contextualized headnote and analysis questions.

The **map** icon refers to maps, many of which are interactive and contain headnotes and questions designed to help students visualize the material they are learning. Printable map activities from Longman's outstanding geography workbooks allow students to interact with maps.

The **video** icon leads students to video clips that focus on the regions, people, or events discussed in the text.

## A Note About Dates and Transliterations

In keeping with current academic practice, *The West: Encounters & Transformations* uses B.C.E. (before the common era) and C.E. (common era) to designate dates. We also follow the most current and widely accepted English transliterations of Arabic. *Qur'an*, for example, is used for *Koran; Muslim* is used for *Moslem.* Chinese words appearing in the text for the first time are written in pinyin, followed by the older Wade-Giles system in parentheses.

# Supplements

## For Qualified College Instructors

### Instructor's Resource Manual
0-321-42735-1
In this manual written by Sharon Arnoult, Midwestern State University, each chapter contains a chapter outline, significant themes, learning objectives, lesson enrichment ideas, discussion suggestions, and questions for discussing the primary source documents in the text.

### Test Bank
0-321-42731-9
Written by Susan Carrafiello, Wright State University, this supplement contains more than 1,200 multiple-choice and essay questions. All questions are referenced by topic and text page number.

### TestGen-EQ Computerized Testing System
0-321-42573-1
This flexible, easy-to-master computerized test bank on a dual-platform CD includes all of the items in the printed test bank and allows instructors to select specific questions, edit existing questions, and add their own items to create exams. Tests can be printed in several different fonts and formats and can include figures, such as graphs and tables.

### Companion Website (www.ablongman.com/levack2e)
Instructors can take advantage of the Companion Website that supports this text. The instructor section includes teaching links, downloadable maps, tables, and graphs from the text for use in PowerPoint, PowerPoint lecture outlines, and a link to the Instructor Resource Center.

### Instructor Resource Center (IRC) (www.ablongman.com/irc)
Through the Instructor Resource Center, instructors can log into premium online products, browse and download book-specific instructor resources, and receive immediate access and instructions to installing course management content. Instructors who already have access to CourseCompass or Supplements Central can log in to the IRC immediately using their existing login and password. First-time users can register at the Instructor Resource Center welcome page at www.ablongman.com/irc.

### MyHistoryLab (www.myhistorylab.com)
MyHistoryLab provides students with an online package complete with the entire electronic textbook and numerous study aids. With several hundred primary sources, many of

which are assignable and link to a gradebook, pre- and post-tests that link to a gradebook and result in individualized study plans, videos and images, as well as map workbook activities with gradable quizzes, the site offers students a unique, interactive experience that brings history to life. The comprehensive site also includes a History Bookshelf with fifty of the most commonly assigned books in history classes and a History Toolkit with tutorials and helpful links. Other features include gradable assignments and chapter review materials; a Test Bank; and Research Navigator.

Delivered in CourseCompass, Blackboard, or WebCT, as well as in a non-course-management version, MyHistoryLab is easy to use and flexible. MyHistoryLab is organized according to the table of contents of this textbook. With the course management version, instructors can create a further customized product by adding their own syllabus, content, and assignments, or they can use the materials as presented.

### PowerPoint Presentations

These presentations contain PowerPoint slides for each chapter and may include key points and terms for a lecture on the chapter, as well as full-color images of important maps, graphs, and charts. The presentations are available for download from www.ablongman.com/levack2e and www.ablongman.com/irc.

### Text-Specific Transparency Set
0-321-42732-7
Instructors can download files with which to make full-color transparency map acetates taken from the text at www.ablongman.com/irc.

### History Video Program
Longman offers more than one hundred videos from which qualified adopters can choose. Restrictions apply.

### History Digital Media Archive CD-ROM
0-321-14976-9
This CD-ROM contains electronic images, interactive and static maps, and media elements such as video. It is fully customizable and ready for classroom presentation. All images and maps are available in PowerPoint as well.

### Discovering Western Civilization Through Maps and Views
0-673-53596-7
Created by Gerald Danzer, University of Illinois at Chicago, and David Buissert, this unique set of 140 full-color acetates contains an introduction to teaching history through maps and a detailed commentary on each transparency. The collection includes cartographic and pictorial maps, views and photos, urban plans, building diagrams, and works of art. Available to qualified college adopters on Longman's Instructor Resource Center (IRC) at www.ablongman.com/irc.

## For Students

### Study Guide
Volume I: 0-321-42733-5
Volume II: 0-321-42734-3
Containing activities and study aids for every chapter in the text, each chapter of the *Study Guide* written by Carron Fillingim, Louisiana State University, includes a thorough chapter outline; timeline; map exercises; identification, multiple-choice and thought questions; and critical-thinking questions based on primary source documents from the text.

## Companion Website (www.ablongman.com/levack2e)

Providing a wealth of resources for students using *The West: Encounters & Transformations,* Second Edition, this Companion Website contains chapter summaries, interactive practice test questions, and Web links for every chapter in the text.

## Research Navigator and Research Navigator Guide

0-205-40838-9

Research Navigator is a comprehensive Website comprising four exclusive databases of credible and reliable source material for research and for student assignments: EBSCO's ContentSelect Academic Journal & Abstract Database, the *New York Times* Search-by-Subject Archive, *Financial Times* Article Archive and Company Financials, and "Best of the Web" Link Library. The site also includes an extensive help section. The Research Navigator Guide provides your students with access to the Research Navigator website and includes reference material and hints about conducting online research. Available to qualified college adopters when packaged with the text.

## Mapping Western Civilization: Student Activities

0-673-53774-9

Created by Gerald Danzer, University of Illinois at Chicago, this FREE map workbook for students is designed as an accompaniment to *Discovering Western Civilization Through Maps and Views.* It features exercises designed to teach students to interpret and analyze cartographic materials such as historical documents. Available to qualified college adopters when packaged with the text.

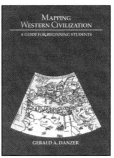

## Western Civilization Map Workbook

Volume I: 0-321-01878-8
Volume II: 0-321-01877-X

The map exercises in these volumes, created by Glee Wilson at Kent State University, test and reinforce basic geography literacy while building critical-thinking skills. Available to qualified college adopters when packaged with the text.

## Study Card for Western Civilization

0-321-29233-2

Colorful, affordable, and packed with useful information, Longman's Study Cards make studying easier, more efficient, and more enjoyable. Course information is distilled down to the basics, helping students quickly master the fundamentals, review a subject for understanding, or prepare for an exam. Because they're laminated for durability, they can be kept for years to come and used whenever necessary for a quick review. Available to qualified college adopters when packaged with the text.

## MyHistoryLab (www.myhistorylab.com)

MyHistoryLab provides students with an online package complete with the entire electronic textbook, numerous study aids, primary sources, and chapter exams. With several hundred primary sources and images, as well as map workbook activities with gradable quizzes, the site offers students a unique, interactive experience that brings history to life. The comprehensive site also includes a History Bookshelf with fifty of the most commonly assigned books in history classes and a History Toolkit with tutorials and helpful links.

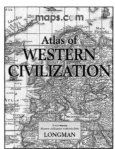

## Longman Atlas of Western Civilization

0-321-21626-1

This fifty-two-page atlas features carefully selected historical maps that provide comprehensive coverage for the major historical periods. Each map has been designed to be colorful, easy to read, and informative, without sacrificing detailed accuracy. This atlas makes history—and geography—more comprehensible.

## A Short Guide to Writing About History, Fifth Edition
0-321-22716-6

Written by Richard A. Marius, late of Harvard University, and Melvin E. Page, Eastern Tennessee State University, this engaging and practical text helps students get beyond merely compiling dates and facts; it teaches them how to incorporate their own ideas into their papers and to tell a story about history that interests them and their peers. Covering both brief essays and the documented resource paper, the text explores the writing and researching processes; identifies different modes of historical writing, including argument; and concludes with guidelines for improving style.

## Penguin-Longman Partnership

The partnership between Penguin Books and Longman Publishers offers a discount on the following titles when bundled with any Longman history survey textbook. Visit www.ablongman.com/penguin for more information.

## Available Titles

Peter Abelard, *The Letters of Abelard and Heloise*
Dante Alighieri, *Divine Comedy: Inferno*
Dante Alighieri, *The Portable Dante*
Anonymous, *Early Irish Myths & Sagas*
Anonymous, *The Epic of Gilgamesh*
Anonymous, *The Song of Roland*
Anonymous, *Vinland Sagas*
Hannah Arendt, *On Revolution*
Aristophanes, *The Birds and Other Plays*
Aristotle, *The Politics*
Louis Auchincloss, *Woodrow Wilson* (Penguin Lives Series)
St. Augustine, *The Confessions of St. Augustine*
Jane Austen, *Emma*
Jane Austen, *Persuasion*
Jane Austen, *Pride and Prejudice*
Jane Austen, *Sense and Sensibility*
Edward Bellamy, *Looking Backward*
Richard Bowring, *Diary of Lady Murasaki*
Charlotte Brontë, *Jane Eyre*
Charlotte Brontë, *Villette*
Emily Brontë, *Wuthering Heights*
Edmund Burke, *Reflection on the Revolution in France and on the Proceedings in Certain Societies in London Relative to that Event*
Benvenuto Cellini, *The Autobiography of Benvenuto Cellini*
Geoffrey Chaucer, *The Canterbury Tales*

Marcus Tullius Cicero, *Cicero: Selected Political Speeches*
Miguel de Cervantes, *The Adventures of Don Quixote*
Bartolome de las Casas, *A Short Account of the Destruction of the West Indies*
René Descartes, *Discourse on Method and Related Writings*
Charles Dickens, *Great Expectations*
Charles Dickens, *Hard Times*
John Dos Passos, *Three Soldiers*
Einhard, *Two Lives of Charlemagne*
Olaudah Equiano, *The Interesting Narrative and Other Writings*
M. Finley (ed.), *The Portable Greek Historians*
Benjamin Franklin, *The Autobiography and Other Writings*
Jeffrey Gantz (tr.), *Early Irish Myths and Sagas*
Peter Gay, *Mozart* (Penguin Lives Series)
William Golding, *Lord of the Flies*
Grimm & Grimm, *Grimms' Fairy Tales*
Thomas Hardy, *Jude the Obscure*
Herodotus, *The Histories*
Thomas Hobbes, *Leviathan*
Homer, *The Iliad*
Homer, *The Iliad* (Deluxe)
Homer, *Odyssey Deluxe*
Homer, *Odyssey: Revised Prose Translation*
*The Koran*

Deborah Lipstadt, *Denying the Holocaust*
Machiavelli, *The Prince*
Bill Manley, *The Penguin Historical Atlas of Ancient Egypt*
Karl Marx, *The Communist Manifesto*
Colin McEvedy, *The New Penguin Atlas of Ancient History*
Colin McEvedy, *The New Penguin Atlas of Medieval History*
John Stuart Mill, *On Liberty*
Jean-Baptiste Molière, *Tartuffe and Other Plays*
Sir Thomas More, *Utopia and Other Essential Writings*
Robert Morkot, *The Penguin Historical Atlas of Ancient Greece*
Sherwin Nuland, *Leonardo Da Vinci*
George Orwell, *1984*
George Orwell, *Animal Farm*
Plato, *Great Dialogues of Plato*
Plato, *The Last Days of Socrates*
Plato, *The Republic*
Plutarch, *Fall of the Roman Republic*
Marco Polo, *The Travels*
Procopius, *The Secret History*
Jean-Jacques Rousseau, *The Social Contract*
Sallust, *The Jugurthine Wars, The Conspiracy of Cataline*
Chris Scarre, *The Penguin Historical Atlas of Ancient Rome*
Desmond Seward, *The Hundred Years' War*
William Shakespeare, *Four Great Comedies: The Taming of the Shrew, A Midsummer's Night Dream, Twelfth Night, The Tempest*

William Shakespeare, *Four Great Tragedies: Hamlet, Macbeth, King Lear, Othello*
William Shakespeare, *Four Histories: Richard II, Henry IV: Part I, Henry IV: Part II, Henry V*
William Shakespeare, *Hamlet*
William Shakespeare, *King Lear*
William Shakespeare, *Macbeth*
William Shakespeare, *The Merchant of Venice*
William Shakespeare, *Othello*
William Shakespeare, *The Taming of the Shrew*
William Shakespeare, *The Tempest*
William Shakespeare, *Twelfth Night*
Mary Shelley, *Frankenstein*
Aleksandr Solzhenitsyn, *One Day in the Life of Ivan Denisovich*
Sophocles, *The Three Theban Plays*
Robert Louis Stevenson, *The Strange Case of Dr. Jekyll and Mr. Hyde*
Suetonius, *The Twelve Caesars*
Jonathan Swift, *Gulliver's Travels*
Tacitus, *The Histories*
Various, *The Penguin Book of Historical Speeches*
Voltaire, *Candide, Zadig and Selected Stories*
Carl von Clausewitz, *On War*
von Goethe, *Faust, Part 1*
von Goethe, *Faust, Part 2*
Edith Wharton, *Ethan Frome*
Willet, *The Signet World Atlas*
Gary Wills, *Saint Augustine* (Penguin Lives Series)
Virginia Woolf, *Jacob's Room*

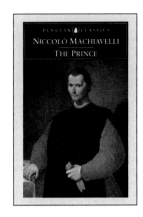

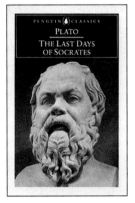

## Longman Library of World Biography Series

Each interpretive biography in the new Library of World Biography series focuses on a figure whose actions and ideas significantly influenced the course of world history. Pocket-sized and brief, each book relates the life of its subject to the broader themes and developments of the time. Longman Publishers offers your students a discount on the titles below when instructors request that they be bundled with any Longman history survey textbook. Series titles include:

*Ahmad al-Mansur: Islamic Visionary* by Richard Smith (Ferrum College)
*Alexander the Great: Legacy of a Conqueror* by Winthrop Lindsay Adams (University of Utah)
*Benito Mussolini: The First Fascist* by Anthony L. Cardoza (Loyola University)
*Fukuzawa Yûkichi: From Samurai to Capitalist* by Helen M. Hopper (University of Pittsburgh)
*Ignatius of Loyola: Founder of the Jesuits* by John Patrick Donnelly (Marquette University)

*Jacques Coeur: Entrepreneur and King's Bursar* by Kathryn L. Reyerson
  (University of Minnesota)
*Katô Shidzue: A Japanese Feminist* by Helen M. Hopper (University of Pittsburgh)
*Simón Bolívar: Liberation and Disappointment* by David Bushnell (University of Florida)
*Vasco da Gama: Renaissance Crusader* by Glenn J. Ames (University of Toledo)
*Zheng He: China and the Oceans in the Early Ming, 1405–1433* by Edward Dreyer
  (University of Miami)

# Acknowledgments

In writing this book we have benefited from the guidance of many members of the superb editorial staff at Longman. We would like to thank our acquisitions editor Janet Lanphier for helping us refine and develop this second edition. David Kear, our development editor, gave us valuable criticisms and helped us keep our audience in mind. Heather Johnson superintended the copyediting and proofreading with skill and efficiency, while Christine Buese helped us locate the most appropriate illustrations. Sue Westmoreland, the executive marketing manager for history, offered many creative ideas for promoting the book.

The authors wish to thank the following friends and colleagues for their assistance: Kenneth Alder, Joseph Alehermes, Karl Appuhn, Sharon Arnoult, Nicholas Baker, Paula Baskovits, Paul-Alain Beaulieu, Kamilia Bergen, Timothy Breen, Peter Brown, Peter Carroll, Shawn Clybor, Jauabeth Condie-Pugh, Patricia Crone, Tracey Cullen, Arthur Eckstein, Susanna Elm, Benjamin Frommer, Cynthia Gladstone, Dena Goodman, Stefka Hadjiandonova, Matthias Henze, Stanley Hilton, Kenneth Holum, Mark Jurdjevic, Werner Kelber, Cathleen Keller, Anne Kilmer, Jacob Lassner, Robert Lerner, Nancy Levack, Richard Lim, David Lindenfeld, Brian Maxson, Sarah Maza, Peter Mazur, Laura McGough, Roderick McIntosh, Susan K. McIntosh, Glenn Markoe, William Monter, Randy Nichols, Scott Noegel, Monique O'Connell, Carl Petry, Michael Rogers, Karl Roider, Sarah Ross, Michele Salzman, Paula Sanders, Regina Schwartz, Ethan Shagan, Julia M. H. Smith, James Sidbury, and Rachel Wahlig.

We would also like to thank the many historians who gave generously of their time to review during the various stages of development of our second edition. Their comments and suggestions helped to improve the book. Thank you:

Melanie A. Bailey, *South Dakota State University*
Brett Berliner, *Morgan State University*
Alfred S. Bradford, *University of Oklahoma*
Linda Charmaine Powell, *Amarillo College*
Daniel Christensen, *California State University, Fullerton*
William L. Cumiford, *Chapman University*
Rebecca Durrer, *Columbia College*
Steven Fanning, *University of Illinois at Chicago*
Sean Farrell, *Northern Illinois University*
Judy E. Gaughan, *Colorado State University*
Jennifer Hedda, *Simpson College*
David Hudson, *California State University, Fresno*
Rebecca Huston, *Hinds Community College*
Barbara A. Klemm, *Broward Community College*
Molly McClain, *University of San Diego*
Randall McGowen, *University of Oregon*

John A. Nichols, *Slippery Rock University*
James T. Owens, *Oakton Community College*
Elizabeth Propes, *Mesa State College*
Miriam Raub Vivian, *California State University, Bakersfield*
Anne Rodrick, *Wofford College*
Jarbel Rodriguez, *San Francisco State University*
Jacquelyn A. Royal, *Lee University*
Jutta Scott, *South Carolina University*
Susan O. Shapiro, *Utah State University*
Steven E. Sidebotham, *University of Delaware*
David Stone, *Kansas State University*
Charles R. Sullivan, *University of Dallas*
Mary C. Swilling, *University of Mississippi*
Larissa Juliet Taylor, *Colby College*
Jonathan Ziskind, *University of Louisville*

We would also like to thank the historians whose careful reviews and comments on the first edition helped us revise the book for its second edition. Our thanks for your contributions:

Henry Abramson, *Florida Atlantic University*
Patricia Ali, *Morris College*
Joseph Appiah, *J. Sergeant Reynolds Community College*
Sharon L. Arnoult, *Midwestern State University*
Arthur H. Auten, *University of Hartford*
Clifford Backman, *Boston University*
Suzanne Balch-Lindsay, *Eastern New Mexico University*
Wayne C. Bartee, *Southwest Miami State University*
Brandon Beck, *Shenandoah University*
James R. Belpedio, *Becker College*
Richard Berthold, *University of New Mexico*
Cynthia S. Bisson, *Belmont University*
Richard Bodek, *College of Charleston*
Melissa Bokovoy, *University of New Mexico*
William H. Brennan, *University of the Pacific*
Morgan R. Broadhead, *Jefferson Community College*
Theodore Bromund, *Yale University*
April A. Brooks, *South Dakota State University*
Nathan M. Brooks, *New Mexico State University*
Michael Burger, *Mississippi University for Women*
Susan Carrafiello, *Wright State University*
Kathleen S. Carter, *High Point University*
William L. Combs, *Western Illinois University*
Joseph Coohill, *Pennsylvania State University–New Kensington*
Richard A. Cosgrove, *University of Arizona*
Leonard Curtis, *Mississippi College*
Miriam Davis, *Delta State University*
Alexander DeGrand, *North Carolina State University*
Marion Deshmukh, *George Mason University*
Janusz Duzinkiewicz, *Purdue University, North Central*
Mary Beth Emmerichs, *University of Wisconsin, Sheboygan*
Steven Fanning, *University of Illinois at Chicago*
Bryan Ganaway, *University of Illinois at Urbana–Champaign*
Frank Garosi, *California State University–Sacramento*
Christina Gold, *Loyola Marymount University*
Ignacio Götz, *Hofstra University*
Louis Haas, *Duquesne University*
Linda Jones Hall, *Saint Mary's College of Maryland*
Paul Halsall, *University of North Florida*
Donald J. Harreld, *Brigham Young University*
Carmen V. Harris, *University of South Carolina at Spartanburg*
James C. Harrison, *Siena College*
Mark C. Herman, *Edison Community College*
Curry A. Herring, *University of Southern Alabama*
Patrick Holt, *Fordham University*
W. Robert Houston, *University of South Alabama*
Lester Hutton, *Westfield State College*

Jeffrey Hyson, *Saint Joseph's University*
Paul Jankowski, *Brandeis University*
Padraic Kennedy, *McNeese State University*
Joanne Klein, *Boise State University*
Theodore Kluz, *Troy State University*
Skip Knox, *Boise State University*
Cynthia Kosso, *Northern Arizona University*
Ann Kuzdale, *Chicago State University*
Lawrence Langer, *University of Connecticut*
Oscar E. Lansen, *University of North Carolina at Charlotte*
Michael V. Leggiere, *Louisiana State University at Shreveport*
Rhett Leverett, *Marymount University*
Alison Williams Lewin, *Saint Joseph's University*
Wendy Liu, *Miami University, Middletown*
Elizabeth Makowski, *Southwest Texas State University*
Daniel Meissner, *Marquette University*
Isabel Moreira, *University of Utah*
Kenneth Moure, *University of California–Santa Barbara*
Melva E. Newsom, *Clark State Community College*
John A. Nichols, *Slippery Rock University*
Susannah R. Ottaway, *Carleton College*
James H. Overfield, *University of Vermont*
Brian L. Peterson, *Florida International University*
Hugh Phillips, *Western Kentucky University*
Jeff Plaks, *University of Central Oklahoma*
Thomas L. Powers, *University of South Carolina, Sumter*
Carole Putko, *San Diego State University*
Barbara Ranieri, *University of Alabama at Birmingham*
Elsa M. E. Rapp, *Montgomery County Community College*
Marlette Rebhorn, *Austin Community College*
Roger Reese, *Texas A&M University*
Travis Ricketts, *Bryan College*
Thomas Robisheaux, *Duke University*
Bill Robison, *Southeastern Louisiana University*
Mark Ruff, *Concordia University*
Frank Russell, *Transylvania University*
Marylou Ruud, *The University of West Florida*
Michael Saler, *University of California–Davis*
Timothy D. Saxon, *Charleston Southern University*
Daniel A. Scalberg, *Multnomah Bible College*
Ronald Schechter, *College of William and Mary*
Philip Skaggs, *Grand Valley State University*
Helmut Walser Smith, *Vanderbilt University*
Eileen Solwedel, *Edmonds Community College*
Sister Maria Consuelo Sparks, *Immaculata University*
Ilicia J. Sprey, *Saint Joseph's College*
Charles R. Sullivan, *University of Dallas*
Frederick Suppe, *Ball State University*

Frank W. Thackery, *Indiana University Southeast*
Frances B. Titchener, *Utah State University*
Katherine Tosa, *Muskegon Community College*
Lawrence A. Tritle, *Loyola Marymount University*

Clifford F. Wargelin, *Georgetown College*
Theodore R. Weeks, *Southern Illinois University*
Elizabeth A. Williams, *Oklahoma State University*
Mary E. Zamon, *Marymount University*

BRIAN LEVACK
EDWARD MUIR
MEREDITH VELDMAN
MICHAEL MAAS

# Meet the Authors

**Brian Levack** grew up in a family of teachers in the New York metropolitan area. From his father, a professor of French history, he acquired a love for studying the past, and he knew from an early age that he too would become a historian. He received his B.A. from Fordham University in 1965 and his Ph.D. from Yale in 1970. In graduate school he became fascinated by the history of the law and the interaction between law and politics, interests that he has maintained throughout his career. In 1969 he joined the history department of the University of Texas at Austin, where he is now the John Green Regents Professor in History. The winner of several teaching awards, Levack teaches a wide variety of courses on British and European history, legal history, and the history of witchcraft. For eight years he served as the chair of his department, a rewarding but challenging assignment that made it difficult for him to devote as much time as he wished to his teaching and scholarship. His books include *The Civil Lawyers in England, 1603–1641: A Political Study* (1973), *The Formation of the British State: England, Scotland and the Union, 1603–1707* (1987), and *The Witch-Hunt in Early Modern Europe* (1987 and 1995), which has been translated into eight languages.

His study of the development of beliefs about witchcraft in Europe over the course of many centuries gave him the idea of writing a textbook on Western civilization that would illustrate a broader set of encounters between different cultures, societies, and ideologies. While writing the book, Levack and his two sons built a house on property that he and his wife, Nancy, own in the Texas hill country. He found that the two projects presented similar challenges: It was easy to draw up the design, but far more difficult to execute it. When not teaching, writing, or doing carpentry work, Levack runs along the jogging trails of Austin, and he has recently discovered the pleasures of scuba diving.

**Edward Muir** grew up in the foothills of the Wasatch Mountains in Utah, close to the Emigration Trail along which wagon trains of Mormon pioneers and California-bound settlers made their way westward. As a child he loved to explore the broken-down wagons and abandoned household goods left at the side of the trail and from that acquired a fascination with the past. Besides the material remains of the past, he grew up with stories of his Mormon pioneer ancestors and an appreciation for how the past continued to influence the present. During the turbulent 1960s, he became interested in Renaissance Italy as a period and a place that had been formative for Western civilization. His biggest challenge is finding the time to explore yet another new corner of Italy and its restaurants.

Muir received his Ph.D. from Rutgers University, where he specialized in the Italian Renaissance and did archival research in Venice and Florence, Italy. He is now the Clarence L. Ver Steeg Professor in the Arts and Sciences at Northwestern University and former chair of the history department. At Northwestern he has won several teaching awards. His books include *Civic Ritual in Renaissance Venice* (1981), *Mad Blood Stirring: Vendetta in Renaissance Italy* (1993 and 1998), and *Ritual in Early Modern Europe* (1997 and 2005).

Some years ago Muir began to experiment with the use of historical trials in teaching and discovered that students loved them. From that experience he decided to write this textbook, which employs trials as a central feature. He lives beside Lake Michigan in Evanston, Illinois. His twin passions are skiing in the Rocky Mountains and rooting for the Chicago Cubs, who manage every summer to demonstrate that winning isn't everything.

**Meredith Veldman** grew up in the western suburbs of Chicago in a close-knit, closed-in Dutch Calvinist community. In this immigrant society, history mattered: the "Reformed tradition" structured not only religious beliefs but also social identity and political practice. This influence certainly played some role in shaping Veldman's early fascination with history. But probably just as important were the countless World War II reenactment games she played with her five older brothers. Whatever the cause, Veldman majored in history at Calvin College in Grand Rapids, Michigan, and then earned a Ph.D. in modern European history, with a concentration in nineteenth- and twentieth-century Britain, from Northwestern University in 1988.

As associate professor of history at Louisiana State University, Veldman teaches courses in nineteenth- and twentieth-century British history and twentieth-century Europe, as well as the second half of "Western Civ." In her many semesters in the Western Civ. classroom, Veldman tried a number of different textbooks but found herself increasingly dissatisfied. She wanted a text that would convey to beginning students at least some of the complexities and ambiguities of historical interpretation, introduce them to the exciting work being done now in cultural history, and, most important, tell a good story. The search for this textbook led her to accept the offer made by Levack, Maas, and Muir to join them in writing *The West: Encounters & Transformations*.

The author of *Fantasy, the Bomb, and the Greening of Britain: Romantic Protest, 1945–1980* (1994), Veldman is also the wife of a Methodist minister and the mother of two young sons. They reside in Baton Rouge, Louisiana, where Veldman finds coping with the steamy climate a constant challenge. She and her family recently returned from Manchester, England, where they lived for three years and astonished the natives by their enthusiastic appreciation of English weather.

**Michael Maas** was born in the Ohio River Valley, in a community that had been a frontier outpost during the late eighteenth century. He grew up reading the stories of the early settlers and their struggles with the native peoples, and seeing in the urban fabric how the city had subsequently developed into a prosperous coal and steel town with immigrants from all over the world. As a boy he developed a lifetime interest in the archaeology and history of the ancient Mediterranean world and began to study Latin. At Cornell University he combined his interests in cultural history and the classical world by majoring in classics and anthropology. A semester in Rome clinched his commitment to these fields—and to Italian cooking. Maas went on to get his Ph.D. in the graduate program in ancient history and Mediterranean archaeology at the University of California at Berkeley.

He has traveled widely in the Mediterranean and the Middle East and participated in several archaeological excavations, including an underwater dig in Greece. Since 1985 he has taught ancient history at Rice University in Houston, Texas, where he founded and directs the interdisciplinary B.A. program in ancient Mediterranean civilizations. He has won several teaching awards.

Maas's special area of research is late antiquity, the period of transition from the classical to the medieval worlds, which saw the collapse of the Roman Empire in western Europe and the development of the Byzantine state in the East. During his last sabbatical, he was a member of the Institute for Advanced Study in Princeton, New Jersey, where he worked on his current book, *The Conqueror's Gift: Ethnography, Identity, and Imperial Power at the End of Antiquity* (forthcoming). His other books include *John Lydus and the Roman Past: Antiquarianism and Politics in the Age of Justinian* (1992), *Readings in Late Antiquity: A Sourcebook* (2000), and *Exegesis and Empire in the Early Byzantine Mediterranean* (2003).

Maas has always been interested in interdisciplinary teaching and the encounters among different cultures. He sees *The West: Encounters & Transformations* as an opportunity to explain how the modern civilization that we call "the West" had its origins in the diverse interactions among many peoples of antiquity.

# THE WEST

# What Is the West?

MANY OF THE PEOPLE WHO INFLUENCE PUBLIC OPINION—POLITI-cians, teachers, clergy, journalists, and television commentators—refer to "Western values," "the West," and "Western civilization." They often use these terms as if they do not require explanation. But what *do* these terms mean? The West has always been an arena within which different cultures, religions, values, and philosophies have interacted, and any definition of the West will inevitably arouse controversy.

The most basic definition of the West is of a place. Western civilization is now typically thought to comprise the regions of Europe, the Americas, Australia, and New Zealand. However, this is a contemporary definition of the West. The inclusion of these places in the West is the result of a long history of European expansion through colonization. In addition to being a place, Western civilization also encompasses a cultural history—a tradition stretching back thousands of years to the ancient world. Over this long period the civilization we now identify as Western gradually took shape. The many characteristics that identify any civilization emerged over this time: forms of government, economic systems, and methods of scientific inquiry, as well as religions, languages, literature, and art.

Throughout the development of Western civilization, the ways in which people identified themselves changed as well. People in the ancient world had no such idea of the common identity of the West, only of being members of a tribe, citizens of a town, or subjects of an empire. But with the spread of Christianity and Islam between the first and seventh centuries, the notion of a distinct civilization in these "Western" lands subtly changed. People came to identify themselves less as subjects of a particular empire and more as members of a community of faith—whether that community comprised followers of Christianity, Judaism, or Islam. These communities of faith drew lines of inclusion and exclusion that still exist today. Starting

**The Temple of Hera at Paestum, Italy** Greek colonists in Italy built this temple in the sixth century B.C.E. Greek ideas and artistic styles spread throughout the ancient world both from Greek colonists, such as those at Paestum, and from other peoples who imitated the Greeks.

about 1,600 years ago, Christian monarchs and clergy began to obliterate polytheism (the worship of many gods) and marginalize Jews. From a thousand to 500 years ago, Christian authorities strove to expel Muslims from Europe. Europeans developed definitions of the West that did not include Islamic communities, even though Muslims continued to live in Europe and Europeans traded and interacted with the Muslim world. The Islamic countries themselves erected their own barriers, seeing themselves in opposition to the Christian West, even as they continued to look back to the common cultural origins in the ancient world that they shared with Jews and Christians. During the Renaissance in the fifteenth century, these ancient cultural origins became an alternative to religious affiliation for thinking about the identity of the West. From this Renaissance historical perspective Jews, Christians, and Muslims descended from the cultures of the ancient Hebrews, Greeks, and Romans. Despite all their differences, the followers of these religions shared a history. In fact, in the late Renaissance a number of thinkers imagined the possibility of rediscovering the single universal religion that they thought must have once been practiced in the ancient world. If they could just recapture that religion they could restore the unity they imagined had once prevailed in the West.

**A Satellite View of Europe**

What is the West? Western civilization has undergone numerous transformations throughout history, but it has always included Europe.

The definition of the West has also changed as a result of European colonialism, which began about 500 years ago. When European powers assembled large overseas empires, they introduced Western languages, religions, technology, and culture to many distant places in the world, making Western identity a transportable concept. In some of these colonized areas—such as North America, Argentina, Australia, and New Zealand—the European newcomers so outnumbered the indigenous people that these regions became as much a part of the West as Britain, France, and Spain. In other European colonies, especially in European trading outposts on the Asian continent, Western culture failed to exercise similar levels of influence.

As a result of colonialism Western culture sometimes merged with other cultures, and in the process both were changed. Brazil, a South American country inhabited by large numbers of indigenous peoples, the descendants of African slaves, and European settlers, epitomizes the complexity of what defines the West. In Brazil, almost everyone speaks a Western language (Portuguese), practices a Western religion (Christianity), and participates in Western political and economic institutions (democracy and capitalism). Yet in Brazil all of these features of Western civilization have become part of a distinctive culture, in which in-

digenous, African, and European elements have been blended. During Carnival, for example, Brazilians dressed in indigenous costumes dance in African rhythms to the accompaniment of music played on European instruments.

For many people today, the most important definition of the West involves adherence to a certain set of values, the "Western" values. The values typically identified as Western today include universal human rights, toleration of religious diversity, equality before the law, democracy, and freedom of inquiry and expression. However, these values have not always been part of Western civilization. They came to be fully appreciated only very recently as the consequence of a long and bloody history. In fact, there is nothing inevitable about these values, and Western history at various stages exhibited quite different ones. For example, the rulers of ancient Rome did not extend the privileges of citizenship to all the inhabitants of the empire until a century after it had reached its greatest size. The extent to which women could participate in public life was limited by law. Rich and powerful people enjoyed more protection under the law than did slaves or humble people. Most medieval Christians were completely convinced that their greatest contribution to society would be to make war against Muslims and heretics and to curtail as much as possible the actions of Jews. Western societies seldom valued equality until quite recently. Before the end of the eighteenth century, few Westerners questioned the practice of slavery; a social hierarchy of birth remained powerful in the West through the entire nineteenth century; most Western women were excluded from equal economic and educational opportunities until well into the twentieth century. Swiss women did not get the vote until 1971 (and in one canton not until 1990). Also in the twentieth century, Nazi Germany and the Soviet Union demonstrated that history could have turned out very differently in the West. These totalitarian regimes in Europe rejected most of the Western values so prized today and terrorized their own populations and millions of others beyond their borders through massive abuses of human rights. The history of the West is riddled with examples of leaders who stifled free inquiry and who censored authors and journalists. These examples testify to the fact that the values of Western societies have always been contended, disputed, and fought over. In other words, they have a history. This text highlights and examines that history, demonstrating how hard values were to formulate in the first place and how difficult they have been to preserve.

# The Shifting Borders of the West

The geographical setting of the West also has a history. This textbook begins about 10,000 years ago in what is now Iraq and it ends in Iraq, but in the meantime the Mesopotamian region is only occasionally a concern for Western history. The West begins with the domestication of animals, the cultivation of the first crops, and the establishment of long-distance trading networks in the Tigris, Euphrates, and Nile River valleys. Cities, kingdoms, and empires in those valleys gave birth to the first civilizations. By about 500 B.C.E., the civilizations that are the cultural ancestors of the modern West had spread from southwestern Asia and North Africa to include the entire Mediterranean basin—areas influenced by Egyptian, Hebrew, Greek, and Roman thought, art, law, and religion. By the first century C.E. the Roman Empire drew the map of what historians consider the heartland of the West: most of western and southern Europe, the coastlands of the Mediterranean Sea, and the Middle East.

The West is now usually thought to include Europe and the Americas. However, the borders of the West have in recent decades come to be less about geography than culture, identity, and technology. When Japan, an Asian country, accepted human rights, democracy, and industrial capitalism after World War II, did it become part of the West? Most Japanese might not think they have adopted "Western" values, but the industrial power and stable democracy of a traditional Asian country that had never been colonized by a European power complicates the idea of what is the West. Or consider the Republic of South Africa, which until 1994 was ruled by the white minority, people descended from European immigrants. The oppressive regime violated human rights, rejected full legal equality for all citizens, and jailed or murdered those who questioned the government. Only when that government was replaced through democratic elections and a black man became president did South Africa fully embrace what the rest of the West would consider Western values. To what degree was South Africa part of the West before and after these developments?

Russia long saw itself as a Christian country with a tradition of cultural, economic, and political ties with the rest of Europe. The Russians have intermittently identified with their Western neighbors, but their neighbors were not always sure about the Russians. After the Mongol invasions of the thirteenth and fourteenth centuries much of Russia was isolated from the rest of the West; during the Cold War from 1949 to 1989, Russian communism and the Western democracies were polarized. When was Russia "Western" and when not?

Thus, when we talk about where the West is, we are almost always talking about the Mediterranean basin and much of Europe (and later, the Americas). But we will also show that countries that border "the West," and even countries far from it, might be considered Western in many aspects as well.

### The Astrolabe

The mariner's astrolabe was a navigational device intended for use primarily at sea. The astrolabe originated in the Islamic world and was adopted by Europeans in the twelfth century— a cultural encounter that enabled Europeans to embark on long ocean voyages around the world.

# Asking the Right Questions

So how can we make sense of the West as a place and an identity, the shifting borders of the West, and Western civilization in general? In short, what has Western civilization been over the course of its long history—and what is it today?

Answering these questions is the challenge this book poses. There are no simple answers to any of these questions, but there is a method for finding answers. The method is straightforward. Always ask the *what, when, where, who, how,* and *why* questions of the text.

## The *What* Question

What is Western civilization? The answer to this question will vary according to time and place. In fact, for much of the early history covered in this book, Western civilization as we know it today did not exist as a single cultural entity. Rather, a number of distinctive civilizations were taking shape in the Middle East, northern Africa, and Europe, each of which contributed to what later became Western civilization. But throughout time the idea of Western civilization slowly began to form. Thus the understanding of Western civilization will change from chapter to chapter. The most extensive change in the place of the West was through the colonial expansion of the European nations between the fifteenth and twentieth centuries. Perhaps the most significant cultural change in the West came with acceptance of the values of scientific inquiry for solving human and philosophical problems, an approach that did not exist before the seventeenth century but became one of the distinguishing characteristics of Western civilization. During the late eighteenth and nineteenth centuries, industrialization became the engine that drove economic development in the West, and during the twentieth century industrialization in both its capitalist and communist forms dramatically gave the West a level of economic prosperity unmatched in the non-industrialized parts of the world.

## The *When* Question

When did the defining characteristics of Western civilization first emerge, and for how long did they prevail? Dates frame and organize each chapter, and there are numerous short chronologies offered. These resources make it possible to keep track of what happened when. Dates have no meaning by themselves, but the connections *between* them can be very revealing. For example, dates show that the agricultural revolution that permitted the birth of the first civiliza-

tions unfolded over a span of about 10,000 years—which is more time than was taken by all the other events and developments covered in this textbook. Wars of religion plagued Europe for nearly 200 years before Enlightenment thinkers articulated the ideals of religious toleration. The American Civil War—the war to preserve the union, as President Abraham Lincoln termed it—took place at exactly the same time as other wars were being fought to achieve national unity in Germany and Italy. In other words, by paying attention to other contemporaneous wars for national unity the American experience seems less peculiarly an American event.

By learning when things happened, one can identify the major causes and consequences of events and thus see the transformations of Western civilization. For instance, the ability to produce a surplus of food through agriculture and the domestication of animals was a prerequisite for the emergence of civilizations. The violent collapse of religious unity after the Protestant Reformation in the sixteenth century led some Europeans to propose the separation of church and state two centuries later. And during the nineteenth century many Western states—in response to the enormous diversity among their own peoples—became preoccupied with maintaining or establishing national unity.

## The *Where* Question

Where has Western civilization been located? Geography, of course, does not change very rapidly, but the idea of where the West is does. The location of the West is not so much a matter of changing borders but of how people identify themselves. The key to understanding the shifting borders of the West is to study how the peoples within the West thought of themselves. These groups include Muslims and the peoples of eastern Europe (such as the Soviet Union during the Cold War), which some people have wanted to exclude from the West. In addition, the chapters trace the relationships between the West (as it was constituted in different periods) and other, more distant civilizations with which it interacted. Those civilizations include not only those of East Asia and South Asia but also the indigenous peoples of sub-Saharan Africa, the Americas, and the Pacific islands.

## The *Who* Question

Who were the people responsible for making Western civilization? Sometimes they were anonymous, such as the unknown geniuses who invented the mathematical systems of ancient Mesopotamia. At other times the makers of the

West were famous—saints such as Joan of Arc, creative thinkers such as Galileo Galilei, or generals such as Napoleon. But history is not made only by great and famous people. Humble people, such as the many millions who migrated from Europe to North America or the unfortunate millions who suffered and died in the trenches of World War I, can also influence the course of events.

Perhaps most often this book encounters people who were less the shapers of their own destinies than the subjects of forces that conditioned the kinds of choices they could make, often with unanticipated results. When during the eleventh century farmers throughout Europe began to employ a new kind of plow to till their fields, they were merely trying to do their work more efficiently. They certainly did not recognize that the increase in food they produced would stimulate the enormous population growth that made possible the medieval civilization of thriving cities and magnificent cathedrals. Answering the who question requires an evaluation of how much individuals and groups of people were in control of events and how much events controlled them.

## The *How* Question

How did Western civilization develop? This is a question about processes—about how things change or stay the same over time. This book identifies these processes in several ways. First, the theme of encounters and transformations has been woven throughout the story. What is meant by encounters? When the Spanish *conquistadores* arrived in the Americas some 500 years ago, they came into contact with the cultures of the Caribs, the Aztecs, the Incas, and other peoples who had lived in the Americas for thousands of years. As the Spanish fought, traded with, and intermarried with the natives, each culture changed. The Spanish, for their part, borrowed from the Americas new plants for cultivation and responded to what they considered serious threats to their worldview. Many native Americans, in turn, adopted European religious practices and learned to speak European languages. At the same time, they were decimated by European diseases to which they had never before been exposed. They also witnessed the destruction of their own civilizations and governments at the hands of the colonial

## Map 1   Core Lands of the West

The geographical borders of the West have changed substantially throughout history.

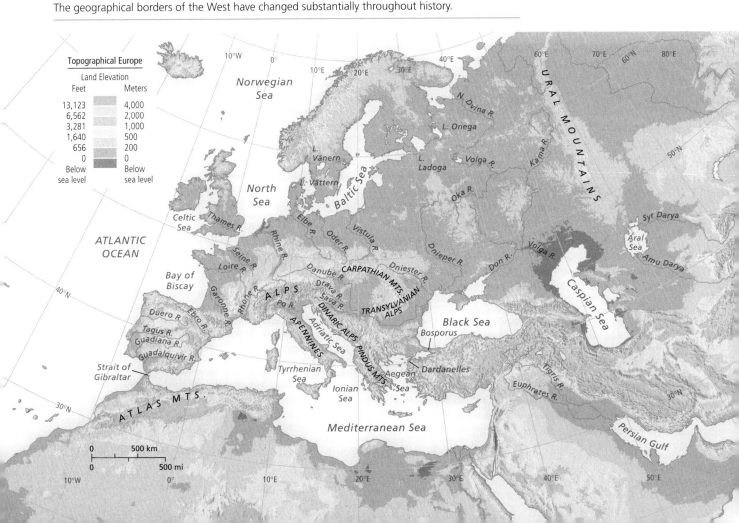

**Cortés Meets Montezuma**

As the Spanish fought, traded, and intermarried with the native peoples of the Americas during the fifteenth and sixteenth centuries, each culture changed.

powers. Through centuries of interaction and mutual influence, both sides became something other than what they had been.

The European encounter with the Americas is an obvious example of what was, in fact, a continuous process of encounters with other cultures. These encounters often occurred between peoples from different civilizations, such as the struggles between Greeks and Persians in the ancient world or between Europeans and Chinese in the nineteenth century. Other encounters took place among people living in the same civilization. These include interactions between lords and peasants, men and women, Christians and Jews, Catholics and Protestants, factory owners and workers, and capitalists and communists. Western civilization developed and changed through a series of external and internal encounters.

Second, features in the chapters formulate answers to the question of how Western civilization developed. For example, each chapter contains an essay titled "Justice in History." These essays discuss a trial or some other episode involving questions of justice. Some "Justice in History" essays illustrate how Western civilization was forged in struggles over conflicting values, such as the discussion of the trial of Galileo, which examines the conflict between religious and scientific concepts of truth. Others show how efforts to resolve internal cultural, political, and religious tensions helped shape Western ideas about justice, such as the

essay on the *auto-da-fé*, which illustrates how authorities attempted to enforce religious conformity. At the end of each "Justice in History" feature are several questions tying that essay to the theme of the chapter.

Some chapters include two other features as well. Essays titled "The Human Body in History" demonstrate that even the body, which is typically understood as a product of genetics and biology, has a history. These essays show that the ways in which Western people understand their bodies, how they cure them, how they cover and uncover them, and how they adorn them tell us a great deal about the history of Western culture. For example, the book explores how the bodies of World War I soldiers afflicted with shell shock were treated differently from women experiencing similar symptoms of hysteria. Shell-shocked soldiers gave people a sense of the horrors of war and stimulated powerful movements in Europe to outlaw war as an instrument of government policy.

The "Encounters and Transformations" features show how encounters between different groups of people, technologies, and ideas were not abstract historical processes but events that brought people together in a way that transformed history. For example, when the Arabs encountered the camel as an instrument of war, they adopted it for their own purposes and were able to conquer their neighbors very quickly and spread Islam far beyond its original home in Arabia.

## The *Why* Question

Why did things happen in the way they did in history? This is the hardest question of all, one that engenders the most debate among historians. To take one persistent example, why did Hitler initiate a plan to exterminate the Jews of Europe? Can it be explained by something that happened to him in his childhood? Was he full of self-loathing that he projected onto the Jews? Was it a way of creating an enemy so that he could better unify Germany? Did he really believe that the Jews were the cause of all of Germany's problems? Did he merely act on the deeply seated anti-Semitic tendencies of the German people? Historians still debate the answers to these questions. These questions raise issues about human motivation and the role of human agency in historical events. Can historians ever really know what motivated a particular individual in the past, especially when it is so notoriously difficult to understand what motivates other people in the present? Can any individual determine the course of history? The *what, when, where, who,* and *how* questions are much easier to answer, but the *why* question, of course, is the most interesting one, the one that cries out for an answer.

This book does not always offer definitive answers to the *why* question, but it attempts to lay out the most likely possibilities. For example, historians do not really know what disease caused the Black Death in the fourteenth century, which killed about one-third of the population in a matter of months. But they can answer many questions about the consequences of that great catastrophe. Why were there so many new universities in the fourteenth and fifteenth centuries? It was because so many priests had died in the Black Death, creating a huge demand for replacements. The answers to the *why* questions are not always obvious, but they are always intriguing, and finding them is the joy of studying history.

# The Age of
# Confessional Division

# 14

O N JULY 10, 1584, CATHOLIC EXTREMIST FRANÇOIS GUION, WITH A brace of pistols hidden under his cloak, surprised William the Silent, the Prince of Orange, as he was leaving the dining hall of his palace and shot him at point-blank range. William had been the leader of the Protestant nobility in the Netherlands, which was in revolt against the Catholic king of Spain. Guion masqueraded as a Protestant for seven years in order to ingratiate himself with William's party, and before the assassination he had consulted three Catholic priests who had confirmed the religious merit of his plan. Spain's representative in the Netherlands, the Duke of Parma, had offered a reward of 25,000 crowns to anyone who killed William, and at the moment of the assassination four other fanatics were in Delft trying to gain access to the Prince of Orange.

The murder of William the Silent exemplified an ominous figure in Western civilization—the religiously motivated assassin. There had been many assassinations before the late sixteenth century, but the assassins tended to be motivated by the desire to gain political power or to avenge a personal or family injury and less often by religious differences. In the wake of the Reformation the idea that killing a political leader of the opposing faith would serve God's plan became all too common. The assassination of William illustrated patterns of violence that have become the modus operandi of the political assassin—the use of deception to gain access to the victim, the vulnerability of leaders who wish to mingle with the public, the lethal potential of easily concealed pistols (a new weapon at that time), the corruption of politics through vast sums of money, and the obsessive hostility of zealots against their perceived enemies. The widespread acrimony among the varieties of Christian faith created a climate of religious extremism during the late sixteenth and early seventeenth centuries. After the Protestant and Catholic Reformations, the various forms of Christianity

**Procession of the Catholic League** During the last half of the sixteenth century, Catholics and Protestants in France formed armed militias or leagues. Bloody confrontations between these militias led to prolonged civil wars. In this 1590 procession of the French Catholic League, armed monks joined soldiers and common citizens in a demonstration of force.

came to be called confessions° because their adherents believed in a particular confession of faith, or statement of religious doctrine.

Religious extremism was just one manifestation of an anxiety that pervaded European society at the time—a fear of hidden forces controlling human events. In an attempt to curb that anxiety, the European monarchs created confessional states. The combined effort of state and church sought to discipline common people, persecute deviants of all sorts, and combat enemies through a religiously driven foreign policy. During this age of confessional division, European countries polarized along confessional lines, and governments persecuted followers of minority religions, whom they saw as threats to public security. Anxious believers everywhere were consumed with pleasing an angry God, but when they tried to find God within themselves many Christians seemed only to find the Devil in others. The bloody history of confessional conflicts during the sixteenth and seventeenth centuries, in fact, eventually stimulated the formation of the modern ethical principles of religious toleration, separation of church and state, and human rights during the eighteenth.

By attempting to discipline the people of Europe and make them better Christians, educated and elite society directly confronted a thriving popular culture. In many respects, the culture they encountered was nearly as alien as the native cultures in the newly discovered America. Certainly, the peoples of early modern Europe considered themselves Christian, but what they meant by Christianity was quite at odds with that of the Protestant and Catholic reformers. In a confused, haphazard, and sometimes violent fashion, members of the elite attempted to blot out many elements of popular culture that they suspected might be remnants of pre-Christian beliefs and practices. One of the most curious consequences of the Reformations during the sixteenth and seventeenth centuries was a dramatic conflict between two cultures, that of the educated elite and that of the ordinary people. However, the disciplining of the people was primarily confined to western Europe. In eastern Europe religious diversity and popular culture thrived largely due to the relative weakness of the monarchs.

The religious controversies of the age of confessional division redefined the West. During the Middle Ages, the West came to be identified with the practice of Roman Catholic Christianity. The Reformation of the early sixteenth century broke up the unity of medieval Christian Europe by dividing westerners into Catholic and Protestant camps. During the late sixteenth and seventeenth centuries, governments reinforced religious divisions and attempted to unify their peoples around a common set of beliefs. By the end of the eighteenth century, these confessional religious identities changed in some places into more secular political ideologies, such as the belief in the superiority of a republic over a monarchy, but the assumption that all citizens of a state should believe in some common ideology re-

mained. The period from about 1500 to 1750—the Early Modern period in European history—produced the lasting division of the West into national camps that were based on either religious confessions or ideological commitments. How did the encounter between the confessions and the state transform Europe into religiously driven camps?

■ How did the expanding population and price revolution exacerbate religious and political tensions?
■ How did religious and political authorities attempt to discipline the people?
■ How did religious differences provoke violence and start wars?
■ How did the countries of eastern Europe during the late sixteenth century become enmeshed in the religious controversies that began in western Europe during the early part of the century?

# The Peoples of Early Modern Europe

■ How did the expanding population and price revolution exacerbate religious and political tensions?

During the tenth century if a Russian had wanted to see the sights of Paris—assuming he had even heard of Paris—he could have left Kiev and walked under the shade of trees all the way to France, so extensive were the forests and so sparse the human settlements of northern Europe. By the end of the thirteenth century, the nomadic Russian would have needed a hat to protect him on the shadeless journey. Instead of human settlements forming little islands in a sea of forests, the forests were by then islands in a sea of villages and farms, and from any church tower the sharp-eyed traveler could have seen other church towers, each marking a nearby village or town. At the end of the thirteenth century, the European continent had become completely settled by a dynamic, growing population, which had cleared the forests for farms.

During the fourteenth century all of that changed. A series of crises—periodic famines, the catastrophic Black Death, and a general economic collapse—left the villages and towns of Europe intact, but a third or more of the population was gone. In that period of desolation, many villages looked like abandoned movie sets, and the cities did not have enough people to fill in the empty spaces between the central market square and the city walls. Fields that had once been put to the plow to feed the hungry children of the thirteenth century were neglected and overrun with bristles and brambles. During the fifteenth century a general European depression and recurrent epidemics kept the population stagnant.

In the sixteenth century the population began to re-bound, but the sudden swell brought dramatic and destabilizing consequences that contributed to pervasive anxiety. An important factor in the population growth was the transformation of European agriculture from subsistence to commercial farming, an uneven transformation that impoverished some villages while it enriched others. Moreover, the expanded population transformed the balance of power, as northern Europe recovered its population more successfully than southern Europe. As the population grew, young men and women flocked to the cities, creating enormous social strains and demands on local governments. Perhaps most disruptive was the price revolution, which brought inflation that ate away at the buying power of everyone from working families to kings and queens. The anxiety produced by these circumstances lasted into the seventeenth century.

## The Population Recovery

During a period that historical demographers call the "long sixteenth century" (ca. 1480–1640), the population of Europe began to grow consistently again for the first time since the late thirteenth century. In 1340, on the brink of the Black Death, Europe had about 74 million inhabitants, or 17 percent of the world's total. By 1400 the population of all of Europe had dropped to 52 million (less than one-fifth of the population of the United States today), or 14 percent of the world's total. Over the course of the long sixteenth century, Europe's population grew from 60.9 million to 77.9 million, just barely surpassing the pre–Black Death level.

The table to the right shows some representative population figures for the larger European countries during the sixteenth century. Two stunning facts emerge from these data. The first is the much greater rate of growth in northern Europe compared to southern Europe. England grew by 83 percent, Poland grew by 76 percent, and even the tiny, war-torn Netherlands gained 58 percent. During the same period Italy grew by only 25 percent and Spain by 19. These trends signal a massive, permanent shift of demographic and economic power from the Mediterranean countries of Italy and Spain to northern, especially northwestern, Europe. The second fact to note from these data is the overwhelming size of France, which was home to about a quarter of Europe's population. Once France recovered from its long wars of religion, its demographic superiority overwhelmed competing countries and made it the dominant power in Europe, permanently eclipsing its chief rival, Spain. Because the Holy Roman Empire and especially its core regions in the German-speaking lands lacked political unity, it was unable to take advantage of its position as the second-largest state.

What explains the growth in the population and the economy? To a large extent, it was made possible by the

### European Population, 1500–1600 (in millions)

|  | 1500 | 1550 | 1600 |
|---|---|---|---|
| England | 2.30 | 3.10 | 4.20 |
| Germany | 12.00 | 14.00 | 16.00 |
| France | 16.40 | 19.00 | 20.00 |
| Netherlands | 0.95 | 1.25 | 1.50 |
| Belgium | 1.25 | 1.65 | 1.30 |
| Italy | 10.50 | 11.40 | 13.10 |
| Spain | 6.80 | 7.50 | 8.10 |
| Austria-Bohemia | 3.50 | 3.60 | 4.30 |
| Poland | 2.50 | 3.00 | 3.40 |

*Source:* Jan de Vries, "Population," in *Handbook of European History 1400–1600: Late Middle Ages, Renaissance and Reformation,* Vol. 1: *Structures and Assertions,* eds. Thomas A. Brady, Jr., Heiko A. Oberman, and James D. Tracy (1994), Table 1, 13.

transformation from subsistence to commercial agriculture in certain regions of Europe. Subsistence farmers, called peasants, had worked the land year in and year out, raising grains for the coarse black bread that fed their families, supplemented only by beer, grain porridge, and occasionally vegetables. Meat was rare and expensive. Peasants consumed about 80 percent of everything they raised, and what little was left over went almost entirely to the landlord as feudal dues and to the church as tithing—the obligation to give to God one-tenth of everything earned or produced. Peasant families lived on the edge of existence. In a bad year some starved to death, usually the vulnerable children and old people. But during the sixteenth century, in areas with access to big cities, subsistence agriculture gave way to commercial crops, especially wheat, which was hauled to be sold in town markets. Profits from this market agriculture stimulated farmers to raise even greater surpluses in the agricultural regions around the great cities—London, Antwerp, Amsterdam, Paris, Milan, Venice, Barcelona, and scattered places in Germany. Commercial crops and the cash income they produced meant fewer starving children and a higher standard of living for those who were able to take advantage of the new opportunities. As commercial agriculture spread, the population grew because the rural population was better fed and more prosperous.

## The Prosperous Villages

Success in commercializing agriculture could make an enormous difference in the lives of peasants. The village of Buia tells the story of many similarly prosperous hamlets.

Situated in Friuli, a region in the northeast corner of Italy, it served as part of the agricultural hinterland of the great metropolis of Venice. For centuries the peasants of hilly and pleasant Buia had lived in thatched hovels surviving at the subsistence level. But during the fourteenth and fifteenth centuries serfdom disappeared in the region and the peasants' legal status changed. Now free to sell their labor to the highest bidder, peasant families contracted with a landlord to lease a plot of land for a certain number of years in exchange for annual rent payments in kind. A typical yearly rent might include two bushels of wheat, two of oats, one of beans, one of millet, three barrels of wine, two chickens, one ham, three guinea hens, thirty eggs, two cartloads of firewood, and two days' work mowing hay. In contrast to the servitude of serfdom, which tied peasants to the land, agricultural leases created a measure of economic freedom. They allowed landlords to find labor at a time when laborers were scarce, and they enabled peasants to negotiate for a better reward for their labor.

Unlike some neighboring villages that were still under the heel of their lords, Buia had incorporated as a town, a status that provided it with more autonomy from its lords, the Savorgnan family. Moreover, Buia had diversified its economy, branching out into cattle raising and marketing its fierce pear brandy and smooth white wine. But Buia's crucial economic advantage derived from its access to capital. The Savorgnan lords liberally lent money to their tenants in Buia, which enabled them to survive hard times and to invest in commercial profit-making enterprises. Unlike other families, the Savorgnans were willing to invest in their tenants, because they had established political and economic ties with the nearby commercial metropolis of Venice, whose bankers were more than happy to bankroll the Savorgnan family. From the commercial banks of Venice, money flowed through the hands of the Savorgnan to the peasants of the little village of Buia, who in turn produced crops that could be sold in the markets of Venice, a flow of money and goods that enriched, although unequally, everyone involved—the peasants, their Savorgnan landlords, and the Venetian bankers. With the increased income from commercial agriculture, Buia even began to look more affluent during the sixteenth century, boasting a substantial church, a tavern, and a simple one-room town hall where citizens could gather to debate their affairs.

The success of commercial agriculture during the sixteenth century depended on a free and mobile labor supply, access to capital for investment, and proximity to the markets of the big cities. What happened in Buia happened in many places throughout Europe, but overall the amount of

**The Rise of Commercial Agriculture**
During the sixteenth century commercial agriculture began to produce significant surpluses for the expanding population of the cities. This scene depicts a windmill for grinding grain and a train of wagons hauling produce from the country to be marketed in a city.

land available could not provide enough work for the growing farm population. As a result, the growth of the rural population created a new class of landless, impoverished men and women, who were forced to take to the road to find their fortunes. These vagabonds, as they were called, exemplified the social problems that emerged from the uneven distribution of wealth created by the new commerce.

## The Regulated Cities

By the 1480s cities began to grow, largely through migration from the more prosperous countryside, but the growth was uneven with the most dramatic growth occurring in the cities of the North, especially London, Antwerp, and Amsterdam (see Map 14.1). The surpluses of the countryside, both human and agricultural, flowed into the cities during the sixteenth century. Compared to even the prosperous rural villages, such as Buia, the cities must have seemed incomparably rich. Half-starved vagabonds from the countryside would have marveled at shops piled high with food (white bread, fancy pies, fruit, casks of wine, roasting meats); they would have wistfully passed taverns full of drunken, laughing citizens; and they would have begged for alms in front of magnificent, marble-faced churches.

Every aspect of the cities exhibited dramatic contrasts between the rich and poor, who lived on the same streets and often in different parts of the same houses. Around 1580 Christian missionaries brought a Native American chief to the French city of Rouen. Through an interpreter he was asked what impressed him the most about European cities, so unlike the villages of North America. He replied that he was astonished that the rag-clad, emaciated men and women who crowded the streets did not grab the plump, well-dressed rich people by the throat.

The wretched human surplus from the farms continuously replenished and swelled the populations of the cities, which were frequently depleted by high urban death rates. As wealthy as the cities were, they were unhealthy places: human waste overflowed from open latrines because there were no sewage systems; garbage, manure, dead animals, and roaming pigs and dogs made the streets putrid and dangerous; and water came from polluted rivers or sat stale in cisterns for months. Under such conditions, entire neighborhoods could be wiped out in epidemics. Both ends of the life span were vulnerable: one in three babies died in the first year of life; old people did not last long in cold, drafty houses. When the epidemics appeared, which they continued to do about every twenty years until 1721, the rich escaped to their country retreats while the poor died in the streets or in houses locked up and under quarantine.

Despite the danger from disease in the cities, rural immigrants were less likely to starve than those who remained in small villages where they lacked land. Every city maintained storehouses of grain and regulated the price of bread and the size of a loaf so that the poor could be fed. The impulse to feed the poor was less the result of humanitarian motives than a recognition that nothing was more dangerous than a hungry mob. Given the contrasts in wealth among its inhabitants, cities guarded carefully against revolts and crime. Even for petty crime, punishment was

## Map 14.1  Population Distribution in the Sixteenth Century

The population of Europe concentrated around the cities of northern Italy, the Danube and Rhine River valleys, Flanders and northern France, and southeastern England. During the late sixteenth century, northwestern Europe began to grow significantly more rapidly than southern Europe.

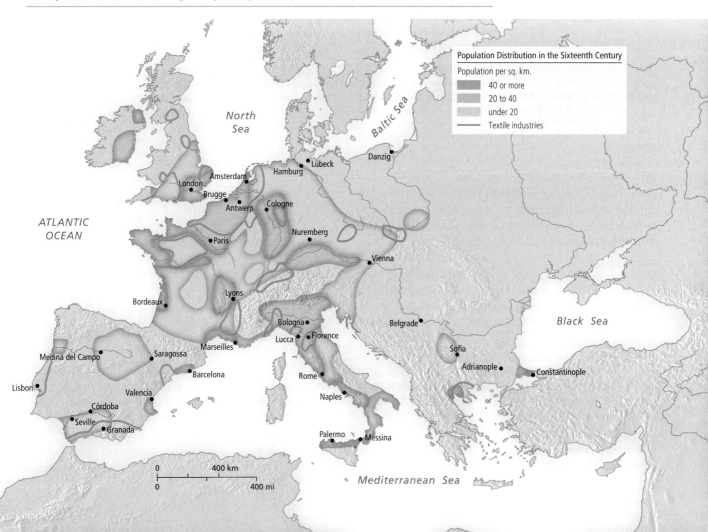

swift, sure, and gruesome. The beggar who stole a loaf of bread from a baker's cart would have his hand amputated on a chopping block in the market square. A shabbily dressed girl who grabbed a lady's glittering trinket would have her nose cut off so that she could never attract a man. A burglar would be tortured, drawn, and quartered, and have his severed head impaled on an iron spike at the town gate as a warning to others.

To deal with the consequences of commerce and massive immigration, European cities attempted to regulate the lives of their inhabitants. Ringing bells measured each working day, and during the sixteenth century many cities erected a large mechanical clock in a prominent place so that busy citizens could keep to their schedules. Municipal officers inspected the weights and measures in the city market, regulated the distribution of produce to guarantee an abundant food supply, and repaired the streets and city walls. However talented or enterprising, new arrivals to the city had very limited opportunities. They could hardly start up their own business because all production was strictly controlled by the guilds, which were associations of merchants or artisans organized to protect their interests. Guilds rigidly regulated their membership; they required an apprenticeship of many years, prohibited technological innovations, guaranteed certain standards of workmanship, and did not allow branching out into new lines. A member of the goldsmiths' guild could not make mirrors; a baker could not sell fruit on the side; a house carpenter could not lay bricks. Given the limited opportunities for new arrivals, immigrant men and women begged on the streets or took charity from the public dole. The men picked up any heavy-labor jobs they could find. Both men and women became servants, a job that paid poorly but at least guaranteed regular meals.

Among the important social achievements of both Protestant and Catholic Reformations were efforts to address the problems of the destitute urban poor, who constituted at least a quarter of the population, even in the best of times. In Catholic countries such as Italy, Spain, southern Germany, and France, there was an enormous expansion of credit banks, which were financed by charitable contributions in order to provide small loans to the poor. Catholic cities established convents for poor young women who were at risk of falling into prostitution and for other women who had retired from the sex trade. Catholic and Protestant cities established orphanages, hospitals for the sick, hospices for the dying, and apartments lent out for a modest rent to poor widows. Both Catholic and Protestant cities attempted to distinguish between the "honest" poor—those who were disabled and truly deserving—and the "dishonest" poor who were thought to be malingerers. Protestant cities established poorhouses, which segregated the poor, subjected them to prisonlike discipline, and forced the able-bodied to work.

The more comfortable classes of the cities enjoyed large palaces and luxurious lifestyles. They hired extensive staffs of servants, feasted on meat and fine wines, and purchased exotic imports such as silk cloth, spices from the East, and, in the Mediterranean cities, slaves from eastern Europe, the Middle East, or Africa. The merchants whose fortunes came from cloth manufacturing, banking, and regional or international trade maintained their status by marrying within their own class, providing municipal offices to those whose fortunes had fallen, and educating their children in the newly fashionable humanist schools. The wealthy of the cities were the bastions of social stability. They possessed the financial resources and economic skills to protect themselves from the worst consequences of economic instability, especially the corrosive wave of price inflation that struck the West after about 1540.

## The Price Revolution

Price inflation became so pervasive during the last half of the sixteenth century that it contributed to the widespread fear that events were being controlled by hidden forces. The effects of inflation are illustrated by the experience of the students at Winchester College in England. These young men were the privileged sons of English aristocrats and country gentlemen, destined for leisured wealth and public responsibility. The curriculum of Winchester emphasized the unchanging values of aristocratic privilege and Christian rectitude, but the dusty account books, kept in meticulous detail by generations of college stewards, reveal that change was very much a fact of college life during the sixteenth century. For example, in 1500 a piece of cloth large enough to make a student's uniform cost forty shillings. By 1580 the cost had doubled, and by 1630 it had tripled. During the sixteenth century the cost of a dozen sheets of parchment doubled, the cost of a dozen candles quadrupled, and the cost of a twelve-gallon barrel of wine (yes, the college served wine to its teenaged students) rose from eight to sixty-four shillings. English masons' experience of price inflation during this period was far more painful. Over the course of the century their wages doubled, but the price of bread increased four- or fivefold, and because the survival of their families depended on the cost of bread, price inflation seriously threatened their lives.

The finances of English college students and masons reveal the phenomenon that historians call the Price Revolution°. After a long period of falling or stable prices that stretched back to the fourteenth century, Europe experienced sustained price increases, beginning around 1540. The inflation lasted a century, forcing major economic and social changes that permanently altered the face of Western society. During this period overall prices across Europe multiplied five- or sixfold.

What caused the inflation? The basic principle is simple. The price paid for goods and services is fundamentally the result of the relationship between *supply* and *demand.* If the number of children who need to be fed grows faster than the supply of grain, the price of bread goes up. This happens simply because mothers who can afford it will be willing to pay a higher price to save their children from hunger. If good harvests allow the supply of grain to increase at a greater rate than the demand for bread, then prices go down. The equation gets somewhat more complicated when taking into account two other factors that can influence price. One factor is the *amount of money in circulation.* If the amount of gold or silver available to make coins increases, there is more money in circulation. When more money is circulating, people have more money to buy more things, which creates the same effect as an increase in demand—prices go up. The other factor is called the *velocity of money in circulation,* which refers to the number of times money changes hands to buy things. When people buy commodities with greater frequency, it has the same effect as increasing the amount of money in circulation or of increasing demand—again, prices go up.

The precise combination of these factors in causing the great Price Revolution of the sixteenth century has long been a matter of considerable debate. Most historians would now agree that the primary cause of inflation was population growth, which increased demand for all kinds of basic commodities, such as bread and woolen cloth for clothing. As Europe's population finally began to recover, it meant that more people needed and desired to buy more things. This explanation is most obvious for commodities that people need to survive, such as grain to make bread. These commodities have what economists call *inelastic demand,* that is, consumers do not have a great deal of discretion in purchasing them. Everybody has to eat. The commodities that people could survive without if the price is too high are said to have *elastic demand,* such as dancing shoes and lace collars. In England between 1540 and 1640 overall prices rose by 490 percent. More telling, however, is that the price of grain (inelastic demand) rose by a stunning 670 percent, whereas the price of luxury goods (elastic demand) rose much less, by 204 percent. Thus, inflation hurt the poor, who needed to feed their children, more than the rich, whose desires were more elastic.

Monetary factors also contributed to inflation. The Portuguese brought in significant amounts of gold from Africa, and newly opened mines in central Europe increased the amount of silver by fivefold as early as the 1520s. The discovery in 1545 of the fabulous silver mine of Potosí (in present-day Bolivia) brought to Europe a flood of silver, which Spain used to finance its costly wars. As inflation began to eat away at royal incomes, financially strapped monarchs all across western Europe debased their money because they believed, mistakenly, that producing more coins

containing less silver would buy more. In fact, the minting of more coins meant each coin was worth less and would buy less. In England, for example, debasement was the major source of inflation during the 1540s and 1550s.

During the sixteenth century, no one understood these causes, however. People only experienced the effects of inflation, and then only gradually. The real wages of workers declined, causing widespread suffering and discontent. Incomes eroded for those dependent on fixed incomes—clergymen, pensioners, government clerks, and landlords who rented out land on long leases. Landlords who were willing to be ruthless and enterprising survived and even prospered. Those who were more paternalistic or conservative in managing their estates often lost their land to creditors.

The Price Revolution severely weakened governments. Most monarchs derived their incomes from their own private lands and from taxes on property. As inflation took hold, property taxes proved dangerously inadequate to cover royal expenses. Even frugal monarchs such as England's Elizabeth I were forced to take extraordinary measures, in her case to sell off royal lands. Spendthrift monarchs faced disaster. Spain was involved in the costly enterprise of nearly continuous war during the sixteenth century. To pay for the wars, Charles V resorted to a form of deficit financing in which he borrowed money by issuing *juros,* which provided lenders an annuity yielding between 3 and 7 percent on the amount of the principal. By the 1550s, however, the annuity payments of the *juros* consumed half of the royal revenues. Charles's son, Philip II, inherited such an alarming situation that in 1557, the year after he assumed the throne, he was forced to declare bankruptcy. Philip continued to fight expensive wars and borrow wildly, and thus failed to get his financial house in order. He declared bankruptcy again in 1575 and 1596. Philip squandered Spain's wealth, impoverishing his own subjects through burdensome taxes and contributing to inflation by borrowing at high rates of interest and debasing the coinage. Although the greatest power of the sixteenth century, Spain sowed the seeds of its own decline by fighting on borrowed money.

Probably the most serious consequence of the Price Revolution was that the hidden force of inflation caused widespread human suffering. During the late sixteenth and early seventeenth centuries, people felt their lives threatened, but they did not know the source and so they imagined all kinds of secret powers at work, especially supernatural ones. The suspicion of religious differences created by the Reformation provided handy, if utterly false, explanations for what had gone wrong. Catholics suspected Protestants, Protestants suspected Catholics, both suspected Jews, and they all worried about witches. Authorities sought to relieve this widespread anxiety by looking in all the wrong

Michel de Montaigne, *Essays* (1575)

places, disciplining the populace, hunting for witches, and battling against enemies from the opposite side of the confessional divide.

# Disciplining the People

■ How did religious and political authorities attempt to discipline the people?

The first generation of the Protestant and Catholic Reformations had been devoted to doctrinal disputes and to either rejecting or defending papal authority. Subsequent generations of reformers in the last half of the sixteenth and the early seventeenth centuries faced the formidable task of building the institutions that would firmly establish a Protestant or Catholic religious culture. Leaders of all religious confessions attempted to revitalize the Christian community by disciplining nonconformists and enforcing moral rigor. Members of the community came to identify responsible citizenship with conformity to a specific Christian confession.

Whether Lutheran, Calvinist, Catholic, or Anglican, godly reformers sought to bring order to society, which meant they often felt obliged to attack popular culture. They reformed or abolished wild festivals, imprisoned town drunks, decreased the number of holidays, and tried to regulate sexual behavior. Many activities that had once been accepted as normal came to be considered deviant or criminal. The process of better ordering society required that the common people accept a certain measure of discipline. Discipline required cooperation between church and secular authorities, but it was not entirely imposed from above. Many people wholeheartedly cooperated with moral correction and even encouraged reformers to go further. Others passively, actively, or resentfully resisted it.

## Establishing Confessional Identities

Between 1560 and 1650 religious confessions reshaped European culture, and loyalty to a single confession governed the relationships between states. A confession consisted of the adherents to a particular statement of religious doctrine—the Confession of Augsburg for Lutherans, the Helvetic Confessions for Calvinists, the Thirty-Nine Articles for Anglicans, and the decrees of the Council of Trent for Catholics. Based on these confessions of faith, the clergy disciplined the laity, exiled nonconformists, and promoted distinct religious institutions, beliefs, and culture.

The process of establishing confessional identities did not happen overnight; it lasted for centuries and had far-reaching consequences. During the second half of the sixteenth century, Lutherans turned from the struggle to survive within the hostile Holy Roman Empire to establishing a confessional identity in the parts of the empire where Lutheranism was the chosen religion of the local prince. They had to recruit Lutheran clergy and provide each clergyman with a university education, which was made possible by scholarship endowments from the Lutheran princes of the empire. Once established, the Lutheran clergy became a branch of the civil bureaucracy, received a government stipend, and enforced the will of the prince. Calvinist states followed a similar process, but where they were in a minority, as in France, Calvinists had to go it alone, and the state often discriminated against them. In those places confessional identities were established in opposition to the state and the dominant confession.

Catholics responded with their own aggressive plan of training new clergymen, educating the laity, and reinforcing the bond between church and state. Just as with the Lutheran princes, Catholic princes in the Holy Roman Empire associated conformity to Catholicism with loyalty to themselves, making religion a pillar of the state. Everywhere in western Europe (except for Ireland, a few places in the Holy Roman Empire, and for a time France) the only openly practiced religion was the religion of the state.

The authorities primarily formed confessional identities among the laity by promoting distinctive ritual systems. These ritual systems embodied ways of acting and even of gesturing that transformed the way people moved their bodies so that a Catholic and a Protestant might be instantly recognized by certain telltale signs of posture, speech, and comportment.

The Catholic and Protestant ritual systems differed primarily in their attitude toward the sacred. Whereas Catholic ritual behavior depended on a repertoire of gestures that indicated reverence in the presence of the sacred, Protestant ritual depended on a demonstration of sociability that identified people as members of a certain congregation or church. For example, until the late sixteenth century Europeans greeted one another either by raising a hand, palm outward, which meant "welcome," or with a bow by which someone of lower status recognized the superiority of another. Some radical Protestants, however, insisted that all gestures of deference, such as bows and curtsies, were an affront to God and introduced a new form of greeting, the handshake. Shaking hands was completely egalitarian, and one could identify English Quakers or Scottish Calvinists, for example, simply by the fact that they shook hands with one another.

A particularly revealing ritual difference can be seen in the contrasting ways that Scottish Calvinists and Spanish Catholics reintegrated repentant sinners into the Church. In Calvinism disciplinary authority rested with the presbytery, a board of pastors and elders elected by the community. If a Scottish Calvinist blasphemed God, the presbytery could discipline him, shun him, or banish him from the community. If he wished to be reinstated and the presbytery agreed, he would be obliged to come before the entire congregation to confess sincerely his wrongs and beg forgiveness. The congregation would make a collective judgment about his acceptability for renewed membership. The pain inflicted on the Calvinist sinner was the social pain of having his transgression openly discussed and evaluated by his friends and neighbors.

If a Spanish Catholic blasphemed, he would be subjected to an extended ritual of penance, the auto-da-fé°, which meant a theater of faith. The auto-da-fé was designed to promote fear and to cause physical pain because, according to Catholic doctrine, bodily suffering in this world was necessary in order to free the soul from worse suffering in the next. An *auto* was a public performance in which dozens or sometimes hundreds of sinners and criminals were paraded through the streets in a theatrical demonstration of the authority of the Church and the power of penance. The *auto* culminated in a mass confirmation of faith in which the repentant sinners utterly subjected themselves to the authority of the clergy, while those who refused to repent or were relapsed heretics were strangled and their corpses burned.

Whereas the punishment of the Calvinist community was primarily a rite of social humiliation, the auto-da-fé involved physical torture as well as social degradation. The nub of the difference was that Calvinists had to demonstrate the sincerity of their social conformity; Catholics had to go through a performance that emphasized the authority of the clergy and that purified sin with physical pain.

## Regulating the Family

One matter on which Calvinists, Lutherans, and Catholics agreed was that the foundation of society should be the authority fathers had over their families. This principle, known as patriarchy, was very traditional. The confessions that emerged from the Reformation further strengthened patriarchy because it so usefully served the needs of church and state to establish social order and encourage morality. According to an anonymous treatise published in 1586 in Calvinist Nassau, the three pillars of Christian society were the church, the state, and the household. This proposition made the father's authority parallel to the authority of clergy and king—a position that all the confessions would have accepted. Enforcing patriarchy led to regulating sexuality and the behavior of children.

### Marriage and Sexuality: The Self-Restrained Couple

However, regional differences in the structure of the family itself meant that despite the near universal acceptance of the theory of patriarchy, the reality of the father's authority varied a great deal. Since the early Middle Ages in northwestern Europe—in Britain, Scandinavia, the Netherlands, northern France, and western Germany—couples tended to wait to marry until their mid- or late twenties, well beyond the age of sexual maturity. When these couples married, they established their own household separate from either of their parents. Husbands were usually only two or three years older than their wives, and that proximity of age tended to make those relationships more cooperative and less authoritarian than the theory of patriarchy might suggest. In northwestern European the couple had to be economically independent before they married, which meant both had to accumulate savings or the husband needed to inherit from his deceased father before he could marry. By contrast, in southern Europe, men in their late twenties or thirties married teenaged women over whom they exercised authority by virtue of their age. In the South patriarchy meant husbands ruled over wives. In eastern Europe, both spouses married in their teens and resided in one of the parental households for many years, which placed both spouses for extended periods under the authority of the husband's parents.

The marriage pattern in northwestern Europe required prolonged sexual restraint by young men and women until they were economically self-sufficient. In addition to individual self-control, sexual restraint required social control by church and secular authorities, who seem to have been more vigilant about regulating sexual behavior than in southern and eastern Europe. Their efforts seem to have been generally successful. For example, in sixteenth-century Geneva, where the elders were especially wary about sexual sins, the rates of illegitimate births were extremely low. The elders were particularly vigilant about disciplining women and keeping them subservient, often making and enforcing highly minute regulations. In 1584 Calvinist elders in another Swiss town excommunicated Charlotte Arbaleste and her entire household because she wore her hair in curls, which the elders thought were too alluring.

Northwestern European families also tended to be smaller. Married couples in northwestern Europe began to space their children through birth control and family planning. These self-restrained couples practiced withdrawal, the rhythm method, or abstinence. When mothers no longer relied on wet nurses and nursed their own infants, often for long periods, they also reduced their chances of becoming pregnant. Thus, limiting family size became the social norm in northwestern Europe, especially among the educated and urban middle classes. Protestant families tended to have fewer children than Catholic families, but Catholics in this region also practiced some form of birth control, even though Church law prohibited all forms except abstinence.

For prospective couples, parental approval remained more important than romantic love. In fact, a romantic attachment between a husband and wife was frowned upon as unseemly and even dangerous. More highly prized in a marriage partner were trust, dependability, and the willingness to work. Many married couples certainly exhibited

# The *Auto-da-Fé:*
# The Power of Penance

Performed in Spain and Portugal from the sixteenth to eighteenth centuries, the auto-da-fé merged the judicial processes of the state with the sacramental rituals of the Catholic Church. An *auto* took place at the end of a judicial investigation conducted by the inquisitors of the Church after the defendants had been found guilty of a sin or crime. The term *auto-da-fé* means "theater of faith," and the goal was to persuade or force a person who had been judged guilty to repent and confess. Organized through the cooperation of ecclesiastical and secular authorities, autos-da-fé brought together an assortment of sinners, criminals, and heretics for a vast public rite that dramatized the essential elements of the sacrament of penance: contrition, by which the sinner recognized and felt sorry for the sin; confession, which required the sinner to admit the sin to a priest; and satisfaction or punishment, by which the priest absolved the sinner and enacted some kind of penalty. The auto-da-fé transformed penance, especially confession and satisfaction, into a spectacular affirmation of the faith and a manifestation of divine justice.

The *auto* symbolically anticipated the Last Judgment, and it provoked deep anxiety among those who witnessed it about how God would judge them. By suffering bodily pain in this life the soul might be relieved from worse punishments in the next. The sinners, convicts, and heretics, now considered penitents, were forced to march in a procession that went through the streets of the city from the cathedral to the town hall or place of punishment. These processions would typically include some thirty or forty penitents, but in moments of crisis they could be

far larger. In Toledo in 1486 there were three *autos*—one parading 750 penitents and two displaying some 900 each.

A 1655 *auto* in Córdoba illustrates the symbolic character of the rites. Soldiers bearing torches that would light the pyre for those to be burnt led the procession. Following them came three bigamists who wore on their heads conical miters or hats painted with representations of their sin, four witches whose miters depicted devils, and three criminals with harnesses around their necks to demonstrate their status as captives. The sinners carried unlit candles to represent their lack of faith. Criminals who had escaped arrest were represented in the procession by effigies made in their likeness, and those who had died before punishment were carried in their coffins. The marching sinners appeared before their neighbors and fellow citizens stripped of the normal indicators of status, dressed only in the emblems of their sins. Among them walked a few who wore the infamous *sanbenitos,* a kind of tunic or vest with a yellow strip down the back, and a conical hat painted with flames. These were the *relajados,* the unrepentant or relapsed sinners who were going to be "relaxed" (released into the hands of the secular authorities) at the culminating moment of the *auto* when they were strangled and burned.

The procession ended in the town square at a platform from which penances were performed as on the stage of a theater. Forced to their knees, the penitents were asked to confess and to plead for readmission into the bosom of the church. For those who did confess, a sentence was an-

nounced that would rescue them from the pains of Purgatory and the flames of the *auto*. The sentence required them to join a penitential procession for a certain number of Fridays, perform self-flagellation in public, or wear a badge of shame for a prescribed period of time. Those who failed to confess faced a more immediate sentence.

The most horrendous scenes of suffering awaited those who refused to confess or who had relapsed into sin or heresy, which meant their confession was not considered sincere. If holdouts confessed prior to the reading of the sentence, then the *auto* was a success, a triumph of the Christian faith over its enemies, and everything that could possibly elicit confessions was attempted, including haranguing, humiliating, and torturing the accused until their stubborn will broke. If the accused finally confessed after the sentence was read, then they would be strangled before burning, but if they held out to the very end, they would be burned alive. From the ecclesiastics' point of view, the refusal to confess was a disaster for the entire Church because the flames of the pyre opened a window into Hell. They would certainly prefer to see the Church's authority acknowledged through confession than to see the power of Satan manifest in such a public fashion.

It is reported that crowds witnessed the violence of the autos-da-fé with silent attention in a mood of deep dread, not so much of the inquisitors, it seems, as for the inevitability of the final day of divine judgment that would arrive for them all. The core assumption of the auto-da-fé was that bodily pain could save a soul from damnation. As one contemporary

...elapsed heretics were burned
...n a pyre.

The conical hats were painted
with the representation of the
sinner's sin.

Sinners wearing the sanbenitos.

A procession conducted the
sinners to the town square.

**Auto-da-fé in Lisbon**

witness put it, the inquisitors removed "through external ritual
[the sinners'] internal crimes." It
was assumed that the public ritual
framework for the sacrament of
penance would have a salutary
effect on those who witnessed the
*auto* by encouraging them to repent before they too faced divine
judgment.

## Questions of Justice

1. How did the auto-da-fé contribute
to the formation of an individual and
collective sense of being a Catholic?
2. In the auto-da-fé, inflicting physical
pain was more than punishment. How
was pain understood to have been
socially and religiously useful?

## Taking It Further

Flynn, Maureen. "Mimesis of the Last
Judgment: The Spanish *Auto da fe,*"
*Sixteenth Century Journal* 22 (1991):
281–97. The best analysis of the
religious significance of the auto-da-fé.

Flynn, Maureen. "The Spectacle of
Suffering in Spanish Streets," in
Barbara A. Hanawalt and Kathryn L.
Reyerson, eds., *City and Spectacle in
Medieval Europe.* 1994. In this fasci-
nating article Flynn analyzes the
spiritual value of physical pain.

signs of affection—addressing one another lovingly in letters, nursing a sick mate, mourning a dead one—but overly sentimental attachments were discouraged as contrary to the patriarchal authority that ideally characterized family life. Most husbands and wives seem to have treated one another with a certain coolness and emotional detachment.

The moral status of marriage also demonstrated regional variations during the early modern period. Protestants no longer considered husbands and wives morally inferior to celibate monks and nuns, and the wives of preachers in Protestant communities certainly had a respected social role never granted to the concubines of priests. But the favorable Protestant attitude toward marriage did not necessarily translate into a positive attitude toward women. In Germany the numerous books of advice, called the Father of the House literature, encouraged families to subordinate the individual interests of servants, children, and the mother to the dictates of the father, who was encouraged to be just but who must be obeyed. Even if a wife was brutally treated by her husband, she could neither find help from authorities nor expect a divorce.

**The Domestic Ideal**

During the late sixteenth and seventeenth centuries, idealized depictions of harmonious family life became very popular, especially in the Netherlands. In this painting by Pieter De Hooch a young child is learning to walk.

## Children: Naturally Evil?

Although families had always cherished their children, during the Reformation both Protestant and Catholic preachers placed even greater emphasis on the welfare, education, and moral upbringing of children. Protestants contributed to this process by emphasizing the family's responsibility for their children's moral guidance and religious education. One of the obligations of Protestant fathers was to read and teach the Bible in the home. This directive may have been more a theoretical ideal than a practical reality, but the rise in literacy among both boys and girls in Protestant countries attests to the increased importance of education.

Discipline also played a large role in the sixteenth-century family. Parents had always demonstrated love toward their children by indulging them with sweets and toys and protecting them from danger. But during the sixteenth century some authors of advice books and many preachers began to emphasize that parental love must be tempered by strict discipline. In effect, the clergy attempted to impose their own authoritarian impulses on the emotional lives of the family. The Protestant emphasis on the majesty of God and a belief in original sin translated into a negative view of human nature. Calvinist theologians who held such a view placed a special emphasis on family discipline. The *Disquisition on the Spiritual Condition of Infants* (1618) pointed out that from a theological point of view, babies were naturally evil. The godly responsibility of the father was to break the will of his evil offspring, taming them so that they could be turned away

from sin toward virtue. The very title of a 1591 Calvinist treatise revealed the strength of the evil-child argument: *On Disciplining Children: How the Disobedient, Evil, and Corrupted Youth of These Anxious Last Days Can Be Bettered.* The treatise also advised that the mother's role should be limited to her biological function of giving birth. It directed fathers to be vigilant so that their wives did not corrupt the children, because women "love to accept strange, false beliefs, and go about with benedictions and witches' handiwork. When they are not firm in faith and the Devil comes to tempt them . . . they follow him and go about with supernatural fantasies."[1]

In order to break the will of their infants, mothers were encouraged to wean them early and turn them over for a strict upbringing by their fathers. The ideal father was to cultivate both love and fear in his children by remaining unemotional and firm. He was to be vigilant to prevent masturbation, to discourage frivolity, and to toughen little children by not allowing them to eat too much, sleep too long, or stay too comfortably warm. Although discouraged from being unnecessarily brutal, the godly father was never to spare the rod on either his children or his wife.

It is clear that disciplining children was an important theoretical guideline in sixteenth- and seventeenth-century Europe. It is less clear whether this was as true in practice as in theory. Historians disagree on the issue. It is likely that then, as now, there were many different ways of raising children, and each family exhibited its own emotional chemistry. And it is also likely that sixteenth-century parents did considered firm discipline loving.

## Suppressing Popular Culture

The family was not the only institution that sixteenth-century educated reformers sought to discipline. Their efforts also targeted many manifestations of traditional popular culture. The reformers or puritans, as they came to be called in England, wanted to purify both the church and society, to transform them into a "godly community" by encouraging and even enforcing moral behavior, particularly in rowdy youths and members of the lower classes. The suppression of popular culture had two aspects. One was a policing effort, aimed at ridding society of presumably un-Christian practices. The other was a missionary enterprise, an attempt to bring the Protestant and Catholic Reformations to the people through instruction and popular preaching.

Overall the reformers sought to encourage an ethic of moderation, which valued thrift, modesty, chastity, and above all self-control. This ethic was neither Protestant nor Catholic but was promoted by clerics of all religious confessions. The traditional popular culture they so distrusted stressed other values such as spontaneity and emotional freedom, values that were hardly subject to control and could have dangerous, often violent consequences.

Once the reformers had cleaned up the churches by eliminating idolatry, unnecessary holidays, and superfluous rituals, they turned to the secular world, and they found much to criticize. The reformers saw impiety in comedians, dancing, loud music, rough sports, dice and card games, public drinking, dressing up in costumes, puppets, and above all actors. The Catholic Bishop of Verona condemned preachers who told stories that made the congregations laugh. To the reformers, these things were despicable because they seemed to be vestiges of pre-Christian practices and because they led people into sin.

The festival of Carnival° came under particularly virulent attack. The most popular annual festival, Carnival took place for several days or even weeks before the beginning of Lent and included all kinds of fun and games—silly pantomimes, bear baiting, bullfights, masquerades, dances, lots of eating and drinking, and illicit sex. The *Discourse Against Carnival* (1607) complained about the temptations to sin and the money wasted in Carnival play. Catholics attempted to reform Carnival by eliminating the most offensive forms of behavior, especially those that led to violence or vice. Other popular festivals and entertainments suffered a similar fate of scornful criticism, regulation, or even abolition.

Pieter Brueghel the Elder's painting *The Battle Between Carnival and Lent* (1559) illustrates the role of festivals in the popular culture. In the painting, a fat man riding on a wine barrel engages in a mock joust with an emaciated, stooped figure of uncertain gender who rides a wheeled cart pulled by a monk and nun. The two figures in the painting symbolize the two festival seasons. The fat man represents Carnival, a time of joyous, gluttonous, drunken feasting; the lean one represents Lent, a period of sexual abstinence and fasting that precedes Easter. During the

### The Battle Between Carnival and Lent

In this allegory, called *The Battle Between Carnival and Lent* (1559) by Pieter Brueghel the Elder, the festive season of Carnival is represented on the left by a fat man riding a wine barrel wielding as a lance a roasted pig on a spit. He is engaged in a mock joust with an emaciated figure holding a paddle of fish representing Lent, the season for fasting and giving up meat. On the Carnival side are cards, dice, and people dressed in the funny costumes of Carnival. On the Lent side are pretzels and flatbread, the unleavened breads of the fasting season.

# The Introduction of the Table Fork: The New Sign of Western Civilization

Sometime in the sixteenth century, western Europeans encountered a new tool that would initiate a profound and lasting transformation in Western society: the table fork. Before people used the table fork and practiced the refined dining manners that accompanied its use, they dined in a way that, to our modern sensibilities, would seem disgusting. Meat was a luxury available only to people in the upper classes, who indulged themselves by devouring it in enormous quantities. Whole rabbits, lambs, and pigs roasted on a spit would be placed before diners. A quarter of veal or venison or even an entire roast beef, complete with its head, might be heaved onto the table. Diners would use knives to cut off a piece of meat that they would then eat with their hands, allowing the juices to drip down their arms. The long sleeves of their shirts were used to wipe meat juices, sweat, and spittle from their mouths and faces. These banquets celebrated the direct physical contact between the body of the dead animal and the bodies of the diners themselves who touched, handled, chewed, and swallowed it.

During the sixteenth century, reformers who were trying to abolish the cruder aspects of popular culture also promoted new table manners that treated the eating of meat as discomforting, if not shameful. Well-mannered people increasingly felt the need to distance themselves from the fact that they were consuming a dead animal. To accomplish this, new implements made certain that diners did not come into direct physical contact with their food

before they placed it in their mouths. In addition to napkins—which came into widespread use to replace shirt sleeves for wiping the mouth—table forks appeared on upper-class tables. It became impolite to transfer food directly from the table or common serving plate to the mouth. Food first had to go onto each individual's plate and then be cut into small portions and raised to the mouth. A French treatise of 1672 warns that "meat must never be touched . . . by hand, not even while eating."[2] This prohibition had nothing to do with cleanliness, because bacteria were not discovered until the end of the nineteenth century. The fear was not of disease, but of direct contact with the bodies of dead animals. The fear, it seems, derived from a growing sense of revulsion with the more physical aspects of human nature, including sexuality, which was regulated by church authorities, and the killing of animals in order to survive, which was regulated by table manners. The table fork made it possible to eat meat without ever touching it. Forks enabled diners to avoid their growing sense of discomfort with the textures and juices of meats that perhaps reminded them of the flesh and blood of the dead animal.

The use of the table fork, therefore, has more to do with civility than hygiene, which can be demonstrated by the fact that certain foods, such as bread, cherries, or chocolates, are always eaten with the hands, even by the Queen of England. In determining when to use a fork it is not cleanliness that matters but the kind of food consumed. Moreover, the civility that resulted from use of the table fork promoted individualism, because everyone—regardless of their social origins—could learn how to use it. A clerk or governess could disguise a humble background simply by learning how to eat properly. In the end, the transformations that occurred in Western society because of its encounter with the table fork—the blurring of class distinctions and creation of a universal code of manners—were so gradual and subtle that few of us who use a table fork daily are even aware of its profound significance.

## For Discussion

How do manners, both good and bad, communicate messages to other people? Does it matter to have good manners?

**The Introduction of the Table Fork**
During the late sixteenth century the refinement of manners among the upper classes focused on dining. No innovation was more revolutionary than the spread of the use of the table fork. Pictured here are the travel cutlery, including two table forks, of Queen Elizabeth I.

sixteenth century contemporaries understood the contrast between Carnival, which was devoted to bodily pleasure, and Lent, during which the bodily desires were ignored to enable repentance, as the battle between two divergent ideas of society. The battle was not just a symbol but a reality that took place through the attempts to suppress popular culture.

What Catholics reformed, Protestants abolished. Martin Luther had been relatively tolerant of popular culture, but later reformers were not. The most famous German Carnival, the *Schembartlauf* of Nuremberg, was abolished; in England the great medieval pageants of York, Coventry, Chester, Norwich, and Worcester disappeared; in Calvinist Holland, the Christmas tradition of giving children gifts was strongly denounced.

The Carnival festival was highly resilient, however. Along with many other forms of popular culture, it persisted, even if less openly public. The moralist attack on popular culture meant that some activities retreated from outside to inside—into sports arenas, taverns, theaters, and opera houses. And some were professionalized by athletes, entertainers, actors, and singers. The attempts of mayors and clerics to abolish fun also provoked open resistance. In 1539 in Nuremberg the Lutheran pastor Andreas Osiander, who had preached against Carnival, found himself lampooned by a float in the shape of a ship of fools, in which he was depicted as the captain.

The attempts to suppress popular culture produced a confrontation between the educated elites of Europe and the workers, peasants, servants, and artisans who surrounded them and served them. Although not entirely successful, by the late sixteenth century the suppression had the effect of broadening the cultural gap between the educated few and the masses. Practices that previously had been broadly accepted forms of public entertainment, in which even members of the clergy participated, came to be seen as unworthy of educated people.

## Hunting Witches

The most catastrophic manifestation of the widespread anxiety of the late sixteenth and seventeenth centuries was the great witch-hunt°. The judicial prosecution of alleged witches in either church or secular courts dramatically increased about the middle of the sixteenth century and lasted until the late seventeenth, when the number of witchcraft trials rapidly diminished and stopped entirely in western Europe.

Throughout this period, people accepted the reality of two kinds of magic°. The first kind was natural magic, such as the practice of alchemy or astrology, which involved the manipulation of occult forces believed to exist in nature. The fundamental assumption of natural magic was that everything in nature is alive. The trained magician could coerce the occult forces in nature to do his bidding. During the Renaissance many humanists and scientific thinkers were drawn to natural magic because of its promise of power over nature. Natural magic, in fact, had some practical uses. Alchemists, for example, devoted themselves to discovering what they called the "philosopher's stone," the secret of transmuting base metals into gold. In practice this meant that they learned how to imitate the appearance of gold, a very useful skill for counterfeiting coins or reducing the content of precious metals in legal coins. Natural magic was practiced by educated men and involved the human manipulation of the occult, but it did not imply any kind of contact with devils. Most practitioners of natural magic desired to achieve good, and many considered it the highest form of curative medicine.

Many people of the sixteenth and seventeenth centuries also believed in a second kind of magic—demonic magic. The practitioner of this kind of magic—usually but not always a female witch—called upon evil spirits to gain access to power. Demonic magic was generally understood as a way to work harm by ritual means. Belief in the reality of harmful magic and of witches had been widespread for centuries, and there had been occasional witch trials throughout the Middle Ages. Systematic witch-hunts, however, began only when ecclesiastical and secular authorities showed a willingness to employ the law to discover and punish accused witches. The Reformation controversies of the late sixteenth century and the authorities' willingness to discipline deviants of all sorts certainly intensified the hunt for witches. Thousands of people were accused of and tried for practicing witchcraft. About half of these alleged witches were executed, most often by burning. Cases of alleged witchcraft rarely occurred in a steady flow, as one would find for other crimes. Typically, witchcraft trials took place during localized hunts when a flare-up of paranoia and torture multiplied allegations against vulnerable members of the community. Most allegations were against women, in particular young unmarried women and older widows, but men and even young children could be accused of witchcraft as well.

People in many different places—from shepherds in the mountains of Switzerland to Calvinist ministers in the lowlands of Scotland—thought they perceived the work of witches in human and natural events. The alleged demonic magic of witchcraft appeared in two forms: *maleficia* (doing harm) and *diabolism* (worshiping the devil). The rituals of *maleficia* consisted of a simple sign or a complex incantation, but what made them *maleficia* was the belief that the person who performed them intended to cause harm to someone or something. There were many kinds of *maleficia,* including coercing an unwilling lover by sprinkling dried menstrual blood in his food, sickening a pig by cursing it, burning a barn by marking it with a hex sign, bringing wasting diarrhea to a child by reciting a spell, and killing an enemy by stabbing a wax statue of him. Midwives and women who specialized in healing were especially vulnerable to accusations of witchcraft. The intention behind a particular action they might have performed was often obscure, making it difficult to distinguish between magic designed to bring beneficial results, such as the cure of a child, and *maleficia* designed to bring harmful ones. With the high infant mortality rates of the sixteenth and seventeenth centuries, performing magical rituals for a sick baby could be very risky. The logic of witchcraft beliefs implied that a bad ending must have been caused by bad intentions.

While some people certainly attempted to practice *maleficia,* the second and far more serious kind of ritual practice associated with demonic magic, diabolism, almost certainly never took place. Diabolism was a fantasy that helped explain events that could not otherwise be explained. The theory behind diabolism asserted that the witch had sold her soul to the Devil, whom she worshiped as her god. These witches had made a pact with the Devil, worshiped the Devil in the ritual of the witches' sabbath, flew around at night, and sometimes changed themselves into animals. The two core beliefs of the pact with the Devil and the witches' sabbath created the intellectual and legal conditions for the great witch-hunts of the sixteenth and seventeenth centuries.

A pact with the Devil was believed to give the witch the ability to accomplish *maleficia,* in exchange for which she was obliged to serve and worship Satan. The most influential witchcraft treatise, *The Hammer of Witches* (1486), had an extensive discussion of the ceremony of the pact. After the prospective witch had declared her intention to enter his service, Satan appeared to her, often in the alluring form of a handsome young man who offered her rewards, including a demonic lover, called an *incubus.* To obtain these inducements, the witch was obligated to renounce her allegiance to Christ, usually signified by stomping on the cross. The Devil rebaptized her in a disgusting substance, guaranteeing that her soul belonged to him. To signify that she was one of his own, the Devil marked her body in a hidden place, creating a sign, which could easily be confused with a birthmark or blemish. To an inquisitor or judge almost any mark on the skin might confirm guilt.

One of the fullest accounts of beliefs in the witches' sabbath comes from the tragic trial of the Pappenheimer family in Bavaria in 1600. The Pappenheimers, consisting of a mother, a father, and their sons, were vagrants arrested for killing babies and cutting off their hands for the purposes of witchcraft. In her confession under torture, Anna Pappenheimer gave a full account of her participation in a fantastic witches' sabbath that supposedly took place at night on a hill outside of the village of Tettenwang. She claimed that witches arrived from near and far flying in on broomsticks and pitchforks. The assembled company largely consisted of women, young and old and most of them naked, but there were a few male witches (known as warlocks) and even some children. With a clap of thunder

## DOCUMENT

### How Women Came to Be Accused of Witchcraft: A Witch's Confession

*Walpurga Hausmännin, an elderly widow and midwife from a small town near Augsburg in the Holy Roman Empire, was accused in 1587 of killing more than forty children. Her confession, extracted out of her through fear and torture, is tragic but typical, complete with lurid details of sexual intercourse with the Devil, the Devil's mark, a pact with the Devil, and riding on a broomstick to a witches' sabbath. This excerpt from her confession, which lists some of her alleged victims, illustrates how the collective fears of the community were channeled into imagined crimes against children.*

[The Devil] also compelled her to do away with and to kill young infants at birth, even before they had been taken to Holy Baptism. This she did, whenever possible. These as follows:

1 and 2. About ten years ago, she had rubbed Anna Hämännin, who dwelt far from Dursteigel, with her salve on the occasion of her first childbirth and also otherwise damaged her so that mother and child remained together and died.

3. Dorothea, the stepdaughter of Christian Wachter, bore her first child ten years before; at its birth she made press on its little brain so that it died. The Devil had specially bidden her destroy the first-born.

5. When, four years ago, the organist's wife was awaiting her confinement, she touched her naked body with her salve whereby the child promptly died and came stillborn.

8. Three years ago when she was called to a mill to the miller's wife there she had let the child fall into the water and drown.

11. When six years ago, she partook of food with Magdalena Seilerin, called *Kammerschreiberin* (wife of the chamber scribe), she had put a salve in her drink, so that she was delivered prematurely. This child she, Walpurga, secretly buried under the doorway of the said wife of the scribe on the pretext that then she would have no other miscarriage. The same she also did with many others. When she was questioned under torture for the reasons of this burial, she admitted that it was done in order to cause disunion between two spouses. This her Devil-Paramour had taught her.

15. She had also rubbed a salve on a beautiful son of the late Chancellor, Jacob by name: this child had lovely fair hair and she had given him a hobby-horse so that he might ride on it till he lost his senses. He died likewise.

Source: From George T. Matthews, ed., *News and Rumor in Renaissance Europe: The Fugger Newsletters,* pp. 137–143. Copyright © 1959 by G. P. Putnam's Sons.

**The Witches' Kitchen**
During the sixteenth and seven-teenth centuries it was widely be-lieved that witches were women who practiced *maleficia* and wor-shiped Satan. Both attractive young and wrinkled old women appear here as witches. From the right an old witch embraces her naked demon lover, a young woman opens her blouse for her approaching lover, another young woman points to the witch's mark on her leg, a hag reads spells from a book in front of a human skull, a witch brews noxious substances in a large kettle, and a kneeling woman worships a satanic idol. In the background is a house fire, the product of the witches' evil work.

and a profusion of smoke, Satan himself suddenly appeared with his eyes glowing, dressed in black and smelling horri-bly. The assembled witches and warlocks bowed low before him, praying in a travesty of the Lord's Prayer, "Our Satan which art in Hell. . . ." There followed an infernal banquet of disgusting foods, including horse meat, ravens, crows, toads, frogs, and boiled and roasted infants. After the feast, an or-chestra of demons played tuneless, screeching dance music that aroused a mad lust in the witches and their demon lovers, who began a wild spinning dance that finally broke

down into a indiscriminate orgy. The family and some other drifters were grotesquely tortured and burned alive.

Between about 1550 and 1650, approximately 100,000 people in Europe were tried for witchcraft. About 50,000 of these were executed. Approximately half of the trials were in the German-speaking lands of the Holy Roman Empire. Prosecutions were also extensive in Switzerland, France, Scotland, Poland, Hungary, Transylvania, and Russia. 10,000 people were tried in Spain and Italy, but these were mostly for minor offenses of *maleficia*, and very few people

**Burning of Witches at Dernberg in 1555**
One of the witches is being taken away by a flying demon to whom she had sold her soul.

were executed, probably none in Italy. As the product of collective beliefs and collective paranoia, witchcraft beliefs could be applied to all kinds of people, but allegations were most commonly lodged against poor, older women in small rural villages. Perhaps most tragic is the fact that these women were the members of the community most dependent on their neighbors for kindness and charity.

# The Confessional States

■ How did religious differences provoke violence and start wars?

The Religious Peace of Augsburg of 1555 provided the model for a solution to the religious divisions produced by the Reformation. According to the principle of *cuius regio, eius religio* (he who rules determines the religion of the land), each prince in the Holy Roman Empire determined the religion to be followed by his subjects, and those who disagreed were obliged to convert or emigrate elsewhere. Certainly, forced exile was economically and personally traumatic for those who emigrated, but it preserved what was almost universally believed to be the fundamental principle of successful rulership—one king, one faith, one law. In other words, each state should have only one church. Except in the notoriously weak states of eastern Europe and a few small troubled principalities in the Holy Roman Empire, few thought it desirable to allow more than one confession in the same state.

The problem with this political theory of religious unity, of course, was the reality of religious divisions created by the Reformation. In some places there were as many as three active confessions—Catholic, Lutheran, and Calvinist—in addition to the minority sects, such as the Anabaptists and the Jewish communities. The alternative to religious unity would have been religious toleration, but hardly anyone in a position of authority was willing to advocate that. Calvin had expelled advocates of religious toleration, and Luther had been aggressively hostile to those who disagreed with him on seemingly minor theological points. After 1542 with the establishment of the Universal Inquisition, the Catholic Church was committed to exposing and punishing anyone who professed a different faith, with the exception of Jews in Italy, who were under papal protection. Geneva and Rome became competing missionary centers, each flooding the world with polemical tracts and specially trained missionaries willing to risk their lives by going behind the enemy lines to console their co-religionists and evangelize for converts.

Wherever there were significant religious minorities within a state, the best that could be hoped for was a condition of anxious tension, omnipresent suspicion, and peri-odic hysteria (see Map 14.2). The worst possibility was civil war in which religious affiliations and political rivalries were intertwined in such complicated ways that finding peaceful solutions was especially difficult. Between 1560 and 1648 several religious civil wars broke out, including the French Wars of Religion, the Dutch revolt against Spain, the Thirty Years' War in Germany, and the English Civil War. (The latter two will be discussed in Chapter 15.)

During the late sixteenth century a new word appeared to describe a personality type that may not have been entirely new but was certainly much more common—the fanatic°. Originally referring to someone possessed by a demon, *fanatic* came to mean a person who expressed immoderate enthusiasm in religious matters, a person who pursued a supposedly divine mission, often to violent ends. Fanatics from all sides of the religious divide initiated waves of political assassinations and engaged in grotesque massacres of their opponents. François Guion, the assassin of William the Silent, whose story began this chapter, was in many ways typical of fanatics in his steadfast pursuit of his victim and his willingness to masquerade for years under a false identity. During the sixteenth and seventeenth centuries, no religious community had a monopoly on fanatics. They presented themselves as serving the pope as well as the Protestant churches.

The sharp confessional divisions that produced fanatics and assassins also stimulated writers, poets, and dramatists to examine the human condition. Perhaps no period in the history of the West produced so many great works of literature as the late sixteenth and early seventeenth centuries.

# The French Wars of Religion

When King Henry II (r. 1547–1559) of France died unexpectedly from a jousting accident, he left behind his widow, the formidable Catherine de Médicis (1519–1589), and a brood of young children—including his heir, Francis II (r. 1559–1560), who was only 15. Henry II had been a peacemaker. He succeeded in keeping France from civil war by carefully pacifying the quarrelsome nobles of the realm, and at the Peace of Cateau-Cambrésis (1559) he finally ended more than sixty years of war with Spain. In contrast, Catherine and her children, including three sons who successively ascended to the throne, utterly failed to keep the peace, and for some forty years France was torn apart by a series of desperate civil wars.

### The Huguenots:
### The French Calvinist Community
By 1560 Calvinism had made significant inroads into predominantly Catholic France. Pastors sent from Geneva had been especially successful in the larger provincial towns, where their evangelical message appealed to enterprising

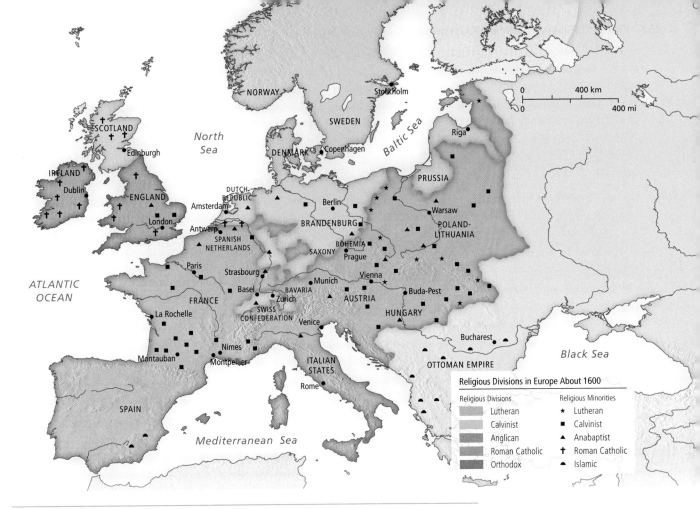

**Map 14.2  Religious Divisions in Europe About 1600**
After 1555 the religious borders of Europe became relatively fixed, with only minor changes in confessional affiliations to this day.

merchants, professionals, and skilled artisans. One in ten of the French had become Calvinists, or Huguenots° as French Protestants were called. The political strength of the Huguenots was greater than their numbers might indicate, because between one-third and one-half of the lower nobility professed Calvinism. Calvinism was popular among the French nobility for two reasons. One involved the imitation of social superiors. The financial well-being of any noble depended on his patron, an aristocrat of higher rank who had access to the king and who could distribute jobs and lands to his clients. When a high aristocrat converted to Protestantism, he tended to bring into the new faith as well his noble clientele, who converted through loyalty to their patron or through the patron's ability to persuade those who were financially dependent on him. As a result of a few aristocratic conversions in southwest France, Calvinism spread through "a veritable religious spider's web,"[3] as one contemporary put it.

Even more important than networks of male patrons was the influence of aristocratic women. The sister of King Francis I of France (r. 1515–1547), Marguerite of

Angoulême (1492–1549), married the King of Navarre (an independent kingdom situated between France and Spain) and created a haven in Navarre for Huguenot preachers and theologians. Her example drew other aristocratic ladies to the Huguenot cause, and many of the Huguenot leaders during the French Wars of Religion were the sons and grandsons of these early female converts. Marguerite's daughter, Jeanne d'Albret, sponsored Calvinist preachers for several years before she publicly announced her own conversion in 1560, and her son, Henry Bourbon, became the principal leader of the Huguenot cause during the French Wars of Religion° and the person responsible for eventually bringing the wars to an end.

## The Origins of the Religious Wars
Like all civil wars, the French Wars of Religion exhibited a bewildering pattern of intrigue, betrayal, and treachery. Three distinct groups constituted the principal players. The first group was the royal family, consisting of Queen Catherine de Médicis and her four sons by Henry II—King Francis II (r. 1559–1560), King Charles IX (r. 1560–1574),

King Henry III (r. 1574–1589), and Duke Francis of Alençon (1554–1584)—and her daughter, Marguerite Valois (1553–1615). The royal family remained Catholic but on occasion reconciled themselves with the Huguenot opposition, and Marguerite married into it. The second group was the Huguenot faction of nobles led by the Châtillon family and the Bourbon family who ruled Navarre. The third group was the hard-line Catholic faction led by the implacable Guise family. These three groups vied for supremacy during the successive reigns of Catherine de Médicis's three sons, none of whom proved to be effective monarchs.

During the reign of the sickly and immature Francis II, the Catholic Guise family dominated the government and raised the persecution of the Huguenots to a new level. In response to that persecution, a group of Protestant nobles plotted in 1560 against the Guises, and some Calvinist ministers provided scriptural justifications for vengeance against tyrants. The Guises got wind of a conspiracy to kill them and surprised the plotters as they arrived in small groups at the royal chateau of Amboise. Some were ambushed, some drowned in the Loire River, and some hanged from the balconies of the chateau's courtyard. A tense two years later in 1562, the Duke of Guise was passing through the village of Vassy just as a large congregation of Protestants was holding services in a barn. The duke's men attacked the worshipers, killing some 740 of them and wounding hundreds of others.

Following the massacre at Vassy, civil war broke out in earnest. For nearly forty years a series of religious wars sapped the strength of France. Most of the battles were indecisive, which meant neither side sustained military superiority for long. Both sides relied for support on their regional bases: The Protestant strength was in the southwest, the Catholic in Paris and the north. Besides military engagements, the French Wars of Religion were characterized by political assassinations and massacres.

## Massacre of St. Bartholomew's Day

After a decade of bloody yet inconclusive combat, the royal family tried to resolve the conflict by making peace with the Protestants, a shift of policy signified by the announcement of the engagement of Marguerite Valois, daughter of Henry II and Catherine de Médicis, to Henry Bourbon, the son of the Huguenot King of Navarre. At age 19, Marguerite—or Queen Margot, as she was known—was already renowned for her brilliant intelligence. But she was renowned also for her wanton morals, and to complicate the situation further, on the eve of the wedding she was having an affair with another Henry, the young new Duke of Guise who was the leader of the intransigent Catholic faction. The marriage between Marguerite and Henry of Navarre was to take place in Paris in August 1572, an event that brought all the Huguenot leaders to the heavily armed Catholic capital for the first time in many years. The gathering of all their ene-

mies in one place presented too great a temptation for the Guises, who hatched a plot to assassinate the Huguenot leaders. Perhaps because she had become jealous of the Huguenots' growing influence on her son, King Charles IX, the mercurial Catherine suddenly switched sides and became implicated in the plot.

Catherine somehow convinced the weak-willed king to order the massacre of the Huguenot nobles gathered in Paris. On August 14, 1572, St. Bartholomew's Day, the people of Paris began a slaughter. Between 3,000 and 4,000 Huguenots were butchered in Paris and more than 20,000 were put to death throughout the rest of France. Henry of Navarre saved his life by pretending to convert to Catholicism, while most of his companions were murdered.

St. Bartholomew's Day Massacre (1572)

## DOCUMENT

### The St. Bartholomew's Day Massacre: Painful Memories

*The Duke of Sully (1560–1641) became an ambassador and finance minister for French King Henry IV and was the principal architect of the Edict of Nantes, which provided a measure of religious toleration for Protestants in France after 1589. During the St. Bartholomew's Day massacre he was 12 years old, but he never forgot what he witnessed. Sully was one of the few members of Henry of Navarre's personal entourage to survive the massacre.*

Intending on that day to wait upon the king my master [Henry of Navarre, later King Henry IV of France], I went to bed early on the preceding evening; about three in the morning I was awakened by the cries of people, and; the alarm-bells, which were everywhere ringing.... I was determined to escape to the College de Bourgogne, and to effect this I put on my scholar's gown, and taking a book under my arm, I set out. In the streets I met three parties of the Life-guards; the first of these, after handling me very roughly, seized my book, and, most fortunately for me, seeing it was a Roman Catholic prayer-book, suffered me to proceed, and this served me as a passport with the two other parties. As I went along I saw the houses broken open and plundered, and men, women, and children butchered, while a constant cry was kept up of, "Kill! Kill! O you Huguenots! O you Huguenots!" This made me very impatient to gain the college, where, through God's assistance, I at length arrived, without suffering any other injury than a most dreadful fright.

Source: From "The Saint Bartholomew's Day Massacre" in Bayle St. John, ed., *Memoirs of the Duke of Sully, Vol. 1* (London: George Bell and Sons, 1877).

**St. Bartholomew's Day Massacre**
This Protestant painter, François Dubois, depicted the merciless slaughter of Protestant men, women, and children in the streets of Paris in 1572. The massacre was the most bloody and infamous in the French Wars of Religion and created a lasting memory of atrocity.

After the massacre of St. Bartholomew's Day, both sides tried to interpret the events to their own advantage. Catholics celebrated. The pope marked the occasion by having a medal struck and frescoes painted in the Vatican. King Philip II of Spain wrote that the massacre "was indeed of such value and prudence and of such service, glory, and honor to God and universal benefit to all Christendom that to hear of it was for me the best and most cheerful news which at present could come to me."[4] For Catholics the massacre was a great service to God. Protestants had a very different reaction, and presented it as a great affront to God.

Catherine's attempted solution for the Huguenot problem failed to solve anything, however. Henry of Navarre escaped his virtual imprisonment in the royal household, set Marguerite up in an isolated castle, returned to Navarre and his faith, and reinvigorated Huguenot resistance. Two Huguenot political thinkers laid out a theory justifying po-

litical revolution: François Hotman in *Francogallia* (1573) and Théodore de Bèze in *Right of Magistrates* (1579). They argued that because the authority of all magistrates, including even low-ranking nobles, came directly from God, the Huguenot nobles had the right and obligation to resist a tyrannical Catholic king. During the same period, Catholic moderates known as the *politiques* rejected the excesses of the Guises and argued for an accommodation with the Huguenots.

The wars of religion continued until the assassination of King Henry III, brother of the late Charles IX. Both Charles and Henry had been childless, a situation that made Henry Bourbon of Navarre the rightful heir to the throne, even though he was a Huguenot. Henry Bourbon became King Henry IV (r. 1589–1610) and recognized that predominantly Catholic France would never accept a Huguenot king, and so in 1593 with his famous quip, "Paris is worth a mass," Henry reconverted to the ancient faith, and most opposition to him among Catholics collapsed. Once he returned to Catholicism he managed to have the pope annul his childless marriage to Marguerite so that he could marry Marie de' Medici and obtain her huge dowry. Affable, witty, generous, and exceedingly tolerant, "Henry the Great" became the most popular king in French history, reuniting the war-torn country by ruling with a very firm hand. With the Edict of Nantes° of 1598, he allowed the Huguenots to build a quasi state within the state, giving them the right to have their own troops, church organization, and political autonomy within their walled towns, but they were banned from the royal court and the city of Paris.

Henry encouraged economic development under his minister the Duke of Sully, who retired the crushing state debt and built up a fiscal surplus by reforming finances and eliminating corruption. Henry declared that his ambition was for even the poorest peasant to be able to afford a chicken in his pot every Sunday, and even though he did not achieve this laudatory goal, his public works included the beautification of Paris and an impressive canal system to facilitate transportation.

Despite his enormous popularity, Henry too fell victim to fanaticism. After surviving eighteen attempts on his life, in 1610 the king was fatally stabbed by a Catholic fanatic, who took advantage of the opportunity presented when the royal coach unexpectedly stopped behind a cart loading hay. Unlike the aftermath of the St. Bartholomew's Day massacre, Catholics all over France mourned Henry's death and considered the assassin mad. Henry's brilliant conciliatory nature and the horrors of the religious wars had tempered public opinion.

## Philip II, His Most Catholic Majesty

France's greatest rivals were the Habsburgs, who possessed vast territories in the Holy Roman Empire, controlled the elections for emperor, and had dynastic rights to the throne of Spain. As archenemies of the Protestant Reformation, they had regularly helped finance the Catholic cause during the French Wars of Religion. During the late sixteenth century, Habsburg Spain took advantage of French weakness to establish itself as the dominant power in Europe. When Emperor Charles V (who had been both Holy Roman Emperor and king of Spain) abdicated his thrones in 1556, the Habsburg possessions in the Holy Roman Empire and the emperorship went to his brother, Ferdinand I, and the balance of his vast domain to his son, Philip II (r. 1556–1598). Philip's inheritance included Milan, Naples, Sicily, the Netherlands, scattered outposts on the north coast of Africa, colonies in the Caribbean, Central America, Mexico, Peru, the Philippines, and most important of all, Spain. In 1580 he also inherited Portugal and its far-flung overseas empire, which included a line of trading posts from West Africa to the Spice Islands and the vast colony of unexplored Brazil.

Ruling over these enormous territories was a gargantuan task that Philip undertook with obsessive seriousness. From the rambling palace of El Escorial, which was also a mausoleum for his father and a monastery, Philip lived in semimonastic seclusion and ruled as the "King of Paper," an office-bound bureaucrat rather than the rule-from-the-saddle warrior his father had been and many of his contemporary monarchs remained. Philip kept himself to a rigid daily work discipline that included endless committee meetings and long hours devoted to poring over as many as 400 documents a day, which he annotated extensively in his crabbed hand. Because of his inability to delegate authority and his immersion in minutiae, Philip tended to lose his grasp of the larger picture, especially the shaky finances of Spain.

This grave, distrustful, rigid man saw himself as the great protector of the Catholic cause and committed Spain to perpetual hostility toward Muslims and Protestants. On the Muslim front he first bullied the Moriscos, the descendants of the Spanish Muslims. The Moriscos had received Christian baptism, but they were suspected of secretly practicing Islam, and in 1568 Philip issued an edict that banned all manifestations of Muslim culture and ordered the Moriscos to turn over their children to Christian priests to educate. The outraged Moriscos of Granada rebelled but were soundly defeated. At first dispersed throughout Spain, the surviving Moriscos were eventually expelled from the country in 1609. Philip hardened his policy toward the Moriscos because he feared, not unreasonably, that they would become secret agents on Spanish soil for his great Mediterranean rivals, the Ottoman Turks. To counter the Turkish threat, Philip maintained expensive fortresses on the North African coast. In 1571 he joined the Venetians and the pope to check Turkish advances after the Ottomans captured Cyprus, Venice's richest colony. The Christian victory at Lepanto in the Gulf of Corinth, which destroyed more than one-third of the enemy's fleet, was heralded as one of the greatest events of the sixteenth century, proving that the Turks could be beaten. Lepanto renewed the crusading spirit in the Catholic world. Although the victory at Lepanto was a valuable propaganda tool, it had slight military significance because the Turks quickly rebuilt their fleet and forced Venice to cede Cyprus to them. The island remains divided between Christian and Muslim populations to this day.

Philip once said he would rather lose all his possessions and die a hundred times than be the king of heretics. His attitude toward Protestants showed that he meant what he said. Through his marriage to Queen Mary I of England (r. 1553–1558), Philip encouraged her persecutions of Protestants, but they got their revenge. After Mary's death her half-sister, Queen Elizabeth I, refused his marriage proposal and in 1577 signed a treaty to assist the Protestant Netherlands, which was in rebellion against Spain. To add insult to injury, the English privateer Sir Francis Drake (ca. 1540–1596) conducted a personal war against Catholic Spain by raiding the Spanish convoys bringing silver from the New World. In 1587 Drake's embarrassing successes culminated with a daring raid on the great Spanish port city of Cadiz, where, "singeing the king of Spain's beard," he destroyed the anchored Spanish fleet and many thousands of tons of vital supplies. Philip retaliated by building a huge fleet of 132 ships armed with 3,165 cannons, which sailed from Portugal to rendezvous with the Spanish army stationed in the Netherlands and launch an invasion of England in 1588. As the Invincible Armada, as it was called, passed through the English Channel, it was met by a much smaller English fleet, assembled out of merchant ships refit for battle. Unable to maneuver as effectively as the English in the fluky winds of the channel and mauled by the rapid-firing

DOCUMENT

John Hawkins Reports on the Spanish Armada (1588)

## Defeat of the Spanish Armada

The smaller English ships on the left outmaneuvered the Spanish Armada arrayed in the formal curved line of galleons in the middle.

English guns, the Spanish Armada° suffered heavy losses and was forced to retreat to the north, where it sustained further losses in storms off the coast of Scotland and Ireland. Barely more than half of the fleet finally straggled home. The defeat severely shook Philip's sense of invincibility.

The reign of Philip II illustrated better than any other the contradictions and tensions of the era. No monarch had at his grasp as many resources and territories as Philip, and yet defending them proved extremely costly. The creaky governmental machinery of Spain put a tremendous burden on a conscientious king such as Philip, but even his unflagging energy and dedication to his duties could not prevent military defeat and financial disaster. Economic historians remember Philip's reign for its series of state bankruptcies and for the loss of the Dutch provinces in the Netherlands, the most precious jewel in the crown of Spain.

## The Dutch Revolt

The Netherlands boasted some of Europe's richest cities, situated amid a vast network of lakes, rivers, channels, estuaries, and tidal basins that periodically replenished the exceptionally productive soil through flooding. The Netherlands consisted of seventeen provinces, each with its own distinctive identity, traditions, and even language. The southern provinces were primarily French-speaking; those in the north spoke a bewildering variety of Flemish dialects. In 1548 Emperor Charles V annexed the northern provinces that had been part of the Holy Roman Empire to the southern provinces he had inherited from his father. His decision meant that when his son, Philip II, became king of Spain, all of the Netherlands was included with the Spanish crown. With his characteristic bureaucratic mentality, Philip treated Dutch affairs as a management problem rather than a political sore spot, an attitude that subordinated the Netherlands to Spanish interests. Foreign rule irritated the Dutch, who had long enjoyed ancient privileges including the right to raise their own taxes and muster their own troops.

Consolidating the Netherlands under the Spanish crown deprived the Dutch princes of the right to chose the official religion of their lands, a right they would have enjoyed had the provinces remained in the Holy Roman Empire, where the Religious Peace of Augsburg granted princes religious freedom. Philip's harsh attitude toward Protestants upset the Netherlands' delicate balance among Catholic, Lutheran, Calvinist, and Anabaptist communities. Huguenot refugees from the French Wars of Religion heightened the anti-Catholic fanaticism of the local Calvinists, who in 1566 occupied many Catholic churches and destroyed paintings and statues.

In response to the rapidly deteriorating situation in the Netherlands, Philip issued edicts against the heretics and strengthened the Spanish Inquisition. The Inquisition in Spain was an arm of the monarchy charged with ensuring religious conformity among the extremely diverse cultures of the Iberian peninsula. The Spanish Inquisition had been preoccupied with investigating the Christian sincerity of former Jews, who after the expulsions of 1492 had converted to Christianity in order to stay in Spain. When introduced in the Netherlands, the Inquisition became an investigating agency devoted to finding, interrogating, and, if necessary, punishing Protestants. Philip also dispatched 20,000 Spanish troops under the command of the Duke of Alba (1508–1582), a veteran of the Turkish campaigns in North Africa and victories over the Lutheran princes in the Holy Roman Empire. Alba directly attacked the Protestants. He personally presided over the military court, the Council of Troubles, which became so notoriously tyrannical that the people called it the Council of Blood. As an example to others, he systematically razed several small villages where there had been incidents of desecrating Catholic images, slaughtering every inhabitant. Alba himself boasted that during the campaign against the rebels, he had 18,000 people executed, in addition to those who died in battle or were massacred by soldiers. The Prince of Orange, William the

Silent (1533–1584), accompanied into exile some 60,000 refugees, who constituted about 2 percent of the population. While abroad William began to organize resistance to Alba.

Alba's cruelty backfired by steeling Protestant opposition to the Spanish. Alba also lost support among otherwise loyal Catholics when he attempted to introduce a 10 percent tax on trade. His policies a failure, Alba was recalled to Spain in 1573. Meanwhile the sea-beggars, as the Dutch Calvinist privateers were called, had begun to achieve some success against the Spanish. Within a few short years, William the Silent seized permanent control of the provinces of Holland and Zealand, which were then flooded by Calvinist refugees from the southern provinces. After Alba's departure, no one kept control of the unpaid Spanish soldiers, who in mutinous rage turned against cities loyal to Spain, including Brussels, Ghent, and most savagely Antwerp, the rich center of trade. Antwerp lost 7,000 citizens and one-third of its houses to the "Spanish fury," which permanently destroyed its prosperity. Alba's replacement, the shrewd statesman and general the Duke of Parma (r. 1578–1592), ultimately subdued the southern provinces, which remained a Spanish colony. The seven northern provinces, however, united in 1579 and declared independence from Spain in 1581 (see Map 14.3). William the Silent became the *stadholder* (governor) of the new United Provinces, and after his assassination his 17-year-old son, Maurice of Nassau, inherited the same title.

The Netherlands' struggle for independence transformed the population of the northern provinces from mixed religions to staunch Calvinism. The Dutch Revolt°

**Map 14.3   The Netherlands During the Dutch Revolt, ca. 1580**

During the late sixteenth century the northern United Provinces separated from the Spanish Netherlands. The independence of the United Provinces was not recognized by the other European powers until 1648.

became ensnared in the French Wars of Religion through Huguenot refugees, and the alliance with England, which provided much-needed financial and moral support, reinforced the Protestant identity of the Dutch. The international Protestant alliance created by the Dutch Revolt and centered in the Netherlands withstood both Philip's fury and Parma's calm generalship. The failure of the Spanish Armada to land Parma's men in England guaranteed the survival of an independent Netherlands. The Dutch carried on a sporadic and inconclusive war against Spain until the end of the Thirty Years' War in 1648, when the international community recognized the independent Republic of the United Provinces.

## Literature in the Age of Confessional Division

Churches and monarchs everywhere demanded religious conformity in word and deed, a situation that would seem to stifle creativity, and yet the late sixteenth and early seventeenth centuries were one of the most remarkable periods in the history of creative literature. During this period the native or vernacular languages of western Europe became literary languages, replacing Latin as the dominant form of expression, even for the educated elite. Italian was the first vernacular to be prized for its literary qualities and considered a worthy alternative to Latin. The availability of cheap printed books and the Bible reading encouraged by the Protestant Reformation stimulated literature in other vernacular languages so that by the late sixteenth century great literary figures were writing in French, Portuguese, Spanish, and English.

## French Literature During the Religious Turmoil

In France royal decrees in 1520 and 1539 substituted French for Latin in official legal and government documents. A century later with the founding of the Académie Française, it became government policy to promote, protect, and refine the French language. The greatest masters of French prose during this crucial period were François Rabelais (ca. 1483–1553) and Michel de Montaigne (1533–1592). Trained as a lawyer, Rabelais became a friar and priest but left the Church under a cloud of heresy to become a physician. Rabelais's satirical masterpiece, a series of novels recounting the fantastic and grotesque adventures of the giants Gargantua and Pantagruel, combined an encyclopedic command of humanist thought with stunning verbal invention that has had a lasting influence on humorous writers to this day. One of Rabelais's most remarkable creations was the imaginary Abbey of Thélème, inhabited by a kind of antimonastic community of monks and nuns for whom "all their life was regulated not by laws, statutes, or rules, but according to their free will and pleasure." This was an abbey for hedonists who lived by the motto, "DO WHAT YOU WILL, because people who are free, well-born, well-bred, and easy in honest company have a natural spur and instinct which drives them to virtuous deeds and deflects them from vice."[5] Rabelais's optimistic vision of human nature represented a startling contrast to the growing anxiety provoked by the religious controversies of his time. Rabelais's controversial work was banned, and he was briefly forced into exile.

It is ironic that Montaigne became a master of French prose. His mother was a Catholic of Spanish-Jewish origins, and the young Michel spoke only Latin for the first six years of his life because his German tutor knew no French. After a modestly successful legal career, Montaigne retired to the family chateau to discover himself by writing essays, a literary form well suited to reflective introspection. In his essays, Montaigne struggled with his lasting grief over the premature death from dysentery of a close friend, reflected on his own experience of the intense physical pain of illness, and diagnosed the absurd causes of the French Wars of Religion. Montaigne's essays are a profound series of

## Men Are the Source of the Epidemic of Violence

*Lucrezia Marinella (1571–1653) was a brilliant, well-educated intellectual who wrote passionately on moral issues of the day. Her masterpiece was* The Nobility and Excellence of Women, and the Defects and Vices of Men, *first published in 1600. The book was an answer to the alleged defects of women in which she argued that morally and in many other ways women are superior to men. Marinella depicts violence as the product of male swagger and feelings of insecurity. She contrasts male bluster with women's use of cosmetics. If women were in charge, she implies, the civil wars and violence of the age would be quickly resolved.*

Since beauty is women's special gift from the Supreme Hand, should she not seek to guard it with all diligence? And when she is endowed with but a small amount of that excellent quality, should she not seek to embellish it by every means possible, provided it is not ignoble? I certainly believe that it is so. When man has some special gift such as physical strength, which enables him to perform as a gladiator or swagger around, as is the common usage, does he not seek to conserve it? If he were born courageous, would he not seek to augment his natural courage with the art of defense? But if he were born with little courage would he not practice the martial arts and cover himself with plate and mail and constantly seek out duels and fights in order to demonstrate his courage rather than reveal his true timidity and cowardice?

I have used this example because of the impossibility of finding a man who does not swagger and play the daredevil. If there is such a one people call him effeminate, which is why we always see men dressed up like soldiers with weapons at their belts, bearded and menacing, and walking in a way that they think will frighten everyone. Often they wear gloves of mail and contrive for their weapons to clink under their clothing so people realize they are armed and ready for combat and feel intimidated by them.

What are all these things but artifice and tinsel? Under these trappings of courage and valor hide the cowardly souls of rabbits or hunted hares, and it is the same with all their other artifices. Since men behave in this way, why should not those women who are born less beautiful than the rest hide their less fortunate attributes and seek to augment the little beauty they possess through artifice, provided it is not offensive?

Source: From Lucrezia Marinella, *The Nobility and Excellence of Women, and the Defects and Vices of Men,* edited and translated by Anne Dunhill, Chicago: University of Chicago Press, 1999, pp. 166–67.

meditations on the meaning of life and death, presented in a calm voice of reason to an age of violent fanaticism. In one essay, for example, he exposed the presumption of human beings: "The most vulnerable and frail of all creatures is man, and at the same time the most arrogant." Montaigne thought it presumptuous that human beings picked themselves out as God's favorite creatures. How did they know they were superior to other animals? "When I play with my cat, who knows if I am not a pastime to her more than she is to me?"[6] His own skepticism about religion insulated him from the sometimes violent passions of his era.

## Stirrings of the Golden Age in Iberia

The literary tradition in the Iberian peninsula differed from that of other regions in Europe in that Iberia is a polyglot region in which several languages are spoken—Basque, Galician, Portuguese, Castilian, and Catalan. The greatest lyric poet of the peninsula, Luís Vaz de Camões (1524–1580), lost an eye in battle and was sent to the Portuguese East Indies after he killed a royal official in a street brawl. When he returned years later, he completed his epic poem *The Lusiads* (1572), which became the national poem of Portugal by celebrating Vasco da Gama's discovery of the sea route to India. This great work was modeled on the ancient epics, especially the *Aeneid*, the greatest Latin epic of ancient Rome, and even included the gods of Olympus as commentators on the human events of Camões's time. In the opening lines, Jupiter spoke of contemporary Portugal:

> *Eternal dwellers in the starry heavens, you will not have forgotten the great valor of that brave people the Portuguese. You cannot therefore be unaware that it is the fixed resolve of destiny that before their achievements those of Assyrians, Persians, Greeks and Romans shall fade into oblivion. Already with negligible forces— you were witnesses—they have expelled the Moslem, for all his strength and numbers . . . while against the redoubtable Castilians they have invariably had heaven on their side. Always, in a word, they have known victory in battle and have reaped, with its trophies, fame and glory too.[7]*

By connecting Portugal directly to the glories of the ancient empires, Camões managed to elevate the adventures of his fellow Portuguese in Asia to an important moment in the history of the world.

Because Spain was unified around the crown of Castile, the Castilian language became the language we now call Spanish. The period when Spain was the dominant power in Europe coincided with the Golden Age of Spanish literature. The greatest literary figure was Miguel de Cervantes Saavedra (1547–1616), an impoverished son of an unsuccessful doctor with little formal education. Like Camões, Cervantes survived many adventures, losing the use of his left hand at the naval battle of Lepanto and spending five years languishing in a Turkish prison after he was captured by Algerian pirates. In order to survive, the disabled veteran

was forced to write plays for the Madrid theater and to work as a tax collector, but he was still imprisoned several times for debts. Desperate to make money, Cervantes published a serial novel in installments between 1605 and 1615. It became the greatest masterpiece in Spanish literature, *Don Quixote*.

The prototype of the modern novel form, *Don Quixote* was a satire of chivalric romances. Cervantes presented reality on two levels, the "poetic truth" of the master and dreamer Don Quixote and the "historic truth" of his squire and realist Sancho Panza. Don Quixote's imagination persistently ran away with him as he tilted at windmills, believing they were fierce dragons. It remained to Sancho Panza to point out the unheroic truth. Cervantes pursued the interaction between these two incongruous views of truth as a philosophical commentary on existence. For Cervantes there was no single, objective truth, only psychological truths revealed through the interaction of the characters, an idea that contrasted with the notion of dogmatic religious truth that dominated the time. Despite the extensive popularity of *Don Quixote*, Cervantes died a pauper, buried in an unmarked grave in Madrid.

## The Elizabethan Renaissance

During the reign of Elizabeth I (r. 1558–1603), the Renaissance truly arrived in England. The daughter of Henry VIII and Anne Boleyn, Elizabeth faced terrible insecurity as a girl. Her father had her mother beheaded, she was declared illegitimate, and her sister Mary imprisoned her for treason in the Tower of London. After she ascended to the throne in 1558, however, she proved to be a brilliant leader. She prevented the kind of religious civil wars that broke out in France by establishing a moderate form of Protestantism as the official religion. She presided over the beginnings of England's rise as a major European power. Perhaps most remarkably, she became the patron and inspiration for England's greatest age of literature. Never married, Elizabeth used her eligibility for marriage as a lure in diplomacy, and even though she may have had real lovers, she addressed her subjects as if they were her only love. Her "golden speech" delivered before a troublesome House of Commons in 1601 exemplifies her ability to inspire exuberant loyalty:

> *Though God hath raised me high, yet this I account the glory of my crown, that I have reigned with your loves. . . . It is not my desire to live or reign longer than my life and reign shall be for your good. And though you have had, and may have, many mightier and wiser princes sitting in this seat, yet you never had, nor shall have any that will love you better.[8]*

Among Elizabeth's courtiers were major literary figures, including the adventurer-poet Sir Walter Raleigh (ca. 1552–1618), the soldier-poet Sir Philip Sidney (1554–1586), and Edmund Spenser (ca. 1552–1599), whose great poem *The Faerie Queen* was a personal tribute to Elizabeth.

**Queen Elizabeth I of England**
Elizabeth presided over the greatest age of English literature.

The principal figure of the Elizabethan Renaissance, however, was not a courtier but a professional dramatist, William Shakespeare (1564–1616). In a series of theaters, including the famous Globe on the south side of the Thames in London, Shakespeare wrote, produced, and acted in comedies, tragedies, and history plays. Shakespeare's enormous output of plays, some of which made veiled allusions to the politics of Elizabeth's court, established him not only as the most popular dramatist of his time but the greatest literary figure in the English language. The power of his plays derives from the subtle understanding of human psychology found in his characters and the stunning force of his language. For Shakespeare, as for Montaigne, the source of true knowledge was self-knowledge. One character advises,

> Neither a borrower nor a lender be,
> For loan oft loses both itself and friend
> And borrowing dulls the edge of husbandry.
> This above all: To thine own self be true,
> And it must follow, as the night the day,
> Thou canst not then be false to any man.
> (Hamlet I, iii, 75–80)

Unlike most contemporary authors, Shakespeare wrote for a broad audience of paying theatergoers that included common workers as well as highly educated members of Elizabeth's court. This need to appeal to a large audience who gave instant feedback helped him hone his skills as a dramatist.

Some of these literary figures found their works banned, as did Rabelais. Some had political or personal troubles with their monarch, as did Montaigne, Camões, Raleigh, and Sidney. But the controversies of the day seemed to have stimulated rather than inhibited these writers. Political and religious turmoil led them to ask penetrating questions about the meaning of life and to rise above the petty squabbles that preoccupied so many of their contemporaries.

# States and Confessions in Eastern Europe

■ How did the countries of eastern Europe during the late sixteenth century become enmeshed in the religious controversies that began in western Europe during the early part of the century?

In contrast to the confessional states of western Europe where rulers demanded religious conformity, the weak states of eastern Europe during the early sixteenth century were less successful in linking religious conformity to political loyalty. Whereas in the West the religious controversies stimulated writers to investigate deeply the human condition but made them cautious about expressing nonconforming religious opinions, writers and creative people in the East during this period were able to explore a wide range of ideas in a relatively tolerant atmosphere. Bohemia and Poland, in particular, allowed levels of religious diversity unheard of in the West. During the last decades of the sixteenth century and early decades of the seventeenth, however, dynastic troubles compromised the relative openness of the eastern states, enmeshing them in conflicts among themselves that had an increasingly strong religious dimension. In the Holy Roman Empire, the weakness of the mad Emperor Rudolf permitted religious conflicts to fester, setting the stage for the disastrous Thirty Years' War (1618–1648) that pitted Catholic and Protestant princes against one another.

Around the Baltic Sea, rivalries among Lutheran Sweden, Catholic Poland-Lithuania, and Orthodox Russia created a state of almost permanent war in a tense standoff among three very different political and religious states. The enormous confederation of Poland-Lithuania struggled to sustain the most decentralized, religiously diverse state anywhere in Europe. By the end of the century, it remained politically decentralized but had become an active theater of the Catholic Reformation where dynastic policy firmly supported the Roman Church. Russia began to strengthen itself from obscurity under the authoritarian rule of the tsars, who began to transform it into a major European power.

## The Dream World of Emperor Rudolf

In Goethe's *Faust*, set in sixteenth-century Germany, drinkers in a tavern sing:

> *The dear old Holy Roman Empire,*
> *How does it hang together?*[9]

Good question. How did this peculiarly decentralized state—neither holy, nor Roman, nor an empire—hang together? In the late sixteenth century the empire consisted of the following components: 1 emperor; 7 electors, comprising 4 secular princes and 3 archbishops; 50 other bishops and archbishops; 21 dukes, margraves, and landgraves; 88 independent abbots and assorted prelates of the Church; 178 counts and other sovereign lords; about 80 free imperial cities; and hundreds of free imperial knights. The emperor presided over all, and the Imperial Diet served as a parliament, but the Holy Roman Empire was, in fact, a very loose confederation of semi-independent, mostly German-speaking states, many of which ignored imperial decrees that did not suit them. During the first half of the sixteenth century the empire faced a number of challenges—the turmoil within the empire created by Lutheranism, endless French enmity on the western borders, and the tenacious Ottoman threat on the eastern frontier. Only the universal vision and firm hand of Emperor Charles V kept the empire together. The universal vision and firm hand disappeared in the succeeding generations of emperors, to be replaced by petty dynastic squabbles and infirm minds.

The crippling weakness of the imperial system became most evident during the reign of Rudolf II (r. 1576–1612).

The Habsburg line had a strain of insanity going back to Joanna "The Mad," the mother of Emperors Charles V (r. 1519–1558) and Ferdinand I (r. 1558–1564), who happened to be Rudolf's two grandfathers, giving him a double dose of Habsburg genes. Soon after his election to the imperial throne, Rudolf moved his court from bustling Vienna to the lovely quiet of Prague in Bohemia. Fearful of noisy crowds and impatient courtiers, standoffish toward foreign ambassadors who presented him with difficult decisions, paranoid about scheming relatives, and prone to wild emotional gyrations from deep depression to manic grandiosity, Rudolf was hardly suited for the imperial throne. In fact, many contemporaries, who had their own reasons to underrate him, described him as hopelessly insane. Rudolf certainly suffered from moments of profound melancholy and irrational fears that may have had genetic or organic causes, but he was probably unhinged by the conundrum of being the emperor, a position that trapped him between the glorious universal imperial ideal and the ignoble reality of unscrupulous relatives and petty rivalries.

Rudolf was not the only sixteenth-century prince in the Holy Roman Empire driven to distraction by the pressures of court life. At least twenty German princes and princesses were confined or deposed due to symptoms of serious mental disorder. Certainly inbreeding within a small pool of princely families contributed to the patterns of madness, but the most unhealthy emotional pressure was produced by the code of manners required of all courtiers, most particularly princes and princesses. This strictly maintained code demanded the repression of all spontaneous feelings, a repression that resulted in a prevailing sense of shame. When religious rigidity and extreme political conflict were mixed into this volatile psychological concoction, it is not surprising that some personalities shattered. Because the entire political system depended on the prince's guidance, a mad prince could seriously disrupt an entire society.

Incapable of governing, Rudolf transmuted the imperial ideal of universality into a strange dream world. In Prague he gathered around him a brilliant court of humanists, musicians, painters, physicians, astronomers, astrologers, alchemists, and magicians. These included an eclectic assortment of significant thinkers—the great astronomers Tycho Brahe and Johannes Kepler, the notorious occult philosopher Giordano Bruno, the theoretical mathematician and astrologer John Dee, and the remarkable inventor of surrealist painting Giuseppe Arcimboldo. Many of these figures are considered the immediate forerunners of the Scientific Revolution, but Rudolf also fell prey to fast-talking charlatans. These included the illusionist and opera-set designer Cornelius Drebber, who claimed to have invented a perpetual-motion machine. This weird court, however, was less the strange fruit of the emperor's hopeless dementia than the manifestation of a striving for universal empire. Rudolf sought to preserve the cultural and political unity of the

**The Strange Court of Emperor Rudolf II**
Among the many creative people in the Emperor Rudolf's court was the Italian surrealist painter Giuseppe Arcimboldo, who specialized in creating images out of fruits, vegetables, flowers, and animals. This is a portrait of the Emperor Rudolf.

empire, to eradicate religious divisions, and to achieve peace at home. Rudolf's court in Prague was perhaps the only place left during the late sixteenth century where Protestants, Catholics, Jews, and even radical heretics such as Bruno could gather together in a common intellectual enterprise. The goal of such gatherings was to discover the universal principles that governed nature, principles that would provide the foundations for a single unifying religion and a cure for all human maladies. It was a noble, if utterly improbable, dream.

While Rudolf and his favorite courtiers isolated themselves in their dream world, the religious conflicts within the empire reached a boiling point. Without a strong emperor, the Imperial Diets were paralyzed by confessional squabbles. In 1607 in the imperial free city of Donauworth in south Germany, a conflict between the Lutheran town council and the substantial Catholic minority gave the Catholic Duke of Bavaria the excuse to annex the city to his own territories. Despite the illegality of the duke's action,

Rudolf passively acquiesced, causing fear among German Protestants that the principles of the Religious Peace of Augsburg of 1555 might be ignored. In the following decade, more than 200 religious revolts or riots took place. In 1609 the insane Duke John William of Jülich-Cleves died without a direct heir, and the most suitable claimants to the Catholic duchy were two Lutheran princes. Were one of them to succeed to the dukedom, the balance between Catholics and Protestants in Germany would have been seriously disrupted. Religious tensions boiled over. As Chapter 15 will describe, in less than a decade the empire began to dissolve in what became the Thirty Years' War.

## The Renaissance of Poland-Lithuania

During the late sixteenth and early seventeenth centuries, Poland-Lithuania experienced a remarkable cultural and political renaissance. It was inspired by influences from Renaissance Italy linked to strong commercial and diplomatic ties to the Republic of Venice and intellectual connections with the University of Padua. As the major power in eastern Europe, Poland-Lithuania engaged in a tug-of-war with Sweden over control of the eastern Baltic and virtually constant warfare against the expansionist ambitions of Russia (see Map 14.4). The most remarkable achievement of Poland-Lithuania during this contentious time was its unparalleled and still controversial experiments in government. Poland-Lithuania had an elected king but called itself a republic. The king was a figurehead, and Poland-Lithuania was a republic in the sense that it was effectively governed by assemblies of nobles.

Very loosely joined since 1336, Poland and Lithuania created a constitutional union in 1569, creating a confederation in which Poland supplied the king, but the Grand Duchy of Lithuania was considered an equal partner and allowed to retain its own laws, administration, and army. The novel feature of the confederation was how the nobles reserved power for themselves through their control of regional assemblies, which in turn dominated the central parliament called the Sejm. These nobles elected the king and treated him, at best, as a hired manager. They resisted all attempts to exert royal power by asserting the legal right to form local armed assemblies against the king and by exercising the principle of unanimity in the Sejm, which prevented the king or a strong faction from dominating affairs. In the last half of the seventeenth century Poland-Lithuania fell into chaos under this system, but for nearly three-quarters of a century it worked well enough—at least for the nobles.

The rule of the nobles in Poland-Lithuania came at a great cost to the Polish peasants, however, who were ruthlessly forced into serfdom and deprived of their legal rights.

Peasants were prohibited from leaving the land without permission from their landlords, and they were denied the ability to appeal the legal judgments of their local lords. In this regard, Poland-Lithuania moved in the opposite direction from western European states, which at this time were extending the right of judicial appeal and allowing serfdom to fade away. Moreover, the Polish kings could not stop the gradual erosion of their authority so that Poland-Lithuania, the greatest power in the East, enfeebled itself through the grasping hands of a notoriously self-interested and proud nobility.

Poland-Lithuania contained an incomparable religious mixture of Roman Catholics, Lutherans, Calvinists, Russian Orthodox, Anabaptists, Unitarians, and Jews, but these communities were strongly divided along geographic and class lines. Lutheranism was a phenomenon of the German-speaking towns, the peasants of Poland remained Catholic, those in Lithuania were Orthodox, and many of the nobles were attracted to Calvinism. During the late sixteenth century, however, Christians in Poland almost completely returned or converted to the Roman Catholic faith. The key to the transformation was the changing attitude of the Polish nobles, who had tolerated religious diversity because they believed that religious liberty was the cornerstone of political liberty. The return to Catholicism owed a great deal to Stanislas Hosius (1504–1579), who had studied in Italy before he returned to Poland to become successively a diplomat, bishop, and cardinal. Imbued with the zeal of the Italian Catholic Reformation, Hosius invited the Society of Jesus into Poland and worked closely with the papal *nuncios* (the diplomatic representatives of the pope), who organized a campaign to combat all forms of Protestantism.

## Map 14.4   Poland-Lithuania and Russia

These countries were the largest in Europe in the size of their territories but were relatively under-populated compared to the western European states.

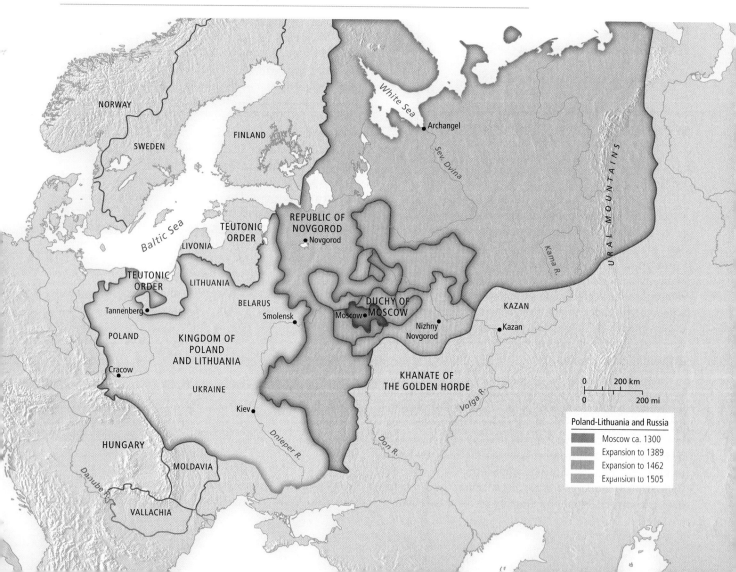

| Poland-Lithuania and Russia |
| --- |
| Moscow ca. 1300 |
| Expansion to 1389 |
| Expansion to 1462 |
| Expansion to 1505 |

Between 1565 and 1586, forty-four young Polish nobles studied at the Jesuit college in Rome and when they returned took up the most influential church and government offices in Poland. Jesuit colleges sprouted up in many Polish towns, attracting the brightest sons of the nobility and urban bourgeoisie. A close alliance between the kings of Poland and the Jesuits enhanced the social prestige of Catholicism.

The cultural appeal of all things Italian helped lure the Polish nobility back to Catholicism. Through the spread of elite education, Catholicism returned to Poland largely through persuasion rather than coercion. But the transformation did not occur without violent repercussions. Lutheran, Calvinist, and Bohemian Brethren churches were burned. In Cracow armed confrontations between Protestant and Catholic militants led to casualties. However, Poland did not degenerate into civil war, as did France or the Netherlands over much the same issues. As the monarchy progressively weakened, the Catholic Church became the only solid institutional pillar of Polish national identity and Polish culture.

## The Troubled Legacy of Ivan the Terrible

While Poland experimented with a decentralized confederation dominated by nobles that severely restricted the king's initiative, Russia evolved in the opposite direction. During the late fifteenth and sixteenth centuries, the grand dukes of Moscow who became the tsars of Russia eclipsed the authority of the great landed nobles and snuffed out the independence of the towns. The authoritarian tendencies of the tsars harmed the Russian peasants, however, just as royal weakness harmed the Polish peasants. After 1454 Moscow's creation of military fiefs (*pomestye*) to supply soldiers against the Tartars (Mongol tribes) allowed the nobles to push the peasants back into serfdom. Refusing to accept enserfment, the peasants fled the fields in massive numbers, depopulating central Russia as they found refuge among the Cossack colonies along the borders to the southeast.

Russia was already well integrated into the European diplomatic community and engaged in trade with its western neighbors. But for more than 300 years Russia had been under the "Tartar Yoke," a term describing the Mongolian tribes that overran the country, pillaging and depopulating it. Ivan III, "The Great" (1462–1505), succeeded in gradually throwing off the Tartar Yoke by refusing to continue to pay tribute to the Mongols. Ivan married Zoë, the niece of the last Greek emperor of Constantinople. The marriage gave him the basis for claiming that the Russian rulers were the heirs of Byzantium and the exclusive protectors of Orthodox Christianity, the state religion of Russia. Following the Byzantine tradition of imperial pomp, Ivan practiced Byzantine court ceremonies, and his advisers developed the theory of the Three Romes. According to this theory, the authority of the ancient Roman Empire had passed first to the Byzantine Empire, which God had punished with the Turkish conquest, and then to Moscow as the third and last "Rome." Ivan celebrated this theory by assuming the title of tsar (or "Caesar"). With his wife's assistance, he hired Italian architects to rebuild the grand ducal palace, the Kremlin. Ivan captured the vast northern territories of the city-state of Novgorod, expanding the Russian state north to the White Sea and east to the Urals. Ivan's invasion of parts of Lithuania embroiled Russia in a protracted conflict with Poland that lasted more than a century. Like his fellow monarchs in western Europe, Ivan began to bring the aristocrats under control by incorporating them into the bureaucracy of the state.

Ivan III's grandson, Ivan IV, "The Terrible" (1533–1584), succeeded his father at age 3 and became the object of innumerable plots, attempted coups, and power struggles among his mother, uncles, and the boyars (the upper-level nobles who dominated Russian society). The trauma of his childhood years and a painful disease of the spine made him inordinately suspicious and prone to acts of impulsive violence. When at age 17 Ivan was crowned, he reduced the power of the dukes and the boyars by forcing them to exchange their hereditary estates for lands that obligated them to serve the tsar in war. In weakening the boyars, Ivan gained considerable support among the common people and was even remembered in popular songs as the people's tsar. Nevertheless, Ivan distrusted everyone. He often arrested people on charges of treason, just for taking a trip abroad. In a cruel revenge on his enemies among the boyars, he began a reign of terror in which he personally committed horrendous atrocities. His massacre in 1570 of the inhabitants of Novgorod, whom he suspected of harboring Polish sympathies, contributed to his reputation as a bloody tyrant. By setting aside half of the realm as his personal domain, he created a strong financial base for the army, which led to military successes in the prolonged wars against Poland-Lithuania and Sweden. During his reign, however, the Polish threat and boyar

---

### CHRONOLOGY

## States and Confessions in Eastern Europe

| | |
|---|---|
| 1480 | Grand Duke and later Tsar Ivan III, "The Great," of Russia refuses to pay tribute to Tartars |
| 1569 | Constitutional Union of Poland and Lithuania |
| 1604–1613 | Time of Troubles in Russia |
| 1613 | Michael Romanov elected Tsar of Russia |

**The Kremlin**

The Kremlin was the seat of government for the Russian tsars until 1712. Originally built in 1156, the present enclosure of the Kremlin dates from the sixteenth century and reflects the influence of Italian architects brought to Moscow as well as traditional Byzantine styles.

opposition to his rule revealed signs of the fragility of Russian unity.

During the "Time of Troubles°" (1604–1613), Russia fell into chaos. Boyar families struggled among themselves for supremacy, the Cossacks from the south led a popular revolt, and Poles and Swedes openly interfered in Russian affairs. Finally, the Time of Troubles ended when in 1613 the national assembly elected Tsar Michael Romanov, whose descendants ruled Russia until they were deposed in 1917. During the seventeenth century the Romanovs gradually restored order to Russia, eroded the independence of local governments, and strengthened the institution of serfdom. By the end of the seventeenth century Russia was strong enough to reenter European affairs as a major power.

# Conclusion

## The Divisions of the West

During the late sixteenth and early seventeenth centuries, hidden demographic and economic pressures eroded the confidence and security of many Europeans, creating a widespread sense of unease. Most people retreated like confused soldiers behind the barricades of a rigid confessional faith, which provided reassurance that was unavailable elsewhere. To compensate for the absence of predictability in daily life, societies everywhere imposed strict discipline—discipline of women, children, the poor, criminals, and alleged witches. The frenzy for social discipline displaced the fear of those things that could not be controlled onto the most easily controllable people, especially the weak, the subordinate, and those perceived to be different in some way.

The union between religion and political authority in the confessional states bolstered official religious faith with the threat of legal or military coercion. Where different religious confessions persisted within one state—most notably France and the Netherlands—the result was riots, assassinations, and civil war. The West had become divided along religious lines in two ways. The first kind of division was within countries with religiously mixed populations, where distinctive religious communities competed for political power and influence. In these countries religion became the cornerstone to justify patriotism or rebellion, loyalty or disloyalty to the monarch. The second kind of division was international. The confessional states formed alliances, crafted foreign policies, and went to war, with religion determining friend and foe. The West split into religiously driven camps. Over the subsequent centuries, religious differences mutated into ideological differences, but the sense that alliances among states should be linked together by a common set of beliefs has persisted to this day as a legacy from the sixteenth century.

During the period of the middle seventeenth to eighteenth centuries, confessional identity and the fear of religious turmoil led monarchs throughout Europe to build absolutist regimes, which attempted to enforce stability through a strengthened, centralized state. The principles of religious toleration and the separation of church and state were still far in the future. They were made possible only as a consequence of the hard lessons learned from the historical turmoil of the late sixteenth and seventeenth centuries.

## Suggestions for Further Reading

For a comprehensive listing of suggested readings, please go to
www.ablongman.com/levack2e/chapter14

Anderson, M. S. *The Origins of the Modern European State System, 1494–1618.* 1998. The best short study for students new to the subject of the evolution of the confessional states in Europe. This book is very good at establishing common patterns among the various states.

Burke, Peter. *Popular Culture in Early Modern Europe.* 1994. This wide-ranging book includes considerable material from eastern Europe and Scandinavia, as well as the more extensively studied western European countries. Extraordinarily influential, it practically invented the subject of popular culture by showing how much could be learned from studying festivals and games.

Davies, Norman. *God's Playground: A History of Poland.* Rev. ed., 2 vols. 1982. By far the most comprehensive study of Polish history, this is particularly strong for the sixteenth and seventeenth centuries. Davies offers a Polish-centered view of European history that is marvelously stimulating even if he sometimes overstates his case for the importance of Poland.

Dukes, Paul. *A History of Russia: Medieval, Modern, Contemporary, ca. 882–1996.* 3rd ed. 1998. A comprehensive survey that synthesizes the most recent research.

Dunn, Richard S. *The Age of Religious Wars, 1559–1715.* 2nd ed. 1980. An excellent survey for students new to the subject.

Evans, R. J. W. *Rudolf II and His World: A Study in Intellectual History, 1576–1612.* 1973. A sympathetic examination of the intellectual world Rudolf created. Evans recognizes Rudolf's mental problems but lessens their significance for understanding the period.

Holt, Mack P. *The French Wars of Religion, 1562–1629.* 1996. A lucid short synthesis of the events and complex issues raised by these wars.

Hsia, R. Po-chia. *Social Discipline in the Reformation: Central Europe, 1550–1750.* 1989. An excellent, lucid, and short overview of the attempts to discipline the people in Germany.

Huppert, George. *After the Black Death: A Social History of Early Modern Europe.* 1986. Engaging, entertaining, and elegantly written, this is the best single study of European social life during the Early Modern period.

Levack, Brian P. *The Witch-Hunt in Early Modern Europe.* 2nd ed. 1995. The best and most up-to-date short examination of the complex problem of the witch-hunt. This is the place to begin for students new to the subject.

Ozment, Steven E. *Ancestors: The Loving Family in Old Europe.* 2001. This comprehensive study of family life demonstrates that families were actually far more loving than the theory of patriarchy would suggest.

Parker, Geoffrey. *The Dutch Revolt.* Rev. ed. 1990. The classic study of the revolt by one of the most masterful historians of the period. This study is especially adept at pointing to the larger European context of the revolt.

Parker, Geoffrey. *The Grand Strategy of Philip II.* 1998. Rehabilitates Philip as a significant strategic thinker.

Wiesner, Merry E. *Women and Gender in Early Modern Europe.* 1993. The best short study of the subject. This is the best book for students new to the subject.

## Notes

1. Quoted in R. Po-Chia Hsia, *Social Discipline in the Reformation: Central Europe, 1550–1750* (1989), 147–148.

2. Quoted in Norbert Elias, *The Civilizing Process,* Vol. 1: *The History of Manners,* trans. Edmund Jephcott (1978), 119.

3. Quoted in R. J. Knecht, *The French Wars of Religion, 1559–1598,* 2nd ed. (1996), 13.

4. Quoted in John Neale, "The Massacre of St. Bartholomew," reprinted in Orest Ranum, ed., *Searching for Modern Times,* Vol. 1, *1500–1650* (1969), 176.

5. François Rabelais, *The Histories of Gargantua and Pantagruel,* trans. J. M. Cohen (1955), 159.

6. Michel de Montaigne, *Essays and Selected Writings,* trans. and ed. Donald M. Frame (1963), 219–221.

7. Luís Vaz de Camões, *The Lusiads,* trans. William C. Atkinson (1952), 42.

8. Quoted in "Elizabeth I," *Encyclopedia Britannica* 8 (1959), 364b.

9. Quoted in Norman Davies, *Europe: A History* (1996), 529.

# Absolutism and State Building, 1618–1715

# 15

N 1651 THOMAS HOBBES, AN ENGLISH PHILOSOPHER LIVING IN EXILE IN France, was convinced that the West had descended into chaos. As he looked around him, Hobbes saw nothing but political instability, rebellion, and civil war. The turmoil had begun in the late sixteenth century, when the Reformation sparked the religious warfare described in the last chapter. In 1618 the situation deteriorated when another cycle of internal political strife and warfare erupted. The Thirty Years' War (1618–1648) began as a religious and political dispute in Germany but soon became an international conflict involving the armies of Spain, France, Sweden, and England as well as those of many German states. The war wreaked economic and social havoc in Germany, decimated its population, and forced governments throughout Europe to raise large armies and tax their subjects to pay for them. The entire European economy suffered as a result.

During the 1640s, partly as a result of that devastating conflict, the political order of Europe virtually collapsed. In England a series of bloody civil wars led to the destruction of the monarchy and the establishment of a republic. In France a civil war over constitutional issues drove the royal family from Paris. In Spain the king faced rebellions in no fewer than four of his territories, while in many European kingdoms peasants had risen in protest against the taxes their governments were collecting. Europe was in the midst of a profound and multifaceted crisis.

Hobbes, a man plagued by anxiety even since he was a child, proposed a solution to this crisis. In 1651 he published a book, *Leviathan,* about the origin and exercise of political power. He began by observing that people had a natural tendency to quarrel among themselves and seek power over each other. If left to their own devices in a hypothetical state of nature, in which government did not exist, they would find themselves in constant conflict. In these circumstances, which Hobbes referred to as a state of war, people would be unable to engage in trade or agriculture or pursue cultural

**Louis XIV** Portrait of Louis XIV in military armor, with his plumed helmet and his crown on the table to the right. The portrait was painted during the period of French warfare. In the background is a French ship.

interests. Life would soon become, in Hobbes's famous words, "solitary, poor nasty, brutish, and short."[1] The only way for people to find peace in this dangerous and unproductive world would be to agree with their neighbors to form a political society, or a state, by surrendering their independent power to a ruler who would make laws, administer justice, and maintain order. In this state the ruler would wield great power, and he would not share it with others. His subjects, having agreed to endow him with such extensive power, and having agreed to submit to his rule, could not resist or depose him.

Hobbes wrote *Leviathan* not simply as an abstract study of political philosophy but as a solution to the problems that plagued the West in the middle of the seventeenth century. He was suggesting that the best way to achieve peace and security was for people to submit themselves to the authority of a single ruler. The term used to designate this type of government is absolutism°. In the most general terms, absolutism means a political arrangement in which one ruler possesses complete and unrivaled power.

The political history of the West during the seventeenth and early eighteenth centuries can be written largely in terms of the efforts made by European monarchs to introduce absolutism. Those efforts were accompanied by policies intended to make the states they ruled wealthier and more powerful. Attempts to introduce absolutism and to strengthen the state took place in almost every country in Europe. In all these countries a succession of encounters took place between rulers who were trying to enlarge the power of the state and those who resisted their efforts. The outcome of these encounters varied from country to country, but for the most part the advocates of state building and absolutism prevailed. By the end of the seventeenth century the West comprised a number of large states, governed by rulers who had achieved unrivaled power and who commanded large, well-equipped armies. The West had entered the age of absolutism, which lasted until the outbreak of the French Revolution in 1789.

Not only did the West acquire a clear political identity during the seventeenth century, but its geographical boundaries also began to shift. Russia, which Europeans thought of as part of the East, began a program of imitating Western governments and became a major player in European diplomacy and warfare. At the same time Russia's southern neighbor, the Ottoman Empire, which had long straddled the boundary between East and West, was increasingly viewed by Europeans as part of a remote, Asian world.

The overarching question that this chapter addresses is: How did Western rulers strengthen the administrative and military capacities of the states they governed during this

**The Frontispiece of Thomas Hobbes's Treatise**
***Leviathan,* Published in London in 1651**
The ruler is depicted as incorporating the bodies of all his subjects, as they collectively authorized him to govern.

period? The individual sections of the chapter will answer the following questions:

■ **What did absolutism mean, both as a political theory and as a practical program, and how was absolutism related to the growth of the power of the state?**

■ **How did the encounters that took place in France and Spain during the seventeenth century result in the establishment of absolutism, and how powerful did those two states become in the seventeenth century?**

■ **What was the nature of royal absolutism in central and eastern Europe, and how did the policies of the Ottoman Empire and Russia help establish the boundaries of the West during this period?**

■ **Why did absolutism fail to take root in England and the Dutch Republic during the seventeenth century?**

# The Nature of Absolutism

■ What did absolutism mean, both as a political theory and as a practical program, and how was absolutism related to the growth of the power of the state?

Seventeenth-century absolutism had both a theoretical and a practical dimension. Theoretical absolutists included writers like Hobbes who described the nature of power in the state and explained the conditions for its acquisition and continuation. Practical absolutists were the rulers who took concrete political steps to subordinate all other political authorities within the state to themselves. Efforts to introduce royal absolutism in Europe began in the late sixteenth and early seventeenth centuries, but only in the late seventeenth century, after the Thirty Years' War and the political turmoil of the 1640s, did many European rulers consolidate their political positions and actually achieve absolute power.

The word *absolutism* usually conjures up images of despotic kings terrorizing every segment of the population, ruling by whim and caprice, and executing their subjects at will. Nothing could be further from the truth. Absolute monarchs succeeded in establishing themselves as the highest political authorities within their kingdoms, but they never attained unlimited power. Nor could they exercise power in a completely arbitrary manner. Theoretical absolutists never sanctioned this type of arbitrary rule, and the laws of European states never permitted it. Even if European monarchs had wished to act in this way, they usually could not because they did not have the political or judicial resources to impose their will on the people. The exercise of royal power in the seventeenth century, even when it was considered absolute, depended on the tacit consent of noblemen, office holders, and the members of local political assemblies. Kings usually could not afford to risk losing the support of these prominent men by acting illegally or arbitrarily, and when they did, they found themselves faced with rebellion.

## The Theory of Absolutism

When seventeenth-century political writers referred to the monarch as having absolute power, they usually meant that he possessed the highest legislative power in his kingdom. In particular, they meant that he did not share the power to make law with representative assemblies such as the English Parliament. The French magistrate Jean Bodin (1530?–1596), who was one of the earliest proponents of absolutist theory, argued in *Six Books of a Commonweal* (1576) that absolute power consisted of several attributes, the most important of which was the power to make law. In similar fashion Hobbes referred to the absolute ruler as

"sole legislator." Absolute monarchs, therefore, were rulers who could make law by themselves.

In order to bolster their authority, absolute monarchs frequently asserted that they received their power directly from God and therefore ruled by divine right. This idea was hardly new in the seventeenth century. The Bible proclaimed that all political authorities were "of God" and that people must therefore be obedient to them. In the fourteenth century European monarchs asserted that because God had given them the right to rule, the pope could not depose them. In the sixteenth century the idea of divine right was used to discourage rebellion, for to resist the king was to attack God's representative on Earth. In the seventeenth century many theorists of absolutism—although not Hobbes—used the idea of divine right to insist that kings were accountable only to God, rather than to their subjects.

Absolute rulers often claimed that they were above the law. This meant that when monarchs acted for reason of state, that is, for the benefit of the entire kingdom, they were not strictly bound by the law of their kingdoms. Being above the law also meant that they could not be held legally accountable for their actions, as they were the highest judges in the land. Being above the law did not mean kings or queens could act arbitrarily, illegally, or despotically, even though some of them did so from time to time. Absolute rulers, no less than those who shared power with representative assemblies, were always expected to observe the individual rights and liberties of their subjects as well as the moral law established by God. They were expected, for example, to try people in a court of law rather than execute them at will. The French preacher Jacques Bossuet (1627–1704), who wrote an absolutist treatise on the authority of kings in 1670, insisted that even though kings were not subject to the penalties of the law, they still were not freed from the obligation to observe that law. No less than their subjects, kings were subject to the "equity of the laws." This meant that they should not rule despotically or arbitrarily.

Theorists of absolutism distinguished between European monarchs and rulers in other parts of the world, such as Turkish sultans, Russian tsars, and the kings of Asian and African lands. In those so-called Eastern countries, according to Bodin, "the prince has become the lord of the goods and the persons of his subjects," by which Bodin meant that the rulers of those lands could seize the possessions of their subjects or execute them without due process of law.[2] Only in the West, wrote Bodin, did royal subjects live under a regime that abided by the rule of law. Bodin exaggerated the powers of both Turkish sultans and Russian tsars, who had much in common with the absolute rulers of western and central Europe. But by emphasizing the rule of law and the king's obligation to abide by it, Bodin identified one of the distinctive features of Western politics during the age of absolutism.

## The Practice of Absolutism

What steps did the European monarchs who claimed absolute power take to establish and maintain themselves as the supreme authorities within the state? The first strategy they employed was the elimination or the weakening of national representative assemblies, such as Parliament in England, Diets in German states, and the Cortes in Spain and Portugal. In France, which is considered to have been the most absolutist state in seventeenth-century Europe, the monarchy stopped summoning its national assembly, the Estates General, in 1614. This assembly did not meet again until the late eighteenth century.

The second strategy of absolutist rulers was to subordinate the nobility to the king and make them dependent on his favor. The political and social power of the nobility often led them to participate in rebellions and conspiracies against the king. Monarchs who aspired to a position of unrivaled power in their kingdoms therefore took steps to keep the nobility in line, not only by suppressing challenges to their authority but also by appointing men from different social groups as their chief ministers, At the same time, however, the king could not afford to alienate these wealthy and high-ranking men, upon whom he still relied for running his government and maintaining order in the localities. Absolute monarchs, therefore, offered nobles special privileges, such as exemption from taxation, positions in the king's household, and freedom to exploit their peasants in exchange for their recognition of the king's superiority and their assistance in maintaining order in the localities. In this way nobles became junior partners in the management of the absolutist state.

The final strategy of absolute monarchs was to gain effective control of the administrative machinery of the state and to use it to enforce royal policy throughout their kingdoms. Absolute monarchs were by nature state builders. They established centralized bureaucracies that extended the reach of their governments down into the smallest towns and villages and out into the most remote regions of their kingdoms. The business conducted by these centrally controlled bureaucracies included collection of taxes, recruitment of soldiers, and operation of the judicial system. Some absolute monarchs used the central machinery of the state to impose and maintain religious conformity. As the seventeenth century advanced, they also used the same machinery to regulate the price of grain, stimulate the growth of industry, and relieve the plight of the poor. In these ways the policies pursued by absolute monarchs had an impact on the lives of all royal subjects, not just noblemen and royal councilors.

## Warfare and the Absolutist State

Much of the growth of European states in the seventeenth century can be related in one way or another to the conduct of war. During the period from 1600 to 1721, European powers were almost constantly at war. The entire continent was at peace for only four of those years. To meet the demands of war, rulers kept men under arms at all times. By the middle of the seventeenth century, after the Thirty Years' War had come to an end, most European rulers had acquired such standing armies. These armies not only served their rulers in foreign wars but also helped them maintain order and enforce royal policy at home. Standing armies thus became one of the main props of royal absolutism.

During the seventeenth and early eighteenth centuries European armies became larger, in many cases tripling in size. In the 1590s Philip II of Spain had mastered Europe with an army of 40,000 men. By contrast, in the late seventeenth century Louis XIV of France needed an army of 400,000 men to become the dominant power on the continent. The increase in the size of these forces can be traced to the invention of gunpowder and its more frequent use in the fifteenth and sixteenth centuries. Gunpowder led to the widespread use of the musket, a heavy shoulder firearm carried by a foot soldier. The use of the musket placed a premium on the recruitment and equipment of large armies of infantry, who marched in square columns with men holding long pikes (long wooden shafts with pointed metal heads) to protect the musketeers from enemy attacks. As the size of these armies of foot soldiers grew, the role of mounted soldiers, who had dominated medieval warfare, was greatly reduced.

Changes in military technology and tactics also necessitated more intensive military training. In the Middle Ages mounted knights had acquired great individual skill, but they did not need to work in precise unison with other men under arms. Seventeenth-century foot soldiers, however, had to learn to march in formation, to coordinate their maneuvers, and to fire without harming their comrades in arms. Therefore they needed to be drilled. The introduction of volley fire, by which each successive line of soldiers stepped forward to fire while the others were reloading, placed an even greater premium on precise drilling. Drilling took place in peacetime as well as during war. The wearing of uniforms, which began when the state assumed the function of clothing its thousands of soldiers, gave further unity and cohesion to the trained fighting force.

The cost of recruiting, training, and equipping these mammoth armies was staggering. In the Middle Ages individual lords often had sufficient financial resources to assemble their own private armies. By the beginning of the seventeenth century the only institution capable of putting the new armies in the field was the state itself. The same was true for navies, which now consisted of heavily armed sailing ships, each of which carried as many as 400 sailors. To build these large armies and navies, as well as to pay the increasing cost of waging war itself (which rose 500 percent between 1530 and 1630), the state had to identify new methods of raising and collecting taxes. In times of war as much as 80 percent of the revenue taken in by the state went for military purposes.

The equipment and training of military forces and the collection and allocation of the revenue necessary to subsidize these efforts stimulated the expansion and refinement of the state bureaucracy. Governments found it necessary to employ thousands of new officials to supervise the collection of new taxes, and in order to make the system of tax collection more efficient, governments often introduced entirely new administrative systems. Some states completely reorganized their bureaucracies to meet the demands of war. New departments of state were created to supervise the recruitment of soldiers, the manufacture of equipment and uniforms, the building of fleets, and the provisioning of troops in time of war. Rulers of European states recognized that the exercise of absolute power greatly facilitated the utilization of state power for these purposes.

# The Absolutist State in France and Spain

■ How did the encounters that took place in France and Spain during the seventeenth century result in the establishment of absolutism, and how powerful did those two states become in the seventeenth century?

The two European countries in which royal absolutism first became a political reality were France and Spain. The histories of these two monarchies in the seventeenth century followed very different courses. The kingdom of France, especially during the reign of Louis XIV (r. 1643–1715), became a model of state building and gradually emerged as the most powerful country in Europe. The Spanish monarchy, on the other hand, struggled to introduce absolutism at a time when the overall economic condition of the country was deteriorating and its military forces were suffering a series of defeats. Spain established the forms of absolutist rule, but the monarchy was not able to match the political or military achievements of France in the late seventeenth century.

## The Foundations of French Absolutism

Efforts to make the French monarchy absolute began in response to the disorder that occurred during the wars of religion in the late sixteenth century. Bodin wrote his treatises during those wars, and the threat of renewed civil war between Protestants and Catholics affected French politics throughout the seventeenth century. The first steps toward the achievement of absolutism were taken during the reign of Henry IV (r. 1589–1610), the Huguenot who converted to Catholicism in 1594 and who ended the wars of religion by granting freedom of worship and full civil rights to

French Protestants by the Edict of Nantes (1598). This decree brought internal religious peace to the kingdom, while the progressive financial and economic policies of Henry's brilliant minister, the Duke of Sully, helped restore the financial strength of the crown and involve the government in a process of commercial recovery and expansion. Despite this success, Henry could not prevent the great nobles from conspiring against him, and his policy of religious toleration encountered resistance from Catholics committed to the suppression of Protestantism. In 1610 a fanatical Catholic, François Ravaillac, stabbed the king to death in his carriage on a Parisian street.

On Henry's death the crown passed to his young son, Louis XIII (r. 1610–1643), while the queen mother, Marie de' Medici, assumed the leadership of a government acting in the king's name during his youth. This period of regency, in which aristocratic factions vied for supremacy at court, exposed the main weakness of the monarchy, which was the rival power of the great noble families of the realm. The statesman who addressed this problem most directly was Louis's main councilor, Cardinal Armand Jean du Plessis de Richelieu (1585–1642). A member of an old and wealthy family, Richelieu rose to power through the patronage of the queen mother and then, after losing her support, maintained his preeminent position with the support of the king himself. He became the king's chief minister in 1628. Richelieu was arguably the greatest state builder of the seventeenth century. He directed all his energies toward centralizing the power of the French state in the person of the king.

Richelieu's most immediate concern was bringing the independent nobility to heel and subordinating their local power to that of the state. This he accomplished by suppressing several conspiracies and rebellions led by noblemen and by restricting the independent power of the provincial assemblies and the eight regional parlements°, which were the highest courts in the country. His great administrative achievement was the strengthening of the system of the intendants°. These paid crown officials, who were recruited from the professional classes and the lower ranks of the nobility, became the main agents of French local administration. Responsible only to the royal council, they collected taxes, supervised local administration, and recruited soldiers for the army. Because they could not come from the districts to which they were assigned, they had no vested interest in maintaining local customs or privileges.

Richelieu also modified the religious policy embodied in the Edict of Nantes. According to that document, Huguenots not only had freedom of worship but could also fortify the towns in which they lived. Richelieu resented the maintenance of these citadels of local power, which represented a challenge to the type of absolutist state he envisioned. He also suspected that rivals of the king from the nobility were using the Huguenot towns as a means of maintaining their independent power. A series of military confrontations between the government and the

**Cardinal Richelieu**
Triple portrait of Cardinal Richelieu, who laid the foundations of French absolutism.

The most challenging task for Richelieu, as for all French ministers in the early modern period, was increasing the government's yield from taxation, a task that became more demanding during times of war. Levying taxes on the French population was always a delicate process, as the needs of the state conflicted with the privileges of various social groups, such as the nobles, who were exempt from taxation, and the estates of individual provinces such as Brittany that claimed the right to tax the people themselves. Using a variety of tactics, including negotiation and compromise, and relying heavily on the support of the provincial intendants, Richelieu managed to increase the yield from the *taille*, the direct tax on land, as much as threefold during the period 1635–1648. He supplemented the taille with taxes on office holding. Even then, the revenue was insufficient to meet the extraordinary demands of war.

Opposition to Richelieu's financial policies lay at the root of the main problem the government faced after the cardinal's death in 1642. The minister who succeeded him was his protégé Jules Mazarin (1602–1661), a diplomat of Italian birth who had entered French government service during Richelieu's administration. Mazarin dominated the government of Louis XIV when the king, who inherited the throne at age 5, was still a boy and while his mother was serving as regent. Mazarin continued the policies of his predecessor, but he was unable to prevent civil war from breaking out in 1648. This challenge to the French state, known as the *Fronde* (a pejorative reference to a Parisian game in which children flung mud at passing carriages), had two phases. The first, the Fronde of the Parlement (1648–1649), began when the members of the Parlement of Paris, the most important of all the provincial parlements, refused to register an edict of the king that had required them to surrender four years' salary. This act of resistance led to demands that the king sign a document limiting royal authority. Barricades went up in the streets of Paris, and the royal family was forced to flee the city. A blockade of the city by royal troops led to an uneasy compromise in 1649. Revolts in three other parlements, each of which had its own dynamic and which were not coordinated with that of Paris, came to a similar resolution. The second and more violent phase was the Fronde of the Princes (1650–1653), during which the Prince de Condé and his noble allies waged war on the government and even formed an alliance with

Protestants in the late 1610s and 1620s brought the country to the brink of civil war. Following the successful siege of the town of La Rochelle in 1627–1628, the government razed the fortifications of the Huguenot cities, melted down their cannons, and disarmed their Protestant citizens. A peace treaty signed in 1629 ratified the government's victory, but it did not deny the Huguenots their right to worship freely.

# CHRONOLOGY

## France in the Age of Absolutism

| | |
|---|---|
| **1598** | The Edict of Nantes grants toleration to French Calvinists, known as Huguenots |
| **1610** | Assassination of Henry IV of France, who was succeeded by Louis XIII (r. 1610–1643) |
| **1628** | Cardinal Richelieu becomes chief minister of Louis XIII of France |
| **1643** | Death of Louis XIII of France and accession of Louis XIV; Louis's mother, Anne of Austria, becomes queen regent with Cardinal Mazarin as his minister |
| **1648–1653** | The Fronde |
| **1661** | Death of Cardinal Mazarin; Louis XIV assumes personal rule |
| **1685** | Revocation of the Edict of Nantes |
| **1715** | Death of Louis XIV of France; succeeded by his grandson, Louis XV |

France's enemy, Spain. Only after Condé's military defeat did the entire rebellion collapse.

The Fronde stands as the great crisis of the seventeenth-century French state. It revealed the strength of the local, aristocratic, and legal forces with which the king and his ministers had to contend. These forces managed to disrupt the growth of the French state, drive the king from his capital, and challenge his authority throughout the kingdom. But in the long run they could not destroy the achievement of Richelieu and Mazarin. By the late 1650s the damage had been repaired and the state had resumed its growth.

## Absolutism in the Reign of Louis XIV

The man who presided over the development of the French state for the next fifty years was the king himself, Louis XIV, who assumed direct control of his government after the death of Mazarin in 1661. In an age of absolute monarchs, Louis towered among his contemporaries. He is widely regarded as the most powerful king of the seventeenth century. This reputation comes as much from the image he conveyed as from the policies he pursued. Artists, architects, dramatists, and members of his immediate entourage helped the king project an image of incomparable majesty and authority. Paintings and sculptures of the king depicted him in sartorial splendor, holding the symbols of power and displaying expressions of regal superiority that bordered on arrogance. At Versailles, about ten miles from Paris, Louis constructed a lavishly furnished palace that became his main residence and the center of the glittering court that surrounded him. The palace was built in the baroque° style, which emphasized the size and grandeur of the structure while also conveying a sense of unity and balance among its diverse parts. The sweeping façades of baroque buildings gave them a dynamic quality that evoked an emotional response from the viewer. The baroque style, criticized by contemporaries for its exuberance and pomposity, appealed to absolute monarchs who wished to emphasize their unrivaled position within society and their determination to impose order and stability on their kingdoms.

Court life at Versailles revolved entirely around the king. Court dramas depicted Louis, who styled himself "the sun king," as Apollo, the god of light. The paintings in the grand Hall of Mirrors at Versailles, which recorded the king's military victories, served as reminders of his unrivaled accomplishments. Louis's formal routine in receiving visitors created appropriate distance between him and his courtiers while keeping his subjects in a state of subservient anticipation of royal favor. His frequent bursts of anger achieved the same effect. When an untitled lady took the seat of a noblewoman at a dinner in his presence, he described the act as one of "incredible insolence" that "had thrown him into such a rage that he had been unable to eat." After rebuking the offending lady for her "impertinence," he became so angry that he left the room.[3]

The image of magnificence and power that Louis conveyed in art and ceremony mirrored and reinforced his more tangible political accomplishments. His greatest

### Versailles Palace, Center of the Court of Louis XIV After 1682

The palace was constructed between 1669 and 1686. Its massiveness and grandeur and the order it imposed on the landscape made it a symbol of royal absolutism.

achievement was to solve the persistent problem of aristocratic independence and rebellion by securing the complete loyalty and dependence of the old nobility. This he achieved first by requiring the members of these ancient families to come to Versailles for a portion of every year, where they stayed in apartments within the royal palace itself. At Versailles Louis involved them in the elaborate cultural activities of court life and in ceremonial rituals that emphasized their subservience to the king. At the same time, he excluded the nobles from holding important offices in the government of the realm, a strategy designed to prevent them from building an independent power base within the bureaucracy. Instead he recruited men from the mercantile and professional classes to run his government. This policy of taming the nobility and depriving them of central administrative power could work only if they received something in return. Like all the absolute monarchs of western Europe, Louis used the patronage at his disposal to grant members of the nobility wealth and privileges in exchange for their loyalty to the crown. In this way the monarchy and the nobility served each other's interests.

In running the actual machinery of government Louis built upon and perfected the centralizing policies of Richelieu and Mazarin. After the death of Mazarin in 1661

**DOCUMENT**

Louis XIV Writes to His Son (1661)

the king, now 23 years old, became his own chief minister, presiding over a council of state that supervised the work of government. An elaborate set of councils at the highest levels of government set policy that was implemented by the department ministers. The provincial intendants became even more important than they had been under Richelieu and Mazarin, especially in providing food, arms, and equipment for royal troops. It was the intendants' job to secure the cooperation of the local judges, city councils, and parish priests as well as the compliance of the local population. If necessary they could call upon royal troops in order to enforce their will, but for the most part they preferred to rely on the more effective tactics of negotiation and compromise with local officials. The system, when it worked properly, allowed the king to make decisions that directly affected the lives and beliefs of his 20 million subjects.

A further manifestation of the newfound power of the French state in the late seventeenth century was the government's active involvement in the economic and financial life of the country. The minister who was most responsible for this series of undertakings was Jean Baptiste Colbert (1619–1683), a protégé of Mazarin who in 1661 became controller general of the realm. Born into a family of merchants, and despised by the old nobility, Colbert epitomized the type of government official Louis recruited into his service. Entrusted with the supervision of the entire system of royal taxation, Colbert managed to increase royal revenues dramatically simply by reducing the cut taken by the agents whom the government hired to collect taxes.

Even more beneficial to the French state was the determination of Colbert to use the country's economic resources for its benefit. The theory underlying this set of policies was mercantilism°, which held that the wealth of the state depended on its ability to import fewer commodities than it exported. Its goal was to secure the largest possible share of the world's monetary supply. In keeping with those objectives, Colbert increased the size of France's merchant fleet, founded overseas trading companies, and levied high tariffs on France's commercial rivals. To make France economically self-sufficient he encouraged the growth of the French textile industry, improved the condition of the roads, built canals throughout the kingdom, and reduced some of the burdensome tolls that impeded internal trade.

The most intrusive exercise of the power of the state during Louis XIV's reign was the decision to enforce religious uniformity. The king always considered the existence of a large Huguenot minority within his kingdom an affront to his sense of order. Toleration was divisive and dangerous, especially to someone who styled himself as "Most Christian King." Even after Richelieu had leveled the walls of the fortified Huguenot towns, the problem of religious pluralism remained. In 1685 Louis addressed this problem by revoking the entire Edict of Nantes, thereby denying freedom of religious worship to about one million of his subjects. The enforcement of this policy was violent and disruptive, with the army being called upon to enforce public conversions to Catholicism. Protestant churches were closed and often destroyed, while large numbers of Huguenots were forced to emigrate to the Netherlands, England, and Protestant German lands. Few exercises of absolute power in the seventeenth century caused more disruption in the lives of ordinary people than this attempt to realize the king's ideal of "one king, one law, one faith."

## Louis XIV and the Culture of Absolutism

A further manifestation of the power of the French absolutist state was Louis's success in influencing and transforming French culture. Kings had often served as patrons of the arts by providing income for artists, writers, and musicians while endowing cultural and educational institutions. Louis took this type of royal patronage to a new level, making it possible for him to control the dissemination of ideas and the very production of culture itself. During Louis's reign royal patronage, emanating from the court, extended the king's influence over the entire cultural landscape. The architects of the palace at Versailles, the painters of historical scenes that hung in its hallways and galleries, the composers of the plays and operas that were performed in its theaters, the sculptors who created busts of the king to decorate its chambers, and the historians and pamphlet

DOCUMENT

## Revocation of the Edict of Nantes, October 25, 1685

*In 1685 King Louis XIV of France revoked the Edict of Nantes, the decree of King Henry IV that had granted freedom of worship to French Protestants in 1598. Before the revocation was published, the government sent dragoons (cavalry who arrived on horseback but fought on foot) to terrorize Protestant households and make them convert to Catholicism. The terms of the revocation were particularly harsh, and despite the prohibition against leaving the country, hundreds of thousands of Huguenots emigrated to England, the Dutch Republic, and North America.*

. . . Therefore we decided that there was nothing better we could do to erase from memory the troubles, the confusion, and the evils that the growth of this false religion had caused in our kingdom and that gave rise to the said Edict and to so many other edicts and declarations that preceded it . . . than to revoke entirely the said Edict of Nantes and the detailed articles attached to it and everything that has been done since on behalf of the said Supposedly Reformed Religion [Calvinism].

1. We therefore for these reasons and in full knowledge, power, and Royal authority, by means of the present perpetual and irrevocable edict, do suppress and revoke the Edict of the king, our grandfather, issued at Nantes in April 1598. . . . As a result we desire and it is our pleasure that all the temples of the Supposedly Reformed Religion situated in our kingdom, county, lands and seigneuries within our obedience be immediately demolished. . . .
2. Our subjects of the Supposedly Reformed Religion are not to assemble for worship in any place or house for any reason.
3. Noble lords are not to hold worship services in their houses or fiefs of any sort on pain of confiscation of goods and property.
4. Ministers of the Supposedly Reformed Religion who have not converted are to leave the kingdom within

fifteen days and are not to preach or perform any functions in the meantime, or they will be sent to the galleys.
5. Ministers who convert, and their widows after their death, are to enjoy the same exemptions from taxes and troop lodgings that they had as ministers. . . .
6. Converted ministers can become lawyers or doctors of law without the usual three years of study and for half the fees usually charged by the universities.
7. Special schools for the children of the Supposedly Reformed Religion are prohibited.
8. Children of [Huguenot] parents are to be baptized by the chief priests of their parishes and raised as Catholics, and local judges are to oversee this.
9. If Protestants who left the kingdom before this edict was issued return within four months, they can regain their property and resume their lives. If, however, they do not return within four months, their goods will be confiscated.
10. All subjects belonging to the Supposedly Reformed Religion and their wives and children are forbidden to leave the country or to send out their property and effects. The penalty for men is the galleys and women confiscation of their persons and property.
11. The declarations already issued concerning those who relapse are to be executed in full.

And, in addition, those who adhere to the Supposedly Reformed Religion, while waiting until it pleases God to enlighten them like the others, may continue to live in the cities and communities of our realm, continue their commerce, and enjoy their property without being bothered or hindered because of the Supposedly Reformed Religion, on condition, however, of not practicing their religion or assembling for prayers or worship or for any other pretext, with the penalties stated above.

Source: Copyright © 2000 by Bedford/St. Martin's. From *Louis XIV & Absolutism: A Brief Study with Documents* by William Beik. Reprinted with permission of Bedford/St. Martin's.

writers who celebrated the king's achievements in print all benefited from Louis's direct financial support.

Much of Louis's patronage went to cultural institutions, thereby enabling the king to influence a wider circle of artists and have a greater effect on the cultural life of the nation. He took over the Academy of Fine Arts in 1661, founded the Academy of Music in 1669, and chartered a theater company, the *Comédie Française*, in 1680. Two great French dramatists of the late seventeenth century,

Jean Baptiste Molière (1622–1673), the creator of French high comedy, and Jean Racine (1639–1699), who wrote tragedies in the classical style, benefited from the king's patronage. Louis even subsidized the publication of a new journal, the *Journal des savants*, in which men of letters advanced their ideas. In 1666 Louis extended his patronage to the sciences with the founding of the *Académie des Sciences*, which had the twofold objective of advancing scientific knowledge and glorifying the king. It also benefited the state by devising improvements in ship design and navigation.

Of all the cultural institutions that benefited from Louis XIV's patronage, the *Académie Française* had the most enduring impact on French culture. This academy, a society of literary scholars, had been founded in 1635 with the support of Cardinal Richelieu. Its purpose was to standardize the French language and serve as the guardian of its integrity. In 1694, twenty-two years after Louis became the academy's patron, the first official French dictionary appeared in print. This achievement of linguistic uniformity, in which words received authorized spellings and definitions, reflected the pervasiveness of Louis's cultural influence as well as the search for order that became the defining characteristic of his reign.

Louis introduced order and uniformity into every aspect of his own life and that of his country. He followed a precise routine in ordering his daily life, created ceremonies that ordered the life of his court, and insisted on the court's adoption of table manners that followed strict rules of politeness. He created a bureaucracy that was organized along rational, orderly principles, and he sought to ensure that all his subjects would practice the same religion. The establishment of a clearly defined chain of command in the army, which Louis's minister the Marquis de Louvois introduced, gave organizational cohesion and hierarchical order to the large military force the king and his ministers assembled. Nearly all areas of French public life were transformed by the king's desire to establish order and uniformity and his use of the power of the state to enforce it.

One indication of the extent of Louis's achievement was the conspicuous attempt of other monarchs to imitate France, even in the eighteenth century. The absolute monarchs in Prussia, Austria, and Russia, as well as aspiring ones in England and Sweden, not only experimented selectively with French political methods but imported many of the features of French culture that Louis had supported. They built palaces in the same architectural style as that of Versailles, designed French gardens to surround them, imported the fashions and decorative styles of the French court, staged French ballets and operas in their capitals, and even spoke French, which had replaced Latin as the language of international diplomacy, when conducting official business. The power of the French monarchy had made French culture the dominant influence in the courts and capitals of Europe.

## The Wars of Louis XIV, 1667–1714

The seventeenth-century French state was designed not only to maintain internal peace and order but also to wage war against other states. Colbert's financial and economic policies, coupled with the military reforms of the Marquis de Louvois, had laid the foundations for the creation of a

formidable military machine. In 1667 Louis XIV began unleashing its full potential. Having assembled an army that was twenty times larger than the French force that had invaded Italy in 1494, Louis deployed this armed force against an array of European powers in four separate wars between 1667 and 1714. His goal in all these wars, as it had been in all French international conflicts since 1635, was territorial acquisition (see Map 15.1). In this case Louis set his sights mainly on the German and Spanish territories in the Rhineland along the eastern borders of his kingdom. Contemporaries suggested, however, that he was thinking in grander terms than traditional French dynastic ambition. Propagandists for the king in the late 1660s claimed that Louis harbored visions of establishing a "universal monarchy" or an "absolute empire," reminiscent of the empires of ancient Rome, Charlemagne in the ninth century, and Charles V in the sixteenth century.

Louis never attained the empire of his dreams, but concerted action by almost all the other European powers was required to stop him. France's acquisition of new territories

**Map 15.1 French Territorial Acquisitions, 1679–1714**
The main acquisitions were lands in the Spanish Netherlands to the north and Franche Comté, Alsace, and Lorraine to the east. Louis thought of the Rhine River as France's natural eastern boundary, and territories acquired in 1659 and 1697 allowed it to reach that limit.

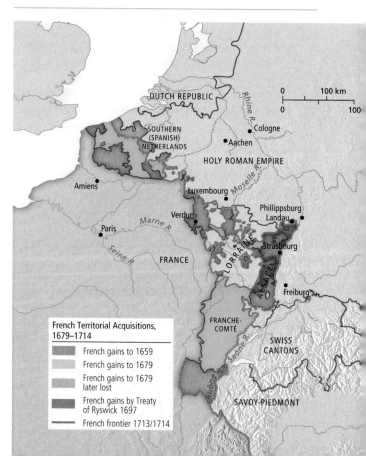

**The French Bourbons and the Spanish Succession 1589–1700**

**Henry IV** = Marie de' Medici
(r. 1589–1610)

**Louis XIII** = Anna of Austria,
(r. 1610–1643)   d. of Philip III of Spain

Maria Theresa = **Louis XIV**      Philip = Elizabeth-Charlotte
of Spain    (r. 1643–1715)    duc d'Orleans

Louis = Maria Anna of Bavaria
(d. 1711)

Louis = Marie Adelaide    Philip, duke of Anjou    Charles,
(d. 1712)  of Savoy    and **Philip V**, king of Spain    duc de Berry
                (r. 1700–1746)

**Louis XV**
(r. 1715–1774)

along its eastern boundaries between 1668 and 1684 confirmed the fears of other European states that the king had imperial ambitions. After Louis had launched an offensive against German towns along the Rhine River in 1688, signaling the beginning of yet another round of European warfare, Great Britain, the Dutch Republic, Spain, and Austria formed a coalition against him. Finally matched by the combined military forces of these allies, forced to wage war on many different fronts (including North America), and unable to provide adequate funding of the war on the basis of its system of taxation, France felt compelled to conclude peace in 1697. The Treaty of Ryswick marked the turning point in the expansion of the French state and laid the groundwork for the establishment of a balance of power° in the next century, an arrangement whereby various countries form alliances to prevent any one state from dominating the others.

The Treaty of Ryswick, however, did not mark the end of French territorial ambition. In 1701 Louis went to war once again, this time as part of an effort to place a French Bourbon candidate, his grandson Duke Philip of Anjou, on the Spanish throne. The impending death of the mentally weak, sexually impotent, and chronically ill King Charles II of Spain (r. 1665–1700) without heirs had created a succession crisis. In 1698 the major European powers had agreed to a treaty in which Spanish lands would be divided between Louis himself and the Holy Roman Emperor, both of whom happened to be Charles's brothers-in-law. By his will, however, Charles left the Spanish crown and all its overseas possessions to Philip. This bequest offered France

more than it would have received on the basis of the treaty. If the will had been upheld, the Pyrenees mountains would have disappeared as a political barrier between France and Spain, and France, as the stronger of the two kingdoms, would have controlled unprecedented expanses of European and American territory.

Dreaming once again of universal monarchy, Louis rejected the treaty in favor of King Charles's will. The British, Dutch, and Austrians responded by forming a Grand Alliance against France and Spain. After a long and costly conflict, known as the War of the Spanish Succession (1701–1713), the members of this coalition were able to dictate the terms of the Treaty of Utrecht (1713). Philip, who suffered from fits of manic depression and went days without dressing or leaving his room, remained on the Spanish throne as Philip V (r. 1700–1746), but only on the condition that the French and Spanish crowns would never be united. Spain ceded its territories in the Netherlands and in Italy to the Austrian Habsburg Monarchy and its strategic port of Gibraltar at the entrance to the Mediterranean to the British. The treaty not only confirmed the new balance of power in Europe but also resulted in the transfer of large parts of French Canada, including Newfoundland and Nova Scotia, to Great Britain.

The loss of French territory in North America, the strains placed on the taxation system by the financial demands of war, and the weakening of France's commercial power as a result of this conflict made France a less potent state at the time of Louis's death in 1715 than it had been in the 1680s. Nevertheless the main effects of a century of

**Map 15.2 The Decline of Spanish Power in Europe, 1640–1714**
Revolts in the United Provinces of the Netherlands and Portugal account for two of the most significant losses of Spanish territory. Military defeat at the hands of the French in 1659 and Austria in 1714 account for the loss of most of the other territories.

French state building remained, including a large, well-integrated bureaucratic edifice that allowed the government to exercise unprecedented control over the population and a military establishment that remained the largest and best equipped in Europe.

## Absolutism and State Building in Spain

The history of Spain in the seventeenth century is almost always written in terms of failure, as the country endured a long period of economic decline that began in the late sixteenth century with a precipitate drop in the size of its population and stretched well into the eighteenth century. The monarchy became progressively weaker during the seventeenth century, as it was occupied by a succession of ineffective kings who exercised far less power than their French counterparts. To make matters worse, Spain in the seventeenth century suffered a long series of military defeats, most of them at the hands of the French, and it lost the position it had held in the sixteenth century as the major

European power (see Map 15.2). By the early eighteenth century Spain was a shadow of its former self, and its culture reflected uncertainty, pessimism, and nostalgia for former imperial greatness. None of this failure, however, should obscure the fact that Spain, like France, underwent a period of state building during the seventeenth century, and that its government, like that of France, gravitated toward absolutism.

The Spanish monarchy in 1600 ruled more territory than did France, and the various kingdoms and principalities that it comprised possessed far more independence than even the most remote and peripheral French provinces. The center of the monarchy was the kingdom of Castile, with its capital at Madrid. This kingdom, the largest and wealthiest territory within the Iberian peninsula, had been united with the kingdom of Aragon in 1479 when King Ferdinand II of Aragon (r. 1479–1516), the husband of Queen Isabella of Castile (r. 1474–1504), ascended the throne. These two kingdoms, however, continued to exist as separate states after the union, each having its own representative institutions and administrative systems. Each of them, moreover, contained smaller, semiautonomous kingdoms and provinces that retained their own distinctive political institutions. The kingdom of Valencia and the principality of Catalonia formed part of the Crown of Aragon, while in the sixteenth century the kingdoms of Navarre and Portugal had been annexed to the Crown of Castile. Outside the Iberian peninsula the Spanish monarchy ruled territories in the Netherlands, Italy, and the New World.

The only institution besides the monarchy itself that provided any kind of administrative unity to all these Spanish territories in the seventeenth century was the Spanish Inquisition, a centralized ecclesiastical court with a supreme council in Madrid and twenty-one regional tribunals in different parts of Spain, Italy, and America. Its function was to enforce religious uniformity and maintain the purity of the Catholic faith.

The great challenge for the Spanish monarchy in the seventeenth century was to integrate the various kingdoms and principalities of Spain into a more highly centralized state while at the same time making the machinery of that state more efficient and profitable. The statesman who made the most sustained efforts at realizing these goals was the energetic and authoritarian Count-Duke of Olivares (1587–1645), the contemporary and counterpart of Richelieu during the reign of the Spanish king Philip IV (1621–1665). The task Olivares faced was more daunting than anything the French cardinal had ever confronted. As a result of decades of warfare, the Spanish monarchy in the 1620s was penniless, the kingdom of Castile had gone bankrupt, and the entire country had already entered a period of protracted economic decline.

To deal with these deep structural problems Olivares proposed a reform of the entire financial system, the establishment of national banks, and the replacement of the main tax, the *millones*, which was levied on the consumption of basic commodities such as meat and wine, with proportional contributions from all the towns and villages in the kingdom. At the same time he tried to address the problem of ruling a disparate and far-flung empire, making all the kingdoms and principalities within the monarchy contribute to national defense on a proportionate basis. His ultimate goal was to unify the entire peninsula in a cohesive Spanish national state, similar to that of France. This policy involved suppression of the individual liberties of the various kingdoms and principalities and direct subordination of each area to the king himself. It was, in other words, a solution based on the principles of absolutism.

Olivares was unable to match the state-building achievement of Richelieu in France. His failure, which was complete by the time he fell from office in 1643, can be attributed to three factors. The first was the opposition he confronted within Castile itself, especially from the cities represented in the Cortes, over the question of taxation. The second, a problem facing Spain throughout the seventeenth century, was military failure, in this case the losses to France during the final phase of the Thirty Years' War. That failure aggravated the financial crisis and prevented the monarchy from capitalizing on the prestige that usually attends military victory. The third and most serious impediment was opposition to the policy of subordinating the outlying Spanish regions to the kingdom of Castile. The kingdoms and provinces on the periphery of the country were determined to maintain their individual laws and liberties, especially the powers of their own Cortes, in the face of the pressures to centralize power in Madrid. The problem became more serious as Olivares, in the wake of military defeat by the French and Dutch, put more pressure on these outlying kingdoms and provinces to contribute to the war effort.

Provincial resistance to a policy of Castilian centralization lay at the root of the Spanish crisis of the seventeenth

## CHRONOLOGY

### International Conflict in the Seventeenth Century

| | |
|---|---|
| **1609** | Truce between the seven Dutch provinces and Spain |
| **1618** | Bohemian revolt against Habsburg rule; beginning of the Thirty Years' War |
| **1620** | Imperial forces defeat Bohemians at Battle of White Mountain |
| **1648** | Treaty of Westphalia, ending the Thirty Years' War; Treaty of Münster, ending the Dutch War of Independence |
| **1667** | Beginning of the wars of Louis XIV |
| **1672** | William III of Orange-Nassau becomes captain-general of Dutch; beginning of the war against France (1672–1678) |
| **1688–1697** | War of the League of Augsburg (Nine Years' War); England and Scotland join forces with Prussia, Austria, the Dutch Republic, and many German states against France |
| **1697** | Treaty of Ryswick |
| **1700–1721** | Great Northern War in which Russia eventually defeated Sweden; emergence of Russia as a major power |
| **1701–1713** | War of the Spanish Succession |
| **1713** | Treaty of Utrecht |

century. This crisis did not throw Castile itself into a state of civil war. Unlike Paris during the Fronde, Madrid itself remained peaceful. Throughout the 1640s the crown managed to maintain order within its main kingdom, probably because it had learned the art of negotiating directly with the thousands of towns and villages that ran local government. Instead, the Spanish crisis took the form of separatist revolts in Portugal, Catalonia, Sicily, and Naples. With the exception of Portugal, which recovered its sovereignty in 1640, the monarchy met this test and managed to maintain control of its provincial and Italian territories. In the aftermath of the revolts, however, the monarchy failed to bring the areas within the sphere of effective central government control.

The relative weakness of the Spanish monarchy, especially in comparison with that of France, became most apparent in the late seventeenth century, the age of Louis XIV. In two important respects the Spanish government failed to match the achievement of the French. First, it could never escape the grip that the old noble families had on the central administration. The unwillingness of the nobility to recruit ministers and officials from the mercantile and professional groups within society (which were small to begin with in Spain) worked against the achievement of bureaucratic efficiency and made innovation virtually impossible. Second, unlike the French government during Colbert's ministry, the Spanish government failed to encourage economic growth. The hostility of the aristocratic ruling class to mercantile affairs, coupled with a traditional Spanish unwillingness to follow the example of foreigners (especially when they were Protestants) prevented the country from stemming its own economic decline and the government from solving the formidable financial problems facing it. To make matters worse, the Spanish government failed to make its system of tax collection more efficient.

The mood that prevailed within the upper levels of Castilian society in the seventeenth century reflected the failure of the government and the entire nation. The contrast between the glorious achievements of the monarchy during the reign of Philip II (r. 1555–1598) and the somber realities of the late seventeenth century led most members of the ruling class to retreat into that past, a nostalgia that only encouraged further economic and political stagnation. The work of Miguel de Cervantes (1547–1616), the greatest Spanish writer of the seventeenth century, reflected this change in the Spanish national mood. In 1605 and 1615 Cervantes published (in two parts) *Don Quixote*, the story of an idealistic wandering nobleman who pursued dreams of an

elusive military glory. This work, which as we have seen in Chapter 14 explored the relationship between illusion and reality, served as a commentary on a nobility that had lost confidence in itself.

Spanish painting, which paradoxically entered its Golden Age at the time the country began to lose its economic, political, and military vitality, was less willing to accept the decline of Spain. There was very little in the paintings of the great Spanish artist Diego de Velázquez (1599–1660) that would suggest the malaise that was affecting Spain and its nobility at the time. Velázquez painted in the baroque style that was in favor at court throughout Europe, depicting his subjects in heroic poses and imbuing them with a sense of royal or aristocratic dignity. One of his historical paintings, *The Surrender of Breda* (1634), commemorated a rare Spanish military victory over the Dutch in 1625 and the magnanimity of the Spanish victors toward their captives. All this was intended to reinforce the prestige

**Diego de Velázquez, Portrait of the Prince Baltasar Carlos, Heir to the Spanish Throne**
The depiction of the six-year-old prince on a rearing horse was intended to suggest military and political power at a time when the monarchy was losing both. The prince died in 1646, before he could succeed to the throne.

**Diego de Velázquez, *The Surrender of Breda*, 1634**
The Spanish victory over the Dutch in 1625 gave Velázquez a rare opportunity to depict Spanish soldiers in a role they had frequently played in the sixteenth century.

of the monarchy, the royal family, and the nation itself at a time when the imperial grandeur of the past had faded. Velázquez's painting reflected the ideals of absolutism but ignored the realities of Spanish political and military life.

# Absolutism and State Building in Central and Eastern Europe

■ What was the nature of royal absolutism in central and eastern Europe, and how did the policies of the Ottoman Empire and Russia help establish the boundaries of the West during this period?

The forces that led to the establishment of absolutism and state building in France and Spain also made an impact on central and eastern Europe. In Germany the Thirty Years' War led to the establishment of two absolutist states, Prussia and the Austrian Habsburg Monarchy. Further to the East, the Ottoman and Russian Empires, both of them on the margins of the West, also developed absolutist political systems that shared many of the same characteristics as those in western and central Europe. Russia, previously thought of as belonging to an Eastern, Asian world, entered upon a program of westernization and staked a claim to be considered a Western power. At the same time the Ottoman Empire, whose political develop-

ment followed a Western pattern in many respects, was increasingly dismissed by Europeans as part of a distant, non-Western world.

## Germany and the Thirty Years' War, 1618–1648

Before 1648 the main political power within the geographical area known as Germany was the Holy Roman Empire. This large political formation was a loose confederation of kingdoms, principalities, duchies, ecclesiastical territories, and cities, each of which had its own laws and political institutions. The emperor, who was elected by a body of German princes, exercised immediate jurisdiction only in his own dynastic possessions and in the imperial cities. He also convened a legislative assembly known as the *Reichstag*, over which he exercised limited influence. But the emperor did not have a large administrative or judicial bureaucracy through which he could enforce imperial law in the localities. The empire was not in any sense a sovereign state, even though it had long been a major force in European diplomacy. It had acquired and maintained that international position by relying on the military and financial contributions of its imperial cities and the lands controlled directly by the Habsburg emperors.

The Thirty Years' War permanently altered the nature of this vast and intricate political structure. That war began as a conflict between Protestant German princes and the Catholic emperor over religious and constitutional issues. The incident that triggered it in 1618 was the so-called Defenestration of Prague, when members of the predominantly Protestant Bohemian legislature, known as the Diet, threw two imperial officials out a castle window as a protest against the religious policies of their recently elected king, the future emperor Ferdinand II. The Diet proceeded to depose Ferdinand, a Catholic, and elect a Protestant prince, Frederick V of the Palatinate, to replace him. The war soon broadened into a European-wide struggle over the possession of German and Spanish territory, as the Danes, Swedes, and French successively entered the conflict against the emperor and his Spanish Habsburg relatives. For a brief period in the late 1620s England also entered the conflict against Spain. The war, which was fought mainly on German soil, had a devastating effect on the country. More than one million soldiers marched across German lands, sacking towns and exploiting the resources of local communities. Germany lost up to one-third of its population, while the destruction of property retarded the economic development of the country for more than fifty years.

The political effects of the war were no less traumatic. By virtue of the Treaty of Westphalia, which ended the war in 1648, the empire was permanently weakened, although it continued to function until 1806 (see Map 15.3). The individual German territories within the empire developed more institutional autonomy than they had before the war.

They became sovereign states themselves, with their own armies, foreign policies, and central bureaucracies. Two of these German states soon surpassed all the others in size and military strength and became major European powers. The first was Brandenburg-Prussia, a collection of various territories in northern Germany that was transformed into the kingdom of Prussia at the beginning of the eighteenth century. In the nineteenth century Prussia would unify Germany under its leadership. The second state was the Austrian Habsburg Monarchy, which in the eighteenth century was usually identified simply as Austria. The Habsburgs had long dominated the Holy Roman Empire and continued to secure election as emperors after the Treaty of Westphalia. In the late seventeenth century, however, the Habsburg Monarchy acquired its own institutional identity, distinct from that of the empire. It consisted of the lands that the Habsburgs controlled directly in the southeastern part of the empire and other territories, including the kingdom of Hungary, which lay outside the territorial boundary of the empire. Both Prussia and Austria developed their own forms of absolutism during the second half of the seventeenth century.

## The Growth of the Prussian State

In 1648, at the end of the Thirty Years' War, Prussia could barely have claimed the status of an independent state, much less that of an absolute monarchy. The core of the

**Defenestration of Prague, May 23, 1618**

The Thirty Years' War was touched off when Protestant nobles in the Bohemian legislature threw two Catholic imperial governors out the window of a castle in Prague.

Map 15.3 Europe After the Treaty of Westphalia, 1648

**Europe After the Treaty of Westphalia, 1648**

- Spanish dominions
- Austrian dominions
- Brandenburg-Prussia
- Swedish dominions
- ——— Boundary of Holy Roman Empire

SCOTLAND

IRELAND

ENGLAND

London

ATLANTIC
OCEAN

North
Sea

DUTCH
REPUBLIC
Amsterdam

SPANISH
NETHERLANDS

Paris

FRANCE

SWITZERLAND

Rhine R.

Rhône R.

PORTUGAL

SPAIN

Madrid

FEZ AND MOROCCO

DENMARK
AND
NORWAY

Copenhagen

Baltic Sea

SWEDEN

POMERANIA

BREMEN
BRANDENBURG
Berlin

SAXONY   SILESIA

BOHEMIA
MORAVIA

BAVARIA

TYROL

Milan

Genoa

Corsica
(Genoa)   Rome

Sardinia

Palermo

Sicily

POLAND

Warsaw

HUNGARY

Vienna
AUSTRIA

Budapest

Danube R.

VENETIAN REPUBLIC

PAPAL
STATES

Naples

Mediterranean Sea

RUSSIA

Black Sea

OTTOMAN   EMPIRE

Constantinople

Athens

Crete
(Venice)

OTTOMAN
VASSALS

0    400 km
0    400 mi

**Map 15.3   Europe After the Treaty of Westphalia, 1648**

The Holy Roman Empire no longer included the Dutch Republic, which was now independent of Spain. Some of the lands of the Austrian Habsburg Monarchy and Brandenburg-Prussia lay outside the boundaries of the Holy Roman Empire. Italy was divided into a number of small states in the north, while Naples, Sicily, and Sardinia were ruled by Spain.

Prussian state was Brandenburg, which claimed the status of an electorate because its ruler cast one of the ballots to elect the Holy Roman Emperor. The lands that belonged to the elector of Brandenburg lay scattered throughout northern Germany and stretched into eastern Europe. As a result of the Thirty Years' War, the archbishoprics of Magdeburg and East Pomerania were annexed to Brandenburg. The Hohenzollern family, in whose line the electorate of Brandenburg passed, also owned or controlled various parcels of German territory in the Rhineland, near the borders of the Spanish Netherlands. In 1618 the Hohenzollerns had acquired the much larger but equally remote duchy of Prussia, a Baltic territory lying outside the boundaries of the Holy Roman Empire. As ruler of these disparate and noncontiguous lands, the elector of Brandenburg had virtually no state bureaucracy, collected few taxes, and commanded only a small army. Most of his territories, moreover, lay in ruins in 1648, having been devastated by Swedish and imperial troops at various times during the war.

The Great Elector Frederick William (r. 1640–1688) began the long process of turning this ramshackle structure into a powerful and cohesive German state (see Map 15.4). His son King Frederick I (r. 1688–1713) and grandson Frederick William I (r. 1713–1740) completed the transformation. The key to their success, as it was for all aspiring absolute monarchs in eastern Europe, was to secure the compliance of the traditional nobility, who in Prussia were known as Junkers°. The Great Elector Frederick William achieved this end by granting the Junkers a variety of privileges, including exemption from import duties and the excise tax. The most valuable concession was the legal confirmation of their rights over the serfs. During the previous 150 years Prussian peasants had lost their freedom, becoming permanently bound to the estates of their lords and completely subject to the Junkers' arbitrary brand of local justice. The Junkers had a deeply vested interest in perpetuating this oppressive system of serfdom, and the lawgiver Frederick was able to provide them with the legal guarantees they required.

## DOCUMENT

# A German Writer Describes the Horrors of the Thirty Years' War

*In 1669 the German writer H. J. C. Grimmelshausen (1625–1676) published an imaginary account of the adventures of a German vagabond, to whom he gave the name Simplicissimus. The setting of the book was the Thirty Years' War in Germany, which Grimmelshausen had experienced firsthand. At age 10 Grimmelshausen, like the character Simplicissimus in the book, was captured by Hessian troops and later became a camp-follower. In this chapter Simplicissimus describes how the palace of his father was stormed, plundered, and ruined.*

The first thing that these troops did was, that they stabbed their horses; thereafter each fell to his appointed task, which task was either more or less than ruin and destruction. For though some began to slaughter and to boil and to roast, so that it looked as if there should be a merry banquet forward, yet others there were who did but storm through the house above and below the stairs. . . . All that they had no mind to take with them they cut in pieces. Some thrust their swords through the hay and straw as if they had not enough sheep and swine to slaughter; and some shook the feathers out of the beds and in their stead stuffed in bacon and other dried meat and provisions as if such were better and softer to sleep upon. Others broke the stove and the windows as if they had a never-ending summer to promise. Housewares of copper and tin they beat flat, and packed such vessels, all bent and spoiled, in with the rest. Bedsteads, tables, chairs and benches they burned, though there lay many cords of dry wood in the yard. . . .

Our maid was so handled in the stable that she could not come out; which is a shame to tell of. Our man they laid bound upon the ground, thrust a gag into his mouth, and poured a pailful of filthy water into his body; and by this, which they called a Swedish draught, they forced him to lead a party of them to another place where they captured men and beasts, and brought them back to our farm, in which company were my dad, my mother, and our Ursula.

And now they began first to take the flints out of their pistols and in place of them to jam the peasants' thumbs in and so to torture the poor rogues as if they had been about the burning of witches. For one of them they had taken they thrust into the baking oven and there lit a fire under him, although he had as yet confessed no crime; as for another, they put a cord round his head and so twisted it tight with a piece of wood that the blood gushed from his mouth and nose and ears. In a word each had his own device to torture the peasants, and each peasant his several torture.

Source: Reprinted from *The Adventurous Simplicissimus: Being the Description of the Life of a Strange Vagabond Named Melchior Sternfels Von Fuchshaim* by H. J. C. Grimmelshausen. Published by the University of Nebraska Press.

---

With the loyalty of the Junkers secure, Frederick William went about the process of building a powerful Prussian state. A large administrative bureaucracy, centralized under a General Directory in Berlin, governed both financial and military affairs throughout the elector's lands. At first it was staffed by members of the nobility, but eventually educated commoners were recruited into the system. The taxes that the government collected, especially from the towns, went in large part to fund a standing army, which had come into being in the late 1650s.

The Prussian army grew rapidly, rising to 30,000 men in 1690 and 80,000 by 1740. It consisted of a combination of carefully recruited volunteers, foreign mercenaries, and, after 1713, conscripts from the general population. Its most famous regiment, known as the Blue Prussians or the Giants of Potsdam, consisted of 1,200 men, each of whom was at least six feet tall. Commanded by officers drawn from the nobility and reinforced by Europe's first system of military reserves, this army quickly became the best trained fighting force in Europe. Prussia became a model military state, symbolized by the transformation of the royal gardens into an army training ground during the reign of Frederick William I.

As this military state grew in size and complexity, its rulers acquired many of the attributes of absolute rule. Most significantly they became the sole legislators within the state. The main representative assembly in the electorate, the Diet of Brandenburg, met for the last time in 1652. Frederick William and his successors, however, continued to consult with smaller local assemblies, especially in the matter of taxation. The elevation of Frederick I's status to that of king of Prussia in 1701 marked a further consolidation of power in the person of the ruler. His son's style of rule, which included physical punishment of judges whose decisions displeased him, suggested that the Prussian monarchy not only had attained absolute power but could occasionally abuse it.

## The Austrian Habsburg Monarchy

The Austrian Habsburgs were much less successful than the Hohenzollerns in building a centralized, consolidated state along absolutist lines. The various territories that made up the Austrian Habsburg Monarchy in the late seventeenth century were larger and more diverse than those that belonged to the king of Prussia. In addition to the collection of duchies that form present-day Austria and that then served as the core of the monarchy, it embraced two subordinate kingdoms, which were themselves composed of various semiautonomous principalities and duchies. The first of these, lying to the north, was the kingdom of Bohemia, which had struggled against Habsburg control for nearly a century and included Moravia and Silesia. The second, lying to the southeast, was the kingdom of Hungary, including the large semiautonomous principality of Transylvania. The Habsburgs regained Hungary from the Ottoman Empire in stages between 1664 and 1718. In 1713 the monarchy also acquired the former Spanish Netherlands and the Italian territories of Milan and Naples.

The Austrian Habsburg monarchs of the seventeenth and early eighteenth centuries never succeeded in integrating these ethnically, religiously, and politically diverse lands into a unified, cohesive state similar to that of France. The

problem was a lack of a unified bureaucracy. The only centralized administrative institutions in this amalgam of kingdoms were the Court Chamber, which superintended the collection of taxes throughout the monarchy, and the Austrian army, which included troops from all Habsburg lands. Like many European military forces it had become a standing army in 1648, and by 1716 it had a troop strength of 165,000 men. Even these centralized institutions had difficulty operating smoothly. The council of the army had trouble integrating units drawn from separate kingdoms, while the Court Chamber never developed a uniform system of tax collection. For all practical purposes the Habsburgs had to rule their various kingdoms separately.

In governing its Austrian and Bohemian lands, this decentralized Habsburg Monarchy nonetheless acquired some of the characteristics of absolutist rule. This development toward absolutism began long before the Treaty of

## Map 15.4  The Growth of Brandenburg-Prussia, 1618–1786

By acquiring lands throughout northern Germany, Prussia became a major European power. The process began during the early seventeenth century, but it continued well into the eighteenth century. The Prussian army, which was the best trained fighting force in Europe in the eighteenth century, greatly facilitated Prussia's growth.

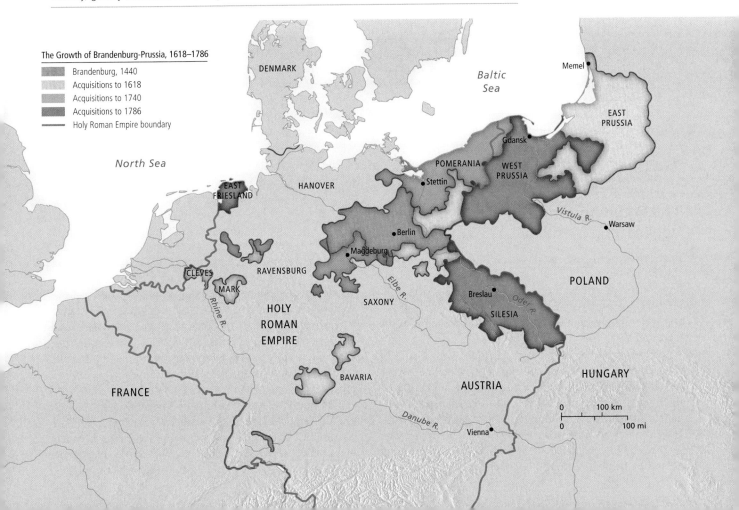

Westphalia in 1648. After defeating the Bohemians at the Battle of White Mountain in 1620 during the Thirty Years' War, Emperor Ferdinand II (r. 1618–1637) had decided to strengthen his authority in the areas under his direct control. Bohemia, which had led the revolt against him, was the main target of this policy, but the emperor used this opportunity to increase his power throughout his territories. After punishing the rebels and exiling many of the Protestant nobility, he undertook a deliberate expansion of his legislative and judicial powers, and he secured direct control over all his administrative officials.

A policy of severe religious repression accompanied this increase in the emperor's authority. Like Cardinal Richelieu of France, Ferdinand assumed that Protestantism served as a justification for rebellion, and he therefore decided that its practice could not be tolerated. Protestants in all the emperor's territories were forced to take a Catholic loyalty oath, and Protestant education was banned. Protestant towns were destroyed at exactly the same time that Richelieu was razing the fortifications of the Huguenot town of La Rochelle. These efforts at reconversion continued right through the seventeenth century. They amounted to a policy of religious or "confessional" absolutism.

While the Habsburgs succeeded in imposing some elements of absolutist rule on the Austrians and the Bohemians in the early seventeenth century, they encountered much more resistance when they attempted to follow the same course of action with respect to Hungary in the late seventeenth and eighteenth centuries. Hungarians had a long tradition of limited, constitutional rule in which the national Diet had exercised powers of legislation and taxation, just as Parliament did in England. Habsburg emperors made some limited inroads on these traditions but they were never able to break them. They also were unable to achieve the same degree of religious uniformity that they had imposed on their other territories. In Hungary the Habsburgs encountered the limits of royal absolutism.

## The Ottoman Empire: Between East and West

In the seventeenth and early eighteenth centuries the southeastern border of the Habsburg monarchy separated the kingdom of Hungary from the Ottoman Empire. This militarized frontier marked not only the political boundary between two empires but a deeper cultural boundary between East and West.

As we have seen in previous chapters, the West is not just a geographical but also a cultural realm, and the people who inhabit this realm, although distinct from one another, share many of the same religious, political, legal, and philosophical traditions. The Ottoman Turks, who posed a recurrent military threat to the Habsburg monarchy and who reached the gates of Vienna in 1683, were generally thought of as not belonging to this Western world. Because the

Ottoman Turks were Muslims, Europeans considered them enemies of Christianity, infidels who were bent on the destruction of Christendom. In the sixteenth century Catholics and Protestants alike claimed that the military victories of the Turks over European forces were signs of divine punishment for the sins European Christians had committed. Ottoman emperors, known as sultans, were considered despots who ruled over their subjects as slaves. The sultans were also depicted in Western literature as cruel and brutal tyrants, the opposite of the ideal Christian prince of Europe. One French play of 1612 depicted the mother of the sultan Mehmed the Conquerer (r. 1451–1481) as drinking the blood of a victim.

These stereotypes of the Turks served the function of giving Europeans a sense of their own Western identity. Turks became a negative reference group with whom Europeans could favorably compare themselves. The realities of Ottoman politics and culture, however, were quite different from the ways in which they were represented in European literature. Turkish despotism, the name Europeans gave to the Ottoman system of government, existed only in theory. Ever since the fourteenth century Ottoman writers had claimed for the sultan extraordinary powers, including the right to seize the landed property of his subjects at will. In practice he never exercised unlimited power. His prerogatives were limited by the spirit of Muslim law, and he shared power with the grand vizier, who was his chief executive officer. In practice there was little difference between the rule of the sultans and that of European absolute monarchs. As far as religious policy is concerned, the Ottoman practice of tolerating non-Muslim religions within the empire made the sultans less absolutist than most of their seventeenth-century European counterparts.

**DOCUMENT**

Venetian Observations on the Ottoman Empire (late 16th c.)

Even the high degree of administrative centralization for which the Ottoman Empire was famous did not encompass all the regions under its control. Many of its provinces, especially those in the Balkans, enjoyed a considerable measure of autonomy, especially in the seventeenth century. The Balkans, which were geographically part of Europe, never experienced the full force of direct Turkish rule. In all the Ottoman provinces there was a complex pattern of negotiation between the central imperial administration and local officials. In this respect the Ottoman Empire was similar to the absolutist monarchies of western and central Europe. The Ottoman Empire bore the closest resemblance to the Spanish monarchy, which also ruled many far-flung territories in Europe. Like the Spanish monarchy, the Ottoman Empire declined in power during the seventeenth century and lost effective control of some of its outlying provinces.

Ottoman Turks and Europeans frequently went to war against each other, but there was a constant pattern of diplomatic, economic, and cultural interaction between them. The Turks had been involved in European warfare since the fifteenth century, and they had formed diplomatic alliances with the French against the Austrian Habsburgs on a number of occasions. Europeans and Ottomans often borrowed military technology from each other, and they also shared knowledge of administrative techniques. Trade between European countries and the Ottoman Empire remained brisk throughout this period. Europe supplied hardware and textiles to the Turks while they in turn shipped coffee, tobacco, and tulips to European ports. Communities of Turks and other Muslims lived in European cities, while numerous European merchants resided in territories under Ottoman control.

These encounters between Turks and Europeans suggest that the militarized boundary between the Habsburgs and the Ottoman Empire was much more porous than its fortifications would suggest. Military conflict and Western contempt for Muslim Turks disguised a much more complex process of political and cultural interaction between the two civilizations. Europeans tended to think of the Ottoman Empire as "oriental," but it is more accurate to view it as a region lying between the East and the West.

## Russia and the West

The other seventeenth-century power that marked the boundary between East and West was the vast Russian Empire, which stretched from its boundary with Poland in the west all the way to the Pacific Ocean in the east. Until the end of the seventeenth century, the kingdom of Muscovy and the lands attached to it seemed, at least to Europeans, part of the Asiatic world. Dominated by an Eastern Orthodox branch of Christianity, Russia drew very little upon the cultural traditions associated with western Europe. Unlike its neighboring Slavic kingdom of Poland, it had not absorbed large doses of German culture. It also appeared to Europeans to be another example of "oriental despotism," a state in which the ruler, known as the tsar, could rule his subjects at will, "not bound up by any law or custom."

Adan Olearius:
A Foreign
Traveler in
Russia (early
17th c.)

During the reign of Tsar Peter I, known as Peter the Great (r. 1682–1725), Russia underwent a process of westernization, bringing it more into line with the culture of European countries and becoming a major European power. This policy began after Peter visited England, Holland, northern Germany, and Austria in 1697 and 1698. Upon his return he directed his officials and members of the upper levels of Russian society to adopt Western styles of dress and appearance, including the removal of men's beards. (Scissors were kept in the customs house for this purpose alone.) Beards symbolized the backward, Eastern, Orthodox culture from whose grip Peter hoped to extricate his country. Young Russian boys were sent abroad for their education. Women began to participate openly in the social

Peter the
Great

and cultural life of the cities, in violation of Orthodox custom. Smoking was permitted despite the Church's insistence that Scripture condemned it. The calendar was reformed and books were printed in modern Russian type. Peter's importation of Western art and the imitation of Western architecture complemented this policy of enforced cultural change. Westernization, however, involved more than a change of manners and appearance. It also involved military and political reforms that changed the character of the Russian state.

During the first twenty-five years of his reign Peter had found himself unable to achieve sustained military success against his two great enemies, the Ottoman Turks to the south and the Swedes to the west. During the Great Northern War with Sweden (1700–1721) Peter introduced a number of military reforms that eventually turned the tide against his enemy. These reforms were based on the knowledge he had acquired of military technology, organization, and tactics of western European states, especially Prussia and, ironically, Sweden itself. Having introduced a program of conscription, Peter assembled a large standing army of more than 200,000 men, which he trained and disciplined in the Prussian manner. All of this was supported by the imposition of new taxes on a variety of commodities, including beards, and the encouragement of Russian industry in much the same way that Colbert had encouraged French industry. A central council, established in 1711, not only directed financial administration but also levied and supplied troops, not unlike the General Directory of the electorate of Brandenburg.

This new military state also acquired many of the centralizing and absolutist features of western European

## CHRONOLOGY

### The Age of Absolutism in Central and Eastern Europe

**1618** Ferdinand II becomes Holy Roman Emperor (r. 1618–1637)

**1640** Beginning of the reign of Frederick William, the Great Elector of Brandenburg Prussia (r. 1640–1688)

**1657** Leopold I becomes Holy Roman Emperor (r. 1657–1705)

**1682** Accession of Tsar Peter the Great of Russia (r. 1682–1725)

**1688** Accession of Frederick as elector of Prussia; becomes king of Prussia in 1701

**1703** Foundation of St. Petersburg, Russia's new capital and "window on the West"

**1705** Joseph I becomes Holy Roman Emperor (r. 1705–1711)

**1711** Charles VI, brother of Joseph I, becomes Holy Roman Emperor (r. 1711–1740)

# St. Petersburg and the West

The major encounter between Russia and the West during the reign of Peter the Great was the building of a new capital city, St. Petersburg, on the marshy delta of the Neva River, which empties into the Gulf of Finland. The land on which the city was located was seized from Sweden during the Northern War. The construction of the city, which first served as a fortress and then a naval base in that conflict, occurred at a tremendous cost in treasure and human life. Using the royal powers that he had significantly augmented earlier in his reign, Peter ordered more than 10,000 workers (and possibly twice that number) from throughout his kingdom to realize this ambitious and risky project. The harsh weather conditions, the ravages of malaria and other diseases, and the chronic shortages of provisions in a distant location resulted in the death of a few thousand workers—numbers that were often greatly exaggerated by foreigners. Beginning in 1710 Peter ordered the transfer of central governmental, commercial, and military functions to the new city. The city became the site for Peter's Winter Palace, the residences of Russia's foreign ambassadors, and the headquarters of the Russian Orthodox Church. The Academy of Fine Arts and the Academy of Sciences were built shortly thereafter. During the 1730s Russia's first bourse, or exchange, fulfilled the prophecy of a British observer in 1710 that the city, with its network of canals, "might one day prove a second Amsterdam or Venice." Thus St. Petersburg came to embody all the modernizing and westernizing achievements of Peter the Great.

Russia's encounter with the West at St. Petersburg was reflected both in the location of the new city and the styles in which the buildings were constructed. As a port with access to the Baltic Sea, the new city, often described as "a window on the West," looked toward the European ports with which Russia increased its commerce and the European powers that Russia engaged in battle and diplomacy. The architects, stonemasons, and interior decorators that Peter commissioned came from France, Italy, Germany and the Dutch Republic, and they constructed the buildings in contemporary European styles. The general plan of the city, drawn up by the French architect Le Blond, featured straight, paved streets with stone paths that are now called sidewalks. St. Petersburg thus became a port through which Western influences entered Russia. The contrast with the old capital, Moscow, which was situated in the center of the country and embodied the spirit of the old Russia that Peter strove to modernize, could not have been clearer.

The construction of St. Petersburg played a central role in transforming Russia from a medieval kingdom on the fringes of Europe into a modern, Western power. It did not, however, eliminate the conflict in Russia between those who held the West up as the cultural standard that Russia should strive to emulate and those who celebrated Russia's cultural superiority over the West. This conflict between westernizers and Slavophiles, which began in the eighteenth century, has continued to the present day. During the period of communism in the twentieth century, when St. Petersburg was renamed Leningrad and Moscow once again became the political capital of the country, the Slavophile tradition tended to prevail. It is no coincidence that the collapse of communism and the disintegration of the Union of Soviet Socialist Republics in 1989 has led to a renewed emphasis on Russia's ties with the West. The celebration of the 300th anniversary of St. Petersburg in 2003 and the restoration of its original name in 1991 constitute one more episode in the effort to integrate Russia more fully into the West.

## For Discussion

How did the founding of St. Petersburg contribute to the growth of the Russian state?

How did Peter the Great's absolute power facilitate the growth of the city?

**A Picture of St. Petersburg (1815)**
This view of St. Petersburg from the quay in front of the Winter Palace reveals the city's Western character. The buildings lying across the Neva River, including the bourse, were designed by European architects. The gondolas, seen in the foreground docking at the quay, enhanced St. Petersburg's reputation as "Venice of the North."

monarchies. Efforts to introduce absolutism in Russia had begun during the reigns of Alexis (r. 1645–1676) and Fedor (r. 1676–1682), who had achieved limited success in strengthening the central administration, controlling the nobility, and brutally suppressing peasant rebellions. Peter built upon his predecessors' achievement. He created an entirely new structure for managing the empire, appointing twelve governors to superintend Russia's forty-three separate provinces. He brought the Church under state control. By establishing a finely graded hierarchy of official ranks in the armed forces, the civil administration, and the court, Peter not only improved administrative efficiency but also made it possible for men of nonaristocratic birth to attain the same privileged status as the old landowning nobility. At the same time he won the support of all landowners by introducing primogeniture (inheritance of the entire estate by the eldest son), which prevented their estates from being subdivided, and supporting the enserfment of the peasants. In dealing with his subjects Peter claimed more power than any other absolute monarch in Europe. During the trial of his own son, Alexis, for treason in 1718, he told the clergy that "we have a sufficient and absolute power to judge our son for his crimes according to our own pleasure."[4]

The most visible sign of Peter's policy of westernization was the construction of the port city of St. Petersburg on the Gulf of Finland, which became the new capital of the Russian Empire. One of the main objectives of Russian foreign policy during Peter's reign had been to secure access to the Baltic Sea, allowing Russia to open maritime trade with Europe and to become a Western naval power. By draining a swamp on the estuary of the Neva River, Peter laid the foundations of a city that became the new capital of his empire. Construction began in 1703, and within twenty years St. Petersburg had a population of 40,000 people. With his new capital city now looking westward, and an army and central administration reformed on the basis of Prussian and French example, Peter could enter the world of European diplomacy and warfare as both a Western and an absolute monarch.

# Resistance to Absolutism in England and the Dutch Republic

■ Why did absolutism fail to take root in England and the Dutch Republic during the seventeenth century?

The kingdom of England and the northern provinces of the Netherlands stand out as the two great exceptions to the dominant pattern of political development in seventeenth-century Europe. Both of these countries successfully resisted the establishment of royal absolutism, and

neither underwent the rigorous centralization of power and the dynamic growth of the state that usually accompanied the establishment of absolutist rule. In England the encounter between the proponents and opponents of absolute monarchy was more pronounced than in any other European country. It resulted in the temporary destruction of the monarchy in 1649 and the establishment of parliamentary supremacy after the Glorious Revolution of 1688. In the northern provinces of the Netherlands, known as the Dutch Republic, an even more emphatic rejection of absolutism occurred. During their long struggle to win their independence from Spain, the Dutch established a republican, decentralized form of government, but that did not prevent them from acquiring considerable military strength and dominating the world's economy during the seventeenth century.

## The English Monarchy

At various times in the seventeenth century English monarchs tried to introduce royal absolutism, but the political institutions and the political culture of the country stood as major obstacles to their designs. As early as the fifteenth century, the English writer and diplomat Sir John Fortescue (ca. 1395–1477) had celebrated England's parliamentary system of government by contrasting it with that of France, where he claimed the king could make laws by himself and impose his will on his subjects. Fortescue's treatise contributed to the pride Englishmen had in what they considered their distinctive set of political and legal traditions. The most important of these traditions was the making of law and the levying of taxes by the two Houses of Parliament, the House of Lords and the House of Commons, with the king holding the power to sign or veto the bills they passed.

In the early seventeenth century the perception began to arise, especially among certain members of the House of Commons, that this tradition of parliamentary government was under attack. The first Stuart king, James I (r. 1603–1625), who succeeded the last Tudor monarch, Elizabeth I, aroused some of these fears as early as 1604, when he called his first parliament. James thought of himself as an absolute monarch, and in a number of speeches and published works he emphasized the height of his independent royal power, which was known in England as the prerogative°. James also spoke often about his divine right to rule, and he claimed that the main function of Parliament was simply to give the king advice, rather than to make law. These statements had the effect of antagonizing members of Parliament, leading them to defend their privileges, including the right they claimed to discuss foreign policy and other affairs of state.

James believed that he was an absolute monarch, but he did not actually try to put his ideas into practice. For

**DOCUMENT**

James I on the Divine Right of Kings (1598)

example, he did not try to make laws or levy taxes without the consent of Parliament or deny men their legal rights, such as freedom from arbitrary imprisonment. The real political fireworks did not begin until James's son, Charles I (r. 1625–1649), succeeded him. Charles believed in absolutism every bit as much as his father, but unlike James, Charles actually put his theories into practice. His efforts to force his subjects to lend money to the government during a war with Spain (1625–1629) and his imprisonment of men who refused to make these loans led Parliament to pass the Petition of Right in 1628. This document declared boldly that subjects possessed fundamental rights that kings could not violate under any circumstances, even when the country was at war.

Charles consented to the Petition of Right, but when Parliament met again in 1629, further conflict between the king and certain members of the House of Commons developed over taxation and the king's religious policies. Charles had been collecting duties on exports without parliamentary approval since 1625. He had also begun to favor conservative clergymen known as Arminians, leading the more zealous English Protestants, the Puritans, to fear that the English Church was leaning in the direction of Catholicism or "popery." Faced with this opposition over constitutional and religious issues, Charles decided to dismiss this parliament and to rule indefinitely without calling another one.

This period of nonparliamentary government, known as the personal rule,° lasted until 1640. During these years Charles, unable to collect taxes by the authority of Parliament, used his prerogative to bring in new revenues, especially by asking all subjects to pay "ship-money" to support the outfitting of ships to defend the country against attack. During the personal rule the king's religious policy fell under the control of William Laud, who was named archbishop of Canterbury in 1633 and who became one of the king's main privy councilors. Laud's determination to restore many of the rituals associated with Roman Catholicism alienated large numbers of Puritans and led to a growing perception that members of the king's government were engaged in a conspiracy to destroy both England's ancient constitution and the Protestant religion.

This period of absolutism might have continued indefinitely if Charles had not once again been faced with the financial demands of war. In 1636 the king tried to introduce a new religious liturgy in his northern kingdom of Scotland. The liturgy included a number of rituals that the firmly Calvinist Scottish population considered popish. The new liturgy so angered a group of women in Edinburgh that they threw their chairs at the bishop when he introduced it. In response to this affront to their religion, the Scots signed a National Covenant (1638) pledging themselves to defend the integrity of their Church, abolished episcopacy (government of the church by bishops) in favor of a Presbyterian system of church government, and mobi-

**The English House of Commons in 1604**
The men elected to sit in the House of Commons were known as Members of Parliament or MPs. In the early seventeenth century many of these men claimed that King James I was denying them their ancient privileges and liberties, including freedom of speech. They also objected to the claims of James that he was an absolute monarch.

lized a large army. To secure the funds to fight the Scots, Charles was forced to summon his English Parliament, thereby ending the period of personal rule.

## The English Civil Wars and Revolution

Tensions between the reconvened English Parliament and Charles led to the first revolution of modern times. The Short Parliament, called in April 1640, lasted only two months, but a Scottish military victory against the English in that year forced the king to call a second parliament. The Long Parliament, which met in November 1640, impeached many of the king's ministers and judges and dismantled the judicial apparatus of the eleven years of personal rule, including the courts that had been active in the prosecution of Puritans. Parliament declared the king's nonparliamentary taxes illegal and enacted a law limiting the time between the meetings of Parliament to three years.

This legislation did not satisfy the king's critics in Parliament. Their suspicion that the king was conspiring against them and their demand to approve all royal appointments created a poisoned political atmosphere in which neither side trusted the other. After the king and his armed guards forced their way into the House of Commons to arrest five members for treason, there was little hope of reconciliation. In August 1642 civil war began between the Parliamentarians, known as Roundheads because many of the artisans who supported them had close-cropped hair styles, and the Royalists or Cavaliers, who often wore their hair in long flowing locks. Parliament, which was supported by the Scots and which benefited from the creation in 1645 of a well-trained, efficient fighting force, the New Model Army, ultimately won this war in 1646 and took Charles prisoner. The king's subsequent negotiations with the Scots and the English Presbyterians, both of whom had originally fought against him, led to a second civil war in 1648. In this war, which lasted only a few months, the New Model Army once again defeated Royalist forces.

This military victory led to a series of revolutionary changes in the English system of government. Believing with some justification that Charles could never be trusted, and eager to bring about an end to years of political uncertainty, members of the army purged Parliament of its Presbyterian members, leaving only a small group of Independents. These men, who favored a form of church government in which the congregations had a high degree of autonomy, had broken off negotiations with Charles I. The remaining members of Parliament were known as the Rump, because they were all that was left of the Long Parliament elected in 1640. This small group of Independents in Parliament, following the wishes of the army, set up a court to try Charles in January 1649. The trial resulted in Charles's conviction and execution, and shortly thereafter the Rump destroyed the House of Lords and the monarchy itself. As Parliament had already abolished the episcopal structure of the English Church in 1646, these actions completed a genuine revolution, a political transformation that destroyed the very system of government and replaced it with new institutions.

The revolution resulted in the establishment of a republic, in which the House of Commons possessed supreme legislative power in the name of the people of England. This change in the system of government, however, did not lead to the introduction of a more democratic form of government. A government of this sort, in which a very large percentage of the adult male population would be allowed to vote, was the goal of a political party, the Levellers, which originated in the New Model Army and attracted consider-

## CHRONOLOGY

### A Century of Revolution in England and Scotland

| | |
|---|---|
| **1603** | James VI of Scotland (r. 1567–1625) becomes James I of England (r. 1603–1625) |
| **1625** | Death of James I and accession of Charles I (r. 1625–1649) |
| **1628** | Parliament passes the Petition of Right |
| **1629–1640** | Personal rule of Charles I |
| **1638** | Scots sign the National Covenant |
| **1640** | Opening of the Long Parliament |
| **1642–1646** | Civil War in England, ending with the capture of King Charles I |
| **1648** | Second Civil War; New Model Army defeats English Presbyterians and Scots |
| **1649** | Execution of Charles I of England and the beginning of the Republic |
| **1653** | End of the Long Parliament; beginning and dissolution of Barebones Parliament; Oliver Cromwell becomes Protector of England, Scotland, and Ireland |
| **1660** | Restoration of the monarchy in the person of Charles II; House of Lords and the Church of England also restored |
| **1685** | Death of Charles II and accession of his brother, James II (r. 1685–1688) |
| **1688–1689** | Glorious Revolution in England and Scotland |
| **1707** | England and Scotland politically joined to form the United Kingdom of Great Britain |

able support in London and the towns. In 1647 at Putney Bridge, near London, the Levellers participated in a debate with more conservative army officers concerning the future constitution of the country. The spokesmen for the Levellers called for annual parliaments, the separation of powers between the executive and legislative branches of government, and the introduction of universal suffrage for men. The army officers argued against this proposed constitution, arguing that the vote should be entrusted only to men who owned property. The officers made sure that the Leveller program would not be accepted. The Levellers eventually mutinied in the army, their leaders were imprisoned, and the party collapsed.

The fate of the Levellers and their program underlines the fact that the English revolution was brought about by men of property, especially by the gentry or lesser aristocracy who sat in the House of Commons and who served as officers in the New Model Army. Although these men defeated and executed the king and secured the right to participate regularly in the governance of the kingdom, they

# The Trial of Charles I

In January 1649, after the New Model Army had defeated Royalist forces in England's second civil war and purged Parliament of its Presbyterian members, the few remaining members of the House of Commons voted by a narrow margin to erect a High Court of Justice to try King Charles I. This trial, which resulted in Charles's execution, marked the only time in European history that a monarch was tried and executed while still holding the office of king.

The decision to try the king formed part of a deliberate political strategy. The men who arranged the proceeding knew that they were embarking upon a revolutionary course by declaring that the House of Commons, as the elected representative of the people, was the highest power in the realm. They also knew that the republican regime they were establishing did not command a large body of popular support. By trying the king publicly in a court of law and by ensuring that the trial was reported in daily newspapers (the first such trial in history), they hoped to prove the legitimacy of their cause and win support for the new regime.

The decision to bring the king to justice created two legal problems. The first was to identify a crime upon which the trial would be based. For many years members of Parliament had insisted that the king had violated the ancient laws of the kingdom. The charge read that he had "wickedly designed to erect an unlimited and tyrannical power" and had waged war against his people in two civil wars. His prosecutors claimed that those activities amounted to the crime of treason. The problem was that treason in England was a crime committed by a subject against the king, not by the king against his subjects. In order to try the king for this crime, his accusers had to construct a new theory of treason, according to which the king had attacked his own political body, which they identified with the kingdom or the state.

The second problem was to make the court itself a legitimate tribunal. According to English constitutional law, the king possessed the highest legal authority in the land. He appointed his judges, and the courts represented his authority. Parliament could vote to erect a special court, but the bill authorizing it would become law only if the king agreed to it. In this case the House of Commons had set up the court by its own authority, and it had named 135 men, most of whom were army officers, to serve as its judges. The revolutionary nature of this tribunal was difficult to disguise, and Charles made its illegality the basis of his defense. When asked how he would plead, he challenged the legitimacy of the court.

*"By what power am I called hither?" he asked. "I would know by what authority—I mean lawful authority. There are many unlawful authorities in the world—thieves and robbers by the highways. And when I know what lawful authority, I shall answer. Remember I am your king, your lawful king. . . . I have a trust committed to me by God by old and lawful descent; I will not betray it to answer to a new unlawful authority."*

By taking this position Charles put himself on the side of the law, and by refusing to enter a plea he also prevented his prosecutors from presenting the evidence against him.

The arguments that King Charles and John Bradshawe, the president of the court, presented regarding the legitimacy of the court reflected the main constitutional conflict in seventeenth-century England. On the one hand was the doctrine of divine-right absolutism, according to which the king received his authority from God. He was therefore responsible to God alone, not to the people. His subjects could neither try him in a court of law nor fight him on the battlefield. "A king," said Charles, "cannot be tried by any superior jurisdiction on earth." On the other hand was the doctrine of popular sovereignty, which held that political power came from the people. As Bradshawe said in response to Charles's objection, "Sir, as the law is your superior, so truly Sir, there is something that is superior to the law, and that is indeed the parent or author of law, and that is the people of England." This trial, therefore, involved not only a confrontation between Charles and his revolutionary judges but an encounter between two incompatible political ideologies.

In 1649 the advocates of popular sovereignty triumphed over those of divine right. Charles was convicted as a "tyrant, traitor, murderer, and public enemy of the good people of this nation." The verdict was never in doubt, although only 67 of the 135 men originally appointed as judges voted to convict the king, and a mere 59 signed the death warrant. The trial succeeded only to the extent that it facilitated the establishment of the new regime. With Charles gone, the Rump could move ahead with the abolition of the monarchy and the establishment of a republic. But in dramatic terms the trial was a complete failure. Charles, a small shy man with a nervous stammer, was expected to make a poor impression, but he spoke eloquently when he refused to plead, and he won support from spectators in the gallery. In the greatest show trial of the seven-

**Trial of Charles I at Westminster Hall, January 1649**
The king is sitting in the prisoner's box in the foreground, facing the commissioners of the High Court of Justice. His refusal to plead meant that a full trial could not take place.

teenth century, the royal defendant stole the show.

When Charles's son, Charles II, was restored to the throne in 1660, Royalists finally had their revenge against the judges of this court. Those who could be found alive were hanged, disemboweled, and quartered. For those who were already dead, there was to be another type of justice. In 1661 Royalists exhumed the badly decomposed corpses of Bradshawe, Henry Ireton, and Oliver Cromwell, the three men who bore the largest responsibility for the execution of the king. The three cadavers were hanged and

their skulls were placed on pikes on top of Westminster Hall. This macabre ritual served as the Royalists' way of vilifying the memory of the judges of this illegal and revolutionary trial, and their unpardonable sin of executing an anointed king.

## Questions of Justice

1. The men who brought King Charles to trial often spoke about bringing him to "justice." How is justice best understood in this context?
2. How does this trial reveal the limitations of divine-right absolutism in England?

## Taking It Further

Peacey, Jason, ed. *The Regicides and the Execution of Charles I*. 2001. A collection of essays on various aspects of this episode and the men who signed the death warrant.

Wedgewood, C. V. *The Trial of Charles I*. 1964. Presents a full account and analysis of the trial by one of the great historical stylists of the twentieth century.

were also determined to keep political power in the hands of their own class.

The republican government established in 1649 did not last. Tension between the army and the Rump, fueled by the belief that the Rump was not creating a godly society, resulted in the army's dissolution of the Long Parliament in 1653 and the selection of a small parliament of zealous Puritans, nominated by the army. Known as the Barebones Parliament for one of its members, Praise-God Barebones, this assembly soon became hopelessly divided between radicals who wished to eliminate state support of the Church, the Court of Chancery, and the universities, and the moderates who opposed these measures. Unable to overcome its divisions, it too was dissolved after sitting for only five months.

At that point Oliver Cromwell (1599–1658), the commander in chief of the army and the most prominent member of the Council of State after 1649, had himself proclaimed Protector of England, Scotland, and Ireland.

Allegorical View of Cromwell as Savior of England

Cromwell had been a leader of the revolution, a zealous Puritan who had provided crucial support for the execution of the king and the establishment of the republic. At the same time, however, Cromwell feared that the Levellers and now the radical Puritans of the Barebones Parliament would destroy the social order. The establishment of the Protectorate, in which Cromwell shared legislative power with Parliament, represented an effort to return to a more traditional system of government. Cromwell would not, however, go so far as to accept a petition of 1657 to make him king. After Cromwell's death in 1658 and the brief rule of his son Richard, the Protectorate collapsed. A period of political instability, in which there was renewed hostility between the army and the members of Parliament, led the army to restore the monarchy in 1660.

## Later Stuart Absolutism and the Glorious Revolution

Charles II (r. 1660–1685) and his brother James II (r. 1685–1688) were both absolutists who admired the political achievement of their cousin, Louis XIV of France. At the same time, however, they realized that they could never return to the policies of their father, much less adopt those of Louis. Neither of them attempted to rule indefinitely without Parliament, as Charles I had. Their main objective was to destroy the independence of Parliament by packing it with their own supporters and use the prerogative to weaken the force of the parliamentary statutes to which they objected.

The main political crisis of Charles II's reign was the attempt by a group of members of Parliament, headed by the Earl of Shaftesbury (1621–1683) and known by their

---

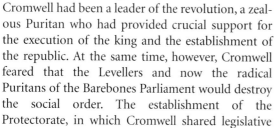

## DOCUMENT

# John Locke Justifies the Glorious Revolution

*John Locke wrote* Two Treatises of Government *between 1679 and 1682, during the reign of Charles II. The main purpose of the book was to justify armed resistance against Charles, who was pursuing absolutist policies, including attacks on the freedom of the English Parliament. Locke did not publish the* Two Treatises, *however, until after the Glorious Revolution of 1688. In order to justify that revolution, Locke wrote two new paragraphs, claiming that when a king abandons his responsibility to enforce the law, as James II had when he fled to France in December 1688, the government was dissolved and the people had the right to form a new one, as they had when they offered the crown to William and Mary in February 1689.*

There is one more way whereby such a government may be dissolved, and that is when he who has the supreme executive power neglects and abandons that charge, so that the laws already made can no longer be put in execution. This is demonstrably to reduce all to anarchy, and so effectually to dissolve the government. For laws not being made for themselves, but to be by their execution the

bonds of the society, to keep every part of the body politic in its due place and function, when that totally ceases, the government visibly ceases, and the people become a confused multitude, without order or connection. Where there is no longer the administration of justice, for the securing of men's rights, nor any remaining power within the community to direct the force, or provide for the necessities of the public, there is certainly no government left. Where the laws cannot be executed, it is all one as if there were no laws, and a government without laws is, I suppose, a mystery in politics, unconceivable to human capacity, and inconsistent with human society.

In these and in the like cases, when the government is dissolved, the people are at liberty to provide for themselves, by erecting a new legislative, differing from the other by the change of persons or form, or both, as they shall find it most for their safety and good. For the society can never, by the fault of another, lose the native and original right it has to preserve itself, which can only be done by a settled legislative and a fair and impartial execution of the laws made by it.

Source: From *Two Treatises of Government* by John Locke, 1698.

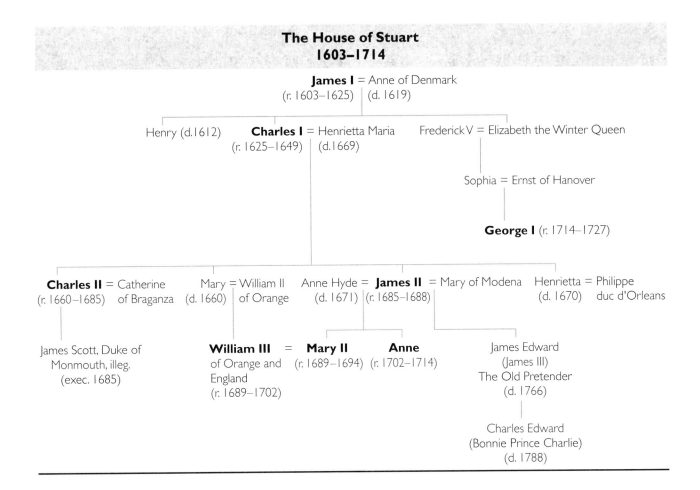

**The House of Stuart**
**1603–1714**

**James I** = Anne of Denmark
(r. 1603–1625) (d. 1619)

Henry (d.1612)   **Charles I** = Henrietta Maria   Frederick V = Elizabeth the Winter Queen
(r. 1625–1649) (d.1669)

Sophia = Ernst of Hanover

**George I** (r. 1714–1727)

**Charles II** = Catherine   Mary = William II   Anne Hyde = **James II** = Mary of Modena   Henrietta = Philippe
(r. 1660–1685) of Braganza   (d. 1660) of Orange   (d. 1671) (r. 1685–1688)   (d. 1670) duc d'Orleans

James Scott, Duke of   **William III** = **Mary II**   **Anne**   James Edward
Monmouth, illeg.   of Orange and   (r. 1689–1694) (r. 1702–1714)   (James III)
(exec. 1685)   England   The Old Pretender
(r. 1689–1702)   (d. 1766)

Charles Edward
(Bonnie Prince Charlie)
(d. 1788)

opponents as Whigs, to exclude the king's brother, James, from the throne on the grounds that he was a Catholic. Charles opposed this strategy because it violated the theory of hereditary divine right, according to which God sanctioned the right of the king's closest heir to succeed him. Those members of Parliament who supported Charles on this issue, whom the Whigs called Tories, thwarted the designs of the Whigs in three successive parliaments between 1679 and 1681.

An even more serious political crisis occurred after James II succeeded to the throne in 1685. James began to exempt his fellow Catholics from the penal laws, which prevented them from worshiping freely, and from the Test Act of 1673, which had denied them the right to hold office under the crown. Catholics began to secure appointments in the army, the court, and local government. These efforts by the monarchy to grant toleration and political power to Catholics revived the traditional English fears of absolutism and popery. Not only the Whigs but also the predominantly Anglican Tories became alarmed at the king's policies. The birth of a Catholic son to James by his second wife, the Italian princess Mary of Modena, in June 1688 created the fear that the king's religious policy might be continued indefinitely. A group of seven Whigs and Tories, including the Bishop of London, drafted an invitation to William III of Orange, the captain-general of the military forces of the

Dutch Republic and James's nephew, to come to England to defend their Protestant religion and their constitution. William was married to James's eldest daughter, the Protestant Princess Mary, and as the king's nephew he also had a claim to the throne himself.

Invading with an international force of 12,000 men, William gathered substantial support from the English population, and when James's army defected, he was forced to flee to France without ever engaging William's forces in battle. The Convention, a special parliament convened by William in 1689, offered the crown to William and Mary while at the same time securing their assent to the Declaration of Rights, a document that later became the parliamentary statute known as the Bill of Rights. This bill, which is considered a cornerstone of the English constitution, corrected many of the abuses of royal power at the hands of James and Charles, especially the practice of exempting individuals from the penalties of the laws made by Parliament. By proclaiming William king and by excluding Catholics from the throne, the Bill of Rights also destroyed the theory of hereditary divine right.

It would be difficult to argue that this sequence of events, which is known as the Glorious Revolution, amounted to a revolution in the full sense of the word, because it did not change the basic institutions of English government. The revolution simply replaced one monarch with a king and queen who were more acceptable to the nation's political elite. But the events of 1688–1689 were decisive in defeating once and for all the absolutist designs of the Stuart kings and in guaranteeing that Parliament would form a permanent and regular place in English government. That Parliament has in fact met every year since 1689, and its legislative power grew considerably when the crown vetoed a bill for the last time in 1707.

For the English aristocracy, the peers and gentry who sat in Parliament, the revolution guaranteed that they would occupy a paramount position within English politics and society for more than a hundred years. The revolution also had profound effects on British and European diplomacy, as it quickly brought England and Scotland into a war against Louis XIV of France, the great antagonist of William III. The main reason William had come to England and secured the crown in the first place was to secure British entry into the European alliance he was building against France.

Even if the Glorious Revolution has been misnamed, it prompted the publication of a genuinely revolutionary political manifesto, John Locke's *Two Treatises of Government* (1690). Locke was a radical Whig; he had written the *Treatises* in the early 1680s as a protest against the absolutist policies of Charles II, but only after the abdication and flight of James II could he safely publish his manuscript. Like Hobbes, Locke argued that men left the state of nature and agreed to form a political society in order to protect their property and prevent the chaos that characterized a state of war. But unlike Hobbes, Locke asserted that the government they formed was based on trust and that governments that acted against the interests of the people could be dissolved. In these circumstances the people, in whom sovereignty was always vested, could establish a new regime. Locke's treatises constituted an uncompromising attack on the system of royal absolutism, which he equated with slavery. His work gave the people permission to take up arms against an oppressive regime even before that regime had consolidated its power. Since its publication, the *Two Treatises of Government* has been pressed into the service of various revolutionary and radical causes, most notably in the Declaration of Independence by the United States of America in 1776.

The Glorious Revolution had a direct bearing on the growth of the English state. As long as Parliament had remained suspicious of the Stuart kings, it had been reluctant to facilitate the growth of the state, which until 1688 was under direct royal control. Once the king's power had been permanently restricted, however, and Parliament had begun to emerge as the highest power within the country, Members of Parliament had less to fear from the executive branch of government. The inauguration of a long period of warfare against France in 1689 required the development of a large army and navy, the expansion of the bureaucracy, government borrowing on an unprecedented scale, and an

increase in taxes. Members of Parliament, especially those in the Whig party, which had formed the main opposition to the monarchy before the revolution and had long opposed standing armies as a threat to English liberty, supported this expansion of the state as well as the war effort itself. By 1720 the kingdom of Great Britain, which had been created by the parliamentary union of England and Scotland in 1707, could rival the French state in military power, wealth, and diplomatic prestige. In fact, with its system of parliamentary government, Great Britain proved to be more successful than absolutist France in tapping the wealth of the people in the form of taxation to support its military establishment.

## The Dutch Republic

In many respects the United Provinces of the Netherlands, known as the Dutch Republic, forms the most striking exception to the pattern of state building in seventeenth-century Europe. Formally established in 1588 during its revolt against Spanish rule, the Dutch Republic was the only major European power to maintain a republican form of government throughout the entire seventeenth century. As a state it also failed to conform to the pattern of centralization and consolidation that became evident in virtually all European monarchies. Having successfully resisted the centralizing policies of a large multinational Spanish monarchy, the Dutch Republic never acquired much of a centralized bureaucracy of its own. The provinces formed little more than a loose confederation of sovereign republican states. Each of the provinces sent deputies to the States General, where unanimity was required on all important issues, such as the levying of taxes, the declaration of war, and the ratification of treaties. Executive power was vested in a Council of State, which likewise consisted of deputies from the provinces. Even the individual provinces, the most important of which was Holland, were themselves decentralized, with the cities and rural areas sending delegates to a provincial assembly known as the States. Only the province of Holland invested one official, known as the grand pensionary, with extraordinary executive power.

This system of decentralized republican rule was much better suited for domestic affairs than the conduct of foreign policy. During most of the seventeenth century the Dutch were at war. After finally securing Spanish recognition of their independence by the Treaty of Münster in 1648, the Republic engaged in three commercial naval wars against England (1652–1654, 1665–1667, 1672–1674) and a much longer struggle against the territorial ambitions and economic policies of Louis XIV of France (1672–1678, 1689–1697, 1701–1713). The conduct of Dutch foreign policy and the coordination of the military forces of the seven provinces required some kind of central direction. During the 1650s John de Witt, the grand pensionary of Holland, assumed an informal presidency of the republic and directed the state's foreign policy in the first two wars against England. After 1672 William III, a prince of the hereditary house of Orange-Nassau, gave further unity and coordination to Dutch state policy. William, who served as the stadholder or governor of each of the seven provinces, became the captain-general of the republic's military forces when war with France began in 1672.

The House of Orange, which had a permanent vote in the States General, represented the royal, centralizing force within the Dutch Republic, and it led a party within the republic that favored a modification of republican rule. These princes never acquired the same type of constitutional authority that monarchs exercised in other European states. William III of Orange, who became William III of England and Scotland in 1689, exercised far more power in his new British kingdoms than he did in the Dutch Republic. Nevertheless the House of Orange played a crucial role in the rise of this tiny republic to the status of a world power. During the period of its influence the size of the Dutch military forces increased dramatically, from 50,000 men in 1670 to 73,000 in 1690 and 130,000 in 1710. During the same period of time the size of the Dutch navy doubled. In this one respect the republican, decentralized United Provinces participated in the same process of state building as the other great powers of Europe. The main reason the government was able to support this large standing army was the enormous wealth it had accumulated by virtue of the country's thriving international trade.

Political power in the Dutch Republic lay mainly with the wealthy merchants and bankers who served as regents in the councils of the towns. These same men represented the towns in the States of each province. The rural areas, which predominated only in the eastern provinces, were represented by the aristocracy. The country was therefore ruled by an oligarchy, but the men who belonged to it represented a predominantly urban, mercantile elite rather than a rural nobility. The members of this bourgeois elite did not tend to seek admission to landed society in the way that successful English merchants often did. Nor were they lured into becoming part of an ostentatious court in the manner of the French nobility. As men completely immersed in the world of commerce, they remained part of mercantile society and used their political power to guarantee that the Dutch state would serve the interests of trade.

The political prominence of Dutch merchants reflected the highly commercial character of the Dutch economy. Shortly after its truce with Spain in 1609, the Dutch cities, especially the rapidly expanding port city of Amsterdam in Holland, began to dominate European and world trade. The Dutch served as middlemen and shippers for all the other powers of Europe, transporting grain from the Baltic, textiles from England, timber from Scandinavia, wine from Germany, sugar from Brazil and Ceylon, silk from Persia and China, and porcelain from Japan to markets throughout the world. The Dutch even served as middlemen for their archenemy Spain, providing food and manufactured goods to the Spanish colonies in the New World in exchange for silver from the mines of Peru and Mexico. As part of this process Dutch trading companies, such as the Dutch East India Company, began to establish permanent outposts in India, Indonesia, North America, the Caribbean, South America, and South Africa. Thus a relatively small country, with one-tenth the population of France and one-third that of Great Britain, became a colonial power.

### The Amsterdam Stock Exchange in 1668

Known as the Bourse, this multipurpose building served as a gathering point for merchants trading in different parts of the world. The main activity was the buying and selling of shares of stock in trading companies during trading sessions that lasted for two hours each day.

To support their dynamic mercantile economy, Dutch cities developed financial institutions favorable to trade. An Exchange Bank in Amsterdam, which had a monopoly on the exchange of foreign currencies, allowed merchants to make international transactions by adding sums to or deducting sums from their accounts whenever they imported or exported goods. The Dutch also developed rational and efficient methods of bookkeeping. A stock market, also situated in Amsterdam, facilitated the buying and selling of shares in commercial ventures. Even lawyers contributed to these commercial enterprises. In *The Freedom of the Sea* (1609), the great legal and political philosopher Hugo Grotius (1583–1645) defended the freedom of merchants to use the open seas for trade and fishing, thereby challenging the claims of European monarchs who wished to exclude foreigners from the waters surrounding their countries. Grotius, who also wrote *The Law of War and Peace* (1625), gained a reputation as the father of modern international law.

One of the most striking contrasts between the Dutch Republic and the kingdom of France in the seventeenth century lay in the area of religious policy. Whereas in France the revocation of the Edict of Nantes represented the culmination of a policy enforcing religious uniformity and the suppression of Protestant dissent, the predominantly Calvinist Dutch Republic gained a reputation for religious toleration. The Dutch Reformed Church did not always deserve this reputation, but secular authorities, especially in the cities, proved remarkably tolerant of different religious groups. Amsterdam, which attracted a diverse immigrant population during its period of rapid growth, contained a large community of Jews, including the

philosopher Baruch Spinoza (1632–1677). The country became the center for religious exiles and political dissidents, accommodating French Huguenots who fled their country after the repeal of the Edict of Nantes in 1685 as well as English Whigs (including the Earl of Shaftesbury and John Locke) who were being pursued by the Tory government in the 1680s. In keeping with this Dutch tradition of toleration, Dutch courts became the first to stop the prosecution of witches, executing the last person for this crime in 1608.

This tolerant bourgeois republic also made a distinct contribution to European culture during the seventeenth century, known as its Golden Age. The Dutch cultural achievement was greatest in the area of the visual arts, where Rembrandt van Rijn (1606–1669), Franz Hals (ca. 1580–1666) and Jan Steen (1626–1679) formed only part of an astonishing concentration of artistic genius in the cities of Amsterdam, Haarlem, and Leiden. Dutch painting of this era reflected the religious, social, and political climate in which painters worked. The Protestant Reformation had brought an end to the tradition of didactic and devotional religious painting that had flourished during the Middle Ages, leading many Dutch artists to adopt more secular themes for their work. At the same time the absence of a baroque court culture, such as that which still flourished in Spain and France as well as in the Spanish Netherlands, reduced the demand for royal and aristocratic portraiture as well as for paintings of heroic classical, mythological, and historical scenes. Instead the Dutch artists of the Golden Age produced intensely realistic portraits of merchants and financiers, such as Rembrandt's famous *Syndics of the Clothmakers of Amsterdam* (1662).

**Rembrandt, *Syndics of the Clothmakers of Amsterdam* (1662)**
Rembrandt's realistic portrait depicted wealthy Dutch bourgeoisie, who had great political as well as economic power in the Dutch Republic.

Realism became one of the defining features of Dutch painting, evident in the numerous street scenes, still lifes, and landscapes that Dutch artists painted and sold to a largely bourgeois clientele. At the same time Dutch engravers perfected the art of political printmaking, much of it highly satirical, an achievement that was encouraged by the political tolerance of the country.

In the early eighteenth century the Dutch Republic lost its position of economic superiority to Great Britain and France, which developed even larger mercantile empires of their own and began to dominate world commerce. The long period of war against France, which ended in 1713, took its toll on Dutch manpower and wealth, and the relatively small size of the country and its decentralized institutions made it more difficult for it to recover its position in European diplomacy and warfare. As a state it could no longer fight above its weight, and it became vulnerable to attacks by the French in the nineteenth century and the Germans in the twentieth. But in the seventeenth century this highly urbanized and commercial country showed that a small, decentralized republic could hold its own with the absolutist states of France and Spain as well as with the parliamentary monarchy of England.

and in two states, England and the Dutch Republic, they ended in failure. Nevertheless, during the seventeenth and eighteenth centuries the absolutist state became the main form of government in the West. For this reason historians refer to the period of Western history beginning in the seventeenth century as the age of absolutism.

The third change was the conduct of a new style of warfare by Western absolutist states. The West became the arena where large armies, funded, equipped, and trained by the state, engaged in long, costly, and bloody military campaigns. The conduct of war on this scale threatened to drain the state of its financial resources, destroy its economy, and decimate its civilian and military population. Western powers were not unaware of the dangers of this type of warfare. The development of international law and the attempt to achieve a balance of power among European powers represented efforts to place restrictions on the conduct of seventeenth-century warfare. These efforts, however, were not completely successful, and in the eighteenth and nineteenth centuries warfare in the West entered a new and even more dangerous phase, aided by the technological innovations that the Scientific and Industrial Revolutions made possible. To the first of those great transformations, the revolution in science, we now turn.

# Conclusion

## The Western State in the Age of Absolutism

Between 1600 and 1715 three fundamental political changes, all related to each other, helped redefine the West. The first was the dramatic and unprecedented growth of the state. During these years all Western states grew in size and strength. They became more cohesive as the outlying provinces of kingdoms were brought more firmly under central governmental control. The administrative machinery of the state became more complex and efficient. The armies of the state could be called upon at any time to take action against internal rebels and foreign enemies. The income of the state increased as royal officials collected higher taxes, and governments became involved in the promotion of trade and industry and in the regulation of the economy. By the beginning of the eighteenth century one of the most distinctive features of Western civilization was the prevalence of these large, powerful, bureaucratic states. There was nothing like them in the non-Western world.

The second change was the introduction of royal absolutism into these Western states. From one end of the European continent to the other, efforts were made to establish the monarch as a ruler with complete and unrivaled power. These efforts achieved varying degrees of success,

## Suggestions for Further Reading

For a comprehensive listing of suggested readings, please go to www.ablongman.com/levack2e/chapter15

Aylmer, G. E. *Rebellion or Revolution.* 1986. A study of the nature of the political disturbances of the 1640s and 1650s.

Beik, William. *Louis XIV and Absolutism: A Brief Study with Documents.* 2000. An excellent collection of documents.

Collins, James B. *The State in Early Modern France.* 1995. The best general study of the French state.

Elliott, J. H. *Richelieu and Olivares.* 1984. A comparison of the two contemporary absolutist ministers and state builders in France and Spain.

Harris, Tim. *Politics Under the Later Stuarts.* 1993. The best study of Restoration politics, including the Glorious Revolution.

Hughes, Lindsey. *Russia in the Age of Peter the Great.* 1998. A comprehensive study of politics, diplomacy, society, and culture during the reign of the "Tsar Reformer."

Israel, Jonathan. *The Dutch Republic: Its Rise, Greatness and Fall, 1477–1806.* 1996. A massive and authoritative study of the Dutch Republic during the period of its greatest global influence.

Lincoln, W. Bruce. *Sunlight at Midnight: St. Petersburg and the Rise of Modern Russia.* 2000. The best study of the building of Peter the Great's new capital city.

Parker, David. *The Making of French Absolutism.* 1983. A particularly good treatment of the early seventeenth century.

Parker, Geoffrey. *The Military Revolution.* 1988. Deals with the impact of the military revolution on the world as well as European history.

Rabb, Theodore K. *The Struggle for Stability in Early Modern Europe.* 1975. Employs visual as well as political sources to illustrate the way in which Europeans responded to the general crisis of the seventeenth century.

Schama, Simon. *The Embarrassment of Riches: An Interpretation of Dutch Culture in the Golden Age.* 1987. Contains a wealth of commentary on Dutch art and culture during its most influential period.

Wilson, Peter H. *Absolutism in Central Europe.* 2000. Analyzes both the theory and the practice of absolutism in Prussia and Austria.

## Notes

1. Thomas Hobbes, *Leviathan,* ed. C. B. Macpherson (1968), 186.

2. Jean Bodin, *The Six Books of the Commonweale* (1606), Book II, Chapter 2.

3. Louis de Rouvroy, duc de Saint-Simon, *Memoirs of Louis XIV and the Regency* trans. Bayle St. John (1901) vol. 2, p. 11.

4. Quoted in Lindsey Hughes, *Russia in the Age of Peter the Great* (1998), 92.

# The Scientific Revolution

I N 1609 GALILEO GALILEI, AN ITALIAN MATHEMATICIAN AT THE UNIVERSITY OF Padua, introduced a new scientific instrument, the telescope, which revealed a wealth of knowledge about the stars and planets that filled the night skies. Having heard that a Dutch artisan had put together two lenses in such a way that magnified distant objects, Galileo built his own such device and directed it toward the heavens. Anyone who has looked through a telescope or seen photographs taken from a satellite can appreciate Galileo's excitement at what he saw. Objects that appeared one way to the naked eye looked entirely different when magnified by his new "spyglass," as he called it. The Milky Way, the pale glow that was previously thought to be a reflection of diffused light, turned out to be composed of a multitude of previously unknown stars. The surface of the moon, long believed to be smooth, uniform, and perfectly spherical, now appeared to be full of mountains, craters, and other irregularities. The sun, which was also supposed to be perfect in shape and composed of matter that could not be altered, was marred by spots that appeared to move across its surface. When turned toward Jupiter, the telescope revealed four moons never seen before. Venus, viewed over the course of many months, appeared to change its shape, much in the way that the moon did in its various phases. This latter discovery provided evidence for the relatively new theory that the planets, including Earth, revolved around the sun rather than the sun and the planets around the Earth.

Galileo shared the discoveries he made not only with fellow scientists but with other Europeans. In 1610 he published *The Starry Messenger,* a treatise in which he described his discovery of the new moons of Jupiter. Twenty-two years later he included the evidence he had gained from his telescope in another book, *Dialogue Concerning the Two Chief World Systems,* to support the claim that the Earth orbited the sun. He also staged a number of public demonstrations of his new astronomical instrument, the first of which took place on top of one of the city gates of Rome in 1611. To convince those who doubted the reality of the images they saw, Galileo turned

**The Telescope** The telescope was the most important of the new scientific instruments that facilitated discovery. This engraving depicts an astronomer using the telescope in 1647.

the telescope toward familiar landmarks in the city. Interest in the new scientific instrument ran so high that a number of amateur astronomers acquired telescopes of their own.

Galileo's observations and discoveries formed one facet of the development that historians call the Scientific Revolution. A series of remarkable achievements in astronomy, physics, chemistry, and biology formed the centerpieces of this revolution, but its effects reached far beyond the observatories and laboratories of seventeenth-century scientists. The Scientific Revolution brought about fundamental changes in Western thought, altering the way in which Europeans viewed the natural world, the supernatural realm, and themselves. It stimulated controversies in religion, philosophy, and politics and brought about changes in military technology, navigation, and economic enterprise. The revolution added a new dimension to Western culture and provided a basis for claims of Western superiority over people in other lands. For all these reasons the Scientific Revolution marked a decisive turning point in the history of Western civilization, and it set the West apart from contemporary civilizations in the Middle East, Africa, and Asia.

The scientific culture that emerged in the West by the end of the seventeenth century was the product of a series of cultural encounters. It resulted from a complex interaction among scholars proposing different accounts of how nature operated. In some cases the scientists who advanced the revolutionary ideas were themselves influenced by ideas drawn from different cultural traditions. Some of these ideas had originated in Greek philosophy, while others came from orthodox Christian sources. Still other ideas came from a tradition of late medieval science, which had in turn been heavily influenced by the scholarship of the Islamic Middle East. A skeptical refusal to rely on any inherited authority whatsoever had its own religious and philosophical sources.

The main question this chapter seeks to answer is how European scientists in the sixteenth and seventeenth centuries changed the way in which people in the West viewed the natural world. Five specific questions, each of which will be addressed in a separate section of the chapter, will structure our exploration of this subject:

■ What were the scientific achievements and discoveries of the late sixteenth and seventeenth centuries that historians refer to as the Scientific Revolution?
■ What methods did scientists use during this period to investigate nature, and how did they think nature operated?
■ Why did the Scientific Revolution take place in western Europe at this particular time?
■ How did the Scientific Revolution influence the development of philosophical and religious thought in the seventeenth and early eighteenth centuries?
■ How did the Scientific Revolution change the way in which seventeenth- and eighteenth-century Europeans thought of their relationship to the natural world?

# The Discoveries and Achievements of the Scientific Revolution

■ What were the scientific achievements and discoveries of the late sixteenth and seventeenth centuries that historians refer to as the Scientific Revolution?

Unlike political revolutions, such as the English Revolution of the 1640s discussed in the last chapter, the Scientific Revolution developed gradually and over a long period of time. It began in the middle and later decades of the sixteenth century and continued into the early years of the eighteenth century. Even though it took a relatively long time to unfold, it was revolutionary in the sense that it brought about a radical transformation of human thought, just as political revolutions have produced fundamental changes in systems of government. The most important changes in seventeenth-century science took place in the fields of astronomy, physics, chemistry, and biology.

## Astronomy: A New Model of the Universe

The most significant change in astronomy was the acceptance of the view that the sun, not the Earth, was the center of the universe. Until the middle of the sixteenth century, most natural philosophers—as scientists were known at the time—subscribed to the writings of the Greek astronomer Claudius Ptolemy (100–170 C.E.). Ptolemy's observations and calculations had given considerable support to the cosmology° (a theory regarding the structure and nature of the universe) proposed by the Greek philosopher Aristotle (384–322 B.C.E.). According to Ptolemy and Aristotle, the center of the universe was a stationary Earth, around which the moon, the sun, and the other planets revolved in circular orbits. Beyond the planets a large sphere carried the stars, which stood in a fixed relationship to each other, around the Earth from east to west once every twenty-four hours, thus accounting for the rising and setting of the stars. Each of the four known elements—earth, water, air, and fire—had a natural place within this universe, with the heavy elements, earth and water, being pulled down toward the center of the Earth and the light ones, air and fire, hovering above it. All heavenly bodies, including the sun and the planets, were composed of a fifth element, called ether, which unlike matter on Earth was thought to be eternal and could not be altered, corrupted, or destroyed.

This traditional view of the cosmos had much to recommend it, and some educated people continued to subscribe to it well into the eighteenth century. The authority

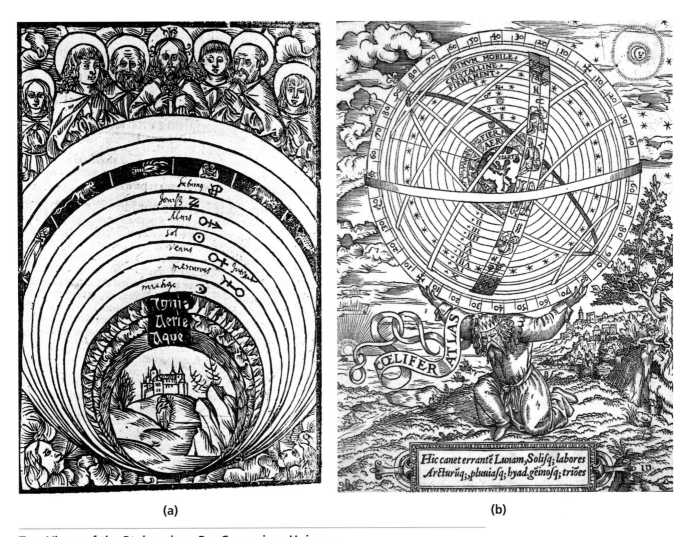

(a)                                                                 (b)

### Two Views of the Ptolemaic or Pre-Copernican Universe

(a) In this sixteenth-century engraving the Earth lies at the center of the universe and the elements of water, air, and fire are arranged in ascending order above the Earth. The orbit that is shaded in black is the firmament or stellar sphere. The presence of Christ and the saints at the top reflects the view that Heaven lay beyond the stellar sphere. (b) A medieval king representing Atlas holds a Ptolemaic cosmos. The Ptolemaic universe is often referred to as a two-sphere universe: The inner sphere of the Earth lies at the center and the outer sphere encompassing the entire universe rotates around the Earth.

of Aristotle, predominant in late medieval universities, was reinforced by the Bible, which in a few passages referred to the motion of the sun. The motion of the sun could be confirmed by simple human observation. We do, after all, see the sun "rise" and "set" every day, while the idea that the Earth rotates at a high speed and revolves around the sun contradicts the experience of our senses. Nevertheless, the Earth-centered model of the universe failed to provide an explanation for many patterns that astronomers observed in the sky, most notably the paths followed by planets. In the sixteenth century natural

philosophers began to consider alternative models of the universe.

The first major challenge to the Ptolemaic system came from a Polish cleric, Nicolaus Copernicus (1473–1543), who in 1543 published *The Revolutions of the Heavenly Spheres,* in which he proposed that the center of the universe was not the Earth but the sun. The book was widely circulated, but it did not win much support for the sun-centered theory of the universe. The mathematical arguments Copernicus presented in the book were so abstruse

**DOCUMENT**

Nicolaus Copernicus, *On the Revolution of Heavenly Spheres* (1500s)

that only the most erudite astronomers could understand them. Even those who could appreciate his detailed plotting of planetary motion were not prepared to adopt the central thesis of his book. In the late sixteenth century the great Danish astronomer Tycho Brahe (1546–1601) accepted the argument of Copernicus that the planets revolved around the sun but still insisted that the sun continued to revolve around the Earth.

Significant support for the Copernican model of the universe among scientists began to materialize only in the seventeenth century. In 1609 a German astronomer, Johannes Kepler (1571–1630), using data that Brahe had collected, confirmed the central position of the sun in the universe. In his treatise *New Astronomy,* Kepler also demonstrated that the planets, including the Earth, followed elliptical rather than circular orbits and that the planets moved in accordance with a series of physical laws. Kepler's book, however, did not reach a large audience, and his achievement was not fully appreciated until many decades later.

Galileo Galilei (1564–1642) was far more successful than Kepler in gaining support for the sun-centered model of the universe. In some respects Galileo was more conservative than Kepler. For example, Galileo never took issue with the traditional idea that the planets followed circular orbits. But Galileo had the literary skill, lacking in Kepler, of being able to write for a broad audience. Using the evidence gained from his observations with the telescope, and presenting his views in the form of a dialogue between the advocates of the two competing worldviews,

**(a)**

**Two Early Modern Views of the Sun-Centered Universe**

(a) The depiction by Copernicus. Note that all the orbits are circular, rather than elliptical, as Kepler was to show they were. The outermost sphere is that of the fixed stars. (b) A late-seventeenth-century depiction of the cosmos by Andreas Cellarius in which the planets follow elliptical orbits. It illustrates four different positions of the Earth as it orbits the sun.

**(b)**

he demonstrated the plausibility and superiority of Copernicus's theory.

The publication of Galileo's *Dialogue Concerning the Two Chief World Systems—Ptolemaic and Copernican* in 1632 won many converts to the sun-centered theory of the universe, but it lost him the support of Pope Urban VIII, who had been one of his patrons. Urban believed that by naming the character in *Dialogue* who defended the Ptolemaic system Simplicio (that is, a simple person), he was mocking the pope himself. In the following year Galileo was tried before the Roman Inquisition, an ecclesiastical court whose purpose was to maintain theological orthodoxy. The charge against him was that he had challenged the authority of Scripture and was therefore guilty of heresy, the denial of the theological truths of the Roman Catholic Church. (See "Justice in History: The Trial of Galileo" later in this chapter.)

As a result of this trial Galileo was forced to abandon his support for the Copernican model of the universe, and *Dialogue* was placed on the Index of Prohibited Books, a list compiled by the papacy of all printed works containing heretical ideas. Despite this setback, support for Copernicanism grew during the seventeenth century, and by 1700 it commanded widespread support among scientists and the educated public. *Dialogue*, however, was not removed from the Index until 1822.

## Physics: The Laws of Motion and Gravitation

Galileo made his most significant contributions to the Scientific Revolution in the field of physics, which deals with matter and energy and the relationship between them. In the seventeenth century the main branches of physics were mechanics (the study of motion and its causes) and optics (the study of light). Galileo's most significant achievement in physics was to formulate a set of laws governing the motion of material objects. His work, which laid the foundation of modern physics, effectively challenged the theories of Aristotle regarding motion.

According to Aristotle, whose views dominated science in the late Middle Ages, the motion of every object except the natural motion of falling toward the center of the Earth required another object to move it. If the mover stopped, the object fell to the ground or simply stopped moving. One of the problems with this theory was that it could not account for the continued motion of a projectile, such as a discus or a javelin, after it left the hand of the person who threw it. Galileo's answer to that

question was a theory of inertia, which became the basis of a radical new theory of motion. According to Galileo, an object continues to move or to lie at rest until something external to it intervenes to change its motion. Thus motion is neither a quality inherent in an object nor a force that it acquires from another object; it is simply a state in which the object finds itself.

Galileo also discovered that the motion of an object occurs only in relation to things that do not move. A ship moves through the water, for example, but the goods carried by that ship do not move in relationship to the moving ship. This insight served the immediate purpose of explaining to the critics of Copernicus how the Earth can move even though we do not experience its motion. Galileo's most significant contribution to the study of mechanics was his formulation of a mathematical law of motion that explained how the speed and acceleration of a falling object are determined by the distance it travels during equal intervals of time.

The greatest achievements of the Scientific Revolution in physics belong to English scientist Sir Isaac Newton (1642–1727). Newton was one of those rare geniuses whose research changed the way future generations viewed the world. As a boy Newton found himself out of place while working on his mother's farm in a small hamlet in

## CHRONOLOGY

### Discoveries of the Scientific Revolution

**1543** Andreas Vesalius publishes *On the Fabric of the Human Body*, the first realistic depiction of human anatomy; Copernicus publishes *The Revolutions of the Heavenly Spheres*, challenging the traditional Earth-centered cosmos

**1609** Johannes Kepler publishes *New Astronomy*, identifying elliptical orbits of the planets

**1628** William Harvey publishes *On the Motion of the Heart and Blood in Animals*, demonstrating the circulation of the blood

**1632** Galileo publishes *Dialogue Concerning the Two Chief World Systems*, leading to his trial

**1638** Galileo publishes *Discourses on the Two New Sciences of Motion and Mechanics*, proposing new laws of motion

**1655** Evangelista Torricelli conducts experiments on atmospheric pressure

**1659** Robert Boyle invents the air pump and conducts experiments on the elasticity and compressibility of air

**1673** Christian Huygens publishes *On the Motion of Pendulums*, developing his theories of gravitation and centrifugal force

**1687** Newton publishes his *Mathematical Principles of Natural Philosophy*, presenting a theory of universal gravitation

Lincolnshire and while attending school in the same county. Fascinated by mechanical devices, he spent much of his time building wooden models of windmills and other machines. When playing with his friends he always found ways to exercise his mind, calculating, for example, how he could use the wind to win jumping contests with his classmates. While he was still an adolescent, it had become obvious to all his acquaintances that the only place where he would be comfortable would be at a university. In 1661 he entered Trinity College, Cambridge, a step that introduced him to the broader world of ideas. In 1667 he became a fellow of the college and two years later, at age 27, he became the Lucasian Professor of Mathematics.

At Cambridge Newton pursued a wide range of intellectual interests, including the study of biblical prophecy. His great discoveries, however, were in the disciplines of mathematics and natural philosophy. During the 1680s Newton formulated a set of mathematical laws that governed the operation of the entire physical world. In 1687 he published his theories in *Mathematical Principles of Natural Philosophy*. The centerpiece of this monumental work was the universal law of gravitation°, which demonstrated that the same force holding an object to the Earth also holds the planets in their orbits. Newton established that any two bodies attract each other with a force that is directly proportional to the product of their masses and inversely proportional to the square of the distance between them. This law represented a synthesis of the work by Kepler on planetary motion, Galileo on inertia, the English physicist Robert Hooke (1635–1703) on gravity, and the Dutch scientist Christian Huygens (1629–1695) on centrifugal force. Newton's *Mathematical Principles* superseded the works of all these scientists by establishing the existence of a single gravitational force and by giving it precise mathematical expression. At the same time it revealed the unity and order of the entire physical world. It provided, in Newton's words, "a system of the world."

Newton extended his study of motion to the science of optics by demonstrating that light consists of small particles that also follow the laws of motion. Newton's theory prevailed until the early nineteenth century, when a series of experiments provided support for a new theory of light, according to which light should be thought of as waves, similar to those that cross a pond after a stone is dropped. Later in the nineteenth century the wave theory itself gave way to the view that light is a form of electromagnetic radiation. The most revolutionary change in our understanding of light, however, came with Newton in the seventeenth century.

## Chemistry: Discovering the Elements of Nature

At the beginning of the seventeenth century, the branch of science today called chemistry had little intellectual respectability. It was not even an independent discipline, because it was considered a part of either medicine or

alchemy°, the magical art of attempting to turn base metals into precious ones. The most famous chemist of the sixteenth century was the Swiss physician and natural magician Paracelsus (1493–1541), who rejected the theory advanced by the Greek physician Galen (129–200 C.E.) that diseases were caused by the imbalance of the four "humors" or fluids in the body—blood, phlegm, black bile, and yellow bile. The widespread medical practice of drawing blood from sick patients to cure them was based on Galen's theory. Paracelsus began instead to treat his patients with chemicals, such as mercury and sulfur, to cure certain diseases. Paracelsus and his followers also believed that chemistry would provide a new basis for the understanding of nature, and he interpreted the biblical account of Creation as the chemical unfolding of nature. Paracelsus is often dismissed for his belief in alchemy, but his prescription of chemicals to treat specific diseases helped give chemistry a respectable place within medical science.

During the seventeenth century chemistry became a legitimate field of scientific research, largely as the result of the

**Sir Isaac Newton**
This portrait was painted by Sir Godfrey Kneller in 1689, two years after the publication of *Mathematical Principles of Natural Philosophy*.

**Portrait of Robert Boyle with His Air Pump in the Background (1664)**
Boyle's pump became the center of a series of experiments carried on at the Royal Society in London.

work of the English natural philosopher Robert Boyle (1627–1691). Boyle destroyed the prevailing idea that all basic constituents of matter share the same structure. He contended that the arrangement of their components, which Boyle identified as corpuscles or atoms, determines their characteristics. Boyle also conducted experiments on the volume, pressure, and density of gas and the elasticity of air. His most famous experiments, undertaken with the help of an air pump, proved the existence of a vacuum. Largely as a result of Boyle's discoveries, chemists won acceptance as legitimate members of the company of scientists.

## Biology: The Circulation of the Blood

The English physician William Harvey (1578–1657) made one of the great medical discoveries of the seventeenth century by demonstrating in 1628 that blood circulates throughout the human body. Harvey, who had studied medicine at the University of Padua and who became the royal physician to both James I and Charles I in England,

challenged the traditional theory regarding the motion of the blood advanced by Galen and perpetuated by medieval philosophers. According to this traditional theory, blood originated in the liver, where it was converted from food and then flowed outward through the veins, providing nourishment to the organs and the other parts of the body. A certain amount of blood was also drawn from the liver into the heart, where it passed from one ventricle to the other and then traveled through the arteries to different parts of the body. During its journey this arterial blood was enriched by a special *pneuma* or "vital spirit" that originated in the atmosphere and was necessary to sustain life. When this enriched blood reached the brain, it became the body's "psychic spirits," which eventually traveled to the nerves and influenced human behavior.

During the late sixteenth century a succession of Italian scientists called specific aspects of Galen's theory into question. It was Harvey, however, who proposed an entirely new framework for understanding the motion of the blood. Through a series of experiments on human cadavers and live animals in which he weighed the blood that the heart pumped every hour, Harvey demonstrated that the blood circulates throughout the body, traveling outward from the heart through the arteries and returning to the heart through the veins. The heart, rather than sucking in blood, performed the essential function of pumping it by means of its contraction and constriction. The only gap in Harvey's theory was the question of how blood goes from the ends of the arteries to the ends of the veins. The answer to this question came in 1661, when scientists, using another new magnifying instrument known as a microscope, could see the capillaries connecting the veins and arteries. Harvey, however, had provided the basis for understanding how blood circulates through the body, and he had set a standard for the conduct of future biological research.

## The Search for Scientific Knowledge

■ **What methods did scientists use during this period to investigate nature, and how did they think nature operated?**

The natural philosophers who made these various scientific discoveries worked in different academic disciplines, and each followed his own procedures for discovering scientific truth. In the sixteenth and seventeenth centuries there was no such thing as a single "scientific method." Many natural philosophers, however, shared similar views regarding the way in which nature operated and the means by which humans could acquire knowledge of it. In searching for scientific knowledge, these scientists engaged in extensive observation and experimentation, used a process of deductive reasoning to solve scientific problems,

# Dissecting the Human Corpse

As medical science developed in the sixteenth and seventeenth centuries, the dissection of human corpses became a standard practice in European universities and medical schools. Knowledge of the structure and composition of the human body, which was central to the advancement of physiology, could best be acquired by cutting open a corpse to reveal the organs, muscles, and bones of human beings. The practice reflected the emphasis scientists placed on observation and experimentation in conducting scientific research. In the sixteenth century the great Flemish physiologist Andreas Vesalius (1514–1564), who published the first realistic drawings of human anatomy in 1543, cut limbs and extracted organs in his lectures on anatomy at the University of Padua. A century later, the English physician William Harvey dissected human cadavers in his path-breaking study of the circulation of the blood.

The physicians who performed dissections had difficulty securing an adequate supply of corpses. A preference developed for the bodies of recently hanged criminals, mainly because rulers claimed jurisdiction over the bodies of the condemned and could dispose of them at will. Criminals, moreover, were generally young or middle-aged and in fairly good health, thus making them desirable specimens for dissection. Demand for corpses became so great in the late seventeenth and eighteenth centuries that surgeons were willing to pay a price for them, thus turning the dead human body into a commodity. In eighteenth-century England the demand for bodies of the hanged often resulted in brawls between the agents whom

the surgeons paid to snatch the bodies from the scaffold and the relatives and friends of the deceased, who wanted to claim the corpses in order to guarantee a decent burial.

During the sixteenth and seventeenth centuries, dissection underwent two transformations. The first was the expansion of the audience from a small group of medical students to a large cross-section of scholars who attended in order to learn more about the relationship between human beings and the natural world. The audiences also began to include artists, who learned from these exercises how to depict the human body more accurately. The second change was the transformation of dissection into a public spectacle, controlled by municipal authorities. During the seventeenth century, the city of Bologna staged dissections every year before crowds of as many as 200 people.

To these public dissections, which took place in many other European cities, people from the lower classes were often admitted together with scholars, students,

and artists. The uneducated men and women who attended were attracted by the entertaining aspects of the event and the eagerness to witness the violence done to the corpse, just as they were at public executions. They were particularly eager to see the dissection of the genital organs, so much so that some authorities restricted access to that part of the dissection in the interest of public decency.

The holding of public anatomy lessons had much less to do with the popularization of science than with the satisfaction of the popular taste for blood and sex. Only in the late eighteenth century, during the age of the Enlightenment, did a new sensitivity to blood and human torment and an unprecedented repugnance toward death bring about an end to public dissections, together with the public executions with which they were closely associated.

## For Discussion

What interests were served by holding public dissections of human corpses in the seventeenth and eighteenth centuries?

**Dissection**
The English surgeon William Cheselden giving an anatomical demonstration to spectators in London ca. 1735.

expressed their theories in mathematical terms, and argued that nature operated like a machine. Taken together, these common features of scientific research ultimately defined a distinctly Western approach to solving scientific problems.

## Observation and Experimentation

The most prominent feature of scientific research in sixteenth- and seventeenth-century Europe was the extensive observation of nature, combined with the testing of hypotheses by means of rigorous experimentation. This was primarily a process of induction°, in which theories emerged only after the systematic accumulation and analysis of large amounts of data. It assumed a willingness to abandon all preconceived notions, whether they were those of Aristotle, Galen, or medieval philosophers, and to base scientific conclusions on experience and observation.

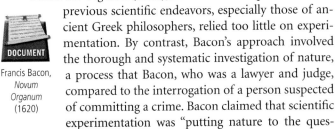

Francis Bacon, *Novum Organum* (1620)

The English philosopher Francis Bacon (1561–1626) promoted this empirical, experimental approach in his book *New Organon* (1620), in which he complained that all previous scientific endeavors, especially those of ancient Greek philosophers, relied too little on experimentation. By contrast, Bacon's approach involved the thorough and systematic investigation of nature, a process that Bacon, who was a lawyer and judge, compared to the interrogation of a person suspected of committing a crime. Bacon claimed that scientific experimentation was "putting nature to the question" in order to obtain the truth, a phrase that referred to questioning a prisoner under torture to determine the facts of a case.

All the great scientists of the sixteenth and seventeenth centuries abandoned preconceived notions and based their theories on the facts of nature, but the most enthusiastic practitioners of carefully planned and controlled experimentation came from England. Two of its most tireless advocates were Boyle, who performed a succession of experiments with an air pump to prove the existence of a vacuum, and Robert Hooke, whose experiments with a pendulum provided one of the foundations for Newton's theory of universal gravitation. Harvey belongs to the same English experimental tradition, although his commitment to this methodology originated at the University of Padua. Galileo and some other Italian scientists matched the English in their insistence on experimentation, but Galileo's experiments were designed more to demonstrate the validity of his theories than to help him establish them in the first place.

## Deductive Reasoning

The second feature of sixteenth- and seventeenth-century scientific research was the application of deductive reasoning to scientific problems. Unlike the inductive experimental approach, which found its most enthusiastic practitioners in England, the deductive approach had its most zealous advocates on the European continent. The men who took this approach were just as determined as Bacon and Boyle to replace the testimony of human authorities with what they discovered from nature itself. Their main method, however, was to establish basic scientific truths or propositions from which other ideas or laws could be deduced logically. The French philosopher and mathematician René Descartes (1596–1650) became the champion of this methodology. In his *Discourse on the Method* (1637) he recommended that in solving any intellectual problem a person should first establish fundamental principles or truths and then proceed deductively from those ideas to more specific conclusions.

The model for deductive reasoning was mathematics, in which one also moves logically from certain premises to conclusions by means of equations. Rational deduction° proved to be an essential feature of scientific methodology, although some scientists relied too heavily on it at the expense of a more experimental approach. The limitations of an exclusively deductive approach became apparent when Descartes and his followers deduced a theory of gravitation from the principle that objects could influence each other only if they actually touched. The theory, as well as the principle upon which it was based, lacked an empirical foundation, which is one based on observation and experience, and eventually had to be abandoned.

## Mathematics and Nature

The third feature of scientific research in the sixteenth and seventeenth centuries was the application of mathematics to the study of the physical world. The mathematical treatment of nature was undertaken by scientists working in both the experimental and the deductive traditions. Descartes shared with Galileo, Kepler, and Huygens the conviction that nature had a geometrical structure and that it could therefore be understood in mathematical terms. The physical dimensions of matter, which Descartes claimed were its only properties, could of course be expressed mathematically. Galileo claimed that mathematics was the language in which philosophy was written in "the book of the universe."

This mathematical way of looking at the physical world had a long history. The Greek philosophers Pythagoras (582–507 B.C.E.) and Plato (ca. 428–348 B.C.E.) had both emphasized the geometric structure of the cosmos and therefore considered numbers to hold the key to its secrets. In the fifteenth century Renaissance philosophers revived this ancient Greek emphasis on mathematics. Copernicus, who was influenced by Platonic thought, criticized the Islamic and western European medieval philosophers who had accepted an Earth-centered universe for their mathematical miscalculations. Copernicus advocated a rigorous application of mathematics to astronomical writing. One of the reasons his book *The Revolutions of the Heavenly Spheres* was so demanding was that he described planetary motion in technical, mathematical terms.

In the seventeenth century Isaac Newton's work provides the best illustration of the application of mathematics to scientific problems. Newton used observation and experimentation to confirm his theory of universal gravitation, but the work in which he presented his theory, *Mathematical Principles of Natural Philosophy,* was written in the language of mathematics. Just as Newton had synthesized previous work in physics to arrive at the law of universal gravitation, he also combined the experimental and deductive approaches to acquire scientific truth. His approach to solving scientific problems, which became a model for future scientific research, involved generalization on the basis of particular examples derived from experiments and the use of deductive, mathematical reasoning to discover the laws of nature.

## The Mechanical Philosophy

Much of the scientific experimentation and deduction undertaken in the seventeenth century proceeded on the assumption that the natural world operated as if it were a machine made by a human being. This philosophy of nature, which is often referred to as the mechanical philosophy°, cannot be attributed to a single person, but its most comprehensive statement can be found in the work of Descartes. The scholastic philosophers of the fourteenth and fifteenth centuries insisted that nature was fundamentally different from a machine or any other object built by humans. According to the scholastics, natural bodies had an innate tendency to change, whereas artificial objects, that is, those constructed by humans, did not. Descartes, Kepler, Galileo, and Bacon all denied that assumption, arguing that nature operated in a mechanical way, just like a clock or some other piece of machinery. The only difference was that we cannot readily observe the structures of natural mechanisms, in the way that we can see the structure of a pump or a wagon.

According to mechanists—scientists who subscribed to the mechanical philosophy—nature consisted of many machines, some of them extremely small. The human body was itself a machine, and the center of that human machine, the heart, was in Harvey's words "a piece of machinery in which, though one wheel gives motion to another, yet all the wheels seem to move simultaneously." Because the human body was made by God, it was superior to any human-made machine, but it was still nothing more than a machine.

According to Descartes, the only part of a human being that was not a machine was the mind, which was completely different from the body and the rest of the material world. Unlike the body, the mind was an immaterial substance that could be neither extended in space nor divided. Nor could it

be measured mathematically, in the way one could record the dimensions of the human body. Because Descartes made this sharp distinction between the mind and the human body, we speak of his philosophy as being dualistic°.

The mechanical philosophy presented just as bold a challenge to the philosophers known as Neoplatonists° as it did to the scholastics. Neoplatonists were inspired by the work of Plotinus (205–270 C.E.), the last great philosopher of antiquity who had synthesized the work of Plato with that of other Greek philosophers. Plotinus also drew on many traditions of ancient Persian religion. Neoplatonic thought experienced a revival in the fifteenth and sixteenth centuries at the time of the Renaissance (see Chapter 11). Neoplatonists believed that the natural world was animistic—that is, it possessed a soul (known to them as a world soul) and was charged with various occult forces and spirits. The English natural philosopher William Gilbert (1544–1603), who wrote extensively on the phenomenon of magnetism, adopted a Neoplatonic worldview when he declared that the Earth and other planets were actually alive. Kepler clearly recognized the incompatibility of this outlook with that of the mechanical philosophy when he insisted that "the machine of the universe is not similar to a divine animated being but similar to a clock."[1]

**René Descartes**

Although Descartes was a scientist who made contributions to the study of biology and optics, he is best known for the method he proposed to attain certain knowledge and his articulation of the mechanical philosophy.

Descartes and other mechanists argued that matter was completely inert or dead. It had neither a soul nor any innate purpose. Its only property was extension, or the physical dimensions of length, width, and depth. Without a spirit or any other internal force directing its action, matter simply responded to the power of the other bodies with which it came in contact. According to Descartes, all physical phenomena could be explained by reference to the dimensions and the movement of particles of matter. He once claimed, "Give me extension and motion and I will construct the universe."[2] Even the human body contained no "vital spirits." It consisted only of flesh and the blood pumped by the mechanism of the heart. The only difference between the human body and other machines was that the mind (or soul) could move it, although how it did so was a matter of great controversy, as we shall see in a later section.

The view of nature as a machine implied that it operated in a regular, predictable way in accordance with unchanging laws of nature. Scientists could use reason to discover what those laws were and thus learn how nature performed under any circumstances. The scientific investigations of Galileo and Kepler were based on those assumptions, and Descartes made them explicit. The immutability of the laws of nature implied that the entire universe was uniform in structure, an assumption that underlay Newton's formulation of the laws of motion and of universal gravitation. Newton's theory of gravity denied Descartes's view of matter as inert, but he nonetheless accepted his view that the universe operated like a machine.

# The Causes of the Scientific Revolution

■ Why did the Scientific Revolution take place in western Europe at this particular time?

Why did the Scientific Revolution take place at this particular time, and why did it originate in western European countries? What prompted natural philosophers in Italy, France, England, and the Dutch Republic to develop new ways of looking at the world? There are no simple answers to these questions. We can, however, identify a number of developments that inspired this remarkable set of scientific discoveries. Some of these developments were internal to science, in the sense that they arose out of earlier investigations conducted by natural philosophers in the late Middle Ages, the Renaissance, and the sixteenth century. Others were external to the development of science, arising out of the religious, political, social, and economic life of Europe during the early modern period.

# Developments Within Science

The three internal causes of the Scientific Revolution were the research into motion conducted by scholastic natural philosophers in the fourteenth century, the scientific investigations conducted by humanists at the time of the Renaissance, and the collapse of the dominant conceptual frameworks that had governed scientific inquiry and research for centuries.

## Late Medieval Science

Modern science can trace some of its origins to the fourteenth century, when the first significant modifications of Aristotle's scientific theories began to emerge. These challenges came not only from theologians, who objected that Aristotle was a pagan philosopher, but from natural philosophers, who refined some of the basic ideas of Aristotle's physics.

The most significant of these refinements was the theory of impetus. Aristotle, as we have seen, had argued that an object would stop as soon as it lost contact with the object that moved it. The scholastic philosophers who modified this principle claimed that objects in motion acquire a force that stays with them after they lose contact with the mover. The theory of impetus did not bring about a full-scale demolition of Aristotle's mechanics, but it did begin to call Aristotle's authority into question. The theory of impetus was known in Galileo's day, and it influenced some of his early thought on motion.

Scholastic philosophers of the fourteenth century also began to recommend direct, empirical observation in place of the traditional scholastic tendency to accept preconceived theories regarding the operation of nature. This approach to answering scientific questions did not result in the type of rigorous experimentation that Bacon demanded three centuries later, but it did encourage scientists to base their theories on the facts that emerged from an empirical study of nature.

The contribution of late medieval science to the Scientific Revolution should not be exaggerated. Scholastic natural philosophers continued to accept the cosmology of Ptolemy. They still perpetuated the anatomical theories of Galen. The restraints that theology exercised over scientific thought in the Middle Ages also prevented the emergence of new scientific ideas.

## Renaissance Science

Natural philosophers during the Renaissance made more tangible contributions to the rise of modern science than the scholastics of the late Middle Ages. Renaissance natural philosophers made those contributions despite the fact that the Renaissance, the revival of classical antiquity in the fifteenth and sixteenth centuries, was not conducive to the type of scientific research that Galileo, Descartes, Boyle, and Newton conducted. Renaissance humanism was mainly a literary and artistic movement, and humanists were not particularly interested in scientific knowledge. Humanism also cultivated a tradition of deferring to the superior wisdom of classical authors, whereas the new science defined itself largely in opposition to the theories of the ancients, especially Aristotle, Ptolemy, and Galen. The main philosophical movement of the Renaissance, moreover, was Neoplatonism, which, as we have seen, promoted an animistic view of nature that mechanists such as Descartes and Kepler rejected.

The natural philosophers of the Renaissance did nonetheless make a number of important contributions to the birth of modern science. Many of the discoveries of the late sixteenth and seventeenth centuries drew their inspiration from Greek scientific works that had been recovered in their original form during the Renaissance. Copernicus found the original idea of his sun-centered universe in the writings of Aristarchus of Samos, a Greek astronomer of the third century B.C.E. whose work had been unknown during the Middle Ages. The theory that matter was divisible into small measurable particles known as atoms was inspired at least in part by the recovery of the texts of the ancient philosophers, most notably Democritus, who flourished around 480 B.C.E. Sixteenth-century editions of the works of Archimedes (287–212 B.C.E.), which had been virtually unknown in the Middle Ages, stimulated interest in the science of mechanics. The recovery and translation of previously unknown texts also made scientists aware that Greek scientists did not always agree with each other and thus provided a stimulus to independent observation and experimentation as a means of resolving their differences.

The Renaissance philosophy of Neoplatonism, despised by mechanists, also played an important role in the Scientific Revolution. In addition to the belief that the natural world had a soul, Neoplatonists adopted a geometric view of the universe and therefore encouraged the application of mathematics to the study of the natural world. Kepler developed his third law of planetary motion by applying to the cosmos the Neoplatonic idea of a harmony between numbers. The Neoplatonic tendency to think in terms of large, general categories also encouraged scientists such as Kepler, Galileo, and Newton to discover universal laws of nature. Even alchemy, which many Neoplatonists practiced during the Renaissance, involved natural philosophers in experiments that gave them a limited sense of control over the operations of nature. The followers of Paracelsus, whose alchemy was tinged with Neoplatonic mysticism, were firm advocates of the observation of nature and experimentation.

Some of the most prominent natural philosophers of the seventeenth century were influenced to some extent by the cultural traditions that we associate with the Renaissance. Kepler became involved in the study of magic at the court of the Holy Roman Emperor Rudolf II. From his reading in Neoplatonic sources, Kepler acquired his belief that the universe was constructed according to geometric principles.

**DOCUMENT**

## Copernicus Proposes His Sun-Centered Theory of the Universe

*In the dedication of his book* On the Revolution of the Heavenly Spheres *(1543) to Pope Paul III, Copernicus explains that in his search for an orderly model of the universe he drew inspiration from a few ancient philosophers who had imagined that the Earth moved. He then explained how he had bolstered his theory through long and frequent observations. Anticipating condemnation from those who based their astronomical theories on the Bible, he appeals to the pope for protection while showing contempt for the theories of his opponents.*

. . . I began to chafe that philosophers could by no means agree on any one certain theory of the mechanism of the Universe, wrought for us by a supremely good and orderly Creator . . . I therefore took pains to read again the works of all the philosophers on whom I could lay my hand to seek out whether any of them had ever supposed that the motions of the spheres were other than those demanded by the mathematical schools. I found first in Cicero that Hicetas had realized that the Earth moved. Afterwards I found in Plutarch that certain others had held the like opinion. . . .

Taking advantage of this I too began to think of the mobility of the Earth; and though the opinion seemed absurd, yet knowing now that others before me had been granted freedom to imagine such circles as they chose to explain the phenomena of the stars, I considered that I also might easily be allowed to try whether, by assuming some motion of the Earth, sounder explanations than theirs for the revolution of the celestial spheres might so be discovered.

Thus assuming motions, which in my work I ascribe to the Earth, by long and frequent observations I have at last discovered that, if the motions of the rest of the planets be brought into relation with the circulation of the Earth and be reckoned in proportion to the circles of each planet . . . the orders and magnitudes of all stars and spheres, nay the heavens themselves, become so bound together that nothing in any part thereof could be moved from its place without producing confusion of all the other parts and of the Universe as a whole. . . .

It may fall out, too, that idle babblers, ignorant of mathematics, may claim a right to pronounce a judgment on my work, by reason of a certain passage of Scripture basely twisted to serve their purpose. Should any such venture to criticize and carp at my project, I make no account of them; I consider their judgment rash, and utterly despise it.

Source: From Nicolaus Copernicus, *De Revolutionibus Orbium Caelestium* (1543), translated by John F. Dobson and Selig Brodetsky in *Occasional Notes of the Royal Astronomical Society*, Vol. 2, No. 10, 1947. Reprinted by permission of Blackwell Publishing.

Bacon gained some of his enthusiasm for experimentation from his interest in natural magic°, which was the use of magical words and drawings to manipulate forces in the physical world without calling on supernatural beings for assistance. Newton was fascinated by the subject of magic and studied alchemy intensively. The original inspiration of Newton's theory of gravitation probably came from his professor at Cambridge, the Neoplatonist Henry More, who insisted on the presence of spiritual and immaterial forces in the physical world.

These contributions of the Renaissance to the new science were so important that some historians have identified the sixteenth century, when learned magic was in vogue and when the mechanical philosophy had not yet taken hold, as the first stage of the Scientific Revolution, to be followed by the mechanical phase when the discoveries of Galileo, Boyle, and Newton took center stage. Modern science resulted not so much from the victory of the mechanical philosophy over its Neoplatonic predecessor but from this encounter between these two worldviews.

### The Collapse of Paradigms
The third internal cause of the Scientific Revolution was the collapse of the intellectual frameworks that had governed the conduct of scientific research since antiquity. The key to understanding this development is the recognition that scientists in all historical periods do not strive to introduce new theories but prefer to work within an established conceptual framework, or what the scholar Thomas Kuhn has referred to as a paradigm°. Scientists strive to solve puzzles that are presented by the paradigm. Every so often, however, the paradigm that has governed scientific research for an extended period of time collapses because it can no longer account for many different observable phenomena. A scientific revolution occurs when the old paradigm collapses and a new paradigm takes its place.[3]

The revolutionary developments we have studied in astronomy and biology can be explained at least in part by the collapse of old paradigms. In astronomy the paradigm that had governed scientific inquiry in antiquity and the Middle Ages was the Ptolemaic system, in which the sun and the planets revolved around the Earth. Whenever ancient or medieval astronomers confronted a new problem as a result of their observations, they tried to accommodate the results to the Ptolemaic model. In the process they had to refine the basic concept that Ptolemy had presented. By the sixteenth century the paradigm had been modified or adjusted so many times that it no longer made sense. As scientists gradually added numerous "epicycles" of planetary motion outside the prescribed spheres, and as they identified numerous "eccentric" or noncircular orbits around the Earth, Ptolemy's paradigm of a harmoniously functioning universe gradually became a confused collection of planets and stars following different motions. Faced with this situation, Copernicus began to look for a simpler and more plausible

model of the universe. The sun-centered theory that he proposed became the new paradigm within which Kepler, Galileo, and Newton all worked.

In the field of biology a parallel development occurred when the old paradigm constructed by Galen, in which the blood originated in the liver and was drawn into the heart and from there traveled through the arteries to the brain and nerves, also collapsed. By the seventeenth century the paradigm of Galen could no longer satisfactorily explain the findings of medical scholars, such as the recognition that blood could not easily pass from one ventricle of the heart to the other. It was left to Harvey to introduce an entirely new paradigm, in which the blood circulated through the body. As in astronomy, the collapse of the old paradigm led to the Scientific Revolution, and Harvey's new paradigm served as a framework for subsequent biological research.

## Developments Outside Science

A number of nonscientific developments also encouraged the development and acceptance of new scientific ideas. These developments outside science include the spread of Protestantism, the patronage of scientific research, the invention of the printing press, military and economic change, and voyages of exploration.

### Protestantism
The growth of Protestantism in the sixteenth and seventeenth centuries encouraged the rise of modern science. Catholics as well as Protestants engaged in scientific research, and some of the most prominent European natural philosophers, including Galileo and Descartes, were devout Catholics. Protestantism, however, encouraged the emergence of modern science in three indirect ways.

First, Protestant countries proved to be more receptive than Catholic ones to new scientific ideas. Protestant churches, for example, did not prohibit the publication of books that promoted novel scientific ideas on the grounds that they were heretical, as the Papal Index did. The greater willingness of Protestant governments, especially those of England and the Dutch Republic, to tolerate the expression of unorthodox ideas helps to explain why the main geographical arena of scientific investigation shifted from the Catholic Mediterranean to the Protestant North Atlantic in the second half of the seventeenth century.

The second connection between Protestantism and the development of science was the emphasis Protestant writers placed on the idea that God revealed his intentions not only in the Bible but also in nature itself. Protestants claimed that individuals had a duty to discover what God had revealed to them in this way, just as it was their duty to read Scripture to gain knowledge of God's will. Kepler's claim that the astronomer was "as a priest of God to the book of nature," a reference to the Protestant idea of the priesthood of all believers, serves as an explicit statement of this Protestant outlook.

The third contribution of Protestantism to the new science was the strong Protestant belief in the millennium, the second coming of Christ predicted in the book of Revelation in the New Testament. Many Protestants believed that the event was about to occur and after Christ's arrival he would rule the world with the saints for a thousand years. In preparation for this climactic event, many English scientists, including Boyle and Newton, called for the use of scientific knowledge to achieve the general improvement of society. They also took seriously the biblical prediction that as the millennium approached, knowledge and understanding would increase.

## Patronage

Although the intellectual problems that scientists grappled with may have inspired them to pursue their research and conduct experiments, they could not have succeeded without some kind of financial and institutional support. Only with the acquisition of an organizational structure could science acquire a permanent status, develop as a discipline, and give its members a professional identity. The universities, which today are known for their support of scientific research, did not serve as the main source of that support in the seventeenth century. One reason was that most universities, which were predominantly clerical institutions, had a vested interest in the defense of scholastic theology and Aristotelian science. They were therefore unlikely to provide the type of free academic atmosphere in which new scientific ideas might flourish. Moreover, within the university the only subject that allowed for the exploration of nature was that of philosophy. As long as science was considered a branch of philosophy, it could not establish its autonomy as a discipline and gain recognition as a legitimate pursuit in its own right.

Given limited support from the universities, scientists became dependent upon the patronage of wealthy and politically influential individuals. For the most part this patronage came from the kings, princes, and great noblemen who ruled European territorial states. During the seven-

teenth century, scientists found this type of patronage in two different types of institutions. The first were the courts of Italian and German princes. Galileo, for example, was the beneficiary of the patronage of Vincenzio Pinelli of Padua, the Venetian patrician Giovanfrancesco Sagredo, the Grand Duke of Tuscany Cosimo II de' Medici, the Roman aristocrat Prince Federico Cesi, and even Pope Urban VIII. These patrons, who were eager to display their interest in and support of learning, were actually responsible for securing Galileo's university appointments.

The terms of these appointments could be very generous. Galileo's appointment as Chief Mathematician at the University of Pisa, which Cosimo II secured for him in 1610, did not even require him to reside or teach there. Galileo's patrons gave him the opportunity to engage in his scientific work, and they circulated his publications at foreign courts. They did not, however, provide him with a permanent institutional base in which he could work.

Patronage from one politically powerful ruler rarely outlived the death of the patron, and the client could also lose the support of his patron, as Galileo did when he fell out of favor with Pope Urban VIII in 1632. Scientists who secured their livelihood at court also had to conduct themselves and their research in such a way as to maintain the favor of their patrons. Galileo referred to the new moons of Jupiter that he observed through his telescope as the Medicean stars in order to add luster to the image of the Medici family. His publications were inspired as much by his obligation to glorify Cosimo as by his belief in the validity of the sun-centered theory.

The second type of scientific institutions that provided patronage to scientists were academies in which groups of scientists could share ideas and work collectively. One of the earliest of these institutions was the Academy of the Lynxes in Rome, founded in 1603 by Prince Cesi. In keeping with the aristocratic values of its founder, it was modeled on an order of knights. Galileo became a member of this academy in 1611, and it published many of his works. In 1657 Cosimo II founded a similar institution, the Academy of Experiment, in Florence. These academies offered a more regular source of patronage than scientists could acquire from individual positions at court, but they still served the function of glorifying their founders, and they depended on patrons for their continued existence. The royal academies established in the 1660s, however, especially the Royal Academy of Sciences in France and the Royal Society in England, reduced that dependence on their patrons. These academies became in effect public institutions; even though they were established by the crown, they operated with a minimum of royal intervention. The royal academies also acquired a permanent location that made possible a continuous program of work.

The mission of the Royal Society in England was the promotion of scientific knowledge through a program of experimentation. It also served the political purpose of placing the results of scientific research at the service of the

## CHRONOLOGY

### The Formation of Scientific Societies

**1603** Prince Cesi founds the Academy of the Lynxes in Rome

**1657** Cosimo II de' Medici founds the Academy of Experiment in Florence

**1662** Founding of the Royal Society of London under the auspices of Charles II

**1666** Founding of the Academy of Sciences in Paris

state, as we shall see shortly. This had been Francis Bacon's objective in his *New Organon,* and many of the members of the society, including Robert Boyle and Robert Hooke, were committed to the implementation of Bacon's plans. The research that members of the Royal Society did on both ship construction and military technology gave some indication of this commitment. These attempts to use scientific technology to strengthen the power of the state show that two of the most important developments of the seventeenth century, the growth of the modern state and the emergence of modern science, were related.

## The Printing Press

The scientific academies and societies of the seventeenth century gave natural philosophers an opportunity to discuss their findings among themselves, but these scientists also needed to communicate the results of their research to scientists in more distant localities. The introduction and spread of printing throughout Europe made it much easier for scientists to share their discoveries with others who were working on similar problems. During the Middle Ages, when books were handwritten, the dissemination of scientific knowledge was limited by the number of copies that could be made of a manuscript. Moreover, errors could easily creep into the text as it was being copied. The advent and spread of printing helped to correct this problem: Scientific achievements could be preserved in a much more accurate form and presented to a broader audience. The availability of printed copies also made it much easier for other scientists to correct or supplement the data that the authors supplied. In this way the entire body of scientific knowledge became cumulative, as it is today. Printing also made possible the reproduction of illustrations, diagrams, tables, and other schematic drawings that helped to convey the author's findings.

It remains uncertain how large a role printed materials played in the development of science. Scientists certainly read the work of others, but they also devoted large amounts of time to their own experiments, and those experiments in the long run were more important than books in the development of scientific knowledge. Printing may have accomplished more by making members of the nonscientific community aware of the latest advances in physics and astronomy than by leading scientists themselves to make new discoveries. In this way printing helped to make science an integral part of the culture of educated Europeans. The printing press also facilitated the growth of opposition to the new science, since it made possible the publication of treatises attacking the theories of Copernicus, Galileo, and Descartes.

## Military and Economic Change

The Scientific Revolution occurred at roughly the same time that both the conduct of warfare and the European economy were undergoing dramatic changes. As territorial states increased the size of their armies and their mili-

tary arsenals, they naturally demanded more accurate weapons with longer range. Some of the work undertaken by physicists during the seventeenth century, especially concerning the trajectory and velocity of missiles, gravitation, and air resistance, had the specific intention of improving military weaponry. Members of the Royal Society in England conducted extensive scientific research on these topics, and in so doing followed Francis Bacon's recommendation that scientists place their research at the service of the state.

The practical needs of capitalist enterprise also had a bearing on the direction of scientific research. The seventeenth century was a formative period in the emergence of a new capitalist economy, one in which private individuals engaged in trade, agriculture, and industry in order to realize ever-increasing profits. Some of the questions discussed at the meetings of the Royal Society suggest that its members undertook research with the specific objective of making such capitalist ventures more productive and profitable. The research did not always produce immediate results, but ultimately it increased economic profitability and contributed to the growth of the English economy in the eighteenth century. Knowledge of the displacement of water by ships led to improvements in methods of ship construction, which benefited merchants engaged in overseas trade. The determination of longitude by means of an accurate measurement of time at sea, a problem with which many seventeenth-century scientists grappled and which was finally solved in the eighteenth century with the invention of the chronometer, improved navigation. The study of mechanics led to new techniques to ventilate mines and raise coal or ore from them, thus making mining more profitable.

## Voyages of Exploration

Closely related to the economic causes of the Scientific Revolution were the oceanic voyages of exploration that European mariners began to make in the late fifteenth century. As these voyages began long before the seventeenth century, they did not exercise an immediate or direct influence on the development of science. Most of the voyages, moreover, were undertaken by Portuguese and Spaniards, who did not play a major role in the Scientific Revolution. Nevertheless, these voyages revealed to mariners a number of natural phenomena that conflicted with the inherited traditions of Greek and late medieval science. They disproved, for example, much of what Ptolemy had written about the moistness of land in the Southern Hemisphere and what Aristotle had written about the difficulty of living in tropical areas. These inconsistencies led European natural philosophers to call into question the inherited authority of the Greeks on a variety of scientific matters and to base their views on the empirical observation of nature. In writing about the experimental method, Bacon frequently cited the body of evidence that had come from these voyages.

# The Intellectual Effects of the Scientific Revolution

■ How did the Scientific Revolution influence the development of philosophical and religious thought in the seventeenth and early eighteenth centuries?

The Scientific Revolution had a profound impact on the intellectual life of educated Europeans. The discoveries of Copernicus, Kepler, Galileo, and Newton, as well as the assumptions upon which their work was based, influenced the subjects that people in the West studied, the way in which they approached intellectual problems, and their views regarding the supernatural realm.

## Education

The philosophy of Aristotle, especially in its Christianized, scholastic form, had proved remarkably durable at European universities during the sixteenth century. It had successfully withstood the challenge of Neoplatonism, but the new science and the mechanical philosophy represented a more potent challenge to its supremacy. Over the course

## CHRONOLOGY

### The Impact of the Scientific Revolution

| | |
|---|---|
| 1620 | Sir Francis Bacon publishes *The New Organon,* arguing for the necessity of rigorous experimentation |
| 1633 | Galileo tried by the Roman Inquisition |
| 1637 | René Descartes publishes *Discourse on the Method,* recommending the solution of intellectual problems through a process of deduction |
| 1670 | Baruch Spinoza publishes *Treatise on Religion and Political Philosophy,* challenging the distinction between spirit and matter |
| 1682 | Edict of Louis XIV ending most witchcraft trials in France |
| 1685 | Last execution for witchcraft in England |
| 1686 | Bernard de Fontenelle publishes *Treatises on the Plurality of Worlds,* a fictional work exploring the possibility of extraterrestial life |
| 1691–1693 | Balthasar Bekker publishes *The Enchanted World* in four volumes, denying the intervention of the Devil in the operation of the natural world |
| 1709 | Thomas Newcomen invents the first steam engine |

of the seventeenth and early eighteenth centuries, especially between 1680 and 1720, science and the new philosophy that was associated with it acquired academic respectability and became an important component of university education. Outside academia, knowledge of science increased as the result of its promotion by learned societies, attendance at public lectures, the discussion of science in coffeehouses, and the publication of scientific textbooks. As this knowledge was diffused among the educated classes, science secured a permanent foothold in Western culture.

The spread of science did not go unchallenged. It encountered academic rivals committed not only to traditional Aristotelianism but also to Renaissance humanism, which had gradually penetrated the curriculum of the universities during the sixteenth and seventeenth centuries. Beginning in the late seventeenth century a conflict arose between "the ancients," who revered the wisdom of classical authors, and "the moderns," who emphasized the superiority of the new scientific culture. The most concrete expression of this conflict was the Battle of the Books, an intellectual debate that raged in England and on the Continent in the late seventeenth and early eighteenth centuries over the question of which group of thinkers had contributed more to human knowledge. The battle accentuated the differences between two distinct components of western European culture. The Battle of the Books ended with no clear winner, and the conflict between the ancients and the moderns has never been completely resolved. The humanities and the sciences, while included within the same curriculum at many universities, are still often regarded as representing two separate cultural traditions.

## Skepticism and Independent Reasoning

One of the most significant intellectual effects of the Scientific Revolution was the encouragement it gave to the habit of skepticism, the tendency to doubt what we have been taught and are expected to believe. This skepticism formed part of the method that seventeenth-century scientists adopted in their efforts to solve philosophical problems. As we have seen, Descartes, Bacon, Galileo, and Kepler all refused to acknowledge the authority of classical or medieval texts, preferring instead to rely upon the knowledge they acquired from the observation of nature and the use of their own rational faculties.

In *Discourse on the Method,* Descartes showed the extremes to which this skepticism could be taken by doubting the reality of his own sense perceptions and even his own existence. He eventually found a way out of this dilemma when he real-

**Baruch Spinoza**

Spinoza was one of the most radical thinkers of the seventeenth century. His followers in the Dutch Republic, who were known as freethinkers, laid the foundations for the Enlightenment in the eighteenth century.

ized that the very act of doubting proved his existence as a thinking being. As he wrote in words that have become famous, "I think, therefore I am."[4] Upon this foundation Descartes went on to prove the existence of God and the material world, thereby conquering the skepticism with which he began his inquiry. In the process, however, Descartes had promoted an approach to solving intellectual problems that asked people to question the authority of others and to think clearly and systematically for themselves. The effects of this method began to become apparent in the late seventeenth century, when Descartes's methodology was invoked in challenging a variety of orthodox opinions regarding the supernatural world.

Some of the most radical of those opinions came from the mind of Baruch Spinoza (1632–1677), who grew up in Amsterdam in a community of Spanish and Portuguese Jews who had fled the Inquisition. Although educated in the Orthodox Jewish manner, Spinoza also studied Latin and read the works of Descartes and other Christian writers of the period. From Descartes, Spinoza had learned "that nothing ought to be admitted as true but what has been proved by good and solid reason." This skepticism and independence of thought led to his excommunication from the Jewish community at age 24, at which time he changed his first name from its Jewish form, Baruch, to Benedict. A skilled lens grinder by trade, Spinoza spent much of his life developing his philosophical ideas.

Spinoza challenged Descartes's separation of the mind and the body and the radical distinction between the spiritual and the material. For Spinoza there was only one substance in the universe, which he equated with nature or God. This pantheism, in which all matter became spirit and was comprehended within God, challenged not only the ideas of Descartes but also a fundamental tenet of Christianity—the distinction between God as pure spirit and the material world that he had created. In his most famous book, *A Treatise on Religion and Political Philosophy* (1670), Spinoza developed these ideas and also called for complete freedom from intellectual restraints.

The type of freethinking that Spinoza advocated aroused considerable suspicion. His followers, most of whom lived in the Dutch Republic, were constantly exposed to the danger of prosecution for atheism and blasphemy. Spinoza's skeptical approach to solving philosophical and scientific problems revealed the radical intellectual potential of the new science. The freedom of thought that Spinoza advocated, as well as the belief that nature followed immutable laws and could be understood in mathematical terms, served as important links between the Scientific Revolution and the Enlightenment of the eighteenth century. Those connections will be studied more fully in Chapter 18.

## Science and Religion

The most profound intellectual effects of the Scientific Revolution occurred in the area of religious thought. The claims of the new science presented two challenges to traditional Christian belief. The first involved the apparent contradiction between the sun-centered theory of the universe and biblical references to the sun's mobility. Because the Bible was considered the inspired word of God, the Church took everything it said, including any passages regarding the operation of the physical world, as literally true. The Bible's reference to the sun moving across the sky served as the basis of the official papal condemnation of sun-centered theories in 1616 and the prosecution of Galileo in 1633.

The second challenge to traditional Christian belief was the implication that if the universe functioned as a machine, on the basis of immutable natural laws, then God apparently played a very small role in its operation. This position, which was adopted by the late-seventeenth- and eighteenth-century thinkers known as Deists°, was considered a denial of the Christian belief that God superintended the operation of the world and was continually active in its governance. None of the great scientists of the seventeenth century actually adopted this position, but the acceptance of the mechanical philosophy made them vulnerable to the charge that they denied Christian doctrine. Because of his support for the mechanical philosophy, Descartes was suspected of atheism.

Although the new science and seventeenth-century Christianity appeared to be on a collision course, a number of scientists and theologians insisted that there was no conflict between them. One argument they made was that religion and science were separate disciplines that had very different concerns. Religion dealt with the relationship between humans and God, while science explained how nature operated. As Galileo wrote in a letter to the Grand Duchess Christina of Tuscany in 1615, "The intention of the Holy Ghost is to teach us how one goes to heaven, not how the heaven goes."[5] Scripture was not intended to explain natural phenomena, but to convey religious truths that could not be grasped by human reason. In making these points Galileo was pleading for the separation of religion and science by freeing scientific inquiry from the control of the

DOCUMENT

Galileo Galilei, *Letter to the Grand Duchess Christina*

Church. To some extent, that separation has taken place over the course of the last three centuries. Theology and science have gradually become separate academic disciplines, each with its own objectives and methodology. Even the papacy eventually accepted the position of Galileo on this question in 1992. Nevertheless, conflicts between the claims of science and those who believe in the literal truth of the Bible have not disappeared, especially regarding the theory of evolution.

Another argument for the compatibility of science and religion was the claim that the mechanical philosophy, rather than relegating God to the role of a retired engineer, actually manifested his unlimited power. In a mechanistic universe God was still the creator of the entire physical world and the formulator of the laws of nature that guaranteed its regular operation. He was still all-powerful and present everywhere. According to Boyle and Newton, moreover, God played a supremely active role in governing the universe. Not only had he created the universe, but, in a theory developed by Boyle, he also continued to keep all matter constantly in motion. This theory served the purpose of redefining God's power without diminishing it in

## DOCUMENT

# Science and the Preternatural

*Thomas Sprat (1635–1713), an English clergyman who rose to be bishop of Rochester, was elected a member of the Royal Society of London in 1663, and in 1667 he published a history of that society. Sprat praised the tradition of experimentation that became the hallmark of the society, and in this passage he claimed that the empiricism of modern science eliminated the imaginary creatures, such as fairies and ghosts, that classical writers had invented and medieval theologians had continued to claim were the causes of unusual phenomena. According to Sprat, all such phenomena can be explained by natural causes and effects, through which God governed the universe. Sprat claims that by showing these creatures to be mere phantasms, science has eliminated the fear that people have had of them from early childhood.*

And as for the terrors and misapprehensions which commonly confound weaker minds and make men's minds to fail and boggle at trifles, there is so little hope of having them removed by speculation alone that it is evident they were first produced by the most contemplative men among the ancients and chiefly prevailed of late years, when that way of learning flourished. The poets began of old to impose the deceit. They to make all things look more venerable than they were devised a thousand false chimeras; on every field, river, grove and cove, they bestowed a phantasm of their own making. With these they amazed the world; these they clothed with what shapes they pleased. By these they pretended that all wars and counsels and actions of men were administered. And in the modern ages these fantastical forms were revived and possessed Christendom in the very height of the schoolmen's time. An infinite number of fairies haunted every house; all churches were filled with apparitions; men began to be frightened from their cradles, which fright continued to their graves, and their names also were made the causes of scaring others. All which abuses if those acute philosophers did not promote, yet they were never able to overcome; nay, even not so much as King Oberon and his invisible army.

But from the time in which the real philosophy [science] appeared, there is scarce any whisper remaining of such horrors. Every man is unshaken at those tales at which his ancestors trembled. The course of things goes quietly along, in its own true channel of causes and effects. For this we are beholden to experiments, which though they have not yet completed the discovery of the true world, yet they have already vanquished those wild inhabitants of the false worlds that used to astonish the minds of men. A blessing for which we ought to be thankful, if we remember, that it is one of the greatest curses that God pronounces on the wicked, that they shall fear where no fear is.

Source: From *History of the Royal Society of London* by Thomas Sprat, 1702, pp. 339–341.

any way. Newton arrived at a similar position in his search for an immaterial agent who would cause gravity to operate. He proposed that God himself, who he believed "endures always and is present everywhere," made bodies move according to gravitational laws. Throughout the early eighteenth century this feature of Newtonian natural philosophy served as a powerful argument for the existence and immanence of God.

As the new science became more widely accepted, and as the regularity and immutability of the laws of nature became more apparent, religion itself began to undergo a transformation. Instead of denying the validity of the new science, many theologians, especially Protestants, accommodated scientific knowledge to their religious beliefs. Some Protestants welcomed the discoveries of science as an opportunity to purify the Christian religion by combating the superstition, magic, and ignorance that they claimed the Catholic Church had been promoting. Clerics who accepted the new science, including those who became members of the Royal Society, argued that because God worked through the processes of nature, human beings could acquire theological knowledge of him by engaging in scientific inquiry. For them religion and science were not so much separate but complementary forms of knowledge, each capable of illuminating the other.

The most widespread effect of the new science on religion was a new emphasis on the compatibility of reason and religion. In the Middle Ages scholastic theologians such as Thomas Aquinas had tried to reconcile the two, arguing that there was a body of knowledge about God, called natural theology, that could be obtained without the assistance of revelation. Now, however, with the benefit of the new science, theologians and philosophers began to expand the role that reason played in religion. In the religious writings of the English philosopher John Locke, the role of reason became dominant. In *The Reasonableness of Christianity* (1695), Locke argued that reason should be the final arbiter of the existence of the supernatural and it should also determine the true meaning of the Bible. This new emphasis on the role of reason in religion coincided with a rejection of the religious zeal that had characterized the era of the Reformation and the wars of religion. Political and ecclesiastical authorities looked down on religious enthusiasm not only as politically dangerous, as it had inspired revolution and rebellion throughout Europe, but as a form of behavior that had no rational basis.

The new emphasis on the reasonableness of religion and the decline of religious enthusiasm are often viewed as evidence of a broader trend toward the secularization of European life, a process in which religion gave way to more worldly concerns. In one sense this secular trend was undeniable. By the dawn of the eighteenth century, theology had lost its dominant position at the universities, the sciences had become autonomous academic disciplines, and religion had lost much of its intellectual authority. Religion also began to exercise less influence on the conduct of politics and diplomacy and on the regulation of economic activity.

Religion had not, however, lost its relevance. Throughout the eighteenth century it remained a vital force in the lives of most European people. Religious books continued to be published in great numbers. Many of those who accepted the new science continued to believe in a providential God and the divinity of Christ. Moreover, a small but influential group of educated people, following the lead of the French mathematician, physicist, and religious philosopher Blaise Pascal (1623–1662), insisted that although reason and science have their place, they represent only one sphere of truth. In his widely circulated book *Reflections,* which lay unfinished at his death but was published in 1670, Pascal argued that religious faith occupied a higher sphere of knowledge that reason and science could not penetrate. Pascal, the inventor of a calculating machine and the promoter of a system of public coach service in Paris, had been an advocate of the new science. He endorsed the Copernican model of the universe and opposed the condemnation of Galileo. But on the question of the relationship between science and religion, Pascal presented arguments that could be used against Spinoza, Locke, and all those who considered reason the ultimate arbiter of truth.

## Magic, Demons, and Witchcraft

The new science not only changed many patterns of religious thought but also led to a denial of the reality and effectiveness of magic. Magic is the use of a supernatural, occult, or mysterious power to achieve extraordinary effects in the physical world or to influence the course of human events. The effects can be beneficial or harmful. Magicians claimed to be able to use their special powers to cure a person or inflict disease, acquire political power, stimulate love or hatred in another individual, predict the future, or produce any number of natural "marvels," including changes in the weather. In the sixteenth and seventeenth centuries men and women believed in and practiced two forms of magic. Natural magic, such as the practice of alchemy, involved the manipulation of occult forces that were believed to exist in nature. As we have seen, many Neoplatonists believed in the possibility of this type of magic, and many of them actually practiced it. Demonic magic°, on the other hand, involved the invocation of evil spirits so that one might gain access to their supernatural power. The men who were most committed to the mechanical philosophy denied the effectiveness of both types of magic. By claiming that matter was inert, they challenged the central notion of natural magic, which is the belief that material objects are animated by occult forces, such as an innate attraction to another object. If matter was not alive, it contained no forces for a magician to manipulate.

# The Trial of Galileo

The events leading to the trial of Galileo for heresy in 1633 began in 1616, when a committee of eleven theologians reported to the Roman Inquisition that the sun-centered theory of Copernicus was heretical. Those who accepted this theory were declared to be heretics not only because they called the authority of the Bible into question but because they denied the exclusive authority of the Catholic Church to determine how the Bible should be interpreted. The day after this report was submitted, Pope Paul V instructed Cardinal Robert Bellarmine, a theologian who was on good terms with Galileo, to warn him to abandon his Copernican views. Galileo had written extensively in support of the sun-centered thesis, especially in his *Letters on Sunspots* (1613) and his *Letter to the Grand Duchess Christina* (1615), although he had never admitted that the theory was proved conclusively. Now he was being told that he should not hold, teach, or defend in any way the opinion of the sun's stability or the Earth's mobility. If he were to ignore that warning, he would be prosecuted as a heretic.

During the next sixteen years Galileo published two books. The first, *The Assayer* (1623), was an attack upon the views of an Italian philosopher regarding comets. The book actually won Galileo considerable support, especially from the new pope, Urban VIII, who was eager to be associated with the most fashionable intellectual trends. Urban took Galileo under his wing and made him the intellectual star of his court. Urban even went so far as to declare that support for Copernicanism was not heretical but only rash.

The patronage of the pope may have emboldened Galileo to exercise less caution in writing his second book of this period, *Dialogue Concerning the Two Chief World Systems* (1632). This treatise was ostensibly an impartial presentation of the rival Ptolemaic and Copernican cosmologies, but in its own quiet way it served the purpose of promoting Copernicanism. Galileo sought proper authorization from ecclesiastical authorities to put the book in print, but he eventually allowed it to be published in Florence before it received official approval from Rome.

The publication of *Dialogue* precipitated Galileo's fall from the pope's favor. Urban, who at this time was coming under criticism for leniency with heretics, ordered the book taken out of circulation in the summer of 1632 and appointed a commission to investigate Galileo's activities. After receiving the report from the committee a few months later, he turned the matter over to the Roman Inquisition, which charged Galileo with heresy.

The Roman Inquisition had been established in 1542 to preserve the Catholic faith. Its main concern was the prosecution of heresy. Like the Spanish Inquisition, this Roman ecclesiastical court has acquired a reputation for being harsh and arbitrary, for administering torture, for proceeding in secrecy, and for denying the accused the right to know the charges in advance of the trial. There is some validity to these criticisms, although the Roman Inquisition did not torture Galileo or deny him the opportunity to present a defense. The most unfair aspect of the proceeding, and of inquisitorial justice in general, was the determination of the outcome of the trial by the same judges who had brought the charges against the accused and conducted the interrogation. This meant that in a politically motivated trial such as

Galileo's, the verdict was a foregone conclusion. To accept Galileo's defense would have been a sign of weakness and a repudiation of the pope.

Although the underlying substantive issue in the trial was whether Galileo was guilty of heresy for denying the sun's motion and the Earth's immobility, the more technical question was whether by publishing *Dialogue* he had violated the prohibition of 1616. In his defense Galileo claimed that the only reason he had written *Dialogue* was to present "the physical and astronomical reasons that can be advanced for one side or the other." He denied holding Copernicus's opinion to be true.

In the end the court determined that by publishing *Dialogue,* Galileo had violated the injunction of 1616. He had disseminated "the false opinion of the Earth's motion and the sun's stability" and he had "defended the said opinion already condemned." Even Galileo's efforts "to give the impression of leaving it undecided and labeled as probable" was still a very serious error, because there was no way that "an opinion declared and defined contrary to divine Scripture may be probable." The court also declared that Galileo had obtained permission to publish the book in Florence without divulging to the authorities there that he was under the injunction of 1616.

Throughout the trial every effort was made to distance the pope from his former protégé. There was real fear among the members of the papal court that because the pope had been Galileo's patron and had given him considerable latitude in developing his ideas, he himself would be implicated in Galileo's heresy. Every step was taken to guarantee

**The Trial of Galileo, 1633**
Galileo is shown here presenting one of his four defenses to the Inquisition. He claimed that his book *Dialogue Concerning the Two Chief World Systems* did not endorse the Copernican model of the universe.

that information regarding the pope's support for Galileo did not surface. The court made sure, for example, that no one from the Medici court, which had provided support for Galileo, would testify on Galileo's behalf. The trial tells us as much about the efforts of Urban VIII to save face as about the Catholic Church's hostility to the new science.

Galileo was required to formally renounce his views and to avoid any further defense of Copernicanism. After making this humiliating submission to the court, he was sent to Siena and later that year was allowed to return to his villa in Arcetri near Florence, where he remained under house arrest until his death in 1642.

## Questions of Justice

1. Galileo was silenced because of what he had put into print. Why had he published these works, and why did the Church consider his publications a serious threat?
2. Is a court of law an appropriate place to resolve disputes between science and religion? Why or why not?

## Taking It Further

Finocchiaro, Maurice, ed. *The Galileo Affair: A Documentary History*. 1989. A collection of original documents regarding the controversy between Galileo and the Roman Catholic Church.

Sharratt, Michael. *Galileo: Decisive Innovator*. 1994. A study of Galileo's place in the history of science that provides full coverage of his trial and papal reconsiderations of it in the late twentieth century.

The denial of the reality of demonic magic was based on a rejection of the powers of demons. Seventeenth-century scientists did not necessarily deny the existence of angelic or demonic spirits, but the mechanical philosophy posed a serious challenge to the belief that those spirits could influence the operation of the physical world. The belief in demons experienced a slow death. Many scientists struggled to preserve a place for them in the physical world, arguing that the Devil, like God, could work through the processes of nature. Ultimately, however, the logic of the mechanical philosophy expelled demons from the worldview of the educated classes. By the beginning of the eighteenth century, scientists and even some theologians had labeled the belief in demons as superstition, which originally had meant false or erroneous religion but which was now redefined to mean ignorance of natural causes.

The denial of the power of magic, together with the rejection of the belief in the power of demonic spirits, also explains why many educated Europeans began to deny the reality of witchcraft in the second half of the seventeenth century. As we have seen in Chapter 14, witches were individuals, mostly women, who stood accused of using magic to harm their neighbors, their animals, or their crops. They were also accused of having made a pact with the Devil, the means by which they received their magical powers. In many cases it was claimed that witches worshiped the Devil collectively at nocturnal orgies known as sabbaths. To someone who subscribed to the mechanical philosophy, this entire set of beliefs about witches was highly questionable. Demons could not intervene in the operation of the physical world, nor could human beings perform magic with or without their assistance.

Science also played a major role in challenging the belief that demons could invade a human body and control the person's movements and behavior. During the seventeenth century Europe experienced a wave of such demonic possessions, in which individuals—often young girls—experienced fits and convulsions, spoke in deep, gruff voices, displayed preternatural strength, vomited foreign objects such as pins, and experienced temporary blindness and deafness. Believing that demons were the cause of these symptoms, clerics attempted to dispossess or exorcise them through either an elaborate ritual in Roman Catholic countries or a program of prayer and fasting in Protestant communities. By the end of the seventeenth century the belief that demons were responsible for such possessions had given way to the assumption that the behavior of the possessed person or demoniac had natural, medical causes. The range of possible maladies afflicting demoniacs included the disease known then as hysteria, in which the body of a person displayed such symptoms as a reaction to unbearable stress.

The most emphatic, comprehensive, and unequivocal attack on the entire body of beliefs regarding the Devil during the seventeenth century came from the pen of a Dutch minister and follower of Descartes, Balthasar Bekker. In his four-volume study, *The Enchanted World* (1691–1693), Bekker denied that the Devil could exercise any jurisdiction over the natural world. The mechanical philosophy was not the only basis for Bekker's skepticism. A biblical scholar, Bekker produced many passages from Scripture indicating that God exercised complete sovereignty over the Devil and had in fact chained him up in Hell. In this way the Devil had been rendered incapable of causing physical destruction in the world, either with or without the assistance of witches.

The skeptical views that many educated people acquired regarding demons and magic were usually not shared by people who remained illiterate. For them magic and witchcraft remained very real, and they continued to suspect and accuse their neighbors of engaging in diabolical practices until the early nineteenth century. In a number of instances they took the law into their own hands, stoning accused witches, drowning them, or burning them alive. All of this served to highlight a widening gap between the views of the educated and those of the common people. There had always been differences between learned and popular culture, but many aspects of culture were shared by educated and uneducated people. Both groups, for example, took part in the same religious services and rituals, and both groups also held some of the same beliefs about magic and witchcraft. In the late seventeenth century, however, this common cultural ground began to disappear, and members of the educated classes began to develop unprecedented contempt for the ignorance and superstition of the common people. The education of the upper classes in the new science and in Descartes's philosophy only aggravated what was already a noticeable trend.

The development of two separate realms of culture became one of the main themes of eighteenth-century history, and it contributed directly to the formation of class divisions. On the one side were the educated upper classes who prided themselves on their rational and enlightened views; on the other were the illiterate peasants who continued to believe in magic, witchcraft, and what the educated referred to as "vulgar superstition."

# Humans and the Natural World

■ How did the Scientific Revolution change the way in which seventeenth- and eighteenth-century Europeans thought of their relationship to the natural world?

The spread of scientific knowledge not only redefined the views of educated people regarding the supernatural realm, but it also led them to reconsider their relationship to nature. This process involved three separate but related inquiries. The first was to determine the place of human beings in a sun-centered universe; the second to investigate how science and technology had given human beings greater control over nature; and the third to reconsider the relationship between men and women in light of new scientific knowledge regarding the human mind and body.

## The Place of Human Beings in the Universe

The astronomical discoveries of Copernicus and Galileo offered a new outlook regarding the position of human beings in the universe. The Earth-centered Ptolemaic cosmos that dominated scientific thought during the Middle Ages was also human-centered. Not only was the planet that human beings inhabited situated at the center of the universe, but on Earth humans occupied a privileged position. This is not to say that the human condition was always viewed in positive terms. Trapped on a stationary Earth, which itself was corruptible, individuals were always vulnerable to the temptations of the demonic spirits that medieval clerics told them were constantly hovering in the atmosphere. But human beings nonetheless remained the absolute physical and moral center of this universe. They were, after all, created in the image of God, according to Christian belief. Renaissance Neoplatonism reinforced this medieval view. By describing human beings as having the characteristics of both angels and beasts, with the capacity to ascend toward God or descend to the level of animals, Neoplatonists accentuated the centrality and importance of humankind in the world.

The acceptance of a sun-centered model of the universe began to bring about a fundamental change in these views of humankind. Once it became apparent that the Earth was not the center of the universe, human beings began to lose their privileged position in nature. The Copernican universe was neither Earth-centered nor human-centered. Scientists such as Descartes continued to claim that human beings were the greatest of nature's creatures, but their habitation of a tiny planet circling the sun inevitably reduced the sense of their own importance. Moreover, as astronomers began to recognize the incomprehensible size of the cosmos, the possibility emerged that there were other habitable worlds in the universe, calling into further question the unique status of humankind.

In the late sixteenth and seventeenth centuries a number of literary works explored the possibility of other inhabited worlds and forms of life. In *The Infinite Universe and World* (1584), the Neoplatonist monk Giordano Bruno (1548–1600), who was eventually burned as a heretic, postulated the existence of other rational beings and suggested that they might be more intelligent than humans. Kepler's *Somnium,* or *Lunar Astronomy* (1634), a book that combined science and fiction, described various species of moon dwellers, some of whom were rational and superior to humans. This was followed by a number of works of fic-

tion on travel to the moon, including Francis Godwin's *The Man in the Moon* (1638) and Cyrano de Bergerac's *The Other World* (1657). The most ambitious and fascinating of all these books was a fictional work by the French dramatist and poet Bernard de Fontenelle, *Conversations on the Plurality of Worlds* (1686). This work, which became immensely popular throughout Europe, was more responsible than any purely scientific discovery of the seventeenth century for leading the general reading public to call into question the centrality of humankind in Creation.

## The Control of Nature

The Scientific Revolution bolstered the confidence human beings had in their ability to control nature. By disclosing the laws governing the operation of the universe, the new science gave humans the tools they needed to make nature serve their own purposes more effectively than it had in the past. This confidence in human mastery over nature found its most articulate expression in the writings of Francis Bacon. Instead of accepting the traditional view that humans were either passively reconciled with nature or victimized by it, Bacon believed that knowledge of the laws of nature could restore the dominion over nature that humans had lost in the biblical Garden of Eden. Bacon believed that nature existed for human beings to control and exploit for their own benefit. His famous maxim, "knowledge is power," conveyed his confidence that science would give human beings this type of control over nature.

In the same spirit Descartes announced that as human beings we had the capacity "to turn ourselves into the masters and possessors of nature."[6] For him nature included animals or beasts, which, unlike human beings, did not have souls and were therefore merely corporal machines. (For this reason, he was not at all reluctant to dissect live animals.) Later in the seventeenth century the members of the Royal Society proclaimed their intention to make scientific knowledge "an instrument whereby mankind may obtain a dominion over things." This optimism regarding human control of nature found support in the belief that God permitted such mastery, first by creating a regular and uniform universe and then by giving people the rational faculties by which they could understand nature's laws.

Many scientists of the seventeenth century emphasized the practical applications of their research, just as scientists often do today. Descartes, who used his knowledge of optics to improve the grinding of lenses, contemplated ways in which scientific knowledge might improve the drainage of marshes, increase the velocity of bullets, and use bells to make clouds burst. In his celebration of the French Academy of Sciences in 1699, Fontenelle wrote that "the application of science to nature will constantly grow in scope and intensity and we shall go on from one marvel to the next; the day will come when man will be able to fly by

**The Founding of the French Acadèmie des Sciences**
Like the Royal Society in England, the French Académie of Sciences was dependent upon royal patronage. Louis XIV, seen sitting in the middle of the painting, used the occasion to glorify himself as a patron of the sciences as well as the arts. The painting also commemorates the building of the Royal Observatory in Paris, which is shown in the background.

fitting on wings to keep him in the air . . . till one day we shall be able to fly to the moon."[7] As we mentioned earlier, members of the Royal Society discussed how their experiments would help miners, farmers, and merchants. They even discussed the possibility of making labor-saving machines. These efforts to apply scientific knowledge to practical problems encouraged the belief, which has persisted to the present day, that science could improve human life.

The hopes of seventeenth-century scientists for the improvement of human life by means of technology remained in large part unfulfilled until the eighteenth century. Only then did the technological promise of the Scientific Revolution begin to be realized, most notably with the innovations that preceded or accompanied the Industrial Revolution. The first steam engine, for example, which utilized the scientific study of atmospheric pressure conducted by a student of Galileo in the 1650s, was not invented until 1709. The great improvements in the construction of canals and the use of water power to drive machinery, which were based upon the study of Newtonian mechanics, likewise did not take place until the eighteenth century. In similar fashion, research on the internal structure of grains and the breeding of sheep did not significantly increase food production until the eighteenth century, at the time of the agricultural revolution.

By the middle of the eighteenth century, the belief that science would lead to an improvement of human life became an integral part of Western culture. Much less apparent at that time, however, was a recognition of the destructive potential of applied science. Governments supported scientific research on ballistics to gain military advantage,

but it was not until the twentieth century, especially with the construction of engines of mass destruction, that people began to recognize technology's potential to cause permanent harm to the human race. In the seventeenth and eighteenth centuries, those who possessed scientific knowledge thought mainly in terms of the benefits that science and technology could confer. Their faith in human progress became one of the main themes of the Enlightenment, which will be discussed in Chapter 18.

## Women, Men, and Nature

The new scientific and philosophical ideas of the seventeenth century challenged ancient and medieval notions regarding women's physical and mental inferiority to men. At the same time the new science left other traditional ideas about the roles of men and women unchallenged.

Until the seventeenth century, a woman's sexual organs were thought to be imperfect versions of a man's, an idea that made woman an inferior version of man and in some respects a freak of nature. During the sixteenth and seventeenth centuries, a body of scientific literature advanced the new idea that women had sexual organs that were perfect in their own right and served distinct functions in reproduction. Another traditional biological idea that came under attack during this period was Aristotle's view that men made a more important contribution to reproduction than did women. The man's semen was long believed to contain the form of the body as well as the soul, while the only contribution the woman was believed to make to the process

## DOCUMENT

# Elisabeth of Bohemia Challenges Descartes

*Elisabeth of Bohemia, the daughter of King Frederick of Bohemia and granddaughter of King James I of England, engaged in a long correspondence with Descartes regarding his philosophy. Privately educated in Greek, Latin, and mathematics, Elisabeth was one of a small group of noblewomen who participated in the scientific and philosophical debates of the day. The letter concerns the relationship between the soul (or mind), which Descartes claimed was immaterial, and the body, which is entirely composed of matter. One of the problems for Descartes was to explain how the mind could move that body to perform certain functions. In the letter Elisabeth plays a deferential, self-effacing role but in the process exposes one of the weaknesses of Descartes's dualistic philosophy.*

The Hague, 20 June 1643

Monsieur Descartes,

. . . The life I am forced to lead does not leave me the disposition of enough time to acquire a habit of meditation according to your rules. So many interests of my family that I must not neglect, so many interviews and civilities that I cannot avoid, batter my weak spirit with such anger and boredom that it is rendered for a long time afterward useless for anything else. All of which will excuse my stupidity, I hope, not to have been able to understand the idea by which we must judge how the soul (not extended and immaterial) can move the body by an idea we have in another regard of heaviness, nor why a power—which we have falsely attributed to things under the name of a quality—of carrying a body toward the center of the Earth when the demonstration of a contrary truth (which you promised in your Physics) confirms us in thinking it impossible. The idea of a separate independent quality of heaviness—given that we are not able to pretend to the perfection and objective reality of God—could be made up out of ignorance of that which truly propels bodies towards the center of the Earth. Because no material cause represents itself to the senses, one attributes heaviness to matter's contrary, the immaterial, which nevertheless I would never be able to conceive but as a negation of matter and which could have no communication with matter.

I confess that it is easier for me to concede the matter and the extension of the soul than to concede that a being that is immaterial has the capacity to move a body and to be moved by it. For if the former is done by giving information, it is necessary that the spirits which make the movement be intelligent, which you do not accord to anything corporal. And although, in your meditations, you show the possibility of the soul being moved by the body, it is nevertheless very difficult to comprehend how a soul, as you have described it, after having had the faculty and habit of good reasoning, would lose all that by some sort of vapors, or that being able to subsist without the body and having nothing in common with it, would allow itself to be so ruled by the body.

Source: From *The Princess and the Philosopher: Letters of Elisabeth of the Palatine to René Descartes* by Andrea Nye. Copyright © 1999 by Rowman & Littlefield Publishers, Inc. Reprinted by permission.

was the formless matter upon which the semen acted. By the beginning of the eighteenth century, a scholarly consensus had emerged that recognized equal contributions from both sexes to the process of reproduction.

Some seventeenth-century natural philosophers also called into question ancient and medieval ideas regarding women's mental inferiority to men. In this regard Descartes supplied a theory that presupposed intellectual equality between the sexes. In making a radical separation between the mind and the human body, Descartes found no difference between the minds of men and women. As one of his followers wrote in 1673, "The mind has no sex."[8] A few upper-class women provided solid evidence to support this revolutionary claim of female intellectual equality. Princess Elisabeth of Bohemia, for example, carried on a long correspondence with Descartes during the 1640s and challenged many of his ideas on the relationship between the body and the soul. The privately educated English noblewoman Margaret Cavendish (1623–1673) wrote scientific and philosophical treatises and conversed with the leading philosophers of the day. In early eighteenth-century France, small groups of women and men gathered in the salons or private sitting rooms of the nobility to discuss philosophical and scientific ideas. In Germany it was not uncommon for women to help their husbands run astronomical observatories.

Although seventeenth-century science laid the theoretical foundations for a theory of sexual equality, it did not challenge other traditional ideas that compared women unfavorably to men. Most educated people continued to ground female behavior in the humors, claiming that because women were cold and wet, as opposed to hot and dry, they were naturally more deceptive, unstable, and melancholic than men. They also continued to identify women with nature itself, which had always been depicted as female. Bacon's use of masculine metaphors to describe science and his references to "man's mastery over nature" therefore seemed to reinforce traditional ideas of male dominance

Eighteenth-Century Midwifery

**Astronomers in Seventeenth-Century Germany**
Elisabetha and Johannes Hevelius working together with a sextant in a German astronomical observatory. More than 14 percent of all German astronomers were female. Most of them cooperated with their husbands in their work.

over women. His language also reinforced traditional notions of men's superior rationality.[9] In 1664 the secretary of the Royal Society, which excluded women from membership, proclaimed that the mission of that institution was to develop a "masculine philosophy."[10] At the same time the tradition of depicting science as a female goddess, such as Minerva, began to disappear.

The new science provided the theoretical foundations for the male control of women at a time when many men expressed concern over the "disorderly" and "irrational" conduct of women. In a world populated with witches, rebels, and other women who refused to adhere to conventional standards of proper feminine behavior, the adoption of a masculine philosophy was associated with the reassertion of patriarchy.

# Conclusion

## Science and Western Culture

The Scientific Revolution was a uniquely Western phenomenon. It had no parallel in the Eastern world. During the Middle Ages the Islamic civilizations of the Middle East produced a rich body of scientific knowledge that had influenced the development of science in western Europe, but by the time of the Scientific Revolution Islamic science had entered a period of decline. Other civilizations, most notably in China and India, also possessed impressive scientific traditions, but they too failed to undergo a transformation similar to that which occurred in western Europe in the seventeenth century.

In all these non-Western civilizations, religious traditions had prevented philosophers from undertaking an objective study of the natural world. Either nature was viewed as an entirely secular (that is, not religious) entity and hence not worthy of study on its own terms, or it was viewed as something so heavily infused with spiritual value that it could not be subjected to rational analysis. Only in Europe did religious and cultural traditions allow the scientist to view nature as both a product of supernatural forces and something that was separate from the supernatural realm. Nature could therefore be studied objectively without losing its religious significance. Only when nature was viewed in this dual way, as both the creation of God and as something independent of the deity, could it be subjected to mathematical analysis and brought under human domination.

The Scientific Revolution gave the West a new source of identity. The West could be distinguished not only by its Christianity, its capitalist economic system, its large bureaucratic states, and its massive standing armies, but also by the scientific content of its education, its approach to the natural world, and its science-based technology. By the beginning of the eighteenth century, modern science became an essential component of Western culture. It also laid the foundations of the Enlightenment, another distinctively Western phenomenon, which will be discussed in Chapter 18.

The rise of Western science and technology had profound implications for the encounters that took place between Western and non-Western peoples in Africa, Asia, and the Americas. By the eighteenth century, European science provided explicit support for European empires, which will be discussed in Chapters 17 and 23. Science gave Western states the military and navigational technology that allowed them to establish their control over non-Europeans. Knowledge of botany and agriculture allowed Western powers to develop the resources of the areas they colonized and to use these resources for the improvement of their own societies. Most important, the possession of scientific knowledge and technology encouraged people in the West to think of themselves as superior to the people they subjugated or controlled. Scientific theories regarding biological and physiological differences between the people who inhabited the West and natives of other countries also contributed to those attitudes. Western imperialism had its roots in the Scientific Revolution of the seventeenth century.

## Suggestions for Further Reading

For a comprehensive listing of suggested readings, please go to www.ablongman.com/levack2e/chapter16

Biagioli, Mario. *Galileo, Courtier: The Practice of Science in the Culture of Absolutism.* 1993. Argues that Galileo's desire for patronage determined the type of research he engaged in and the scientific questions he asked.

Cohen, H. Floris. *The Scientific Revolution: A Historiographical Inquiry.* 1995. A thorough account of all the different interpretations of the causes and significance of the Scientific Revolution.

Dear, Peter. *Discipline and Experience: The Mathematical Way in the Scientific Revolution.* 1995. Explains the importance of mathematics in the development of seventeenth-century science.

Debus, Allen G. *Man and Nature in the Renaissance.* 1978. Deals with the early history of the Scientific Revolution and develops many of its connections with the Renaissance.

Drake, Stillman, ed. *Discoveries and Opinions of Galileo.* 1957. Includes four of Galileo's most important writings, together with a detailed commentary.

Easlea, Brian. *Magic, Witch-Hunting and the New Philosophy.* 1980. Relates the end of witch hunting to the spread of the mechanical philosophy.

Feingold, Mordechai. *The Newtonian Moment: Isaac Newton and the Making of Modern Culture.* 2004. A richly illustrated volume that contains valuable material on the reception of Newtonian ideas in the eighteenth century as well as a chapter on Newtonian women.

Kuhn, Thomas S. *The Copernican Revolution.* 1957. The most comprehensive and authoritative study of the shift from an Earth-centered to a sun-centered model of the universe.

Popkin, Richard. *The History of Scepticism from Erasmus to Spinoza.* 1979. Discusses skepticism as a cause as well as an effect of the Scientific Revolution.

Schiebinger, Londa. *The Mind Has No Sex? Women in the Origins of Modern Science.* 1989. Explores the role of women in all aspects of scientific endeavor.

Shapin, Steven. *The Scientific Revolution.* 1996. A study of the origins of the modern scientific worldview that emphasizes the social influences on the production of knowledge and the social purposes for which scientific knowledge was intended.

Shapin, Steven, and Simon Schaffer. *Leviathan and the Air Pump.* 1989. Discusses the difference between Robert Boyle and Thomas Hobbes regarding the value of experimentation.

Thomas, Keith. *Man and the Natural World: A History of the Modern Sensibility.* 1983. A study of the shifting attitudes of human beings toward nature during the period from 1500 to 1800.

Webster, Charles. *The Great Instauration: Science, Medicine and Reform, 1626–1660.* 1975. Explores the relationship between Puritanism and the Scientific Revolution in England.

Westfall, Richard S. *Never at Rest: A Biography of Isaac Newton.* 1980. A superb biography of the most influential scientist in the history of the West.

## Notes

1. Quoted in Steven Shapin, *The Scientific Revolution* (1996), 33.

2. René Descartes, *Le Monde,* Book VI.

3. Thomas S. Kuhn, *The Structure of Scientific Revolutions* (1970).

4. René Descartes, *Discourse on the Method and Meditations on First Philosophy,* ed. David Weissmann (1996), 21.

5. Galileo, "Letter to the Grand Duchess Christina," in *Discoveries and Opinions of Galileo,* ed. Stilman Drake (1957), 186.

6. Descartes, *Discourse on the Method,* 38.

7. Quoted in W. Hazard, *The European Mind, 1680–1715* (1964), 362.

8. François Poullain, *De l'égalite des deux sexes* (1673), 85.

9. Francis Bacon, *The Works of Francis Bacon,* ed. J. Spedding (1857–1874), vol. 3, 524–539.

10. Henry Oldenburg, "To the Reader," in Robert Boyle, *Experiments and Considerations in Touching Colours* (1664).

# The West and the World: Empire, Trade, and War, 1650–1815

# 17

I N 1789 OLAUDAH EQUIANO, A FREED SLAVE LIVING IN GREAT BRITAIN, published an autobiographical account of his experiences in captivity. In this narrative Equiano recounted his seizure in the Gambia region of Africa and his transportation on a slave ship to the British Caribbean colony of Barbados. He described the unmerciful floggings to which the Africans on his ship were subjected, the unrelieved hunger they experienced, and the insufferable heat and smells they endured in the hold of the ship. He witnessed the suicide of those who threw themselves into the sea in order to avoid further misery. He was terrified that his white captors would eat him, and he wished for a merciful death.

Once the ship had reached its destination Equiano related how the Africans were herded into pens where white plantation owners examined, purchased, and branded them. The most moving part of Equiano's narrative is his account of the cries he heard as family members were sold to different masters. "O you nominal Christians," wrote Equiano, "might not an African ask you, learned you this from your God? Is it not enough that we are torn from our country and friends to toil for your luxury and lust of gain? Must every tender feeling be sacrificed to your avarice? Surely this is a new refinement in cruelty, which, while it has no advantage to atone for it, thus aggravates distress and adds fresh horrors to the wretchedness of slavery."[1]

The journey that Equiano was forced to take across the Atlantic Ocean and the emotions he described were experienced by millions of African men and women during the period from 1650 to 1815. The forced emigration of Africans from their homelands, their sale to white landlords, and their subjection to inhumane treatment number among the abiding horrors of Western civilization. To understand how these horrors could have occurred, especially at the hands of men who proclaimed a commitment to human freedom, we must study the growth of European empires during these centuries.

As European states grew in size, wealth, and military power in the sixteenth and seventeenth centuries, the most powerful of them acquired large

## CHAPTER OUTLINE

- European Empires in the Americas and Asia

- Warfare in Europe, North America, and Asia

- The Atlantic World

- Encounters Between Europeans and Asians

- The Crisis of Empire and the Atlantic Revolutions

---

**Samuel Scott, *A Thames Wharf* (1750s)** British merchants conducted a brisk trade with Asia and the Americas in the eighteenth century.

**541**

overseas empires. By the end of the seventeenth century the British, French, and Dutch had joined the Portuguese and the Spanish as overseas imperial powers. As we discussed in Chapter 12, the first stage of empire building, which lasted from 1500 until about 1650, had many different motives. The search for gold and silver, the mission to Christianize the indigenous populations, the desire of some colonists to escape religious persecution, the urge to plunder, the efforts of monarchs to expand the size of their dominions, and the desire to profit from international trade all figured in the process. In 1625 the English government recognized many of these motives when it declared the purpose of the colony of Virginia to be "the propagation of the Christian religion, the increase of trade, and the enlarging of the royal empire."[2]

During the second stage of empire building, which lasted from roughly 1650 to 1815, the economic motive for acquiring overseas possessions became dominant. More than anything else, imperial policy was shaped by the desire for profit within a world economy. As far as the governments of western Europe were concerned, all colonies were economic enterprises. Whether these colonies were primarily involved in commerce or agriculture or mining was only a minor distinction. The main consideration was that they provided economic benefits to the European countries. They supplied the parent country, often referred to as the metropolis°, with agricultural products, raw materials, and minerals. Overseas colonies also provided the metropolis with markets for its manufactured goods.

The growth of these empires resulted in the expansion of the geographical boundaries of the West. It also resulted in the spread of Western ideas, political institutions, and economic systems to Asia and the Americas. At the same time, encounters between Europeans and non-Western peoples, especially those of Asia, brought about significant changes in the cultures of the West.

The main question that this chapter will address is how the growth of European empires in Asia and the Americas, the expansion of international trade, and the wars fought over empire and trade during the period 1650–1815 changed Western culture and politics. More specifically, the individual sections of the chapter will ask the following questions:

- How did the composition and organization of European empires change during the seventeenth and eighteenth centuries?
- In what ways did the wars waged by European powers during this period involve competition for overseas possessions and trading routes?
- How did European empires create an Atlantic economy in which the traffic in slaves was a major feature?
- What cultural encounters took place between European and Asian peoples during this period of empire building, and how did these encounters change Western attitudes toward outsiders?

- Why did European powers begin to lose control of some of their colonies, especially those in the Americas, between 1775 and 1825?

# European Empires in the Americas and Asia

- How did the composition and organization of European empires change during the seventeenth and eighteenth centuries?

The main political units in Europe during this long period of history are usually referred to as states°. A state is a consolidated territorial area that has its own political institutions and recognizes no higher authority. Thus we refer to France, England (which became Great Britain after its union with Scotland in 1707), Prussia, the Dutch Republic, and Portugal as states. As we have discussed in Chapter 15, most of these states acquired larger armies and administrative bureaucracies during the sixteenth and seventeenth centuries, mainly to meet the demands of war. Consequently they became more highly integrated and cohesive political structures.

Many European states formed the center or core of much larger political formations known as empires°. The main characteristic of an empire in the seventeenth and eighteenth centuries was that it comprised many different kingdoms or territorial possessions outside the geographical boundaries of the state itself. These imperial territories were controlled by the metropolis, but they were not fully integrated into its administrative structure. Some of the territories that formed a part of these empires were located in Europe. The Austrian Habsburg monarchy, for example, had jurisdiction over a host of separate kingdoms and principalities in central and eastern Europe, including Hungary and Bohemia. This arrangement made Austria an empire, a designation it formally acquired in 1806. In like manner the Spanish monarchy, which also was an empire, controlled many different kingdoms and provinces in the Iberian peninsula as well as territories in southern Italy and the Netherlands. On the eastern and southeastern periphery of Europe lay two other empires: the Russian and the Ottoman, which controlled vast expanses of land not only in eastern Europe but also in the adjacent areas of Asia. As in previous centuries, the Russian and Ottoman empires marked the ever-shifting and often blurred boundaries between East and West.

Beginning in the fifteenth century, as the result of transoceanic voyages of exploration and the establishment of overseas colonies, western European states acquired, settled, or controlled territories in the Americas, Africa, and Asia. Mastery of these lands came much more quickly in the

New World than in Asia. The peoples of North and South America whom the Europeans encountered when they arrived were able fighters, but they were not organized politically, and diseases introduced by the Europeans drastically reduced their numbers. European settlers, who had the added advantage of superior military technology, were able to gain the upper hand in battle, seize or purchase their lands, and force those who survived to retreat into less inhabited areas.

When Europeans started to develop extensive trading routes in Asia, however, that continent was already highly developed politically and militarily. Three Muslim empires—the Ottoman, the Safavid (Persia), and the Mughal (India)—as well as the neighboring Chinese Empire in East Asia occupied the mass of land from the Balkans to the Pacific Ocean. Only when these Asian empires began to fall apart, giving greater autonomy to the smaller, subordinate states within their boundaries, were Europeans able to exploit the situation and secure favorable trading arrangements and ultimately control of Asian territory itself.

Until the late eighteenth century European governments usually allowed their colonies a considerable degree of political autonomy. Although monarchs claimed sovereignty over all their imperial possessions, the distance of these lands from the metropolis made direct rule difficult. The solution to this problem was to delegate the functions of government either to officials who represented royal authority in the colony or to some corporate body. In the British, Dutch, and French empires, trading companies that engaged in commerce with the East Indies assumed many of these functions. These companies could negotiate treaties, raise military forces, and govern the population of the colonies. In many ways the companies became small states themselves, operating under the authority of the Crown. In North America and the Caribbean, imperial governments usually granted charters to their colonies, authorizing them to establish their own legislative assemblies.

Colonists were granted considerable autonomy as long as they conducted trade exclusively with the metropolis. Metropolitan governments were determined to use the colonies to realize the objectives of gaining the largest possible share of world trade, acquiring a supply of gold and other precious metals, and collecting import and export duties on the colonial trade. To accomplish these ends they passed legislation forcing the colonists to trade exclusively with the metropolis. When colonists tried to break this monopoly by trading with other nations or colonies, they came into direct conflict with their own governments in Europe.

The earliest of the European overseas empires were established by the Spanish and the Portuguese. During the period under consideration, three rising European powers—Great Britain, France, and the Dutch Republic—began to rival the older empires. By the end of the period the British had emerged as the dominant imperial power. During the third period of imperial expansion in the late nineteenth and

early twentieth centuries, the imperial rivalries that had developed in earlier years continued in different forms, and new European powers, most notably Germany and Italy, joined in the competition.

## The Rise of the British Empire

The fastest-growing of these new European overseas empires during this period was that of Great Britain. England had begun its overseas empire in the late twelfth century, when it conquered the neighboring island of Ireland, but only in the seventeenth century did it begin to acquire lands in the New World and Asia. Attempts to establish colonies on the Atlantic coast of North America in the late sixteenth century had failed, most notably at Roanoke (in present-day North Carolina) in 1584. After Spain agreed not to contest English claims of territory north of Florida, the English succeed in settling a series of colonies along the Atlantic seaboard, the first of which was at Jamestown, Virginia, in 1607.

By 1700 this English empire in the New World included a number of colonies on the North American mainland, a vast territory in the northern part of Canada, and a cluster of islands in the Caribbean, most notably Barbados, Jamaica, and the Bahamas. These West Indian colonies developed an economy that used slave labor, and therefore blacks brought there from Africa soon outnumbered Europeans by a significant margin. In the colonies on the mainland of North America, however, most of the colonists were white. This was true even in the southern colonies, where slave labor was also introduced. Only in South Carolina, which was settled by Caribbean planters, did the black population exceed 50 percent.

A number of English colonists, especially in the northern colonies, had emigrated so that they might practice their religion without legal restraint. During the 1630s communities of English Protestants known as Puritans settled in New England. They objected to the control of the English Church by bishops, especially during the period from 1633 to 1641, when William Laud served as archbishop of Canterbury. Their main complaint was that the church services authorized by Laud too closely resembled those of Roman Catholicism. At the same time small groups of English Catholics, who often faced prosecution in English courts for practicing their religion, had taken refuge in Maryland. In the late seventeenth century a dissenting Protestant sect known as Quakers (so called because their founder, George Fox, told them to quake at the word of the Lord), smarting under legislation that denied them religious freedom and political power, emigrated to Pennsylvania.

Many other British colonists had come to America as indentured servants, usually serving for seven years in order to gain their freedom. By this time the size of the indigenous American population in the colonies had become negligible. The Indians of North America either had been pushed westward beyond the frontiers of these colonies, had died of diseases to which they were highly vulnerable, or had been killed in skirmishes with the English.

During the seventeenth century the English also established a number of trading posts, known as factories°, along the coast of India. The first of these factories was Surat, which was settled in 1612, and it was soon followed by Madras (1640), Bombay (1661), and Calcutta (1690). There were significant differences between these mercantile outposts and the colonies in the Caribbean and the North American mainland. The number of British settlers in India, most of whom were members of the East India Company, remained extremely small, and they did not establish large plantations like those in the Caribbean colonies and the southern mainland colonies. Consequently they did not introduce slave labor into these countries.

In contrast to the situation in North America and the Caribbean, the British in India had to deal with a large native population. At first they had contact with that population only when they were engaged in trade. In the second half of the eighteenth century, however, the British began to gain direct political control of Indian provinces, and by 1850 they controlled a large portion of the South Asian subcontinent. Not only did the British eventually subject the Indians to their rule, but they also drove out their French and Dutch commercial rivals, who had established their own factories along the coast.

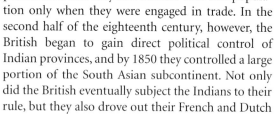

DOCUMENT

Arrival of
the British in
the Punjab
(mid-19th c.)

In addition to their settlements in America and India, the British acquired influence and ultimately political control of the area from Southeast Asia stretching down into the South Pacific. In the late seventeenth century the British began to challenge the Dutch and the Portuguese for control of the trade with Indonesia, and in the second half of the eighteenth century British merchants established a thriving trade with the countries on the Malay peninsula. In the late eighteenth century the British also began to explore the South Pacific, which remained the last part of the inhabited world that Europeans had not yet visited and settled. In 1770 the British naval officer and explorer Captain James Cook (1728–1779) claimed the entire eastern coast of Australia for Great Britain, and in 1788 the British established a penal colony in the southeastern corner of the continent at Botany Bay. Cook also visited New Zealand and many of the islands in the South Pacific, including Fiji, but colonies were not established at those locations until the middle of the nineteenth century.

The British Empire of the late seventeenth and eighteenth centuries possessed little administrative coherence; it was a hodgepodge of colonies, factories, and territories that had different relationships to the royal government in Britain (see Map 17.1). In India the provinces brought un-

## Map 17.1  European Empires in 1763

This map shows the overseas possessions of Britain, France, the Dutch Republic, Spain, and Portugal. Russian overseas expansion into North America had not yet begun.

der British control were run by a trading corporation that exercised many functions of government. Some colonies in America, such as Maryland and Pennsylvania, operated under charters granted to members of the aristocracy. Most of the colonies on the North American mainland and in the Caribbean had their own legislatures. None of these colonies, however, sent representatives to the British Parliament. The only bond of unity among all the colonists is that they, like British subjects living in England or Scotland, owed their allegiance to the monarch and were under the monarch's protection. All of these colonists were therefore British subjects.

## The Scattered French Empire

French colonization of North America and India paralleled that of Great Britain, but it never achieved the same degree of success. As the British were establishing footholds in the West Indies and the mainland of North America, the French acquired their own islands in the Caribbean and laid claim to large sections of Canada and the Ohio and Mississippi River valleys in the present-day United States. In the West Indies the French began the process of colonization by introducing indentured servants for periods of three years, but in the eighteenth century they began to follow the British and Spanish pattern of importing slaves to provide the labor for the sugar plantations. In North America French settlers did not require a large labor supply, as their main economic undertakings were the fur trade and fishing. Consequently slaves were not introduced to those areas. The European population of French possessions in North America also stayed well below that of the British colonies.

The parallel between French and British overseas expansion extended to India, where in the early eighteenth century the French East India Company established factories at Pondicherry, Chandenagar, and other locations. Rivalry with the British also led the French to make alliances with native governors of Indian provinces, and with this support the French fought the British both on land and at sea at different critical times between 1744 and 1815. The British ultimately prevailed in this struggle, and by the turn of the nineteenth century the French presence in India had been reduced to a few isolated factories.

The waning of French influence in India coincided with a series of territorial losses in the New World. Defeats suffered at the hands of the British during the Seven Years' War (1756–1763) resulted in the transfer of French Canada and the territory east of the Mississippi River to Great Britain. During that conflict France also ceded the vast region of Louisiana between the Mississippi River and the Rocky Mountains to Spain. France regained Louisiana in 1801 but then promptly sold the entire territory to the United States in 1803. The following year the French Caribbean colony of Saint Domingue became independent, although France retained possession of its other West Indian colonies.

The only overseas area where France continued to expand after 1800 was much closer to home, on the Mediterranean shores of North Africa. French influence in this area had begun in the seventeenth century, and it persisted until the twentieth century. France occupied Egypt briefly from 1798 until 1801, and it acquired Algeria in 1830. It was not until the third stage of imperialism in the late nineteenth century that France took possession of large territories in the interior of Africa and in Asia (see Chapter 23).

## The Commercial Dutch Empire

The tiny Dutch Republic acquired almost all of its overseas possessions in the first half of the seventeenth century, at about the same time that the British and French were establishing their first colonies in Asia and the New World. The formation of the Dutch empire went hand in hand with the explosive growth of the Dutch economy in the seventeenth century. At that time the Dutch Republic became the center of a global economy, and its overseas colonies in the New World, Asia, and Africa helped the republic maintain its commercial supremacy. Dutch overseas settlements, just like the port cities of the metropolis, were dedicated almost exclusively to serving the interests of trade.

The Dutch were more eager than other European powers to use military and naval power to acquire and fortify trading depots. They also used military force to seize factories that had been established earlier by other countries, especially Portugal. With more than 1,400 vessels that could be used as warships and 250,000 sailors, they had a distinct military advantage over the Portuguese, who could not muster half those numbers. They seized two trading posts from the Portuguese on the West African coast in 1637, and in 1641 they also acquired from Portugal the African islands of São Tomé and Principe. In 1624 the Dutch, operating through their West Indian Company, seized the northern coast of Brazil, and after its return to Portugal in 1654 they acquired two small West Indian islands and a number of small plantation colonies on the Guiana coast of South America, mainly in present-day Surinam. From these small settlements in Africa and the Caribbean the Dutch carried on trade with the Spanish, Portuguese, French, and British colonies. Through these ports the Dutch brought more than 500,000 slaves to Brazil, the Spanish colonies, and the French and British West Indies.

In addition to their African and Caribbean possessions, the Dutch established a presence in three other parts of the world. In the early seventeenth century they settled a colony in the Hudson River valley on the North American mainland. They named the colony New Netherland and its main port, at the mouth of the river, New Amsterdam. In 1664 the Dutch lost the colony to the English, who renamed the colony and the port New York. The second area was in Asia, where the Dutch East India Company established a fort at Batavia (now Jakarta in Indonesia) and factories in India,

# The Trial of the Mutineers on the *Bounty*

In December 1787 a British ship named the *Bounty,* under the captainship of William Bligh, left Portsmouth, England, on a momentous journey to Tahiti, an island in the South Pacific that Captain James Cook had first visited in 1769. The goal of the voyage of the *Bounty* was neither exploration nor colonial expansion but to bring home breadfruit trees that Cook had discovered on his second trip to the island in 1773. The trees, so it was hoped, would be introduced to the West Indies as a source of food for the slaves and hence the survival of the plantation economy. The voyage of the *Bounty* was therefore part of the operation of the new global economy that European expansion had made possible. The total size of the crew, all of whom had volunteered for service, was forty-six. The master's first mate, who became the main leader of a mutiny against Bligh, was Fletcher Christian.

The mutiny did not take place until after the ship had remained at Tahiti for a number of months, loaded its cargo of more than a thousand breadfruit plants, and begun its return voyage. The main reason for the mutiny was Captain Bligh's abusive and humiliating language. Unlike many other officers who faced the task of maintaining order on their ships and commanding the obedience of their crews, Bligh did not flog his men. In that regard Bligh's behavior was mild. Instead he went into tantrums and verbally abused them, belittling them and calling them scoundrels. Just before the mutiny Bligh called Fletcher Christian a cowardly rascal and falsely accused him of stealing from him. On the morning of April 28, 1788, Christian arrested Bligh at bayonet point, tied his hands

behind his back, and threatened him with instant death if he should speak a word. Claiming that "Captain Bligh had brought all this on himself," Christian and his associates put Bligh and eighteen other members of the crew into one of the ship's small launch boats and set them adrift, leaving them to reach a nearby island by their own power.

The mutineers sailed on to the island of Tubuai, where after a brief stay they split into two groups. Nine of them, headed by Christian and accompanied by six Tahitian men and twelve women, established a settlement on Pitcairn Island. The remaining sixteen mutineers returned to Tahiti. All but two of these men were apprehended in 1791 by Captain Edwards of the H.M.S. *Pandora,* which had been sent to Tahiti with the objective of arresting them and returning them to England for trial. At the beginning of its return voyage the *Pandora* was shipwrecked, and four of the prisoners drowned. The rest reached England aboard another ship in 1792. They were

promptly charged before a navy court-martial with taking the *Bounty* away from its captain and with desertion, both of which were offenses under the Naval Discipline Act of 1766.

The trial took place aboard a British ship, H.M.S. *Duke,* in Portsmouth harbor in September 1792. The proceeding had all the markings of a state trial, one initiated by the government for offenses against the Crown. Mutiny and desertion represented challenges to the state itself. During the second period of imperial expansion navies became major instruments of state power. Even when ships were used for purposes of exploration rather than naval combat, they served the interests of the state. The captain of the ship represented the power of the sovereign at sea. Because of the difficulty of maintaining order in such circumstances, he was given absolute authority. He could use whatever means necessary, including the infliction of corporal punishment, to preserve order. To disobey or challenge

**Sextant**
Eighteenth-century ships like the *Bounty* used this instrument to determine nautical position by means of the stars.

**The Mutineers Casting Bligh Adrift in the Launch,** Engraving by Robert Dodd (1790)
This was the central act in the mutiny led by Fletcher Christian. Captain Bligh is standing in the launch in his night-clothes. Some of the breadfruit trees loaded on the ship at Tahiti can be seen on the top deck.

him was interpreted as an act of rebellion.

The trial was based on the assumption that the mutiny was illegal and seditious. The only question was the extent of individual involvement in the act itself. The degree of involvement was measured by evidence of one's co-operation with Christian or his loyalty to Bligh. The mere fact that some men had remained with Christian on the *Bounty* did not prove that they had supported the mutiny. Four of those men gave little evidence of having voluntarily cooperated with Christian, and those four men were eventually acquitted. The testimony of Captain Bligh, who declared that those four crew members had been reluctant to put him in the launch boat, was decisive in securing their nonguilty verdicts.

The remaining six men were convicted and sentenced to die by hanging. Three of those men were eventually spared their lives. Peter Heywood and James Morrison were well connected to influential people in the navy and the government and received royal pardons. William Muspratt, one of only three mutineers to hire a lawyer, entered a protest against the procedures of the court. In a court-martial, unlike a criminal trial at the common law, a prisoner could not call witnesses in his own defense. At the time of his conviction Muspratt protested that he had been "debarred calling witnesses whose evidence I have reason to believe would have tended to prove my innocence." The difference between the two systems of criminal justice, he claimed, "is dreadful to the subject and fatal to me." On this ground Muspratt was reprieved.

The three men who were executed died as model prisoners, proclaiming the illegality of their rebellion. Although the government had executed only a small minority of the mutineers, by securing their conviction and dramatizing it with a widely publicized hanging, it had upheld its authority and thus reinforced the power of the Crown.

## Questions of Justice

1. How would you characterize the different ideals of justice adhered to by the mutineers on the *Bounty* and the British admiralty court that tried them?
2. What does the journey of the *Bounty* tell us about the role of the British navy in the process of imperial expansion? What problems were inherent in using British ships for these purposes?

## Taking It Further

Rutter, Owen, ed. *The Court-Martial of the "Bounty" Mutineers.* 1931. Contains a full transcript of the trial.

**The Dutch Factory of Batavia in Indonesia, ca. 1665**
The Dutch Republic dominated the Asian trade in the seventeenth century. Batavia (now Jakarta) was the most important of their settlements in Southeast Asia. The efforts of the Dutch to transplant their culture is evident in this building's Dutch style of architecture.

China, and Japan. These possessions allowed the Dutch to engage in trade throughout Asia. In the eighteenth century, however, the British began to take control of Dutch trading routes.

The third area was the southern tip of Africa, where in 1652 the Dutch settled a colony at the Cape of Good Hope, mainly to provide support for ships engaged in commerce with the East Indies. In this colony some 1,700 Dutch settlers, most of them farmers known as boers°, developed an agricultural economy on plantations that employed slave labor. The loss of this colony to the British at the end of the eighteenth century reflected a more general decline of Dutch military and imperial strength.

## The Vast Spanish Empire

Of all the European overseas empires, the lands under the control of the Spanish monarchy were the most extensive. At the height of its power in 1650, the Spanish Empire covered the western part of North America from California to Mexico and from Mexico down through Central America.

It also included Florida and the Caribbean islands of Cuba, San Domingo, and Puerto Rico. It embraced almost all of South America except Brazil, which was under Portuguese control. In Asia the main Spanish possessions were the Philippine Islands, named for the future King Philip II in 1542 and conquered with little bloodshed after 1564. The Philippines served as the main base from which the Spanish engaged in trade with other Asian countries.

Spanish overseas possessions were never ruled as closely as the royal government in Madrid ruled the smaller kingdoms and principalities on the Iberian peninsula. Spanish overseas possessions were, however, integrated into a much more authoritative imperial system than were those of the British. Until the eighteenth century a hierarchy of councils, staffed by men appointed by the Crown, exercised political control of the various large territories or viceroyalties into which the empire was divided. Like all mercantilist enterprises, the Spanish colonial empire was designed to serve the purposes of trade. Until the eighteenth century a council known as the House of Trade, situated in Seville, exercised a monopoly over all colonial commerce. It funneled trade with the colonies from the southwestern Spanish port of Cadiz and to selected ports on the eastern coasts of Spanish America, from which it was then redirected to other ports. The ships returned to Spain carrying the gold and silver that had been extracted from the mines of Mexico and Peru. The entire journey was made under the protection of Spanish warships.

The Bourbon kings of Spain, who were installed on the throne in 1700, introduced a number of political reforms that were intended to increase the volume of the colonial trade and prevent the smuggling that had always threatened to undermine it. On the one hand, they opened up the colonial trade to more Spanish and American ports and also permitted more trade within the colonies. On the other hand, the Bourbons, especially Charles III (r. 1759–1788), brought the viceroyalties under more direct control of Spanish royal officials and increased the efficiency of the tax collection system. These Bourbon reforms made the empire more manageable and profitable, but they also created tension between the Spanish-born bureaucrats and the creoles°, the people of Spanish descent who had been born in the colonies. These tensions eventually led in the early nineteenth century to a series of wars of independence from Spain that we shall discuss in a later section.

## The Declining Portuguese Empire

The Portuguese had been the first European nation to engage in overseas exploration and colonization. During the late fifteenth and sixteenth centuries they had established colonies in Asia, South America, and Africa (see Chapter 12). By the beginning of the eighteenth century, however, the Portuguese Empire had declined in size and wealth in relation to its rivals. The Portuguese continued to hold a few ports in India, most notably the small island of Goa. They also retained a factory at Macao off the southeastern coast of China. In the New World the major Portuguese plantation colony was Brazil, which occupied almost half the land mass of South America and which supplied Europe with sugar, cacao (from which chocolate is made), and other agricultural commodities. Closely linked to Brazil were the Portuguese colonies along and off the West African coast. These possessions were all deeply involved in the transatlantic trade, especially in slaves. The Portuguese also had a series of trading stations and small settlements on the southeastern coast of Africa, including Mozambique.

The contraction of the Portuguese Empire in the seventeenth and eighteenth centuries resulted in the transfer of land to other European countries. A relatively weak European power, Portugal did not fare well in the fierce military conflicts that ensued in South America and Asia over control of the colonial trade. Portugal's main military and economic competition came from the Dutch, who seized many of its Asian, African, and South American colonies, and who acquired many Portuguese trading routes. Most of those losses took place in Asia between 1600 and 1670. The Portuguese Empire suffered further losses when the crown relinquished Bombay and the northern African port of Tangier to the English as part of the dowry for the Portuguese princess Catherine of Braganza when she married King Charles II in 1661.

Brazil remained by far the most important of the Portuguese possessions during the late seventeenth and eighteenth centuries. The colony suffered from an unfavorable balance of trade with Portugal, but it expanded in population and wealth during this period, especially after the discovery of gold and diamonds led to large-scale mining in the interior. The slave trade increased in volume in order to provide additional labor in the mines and on the sugar plantations. In the first quarter of the nineteenth century, as the British slave trade declined and came to an end, Portuguese ships carried 871,600 slaves to Brazil. Between 1826 and 1850 the number increased to an astonishing 1,247,700. As a result of this massive influx of Africans, slaves accounted for approximately 40 percent of the entire Brazilian population by the beginning of the nineteenth century.

Like most other European countries, Portugal tightened the control of its imperial possessions during the second half of the eighteenth century. During the ministry of the dictatorial Marquis of Pombal from 1755 to 1777, efforts were made to increase the control exercised by the Crown over all aspects of colonial life. Pombal also took steps to encourage the growth of the colonial trade, and he legalized intermarriage between whites and indigenous peoples. Like the Bourbon reforms in Spanish America, this legislation created considerable resentment among the creoles against the Portuguese bureaucrats who controlled the government. As in Spanish America, these tensions led to demands for Brazil's autonomy in the nineteenth century.

## The Russian Empire in the Pacific

The only eastern European state that established an overseas empire during the eighteenth century was Russia. Between the fifteenth and the early eighteenth centuries Russia had gradually acquired a massive overland empire stretching from St. Petersburg in the west across the frigid expanse of Siberia to the Pacific Ocean. The main impulse of Russian expansion had been the search for exotic furs that were in high demand in the colder climes of Russia and northern Europe. During the reign of the empress Catherine the Great (r. 1762–1796), Russia entered a period of further territorial expansion. On its western frontier it took part in the successive partitions of Poland between 1772 and 1795, while to the south it held the Crimean region within the Ottoman Empire between 1783 and 1792.

During the late eighteenth and early nineteenth centuries Russia also extended its empire overseas. Russian traders and explorers undertook numerous expeditions to Hawaii and other islands in the Pacific Ocean, sailing as far south as Mexico. They did not, however, establish colonies in these locations. Further expeditions brought Russia across the northern Pacific, where they encroached upon the hunting grounds of the native Aleuts in Alaska. The Russian-American Company, established in 1789, built a number of trading posts along the Pacific seaboard from Alaska down to Fort Ross in northern California. These claims led to a protracted territorial dispute with Spain, which had established a string of missions and settlements on the California coast as far north as San Francisco. In this way the two great European empires of Russia and Spain, advancing from opposite directions, confronted each other on the western coast of North America. Russian expansion into Alaska and California also led to territorial disputes with the United States, which was engaged in its own process of territorial expansion westward toward the Pacific during the nineteenth century.

# Warfare in Europe, North America, and Asia

■ In what ways did the wars waged by European powers during this period involve competition for overseas possessions and trading routes?

Until the middle of the seventeenth century, European states engaged each other in battle almost exclusively within their own continent. The farthest their armies ever traveled was to the Middle East to fight the Turks or to Ireland to conquer the native Celts. The acquisition of overseas empires and the conflicts that erupted between European powers over the control of global trade brought those European conflicts to new and distant military theaters. Wars that began over territory in Europe were readily extended to America in one direction and to Asia in the other. The military forces that fought in these imperial battles consisted not only of metropolitan government troops but also those of the colonists. These colonial forces were often supplemented by the troops drawn from the local population, such as when the French recruited Native Americans to fight with them against the British in North America. This pattern of recruiting soldiers from the indigenous population, which began in the eighteenth century, became the norm during the third and final phase of empire building in the nineteenth and early twentieth centuries.

Wars fought overseas placed a premium on naval strength. Ground troops remained important, both in Europe and overseas, but naval power increasingly proved to be the crucial factor. All of the Western imperial powers either possessed or acquired large navies. Great Britain and the Dutch Republic rose to the status of world powers on the basis of sea power, while the French strengthened their navy considerably during the reign of Louis XIV. The Dutch used their naval power mainly against the Portuguese and the British, while the British directed theirs against the French and the Spanish as well as the Dutch. The overwhelming success that the British realized in these conflicts resulted in the establishment of British maritime supremacy.

## Mercantile Warfare

An increasingly important motive for engaging in warfare in the late seventeenth and eighteenth centuries was the protection and expansion of trade. The theory that underlay and inspired these imperial wars was mercantilism. As we discussed in Chapter 15, those who subscribed to this theory, such as Louis XIV's minister Jean-Baptiste Colbert, believed that the wealth of the state depended on its ability to import fewer commodities than it exported and thus to acquire the largest possible share of the world's monetary supply. In order to achieve this goal, mercantilists encouraged domestic industry and placed heavy customs duties or tariffs on imported goods. Mercantilism was therefore a policy of protectionism°, the shielding of domestic industries from foreign competition. Mercantilists also sought to increase the size of the country's commercial fleet, establish colonies in order to promote trade, and import raw materials from the colonies to benefit domestic industry. The imperial wars of the seventeenth and eighteenth centuries, which were fought over the control of colonies and trading routes, thus formed part of a mercantilist policy.

Of course the older, more traditional motives for waging war, especially the desire of rulers for territorial expansion, did not disappear. The acquisitive impulses of France, Prussia, Austria, and Russia remained a recurrent source of international conflict throughout this period. But the mercantile motive, which began to emerge only in the 1650s, soon became a major feature of European warfare, and it explains why military conflict was extended from Europe to the colonies. As this motive for going to war became more important, wars fought primarily for religious or ideological reasons, which had been the norm during the period of the Reformation, virtually disappeared.

The first of the great mercantile wars that involved conflict overseas arose between England and the Dutch Republic in the middle and late seventeenth century (1652–1654, 1664–1667, 1672–1675). As these wars were fought between two Protestant powers, little about these conflicts could be attributed to religious zeal. Instead they were fought mainly for mercantile advantage between the two emerging commercial giants of Europe. The two countries were engaged in heated competition for control of the transatlantic trade, and the Dutch resented the passage of English laws, known as the Navigation Acts, that excluded them from trade with the English colonies. The Dutch claimed the right to trade with all ports in the world as well as to fish in the waters off British shores. Not surprisingly, many of the engagements in these wars took place at sea and in the colonies. The most significant outcome of these Anglo-Dutch wars was the loss of the port city of New Amsterdam to the English. That city, renamed New York, later became the leading port and financial center in the Western Hemisphere.

Shortly after the first Anglo-Dutch War, England also went to war against Spain (1655–1657). Although this conflict pitted a Protestant against a Catholic power, it too reflected the new emphasis on mercantile objectives. The main battles of this war were not fought in the English Channel, as they had been when the Spanish Armada had descended on England in 1588, but in the Caribbean. The war resulted in the British acquisition of one of its most important Caribbean colonies, Jamaica, in 1655. The Anglo-Spanish tensions that surfaced in this conflict continued into the eighteenth century, when Britain tried to smuggle more goods than it was allowed by the Treaty of Utrecht (1713) into the Spanish trading post of Portobelo on the isthmus of Panama. The Spanish retaliated by cutting off the ear of Robert Jenkins, an English captain, and this incident led to the War of Jenkins' Ear in 1739. In 1762, during another war against Spain (as well as France), armed forces from Britain and the North American colonies seized the Cuban port of Havana as part of an effort to monopolize the Caribbean trade. The following year, however, Britain returned the city to Spain in exchange for Florida. This acquisition gave the British control of the entire North American eastern seaboard.

## Anglo-French Military Rivalry

Anglo-Spanish conflict paled in comparison with the bitter commercial rivalry between Great Britain and France during the eighteenth century. Anglo-French conflict was one of the few consistent patterns of eighteenth-century European warfare. It lasted so long and had so many different phases that it is known as the second Hundred Years' War, a recurrence of the bitter period of warfare between England and France from the middle of the fourteenth to the middle of the fifteenth century. The great difference between the two periods of warfare was that the first Hundred Years' War involved military conflicts in France, while the second was marked by periodic naval and military engagements not only in Europe but in Asia and North America as well.

### The Wars of the Spanish and Austrian Successions, 1701–1748

This eighteenth-century Anglo-French rivalry had its roots in the war of the Spanish Succession (1701–1713). The war began as an effort to prevent France from putting Louis XIV's grandson, Philip, on the Spanish throne (see Chapter 15). The implications of this dynastic conflict for the British and French colonial empires were monumental. By uniting French and Spanish territory the proposed succession would have created a massive French-Spanish empire not only in Europe but in the Western Hemisphere as well. This combination of French and Spanish territory and military power threatened to eclipse the British colonies along the North American coast and deprive British merchants of much of their valuable trade.

The ensuing struggle in North America, known by British colonists as Queen Anne's War, was settled in Britain's favor by the Treaty of Utrecht in 1713. Philip V, the first Spanish king from the Bourbon dynasty (r. 1700–1746), was allowed to remain on the throne, but French and Spanish territories in Europe and America were kept separate. Even more important, the French ceded their Canadian territories of Newfoundland and Nova Scotia to the British. The treaty, which also gave Britain the contract to ship slaves to the Spanish colonies for thirty years, marked the emergence of Britain as Europe's dominant colonial and maritime power.

The next phase of Anglo-French warfare, the War of the Austrian Succession (1740–1748), formed part of a European conflict that engaged the forces of Austria, Prussia, and Spain as well as those of Britain and France. In this conflict European dynastic struggles once again intersected with competition for colonial advantage overseas. The ostensible cause of this war was the impetuous decision by the new king of Prussia, the absolutist

Frederick II (r. 1740–1786), to seize the large German-speaking province of Silesia from Austria upon the succession of Maria Theresa (r. 1740–1780) as the ruler of the hereditary Habsburg lands (see Map 17.2). Using the large army that his militaristic father Frederick William I had assembled, Frederick struck with devastating effectiveness, and by terms of the treaty that ended the war he acquired most of the province.

Frederick's aggression enticed other European powers to join the conflict. Eager to acquire some of the Habsburg territories in different parts of Europe, France and Spain both declared war on Austria. Britain then entered the war against France, mainly to keep France from acquiring Austria's possessions in the Netherlands. Britain's main concern in the European phase of this war, as it had been in the War of the Spanish Succession, was to maintain the balance of power among European states.

The colonial phase of this war, known in British North America as King George's War, opened in 1744, when the French supported the Spanish in a separate war that Spain had been waging against Britain since 1739 over the Caribbean trade. Clashes between French and British trading companies in India also began in the same year. The main military engagement of this war was the seizure of the French port and fortress of Louisbourg on Cape Breton Island in Canada by 4,000 New England colonial troops and a large British fleet. At the end of the war, however, the British returned Louisbourg to the French in exchange for

**Map 17.2  The War of the Austrian Succession, 1740–1748**
Austria lost Silesia to Prussia during the War of the Austrian Succession in 1742. Maria Theresa's efforts to regain the province in the Seven Years' War were unsuccessful.

the factory of Madras in India, which the French had taken during the war.

## The Seven Years' War, 1756–1763

European and colonial rivalries became even more entangled in the next round of Anglo-French warfare, known as the Seven Years' War (1756–1763) in Europe and the French and Indian War (1754–1763) in North America. In Europe the conflict arose as a result of Maria Theresa's eventually unsuccessful attempt to regain Silesia. In this encounter, however, she joined forces with her former enemies, France and Russia, after Great Britain signed a defensive alliance with Prussia. This "diplomatic revolution" of 1756 shifted all the traditional alliances among European powers, but it did not affect Anglo-French rivalry in the colonies, which continued unabated.

The fighting in this North American theater of the war was particularly brutal and inflicted extensive casualties. In their struggle to gain control of eastern port cities and interior lands, the British and the French secured alliances with different Indian tribes. Among the many victims were some

of France's Indian allies who contracted smallpox when British-American colonists sold them blankets deliberately contaminated with the disease—the first known use of germ warfare in the West. This colonial war also had an Asian theater, in which French and British forces, most of them drawn from the trading companies of their respective countries, vied for mercantile influence and the possession of factories along the coast of the Indian Ocean. This conflict led directly to the British acquisition of the Indian province of Bengal in 1765.

The Treaty of Paris, which ended this round of European and colonial warfare in 1763, had more profound implications in the colonies than in Europe. In Europe, Prussia managed to hold on to Silesia, although its army incurred heavy casualties and its economy suffered from the war. In North America, however, monumental changes occurred. As a result of British naval victories, all of French Canada east of the Mississippi, including the entire province of Quebec, with its predominantly French population and French system of civil law, passed into British control (see Map 17.3). Even more important, the treaty secured British naval and mercantile superiority in the Atlantic, Caribbean, and Indian oceans. By virtue of its victories over France, Britain gained control of the lion's share of world commerce. This commercial superiority had profound implications for the economic development of Britain. Partially because of its ability to acquire raw materials from its colonies and to market its products throughout the world, Britain became the first country to experience the Industrial Revolution, as shall be discussed fully in Chapter 20.

## The American and French Revolutionary Wars, 1775–1815

Despite the British victory over the French in 1763, the long conflict between the two countries continued into the early nineteenth century. During the American War of Independence (1775–1783), which we shall consider later, the North American colonists secured French military aid. During that war a British fleet attacked the French colony of Martinique, while the French dispatched an expedition against the British at Savannah that included hundreds of Africans and mulattos, or people of mixed race, drawn from the population of the West Indies. In India further conflicts between the French and British occurred, mainly between 1781 and 1783. These simultaneous military engagements in various parts of the world turned this phase of Anglo-French conflict into the first truly global war.

Anglo-French rivalry entered yet another phase between 1792 and 1815, during the era of the French Revolution (see Chapter 19). The British were able to

## Map 17.3   British Possessions in North America and the Caribbean After the Treaty of Paris, 1763

The British acquisition of French territory marked a decisive moment in the expansion of the British Empire.

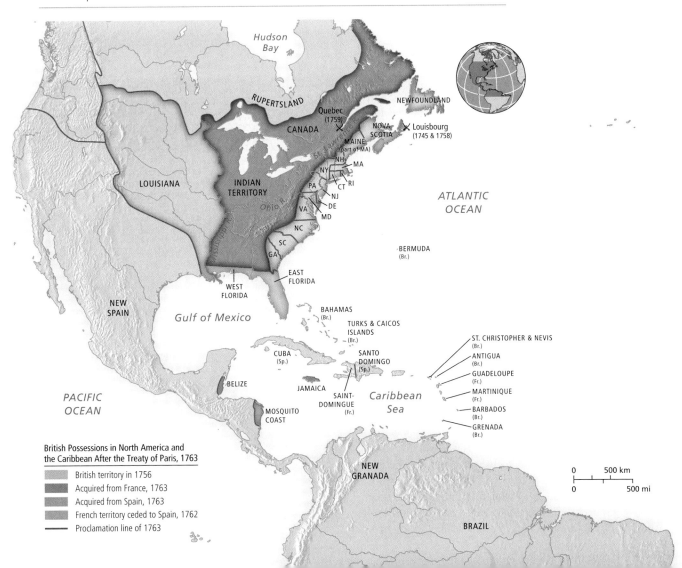

British Possessions in North America and the Caribbean After the Treaty of Paris, 1763

- British territory in 1756
- Acquired from France, 1763
- Acquired from Spain, 1763
- French territory ceded to Spain, 1762
- —— Proclamation line of 1763

maintain their military and naval superiority, although once again it required an alliance with many European powers and the creation of a new balance of power against France. Even during this later phase of this French-British rivalry the British pursued imperial objectives. They expanded their empire in India and consolidated their territory there under the governorship of Richard Wellesley (1760–1842). In 1795, in the midst of the war against France, the British also acquired the Dutch colony at the Cape of Good Hope, giving them a base for their claims to much larger African territories in the nineteenth century.

# The Atlantic World

■ How did European empires create an Atlantic economy in which the traffic in slaves was a major feature?

By the beginning of the eighteenth century, the territorial acquisitions of the five European maritime powers had moved the geographical center of the West from the European continent to the Atlantic Ocean itself. The Atlantic, rather than separating large geographical land masses, became a central, unifying geographical entity. The boundaries of this new Western world were the four continents that bordered the Atlantic: Europe, Africa, North America, and South America. The main thoroughfares that linked them were maritime routes across the Atlantic and up and down its coasts. The main points of commercial and cultural contact between the four continents, until the end of the eighteenth century, were the coastal areas and ports that bordered on the ocean. Within this Atlantic world arose new patterns of trade and economic activity, new interactions between ethnic and racial groups, and new political institutions. The Atlantic world also became the arena in which political and religious ideas were transmitted across the ocean and developed within a new environment.

## The Atlantic Economy

The exchange of commercial goods and slaves between the western coasts of Europe, the African coasts, and the ports of North and South America created an economic enterprise that became one of the most active in the entire world (see Map 17.4). The ships that had brought the slaves from Africa to the Americas used the profits gained from their transactions to acquire precious metals and agricultural products for the European market. They then returned to western European Atlantic ports, where the goods were sold.

This Atlantic economy was fueled ultimately by the demand of a growing European population for agricultural products that could not be obtained in Europe and were more costly to transport from Asia. Sugar was the most important of these commodities, but tobacco, cotton, rice,

cacao, and coffee also became staples of the transatlantic trade. At the same time the North and South American colonists created a steady demand for manufactured goods, especially cutlery and metal tools, that were produced in Europe.

Two of the commodities that were imported from the colonies, tobacco and coffee, were criticized for the harmful effects they had on the human body. Tobacco, which came from the Americas, was the target of a number of criticisms in the seventeenth century. Even at that early date critics recognized the adverse physical effects of this product, which had been used widely among Native Americans. "Tobacco, that outlandish weed," read one popular rhyme, "It spends the brain and spoils the seed." Critics also believed that it had a hallucinatory effect on those who inhaled its smoke.

Coffee was a stimulant that originally came exclusively from the Middle East but later began to be shipped from Haiti and after 1809 from Brazil. Like tobacco, coffee was controversial because of the effects it had on the human

**A Satire Against Coffee and Tobacco**
A seventeenth-century satirical depiction of two European women smoking tobacco and drinking coffee. Turkey, represented by the figure to the right, was the main source of coffee in the seventeenth century. An African servant, to the left, pours the coffee. Tobacco came from the Americas.

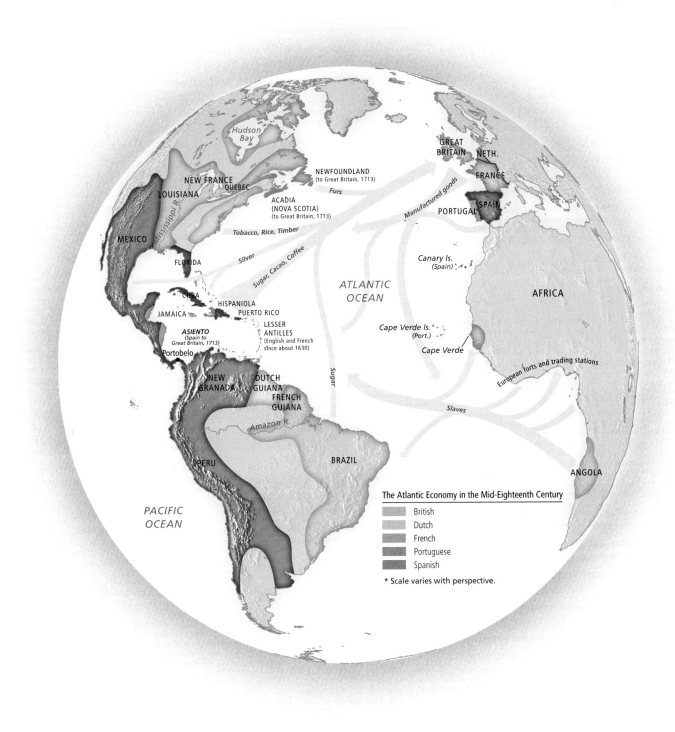

**Map 17.4   The Atlantic Economy in the Mid-Eighteenth Century**
Commodities and African slaves were exchanged between the four continents of North America, South America, Europe, and Africa.

body. In the late seventeenth and eighteenth centuries it was believed to be a source of political radicalism, probably because the coffeehouses where it was consumed served as gathering places for political dissidents. Contemporaries also identified coffee's capacity to produce irritability and depression.

The Atlantic economy had its own rhythms, but it was also part of a global economy that had taken shape during the seventeenth century. As Europeans had expanded the volume of their imports from Asia, those markets were fully integrated into this world system. The system was capitalist in the sense that the production and distribution of

# Chocolate in the New World and the Old

One product of the encounters that took place between Spaniards and the indigenous people of the New World was the widespread consumption of chocolate among western Europeans in the seventeenth century. Chocolate was produced from the seeds of the cacao tree, which was indigenous to South America. Consumed mainly as a beverage, chocolate had been in widespread use among Aztecs and Mayans for centuries before the Spanish Conquest in the sixteenth century; like another native American plant, tobacco, it was used in religious and political ceremonies as well as for medicinal purposes. Spanish colonists received gifts of chocolate from Indians and soon began to enjoy the pleasurable physiological effects of this commodity, which contains chemical agents that act like amphetamines. Because it had such pleasurable effects, it was used in rituals of worship, friendship and courtship.

By the beginning of the seventeenth century, chocolate made its way from colonial America across the Atlantic to Spain. Shortly thereafter it became available in other western European countries. Its widespread use prepared the way for the introduction of two stimulants that came originally from the Middle East and Asia in the latter half of the seventeenth century: coffee and tea.

Because chocolate was grown in non-Christian lands where Spaniards believed that demons inhabited the landscape, and because it was associated with sexual pleasure, it met with harsh disapproval. Clerics denounced it—together with tobacco—as an inducement to vice and the work of Satan. Gradually, however, chocolate came to be viewed in purely secular terms as a commodity, without any religious significance.

The European demand for chocolate contributed to three major transformations of Western life. The first was the growth of the Atlantic trade and a global economy. Among the products that were shipped from the Americas to Europe in exchange for slaves and manufactured goods, cacao was second only to sugar in volume. In preconquest America cacao had often served as an exchange currency; now it was assigned a specific value in the world marketplace. As the price of chocolate escalated Spain established a monopoly over the trade, thus integrating it into the mercantilist system.

Second, the introduction of chocolate into Europe transformed the drinking patterns of Europeans. There had been nothing like chocolate in the diets of Europeans before its arrival, and when it was introduced, new rituals of consumption developed around its use. Cups with handles were designed specifically for drinking the hot beverage, the same cups later used for coffee and tea. The Aztec custom of scooping the foam from the top of a chocolate drink was adopted in Europe. The European desire to sweeten chocolate, as well as coffee and tea, increased the demand for sugar, which in turn encouraged the growth of slavery on the sugar plantations in the West Indies. Sweetened chocolate eventually began to be served as a candy, and by the nineteenth century chocolate candy became the main form in which the commodity was consumed.

Finally, chocolate became a part of the emerging bourgeois sexual culture of eighteenth-century France and England. Just as in preconquest Spanish America, it began to play a role in rituals of sexual seduction. It is no accident that boxes of chocolate are popular gifts on Valentine's Day and that the most well-known chocolate candy in the United States, Godiva, features the English noblewoman who rode naked through the streets of Coventry in 1140. The sustained exchange of a delectable commodity between the New World and the Old World thus contributed to a transformation of Western culture.

## For Discussion

To what extent did the tastes of European consumers determine the nature of the Atlantic economy in the seventeenth and eighteenth centuries?

**The Chocolate House** (1787)
Men and women drinking chocolate, tea, and coffee at the White Conduit House, Islington, London.

commodities were undertaken by private individuals, in a systematic way, for the purposes of profit. European governments had an interest in this capitalist economy because as mercantilists they wanted their countries to acquire the largest possible share of world trade, but they did not control the actual operations of the marketplace. Their role was mainly to authorize individuals or trading companies to conduct trade in a particular geographical area.

## The Atlantic Slave Trade

The slave trade became the very linchpin of the Atlantic economy, and all five Western European imperial powers—Britain, France, the Dutch Republic, Spain, and Portugal—engaged in it. The trade arose to meet the demand of plantation owners in the New World for agricultural labor. In the seventeenth century, after the indigenous Indian population had been ravaged by disease and the indentured whites who had emigrated from Europe in search of a more secure future had gained their freedom, this demand became urgent. Slave labor possessed a number of advantages over free labor. Slaves could be disciplined more easily, they could be forced to work longer hours, and they could be used to build a plantation economy in which the growing, harvesting, and processing of sugar and other agricultural commodities could be directed by one authority. The use of slave labor also allowed the economies of

European countries, especially Great Britain, to develop. Those who had invested in the colonial trade received attractive returns on their investment, while agricultural profits acquired from crops produced by slaves encouraged the growth of domestic manufacturing.

The slave trade formed the crucial link in the triangular pattern of commercial routes that began when European vessels traveled to ports along the western coast of Africa. There they exchanged European goods, including guns, for slaves that African merchants had captured in the interior and had marched to the sea. At these ports the slaves were branded with initials indicating to which nation they belonged. They were then crowded into ships that transported them across the Atlantic to the coast of South America, to the Caribbean, or as far north as Maryland. This was the famous and often deadly Middle Passage, the second leg of the triangular journey, which was completed when the ships returned to their point of origin. Once they had arrived in the Americas, the slaves were sold to the owners of plantations in the tropical areas of the Caribbean and the south Atlantic and in the more moderate climates of the North American mainland.

**DOCUMENT**

Mungo Park on Slavery in the Atlantic (late 1700s)

Slavery has been present throughout world history. It was a major feature of classical civilization and it was also present in medieval Europe before 1200. In Greece and Rome it had often been the result of captivity in war, whereas in the Middle Ages it was reserved for individuals

---

**DOCUMENT**

## A Former Slave Protests African Slavery

*In 1787 Quobna Ottobah Cugoano (1757–1791), a former slave, published an abolitionist treatise,* Thoughts and Sentiments on the Evil and Wicked Traffic of the Slavery and Commerce of the Human Species. *Like the narrative written by Olaudah Equiano quoted at the beginning of this chapter, Cugoano's account describes the horrors of the African slave trade that he himself had experienced. In this passage Cugoano deplores the effect that the slave trade had on his native Africa.*

That base traffic of kid-napping and stealing men was begun by the Portuguese on the coast of Africa, and as they found the benefit of it for their own wicked purposes, they soon went on to commit further depredations. The Spaniards followed their infamous example, and the African slave trade was thought most advantageous for them, to enable themselves to live in ease and affluence by the cruel subjection and slavery of others. The French and English, and some other nations in Europe, as they founded

settlements or colonies in the West Indies or in America, went on in the same manner, and joined hand in hand with the Portuguese and Spaniards to rob and pillage Africa as well as to waste and desolate the inhabitants of the western continent. But the European depredators and pirates have not only robbed and pillaged the people of Africa themselves; but, by their instigation, they have infested the inhabitants with some of the vilest combinations of fraudulent and treacherous villains, even among their own people, and have set up their forts and factories as a reservoir of public and abandoned thieves and as a den of desperadoes, where they may ensnare, entrap and catch men. So that Africa has been robbed of its inhabitants, its freeborn sons and daughters have been stole, and kid-napped and violently taken away and carried into captivity and cruel bondage. And it may be said in respect to that diabolical traffic which is still carried on by the European depredators, that Africa has suffered as much and more than any other quarters of the globe.

Source: Quobna Ottobah Cugoano, *Thoughts and Sentiments on the Evil and Wicked Traffic of the Slavery and Commerce of the Human Species* (London, 1787).

who had been denied certain liberties. As Islam expanded in the ninth century, Arabs began the enslavement of foreign peoples, including black slaves from eastern Africa, and they continued that traffic into the early modern period. In the sixteenth and seventeenth centuries Barbary pirates in the Mediterranean captured approximately 850,000 white Europeans during sea raids and forced them into slavery in Muslim North Africa.

Within this long history of world slavery, the African slave trade conducted by Europeans is unique in three respects. The first distinction is its size. As a demographic phenomenon this involuntary transportation of Africans to the New World is without parallel in world history. It is the largest transoceanic migration recorded in written documents. Between 1519 and 1867 more than 11 million slaves were shipped from Africa to the New World. Deaths at sea reduced the number of slaves who actually arrived in the Americas to about 9.5 million. The peak years of the trade were from 1751 to 1800, when nearly four million slaves left African shores. As the volume of the slave trade increased during the eighteenth century, the percentage of African slaves among all immigrants arriving in the New World rose to more than 75 percent. Nine out of every ten slaves were sent to Brazil or the Caribbean region, including the northern coast of South America. The great majority of these slaves were sold to the owners of sugar and coffee plantations. Only about 4 percent of all slaves were destined for the British colonies on the North American mainland (after 1776 the United States), and almost all of those slaves were sent to the southern colonies.

The second distinctive feature of African slavery in the Americas was its racial character. It differed from the forms of slavery that had existed in ancient Greece and Rome as well as in medieval Europe, in which people of different races and ethnicities had been enslaved. It even differed from Muslim slavery, which involved the enslavement of European Christians as well as black Africans. As the slave trade brought millions of Africans into the Americas, and as indigenous Indian slavery diminished in size, slavery came to be equated with being black, while race was used to justify the inferiority of all African slaves.

The third distinctive feature of the Atlantic slave trade was its commercial character. Its sole function was to provide slave traders with a profit and slave owners with a supply of unfree labor. From the very beginning of their captivity African slaves were considered objects to be sold and their labor exploited. Acting in concert with African chieftains, European slave traders seized people who had performed no acts of aggression in their homelands, transported them overseas, and sold them to the highest bidders. Theories of private property developed in Europe in the seventeenth and eighteenth centuries established the right of slave masters to own their slaves as they would other pieces of property. In this way African slaves were turned into commercial commodities and treated in a manner that

### Volume of the Transatlantic Slave Trade from Africa, 1519–1867

| | |
|---|---|
| 1519–1600 | 266,100 |
| 1601–1650 | 503,500 |
| 1651–1675 | 239,800 |
| 1676–1700 | 510,000 |
| 1701–1725 | 958,600 |
| 1725–1750 | 1,311,300 |
| 1751–1775 | 1,905,200 |
| 1776–1800 | 1,921,100 |
| 1801–1825 | 1,645,100 |
| 1826–1850 | 1,621,000 |
| 1851–1867 | 180,800 |
| Total | 11,062,000 |

Source: David Eltis, "The Volume and Structure of the Transatlantic Slave Trade: A Reassessment," *William and Mary Quarterly,* 3rd series, 58 (2001), Table II.6.

deprived them of all human dignity. To justify such treatment their owners insisted that they "were beasts and had no more souls than beasts."[3] Slaves have never been treated well in any society, but slavery in the Americas acquired a reputation for being particularly exploitative and barbaric, and this has much to do with its commercial character.

One harrowing incident on the British slave ship *Zong* reveals the way in which financial calculations determined the fate of slaves. The *Zong* set sail in 1781 from the African island of São Tomé with 442 African slaves on board. When the slaves began to fall ill and die from malnutrition and disease, the captain of the ship, Luke Collingwood, feared that the owners of the ship would suffer a financial loss. If, however, the slaves were to be thrown overboard on the pretext that the safety of the crew was in jeopardy, the loss would be absorbed by those who had insured the voyage. Accordingly Collingwood decided to tie 132 slaves together, two by two, and fling them into the sea. When the ship owners went to court to collect the insurance, they argued that slaves were no different from horses and that they had a perfect right to throw the slaves overboard in order to preserve the safety of the ship.

Differences in the treatment and survival of slaves in the various parts of the New World had more to do with economic conditions, climate, and population trends than with the nationality or the religion of the slave masters. The crucial factor was the nature of the labor to which the slaves were subjected. Slaves who worked on plantations, especially those growing sugar, usually died within a few years. They were—simply said—worked to death. In the French colony of Saint Domingue, more than 500,000 of the 800,000 slaves brought to the colony between 1680 and 1780 perished. As long as the slave trade was still open, it was more profitable simply to replace those who died with new slaves than to try to extend the life of those the plantation owners already had. It was for this reason that the slave population did not start to grow internally in most areas until the slave trade ended in the nineteenth century.

Another factor influencing the treatment and survival of slaves was the ratio of the black to the white populations. When that ratio was high, as in all the Caribbean colonies, the codes regulating slave life were particularly harsh and created a reign of terror within the slave community. Yet another factor was climate. The absence of tropical diseases in the more temperate zone of the North American colonies provides the best explanation why in these colonies the numbers of births equaled and eventually exceeded the number of deaths long before they did in the Caribbean and South American colonies.

The slave trade itself became the object of intense competition, as each country tried to establish a monopoly over certain routes. During the seventeenth century the British managed to make inroads into the French slave trade, and eventually they surpassed the Portuguese and the Dutch as well. By 1700 British ships were transporting more than 50 percent of all slaves to the Americas. The dominance that Britain established in the slave trade was closely related to its growing maritime and commercial strength. With an enormous merchant marine and a navy that could support it, the British came to dominate the slave trade in the same way they came to dominate the entire world economy. Both revealed how far mercantile capitalism had triumphed in Britain and its overseas possessions.

For the British merchants who engaged in this trade there was no conflict between their traditional beliefs in individual liberty and their subjugation of African slaves. Theories of racial and national superiority removed Africans as well as other non-Europeans from the category of human beings who lived in a free society and who enjoyed individual rights. As long as those rights were tied to a particular national or racial group, such as freeborn Englishmen, slavery presented no challenge to British political ideas.

Not until the late eighteenth century did the enslavement of black Africans become a source of widespread moral concern. The movement to end the slave trade and slavery itself arose almost simultaneously in all European countries. It was inspired mainly by religious zeal, especially from evangelical Protestants in Great Britain and

***The Slave Ship* by J. M. W. Turner (1840)**
The English painter J. M. W. Turner captured the horror of the incident that took place aboard the slave ship *Zong,* when the crew threw 132 slaves overboard in 1781.

the Jesuits in Spain and Portugal. Societies were formed to campaign for the legislative prohibition of the transportation and sale of slaves. These appeals found support in the calculations by European capitalists, especially in Britain, that slavery was no longer economically advantageous. Goods produced by free labor, especially by machine, made slavery appear less cost-effective than in the past, and the entire system of slavery began to be viewed as a costly encumbrance.

By the first decade of the nineteenth century opposition to slavery began to achieve limited success, and by 1851 it had brought about an end to the entire slave trade. The United States refused to allow any of its ports to accept slave ships after 1808, the same year in which the British parliament legislated an end to the trade within its empire. The Dutch ended their slave trade in 1814, the French in 1815, and the Spanish in 1838. The Portuguese continued to import slaves to Brazil until 1851 and ended the practice only because the British were subjecting Portuguese slave traders to constant harassment. Liberation of the slaves generally came later, except in Haiti (formerly Saint Domingue), where slavery was abolished in 1794. The British dismantled the system within their empire between 1834 and 1838. Slavery persisted until 1848 in the French Caribbean, 1863 in the southern United States, 1886 in Cuba, and 1888 in Brazil.

**Carlos Julião, *Extraction of Diamonds***
In addition to their labor on plantations, slaves in Latin America were put to work mining precious metals and jewels. This water-color depicts African slaves mining diamonds in eighteenth-century Brazil.

The ethnicity of colonial populations was more varied in Latin American colonies than in North America. The higher proportion of Africans in those colonies, more extensive patterns of intermarriage, and the free status achieved by large numbers of blacks and mulattos created highly stratified societies by the end of the eighteenth century. In these colonies divisions arose not only between the recently arrived Europeans and the creoles, but between the various groups considered by Europeans to be below them. The social structure of Brazil was more complex than that of any other country in the New World. At the top of the social hierarchy were Portuguese bureaucrats and below them was a large and wealthy group of planter creoles. These two elite groups dominated a lower-class social hierarchy of mestizos (people of mixed white and Indian ancestry), indigenous people, mulattos, freed blacks, and slaves.

Encounters between Europeans and Africans in the New World fostered the growth of ideas of white racial superiority that were grounded in the unbalanced power relationship between the dominant white and subordinate black populations. The circumstances under which physical contact between the races took place made the imbalance of this relationship readily apparent. Blacks appeared at the slave-trading stations having already been beaten into submission by their captives and forced to march hundreds of miles. The demeaning medical exams to which the slaves were subjected and their reduction to the status of a commodity for sale could readily deprive them of any sense of pride or self-respect. Their lack of formal education and literacy put them in a position of cultural inferiority, further reducing them to the status of beasts in the eyes of their white masters. In such circumstances references to the reputed blackness of the biblical Cain (Adam and Eve's first son, who murdered his brother Abel) only confirmed or reinforced the sense of superiority that white people took for granted.

## Cultural Encounters in the Atlantic World

European countries had always possessed some ethnic diversity, but the emigration of people from many different parts of Europe and Africa to America, followed by their intermarriage, created societies of much greater complexity. Even the composition of the white European communities in the colonies was more varied than in the metropolis. In the British colonies, for example, English, Scots, and Irish were joined by large numbers of Germans, French, and Swiss. In 1776 Thomas Paine argued that all of Europe, rather than just England, was the true parent country of North American colonists. Ethnic divisions were further complicated by those of religion, especially in North America, where Protestants of many different denominations, as well as Roman Catholics, lived in close proximity to each other.

## The Transmission of Ideas

The Atlantic Ocean became a corridor for the transmission of political and religious ideas. Political ideologies that developed in Europe were spread from the Old World to the New World mainly by the large volume of printed works that were exported during the eighteenth century. The ancient idea that a republic was the best form of government, which had found widespread support in Renaissance Italy and in seventeenth-century England, appealed to many political leaders in colonial North America. Eighteenth-century French and Scottish ideas regarding the rights of man and the responsibility of the government to bring about the improvement of society found fertile ground in many parts of North and South America. At the time of the French Revolution, ideals of liberty and equality spread not only throughout Europe but in the Americas as well. Legal ideas embodied in English common law, French civil law, and Spanish customary law were also transported to the New World and became the legal foundation of the new societies that were formed there.

The traffic in political ideas did not flow in only one direction. Political ideologies that were formed out of British and European ideas of liberty at the time of the American Revolution were sent back to European countries in a new form, where they inspired reform and revolution in Britain, France, and Ireland. These same ideas of liberty exerted a powerful influence in the Caribbean colonies and in South America. In Haiti, where French and American ideas of liberty inspired a revolution in the 1790s, radical ideas of racial equality developed within the new republic and then spread outward to other colonies and the United States.

Religious ideas experienced a similar transmission and transportation. The Calvinist belief in predestination, which had been formulated in Switzerland and modified by Puritans in England during the sixteenth century, was adopted and further modified by colonists in New England during the seventeenth century. Catholic theological ideas that were introduced into Spanish and Portuguese America, including those regarding the role of the Devil in human society, interacted with those of indigenous peoples and African slaves and produced new religious syntheses. In religion as well as politics, these exchanges of ideas enriched the intellectual worlds of Europeans and colonists alike.

# Encounters Between Europeans and Asians

■ What cultural encounters took place between European and Asian peoples during this period of empire building, and how did these encounters change Western attitudes toward outsiders?

The period from 1650 to 1815 was decisive in the development of European empires in Asia. These overseas possessions, like the American colonies, formed important components of the empires of European states and were also essential to the operation of the global economy. European dominance of world trade was exercised not only in the Atlantic world but also in the Middle East and Asia. The history of the European presence in these areas, however, is very different from that which occurred in the New World. A first difference was that of simple numbers. Prior to the eighteenth century the European presence in Asia had been limited to the activities of missionaries and merchants in places such as Jakarta, Macao, and Manila. During the eighteenth century the number of European colonists in Asia, even in India, remained relatively small in comparison with the numbers who settled in America, especially in British North America.

A second major difference between European empires in the East and in the West during the period from 1650 to 1850 is that in Asia European powers initially did not try to acquire and govern large land masses and subjugate their populations. Europeans first came to Asia to trade, not to conquer. They did not engage in fixed battles with Asians, take steps to reduce the size of their populations, or force them to migrate, as they did in the New World. Only in a handful of Southeast Asian islands did a pattern of conquest, similar to that which had occurred in the New World, take place. When Europeans used military force in Asia, it was almost always against rival European powers, not the indigenous population. When European countries did eventually use force against Asians, they discovered that victory was much more difficult than it had been in the New World. Indeed, Asian peoples already possessed or were acquiring sufficient military strength to respond to European military might. In China and Japan the possession of this military power prevented Europeans from even contemplating conquest or exploitation until the nineteenth century. Establishment of European hegemony in Asia, therefore, took longer and was achieved more gradually than in the Americas.

## Political Control of India

Despite their original intentions, Europeans eventually began to acquire political control over large land masses in Asia and subject Asians to European rule. The first decisive steps in this process took place in India during the second half of the eighteenth century. Until that time the British in India, most of whom were members of the British East India Company, remained confined to the factories that were established along the Indian coast. The main purpose of these factories was to engage in trade not only with Europe but also with other parts of Asia. In conducting this trade the British had to deal with local Indian merchants and to compete with the French, the Portuguese and the Dutch, who had established factories of their own. They also found it advantageous to make alliances with the provincial governors, known as nawabs°, who controlled the interior of the country. It became customary for each European power to have its own candidate for nawab, with the expectation that he would provide favors for his European patrons once he took office.

### Military Conflict and Territorial Acquisitions, 1756–1856

In 1756 this pattern of trading and negotiating resulted in armed military conflict in the city of Calcutta in the northeastern province of Bengal. The British had established a factory at Calcutta in 1690, and they continued to carry on an extensive trade there with Indian merchants, many of whom were Hindus. The nawab of Bengal, the Muslim

**Warren Hastings**

Warren Hastings (1732–1818), who was appointed the first governor-general of India in 1773, represented the ambiguities of early British rule in that country. An officer in the British East India Company, he was sympathetic to Indian culture. He was, however, accused of gross misconduct in the management of Indian affairs. His impeachment by the British Parliament in 1786 for corruption in his administration and cruelty toward some of the native people in Bengal lasted 145 days but resulted in an acquittal in 1787.

Siraj-ud-Daulah, had contempt for all Europeans, especially the British, and he was determined that he would not be beholden to any of them. He was also deeply hostile to the Hindu merchants who were trading with the British. In June 1756 he sent an army of 50,000 Muslims against Calcutta, burning and plundering the city and beginning a siege of the East India Company's Fort William, which was manned by 515 troops in the service of the company. The entire British population of the city, together with more than 2,000 Hindus, had taken refuge in the fort. After a long struggle, which resulted in the death of hundreds of Indians, the fort fell to the nawab's forces, and some of the British officers and magistrates, including the governor of Calcutta, fled by sea.

During this siege the shooting death of a Bengali guard led to an incident that became permanently emblazoned on the emerging imperial consciousness of the British people. Officers in the nawab's army crammed the entire remaining British contingent, a total of 146 men and women, into the fort's lockup or prison, known as the Black Hole of Calcutta. Measuring 18' × 14' 10", it was meant to hold only three or four prisoners overnight. The British prisoners were stifled by the insufferable heat and a lack of water and air. The stench was so bad that many prisoners vomited on the people squeezed next to them. Only twenty-two men and one woman survived until the next morning, when the nawab released them. The remainder either had been trampled to death or had asphyxiated.

The deaths of these British men and women in the Black Hole of Calcutta led the British to seek swift and brutal retribution against the nawab. In 1757, under the direction of the British military officer Robert Clive, a force of 800 British troops and 2,000 native Indian soldiers known as sepoys° retook Calcutta and routed Siraj-ud-Daulah's army of 50,000 men at the battle of Plassey. Siraj-ud-Daulah was executed and replaced by a nawab more amenable to the British. A few years later the British East India Company secured the right to collect taxes and thus exercised political control over the entire province of Bengal. The enormous revenue from these taxes enabled the company to acquire a large army, composed mainly of sepoys. This force grew to 115,000 men by 1782. The British then used these military forces, which were equipped with Western military technology, to gain control of other provinces in India as well as to defeat their French rivals in subsequent engagements during the early nineteenth century.

These further acquisitions of Indian territory led to the eventual establishment of British rule throughout the South Asian subcontinent (see Map 17.5). New territories were brought under British control in the early years of the nineteenth century, and during the tenure of Lord Dalhousie as governor-general of India from 1848 to 1856 the British annexed eight Indian states, including the great Muslim state of Oudh in 1856. This policy of annexation went hand in hand with the introduction of Western technology and literature, the English language, and British criminal procedure.

## The Sepoy Mutiny

The British policy of annexation in India, coupled with the attitude of cultural superiority it encouraged, lay at the root of the greatest act of rebellion by Indians against British rule in the nineteenth century. This rebellion, which began in 1857, is often known as the Sepoy Mutiny, because it originated in the ranks of the Indian troops serving in the armed forces of the British East India Company. The main source of resentment was the British annexation

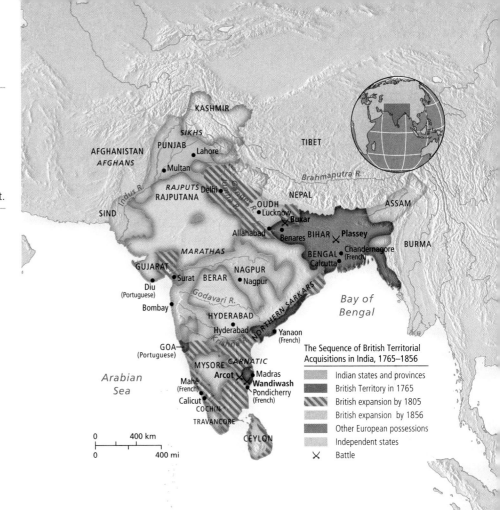

## Map 17.5 The Sequence of British Territorial Acquisitions in India, 1765–1856

British political control of large territories on the South Asian subcontinent began more than a century after the establishment of the first factories along the coast.

**The Sequence of British Territorial Acquisitions in India, 1765–1856**

- Indian states and provinces
- British Territory in 1765
- British expansion by 1805
- British expansion by 1856
- Other European possessions
- Independent states
- ✕ Battle

of Oudh, which many sepoys considered their homeland. The incident that actually provoked the rebellion was the issue of rifle cartridges coated with beef fat, which violated Hindu law, and pork fat, which violated Muslim law. Although this insensitivity to native Indian culture was not unprecedented, in this case it struck a particularly raw nerve and led to a mutiny by the Bengali army. The cities of Delhi and Lucknow came under siege, and dreadful atrocities, including the hacking to death of British women and children, occurred. British reprisals were equally savage and eventually succeeded in suppressing the rebellion.

In the wake of the mutiny the British government abolished the British East India Company and assumed direct rule of India. Queen Victoria (r. 1837–1901), the constitutional monarch of the United Kingdom, acquired much greater power over her Indian empire. Although the British government did take steps to confirm the lands and titles of Indian princes and to give them local power, their relationship with their British overlords remained one of strict subordination.

## Changing European Attitudes Toward Asian Cultures

This second phase of European imperialism in Asia played a crucial role in the formation of Western identity. The steadily increasing numbers of Europeans who had contact with these lands—merchants, missionaries, writers, and colonial administrators—and to a lesser extent the public who read about these foreign places gained a clearer sense of who they were once they compared themselves to Indians, Chinese, and Polynesians. Until the seventeenth century Europeans thought of "the East" mainly as the Middle East, an area that was largely subsumed within the Ottoman Empire. Europeans expressed a generally negative

view of the culture of this region (see Chapter 15), and over the years that perception had not changed. The political system of the Ottoman Empire was considered despotic and its religion, Islam, the antithesis of Christianity. The Far East, comprising South Asia (India), East Asia (China, Japan), and Southeast Asia (Burma, Siam, Indonesia), generally did not enter into these perceptions of "the Orient." There was little contact with this part of the world, and much of what was known about it was shrouded in mystery. During this period Europeans viewed the Far East mainly as an exotic land, rich in spices, silk, and other luxury commodities.

As Western missionaries and merchants made more frequent contacts with Asian society, Europeans developed more informed impressions of these distant lands and peoples. Some of those impressions were negative, especially when the power of Asian rulers was discussed, but many other characterizations of the East were positive. Interest in and admiration for both Indian and Chinese culture were most widespread during the middle years of the eighteenth century. The systematic study of Asian languages, especially Chinese and Sanskrit, began during this period. A preference for things Asian became characteristic of Enlightenment thinkers such as Voltaire (1694–1778), who regarded Asian cultures as superior to

**DOCUMENT**

## The East India Company and the British Government

*In the eighteenth century the control of British factories in India was entrusted to the East India Company, which had its own administrative bureaucracy and armed forces. Responding to reports of widespread corruption and other abuses by the company, the British Parliament passed an act regulating the company's affairs in 1773. This arrangement did not satisfy many critics of the company, who demanded that the British government assume direct rule of its Indian territories, at a time when the company was acquiring new provinces. The government, however, was reluctant to assume these responsibilities, and in this paper, written in 1778, John Robinson, the secretary to the treasury, set down his reasons for leaving the government of British India in the hands of the East India Company.*

As far as I am hitherto informed, my opinion is that the government should not take the management of these acquisitions in their own hands but should leave them in the hands of the company, reforming and altering the government of the company, so as to make it more fit than it is at present for the management of such a concern.

My reasons . . . are as follows:

First, I have never yet seen any plan to my satisfaction by which these acquisitions can be properly transferred from the Company to the government in a better manner than they may be by the Company, provided the government of it be amended and made subject to the superintendence and frequent control of the legislature.

Secondly, the change itself would be very difficult and even dangerous in the present moment when we have a rebellion in our colonies, a foreign war and many other difficulties to contend with. . . .

Fourthly, I am violently against pledging the revenues and substance of this country for the security of these acquisitions, in return for any advantage by way of revenue that may be derived from them; and yet this must be the case, if the government take the management of them into their own hands.

Fifthly, I think that the errors which must be committed in the management of such acquisitions, at so great a distance from the seat of government, had better fall upon the directors of the Company than fall directly upon the ministers of the king, who in the midst of the difficulties that at present surround them, and of the calumnies to which they are necessarily subject, can hardly now retain a sufficient degree of authority and respect for the government of this country.

Source: British Library, Additional Manuscript 38398, folios 108–17.

those of a corrupt Europe in many respects. Voltaire also found the East unaffected by the superstition and the fanaticism that characterized Western Christianity, which he loathed. To him, the main philosophical tradition of China, Confucianism, which embodied a strict moral code, was a more attractive alternative. Eastern religion, especially Hinduism, was also admired for its ethical content and its underlying belief in a single deity.

This mid-eighteenth-century admiration of Asian culture even extended to Chinese and Indian political institutions. The despotic Chinese Empire was transformed through Voltaire's perceptions into an enlightened monarchy. There was less to admire in the Mughal Empire in India, but in his history of European colonialism the French Jesuit priest Guillaume Thomas Raynal (1713–1796) idealized the "purity and equity" of the ancient Indian political system. Comparison of contemporary Indian politics with the corruption of governments in Europe made native Asian political systems look good by comparison. In Britain there was more disrespect for the members of the East India Company known as nabobs°, who returned to England to flaunt the wealth they had recently acquired in India, than there was for native Indian officials. There was also more interest in reforming the British East India Company than in reforming Indian politics.

This intellectual respect for Asian philosophy and politics coincided with a period of widespread Asian influences on Western art, architecture, and design. Eastern themes began to influence British buildings, such as in the Brighton Pavilion, designed by John Nash. Small cottages, known as bungalows, owed their inspiration to Indian models. French architects built pagodas (towers with the roof of each story turning upward) for their clients. Chinese gardens, which unlike classical European gardens were not arranged geometrically, became popular in England and France.

A new form of decorative art that combined Chinese and European motifs, known in French as chinoiserie°, became highly fashionable. Wealthy French people furnished their homes with Chinese wallpaper and hand-painted folding screens. The demand for Chinese porcelain, known in English simply as china, was insatiable. Vast quantities of this porcelain, which was technically and aesthetically superior to the stoneware produced in Germany and England, left China for the ports of western Europe. Even the dress of Europeans was influenced by Asian styles. Indian and Chinese silks were in high demand, and Europeans ex-

**Brighton Pavilion**

This building, designed by John Nash, reflected the incorporation of Eastern styles into English architecture, and was inspired by the description of Kubla Khan's palace in Samuel Taylor Coleridge's poem "Kubla Khan" (1816).

pressed a preference for Indian cotton over that produced in the New World. A style of Indian nightwear known as pajamas became popular in England. Even a new sport, polo, which had originated to India, made its entry into upper-class European society at this time.

During the late eighteenth and early nineteenth centuries the high regard in which many Europeans held Asian culture began to wane. As the European presence in Asia became larger and more powerful, as the British began to exercise more control in India, and as merchants began to monopolize the Asian trade, Western images of the East became more unfavorable. Chinese philosophy, instead of being viewed as a repository of ancient ethical wisdom, was labeled as irrational when compared with that of the West. Confucianism fell out of favor, and Eastern religion in general was despised as being inferior to Christianity. Enlightenment thinkers ranked Asian political systems below those of the more "advanced" countries of Europe. The English scholar George Anson claimed that the Chinese reputation for industry and ingenuity was undeserved and that their scientific thought was inferior to that of Europeans. The English writer Samuel Johnson (1709–1784) expressed this

DOCUMENT

Thomas Babington Macaulay's "Minute on Education" (1834)

sense of Western intellectual superiority when he had an Arab poet in his novel *Rasselas* (1759) state that Europeans "are more powerful ... than we, because they are wiser; knowledge will always predominate over ignorance."[4]

Expressions of Western superiority over Asians were reinforced by emerging ideas of racial difference. Sixteenth- and seventeenth-century ideas of Europeans' superiority over black Africans and the indigenous peoples of the Americas on the basis of differences in skin color and facial features were now extended to the Chinese, dark-skinned South Asians, and Polynesians. Intellectual theories of race, which are a distinctly Western creation and were developed mainly during the late eighteenth century, provided an apparently empirical and scientific foundation for these assumptions. The color of one's skin in India, which had determined the position of a person in the Hindu caste system, was now used by Westerners to identify South Asians as "coloreds."

By the same token Chinese people, previously described as white by Westerners who admired China, were now referred to as being nonwhite or yellow. By the beginning of the nineteenth century, Westerners had acquired an ideology of superiority over Asians as well as Africans and indigenous

American people that included racial difference as one of its main components. This ideology prepared Europeans intellectually and emotionally for the conquest of numerous countries in Asia and Africa in the second half of the nineteenth century. This third and final period of European imperial expansion, which began around 1870 and reached its peak around 1900, brought 84 percent of the Earth's surface under Western control.

# The Crisis of Empire and the Atlantic Revolutions

■ **Why did European powers begin to lose control of some of their colonies, especially those in the Americas, between 1775 and 1825?**

During the period from 1780 to 1825, European empires experienced a crisis that marked the end of the second stage of European overseas expansion. As a result of this crisis British, French, and Spanish governments lost large segments of their empires, all in the Americas. New states and nations were carved out of the older sprawling empires. The crisis was to some extent administrative. Having acquired large expanses of territory overseas, European states were faced with the challenging problem of governing them from a distance. They not only had to rule large areas inhabited by non-European peoples (Indians and African slaves), but they also faced the difficulty of maintaining the loyalty of people of European descent who were born in the colonies.

These European colonials or creoles became the main protagonists in the struggles that led to the independence of the North American colonies from Britain in 1776 and the South American colonies from Spain a generation later. In the French colony of Saint Domingue, the location of the only successful revolution in the Caribbean region during this period, a very different set of pressures led to independence. In this colony, which became the republic of Haiti in 1804, the revolution was led not by white creoles but by people of color, including the slaves who worked on the plantations. In Britain's European colony of Ireland, where an unsuccessful revolution against British rule took place in 1798, the urge for independence came both from settlers of British descent and the native Irish population.

## The American Revolution, 1775–1783

The first Atlantic revolution was the revolt of the thirteen North American colonies and the establishment of their independence from British rule. During the second half of the eighteenth century, a number of tensions arose between the British government and its transatlantic colonies. All of

these overseas colonies had developed traditions of self-government, and all of them had their own representative assemblies. At the same time the colonies were controlled by various governmental bodies responsible to the British Parliament, such as the Board of Trade. The colonies had their own militias, but they also received protection from British troops when conflicts developed with the French or other hostile powers.

The crisis that led to the American Revolution had its roots in the situation that emerged at the end of the French and Indian War. In order to maintain the peace agreed to in 1763, the government stationed British troops on the frontiers of the colonies. It argued that because the troops were protecting the colonists, they should contribute financially to their own defense. To this end the government began imposing a number of new taxes on the colonists. In 1765 the British Parliament passed the Stamp Act, which forced

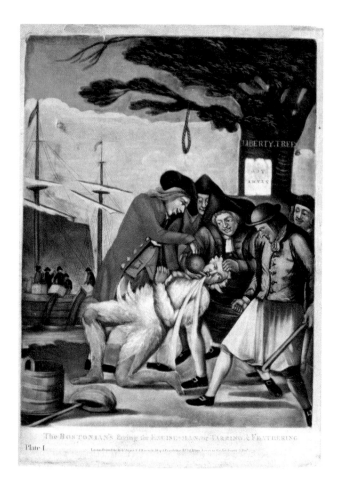

**The Bostonian's Paying the Excise Man or Tarring and Feathering (1774)**
This satirical engraving reflects the hatred of colonial Americans at the collection of taxes levied on them without their consent. The Boston Tea Party is depicted in the background. The colonists are forcing the tax collector to drink the tea on which he is trying to collect taxes.

**The British Surrender at Yorktown in 1781**
This battle ended the American War of Independence, although the peace treaty was not signed
for another two years.

colonists to purchase stamps for almost anything that was printed. This piece of legislation raised the central constitutional issue of whether Parliament had the power to legislate for British subjects in lands that did not elect members of that Parliament. "Taxation without representation is tyranny" became the main rallying cry of the colonists. Opposition to the Stamp Act was so strong that Parliament repealed the act the following year, but at the same time it passed a statute declaring that it had the authority to tax the colonists as it pleased. When the government imposed new taxes on the tea imported from Britain in 1773, a number of colonists, dressed as Indians, threw the tea into the Boston Harbor.

The government responded to this "Boston Tea Party" by passing a series of statutes, known in the colonies as the Intolerable Acts, in 1774. One of these acts specified that the port of Boston be closed until the colonists had repaid the cost of the tea. The Intolerable Acts led to organized resistance to British rule, and in the following year military conflict broke out at Lexington and Concord in Massachusetts. On July 4, 1776, thirteen of the colonies on the North American mainland, stretching from New Hampshire to

Georgia, approved a Declaration of Independence from Great Britain. A long revolutionary war, in which the colonists received assistance from France in 1778, ended with the defeat of British troops at Yorktown in 1781 and the recognition of the republic of the United States of America in the Treaty of Paris in 1783.

The case that the American colonists made for independence from Britain drew upon the political theories of John Locke, who justified resistance against the Stuart monarchy at the time of the Glorious Revolution. Locke, who placed limits on legislative as well as executive power, became the main inspiration of the Declaration of Independence, which was drafted by Thomas Jefferson. The Revolution also found support in the customs and traditions embodied in the English common law, especially the principle that men could not be deprived of their rights without their own consent. Republican ideas, drawn both from ancient Greece and Rome and revived at the time of the Renaissance, gave colonists a model of a community of virtuous men joined in a commitment to the body politic, which they defined in colonial terms. Finally there was the influence of the ideas of the Enlightenment, which empha-

## DOCUMENT

## Thomas Paine Supports the American Cause

*Thomas Paine (1737–1809) was a radical Whig reformer who supported the cause for American independence. In* Common Sense *(1776), a pamphlet written to support the American cause in the year of the Declaration of Independence, Paine refutes the arguments of the British that they served the interests of the American colonists. Paine protests not only the commercial exploitation of the colonies but also the way in which Great Britain has involved them in warfare with continental rivals.*

I have heard it asserted by some, that as America has flourished under her former connection with Great Britain, the same connection is necessary towards her future happiness, and will always have the same effect. Nothing can be more fallacious than this kind of argument. We may as well assert that because a child has thrived upon milk, that it is never to have meat, or that the first twenty years of our lives is to become a precedent for the next twenty. But even this is admitting more than is true; for I answer roundly that America would have flourished as much, probably much more, had no European power taken

any notice of her. The commerce by which she hath enriched herself are the necessaries of life and will always have a market while eating is the custom of Europe.

But she has protected us, say some. That she hath engrossed us is true, and defended the Continent at our expense as well as her own, is admitted; and she would have defended Turkey from the same motive, *viz.* for the sake of trade and dominion.

Alas! We have been long led away by ancient prejudices and made large sacrifices to superstition. We have boasted the protection of Britain without considering that her motive was *interest,* not *attachment;* and that she did not protect us from *our enemies* on *our account* but from *her enemies* on *her own account,* from those who had no quarrel with us on any *other account,* and who will always be our enemies on the *same account.* Let Britain waive her pretensions to the Continent, or the Continent throw off the dependence, and we should be at peace with France and Spain, were they at war with Britain. The miseries of Hanover last war ought to warn us against connections.

Source: From Thomas Paine, *Common Sense* (Philadelphia: W. T. Bradford, 1776).

sized the natural right of all men to life, liberty, and the pursuit of happiness (see Chapter 18).

Although the American Revolution was inspired by many of the ideas that had originated in the two English revolutions of the seventeenth century, it differed from those earlier revolutions in that it was directed more against the British Parliament than the king. The Declaration of Independence severed the bonds between the colonists and King George III, to whom they formally owed allegiance, but the constitutional powers against which they protested, especially that of taxation, were those of Parliament. It was taxation by the British Parliament, rather than nonparliamentary taxes like those levied in the 1640s, that led to the American Revolution.

## The Haitian Revolution, 1789–1804

The second successful revolution in the Atlantic world took place in the French Caribbean colony of Saint Domingue, known later as Haiti, which occupied the western portion of the island of Hispaniola. This revolution resulted in the establishment of the colony's independence, but the revolt was directed not so much against French rule as against the island's white planters. Just like their counterparts in Spanish and British Caribbean colonies, these planters, known in Haiti as colons°, had little desire for national in-

dependence. They wished to remain within the protective custody of the French state. Because they formed a distinct minority of the total population, they did not think of themselves as constituting a separate national community. Any resistance to imperial rule, moreover, would have required that they arm their slaves in order to make the movement succeed, and that would have threatened their control of the black population.

The real threat of revolution in all the Caribbean colonies came not from the elite or ruling class but from the subordinate members of the population. In Saint Domingue the revolution began in 1789 with a rebellion of people defined legally as free coloreds, most of whom were mulattos. The development that triggered this revolt, organized under the leadership of Vincent Ogé, was the refusal of the white planters, who were creoles, to give the free coloreds representation in the revolutionary French National Assembly as well as in local assemblies in Saint Domingue.

The free colored rebellion of 1789 led directly to a massive slave revolt in 1791. At that time slaves constituted about 90 percent of the population. Their uprising took place after the French National Assembly voted to abolish slavery in France but not in the French colonies. In this revolt 12,000 African slaves, armed with machetes and reacting to their brutal treatment by their masters, destroyed a thousand plantations and killed hundreds of whites. Their tactics, which included cutting white planters in half, raping their wives and daughters, and decapitating their children, were matched by those of the planters, who retaliated by torturing blacks and hanging them in the streets.

Spanish and British armies, frightened that this slave rebellion would spread to their colonies, occupied Saint Domingue and massacred thousands of slaves, many of them after they surrendered. In 1795, however, the Spanish withdrew from Saint Domingue and ceded their portion of the island of Hispaniola to France. The British were likewise forced to leave the colony in 1798, having lost as many as 40,000 soldiers, most of them from disease. The man who had assumed the leadership of the slave revolt, the freed slave Toussaint L'Ouverture, then proceeded to conquer the entire island in 1801, abolish slavery, and proclaim himself the governor-general of an autonomous province.

In 1801, after Napoleon had assumed control of the French government and the idealism of the French Revolution had evaporated, a French army of 20,000 men occupied Saint Domingue. The purpose was to make the colony the centerpiece of a restored French Empire, including Florida, Louisiana, French Guiana, and the French West Indies. This assertion of French imperial control secured the surrender of L'Ouverture. When it was learned that the French were planning to reintroduce slavery, however, two black generals, Jean-Jacques Dessalines and Henri Christophe, whom the French had enlisted to suppress the revolt, united freed blacks and slaves against the French forces. In 1803 these united forces drove the French out of the colony, and in 1804 they established an independent state of Haiti.

This new state of Haiti was far different from the United States, in that it was governed entirely by people of color and it banned slavery. It proclaimed racial equality by defining all Haitians as black. The plantation system was destroyed and the land was redistributed among free blacks; foreigners were forbidden to hold property. Deciding upon the form of government took time, however, as the new rulers of the country were divided between those who wished to establish a monarchy and those who favored a republic. Those divisions led to a prolonged civil war from 1807 until 1822, when the warring northern and southern provinces were integrated into a single republic.

The Haitian revolution was the most radical and egalitarian of the Atlantic revolutions of the late eighteenth and early nineteenth centuries. Whereas the American Revolution was mainly a political movement that established a new republic, the Haitian revolution was a genuine social and economic revolution as well. Its unqualified declaration of human equality and its abolition of slavery served as an inspiration to abolitionist movements in other countries, including the United States, throughout the nineteenth century. The destruction of the plantation system, however, brought about a revolutionary transformation of the country's economy. As a French possession Saint Domingue was quite possibly the richest colony in the world, producing about two-fifths of the world's sugar and half of its coffee. After the revolution, with its economy severed from that of France, the country could no longer compete successfully in the Atlantic economy.

## The Irish Rebellion, 1798–1799

Within the British Empire the country that was most directly inspired by the success of the American Revolution was the kingdom of Ireland. Unlike the residents of the thirteen colonies in North America, the Gaelic people of Ireland had long thought of themselves as a distinct nation. The English, however, had begun a conquest of this Irish nation in the twelfth century, and during the next 500 years they had struggled to rule it effectively. One of their methods was to settle English landlords on Irish lands. They had done this in the Middle Ages by giving large estates to English feudal lords, but those old Anglo-Irish families had gradually begun to think of themselves as Irish, and after the Reformation they had remained Catholic, while most English people had become Protestant.

In the sixteenth century the English government had begun to settle colonies of English Protestants on plantations in various parts of Ireland. The purpose of this policy was to gain tighter control over the country and to promote the loyalty of Irish landowners to the English government. In the early seventeenth century James VI of Scotland (who had also become James I of England in 1603) had settled both Scottish Presbyterians, later known as the Scots Irish, as well as English Anglicans, in the northern Irish province of Ulster. These Protestants of Scottish and English descent had become the core of the ruling establishment throughout Ireland, especially after Catholic rebellions in 1641–1649 and again in 1689–1690 had failed.

In the eighteenth century Irish Protestants began to resent their subservient relationship to the British government. Just like the American colonists, they recognized the way in which the Irish economy was serving British rather than Irish interests, and they resented the control that Britain had over the Irish parliament. A reform association known as the Society of United Irishmen, led by the Protestant Ulsterman Wolfe Tone, succeeded in building common ground between Protestants and Catholics. The United Irishmen demanded the repeal of the laws that denied Catholics the right to hold office and sit in the Irish parliament.

The ideals of the United Irishmen drew on many different sources. A long tradition of Presbyterian republican radicalism found reinforcement in the ideals of the American Revolution. The Irish objected to paying tithes to the established Anglican church, and like the American colonists in the 1760s they resented the taxes they were asked to pay to aid in the British war against the French during the 1790s.

French revolutionary ideas of liberty, equality, and fraternity had a pervasive influence in Ireland as well.

In 1798 the United Irishmen aligned themselves with lower-class Catholic peasants known as Defenders, and these Irish groups staged a rebellion against British rule with the intention of establishing an Irish republic. Like the American colonists, the Irish revolutionaries sought French aid, but it came too little and too late, and the rebellion failed. The revolt, which was marred by atrocities on both sides, resulted in the deaths of 30,000 people.

The British government recognized that its arrangement for ruling Ireland, in which the nationalist republican movement had originated, could no longer work. The British government decided therefore to bring about a complete union between Great Britain and Ireland. By the terms of this arrangement, which took effect in 1801, Ireland's parliament ceased to meet; instead the Irish were to elect a limited number of representatives to sit in the British parliament. Ireland thus became a part of the United Kingdom, just as Scotland had done in 1707. The proximity of Ireland to Britain, which made the prospect of Irish independence much more dangerous, was a major factor in making the British determined to hold on to this "internal colony." The forces of Irish nationalism could not be contained, however, and during the nineteenth century new movements for Irish independence arose.

# National Revolutions in Spanish America, 1810–1824

The final set of revolutions against European imperial powers occurred between 1810 and 1824 in a number of Spanish American colonies. These struggles, like the American Revolution, turned colonies into new states and

## CHRONOLOGY

## The Atlantic Revolutions, 1775–1824

| | |
|---|---|
| 1775–1783 | United States of America |
| 1789–1804 | Haiti |
| 1798–1799 | Ireland |
| 1810–1821 | Mexico |
| 1810–1819 | Colombia |
| 1810–1821 | Venezuela |
| 1810–1816 | Argentina |
| 1810–1818 | Chile |
| 1821–1824 | Peru |

led to the building of new nations. The first of these revolutions began in Mexico in 1810; others soon arose in Argentina, Colombia, Chile, and Peru. In these revolutions creoles played a leading role, just as they had in the American War of Independence. The main sources of creole discontent were the Bourbon reforms, which ironically had been intended to make the Spanish Empire more efficient and thus to preserve it. The reforms had achieved this goal, however, by favoring commercial interests at the expense of the traditional aristocracy, thereby reversing or threatening the position of many creole elites. The creoles also faced increasingly heavy taxation, as the Spanish government sought to make them support the expenses of colonial administration.

During the late eighteenth century Spanish creole discontent had crystallized into demands for greater political autonomy, similar to the objectives of British American colonists. South American creoles began to think of themselves as Spanish Americans and sometimes simply as Americans. Like British American colonists, they also read and were inspired by the works of Enlightenment political philosophers. They protested against the Bourbon reforms. Nevertheless, the Spanish creole struggle against imperial rule did not commence until some thirty years after the North American colonies had won their independence. One reason for this slow development of revolutionary action was that Spanish American creoles still looked to the Spanish government to provide them with military support against the threat of lower-class rebellion. When, for example, a rebellion of this sort against Spanish rule occurred in Peru in 1780, creole planters not only refused an invitation to join the revolt but also supported the Spanish forces that crushed it. Faced with this lower-class threat, which continued to plague them even after independence, creoles were cautious about abandoning the military and police support provided by the metropolis.

The event that eventually precipitated these wars for national independence was the collapse of the Spanish monarchy after Napoleon's French army invaded Spain in 1808 (see Chapter 19). This development left the Spanish Empire, which had always been more centralized than the British Empire, in a weakened position. In an effort to reconstitute the political order in their colonies, creoles sought to establish greater autonomy. Once the monarchy was restored, this demand for autonomy led quickly to armed resistance. This resistance began in Mexico, but it soon spread throughout Spanish America and quickly acquired popular support.

The man who took the lead in these early revolts against Spanish rule was the fiery Venezuelan aristocrat Símon Bolívar (1783–1830). Educated in the ideas of the Enlightenment, Bolívar led uprisings in his homeland in 1812 and 1814 and eventually defeated the Spanish there in 1819. Unlike most creoles, Bolívar was not afraid to recruit free coloreds and blacks into his armies. His hatred of European

DOCUMENT

The Plan of Iguala (1821)

**Símon Bolívar Presenting the Flag of Liberation to Soldiers After the Battle of Carabobo, 1821**
Bolívar was the man most directly responsible for liberating South American countries from Spanish rule. He liberated his native Venezuela in 1821 and defeated Spanish forces in Peru in 1824.

colonial governors knew few boundaries. At one point he reportedly commanded his soldiers to shoot and kill any European on sight. He vowed never to rest until all of Spanish America was free. Bolívar carried the struggle for liberation to Peru, which became independent in 1824, and created the state of Bolivia in 1825. Often compared to George Washington, he was more responsible than any one individual for the liberation of Spanish America from Spanish rule. Independent states were established in Argentina in 1816, Chile in 1818, Colombia in 1819, and Mexico in 1821. By then the Spanish, who in the sixteenth century had the largest empire in the world, retained control of only two colonies in the Western Hemisphere: Puerto Rico and Cuba.

# Conclusion

## The Rise and Reshaping of the West

During the second period of European empire building, the West not only expanded geographically but also acquired a large share of the world's resources. By dominating the world's carrying trade, and by exploiting the agricultural and mineral resources of the Americas, Western states gained control of the world economy. The slave trade, with all its horrors, formed an important part of

this economy and served as one of the main sources of Western wealth.

Western economic power laid the foundations for Western political control. In Asia European states assumed political control over territories slowly and reluctantly, as Britain's gradual and piecemeal acquisition of territory in India revealed. In the Americas, European powers acquired territory with relative ease, and European possessions in the New World soon became part of the West. By 1700, as we have seen, the geographical center of the West had become the Atlantic Ocean.

The American territories that were brought under European political control also became, at least to some extent, culturally part of the West. The European colonists who settled in the Americas preserved the languages, the religions, and many of the cultural traditions of the European countries from which they came. When some of the British and Spanish colonies in the Americas rebelled against European regimes in the late eighteenth and early nineteenth centuries, the identity of the colonists who led the resistance remained essentially Western. Even the political ideas that inspired national resistance to European regimes had their origins in Europe.

The assertion of Western political and economic power in the world cultivated a sense of Western superiority. The belief that Europeans, regardless of their nationality, were superior to those from other parts of the world originated in the encounters that took place between Europeans and both African slaves and the indigenous peoples in the

Americas. In the late eighteenth century a conviction also developed, although much more slowly, that the West was culturally superior to the civilizations of Asia. This belief in Western superiority became even more pronounced when the economies of Western nations began to experience more rapid growth than those of Asia. The main source of this new Western economic strength was the Industrial Revolution, which will be the subject of Chapter 20.

## Suggestions for Further Reading

For a comprehensive listing of suggested readings, please go to www.ablongman.com/levack2e/chapter17

Bailyn, Bernard. *Ideological Origins of the American Revolution.* 1967. A probing analysis of the different intellectual traditions upon which the American colonists based their arguments for independence.

Blackburn, Robin. *The Making of New World Slavery: From the Baroque to the Modern, 1492–1800.* 1997. Places European slavery in a broad world perspective.

Boxer, C. R. *The Dutch Seaborne Empire, 1600–1800.* 1965. A thorough account covering the entire period of Dutch expansion.

Davis, Ralph. *The Rise of the Atlantic Economies.* 1973. A readable study of economic development on both sides of the Atlantic.

Eltis, David, *The Rise of African Slavery in the Americas.* 2000. An analysis of the different dimensions of the slave trade based on a database of slave ships and passengers.

Goody, Jack. *The East in the West.* 1996. Challenges the idea that Western cultures are more rational than those of Asia.

Greene, Jack P. *Peripheries and Center: Constitutional Development in the Extended Polities of the British Empire and the United States, 1607–1788.* 1986. A study of the composition of the British Empire and its disintegration in North America.

Kamen, Henry. *Empire: How Spain Became a World Power.* 2003. Explains how Spain established the most extensive empire the world had ever known.

Langley, Lester D. *The Americas in the Age of Revolution, 1750–1850.* 1996. A broad comparative study of revolutions in the United States, Haiti, and Latin America.

Liss, Peggy K. *The Atlantic Empires: The Network of Trade and Revolutions, 1713–1826.* 1983. Places the American Revolution in a broader comparative setting and includes material on early Latin American independence movements.

Mungello, D. E. *The Great Encounter of China and the West, 1500–1800.* 1999. Studies China's acceptance and rejection of Western culture as well as the parallel Western reception of China.

Pagden, Anthony. *Lords of All the World: Ideologies of Empire in Spain, Britain and France, ca. 1500–ca. 1800.* 1996. Discusses the theoretical foundations of the Atlantic Empires.

Said, Edward. *Orientalism.* 1979. A study of the way in which Western views of the East have assumed its inferiority.

## Notes

1. Olaudah Equiano, *The Interesting Narrative of the Life of Olaudah Equiano, or Gustavus Vassa the African* (1789).

2. Thomas Rymer (ed.), *Foedera* (1704–1735), vol. 18, 72.

3. Quoted in Robin Blackburn, *The Making of New World Slavery* (1997), 325.

4. Samuel Johnson, *Rasselas* (1759), 47.

# Eighteenth-Century Society and Culture

# 18

I N 1745 THOMAS BROWN AND ELEVEN OTHER MEN LIVING ON THE ESTATE OF the Earl of Uxbridge, an English nobleman, were jailed for up to one year for shooting deer and rabbits on the earl's land. All twelve defendants were poor. Brown eked out a living as a coal miner in the earl's mines and rented a cottage and five acres of land from him. Like many of his fellow villagers, Brown supplemented his family's diet by shooting game from time to time, usually as he was walking to work through the earl's vast estate. This poaching violated a set of English parliamentary statutes known as the game laws, which restricted the shooting or trapping of wild animals to the members of the landed class.

The earl and other noblemen defended the game laws on the grounds that they were necessary to protect their property. The laws, however, served the even more important purpose of maintaining social distinctions between landowners and the common people. Members of the landed class believed that only they should have the right to hunt game and to serve deer, pheasants, and hares at lavish dinners attended by their social equals. For a poor person like Thomas Brown, who was described in a court document as "a rude disorderly man and a most notorious poacher," to enjoy such delicacies was a challenge to the social order.

This mid-eighteenth-century encounter between the Earl of Uxbridge and his tenants, which took the form of a criminal prosecution, reflected the tensions that simmered beneath the calm surface of eighteenth-century European society. These tensions arose between the members of the aristocracy, a small but wealthy governing elite, and the masses of tenants and laborers who formed the overwhelming majority of the European population. The aristocracy occupied a dominant position in eighteenth-century society. They controlled an enormous portion of the wealth in their countries, much of it in land. They staffed the state bureaucracies, the legislative assemblies, the military officer corps, and the judiciaries of almost all European states. They dominated and set the tone of high cultural life in Europe. Together

**First Lecture in the Salon of Madame Geoffrin, 1755** The speaker is lecturing on Voltaire's *The Orphan of China* before a predominantly aristocratic audience of men and women.

with the monarchy and the church, with which they were socially and politically linked, the aristocracy formed what today is often referred to as "the Establishment."

By 1800 the social and political dominance of the aristocracy had begun to wane. Their legitimacy as a privileged elite was increasingly called into question. In a few countries political power began to pass from them to different social groups. The aristocracy did not surrender all their power, but they lost their stranglehold over society. This change began during a period of political stability between 1750 and the outbreak of the French Revolution in 1789.

The decline of the aristocracy was the result of a series of cultural encounters. The first were the tense and occasionally violent interactions between landowners and peasants who resented the repressive features of upper-class rule. The second were criticisms of the aristocracy and the demands for reform that came from the increasingly literate, politically active people from the middle ranks of society, such as merchants, financiers, industrialists, and skilled artisans. The third was the cultural and intellectual movement known as the Enlightenment. Even though many of the Enlightenment's most prominent thinkers came from the ranks of the aristocracy, they advanced a set of political, social, economic, and legal ideas that ultimately inspired the creation of a more egalitarian society.

The aristocracy did not relinquish power willingly or quickly. Although they faced severe criticism and challenges to their dominance, they managed to preserve much of their wealth and maintain at least some of their political influence. To insulate themselves from criticisms from less powerful social groups, they adopted many of the values of the people who occupied the middle ranks of society and subscribed to many of the ideas of the Enlightenment, including those that criticized their own class. Internal encounters between different social groups, just like external encounters between Western and non-Western peoples, rarely result in total domination of one group over the other. Instead both parties change their thinking and behavior as a result of their interaction.

These encounters, especially those that took place at the time of the Enlightenment, resulted in a redefinition of the West. In Chapter 16 we saw how the Scientific Revolution completely changed the face of Western culture. In the eighteenth century the Enlightenment, which was inspired to a great extent by the ideas of the Scientific Revolution, produced a set of political and social ideals that served as the basis for a new Western identity.

This chapter will explore the ways in which these social and cultural encounters changed the political and intellectual culture of the West. In doing this the individual sections of the chapter will address the following questions:

- **What social groups belonged to the aristocracy and how did they exercise their power and influence during the eighteenth century?**

- **How did subordinate social groups, most notably the rural peasantry and those who lived in the towns, challenge the aristocracy during the late eighteenth century?**
- **What were the main features of Enlightenment thought and how did it present a threat to the old order?**
- **What impact did the Enlightenment have on Western culture and politics?**

# The Aristocracy

- **What social groups belonged to the aristocracy and how did they exercise their power and influence during the eighteenth century?**

During the eighteenth century a relatively small, wealthy group of men dominated European society and politics. This social and ruling elite is often referred to as the aristocracy°, a term derived from a Greek word meaning the people who were the most fit to rule. In the eighteenth and nineteenth centuries the term *aristocracy* began to be applied not just to those few men who exercised political power but to the wealthiest members of society, especially those who owned land.

Within the aristocracy those who received official recognition of their hereditary status, including their titles of honor and special legal privileges, were known as the nobility°. In the Middle Ages the nobility consisted mainly of warriors who prided themselves on their courage and military skill. Over the course of many centuries these military functions became less important, although many noblemen, especially in central and eastern Europe, continued to serve as military officers in the armies of the state during the eighteenth century.

The aristocracy for the most part lived on their estates in the countryside, but they also spent time in the cities and towns, where many of them maintained townhouses or even large palaces. In cities that were centers of national government, such as Madrid and Berlin, aristocrats were prominent members of the royal court. As royal judges, some members of the aristocracy also took an active part in the administration of the law in the cities, just as they did in the provinces. The aristocracy, therefore, maintained a visible and powerful presence in urban society.

By the eighteenth century most European aristocracies included a relatively small group of titled noblemen (such as dukes and counts) who possessed great wealth and political influence and a much larger group of lesser aristocrats, occasionally referred to as gentry, who sometimes did not even bear hereditary titles. In Spain a vast gulf separated a few hundred titled noblemen, the *titulos,* and thousands of sometimes poverty-stricken *hidalgos.* In Britain a few hun-

# Merchants Become Members of the Aristocracy in England

*Daniel Defoe is most famous for his novels, such as* Robinson Crusoe *(1719) and* Moll Flanders *(1722), but he also wrote commentaries on contemporary English politics and society. In* The English Tradesman *(1726), which is excerpted here, Defoe argued that the wealth of England "lies mainly among the trading part of the people." To support his argument he presented evidence that many members of the English aristocracy came from trading backgrounds. England was unusual in the opportunities it offered for this type of upward social mobility, but Defoe nonetheless overstated his case. Even the English aristocracy of the eighteenth century was not open to such frequent entry from below.*

This being the case in England, and our trade being so vastly great, it is no wonder that the tradesmen in England fill the lists of our nobility and gentry; no wonder that the gentlemen of the best families marry tradesmen's daughters, and put their younger sons' apprentices to tradesmen; and how often do these younger sons come to buy the elder sons' estates, and restore the family, when the elder and head of the house, proving rakish and extravagant, has wasted his patrimony, and is obliged to make out the blessing of Israel's family, where the younger son brought the birthright, and the elder was doomed to serve him?

Trade is so far here from being inconsistent with a gentleman, that in short trade in England makes gentlemen, and has peopled this nation with gentlemen; for after a generation or two the tradesmen's children, or at least their grand-children, come to be as good gentlemen, statesmen, parliament-men, privy counselors, judges, bishops and noblemen, as those of the highest birth and the most ancient families; and nothing too high for them. Thus the earl of Haversham was originally a merchant; the late Secretary Craggs was the son of a barber; the present Lord Castlemaine's father was a tradesman, the great grandfather of the present Duke of Bedford the same, and so of several others. . . .

We see the tradesmen of England, as they grow wealthy, coming every day to the herald's office, to search for the coats of arms of their ancestors, in order to paint them upon their coaches, and engrave them upon their furniture, or carve them upon the pediments of their new houses; and how often do we see them trace the registers of their families up to the prime nobility, or the most ancient gentry of the kingdom?

Source: From Daniel Defoe, *The Complete English Tradesman,* Volume I, 1726.

dred titled noblemen, known as peers, took precedence over some 50,000 families that belonged to the gentry. In Poland the nobility, known as the *szlachta,* was divided between a tiny, powerful group of magnates and some 700,000 noblemen of much more modest means who constituted more than 10 percent of the entire population.

The aristocracy was not completely closed to outsiders. Commoners could gain entrance to it, especially its lower ranks, on the basis of acquired wealth or government service. It was not unusual for lawyers, wealthy merchants, or accomplished state servants to accumulate wealth during their careers, use that wealth to purchase land, and then receive a recognition of their new status in the form of a title of nobility. Many of the men to whom Peter the Great of Russia gave titles of nobility in the early eighteenth century were commoners. In France, where the old "nobility of the sword" could be distinguished from the "nobility of the robe" that ascended through state service, more than 20 percent of mid-eighteenth-century noblemen could not trace their noble status back further than two generations.

It was also possible for prosperous farmers to enter the aristocracy by purchasing land, hiring manual laborers to perform agricultural work, and then adopting the leisured lifestyle, dress, and manners of aristocrats. These men did not bear titles, but they expected to be regarded as having the same status as other members of the lesser aristocracy. Occasionally women of nonnoble birth gained entry into aristocratic society by marriage. This usually occurred when a nobleman who was greatly in debt arranged to marry his son to the daughter of a wealthy merchant in order to secure the dowry from the father of the bride. The dowry became the price of the daughter's admission to the nobility.

In the sixteenth and seventeenth centuries the size of the aristocracy had grown faster than the general population, as a result of both economic prosperity and the expansion of the state bureaucracy. In eastern Europe monarchs had increased the number of hereditary noblemen in order to gain their services for the state. In the eighteenth century the size of the aristocracy stabilized and in many countries declined, as nobles took steps to restrict the number of newcomers from the lower orders. It was never a very large social group. The number of titled nobles was almost always less than 1 percent of the total population, and even when lesser nobles or gentry are taken into account, their total numbers usually amounted to no more than 4 percent. Only in Poland and Hungary did the percentages climb to more than 10 percent. Because of the small size of this social group, many nobles knew each other, especially those who were members of the same political assembly or who served together at court. The aristocracy was in fact the only real class° in European society before the early nineteenth century, in the sense that they formed a cohesive social group with similar economic and political interests, which they were determined to protect.

## The Wealth of the Aristocracy

The aristocracy was without question the wealthiest social group in all European countries, and during the eighteenth century many members of this group became even wealthier. The most prosperous aristocratic families lived in stupendous luxury. They built magnificent homes on their country estates and surrounded them with finely manicured gardens. In the cities, where service at court demanded more of their time, they built spacious palaces, entertained guests on a lavish scale, and purchased everything from expensive clothes to artistic treasures. They consumed the best food and wines they could find at home or abroad. This ostentatious display of wealth was intended to confirm their social importance and status.

Most of the income that supported the lifestyle of the aristocracy came directly or indirectly from land. In all European countries the aristocracy owned at least one-third of all the land, and in some countries, such as England and Denmark, they owned more than four-fifths of it. Even in the Italian states, where many of the nobility had come from families of merchants, they controlled large estates. Land provided the aristocracy with either feudal dues or rents from the peasants who lived and worked on their estates. Because noblemen did not engage in manual labor themselves, it is not surprising that they later came to be seen as unproductive parasites living off the labor of others.

During the first half of the eighteenth century the collective wealth of the European aristocracy reached new heights. In eastern Europe that increase in wealth derived mainly from the dramatic increase in the size of the population. With more serfs under their control, the landed nobility could increase the wealth they gained from their labor and dues. In western European countries, most notably Britain and France, the members of the aristocracy increasingly participated in other forms of economic activity. They operated rural industries such as mining and forestry. They entered the financial world by lending money to the government, thus serving the state in the process. They became involved in urban building projects and in the economic development of overseas colonies. Those who came from old families considered these pursuits to be beneath the status of a nobleman, but by investing at a distance nobles could give the impression that they were not actually engaged in the sordid transactions of the marketplace.

### Size of the Aristocracy in European States in the Eighteenth Century

| Country | Date | Number of Nobles and Lesser Aristocrats | Percent of the Population |
|---|---|---|---|
| Austria | 1800 | 90,000 | 1.15% |
| France | 1775 | 400,000 | 1.60 |
| Great Britain & Ireland | 1783 | 50,000 | 3.25 |
| Hungary | 1800 | 400,000 | 11.25 |
| Poland | 1800 | 700,000 | 11.66 |
| Russia | 1800 | 600,000 | 1.66 |
| Spain | 1797 | 402,000 | 3.80 |
| Sweden | 1757 | 10,000 | 0.50 |
| Venice | 1797 | 1,090 | 0.80 |

*Sources:* A. Corvisier, *Armies and Society in Europe, 1494–1789* (1976), pp. 113, 115; J. Meyer, *Noblesses et pouvoirs dans l'Europe d'Ancien Régime* (1973); M. Reinard and A. Armenguard, *Histoire Générale de la Population Modiale* (1961); J. Dewald, *The European Nobility* (1996), pp. 22–27.

The members of the eighteenth-century aristocracy are often described as social and economic conservatives who were unable or unwilling to act in an entrepreneurial manner. The financial and commercial projects that many noblemen engaged in suggest that this reputation of the aristocracy is not fully deserved. Even on their landed estates, the aristocracy often behaved in a capitalistic manner during the seventeenth and eighteenth centuries. Many members of the aristocracy, both titled and untitled, adopted capitalist techniques of estate management to make their lands more productive. In England a nobleman, Charles Townshend, became widely known as "Turnip Townshend" when he introduced a crop rotation that included the lowly turnip. This type of agrarian entrepreneurship accounts for the accumulation of many great eighteenth-century aristocratic fortunes.

## The Political Power of the Aristocracy

The mid-eighteenth century also marked the apex of political power for the aristocracy in Europe. Having recovered from the economic and political turmoil of the mid-seventeenth century, when they suffered economic losses and experienced a temporary eclipse of their power, noblemen pursued various strategies to increase or preserve their share of local and national political power. In

**Marriage into the Nobility**

This painting by William Hogarth, in a series titled *Marriage à la Mode,* depicts the negotiation of a marriage contract between an English earl and a wealthy London merchant. The earl, seated to the left and pointing to his family tree, is negotiating with the merchant sitting across the table. The marriage will take place between the earl's vain son, sitting to the far right, and the distracted daughter of the merchant, sitting next to him. The two individuals who are about to be married have no interest in each other. The earl has incurred large debts from building the large mansion depicted in the rear, and he intends to use the dowry to recover financially. By virtue of this transaction the daughter will enter aristocratic society.

England, where royal power was greatly restricted as a result of the Glorious Revolution, the aristocracy gained political dominance. A small group of noblemen sat in the House of Lords, while the gentry formed the large majority of members of the House of Commons. After 1689 the English king could not rule without the cooperation of these two Houses of Parliament. The monarchy tried to control the proceedings of that assembly by creating parties of royal supporters within both houses. Because those parties were controlled by the king's ministers, who were themselves members of the nobility, the system allowed the aristocracy to dominate.

A similar situation prevailed in Poland and Hungary, where only the nobility were represented in the legislative assemblies of those countries. In Sweden and most German states the nobility formed a separate group that voted by themselves within the representative assemblies of those kingdoms. The country in Europe where members of the aristocracy exercised the least power and influence was the Dutch Republic. The traditional Dutch landed nobility remained a force to be reckoned with in eighteenth-century politics, but wealthy merchants and bankers held the balance of power in the seven Dutch provinces.

In absolute monarchies, where rulers had succeeded in restricting independent aristocratic power, members of the aristocracy exercised political power by controlling the institutions through which royal power was exercised. As we have seen in Chapter 15, absolute monarchs appeased the aristocracy by giving them control over provincial government and by recruiting them to occupy offices in the central bureaucracy of the state. The large bureaucracy of the eighteenth-century French state, for example, was run mainly by noblemen of the robe, a privileged group of approximately 2,000 officials who owed their noble status to their appointment to office rather than to heredity. In Russia during the early eighteenth century, tsars granted the nobility privileges and strengthened their powers over their serfs in order to secure the assistance the tsars needed to administer the Russian state at the local level.

The aristocracy also exercised political power through the judiciary. Members of the aristocracy often served as judges of the law courts of their kingdoms. In England noblemen and gentry served as the judges of almost all the common law courts, hearing cases both at the center of government at Westminster and in the provinces. In France noblemen staffed the nine regional *parlements* that registered royal edicts and acted as a court of appeal in criminal cases. The nobility controlled the central tribunals of the German kingdoms and principalities. At the local level the nobility exercised either a personal jurisdiction over the peasants who lived on their lands or an official jurisdiction as magistrates, such as the justices of the peace in each English county.

Britain provides a vivid example of the way in which the members of the landed class could use their judicial power to keep the lower classes in line: punishing petty crimes with harsh penalties. During the eighteenth century the incidence of crimes against property increased, especially when war created shortages of basic commodities. Those who occupied the middle ranks of society were the most frequent victims of these crimes, but as men of great wealth the aristocracy believed that all crimes against property threatened them as well. The aristocracy responded to this threat by passing legislation making even minor crimes against property, such as petty theft, capital offenses punishable by death. One victim of this harsh policy was John Burton, a lowly paid wagon driver who was hanged in 1744 for stealing two woolen caps.

Not all those convicted of such petty crimes suffered the same punishment as Burton. A few public executions every year were deemed sufficient to deter crime in a country that did not have a police force. Most convicted criminals were pardoned or had their sentences reduced. These displays of judicial mercy also served the purposes of the aristocracy by making people from the lower ranks of society dependent upon them for their lives. Exercising the power of pardon also strengthened their authority and made them appear sympathetic to the poor. In this way the British aristocracy helped to maintain the traditional deference paid to them from the lower ranks of society.

## The Cultural World of the Aristocracy

During the eighteenth century the aristocracies in western European countries followed a lifestyle that emphasized their learning, refinement, and appreciation of the fine arts. It had not always been that way. As late as the fifteenth century the aristocracy, which in the Middle Ages had been a warrior class, had a reputation for their indifference or

even hostility to learning, and their conduct was often uncouth if not boorish. In eastern Europe a tradition of aristocratic illiteracy persisted into the eighteenth century. In western and central Europe, however, the pattern began to change in the sixteenth century, when members of the aristocracy started providing for the education of their children either at universities or in private academies. Even more important, aristocratic families began to acquire the manners and social graces that would be acceptable at court. By the eighteenth century the aristocracy, especially its upper ranks, became the backbone of what was then called "polite society."

The aristocracy also developed a sophisticated appreciation of high culture. Their homes housed large private collections of artwork that occasionally rivaled or even surpassed those of contemporary European monarchs. They were the main participants in the cultural life of European cities, especially Paris, London, Rome, Vienna, and Berlin. They formed the audiences of musical recitals, attended plays and operas in large numbers, and frequented the art galleries that were established in all the capitals of Europe. They also became the patrons of musicians, writers, and artists.

The homes of the eighteenth-century aristocracy reflected their preference for classicism°, a style in art, architecture, music, and literature that emphasizes proportion, adherence to traditional forms, and a rejection of emotion and enthusiasm. The classicism of the eighteenth century marked a step away from the more dynamic, imposing baroque style, which had flourished in the seventeenth century. Classicism celebrated the culture of ancient Greece and Rome. The revival of that culture in the eighteenth century in art and architecture is often referred to as neoclassicism°. The residences of the eighteenth-century aristocracy built in the classical style were perfectly proportioned and elegant without being overly decorated. Their Greek columns and formal gardens, lined with statues of classical figures, served as symbols of their cultural heritage. The classical architecture of the eighteenth century reflected the quiet confidence of the aristocracy that they, like their Greek and Roman forebears, occupied a dominant position in society.

Eighteenth-century music, which is likewise referred to as classical, reflected a concern for formal design, proportion, and concise melodic expression. The two greatest composers of the eighteenth century, Franz Joseph Haydn (1732–1809) and Wolfgang Amadeus Mozart (1756–1791), whose music was played before predominantly aristocratic audiences, became the most famous composers in this tradition. Classical music appealed less to the emotions than either the baroque music of the seventeenth century or the romantic music of the nineteenth century. The dominance of classicism in music as well as architecture during the eighteenth century reflected broader cultural currents in

**Chiswick House**

This house was built by Lord Burlington as a library and reception hall on his estate near London about 1725. Symmetrical, balanced, and restrained, the building embodies many of the features of classicism. Chiswick House was modeled on the architecture of the Italian Andrea Palladio (1518–1580), who in turn drew his inspiration from the buildings of ancient Rome.

European intellectual life, when science and philosophy placed the highest value on the rationality and order of all material and human life.

in the French Revolution, and they also showed their resourcefulness by accommodating themselves to the new order, but they never recovered the dominant position they had held in the eighteenth century.

# Challenges to Aristocratic Dominance

■ How did subordinate social groups, most notably the rural peasantry and those who lived in the towns, challenge the aristocracy during the late eighteenth century?

Starting around the middle of the eighteenth century, the aristocracy endured increasingly acrimonious challenges to their power and criticisms of their values and lifestyles. They gradually lost the respect that they commanded from the lower ranks of society. By the end of the century European aristocracies had been significantly weakened. Their values had been called into question, while their political power and privileges had been eroded. A claim of nobility began to be viewed more as a sign of vanity than as a natural right to rule. The revolution that took place in France in the last decade of the eighteenth century, followed by the reform movements that developed in its wake throughout Europe in the early nineteenth century, brought the age of aristocracy to an end. Members of the aristocracy managed to regain some of what they had lost

## Encounters with the Rural Peasantry

One set of challenges to the aristocracy came from the peasants and serfs who lived and worked on landed estates. This was the social group over whom the aristocracy exercised the most direct control. The control was most oppressive in central and eastern Europe, where the rural masses were serfs and therefore had no personal freedom. Landlords not only determined where serfs lived and when they married, but they also collected burdensome financial duties from them. Their plight was relieved only partially by the elimination of some of the burdens of serfdom. In Prussia and Austria these obligations were abolished by royal edict. The monarchs who instituted these reforms may have been responding to the demands of philosophes°, the intellectuals and writers of the age, who condemned the institution of serfdom for its cruelty and inefficiency. (See the section on the Enlightenment later in this chapter.) A more powerful motive, however, was the desire of monarchs to collect taxes from a peasantry that was spending the greater part of its income on financial duties owed to aristocratic landowners. Because the peasants still remained overburdened by financial obligations, emancipation did little to improve their lot.

In western Europe, where serfdom had for the most part given way to tenant ownership and leasehold tenure, the condition of the rural masses was only marginally better. After 1720, famines became less common than they had been in the late seventeenth century, making it possible for peasants to eke out an existence, but other economic pressures, including the elimination of common pasture rights and an increase in taxation, continued to weigh down on them. Over the course of the eighteenth century the number of peasants owning small plots of land declined. Many of those who leased land were forced to sell it as landowners consolidated their holdings. Consequently the number of landless laborers who worked for wages increased. By 1789 almost half the peasants in France had no land at all.

Under these circumstances the relationship between peasants and landowners continued to deteriorate. The realities of the marketplace gradually eroded the paternalistic concern that the nobility had traditionally shown for the welfare of their serfs or tenants. As the relationship between landlord and peasant became predominantly economic, the two parties became more distant. At the same time the gap between the culture of the elite and that of the common people, which as we have seen in Chapter 16 began in the seventeenth century, became more pronounced. The distance between landlord and peasant assumed real geographical form as landlords built their mansions away from the local village. By surrounding their homes with acres of parkland and gardens, they shielded themselves from the sight of the peasants working in the fields. Visual and personal contact between lord and peasant therefore became less frequent. The most direct contact a landlord made with the members of the lower classes was with the servants who worked in their homes.

As economic pressures on the peasants mounted, conflict between them and the aristocracy increased. Peasant resistance to their landlords could take a number of different forms. In some countries, most notably France, peasants could bring their grievances before village assemblies. These democratic institutions often succeeded in upholding peasants' demands, especially when royal officials in the provinces, who wished to collect their own taxes from the peasants, sided with them against the nobility.

Another option was to file a lawsuit against the lord, often with the assistance of the royal government. In Burgundy numerous peasant communities hired lawyers to take their seigneurs° or lords to court in order to prevent the imposition of new financial dues or the confiscation of communal village land. They were often aided in these efforts by the agents of the royal government, who wanted the peasants to be able to pay higher taxes imposed by the king. In these lawsuits, which became very common in the second half of the eighteenth century, peasants challenged not only the imposition of seigneurial dues but the very institution of aristocratic lordship. In 1765 one lawyer representing a peasant community in Champagne argued that the

rights claimed by landowners "derive from the violence of seigneurs" and had always been "odious." The language used in these cases inspired much of the rhetoric employed in the abolition of feudal privilege at the time of the French Revolution (see Chapter 19).

Peasants occasionally took more direct action against their landlords. In eastern France the number of incidents of rural violence against the property of seigneurs who tried to collect new duties increased toward the end of the eighteenth century. In Ireland a group known as the Whiteboys maimed cattle and tore down fences when landowners denied tenants their common grazing rights. Other forms of peasant action included poaching on the lands of landowners who claimed the exclusive right to hunt or trap game on their estates. The hunting activities of the tenants of the Earl of Uxbridge discussed at the beginning of this chapter are just one example of this type of lower-class resistance to aristocratic privilege.

In western Europe these acts of resistance did not develop into widespread peasant rebellion until the outbreak of the French Revolution in 1789. During the late eighteenth century incidents of rural violence were largely confined to individual villages. The reduction in the incidence of famine in the eighteenth century provides one possible explanation for this pattern of isolated, localized resistance. Without recurrent subsistence crises, the plight of the rural masses was not sufficiently desperate to provoke large-scale rebellion. The only expressions of collective unrest over the supply of food in western Europe during the eighteenth century were urban riots. These food riots usually took place in market towns or ports where grain was being exported. The violence was not directed against landlords but merchants or officials who were suspected of hoarding grain or fixing the price of bread.

The economic and social situation in eastern Europe differed from that of France, Britain, and other western European countries. In the east the deteriorating economic condition of the peasantry led to large-scale rebellion. Bohemia, Hungary, and Croatia, all of which lay within the boundaries of the Austrian Habsburg monarchy, witnessed large peasant revolts in the 1780s. The bloodiest of these revolts occurred in the province of Transylvania in 1784, when 30,000 peasant rebels butchered hundreds of noblemen and their families after those landowners had raised the dues owed to them as much as 1,000 percent.

The largest eastern European rural rebellion took place in Russia between 1773 and 1774. Pretending to be the murdered Tsar Peter III (d. 1762), the Cossack Emelian Pugachev (1726–1775) set out to destroy the Russian government of Catherine the Great and the nobility that served it. Pugachev assembled an army of 8,000 men, which staged lightning raids against government centers in the southern Urals. The most serious phase of this uprising took place when these troops marched into the agricultural regions of the country and inspired as many as three million serfs to revolt. Pugachev promised to abolish serfdom, end taxation, and eliminate the lesser aristocracy. The rebellion took a heavy toll, as the serfs and soldiers murdered some 3,000 nobles and officials. The Russian upper class feared that the rebellion would spread and destroy the entire social order, but government troops prevented that from happening by brutally suppressing the rising. Pugachev was transported to Moscow in an iron cage, where he was hanged, quartered, and burned.

Neither Pugachev nor the serfs who joined his rebellion envisioned the creation of a new social order. They still spoke in conservative terms of regaining ancient freedoms that had been lost. But this massive revolt, like others that resembled it, reflected the depth of the tension that prevailed between landlord and peasant, between nobleman and serf, in the apparently stable world of the eighteenth century. That tension serves as one of the most striking and ominous themes of eighteenth-century social history.

## The Social Position of the Bourgeoisie

In the cities and towns the most serious challenges to the aristocracy came not from the urban masses, who posed an occasional threat to all urban authorities, but from the bourgeoisie°. This social group was more heterogeneous than the aristocracy. It consisted of untitled people of property who lived in the cities and towns. The word *bourgeoisie* refers to those who were burghers—or those who had voting rights in the towns. Prosperous merchants and financiers formed the upper ranks of the bourgeoisie, while members of the legal and medical professions, second-tier government officials, and emerging industrialists occupied a social niche just below them. The bourgeoisie also included some skilled artisans and shopkeepers, sometimes referred to as the "petty bourgeoisie," who were far more prosperous than the large mass of urban laborers. The size of the bourgeoisie grew as the urban population of Europe expanded during the eighteenth century, even before the advent of industrialization. This social group was far more numerous in the North Atlantic countries of France, the Dutch Republic, and Britain than in the states of central and eastern Europe. In England the bourgeoisie accounted for about 15 percent of the total population in 1800, whereas in Russia they constituted no more than 3 percent.

Because it was possible for some members of the bourgeoisie to achieve upward social mobility and join the ranks of the aristocracy, the social and economic boundaries separating these wealthy townsmen from the lower ranks of the nobility could become blurred. In French towns it was often difficult to distinguish between wealthy financiers and noble bureaucrats. Although the two groups received their income from different sources, they both belonged to a wealthy, propertied elite. The middle and lower ranks of the

**Joshua Reynolds, *Mary, Duchess of Richmond* (ca. 1765)**
At a time when most European noblewomen were attracting criticism for their luxury and vanity, this prominent English duchess was depicted as being engaged in the simple domestic task of needlepoint. Some members of the aristocracy were able to deflect criticism of their lifestyle by adopting the habits of the bourgeoisie.

bourgeoisie, however, gradually emerged as a social group that acquired its own social, political, and cultural identity distinct from that of the aristocracy.

Bourgeois identity was rooted in the towns, which had their own political institutions and their own social hierarchies. The bourgeoisie also possessed the means of effectively communicating with each other and thus were capable of forming common political goals. Their high rates of literacy made them the core of the new political force of public opinion that emerged in the cities and towns in the eighteenth century. The bourgeoisie made up the main audience of the thousands of newspapers, pamphlets, and books that rolled off the presses during the eighteenth century. A "public sphere" of activity, in which politically conscious townsmen participated, became a peculiar feature of bourgeois society. During the eighteenth and early nineteenth centuries the bourgeoisie became the leaders of movements seeking political change. They organized and became the main participants in the protest movements,

# Bathing in the West

One of the personal habits that members of the European aristocracy and bourgeoisie began to adopt in the eighteenth century was frequent bathing. Until that time people in the West had been reluctant to immerse their bodies in water. In this respect there was a clear difference between Western and Eastern practice. Among Asians who practiced the Hindu religion, bathing had deep religious significance and was a daily ritual. The same was true for Muslims, for whom water possessed a sacred purifying role and prepared the bather for prayer or sacrifice. In the West bathing was not invested with similar religious significance. Christianity had emphasized purity of heart, not of the body. Without a religious inspiration, bathing the body rarely occurred in Western nations during the early modern period. Europeans might wash various parts of their body, especially the hands and face, but total immersion was almost unheard of. The few who did bathe usually did so no more than once a year, and tubs and basins were not widely available. Swimming in rivers and lakes was dangerous and often resulted in drowning. Even medical opinion conspired against bathing. According to one seventeenth-century French doctor, "bathing outside the practice of medicine was not only superfluous but very damaging to health."

By the beginning of the nineteenth century, many Europeans had begun to take regular baths. The sale of washbasins and commercially produced soap soared. This change occurred as a result of three distinct factors. The first was the insistence by many eighteenth-century Protestants that Christianity did indeed demand a clean body as well as a clean soul. The eighteenth-century founder of Methodism, the English preacher John Wesley, coined a new proverb when he declared that "cleanliness is indeed next to godliness."

A second reason was that cleanliness became associated with gentility and good manners. Bodily cleanliness became one of the ways in which members of society who considered themselves civilized made themselves attractive to the people with whom they associated. This explains why bathing the body all over was first adopted by the upper classes, who contrasted themselves with the dirty lower classes. It also became more common among women than men. The third reason was a change in medical opinion, which began to view bathing as a means to keep the pores of the skin open and thus promote perspiration. Bathing came to be viewed as a means of curing numerous diseases and as a key to long life.

The acceptance of bathing in the West owed something to Eastern influence. Eighteenth-century Western writers often commented on the daily bathing of Turks and Hindus, and Europeans who lived in the East had the opportunity to witness firsthand a custom that contrasted strikingly with their own. The period of most pronounced influence was the mid-eighteenth century, when many other features of Eastern culture penetrated the West. In the early nineteenth century a Hindu noted that bathing in the West was still very different from that practiced in his own country. Nevertheless, the reluctant European adoption of immersing the body in water had brought about a minor accommodation between Eastern and Western practice.

## For Discussion

What does the widespread practice of bathing in Asia and the reluctance of Europeans to adopt this practice tell us about the differences between Eastern and Western cultures in the eighteenth century?

**Jean-Jacques Henner, *Chaste Susanna at Her Bath* (1865)**
By the nineteenth century, Europeans had adopted the practice of bathing the entire body.

petitioning drives, and ultimately the revolutionary steps taken to challenge and replace established regimes.

## The Bourgeois Critique of the Aristocracy

At the core of bourgeois identity lay a set of values that contrasted with those attributed to the aristocracy, especially the noblemen and noblewomen who gathered at court. Not all members of the bourgeoisie shared these values, nor did all members of the nobility embody those attributed to them. Nonetheless, the bourgeois critique of aristocratic society, which flourished mainly among the lower or petty bourgeoisie rather than the great merchants and financiers, contributed to the formation of bourgeois identity and helped to erode respect for the traditional aristocracy.

The bourgeois critique of the aristocracy consisted of three related themes. First was the allegation that the aristocracy lived a life of luxury, hedonism, and idleness that contrasted with the thrifty, sober, hardworking petty bourgeoisie. Unlike the aristocracy, the bourgeoisie did not display their wealth. Second, court nobles were accused of being sexually promiscuous and immoral, while their wives were depicted as vain flirts. There was some foundation to this charge, especially because the predominance of arranged marriages within the nobility had induced many noble husbands and wives to seek sexual partners outside marriage, a practice that was widely tolerated within aristocratic circles. By contrast, the bourgeoisie tended to enter into marriages in which both partners remained faithful to each other. Third, the members of the aristocracy were considered participants in a decadent international culture that often ignored or degraded the more wholesome, patriotic values of the bourgeoisie.

This critique of the aristocracy had profound political implications. It laid the foundation for the demands for equal political rights and the advancement of careers on the basis of talent rather than inherited wealth. These demands came not from the wealthy financiers, merchants, and capitalists who had the opportunity to ascend into the ranks of the nobility but from men of more modest wealth: holders of minor political offices, shopkeepers, and even skilled artisans. These people from the middle ranks of society, especially those who lived in the cities and towns, were most responsible for eventually reducing the influence of the aristocracy in European political and social life.

Criticism of aristocratic values and demands for liberty and equality received support from intellectuals who are usually identified with the movement known as the Enlightenment°. Not all of these thinkers and writers came from the middle ranks of society. Many of them were in fact members of the aristocracy or the beneficiaries of aristocratic patronage. Nevertheless their goal was to bring about the reform of society, and that inevitably led to a critique of aristocratic values and practices.

# The Enlightenment

■ What were the main features of Enlightenment thought and how did it present a threat to the old order?

The Enlightenment was the defining intellectual and cultural movement of the eighteenth century. This complex movement had roots in the seventeenth century; the Scientific Revolution and the growth of philosophical skepticism were particularly important influences (see Chapter 16). Contemporaries used the word *Enlightenment* to describe their own intellectual outlook and achievements. For Immanuel Kant (1724–1804), the renowned German philosopher and author of *Critique of Pure Reason* (1781), enlightenment was the expression of intellectual maturity, the attainment of understanding solely by using one's reason without being influenced by dogma, superstition, or another person's opinion. For Kant enlightenment was both the process of thinking for oneself and the knowledge of human society and human nature that one achieved as a result. His famous exhortation, "Have the courage to know!" could serve as a slogan for the entire Enlightenment.

The Enlightenment is often referred to as a French movement, and it is true that the most famous of the European writers and thinkers of the Enlightenment, known as philosophes, were French. It was also in France that the Enlightenment first became a campaign to change people's minds and reform institutions. But French philosophes were inspired by seventeenth-century English sources, especially the writings of Isaac Newton (1647–1727) and John Locke (1632–1704), while German, Scottish, Dutch, Swiss, and Italian writers made their own distinctive contributions to Enlightenment thought. The ideas of the Enlightenment also spread to the Americas, where they inspired movements for political reform and national independence. The men and women of the Enlightenment thought of themselves not so much as French, British, or Dutch but as members of an international Republic of Letters, not unlike the international community of scholars that had arisen within the ancient Roman Empire and again at the time of the Renaissance. This cosmopolitan literary republic knew no geographical boundaries, and it was open to ideas from all lands (see Map 18.1). Its literary achievements, however, bore a distinctly Western stamp, and the ideas its members promoted became essential components of Western civilization.

## Themes of Enlightenment Thought

Because the Enlightenment spanned the entire continent and lasted for more than a century, it is difficult to establish characteristics that all its participants shared. The Enlightenment was more a frame of mind, an approach to

**Map 18.1   The European Enlightenment**

The map shows the birthplaces of thinkers and writers of the Enlightenment. The greatest number of them came from France and Britain, but all European countries were represented, and the men and women of the Enlightenment thought of themselves as belonging to an international "Republic of Letters" that knew no political boundaries.

obtaining knowledge, as Kant claimed, than a set of clearly defined beliefs. Enlightenment writers, however, emphasized several intellectual themes that gave the entire movement a certain degree of unity and coherence.

### Reason and the Laws of Nature

The first theme emphasized by Enlightenment thinkers was the elevation of human reason to a position of paramount philosophical importance. Enlightenment thinkers placed almost unlimited confidence in the ability of human beings to understand how the world operates. In previous ages philosophers had always found a place for human reason, but they also placed limits on it, especially when it came into conflict with religious faith. Medieval scholastic philosophers had tried to reconcile faith and reason, and that effort continued through the seventeenth century, par-

ticularly in scientific circles. In the eighteenth century, however, greater emphasis was placed on reason alone, which was believed to be superior to religious faith and the final arbiter of all disputes.

Confidence in human reason was closely associated with the belief that the operation of the entire universe was governed by natural laws that human reason could discover. This belief in natural law can be traced back to the ancient Greeks and to its revival and assimilation to Christian theology by the scholastics in the Middle Ages. Natural law acquired a distinctive character at the time of the Scientific Revolution. The search for and discovery of the laws governing such phenomena as gravitation, the circulation of the blood, and dynamics gradually led to the belief that all activity, including the behavior of human beings, was governed by similar laws.

The application of natural law to human society was the most novel and distinctive feature of Enlightenment thought. According to Enlightenment thinkers, scientific laws governed the functioning of society. There were even laws governing the passions and the operation of the human psyche. In his *Treatise of Human Nature* (1739–1740), the Scottish philosopher David Hume (1711–1776) offered a science of the human mind, which could be applied to politics and other human endeavors. Economics, too, received the same treatment. The Scottish economist Adam Smith (1723–1790), who described the operation of economic life in *The Wealth of Nations* (1776), believed that the economy was subject to inviolable laws, just like those that governed the movement of the heavens. The Enlightenment therefore gave birth to modern social science. Economics, political science, sociology, anthropology, and psychology all trace their origins as intellectual disciplines to this time. They were all based on the premise that reason could discover the laws or principles of human nature.

**DOCUMENT**

Adam Smith, Introduction to *The Wealth of Nations* (1776)

The search for natural laws governing all human life provides one explanation for the unprecedented interest of eighteenth-century writers in non-European cultures. During the Enlightenment a vast literature subjected the peoples of the world to detailed description, classification, and analysis. The first thorough, scholarly studies of Indian, Chinese, and Arab cultures were published during the middle and late eighteenth century. Egypt, a country that had been a part of the Ottoman Empire and isolated from the West since the sixteenth century, became the subject of a sizable literature, especially after the French occupied the country in 1798. There also was an increase in travel literature describing the societies that Europeans were encountering, some of them for the first time. Descriptions of the indigenous peoples of northwestern Canada, Australia, and Tahiti became readily available in the bookshops of Paris and London.

This cross-cultural scholarship, which was facilitated by the rapid growth of overseas empires after 1660, served the purpose of providing intellectuals with information enabling them to discover laws governing the behavior of all people. Some of the non-European countries that these scholars studied, such as China, had highly developed civilizations, whereas those of Native Americans and the indigenous people of the South Sea islands were far less developed. In both cases, however, educated people in the West began to consider these non-Western societies valid subjects of intellectual inquiry.

## Religion and Morality

The spread of scientific knowledge in the eighteenth century gave the thinkers of the Enlightenment a new understanding of God and his relationship to humankind. The Christian God of the Middle Ages and the Reformation period was an all-knowing, personal God who often intervened in the life of human beings. He could be stern and severe or gentle and merciful, but he was always involved in the affairs of humankind, which he governed through Providence. The gradual recognition that the universe was of unfathomable size and that it operated in accordance with natural laws made God appear more remote. Most philosophes believed that God was still the creator of the universe and the author of the natural laws that governed it, but they did not believe that he was still actively involved in its operation. God was the playwright of the universe, but not its director. This belief that God had created the universe, given it laws, and then allowed it to operate in a mechanistic fashion is known as deism°. In deism there was no place for the traditional Christian belief that God became human in order to redeem humankind from original sin.

Enlightenment thinkers, especially those who were deists, believed that human beings could use reason to discover the natural laws God had laid down at the time of creation. This inquiry included the discovery of the principles of morality, which no longer were to be grounded in Scripture. To observe the laws of God now meant not so much keeping his commandments but discovering what was natural and acting accordingly. In a certain sense God

**David Hume, Scottish Philosopher**
Like John Locke, Hume explored the process by which the human mind reaches an understanding of the material world. Hume was committed to the application of science to the human psyche.

was being remade in a human image and was being identified with the natural instincts of human beings. In this way religion could become equated with the pursuit of human happiness.

If one believed that God established natural laws for all humanity, then doctrinal differences between religions became less important. All religions were valid to the extent that they led to an understanding of natural law. There was no one true religion, a point that the German dramatist and philosopher Gotthold Lessing (1729–1781) made in his play *Nathan the Wise* (1779) in response to the persistent questioning of a fictional Turkish sultan. This denial of the existence of one true religion led naturally to a demand for toleration of all religions, including those of non-Western peoples.

Enlightenment thinkers were highly critical of the superstitious and dogmatic character of contemporary Christianity, especially Roman Catholicism. French philosophes in particular had little use for priests, whom they castigated relentlessly in their letters and pamphlets. They minimized the importance of religious belief in the con-

duct of human life and substituted rational for religious values. They had little respect for the academic discipline of theology. The German-born Parisian writer Baron d'Holbach (1723–1789), one of the few philosophes who could be considered an atheist—denying the existence of God at all—dismissed theology as a "pretended science." He claimed that its principles were "only hazardous suppositions, imagined by ignorance, propagated by enthusiasm or knavery, adopted by timid credulity, preserved by custom which never reasons, and revered solely because not understood."[1]

Epitomizing the new religious outlook of the Enlightenment was the Scottish moral philosopher David Hume, who is most famous for his treatise *An Enquiry Concerning Human Understanding* (1748). In that work he challenged the argument of the great rationalist philosopher René Descartes that God implants a number of clear and distinct ideas in our minds, from which we are able to deduce other truths. Hume's position was that our understanding derives from sense perceptions, not innate ideas. Even more important, he denied that there was any certain knowledge,

Hogarth pinx<sup></sup>                                                                T. Oole sculp<sup></sup>

CREDULITY, SUPERSTITION, & FANATICISM.

*Published by Longman, Hurst, Rees, & Orme, Jan<sup>y</sup> 1<sup>st</sup> 1809.*

### William Hogarth, *Credulity, Superstition, and Fanaticism* (1762)

Hogarth was a moralist who embodied the rationalism and humanitarianism of the Enlightenment. In this engraving he exposes the effects of fanatical religion, witchcraft, and superstition. The sermon has whipped the entire congregation into a highly emotional state. The woman in the foreground is Mary Tofts, who was believed to have given birth to rabbits. The boy next to her, allegedly possessed by the Devil, vomits pins. The Protestant preacher's wig falls off, exposing the shaven head of a Roman Catholic monk. An unemotional Turk observes this scene from outside the window.

thereby calling into question the authority of revealed truth and religious doctrine.

Hume's writing on religion reflected his skepticism. Raised a Presbyterian, he nevertheless rejected the revealed truths of Christianity on the ground that they had no rational foundation. The concept of Providence was completely alien to his philosophical position. An avowed deist, he expressed contempt for organized religion, especially Catholicism in France and Anglicanism in England. Organized religion, according to Hume, "renders men tame and submissive, is acceptable to the magistrate, and seems inoffensive to the people; till at last the priest, having firmly established his authority, becomes the tyrant and disturber of human society."[2]

## Progress and Reform

Theories regarding the stages of human development, coupled with the commitment of philosophes to the improvement and ultimate transformation of society, contributed to a belief in the progress of civilization. Until the eighteenth century the very notion of progress was alien to even the most highly educated Europeans. Those who held political power had dedicated themselves to maintaining the social and political order, not its transformation. Programs of reform were almost always associated with the restoration of a superior golden age rather than the realization of something new and different. If movement took place, it was cyclical rather than progressive. Even the original meaning of the word *revolution* was the path of a planet that came full circle in its orbit, not the creation of a new order. Now, however, the possibility of improvement began to dominate philosophical and political discussion. The Enlightenment was largely responsible for making this belief in progress, especially toward the attainment of social justice, a prominent feature of modern Western culture.

Some Enlightenment thinkers, using evidence gained from encounters with non-Western people, argued that all civilizations progressed gradually from relatively simple to more complex economies and societies. David Hume, Adam Smith, and their fellow Scotsman Adam Ferguson (1723–1816) identified four stages of human development. The first was characterized by hunting and gathering, the second by pastoral farming, the third by agriculture, and the last by commerce. The French philosophe the Marquis de Condorcet (1743–1794) focused more on intellectual progress. In *A Sketch for a Historical Picture of the Progress of the Human Mind* (1795), Condorcet identified nine distinct epochs in human history. He predicted that in the tenth and final epoch humankind would achieve a state of perfection in which rational moral judgments would inform efficient government policy.

Another source of the Enlightenment's belief in progress was the conviction that corrupt institutions could be reformed, thereby allowing societies to advance to a higher level and realize their full potential. The system of taxation, bureaucratic institutions, established churches, and the institution of monarchy itself all became the targets of Enlightenment reformers. The judicial institutions of government were particularly susceptible to this type of reforming zeal. Campaigns arose to eliminate the administration of judicial torture as well as capital punishment. All of this was intended to establish a more humane, civilized society.

The intellectual inspiration to this movement for legal reform was the work of the Italian jurist Cesare Beccaria (1738–1794). In his *Essay on Crimes and Punishments* (1764), Beccaria argued that punishment should be used not to exact retribution for crimes but to rehabilitate the criminal and to serve the interests of society. "In order that every punishment may not be an act of violence committed by one or by many against a private member of society," wrote Beccaria, "it should be above all things public, immediate, and necessary, the least possible in the case given, proportioned to the crime, and determined by the laws."[3] He called for the abolition of capital punishment and the imprisonment of convicted felons. The prison, which prior to the eighteenth century had been little more than a jail or holding facility, was now to become a symbol of the improvement of society.

## Voltaire and the Spirit of the Enlightenment

The philosophe who captured all the main themes as well as the spirit of the Enlightenment was the writer and philosopher François Marie Arouet (1694–1778), known universally by his pen name, Voltaire. Born into a French bourgeois family, Voltaire became one of the most prominent and prolific writers of the eighteenth century. Although he wrote for a fairly broad, predominantly bourgeois audience, and although he waged war against the injustices of aristocratic society, he was comfortable in the homes of the nobility and at the courts of European monarchs, especially that of Frederick the Great of Prussia. Voltaire's main career was as an author. He wrote plays and novels as well as poems, letters, essays, and history. These writings revealed his commitment to scientific rationality, his contempt for established religion, and his unflagging pursuit of liberty and justice.

**DOCUMENT**

Voltaire on the Relations Between Church and State (mid-18th c.)

Like many men of the Enlightenment, Voltaire developed a deep interest in science. He acquired much of his scientific knowledge from a learned noblewoman, Madame du Châtelet (1706–1749), a scientist and mathematician who translated the works of Newton into French. Madame du Châtelet became Voltaire's mistress, and the two lived together with her tolerant husband in their country estate in eastern France. The sexual freedom they experienced was characteristic of many Enlightenment figures, who rejected the Christian condemnation of

# A Case of Infanticide in the Age of the Enlightenment

A mid-eighteenth-century trial of a young French woman charged with killing her newborn child provides a window into the life of women who occupied the lower rungs of French society, in contrast to those who frequented the court and met in salons. The trial also raises the larger questions, debated in French and European judicial circles during the time of the Enlightenment, of how society should deal with the mothers of illegitimate children and whether the punishments prescribed for infanticide, or the killing of a young child, were proportionate to the crime.

In August 1742 Marie-Jeanne Bartonnet, a 21-year-old unmarried woman from a small French village in Brie, moved to Paris, where she took up residence with Claude le Queux, whom she had known in her youth, and Claude's sister. At that time Bartonnet was seven months pregnant. On October 22 Bartonnet caused a ruckus in the middle of the night when she went to the toilet and began groaning loudly and bleeding profusely. When her neighbors found her, and when she asked for towels for the blood, they suspected that she had had a miscarriage and called for a midwife. By the time the midwife arrived, it was clear that the delivery had already taken place and that the infant had fallen down the toilet to the cesspool five stories below. Suspecting that Bartonnet had killed the baby, the proprietress of the building reported her to the nearest judicial officer. The next day judicial authorities returned to the building and found the dead infant in the cesspool. An autopsy revealed that the child's skull had been dented by either a blunt instrument or a fall. After a med-

ical examination of Bartonnet revealed the signs of having just delivered a baby, she was arrested and imprisoned for the crime of infanticide.

Bartonnet came very close to being executed, but the strict procedures of French justice saved her from paying the ultimate price for her apparent crime. In the seventeenth and eighteenth centuries French criminal justice had established clear criteria for determining the guilt or innocence of a person accused of a crime. These procedures involved a systematic interrogation of the accused (only rarely under torture), the deposition of witnesses, the evaluation of physical evidence, and the confrontation of the accused with the witnesses who testified against her. There also was a mandatory review of the case, which involved a further interrogation of the defendant, before the Parlement of Paris, the highest court in northern France.

The interrogations of Bartonnet did not give her judges much evidence on which they could convict her. When asked the name of the village where she had lived in Brie, she told her interrogators, "It's none of your business." She denied that she had even known she was pregnant, refused to name the man with whom she had had intercourse, and claimed that she had mistaken her labor pains for colic or diarrhea. She denied picking her baby off the floor of the toilet after the delivery and throwing it into the cesspool. When presented with the baby's corpse, she claimed she did not recognize it.

After this interrogation, Bartonnet was given the opportunity to challenge the testimony of the witnesses who had seen her

the night of the delivery. The most damning testimony came from Madame Pâris, the wife of the proprietor, who had found Bartonnet on the toilet and thus could verify the circumstances of the clandestine delivery. Bartonnet's inability to challenge the testimony of Madame Pâris led directly to her initial conviction. After reviewing the entire dossier of evidence, the king's attorney recommended conviction for concealing her pregnancy, hiding her delivery, and destroying her child. French criminal procedure entrusted the decision of guilt or innocence to the judges themselves, and on November 27 they voted that Bartonnet should be executed by hanging.

Marie-Jeanne Bartonnet's fate, however, was not yet sealed. When her case went on appeal to the Parlement of Paris, Bartonnet repeated her statement that she had gone to the toilet but did not know whether she had given birth. Even though her execution was warranted by terms of an edict of 1557 that defined the crime of infanticide, the judges of this court voted to commute her sentence to a public whipping, banishment from the jurisdiction of the Parlement of Paris, and confiscation of her property. The basis of this decision appears to have been the absence of any proof that she had deliberately killed her baby. Indeed, its injuries could have been caused by its fall down the drain pipe into the cesspool. There was also the persistent refusal of the defendant to make a confession. She may have been lying, but it is equally possible that once she had delivered the baby, which happened very quickly, she convinced herself that it had not happened.

Bartonnet's trial for infanticide stands at the end of a long period of intense prosecution of this crime. Trials of this sort declined as cities and towns built foundling hospitals for abandoned infants and as the moral outrage for illegitimacy was redirected from the pregnant mother to the illegitimate father. The new legal values promoted at the time of the Enlightenment, moreover, made it less likely that any woman or man would be executed for this or any other crime.

## Questions of Justice

1. As in many trials, the facts of this case can be used to support different claims of justice. If you had been the prosecutor in this trial, what position would you have taken to prove the crime of infanticide? If you had been defending Marie-Jeanne Bartonnet, what arguments would you have used in her defense?

2. In his *Essay on Crimes and Punishments* (1764), Beccaria recommended that punishments be determined strictly in accordance with the social damage committed by the crime. What would Beccaria have said about the original sentence of death in this case? What would he have said about the modified sentence handed down by the Parlement of Paris?

## Taking It Further

Michael Wolfe, ed. *Changing Identities in Early Modern France.* 1997. Gives a full account of Marie-Jeanne Bartonnet's trial for infanticide.

**A Woman Accused of Murder in the Eighteenth Century**
With the exception of infanticide—the crime for which Marie-Jeanne Bartonnet was tried and convicted—few women were tried for capital crimes in the eighteenth century. One exception was Sarah Malcolm, a 22-year-old Englishwoman, shown here in a portrait by William Hogarth (1733). Malcolm was executed for slitting the throat of a wealthy lady in London.

sexual activity outside marriage and who justified their behavior on the basis of natural law and the pursuit of happiness. From Madame du Châtelet, Voltaire acquired not only an understanding of Newton's scientific laws but also a commitment to women's education and equality. Voltaire lived with her until she died in 1749 while giving birth to a child that was fathered neither by Voltaire nor her husband.

Voltaire's belief in a Newtonian universe—one governed by the universal law of gravitation—laid the foundation for his deism and his attacks on contemporary Christianity. In his *Philosophical Dictionary* (1764), he lashed out at established religion and the clergy, Protestant as well as Catholic. In a letter to another philosophe attacking religious superstition he pleaded, "Whatever you do, crush the infamous thing." In Voltaire's eyes Christianity was not only unreasonable; it was vulgar and barbaric. He condemned the Catholic Church for the slaughter of millions of indigenous people in the Americas on the grounds that they had not been baptized, as well as the executions of hundreds of thousands of Jews and heretics in Europe. All of these people were the victims of "barbarism and fanaticism."[4]

Voltaire's indictment of the Church for these barbarities was matched by his scathing criticism of the French government for a series of injustices, including his own imprisonment for insulting the regent of France. While living in England for three years, Voltaire became an admirer of English legal institutions, which he considered more humane and just than those of his native country. Using England as a model, he appealed for the implementation of various political reforms in France. He deplored those "who reduce men to a state of slavery by force and downright violence." A tireless advocate of individual liberty, he became a regular defender of victims of injustice, including Jean Calas, a Protestant shopkeeper from Toulouse who had been tortured and executed for allegedly murdering his son because he had expressed a desire to convert to Catholicism. The boy had in fact committed suicide.

Voltaire showed a commitment to placing his knowledge in the service of humanitarian causes. In his most famous novel, *Candide* (1759), the character by that name challenges the smug confidence of Dr. Pangloss, the tutor who repeatedly claims that they lived in "the best of all possible worlds." At the end of the novel Candide responds to this refrain by saying that "we must cultivate our garden." Voltaire, instead of being content with the current condition of humankind, was demanding that we work actively to improve society.

**Madame du Châtelet**

In her *Institutions de physique* (1740) this French noblewoman, the mistress of Voltaire, made an original and impressive attempt to give Newtonian physics a philosophical foundation.

## Enlightenment Political Theory

Enlightenment thinkers are known most widely for their political theories, especially those that supported the causes of liberty and reform. The men and women of the Enlightenment did not, however, share a common political ideology, nor did they agree on the most desirable type of political society. They did share a belief that politics was a science that, like the cosmos, had its own natural laws. The title of one of David Hume's treatises, *That Politics May Be Reduced to a Science* (1741), reflects a belief that most Enlightenment political writers endorsed. They also thought of the state in secular rather than religious terms. There was little place in Enlightenment thought for the divine right of kings. Nor was there a place for the Church in the government of the state. On other issues, however, there was little consensus. Three thinkers in particular illustrate the range of Enlightenment political thought: Montesquieu, Rousseau, and Paine.

## Baron de Montesquieu: The Separation of Powers

The most influential political writer of the Enlightenment was the French philosophe Charles-Louis de Secondat, Baron de Montesquieu (1689–1755). The son of a nobleman of the robe from Bordeaux, Montesquieu had a legal education and also developed an early interest in science. His political thought owed as much to his study of history and anthropology as to the study of law and science. His first book, *The Persian Letters,* published anonymously in Holland in 1721, was a brilliant satire of Western government and society through the eyes of two Persian aristocrats traveling in Europe. It laid the groundwork for a much more scholarly and substantial contribution to political theory, *Spirit of the Laws* (1748). Often compared to Aristotle because of the range of his thought, Montesquieu interwove commentaries on natural law, religion, morals, virtue, climate, and liberty. Unlike Hobbes, Locke, and the other natural-law philosophers who preceded him, Montesquieu was not concerned with the origin of government or with the establishment of a universal model of politics. Rather, he treated the laws of a country in historical perspective and within the context of that country's religion, morality, climate, geography, and culture. His political writing was scientific mainly in its empirical approach to its subject, and in the comparisons it made between politics on the one hand and Newtonian physics on the other.

Montesquieu argued that there were three forms of government: republics, monarchies, and despotisms, each of which had an activating or inspirational force. In republics that force was civic virtue, in monarchies it was honor, and in despotisms it was fear. In each form of government there was a danger that the polity could degenerate: The virtue of republics could be lost, monarchies could become corrupt, and despotisms could lead to repression. The key to maintaining moderation and preventing this degeneration of civil society was the law of each country. Ideally the law of a country should provide for the separation and balance of political powers. Only in that way could degeneration be avoided and moderation ensured.

Montesquieu used his knowledge of the British political system, which he had studied firsthand while living in England for two years, to propose that the key to good government was the separation of executive, legislative, and judicial power. He was particularly concerned about the independence of the judiciary. Montesquieu was unaware of

## CHRONOLOGY

## Literary Works of the Enlightenment

**1687**  Isaac Newton, *Mathematical Principles of Natural Philosophy*

**1690**  John Locke, *An Essay Concerning Human Understanding*

**1721**  Baron de Montesquieu, *The Persian Letters*

**1738**  Voltaire, *Elements of the Philosophy of Newton*

**1739**  David Hume, *Treatise of Human Nature*

**1748**  Baron de Montesquieu, *Spirit of the Laws*

**1748**  David Hume, *An Enquiry Concerning Human Understanding*

**1751**  First volume of Diderot and d'Alembert's *Encyclopedia*

**1755**  Jean-Jacques Rousseau, *Discourse on the Origin of Inequality Among Men*

**1759**  Voltaire, *Candide*

**1762**  Jean-Jacques Rousseau, *The Social Contract* and *Emile, or on Education*

**1763**  Voltaire, *Treatise on Toleration*

**1764**  Cesare Beccaria, *Essay on Crimes and Punishments*

**1764**  Voltaire, *Philosophical Dictionary*

**1776**  Adam Smith, *The Wealth of Nations*

**1781**  Immanuel Kant, *Critique of Pure Reason*

**1791**  Thomas Paine, *The Rights of Man*

**1792**  Mary Wollstonecraft, *A Vindication of the Rights of Woman*

**1795**  Marquis de Condorcet, *Progress of the Human Mind*

how legislative and executive powers actually overlapped in eighteenth-century Britain, but his emphasis on the importance of a separation of powers became the most durable of his ideas. It had profound influence on the drafting of the Constitution of the United States of America in 1787.

## Jean-Jacques Rousseau: The General Will

Also influential as a political theorist was the Swiss philosophe Jean-Jacques Rousseau (1712–1778), who as a young man moved from Geneva to Paris and became a member of a prominent intellectual circle. Rousseau does not conform to the model of the typical Enlightenment thinker. His distrust of human reason and his emotionalism separated him from Hume, Voltaire, and another

**Differences Among the Philosophes**
This satirical print shows Rousseau, to the left, and Voltaire engaged in heated debate. The two men were both major figures in the Enlightenment, but they differed widely in temperament and in their philosophical and political views. Rousseau was very much the rebel; unlike Voltaire, he distrusted reason and articulated highly egalitarian political principles.

great French philosophe, Denis Diderot (1713–1784). That distrust laid the foundations for the romantic reaction against the Enlightenment in the early nineteenth century (see Chapter 21). Instead of celebrating the improvement of society as it evolved into higher forms, Rousseau had a negative view of the achievements of civilization. In his novel *Emile, or on Education* (1762) he wrote, "All our wisdom consists of servile prejudices, all our customs are but enslavement, constraint, or bondage. Social man is born, lives and dies enslaved. At birth he is bound up with swaddling clothes; at his death he is nailed down in a coffin. For the whole of his existence as a human being he is chained up by our institutions."[5] Rousseau idealized the uncorrupted condition of human beings in the state of nature, supporting the theory of the "noble savage." Human beings could not ever return to that original natural state, but Rousseau held out the hope

of recreating an idealized golden age when they were not yet alienated from themselves and their environment.

Rousseau's political theories were hardly conventional, but they appealed to some segments of the reading public. In his *Discourse on the Origin of Inequality Among Men* (1755) and *The Social Contract* (1762) he challenged the existing political and social order with an uncompromising attack on aristocracy and monarchy. He linked absolute monarchy, which he referred to as despotism, with the court and especially with the vain, pampered, conceited, and overdecorated aristocratic women who wielded political influence with the king and in the salons. As an alternative to this aristocratic, monarchical, and feminized society Rousseau proclaimed the sovereignty of the people. Laws were to be determined by the General Will, by which he meant the consensus of a community of citizens (but not necessarily the vote of the majority).

As a result of his writings Rousseau became associated with radical republican and democratic ideas that flourished at the time of the French Revolution. One indication of that radicalism was the fact that *The Social Contract* was banned not only in absolutist France but in the republics of the Netherlands and Switzerland as well. Rousseau was also criticized for justifying authoritarian rule. His argument that the General Will placed limits on individual civil liberty encouraged autocratic leaders, such as the radical Maximilien Robespierre at the time of the French Revolution, to claim that their dictatorial rule embodied that General Will.

## Thomas Paine: The Rights of Man
Of all the Enlightenment political theorists, the English publicist and propagandist Thomas Paine (1737–1809) was arguably the most radical. Paine was influenced by Rousseau, Diderot, and Voltaire, but his radicalism was cultivated mainly by his intense involvement in the political world of revolutionary America, where he became politically active in the 1770s. In *Common Sense* (1776) Paine presented the case for American independence from Britain. This included a passionate statement of human freedom, equality, and rationality. It also involved a vicious attack on hereditary monarchy and an eloquent statement for the sovereignty of the law. At the time of the French Revolution, Paine continued to call for the establishment

## DOCUMENT

## Rousseau Places Limits on Civil Liberty

*In his Social Contract (1762) Rousseau discussed the effect that the formation of the civil state had on individual liberty. Rousseau is careful to distinguish between the liberty one enjoys in the state of nature and the liberty one acquires by entering civil society. As he explains in this passage, the establishment of the civil state limits one's natural liberty, but contrary to what some scholars have maintained, he does not justify totalitarian rule. Passionately committed to human liberty, Rousseau claims that the democratic and egalitarian society he envisions would serve as an alternative to the despotic systems of government that existed in late-eighteenth-century Europe.*

The passage from the state of nature to the civil state produces a very remarkable change in man, by substituting justice for instinct in his conduct and giving his actions the morality they had formerly lacked. Then only, when the voice of duty takes the place of physical impulses and right of appetite, does man who so far had considered only himself, find that he is forced to act on different princi-

ples, and to consult his reason before listening to his inclinations. Although in this state he deprives himself of some advantages which he got from nature, he gains in return others so great, his facilities are so stimulated and developed, his ideas so extended, his feelings so ennobled, and his whole soul so uplifted that, did not the abuses of this new condition often degrade him below that which he left, he would be bound to bless continually the happy moment which took him from it forever and, instead of a stupid and unimaginative animal, made him an intelligent being and a man.

Let us draw up the whole account in terms easily commensurable. What man loses by the social contract is his natural liberty and an unlimited right to everything he tries to get and succeeds in getting; what he gains is civil liberty and the proprietorship of all he possesses. If we are to avoid mistake in weighing one against the other, we must clearly distinguish natural liberty, which is bounded only by the strength of the individual, from civil liberty, which is limited by the general will; and possession, which is merely the effect of force or the right of the first occupier, from property, which can be founded only on a positive title.

Source: Jean-Jacques Rousseau, *The Social Contract* (1762).

of a republic in France and in his native country. In his most widely circulated work, *The Rights of Man* (1791), he linked the institution of monarchy with the aristocracy, which he referred to as "a seraglio of males, who neither collect the honey nor form the hive but exist only for lazy enjoyment."

The title of *The Rights of Man* identified a theme that appeared in much Enlightenment writing. Like Diderot and Rousseau, Paine spoke the language of natural rights. Until the Enlightenment, rights were considered legal privileges acquired by royal charter or by inheritance. One had a right, for example, to a particular piece of land or to elect representatives from one's county or town. Those rights could be surrendered under certain circumstances, such as when a person sold land. The new emphasis on natural law, however, led to the belief that simply by being a human being one acquired natural rights that could never be taken away. The American Declaration of Independence (1776), drafted by Thomas Jefferson, presented an eloquent statement of these God-given inalienable rights, which included "life, liberty and the pursuit of happiness." In defending that independence, Paine claimed that "a government of our own is our natural right." Since the eighteenth century those rights have been extended to include newly defined activities, such as the right to privacy, but the language in which such rights are asserted is a legacy of the Enlightenment.

## Women and the Enlightenment

The claim advanced by Enlightenment thinkers that all human beings are equal in a state of nature did not lead to a widespread belief that on the basis of natural law men and women are equal. Quite to the contrary, many philosophes, including Diderot and Rousseau, argued that women are different in nature from men and that they should be confined to an exclusively domestic role as chaste wives and mothers. Rousseau also insisted on the separate education of girls.

This patriarchal argument supported the emerging theory of separate spheres°, which held that men and women should conduct their lives in different social and political environments. The identification of women with the private, domestic sphere laid the foundation for the ideology of female domesticity, which became popular in bourgeois society in the nineteenth century. But it denied them the freedom that aristocratic women in France had acquired during the eighteenth century, especially those who participated in polite society. It also continued to deny them civil rights. Like women in ancient Sparta, whose situation served as the model for a number of Enlightenment thinkers, eighteenth-century women could not vote and could not initiate lawsuits on their own authority. They were not full members of civil society.

## DOCUMENT

# Montesquieu Satirizes European Women

*Montesquieu's first publication,* The Persian Letters *(1721), is a clever satire on French society. The book consists of a series of letters written to and from two fictional Persian travelers, Usbek and Rica. Because the characters come from a radically different culture, Montesquieu was able to avoid official censure for presenting his irreverent views. The Persians refer to the king as a great magician who has the power to persuade men to kill one another though they have no quarrel, and to the pope as "an old idol worshipped out of habit." Montesquieu's satire was all the more biting because Europeans harbored deep contempt for the world of the Middle East, which they thought of as a region ruled by oriental despots and inhabited by people with lax standards of sexual morality. In this passage from one of Usbek's early letters to one of his wives in the harem, Montesquieu presents a favorable image of the oriental harem to contrast with the aristocratic women of eighteenth-century France.*

Usbek to Roxana, at the seraglio in Ispahan

How fortunate you are, Roxana, to live in the gentle land of Persia and not in these poisoned regions where neither shame nor virtue are known! You live in my seraglio as in the bower of innocence, inaccessible to the assaults of mankind; you rejoice in the good fortune that makes it impossible for you to fall. No man has sullied you with lascivious glances;

even your father-in-law, during the freedom of the festivals, has never seen your lovely mouth, because you have never failed to cover it with a sacred veil . . . .

If you had been raised in this country, you would not have been so troubled. Women here have lost all restraint. They present themselves barefaced to men, as if inviting conquest; they seek attention, and they accompany men to the mosques. On walks, even to their rooms; the service of eunuchs is unknown. In place of the noble simplicity and charming modesty which is the rule among you, one finds here a barbaric impudence, to which one cannot grow accustomed. . . .

When you enhance the brilliance of your complexion with lovely coloring, when you perfume all your body with the most precious essences, when you dress in your most beautiful garments, when you seek to distinguish yourself from your companions by the charm of your dancing or the delight of your song, when you graciously compete with them in beauty, sweetness and vivacity, then I cannot imagine that you have any other object than that of pleasing me. . . .

But what am I to think of European women? Their art in making up their complexions, the ornaments they display, the care they give to their bodies, their preoccupation with pleasing are so many stains on their virtue and outrages to their husbands.

Source: From Baron de Montesquieu, *The Persian Letters,* translated by George R. Healy (Hackett, 1999), Letter 26. Reprinted by permission of Hackett Publishing Company, Inc. All rights reserved.

---

Only in the 1790s did writers begin to use the language and ideas of the Enlightenment to advance the argument for the full equality of men and women. The first of these appeals came from Condorcet, who published *On the Admission of Women to the Rights of Citizenship* in 1789. In that pamphlet he proposed that all women who own property be given the right to vote. He later called for universal suffrage for all men and women on the grounds that they all shared a common human nature. A similar appeal came from the French dramatist and revolutionary activist Marie Olympe Aubrey de Gouges (1748–1793). At the very beginning of the French Revolution, de Gouges, the daughter of a butcher, proposed that the revolutionary manifesto adopted by the French National Assembly, *Declaration of the Rights of Man and Citizen* (1789), be extended to include women as well as men.

De Gouges drafted her most famous publication, *The Rights of Woman* (1791), as a proposed appendix to that constitutional document. She took the authors of the *Declaration* to task for their failure to address the problem of women's civil rights and responsibilities with the same

determination and enthusiasm they had manifested in proclaiming the rights of men. Revealing her debt to Rousseau, she proposed in Article VI of her document that "the law must be the expression of the general will. All citizens, men and women, must concur, personally or through their representatives, in its creation. It must be the same for everyone: every citizen, man and woman, being equal in its eyes, must be equally eligible for all high honors, public offices, and positions according to their merits. . . . " Using more of Rousseau's language, she went on to propose a "social contract" between man and woman that recognized, among other things, common ownership of property. None of de Gouges's proposals were implemented by the French government, but she did succeed in drawing attention to the contradictions between the rhetoric and the reality of natural rights.

De Gouges's English contemporary, Mary Wollstonecraft (1759–1797), was the most famous of the Enlightenment's advocates of women's rights. Inspired by the events of the French Revolution and angered by the conservative English response to the events taking place in France,

Wollstonecraft wrote *A Vindication of the Rights of Woman* (1792). This treatise, which embodies a stinging critique of eighteenth-century polite society, has become a founding document of modern feminism. In it Wollstonecraft made an eloquent appeal for extending civil and political rights to women and even proposed that women elect their own representatives to legislatures. Her most original and innovative proposals, however, dealt with education. She claimed that in order for women to take control of their lives and to become the full equals of men within marriage and in the political realm, girls had to acquire greater knowledge and skill and learn how to support themselves. Wollstonecraft insisted that the education of women must be made equal and identical to that of men. In this way she challenged the arguments presented by Rousseau and many other male Enlightenment thinkers that cultural and social differences between men and women should be maintained because they were "natural."

## The Enlightenment and Sexuality

One facet of Enlightenment thought that had a profound effect on the position of women in society was the appeal for greater sexual permissiveness. Many philosophes, including Voltaire, Diderot, and Holbach, remained openly critical of the strict standard of sexual morality enforced by Christian churches. The basic argument of the philosophes was that sexual activity should not be restricted, because it was pleasurable and a source of happiness. The arbitrary prohibitions imposed by the Church contradicted human nature. European encounters with pagan natives of the South Pacific, who were reported to have enjoyed great sexual permissiveness, were used to reinforce this argument based on human nature. Diderot appealed to the sexual code of the Tahitians in his attack on Christian sexual morality.

Many philosophes, including Voltaire, practiced what they preached and lived openly with women out of wedlock. Other members of wealthy society adopted an even more libertine lifestyle. The Venetian adventurer and author Giacomo Casanova (1725–1798), who was expelled from a seminary for his immorality, gained fame for his life of gambling, spying, and seducing thousands of women. To one young Spanish woman, who resisted his advances in order to protect her virginity, he said: "You must abandon yourself to my passion without any resistance, and you may rest assured I will respect your innocence." Casanova's name soon became identified with sexual seduction.

The violent excesses to which this type of eighteenth-century sexual permissiveness could lead can be seen in the career of Alphonse Donatien François, the Marquis de Sade (1740–1814). The author of licentious libertine narratives, including his own memoirs and an erotic novel, *Justine* (1793), de Sade described the use of violence in sexual en-counters and thus gave rise to the word *sadism* to describe the pleasurable administration of pain. He spent twenty-seven years in prison for his various sexual offenses.

It makes sense that noblemen like Casanova and de Sade would have adopted the libertine values of the Enlightenment thinkers. Somewhat more remarkable was the growth of public sexual permissiveness among all social groups, including the rather prim and proper bourgeoisie and the working poor. Erotic literature, such as John Cleland's *Memoirs of a Woman of Pleasure* (1749), and pornographic prints achieved considerable popularity in an increasingly commercialized society, while prostitution became more open and widespread. Voltaire and Diderot might not have approved of this literature or these practices, but their libertine, anti-Christian, materialist outlook helped to prepare the ground for their acceptance.

# The Impact of the Enlightenment

■ **What impact did the Enlightenment have on Western culture and politics?**

The ideas of the Enlightenment spread to every country in Europe as well as to the Americas. They inspired programs of reform and radical political movements. Enlightenment thought, however, did not become the property of the entire population. It appealed mainly to the educated and the relatively prosperous and failed to penetrate the lower levels of society.

## The Spread of Enlightened Ideas

The ideas of the Enlightenment spread rapidly among the literate members of society, mainly by means of print. During the eighteenth century, print became the main medium of formal communication. The technology of printing allowed for the publication of materials on a scale unknown a century before. Pamphlets, newspapers, and books poured off presses, not only in the major cities but in provincial towns as well. Literacy rates increased dramatically throughout western Europe. The highly educated still constituted a minority of the population, but the better part of the aristocracy and many of those who occupied the middle ranks of society could read and write. By 1750 more than half the male population of France and England could read basic texts. The foundation of public libraries in all the major cities of western Europe made printed materials more widely available. In many bookshops, rooms were set aside for browsing in the hope that readers would eventually purchase the books they consulted.

One of the most widely circulated publications of the Enlightenment was the *Encyclopedia* compiled by the philosophe Denis Diderot and the mathematician Jean le Rond d'Alembert. This massive seventeen-volume work,

Diderot's *Encyclopedia*, Plate Illustrating Agricultural Techniques

which was published between 1751 and 1765, contained thousands of articles on science, religion, politics, and the economy. The entries in the *Encyclopedia* were intended not only to promote knowledge but also to advance the ideas of the Enlightenment. Included, for example, were two entries on natural law, which was described as being "perpetual and unchangeable." The entry on intolerance makes a passionate plea against religious persecution, asserting that "If we may tear out one hair of anyone whose opinions differ from ours, we could also claim the whole head, for there is no limit to injustice." Other articles praised the achievements of science and technology and gave special attention to industrial crafts and trades. Underlying the entire enterprise was the belief that knowledge was useful, that it could contribute to the improvement of human life. In these respects the *Encyclopedia* became the quintessential statement of the worldview of the Enlightenment, and its publication stands as a crowning achievement of the entire movement.

Encyclopedias, pamphlets, newspapers, and novels were not the only means by which the ideas of the Enlightenment spread. A number of informal institutions promoted the exchange of ideas. Literary societies and book clubs, which proliferated in the major cities of western Europe, encouraged the public reading and discussion of the latest publications. Scientific societies sponsored lectures on the latest developments in physics, chemistry, and natural history. One of the most famous of these lectures demonstrated the power of electricity by charging a young boy, suspended from the ground, with static electricity. This "electrified boy," who was not harmed in the process, attracted objects from a stool placed below him. Lectures like this one attracted large crowds.

Equally important in the spread of the scientific and cultural ideas of the Enlightenment were museums, where scientific and cultural artifacts, many of them gathered from around the world, could be viewed by an increasingly curious and educated public. The museums often sponsored exhibits and lectures. Paris became home to a number of these museums in the 1780s, and they could be found in all the major cities of Europe by the end of the eighteenth century. A more informal set of cultural institutions were the coffeehouses that sprang up in cities across Europe. These commercial

establishments were open to everyone who could pay the fare, and therefore they proved immensely successful in facilitating the spread of ideas within the bourgeoisie. Newspapers were often read aloud at coffeehouses, and they became the setting for many political debates.

Another set of institutions that promoted the ideas of the Enlightenment were the secret societies of men and women known as freemasons°. Freemasons strove to create a society based on reason and virtue, and they were committed to the principles of liberty and equality. Freemasonry first appeared in England and Scotland in the seventeenth century and then spread to France, the Dutch Republic, Germany, and as far east as Poland and Russia during the eighteenth century. Some of the most famous figures of the Enlightenment, including Voltaire, belonged to masonic lodges. In the 1770s there were more than 10,000 freemasons in Paris alone. The lodges were places where philosophes interacted with merchants, lawyers, and government leaders. The pope condemned the freemasons in 1738, and many civil authorities expressed deep suspicion of the political and religious ideas they fostered.

The most famous informal cultural institutions of the Enlightenment were the salons, the private sitting rooms or parlors of wealthy women where discussions of philosophy, science, literature, and politics took place. Salons became particularly prominent in Paris, where the salons of Madame Geoffrin and Madame du Deffand won international fame. The women who hosted these meetings invited the participants, entertained those who attended, and used their conversational skills to direct and facilitate the discussions that took place in the salons. They also used their influence to secure aristocratic patronage of the young male writers and scientists whom they cultivated. The success of a new book was often determined by its initial reception in the salon. Most of the prominent male figures of the French Enlightenment participated in these meetings, at least during the early years of their careers. (See the illustration at the beginning of this chapter.)

**Madame Geoffrin**
Her salon was called "one of the wonders of the social world."

The salons became the target of contemporary criticism not only because they allowed women to participate in public life but also because they were bastions of aristocratic society. While most of the salon women came from the aristocracy, many of their fathers had recently risen into the nobility or had merely purchased their noble status. The men who attended the meetings had even fewer ties to the traditional aristocracy. The salons were places where old and new noble blood intermingled, where social refinement was even more important than inherited nobility. What mattered most in the salons was the quickness of one's wit, the quality of one's conversational skills, and the appeal of one's views. Thus the salon succeeded in opening elite society to the talented. In this way the salons helped to dissolve the bonds that held together the Old Regime and contributed to the creation of a society based on merit rather than birth alone.

## The Limits of the Enlightenment

The ideas of the Enlightenment spread rapidly across Europe, but their influence was limited. The market for books by philosophes such as Voltaire and Rousseau was quite small. Diderot and d'Alembert's *Encyclopedia* sold a remarkable 25,000 copies by 1789, but that was exceptional, and many sales were to libraries. Paine's *The Rights of Man* also reached a fairly broad audience, mainly because it was written in a simple direct style and its price was deliberately kept low. Most books on social and political theory, however, like scholarly works on science, did not sell very well. Rousseau's *The Social Contract* was a commercial failure.

Books on other topics had much better sales. Inspirational religious literature continued to be published in large quantities, indicating the limits of Enlightenment secularism. Novels, a relatively new genre of fiction that appealed to the bourgeoisie, were almost as successful. We can readily see why Rousseau and Voltaire both used novels to advance their radical social views. In France, books that were banned because of their pornographic content or their satirical attacks on the monarchy, the clergy, or ministers in the government also proved to be best-sellers in the huge underground French book market.

One segment of the popular press that revealed a limited influence of the Enlightenment was the literature on popular science. The reading public did not show much interest in technical scientific books, but they did purchase publications on such technological developments as hot-air balloons, which became a new fad in the 1780s. Descriptions of monsters found in distant lands and other extraordinary natural occurrences also sold thousands of copies. Some of this interest in the preternatural originated in the work of highly educated scholars, but the reports of new discoveries increasingly lent themselves to sensational treatment in the popular press.

Another subject of popular literary interest was mesmerism°. The Viennese physicist and physician Franz Anton Mesmer (1734–1815), who moved to Paris in 1778, claimed that he had discovered a fluid that permeated and surrounded all bodies and was the source of heat, light, electricity, and magnetism. Sickness was caused by the obstruction to the flow of this fluid in the human body. To restore this flow patients were massaged, hypnotized, or "mesmerized" with the intention of producing a convulsion or crisis that restored health. Mesmerism developed into a form of spiritualism in which its patients engaged in séances with spirits, and its practitioners dabbled in the occult. This pseudoscience, which was rejected by the French Academy of Science as a hoax, became the subject of numerous pamphlets and newspaper articles that fascinated the reading public.

Those who read books about mesmerism had only a tenuous connection with the learned world of the Enlightenment. Among those who were illiterate or barely literate, Enlightened ideas made even fewer inroads. The only exposure these people may have had to the ideas we associate with the Enlightenment would be through the actions and attitudes of their social superiors. From the elitist perspective of the philosophes, the intellectual world of the illiterate was characterized by the superstition and ignorance that the philosophes were determined to eliminate.

The growing gap between a learned culture shared by philosophes and members of salons on the one hand and the popular culture of the lower classes on the other can be seen in the perpetuation of beliefs regarding magic and witchcraft among the uneducated. During the late seventeenth and eighteenth centuries, educated people in Europe gradually abandoned their belief in magic and witchcraft. As we have seen in Chapter 16, belief in the operation of a mechanical universe, religious skepticism, and rationalism had gradually eroded many beliefs regarding the operation of a supernatural realm, especially the possibility of demonic intervention in the natural world. Among the lower classes, however, this skeptical outlook found very little fertile ground. Popular belief in a world charged with supernatural and magical forces continued to lead villagers to accuse their neighbors of having harmed them by means of witchcraft. After European courts stopped prosecuting witches in the late seventeenth and early eighteenth centuries, local communities often took justice into their own hands and lynched the suspects themselves. It was left to the government to prosecute those who engaged in this illegal form of local justice.

The gap between the high culture of the Enlightenment and that of the lower classes can also be seen in the condemnations of certain sports and amusements. Popular culture was known for its blood sports, especially cockfighting, and the baiting of bulls, bears, and badgers by tying the animals down and allowing dogs to attack them. These blood sports, which could attract thousands of spectators at a single event, resulted in the serious injury or death of animals. Enlightenment thinkers, especially those from the bourgeoisie, condemned this activity for its cruelty and its barbarism. Just like the torture and execution of criminals, these "barbarous" pastimes had no place in polite society. Popular sports, however, could not be easily eradicated. It was not until the nineteenth century that they began to disappear, often as the result of campaigns conducted by clergymen rather than philosophes. The persistence of blood sports reveals the strength of popular culture and the inability of the Enlightenment to transform it.

## Enlightened Absolutism

When we turn to Enlightened political ideas, we confront an even more difficult task of determining the extent of their impact. The main figures of the Enlightenment were intellectuals—men of letters who did not occupy positions of great political importance and who did not devote much thought to the challenging task of putting their theories into practice. The audience for their books did not always include people with the power to implement their proposals. Rulers often treated Enlightenment thinkers with suspicion, if only because they criticized established authority. Nevertheless, Enlightenment thought did make its mark on eighteenth-century politics in two strikingly different ways.

The first was through the reforms enacted by rulers who are often referred to as enlightened despots°. These rulers exercised absolute power and used that power to implement changes that Enlightenment thinkers had proposed. The term *despot* is misleading, as these enlightened rulers were rarely despotic in the sense of exercising power cruelly and arbitrarily. The connection between Enlightenment and royal absolutism is not as unnatural as it might appear. It is true that philosophes tended to be critical of the Old Regime°, the eighteenth-century political order that was dominated by an absolute monarch and a privileged nobility and clergy. But many of them, including Voltaire, had little sympathy with democracy and social equality, and preferred to entrust absolute monarchs with the implementation of the reforms they advocated. Among the philosophes the prospect of a philosopher-king had widespread appeal.

Rulers of central and eastern European countries were particularly open to Enlightenment thought. These monarchs had read widely in the literature of the Enlightenment and introduced Western intellectuals to their courts. The most famous of the enlightened absolutists was King Frederick II of Prussia, known as Frederick the Great (r. 1740–1786). Frederick, a deist who wrote poetry and played the flute, was enamored of all things French. When the French philosophe d'Alembert visited his court, the king hosted a dinner at which he spoke only French, leav-

ing many of the Prussian guests to sip their soup in stunned silence. Frederick corresponded extensively with Voltaire and invited him to take up residence at his French-style royal palace, "Sans Souci," at Potsdam. The relationship between king and philosopher, however, was often stormy, and when Frederick publicly burned a publication in which Voltaire had lampooned a royal favorite, Voltaire left Potsdam in 1752.

The departure of Voltaire did not weaken Frederick's determination to implement a number of policies that reflected the ideals of the Enlightenment. The most noteworthy of these was the introduction of religious toleration throughout his predominantly Lutheran kingdom. Protestants of all denominations and Catholics (but not Jews) received the protection of the law and even benefited from royal patronage. Frederick also introduced a number of legal reforms with the intention of realizing the Enlightenment ideal of making the law both rational and humane. He authorized the codification of Prussian law (which was completed after his death in 1794), abolished judicial torture, and eliminated capital punishment. In order to provide for the training of future servants of the state, he began a system of compulsory education throughout the country. Like most enlightened rulers, Frederick never abandoned his commitment to absolute rule, which he strengthened by winning the support of the nobility. He also remained committed to the militaristic and expansionist policies of his father, Frederick William I. For him there was no contradiction between his style of rule and his commitment to Enlightenment ideals.

In neighboring Austria two Habsburg rulers, Maria Theresa (r. 1740–1780) and her son Joseph II (r. 1780–1790), pursued reformist policies that gave them the reputation of being enlightened monarchs. Most of Maria Theresa's reforms were of an administrative nature. Stunned by the Prussian invasion and occupation of the Habsburg province of Silesia in 1740, Maria Theresa set out to strengthen the Habsburg monarchy by gaining complete control over taxation and by reorganizing the military and civil bureaucracy. She also took steps to make the serfs more productive, mainly by restricting the work they performed on their lords' lands and by abolishing the feudal dues they paid.

These efforts won the applause of philosophes, but the policies of Maria Theresa's that most clearly bore the stamp of the Enlightenment were her legal reforms. Inspired by Beccaria and Montesquieu, she established a commission to reform the entire corpus of Austrian law. A new code of criminal law was promulgated in 1769, and seven years later Maria Theresa issued an edict abolishing judicial torture. Joseph continued this program of legal reform by reorganizing the entire central court system and by eliminating capital punishment. He also revealed the influence of the Enlightenment by granting religious toleration, first to Protestants and eastern Orthodox

**Torture**

The torture of a defendant as depicted in the published version of the criminal code promulgated by Empress Maria Theresa in 1769. This form of torture, the *strappado,* used a pulley to hang the accused from the ceiling. Weights could be attached to the feet to make the pain more excruciating. The purpose of judicial torture was to extract a confession. Torture was eliminated from the law codes of most continental European countries during the Enlightenment.

Christians in 1781, and then to Jews in 1782. With respect to social issues, he completed his mother's work of abolishing serfdom altogether.

The efforts of Catherine II of Russia (r. 1762–1796) to implement the ideas of the Enlightenment followed a different course from those of Maria Theresa and Joseph. The daughter of a German prince, Catherine received an education grounded in a traditional curriculum of history, geography, and Lutheran theology. In 1745 she was married to a distant cousin, Peter, who was in line to inherit the Russian throne from his aunt, the childless Empress Elizabeth (r. 1741–1762). After arriving in St. Petersburg Catherine

not only acquired a knowledge of Russian language, literature, and religion but also read widely in western European sources, including the works of Enlightenment thinkers. She later corresponded with Voltaire and d'Alembert and employed the famous salon hostess Madame Geoffrin at her court. At Catherine's invitation Diderot visited St. Petersburg for six months.

Early in her reign, Catherine embarked on a program of reform similar to those of other enlightened absolutists. In 1767 she appointed a commission to codify Russian law on the basis of western European principles. Her recommendations to the commission included the abolition of torture and inhumane punishment and the establishment of religious toleration. She was eventually forced to disband the commission, which could not agree on a new code, but she later abolished torture and capital punishment on her own authority. Like Maria Theresa, she instituted a number of administrative and educational reforms, including the introduction of primary schooling in the provinces. Catherine, who became known as Catherine the Great, also tried unsuccessfully to provide for the education of girls as well as boys.

DOCUMENT

Catherine the Great's Constitution (1767)

Catherine gained a reputation for being an enlightened European monarch, but her acceptance of traditional Russian culture and the need to maintain her rule prevented her from fully embracing the ideals of the Enlightenment. She even admitted that it was much easier to subscribe to the ideals of the Enlightenment than actually to implement them. The strength of vested interests within Russian society accounted for the failure of the law commission of 1767. After putting down the Pugachev rebellion in 1774, she began to question the desirability of social reform, and the experience of the French Revolution in the 1790s (see Chapter 19) led her to disavow the ideals of the Enlightenment.

On the issue of serfdom, which most Enlightenment thinkers wished to see abolished, she would not yield. She preserved that social system in order to secure the loyalty of the Russian nobility, and she extended it to Ukraine and parts of Poland after Russia incorporated those regions into the empire. Catherine also catered to the imperialistic ambitions of the Russians, gaining vast territories in eastern Europe, East Asia, and Alaska. Thus she expanded the Russian Empire at the very time when the ideals of the Enlightenment were leading some philosophes to call for the dissolution of large imperial structures.

## The Enlightenment and Revolution

The second mark that Enlightenment thought made on eighteenth-century politics was the inspiration it gave to movements for reform and revolution in western Europe and the Americas. The emphasis placed by Enlightenment

**Catherine the Great**

Catherine II of Russia on the day she succeeded in taking the throne from her husband, Peter III, at Peterhof in 1762. Catherine, who despised her husband, joined a conspiracy against him right after his accession to the throne. Catherine, like Peter, had a number of lovers, and her two children, including the future emperor Paul, were reputedly conceived by members of the nobility.

thinkers on individual liberty, natural rights, and political reform put pressure on both monarchs and the traditional nobility either to make concessions or to relinquish power altogether.

In Britain, for example, the movement for parliamentary reform and the expansion of the franchise°, as well as the first appeals for women's rights, were partially inspired by the Enlightenment. The radical democrat Thomas Paine, the feminist Mary Wollstonecraft, and the parliamentary reformer Joseph Priestley all based their demands for political reform on Enlightenment ideas of natural rights and civil liberty. It took considerable time, however, for these reforms to be realized. Only in 1832 did the British Parliament agree to a modest extension of the franchise, and women did not receive the vote until the early twentieth century. Nevertheless the movements to achieve these reforms were inspired by ideals born of the Enlightenment.

In France the influence of the Enlightenment on the momentous changes that took place during the French Revolution (1789–1799) has been a matter of debate among historians. The complexity of the revolution, which will be discussed in Chapter 19, and the diversity of Enlightenment thought make this a particularly difficult debate to resolve. Many of the revolutionaries of the 1790s were steeped in the ideas of the Enlightenment, but those ideas did not necessarily inspire the revolution itself. The French philosophes of the eighteenth century denounced the evils of the Old Regime and proposed many ideas about how governments should function, but they did not make serious efforts to introduce actual reforms, much less topple the government. Many philosophes, including Voltaire, had personal connections with aristocratic society, and very few shared the democratic and egalitarian ideas that came to the fore at the time of the Revolution. Some lesser journalists and literary hacks were more successful than the most renowned philosophes in fostering contempt for the Old Regime before the Revolution. Their merciless satires of the court and the clergy were more responsible than the grand treatises of the philosophes for stimulating a crisis of confidence in the French government and eroding the traditional respect for authority that made possible the violent overthrow of the Old Regime.

We can nevertheless establish some connections between the ideas and programs of the philosophes and the events that transpired in France during the 1790s. Some of the figures of the Enlightenment contributed to the new critical spirit evident after 1750 or provided some inspiration for the creation of a new political culture once the revolution began. The towering reputation of Voltaire during the French Revolution—and the anger of conservatives who exhumed and burned his bones after it had ended—suggest that his passionate criticisms of the Old Regime and his pleas for human freedom at the very least helped to set the stage for the revolutionary events of the 1790s. The same is true of the radical Rousseau, whose concept of the General Will served as the basis of a revolutionary ideology. Rousseau's democratic and republican ideas were used to justify some of the most important changes that took place during the revolution. Contemporaries glorified or attacked him, depending on their political philosophy, for having actually caused the revolution. One book published in 1791 was titled *On Jean-Jacques Rousseau Considered as One of the First Authors of the Revolution.*

Yet another application of enlightened ideas to politics took place in the Americas. The advocates of colonial independence from their mother countries, such as Thomas Jefferson in Virginia and Símon Bolívar in Venezuela and Colombia, were all deeply influenced by the Enlightenment concepts of natural law, natural rights, liberty, and popular sovereignty. The Declaration of Independence, which was written by Jefferson, betrayed its debt to the Enlightenment in its reference to the inalienable rights of all men and to the foundation of those rights in "the law of nature and Nature's God." Of course the American Revolution cannot be explained solely in terms of these Enlightenment ideas. The colonists found inspiration in many different sources, including English common law. But the American colonists did wish to create an entirely new world order, just as did many Enlightenment thinkers. They also adopted some of the most radical political ideas of the Enlightenment, which identified the people as the source of political power.

More generally, the Enlightenment fostered a critique of all efforts to establish overseas empires. The French priest Guillaume Thomas Raynal, mentioned in Chapter 17, wrote a condemnation of colonialism titled *The Philosophical and Political History of the Settlement and Commerce of Europeans in the Two Indies* (1770). Diderot and a number of lesser-known philosophes contributed to the final version of this massive work, which was published at Geneva in 1780. The book, which was the first to treat European imperialism in both hemispheres in the same context, praised the civilizing effects of commerce but condemned colonialism for the effects it had on those who emigrated. Cut off from their homeland, colonists brought with them only the prejudices of the civilizations they left behind and became hopelessly corrupt and degenerate. The English political theorist Richard Price developed a similar critique of all overseas empires, claiming that simply by their size and their diversity they could not promote the happiness of a community and the "fellow-feeling that takes place between persons in private life." According to Price, sprawling overseas empires by their very nature violated the standards of humanity.

# Conclusion

## The Enlightenment and Western Identity

The Enlightenment was a distinctly Western phenomenon. It arose in the countries of western Europe and then spread to central and eastern Europe (Germany, Austria, Poland, and Russia) and to the Americas. Most traditions that are identified today as "Western values" either had their origin or received their most cogent expression in the Enlightenment. In particular, the commitment to individual liberty, civil rights, toleration, and rational decision making all took shape during this period.

It would be misleading to make a simple equation between the ideas of the Enlightenment and the Western intellectual tradition. First, the ideals of the Enlightenment have never been fully accepted within Western societies. Ever since their original formulation, the ideas of the philosophes and publicists of the Enlightenment have been challenged by conservatives who argued that those ideas would lead to the destruction of religion and the social order. Those conservative criticisms, which are voiced even today, became intense at the time of the French Revolution and during the early years of the nineteenth century, and we shall discuss them in Chapters 19 and 21. Second, claims that the ideas promoted by the Enlightenment are exclusively Western can also be disputed. A celebration of reason and an insistence on religious tolerance, for example, can be found in the cultures of ancient India and China. The claim that the West is more rational than the East is itself a product of long-standing Western prejudice, an assertion that studies of other cultures undertaken by Enlightenment writers only served to strengthen.

Nevertheless, the ideas and traditions of the Enlightenment, despite the challenges they have endured, have become deeply ingrained in Western law and politics. They are less often found embedded in the political and legal traditions of non-Western lands, and when they are, such as in the twentieth-century socialist legal system of China, their presence is more often the result of Western influence than the legacy of native Eastern thought.

The acquisition of the values of the Enlightenment, even though they were never universally adopted, gave Europeans a clear sense of their own identity with respect to the rest of the world. Educated people who prided themselves on being enlightened knew that their scientific, rational worldview was not shared by Asians, Africans, indigenous Americans, or South Pacific islanders. It did not matter whether Enlightenment thinkers had a positive view of those other cultures, like Voltaire or Rousseau, or a negative one, like Montesquieu. What mattered was that they shared a similar mental outlook and a commitment to individual liberty, justice, and the improvement of civilization. For all of them religious faith was less important, both as an arbiter of morality and as a source of authority, than it was in these other cultures. The men and women of the Enlightenment all looked to the law as a reflection of natural law and as the guardian of civil liberty. Their writings helped their European and colonial public audiences think of themselves as even more distinct from non-Western people than they had in the past.

As these enlightened Western cultural values were spreading, the boundaries between East and West remained fluid and contested. The geographical region where this contest took place was what we now call eastern Europe. As we have seen in Chapter 15, the countries that occupied this buffer zone between East and West had long-standing cultural ties with Asia, especially the Middle East, but they also developed an attraction to Western culture beginning in the late seventeenth century. In Russia, this process of westernization began with Peter the Great, who integrated his country into European social, political, and diplomatic life. But it was carried further by Catherine the Great, who invited *philosophes* to her court and introduced Western reforms. This adoption of Western ideas made her appear to be a model Enlightened ruler and her country part of the Western world, but Russia's inclusion became and has remained a matter of debate. The very term "eastern Europe," which was coined during the Enlightenment, reflected the ambiguous relationship between this part of the world and the West. It provides a further illustration of the fact that the West was a cultural realm whose geographical boundaries have frequently changed.

## Suggestions for Further Reading

For a comprehensive listing of suggested readings, please go to www.ablongman.com/levack2e/chapter 18

Alexander, John T. *Catherine the Great: Life and Legend.* 1989. A lively biography of the remarkable "enlightened despot."

Beckett, J. V. *The Aristocracy in England, 1660–1914.* 1986. A comprehensive study of this landholding and governing elite. Makes the important distinction between the aristocracy and the nobility.

Darnton, Robert. *The Forbidden Best-Sellers of Pre-Revolutionary France.* 1995. A study of the salacious, blasphemous, and subversive books that sold more copies than those of the philosophes in eighteenth-century France.

Dewald, Jonathan. *The European Nobility, 1500–1800.* 1996. A comprehensive study of this social class that emphasizes its adaptability.

Doyle, William. *The Old European Order, 1660–1800.* 2nd ed. 1999. The best general study of the period.

Houston, R. A. *Literacy in Early Modern Europe: Culture and Education.* 1991. The best survey of the subject for the entire period.

Lugee, Carolyn. *Le Paradis des Femmes: Women, Salons and Social Stratification in 17th-Century France.* 1976. A social study of the women of the salons.

Outram, Dorinda. *The Enlightenment.* 1995. A balanced assessment of the major historiographical debates regarding the Enlightenment.

Root, Hilton. *Peasants and King in Burgundy: Agrarian Foundations of French Absolutism.* 1979. A study of peasant communal institutions and their relationship with the crown as well as the nobility.

Williams, David, ed. *The Enlightenment.* 1999. An excellent collection of political writings with a long introduction.

## Notes

1. Baron d'Holbach, *Good Sense* (1753).

2. David Hume, *Essays Moral, Political, and Literary* (1742), Essay X: "Of Superstition and Enthusiasm."

3. Cesare Beccaria, *An Essay on Crimes and Punishments* (1788), Chapter 47.

4. Voltaire, "Religion," in *The Philosophical Dictionary* (1802).

5. Jean-Jacques Rousseau, *Emile, or on Education* (1762).

# The Age of the French Revolution, 1789–1815

# 19

O N July 12, 1789, the French journalist Camille Desmoulins addressed an anxious crowd of Parisian citizens gathered outside the Palais-Royal, where public debate often took place. Playing upon fears that had been mounting during the past two months, Desmoulins claimed that the royal government of Louis XVI was preparing a massacre of Parisians. "To arms, to arms," Desmoulins cried out, as he roused the citizens to their own defense. That night Parisians responded to his call by invading arsenals in the city in anticipation of the violence they thought was about to descend upon them. The next day they continued to seize weapons and declared themselves members of the National Guard, a volunteer militia of propertied citizens.

On the morning of July 14, crowds of Parisians moved into a district of the city where royal troops were stationed in an ancient fortress known as the Bastille. The Parisians feared that the troops in the Bastille would take violent action against them, and they also wanted to capture the ammunition stored inside the building, which served as both an arsenal and a prison. Negotiations with the governor of the Bastille were interrupted when some of the militia, moving into the courtyard of the fortress, demanded the surrender of the troops. Shots were fired from both sides, and the exchange led to a full-scale assault upon the Bastille by the National Guard.

After three hours of fighting and the death of eighty-three people, the governor surrendered. He was then led by his captors, bearing the arms they had seized, to face charges before the officers of the city government. The crowd, however, crying for vengeance against their oppressors, attacked the soldiers and crushed some of them underfoot. The governor was stabbed hundreds of times, hacked to pieces, and decapitated. The chief magistrate of the city suffered the same fate for his reluctance to issue arms to its citizens. The crowd then placed the heads of the two men on pikes and paraded through the city.

## CHAPTER OUTLINE

- The First French Revolution, 1789–1791

- The French Republic, 1792–1799

- Cultural Change in France During the Revolution

- The Napoleonic Era, 1799–1815

- The Legacy of the French Revolution

**Jacques-Louis David, *The Oath of the Tennis Court*** The oath taken by the members of the Third Estate not to disband until France had a constitution led to the creation of the National Assembly and the legislation that destroyed royal absolutism and feudalism.

The storming of the Bastille was the first of many violent episodes that occurred during the sequence of events called the French Revolution. That revolution brought about some of the most fundamental changes in European political life since the end of Roman rule. It heralded the destruction of the Old Regime, the eighteenth-century political order that had been dominated by an absolute monarch and a privileged nobility and clergy. It led to the submission of the Catholic Church to state control. A more radical phase of the revolution, beginning in 1792, resulted in the destruction of the French monarchy and the declaration of a republic. It also led to a period of state-sponsored terrorism in 1793 and 1794, during which one group of revolutionaries engaged in a brutal campaign to eliminate their real and imagined enemies.

The excesses of the revolution led to a conservative reaction. Between 1795 and 1799 a moderate republican government, known as the Directory, modified the egalitarianism of the revolution by limiting the right to vote to men of property. Between 1799 and 1814 the reaction continued under the direction of Napoleon Bonaparte, a military officer who dominated the Consulate, a new political structure established in 1799, and then proclaimed himself emperor in 1804. Although Napoleon declared his loyalty to many of the principles of the revolution, his authoritarian rule undermined or reversed many of its achievements. In 1815 Napoleon fell from power and the monarchy was restored, marking the end of the revolutionary period. The ideas of the revolution, however, especially its commitment to democratic republicanism and its concept of the nation, continued to dominate politics in the West for the next hundred years. The French Revolution permanently changed the political culture of the West.

This chapter will address the question of how the encounters between different political and social groups in France at the end of the eighteenth century brought about some of the most important and far-reaching changes in the history of the West. In pursuing this broad objective, the individual chapter sections will address the following questions:

**The Storming of the Bastille, July 14, 1789**
The Bastille was attacked not because it was a symbol of the Old Regime, but because it contained weapons that the Parisian citizens needed to protect themselves from royalist troops.

- Why did the Old Regime in France collapse in 1789, and what revolutionary changes took place in French government and society during the next two years?
- How did a second, more radical revolution, which began with the establishment of the Republic in 1792, lead to the creation of a regime that used the power of the state to institute the Reign of Terror?
- In what ways did the political events of the revolution change French cultural institutions and create a new political culture?
- How did the authoritarian rule of Napoleon Bonaparte from 1799 to 1814 confirm or betray the achievements of the French Revolution, and what impact did his military conquests have on Europe and the world?

■ What did the French Revolution ultimately achieve and in what ways did it change the course of European and Western history?

# The First French Revolution, 1789–1791

■ Why did the Old Regime in France collapse in 1789, and what revolutionary changes took place in French government and society during the next two years?

One of the main characteristics of political revolutions is that they involve a fundamental change in the political *system*, not simply in the personnel of government. On the basis of this criterion the French Revolution consisted of two distinct revolutions. The first revolution, which began in 1789, resulted in a destruction of royal absolutism and the drafting of a constitution. The second and more radical revolution began in 1792 with the abolition of the monarchy and the formation of the French Republic.

Like all revolutions, the first French revolution had deep-seated causes. As we discussed in Chapter 18, a constant barrage of satirical literature directed at the royal family and the court lowered the prestige of the government and thus weakened its authority. The publication of thousands of pamphlets advocating reform, including many written by philosophes of the Enlightenment, fostered a critical attitude toward the French government and led to demands for political and economic change. Conflicts between the nobility and the crown over constitutional issues, a source of tension throughout the age of absolutism, led to charges that the government was acting despotically. Encounters between the landowning nobility and the peasantry, which increased in the last half of the eighteenth century, also contributed to the disaffection with the Old Regime and played a major role in stimulating demands for a restriction of the privileges enjoyed by the nobility. Ongoing food shortages in the cities created a militant citizenry ready to take action against authorities they considered responsible for the high price of bread.

The immediate cause of the revolution was a major economic crisis that bankrupted the monarchy and deprived it of its authority. This crisis led to a revolt of the nobles against the crown and brought down the entire system of royal absolutism. Only after this collapse of royal government did various groups that had had long-standing grievances against the regime take the initiative and establish a new political system. These groups never actually planned the revolution; they simply filled a void created by the absence of effective governmental power.

**DOCUMENT**
De Stael on the Ancien Regime (1789)

## The Beginning of the Revolution

The financial crisis that brought about the collapse of the French government peaked in the late 1780s. The government of Louis XVI (r. 1774–1792) had inherited considerable debts from that of his grandfather, Louis XV (r. 1715–1774) as a result of protracted periods of warfare with Great Britain. The opening of a new phase of this warfare in 1778, when France intervened in the American War of Independence on the side of the United States, pushed the government further into debt and put a strain on the entire French economy. Attempts to solve the crisis by implementing financial reforms made the situation only worse. In 1787 the government had a revenue of 475 million livres and expenses of just under 600 million livres. More than half of the revenue went to pay interest on the accumulated debt. As the crisis deepened, protests from the ranks of the nobility against royal policy became more vocal.

In 1787 the king made efforts to win the support of the nobility by convening an Assembly of Notables, a handpicked group of 144 nominees, the great majority of whom were noblemen. The purpose of the meeting was to gain approval for a new system of taxation that would include a direct tax on all landowners. These proposals encountered formidable opposition from the members of the assembly, and the meeting was adjourned. Some of the nobles in the assembly had been willing to pay the taxes, but only if the king would convoke the Estates General, a national legislative body that had not met since 1614. Convening the Estates General, they argued, would provide them with guarantees against royal despotism. Louis resisted these pressures because he did not want to give up the right to make law by his own authority.

The king then tried to gain approval of new taxes from the regional parlements, the provincial law courts whose powers included the registration of royal edicts. There too the crown met resistance. The Parlement of Paris, which was the most important of all the parlements, refused to comply with the king's request. The other parlements followed suit, claiming that only the Estates General had the power to approve new taxes. Constitutional tension was heightened when the king demanded the registration of edicts for new loans without the approval of the parlements, a step that even he acknowledged was illegal. He then suspended the parlements, thereby deepening the constitutional crisis.

The deterioration of the government's financial condition finally forced the king to yield to the demands of the nobles and the increasingly hostile popular press. When tax returns dried up as the result of an agricultural crisis in the summer months of 1788, the government could no longer pay its creditors. In a desperate effort to save his regime, Louis announced that he would convene the Estates General. By this time there was little hope for Louis. His absolutist government had completely collapsed.

## CHRONOLOGY

## The First French Revolution, 1789–1791

**1787**

| February 22 | Convening of the Assembly of Notables |

**1788**

| August 8 | Announcement of the meeting of the Estates General |

**1789**

| May 5 | The Estates General opens at Versailles |
| June 17 | The Third Estate adopts the title of the National Assembly |
| June 20 | Oath of the Tennis Court |
| July 11 | The king dismisses his finance minister, Jacques Necker |
| July 14 | The storming of the Bastille |
| Late July | The Great Fear in rural areas |
| August 4 | Abolition of feudalism and privileges |
| August 26 | *Declaration of the Rights of Man and Citizen* |
| October 5 | March to Versailles; Louis XVI and National Assembly move to Paris |
| November 2 | Church property is nationalized |

**1790**

| July 12 | Civil Constitution of the Clergy |
| July 14 | Feast of the Federation |
| November 27 | Decree requiring oath of loyalty from the clergy |

**1791**

| June 20 | Royal family flees to Varennes, is apprehended by the National Guard |
| October 1 | Newly elected Legislative Assembly opens |

The meeting of the Estates General was set for May 1789, and during the months leading up to its opening, public debates arose over how the delegates should vote. The Estates General consisted of representatives of the three orders or social groups, known as estates, that made up French society: the clergy, the nobility, and the Third Estate. The Third Estate technically contained all the commoners in the kingdom (about 96 percent of the population), ranging from the wealthiest merchant to the poorest peasant. The elected representatives of the Third Estate, whose num-

bers had doubled by a recent order of the king, were propertied nonnoble elements of lay society, including many lawyers and military officers.

Before the meeting a dispute arose among the representatives whether the three groups would vote by estate, in which case the first two estates would dominate the assembly, or by head, in which case the Third Estate would have numerical parity. Each side claimed that it was the best representative of the "nation," a term meaning the entire body of French people. The nobles maintained that the nation was represented by the nobility and clergy from all the provinces, especially the members of the provincial parlements, who had been critical of royal power during the past few decades. The members of the Third Estate advanced the claim that *they* represented the nation. The cleric Emmanuel-Joseph Sieyès (1748–1836), who joined the Third Estate during this dispute, claimed that it "has within itself all that is necessary to constitute a nation. . . . Nothing can go on without it, and everything would go on far better without the others. . . . This privileged class (nobility and clergy) is assuredly foreign to the nation by its do-nothing uselessness."[1]

The question of voting within the Estates General was not resolved when that body met at Versailles on May 5, 1789. After the king indicated that he would side with the clergy and nobility, the Third Estate took the dramatic step of declaring itself a National Assembly and asking members of the other estates to vote with them on the basis of "one man, one vote." Many members of the lower clergy and a few noblemen accepted this invitation. In a conciliatory response to this challenge, the king planned to summon all three estates to a special "royal session" to announce some concessions. In preparation for this meeting, however, he locked the Third Estate out of its meeting hall without explanation. The outraged members of the Third Estate went to a nearby indoor tennis court and took a solemn oath that they would not disband until the country had been given a constitution. One week later, after more clerics and noblemen had joined the ranks of the Third Estate, the king ordered the nobility and the clergy to join the National Assembly.

As this political crisis was reaching a climax, a major social crisis fueled by the high price of bread was causing a breakdown of public order. For many years French agriculture had had difficulty meeting the demands of an expanding population. These problems, aggravated in the 1780s by a succession of poor harvests, climaxed in a widespread harvest failure in 1788. As the price of bread soared, demand for manufactured goods shrank, thus causing widespread unemployment among artisans. An increasing number of bread riots, peasant revolts, and urban strikes contributed to a sense of panic at the very time that the government's financial crisis deepened. In Paris the situation reached a critical point in June 1789.

At this point the king, a man with little political sense, made two ill-advised decisions. The first was to send 17,000 royal troops to Paris to restore order. The arrival of the troops gave the impression that the government was planning an attack on the people of the city. The second decision was the dismissal of the king's popular finance minister, Jacques Necker, who had favored the meeting of the Estates General and demonstrated real concern for the welfare of the populace. His dismissal sent a signal that the king was contemplating a move against the National Assembly. It was in this atmosphere of public paranoia that Parisians formed the National Guard and stormed the Bastille.

The fall of the Bastille unnerved the king. When he asked one of his aides, "Is it a revolt?" the aide replied, "No, sire, it is a revolution." The revolution had just begun. It moved into high gear two weeks later when the National Assembly responded to the outbreak of social unrest in the provinces. The scarcity of grain in the countryside gave rise to false rumors that the nobles were engaged in a plot to destroy crops and starve the people into submission. Peasants armed themselves and prepared to fight off the hired agents of the nobility. Some of these peasants burned the mansions of noblemen, together with the deeds that gave the nobles title to their lands and the right to collect dues from their tenants. A widespread panic, known as the "Great Fear," gripped many parts of the country. Townspeople and peasants amassed in large numbers to defend themselves and save the harvest. In response to this panic, which reached its peak in the last two weeks of July, the National Assembly began to pass legislation that destroyed the Old Regime and created a new political order.

## The Creation of a New Political Society

Between August 1789 and September 1790 the National Assembly took three revolutionary steps. The first was the elimination of noble and clerical privilege. In August the assembly abolished the feudal dues that peasants paid their lords, the private legal jurisdictions of noblemen, the collection of tithes by the clergy, and the exclusive rights of noblemen to hunt game on their lands. The privileges of provinces and local towns met the same fate, and ten months later the nobility lost their titles. Instead of a society divided into various corporate groups, each with its own privileges, France would now have only citizens, all of them

equal at law. Social distinctions would be based on merit rather than birth. There were no longer any intermediary powers between the king and the individual subject.

The second step, taken on August 26, was the promulgation of the *Declaration of the Rights of Man and Citizen.* This document reveals the main influence of the Enlightenment on the revolution. It declared that all men, not just Frenchmen, had a natural right to liberty, property, equality before the law, freedom from oppression, and religious toleration. The statement that the "law is the expression of the general will" reflects the influence of Rousseau's *The Social Contract* (1762), while the statement that every citizen has the right to participate in the formation of that law either personally or through a representative embodies the basic principle of democracy. The *Declaration* differed from the English Bill of Rights of 1689 by grounding the rights it proclaimed in natural law rather than in the law of one country. The provisions of the French document therefore serve as statements of broad principle rather than as confirmations of specific rights that the government had allegedly been violating.

The third step in this revolutionary program was a complete reorganization of the Church. In order to solve the problem of the national debt, the National Assembly placed land owned by the Church (about 10 percent of all French territory) at the service of the nation. The Civil Constitution of the Clergy of July 1790 in effect made the Church a department of the state, with the government paying the clergy directly. In order to retain their positions, the clergy were required to take an oath of loyalty to the nation. At the same time the Church was reorganized into eighty-three dioceses, one for each of the departments or administrative units into which the country was also now divided. The bishops of these dioceses were to be elected by laymen. The parishes, which were the basic units of ecclesiastical administration, would become uniform in size, each administering to some 6,000 parishioners.

In 1791 a newly elected Legislative Assembly—replacing the National Assembly—confirmed and extended many of these changes. A constitution, put into effect in October, formalized the end of royal absolutism. The king became a constitutional monarch, retaining only the power to suspend legislation, direct foreign policy, and command the armed forces. The constitution did not, however, give all men the right to vote. Only "active citizens," who paid the equivalent of three days' wages in direct taxes, had the right to vote for electors, who in turn chose representatives to the legislature.

The new constitution formally abolished hereditary legal privileges, thus providing equality of all citizens before the law. Subsequent legislation granted Jews and Protestants full civil rights and toleration. A law eliminating primogeniture (inheritance of the entire estate by the eldest son) gave all heirs equal rights to inherited property.

## DOCUMENT

### *Declaration of the Rights of Man and Citizen* (1789)

*The passage of the Declaration of the Rights of Man and Citizen by the National Assembly on August 26, 1789, is one of the earliest and most enduring acts of the French Revolution. A document of great simplicity and power, it was hammered out during many weeks of debate. Its concern with the natural rights of all people and equality before the law reflected the ideas of the Enlightenment.*

1. Men are born free and remain free and equal in rights. Social distinctions may be founded only on the common good.

2. The aim of all political association is the preservation of the natural and imprescriptible rights of man. These rights are liberty, property, security and resistance to oppression.

3. The principle of all authority rests essentially in the nation. No body nor individual may exercise any authority which does not emanate expressly from the nation.

4. Liberty consists in the freedom to do whatever does not harm another; hence the exercise of the natural rights of each man has no limits except those which assure to the other members of society the enjoyment of the same rights. These limits can only be determined by law. . . .

6. Law is the expression of the general will. Every citizen has the right to participate personally or through his representative in its formation. It must be the same for all, whether it protects or punishes. All citizens, being equal in the eyes of the law, are equally eligible to all dignities and to all public positions and occupations, according to their abilities, and without distinction except that of their virtues and talents.

7. No man may be indicted, arrested, or imprisoned except in cases determined by the law and according to the forms prescribed by law. . . .

10. No one should be disturbed for his opinions, even in religion, provided that their manifestation does not trouble public order as established by law.

11. The free communication of thoughts and opinions is one of the most precious of the rights of man. Every citizen may therefore speak, write, and print freely, but shall be responsible for any abuse of this freedom in the cases set by the law. . . .

17. Property being an inviolable and sacred right, no one may be deprived of it except when public necessity, determined by law, obviously requires it, and then on the condition that the owner shall have been previously and equitably compensated.

Source: From P.-J.-B. Buchez and P.-C. Roux, *Histoire parlementaire de la Révolution française.* (Paris: Paulin, 1834).

The establishment of marriage as a civil contract and the right to end a marriage in divorce supported the idea of the husband and wife as freely contracting individuals. The largely symbolic abolition of slavery in France was consistent with the proclamation of equality of all men, but the failure to extend that emancipation to French colonies suggests that there were limits to the concept of liberty proclaimed by the assembly.

This body of legislation amounted to nothing less than a revolution. The Old Regime had been destroyed and a new one had taken its place. Although the form of government remained a monarchy, the powers of that monarchy were drastically curtailed. Unlike the English revolutions of the 1640s and 1688, this revolution did not disguise the extent of the changes that had transpired by using the language of conservatism, claiming that the revolution had recovered lost freedoms. It did not appeal to the French past at all. It promoted a new view of French society as a nation composed of equal citizens possessing natural rights, in place of the older concept of a society consisting of different corporate groups, each with its own privileges. Contemporaries recognized the significance of these changes. The Portuguese ambassador to France, who witnessed the events of 1789 firsthand, reported back to his government, "In all the world's annals there is no mention of a revolution like this."

## Responses to the First French Revolution

During the early years of the revolution, events in Paris and Versailles dominated the political scene. The revolution was not confined, however, to the metropolis. In the provinces groups of ordinary townspeople and peasants, frightened that the members of the nobility might be taking counteraction against them, took the law into their own hands and brought about a new revolutionary political and social order. In many places the local rulers who had exercised political power in towns and villages were overthrown and replaced by supporters of the new regime. At the same time there was considerable opposition to the revolutionary government. In many parts of the country the clergy's refusal to take the oath of loyalty to the nation led to violent clashes with the provincial authorities. In the south nobles began to organize resistance to the new regime, while militant Catholics attacked Protestants, who had been granted toleration and who generally supported the revolution.

The revolutionary events of 1789–1791 quickly gained the attention of countries outside France. In England the nonconformist Protestant minister Richard Price urged members of the British Parliament to follow the example of their French neighbors and abolish the laws that restricted

## DOCUMENT

### Edmund Burke Deplores the Events of the French Revolution

*The first French Revolution met with both praise and criticism abroad. The strongest attack came from Edmund Burke, an Irish-born lawyer who sat in the British Parliament. Burke, who is recognized as the father of modern conservatism, attacked the leaders of the revolution for destroying religion and the social order in the interests of an abstract philosophy, subverting the law, and introducing a new tyranny.*

. . . France has bought undisguised calamities at a higher price than any nation has purchased the most unequivocal blessings. France has bought poverty by crime. France has not sacrificed her virtue to her interest; but she has abandoned her interest that she might prostitute her virtue. All other nations have begun the fabric of a new government, or the reformation of an old, by establishing originally, or by enforcing with greater exactness, some rites or other of religion. All other people have laid the foundation of civil freedom in severer manners and a system of a more austere and masculine morality. France, when she let loose the reins of regal authority, doubled the license of a ferocious dissoluteness in manners, and of an insolent religion in opinions and practices; and has extended through all ranks of life, as if she were communicating some privilege or laying open some secluded benefit, all the unhappy corruptions that usually were the disease of wealth and power. This is one of the new principles of equality in France.

France, by the perfidy of her leaders, has utterly disgraced the tone of lenient council in the cabinets of princes, and disarmed it of its most potent topics. She has sanctified the dark, suspicious maxims of tyrannous distrust, and taught kings to tremble at . . . the delusive plausibilities of moral politicians. Sovereigns will consider those who advise them to place an unlimited confidence in their people as subverterrs of their thrones—as traitors who aim at their destruction, by leading their easy good—nature, under specious pretenses, to admit combinations of bold and faithless men into a participation of their power. . . . They have seen the French rebel against a mild and lawful monarch, with more fury, outrage, and insult than ever any people has been known to rise against the most illegal usurper or the most sanguinary tyrant. . . .

They have found their punishment in their success. Laws overturned; tribunals subverted; industry without vigour; commerce expiring; the revenue unpaid, yet the people impoverished; a church pillaged, and a state not relieved; civil and military anarchy made the constitution of the kingdom; everything human and divine sacrificed to the idol of public credit, and national bankruptcy the consequence. . . .

Were all these dreadful things necessary? Were they the inevitable results of the desperate struggle of determined patriots, compelled to wade through blood and tumult to the quiet shore of a tranquil and prosperous liberty? No! Nothing like it. The fresh ruins of France, which shock our feelings wherever we can turn our eyes, are not the devastation of civil war: they are the sad, but instructive monuments of rash and ignorant counsel in a time of profound peace. . . .

Source: Edmund Burke, *Reflections on the Revolution in France* (1790).

hunting on aristocratic lands. Prussian reformers took heart that the events of the revolution would portend the destruction of absolutism in their country and in other European lands. A Prussian official who had studied with the philosopher Immanuel Kant called the revolution "the first practical triumph of philosophy . . . the hope and consolation for so many of those ancient ills under which mankind has suffered."

Not all foreign assessments of the revolution were positive. In November 1790 the British politician Edmund Burke published *Reflections on the Revolution in France,* in which he expressed horror at the way in which abstract philosophy had destroyed the traditional social order in France. Pope Pius VI condemned the *Declaration of the Rights of Man and Citizen* and then, outraged at the attack upon the Roman Catholic Church, issued a sweeping condemnation of the Civil Constitution of the Clergy. The absolute monarchs of western Europe, sensing rightly that their regimes were in danger of a contagious revolutionary ideology, not only

planned an invasion of France to restore the old order but took action against dissent in their own territories. When Polish legislators wrote a new constitution in 1791, modeled on that of France, Catherine the Great of Russia, who controlled a portion of Poland at the time, claimed that it was the product of French radicalism. She shut down the presses, revived censorship, turned against the philosophes whom she had admired, and banned the works of Voltaire.

## The French Republic, 1792–1799

■ How did a second, more radical revolution, which began with the establishment of the Republic in 1792, lead to the creation of a regime that used the power of the state to institute the Reign of Terror?

Beginning in 1792 France experienced a second revolution that was much more radical than the first. During this revolution France was transformed from a constitutional monarchy into a republic. The state claimed far greater power than it possessed under the constitutional monarchy established in 1791, and it used that power to bring about a radical reform of French society.

## The Establishment of the Republic, 1792

During the first two years of the revolution it appeared that the building of a new French nation would take place within the framework of a constitutional monarchy. Absolutism had suffered an irreversible defeat, but there was little sentiment among the members of the Legislative Assembly, much less among the general population, in favor of abolishing the institution of monarchy. The only committed republicans—those supporting the establishment of a republic—in the Legislative Assembly belonged to a party known as the Jacobins°, who found support in political clubs in Paris and in other parts of the country. By the late summer of 1792 this group of radicals, drawing upon the support of militant Parisian citizens known as *sans-culottes* (literally, those without breeches, the pants worn by noblemen), succeeded in bringing about the second, more radical revolution.

King Louis himself was in part responsible for this destruction of the monarchy. The success of constitutional monarchy depended on the king's willingness to play the new role assigned to him as a constitutional figurehead. In October 1789 Louis had agreed, under considerable pressure, to move his residence from Versailles to Paris, where the National Assembly had also relocated. The pressure came mainly from women, who formed the large majority of 10,000 demonstrators who marched from Paris to Versailles demanding a reduction in the price of bread. The king yielded to their demands and came to Paris. As he entered the city, accompanied by soldiers, monks, and women carrying guns and pikes, he reluctantly agreed to wear the tricolor cockade (a badge) to symbolize his acceptance of the revolution. Louis, however, could not disguise his opposition to the revolution, especially to the ecclesiastical settlement. This opposition led many people to suspect that he was encouraging the powers of Europe to invade France to restore the Old Regime.

Louis XVI had few personal resources upon which he might draw to win the confidence of his subjects. He was not as intelligent as his grandfather, Louis XV, nor did he have the skills necessary to dispel his subjects' growing distrust of him. Neither Louis nor his Austrian wife, Marie Antoinette, commanded much respect among the people. For many years the royal couple had been the object of relentless, sometimes pornographic satire. He had been lampooned for his rumored sexual inadequacies and she for a series of alleged infidelities with the king's brother and a succession of female partners. Whatever confidence Parisian citizens might have retained in the royal couple evaporated in June 1791, when the king and queen attempted to flee the country. The National Guard apprehended them at Varennes, close to the eastern French border, and forced them to return to Paris, where they were kept under guard at the palace of the Tuileries. Even that development, however, failed to destroy the monarchy,

### Sans-Culottes
Male and female dress of the *sans-culottes,* the armed Parisian radicals who supported the Republic. The men did not wear the breeches (*culottes*) that were in style among the members of the French nobility.

which had been preserved in the constitution implemented in October.

The development that actually precipitated the downfall of the monarchy and led to the establishment of a republic was the decision to go to war. Until the summer of 1791 European powers had been involved in various conflicts and had resisted pleas from French émigrés to support a counterrevolutionary offensive against the new French regime. After the flight to Varennes and the capture of the royal family, however, Frederick William II of Prussia (r. 1786–1797) and Emperor Leopold II of Austria (r. 1790–1792), the brother of Marie Antoinette, signed an alliance and called upon the other monarchs of Europe "to restore to the King of France complete liberty and to consolidate the bases of monarchical government." No action would be taken, however, unless all European sovereigns agreed to cooperate.

The actual declaration of war came not from the monarchs of Europe but from the French Legislative Assembly. A small group of republicans, headed by the eloquent orator Jacques-Pierre Brissot (1754–1793), convinced the assembly that an international conspiracy against the revolution would end in an invasion of their country. Brissot and his supporters also believed that if France could be lured into a foreign war, the king and queen would be revealed as traitors and the monarchy would be destroyed. Exploiting xenophobic as well as revolutionary sentiment, and claiming that the strength of a citizen army would win a quick and decisive victory, Brissot and his allies won the support of the entire assembly. They also appealed to the international goals of the revolution, claiming that the French army would inspire revolution against "the tyrants of Europe" everywhere they went.

The Legislative Assembly declared war on Austria in April 1792. Instead of a glorious victory, however, the war resulted in a series of disastrous defeats at the hands of Austrians and their Prussian allies in the Netherlands. This military failure contributed to a mood of paranoia in France, especially in Paris. Fears arose that invading armies, in alliance with nobles, would undermine the revolution. In May members of the assembly learned that the Austrian minister, in cooperation with a group of the king's advisers, was plotting the destruction of the assembly itself. In July the assembly officially proclaimed the nation to be in danger, calling for all citizens to rally against the enemies of liberty at home and abroad. Women petitioned for the right to bear arms. When the Austrians and Prussians threatened to

**Tricolor Cockade**
Louis XVI wearing the red liberty bonnet with the tricolor cockade on October 20, 1792. Refusing to be intimidated by a crowd of 20,000 people outside the royal palace, he donned the cap and proclaimed his loyalty to the constitution.

torch the entire city of Paris and slaughter its population if anyone laid a hand on the royal family, citizens in Paris immediately demanded that the king be deposed.

On August 10 a radical republican committee overthrew the Paris commune, the city government that had been installed in 1789, and set up a new, revolutionary commune. A force of about 20,000 men, including volunteer troops from various parts of the kingdom, invaded the Tuileries, which was defended by about 900 Swiss guards. When the members of the royal bodyguard fled, they were pursued by members of the Paris crowds, who stripped them of their red uniforms and hacked 600 of them to death with knives, pikes, and hatchets. The attack on the Tuileries forced the king to take refuge in the nearby Legislative Assembly. The assembly promptly suspended the monarchy and turned the royal family over to the commune, which imprisoned them in the Temple, a medieval fortress in the northeastern part of the city. The assembly then ordered its own dissolution and called for the election of a new legislative body that would draft a new constitution.

The fall of the monarchy did nothing to allay the siege mentality of the city, especially after further Prussian victories in early September escalated fears of a Prussian invasion. Individuals suspected of plotting against the regime were imprisoned, and when it was rumored that they would escape and support the Prussian enemy, angry crowds pulled 1,200 prisoners (most of whom were being held for nonpolitical crimes) from their cells and killed them. The feared foreign invasion that had inspired this "September Massacre" never did materialize. On September 20, 1792, a surprisingly well-disciplined and well-trained army of French citizens, inspired by dedication to France and the revolution, repulsed the armies of Austria and Prussia at Valmy. This victory saved the revolution. The German poet Johann Wolfgang von Goethe (1749–1832) claimed that the battle marked the beginning of "a new epoch in the history of the world." Delegates to a new National Convention, elected by universal male suffrage°, had already arrived in

**The Attack on the Palace of the Tuileries**

On the night of August 10, 1792, Parisian crowds and volunteer soldiers attacked the royal palace in Paris. The puffs of smoke in the building are coming from the Swiss guards, who were entrusted with the defense of the royal family and the palace. The royal family escaped and took refuge in the Legislative Assembly, but 600 of the Swiss guards were killed. Those that retreated were hunted down in the streets of Paris and stripped of their uniforms, and their heads were placed on the ends of pikes.

Paris to write a new constitution. On September 22 the convention declared that the monarchy was formally abolished and that France was a republic. France had now experienced a second revolution, more radical than the first, but dedicated to the same principles of liberty, equality, and fraternity.

## The Jacobins and the Revolution

Before the Republic was established, different political factions had begun to vie for power, both in the Legislative Assembly and in the country at large. The first major division to emerge was between the Feuillants, who supported a constitutional monarchy, and the Jacobins, many of whom favored the creation of a democratic republic. By the time the Republic had been declared, the Jacobins had become the major political party. Soon, however, factional divisions began to develop within Jacobin ranks. The main split occurred between the followers of Brissot, known as Girondins°, and the radicals known as Montagnards°, or "the Mountain." The latter acquired their name because they occupied the benches on the side of the convention hall, where the floor sloped upward. The Girondins occupied the lower side of the hall, while the uncommitted deputies, known as "the Plain," occupied the middle. Both the Mountain and the Girondins claimed to be advancing the goals of the revolution, but they differed widely on which tactics to pursue. The Mountain took the position that as long as the state was endangered by internal and external enemies, the government needed to centralize authority in the capital. The Mountain thought of themselves as the representatives of the common people, especially the *sans-culottes* in Paris. Many of their leaders, including

Georges-Jacques Danton (1759–1794), Jean-Paul Marat (1743–1793), and Maximilien Robespierre (1758–1794), were in fact Parisians. Their mission was to make the revolution even more egalitarian and to establish a republic characterized by civic pride and patriotism, which they referred to as the Republic of Virtue.

The Girondins, known as such because many of their leaders came from the southwestern department of Gironde, took a more conservative position than the Mountain on these issues. Favoring the economic freedom and local control desired by merchants and manufacturers, they were reluctant to support further centralization of state power. They believed that the revolution had advanced far enough and should not become more radical. They were also afraid that the egalitarianism of the revolution, if unchecked, would lead to a leveling of French society and result in social anarchy.

The conflict between the Girondins and the Mountain became apparent in the debate over what to do with the deposed king. Louis had been suspected of conspiring with the enemies of the revolution, and the discovery of his correspondence with the Austrian government led to his trial for treason against the nation. The Girondins had originally expressed reluctance to bring him to trial, preferring to keep him in prison. Once the trial began, they joined the entire National Convention in voting to convict him, but they opposed his execution. This stance led the Mountain to accuse the Girondins of being secret collaborators with the monarchy. By a narrow vote the convention decided to put the king to death, and on January 21, 1793, Louis was executed at the Place de la Révolution.

The instrument of death was the guillotine, an efficient and merciful but nonetheless terrifying decapitation machine first pressed into service in April 1792. It took its name from Dr. Joseph-Ignace Guillotin, who had the original idea for such a device, although he did not invent it. The guillotine was inspired by the conviction that all criminals, not just those of noble blood, should be executed in a swift, painless manner. The new device was to be put to extensive use during the next eighteen months, and many Girondins fell victim to it.

The split between the Mountain and the Girondins became more pronounced as the republican regime encountered increasing opposition from foreign and domestic enemies. Early in 1793 Great Britain and the Dutch Republic allied with Prussia and Austria to form the First Coalition against France, and within a month Spain and the kingdoms of Sardinia and Naples joined them. The armies of these allied powers defeated French forces in the Austrian Netherlands in March of that year, and once again an invasion seemed imminent. At the same time internal rebellions against the revolutionary regime took place in various outlying provinces, especially in the district of the Vendée in western France. These uprisings were led by noblemen and clerics, but they also had popular support, especially from tenant farmers who resented the increased taxation imposed by the new revolutionary government.

In the minds of Robespierre and his colleagues, the Girondins were linked to these provincial rebels, whom they labeled as federalists° because they opposed the centralization of the French state and thus threatened the unity of the nation. In June twenty-nine Girondins were expelled from the convention for supporting local officials accused of hoarding grain. This purge made it apparent that any political opponent of the Mountain, even those with solid republican credentials, could now be identified as an enemy of the revolution.

## CHRONOLOGY

## The French Republic and the Terror, 1792–1794

**1792**

| | |
|---|---|
| April 20 | Declaration of war against Austria |
| August 10 | Attack on the Tuileries; monarchy is suspended |
| September 2–6 | September Massacre of prisoners in Paris |
| September 20 | French victory at the Battle of Valmy |
| September 21 | National Convention meets |
| September 22 | Abolition of the monarchy and establishment of the Republic |

**1793**

| | |
|---|---|
| January 21 | Execution of Louis XVI |
| February 1 | Declaration of war against Great Britain and the Dutch Republic |
| March 11 | Beginning of rebellion in the Vendée |
| June 2 | Purge of Girondins from the Convention |
| June 24 | Ratification of a republican constitution |
| July 27 | Robespierre elected to the Committee of Public Safety |
| August 23 | The Convention decrees the *levée en masse* |
| October 5 | Adoption of the revolutionary calendar |
| October 16 | Execution of Marie Antoinette |

**1794**

| | |
|---|---|
| July 28 | Tenth of *Thermidor;* execution of Robespierre |
| November 12 | Jacobin clubs are closed |

# The Trial of Louis XVI

After the abolition of the monarchy and the proclamation of the French Republic in September 1792, the National Convention considered the fate of the deposed king. There was a broad consensus that Louis was guilty of treason against the nation and that he should answer for his crimes, but how he should do so was a matter of heated debate. The convention was divided between the Girondins and the Mountain. Of the two, the Girondins were more inclined to follow legal forms, whereas those of the Mountain considered themselves to be acting as a revolutionary tribunal that should adhere to standards of justice not specifically included in the law of the land. The convention thus became a forum where Louis's accusers expressed competing notions of revolutionary justice.

The most divisive and revealing issue was whether there should be a trial at all. The Mountain originally took the position that because the people had already judged the king on August 10, when the monarchy had fallen and the king taken prisoner, there was no need for a second judgment. They should proceed immediately to carrying out the death sentence. Robespierre argued that to have a trial would be counter-revolutionary, for it would allow the revolution itself to be brought before the court to be judged. A centrist majority, however, decided that the king had to be charged with specific offenses in a court of law and found guilty by due process before being sentenced.

A second issue, closely related to the first, was the technical legal question of whether the king could be subject to legal action. Even if the legislative branch of the government was considered the equal of the king in a constitutional monarchy, it did not possess authority over him. A further argu-

ment was that the king could not be tried for actions for which he had already suffered abdication. This claim was challenged on the most basic principle of the revolution—that the nation was higher than the king and his crimes were committed against that nation, which is the people. The king, moreover, was no longer king but was now a citizen and therefore subject to the law in the same way as anyone else.

The third issue was Louis's culpability for the specific charges in the indictment. These crimes included refusing to call the Estates General, sending an army to march against the citizens of Paris, and conducting secret negotiations with France's enemies. The journalist and deputy Jean-Paul Marat added that "he robbed the citizens of their gold as a subsidy for their foes" and "caused his hirelings to hoard, to create famine, to dry up the sources of abundance that the people might die from misery and hunger."

Nonetheless the king, who appeared personally to hear the indictment and then to respond to the charges on December 26, presented a plausible defense. He based it on the laws in force at the various times he was supposed to have committed his crimes. Thus he defended his sending of troops to Paris on the grounds that in June and July 1789 he could order troops wherever he wanted. In the same vein he argued that he had used force solely in response to illegal intimidation. These legalisms, however, only made the members of the convention more contemptuous of the king. His defense failed to persuade a single convention deputy. He was convicted of treason by a vote of 693–0.

This unanimous conviction of the king did not end the factional debates over the king's fate. Knowing that there was extensive

support for the king in various parts of the country, the Girondins asked that the verdict be appealed to the people. Their argument was that the convention, dominated by the Mountain and supported by militants in Paris, had usurped the sovereignty of the people. Pierre-Victurnien Vergniaud, a lawyer from Bordeaux, pleaded that "To take this right from the people would be to take sovereignty from them, to transfer it . . . to the hands of the representatives chosen by the people, to transform their representatives into kings or tyrants." Vergniaud's motion to submit the verdict to the people for ratification lost by a vote of 424–283.

The last vote, the closest of all, determined the king's sentence. Originally it appeared that a majority might vote for noncapital punishment. The Marquis de Condorcet, for example, argued that although the king deserved death on the basis of the law of treason, he could not bring himself to vote for capital punishment on principle. The radical response to this argument came from Robespierre, who appealed to the "principles of nature" in stating that the death penalty could be justified "only in those cases where it is vital to the safety of private citizens or of the public." Robespierre's impassioned oratory carried the day. By a vote of 361–334 the king was sentenced to "death within 24 hours" rather than the alternatives of imprisonment followed by banishment after the war or imprisonment in chains for life. The following day Louis was led to the guillotine.

All public trials, especially those for political crimes, are theatrical events, in that the various parties play specific roles and seek to convey certain messages to their audiences. The men who voted to put Louis XVI on trial

**Execution of Louis XVI, January 21, 1793**
Although the king was convicted of treason by a unanimous vote, the vote to execute him carried by a slender majority of only twenty-seven votes.

wanted to create an educational spectacle in which the already deposed monarch would be stripped of any respect he might still have commanded among the people. Louis was to be tried like any other traitor, and he was to suffer the same fate, execution by the guillotine. The attempt to strip him of all privilege and status continued after his death. His corpse, with his head placed between his knees, was taken to a cemetery, placed in a wooden box, and buried in the common pit. The revolutionaries were determined to guarantee that even in death the king would have the same position as the humblest of his former subjects.

## Questions of Justice

1. How would you describe the standard of justice that the members of the National Convention upheld in voting to execute the king? How did this standard of justice differ from the standard to which King Louis XVI appealed?

2. Evaluate the argument of Robespierre that the death penalty can be justified only in cases of public safety. Compare his argument to that of Enlightenment thinkers such as Cesare Beccaria that capital punishment was an unjust, unnecessary, and uncivilized punishment.

## Taking It Further

Jordan, David P. *The King's Trial: The French Revolution vs. Louis XVI.* 1979. The most thorough account of the trial.

Walzer, Michael, ed. *Regicide and Revolution: Speeches at the Trial of Louis XVI.* 1974. A valuable collection of speeches with an extended commentary.

In order to repel the coalition of foreign powers, the convention ordered a *levée en masse,* a conscription of troops from the entire population. This step, taken in August 1793, created an unprecedented military force, a massive citizen army drawn from all segments of the population and committed to the prosecution of the war. In the past the rank and file of European armies, whether mercenaries or regular troops, had been filled with men on the margins of society: the poor, the unemployed, and even criminal outcasts. The conscription of males from all ranks of society might have promoted a sense of national unity among the troops, but it also caused resentment and resistance against this use of state power. It led to increased federalist resistance to the radical Jacobin government.

## The Reign of Terror, 1793–1794

In order to deal with its domestic enemies, the republican government claimed powers that far exceeded those exercised by the monarchy in the age of absolutism. The convention passed laws that set up special courts to prosecute enemies of the regime and authorized special procedures that deprived those accused of their legal rights. These laws laid the legal foundation for the Reign of Terror°, a campaign to rid the state of its internal enemies. A Committee of Public Safety, consisting of twelve members entrusted with the executive power of the state, superintended this process. Although technically subordinate to the convention, the Committee of Public Safety became in effect a revolutionary dictatorship.

The man who emerged as the main figure on the Committee of Public Safety was Maximilien Robespierre. A brilliant student as a youth, Robespierre was affronted when the king's carriage splashed him with mud as he was waiting to read an address to the king. A man with little sense of humor, he was passionate in his quest for justice. As a lawyer who defended indigent clients, Robespierre was elected to the Third Estate in 1789 and became a favorite of the *sans-culottes,* who called him "The Incorruptible." That

**DOCUMENT**

Saint-Just on Democracy, Justice and the Terror (1790s)

he may have been, but he was also susceptible to the temptation to abuse power for partisan political purposes. Like Rousseau, whose work he admired, he was also willing to sacrifice individual liberty in the name of the collective General Will. His logic was that since the General Will was indivisible, it could not accommodate dissent. Robespierre was primarily responsible for pushing the revolution to new extremes and for establishing the program of state repression that began in the autumn of 1793.

The most intense prosecutions of the Terror took place between October 1793 and June 1794, but they continued until August 1794. By that time the revolutionary courts had executed 17,000 people, while 500,000 had suffered imprisonment. Another 20,000 either died in prison or were

killed without any form of trial. Among the victims of the Terror were substantial numbers of clergy and nobility, as we might expect, but the overwhelming majority were artisans and peasants. One Parisian stableboy was guillotined for having said "f . . . the Republic," while a baker from Alsace lost his head for predicting that "the Republic will go to hell with all its partisans."[2] Many of the victims came from the outlying regions of the country, especially the northeast, where foreign armies were threatening the Republic, and the west, where a brutal civil war between the French army and Catholics and Royalists was raging. These provincial enemies of the regime were identified by special surveillance committees and then were tried by revolutionary tribunals. The guillotine was by no means the only method of execution. In November and December 1793, about 1,800 rebels captured during the uprising in the Vendée were tied to other prisoners, placed in sinking boats, and drowned in the chilly waters of the Loire River.

The most visible and alarming of the executions took place in the capital. The execution of Marie Antoinette and other royalists might have been justified on the basis of their active subversion of the regime, but trumped-up charges against Girondins exposed a process that would destroy republicans as well. As one Girondin said in a speech to the Convention, the revolution, like the mythical Roman god Saturn, devoured its own children. Some of the most prominent figures of the Enlightenment fell victim to this paranoia. Among them was the Marquis de Condorcet, who believed passionately that all citizens, including women, had equal rights. Having campaigned against capital punishment, he committed suicide in a Parisian prison, just before he was to be executed. Another figure of the Enlightenment, the famous chemist Antoine Lavoisier (1743–1794), who had devoted himself to improving social and economic conditions in France, was executed at the same time. So too was the feminist Olympe de Gouges, who as we discussed in Chapter 18 had petitioned for the equal political rights of women. Many French revolutionaries, including Robespierre, used the political ideas of the Enlightenment to justify their actions, but the Terror struck down some of the most distinguished figures of that movement. In that sense the Terror marked the end of the Enlightenment in France.

The Committee of Public Safety then went after Danton and other so-called "Indulgents," who had decided that the Terror had gone too far. Danton's execution made everyone, especially moderate Jacobins, wonder who would be the next victim of a process that had spun completely out of control. In June 1794 the Terror reached a climax, as 1,300 people were sent to their deaths. In order to stop the process, a group of Jacobins in the convention, headed by Joseph Fouché (1759–1820) and Paul Barras (1755–1829), organized a plot against Robespierre. Calling him a tyrant, they arrested him and more than 100 of his followers and guillotined them in late July 1794. An equally swift retaliation was exacted against the Jacobins in the provinces, when members of the White Terror, so named for the white Bourbon flag they displayed, executed leaders of the local revolutionary tribunals. With these reprisals, which used the very same methods that had been perfected by Robespierre and his followers, the most violent and radical phase of the French revolution came to an end.

The Reign of Terror had ended, but its memory would never be extinguished. Its horrors served as a constant warning against the dangers inherent in revolutionary movements. The guillotine, the agent of a dysfunctional and indiscriminate state terrorism, became just as closely identified with the French Revolution as its famous slogan of "Liberty, Equality, Fraternity." The contrast between those two symbols, each of them emblematic of a different stage of the revolution, helps to explain how both conservatives and liberals in the nineteenth century would be able to appeal to the experience of the revolution to support their contradictory ideologies.

## The Directory, 1795–1799

A desire to end the violence of the Terror allowed moderates in the National Convention to regain control of the state apparatus that Robespierre and his allies had used to such devastating effect. The Paris Commune was dismantled and the Committee of Public Safety stripped of most of its powers. In November 1794 the Jacobin clubs throughout the country, which had provided support for the Terror, were closed. The moderates who now controlled the government still hoped to preserve the gains of the revolution, while returning the country to more familiar forms of authority. A new constitution of 1795 bestowed executive power on a five-man Directorate, while an assembly consisting of two houses, the Council of Elders and the Council of Five Hundred, proposed and voted on all legislation. The franchise was limited to property holders, allowing only 2,000,000 men out of an adult male population of 7,000,000 to vote. A system of indirect election, in which a person voted for electors who then selected representatives, guaranteed that only the wealthiest members of the country would sit in the legislative assembly.

The establishment of the Directory formed part of a more general reaction against the culture of the republic. The austere, egalitarian dress of the *sans-culottes* gave way once again to fancy and opulent clothes, at least among the bourgeoisie. Low

necklines, officially out of favor during the Reign of Terror, once again came back into fashion among wealthier members of society. The high social life of the capital experienced a revival. Some dances took place on the sites of churches that Jacobins had desecrated. Jacobin theaters were shut down and Jacobin works of art destroyed. France was still a republic, but it was no longer Robespierre's Republic of Virtue.

Some of the more entrepreneurial citizens of Paris welcomed the new regime, but opposition soon arose, mainly from Jacobins and *sans-culottes*. When the government relaxed the strict price controls that had been in effect under the Jacobins, the soaring price of bread and other commodities caused widespread social discontent among the population. This situation was aggravated by the continuation of the interminable war against the foreign powers in the First Coalition. Wherever French troops went, their constant need of food and other goods resulted in serious shortages of these commodities.

By the end of 1798 conditions had grown even worse. Inflation was running out of control. The collection of taxes was intermittent at best. The paper money known as *assignats*, first issued by the government in 1791 and backed by the value of confiscated church lands, had become almost worthless. Late in 1797 the Directory had been forced to cancel more than half the national debt, a

**CHRONOLOGY**

## The Directory, 1795–1799

**1795**

| | |
|---|---|
| August 22 | The National Convention approves a new constitution |
| October 5 | Napoleon suppresses a royalist insurrection in Paris |
| October 26 | End of the Convention; beginning of the Directory |
| **1796** | |
| February 19 | The issuing of *assignats* is halted |
| April 12 | Beginning of a series of victories by Napoleon in Italy |
| **1798** | |
| May 13 | Napoleon's expedition departs for Egypt |
| May | Second Coalition (Britain, Austria, Russia, Naples, and Turkey) is formed against Napoleon |
| July 21 | Napoleon wins the Battle of the Pyramids |
| August 1 | Nelson destroys the French fleet at the Battle of the Nile |
| **1799** | |
| November 9–10 | Napoleon's coup on the eighteenth of *Brumaire*; Consulate is established |

### The 25th December 1799. The Three Consuls: Bonaparte, Cambecérès and Lebrun (1856)

This painting by Louis-Charles-Auguste Couder shows the three consuls taking the oath of office before the presidents of the Assembly on December 25, 1799. Napoleon, the First Consul, stands at the center of the three to the left.

step that further alienated wealthy citizens who had lent money to the government. Military setbacks in 1798 and 1799 brought the situation to a critical point. An expedition to Egypt, which was intended to gain for France a foothold in the Middle East, had resulted in a number of victories against the Turks, but the British destroyed the French fleet at the Battle of the Nile in 1798. The next year a series of revolts against French rule in Italy and in the Austrian Netherlands pushed the French armies back to France's earlier boundaries. The formation of a Second Coalition of European powers in 1799, which included Russia, Naples, and Turkey as well as Britain and Austria, represented a formidable challenge to French power and ensured that the war would not end soon. These military events produced a swing to the political left and raised the specter of another Jacobin coup.

In the face of this instability, Emmanuel-Joseph Sieyès, who had been elected as one of the directors two years earlier, decided to overthrow the government. Sieyès provided a link between the early years of the revolution, when he had defended the Third Estate, and the current government of the Directory. Unlike many other prominent political figures, he had managed to avoid prosecution as the revolution had become more radical. When asked what he had done during the Reign of Terror, Sieyès replied, "I survived." The goal of the planned coup was to provide the country with strong government, its greatest need in a period of political, economic, and social instability. The person Sieyès selected as his partner in this enterprise, and the man who immediately assumed leadership of the coup, was Napoleon Bonaparte (1769–1821), a 30-year-old general who in 1795

had put down a royalist rebellion in Paris with a "whiff of grapeshot."

Napoleon had already established impressive credentials as a military leader. In 1796 and 1797 he had won major victories in Italy, leading to the Treaty of Campo Formio with Austria in 1797. Those victories and his short-lived success at the Battle of the Pyramids in Egypt had made him enormously popular in Paris, where he was received as a hero when he assumed command of the armed forces in the city in 1799. His popularity, his demonstrated military leadership, and his control of a large armed force made this "man on horseback" appear to have the best chance to replace the enfeebled civilian regime of the Directory.

On November 9, 1799, Napoleon addressed the two legislative councils. He reported that another Jacobin conspiracy had been uncovered and that in order to deal with such insurrections a new constitution must be written to give the executive branch of the government more authority. Napoleon encountered resistance from some members of the Council of Five Hundred, who demanded that he be declared an outlaw. At this stage the president of the council, Napoleon's brother Lucien, intervened and called in troops to evict the members who opposed him. The following day France had a new government, known as the Consulate.

Executive power in the new government was to be vested in three consuls. It soon became clear, however, that Napoleon would be the dominant member of this triumvirate, and in the new constitution of December 1799, which the electorate ratified by means of a plebiscite, Napoleon was named First Consul. This appointment made him the most powerful man in France and for all practical purposes a military dictator. Republican forms of government were preserved in the new constitution, but they were easily manipulated to produce what the consuls desired. A Senate appointed by the consuls chose men from a list of 6,000 "notables" to form a body known as the Tribunate, which would discuss legislation proposed by the consuls. Another assembly, the Legislative Body, would vote on those measures without debate.

With the establishment of the Consulate the French Republic was a thing of the past. It had been replaced by a military dictatorship in all but name. This transformation of the republic into a military dictatorship had been predicted by both the radical democrat Robespierre and the British conservative Edmund Burke many years before. The dictatorship became more apparent in 1802, when Napoleon was named Consul for Life, and in 1804, when he crowned himself emperor of the French.

# Cultural Change in France During the Revolution

■ In what ways did the political events of the revolution change French cultural institutions and create a new political culture?

The French Revolution was primarily a political revolution. It brought about fundamental change in the system of government. It resulted in the destruction of the monarchy and the establishment of a republic. It inspired the drafting of new constitutions, led to the creation of new legislative assemblies, and endowed the state with unprecedented power. The French revolution also brought about profound changes in French culture. It transformed the cultural institutions of the Old Regime and created a new revolutionary culture.

## The Transformation of Cultural Institutions

Between 1791 and 1794 most of the cultural institutions of the Old Regime were either destroyed or radically transformed, and new institutions under the control of the state took their place.

## Schools

The confiscation of church property in 1790, followed by the abolition of the monastic religious orders, had a devastating effect on the traditional parish schools, colleges, and universities, most of which were run by the clergy. Without sufficient endowments, many of these schools were forced to close. During the Terror, schools suspected of having

aristocratic associations and teaching counterrevolutionary doctrines came under further assault. Thousands of teachers lost their salaries and sought employment elsewhere. In September 1793 the universities were suppressed.

The government gradually realized that the entire educational process was collapsing. Recognizing the necessity of using education to encourage loyalty to the republican regime, the National Convention established a system of universal primary education. Instruction would be free, and the teachers would receive their salaries from the state. Unfortunately, the state did not have enough money to pay for the system, so the schools continued to languish.

The state was only slightly more successful in providing secondary education by converting abandoned colleges, monasteries, and libraries into "central schools," which were intended to provide a standardized form of state education. By 1799, the central schools had 10,000 students, 40,000 fewer than were in the colleges in 1789. The system was improved significantly during the Napoleonic period when the government established thirty-six secondary schools known as *lycées* while also allowing private and religious schools to continue to function.

### Academies

The Parisian scientific and artistic academies established by Louis XIV (see Chapter 15) had a monopoly over the promotion and transmission of knowledge in the sciences and the visual arts. The academies were the epitome of privilege. They controlled their own membership, determined the recipients of their prizes, and had a monopoly of their particular branch of knowledge. They were also heavily aristocratic institutions; as many as three-quarters of their members were nobles or clergy.

During the revolution the academies were abolished as part of a general attack on corporate bodies. The work they did was taken over by various government committees. For example, the Commission on Weights and Measures, which had been part of the Academy of Science, became an independent commission. Its task had been to provide uniform weights and measures for the entire kingdom. In 1795 it established the meter, calculated as one ten-millionth of the distance from the North Pole to the equator, as the standard measure of distance. The metric system and the decimal system, which were introduced at the same time, have subsequently been adopted as universal standards in all European countries except Great Britain.

The Royal Academy of Arts, dissolved by a vote of the National Convention in 1793, was replaced by the Popular and Republican Society of the Arts. The inspiration for this new republican society, which was open to artists of all social ranks, was Jacques-Louis David (1748–1825), the greatest painter of his generation. Employed at the court of Louis XVI, David became a vocal main critic of the academy at the time of the revolution. He painted some of the most memorable scenes of the revolution, including the oath taken at the tennis court by the members of the National Assembly in 1789. During the Republic David depicted heroes of the revolution such as Jean-Paul Marat, and after the empire was established he was appointed First Painter to Napoleon. David presided over a revival of classicism in French painting, employing Greek and Roman motifs and exhibiting a rationalism and lack of sentiment in his work.

## Libraries

Shortly after the revolution had begun, thousands of books and manuscripts from the libraries of monasteries, royal castles, residences of the nobility, and academies came into the possession of the state. Many of these were funneled into the Royal Library, which grew five times in size between 1789 and 1794 and was appropriately renamed the National Library. The government also intended to inventory and catalog all the books held in libraries throughout the country. This effort to create the General Bibliography of France was never completed, and while the books were being cataloged, the government decided to get rid of those that dealt with "theology, mysticism, feudalism, and royalism" by sending them to foreign countries. This decision did not lead to the export of books to other parts of Europe, but it initiated a frenzy of book sales, mainly to private individuals. Altogether about five million books were lost or sold during these years.

## Museums and Monuments

The day after the abolition of the monarchy the National Assembly created a Commission of the Museum, whose function was "to collect paintings, statues and other precious objects from the crown possessions" as well as from the churches and houses of the émigrés. The museum was to be located in the Louvre, a royal palace that also served as an art gallery. When it opened in August 1793 the Louvre included a majority of paintings with religious themes, most of them confiscated from royal and émigré residences. The incompatibility of these religious works of art with the republican rejection of Christianity can be explained only by the assumption that this museum was intended to be entirely historical and to have no relevance to contemporary politics. The Louvre and the Museum of French Monuments represented an attempt to quarantine the religious French past from its secular present, lest it contaminate the revolution itself.

The revolutionaries did not have the same respect for the bodies of their former kings. On August 10, 1793, the first anniversary of the deposition of Louis XVI, the National Convention ordered the destruction of all the tombs of past French kings. One by one the tombs were opened and the corpses, embalmed in lead, were removed. Metals and valuables were melted down for use in the war effort. The corpses were either left to disintegrate in the atmosphere or dragged unceremoniously to the cemetery, where they were

**Destruction of the Statue of Louis XIV in the Place de Victoires, August 11, 1792**

The leaders of the Republic attempted to eliminate the memory of the institution of monarchy by destroying statues as well as the tombs of France's kings.

thrown into the common pit. The corpse of Louis XIV landed on top of that of Henry IV. This disrespectful treatment of the remains of France's former kings was intended to erase the memory of monarchy.

## The Creation of a New Political Culture

As the state was taking over and adapting the cultural institutions of the Old Regime, revolutionaries engaged in a much bolder and original undertaking: the production of a new, revolutionary political culture. Its sole purpose was to legitimate and glorify the new regime. It symbolized the political values of that regime: liberty, equality, and fraternity in 1789 and republicanism after 1792. This culture was almost entirely political; all forms of cultural expression were subordinated to the realization of a pressing political agenda.

One of the main characteristics of this culture was that it was popular—it was shared by the entire populace, not simply by a small upper-class or literate elite. The fundamental political doctrine of the revolution was popular sovereignty°: the claim that the people were the highest political power in the state. The revolutionaries claimed that this power could never be alienated. The move of the National Assembly from Versailles to Paris actually enabled the people to be present in the gallery during political debate, and deputies were always conscious of their presence. "Learn," claimed one of them in 1789, "that we are deliberating here in front of our masters and we are answerable to them for our opinions." The political culture that emerged—the textual and literary symbols spoken, written, and drawn to reflect this sovereignty of the people—would become the property of the entire population, especially in Paris, where the revolutionary cause found its most passionate popular support. The very words used to identify revolutionary institutions, such as the National Assembly and the National Guard, formed the texture of this new political culture.

The common people who embraced this new culture most enthusiastically were the *sans-culottes*—the radical shopkeepers, artisans, and laborers of Paris. The dress of these people influenced a change in fashion among the wealthier segments of society. A simple jacket replaced the ruffled coat worn by members of the upper classes, their powdered wigs gave way to natural hair, and they too now wore long trousers. They also donned the red liberty cap, to which a tricolor cockade was affixed. The tricolor, which combined the red and blue colors of Paris with the white symbol of the Bourbon monarchy, identified the adherents of the revolution.

Symbols of revolution could be found everywhere. The commercialization of the revolution guaranteed that the tricolor flag, portraits of revolutionary figures, and images of the Bastille would appear on household objects as constant reminders of the public's support for the revolution. By an order of the government in 1792 all men were required to wear the tricolor cockade. Liberty trees, first planted by peasants as protests against local landlords, became a symbol of the revolution. By May 1792 more than 60,000 had been planted throughout the country.

The press, no longer tightly controlled by the government and the printers' guild, became a crucial agent of revolutionary propaganda and a producer of the new culture. Pamphlets, newspapers, brochures, and posters all promoted a distinctive revolutionary language, which became one of the permanent legacies of the revolution. Political leaders used the same rhetoric in their political speeches. *Sans-culottes* sang satirical songs and ballads, many of them to the same tunes well known in the Old Regime. The most popular of the songs of the revolutionary period was the *Marseillaise,* first sung by soldiers preparing for battle against the Austrians but soon adopted by the civilian population and sung at political gatherings. The theaters, which had been privileged corporations in the Old Regime but also carefully regulated, were now free to engage in political satire that strengthened the ties of the people to the revolution.

Much of this new political culture stemmed from the conviction that the doctrine of popular sovereignty should be practiced in everyday life. *Sans-culottes* did this by joining the political clubs organized by different factions within the National Assembly, by addressing others as citizens, and by using the more familiar form of the pronoun *you* (*tu* rather than *vous*) in all conversations. They also participated in the revolution by taking public oaths. On the first anniversary of the fall of the Bastille, as many as 350,000 people, many of them members of the "federations" of National Guards throughout the country, gathered on the royal parade ground outside Paris to take an oath "to the Nation, to the Law, to the King." Direct democracy was not possible in a society of 27 million people, but these cultural practices allowed people to believe that they were participating actively in the political process.

The new revolutionary culture was emphatically secular. In its most extreme form, it was blatantly anti-Christian. In September 1793 the radical Jacobin and former priest Joseph Fouché inaugurated a program of de-Christianization°. Under his leadership, radical Jacobins closed churches and removed religious symbols such as crosses from cemeteries and public venues. In an effort to establish a purely civic religion, they forbade the public practice of religion and renamed churches "temples of reason." In their public pronouncements the architects of de-Christianization avoided reference to the Christian period of French history, which covered the entire national past.

This de-Christianization campaign became the official policy of the Paris Commune, and the National Convention issued a few edicts to enforce it. The program, however, did not win widespread support, and even some Jacobins

**Oath Taking**

On July 14, 1790, the first anniversary of the fall of the Bastille, as many as 350,000 people gathered on a field outside Paris to take an oath of loyalty to the new French nation. The event was referred to as the Feast of the Federation, because most of the oath takers were members of the regional federations of National Guards. The oath taking, which had many characteristics of a religious gathering, was led by the king himself, and it marked the most optimistic period of the revolution.

claimed that in rejecting Christianity it had undermined a belief in God and the afterlife. In 1794 Robespierre attempted to modify the excesses of de-Christianization by launching the Cult of the Supreme Being. He promoted a series of festivals acknowledging the existence of a deity and the immortality of the soul. This new cult paid lip service to traditional religious beliefs, but it still served secular purposes. In fact, the cult was designed to direct the spiritual yearnings of the French people into patriotic undertakings and promote republican virtue.

The new secular revolutionary culture incorporated many elements of the Christian culture that had prevailed before the revolution began. The new pageants and festivals designed to promote a civic religion were modeled on traditional Catholic processions. Revolutionaries co-opted some of the religious holy days for their own purposes. Churches were converted to temples honoring revolutionary heroes. An effigy of Jean-Paul Marat, who was murdered in 1793, appeared on the altar of a Parisian church, next to a female statue of liberty. Jacques-Louis David's portrait of the murdered Marat depicted the slain victim in the manner of the dead Christ in Michelangelo's *Pietà*. Meetings of revolutionaries often took on the atmosphere of religious revivals, as men and women wept in response to orations. Secular catechisms taught young children the virtues of republicanism in the same way that they had in-

**Jacques-Louis David, *The Death of Marat* (1793)**
The Jacobin journalist Jean-Paul Marat was stabbed to death in his bathtub by a noblewoman, Charlotte Corday, in July 1793. The painting depicts Marat as having suffered a martyr's death. Marat holds the letter from his murderer that gave her entrance to his residence.

structed them in Christian doctrine during the Old Regime.

In order to destroy all vestiges of the Old Regime, the government also instituted a new calendar in October 1793. The dates on the calendar began with September 22, 1792, the day the Republic was established. That became the first day of the year I, while the weeks now had ten days instead of seven. The new months were given names to evoke the different seasons, such as *Brumaire* for the first month of wintry weather, *Germinal* for the season of planting, and *Thermidor* for the warmest month of the summer. Hostile British contemporaries gave their own humorous renditions of these names, translating them as Freezy, Flowery, Heaty, and so on. The new calendar was intended to make the revolution a part of people's everyday consciousness. It remained in effect until the last day of 1805.

The new revolutionary culture was disseminated widely, but it was always contested. Royalists trampled on the tricolor cockade, refused to adopt the new style of dress, and pulled up the liberty trees. This resistance from counterrevolutionary forces guaranteed that when the revolution was reversed, much of the new political culture would disappear. Napoleon did little to perpetuate it, and the restored monarchy was openly hostile to it. Like the political revolution, however, some elements of revolutionary culture, such

as the tricolor and the rhetoric of the revolutionary press, could never be suppressed. Not only did these cultural innovations inspire revolutionaries for the next hundred years, but they also became part of the mainstream of Western civilization.

## Cultural Uniformity

One of the most striking features of the new revolutionary culture was its concern for standardization and simplicity. The division of France into *départements,* all roughly equal in size, population, and wealth, and the further subdivision of each *département* into uniform districts and communes, serves as one manifestation of this compulsion. The establishment of a national school system, at least on paper, serves as another. When the *lycées* were founded by Napoleon, each of the schools was given the exact same curriculum, and the same 3,000 books, chosen by a central committee, were deposited in all *lycée* libraries. The adoption of the metric system and the decimal system and the plan to establish one body of French law for the entire country, eventually brought to fruition by Napoleon, reflected the same impulse. So too did the efforts begun during the Terror to make French the official language in regions of the country that spoke Breton, Occitan, Basque, or other regional dialects.

The main source of this drive toward cultural uniformity was the desire to build a new French nation composed of equal citizens. Linguistic, legal, educational, or administrative diversity only made the realization of that program more difficult. The quest for cultural and political standardization did not, however, originate during the revolution. Many of the projects of the 1790s, especially the desire to establish standard weights and measures, began during the Old Regime. They were often the product of the rationalism of the Enlightenment, which, as we have seen in Chapter 18, sought to make society conform to the operation of universal laws.

## The Napoleonic Era, 1799–1815

■ **How did the authoritarian rule of Napoleon Bonaparte from 1799 to 1814 confirm or betray the achievements of the French Revolution, and what impact did his military conquests have on Europe and the world?**

The coup d'état on November 9, 1799, or the eighteenth of *Brumaire* on the revolutionary calendar, marked a turning point in the political history of France. The Consulate ushered in a period of authoritarian rule. Liberty was restricted in the interest of order; republicanism gave way to dictatorship. The French Revolution had apparently run its course. But the period between 1799 and 1815 was also a time of considerable innovation, especially in the realm of politics and diplomacy. Those innovations were primarily the work of one man, Napoleon Bonaparte, who controlled the French government for the next fifteen years.

## Napoleon's Rise to Power

Napoleon Bonaparte was born on the Mediterranean island of Corsica. His father, Charles-Marie de Buonaparte, was an attorney who had supported the Corsican patriot Pascale de Paoli in winning the independence of the island from the Italian state of Genoa. His mother, Letizia, had come from an old noble family from Lombardy in Italy. In 1770 the new French government, which had gained control of the island the previous year, accepted the Buonaparte family as nobility. In 1779 the young Napoleon, whose native language was Corsican, received an appointment to a French military school. He survived both the rigors of the course of study and the taunting of his classmates, who mocked him for his accent and his poverty. Displaying a natural gift for military science, he won a position in the artillery section of the national military academy in Paris.

Until the beginning of the French Revolution, Napoleon seemed destined to pursue a successful but unspectacular career as an officer in the royal army. The events of the revolution made possible his rapid ascent to military prominence and political power. When the revolution broke out, Napoleon returned to Corsica, where he organized the National Guard and petitioned the government to grant full rights of citizenship to his people. As the revolution became more radical he became a Jacobin, and he was commissioned to attack federalist and royalist positions in the south of France. Unlike many of his fellow Jacobins, he managed to survive the Terror and then found favor with the Directory. In 1796 Napoleon was given command of the Army of Italy, at which time he abandoned the Italian spelling of his name for Bonaparte. His decisive victories against the Austrians and his popularity in Paris attracted the attention of Sieyès and others who wished to give the country strong, charismatic leadership.

Napoleon's personality was ideally suited to the acquisition and maintenance of political power. A man of unparalleled ambition, he was driven by an extraordinarily high assessment of his abilities. After one of his military victories he wrote, "I realized I was a superior being and conceived the ambition of performing great things." To the pursuit of his destiny he harnessed a determined and a stubborn will. Temporary setbacks never seemed to thwart his single-minded pursuit of glory. He brought enormous energy to his military and political pursuits. He wrote more than 80,000 letters during his life, many of them transmitting orders to his officers and ministers. Authoritarian by nature, he used intimidation as well as paternal concern to cultivate the loyalty of his subordinates. Like many authoritarian leaders, he had difficulty delegating authority, a trait that was to weaken his regime. Finally, in an age dominated by high-minded causes, he exhibited an instinctive distrust of ideology and the doctrinaire pronouncements of philosophes such as Rousseau. Napoleon's military training led him to take a pragmatic, disciplined approach to politics, in which he always sought the most effective means to the desired end.

Napoleon's acquisition of power was systematic and shrewd. Playing on the need for a strong leader, and using the army he controlled as his main political tool, he maneuvered himself into the position of first consul in 1799. In 1802 he became consul for life, and two years later he crowned himself emperor of the French and his wife Josephine empress. The title of emperor traditionally denoted the height of monarchical power. It identified a ruler who not only ruled more than one kingdom or state but also did not share power with any other political authority. That was certainly the case with Napoleon. During his rule the Legislative Body, the Senate, and the Tribunate, all of which had been instituted during the Consulate, were reduced to performing only ceremonial functions.

It is certainly ironic that Napoleon, while continuing to hunt down and execute royalists, accepted a title of royalty himself and made his position, just like the French kingship, hereditary. In 1804 a group of royalists, including the members of the Bourbon family, were convicted of and executed for trying to assassinate Napoleon. One of them declared ironically, "We have done more than we hoped. We meant to give France a king, and we have given her an emperor." That emperor, moreover, appeared to the royalists and to many others to be a tyrant who would trample on the rights of the French people. Napoleon's coronation also made a negative impression outside France. The great German composer Ludwig van Beethoven, having dedicated his *Third Symphony* (1803) to Napoleon for overthrowing tyranny in France, scratched Napoleon's name from the dedication after Napoleon assumed his new position as emperor.

## Napoleon and the Revolution

What was the relationship between Napoleon's rule and the French Revolution? Did Napoleon consolidate the gains of the revolution or destroy them? Did he simply redirect the revolutionary commitment to liberty, equality, and fraternity into new and more disciplined channels of expression after 1799? Or did he reverse the political trends that had prevailed from 1789 to 1799, crushing liberty in all its forms and establishing a ruthless, authoritarian dictatorship? Napoleon always thought of himself as the heir of the

**Emperor Napoleon Crowning His Wife, Josephine, Empress of the French
in the Cathedral of Notre Dame, 1804**

This painting by Jacques-Louis David depicts secular and religious figures gathered around
Napoleon not as members of privileged orders but as representatives of the nation. Pope Pius VII
remains seated as Napoleon places the crown on Josephine's head. Napoleon had already crowned
himself emperor of the French.

revolution rather than its undertaker. Certainly he was able to use the radical vocabulary of the revolution to characterize his domestic programs and his military campaigns. He presented himself as the ally of the common man against entrenched aristocratic privilege. He proclaimed a love for the French people and gave his support to the doctrine of popular sovereignty. He often referred to the rulers of other European countries as tyrants and presented himself as the liberator of their subjects.

This view of Napoleon as a true revolutionary, however, ignores the fact that his commitment to liberty was almost entirely rhetorical. Behind the appeals to the slogans of the revolution lurked an authoritarian will that was far stronger than that of any eighteenth-century absolute monarch. He used the language of liberty and democracy to disguise a thoroughgoing authoritarianism, just as he used the rhetoric of republicanism to legitimize his own dictatorial regime. The practice of holding carefully orchestrated and controlled elections to ratify the changes he made in French government guaranteed that his rule would appear to have

emanated from the will of the people. At the establishment of the Consulate, Napoleon paid lip service to representative forms of government, which he maintained but then proceeded to render totally ineffective. When the empire was established he told his troops that they had the freedom to vote for or against the new form of government but then told them that if they voted against it, they would be shot.

We can make a stronger case for Napoleon's egalitarianism. He spoke of equality of opportunity. He synthesized the egalitarianism of the revolution with the authoritarianism of the Old Regime. He supported the equality of all Frenchmen (but not Frenchwomen) before the law. This egalitarianism laid the foundation for the support he received from the peasants, soldiers, and workers. It might be said that he brought both equality and political stability to France in exchange for political liberty.

There are two other ways in which we might legitimately consider Napoleon the heir of the revolution. The first is that he continued the centralization and growth of state power and the rational organization of the administration

## DOCUMENT

### The French People Accept Napoleon as Emperor, 1804

*The Countess de Rémusat was the wife of one of Napoleon's chamberlains. In this letter she explains why the French people accepted Napoleon as their emperor. Her comments reflect the fear of disorder that permeated French society at the end of the eighteenth century.*

I can understand how it was that men worn out by the turmoil of the Revolution, and afraid of that liberty which had long been associated with death, looked for repose under the dominion of an able ruler on whom fortune was seemingly resolved to smile. I can conceive that they regarded his elevation as a decree of destiny and fondly believed that in the irrevocable they should find peace. I may confidently assert that those persons believed quite sincerely that Bonaparte, whether as Consul or Emperor, would exert his authority to oppose the intrigues of faction and would save us from the perils of anarchy.

None dared to utter the word Republic, so deeply had the Terror stained that name, and Directorial Government had perished in the contempt with which its chiefs were regarded. The return of the Bourbons could only be brought about by the aid of a revolution; and the slightest disturbance terrified the French people, in whom enthusiasm of every kind seemed dead. Besides, the men in whom they had trusted had one after the other deceived them; and as, this time, they were yielding to force, they were at least certain that they were not deceiving themselves.

The belief, or rather the error, that only despotism could at that epoch maintain order in France, was very widespread. It became the mainstay of Bonaparte; and it is due to him to say that he also believed it. The factions played into his hands by imprudent attempts which he turned to his own advantage; he had some grounds for his belief that he was necessary; France believed it too; and he even succeeded in persuading foreign sovereigns that he constituted a barrier against Republican influences which, but for him, might spread widely. At the moment when Bonaparte placed the imperial crown upon his head, there was not a king in Europe who did not believe that he wore his own crown more securely because of that event. Had the new emperor granted a liberal constitution, the peace of nations and of kings might, in sober seriousness, have been for ever secured.

Source: *Memoirs of Madame de Rémusat,* translated by C. Hoey and John Lillie (D. Appleton and Co., 1880).

---

that had begun in 1789. Each of the successive regimes between 1789 and 1815, even the Directory, had contributed to this pattern of state building, and Napoleon's contribution was monumental. The second was his continuation and extension of France's military mission to export the revolution to its European neighbors. The two achievements are related to each other, because the war effort necessitated the further growth and centralization of state power.

## Napoleon and the French State

Once Napoleon had gained effective control of the French state, he set about the task of strengthening it, making it more efficient, highly organized, and powerful. In addition to turning the government into a de facto dictatorship, he settled the long struggle between Church and state, laid down an entirely new law code that imposed legal uniformity on the entire country, and made the civil bureaucracy more centralized, uniform, and efficient. All of this was done with the intention of making the state an effective instrument of social and political control.

### Concordat with the Papacy

Napoleon's first contribution to the development of the French state, achieved during the Consulate, was to bring about a resolution of the bitter struggle between Church and state. A committed secularist, Napoleon was determined to bring the Church under the direct control of the state. This had been the main purpose of the Civil Constitution of the Clergy of 1790. Napoleon also realized, however, that this policy had divided the clergy between those who had taken an oath to the nation and those who had refused. Clerical independence had also become a major rallying cry of royalists against the new regime, thereby threatening the stability of the country.

Napoleon's solution to this problem was to reach an agreement with the Church that would satisfy clerics and royalists yet not deprive the state of its authority over the Church. With the Church safely under state control, Napoleon could also use religion to maintain respect for authority and to encourage loyalty and service to the state. "In religion," he wrote, "I do not see the mystery of the Incarnation but the mystery of the social order." In a new catechism published after Napoleon became emperor, children were taught: "Christians owe to the princes who govern them, and we owe in particular to Napoleon I, our Emperor, love, respect, obedience, fidelity, military service, and the tributes laid for the preservation and defense of the Empire."

The death of Pope Pius VI (r. 1775–1799), the implacable foe of the revolution, gave Napoleon the opportunity to address this problem. The new pope, Pius VII (r. 1800–1823), who was more sympathetic to liberal causes, was eager to come to terms with a French government that had become more moderate under the Consulate. The Concordat, which Napoleon and Pope Pius agreed to in 1801 and which was published the following year, gave something to both sides, although Napoleon gained more than he conceded. The pope agreed that all the clergy who refused to swear their loyalty to the nation would resign their posts, thus ending the bitter divisions of the past twelve years. The pope would appoint new bishops, but only with the prior approval of Napoleon. The state would pay all clerical salaries, and the Church would abandon any claims it still had to the ecclesiastical lands seized by the state at the beginning of the revolution.

These provisions represented formidable concessions to state power, and many French bishops found the terms of the Concordat too unfavorable to the Church. But the pope did manage to secure a statement that Roman Catholicism was the religion of the majority of citizens, and Napoleon agreed to scrap the secular calendar introduced in 1793, thereby restoring Sundays and holy days. Church attendance began to increase, having reached historic lows during the period of the Republic. The Church regained its respect as well as its legitimacy and its freedom to function in French society. More young recruits joined the clergy. Napoleon did not make many concessions to the Church, but they were significant enough to alienate a group of liberal philosophers and writers known as the Ideologues°, who objected to what they saw as the return of "monkish superstition."

With the pope at least somewhat appeased, Napoleon took unilateral steps to regulate the administration of the French Church. In a set of regulations known as the Organic Articles, which were added to the Concordat in 1802, the French church became a department of state, controlled by a minister of religion, just like the treasury or any other bureaucratic ministry. Pronouncements from the pope required prior government approval, and the clergy were obliged to read government decrees from the pulpit. Protestant congregations, which were also given freedom of worship and state protection by the terms of the Concordat, were likewise brought under state control, and their ministers were paid by the state. Jews received the protection of the state, but the government did not pay the salaries of rabbis.

## The Civil Code

Napoleon's most enduring achievement in the realm of state building was the promulgation of a new legal code, the Civil Code of 1804, later known as the Napoleonic Code°. A legal code is an authoritative and comprehensive statement of the law of a particular country. The model for modern legal codes in Europe was the *Corpus Juris Civilis* of the Roman Empire, which Justinian decreed at Constantinople

between 529 and 534 C.E. That code had replaced the thousands of constitutions, customs, and judicial decisions that had been in effect during the Roman Republic and Empire. In compiling the new French code Napoleon, who had just proclaimed himself emperor of the French, was imitating Justinian's legal achievement.

The Napoleonic Code also met a long-standing set of demands to reform the confusing and irregular body of French law. Ever since the Middle Ages, France had been governed by a multiplicity of laws. In the southern provinces of the country, those closest to Italy, the law had been influenced by Roman law. The *Corpus Juris Civilis* had been revived in the Middle Ages and had been incorporated into the written law of these southern French provinces and municipalities. In the north the law was based on local or provincial customs that had not originally existed in written form. France needed a common law for all its people. Efforts to produce an authoritative written code began during the revolution, but Napoleon completed the project and published the code.

The Civil Code, which consisted of more than 2,000 articles, reflected the values that were ascendant in Napoleonic French society. The ideals of the revolution were enshrined in the articles guaranteeing the rights of private property, the equality of all people before the law, and freedom of religion. The values it promoted, however, did not include the equality of the sexes. It granted men control of all family property. Women could not buy or sell property without the consent of their husbands. Only adult men could witness legal documents. All male heirs were entitled to inherit equal shares of a family estate, but daughters were excluded from the settlement.

The Civil Code, which dealt only with the rights and relationships of private individuals, was the first and most important of six law codes promulgated by Napoleon. Others dealt with civil procedure (1806), commerce (1807), and criminal law (1811). Renamed the Napoleonic Code in 1806, the Civil Code had an impact on the law of several countries outside France. It became the basis for the codification of the laws of Switzerland, northern Italy, and the Netherlands, and it served as a model for the numerous codes that were compiled in the German territories controlled by France during the Napoleonic period. The Napoleonic Code also influenced the law of French-speaking North America, including the civil law of the state of Louisiana, which bears signs of its influence even today.

## Administrative Centralization

Napoleon laid the foundation of modern French civil administration, which acquired the characteristics of rational organization, uniformity, and centralization. All power emanated from Paris, where Napoleon presided over a Council of State. This body consisted of his main ministers, who handled all matters of finance, domestic affairs, and war and oversaw a vast bureaucracy of salaried,

## The Consulate and the Early Years of the Empire, 1799–1806

**1799**

December 15    Proclamation of the Constitution of the Consulate

**1801**

July 15    Signing of the Concordat with the Papacy

**1802**

March 27    Peace of Amiens

April 8    Organic Articles added to the Concordat

**1803**

May    Renewal of the war with Britain

**1804**

March 21    The Civil Code is promulgated

December 2    Napoleon is crowned emperor of the French

**1805**

August    Third Coalition (Britain, Austria, and Russia) is formed against France

October 21    Defeat of the French navy in the Battle of Trafalgar

October 29    The French defeat the Austrian army at Ulm

December 2    The French defeat Russian and Austrian armies at Austerlitz

December 31    End of the revolutionary calendar

**1806**

October 14    French victories at the battles of Jena and Auerstädt

November 21    Proclamation of the Continental Blockade of British goods

August 6    Formal dissolution of the Holy Roman Empire

trained officials. The central government also exercised direct control over the provinces, which lost the local privileges they had possessed under the Old Regime. In each of the departments an official known as a *prefect*, appointed by the central government, implemented orders emanating from Paris. Paid the handsome annual salary of 20,000 francs, the prefects were responsible for the maintenance of public order. The power of the prefects was far greater than that of the *intendants* of the Old Regime. The prefects enforced conscription, collected taxes, and supervised local public works, such as the construction and improvement of roads.

The men who served in the government of the French Empire belonged to one of two elaborate, hierarchical institutions: the civil bureaucracy and the army officer corps. The two were closely related, because the main purpose of the administrative bureaucracy was to prepare for and sustain the war effort. Both institutions were organized hierarchically, and those who held positions in them were trained and salaried. Appointment and promotion were based primarily on talent rather than birth.

The idea of "a career open to all talents," as Napoleon described it, ran counter to the tradition of noble privilege. This was one of the achievements of the revolution that Napoleon perpetuated during the empire. All of the twenty-six marshals who served under him in the army were of nonnoble blood. Three of them had been sergeants in the army before 1789 and another three had been privates. The new system did not amount to a pure meritocracy, in which advancement is determined solely by ability and performance, because many appointments were made or influenced by Napoleon himself on the basis of friendship or kinship. Napoleon's brother, Lucien, for example, became minister of the interior. The system did, however, allow people from the ranks of the bourgeoisie to achieve rapid upward social mobility. In order to recognize their new status, Napoleon created a new order of nonhereditary noblemen, known as *notables*. As men ascended through the ranks of the bureaucracy and army they were given the titles of duke, count, baron, and chevalier. Instead of earning status based on their ancestry, these men acquired their titles by virtue of their service to the state. Napoleon created more than 3,500 notables during his rule. In this way he encouraged service to the state while also strengthening loyalty to it.

## Napoleon, the Empire, and Europe

Closely related to Napoleon's efforts to build the French state was his creation of a massive European empire. The French Empire was the product of a series of military victories against the armies of Austria, Prussia, Russia, and Spain between 1797 and 1809. By the latter date France controlled, either directly or indirectly, the Dutch Republic, the

Austrian Netherlands, Italy, Spain, and large parts of Germany and Poland. The instrument of these victories was the massive citizen army that Napoleon assembled. Building on the *levée en masse* of 1793, which he supplemented with soldiers from the countries he conquered, Napoleon had more than one million men under arms by 1812. More than three times the size of Louis XIV's army in 1700, it was the largest military force raised under the control of one man up to this time in European history.

These troops engaged in a military offensive that was more massive, wide-ranging, and sustained than Alexander the Great's invasion of Egypt, Persia, and northern India between 334 and 326 B.C.E. Napoleon's invasion began with the great victories against Austria and Prussia in 1797. Two years later, shortly after Napoleon had become first consul, he directed his army to further military successes that paved the way to French dominance of Europe. The defeat of Austria in 1800 confirmed earlier territorial gains in Italy as well as French control over the southern Netherlands, now called Belgium. With Austria defeated and Russia involved with the Ottoman Turks, France and Britain concluded peace at Amiens in 1802. This peace gave Napoleon free rein to reorganize the countries that bordered on France's eastern and southeastern boundaries. In Italy he named himself the president of the newly established Cisalpine Republic, and he transformed the cantons of Switzerland into the Helvetic Republic. These acquisitions gave substance to the title of emperor that he assumed in 1804, because now he controlled many different kingdoms. France had not had an emperor since the ninth century, when Charlemagne and his heirs had ruled as Roman emperors, and Napoleon's territories were more extensive than those under Charlemagne's jurisdiction.

These stunning military successes as well as those that were to follow have secured Napoleon's reputation as one of the most brilliant and successful military leaders in modern history. The reasons for that reputation are a matter of some controversy. Napoleon made terrible strategic blunders in many of his campaigns and tactical mistakes in many of his battles. Somehow he seemed to make up for these mistakes by his careful planning, unbounded energy, and decisive moves. He spent hours studying his opponents' position beforehand but made quick decisions once the battle had begun. "Everything," he once said, "is in the execution." The combination of infantry, artillery, and cavalry in the same units or *corps* allowed him to move these forces easily on the battlefield. He struck quickly, usually at the center of enemy lines, using superior numbers to overwhelm his opponent. Attacks on enemy lines of communication often prevented his opponents from calling up reinforcements. Once they began their retreat, he would pursue them rather than stop to celebrate. In his campaigns he benefited from the loyalty of his troops and the ideological zeal that continued to inspire them, even as his wars lost their ideological purpose of exporting the ideals of the revolution.

Napoleon was far less successful at sea than on land. With no real experience in naval warfare, he could not match the dominance of the British navy, which retained its mastery of the seas throughout the entire revolutionary period. Only in the West Indies, where Britain was never able to send sufficient naval forces, did the French navy manage to hold its own. This naval weakness also explains Napoleon's failure to build or regain an overseas empire. His expedition to Egypt in 1798, which was dominated by dreams of colonial conquest in the Middle East and South Asia, was checked by the British destruction of the French fleet at the Battle of the Nile. In the Western Hemisphere financial problems and a false hope of limiting British power induced Napoleon to sell the vast North American territory of Louisiana, which he had regained from Spain in 1800, to the United States in 1803. The following year the French Caribbean colony of St. Domingue became independent as the result of the violent revolution staged by free blacks and slaves, as discussed in Chapter 17. Informed of that loss, Napoleon shouted "Damn sugar, damn coffee, damn colonies!"

The most significant French naval defeat came in 1805, shortly after Britain, Austria, and Russia had formed the Third Coalition against France. As Napoleon was preparing for an invasion of Britain from northern French ports, the British navy, under the command of the diminutive, one-eyed Admiral Horatio Nelson, won one of the most decisive battles in the history of naval warfare. Nelson broke the line of a Franco-Spanish fleet that was preparing to strike off the Cape of Trafalgar near Gibraltar. The British destroyed or captured half the enemy ships, thus breaking the back of French sea power. The battle is commemorated at Trafalgar Square in London, which is overlooked by a towering statue of Nelson, who died of wounds inflicted during the battle. Nelson might have survived if he had not insisted on wearing glimmering medals on his uniform, thereby attracting the notice of French marksmen.

The monumental naval defeat at Trafalgar did not prevent Napoleon from continuing his wars of conquest in central Europe. In October 1805 he defeated an Austrian army at Ulm, and in December of that year he overwhelmed the combined forces of Austria and Russia at Austerlitz. These victories brought him new German and Italian territory, which he ceded to some of the larger German states; the smaller German states became satellites of France and fought with him until the collapse of his empire. A defeat of Prussian forces at Jena and Auerstädt in 1806 and the subsequent occupation of Berlin gave him the opportunity to carve the new German kingdom of Westphalia out of Prussian territory in the Rhineland and to install his brother Jerome as its ruler. In the East he created the duchy of Warsaw out of Polish lands controlled by Prussia. In 1806

Encounters & Transformations

# The French Encounter the Egyptians, 1798–1801

Napoleon's expedition to Egypt in 1798 marked one of the few times during the revolutionary period that the French came in direct contact with non-Western peoples. The expedition resulted in the military occupation of the country for three years and set the stage for the first extensive encounters between Egyptians and Europeans since the Ottoman conquest of Egypt in the sixteenth century. At that time Egypt had become a semiautonomous province of the Ottoman Empire and had very little contact with the West. Egypt's isolation from the West meant that it had little exposure to the scientific and technological discoveries that had taken place in western Europe during the previous 300 years.

In addition to 38,000 soldiers, Napoleon brought with him 165 scholars who were organized in a Commission of Science and Arts. These men came from virtually every branch of learning: surveyors, cartographers, civil engineers, architects, botanists, physicians, chemists, and mineralogists. The commission also included artists, archaeologists, writers, and musicians. Their purpose was to give Napoleon information on the people and the resources of the country so that he could more easily subject it to French domination. A small group of these scholars set up an Institute of Egypt, whose mission was to propagate the Enlightenment and to undertake research on the history, people, and the economy of the country. This involved the scholarly study of Egyptian antiquities, including the pyramids.

This work of the institute ushered in a long period in which many artifacts of Egyptian antiquity were taken from the country and transported to European museums and palaces. Members of the institute encouraged this cultural plundering, arguing that their addition to the collections of the Louvre would embellish the glory of France. This plundering of native Egyptian antiquities represented a form of cultural imperialism that continued unabated during the nineteenth century.

Cultural imperialism of a different sort can be found in a widely disseminated description of Egypt, *Travels in Upper and Lower Egypt* (1802), by a member of the institute, Dominique Vivant-Denon. This two-volume work contained extensive descriptions of the different "races" of people in Egypt whom the expedition encountered in the thriving port town of Rosetta. Vivant-Denon described the Copts, the most ancient Egyptians, as "swarthy Nubians" with flat foreheads, high cheekbones, and short

broad noses. They displayed the moral qualities of "ignorance, drunkenness, cunning, and finesse." The Arabs, who were the most numerous group, and the Turks had more appealing physical and personal characteristics, although they were often reduced to the "degraded state of animals."

Expressions of French cultural superiority permeate other contemporary accounts of Napoleon's expedition. A multivolume work, *The Description of Egypt,* claimed that Napoleon wanted to procure for Egyptians "all the advantages of a perfected civilization." It praised him for bringing modern knowledge to a country that had been "plunged into darkness." These attitudes provided a justification for the subsequent economic exploitation of Egypt, first by the French and later by the British, during the nineteenth century.

## For Discussion

In what ways did Vivant-Denon's work reflect the values that were cultivated during the Enlightenment?

**Jean Charles Tardieu, *The French Army Halts at Syene, Upper Egypt, on February 2, 1799***
This painting depicts a cultural encounter between French soldiers and Egyptians in the city of Syene (now Aswan) during the Egyptian campaign of 1798–1799. The soldiers are scribbling on the ruins of ancient Egypt, indicating a lack of respect for Egyptian culture.

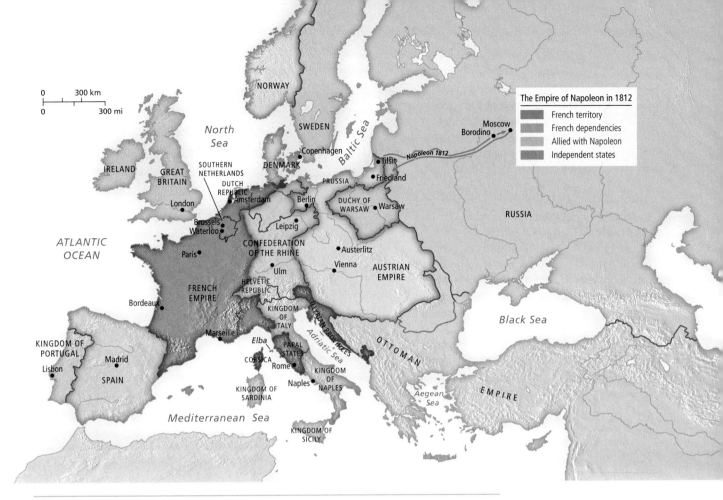

**Map 19.1  The Empire of Napoleon in 1812**
By establishing dependent states in Spain, Italy, Germany, and Poland, France controlled far more territory than the areas technically within the French Empire.

he formally dissolved the ancient Holy Roman Empire and replaced it with a loose association of sixteen German states known as the Confederation of the Rhine. By 1807, in the words of one historian, Napoleon had "only allies and victims" on the Continent (see Map 19.1).

Napoleon inserted the last piece in this imperial puzzle by invading and occupying the kingdom of Spain in 1808. This campaign began as an effort to crush Portugal, the ally of Britain, which he was never able to defeat. In May 1808, as French armies marched through Spain en route to Lisbon, the Portuguese capital, a popular insurrection against Spanish rule occurred in Madrid. This spontaneous revolt, which led to the abdication of King Charles IV and the succession of his son Ferdinand VII, was the first of many developments that caused the collapse of the Spanish Empire in America. In Europe it led to the absorption of Spain into the French Empire. Sensing that he could easily add one more territory to his list of conquests, Napoleon forced Ferdinand to abdicate and summoned his own brother, Joseph Bonaparte, who was then ruling the dependent kingdom of Naples, to become king of Spain.

Joseph instituted some reforms in Spain, but the abolition of the Spanish Inquisition and the closing of two-thirds of the Spanish convents triggered a visceral reaction from the Spanish clergy and the general populace. Fighting for Church and king, small bands of local guerillas subjected French forces to intermittent and effective sabotage. An invasion by British forces under the command of Arthur Wellesley, later the Duke of Wellington (1769–1852), in what has become known as the Peninsula War (1808–1813), strengthened Spanish and Portuguese resistance.

The reception of the French in Spain revealed that the export of revolution, which had begun with the French armies of 1792, was a double-edged sword. The overthrow of authoritarian regimes in other European states won the support of progressive, capitalist, and anticlerical forces in those countries, but it also triggered deep resentment against French rule. The ideology of nationalism in Germany and Italy arose more because of a reaction against French rule than because the armies of France had tried to stimulate it. In Italy during the 1790s young educated *patrioti*, imbued with enthusiasm for liberty, equality, and progress, supported the newly proclaimed republics and envisioned the establishment of a single Italian state, at least in the north of Italy. By the middle of the Napoleonic years that vision had changed. Many of the *patrioti* had become disillusioned and joined secret societies to press for further political and social change and to plot insurrections against the new republics.

In Germany many of those who supported the French cause during the early years of the Republic turned away from it during Napoleon's wars of expansion. In 1809 a German student who attempted to assassinate Napoleon shouted "Long live Germany!" at his execution. In 1813 the German writer Johann Gottlieb Fichte (1762–1814) appealed to the German nation to resist Napoleon in order to regain their liberty. For all his political astuteness, Napoleon could not comprehend that his own policies were responsible for the growth of this reactive sentiment, which formed one of the foundations of nineteenth-century nationalism. We shall discuss this topic more fully in Chapter 21.

## The Downfall of Napoleon

The turning point in Napoleon's personal fortunes and those of his empire came in 1810. After securing an annulment of his marriage to Josephine in late 1809, he married Marie-Louise, the daughter of the Habsburg emperor. This marriage, which the following year produced a son and heir to the throne, should have made the French Empire more secure, but it had the opposite effect. For the first time during his rule, dissent from both the right and the left became widespread. Despite the most stringent efforts at censorship, royalist and Jacobin literature poured off the presses. The number of military deserters and those evading conscription increased. Relations with the papacy reached a breaking point when Napoleon annexed the Papal States, at which point Pope Pius VII, who had negotiated the Concordat of 1801, excommunicated him.

Dissent at home had the effect of driving the megalomaniacal emperor to seek more glory and further conquests. In this frame of mind Napoleon made the ill-advised decision to invade Russia. The motives for engaging in this overly ambitious military campaign were not completely irrational. Victory over Russia promised to give France control of the Black Sea, and that in turn would ultimately lead to the control of Constantinople and the entire Middle East. More immediately, defeating Russia would be necessary to enforce the French blockade of British goods, which Russia had refused to support.

The problem with a Russian invasion was that it stretched Napoleon's lines of communication too far and his resources too thin, despite the support of the Austrians and Prussians whom he had defeated. Even before the inva-

### Francisco Goya, *The Third of May 1808*

This painting of the suppression of the popular revolt in Madrid in 1808 captures the brutality of the French occupation of Spain. A French unit executes Spanish citizens, including a monk in the foreground. Goya was a figure of the Enlightenment and a Spanish patriot.

VIDEO

The Art of Francisco Goya

sion it was becoming increasingly difficult to feed, equip, and train the huge army he had assembled. The Grand Army that crossed from Poland into Russia in 1812 was not the efficient military force that Napoleon had commanded in the early years of the empire. Many of his best soldiers were fighting in the guerilla war in Spain. Casualties and desertions had forced Napoleon to call up new recruits who were not properly trained. Half the army, moreover, had been recruited from the population of conquered countries, making their loyalty to Napoleon uncertain.

The tactics of the Russians contributed to the failure of the invasion. Instead of engaging the Grand Army in combat, the Russian army kept retreating, pulling Napoleon further east toward Moscow. On September 7 the two armies clashed at Borodino, suffering a staggering 77,000 casualties in all. The Russian army then continued its retreat eastward. When Napoleon reached Moscow he found it deserted, and fires deliberately set by Muscovites had destroyed more than two-thirds of the city. Napoleon, facing the onset of a dreaded Russian winter and rapidly diminishing supplies, began the long retreat back to France. Skirmishes with the Russians along the way, which cost him 25,000 lives just crossing the Beresina River, conspired with the cold and hunger to destroy his army. During the entire Russian campaign his army lost a total of 380,000 men to death, imprisonment, or desertion. In the midst of this horror Napoleon, oblivious to the suffering of his troops, reported back to Paris, "The health of the emperor has never been better."

Not to be discouraged, Napoleon soon began preparing for further conquests. Once again his enemies formed a coalition against him, pledging to restore the independence of the countries that had become his satellites or dependents. Napoleon scored a few victories in the late summer of 1813, but in October allied forces inflicted a crushing defeat on him in the Battle of the Nations at Leipzig. Austrian troops administered another blow to the French in northern Italy, and the British finally drove them out of Spain. As a result of these defeats, Napoleon's army was pushed back into France. A massive allied force advanced into Paris and occupied the city. After extensive political maneuvering, including a vote by the Senate to depose Napoleon, the emperor abdicated on April 6, 1814. The allies promptly exiled him to the Mediterranean island of Elba. As he made the journey to the coast, crowds surrounding his coach shouted "Down with the tyrant!" while some villagers hanged him in effigy.

This course of events led to the restoration of the Bourbon monarchy. By the terms of the first Treaty of Paris of May 1814, the allies restored the brother of Louis XVI, the Count of Provence, to the French throne as Louis XVIII (r. 1814–1824). Louis was an implacable foe of the revolution, and much of what he did was intended to undermine its achievements. The white Bourbon flag replaced the revolutionary tricolor. Catholicism was once again recognized as the state religion. Exiled royalists returned to their high-ranking positions in the army. Nonetheless, Louis accepted a Constitutional Charter that incorporated many of the changes made between 1789 and 1791. Representative government, with a relatively limited franchise, replaced the absolutism of the Old Regime. Equality before the law, freedom of religion, and freedom of expression were all reaffirmed. Even more important, the powers of the state that the National Assembly and the Directory had extended and Napoleon had enhanced were maintained. The administrative division of France into departments continued, and the Napoleonic Code remained in force. France had experienced a counterrevolution in 1814, but it did not simply turn the political clock back to 1788. Some of the political achievements of the previous twenty-five years were indeed preserved.

Despite his disgrace and exile, Napoleon still commanded loyalty from his troops and from large segments of the population. While in power he had constructed a legend that drew on strong patriotic sentiment. Supporters throughout France continued to promote his cause in the same way that royalists had maintained that of the Bourbon monarchy since 1792. The Napoleonic legend held great appeal among the lower classes, who were per-

## CHRONOLOGY

### The Downfall of Napoleon, 1807–1815

**1807**

| November–December | French military intervention in Spain and Portugal begins |
|---|---|

**1808**

| May | Beginning of the Spanish rebellion |
| July 20 | Joseph Bonaparte appointed king of Spain |

**1809**

| December 15 | Annulment of marriage of Napoleon and Empress Josephine |

**1810**

| April 2 | Marriage of Napoleon to Marie-Louise |

**1812**

| September 7 | Battle of Borodino |
| September 14 | Napoleon enters Moscow |
| October | Retreat from Moscow begins |

**1813**

| October 16–19 | Battle of the Nations at Leipzig |

**1814**

| April 6 | Abdication of Napoleon |
| May 30 | First Treaty of Paris |
| September | Congress of Vienna assembles |

**1815**

| March | Napoleon escapes from Elba |
| June 18 | Battle of Waterloo |
| November 20 | Second Treaty of Paris |

suaded that Napoleon, the patriot and the savior of the revolution, had made it possible for every Frenchman to achieve wealth and fame. The strength of the Napoleonic legend became apparent in March 1815, when Napoleon escaped from Elba and landed in southern France. Promising to rid the country of the exiled royalists who had returned and to save the revolutionary cause that he claimed had been abandoned, he won over peasants, workers, and soldiers. Regiment after regiment joined him as he marched toward Paris. By the time he arrived, Louis XVIII had gone into exile once again, and Napoleon found himself back in power.

But not for long. The allied European powers quickly began to assemble yet another coalition. Fearing that the allies would launch a massive invasion of France, Napoleon decided to strike first. He marched an army of 200,000 men into the Austrian Netherlands, where the allies responded by amassing 700,000 troops. Near the small village of Waterloo, south of Brussels, he met the British forces of the Duke of Wellington, who had turned the tide against him during the Peninsula War. Reinforced by Prussian troops, Wellington inflicted a devastating defeat on the French army, which lost 28,000 men and went into a full-scale retreat. Napoleon, captured in the battle, abdicated once again. He was exiled to the remote South Atlantic island of St. Helena, from which escape was impossible. He died there in 1821.

Even before the battle of Waterloo, the major powers of Europe had gathered in Vienna to redraw the boundaries of the European states that had been created, dismembered, or transformed during the preceding twenty-five years (see Map 19.2). Under the leadership of the Austrian foreign minister, Prince Clemens von Metternich (1773–1859), this conference, known as the Congress of Vienna°, worked out a settlement that was intended to preserve the balance of power in Europe and at the same time uphold the principle of dynastic legitimacy. By the terms of a separate Treaty of Paris (the second in two years) the boundaries of France

DOCUMENT

Napoleon's Exile to St. Helena (1815)

## Map 19.2   Europe After the Congress of Vienna, 1815

The four most important territorial changes that took place in 1815 were the scaling back of the boundaries of France to their status in 1790, the Austrian acquisition of territory in western and northeastern Italy, the establishment of the new kingdom of the Netherlands, and the formation of the new German Confederation.

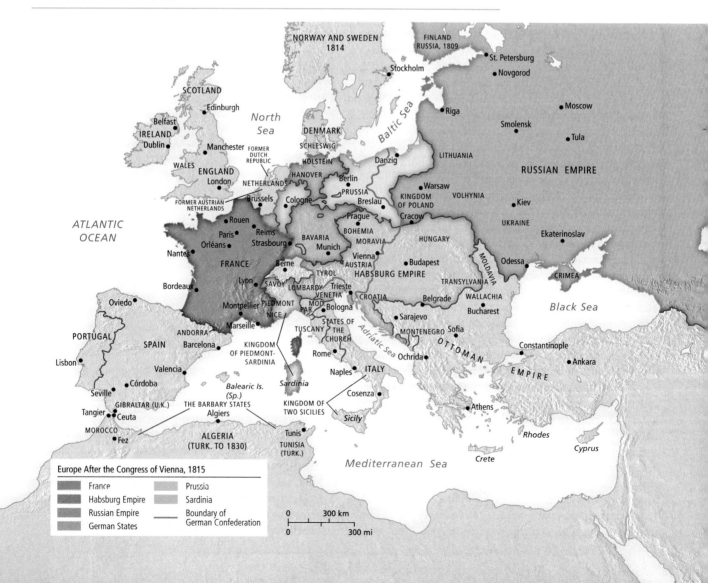

were scaled back to what they had been in 1790, before it had begun its wars of expansion. To create a buffer state on the northern boundary of France, the Congress annexed the Austrian Netherlands to the Dutch Republic, which now became the kingdom of the Netherlands with William I, a prince of the House of Orange, as its king. Territory along the Rhineland in the state of Westphalia was ceded to Prussia, while Austria gained territory in Italy, both along the French border in the west and in northern Italy to the east. In place of the defunct Holy Roman Empire, the Congress established a new German Confederation, a loose coalition of thirty-nine separate territories with a weak legislative assembly, whose members were appointed and instructed by their governments. The five major powers that had drawn this new map of Europe—Britain, Austria, Prussia, Russia, and France—agreed to meet annually to prevent any one country, especially France but also Russia, from achieving military dominance of the European Continent.

# The Legacy of the French Revolution

■ What did the French Revolution ultimately achieve and in what ways did it change the course of European and Western history?

With the conclusion of the Congress of Vienna a tumultuous period of European and Western history finally came to an end. Not only had France experienced a revolution, but every country in Europe and America had felt its effects. Governments were toppled in countries as far apart as Poland and Peru. Added to this turbulence was the experience of incessant warfare. France was at war for more than twenty years during the period of the Republic and the empire, and it had brought almost all European powers into the struggle. With armies constantly in need of provisions and supplies, high taxation, galloping inflation, and food shortages inflicted economic hardship on a large portion of the European population.

The cost of all this instability and warfare in terms of human life was staggering. Within the space of one generation almost two million European soldiers were killed in action, wasted by disease, or starved or frozen to death. In France alone just under 500,000 soldiers died during the revolutionary wars of 1792–1802 and another 916,000 during the wars of the empire. Internal political disturbances took the lives of hundreds of thousands of civilians from all ranks of society, not only in France but throughout Europe. The violence was fed at all levels by unprecedented fears of internal and external subversion. Government officials, col-

laborators, counterrevolutionaries, and imagined enemies of the state were all executed. This spate of violence and death—much of it in the name of liberty—was inflicted almost entirely by the state or its enemies.

What was achieved at this extraordinary price? How did the France of 1815 differ from the France of 1788? What on balance had changed? For many years historians, especially those who believed that economic forces determined the course of history, claimed that as a result of the revolution the bourgeoisie, composed of merchants, manufacturers, and other commoners of substantial wealth, had replaced the nobility as the dominant social and political class in the country. The bourgeoisie, so they argued, had started the revolution in order to acquire political power that was commensurate with their economic power, and they had ultimately prevailed.

This assessment can no longer be sustained. The nobility certainly lost many of their privileges in 1789, and many of them went into exile during the revolutionary period, but the position they had in French society in 1815 did not differ greatly from what it had been under the Old Regime. In both periods there was considerable blurring of the distinctions between nobility and bourgeoisie. Nor did the revolutionary period witness the emergence of a new class of industrial entrepreneurs. The only group who definitely profited from the revolution in the long run were men of property, regardless of their membership in any social category or "class." Men of property emerged triumphant in the Directory, found favor during the Napoleonic period, and became the most important members of political society after the monarchy was restored.

It would be difficult to argue that *women* of any social rank benefited from the revolution. During the early years of the revolution, women participated actively in public life. They were involved in many demonstrations in Paris, including the storming of the Bastille and the march to Versailles to pressure the king to move to Paris. Women as well as men filled the ranks of the *sans-culottes,* and women donned their own female version of nonaristocratic dress. During the early years of the revolution, many women joined patriotic clubs, such as the Club of Knitters or the unisex Fraternal Society of Patriots of Both Sexes. In 1790 the Marquis de Condorcet published *On the Admission of Women to the Rights of Citizenship,* and the following year Olympe de Gouges published *The Rights of Women,* in which she called for the granting of women's equal rights. Both of these advocates of women's rights had been influenced by Enlightenment thought, as we have discussed in Chapter 18.

The goal advanced by Condorcet and de Gouges was not to be realized. The radical Jacobins dealt it a terrible setback when they banned all women's clubs and societies on the grounds that their participation in public life would harm the institution of the family. This action, coupled with the imprisonment and death of both de Gouges and Condorcet during the Terror, signaled an end to the extensive participation of women in political life, which had begun during the eighteenth century, especially in the salons. During the nineteenth century women were generally considered to occupy a separate sphere of activity from that of men. They were expected to exercise influence in the private sphere of the home, but not in the public sphere of politics. As we shall discuss in Chapter 20, the changes wrought by the Industrial Revolution reinforced this segregation of men and women by excluding many married women from the workforce.

It is even more difficult to identify permanent economic changes as a result of the revolution. The elimination of the remnants of feudalism may have made France marginally more capitalist than it had been before the revolution, but agricultural and mercantile capitalism had long been entrenched in French society. Nor did the Continental System, the blockade of British goods from all European ports initiated in 1806, allow French industry to catch up with that of Great Britain. Whatever economic gains were made under the protective shield of the state were offset by the adverse economic effects of twenty-two years of nearly continuous warfare. In the long run the revolutionary period delayed the process of industrialization that had entered its preliminary stages in France during the 1780s and retarded the growth of the French economy for the remainder of the nineteenth century.

The permanent legacy of the French Revolution lies in the realm of politics. First, the period from 1789 to 1815 triggered an enormous growth in the competence and power of the state. This trend had begun before the revolution, but the desire of the revolutionaries to transform every aspect of human life in the service of the revolution, coupled with the necessity of utilizing all the country's resources in the war effort, gave the state more control over the everyday life of its citizens than ever before. Fifteen years of Napoleonic rule only accentuated this trend, and after 1815 many of those powers remained with the government.

An even more significant and permanent achievement of the French Revolution was the promotion of the doctrine of popular sovereignty. The belief that the people constituted the highest political authority in the state became so entrenched during the revolution that it could never be completely suppressed, either in France or in the other countries of Europe. Napoleon recognized its power when he asked the people to approve political changes he had already made by his own authority. He also arranged for such plebiscites to secure approval of the new states he had set up in Europe. After the restoration of the monarchy the doctrine of popular sovereignty was promoted mainly by the press, which continued to employ the new revolutionary rhetoric to keep alive the high ideals and aspirations of the revolution. The doctrine also contributed to the forma-

tion of two nineteenth-century ideologies, liberalism and nationalism, which will be discussed in Chapter 21.

The third permanent political change was the active participation of the citizens in the political life of the nation. This participation had been cultivated during the early years of the revolution, and it had been accompanied by the creation of a new political culture. Much of that culture was suppressed during the Napoleonic period, but the actual habit of participating in politics was not. The franchise was gradually expanded in Europe during the nineteenth century. The press spread political ideas to a large segment of the population. People from all walks of life participated in marches, processions, and demonstrations. All of this followed from the acceptance of the French revolutionary doctrine that the people are sovereign and have a right therefore to participate in the political life of the state.

# Conclusion

## The French Revolution and Western Civilization

The French Revolution was a central event in the history of the West. It began as an internal French affair, reflecting the social and political tensions of the Old Regime, but it soon became a turning point in European and Western history. Proclamations of the natural rights of humanity gave the ideals of the revolution widespread appeal, and a period of protracted warfare succeeded in disseminating those ideals outside the boundaries of France.

Underlying the export of French revolutionary ideology was the belief that France had become the standard-bearer of Western civilization. French people believed they were *la grande nation,* the country that had reached the highest level of political and social organization. They did not believe they had acquired this exalted status by inheritance. Unlike the English revolutionaries of the seventeenth century, they did not claim that they were the heirs of a medieval constitution. French republicans of the 1790s attributed none of their national preeminence to the monarchy, whose memory they took drastic steps to erase. They considered the secular political culture that emerged during the French Revolution to be an entirely novel development.

The export of French revolutionary political culture during the Republic and the empire brought about widespread changes in the established order. Regimes were toppled, French puppets acquired political power, boundaries of states were completely redrawn, and traditional authorities were challenged. Liberal reforms were enacted, new constitutions were written, and new law codes were promulgated. The Europe of 1815 could not be mistaken for the Europe of 1789.

The ideas of the French Revolution, like those of the Enlightenment that had helped to inspire them, did not go unchallenged. From the very early years of the revolution they encountered determined opposition, both in France and abroad. As the revolution lost its appeal in France, the forces of conservatism and reaction gathered strength. At the end of the Napoleonic period, the Congress of Vienna took steps to restore the legitimate rulers of European states and to prevent revolution from recurring. It appeared that the revolution would be completely reversed, but that was not the case. The ideas born of the revolution would continue to inspire demands for political reform in Europe during the nineteenth century, and those demands, just like those in the 1790s, would meet with fierce resistance.

## Suggestions for Further Reading

For a comprehensive listing of suggested readings, please go to www.ablongman.com/levack2e/chapter19

Andress, David. *The French Revolution and the People.* 2004. Focuses on the role played by the common people of France—the peasants, craftsmen and those living on the margins of society—in the revolution.

Blanning, T. C. W. *The French Revolutionary Wars, 1787–1802.* 1996. An authoritative political and military narrative that assesses the impact of the wars on French politics.

Chartier, Roger. *The Cultural Origins of the French Revolution.* 1991. Explores the connections between the culture of the Enlightenment and the cultural transformations of the revolutionary period.

Cobban, Alfred. *The Social Interpretation of the French Revolution.* 1964. Challenges the Marxist interpretation of the causes and effects of the revolution.

Doyle, William. *The Oxford History of the French Revolution.* 1989. An excellent synthesis.

Ellis, Geoffrey. *Napoleon.* 1997. A study of the nature and mechanics of Napoleon's power and an analysis of his imperial policy.

Furet, François. *The French Revolution, 1770–1814.* 1992. A provocative narrative that sees Napoleon as the architect of a second, authoritarian revolution that reversed the gains of the first.

Hardman, John. *Louis XVI: The Silent King.* 2000. A reassessment of the king that mixes sympathy with criticism.

Higonnet, Patrice. *Goodness Beyond Virtue: Jacobins During the French Revolution.* 1998. Explores the contradictions of Jacobin ideology and its descent into the Terror.

Hunt, Lynn. *Politics, Culture and Class in the French Revolution.* 1984. Analyzes the formation of a revolutionary political culture.

Kennedy, Emmet. *The Culture of the French Revolution.* 1989. A comprehensive study of all cultural developments before and during the revolution.

Landes, Joan B. *Women and the Public Sphere in the Age of the French Revolution.* 1988. Explores how the new political culture of the revolution changed the position of women in society.

Lefebvre, Georges. *The Great Fear of 1789: Rural Panic in Revolutionary France.* 1973. Shows the importance of the rural unrest of July 1789 that provided the backdrop of the legislation of August 1789.

Schama, Simon. *Citizens: A Chronicle of the French Revolution.* 1989. Depicts the tragic unraveling of a vision of liberty and happiness into a scenario of hunger, anger, violence, and death.

## Notes

1. Emmanuel-Joseph Sieyès, *What Is the Third Estate?* (1789).

2. H. Wallon, *Histoire du tribunal révolutionnaire de Paris* (1880–1882), Vol. 4, 511.

# The Industrial Revolution

I N 1842 A 17-YEAR-OLD GIRL, PATIENCE KERSHAW, TESTIFIED BEFORE A BRITISH parliamentary committee regarding the practice of employing children and women in the nation's mines. When the girl made her appearance, the members of the committee observed that she was "an ignorant, filthy, ragged, and deplorable-looking object, such as one of uncivilized natives of the prairies would be shocked to look upon." Patience, who had never been to school and could not read or write, told the committee that she was one of ten children, all of whom had at one time worked in the coal mines, although three of her sisters now worked in a textile mill. She went to the pit at five in the morning and came out at five at night. Her job in the mines was to hurry coal, that is, to pull carts of coal through the narrow tunnels of the mine. Each cart weighed 300 pounds, and every day she hauled eleven of them one mile. The carts were attached to her head and shoulders by a chain and belt, and the pressure of the cart had worn a bald spot on her head. Patience hurried coal for twelve hours straight, not taking any time for her midday meal, which she ate as she worked. While she was working, the men and boys who dug the coal and put it in the carts would often beat her and take sexual liberties with her. Patience told the committee, "I am the only girl in the pit; there are about 20 boys and 15 men. All the men are naked. I would rather work in a mill than a coal pit."[1]

Patience Kershaw was one of the human casualties of an extraordinary development that historians usually refer to as the Industrial Revolution. This process, which brought about a fundamental transformation of human life, involved the extensive use of machinery in the production of goods. Much of that machinery was driven by steam engines, which required coal to produce the steam. Coal mining itself became a major industry, and the men who owned and operated the mines tried to hire workers, many of them children, at the lowest possible wage. It was this desire to maximize profits that led to the employment, physical hardship, and abuse of girls like Patience Kershaw.

## CHAPTER OUTLINE

- The Nature of the Industrial Revolution

- Conditions Favoring Industrial Growth

- The Spread of Industrialization

- The Effects of Industrialization

- Industry, Trade, and Empire

---

**Exhibit of Machinery at the Crystal Palace Exhibition in London in 1851**
During the Industrial Revolution the manufacture of heavy machinery itself became an industry.

**Child Labor in the Mines**
A child hurrying coal through a tunnel in a mine.

The story of the Industrial Revolution cannot be told solely in terms of the exploitation of child or even adult workers. Many of its effects can be described in positive or at least morally neutral terms. The Industrial Revolution resulted in a staggering increase in the volume and range of products made available to consumers, from machine-produced clothing to household utensils. It made possible unprecedented and sustained economic growth. The Industrial Revolution facilitated the rapid transportation of passengers as well as goods across large expanses of territory, mainly on the railroads that were constructed in all industrialized countries. It brought about a new awareness of the position of workers in the economic system, and it unleashed powerful political forces intended to improve the lot of these workers.

The Industrial Revolution played a crucial role in redefining and reshaping the West. Until the late nineteenth century industrialization took place only in Western nations. During that century "the West" gradually became identified with countries that had industrial economies. When some non-Western countries introduced mechanized industry in the twentieth century, largely in imitation of Western example, the geographical boundaries of the West underwent a significant alteration.

The main question this chapter sets out to answer is why this fundamental transformation of Western civilization began in Europe in the late eighteenth and nineteenth centuries. The individual sections of the chapter will address the following questions:

- **What do historians mean when they refer to the Industrial Revolution of the late eighteenth and nineteenth centuries?**
- **What social and economic changes made industrial development possible?**
- **How did industrialization spread from Great Britain to the European continent and America?**
- **What were the economic, social, and cultural effects of the Industrial Revolution?**
- **What was the relationship between the growth of industry and Britain's dominance in trade and imperial strength during the middle years of the nineteenth century?**

# The Nature of the Industrial Revolution

- **What do historians mean when they refer to the Industrial Revolution of the late eighteenth and nineteenth centuries?**

The Industrial Revolution was a series of economic and social changes that took place in Great Britain during the late eighteenth and early nineteenth centuries and on the European continent and in the United States after 1815. Some economic historians claim that the use of the term *revolution*, which suggests radical and abrupt change, is misleading in this context, because the economic and social changes to which the term refers occurred gradually over a long period of time. Even so, the term is still appropriate because it conveys the radical nature and profound significance of the changes it identifies. Like the Scientific Revolution of the seventeenth century, which also took place gradually, the Industrial Revolution reshaped Western civilization.

The Industrial Revolution consisted of four closely related developments: the introduction of new industrial technology, the utilization of mineral sources of energy, the concentration of labor in factories, and the development of new methods of transportation.

# New Industrial Technology

The Industrial Revolution ushered in the machine age, and to this day machines are the most striking feature of modern industrial economies. In countries that have become industrialized, virtually every human-made commodity can be mass-produced by some kind of machine. In the late eighteenth century such machines were novelties, but their numbers increased dramatically in the early nineteenth century. For example, the power loom, a machine used for weaving cloth, was invented in Britain in 1787 but not put into widespread use until the 1820s. By 1836 there were more than 60,000 power looms in just one English county.

Machines became so common in Britain that machine making itself became a major industry, supplying its products to other manufacturers rather than to individual consumers. Machines were introduced in the textile, iron, printing, papermaking, and engineering industries and were used in every stage of manufacture. Machines extracted minerals that were used as either raw materials or sources of energy, transported those materials to the factories, saved time and labor in the actual manufacturing of commodities, and carried the finished products to market. Eventually machines were used in agriculture itself, facilitating both the plowing of fields and the harvesting of crops.

The most significant of the new machines, which changed the entire industrial process, were those used for spinning and weaving in the textile industry and the steam engine, first used in mining and the iron industry. These pieces of machinery became almost synonymous with the Industrial Revolution, and their invention in the 1760s appropriately marks its beginning.

## Textile Machinery

Until the late eighteenth century, the production of textiles throughout Europe, which involved both the spinning of yarn and the weaving of cloth, was done entirely by hand, on spinning wheels and hand looms respectively. This was the practice for wool, which was the main textile produced in Europe during the early modern period, as well as for a new material, cotton, which became immensely popular in the early eighteenth century, mainly because of its greater comfort. The demand for cotton yarn was greater than the quantities spinners could supply. To meet this demand a British inventor, James Hargreaves, in 1767 constructed a new machine, the spinning jenny, which greatly increased the amount of cotton yarn that could be spun and thus made available for weaving. The original jenny, a hand machine used in the homes of spinners, consisted of only eight spindles, but it later accommodated as many as 120.

The spinning of yarn on the jenny required a stronger warp, the yarn that ran lengthwise on a loom. A power-driven machine, the water frame, introduced by the barber and wigmaker Richard Arkwright in 1769, made the production of this stronger warp possible. In 1779 Samuel Crompton, using tools he had purchased with his earnings as a fiddle player at a local theater, combined the jenny and the frame in one machine, called the mule. Crompton worked on his machine only at night, in order to keep it secret, and the strange noises that came out of his workshop made his neighbors think his house was haunted. The mule, which could spin as much as 300 times the amount of yarn produced by one spinning wheel, became the main spinning machine of the early Industrial Revolution. Both the water frame and the mule required power, and that requirement led to the centralization of the textile industry in large rural mills located near rivers so that their water wheels could drive the machinery.

The tremendous success of the mule eventually produced more yarn than the weavers could handle on their hand

**Broadlie Mill in the 1790s**
The earliest textile mills were built in the rural areas, near rivers that supplied water power. This mill was built on the Broadlie farm, near the village of Neilston in southwestern Scotland, about twelve miles from Glasgow. The power to run the mill came from the Levern River. By 1815 there were six cotton mills in the area, supporting a community of about 1,500 workers. Housing for the workers, including some houses for single women, was constructed near the mills.

looms. Edmund Cartwright, an Oxford-educated clergyman, supported by monies from his heiress wife, addressed that need with the invention of the power loom in 1787. In that same year he put his new invention to use in a weaving mill he built near the town of Doncaster. The power loom, like the spinning jenny, the water frame, and the mule, met a specific need within the industry. It also gave the producer a competitive advantage by saving time, reducing the cost of labor, and increasing production. Two power looms run by a 15-year-old boy, for example, could produce more than three times what a skilled hand loom weaver could turn out in the same time using only the old hand device, the flying shuttle. The net effect of all these machines was the production of more than 200 times as much cotton cloth in 1850 as in 1780. By 1800 cotton became Britain's largest industry, producing more than 20 percent of the world's cloth, and by 1850 that percentage had risen to more than 50 percent. Indeed, by midcentury, cotton accounted for 70 percent of the value of all British exports.

### The Steam Engine

The steam engine was even more important than the new textile machinery because it was used in almost every stage of the productive process, including the operation of textile machinery itself. The steam engine was invented by a Scottish engineer, James Watt, in 1763. It represented an improvement over the engine invented by Thomas Newcomen in 1709, which had been intended mainly to drain water from deep mines. The problem with Newcomen's engine was that the steam, which was produced in a cylinder heated by coal, had to be cooled in order to make the piston return, and the process of heating and cooling had to be repeated for each stroke of the piston. The engine was therefore inefficient and expensive to operate. Watt created a separate chamber where the steam could be condensed without affecting the heat of the cylinder. The result was a more efficient and cost-effective machine that could pro-

vide more power than any other source. Watt's pride in his invention was matched only by his pride in his Scottish nationality. Upon receiving a patent for the new device, he boasted, "This was made by a Scot."

After designing the steam engine, Watt teamed up with a Birmingham metal manufacturer, Matthew Boulton, to produce it on a large scale. Boulton provided the capital necessary to begin this process and to hire the skilled laborers to assemble the machines. He also had ambitious plans for marketing the new invention throughout the world. "It would not be worth my while to make for three countries only," Boulton said, "but I find it well worth my while to make for the whole world."

The steam engine soon became the workhorse of the Industrial Revolution. Not only did it pump water from mines, but it helped raise minerals such as iron ore that were extracted from those mines. It provided the intense blast of heat that was necessary to resmelt pig iron into cast iron, which in turn was used to make industrial machinery, buildings, bridges, locomotives, and ships. Once the engine was equipped with a rotating device, it was used to drive the factory machinery in the textile mills, and it eventually powered the railroad locomotives that carried industrial goods to market.

The widespread adoption of steam power came fairly late in the Industrial Revolution. Only in the 1840s and 1850s, after its efficiency had been greatly improved, did it become the main source of energy in the textile industry. Until then rural water power was the preferred method of running the cotton mills. Only after the introduction of coal-driven steam power did the factories locate in the cities, especially those of northern England, such as Manchester. The 1840s and 1850s were also the decades when the railroads, using the steam locomotive invented by the English engineer George Stephenson in 1815, began to crisscross the European continent. By midcentury the steam engine had become the predominant symbol of the Industrial Revolution.

## Mineral Sources of Energy

Until the late eighteenth century, most economic activity, including the transportation of goods, was powered by either humans or beasts. Either people tilled the soil themselves, using a spade, or they yoked oxen to pull a plow. Either they carried materials and goods on their backs or they used horses to transport them. In either case the energy for these tasks came ultimately from organic sources, the food that was needed to feed farmers or their animals. If workers needed heat, they had to burn an organic material, wood or charcoal, to produce it. The amount of energy that could be generated in a particular region was therefore limited by its capacity to produce sufficient wood, charcoal, or food. By the middle of the eighteenth

**Philippe Jacques de Loutherbourg,** *Coalbrookdale by Night* **(1801)**
This painting depicts the intense heat produced by the coal bellows used to smelt iron in
Coalbrookdale, an English town in the Severn Valley that was one of the key centers of industrial
activity at the beginning of the nineteenth century.

century, for example, the forests in Britain were no longer
capable of producing sufficient quantities of charcoal for
use in the iron industry.

Organic sources of energy were of course renewable, in
that new crops could be grown and forests replanted, but
the long periods of time that these processes took, coupled
with the limited volume of organic material that could be
extracted from an acre of land, made it difficult to sustain
economic growth. The only viable alternatives to these organic sources of energy before the eighteenth century were
those that tapped the forces of nature: windmills, which
were used mainly in the Netherlands for purposes of field
drainage, and water wheels, which were driven by water
pressure from river currents, waterfalls, or human-made
channels that regulated the flow of water. The potential of
those natural sources of energy was both limited and difficult to harness, and it could be tapped only in certain locations or at certain times. Moreover, those sources could not
produce heat.

The decisive change in the harnessing of energy for industrial purposes was the successful use of minerals, originally coal but in the twentieth century oil and uranium as
well, as the main sources of energy used in the production
and transportation of goods. These minerals were not inex-

haustible, as the decline of coal deposits in Europe during
the twentieth century has shown, but the supplies could last
for centuries, and they were much more efficient than any
form of energy produced from organic materials, including
charcoal and peat. Coal produced the high combustion
temperatures necessary to smelt iron, and unlike charcoal it
was not limited by the size of a region's forests. Coal therefore became the key to the expansion of the British iron industry in the nineteenth century. That industry's dependence on coal was reflected by the relocation of iron works
from the mines that supplied the ore itself to the coal fields
that supplied the energy. Coal also became the sole source
of heat for the new steam engine.

As the Industrial Revolution progressed, it relied increasingly on coal as its main fuel. The change, however, occurred gradually. In 1830 a majority of factories still used
water power, and steam power did not realize its most spectacular increases until after 1870. Nevertheless, largely because of the demands of the mining, textile, and metal industries, coal mining became a major industry itself with
an enormous labor force. By 1850 British mines employed
about 5 percent of the entire national workforce. These
miners were just as instrumental as textile workers in making Britain an industrial nation.

## The Growth of Factories

One of the most enduring images of the Industrial Revolution is that of the large factory, filled with workers laboring amid massive machinery driven by either water or steam power. Mechanized factory production evolved out of forms of industry that had emerged only during the early modern period (1500–1750). In the Middle Ages virtually all industry in Europe was undertaken by skilled craftsmen who belonged to urban guilds. These artisans, working either by themselves or with the assistance of apprentices or journeymen, produced everything from candlesticks and hats to oxcarts and beds. During the early modern period the urban craftsman's shop gave way to two different types of industrial workplaces, the rural cottage and the large handicraft workshop. Both of these served as halfway houses to the large factory.

Beginning in the sixteenth century, entrepreneurs began employing families in the countryside to spin and weave cloth and make nails and cutlery. By locating industry in the countryside the entrepreneurs were able to escape the regulations imposed by the guilds regarding employment and the price of finished products. They also paid lower wages, because the rural workers, who also received an income from farming, were willing to work for less than the residents of towns. Another attraction of rural industry was that all the members of the family, including children, participated in the process. In this "domestic system" a capitalist entrepreneur provided the workers with the raw materials and sometimes the tools they needed. He later paid them a fixed rate for each finished product. The entrepreneur was also responsible for having the finished cloth dyed and for marketing the commodities in regional towns.

Rural household industry was widespread not only in certain regions of Britain but also in most European countries. In the late eighteenth century it gradually gave way to the factory system. The great attraction of factory production was mechanization, which became cost-efficient only when it was introduced in a central industrial workplace. In factories, moreover, the entrepreneur could reduce the cost of labor and transportation, exercise tighter control over the quality of goods, and increase productivity by concentrating workers in one location. Temporary labor shortages sometimes made the transition from rural industry to factory production imperative.

---

## DOCUMENT

## Adam Smith Describes the Division of Labor

*Adam Smith, a Scottish economist who is considered the founder of the classical school of economics, was the great theorist of modern* laissez-faire *capitalism. In* An Inquiry into the Nature and Causes of the Wealth of Nations *(1776), he challenged the mercantilist assumption that there was only a fixed supply of wealth for which nations had to compete. He also argued that in an unregulated economy, the pursuit of self-interest would work in the interest of the public welfare. In this selection Smith discusses the division of labor. Smith wrote* The Wealth of Nations *during the very early stages of industrialization. The place of production that he uses in this example is not a large mechanized factory but a small urban workshop, often referred to as a manufactory.*

To take an example, therefore, from a very trifling manufacture; but one in which the division of labour has been very often taken notice of, the trade of the pin-maker; a workman not educated to this business (which the division of labour has rendered a distinct trade), nor acquainted with the use of the machinery employed in it (to the invention of which the same division of labour has probably given occasion), could scarce, perhaps, with his utmost industry, make one pin in a day, and certainly could not make twenty. But in the way in which this business is now carried on, not only the whole work is a peculiar trade, but it is divided into a number of branches, of which the greater part are likewise peculiar trades. One man draws out the wire, another straits it, a third cuts it, a fourth points it, a fifth grinds it at the top for receiving the head; to make the head requires two or three distinct operations; to put it on is a peculiar business, to whiten the pins is another; it is even a trade by itself to put them into the paper; and the important business of making a pin is in this manner, divided into about eighteen distinct operations, which in some manufactories, are all performed by distinct hands, though in others the same man will sometimes perform two or three of them. I have seen a small manufactory of this kind where ten men only were employed, and where some of them consequently performed two or three distinct operations. But though they were very poor and indifferently accommodated with the necessary machinery, they could, when they exerted themselves, make about twelve pounds of pins a day. There are in a pound upwards of four thousand pins of a middling size. Those ten persons, therefore, could make among them upwards of forty-eight thousand pins in a day. Each person, therefore making a tenth part of forty-eight thousand pins, might be considered as making four thousand eight hundred pins in a day.

Source: From Adam Smith, *An Inquiry into the Nature and Causes of the Wealth of Nations*, 5th Edition, 1789, Book I, Chapter 1.

**Mule Spinning**

A large mechanized spinning mill in northern England, about 1835. The workers did not require
any great skill to run the machinery.

The second type of industrial workplace that emerged during the early modern period was the large handicraft workshop. Usually located in the towns and cities, rather than in the countryside, these workshops employed relatively small numbers of people with different skills who worked collectively on the manufacture of a variety of items, such as pottery and munitions. The owner of the workshop supplied the raw materials, paid the workers' wages, and gained a profit from selling the finished products.

The large handicraft workshop made possible a division of labor°—the assignment of one stage of production to each worker or group of workers. The effect of the division of labor on productivity was evident even in the manufacture of simple items such as buttons and pins. In *The Wealth of Nations* (1776), the economist Adam Smith (1723–1790) used a pin factory in London to illustrate how the division of labor could increase per capita productivity from no more than twenty pins a day to the astonishing total of 4,800.

Like the cottages engaged in rural industry, the large handicraft workshop eventually gave way to the mechanized factory. The main difference between the workshop and the factory was that the factory did not require a body of skilled workers. When production become mechanized, the worker's job was simply to tend to the machinery. The only skill factory workers needed was manual dexterity to operate the machinery. Only those workers who made industrial machinery remained craftsmen or skilled workers in the traditional sense of the word.

With the advent of mechanization, factory owners gained much tighter control over the entire production process. Indeed, they began to enforce an unprecedented discipline among their workers, who had to accommodate themselves to the boredom of repetitive work and a timetable set by the machines. Craftsmen who had been accustomed to working at their own pace now had to adjust to an entirely new and more demanding schedule. "While the engine runs," wrote one critical contemporary, "the people must work—men, women, and children yoked together with iron and steam. The animal machine—breakable in the best case, subject to a thousand sources of suffering—is chained fast to the iron machine which knows no suffering and no weariness."[2]

Despite the growth and development of the factory system, the factory did not become the most common type of industrial workplace until the early twentieth century. In Britain, Germany, France, and the United States most manufacturing continued to take place in handicraft workshops in the cities or in rural households. Indeed, many of the industries that became mechanized spawned a variety of secondary crafts and trades, such as the dyeing and finishing of cloth and the sewing of clothes, which were conducted mainly in rural households.

## New Methods of Transportation

As industry became more extensive and increased its output, transport facilities, such as roads, bridges, canals, and eventually railroads, grew in number and quality. Increased industrial productivity has always depended on efficient movement of raw materials to places of production and transportation of finished products to the market. During the early phase of the Industrial Revolution in Britain, water transportation supplied most of these needs. A vast network of navigable rivers and human-made canals, eventually more than 4,000 miles in length, was used to transport goods in areas that did not have access to the coast. The canals that were built after 1760, with their systems of locks and their aqueducts spanning roads and rivers, were a product of the technology that the Scientific Revolution had made possible. For routes that could not be reached by water, the most common method of transportation was by horse-drawn carriages on newly built turnpikes or toll roads, many of them made of stone so that they were passable even in wet weather.

The most significant innovation in transport during the nineteenth century was the railroad. Introduced as the Industrial Revolution was gaining momentum, the railroad provided quick, cheap transportation of heavy materials such as coal and iron over long distances. Its introduction in Britain during the 1820s and throughout Europe and America during the following decades serves as one of the best illustrations of the transition from an economy based on organic sources of energy to one based on mineral sources of energy. Driven by coal-burning, steam-powered locomotives, the railroads freed transport from a dependence on animal power, especially the horses that were used to pull coaches along turnpikes, barges along canals, and even carts along parallel tracks in mines. Railroads rapidly became the main economic thoroughfares of the industrial economy. They linked towns and regions that earlier had not been easily accessible to each other. They also changed the travel habits of Europeans by making it possible to cover distances in one-fifth the time it took by coach.

The construction and operation of railroads became a major new industry, employing thousands of skilled and unskilled workers and providing opportunities for investment and profit. The industry created an unprecedented demand for iron and other materials used to build and equip locomotives, tracks, freight cars, passenger cars, and signals, thus giving a tremendous boost to the iron industry and the metalworking and engineering trades. By the 1840s the railroads had become the main stimulus to economic growth throughout western Europe and the United States. Transport in industrialized economies continues to experience frequent innovation. During the twentieth century, for example, new methods of transportation, including automobiles, airplanes, and high-speed rails, have sustained economic growth in all industrialized countries, and like the railroads they have become major industries themselves.

Transport facilities, unlike factories, can seldom be built entirely by their individual owners. The cost of building locomotives and laying railroad tracks is almost always too great to come from the profits accumulated in the normal conduct of one's business. The funds for these facilities must come from either private investment, governments, or international financial institutions. In Britain the capital for

**The Stockton and Darlington Railway**

A locomotive and two cars used on the first major railroad in Britain, which opened in 1825. The railroad carried materials and goods to and from towns producing iron in the northern counties of England.

the railroads came entirely from individual investors. In the United States, which built the world's largest railroad system in the nineteenth century, most of the capital also came from private investment, but many state and city governments helped finance early railroads. In other industrialized countries, governments played a more important role. In Belgium, which was the second European country to experience an Industrial Revolution, and in Russia, which was one of the last, the governments of those countries assumed the responsibility for building a national railroad system.

# Conditions Favoring Industrial Growth

■ What social and economic changes made industrial development possible?

The immediate causes of the Industrial Revolution were the competitive pressures that encouraged technological innovation, the transition to coal power, the growth of factories, and the building of the railroads. These developments, however, do not provide a full explanation for this unprecedented economic transformation. Certain social and economic conditions were present in Britain that allowed industrialization to progress—a large population, improved agricultural productivity, the accumulation of capital, a group of people with scientific knowledge and entrepreneurial skill, and sufficient demand for manufactured goods. In this section we will look at the historical experience of Great Britain, which was the first country to industrialize, to see how these conditions made industrial economic development possible.

## Population Growth

Industrialization requires a sufficiently large pool of labor to staff the factories and workshops of the new industries. One of the main reasons why the Industrial Revolution occurred first in Britain is that its population during the eighteenth century increased more rapidly than that of any country in continental Europe. Between 1680 and 1820 the population of England more than doubled, while that of France grew at less than one-third that rate, and that of the Dutch Republic hardly grew at all. One of the reasons this growth took place was that famines, which had occurred periodically throughout the early modern period, became less frequent during the eighteenth century. The last great famine in Britain took place in 1740, only a generation before industrialization began. There was also a decrease in mortality from epidemic diseases, especially typhus, influenza, and smallpox. Bubonic plague, which had deci-

### Increase in European Population, 1680–1820

**Population Totals (millions)**

|  | 1680 | 1820 |
| --- | --- | --- |
| France | 21.9 | 30.5 |
| Italy | 12.0 | 18.4 |
| Germany | 12.0 | 18.1 |
| Spain | 8.5 | 14.0 |
| England | 4.9 | 11.5 |
| Netherlands | 1.9 | 2.0 |
| Western Europe | 71.9 | 116.5 |

**Percentage Growth Rates, 1680–1820**

| England | 133% |
| --- | --- |
| Spain | 64 |
| Italy | 53 |
| Germany | 51 |
| France | 39 |
| Netherlands | 8 |
| Western Europe | 73 |

*Source:* E. A. Wrigley, "The Growth of Population in Eighteenth-Century England: A Conundrum Resolved," *Past and Present* 98 (1983): 122.

mated the European population periodically since the fourteenth century, struck England for the last time in the Great Plague of London of 1665. It made its last European appearance at Marseilles in 1720 but did not spread beyond the southern parts of France.

Even more important than this reduction in mortality was an increase in fertility. More people were marrying, and at a younger age, which increased the birth rate. The spread of rural industry seems to have encouraged this early-marriage pattern. Wage-earning textile workers tended to marry a little earlier than agricultural workers, probably because wage earners did not have to postpone marriage to inherit land or to become self-employed, as was the case with farm workers.

This increase in population facilitated industrialization in two ways. First, it increased demand for the goods that were being manufactured in large quantities in the factories. The desire for these products, especially the new cottons, played an important role in enlarging the domestic market for manufactured goods, as we shall see shortly. Second, it increased the supply of labor, freeing a substantial portion of the population for industry, especially for factory labor. At the same time, however, this increase was not so large as to have had a negative effect on industrialization, as it did in a number of underdeveloped countries in the twentieth century. If population growth is too rapid, it can lead to declining incomes, put pressure on agriculture to feed more people than is possible, and prevent the accumulation of wealth. Most important, it can discourage factory owners from introducing costly machinery, because if labor is plentiful and cheap, it might very well cost less for workers to produce the same volume of goods by hand. Industrialization therefore requires a significant but not too rapid increase in population—the exact scenario that occurred in Britain during the eighteenth century.

## Agricultural Productivity

Between 1700 and 1800 British agriculture experienced a revolution, resulting in a substantial increase in productivity. A major reason for this increase was the consolidation of all the land farmed by one tenant into compact fields. During the Middle Ages and most of the early modern period, each tenant on a manorial estate leased and farmed strips of land that were scattered throughout the estate. The decisions regarding the planting and harvesting of crops in these open fields were made collectively in the manorial court. Beginning in the sixteenth century, some of the wealthier tenants on these estates agreed to exchange their strips of land with their neighbors in order to consolidate their holdings into large compact fields, whose boundaries were defined by hedges, bushes, or walls. The main benefit of this process of enclosure° was that it allowed individual farmers to exercise complete control over the use of their land. In the eighteenth and nineteenth centuries the number of these enclosures increased dramatically, as the British Parliament passed legislation that divided entire estates into a number of enclosed fields. This legislation benefited all landowners, including the members of the aristocracy who passed the legislation.

With control of their lands, farmers could make them more productive. The most profitable change was to introduce new crop rotations, often involving the alternation of grains such as rye or barley with root crops such as turnips or grasses such as clover. These new crops and grasses restored nutrients to the soil and therefore made it unnecessary to let fields lie fallow once every three years. Farmers also introduced a variety of new fertilizers and soil additives that made harvests more bountiful. Farmers who raised sheep took advantage of discoveries regarding scientific breeding that improved the quality of their flocks.

More productive farming meant that fewer agricultural workers were required to feed the population. This made it possible for more people to leave the farms to work in the factories and mines. The expanded labor pool of industrial workers, moreover, was large enough that factory owners did not have to pay workers high wages; otherwise the prospect of industrializing would have lost much of its appeal. The hiring of children and women to work in the factories and mines also kept the labor pool large and the costs of labor low.

## Capital Formation and Accumulation

The term capital° refers to all the assets used in production. These include the factories and machines that are used to produce other goods (fixed capital) as well as the raw materials and finished products that are sent to market (circulating capital). Other forms of capital are the railroads and barges used for transporting raw materials to the place of production and finished products to market. Mechanized industry involves the extensive and intensive use of capital to do the work formerly assigned to human beings. An industrial economy therefore requires large amounts of capital, especially fixed capital.

Capital more generally refers to the money that is necessary to purchase these physical assets. This capital can come from a number of different sources: It can come from individuals, such as wealthy landlords, merchants, or industrialists who invest the profits they have accumulated in industrial machinery or equipment. In many cases the profits derived from industrial production are reinvested in the firm itself. Alternatively, capital can come from financial institutions in the form of loans. Very often a number of individuals make their wealth available to an industrial firm by buying shares of stock in that company's operations. This of course is the main way in which most capital is accumulated today. In countries that have only recently begun to industrialize in Latin America and Southeast Asia, capital often comes from public sources, such as governments, or from international institutions, such as the International Monetary Fund.

In Great Britain the capital that was needed to achieve industrial transformation came almost entirely from private sources. Some of it was raised by selling shares of stock to people from the middle and upper levels of society, but an even larger amount came from merchants who engaged in domestic and international trade, landowners who profited from the production of agricultural goods (including those who owned plantations in America), and the industrial entrepreneurs who owned mines, ironworks, and factories. In Britain, where all three groups were more successful than in other parts of Europe, the volume of capital made available from these sources was substantial. These people could invest directly in industrial machinery and mines or, more commonly, make their wealth available to others indirectly in the form of loans from banks where they kept their financial assets.

Banks supplied a considerable amount of the funds necessary for industrialization. In Britain the possibilities for such capital were maximized in the late eighteenth century when financial institutions offered loans at low interest rates and when the development of a national banking system made these funds readily available throughout the country, especially in the new industrial cities such as Leeds, Sheffield, and Manchester. The number of English banks went from a mere dozen in 1750 to more than 300 in 1800. Many bankers had close ties with industrialists, thereby facilitating the flow of capital from the financial to the industrial sector of the economy. Banks played an even more central role in the industrialization of Germany, which was economically not as advanced as Britain and less capable, therefore, of generating capital through the accumulation of profits.

## Technological Knowledge and Entrepreneurship

The process of industrialization involves the application of technological knowledge to the manufacturing process. It also involves entrepreneurship, the ability to make business ventures profitable. The mechanization of industry demanded scientifically trained people not only to introduce new forms of machinery but also to mass-produce that machinery for other manufacturers. The development of new modes of transportation required the skill of an entire class of civil engineers who could design and construct locomotives, ships, canals, railroads, and bridges. At the same time, industrialization required a group of business experts who knew how to run the factories and market their products. These requirements help explain why countries that are industrializing today often import technological and financial personnel from other countries to assist them in the process of industrialization and take steps to train and educate people from their own countries to carry on this work.

As we have discussed in Chapter 16, the geographical center of the Scientific Revolution shifted from the Mediterranean to the North Atlantic, especially to England, in the late seventeenth century. At the same time, England took the lead in making science an integral part of the nation's culture. In no other European country was so much attention given to the dissemination of scientific knowledge in public lectures, the meetings of local scientific societies, and the publication of scientific textbooks. Much of this popular scientific education focused on Newtonian mechanics and dynamics. These were precisely the areas of science that lent themselves most readily to technological application. The only area that was developed more fully in France than in Britain was thermodynamics, the branch of physics dealing with heat and its conversion into other forms of energy, such as steam power. To some extent the technological innovations and engineering achievements that took place in Britain during the Industrial Revolution can be considered the product of this unparalleled diffusion of scientific knowledge. Those who made these innovations also required extensive mathematical skill. The education given to British schoolchildren in the eighteenth century included more instruction in mathematics than was given in any other European country.

Industrial entrepreneurs, the people who actually ran the factories and superintended the industrial process, also needed a certain level of technological and mathematical skill, but their talents lay much more in their ability to run a variety of capitalist enterprises for a profit. Britain had no shortage of this type of talent in the eighteenth century. Even before the advent of mechanization there had developed an entire class of merchant capitalists who had organized the domestic system of rural industry or run the large handicraft workshops in London and other towns.

The invention and production of the steam engine readily illustrate the way in which technological and entrepreneurial skills reinforced and complemented each other. The partnership between the Scotsman James Watt, who invented the steam engine, and the Englishman Matthew Boulton represented a dynamic British alliance of science and capitalism. Of the two men, Watt had more scientific and mathematical knowledge, having taught himself geometry and trigonometry as well as having read textbooks on mechanics. He was familiar with the work of Joseph Black, the chemist at the University of Glasgow who studied steam, and he had acquired a knowledge of scientific instruments from his father's business as an outfitter of ships. Even though he was not an academic, he thought he was as smart as the famous French chemist Antoine Lavoisier. He was also a shrewd businessman who figured out various ways to use his knowledge of engineering to turn a profit and acquire a competitive advantage over others. Boulton was the classic eighteenth-century English entrepreneur who manufactured a variety of small metal objects from toys and buttons to teakettles and watch chains. His contribution to the partnership was assembling workers with the requisite skills to mass-produce the engine. Boulton was also scientifically knowledgeable, and both he and Watt were members of the Lunar Society of Birmingham, a voluntary scientific society in which they shared similar interests. Both men thought of themselves as scientists, just as both of them acted as entrepreneurs.

## Demand from Consumers and Producers

The conditions for industrialization that we have discussed so far all deal with supply°, that is, the amounts of capital, labor, food, and skill that are necessary to support the industrial process. The other side of the economic equation is demand°, that is, the desire of consumers to purchase industrial goods and of producers to acquire raw materials and machinery. Much of the extraordinary productivity of the Industrial Revolution arose from the demand for industrial products. Many of the technological innovations that occurred at the beginning of the revolution also origi-nated as responses to the demand for more goods. For ex-ample, the demand for more cotton goods spurred the in-troduction of the spinning jenny, the water frame, and the mule. Likewise the demand for coal for industrial and do-mestic use led to the development of an efficient steam engine in order to drain mines so that those supplies of coal could be extracted.

During the early years of industrialization, only about 35 percent of all British manufactured goods were exported. This statistic indicates that as the Industrial Revolution was taking hold, the domestic market was still the main source of demand for industrial products. The demand was espe-cially strong among the bourgeoisie. Within that group a "consumer revolution" had taken place during the eigh-teenth century. This revolution was based on an unprece-dented desire to acquire goods of all sorts, especially clothing and housewares, such as pottery, cutlery, furni-ture, and curtains. The consumer revolution was fueled in large part by a desire to imitate the spending habits of the aristocracy. It was assisted by commercial manipulation of all sorts, including newspaper advertising, warehouse dis-plays, product demonstrations, and the distribution of samples. An entirely new consumer culture arose, one in which women played a leading role. Advertisements pro-moting the latest female fashions, housewares, and chil-dren's toys became more common than those directed at adult male consumers. One ad in a local British paper in 1777, capitalizing on reports that mice were getting into ladies' hair at night, promoted "night caps made of silver wire so strong that no mouse or even a rat can gnaw through them." Advertisements therefore created a demand for new products as well as increasing the demand for those already on the market.

If this consumer revolution had been restricted to the middle class, it would have had only a limited effect on the Industrial Revolution. The bourgeoisie in the eighteenth century constituted at most only 20 percent of the entire population of Britain, and most of the goods they craved, with the exception of the pottery produced in Josiah Wedgwood's factories (which is still made today), were lux-ury items rather than the types of products that could be easily mass-produced. A strong demand for manufactured goods could develop only if workers were to buy consumer goods such as knitted stockings and caps, cotton shirts, earthenware, coffeepots, nails, candlesticks, watches, lace, and ribbon. The demand for these products came from small cottagers and laborers as well as the middle class. The demand for stockings for both men and women was partic-ularly strong. In 1831 the author of a study of the impact of machinery on British society declared, "Two centuries ago not one person in a thousand wore stockings; one century ago not one person in five hundred wore them; now not one person in a thousand is without them."

Demand for manufactured products from the lower classes was obviously limited by the amount of money that wage earners had available for nonessential goods, and real wages did not increase very much, if at all, during the eigh-teenth century. Nevertheless the income of families in which the wife and children as well as the father worked for wages did increase significantly both during the heyday of rural industry and during the early years of industrializa-tion. With these funds available, a substantial number of workers could actually afford to buy the products they de-sired. As the population increased, so too did this lower-class demand, which helped sustain an economy built around industrial production.

# The Spread of Industrialization

■ How did industrialization spread from Great Britain to the European continent and America?

The Industrial Revolution, like the Scientific Revolution of the sixteenth and seventeenth centuries, did not oc-cur in all European countries at the same time. As we have seen, it began in Britain in the 1760s and for more than four decades was confined exclusively to that country (see Map 20.1). It eventually spread to other European and North American countries, where many industrial innova-tions were modeled on those that had taken place in Britain. Belgium, France, Germany, Switzerland, Austria, Sweden, and the United States all experienced their own Industrial Revolutions by the middle of the nineteenth cen-tury. Only in the late nineteenth century did countries out-side the traditional boundaries of the West, mainly Russia and Japan, begin to industrialize. By the middle of the twentieth century, industrialization had become a truly global process, transforming the economies of a number of Asian and Latin American countries.

## Great Britain and the Continent

Industrialization occurred on the European continent much later than it did in Great Britain. Only after 1815 did Belgium and France begin to industrialize on a large scale, and it was not until 1840 that Germany, Switzerland, and Austria showed significant signs of industrial growth. Other European countries, such as Italy and Spain, did not begin serious efforts in this direction until the late nineteenth century. It took continental European nations even longer to rival the economic strength of Britain. Germany, which emerged as Britain's main competitor in the late nineteenth century, did not match British industrial output until the twentieth century.

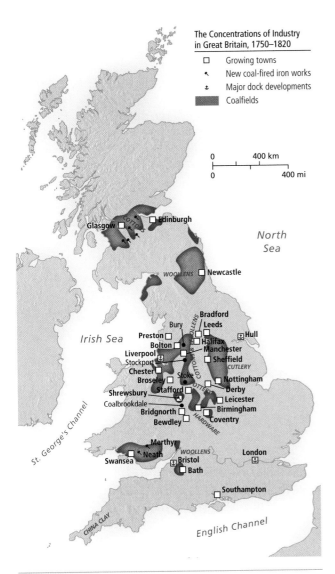

**Map 20.1  The Concentrations of Industry in Great Britain, 1750–1820**

The most heavily industrialized regions were in northern England, where the population of cities such as Manchester, Liverpool, and Sheffield grew rapidly.

cially in France. Nonetheless, industrialization on the Continent, especially in heavy industry, lagged far behind that of Great Britain, and the process was for the most part painfully slow.

One explanation for the slower development of industrialization on the Continent relates to the political situations in those countries. Well into the nineteenth century, most continental European countries had numerous internal political barriers that could impede the transportation of raw materials and goods from one part of the country to another. In Germany, for example, which was not politically united until 1871, scores of small sovereign territorial units charged tariffs whenever goods crossed their territorial boundaries. Only in 1834 was a customs union, the *Zollverein,* created to eliminate some of these barriers. In France, which had achieved a formal territorial unity during the reign of Louis XIV, local rights and privileges impeded internal trade until the early nineteenth century. This political situation was aggravated by the relatively poor state of continental roads and the inaccessibility of many seaports from production sites.

The contrast between the situation on the Continent and that which prevailed in Great Britain is striking. After 1707, when Scotland was united to England and freedom of internal trade was established between the two countries, the United Kingdom of Great Britain constituted the largest free-trade zone in Europe. Thus raw materials and finished products could pass from one place within Great Britain to another, up to a distance of more than 800 miles, without payment of any internal customs or duties. The system of inland waterways was complete by 1780, and seaports were accessible from all parts of the country.

The industrial potential of many continental European countries was also weakened by the imposition of protective tariffs on goods imported from other countries. The purpose of this mercantilist policy was to develop national self-sufficiency and to maintain a favorable balance of trade, but it also had the negative effect of limiting economic growth. For example, in the Dutch Republic (the kingdom of the Netherlands after 1815) a long tradition of protecting established industries prevented that country from importing the raw materials and machines needed to develop new industries. Because protectionism invited retaliation from trading partners, it also tended to shrink the size of potential overseas markets. Britain adopted a policy of free trade during the 1840s, and it pressured other European countries to adopt the same policy.

A further obstacle to European industrialization was aristocratic hostility, or at least indifference, to industrial development. In Britain the aristocracy, which consisted of noblemen and gentry, were themselves often involved in capitalist enterprise and did not have the same suspicion of industry and trade that their counterparts in France and Spain often harbored. Many members of the British aristocracy, such as

Why did it take so long for other countries to industrialize? Virtually all of them had developed extensive rural industry in the late eighteenth century. The governments of European countries, in keeping with mercantilist philosophy, had a long tradition of encouraging the development of domestic industry. Population growth on the Continent during the late eighteenth century, while less dramatic than in Great Britain, should have been sufficient to stimulate consumer demand and increase the supply of labor. Overall economic growth in France during that time almost matched that of Great Britain. Scientific education, while not as widespread as in Britain, was hardly lacking, espe-

customs union
1853

NORWAY
& SWEDEN
customs union
1874–1890

DENMARK

joined German
customs union
1888

SCHLESWIG
HOLSTEIN

Hamburg

Bremen
*Tax union*

RUSSIA
*Russo-Polish
customs frontier
abolished 1851*

CONGRESS
POLAND

LUXEMBOURG

ZOLLVEREIN 1834
*united with the
Tax Union
1854*

FRANCE
*internal
duties
abolished
1790*

HABSBURG
EMPIRE
*Austro-Hungarian
customs frontier
abolished 1850*

SWITZERLAND

*internal duties
abolished 1848–1874*

MOLDAVIA-
WALLACHIA
*customs union
1847*

*Black
Sea*

ITALY

*political and economic
unification 1860–1870*

*Mediterranean Sea*

0    300 km
0    300 mi

**Map 20.2   Customs Unions in
Continental Europe**
One of the reasons for the relatively slow progress of industrialization on the European continent was the existence of internal tariff barriers. This map shows the dates when customs unions, such as the *Zollverein* of 1834 in the German Confederation, were established or the customs barriers were eliminated. By contrast, all internal customs duties within Great Britain had been eliminated more than a century earlier when England and Scotland were united in 1707.

the entrepreneur "Turnip Townshend" (see Chapter 18), were agricultural capitalists who improved the productivity of their estates. Others were involved in mining. The Duke of Devonshire encouraged the exploitation of the copper mines on his estate, while the Duke of Bridgewater employed the engineer James Brindley to build a canal from the duke's coal mines in Worsley to Manchester in 1759. He later had Brindley extend the canal from Manchester to the mouth of the Mersey River, connecting the textile region of Manchester with the large northern industrial city of Liverpool.

One reason for the British aristocracy's support for economic growth was that many of its members, especially the gentry, rose into its ranks from other social and economic groups. These individuals tended to be sympathetic to the values of a commercial and an industrial society. The same attitude toward commerce and industry simply did not exist among the nobility in France before the revolution, much less among German *Junkers*. These groups had little connection with industrial or commercial society, whose values they held in very low regard. Consequently they rarely invested in industry.

Even among the European middle classes, the same type of competitive entrepreneurial spirit that was exhibited by men like Matthew Boulton seems to have been in large part lacking. Capitalism was by no means absent in European countries, but the conduct of business was characterized by

greater caution and less willingness to obtain new capital from loans or the sale of stock to investors. This went hand in hand with a reluctance to innovate as well as a distaste for competition and the maximizing of profits. Consequently continental European countries failed to produce many counterparts to the captains of industry who had contributed much of the capital, technology, and entrepreneurial spirit to the Industrial Revolution in Britain.

A final reason for the slow industrialization of continental European countries was that they lacked the abundant raw materials that were readily accessible in Britain. The natural resources that Britain had in greatest quantities were coal and iron ore, both of which were indispensable to industrialization. At the same time British farms provided ample supplies of raw materials for the wool and leather industries. The French and the Germans had some coal deposits, but they were more difficult to mine, and they were not located near ocean ports. Continental countries also lacked the access to other raw materials that Britain could import through its vast trading network, and in particular from its overseas colonies. With a large empire on four continents and the world's largest merchant marine, Britain had abundant supplies of raw materials such as cotton as well as the capacity to import them cheaply and in large quantities. The greater difficulty European countries had in obtaining these raw materials did not prevent them from industrializing; it simply made the process slower.

# Features of Continental Industrialization

During the first half of the nineteenth century, especially after 1830, Belgium, France, Switzerland, Germany, and Austria began to introduce machinery into the industrial process, use steam power in production, concentrate labor in large factories, and build railroads. This continental European version of the Industrial Revolution is usually described as an imitative process, one in which entrepreneurs or government officials simply tried to duplicate the economic success that Britain had achieved by following British example. Continental European nations did indeed rely to some extent on British industrial machinery. Some of them also relied on British skilled labor when they began to build their first factories and ironworks. In a few instances, in violation of British law, foreign agents actually smuggled blueprints, models, or machine parts out of Britain. British engineers, entrepreneurs, and managers were also occasionally hired to run British-style factories in France and Germany. But each European nation, responding to its own unique combination of political, economic, and social conditions, followed its own course of industrialization.

One distinctive feature of continental European industrialization was that once countries such as Belgium and Germany began to industrialize, their governments played a much more active role in encouraging and assisting in the process. In contrast to Britain, whose government allowed private industry to function with few economic controls, continental governments became active partners in the industrial process. They supplied capital for many economic ventures, especially the railroads and roads. In Prussia the state owned a number of manufacturing and mining enterprises. Many continental governments also imposed protective tariffs to prevent an influx of cheap British goods from underselling the products of their own fledgling industries. In a few cases continental European governments even provided financial support for investors in an effort to encourage capital formation. In some places, such as Austria, the state eliminated the regulations of urban guilds that had restricted industrial development in rural regions.

A second major feature of continental European industrialization was that banks, particularly in Germany and Belgium, played a central role in industrial development. This was necessitated by the low level of capital formation on the Continent and the reluctance of entrepreneurs to take risks by investing money themselves. Banks in Germany and Belgium played a particularly active role in stimulating industry. Drawing on the resources of both small and large investors, these corporate banks became in effect industrial banks, building railroads and factories themselves in addition to making capital available for a variety of industrial ventures.

A third distinct feature of continental European industrialization was that the railroads actually contributed to the beginning of industrial development. In Great Britain the railroads were introduced some sixty years after industrialization had begun and thus helped sustain a process of economic development that had been long afoot. By contrast the railroads on the Continent provided the basic infrastructure of its new economy and became a major stimulus to the development of all other industries. Railroads also gave continental European governments the ability to transport military troops quickly in time of war, which helps to explain why governments supported railroad construction with such enthusiasm. In Belgium, which was the first continental European nation to industrialize, the new government built a national railroad system during the 1830s and 1840s, not only to stimulate industry but also to unify the newly independent nation.

Of all the European countries that industrialized, only Belgium appears to have followed the British model closely by developing coal, iron, and textiles as the three main sectors of the new economy. Other countries tended to concentrate their activity in one specific area. France emphasized textiles, especially those such as worsted woolens that did not compete with British cottons. France's coal production and consumption never matched that of Great Britain or Belgium, and after 1850 it fell behind that of Germany as well. In 1860 France was importing 43 percent of its coal, and it was still relying on charcoal rather than coal to smelt pig iron. In Germany the main economic advances, which did not begin until 1850, occurred mainly in the area of heavy industry, that is, coal, iron, and engineering rather than

**Medal Struck in 1835 to Commemorate the First German Railroad, from Nuremberg to Fürth**

Industry is depicted as a female figure with her arm resting on a winged wheel. The first railroad in Europe had opened in England in 1825. German engineers had modeled their first locomotive on that of George Stephenson.

**A Colossal Steam-Driven Hammer, Nicknamed "Fritz," Installed by Alfred Krupp at His Steelworks in Essen in 1861**
Krupp's factory was located in the Ruhr region of Germany, the main center in that country for heavy industry.

textiles. Together with the United States, Germany began to offer the main economic competition to the British economy by the end of the nineteenth century.

## Industrialization in the United States

Industrialization in the United States began during the 1820s, not long after Belgium and France had begun to experience their own industrial revolutions. It occurred first in the textile industry in New England, where factories using water power produced goods for largely rural markets. New England also began producing two domestic hardware products—clocks and guns—for the same market. Between 1850 and 1880 a second region between Pittsburgh and Cleveland became industrialized. This region specialized in heavy industry, especially steelmaking and the manufacture of large machinery, and it relied on coal for fuel.

American industrialization followed both British and continental European patterns. As in Britain and France, the development of cottage industry in the United States

preceded industrialization. Most of the industrial machinery used in the United States during the nineteenth century was modeled on imports from Britain. The most significant American technological innovation before 1900 was the sewing machine, which was patented by Elias Howe in 1846 and then developed and improved upon by Isaac Singer in the 1850s. This new machine was then introduced in Europe, where it was used in the production of ready-to-wear garments.

The state played an ambivalent role in early American industrialization. The U.S. federal government, whose powers were greatly limited, especially during the early nineteenth century, followed a policy of nonintervention in the economy, similar to the policy followed by the British government. The individual states in America, however, played a much more active role, especially in facilitating the growth of railroads. One of the ironies of early industrialization is that Prussia, with its tradition of strong state government and its control of the mines, did far less to promote the building of railroads than did the individual states in America.

After 1865, when American industrialization began to spread rapidly across the entire country, American entrepreneurs made a distinctive contribution to the industrial process in the area of business organization, especially the operation of international firms. Toward the beginning of the twentieth century, American manufacturers streamlined the production process by introducing the assembly line, a division of labor in which the product passes from one operation to the next until it is fully assembled. The assembly line required the production of interchangeable parts, another American innovation, first used in the manufacture of rifles for the U.S. government.

Like Great Britain, the United States possessed vast natural resources, including coal. It also resembled Britain in the absence of governmental involvement in the process of industrialization. The main difference between the industrializations of the two countries is that during the nineteenth century labor in America was in relatively short supply. This placed workers in a more advantageous situation in dealing with their employers and prevented some of the horrors of early British industrialization from recurring on the other side of the Atlantic. Only with the influx of European immigrants in the late nineteenth century did the condition of American workers deteriorate and begin to resemble the early-nineteenth-century British pattern.

## Industrial Regionalism

Although we have discussed the industrialization of entire nations, the process usually took place within smaller geographical regions. There had always been regional specialization in agriculture, with some areas emphasizing crops and others livestock. During the Industrial Revolution, however, entire economies acquired a distinctly regional character. Regional economies began to take shape during the days of the domestic system, when merchants employed families in certain geographical areas, such as Lancashire in England, to produce textiles. In these regions there was a close relationship between agricultural and industrial production, in that members of the same household participated in both processes. Related industries, such as those for finishing or dyeing cloth, also sprang up close to where the cotton or wool yarn was spun and the cloth woven.

As industrialization spread outside Britain, this regional pattern became even more pronounced. In France the centers of the textile industry were situated near the northeastern border near Belgium and in the area surrounding Lyons in the east-central part of the country. Both of these areas had attracted rural household industry before the introduction of textile machinery. In Germany the iron industry was centered in the Ruhr region, where most of the country's coal was mined. In the city of Essen on the Ruhr River the industrialist Alfred

Krupp (1812–1887) established an enormous steelmaking complex that produced industrial machinery, railroad equipment, and guns for the Prussian army. Within the Habsburg Empire most industry was located in parts of Bohemia (now the Czech Republic).

The development of regional economies did not mean that markets were regional. The goods produced in one region almost always served the needs of people outside that particular area. Markets for most industrial goods were national and international, and even people in small agricultural villages created a demand for manufactured goods. The French iron industry, for example, was centered in the eastern part of the country, but it catered to the needs of the wealthier segments of its own and other European populations, as did the iron industry in the Ruhr region in Germany and the textile industry in the north of England.

The development of regional industrial economies helps to explain the striking contrast that persisted well into the twentieth century between the parts of countries that had become heavily industrialized and those that retained at least many of the appearances of a preindustrial life. In Britain and the rest of Europe industrial machinery and factories were not introduced into every village. Some areas remained exclusively agricultural, while others continued a tradition of rural industry. This pattern was particularly evident in France, where mechanized industry was concentrated in a limited number of centers in the northeastern half of the country. In 1870 more than two-thirds of the French population still lived in rural areas. As economic growth and industrial development continued, however, agricultural regions eventually began to lose their traditional character. Even if industry itself did not arrive, the larger industrial economy made its mark. Agriculture itself became mechanized, while railroads and other forms of mechanized transport integrated these areas in a national economy.

# The Effects of Industrialization

■ What were the economic, social, and cultural effects of the Industrial Revolution?

The Industrial Revolution had a profound impact on virtually every aspect of human life. It encouraged the growth of the population and the economy, affected the conditions in which people lived, changed family life, created new divisions within society, and transformed the traditional rural landscape. The changes that it brought about were most evident in Britain, but in time they have occurred in every country that has industrialized, including the United States.

## Population and Economic Growth

The most significant of these changes was the sustained expansion of both the population and the economy. As we have seen, the Industrial Revolution in Britain was facilitated by a significant population increase in the eighteenth century. That growth had created a plentiful supply of relatively cheap labor, which in turn had helped to bring about a marked increase in industrial output. As industry grew, population kept pace, and each provided a stimulus to the growth of the other.

Most contemporary observers in the late eighteenth century did not believe that this expansion of both the population and the economy could be sustained indefinitely. The most pessimistic of these commentators was Thomas Malthus (1766–1834), an English cleric who wrote *An Essay on the Principle of Population* in 1798.

Thomas Malthus, *Laws of Population Growth* (1798)

Malthus argued that population had a natural tendency to grow faster than the food supply. Thus, unless couples exercised restraint by marrying late and producing fewer children, the population would eventually outstrip the resources necessary to sustain it, resulting in poor nutrition, famine, and disease. These "positive checks" on population growth, which sometimes were initiated or aggravated by war, would drive population back to sustainable levels. These checks would also end periods of economic expansion, which generally accompany increases in population. For example, in the fourteenth century the Black Death, which killed about one-third of the European population, also ended a significant period of economic growth. A similar but less severe contraction of the European population and economy occurred in the second half of the seventeenth century, marking the end of the economic expansion that had begun in the sixteenth century. In both these instances the increase in population put pressure on the food supply, raised the price of food, reduced employment, and lowered wages. The scarcity of food and the reduced nutritional levels that followed had made the population vulnerable to disease. If these demographic and economic patterns were to recur, we might expect that the significant expansion of the population and the economy that took place in eighteenth-century England would likewise reach its limits, just around the time that Malthus was writing.

This predicted cyclical contraction of both the population and the economy did not take place. Europe for the first time in its history managed to escape the "Malthusian population trap." Instead of being sharply reduced after 1800, the population continued to expand at an ever-faster rate, doubling in Great Britain between 1800 and 1850 and following a similar pattern of rapid growth in all other countries that had industrialized. At the same time the economy, instead of contracting or collapsing, continued to grow and diversify.

It is not absolutely clear how Europe avoided the Malthusian trap in the nineteenth century. Part of the answer lies in the greater productivity of agriculture, which resulted from either private initiative, as in Britain, or governmental agrarian reforms, as in Austria. The importation of grain from central and eastern Europe also helped to feed the larger, more urbanized population. Improvements in medicine and public health reduced mortality during the nineteenth century, helping to maintain the size of the industrial population. But it was mainly developments in industry itself, especially the increased accumulation of capital, that kept Europe from succumbing to yet another cycle of depopulation and economic contraction. The accumulation of capital over a long period of time was so great that industry was able to employ large numbers of workers even during the 1790s and 1800s, when Europe was at war. Because they had income from wages, workers were willing to marry earlier and have larger families, and with lower food prices because of higher agricultural productivity they could afford to maintain a healthier diet and purchase more manufactured goods as well. Thus the Industrial Revolution itself, coupled with the changes in agriculture that accompanied it, proved Malthus wrong.

While the rapid growth of population in industrialized societies up until the late twentieth century is incontestable, the record of economic growth is not so clear. In order to claim that the Industrial Revolution has resulted in sustained economic growth, we have to take a broad view, looking at an overall pattern of growth and ignoring certain cyclical recessions and depressions. Nations that have industrialized, beginning with European countries in the nineteenth century, have all experienced a significant increase in both gross national product and per capita income over the long run. Although the contrast between the size of these industrial economies and those of preindustrial, agrarian countries is staggering, economic growth in industrialized countries was not always rapid or continuous. During the first six decades of industrialization in Britain, for example, economic growth was actually fairly slow, mainly because so much capital went into subsidizing the long war against France (1792–1802; 1804–1815). During this period Britain spent an average of 60 million English pounds, or 25 percent of its national income, on war. Nevertheless, there still was steady growth, and more important, the type of Malthusian economic contraction or collapse that had followed all previous periods of expansion did not occur. To that extent we can say that the Industrial Revolution has resulted in sustained economic growth in the West.

## Standards of Living

Ever since the early years of the Industrial Revolution, a debate has raged over the effect of industrialization on the standard of living and the quality of life of the laboring population. The supporters of the two main schools of thought on this issue have been called the optimists and the

## DOCUMENT

# A French Geologist's Impressions of Birmingham, 1784

*Barthélemy Faujas de Saint-Fond (1741–1819), a French scientist who rose to become professor of geology at the Muséum d'Histoire Naturelle in Paris, recorded the following impressions of the industrial city of Birmingham on a journey through England and Scotland in 1784. He was especially impressed by the variety of products made there, the number of workers in the various industries, and the dramatic increase in the city's population,*

From the activity of its manufactures and its commerce, Birmingham is one of the most curious towns in England. If any one should wish to see in one comprehensive view the most numerous and varied industries, all combined in contributing to the arts of utility, of pleasure, and of luxury, it is hither that he must come. Here all the resources of industry, supported by the genius of invention and by mechanical skill of every kind are directed towards the arts and seem to be linked together to cooperate for their mutual perfection.

I know some travelers who have not given themselves the trouble to reflect on the importance and advantage of these kinds of manufactures in such a country as England have disapproved of most of these industrial establishments. I know that even an Englishman who has only taken a hasty, I would almost say an inconsiderate view of these magnificent establishments, William Gilpin, has said that it was difficult for the eye to be long pleased in the midst of so many frivolous arts, where a hundred men may be seen, whose labours are confined to the making of a tobacco box. But

besides that this statement is exaggerated and ill-considered, the author has not deigned to cast his eyes over the vast works where steam-pumps are made, these astonishing machines, the perfecting of which does so much honour to the talents and knowledge of Mr. Watt; over the manufactories in constant activity making sheet-copper for sheathing ships' bottoms; over those of plate-tin and plate-iron, which make France tributary to England, nor over that varied and extensive hardware manufacture which employs to so much advantage more than thirty thousand hands and compels all Europe, and a part of the New World, to supply themselves from England, because all ironmongery is made here in greater perfection, with more economy, and in greater abundance than anywhere else. Once more I say with pleasure, and it cannot be said too often to Frenchmen, that it is the abundance of coal which has performed this miracle and has created, in the midst of a barren desert, a town with forty thousand inhabitants, who live in comfort and enjoy all the conveniences of life. . . .

The population of Birmingham has made such an advance that during the war with the United States of America, a war which weakened the resources of England, at least three hundred new homes were added annually to the town, and this rate doubled as soon as peace was concluded. A well-informed person assured me that this was true, and he showed me, during my stay in the town, a whole street which was in process of erection with such rapidity that, all the houses being built on a given plan at the same time, one could believe that the street would be entirely completed in less than two months.

Source: From Faujas de Saint-Fond, *A Journey through England and Scotland to the Hebrides in 1784* (1907), pp. 345–50.

---

pessimists. The optimists have always emphasized the positive effects of both the process of mechanization and the system of industrial capitalism that arose during the revolution. They have focused on the success that industrialized nations have achieved in escaping the Malthusian trap and in achieving sustained economic growth. The Industrial Revolution, so they argue, has resulted in an unprecedented rise in individual income, which has made it possible for the mass of a country's population to avoid poverty for the first time in human history. In the second half of the twentieth century many optimists claimed that the industrialization of Western nations provided a blueprint for African, Asian, and Latin American countries that wished to escape from the poverty of a predominantly agrarian economy relying on organic sources of energy.

The main yardstick that the optimists have used to measure the improvement in living standards is per capita real income, that is, income measured in terms of its actual purchasing power. Real income in Great Britain rose about

50 percent between 1770 and 1850 and more than doubled during the entire nineteenth century. This increase in income allowed workers to improve their diets as well as to purchase more clothing and other basic commodities. These improvements, however, did not affect the lives of most workers for a long period of time—in Great Britain not until 1820, about sixty years after the beginning of industrialization. The increases that occurred after that date, moreover, were only averages, concealing disparities among workers with different levels of skill. Only in the late nineteenth and twentieth centuries did industrialization raise the real income of all workers to a level that made the benefits of industrialization apparent.

Even if the pessimists concede a long-term increase in real income, it has never been substantial enough to persuade them that industrialization was on balance a positive good, at least for the working class. The pessimists have always stressed the negative effects of industrial development on the life of the lower classes. In their way of thinking, industrialization was an unmitigated disaster. The cause of this disaster in their eyes was not the process of mechanization but the system of industrial capitalism°. This form of capitalism is characterized by the ownership of factories by private individuals and by the employment of wage labor. Like earlier forms of mercantile and agricultural capitalism, it involved a systematic effort to reduce costs and maximize profits. In the pursuit of this goal, employers tried to keep wages as low as possible and to increase production through labor-saving technology, thus preventing workers from improving their lot.

Pessimists regarding the Industrial Revolution over the past two centuries have usually claimed a moral basis for their position. In this respect they follow in a tradition begun by the poet William Blake (1757–1827), who referred to the new factories as "satanic mills," and the socialist Friedrich Engels, who in *The Condition of the Working Class in England in 1844* (1845) accused the factory owners in England of mass murder and robbery. Much pessimist writing has also been used to support a program of social or political reform. The German social philosopher Karl Marx (1818–1883), with whom Engels often collaborated and whose views we shall discuss more fully in Chapter 21, used his critique of industrial capitalism to call for a communist revolution in which the working class would seize political power and acquire ownership of the means of production.

Most of the evidence that social critics have used to support the pessimist position has come from the early period of industrialization in Britain, when incomes were either stagnant or declining and when conditions in factories and industrial and mining towns were most appalling. It

is difficult to measure these living standards statistically, but the weight of qualitative evidence suggests that they deteriorated during the nineteenth century. Working-class housing was makeshift and crowded, and there were few sanitary facilities. A new word, *slum,* was coined to refer to these poverty-stricken working-class neighborhoods. Poor drainage and raw sewage gave rise to a host of new hygienic problems, especially outbreaks of typhus and cholera. Between 1831 and 1866 four epidemics of cholera killed at least 140,000 people in Britain, most of whom lived in poorer districts.

The impact of industrialization and urbanization on the environment was no less harrowing. The burning of coal and the use of industrial chemicals polluted the urban atmosphere. The famous London fogs, which were actually smogs caused by industrial pollutants, presented a serious public health problem throughout the nineteenth century and did not begin to disappear until the introduction of strict regulations on the burning of coal in the 1950s.

While life in the city was bleak and unhealthy, working conditions in the factory were monotonous and demeaning. Forced to submit to a regimen governed by the operation of the machine, workers lost their independence as well as any control whatsoever over the products of their labor.

They were required to work long hours, often fourteen hours a day, six days a week, with few breaks. Factory masters locked the doors during working hours, and they assessed fines for infractions such as opening a window when the temperature was unbearable, whistling while working, and having dirty hands while spinning yarn. Work in the mines was a little less monotonous, but it was physically more demanding and far more dangerous.

## Women, Children, and Industry

During the early Industrial Revolution in Great Britain, large numbers of children and women were recruited into the workforce, especially the textile and mining industries. In the woolen industry in the western part of England, for example, female and child labor together accounted for 75 percent of the workforce. Children under age 13 made up 13 percent of the cotton factory workforce, and those under age 18 made up 51 percent. This pattern of employment reflects the demands of industrialists, who valued the hand skills and dexterity that children possessed as well as the greater amenability of both children and women to the discipline of factory labor. Some of the machines that were introduced into the textile industry in the late eighteenth century were specifically designed for women and children.

Female and child labor was both plentiful and cheap. Children received only one-sixth to one-third the wages of a grown man, while women generally took home only one-third to one-half of that adult male income. There was no lack of incentive for women and children to take one of these low-paying jobs. In a family dependent on wages, everyone needed to work, even when a large labor pool kept wages depressed.

The participation of both women and children in the workforce was not new. In an agricultural economy all members of the family contributed to the work, with parents and children, young and old, all being assigned specific roles. Rural industry also involved the labor of all members of the family. When people began working in the factories, however, they were physically separated from the home, making it impossible for workers to combine domestic and occupational labor.

As the workplace became distinct from the household, family life underwent a fundamental change, although this change did not occur immediately. During the early years of the Industrial Revolution, members of many families found employment together in the factories and mines. Factory owners also tried to perpetuate many aspects of family life in the new industrial setting, defining the entire factory community as an extended family, in which the factory owner played the paternalistic role. Gradually, however, mothers found it impossible to care for their youngest chil-

**DOCUMENT**

## The Employment of Women

*The German social philosopher Friedrich Engels (1820–1895) was one of the founders of modern socialism. He and Karl Marx collaborated in writing* The Communist Manifesto *(1848), and he edited the final two volumes of Marx's* Capital *after Marx died. Having served as a manager in a factory in Manchester, Engels described these conditions throughout Britain in one of his earliest works,* The Condition of the Working Class in England in 1844 *(1845). He emphasized the exploitation and brutalization of the lower classes as they were turned into a wage-earning proletariat. In this passage Engels describes the negative effects of factory labor on women and the family.*

The employment of women at once breaks up the family; for when the wife spends twelve or thirteen hours every day in the mill, and the husband works the same length of time there or elsewhere, what becomes of the children? They grow up like weeds; they are put out to nurse for a shilling or eighteen pence a week, and how they are treated may be imagined. Hence the accidents to which little children fall victims in the factory districts multiply to a terrible extent. . . . Women often return to the mill three or four days after confinement, leaving the baby of course; in the dinner hour they must hurry home to feed the children and eat something, and what kind of suckling that can be is also evident. Lord Ashley repeats the testimony of several work women: "M.H., twenty years old, has two children, the youngest a baby, that is tended by the other, a little older. The mother goes to the mill shortly after five o'clock in the morning, and comes home at eight at night; all day the milk pours from her breasts so that her clothing drips with it". . . . The use of narcotics to keep the children still is fostered by this infamous system and has reached a great extent in the factory districts. Dr. Johns, Registrar in Chief for Manchester, is of opinion that this custom is the chief source of the many deaths from convulsions. The employment of the wife dissolves the family utterly and of necessity, and this dissolution in our present society, which is based upon the family, brings the most demoralising consequences for parents and children. A mother who has no time to trouble herself about her child, to perform the most ordinary loving services for it during its first year, who scarcely indeed sees it, can be no real mother to the child, must inevitably grow indifferent to it, treat it unlovingly like a stranger. The children who grow up under such conditions are utterly ruined for later family life, can never feel at home in the family which they themselves found, because they have always been accustomed to isolation, and they contribute therefore to the already general undermining of the family in the working-class.

Source: From Friedrich Engels, *The Condition of the Working Class in England in 1844,* translated by F. K. Wischnewtzky (London: S. Sonnenshein, 1892).

dren on the job, and most of them dropped out of the full-time workforce. The restriction of child labor by the British Factory Act of 1833 reinforced this trend and led to the establishment of a fairly common situation in which the male wage earner worked outside the home while his wife stayed home with the children. As one young girl who worked in the mines testified before a parliamentary commission investigation of child labor in 1842, "Mother takes care of the children."

As more and more mothers left the factories, the female workforce became increasingly dominated by those who were unmarried. The few female workers who were married with children either came from the very poorest segments of society or took jobs only because their husbands were ill or unemployed. Neither the pay these women received nor the jobs they performed gave them financial autonomy or social prestige. Becoming an independent wage earner meant little when women's wages were on average one-third to one-half those of men. The jobs assigned to women within industry, such as operating textile machinery, generally required the least skill. When men and women were employed in the same workplace, the women were invariably subordinated to the authority of male workers or foremen, thereby perpetuating the patriarchal patterns that prevailed in preindustrial society. The Industrial Revolution did nothing to improve the status of women, and even their exclusion from certain occupations, such as mining by an act of Parliament in 1842, only reinforced a new sexual division of labor that was even more rigid than that which had prevailed in preindustrial society.

## Class and Class Consciousness

As Europe became more industrialized and urbanized, and as the system of industrial capitalism became more entrenched, writers began to use a new terminology to describe the structure of society. Instead of claiming that society consisted of a finely graded hierarchy of ranks to which individuals belonged by virtue of their occupations or their legal status, they divided society into three classes that could be distinguished by the type of property people owned and the manner in which they acquired it. At the top of this new social hierarchy was the aristocracy, consisting

# The Sadler Committee on Child Labor

The widespread use of child labor in Britain during the early decades of the Industrial Revolution led to efforts by social reformers and members of Parliament to regulate the conditions under which children worked. Parliament passed legislation restricting the number of hours that all children could work in textile mills in 1819 and 1829, but neither of these laws was enforced effectively, and they did not apply to all industries. Complaints of inhumane treatment, moral degradation, and exploitation of child workers continued to surface. In 1831 Michael Sadler (1780–1835), a Tory member of the British Parliament, introduced a bill in Parliament to limit the number of hours that all children could work to ten hours per day. Like many social reformers, Sadler was inspired by what he considered his Christian duty to protect dependent members of the community.

Sadler chaired the committee to which his bill was referred. In order to muster support for the bill, Sadler held hearings in which child workers themselves came before the committee to report on the conditions under which they lived and worked. The success of his bill was by no means guaranteed. Many members of Parliament were deeply committed to the policy of *laissez-faire,* according to which the government should not intervene in the operation of the economy, treating it instead as a self-regulating machine. Sadler had to convince his colleagues that they should modify that policy in the case of children, on the grounds that the state was obliged to provide for the welfare of children when their parents were unable to do so. He also needed to make the members of Parliament and the broader public aware of the brutality of the conditions under which the children worked.

The hearings that took place were not a trial in the strict sense of the word, but they possessed many of the features of a judicial investigation, not unlike those conducted by grand juries in criminal cases. The committee's proceedings were intended to expose, condemn, and ultimately remedy misconduct by the factory owners. Procedurally the committee members had more latitude than did courts of law. Because these parliamentary committees were designed to extract information rather than to bring offenders to trial, they did not need to adhere to any established judicial guidelines. There was no cross-examination of witnesses, nor could factory owners present a defense. The witnesses in this investigation were chosen because Sadler knew they would reveal the evils of the factory system.

The testimony presented to the Sadler Committee produced abundant evidence of the exploitation and physical abuse of child workers. Some of the most harrowing testimony came from the examination of a 17-year-old boy, Joseph Hebergam, on July 1, 1832. Hebergam revealed that he had begun the work of worsted spinning at age 7, that he worked at the factory from five A.M. until eight P.M., and that he had only thirty minutes for lunch at noon, leaving him to eat his other meals while standing on the job. In the factory there were three overlookers, one of whom was responsible for greasing the machinery and another for whipping the workers. The latter overlooker walked continually up and down the factory with whip in hand.

When asked where his brother John was working, Joseph replied that he had died three years before at age 16. Sadler then inquired into the cause of his brother's death. The boy responded, "It was attributed to this, that he died from working such long hours and that it had been brought on by the factory. They have to stop the flies [part of the textile machinery] with their knees, because they go so swift they cannot stop them with their hands; he got a bruise on the shin by a spindle-board, and it went on to that degree that it burst; the surgeon cured that, then he was better; then he went to work again; but when he had worked about two months more his spine

**Child Workers**
These children are on their way to work in the Yorkshire textile mills.

**Child Labor in the Textile Industry**
Factory girls operate machinery in a textile mill under the tight supervision of the factory owner.

became affected, and he died." The witness went on to explain that his own severe labor had damaged his knees and ankles so much so that he found it painful to walk. His brother and sister would help carry him to the factory, but when they arrived late, even by as little as five minutes, the overlooker beat all three of them "till we were black and blue."[3] At the request of the committee, Joseph then stood up to show the condition of his limbs. He reported the death of another boy who had sustained massive injuries when he was caught in the shaft of the machinery he was running. Joseph concluded his testimony by recounting how the factory owners had threatened him and his younger brothers

with losing their jobs if they testified before the committee.

The hearings of the Sadler Committee were widely publicized, but they fell short of realizing their original objective. The bill, which eventually was approved by Parliament as the Factory Regulations Act of 1833, prohibited the employment of children under age 9 in all factories. Boys and girls were allowed to work up to nine hours a day from age 9 until their thirteenth birthday, and up to twelve hours a day from age 13 until their eighteenth birthday. The long-term effect of this legislation was to establish in Western industrialized countries the principle that early childhood was a period of life set aside for education rather than work.

## Questions of Justice

1. This investigation was concerned with the achievement of social justice rather than the determination of criminal culpability. What were the advantages of using legislative committees in such an undertaking?
2. Child labor was not a new phenomenon in the early eighteenth century. Why did the Industrial Revolution draw attention to this age-old practice?

## Taking It Further

Horn, Pamela. *Children's Work and Welfare, 1780–1890.* 1996. An examination of the scale and nature of child employment in Britain and changing attitudes toward the practice.

of those who owned land and received their income in the form of rent. The middle class or bourgeoisie, which included the new factory owners, possessed capital and derived their income from profits, whereas the working class owned nothing but their own labor and received their income from wages.

This new model of society served a number of different purposes. Marx and Engels used it to construct a comprehensive theory of historical development. According to this theory, the middle class had struggled for centuries to seize power from the aristocracy, while the working class would eventually take power from the middle class. For Marx and Engels, conflicts over control of the means of production created a state of continuous class conflict. David Ricardo (1772–1823), an English social philosopher whose political and social allegiances were very different from those of Marx, used a similar model of society to illustrate the crucial role that the middle class played in the economy. Ricardo compared society to a coach in which the middle class was the driver guiding the vehicle, the working class was the horse that provided the labor, and the aristocracy was the nonpaying passenger.

Historians and social scientists disagree over the extent to which men and women in the nineteenth century were actually conscious of their membership in these classes. Marxist historians have claimed that the growth of wage labor, the exploitation of the working class, and conflicts between capital and labor encouraged workers to think of themselves not so much as individuals who claimed a certain social status but as members of a large class of workers who shared the same relationship to the means of production. These historians have pointed to the growth of trade unions, political campaigns for universal male suffrage, and other forms of working-class organization and communication as evidence of this awakening of class consciousness.

Other historians have claimed that people were less conscious of their class position. True, at certain times in the early nineteenth century some workers thought of themselves as members of a class whose interests conflicted with those of factory owners and financiers. It was much more common, however, for them to think of themselves primarily as practitioners of a particular craft, as members of a local community, or as part of a distinct ethnic minority, such as the Irish. When they demanded the right to vote, workers based their claim on their historic constitutional rights, not on the interests of all wage earners. When they demonstrated in favor of the ten-hour working day, they did so to improve the conditions in which they worked, not to advance the struggle of all workers against the middle class. The work experiences of laborers were too varied to sustain an awareness among most of them that they belonged to one homogeneous group.

The various capitalists, shopkeepers, and factory owners who belonged to the bourgeoisie also lacked a clear sense of their membership in a single middle class. These people were capable of achieving solidarity on certain occasions, such as when they feared that workers threatened their interests. As we discussed in Chapter 18, the bourgeoisie often criticized the lifestyle and values of the landed aristocracy in print. But like the working class, the bourgeoisie was too diverse to allow for the development of a unifying class consciousness inspired by an identity of economic interest

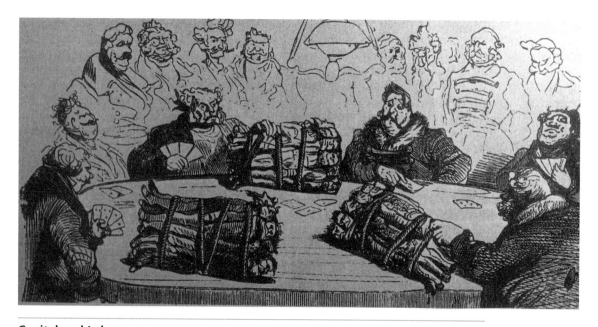

**Capital and Labor**
This cartoon, drawn by the illustrator Gustave Doré, depicts wealthy industrialists gambling with workers tied together as chips.

**The Industrial City of Birmingham in 1829**
Factories dominated the landscape of the city of Birmingham in this watercolor attributed to Frederick Calvert. By this time contemporaries were already complaining about the poor quality of air caused by the smelting of iron.

against those who occupied social positions either above or below them.

Working men and women showed a marked reluctance to engage in militant or violent action against their employers. Appeals for working-class solidarity to a large extent fell on deaf ears. It is true that on certain occasions workers took violent action against their employers. In 1812 groups of hand loom weavers in the highly industrialized Midland region of England engaged in a determined campaign to destroy the new power looms that they blamed for rising unemployment and low wages. Often disguised and operating at night, these "Luddites," who took their name from their mythical leader Ned Ludd, smashed the new textile machinery that factory owners had introduced. (Even today people who object to the introduction of new technology are referred to as Luddites.) The government sent an army of 12,000 men to suppress the Luddites, a task made difficult by the protection given them by their communities.

The Luddites did not, however, represent the majority of the English working class. Factory workers in particular seemed reluctant to join working-class organizations. Most of the workers who participated in these associations and who campaigned for the rights of the workers were independent artisans who had little interest in the struggle that Marx and Engels had predicted would result in the victory of the working class.

Nevertheless, the growing tensions between industrial capitalists and labor, coupled with the recognition that those who had political power were reluctant to give workers the right to vote, led to the gradual emergence of class consciousness in England. A violent encounter between workers demonstrating for the right to vote and better working conditions in Manchester in 1819, described in detail in the Encounters & Transformations feature in this chapter, contributed to a growing awareness among workers and the members of the bourgeoisie alike that British society was divided into classes that were engaged in continual conflict with each other.

## The Industrial Landscape

As industry spread throughout Europe and reached into areas that previously had been untouched by mechanization, urban and rural areas underwent dramatic changes. The most striking of these changes took place in the new industrial towns and cities, some of which had been little more than country towns before the factories were built. Manchester, for example, grew from a modest population of 23,000 people in 1773 to a burgeoning metropolis of 105,000 by 1820. Large factories with their smokestacks and warehouses, ringed by long rows of houses built to accommodate the armies of new industrial workers, gave these cities an entirely new and for the most part a grim appearance.

Cities experienced the most noticeable changes in physical appearance, but the countryside also began to take on a new look, mainly as a result of the transport revolution. The tunnels, bridges, and viaducts that were constructed to accommodate the railroad lines and the canals that were built to improve inland water transportation made an indelible imprint on the traditional terrain. In many ways this alteration of the landscape served as a statement of the mastery over nature that human beings had achieved at the time of the Scientific Revolution. The Industrial Revolution finally fulfilled the technological promise of that earlier revolution, and one of its effects was the actual transformation of the physical world.

# The Peterloo Massacre, 1819

The most dramatic encounter between the middle class and the working class in early nineteenth-century Britain took place in the northern industrial city of Manchester. During the first fifty years of the Industrial Revolution Manchester had grown into a major textile-producing metropolis—known to some as "Cottonopolis"—with a population of some 120,000 people. With thousands of workers finding employment in the mills, the city provided an environment in which demands for a wide suffrage and an improvement in working-class conditions attracted widespread support. In August 1819 some 60,000 people, most of them workers and their families, gathered at St. Peter's Field to demonstrate support for universal male suffrage, annual parliaments, and relief from low wages, high prices, and long working hours. The fact that many of the workers had served in the Napoleonic wars and had been preparing for the demonstration by marching in military style had raised the fears of the middle-class establishment. Shortly after the meeting began, a violent confrontation took place between the demonstrators and the volunteer cavalry (known as yeomen), who belonged to the city's bourgeoisie. Frightened by the size of the demonstration and determined to prevent concessions that would reduce their profits, the yeomen decided to disperse the meeting by force. In the confrontation that ensued, the yeomen trampled hundreds of demonstrators and slashed many others with their swords, killing eleven people and wounding more than 400. "Over the whole field," wrote one observer, "were strewed caps, bonnets, hats, shawls, and shoes, and other parts of male and female dress, trampled, torn and bloody."

The violence that erupted at St. Peter's Field may have occurred too spontaneously to claim that the middle class deliberately attacked the workers who had assembled, but there is little doubt that the demonstration and the brutal response to it contributed to the growth of class solidarity, especially among the workers. The massacre inspired a number of calls for working class revolution. The young poet Percy Shelley (1792–1822), who was in Italy at the time, upon hearing of what had occurred in Manchester, called the working class to action:

> Rise like lions after slumber
> In unvanquishable numbers
> Shake your chains to earth
>  like dew
> Which in sleep had fallen on
>  you.
> You are many—they are few.

The British working class did not respond to Shelley's summons. The Peterloo Massacre did not lead to a working-class revolution in Britain. It did, however, lead to the transformation of Britain into a society that was increasingly divided along class lines. It led directly to the organization of British labor in unions as well as to the birth of the Chartist movement, which staged a number of demonstrations in favor of parliamentary reform and the improvement of working conditions in the 1830s and 1840s. The Peterloo Massacre also contributed to the growth of class consciousness. British workers did not always identify themselves as members of a single class, but incidents such as this violent clash encouraged them to think in such terms. Consequently Britain, the first country in the West to industrialize, gained a reputation, which it has not completely lost today, of being a society in which one's identity is based more on class than the place of one's origins.

## For Discussion

The historian E. P. Thompson has referred to the Peterloo Massacre as class warfare. Is this an appropriate characterization of the events that transpired at St. Peter's Field?

**The Peterloo Massacre, 1819**
This drawing of the Peterloo Massacre shows the mounted yeomen with drawn swords attacking the demonstrators, who had gathered to hear the speeches by the reformers on the platform above.

**Joseph M. W. Turner,
*Rain, Steam and Speed:
The Great Western
Railway* (1844)**
This was one of the first oil
paintings that had the railroad
locomotive as its theme.

The advent of modern industry also brought about a change in attitudes toward the landscape. The destruction of natural beauty in the interest of economic progress stimulated an appreciation of nature that had not been widespread during the medieval and early modern periods. Before the Industrial Revolution many features of the countryside, especially mountains, were viewed as obstacles to either travel or human habitation, not as sources of aesthetic appreciation. Urbanization and industrialization changed those perceptions, triggering a nostalgic reaction that became one of the sources of the romantic movement, which we shall consider in greater detail in the next chapter. Some of the idyllic landscapes of the English romantic painter John Constable (1776–1837), for example, represented an imaginative recreation of a countryside that had already been transformed by the advent of industry by the time he painted them.

Industry did not always form a blight on the landscape or offend artistic sensibilities. Some of the new industrial architecture, especially the viaducts and aqueducts that traversed valleys in the mountainous regions of the country, were masterpieces of modern engineering and architecture. Sir Walter Scott (1771–1832), the Scottish romantic novelist, claimed that the cast-iron Pont Cysyllte aqueduct in Wales, which carried the waters of the Caledonian Canal 127 feet above the River Dee, was the most beautiful work of art he had ever seen. The railroads also had the ability to inspire the artistic imagination, as they did in Joseph Turner's (1775–1851) romantic painting *Rain, Steam and Speed*, which captured the railroad's speed and beauty.

# Industry, Trade, and Empire

■ What was the relationship between the growth of industry and Britain's dominance in trade and imperial strength during the middle years of the nineteenth century?

As the middle of the nineteenth century approached, Britain towered above all other nations in the volume of its industrial output, the extent of its international trade, and the size of its empire. In industrial production it easily outpaced all its competitors, producing two-thirds of the world's coal, about half of its cotton cloth, half of its iron, and 40 percent of its hardware. Little wonder that Britain became known as "the workshop of the world." Britain controlled about one-third of the world's trade, and London had emerged as the undisputed financial center of the global economy. Britain's overseas empire, which included colonies in Canada, the Caribbean, South America, India, Southeast Asia, and Australia, eclipsed that of all other European powers and would continue to grow during the second half of the century.

These three great British strengths—industry, trade, and empire—were closely linked. Britain's colonies in both Asia and the Americas served as trading depots, while the promotion of trade led directly to the acquisition of new imperial possessions. Even when Britain did not formally acquire territory, it often established exclusive trading relationships with those countries, thereby creating an informal "empire of trade." Trade and empire in turn served the purposes of industry. Many of the raw materials used in industrial production, especially cotton, came from Britain's imperial possessions. At the same time, those possessions provided markets for Britain's mass-produced manufactured goods. Such imperial markets proved immensely valuable when France blockaded its ports during the Napoleonic wars and thereby cut into British trade with the entire European continent (see Chapter 19).

The great challenge for Britain during the nineteenth century was to find new markets for its industrial products. Domestic demand had been strong at the beginning of the Industrial Revolution, but by the 1840s British workers did not possess sufficient wealth to purchase the increasingly large volume of hardwares and textiles manufactured in the mills and factories. Britain had to look overseas to find markets in which to sell the bulk of its industrial products. One possibility was to market them in other European countries, such as France and Germany, where demand for manufactured goods was high. These countries, however, were in the midst of their own industrial revolutions, and their governments had often legislated high protective tariffs against British goods to encourage the growth of their own industries. Britain therefore chose instead to market its goods in the less economically developed parts of the world, including its own colonies. We can see this trading pattern in the relationships that Britain had with three different regions: East Asia, India, and Latin America. In all three areas, moreover, British military power and diplomatic influence were enlisted in the cause of industry, trade, and empire.

## East Asia: The Opium War, 1839–1842

British conflict with China provides the best illustration of the way in which the British desire to promote trade led to the acquisition of new colonies. For three centuries the Chinese had tightly controlled their trade with European powers. By 1842, however, British merchants, supported by the British government, managed to break down these barriers and give Britain a foothold in China, allowing it to exploit the East Asian market.

The conflict arose over the importation of opium, a narcotic made from poppy seeds and produced in great quantities in India. This drug, which numbed pain but also had hallucinogenic effects and could cause profound lethargy, was in widespread use in Europe and had an even larger market in Asia. In China opium had become a national addiction by the middle of the eighteenth century, and the situation became much worse when British merchants increased the volume of illegal imports from India to China in the early nineteenth century. The Chinese government prohibited the use of opium, but because it had difficulty

enforcing its own edicts, it decided to put an end to the opium trade.

Chinese efforts to stop British merchants from importing opium led to an increase in tensions between China and Britain. The situation reached a climax in 1839, when the Chinese seized 20,000 chests of opium in the holds of British ships and spilled them into the China Sea. It is unknown what effect the opium had on the fish, but the incident led to a British attack on Chinese ports. In this conflict, the first Opium War (1839–1842), the British had the advantage of superior naval technology, itself a product of the Industrial Revolution. The first iron-clad, steam-driven gunboat used in combat, the *Nemesis,* destroyed Chinese batteries along the coast, and an assault by seventy-five British ships on Chinkiang forced the Chinese to come to terms. In a treaty signed in 1842 China ceded the island of Hong Kong to the British, reimbursed British merchants for the opium it had destroyed, and opened five Chinese ports to international trade. As part of this settlement, each of these ports was to be governed by a British consul who was not subject to Chinese law. In this way Britain expanded its empire, increased its already large share of world trade, and found new markets for British manufactured goods in East Asia.

## India: Annexation and Trade

The interrelationship of industry, trade, and empire became even clearer in India, which became known as the jewel in Britain's imperial crown. As we have seen in Chapter 17, Britain gained control of the Indian province of Bengal in the eighteenth century and subsequently acquired a number of other Indian states. After the Sepoy Mutiny of 1857 the British government brought all of India under its direct control.

Political control of India during the nineteenth century served the interests of British trade in two ways. First, it gave British merchants control of the trade between India and other Asian countries. Second, Britain developed a favorable balance of trade with India, exporting more goods to that country than it imported. Taxes paid to the British government by India for administering the country and interest payments on British loans to India increased the flow of capital from Calcutta to London. The influx of capital from India was in large part responsible for the favorable balance of payments that Britain enjoyed with the rest of the world until World War I. The capital that Britain received from these sources as well as from trade with China was funneled into the British economy or invested in British economic ventures throughout the world.

Control of India also served British interests by supplying British industries with raw materials while giving them access to the foreign markets they needed to make a profit. This promotion of British industry was done at the expense of the local Indian economy. The transportation of cotton grown in India to British textile mills only to be returned to India in the form of finished cloth certainly retarded, if it did not destroy, the existing Indian textile industry. Resentment of this economic exploitation of India became one of the main sources of Indian nationalism in the late nineteenth century.

## Latin America: An Empire of Trade

British policy in Latin America developed differently from the way it had in China and India, but it had the same effect of opening up new markets for British goods. Great Britain was a consistent supporter of the movements for independence that erupted in South America between 1810 and 1824 (see Chapter 17). Britain supported these movements not simply because it wished to undermine Spanish and Portuguese imperialism, but because it needed to acquire new markets for its industrial products. Britain did not need to use military force to open these areas to British trade, as it did in China. Once the countries became independent, they attracted large volumes of British exports. In 1840 the British cotton industry shipped 35 percent of all its exports to Latin American countries, especially to Argentina, Brazil, Uruguay, Mexico, and Chile. Britain also exported large amounts of capital to these Latin American countries by investing vast sums of money in their economies. Britain thus established an informal "empire of trade" in Latin America. These countries were not controlled by Britain, but they had the same economic relationship with Britain as other parts of the British Empire.

British investment and trade brought the newly independent nations of Latin America into the industrial world economy. In so doing, however, Britain assigned these countries to a dependent position in that economy, not unlike the position that India occupied in Asia about the same time. One effect of this dependence was to transform the small, self-sufficient village economies that had developed alongside the large plantations in Central and South America. Instead of producing goods themselves and selling them within their own markets, these villages now became suppliers of raw materials for British industry. At the same time the Latin American population became more dependent upon British manufactured goods. This transformation not only retarded or destroyed native Latin American industry but also created huge trade deficits for Latin American countries by the middle of the nineteenth century.

## Ireland: The Internal Colony

Of all the imperial possessions with which Britain engaged in trade, the position of Ireland was the most anomalous. Despite its proximity to England, Ireland had always been treated as a colony. In 1801, after the unsuccessful Irish rebellion of 1798 discussed in Chapter 17, Ireland was incorporated into the United Kingdom, the Irish parliament was abolished, and Irishmen elected representatives to sit in the British Parliament at Westminster. Even though Ireland thus became formally a part of the British state, Britain nonetheless continued to treat the country as an imperial possession, especially with respect to its economy.

Throughout the nineteenth century Ireland remained almost entirely agricultural; only in the north, in the province of Ulster, which produced ready-to-wear undergarments for women and shirts for men, did industrialization take place, and that usually took the form of cottage industry. At the same time, large agricultural estates in Ireland, many of them owned by absentee British landlords, provided Britain with large imports of grain. Unable to afford the high cost of grain, which British protectionist legislation kept artificially high, and without the opportunity to find employment in industry, Irish tenants eked out an existence on the land, relying on a diet consisting almost entirely of potatoes. When a blight destroyed the potato crop in 1845, the country experienced a devastating famine that killed more than one million Irish people and forced another million to emigrate—many of them to the United States and Canada—between 1845 and 1848. The famine occurred despite the fact that Irish lands produced enough grain to feed the entire population. As the Lord Mayor of Dublin complained in 1845, British commercial policy inflicted on the Irish "the abject misery of having their own provisions carried away to feed others, while they themselves are left contemptuously to starve."[4] Thus, even in this internal colony, the British government's policy of promoting industry at home while importing resources from its imperial possessions promoted British economic interests at the expense of the countries under its control.

# Conclusion

## Industrialization and the West

By 1850 the Industrial Revolution had begun to bring about some of the most dramatic changes in human life recorded in historical documents. Not since the Neolithic Age, when people began to live in settled villages, cultivate grains, and domesticate animals, did the organization of society, the patterns of work, and the landscape undergo such profound changes. In many ways the Industrial Revolution marked the watershed between the old way of life and the new. It gave human beings unprecedented technological control over nature, made employment in the home the exception rather than the rule, and submitted industrial workers to a regimentation unknown in the past. It changed family life, gave cities an entirely new appearance, and unleashed new and highly potent political forces, including the ideologies of liberalism and socialism, which shall be discussed in depth in the next chapter.

Industrialization changed the very definition of the West. In the Middle Ages the predominant cultural values of Western countries were those of Christianity, while in the eighteenth century those values were more often associated with the rational, scientific culture of the Enlightenment. Now, in the nineteenth century, the West was increasingly becoming identified with industrialization and the system of industrial capitalism it had spawned. In discussing the prospects of industrialization in the Ottoman Empire in 1856, a British diplomat wrote that "Europe is at hand, with its science, its labor, and its capital," but that the Qur'an and other elements of traditional Turkish culture "are so many obstacles to advancement in a Western sense."[5] The Industrial Revolution was creating new divisions between the West and the non-Western world.

Until the late nineteenth century, industrialization took place only in nations that have traditionally formed a part of the West. Beginning in the 1890s, however, countries that lay outside the West or on its margins began to introduce industrial technology and methods. Between 1890 and 1910 Russia and Japan underwent a period of rapid industrialization, and in the second half of the twentieth century a number of countries in Asia and Latin America, as well as Turkey, followed suit. This process of industrialization and economic development is often described as one of westernization, and it has usually led to conflicts within those countries between Western and non-Western values. The industrialization of these nations has not always been fully successful, and even when it has, doubt remains as to whether those nations should now be included within the West. Industrialization outside Europe and the United States reveals once again that the composition of the West changes from time to time and that its boundaries are often difficult to define.

## Suggestions for Further Reading

For a comprehensive listing of suggested readings, please go to www.ablongman.com/levack2e/chapter20

Ashton, T. A. *The Industrial Revolution*, reprint edition with preface by P. Hudson. 1992. The classic statement of the optimist position, identifying the benefits of the revolution.

Berg, Maxine. *The Age of Manufactures, 1700–1820: Industry, Innovation and Work in Britain.* 1994. A study of the process and character of specific industries, especially those employing women.

Brinley, Thomas. *The Industrial Revolution and the Atlantic Economy: Selected Essays.* 1993. Essays challenging the view that Britain's Industrial Revolution was a gradual process.

Deane, Phyllis. *The First Industrial Revolution.* 1967. The best study of technological innovation in Britain.

Gutmann, Myron. *Toward the Modern Economy: Early Industry in Europe, 1500–1800.* 1988. A study of cottage industry, especially in France.

Hobsbawm, E. J. *Industry and Empire.* 1968. A general economic history of Britain from 1750 to 1970 that analyzes the position of Britain in the world economy.

Jacob, Margaret. *Scientific Culture and the Making of the Industrial West.* 1997. An exploration of the spread of scientific knowledge and its connection with industrialization.

Morris, R. J. *Class and Class Consciousness in the Industrial Revolution, 1780–1850.* 1979. A balanced treatment of the link between industrialization and class formation.

Pollard, Sidney. *Peaceful Conquest: The Industrialization of Europe, 1760–1970.* 1981. A linking of coal supplies to economic development.

Rule, John. *The Vital Century, England's Developing Economy, 1714–1815.* 1992. A general economic history establishing the importance of early eighteenth-century developments.

Stearns, Peter. *The Industrial Revolution in World History.* 2nd ed. 1998. The best study of industrialization in a global context.

Teich, Mikulas, and Roy Porter, eds. *The Industrial Revolution in National Context: Europe and the USA.* 1981. Essays illustrating similarities as well as national differences in the process of industrialization.

Wrigley, E. A. *Continuity, Chance and Change: The Character of the Industrial Revolution in Britain.* 1988. Includes the best discussion of the transition from an advanced organic economy to one based on minerals.

## Notes

1. Lord Ashley's Commission on Mines, *Parliamentary Papers*, Vols. 15–17 (1842), Appendix 1, Note 26.

2. Sir James Kay-Shuttleworth (1832), quoted in John Rule, *The Labouring Classes in Early Industrial England* (1986).

3. "Report of the Select Committee on the Factories Bill," *Parliamentary Papers*, Vol. 20 (1833).

4. John O'Rourke, *The History of the Great Irish Famine of 1847* (1902).

5. David Gillard, ed., *British Documents on Foreign Affairs*, Vol. 1: *The Ottoman Empire in the Balkans, 1856–1875* (1984–1985), 20.

# Ideological Conflict and National Unification, 1815–1871

# 21

O<small>N MARCH 18, 1871, THE PRESIDENT OF THE FRENCH GOVERNMENT,</small> Adolphe Thiers, sent a small unit of troops to Paris to seize cannons that had been used against Prussian forces during their siege of the city a few months before. The artillery was in the possession of the National Guard, the citizen militia of Paris. The members of the National Guard felt that the government had abandoned them by recently concluding an armistice with the Prussians, who were still camped outside the city. They also believed that the government was determined to gain control of the city, which had refused to comply with the orders of the national government. When the troops reached the city, they encountered a hostile crowd of Parisians, many of whom were armed. The crowd surrounded the two generals who led the detachment, placed them up against a wall, and executed them.

This action led to a full-scale siege of Paris by government troops. In the city a committed group of radicals formed a new municipal government, the Paris Commune, which was a revival of the commune established during the French Revolution in 1792. The Commune took steps to defend the city against the government troops, and during its short life it implemented several social reforms. The Communards, as the members were known, set up a central employment bureau, established nurseries for working mothers, and recognized women's labor unions. For many decades the Commune served as a model of working-class government.

The Paris Commune lasted only a few weeks. On May 21 the troops of the provisional government poured through the gates of the city, and during the "bloody week" that followed they took the city street by street, demolishing the barricades and executing the Communards. The Communards retaliated by executing a number of hostages, including the archbishop of Paris. They also burned down the Tuileries Palace, the hall of justice, and the city

**Eugene Delacroix, *Liberty Leading the People* (1830)** The romantic representation of Liberty carrying the French tricolor during the Paris revolution of 1830 conveys the ideological inspiration as well as the violence of that armed uprising.

hall. During this one week at least 25,000 Communards were killed, and because many bodies were burned in the fires that consumed the city, the numbers were probably much higher.

The short life of the Paris Commune marks the climax of a tumultuous period of European history. Between 1815 and 1871 Europe witnessed numerous movements for reform, periodic uprisings, and several revolutions. The people who participated in these momentous developments were inspired in large part by ideologies°, theories of society and government that lay at the basis of political programs. The ideologies that developed during this period—liberalism, conservatism, socialism, and nationalism—were the product of historical developments that had arisen in the West, and they endowed the West with a distinctive political culture. These four ideologies also provide a framework for understanding the complex and often confusing political and social history of the West from 1815 until 1871.

The main question that this chapter will address is how the ideological encounters of this period influenced the course of Western political development. More specifically, the individual sections of the chapter will address the following questions:

- What were the main features of the ideologies that inspired people to political action during the period from 1815 to 1871?
- How did the encounters among the people who espoused these ideologies shape the political history of Europe between 1815 and 1848?
- How did liberal and conservative leaders use the ideology of nationalism as a tool to unite the people of various territories into nation-states between 1848 and 1871?
- What role did ideology play in international warfare and diplomacy, especially in efforts to maintain the balance of power during this period?

# New Ideologies in the Early Nineteenth Century

- What were the main features of the ideologies that inspired people to political action during the period from 1815 to 1871?

In the wake of the French Revolution, four new ideologies—liberalism, conservatism, socialism, and nationalism—led thousands of Europeans to call for profound changes in the established political order. These ideologies had their roots in the works of eighteenth-century writers, but they developed into integrated systems of thought and

inspired political programs in the first half of the nineteenth century. All four were influenced by the two great transformations of the West that we have discussed in the last two chapters: the French Revolution and the Industrial Revolution.

## Liberalism: The Protection of Individual Freedom

Liberalism° is anchored in the beliefs that political, social, and economic freedoms are of supreme importance and that the main function of government is to protect those freedoms. The political agendas of nineteenth-century liberals varied from one country to another, but they all pursued three main objectives. The first objective was to establish and protect individual rights, such as the freedom of the press, freedom of religion, and freedom from arbitrary arrest and imprisonment. Liberals sought to guarantee these rights by having them enumerated in written constitutions. Opposed to aristocratic privilege, liberals supported the principle of equality before the law. They also tended to be anticlerical, a position that led to frequent tension between them and the Roman Catholic Church. As defenders of individual freedom they often campaigned to end slavery and serfdom.

The second objective of liberals was the extension of the franchise (the right to vote) to all property owners, especially those in the middle class. For the most part liberals were opposed to giving the vote to the lower classes, on the grounds that poor people, with little property of their own, could not be trusted to elect representatives who would protect property rights. Liberals also were opposed to giving the vote or any other form of political power to women. They justified the exclusion on the grounds that the proper arena for female activity was the home, where women occupied their natural domain. In this way liberals subscribed to the theory of separate spheres, which assigned men and women different gender roles. As we know from Chapter 18, this theory was based on the belief that women were different in nature from men and that they should be confined to an exclusively domestic role as chaste wives and mothers. Liberals believed that only male property holders should be allowed to participate in public affairs.

The third objective of liberals was to promote free trade with other nations and to resist government regulation of the domestic economy. This economic dimension of liberal ideology, which is grounded in the writings of the Scottish economist Adam Smith and other advocates of free-market capitalism, is usually referred to as laissez-faire°, a phrase that means "let (people) do (as they choose)." Advocates of *laissez-faire* held that the government should intervene in the economy only if it is necessary to maintain public order and protect property rights. As merchants and manufacturers, liberals favored a policy of *laissez-faire* because it offered them the freedom to pursue their own self-interest without governmental interference and thereby realize greater profits.

Some of the earliest expressions of liberal ideology appear in the works of John Locke and his fellow Whigs in England during the late seventeenth century (see Chapter 15). In arguing against the absolutist policies of Charles II and James II, the Whigs emphasized the inviolability of private property rights, freedom from state economic control, and the rights of those who held property to participate in government. In the eighteenth century these ideas were developed by Enlightenment thinkers who defended natural rights, and they found eloquent expression at the time of the American Revolution and the early years of the French Revolution. Liberal ideas were also embodied in the constitutions implemented in France, Germany, and Spain at the

end of the Napoleonic period. When those constitutions and their principles came under attack after 1815, liberals sought to restore the freedoms they had lost without destroying public order. At that time liberalism became a distinct ideology.

Some liberals sought to realize their goals through the establishment of a republic, but the ideal form of government for most early nineteenth-century liberals was a limited monarchy—one in which the ruler did not act arbitrarily and suppress representative assemblies. As we shall see, liberal reformers in Britain during the 1830s wished to preserve the monarchy, and in France Louis-Philippe, the bourgeois citizen king installed during the Revolution of 1830, sought to implement liberal programs. In Germany, Belgium, and Greece, liberal revolts ended in the establishment of a constitutional monarchy.

## DOCUMENT

## John Stuart Mill Argues for the Sovereignty of the Individual in the Liberal State

*John Stuart Mill (1806–1873) belonged to a group of British utilitarian social philosophers who gave liberalism its classic definition. In his most famous work,* On Liberty *(1859), Mill discusses the nature and limits of the power that can be legitimately exercised over the individual. Mill recognized that this issue, the balance between freedom and authority, "has divided mankind almost from the remotest ages." His solution, which lies at the core of nineteenth-century liberalism, is that while the state can restrict one's liberty for the benefit of society, such as by compelling a person to pay taxes or to testify in court, in all undertakings that do not affect others, the individual has complete freedom over his actions and his opinions.*

The object of this essay is to assert one very simple principle, as entitled to govern absolutely the dealings of society with the individual in the way of compulsion and control, whether the means used be physical force in the form of legal penalties or the moral coercion of public opinion. That principle is that the sole end for which mankind are warranted, individually or collectively, in interfering with the liberty of action of any of their number, is self-protection. That the only purpose for which power can be rightfully exercised over any member of a civilized community, against his will, is to prevent harm to others. His own good, either physical or moral, is not a sufficient warrant. He cannot rightfully be compelled to do or forbear because it will be better for him to do so, because it will make him happier, because in the opinion of others to do so would be wise or even right. . . . The only part of the con-

duct of any one, for which he is amenable to society, is that which concerns others. In the part which merely concerns himself, his independence is, of right, absolute. Over himself, over his own body and mind, the individual is sovereign. . . .

But there is a sphere of action in which society, as distinguished from the individual, has, if any, only an indirect interest; comprehending all that portion of a person's life and conduct which affects only himself, or, if it also affects others, only with their free, voluntary, and undeceived consent and participation. . . . This, then, is the appropriate region of human liberty. It comprises, first, the inward domain of consciousness; demanding liberty of conscience, in the most comprehensive sense; liberty of thought and feeling; absolute freedom of opinion and sentient on all subjects, practical or speculative, scientific, moral or theological. The liberty of expressing and publishing opinions may seem to fall under a different principle, since it belongs to that part of the conduct of an individual which concerns other people; but, being almost of as much importance as the liberty of thought itself, and resting in great part on the same reasons, is practically inseparable from it. Secondly, the principle requires liberty of tastes and pursuits; of framing the plan of our life to suit our own character; of doing as we like, subject to such consequences as may follow; without impediment from our fellow creatures, so long as what we do does not harm them, even though they should think our conduct foolish, perverse, or wrong. Thirdly, from this liberty of each individual follows the liberty, within the same limits, of combination among individuals; freedom to unite for any purpose not involving harm to others: the persons combining being supposed to be of full age, and not forced or deceived.

Source: John Stuart Mill, *On Liberty* (1901).

Liberalism found its greatest strength among the urban middle class: merchants, manufacturers, and members of the professions. These people formed the group that felt most aggrieved by their exclusion from political life during the eighteenth and early nineteenth centuries and most eager to have government protect their property. Their substantial wealth provided the basis for their claim to acquire a share of political power, and as manufacturers and merchants they had the most to gain from an economy unfettered by government regulations.

Liberal economic theory found its most articulate proponents in England, where industrial capitalism achieved its earliest and most significant successes. Two of the most prominent liberals in early nineteenth-century Britain were the utilitarians Jeremy Bentham and David Ricardo. Utilitarians° advocated economic and social policies that in their view would provide the greatest good to the greatest number of people. In pursuit of that goal, Bentham (1748–1832), a legal scholar and political philosopher, proposed that a government should give its people as much freedom as possible and impose only those laws that were socially useful. The economist Ricardo (1772–1823), the son of a Dutch Jewish banker, argued that the absence of government intervention would spur economic growth and thus contribute to the benefit of all people. This *laissez-faire* argument was far more persuasive to manufacturers than to workers. In *Principles of Political Economy and Taxation* (1819), Ricardo argued that if wages were left to the law of supply and demand, they would fall to near subsistence levels. This "iron law of wages" made it clear that *laissez-faire* liberalism would not benefit the working class.

## Conservatism: Preserving the Established Order

Throughout human history people have demonstrated a desire to maintain the established order and to resist change. In the early nineteenth century, however, the ideals of the Enlightenment and the radical changes ushered in by the French Revolution led to the formulation of a new ideology of conservatism°, a set of ideas intended to prevent a recurrence of the revolutionary changes of the 1790s. The main goal of conservatives after 1815 was to preserve the monarchies and aristocracies of Europe against liberal and national movements.

The new conservatism justified the existing political order as the product of gradual change. This defense was most clearly expressed in the writings of the fiery, Irish-born parliamentary orator Edmund Burke (1729–1797). Burke was no reactionary; he advocated a number of changes in British public life, including electoral reform and a reorganization of the British Empire. But Burke, who is regarded as the founder of modern conservatism, had enormous respect for the existing social order, which he

considered the handiwork of God. Society according to Burke was a partnership between the living, the dead, and those who had yet to be born. Only within this historical partnership could change take place, and all changes would have to be gradual.

On the basis of this view of the social order, Burke attacked the liberal and radical ideas that had inspired the French Revolution. In *Reflections on the Revolution in France* (1790), he asserted that equality was a dangerous myth; its effect would be to allow those at the bottom to plunder those at the top and thus destroy the hierarchical order of society. Unlike the French revolutionaries, Burke had no faith in the people, whom he referred to as the "swinish multitude." In Burke's view rights did not derive from human nature, as they did for the philosophes of the Enlightenment; rights were privileges that had been passed down through the ages and could be preserved only by a hereditary monarchy. By claiming abstract rights for all men, the French had rejected their inheritance.

Conservative ideology justified the institution of monarchy on the basis of religion. The French writer Louis de Bonald (1754–1840) argued that Christian monarchies were the final creation in the development of both religious and political society. Only monarchies of this sort could preserve public order and prevent society from degenerating into the savagery witnessed during the French Revolution. De Bonald and his fellow French writer, Joseph de Maistre (1754–1821), rejected the entire concept of natural rights and reiterated the traditional doctrine of divine right, by which all political power came from God. De Maistre also reinforced the alliance between the throne and the altar by considering the monarchy and the Church as the foundations of the social order. In the nineteenth century, conservatives throughout Europe thought of religion as the basis of society. This view was especially strong in Catholic countries such as France and Austria, but Burke had put forth the same argument in Protestant England.

A fine line separates conservatism, which allows for gradual change, and reaction, which is the effort to reject any changes that have taken place and return to the old order. Early nineteenth-century conservatism provided an ideological foundation for the reactionary movements that arose throughout Europe after 1815. These movements had both national and international dimensions. In all western European countries, groups of influential and powerful individuals, usually nobles and churchmen, were determined to return to the days when they had more power. Internationally, the rulers of Europe, under the leadership of the Austrian foreign minister Clemens von Metternich, established a mechanism known as the Concert of Europe° to preserve the map of Europe as it was drawn at the Congress of Vienna (see Chapter 19). To do so meant taking concerted action against liberals and nationalists who attempted to unseat dynastic rulers.

In keeping with the identification of conservatism with religion, three of the four original powers in the Concert of Europe—Prussia, Russia, and Austria—gave their alliance a religious mission. At the Congress of Vienna Tsar Alexander I drafted a document in which the cooperation among European monarchs, whom he referred to as "the delegates of Providence," would be based "upon the sublime truths which the holy religion of Our Savior teaches." The British refused to subscribe to this document, claiming that it was "sublime mysticism and nonsense." So too did the future Louis XVIII of France (which was only a probationary member of the Concert of Europe until 1818) and even the pope. But Alexander's commitment to defend Christian values in what he called the Holy Alliance provided a religious foundation for the reactionary and repressive policies that Russia, Prussia, and Austria took steps to implement.

## Socialism: The Demand for Equality

Socialism, the third new ideology of the early nineteenth century, arose in response to the development of industrial capitalism and the liberal ideas that justified it. Socialism calls for the ownership of the means of production (such as factories, machines, and railroads) by the community, with the purpose of reducing inequalities of income, wealth, opportunity, and economic power. In small communities, such as some early nineteenth-century socialist settlements, ownership could be genuinely collective. In a large country, however, the only practical way to introduce socialism would be to give the ownership of property to the state, which represents the people.

The main appeal of socialism was the prospect of remedying the deplorable social and economic effects of the Industrial Revolution. As we have seen in Chapter 20, the short-term effects of industrialization included wretched working conditions, low wages, a regimentation of the labor force, and a declining standard of living. Socialists did not object to the mechanization of industry as such. Like liberals, they wanted society to be as productive as possible. They did, however, object to the system of industrial capitalism that accompanied industrialization and the liberal economic theory that justified it.

The earliest socialists were known as Utopian socialists, a name given to them because they envisioned the creation of ideal communities in which perfect social harmony and cooperation would prevail. One of these Utopian socialists, the British industrialist and philanthropist Robert Owen (1771–1858), actually turned his mill in New Lanark, Scotland, into a model socialist community in which the principles of cooperation prevailed and where the workers were housed and their children were educated. In 1825 he established a similar community in New Harmony, Indiana. Utopian socialism was not particularly concerned with the

granting of political rights to workers, nor did it encourage class consciousness or class tensions.

A second generation of socialists became more concerned with using the power of the state to improve their lot. The most influential of these socialists was the French democrat Louis Blanc (1811–1882), who proposed that the state guarantee workers' wages as well as employment in times of economic depression. He also wanted the state to support the creation of workshops in which workers would sell the product of their labor directly without an intermediary. The principle underlying Blanc's concept of the social order was, "From each according to his abilities; to each according to his needs." Blanc's brand of socialism began a long tradition in which workers tried to improve their lot by influencing government. This initiative was closely related to the radical democratic goal of universal male suffrage, which became one of the main objectives of many socialists after 1840.

The most radical form of nineteenth-century socialism was formulated by the German social philosopher Karl Marx (1818–1883). Marx was much more preoccupied than

**Karl Marx**
Karl Marx, the German social philosopher who developed the revolutionary socialist doctrine of communism.

## DOCUMENT

# Karl Marx and Friedrich Engels, *The Communist Manifesto* (1848)

*These excerpts from the final pages of* The Communist Manifesto *summarize the communist plan for establishing a socialist society by means of revolution. They reveal Marx's view of history as a succession of class conflicts and his prediction that the proletariat will become the ruling class. The appeal for working-class solidarity and revolution illustrates the power of socialist ideology to inspire people to action.*

The history of all past society has consisted in the development of class antagonisms, antagonisms that have assumed different forms at different epochs. But whatever form they may have taken, one fact is common to all past ages, viz., the exploitation of one part of society by the other. . . .

We have seen above that the first step in the revolution by the working class is to raise the proletariat to the position of ruling class, to win the battle of democracy. The proletariat will use its political supremacy to wrest, by degrees, all capital from the bourgeoisie, to centralize all means of production in the hands of the state, i.e., of the proletariat organized as the ruling class, and to increase the total of productive forces as rapidly as possible.

If the proletariat during its contest with the bourgeoisie is compelled by the force of circumstances, to organize itself as a class, if by means of a revolution it makes itself the ruling class, and as such sweeps away by force the old conditions of production, then it will, along with these conditions, have swept away the conditions for the existence of class antagonisms and of classes generally, and will thereby have abolished its own supremacy as a class. . . .

Communists disdain to conceal their views and aims. They openly declare that their ends can be attained only by the violent overthrow of all existing social conditions. Let the ruling classes tremble at a Communist revolution. The proletarians have nothing to lose but their chains. They have a world to win. WORKING MEN OF ALL COUNTRIES UNITE!

Source: From Karl Marx and Friedrich Engels, *The Communist Manifesto*, 1848, translated in English by Friedrich Engels in 1888.

other socialists with the collective identity and political activities of the working class. Reading about working conditions in France during the early 1840s, he became convinced that workers in industrial society were the ultimate example of human alienation and degradation. In 1844 he began a lifetime association with another German-born philosopher, Friedrich Engels (1820–1895), who as we have seen in the preceding chapter exposed the wretchedness of working-class life in Manchester. Marx and Engels began to think of workers as part of a capitalist system, in which they owned nothing but their labor, which they sold to capitalist producers for wages.

Marx and Engels worked these ideas into a broad account of historical change in which society moved inevitably and progressively from one stage to another. They referred to the process by which history advanced as the dialectic°. Marx acquired the idea of the dialectic from the German philosopher Georg Wilhelm Friedrich Hegel (1770–1831), who believed that history advanced in stages as the result of the conflict between one idea and another. Marx disagreed with Hegel on the source of historical change, arguing that material or economic factors rather than ideas determined the course of history. Hence Marx's socialist philosophy became known as dialectical materialism°.

According to Marx and Engels, the first stage of the dialectic had taken place when the bourgeoisie, who received their income from capital, seized political power from the aristocracy, who received their income from land, during the English and French revolutions. Marx and Engels predicted that the next stage of the dialectic would be a conflict between the bourgeoisie and the working class or proletariat°, which received its income from wages. This conflict, according to Marx and Engels, would result in the triumph of the working class. Led by a committed band of revolutionaries, the proletariat would take control of the state, establish a dictatorship so that they could implement their program without opposition, and usher in a classless society.

Marx and Engels issued this call to action in *The Communist Manifesto* (1848), which ended with the famous words, "Working men of all countries unite!" Marx's brand of socialism, communism°, takes its name from this book. Communism is a revolutionary ideology that advocates the overthrow of "bourgeois" or capitalist institutions and the transfer of political power to the proletariat. Communism differs from other forms of socialism in its call for revolution, its emphasis on class conflict, and its insistence on complete economic equality. Communism belongs to a tradition that originated among members of the extreme wing of the democratic movement at the height of the French Revolution. One of those radicals, François-Noël Babeuf (1760–1797), demanded economic as well as political equality, called for the common ownership of land, and

DOCUMENT

Karl Marx, On the Question of Free Trade (1848)

spoke in terms of class warfare. Marx's achievement was to place Babeuf's radical ideas in a new philosophical and historical framework. That framework, dialectical materialism, was explained in great detail in Marx's monumental three-volume work, *Das Kapital,* or *Capital* (1867–1894).

## Nationalism: The Unity of the People

Nationalism, the fourth new ideology of the early nineteenth century, also took shape during and after the French Revolution. A nation° in the nineteenth-century sense of the word refers to a large community of people who possess a sense of unity based on a belief that they have a common homeland and share a similar culture. The ideology of nationalism° is the belief that the people who form this nation should have their own political institutions and that the interests of the nation should be defended and promoted at all costs.

The geographical boundaries of nations do not often correspond to the geographical boundaries of states, which are administrative and legal units of political organization. For example, in the early nineteenth century Germans often referred to their nation as comprising all people who spoke German. At that time, however, there were several German states, such as Prussia, Bavaria, and Baden, and there were also many German speakers living in non-German lands, such as Bohemia. A primary goal of nationalists is to create a nation-state°, a single political entity that governs all the members of a particular nation. The doctrine that justifies this goal is national self-determination°, the claim that any group that considers itself a nation has the right to be ruled only by members of its own nation and to have all the members of the nation included in this state.

The ideology of nationalism had roots in the French Revolution. Most of the revolutionary steps taken in France during the 1790s were undertaken in the name of a united French people. Article 3 of the *Declaration of the Rights of Man and Citizen* (1789) declared that "the principle of all authority rests essentially in the nation." The French Republic was constructed as the embodiment of the French nation. It gave an administrative unity to the French people and encouraged them to think of themselves as sharing a common cultural bond. Instead of a collection of regions, France had become *la patrie,* or the people's native land.

Nationalists emphasized the antiquity of nations, arguing that there had always been a distinct German, French, English, Swiss, or Italian people living in their respective homelands. This claim involved a certain amount of fiction, because in the past the people living in those lands possessed little cultural unity. There was little uniformity, for example, in the languages spoken by people who were identified as German, French, or Italian. Until the eighteenth century most educated Germans wrote in French, not German. Only a small percentage of Italians spoke Italian, and the main language of many Italian nationalists of the nineteenth century was French. Even after nation-states were formed, a large measure of linguistic, religious, and ethnic diversity has persisted within those states and has made true cultural unity impossible. The nation is therefore something of a myth—an imagined community to which nationalists believe they belong, but which in reality has never existed.

The ideal of the nation-state has proved almost impossible to realize. The boundaries of nations and states have never fully coincided. Patterns of human settlement are too fluid to prevent some members of a particular cultural group from living as a minority in a neighboring state. Germans, for example, have always lived in Poland, Spaniards in Portugal, and Italians in Switzerland. France at the time of the French Revolution probably came closest to realizing the ideal of a nation-state, claiming jurisdiction over most French people. Nevertheless, different regional identities and languages, such as that of the people of the southern province of Languedoc who spoke their own dialect, prevented the emergence of a powerful sense of national identity in all parts of France until the late nineteenth or early twentieth century.

In Britain the creation of a nation-state has been a complicated process. National consciousness, which is a people's belief that they belong to a nation, developed earlier in England than in any other country in Europe. In the sixteenth century almost all English people spoke the same language, and they were also subject to the same common law. In 1536, however, Wales was united to the kingdom of England, thereby including two nations, the English and the Welsh, in the same state. In 1707 England and Scotland were united in a new state, the United Kingdom of Great Britain, and in 1801 Ireland was brought into the United Kingdom as well. Thus the United Kingdom now included four nations: the English, the Welsh, the Scots, and the Irish. The task of building a British, as opposed to an English or a Scottish, nation in this multinational state has taken time, and to this day Britons are more accustomed to think of themselves as primarily English or Scottish than as British.

Other peoples have faced even more daunting obstacles than the British in constructing nation-states. Many nations have been subsumed within large empires, such as Hungarians and Croatians in the Habsburg Empire and Greeks and Serbs in the Ottoman Empire. In those empires, nationalist movements have often taken the form of separatist revolts or wars of independence, in which a nationalist group attempted to break off and form a nation-state of its own. A very different situation prevailed in Germany and Italy, where people who shared some linguistic and cultural traditions lived under the control of many different sovereign states of varying size. In these cases nationalist movements have sought to unite the smaller states into a larger nation-state.

One of the great paradoxes of nationalism is that the acquisition of colonies overseas often strengthened nationalist sentiment at home. The military conquest of these lands became a source of pride for the people in the metropolis, and also gave them a sense of cultural superiority. The main source of British national pride was the rapid spread of British control over one-quarter of the world's surface during the eighteenth and nineteenth centuries. Nationalism could also promote the supremacy of one's own nation over others. The French revolutionaries who conquered a large part of the European continent in the early nineteenth century justified their expansion on the grounds that they were superior to the rest of the human race. In 1848 a fervent German nationalist declared his support for "the preponderance of the German race over most Slav races." The Italian national leader Giuseppe Mazzini (1805–1872), whom we shall discuss in detail shortly, preferred to be called a patriot rather than a nationalist on the grounds that nationalists were imperialists who sought to encroach on the rights of other peoples.

Nationalism was often linked to liberalism during the early nineteenth century, when both movements supported revolutionary programs to realize the goal of national self-determination. Liberals believed that representative government and a limited expansion of the franchise would provide a firm foundation for the establishment of the nation-state, both in nations like Spain with a long tradition of self-rule and in countries like Greece that were seeking their independence from autocratic rulers. In Germany and Italy, where there was no central state, nationalists and liberals joined together to create one. There was, however, a difference of emphasis between the two ideologies, even in the early years of the nineteenth century. Liberalism stressed individual freedom, whereas nationalism was more concerned with political unity. At times those different ideals came into conflict with each other. The liberal doctrine of free trade, for example, ran into conflict with the doctrine of economic nationalism, which encouraged the protection of national industries. The nationalist German economist Friedrich List (1780–1846) claimed that free trade benefited only the wealthy and the powerful; he advocated instead protective tariffs to benefit German businesses.

Nationalism was just as capable of supporting conservatism as liberalism in the early nineteenth century. Because the nation was often viewed as having deep roots in the distant past, some nationalists glorified the monarchical and hierarchical political arrangements that prevailed in the Middle Ages. In 1848 conservative Prussian landlords rallied around the cause of "God, King, and Fatherland." Later in the nineteenth century, nationalism became identified almost exclusively with conservatism when the lower middle classes began to prefer the achievement of national glory, either in warfare or in imperialistic pursuits, to the establishment of individual freedom.

# Culture and Ideology

As the four great ideologies of the Western world were developing during the nineteenth century, they were influenced by two powerful cultural traditions: scientific rationalism and romanticism. These two traditions represented two sharply divergent sides of modern Western culture.

## Scientific Rationalism

Scientific rationalism is a manner of thinking that traces its origins to the Scientific Revolution and reached its full flowering in the Enlightenment. This tradition has provided a major source of Western identity ever since the late eighteenth century. It has stressed the powers of human reason and considered science superior to all other forms of knowledge. Scientific rationalism is essentially a secular tradition, in that it does not rely on theology or Christian revelation for its legitimacy. The effort to construct a science of human nature, which was central to Enlightenment thought, belongs to this tradition, while the Industrial Revolution, which involved the application of scientific knowledge to production, was one of its products.

During the nineteenth century, scientific rationalism continued to have a powerful influence on Western thought and action. As scientific knowledge continued to grow, and as more people received a scientific education, the values of science and reason were proclaimed more boldly. Scientific knowledge and an emphasis on the importance of empirical data (that which can be tested) became essential components of much social thought. The clearest statement that science was the highest form of knowledge and would lead inevitably to human progress was the secular philosophy of positivism°.

The main elements of positivism were set forth by the French philosopher Auguste Comte (1798–1857). Like many thinkers in the Enlightenment tradition, Comte argued that human society passed through a succession of historical stages, each leading to a higher level. It had already passed through two stages, the theological and the metaphysical, and it was now in the third, the positive or scientific stage. The word *positive* in this context means that which has substance or concrete reality, as opposed to that which is abstract or speculative. Comte predicted that in the final positive stage of history the accumulation of factual or scientific knowledge would enable thinkers, whom we now call sociologists, to discover the laws of human behavior and thus make possible the improvement of society. This prediction of human progress, and Comte's celebration of the liberation of knowledge from its theological shackles, had particular appeal to liberals, especially those who harbored hostility to the Roman Catholic Church.

The values of science and the belief in its inevitable advance also influenced the social thought of Karl Marx. His ideology of communism has been referred to as scientific socialism, in that it too is based on a vision of history determined solely by positive, in this case material or economic, developments. Marxism rejects the metaphysical, idealistic world of Hegel and the theology of all Christian religion and thus fits into the same scientific tradition to which positivism and earlier Enlightenment thought belongs.

## Romanticism

The cultural tradition that posed the greatest challenge to scientific rationalism was romanticism°. This tradition originated as an artistic and literary movement in the late eighteenth century, but it soon developed into a more general worldview. The artists and writers who identified themselves as romantics recognized the limits of human reason in comprehending reality. Unlike scientific rationalists, they used intuition and imagination to penetrate deeper levels of being and to comprehend the entire cosmos. Romantic art, music, and literature therefore appealed to the passions rather than the intellect.

Romantics did not think of reality as being simply material, as did the positivists. For them it was also spiritual and emotional, and their purpose as writers and artists was to communicate that nonempirical dimension of reality to their audiences. Romantics also had a different view of the relationship between human beings and nature. Instead of standing outside nature and viewing it objectively, in the manner of a scientist analyzing data derived from experiments, they considered themselves a part of nature and emphasized its beauty and power.

As an art form, romanticism was a protest against classicism and in particular the classicism that prevailed in the late eighteenth century. As we discussed in Chapter 18, classicism reflects a worldview in which the principles of orderliness and rationality prevail. Classicism is a disciplined style that demands adherence to formal rules that governed the structure as well as the content of literature, art, architecture, and music. By contrast, romanticism allows the artist much greater freedom. In literature the romantic protest against classicism led to the introduction of a new poetic style involving the use of imagery, symbols, and myth. One example of this new approach is "Rime of the Ancient Mariner" (1798) by the English romantic poet Samuel Taylor Coleridge (1772–1834), which uses the sun and moon as powerful symbols in describing a nightmarish sea voyage.

Many romantic works of literature, such as the novels of the Scottish author Sir Walter Scott (1771–1832), were set in the Middle Ages, a period often associated with superstition rather than science and enlightenment. Other romantic prose works explore the exotic, the weird, the mysterious, and even the satanic elements in human nature. Mary Shelley's introspective novel *Frankenstein* (1818), an early example of science fiction that embodies a critique of scientific rationalism, incorporates many of these themes.

Within the visual arts, romanticism also marked a rebellion against the classicism that had dominated eighteenth-century culture. Classicism emphasized formality and symmetry in art, and it celebrated the culture of an ideal Greek

**F. G. Lardy, *Entrance to Chamonix Valley***
This painting reflects the romantic concern with the majesty and power of nature.

# Mary Shelley's *Frankenstein:* The Body in Romantic Literature

In 1818, Mary Shelley, the 20-year-old daughter of the feminist Mary Wollstonecraft and the wife of the poet Percy Shelley, published a novel, *Frankenstein: or, The Modern Prometheus,* that became a literary sensation in contemporary England and has inspired books and films down to the present day. The depiction of the human body in the novel reflects the attitude of romantic writers toward nineteenth-century science.

The novel tells the story of an idealistic Swiss scientist, Victor Frankenstein, who discovers the secret of giving life to inanimate matter. Using his knowledge of chemistry, anatomy, and physiology, Frankenstein pieces together bones and flesh from corpses to construct the frame of a human being, which he then infuses with life. The creature turns out to be a freak of nature: a gigantic, ugly, and deformed monster with watery eyes, yellow shriveled skin, and straight black lips. Frankenstein is horrified by what he has wrought, and his rejection leads the monster to turn on his creator, eventually killing his brother, his friend, and his wife on their wedding night. Frankenstein pursues the creature to the Arctic region, but the monster brings about Frankenstein's death. Filled with self-loathing for having murdered "the lovely and the helpless," the monster declares that Frankenstein will be his last victim and sets off to throw himself on his own funeral pyre.

The body of the monster created by Frankenstein is unnatural in the manner of creation, its size, its features, and its preternatural strength. The depiction of monstrous creatures in literature was common during the early modern period, as a way of indicating supernatural intervention in the world. Shelley's depiction of this monster, which reflects the preoccupation of romantic literature with the exotic and the mysterious, differs from that older tradition in that it identifies modern science, not supernatural forces, as the source of the monster's abnormality. In trying to unite the body and the soul, Frankenstein produced a creature he called a daemon, a body inhabited by an evil spirit who commits multiple murders. Science had produced a moral and a physical aberration.

One of the important theological questions in the history of Christianity has been whether an evil spirit or demon can inhabit or possess a human body. Shelley was preoccupied by this issue, as evidenced by Victor Frankenstein's deep interest in the figure of Satan in the novel. Frankenstein's monster was a demonic figure, but unlike the Satan of the Bible, he was the product of science and its attempt to control nature. The real monster becomes science itself, whose power nineteenth-century intellectuals desired but at the same time feared.

Mary Shelley, like many romantic writers, thought of nature as a life force with which human beings should be in harmony. The novel reinforces this theme by showing how a human being's attempt to control nature leads to nature's revenge. Frankenstein's loss of physical and mental health, the thwarting of his ability to have children with his wife, and his eventual death are all penalties for his violation of nature.

## For Discussion

How does *Frankenstein* reflect the themes of romanticism and in particular its critique of scientific rationalism?

**Depiction of the Monster Created by Victor Frankenstein**
The creation of the monster in Mary Shelley's novel embodied a critique of scientific rationalism.

and Roman past. By contrast, romantic painters depicted landscapes that evoked a mood and an emotion rather than an objective pictorial account of the surroundings. Romantic paintings were intended to evoke feeling rather than to help the viewer achieve intellectual comprehension. Some of them conveyed the power of nature while others depicted its majesty and grandeur.

Romantic music, which also appealed to the emotions, marked a similar but more gradual departure from the formal classicism that was triumphant during the eighteenth century. The inspirational music of Ludwig van Beethoven (1770–1827), the son of a German court musician from Bonn, marked the transition from classical to romantic forms. Beethoven's early work conformed to the conventions of classical music, but his later compositions, which were completed as he became progressively deaf and which defied traditional classical harmonies, were intended to evoke an emotional response. His famous "Ode to Joy," in his ninth and final symphony, remains unequaled in its ability to rouse the passions. In the view of one critic, Beethoven's music "opens the floodgates of fear, of terror, of horror, of pain, and arouses that longing for the eternal which is the essence of romanticism."

Another early romantic composer, Franz Schubert (1797–1828), who was born in Vienna, blended classical forms with romantic themes by incorporating Hungarian and gypsy folk music into his compositions. The emotionally powerful operas of the German composer Richard Wagner (1813–1883), which were set in the mythical German past, marked the height of the romantic movement in music. That style attained its greatest popularity during the second half of the nineteenth century with the lyrical symphonies and concertos of Johannes Brahms (1833–1897) in Germany and the symphonies, ballets, and operas of Peter Tchaikovsky (1840–1893) in Russia.

Romanticism, like the rational and scientific culture it rejected, had powerful political implications, leaving its mark on the ideologies of the modern world. In the early nineteenth century, romanticism appealed to many liberals because it involved a protest against the established order and emphasized the freedom of the individual. Romantic writers were themselves often outsiders, and therefore their protests took many different forms. The French romantic author Victor Hugo (1802–1885), whose epic novels *The Hunchback of Notre Dame* (1831) and *Les Misérables* (1862) depicted human suffering with great compassion, identified romanticism as "liberalism in literature." For Hugo a relationship existed between liberty in art and liberty in society. In France wealthy liberal bourgeoisie generally patronized romantic music and literature, while nobles and clerics denounced them. Romanticism could, however, support conservatism by idealizing the traditional social and political order of the Middle Ages and the central importance of religion in society. The hostility of romantics to the culture of the Enlightenment could also lead to political conser-

vatism. Sir Walter Scott and Samuel Taylor Coleridge were both conservatives, while the German writer Johann Wolfgang von Goethe (1749–1832), whose poems reflected many of the themes of romantic literature, opposed all liberal and republican movements in Germany.

Romanticism has a closer association with nationalism than with any other ideology. In the most general sense romanticism invested the idea of "the nation" with mystical qualities, thus inspiring devotion to it. Romantics also had an obsessive interest in the cultural, literary, and historical roots of national identity. This connection between romanticism and nationalism can be seen in the work of the German philosopher and literary critic Johann Gottfried von Herder (1744–1803), who was one of the leaders of the *Sturm und Drang* (storm and stress) literary movement. This movement, which developed in the 1770s and 1780s and included works by Goethe and Friedrich von Schiller (1759–1805), encouraged subjectivity and the youthful revolt of genius against accepted classical standards. Herder promoted the study of German language, literature, and history with the explicit purpose of giving the German people a common sense of national unity. He claimed that "a people may lose its independence, but it will survive as long as its language survives." Like many romantics, Herder idealized the Middle Ages and cultivated many of the myths that surrounded that epoch in Germany's history.

In other parts of Europe, especially in Poland and the Balkans, romantic writers and artists gave nationalists the tools necessary to construct a common culture and history of their nations. The Polish romantic composer Frédéric Chopin (1810–1849), who emigrated to Paris in 1831, inspired Polish nationalists by drawing on native Polish dances in his works for the piano. At the same time the romantic poet Adam Mickiewicz (1798–1855), another Polish exile in Paris, wrote *The Books of the Polish Nation* (1832), exalting his country as the embodiment of freedom and predicting that by its long suffering it would eventually liberate the human race.

# Ideological Encounters in Europe, 1815–1848

■ How did the encounters among the people who espoused these ideologies shape the political history of Europe between 1815 and 1848?

The four new ideologies of the nineteenth century—liberalism, conservatism, socialism, and nationalism—interacted in a variety of ways, sometimes reinforcing each other and at other times leading to direct and violent political conflict. During the years between 1815 and 1831 the main ideological encounters occurred between liberalism, sometimes infused with nationalism, and conservatism. In 1815, at the time of the Congress of Vienna, it appeared that conservatism would carry the day. The determination of Metternich, the Austrian minister, to employ all the resources of the Holy Alliance to suppress any signs of revolutionary activity made the future of liberalism and nationalism appear bleak. The power of the new ideologies, however, could not be completely contained. Liberal and nationalist revolts took place in three distinct periods: the early 1820s, 1830, and 1848. During the latter two periods the demands of workers, sometimes expressed in socialist terms, added to the ideological mixture. In all these encounters conservatives had their say, and in most cases they emerged victorious.

## Liberal and Nationalist Revolts, 1820–1825

Between 1820 and 1825 a sequence of revolts in Europe revealed the explosive potential of liberalism and nationalism and the determination of conservatives to crush those ideologies. These revolts also reflected the strength of movements for national self-determination. The three most significant revolts took place in Spain, Greece, and Russia.

### The Liberal Revolts of 1820 in Spain and Portugal

The earliest clash between liberalism and conservatism occurred in Spain, where liberals ran into determined opposition from their king, Ferdinand VII (r. 1808–1833). Ferdinand had been restored to power in 1814 after his forced abdication in 1808. In 1812, during the rule of Joseph Bonaparte, the Spanish *cortes*—the representative assembly in that kingdom—had approved a liberal constitution. This constitution provided a foundation for a limited monarchy and the protection of Spanish civil liberties. In keeping with the ideas of the French Revolution, it also declared that the Spanish nation, not the king, possessed sovereignty. The tension began when King Ferdinand declared that he would not recognize this constitution. Even worse for the disheartened liberals was Ferdinand's decision to reestablish the Spanish Inquisition, invite exiled Jesuits to return, and refuse to summon the *cortes*. In 1820, when the Spanish Empire in the New World had already begun to collapse (see Chapter 17), liberals in Madrid, in alliance with some military officers, seized power.

This liberal revolt proved to be a test for the Concert of Europe. Metternich urged intervention, and although the British refused because they wanted to protect their trading interests with the Spanish colonies, the members of the Holy Alliance supported the invasion of Spain by a French army of 200,000 men. Ferdinand was restored once again to the throne, and once again he renounced the liberal consti-

tution of 1812. The liberals not only lost this struggle, but they also suffered bitter reprisals from the government, which tortured and executed their leaders. The situation became only marginally better in 1833, when Ferdinand died and the liberal ministers of his young daughter, Queen Isabella II (r. 1833–1868), drew up another constitution. Her reign was marked by civil war, instability, and factional strife in which liberals made few substantial gains.

Shortly after the Spanish revolt of 1820, a similar rebellion based on liberal ideas took place in Portugal. The royal family had fled to Brazil during the Napoleonic wars, leaving Portugal to be governed by a regent. A group of army officers removed the regent and installed a liberal government, which proceeded to suppress the Portuguese Inquisition, confiscate church lands, and invite King John (r. 1816–1826) to return to his native land as a constitutional monarch. After the king returned in 1822, his enthusiasm for liberal government waned. His granddaughter, Maria II (r. 1826–1853), kept the liberal cause alive, relying on support from Portugal's traditional ally, Britain, but she struggled against the forces of conservatism and had only limited success.

### The Nationalist Revolt of 1821 in Greece

A revolt in Greece in 1821, inspired more by nationalism than liberalism, achieved greater success than did the rebellions of 1820 in Spain and Portugal. It succeeded because other members of the Concert of Europe, not just Britain, lent their support to the revolt. Greece had long been a province in the sprawling Ottoman Empire, but a nationalist movement, organized by Prince Alexander Ypsilantis (1792–1828), created a distinct Greek national identity and inspired the demand for a separate Greek state. In 1821 a series of revolts against Ottoman rule took place on the mainland of Greece and on some of the surrounding islands. These rebellions received widespread support in Europe from scholars who considered Greece the cradle of Western civilization and from religiously inspired individuals who saw this as a struggle of Christianity against Islam. Hundreds of European volunteers joined the Greek rebel forces. Thus the insurrection became not only a liberal and national revolt but a broad cultural encounter between East and West. The English romantic poets George Lord Byron (1788–1824) and Percy Shelley (1792–1822) became active and passionate advocates for Greek independence, while the romantic painter Eugène Delacroix (1798–1863) depicted the horror of the Turkish massacre of the entire population at the island of Chios in 1822. The link between nationalism and romanticism could not have been made more explicit.

The Greek revolt placed the powers allied in the Concert of Europe in a quandary. On the one hand they were committed to intervene on behalf of the established order to crush any nationalist or liberal revolts, and they condemned the insurrection on those grounds when it crush nationalist and liberal revolts, the Concert had in this case helped one succeed.

## The Decembrist Revolt of 1825 in Russia

The least successful of the early liberal revolts took place in Russia, where a number of army officers, influenced by liberal ideas while serving in western Europe during the Napoleonic wars, staged a rebellion against the government of Tsar Nicholas I (r. 1825–1855) on the first day of his reign. The officers, together with other members of the nobility, had been meeting for almost a decade in political clubs, such as the Society of True and Faithful Sons of the Fatherland in St. Petersburg. In these societies they articulated their goals of establishing a constitutional monarchy and emancipating the serfs.

The rebels, known as Decembrists° for the month in which their rebellion took place, could not agree on the precise form of government they wished to institute. That disagreement, coupled with a reluctance to take action at the critical moment, led to their failure. When Tsar Alexander I died suddenly in 1825, the Decembrists hoped to persuade his brother Constantine to assume the throne and establish a representative form of government. Their hopes were dashed when Constantine refused to tamper with the succession and accepted the reign of his brother Nicholas. The reactionary Nicholas had no difficulty suppressing the revolt, executing its leaders, and leaving Russian liberals to struggle against police repression for the remainder of the nineteenth century.

**Eugène Delacroix, *The Massacre at Chios* (1824)**
In 1821 the Greeks on the Aegean Islands rebelled against their Turkish rulers, and in April 1822 Turkish reprisals reached their peak in the massacre of the inhabitants of Chios. Romantic paintings were intended to evoke feelings, in this case horror, at the genocide perpetrated by the Turks against the Greek rebels. The painting reveals the close association of romantic art with the causes of liberalism and nationalism.

first erupted. On the other hand they were Western rulers who identified the Ottoman Turks with everything that was alien to Christian civilization. Moreover, Russia wanted to use this opportunity to dismember its ancient enemy, the Ottoman Empire. The European powers eventually took the side of the Greek rebels. In 1827 Britain, France, and Russia threatened the Turks with military intervention if they did not agree to an armistice and grant the Greeks their independence. When the Turks refused, the combined naval forces of those three countries destroyed the fleet of the Turks' main ally, Egypt, at Navarino off the Greek coast. This naval action turned the tide in favor of the Greeks, who in 1833 finally won their independence and placed a Bavarian prince, Otto I (r. 1833–1862), on the throne. Thus the Greek war of independence effectively ended the Concert of Europe. Originally intended to

## Liberal and Nationalist Revolts, 1830

A second cluster of early-nineteenth-century liberal and national revolts in 1830 achieved a greater measure of success than the revolts of the early 1820s. These revolutions took place in France, the kingdom of the Netherlands, and the kingdom of Poland.

### The French Revolution: The Success of Liberalism

The most striking triumph of liberalism in Europe during the early nineteenth century occurred in France, where a revolution took place fifteen years after the final defeat of Napoleon at Waterloo. This liberal success did not come easily. During the first few years of the restored monarchy conservatives had their way, as they did elsewhere in Europe. Louis XVIII had approved a Charter of Liberties in 1814, but he was hardly receptive to any further liberal reforms.

## Liberal and Nationalist Revolts, 1820–1833

**1820**   Liberal revolt in Spain; liberal army officers seize power in Portugal

**1821**   Beginning of Greek revolt against the Ottoman Empire

**1825**   Decembrist revolt in Russia against Nicholas I

**1829**   Liberals gain majority in French Chamber of Deputies

**1830**   Revolution in Paris, Louis-Philippe I becomes king of France; Belgium becomes independent and adopts a liberal constitution; beginning of the Polish rebellion against Nicholas I of Russia

**1833**   Greece becomes independent; Otto I becomes king

Between 1815 and 1828 French politics was dominated by the ultraroyalists, who sponsored a "white terror" (so called because they displayed the white flag of the Bourbon monarchy) against liberals and Protestants. The terror was led by two men nicknamed Three Slices and Four Slices, indicating the number of pieces into which they butchered their Protestant enemies.

In 1824, when the conservative Charles X (r. 1824–1830) ascended the throne and took steps to strengthen the Church and the nobility, there appeared to be little hope for liberalism. Nevertheless liberal opposition to the monarchy gained support from merchants and manufacturers, as well as from soldiers who still kept the memory of Napoleon alive. When liberals feared that Charles would claim absolute power, and when a serious economic crisis afflicted the country in 1829, liberals at last gained a majority in the Chamber of Deputies, the French legislature.

Charles then embarked upon a perilous course. In what became known as the July Ordinances he effectively undermined the principles of the Charter of 1814. These ordinances dissolved the new Chamber of Deputies, ordered new elections under a highly restrictive franchise, and censored the press. The public reaction to this maneuver caught the king by surprise. Thousands of students and workers, liberals and republicans alike, poured onto the streets of Paris to demonstrate. Skirmishes with the king's troops only made the situation worse, and when the tricolor flag of the French Revolution appeared on top of Notre Dame Cathedral, protesters blocked the streets with barricades. Unable to restore order, the king abdicated in favor of his grandson, but the liberals offered the crown in-

stead to the Duke of Orléans, who was crowned as Louis-Philippe I (r. 1830–1848).

Louis-Philippe accepted a revised version of the Charter of 1814 and doubled the franchise, giving the vote to middle-class merchants and industrialists. The king catered to this bourgeois constituency by encouraging economic growth and restricting noble privilege. His reign, which is often referred to as the "bourgeois monarchy," also achieved a measure of secularization when the Chamber of Deputies declared that Roman Catholicism was no longer the state religion. In keeping with mainstream liberal ideals, however, he did nothing to encourage republicanism or radical democracy, much less socialism. Efforts to depict him as the heir to the French Revolution did not persuade the bulk of the population. When the government brought the ashes of Napoleon from St. Helena to Paris, thousands of French men and women turned out to pay homage to the former emperor. Much to his disappointment, Louis-Philippe gained little political benefit from the move. France had acquired a liberal monarchy, but it stood on a precarious foundation.

## The Belgian Revolution: The Success of Nationalism

The French Revolution of 1830 triggered the outbreak of a liberal and nationalist revolution in the neighboring country of Belgium. At the Congress of Vienna the Austrian Netherlands were united with the Dutch Republic in a new kingdom of the Netherlands. This union of the Low Countries did not work out, and soon after the formation of the new kingdom the Belgians began pressing for their independence as a nation. With a Dutchman, William I, as king and with the seat of government in Holland, the Dutch were the dominant partner in this union, a situation that caused considerable resentment in Belgium. Belgians spoke Flemish or French rather than Dutch, which had become the kingdom's official language. Moreover, most Belgians were Catholics, whereas the majority of Dutch people were Protestants. With their own language, religion, and culture, as well as their own history, Belgians thought of themselves as a separate nation. They also were more liberal than their Dutch neighbors, advocating free trade and the promotion of industry, while resenting the high tariffs imposed by the Dutch government.

The two main political parties in Belgium, the Liberals and the Clericals, joined forces to achieve autonomy. When the news of the Revolution in Paris reached Brussels, fighting broke out between workers and government troops. A national congress gathered to write a new constitution, and when the Dutch tried to thwart the rebellion by bombarding the Belgian city of Antwerp, Britain assembled a conference of European powers to devise a settlement. The powers agreed to recognize Belgium's independence, and they arranged for a German prince,

**Scene from the French Revolution of 1830 in Paris**
Demonstrations by students and workers led to the abdication of King Charles X and the establishment of a liberal government. Tricolor flags of the French Revolution hang from the windows.

Leopold of Saxe-Coburg, uncle of the future British Queen Victoria, to become king. The Dutch, however, refused to recognize the new government, and they renewed their military attacks on Belgium. Only in 1839 did all sides accept the new political arrangement.

## The Polish Rebellion: The Failure of Nationalism

The French Revolution of 1830 triggered a second uprising, this one unsuccessful, in the kingdom of Poland (see Map 21.1). Poland had suffered many partitions at the hands of European powers during the eighteenth century, and in 1815 the Congress of Vienna had redefined its borders once again. After incorporating much of the eastern portion of the country into the Russian Empire, the Congress established a separate Polish kingdom, with Warsaw as its capital and the Russian tsar, Alexander I (r. 1815–1825), as its king.

With a Russian king the independence of Poland was a mere fiction, but Alexander had approved a liberal Polish constitution in 1815. He grew to regret this decision, and his rule as king of Poland gradually alienated Polish liberals

within the national legislature, the *sejm*. The accession of Nicholas in 1825 only aggravated those tensions. An uncompromising conservative, Nicholas accused the Polish opposition of complicity with the Russian Decembrist rebels, and he brought them to the brink of rebellion when he made plans to send the Polish army, together with Russian troops, to suppress the French Revolution of 1830 and to prevent the Belgians from receiving their independence.

The revolt began within the school of army cadets, who attacked the residence of the Grand Duke Constantine, but it quickly gained the support of the entire army and the urban populace. The revolt appealed to both liberals and nationalists, and it drew inspiration from a group of romantic poets who celebrated the achievements of the Polish past. A provisional government was established at Warsaw, but the liberal members of the elected national assembly were unwilling to enlist the peasantry in the conflict, fearful that they would rise against Polish landlords rather than the Russians. When the powers of western Europe refused to intervene on behalf of this liberal cause, Nicholas was able to crush the rebellion, abolish the *sejm*, and deprive the

**DOCUMENT**

Adam Mickiewicz, Excerpts from *The Books of the Polish Nation*

Map 21.1 European Centers of Rebellion and Revolution, 1820–1848

**Map 21.1  European Centers of Rebellion and Revolution, 1820–1848**
All these political disturbances were inspired by ideology.

*[Map of Europe with labels: North Sea, Baltic Sea, St. Petersburg, RUSSIA, UNITED KINGDOM, BELGIUM, GERMAN CONFEDERATION, Berlin, Brussels, Frankfurt, Dresden, Warsaw, POLAND, Cracow, Prague, Vienna, Budapest, AUSTRIA-HUNGARY, ATLANTIC OCEAN, Paris, FRANCE, Lyon, Milan, Turin, Bucharest, Madrid, Barcelona, Lisbon, SPAIN, Naples, Palermo, GREECE, Cadiz, Mediterranean Sea, Morea (Battle of Navarino 1827)]*

European Centers of Rebellion and Revolution, 1820–1848
✳  Centers of revolution, 1820s and 1830s
✳  Centers of revolution, 1848

0    500 km
0    500 mi

kingdom of Poland of its autonomous status. Nicholas visited a terrible revenge upon the leaders of the revolt, confiscated the lands of those who had emigrated, and shut down the University of Warsaw. His brutal repression set back the cause of liberalism and nationalism in Poland for another two generations.

# Liberal Reform in Britain, 1815–1848

The challenges that liberals faced in Britain were somewhat different from those they confronted in most other European countries. Having maintained the status quo during the era of the French Revolution, the forces of British conservatism, which bore the ideological stamp of Edmund Burke, remained formidable. At the same time, however, Britons already enjoyed many of the rights that liberals on the European continent demanded, such as freedom of the press and protection from arbitrary imprisonment. The power of the British monarchy was more limited than in almost any other European country. The ideology of liberalism, which originated in England and had deep roots in British political and social philosophy, defined the political creed of many Whigs, who formed the main opposition to the ruling Conservative or Tory party after 1815.

In this relatively favorable political climate, British liberals pursued three major goals, which amounted to a program for reform rather than revolution. The first was parliamentary reform and the expansion of the franchise. The British had a long tradition of representative government, which had been secured by the Glorious Revolution of 1688, but the titled nobility in the House of Lords effectively controlled elections to the House of Commons, while the members of the gentry or lesser aristocracy held most of the seats in the House of Commons. In some boroughs real representation was a sham; the electorate consisted entirely of the borough councils, who elected the nominees of the noblemen who controlled them. Very few people lived in some of these "rotten boroughs"—one was nothing but a

pasture—whereas large segments of the population in the recently industrialized north had no representation at all in Parliament.

The Great Reform Bill of 1832, which was pushed through Parliament by the Whig prime minister, Lord Grey, marked a victory for British liberalism. The bill expanded the franchise to include most of the urban middle class. It eliminated the rotten boroughs and created a number of new ones in heavily populated areas. It also established a uniform standard for the right to vote in all parliamentary boroughs. In keeping with the principles of liberalism, however, the bill restricted the vote, and hence active citizenship, to property owners. It rejected the demands of radicals for universal male suffrage, and by using the phrase "male person" to identify eligible voters, the bill denied all women the vote.

Reform Bill of 1832 Cartoon

The second liberal cause was the repeal of legislation that denied political power to Catholics and also to Protestants who did not attend the services of the Anglican Church. In the seventeenth century a body of legislation had denied both of these religious minorities the right to hold national or local political office. Catholics suffered the additional liability of being denied the right to sit in Parliament. Liberals provided the basis of support for the political "emancipation" of Catholics and Protestant nonconformists. Liberals were opposed on principle to religious discrimination, and many of them belonged to Protestant nonconformist congregations. Conservatives opposed the repeal of this legislation, but they feared a civil war in Ireland if Catholics were not allowed to sit in the British Parliament. The Tory prime minister, the Duke of Wellington, who had defeated Napoleon at Waterloo, eventually agreed to liberal demands. The Protestant nonconformists were emancipated in 1828, while the Catholics had to wait until one year later. One of the first Catholics elected to Parliament in 1830 was Daniel O'Connell (1775–1847), an Irishman who worked tirelessly to improve the lot of his countrymen within the limits of the Irish union with Britain.

The third liberal cause was free trade. The target of this campaign was a series of protective tariffs on the import or export of hundreds of commodities, including raw materials used in production. The most hated protective tariff was on grain (known in Britain as corn), which kept the price of basic food commodities high in order to protect the interests of landlords and farmers. In this respect the determination of liberals for free trade conflicted with the determination of Parliament to defend the economic interests of its largely aristocratic membership. In 1837 a group of industrialists and radical reformers formed the Anti-Corn Law League with the purpose of bringing about the repeal of the Corn Law of 1815, which greatly restricted the importation of foreign grain into Britain. This campaign against protectionism did not succeed until 1845, when the Conservative prime minister, Sir Robert Peel, brought about repeal by securing the votes of some of his own party and combining them with those of the Whigs, all of whom favored free trade. Peel took this action only after the potato famine in Ireland, which was discussed in Chapter 20, had begun to cause widespread starvation. The repeal of the corn laws allowed the importation of foreign grain into Ireland, but this change in government policy occurred too late to alleviate the suffering of the Irish people.

Unlike the liberals, socialists and radical democrats achieved little success in Britain during the first half of the nineteenth century. In 1834 the Utopian socialist Robert Owen established the Grand National Consolidated Trades Union, the purpose of which was to unite all workers in a peaceful struggle to realize his idealist goals. One of Owen's supporters hoped that the union would give "the productive classes a complete dominion over the fruits of their own industry." The refusal of many unions to join this association, coupled with opposition from the government, led to its disintegration. In its wake workers and radicals decided that economic improvement could come only through political means. In 1837 the newly formed London Workingman's Association, in collaboration with a few radical Members of Parliament, drew up a People's Charter, calling for the implementation of a program of radical democracy. Their demands included universal male suffrage, annual parliaments, voting by secret ballot, equal electoral districts, the elimination of property qualifications for Members of Parliament, and the payment of salaries to those same members. The workers who supported this cause became known as Chartists.

### The Last Great Chartist Rally in Britain, April 10, 1848

Government precautions, including the appointment of special constables to handle the crowd, and rain kept the number of demonstrators in London lower than anticipated. The government ordered the leader of the movement, Feargus O'Connor, to stop the planned march to Parliament.

The strength of the Chartist movement fluctuated between 1837 and 1848, gaining the greatest popular participation when economic conditions deteriorated. Most Chartists restricted their activities to meetings to support candidates for Parliament and petitioning Parliament. A few of the more militant, such as the Irish immigrant Feargus O'Connor, called for "a holy and irresistible crusade" against the government. The British government and the upper classes became most frightened in 1848, when revolution broke out in France, Italy, and Germany, and when the Chartists decided to draft a new charter and threatened to form a revolutionary national assembly like that of France if Parliament were to reject the new document.

Within the next few years the Chartist movement died. British workers revealed, as they would throughout the remainder of the nineteenth century, that they had little inclination to take to the streets, especially after good economic times returned. The government's reduction of indirect taxes during the 1840s, coupled with the effective use of the police force and the strict enforcement of the criminal law, also helped prevent Britain from experiencing revolution in 1848. The price of this failure was that further liberal reforms, such as the extension of the franchise, did not take place in Britain for another two decades.

## The Revolutions of 1848

Unlike Britain, almost every country in Europe experienced revolution in 1848. A wave of revolutionary activity spread rapidly throughout the Continent. The revolutions took place during a period of widespread economic discontent. European countries had suffered bad harvests in 1845 and 1846 and an economic recession in 1847, leading to a temporary decline in the standard of living among industrial as well as agricultural workers. Discontent took the form of mass protests and demonstrations, which increased the likelihood of violent confrontation. The revolutions of 1848 were more widespread than the revolts of the 1820s and 1830, and they involved greater popular participation. These revolutions also gave greater attention to both nationalist and socialist issues.

### The French Revolutions of 1848

The first of the revolutions of 1848 took place in France, where the liberal government of Louis-Philippe faced mounting criticism. Declining economic conditions, which prevailed throughout Europe during the 1840s, provided an environment that brought the country to a crisis point. A series of demonstrations in Paris in favor of the right of workers to vote and to receive state assistance for their trades was the final precipitant. When troops from the Paris National Guard fired on the demonstrators and killed forty people, the barricades once again appeared in the streets and the rebels seized government buildings. France was experiencing its third revolution in sixty years. In an effort to save his regime, Louis-Philippe abdicated in favor of his grandson, but the revolutionaries abolished the monarchy and declared the Second French Republic.

A provisional government selected by the Chamber of Deputies was headed by nine republicans, but it included liberals and radical democrats. Most significantly it also included two socialists, Louis Blanc and a worker who preferred to be called by

## CHRONOLOGY

### The Revolutions of 1848

**1848**

| | |
|---|---|
| February | Revolution in Paris |
| March | Insurrection in Berlin, peasant unrest in the countryside, formation of liberal governments in Prussia and other German states; revolutions in Milan and Venice, Ferdinand II issues a new constitution in Naples |
| April | Elections for a new National Assembly in France |
| May | Meeting of the Frankfurt Parliament; meeting of the Prussian Assembly |
| June | Suppression of working-class resistance in Paris; Pan-Slav Congress in Prague; suppression of the rebellion in Prague |
| October | Suppression of revolution in Vienna |
| December | Election of Louis-Napoleon as president of the Second French Republic; Frankfurt Parliament issues *Declaration of the Basic Rights of the German People;* Frederick William dissolves Prussian Assembly |

**1849**

| | |
|---|---|
| March | King Frederick William rejects the German crown offered by the Frankfurt Parliament |
| April | Frankfurt Parliament promulgates a new constitution; Hungarian Diet proclaims Magyar independence |
| May–June | Fall of the liberal ministries in German states |
| August | Venetian Republic surrenders to Austrian forces; suppression of the Hungarian movement for independence |

the single name of Albert. The French Revolution of 1848 offered the socialists the first opportunity to realize their goal of a democratic and socialist republic. Many of the 200 clubs formed in Paris at this time, some of which were exclusively female, were either republican or socialist in their orientation. The socialist agenda included not only universal male suffrage, which was granted immediately by the government, but also active support for the masses of unemployed workers. Louis Blanc secured the establishment of national workshops to give the unemployed jobs on public projects. Ordinances reduced the length of the workday to ten hours in the city and twelve hours in rural areas, and the government authorized a commission to study working conditions.

These bold socialist initiatives did not last long. By the summer the euphoria of the revolution had dissipated and the aspirations of workers had been crushed. The elections held in April 1848 to constitute a new National Assembly and write a new constitution seated an overwhelming majority of conservative monarchists and only a small minority of republicans and socialists. Resentment of the provisional government's assistance to urban workers and anger at the levying of a surtax to pay for government programs revealed the lack of broad popular support for radical political programs. Tension between the new conservative assembly and the forces of the left mounted when the government closed the workshops and Parisian workers were either drafted into the army or sent to the provinces.

These newly adopted policies led to further working-class violence in Paris in June 1848. When General Louis Cavaignac, known as "the butcher," was called in to suppress this insurgency with regular army troops, there was a devastating loss of life. No fewer than 1,500 insurgents were killed in the streets or in summary executions, while another 4,000 were sent into exile in French colonies. These confrontations appeared to Karl Marx to constitute class warfare, a prelude to the proletarian revolution he predicted for the future. Louis Blanc, who was implicated in these uprisings, fled to England, where Marx himself would soon arrive and spend the rest of his life.

The revolution ended with the election of Napoleon's nephew, Louis-Napoleon Bonaparte (1808–1873), as the president of the Second French Republic in December 1848. Until the February Revolution it seemed highly unlikely that Louis-Napoleon, an impetuous adventurer and conspirator, would ever come to power. After staging two unsuccessful coups against the government of Louis-Philippe in 1836 and 1840, he was sentenced to life imprisonment. He managed to escape to England, however, and the events of February 1848 gave him the opportunity to return to France. He became a member of the new National Assembly, and then easily defeated Cavaignac in the presidential election.

Louis-Napoleon v. General Cavaignac— British Cartoon, 1848

As president, Louis-Napoleon drew support from conservatives, liberals, and moderate republicans. He also benefited from the legend that his uncle had created and the nationalist sentiment it inspired. Because the first Napoleon had become emperor, even those who preferred an empire to a republic could vote for his nephew. The younger Napoleon followed in his uncle's footsteps, dissolving the National Assembly in December 1851 and proclaiming himself emperor of the French one year later. This step brought the Second Republic to an end and established the Second Empire. The new emperor called himself Napoleon III, in deference to the dynastic rights of the uncrowned Napoleon II, the son of Napoleon I who had died in 1823.

## The Revolutions of 1848 in Germany, Austria, Hungary, and Bohemia

Until French revolutionaries built barricades in the streets of Paris in 1848, liberalism and nationalism had achieved little success in Germany. German university students, inspired by the slogan "Honor, Freedom, Fatherland," had staged a number of large rallies during the early years of the nineteenth century, but the forces of conservatism had kept them in check. The Carlsbad Decrees of 1819, intended to suppress university radicalism, inaugurated a period of severe repression throughout Germany. The only success achieved by German liberals and nationalists prior to 1848 was the establishment of the *Zollverein,* a customs union of the various German states, in 1834. Even that project, which promoted free trade within German lands, did not attract support from all liberals.

A major opportunity for the liberal cause in Germany came in 1848 in the immediate wake of the February Revolution in France. As in France, however, this opportunity was complicated by the more radical demands of democrats and socialists for universal suffrage, including equal rights for women. German radicals also demanded government assistance for artisans and workers who had suffered economic hardship as a result of industrialization. In Berlin, the capital of Prussia, these discontents led radicals to barricade the streets. The situation became more serious after troops fired into the crowd, killing some 250 people. The violence spread to the countryside, where peasants demanded that landlords renounce their privileges and grant them free use of their lands. In response to these pressures, King Frederick William IV summoned an assembly, elected by universal male suffrage, to write a new Prussian constitution. Other German states also yielded to liberal pressure, establishing liberal governments known as the "March ministries."

As these events were unfolding, the contagion of revolution spread to Austria, the other major German kingdom, which formed the nucleus of the sprawling Habsburg Empire. News of the revolution in Paris led to demonstrations by students and workers in Vienna. An assortment of

## DOCUMENT

# The Carlsbad Decrees, 1819

*The main source of liberal and national ideas in Germany after 1815 were university students, who often belonged to secret societies or fraternities. Conservatives considered these students dangerous revolutionaries and tried to expel them from the universities. When a student assassinated a conservative writer in 1819, the princes of the German Confederation issued a set of decrees that called for the monitoring of the lectures given at the universities, the removal of liberal professors, the expulsion of students, and the censorship of the press.*

2. The confederated governments mutually pledge themselves to remove from the universities or other public educational institutions all teachers who, by obvious deviation from their duty, or by exceeding the limits of their functions, or by the abuse of their legitimate influence over youthful minds, or by propagating harmful doctrines hostile to public order or subversive to existing governmental institutions, shall have unmistakably proven their unfitness for the important office entrusted to them. No teacher who shall have been removed in this manner shall be again appointed to a position in any public institution of learning in another state of the Confederation.

3. Those laws which have for a long period been directed against secret and unauthorized societies in the universities shall be strictly enforced. The governments mutually agree that such persons as shall hereafter be shown to have remained in secret or unauthorized associations, or shall have entered such associations, shall not be admitted to any public office.

4. No student who shall be expelled from a university by a decision of the university senate which was ratified or prompted by the agent of the government, or shall have left the institution in order to escape expulsion, shall be received in any other university.

So long as this decree shall remain in force no publication which appears in the form of daily issues, or as a serial not exceeding twenty sheets of printed matter, shall go to press in any state of the union without the previous knowledge and approval of the state officials.

Source: From *Readings in European History: 1789 to the Present,* 2nd Edition by John L. Heineman. Copyright © 1994 by Kendall/Hunt Publishing Company. Used with permission.

---

Austrian liberal aristocrats, middle-class professionals, and discontented workers demanded an end to the long rule of the conservative minister, Clemens von Metternich. In response to the demands of these groups, Emperor Ferdinand I (r. 1835–1848) summoned a constitutional assembly and installed a moderate government. A conservative Prussian observer feared that these concessions had broken "the most secure dam against the revolutionary tide."

The main difference between the revolutions of 1848 in Austria and the other German lands was that events in Vienna awakened demands of Hungarians and Czechs for national autonomy within the empire. In Hungary the nationalist leader Lajos Kossuth (1802–1894) pushed for a program of liberal reform and national autonomy. This initiative created further tensions between the Magyars and the various national minorities within the kingdom of Hungary. Similar problems arose in Bohemia, where a revolution in Prague led to demands from the Czechs for autonomy within the Habsburg Empire. In June 1848 the Czech rebels hosted a Pan-Slav Congress in Prague to advance a nationalist plan for achieving unity of all Slavic people within the empire. This idealistic proposal could not be realized, for there were many distinct Slavic nationalities, each of which had a desire to preserve its autonomy. In addition, there was a large German-speaking population within Bohemia that identified with other German territories in the Confederation.

The most idealistic and ambitious undertaking of the revolution in central Europe was the meeting of the Frankfurt Parliament in May 1848. Some 800 middle-class liberals, many of whom were lawyers, officials, and university professors, came from all the German states to draft a constitution for a united Germany. The parliament produced powerful speeches in support of both liberal and nationalist ideals, and in December 1848 it promulgated a *Declaration of the Basic Rights of the German People.* This document recognized the equality of all German people before the law; freedom of speech, assembly, and religion; and the right to private property. Like so many liberal assemblies, however, the Frankfurt Parliament failed to address the needs of the workers and peasants. The delegates rejected universal male suffrage as a "dangerous experiment" and refused to provide protection for artisans who were being squeezed out of work by industrialization. For these reasons the parliament failed to win broad popular support.

In April 1849 the Frankfurt Parliament drafted a new constitution for a united Germany, which would have a hereditary "emperor of the Germans" and two houses of parliament, one of which would be elected by universal male suffrage. Austria, however, voted against the new plan, and without Austrian support the new constitution had little hope of success. The final blow to German liberal hopes came when King Frederick William of Prussia refused the Frankfurt Parliament's offer of the crown, which he referred to as coming from the gutter and "reeking of the stench of revolution." At that point the Frankfurt Parliament disbanded and the efforts of German liberals to unite their country and give it a new constitution came to an inglorious end.

By the middle of 1849, conservative forces had triumphed in the various German territories and the Habsburg Empire. In Prussia the efforts of the newly elected assembly to restrict noble privilege triggered a reaction from the conservative nobles known as Junkers. Frederick William dismissed his liberal appointees, sent troops to Berlin, and disbanded the assembly. A similar fate befell the other German states, such as Saxony, Baden, and Hanover, all of which had installed liberal governments in the early months of the revolution. In Austria Prince Alfred Windischgrätz, who had crushed the Czech rebels in June, dispersed the rebels in Vienna in October. When Hungary proclaimed its independence from the empire in April 1849, Austrian and Russian forces marched on the country and crushed the movement.

## The Revolutions of 1848 in Italy

The revolutions of 1848 also spread to Austrian possessions in the northern Italian territories of Lombardy and Venetia. In Milan, the main city in Lombardy, revolutionary developments followed the same pattern as those in Paris, Berlin, and Vienna. When the barricades went up,

some of the Milanese insurgents used medieval pikes stolen from the opera house to fight off Austrian troops. Their success triggered rebellions in other towns in Lombardy, in Venice, and in the southern Kingdom of the Two Sicilies. In that kingdom the Spanish Bourbon king, Ferdinand II (r. 1830–1859), after suppressing a republican revolt in January, was forced to grant a liberal constitution. The spread of these revolts inspired the hope of bringing about the unification of all Italian people in one state.

This Italian nationalist dream had originated among some liberals and republicans during the first half of the nineteenth century. Its most articulate proponent was Giuseppe Mazzini, a revolutionary from Genoa who envisioned the establishment of a united Italian republic through direct popular action. In his youth Mazzini had been a member of the *Carbonari*, a secret conspiratorial society pledged to drive foreigners out of the Italian states, to secure constitutional liberties, and to bring about some form of Italian unity. His arrest led to one of many periods of exile in London, where he continued to pursue the cause of republicanism and democracy. In 1831 Mazzini founded Italy's first organized political party, Young Italy, which was pledged to realize national unification, democracy, and greater social equality. Mazzini combined a passionate commitment to the ideals of liberalism, republicanism, and nationalism. For him the nation was the highest ideal to which one could pledge devotion, one possessing almost

**The German National Assembly Gathered in St. Paul's Church in Frankfurt, 1848**
The parliament ultimately failed in its goal to give a liberal constitution to a united Germany.

# Prostitution, Corporal Punishment, and Liberalism in Germany

In March 1822 Gesche Rudolph, a poor, uneducated 25-year-old woman from the northern German city of Bremen, was arrested by municipal authorities for engaging in prostitution without registering with the police. Ever since the days when troops from five different European nations had occupied her neighborhood, Rudolph had been selling her sexual services as her only form of livelihood. After her arrest she was not given a formal trial but was summarily expelled from the city and banned from ever returning. Unable to earn a living through prostitution in a village outside the city, where she resided with a brother who physically abused her, Rudolph returned to the city, where she was arrested once again for prostitution. This time she was sentenced to fifty strokes of the cane and six weeks in jail, after which she was once again expelled from the city. Returning again to Bremen, she was arrested in a drunken stupor in a whorehouse and subjected to a harsher sentence of three months' imprisonment and 150 strokes before another expulsion. This pattern of arrest, punishment, expulsion, and return occurred repeatedly during the next two decades, with the number of strokes rising to 275 and the period of imprisonment to six years. During a portion of her prison sentence she was given only bread and water for nourishment.

Rudolph's arrest in 1845 at the end of a six-year imprisonment and her subsequent expulsion and return to Bremen led to the appointment of a liberal lawyer, Georg Wilhelm Gröning, to represent her. After reviewing her case and calculating that she had been whipped a total of 893 times and imprisoned for a cumulative period of eighteen years, Gröning

appealed her sentence to the senate of Bremen on the grounds that her treatment was not only futile but immoral. His appeal addressed an issue that went far beyond this particular case or even the prosecution of the crime of prostitution. Gröning's action raised the highly controversial issue of the legitimacy and value of corporal punishment, an issue that divided liberals and conservatives, who had different notions of justice.

Until the eighteenth century the penal systems of Europe had prescribed corporal punishments, administered publicly, for most crimes. These punishments ranged from whippings and placement in the stocks for minor offenses to mutilation, hanging, and decapitation for felonies. They were justified mainly on the grounds that they provided retribution for the crime and deterred the criminal and those who witnessed the punishment from committing further crimes. These two main functions of retribution and deterrence are the same functions that capital punishment allegedly serves today. Corporal punishments were also intended to humiliate the criminal both by violating the integrity of the body and by subjecting the prisoner to the mockery and sometimes the maltreatment of the crowd. The torture of suspects to obtain evidence also served some of these functions, although judicial torture took place during the trial, not as part of the sentence.

The entire system of corporal punishment, as well as that of torture, came under attack during the eighteenth century. In Prussia torture was abolished in 1754, and the General Law Code of 1794 eliminated many forms of corporal punishment. The General Law Code reflected the concern of Enlightenment thinkers that all

such assaults on the body were inhumane and a denial of the moral dignity of the individual. Because corporal punishments in Prussia and elsewhere were administered mainly against people from the lower classes, they also were a violation of the liberal principle of equality before the law.

Despite these efforts at reform, the illegal administration of corporal punishment by public and private authorities continued in Prussia and the other German states. Conservatives, who had a different notion of justice from that of the liberals, defended these sentences on the grounds that all punishment, including imprisonment, was intended to deny the criminal freedom and hence his or her dignity. For them any reference to natural rights and human dignity were "axioms derived from abstract philanthropic speculation." The president of the Prussian police, Julius Baron von Minutoli, expressing the conservative position on the issue, claimed that corporal punishment was more effective than imprisonment in preventing crime, as it alone could instill terror in the criminal.

It was apparent that in the case of Gesche Rudolph, 893 strokes had not instilled terror in her or brought about any transformation of her spirit. The Senate made the young woman Gröning's ward and suspended her sentence. Gröning arranged for Rudolph to live in the countryside under the strict supervision of a competent countryman. This compromise solution at least broke the cycle of expulsion, return, and punishment that had failed to reform her. We do not know whether she gave up her life of prostitution.

Soon after Gesche Rudolph became Gröning's ward, the liberal critics of corporal punishment in

Germany celebrated a victory. King Frederick William IV of Prussia formally abolished the practice in his kingdom in May 1848. Shortly thereafter the Frankfurt Parliament included freedom from physical punishment by the state in its *Declaration of the Basic Rights of the German People*. Most German states and municipalities, including Bremen, wrote this right into law in 1849. The failure of the Frankfurt Parliament, however, and the more general failure of liberalism in Germany after 1849 led to a strong conservative campaign to reinstate corporal punishment in the 1850s. They succeeded only in maintaining corporal punishment within the family, on manorial estates, and in the prisons. Liberalism had not succeeded in completely establishing its standard of justice, but it did end exposure to public shame as a punishment for crime.

## Questions of Justice

1. What elements of liberalism led those who adhered to this ideology in the nineteenth century to object to corporal punishment?
2. In addition to inflicting physical pain, corporal punishment produces social shame. What is the difference between social shame and legal guilt? In what ways does shame still play a role in punishments today?

## Taking It Further

Evans, Richard. *Tales from the German Underworld: Crime and Punishment in the Nineteenth Century.* 1998. Provides a full account of the prosecution of Gesche Rudolph.

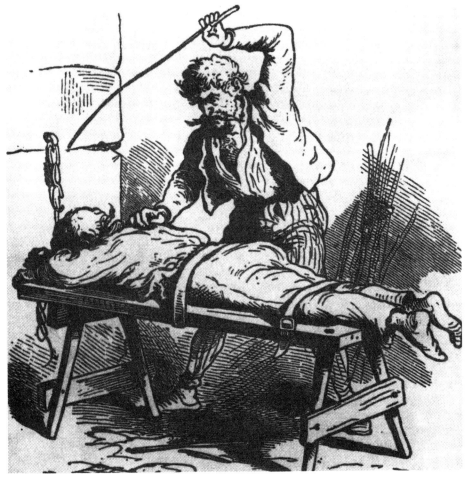

**Corporal Punishment in Nineteenth-Century Germany**
Whipping in prisons continued long after public corporal punishment was abolished in the middle of the nineteenth century.

mystical qualities. "We have beheld in Italy," he wrote, "the purpose, the soul, the consolidation of our thoughts, the country chosen of God and oppressed by men."

The ruler who assumed the nationalist mantle in 1848 was Charles Albert of Piedmont-Sardinia, the most economically advanced of the Italian states. This initiative began successfully, as Charles Albert's army, which included volunteers from various parts of Italy, marched into Lombardy and defeated Austrian forces. Instead of moving forward against Austria, however, Charles Albert decided to consolidate his gains, hoping to annex Lombardy to his own kingdom. This decision alienated republicans in Lombardy and in other parts of Italy as well as the rulers of the other Italian states, who feared that Charles Albert's main goal was to expand the limits of his own kingdom at their expense. By August 1848 the military tide had turned. Fresh Austrian troops defeated the Italian nationalists outside Milan. The people of that city turned against Charles Albert, forcing him to return to his own capital of Turin. The Italian revolutions of 1848 had suffered a complete defeat.

### The Failure of the Revolutions of 1848

The revolutions of 1848 in France, Germany, the Habsburg Empire, and Italy resulted in victory for conservatives and defeat for liberals, nationalists, and socialists. All the liberal constitutions passed during the early phase of the revolutions were eventually repealed or withdrawn. The high hopes of national unity in Germany, Italy, and Hungary were dashed. Workers who built the barricades in the hope of achieving improvements in their working conditions gained little from their efforts.

Divisions among the different groups that began the revolutions were in large part responsible for their failure. The most serious division—in fact, one that was fatal—was the split between the liberals who formulated the original goals of the revolution and the lower-class participants who took to the streets. Liberals used the support of the masses to bring down the governments they opposed, but their ideological opposition to broad-based political movements and their fear of further disorder sapped their revolutionary fervor. Divisions also emerged between liberals and nationalists, whose goals of national self-determination required different strategies from those of the liberals who supported individual freedom.

The failure of the revolutions of 1848 did not, however, portend the death of the ideologies of liberalism, nationalism, and socialism. They all continued to manifest strength during the following two decades, and they often influenced the policies of the conservative governments that returned to power after the revolutions. In Germany, for example, the goal of nationalists was realized under conservative auspices and even mustered a measure of liberal support, while in France liberalism made some inroads

into the conservative and nationalist government of the Second French Empire after 1860.

# National Unification in Europe and America, 1848–1871

■ How did liberal and conservative leaders use the ideology of nationalism as a tool to unite the people of various territories into nation-states between 1848 and 1871?

Prior to 1848 the forces of nationalism, especially when combined with those of liberalism, had little to show for their efforts. Besides the Greek rebellion of 1821, which succeeded largely because of international opposition to the Turks, the only successful nationalist revolution in Europe took place in Belgium. Both of these nationalist movements were secessionist in that they involved the separation of smaller states from larger empires. Efforts in 1848 to form nations by combining smaller states and territories, as in Italy and Germany, or by uniting all Slavic people, as proposed at the Pan-Slav Congress, had failed. Between 1848 and 1871, however, movements for national unification succeeded in Italy, Germany, and the United States, each in a different way. In the vast Habsburg Empire a different type of unity was achieved, but it did little to promote the cause of nationalism.

## Italian Unification: Building a Fragile Nation-State

The great project of Italian nationalists, the unification of Italy, faced formidable obstacles. Austrian military control over the northern territories, which in the end had thwarted the nationalist movement of 1848, meant that national unification would not be achieved peacefully. The dramatic economic disparities between the prosperous north and the much poorer south posed a challenge to any plan for economic integration. A long tradition of local autonomy within the kingdoms, states, and principalities made submission to a strong central government unappealing. The unique status of the papacy, which controlled its own territory and which influenced the decisions of many other states, served as another challenge. Despite these obstacles, the dream of a resurgence of Italian power, reviving the achievements of ancient Rome, had great emotive appeal. Hatred of foreigners who controlled Italian territory, which dates back to the fifteenth century, gave further impetus to the nationalist movement.

The main question for Italian nationalism after the failure of 1848 was who could provide effective leadership of the movement. It stood to reason that Piedmont-Sardinia, the strongest and most prosperous Italian kingdom, would be central to that undertaking. Unfortunately the king, Victor Emmanuel II (r. 1849–1861), was more known for his hunting, his carousing, and his affair with a teenage mistress than his statesmanship. Victor Emmanuel did, however, appoint as his prime minister a nobleman with liberal leanings, Count Camillio di Cavour (1810–1861). Cavour displayed many of the characteristics of nineteenth-century liberalism. He favored a constitutional monarchy, the restriction of clerical privilege and influence, and the development of a capitalist and industrial economy. He was deeply committed to the unification of the Italian peninsula, but only under Piedmontese leadership, and preferably as a federation of states. In many ways he was the antithesis of the republican Mazzini, the other central figure in Italian unification. Mazzini's idealism and romanticism led him to think of national unification as a moral force that would lead to the establishment of a democratic republic, which would then undertake an extensive program of social reform. Mazzini often wore black, claiming that he was in mourning for the unrealized cause of unification.

Mazzini's strategy for national unification involved a succession of uprisings and invasions. Cavour, however, adopted a diplomatic course of action intended to gain the military assistance of France against Austria. In 1859 French and Piedmontese forces defeated the Austrians at Magenta and Solferino and drove them out of Lombardy. One year later Napoleon III signed the Treaty of Turin with Cavour, allowing Piedmont-Sardinia to annex Tuscany, Parma, Modena, and the Romagna, while ceding to France the Italian territories of Savoy and Nice. This treaty resulted in the unification of all of northern and central Italy except Venetia in the northeast and the Papal States in the center of the peninsula (see Map 21.2).

The main focus of unification efforts now turned to the Kingdom of the Two Sicilies in the south. A rebellion against the Bourbon monarch Francis II, protesting new taxes and the high price of bread, had taken place there in 1860. At that point the militant republican adventurer Giuseppe Garibaldi (1807–1882) intervened with decisive force. Garibaldi, who was born in Nice and spoke French rather than Italian as his main language, was determined no less than Cavour and Mazzini to drive all foreigners out of Italy and achieve its unification. Originally a supporter of Mazzini's republican goals, Garibaldi gave his support in the 1860s for Italian unification within the framework of a monarchy. A charismatic military leader, Garibaldi put together an army of volunteers, known as the Red Shirts for their colorful makeshift uniforms. In 1860 he landed in Sicily with an army of 1,000 men, took the main Sicilian

Garibaldi Surrendering Power—British Cartoon, 1860

city of Palermo, and established a dictatorship on behalf of King Victor Emmanuel. He then landed on the mainland and took Naples. Shortly thereafter the people of Naples, Sicily, and most of the Papal States voted their support for union with Piedmont-Sardinia. In March 1861 the king of Sardinia assumed the title of King Victor Emmanuel of Italy (r. 1861–1878). Complete unification was achieved when Austria ceded Venetia to Italy in 1866 and when French troops, which had been protecting a portion of the Papal States, withdrew from Rome in 1870.

The unification of Italy owed more to the statecraft of Cavour than the passion of Mazzini and Garibaldi. Their achievement did not fully realize the lofty nationalist goals of creating a culturally unified people or a powerful central state. Economic differences between northern and southern Italy became even greater after unification than before. The overwhelming majority of the people continued to speak their local dialects or even French rather than Italian. Traditions of local political autonomy and resentment

**Giuseppe Garibaldi**
The uniform he is wearing was derived from his days as a guerilla fighting in the civil war in Uruguay (1842–1846). Garibaldi also spent two years in asylum in the United States.

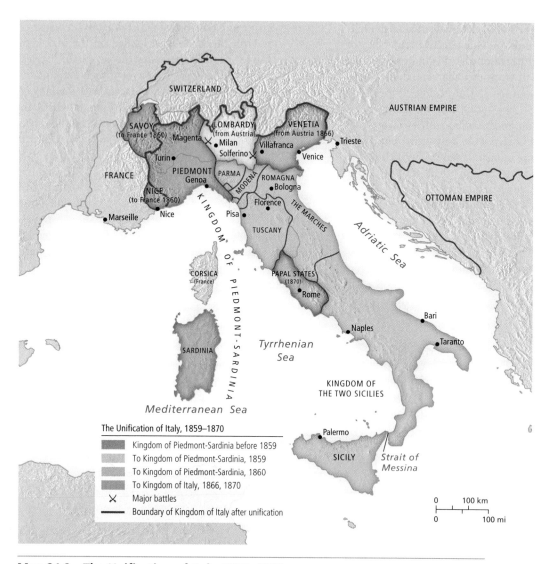

**Map 21.2 The Unification of Italy, 1859–1870**
The main steps to unification took place in 1860, when Piedmont-Sardinia acquired Tuscany, Parma, Modena, and the Romagna and when Garibaldi seized control of the Kingdom of the Two Sicilies in the name of King Victor Emmanuel of Piedmont-Sardinia.

against the concentration of wealth in the north retarded the development of loyalty to the new Italian state and inspired a series of bloody rebellions in the former Kingdom of the Two Sicilies during the 1870s and 1880s.

This instability was aggravated by the widespread practice of banditry in the southern mainland. Bandits were peasants who, in the hope of maintaining a world that appeared to be vanishing, swept through towns, opened jails, stole from the wealthy, and sacked their houses. Closely related to banditry was the growth in Sicily of the Mafia°, organizations of armed men who took control of local politics and the economy. The Mafia originated during the struggle for unification in the 1860s and strengthened their position in Sicily once the country had been unified.

Their power, the prevalence of banditry, and the enduring strength of Italian loyalty to the local community all made it difficult for the new Italian state to flourish. The movement for national unification had driven the French and the Austrians out of the peninsula, but it had failed to create a model nation-state.

## German Unification: Conservative Nation-Building

Like Italy, Germany experienced a successful movement for national unification after the disappointments of 1848. The German movement, like the Italian, benefited from the actions of crafty statesmen and from the decisions made by other states. Unlike Italy, however, Germany achieved unification under the direction of highly conservative rather than liberal forces. One reason for this was that the severity of the reaction to the Revolution of 1848 had forced the emigration of many German liberals and nationalists to Great Britain and the Netherlands and as far west as the hill country of central Texas. Nevertheless a number of liberals, such as those who belonged to a Pan-German association known as the National Union, still kept alive the hopes of the Frankfurt Parliament for a German constitutional republic.

The main dilemma regarding German unification was whether Prussia or Austria would form the nucleus of any new political structure. In the end, Prussia, with its almost entirely German-speaking population, its wealth, and its strong army, assumed leadership of the movement. The key figure in this process was Count Otto von Bismarck (1815–1898), a lawyer and bureaucrat from an old Junker family whom King William I of Prussia appointed as his prime minister in 1862. By birth, training, and instinct Bismarck was an inflexible conservative, determined to preserve and strengthen the Prussian nobility and monarchy and to make the Prussian state strong and powerful. In the words of the liberal British ambassador to Berlin, Robert Morier, "not one mustard seed of faith in liberal principles exists in Count Bismarck's nature." Bismarck did not hesitate, however, to make alliances with any political party, including the liberals, to achieve his goals. This subordination of political means to their ends, and Bismarck's willingness to use whatever tactics were necessary, regardless of any moral considerations, made him a proponent of *Realpolitik,* the adoption of political tactics solely on the basis of their realistic chances of success.

**The Proclamation of the German Empire in the Hall of Mirrors at Versailles, January 21, 1871**
King William I of Prussia, standing on the dais, is being crowned emperor of Germany. At the center of the picture, dressed in a white uniform jacket, is Otto von Bismarck, the person most responsible for the unification of all German territory in one empire.

Bismarck pursued the goal of national unification through the exercise of raw military and political power. "The great questions of the day," he said in 1862, "will not be settled by speeches and majority decisions—that was the error of 1848 and 1849—but by iron and blood." Bismarck did not share the romantic devotion of other German nationalists to the Fatherland or their desire to have a state that embodied the spirit of the German people. His determination to achieve German national unification became synonymous with his goal of strengthening the Prussian state. This commitment to the supremacy of Prussia within a united Germany explains his steadfast exclusion of the other great German power, Austria, from his plans for national unification.

Bismarck's achievement of German unification was based mainly on Prussian success in two wars (see Map 21.3). The first, the Austro-Prussian War of 1866, resulted

in the formation of a new union of twenty-two states, the North German Confederation. This new structure replaced the old German Confederation, the loose association of thirty-nine states, including Austria, that had been established in 1815 by the Congress of Vienna. The North German Confederation had a centralized political structure with its own legislature, the *Reichstag;* the king of Prussia became its president and Bismarck its chancellor. The foundation of the North German Confederation was, however, only one step toward the unification of all Germany. Bismarck laid the foundation for the realization of this larger goal by strengthening the *Zollverein,* which included the southern German states. By encouraging free trade among all the German states he also won support for unification from German liberals.

The second war, which completed the unification of Germany, was the Franco-Prussian War of 1870–1871. This

**Map 21.3 The Unification of Germany, 1866–1871**
Prussia assumed leadership in uniting all German territories except Austria. Prussia was responsible for the formation of the North German Confederation in 1866 and the German Empire in 1871.

conflict began when Napoleon III, the French emperor, challenged Prussian efforts to place a member of the Prussian royal family on the vacant Spanish throne. Bismarck welcomed this opportunity to take on the French, who controlled German-speaking territories on their eastern frontier and who had cultivated alliances with the southern German states. Bismarck played his diplomatic cards brilliantly, guaranteeing that the Russians, Austrians, and British would not support France. He then used the army that he had modernized to invade France and seize the towns of Metz and Sedan. The capture of Napoleon III

during this military offensive precipitated the end of France's Second Empire and the establishment of the Third French Republic in September 1870.

As a result of the war Prussia annexed the predominantly German-speaking territories of Alsace and Lorraine. Much more important, it led to the proclamation of the German Empire with William I of Prussia as emperor. Officially the structure of the new empire, a term used to indicate that it embraced many separate states, was that of a federation, just like that of the North German Confederation that preceded it. In fact the government of the empire, like that of

Prussia, was highly centralized as well as autocratic, and the liberal middle classes did not participate in it, as they did in the governments of Britain, France, and Italy. The German imperial government won the support of the middle class by adopting policies supporting free trade, but the ideologies that underpinned the new German Empire were those of conservatism and nationalism, which encouraged devotion to "God, King, and Fatherland."

## Unification in the United States: Creating a Nation of Nations

At the same time that Italy and Germany were achieving national unification, the United States of America engaged in a bitter process that preserved and strengthened the federal union it had instituted in 1787. The thirteen colonies that proclaimed their independence from Great Britain in 1776 shared common constitutional grievances against the mother country or metropolis, but each colony had its own identity. The U.S. Constitution, drawn up in 1787, sought to preserve this balance between the states and the federal government by dividing sovereignty between them, leaving to the states control over all matters it had not specifically given to the federal government. This arrangement generated friction and debate between the Federalists, who wished to strengthen the central government, and the Anti-Federalists, who feared that a strong central government would lead to corrupt, arbitrary rule. The Federalists won some early victories, including the establishment of a national bank, but they were unable to create a truly united people. The great victory of the Anti-Federalists was the Bill of Rights, the first ten amendments to the U.S. constitution, which was ratified by the states in 1791. By enumerating the rights of the citizens in a formal constitution, including freedom of speech and freedom of assembly, the Bill of Rights embodied one of the main elements of liberal ideology.

Throughout the early years of the republic Americans continued to think of themselves as citizens of particular states more than as members of a single national community. In the early nineteenth century, President Thomas Jefferson (1801–1809) imagined a new American nation, a people "with one heart and one mind," but nationalist sentiment, such as had developed in European countries on the basis of a common language and culture, had difficulty materializing in the United States. The American republic was originally the product of English-speaking colonists who shared the same language and culture as the British against whom they had rebelled. After the revolution, efforts were made to build a new nation on the basis of a distinctly American culture. *The American Dictionary of the English Language,* compiled by Noah Webster (1758–1843) in 1812, made one contribution to this endeavor by listing hundreds of American words that had never been included in English dictionaries. Patriotic sentiment, especially after the defeat

of British forces at the Battle of New Orleans in 1815, also helped give Americans a sense of common purpose and destiny.

These efforts at building an American nation became more challenging as the young republic began to incorporate Western territories into the federal union. Lands acquired by purchase or conquest were formed into territories and then gradually admitted into the union as states. This process of unification, which proceeded in a piecemeal fashion, took much longer than the unifications of Italy and Germany in the 1860s. It was marked by sustained military action against the Native American population and a war against Mexico between 1846 and 1848. Florida was annexed in 1819, while Texas, an independent republic for nine years, was admitted in 1845 and California in 1850. This process of gradual unification did not end until 1912, when New Mexico and Arizona, the last territories in the contiguous forty-eight states, were admitted to the union.

As the United States expanded westward into the Spanish-speaking Southwest, and as immigrants from various European nations swelled the population of the eastern as well as the western states, the country became more rather than less culturally diverse. Assimilation to a dominant Protestant English-speaking culture, even one that was gradually becoming distinct from that of Great Britain, could not provide the same commitment to the homeland that inspired Italians and Germans to support national unification. Americans might be patriotic, in that they proclaimed their allegiance to the federal republic, but they had more difficulty thinking that they shared a common culture with the people from different parts of the country. Building a nation-state in America was a task fraught with obstacles.

The great test of American national unity came during the 1860s, when eleven southern states, committed to the preservation of the economic system of slavery, and determined that it should be extended into new territories acquired by the federal government, seceded from the union and formed a confederation of their own. The issue of slavery had helped to polarize North and South, creating deep cultural and ideological divisions that made the goal of national unity appear even more distant. America had its own ideological and cultural encounters that paralleled those that prevailed in European countries.

The constitutional issue underlying the civil war was the preservation of the union. In a famous speech President Abraham Lincoln (1861–1865) declared that "a house divided against itself cannot stand . . . this government cannot endure permanently half slave and half free." When the war ended and slavery was abolished, that union was not only preserved but strengthened. Amendments to the U.S. Constitution provided for equal protection of all citizens under the law. The South, which had its own regional economy, was integrated into the increasingly commercial and industrial North. The whole process of national unification, both economic and social, was greatly facilitated by the building of railways. In the United States, even more than in Europe, railroads linked otherwise isolated communities and facilitated the spread of products and ideas across vast distances. Gradually the people of the United States began to think of themselves as a united people, drawn from many different nations of the world. The United States became "a nation of nations."

## Nationalism in Eastern Europe: Preserving Multinational Empires

The national unifications that took place in Germany, Italy, and the United States formed part of a *western* European pattern in which the main units of political organization would be nation-states. Ethnic minorities would of course always live within the boundaries of these states, but the state itself would encourage the growth of a national identity among all its citizens. We can observe this process at work in France, Britain, and Spain, all of which had undergone a process of national unification before the nineteenth century. Minority populations within these large western European states have occasionally threatened to establish a separate political identity as nations, but with the one notable exception of Ireland, the southern portion of which became independent of Britain in the twentieth century, the

large states of western Europe have maintained their unity and promoted nationalist sentiment to sustain it.

In *eastern* Europe a very different pattern prevailed, especially in the Habsburg and Russian Empires. Instead of becoming unified nation-states, these two empires remained large, multinational political formations, embracing many different nationalities. This pattern was most obvious in the large, sprawling Habsburg Empire, which encompassed no fewer than twenty different ethnic groups, each of which thought of itself as a nation (see Map 21.4). The largest of these nationalities were the Germans in Austria and Bohemia and the Magyars in Hungary, but the Czechs, Slovaks, Poles, Slovenes, Croats, Rumanians, Bulgarians, and Italians (before 1866) all formed sizable minority populations. Map 21.4 only begins to reveal the full complexity of this diversity. The various nationalities within the empire had little in common except loyalty to the Habsburg emperor, who defended the Catholic faith and the privileges of the nobility. National unification of the empire would have presented a much more formidable task than the ones that confronted Cavour and Bismarck.

During the era of national unification the ideology of nationalism threatened to tear apart this precariously unified empire. It awakened demands of Hungarians, Czechs, and others for national autonomy and also spawned a movement for the national unity of all Slavs. The emperor,

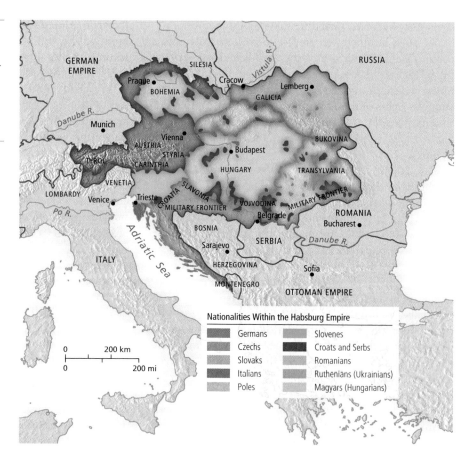

**Map 21.4 Nationalities Within the Habsburg Empire**
The large number of different nationalities within the Habsburg Empire made it impossible to accommodate the demands of all nationalities for their own state.

Nationalities Within the Habsburg Empire

Germans
Czechs
Slovaks
Italians
Poles
Slovenes
Croats and Serbs
Romanians
Ruthenians (Ukrainians)
Magyars (Hungarians)

Francis Joseph (r. 1848–1916), recognized the danger of nationalist ideology. He also feared that liberalism, which was often linked to nationalism, would at the same time undermine his authority, which he had reasserted with a vengeance after the failure of the revolutions of 1848. He therefore repressed these nationalist aspirations at every turn. This policy had disastrous consequences for the future history of Europe, as Slavic nationalism and separatism have remained a source of political instability of southeastern Europe until the present day.

The one concession that Francis Joseph did make during this volatile period was to establish the Dual Monarchy of Austria-Hungary in 1867. This significant increase of Hungarian power within the empire came in the wake of the disastrous defeats of Austrian forces by the French and Piedmontese in 1859 and the Prussians in 1866. Austrian liberals took this opportunity to call for the introduction of constitutional government, while the second-largest ethnic group within the empire, the Magyars, demanded more autonomy for Hungary. The *Ausgleich* (Settlement) of 1867, which was proposed by the wealthy Hungarian nobleman and lawyer Ferenc Deák (1803–1876), created a dual monarchy in which Francis Joseph would be both king of Hungary and emperor of Austria. Each monarchy would have its own parliament and bureaucracy, although matters of foreign policy and finance would be handled in Vienna. This arrangement represented a concession to Magyar nationalism but gave very little to all the other nationalities within both kingdoms. The *Ausgleich* officially recognized the equality of all nationalities within the empire and allowed schooling to be conducted in the local language, but it permitted only Germans in Austria and Magyars in Hungary to acquire their own political identity. Instead of a unified nation-state the emperor now presided over two multinational monarchies.

# Ideology, Empire, and the Balance of Power

■ What role did ideology play in international warfare and diplomacy, especially in efforts to maintain the balance of power during this period?

The new ideologies of the early nineteenth century, and the movements for national unification to which they gave rise, had a disruptive impact on the conduct of international affairs. The original framework for international action after 1815 was the Concert of Europe, which was intended to prevent the recurrence of revolution and preserve the balance of power. It achieved much greater success in pursuing the second goal than it did the first. The five European powers in the Concert—Britain, Austria, Russia, Prussia, and France—could never contain the liberal and national forces that the French Revolution had unleashed, but as a group the five powers prevented any one of them from establishing a dominant position in Europe.

Challenges to the balance of power during this period came mainly from governments engaged in a process of imperial expansion. The first of these challenges arose in the Western Hemisphere during the 1820s, the second occurred in the 1850s in the Balkans, and the third took place after the Franco-Prussian War of 1870–1871.

## Britain, the United States, and the Monroe Doctrine of 1823

In North America a clash of empires threatened to engulf European powers in a new round of imperial expansion and warfare during the early 1820s. As Spanish power in the Western Hemisphere began to collapse, the young republic of the United States feared that Austria or France might intervene in the new Latin American nations. The United States was also alarmed about Russian expansion down the western coast of North America, as we have discussed in Chapter 17. In order to prevent imperial expansion by any of these European powers, the United Sates found an ally in Britain, which even after the loss of the thirteen North American colonies still ruled a large empire of its own in Canada, the Caribbean, and South America. Britain did not wish to compromise the dominant influence it exercised in this area.

British and U.S. resistance to continental European imperialism in the Western Hemisphere had a foundation in liberal ideology. The United States, with its constitutional protection of individual liberty and its success in achieving national self-determination in the American Revolution, had become the very embodiment of European liberalism. No wonder it supported the independence of Latin American nations on ideological as well as diplomatic grounds. In Britain, as we have already seen, the liberal tradition was stronger than in other parts of Europe. Britain's liberal heritage also helps to explain its refusal to join the Holy Alliance of 1815. The British government viewed the Concert of Europe as a mechanism for preserving the balance of power, not for supporting autocratic regimes.

In 1823, President James Monroe (1817–1825) declared that the United States would consider any future attempts by European powers to colonize the Americas as hostile acts. The enforcement of this policy, which became known as the Monroe Doctrine, depended mainly on the support of the British navy, because the United States was not yet capable of taking on the powers of Europe by itself. During the next ten years Britain provided that naval support.

The main effect of the Monroe Doctrine, and Britain's enforcement of it, was to preserve the balance of power in the Western Hemisphere. The doctrine also created the concept of two hemispheres, one old and one new, each refraining from interference in each other's affairs. The broader ideological significance of the Monroe Doctrine was that it provided support for liberalism and nationalism both in Europe and in the Americas. Monroe's speech made explicit reference to the opposition of the United States to the repressive political systems of the allied powers, support for the liberal revolutions that had taken place in Spain and Portugal in 1820, and approval of the revolutions against Spanish rule in Latin America.

## Russia, the Ottoman Empire, and the Crimean War, 1853–1856

The second major challenge to the balance of power occurred as a result of Russian imperial ambitions in the Balkans, resulting in the first major war among European powers since the defeat of Napoleon at Waterloo in 1815. The Crimean War (1853–1856), which claimed almost a million casualties on all sides, was the direct result of Russian imperial expansion. It began when Russia occupied the principalities of Moldavia and Wallachia (present-day Romania) in the Ottoman Empire in order to gain access to

---

**CHRONOLOGY**

### French Politics, 1848–1871

**1848**

| February 25 | Establishment of the Second Republic |
| December | Election of Louis-Napoleon as president of the Second Republic |

**1851**

| December 2 | Louis Napoleon dissolves the National Assembly |

**1852**

| November | Establishment of the Second Empire under Napoleon III |

**1870**

| July 19 | Beginning of the Franco-Prussian War |
| September 2 | Surrender of Napoleon III to Prussia at Sedan |
| September 4 | End of the Second Empire and proclamation of the Third Republic |

**1871**

| February | National Assembly meets at Bordeaux |
| March | Rising of the Paris Commune |
| May 10 | End of the Franco-Prussian War |
| May 21–27 | "Bloody Week"; suppression of the Paris Commune |

---

the Straits of Constantinople and thus to the Aegean and Mediterranean seas. The weakness of the Ottoman Empire had invited Russian expansion into this area, which Russians justified by claiming they were protecting the Orthodox Christianity of people in the Balkans from their Turkish Muslim oppressors. They also claimed that they were promoting the national unity of all Slavic people under Russian auspices. This Russian version of Pan-Slavism differed from that developed by Czech Slavs at the Pan-Slav Congress of 1848. In effect it was an extreme form of Russian imperialism that rivaled the nationalism of individual Slavic nationalities.

Britain resisted the Russian occupation of Moldavia and Wallachia, ostensibly to protect its trade with the Turks but more urgently to prevent Russia from becoming too powerful. In this respect it was adhering to the principles of the Concert of Europe by trying to preserve the balance of power in Europe. The underlying British fear was that Russia might invade India, Britain's most important colony. When the Turks declared war on the Russians, therefore, the British followed suit and were joined by the French. Both powers sent large armies to begin a siege of the port of Sebastopol on the Black Sea.

The poorly trained British forces, commanded by officers who had purchased their commissions and who had no sound knowledge of military tactics, suffered staggering losses, more of them from disease than from battle. The most senseless episode of the war occurred when a British cavalry unit, the Light Brigade, rode into a deep valley, only to be cut down by Russian artillery perched on the surrounding hills. The slaughter was memorialized in a poem by the British poet Alfred Lord Tennyson (1850–1892), "The Charge of the Light Brigade."

Nevertheless, the British, French, and Turks prevailed, handing Russia its most humiliating defeat of the nineteenth century. The defeat led to a curtailment of Russian expansion for the next twenty years and preserved the balance of power in Europe. Within Russia the defeat contributed to a crisis that led to a series of liberal reforms during the rule of Tsar Alexander II (1855–1881). Alexander, an indecisive man who had inherited the throne in the middle of the Crimean War, was hardly a liberal (he once referred to the French system of government as "vile"), but he did yield to mounting liberal pressure to emancipate the serfs in 1861, a step that occurred two years before the emancipation of slaves in the United States.

## The German Empire and the Paris Commune, 1870–1871

A third, and in the long run the most serious, challenge to the balance of power in Europe came from Prussia. As we have seen, Prussian victories over

**Execution of Paris Communards, May 1871**
Troops of the provisional French government killed at least 25,000 Parisians during the uprising.

Austria in 1866 and France in 1871 allowed Bismarck to complete the unification of Germany. The newly created German Empire, which now possessed the strongest army in Europe, replaced Austria as the predominant power in central Europe. The growth of German military power, coupled with its expansionist territorial ambitions, soon made it a formidable rival to other European countries and threatened to upset the delicate balance of power. In the twentieth century Germany's territorial ambitions led ultimately to two world wars.

German military success in the Franco-Prussian War of 1870–1871 played a crucial role in French politics, exposing the complex ideological contradictions of the Second French Empire and laying the groundwork for the Third French Republic. After Napoleon III had established the Second Empire in 1852, he tried to mask his usurpation of power by preserving the tradition of universal male suffrage and by submitting his rule to popular ratification, just as his uncle had done. During the 1860s his government became known as "the Liberal Empire," a strange mixture of conservatism, liberalism, and nationalism. Although "the little Napoleon" ruled as an emperor, he gradually allowed a semblance of real parliamentary government to return, relaxed the censorship of the press, and encouraged industrial development. To this mixture he added a strong dose of nationalist sentiment by evoking the memory of Napoleon I.

These efforts failed to save Napoleon III's regime. His moderate liberal policies angered conservatives on the one hand and failed to satisfy the demands of republicans and socialists on the other. These complex ideological encounters came to a head in 1870 during the Franco-Prussian War, which Napoleon himself was in large part responsible for starting. Napoleon took the field at the Battle of Sedan and was captured. The Prussians allowed him to go into exile in England, where he lived until his death in 1873. On September 4, 1870, a large crowd invaded the Legislative Assembly in Paris and forced the deputies who still remained to join them in declaring the end of the Second Empire and the beginning of the Third Republic. Shortly thereafter Prussian troops surrounded Paris and began a long siege of the city, forcing hungry city dwellers to eat cats and dogs roaming the streets and an elephant seized from the Paris zoo.

In January 1871 Adolphe Thiers (1797–1877), a veteran statesman who had served as prime minister during the liberal government of the 1830s, negotiated an armistice with Bismarck. Thiers hoped to establish a conservative republican regime or possibly a restoration of the monarchy at the conclusion of the war. This prospect gained strength when elections to the new National Assembly, which Bismarck permitted so that the French legislature could conclude a formal peace treaty, returned a majority of monarchists.

The National Assembly then elected Thiers as president of the provisional government.

The National Assembly, which sat at Bordeaux, and the provisional government, which took up residence at Versailles, were determined to assert their authority over the entire French nation. In particular, they wanted to curb the independence of the city of Paris, which was determined to carry on the struggle against Prussia and to keep alive the French radical tradition that had flourished in the city in 1792 and again in 1848. The radicalism of the Paris Commune drew its strength from the large working-class population in the industrialized districts on the northern, eastern, and southern edges of the city. The socialist and republican ideals of the Commune's leaders, coupled with their determination to preserve the independence of the city, culminated in the bloodshed described at the beginning of this chapter. The crushing of the Commune marked a bitter defeat for the forces of French socialism and radicalism. The Third French Republic that was established in September 1870 endured, but its ideological foundation was conservative nationalism, not liberalism or socialism.

# Conclusion

## The Ideological Transformation of the West

The ideological encounters that took place between 1815 and 1871 resulted in significant changes in the political culture of the West. As the early nineteenth-century ideologies of liberalism, conservatism, socialism, and nationalism played out in political movements and revolutions, the people who subscribed to these ideologies often redefined their political objectives. Many British and French socialists, for example, recognizing the necessity of assistance from liberals, abandoned their call for creating a classless society and sought instead to increase wages and improve working conditions of the lower classes. The demands of socialists for greater economic equality pressured liberals to accept the need for more state intervention in the economy. The realities of conservative politics led liberal nationalists in Germany and Italy to accept newly formed nation-states that were more authoritarian than they had originally hoped to establish. Recognizing the strength of the ideologies to which they were opposed, conservative rulers such as Emperor Napoleon III and Tsar Alexander II agreed to adopt liberal reforms. Liberals, conservatives, socialists, and nationalists would continue to modify and adjust their political and ideological positions during the period of mass politics, which began in 1870 and which will be the subject of the next chapter.

The Western ideologies that underwent this process of adaptation and modification had a broad influence on world history. In the twentieth century, three of the four ideologies discussed in this chapter have inspired political change in parts of the world that lie outside the geographical and cultural boundaries of the West. Liberalism has provided the language for movements seeking to establish fundamental civil liberties in India, Japan, and several African countries. In its radical communist form, socialism inspired revolutions in Russia, a country that for many centuries had straddled the boundary between East and West, and in China. Nationalism has revealed its explosive potential in countries as diverse as Nepal, Thailand, and Zaire. Ever since the nineteenth century, Western ideologies have demonstrated a capacity both to shape and to adapt to a variety of political and social circumstances.

## Suggestions for Further Reading

For a comprehensive listing of suggested readings, please go to www.ablongman.com/levack2e/chapter21

Anderson, Benedict. *Imagined Communities: Reflections on the Origin and Spread of Nationalism.* 1991. A discussion of the ways in which people conceptualize the nation.

Clark, Martin. *The Italian Risorgimento.* 1999. A comprehensive study of the social, economic, and religious context of Italian unification as well as its political and diplomatic dimensions.

Gellner, Ernest. *Nations and Nationalism.* 1983. An interpretive study that emphasizes the social roots of nationalism.

Hamerow, Theodore S. *Restoration, Revolution, Reaction: Economics and Politics in Germany, 1815–1871.* 1966. An investigation of the social basis of ideological encounters in Germany.

Honour, Hugh. *Romanticism.* 1979. A comprehensive study of romantic painting.

Hunczak, Tara, ed. *Russian Imperialism from Ivan the Great to the Revolution.* 1974. A collection of essays that illuminate Russian nationalism as well as imperialism over a long period of time.

Lichtheim, George. *A Short History of Socialism.* 1970. A good general treatment of the subject.

Nipperdey, Thomas. *Germany from Napoleon to Bismarck, 1800–1866.* 1996. An exploration of the creation of German nationalism as well as the failure of liberalism.

Onuf, Peter S. *Jefferson's Empire: The Language of American Nationhood.* 2000. A study of Jefferson's expansionary nationalism.

Pflanze, Otto. *Bismarck and the Development of Germany: The Period of Unification, 1815–1871.* 1963. The classic study of both Bismarck and the unification movement.

Pinckney, David. *The French Revolution of 1830.* 1972. The best treatment of this revolution.

Seton-Watson, Hugh. *Nations and States.* 1977. A clearly written study of the nation-state.

Sperber, Jonathan. *The European Revolutions, 1848–1851.* 1994. The best study of the revolutions of 1848.

Tombs, Robert. *The War Against Paris, 1871.* 1981. A narrative history of the Paris Commune.

# The Coming of Mass Politics: Industrialization, Emancipation, and Instability, 1870–1914

## 22

I N THE SPRING OF 1881, A HARROWING SCENE TOOK PLACE IN ST. PETERSBURG, capital of the vast Russian Empire. A 28-year-old woman, Sofiia Perovskaia, was scheduled to be executed for her part in the assassination of Tsar Alexander II. Born into the ranks of wealth and privilege, Perovskaia had rejected her traditional role in order to join the revolutionary socialist movement. She became a leader of the People's Will, a small revolutionary group that sought to undermine the tsarist regime through a program of sabotage and assassination. These revolutionaries dared to set their sights on assassinating the tsar himself, and on March 1, 1881, they achieved this goal. Led by Perovskaia, six People's Will members (all under age 30) stationed themselves at prearranged points along the streets of St. Petersburg. At Perovskaia's signal, they released their bombs and assassinated one of the most powerful men in Europe.

Despite the death of the tsar and the audacity of the crime, however, the tsarist regime did not crumble. The six assassins were quickly arrested and sentenced to death by hanging. (One of the six was pregnant and therefore allowed to live.) On the day of Perovskaia's execution, she mounted the scaffold calmly, but when the noose was placed around her neck, she grabbed hold of the platform below with her feet. It took the strength of two men to pry her feet loose so that she could hang.

The image of Sofiia Perovskaia clinging to the platform with her bare feet while her two executioners strained to push her to her death captures the ferocity of political struggle not only in Russia but throughout Europe at the end of the nineteenth century. As Chapter 21 explained, the ideological

**Mass Society at Play** Pierre Auguste Renoir, *Le Moulin de la Galette* (1876). The growing cities offered both middle- and working-class men and women new opportunities for leisure and relaxation.

competition among liberals, conservatives, socialists, and nationalists shaped the political culture of the West in the nineteenth century. Economic developments after 1870 both intensified and widened this competition. Individuals and groups that had traditionally been excluded from power demanded a voice in political affairs. Even in authoritarian Russia, the political nation could not long remain the preserve of the titled and wealthy. Neither economic modernization nor the coming of mass politics ensured the victory of democracy, however. Like Sofiia Perovskaia's executioners, the governing classes often struggled hard to pry newcomers off the platform of political power—and they often won.

How did the new mass politics reshape definitions of the West by the beginning of the twentieth century? Four questions will structure our exploration of mass politics and its impact:

■ How did the economic transformation of Europe after 1870 help shape the encounters between established political elites and newcomers to the political process?
■ How did the ruling classes of the Western powers respond to the new threats and opportunities provided by mass political participation?
■ What forms did mass politics assume during this time of industrial expansion and the spread of modern nationalist ideology?
■ In what ways did the emergence of feminism in this period demonstrate the potential as well as the limits of political change?

# Economic Transformation

■ How did the economic transformation of Europe after 1870 help shape the encounters between established political elites and newcomers to the political process?

Europe's political development between 1870 and 1914 is inextricably linked to its economic transformation. Four important economic developments helped shape European actions and attitudes during these years: the onset of economic depression in 1873, the expansion of the Industrial Revolution into new geographic regions and economic sectors, the emergence of new patterns in the production and consumption of industrial goods, and accelerated urbanization and immigration. Together, these developments not only altered the daily life of the ordinary European, they also exacerbated social tensions and accelerated political change. The resulting series of often violent encounters within societies helped transform the political structures and ideologies of the West.

## Economic Depression

In 1873, Europe's economy tilted sharply downward—prices, interest rates, and profits all fell, and remained low in many regions until the mid-1890s. Contemporaries referred to this as the Great Depression in Trade and Agriculture°. In hindsight, "Great Depression" may seem an inaccurate label for a period that saw a continuing rise in world production and growing levels of foreign investment in new industrial economies, but to many Europeans living in these decades, this Great Depression seemed depressing indeed. Agriculture was hardest hit of all economic sectors. By the 1890s, the price of wheat had fallen to only one-third of what it had been in the 1860s. Farm owners and laborers across Europe found it difficult to remain on the land and make a living. Business, too, faced hard times after 1873. Profit margins were squeezed as the prices of finished products fell, often by as much as 50 percent, while labor and production costs tended to remain much more static.

What caused this depression? Ironically, it was rooted in the very success of the Industrial Revolution. The development of the steamship and the expansion of railway lines across Europe and the United States sharply reduced the cost of transporting both agricultural and industrial goods. Cheaper transportation costs opened the breadbaskets of the American Midwest and Ukraine to European consumption. With wheat and other agricultural goods now flooding the market, farmers were forced to accept increasingly lower prices for their products. More generally, as regions and nations industrialized, they of course produced more goods. Yet many industrial workers, agricultural laborers, and landowning peasants still stood on the very edge of subsistence, with little money to spend on industrial products. In other words, by the 1870s, a mass consumer society had not yet emerged. Thus in many regions of Europe production exceeded consumption, and the result was a long-term agricultural and industrial depression.

## Industrial Expansion

The onset and impact of economic depression is, then, closely linked to the second important economic development of this period—the continued expansion of the Industrial Revolution. As Chapter 20 detailed, the period between 1760 and 1860 saw gradual, spotty, but still dramatic changes in economic production, first in Britain, then in portions of western Europe. But throughout much of the nineteenth century many of the inhabitants of central, eastern, and southern Europe continued to live and work in ways not far removed from those of their great-grandparents. They used simple horse- or oxen-drawn plows, they harvested with scythes fueled by their own arms and backs, they celebrated births and mourned deaths with

**Pre-Industrial Continuities**

This photograph of French peasant women taking time off for a meal highlights the patchy nature of industrialization even in western Europe. Not until the 1880s and 1890s did many rural regions come within the embrace of the modern industrial economy.

rituals embedded in centuries-old peasant cultures. And they had little contact with unsettling ideas as high rates of illiteracy continued—almost 90 percent in some rural regions of the Austrian Empire, for example.

This cultural and economic isolation was breaking down by the time World War I erupted in 1914. Railways, which increasingly linked Europe's diverse regions into a single economic network, played a crucial role. Between 1870 and 1914 the world's rail network grew by 500 percent. In the 1880s, agriculture still employed the majority of Europe's population in all countries except Britain, Belgium, France, the Netherlands, and Switzerland, but even peasants still farming in traditional ways were caught up in the momentum of the industrial economy.

Imperial Russia serves as a good example of the breakdown of social and cultural isolation. By 1914 Russia had developed a significant industrial zone, one that tied it more closely than ever before to Western economic structures. In the 1890s, Russia underwent dramatic industrialization under the leadership of Sergei Witte (1849–1915), Alexander III's finance minister. Before serving the tsar in this capacity, Witte had a successful career in the railway industry. He used this experience to carry out a program of planned economic development. The state-owned railway network doubled in size. This impressive engineering achievement, which included the 5,000-mile trans-Siberian railway (begun in 1891), accelerated the movement of both goods and laborers across the vast expanse of Russian territory. Witte also placed Russia on the gold standard, making the Russian ruble easily convertible into other curren-

cies and so fostering international trade. High taxes and protective tariffs generated some of the capital to fuel industrial expansion, but foreign investment was also crucial. French, British, German, and Belgian capital poured into Russia, up from 98 million rubles in 1880 to 911 million by 1900. By the turn of the century, as a result of such policies, Russian steel production was ranked fourth worldwide—behind only Britain, Germany, and the United States—and Russia supplied 50 percent of the oil used by the industrialized world. Coal mines and steel mills dotted Ukraine, and huge state-run factories dominated Moscow and St. Petersburg.

## The Second Industrial Revolution

The expansion of the Industrial Revolution coincided with a shift in the processes of industrialization itself. The decades after 1870 witnessed a new phase in the techniques and technologies of both production and consumption, a phase that some historians regard as so important that they call it the "Second Industrial Revolution°." Mechanical processes were altered with the development of more specialized lathes and the mechanization of tasks such as grinding that had previously been completed by hand. By the late 1870s, a series of technological innovations ensured that for the first time steel could be produced cheaply and in huge quantities. The availability of steel, more durable and more flexible than iron, expanded production in industries such as railroads, shipbuilding, and construction.

**The Eiffel Tower Reaches to the Sky**

Engineer Gustave Eiffel designed the Eiffel Tower for the Paris Universal Exposition of 1889. French politicians intended the exposition to highlight the "progress resulting from one hundred years of freedom," yet many of its displays featured artifacts from cultures France had conquered.

The construction industry itself was transformed. New technological advances in the production of not only steel but also iron, cement, and plate glass, combined with the inventions of the mechanical crane and stone cutter, allowed architects and builders to reach to the skies. Cityscapes changed dramatically as these spectacular new constructions thrust upward. In 1885, the engineering firm of Gustave Eiffel (1832–1923) proposed the construction of an iron and steel tower to celebrate the Paris World's Fair of 1889. Modeled on the structural supports of railway viaducts, the Eiffel Tower was ridiculed by critics as a "truly tragic street lamp" and a "half-built factory pipe," but it soon came to symbolize both Paris and the new age of modernity.

This same era saw the development of electric power. In 1866 the English scientist Michael Faraday (1791–1867) designed the first electromagnetic generator. Four years later the first commercially viable generator was produced. Once electricity could be cheaply generated and delivered to homes and shops, it then needed to be converted into usable forms. In 1879, the American Thomas Edison (1847–1931) invented the lightbulb and illuminated the practical possibilities of electric power. These developments created a huge new energy-producing industry. They also accelerated the production and distribution of other industrial goods as factories and shops, as well as the train and tram lines that serviced them, were linked to the city power grid.

One important characteristic that distinguished this new phase of industrialization was the role of the state in encouraging economic modernization. Governments implemented policies of economic regulation and intervention, such as the construction of state-owned and -operated railway networks and the provision of financial assistance to private business ventures. The challenge posed by the Great Depression hastened the retreat from the free-trade principles of economic liberalism. Faced with declining profits and increased competition, businessmen demanded that their governments act to protect domestic industries from foreign competition. In this period, only Britain, Denmark, and the Netherlands retained the liberal commitment to free trade and refused to construct tariff walls designed to overprice the goods of outside competitors.

The emergence of much larger and more complicated organizational structures also characterized this new industrial phase. As a result of the economic pressures of the Great Depression, businesses grew much bigger. Faced with the necessity of trimming production costs in a time of declining profits, business owners developed new organizational forms, including both *vertical integration*—buying up the companies that supplied their raw materials and those that bought their finished products—and *horizontal integration*, linking up with companies in the same industry to fix prices, control competition, and ensure a steady profit. The Standard Oil Company exemplifies both trends. Formed in 1870 by the American industrialist John D. Rockefeller (1839–1937), Standard Oil monopolized 75 percent of the petroleum business in the United States by the 1890s, and in addition controlled iron mines, timberland, and various manufacturing and transportation businesses.

Within these new, huge, often multinational companies, organization grew more complex and impersonal. The small family firm run by the owner who knew the name of every employee grew increasingly rare as an ever-expanding layer of managers and clerical staff separated worker from owner. Moreover, identifying "the owner" grew increasingly difficult. The need for capital to fuel these huge enterprises drove businesses to incorporation—the sale of "shares" in the business to numerous stockholders, each of whom now shared ownership in the company.

The development of more complicated organizational patterns at the production end of the economic process interacted with changes in the way goods were marketed.

**DOCUMENT**

## The Ladies' Paradise

*The French novelist Émile Zola recognized in the new department store a revolutionary force of modernization. His novel* The Ladies' Paradise, *first published in 1883, explored the social and economic changes associated with this retail revolution. As this excerpt makes clear, Zola, through his fictional character Mouret, the fiercely competitive department store owner, saw women as playing a central role in the revolution.*

It was the cathedral of modern business, strong and yet light, built for vast crowds of customers. In the central gallery on the ground floor, after the bargains near the door, came the tie, glove, and silk departments; the Monsigny Gallery was occupied by the household linen and the printed cotton goods, the Michodiere Gallery by the haberdashery, hosiery, cloth, and woolen departments. Then, on the first floor, there were the ready-made clothes, lingerie, shawls, lace, and other new departments, while the bedding, carpets, and furnishing materials, all the bulky goods and those which were difficult to handle, had been relegated to the second floor. By this time there were thirty-nine departments and eighteen hundred employees, of whom two hundred were women. A whole world was springing up amidst the life echoing beneath the high metal naves.

Mouret's [the department store owner's] sole passion was the conquest of Woman. He wanted her to be the queen in his shop; he had built this temple for her in order to hold her at his mercy. His tactics were to intoxicate her with amorous attentions, to trade on her desires, and to exploit her excitement. He racked his brains night and day for new ideas. Already, to spare delicate ladies the trouble of climbing the stairs, he had installed two lifts lined with velvet. In addition, he had just opened a buffet, where fruit cordials and biscuits were served free of charge, and a reading-room, a colossal gallery decorated with excessive luxury, in which he even ventured to hold picture exhibitions. But his most inspired idea, which he deployed with women devoid of coquetry, was that of conquering the mother through the child; he exploited every kind of force, speculated on every kind of feeling, created departments for little boys and girls, stopped the mothers as they were walking past by offering pictures and balloons to their babies. Presenting a balloon as a free gift to each customer who bought something was a stroke of genius; they were red balloons, made of fine indiarubber and with the name of the shop written on them in big letters; when held on the end of a string they traveled through the air, parading a living advertisement through the streets!

Source: Émile Zola, *The Ladies' Paradise* (1883; NY: Oxford University Press, 1995), pp. 232–3. Translation by Brian Nelson.

During these decades, a revolution in retailing occurred, one that culminated in a new type of business aimed at middle-class customers—the department store. In a traditional shop, the retailer (who was often also the producer) offered a single product—gloves, for example—in limited quantity at a fairly high price. Often, this price was not set. The customer haggled with the tradesperson until they agreed on a price. "Browsing" was unheard of; an individual who entered a shop was expected to make a purchase. The department stores changed these practices. These new commercial establishments—Bon Marche in Paris, Macy's in New York, Marshall Field's in Chicago, Whiteley's in London—offered a vast array of products in huge quantities. They made their profits not from high prices, but from a quick turnover of a very large volume of low-priced goods. To stimulate sales, they sought to make shopping a pleasant experience. Thus, they provided huge, well-lighted expanses filled with appealing goods sold by courteous, well-trained clerks. In-store reading rooms and restaurants pampered the weary shopper. Another innovation, mail-order catalogs, offered the store's delights to potential customers stranded in distant rural regions and traditionally reliant for their goods on the itinerant peddler and the seasonal fair. Advertising became a crucial industry in its own

right, as business sought to persuade potential customers of new needs and desires.

## On the Move: Emigration and Urbanization

These three economic developments—the onset of the Great Depression, the expansion of industrialization, and the Second Industrial Revolution—accelerated already existing patterns of urbanization and immigration, and so helped widen the borders of local, regional, and national communities across Europe. The Great Depression hit agricultural regions particularly hard, at just the same time that continuing population growth exerted greater pressure on land and jobs. In addition, industrial expansion undercut rural manufacturing and handicraft production, crucial sources of income for rural populations. As a result, men and women from traditional villages sought new economic opportunities in the industrializing cities of Europe, or further abroad, in the United States, Canada, South America, and Australia.

European cities grew dramatically after 1870. In 1800, only 23 European cities had more than 100,000 inhabitants.

### The Bicycle Revolution

The bicycle revolutionized daily life for ordinary Europeans. The introduction of equal-sized wheels in 1886 and of pneumatic tires in 1890 allowed for a far more comfortable ride than had been the case with the bone-breaking cycles built earlier. Mass industrial production made the bicycle affordable; for the first time, ordinary individuals, far too poor to afford a horse or motorcar, could dare to purchase their own private means of transportation that would get them where they wanted to go in one-quarter of the time that walking required. No longer confined to their village for work opportunities or social contacts, bicycle owners discovered that their daily world had widened fourfold. As this engraving shows, the bicycle also contributed to the expansion of the woman's sphere.

By 1900, 135 cities of such a size had sprung up. The European population as a whole continued to expand in this period, but the cities increased at a much faster pace. For example, in 1800 the city of Odessa in Ukraine held 6,000 inhabitants. By 1914, Odessa contained 480,000 people. In the same period, Hungary's Budapest expanded from 50,000 to 900,000 inhabitants.

The migration flow was not all one-way. Farm laborers moved to the cities when times were tough and then moved home again after they had earned some money. Most urban immigrants came to the cities from the surrounding countryside, and often stayed for less than a year. Duisberg, a steel- and tool-making center located in Germany's Ruhr Valley, grew in population from 8,900 to 106,700 between 1848 and 1904. Almost one-third of its newcomers in the 1890s came from villages less than fifteen miles away. No fewer than two-thirds of these immigrants eventually returned to their rural villages.

By 1910, however, one-sixth of Duisberg's immigrants came from other countries, particularly Italy and the Netherlands. The combined impact of agricultural crisis and urban industrial expansion broke down national boundaries to create an international industrial workforce by 1914. Inhabitants of industrially underdeveloped regions were drawn to more economically advanced areas. Italians headed to France and Switzerland, while the Irish poured across the Irish Sea into Liverpool and Glasgow.

Some immigrants headed not for the nearest city, but for an entirely different continent. Between 1860 and 1914, more than 52 million Europeans crossed the ocean in quest of a better life. Seventy-two percent of these transoceanic immigrants traveled to North America, 21 percent to South America, and the rest to Australia and New Zealand.[1] Irish and English immigration to the United States remained high throughout this period, but after the 1880s eastern Europeans accounted for an ever-larger share of those bound for America. One hundred thousand Poles moved to the United States over the course of the 1880s; in the first decades of the twentieth century, between 130,000 and 175,000 Poles were immigrating to the United States each year.

By the 1890s, a truly global labor market had developed. Both technological developments (primarily the shift from sailing to steam ships) and competition among shipping firms considerably reduced the cost of transoceanic travel. As a result, men from villages in southern Italy and Spain could cross the Atlantic in time for the fall harvest of wheat in Argentina, travel to Brazil to pick coffee beans, and then head back home in May. Clearly, in such societies, the borders between local villages and the rest of the world had become permeable.

## Growing Social Unrest

Rapid economic change, combined with accelerated urbanization and immigration, heightened social tensions and destabilized political structures. The freefall in prices that characterized the Great Depression eroded capitalist profit margins, shattered business confidence, and increased middle-class resistance to workers' demands. Class hostilities

**DOCUMENT**

M. I. Pokzovskaya on Working Conditions of Women in the Factories (early 20th c.)

rose as workers responded angrily to businessmen's efforts to protect their profit margins by reducing the number of their employees and increasing labor productivity.

In rural regions such as Spain and Ireland, the devastating collapse in agricultural prices fostered serious social and economic crises. Increasingly desperate, agricultural laborers and peasants turned to violence to enforce their calls for a fairer distribution of land. The spread of industrialization into southern and eastern Europe also led to social unrest as handicraft producers and independent artisans fought to maintain their traditional livelihoods in the face of the industrial onslaught.

In regions such as Britain and parts of Germany, traditional producers had lost that battle against industrialization in the preceding generation, but the onset of the Second Industrial Revolution brought new social strains. The expansion of office and sales jobs widened the ranks of the lower middle class (or *petty bourgeoisie*). This increasingly important social group exhibited extreme class consciousness and an often fierce hostility toward the working class. With an income no higher than that of a skilled worker, the clerk had to fight hard to maintain middle-class status. The erosion of objective differences such as income levels accentuated the importance of subjective differences—wearing the correct clothing, speaking with the proper accent, living on the right street, keeping the children in school.

The flow of immigrants into Europe's cities also sent social and ethnic tensions soaring. Cities were often unable to cope with the sudden and dramatic increases in population, despite the spread of public health provisions such as water and sewer systems. Housing shortages and poor living conditions exacerbated social tensions as newcomers battled with established residents for jobs and apartments. The mixture of different nationalities and ethnic groups often proved particularly explosive.

# Defining the Political Nation

■ How did the ruling classes of the Western powers respond to the new threats and opportunities provided by mass political participation?

The economic and social changes examined in the last section helped create mass politics—a new political culture characterized by the participation of men (but not yet women) outside the upper and middle classes. Mass politics was in many ways an industrial product. In general terms, industrial expansion broke down local and regional cultures, loyalties, and mindsets; it thus cleared the way for the development of national political identities and interests. More specifically, the new transportation and communication technologies introduced by industrializa-

tion made mass political participation possible. The railroads, telegraph, and telephone, for example, shattered the barriers of distance between province and capital, while new printing technologies made newspapers cheap and available to ordinary people. With access to information, they could now form opinions and participate in national and international debate as never before. At the same time, the dramatic growth of cities associated with industrialization created the environments in which mass political movements could grow.

Faced with the challenge of adapting to this new political culture, political leaders sought ways to quell social discontent and ensure the loyalty of their populations. They did so in the context of the turbulent international climate created not only by the spread of industrialization but also by the national unification of both Italy and Germany and the continuing decline of the Ottoman Empire (see Chapter 21). As the European balance of power shifted, governments scrambled to create policies that would strengthen their states both at home and abroad.

## Nation Making

After 1870, all but the most authoritarian of European political leaders recognized the importance of "nation-making," of creating a sense of national identity powerful enough to overcome the conflicting regional, social, and political loyalties that divided their citizens and subjects. But while European political elites sought to make ordinary men feel a part of political life, they endeavored, through such nation-making policies, to retain their dominant social and political position. As socialism mounted an increasingly powerful challenge to both liberal and conservative regimes, those in power had to figure out how to stay there.

### Franchise Expansion

One way to stay in power was by sharing power. The British political system proved the most flexible in this regard. In the first half of the nineteenth century, Britain's landed elite had accommodated middle-class demands for greater influence without relinquishing its own political dominance. Aristocrats and landed gentlemen played leading roles in both major political parties—the Liberals and the Conservatives (also called "Tories")—but both parties also pursued policies that encouraged industrial growth and benefited the middle classes. In the last third of the century, this system expanded to include working-class men. In 1867, many urban working men won the right to vote, and in 1884 this right was extended to rural male laborers. Although Britain did not achieve universal male suffrage until after World War I, these gradual measures of franchise expansion convinced many British working-class men that they could be a part of the political nation and that the political system did respond to demands for reform.

Across Europe in the last third of the nineteenth century and the opening decades of the twentieth century, we see similar patterns as both aristocratic and middle-class politicians enacted measures extending the vote to lower-class men. These political leaders regarded franchise reform as a preventive measure, a way to avoid socialist revolution by incorporating potential revolutionaries within the system. Even strongly conservative politicians came to realize that mass suffrage did not always mean radical political change, as the political structure of Germany attested. The new German state remained politically authoritarian, despite its democratic appearance. All adult males had the right to elect representatives to the German Reichstag (the lower house of parliament) but the Reichstag was fairly powerless. Real power lay in the hands of William I (r. 1861–1888), the first emperor (or *kaiser*) of the unified Germany, and his chancellor, the conservative aristocrat Otto von Bismarck.

Regardless of conservative or liberal intentions, however, the widened franchise was a key development in the creation of mass politics. New voters had to be wooed and wowed; they had to be persuaded to vote the way their leaders, or aspiring leaders, wished. Again, Germany provides a potent example. Even Bismarck could not entirely ignore the democratically elected Reichstag, because it possessed the power of the purse: It approved the budget and appropriated the funds necessary to run the government.

## Social Reform

To attract workers' votes, but more important, to ensure working-class loyalty to the nation and its political leaders, political parties turned to social welfare legislation. In the

## Map 22.1 Europe at the End of the Nineteenth Century

A comparison of this map with Map 19.2 ("Europe After the Congress of Vienna in 1815," page 638) shows the impact of modern nationalism on European political geography. The most striking change is the formation of the new states of Italy and Germany (the German Empire). In addition, nationalist movements succeeded in carving away large chunks of the Ottoman Empire's European territories. By the 1880s, Bosnia and Herzegovina were under Austrian administration, and Greece, Serbia, Montenegro, Rumania, and Bulgaria had all achieved independence.

1880s, for example, Bismarck introduced to Germany some of the most thoroughgoing social welfare measures yet seen in Europe. He initiated sickness benefits in 1883, coverage for industrial accidents in 1884, and old-age pensions and disability insurance in 1889. Bismarck, a fiercely conservative aristocrat, might seem an unlikely social welfare crusader, but his policies suited his overall goal of ensuring German stability, prosperity, and international power. Alarmed by the growing popularity of the German Social Democratic Party (SPD), Bismarck had outlawed it in 1878 and authorized the federal police to disband all socialist meetings and organizations. This attack on the SPD appealed to antisocialist groups such as conservative landowners, Roman Catholics, and liberal businessmen, but risked alienating the growing urban working class. To attract the support of this vital social segment and weaken the appeal of the SPD's call for violent revolution at the same time, Bismarck turned to social welfare legislation.

Bismarck was not the only or even the first conservative political leader to advocate social welfare as a means of winning the loyalty of the expanding industrial working classes. In Britain, the Conservative Party leader Benjamin Disraeli (1804–1881) argued that the traditional aristocratic policy of *noblesse oblige*, of the privileged caring for those below them, made the Conservatives the natural party of social reform. In the 1870s, his government strengthened trade union rights, established the beginnings of a public housing program, expanded the state's program of inspecting factories, and assumed some responsibility for the population's safety by beginning to monitor the sale of food and drugs.

The most substantial foundations of Britain's welfare state were, however, constructed in the early twentieth century by a Liberal government. Between 1906 and 1912, the Liberals enacted a series of welfare measures, including state-funded lunches for schoolchildren, pensions for the elderly, and sickness and unemployment benefits for some workers. This legislation, like Bismarck's two decades earlier, was a direct response to the political threat posed by working-class socialism. In 1906, British trade unionists and socialists allied together to form the Labour Party. Seeking to maintain their hold on working-class voters, the Liberals turned to social welfare measures.

A similar process occurred in Italy. Alarmed by the growing appeal of Italy's revolutionary socialist parties, the liberal leader Giovanni Giolitti (1842–1928) embarked on a conscious policy of improving workers' lives and so convincing their political leaders that real change did not require revolution. Giolitti legalized trade unions, nationalized the railroads, established public health and life insurance programs, cracked down on child labor, and established a six-day workweek.

## Schooling the Nation
Social welfare was part of a broader nation-making agenda that sought to unite the masses with the elite in a strong national community. In this nation-making effort, schools

also played an essential role. State elementary schools served as important tools in the effort to build internally united and externally competitive nation-states. During the last third of the nineteenth century, most of the nations of western and central Europe established free public elementary education systems. In Austria-Hungary, for example, free and compulsory education was decreed in 1869.

Of course, passing legislation is one thing, ensuring compliance another. Because children's wages contributed to the family income, many poor families deeply resented the laws that made school attendance mandatory. In poorer districts of Austria-Hungary such as Bukovina, only 36 percent of children attended school, despite the law. In Italy communities were required to provide free education to needy children as early as 1859, but as late as 1912 only 31 percent of the children in the southern region of Calabria were in school.

Despite these difficulties, the schools constituted an essential link in the chain of national identity. Schools broke the cultural barriers imposed by illiteracy. Individuals who could read had access to newspapers, magazines, and books that drew them far beyond the borders of their local village or neighborhood. Both political leaders and intellectuals recognized the power of education in creating a national community. In the 1880s, for example, French student teachers were instructed that "their first duty is to make [their pupils] love and understand the fatherland."[2]

Schools thus helped forge a national identity in very specific ways. First, they ensured the triumph of the national language. Required to abandon their regional dialect (and sometimes brutally punished if they did not), children learned to read and write in the national language. Second, history and geography lessons taught children particular versions of the past that buttressed their sense of belonging to a superior people and often served a specific political agenda. For example, French classrooms after 1870 displayed wall maps of France—maps that clearly included the provinces of Alsace and Lorraine, even though these regions belonged to Germany, which had seized them as the spoils of victory after the Franco-Prussian War. Finally, the schools, with their essentially captive populations, participated fully in newly designed nationalistic rituals, including singing aggressive patriotic songs such as "*Deutschland Über Alles*" ("Germany Over All") or "Rule Britannia," and observing special days to commemorate military victories or national heroes.

## Inventing Traditions
Nationalistic ritual was not confined to the schoolroom and playground. Making nations often meant *inventing* traditions to captivate the imagination and capture the loyalty of the mass electorate. German policymakers, for example, developed "Sedan Day." This national holiday, which celebrated the battle that helped create the new German state, featured parades, flag raisings, and special services to foster a sense of German nationalism among its citizens. At the

**German Emperor
William II and
His Entourage**
William preferred to wear military regalia when he appeared in public. In this way, William himself symbolized the link between the German state and Germany's military might.

same time, the person of the emperor, or *kaiser*, became the center of nationalistic ceremony and loyalty, particularly after the accession of William II (r. 1888–1918), the first emperor to identify himself as truly German rather than Prussian. William used personal appearances, militaristic pageantry, and civic ritual to link together monarchy and subjects in a sturdy chain of nationalism.

The monarchy was even more central to British nationalism. Whereas Queen Victoria's coronation in 1837 had been a small, disorganized affair, by the final decades of the century the anniversaries of her accession to the throne (the Silver Jubilee of 1887 and the Diamond Jubilee of 1897) were dramatically different. Elaborately staged, beautifully costumed, and carefully orchestrated, these events were designed to make ordinary individuals feel part of a wider, powerful, meaningful national community. The new technologies of mass printing and mass production helped support this new mass politics of nationality. At the Jubilees, participants could purchase colorfully illustrated commemorative pamphlets, ceramic plates etched with the queen's silhouette, teapots in the shape of Victoria's head, or even an automated musical bustle that played "God Save the Queen" whenever the wearer sat down.

## Crisis, Revolution, and Civil War: The Examples of France, Russia, and Ireland

In the climate of heightened international competition that followed Germany's unification and the spread of industrialization, political leaders recognized domestic unity as a vital ingredient of national strength as well as a strong bul-

wark against revolution. The very different examples of France, Russia, and Ireland demonstrate both the crucial importance and the complexity of creating a sense of national identity and fostering national unity in the years before World War I.

### France: A Crisis of Legitimacy

A century of almost continuous political revolution ensured that in the final decades of the nineteenth century no consensus existed on who or what France actually was. After Napoleon III's capture by Prussian troops in 1871, his empire collapsed and the French returned to a republican form of government, based on universal manhood suffrage (see Chapter 21). Born in the humiliation of military defeat, the Third Republic faced a crisis of legitimacy. Key sectors of the population argued that the Republic had been foisted on the French by their Prussian conquerors, and that it was therefore not a legitimate state and not worthy of their loyalty or support.

This crisis of legitimacy was worsened by the failure of French politicians to generate much enthusiasm. A dozen different parties jostled for control of the legislature. Because no single party controlled a majority, the only way to form a government was through forging coalitions, and thus compromise, political wheeling and dealing, financial corruption, and constant reshuffling of office holders became the common tools of parliamentary politics.

The lackluster nature of French politics accentuated the appeal of those who wished to destroy the French Republic—monarchists who wanted a king back on the throne, Bonapartists longing for the glory days of Napoleonic empire, Roman Catholics disturbed by republican efforts to curb the political power of the Church, aristocrats opposed to democracy. To perceive the

**The Mass Marketing of National Identity**
Advertising and mass production allowed ordinary Britons to participate in the glamour of royalty by purchasing inexpensive trinkets, such as this 1902 coronation souvenir.

depth of opposition to the Republic, it is essential to understand that "republicanism" in France meant more than "no king, no emperor." Rooted in the radical Jacobin Republic of 1792, republicanism rested on a vision of an ideal France consisting of male equals—small shopkeepers and independent artisans, governed by reason rather than religion. Such a vision directly conflicted with the interests and ideals of monarchists, Bonapartists, and Roman Catholics, as well as of the growing number of working-class socialists. The encounter of these rival ideologies generated chaos in French politics throughout this era.

This fundamental lack of consensus about the nature or shape of France was strikingly revealed by the eruption of the Dreyfus Affair°. In 1894, on the basis of hearsay evidence and forged documentation, a French military court convicted Captain Alfred Dreyfus (1859–1935) of espionage. Prominent French intellectuals took up Dreyfus's case, and it became a full-fledged "affair," as supporters and opponents of Dreyfus battled in the streets and in the legislature. Support for Dreyfus, who was Jewish, became linked to support for the secular and egalitarian ideals of the Republic; the anti-Dreyfusards, in contrast, saw Dreyfus's Jewishness as a threat to France's Catholic identity and argued that to question the army hierarchy was to undermine France's military might. The Dreyfus Affair so dominated French politics that in 1899, when René Waldeck-Rousseau, a prominent politician, formed a governing coalition comprising members of a number of political parties, its unifying principle was support for Dreyfus.

Dreyfus was finally declared not guilty in 1906, but the consequences of the affair were far-reaching. The Dreyfus Affair revealed the strength of antirepublicanism in France, and so drove the Republic's supporters to seize the offensive. The government pushed through measures placing the army under civilian control, prohibiting members of Catholic religious orders from teaching in public *or private* schools, and removing the Catholic Church from its privileged position in French political life. With these measures politicians aimed to separate citizenship from religious affiliation and social rank and to redefine France in republican terms.

In 1914 on the eve of World War I, the success of this effort at redefinition remained unclear. National political life was dominated by the Radical Party, which represented the interests of small shopkeepers and independent artisans, not industrial workers, and drew its support from rural and small-town constituencies, not the growing cities. The Radicals' grip on power thwarted any significant efforts to address the grievances of the urban working class. Radicals opposed the high taxes necessary to establish social welfare programs and dragged their feet on social legislation such as the ten-hour workday (not passed until 1904) and old-age provisions (not established until 1910). As a result, workers increasingly turned to violent ideologies and actions, such as anarchism and sabotage. Although by 1914 the Third Republic was far stronger than it had been in the early 1870s, it clearly had not yet gained the approval of all segments of French society.

### Russia: Revolution and Reaction

The success of French republican efforts to redefine the French nation may have remained unclear in 1914, but no one could have doubted the failure of the Russian imperial regime to construct any sense of national identity among the Russian masses at all. Convinced that God had appointed them to rule, Russia's tsars clung to absolutism. To catch up with the West, the tsarist regime adopted Western industrialization but it had no intention of accepting Western ideas of representative government. It could not, however, completely block the flow of these ideas into the Russian Empire. By the 1880s, many members of Russia's small but growing middle class espoused liberal political goals such as a written constitution and limited representational government. Other Russians went further and embraced socialism. Both liberalism and socialism constituted revolutionary ideological challenges to tsarist absolutism, and both liberals and socialists met with fierce repression.

As we saw at the opening of this chapter, some of these political dissenters turned to terrorism. In 1881, the revolutionary People's Will succeeded in assassinating Tsar Alexander II, but not in toppling the tsarist regime. With the use of repressive legislation and an ever-expanding

# The Dreyfus Affair:
## Defining National Identity in France

On September 27, 1894, the five officers who made up the counterespionage section of France's War Ministry examined a disturbing document—an unsigned, undated, torn piece of paper that had clearly served as a cover letter for a packet of documents containing information on French military equipment and training. The officers found no envelope, but they concluded that the letter was intended for Lieutenant Colonel Maximilian von Schwartzkoppen, the German military attaché in Paris. Thus, this torn piece of paper constituted evidence of treason. Someone in the French officer corps was selling military secrets to the Germans.

After a brief investigation and a cursory comparison of handwriting samples, the French investigators concluded that the traitor was Captain Alfred Dreyfus, a candidate officer on the General Staff. An unlikely traitor, Dreyfus had compiled a strong record during his military career and, by all accounts, was a staunch French patriot. Moreover, because of his marriage to a wealthy woman, he had no need to sell his country for money. He was, however, an aloof and arrogant man, disliked by most of his fellow officers and without a strong backer among his superiors. He was also a Jew.

Despite the lack of solid evidence, Dreyfus was convicted of treason. After a ceremony of military degradation, he was exiled in 1895 to a specially constructed prison hut on Devil's Island, a former leper colony twelve miles off the coast of French Guyana. Many French men and women believed he had gotten off too lightly. Both public and press clamored for his execution.

With Dreyfus safely imprisoned on his island, his case seemed closed. But in July 1895, Major

Marie-Georges Picquart was named chief of the Intelligence Bureau. An ambitious man determined to make a name for himself, Picquart soon discovered that the sale of military secrets to the Germans had continued even after Dreyfus's imprisonment. Ignoring his superiors' instructions to leave the Dreyfus case alone, Picquart set out to trap the man he first believed to be Dreyfus's accomplice. The evidence he uncovered, however, led him to conclude that Dreyfus was in fact innocent.

Picquart's investigations raised serious doubts about Dreyfus's conviction. These doubts were transformed into sensational charges on January 13, 1898, when one of France's most famous authors, Émile Zola, alleged in a Paris daily newspaper that the French military was engaged in a colossal cover-up. In an article headlined *"J'accuse!"* ("I accuse!"), Zola charged that the General Staff had knowingly convicted an innocent man. Zola's accusations aroused enormous public attention, and over the next six weeks, riots broke out in French cities.

Retried before a second military court in 1899, Dreyfus was again found guilty—although this time "with extenuating circumstances," a ridiculous verdict (there are no extenuating circumstances for the crime of treason) concocted to salvage the military's position despite Dreyfus's obvious innocence. In the subsequent riots that broke out in Paris, 100 people were wounded and 200 jailed. Ten days later, the French president pardoned Dreyfus in an effort to heal the divisions opened by the trial. Finally, in 1906, a French high court set aside the court-martial verdict and exonerated Dreyfus. Not until 1995, however, did the French military acknowledge the captain's innocence.

The Dreyfus Affair drew international attention, polarized French politics, and tore apart Parisian society. It sparked not only violent protests but also numerous duels and a series of related trials for assault, defamation, and libel. To uphold Dreyfus's conviction, high-ranking military officials falsified evidence, even to the point of forging entire documents. The question "Are you for or against Dreyfus?" divided families and destroyed friendships. During the height of the controversy, for example, the painter Edgar Degas spoke contemptuously of paintings by Camille Pisarro. When reminded that he had once admired these very same works, Degas said, "Yes, but that was before the Dreyfus Affair." Degas was a passionate anti-Dreyfusard; Pisarro believed Dreyfus was innocent.[3]

What about the Dreyfus Affair so aroused personal passion as to alter one painter's perception of another's work? What made this trial not simply a case, but an *affair*, a matter of public debate and personal upheaval, a cause of violent rioting and political turmoil?

To comprehend the Dreyfus Affair, we must understand that it was less about Captain Alfred Dreyfus than about the very existence of the French Third Republic, founded in 1871 in the wake of military defeat in the Franco-Prussian War and the collapse of Napoleon III's empire. The intellectuals and politicians who rallied in support of Dreyfus were defenders of the Republic, men and women who sought to limit the army's involvement in France's political life, who linked both monarchy and empire to national disaster rather than national glory, and who believed in a secular definition of the nation that would treat Roman Catholics no differently from Protestants, Jews, or atheists.

**The Dreyfus Affair**
Captain Alfred Dreyfus before his judges, 1899.

Dreyfus's opponents, in contrast, regarded the establishment of the Third Republic as a betrayal of the true France—a hierarchical, Roman Catholic, imperial state, steeped in military traditions. Defending the military conviction of Dreyfus became a way to express support not only for the army, but also for the authoritarian traditions that the Republic had jettisoned. The Dreyfus Affair was thus an encounter between competing versions of French national identity.

The question "What is France?," however, could not be answered without considering a second question: "Who belongs in France?"—or more specifically, "What about Jews?" France's small Jewish community (less than 1 percent of the total population) had enjoyed the rights of full citizenship since 1791—much longer than in most of Europe. Yet the Dreyfus Affair clearly demonstrated that even in France, the position of Jews in the national community was far from assured. Although anti-Semitism probably played little role in the initial charges against Dreyfus, it quickly became a dominating feature of the affair. More than seventy anti-Semitic riots ravaged France during this period. Anti-Semitic politicians and publications placed themselves in the vanguard of the anti-Dreyfus forces. For many anti-Dreyfusards,

Dreyfus's Jewishness explained everything. The highly acclaimed novelist and political theorist Maurice Barres insisted, "I have no need to be told why Dreyfus committed treason. . . . That Dreyfus is capable of treason I conclude from his race."[4]

Anti-Semites such as Barres regarded Jewishness as a kind of genetic disease that made Jews unfit for French citizenship. To the anti-Semitic nationalist, the Jew was a person without a country, unconnected by racial or religious ties to the French nation—the very opposite of a patriot. As a symbol of rootlessness, "the Jew" came to represent for many anti-Dreyfusards the forces of unsettling economic and political change that appeared to be weakening the French nation. Anti-Semites pointed to the successes of assimilated Jews such as Dreyfus—not only in the army but also in the universities, the professions, and business life—as evidence of what they perceived as the threat of Jewish "domination" of French culture.

Declared innocent in 1906, Dreyfus resumed his military career and served his country with distinction in the First World War. Like Dreyfus, the Third Republic survived the Dreyfus Affair. It was probably even strengthened by it. Outrage over the army's cover-up

led republican politicians to limit the powers of the military and so lessened the chances of an anti-republican military coup. Anti-Semitism, however, remained a pervasive force in French politics and cultural life well into the twentieth century.

## Questions of Justice

1. What does the Dreyfus Affair reveal about definitions of national identity in late-nineteenth-century Europe?
2. Once Dreyfus was convicted, many French men and women believed that for the sake of the national interest, his conviction had to be upheld—whether he was actually guilty or not. In what situations, if any, should "national interest" override an individual's right to a fair trial?

## Taking It Further

Cahm, Eric. *The Dreyfus Affair in French Society and Politics.* 1994. A wide-ranging history.

Kleeblatt, Norman, ed. *The Dreyfus Affair: Art, Truth, and Justice.* 1987. This richly illustrated collection of essays explores the cultural as well as political and legal impact of the case.

Lindemann, Albert S. *The Jew Accused: Three Anti-Semitic Affairs (Dreyfus, Beilis, Frank), 1894–1915.* 1991. An illuminating comparative study.

Snyder, Louis L. *The Dreyfus Case: A Documentary History.* 1973. An accessible collection of primary documents.

# CHRONOLOGY

## Instability Within the Russian Empire

| | |
|---|---|
| **1881** | Assassination of Tsar Alexander II; accession of Alexander III |
| **1882** | May Laws reimpose restrictions on Russian Jews |
| **1890s** | Industrialization accelerates under Witte |
| **1894** | Accession of Nicholas II |
| **1904** | Outbreak of Russo-Japanese War |
| **1905** | Revolution |
| **1906–1910** | Nicholas II stifles political revolution |

secret police force, both Alexander III (r. 1881–1894) and Nicholas II (r. 1894–1917) drove aspiring revolutionaries underground or into exile. They could not, however, quell the social unrest produced by economic change. By the turn of the century, rapid, state-sponsored industrialization had built an industrial structure in Russia, but it stood on a very faulty foundation. Russia remained a largely agricultural nation, with peasants still accounting for more than 75 percent of the population. Heavy taxation and rapid population growth, which increased competition for land, heightened social and economic anxiety among the peasant masses.

Within the industrial cities, social unrest also simmered. Factory workers labored more than twelve hours a day in wretched working conditions for very little pay. Any protest against these conditions was regarded as protest against the tsar and was quickly repressed. The workers themselves remained peasants in their loyalties and mindset. Separated from their families, who remained behind in the village, they lived in crowded state dormitories and traveled regularly back to their villages to plant and harvest. They had little sense of belonging to the Russian nation or of participating in the political structures that governed their lives.

In 1905, popular discontent flared into revolution. That year Japan trounced Russia in a war sparked by competition for territory in Asia. The military debacle of the Russo-Japanese War revealed the incompetence of the tsarist regime and provided an opening for reformers to demand political change. On a day that became known as "Bloody Sunday" (January 22, 1905), a group of 100,000 workers and their families attempted to present to the tsar a petition calling for higher wages, better working conditions, and the right to participate in political decision making. Government troops opened fire on the unarmed crowd; at least 70 people were killed and more than 240 were wounded.

The massacre horrified and radicalized much of Russian society. Across the Russian Empire, cities came to a standstill as workers went on strike and demanded both economic and political rights. In June, portions of the navy mutinied. By the fall, the empire was in chaos, with transportation, communications, energy, and water supplies all facing disruption. Taking advantage of this upheaval, states on the fringes of the empire, such as the Baltic regions, rose up in revolt against imperial rule, and middle-class liberals demanded limited representative government. In October, Tsar Nicholas II gave in and acceded to demands for the election of a legislative assembly. The Revolution of 1905 appeared to be a success.

**The Revolution of 1905 in the Movies**
On Bloody Sunday, January 22, 1905, Russian troops opened fire on more than 100,000 citizens who had gathered in St. Petersburg to present a petition to the tsar. Rather than subduing the revolt, the massacre sparked a revolution. This photograph, supposedly of the moment when the tsar's troops began to shoot the demonstrators, is one of the most familiar images of the twentieth century—yet it is *not* in fact a documentary record. Instead, it is a still taken from *The Ninth of January*, a Soviet film made in 1925.

By 1910, however, the tsar had regained much of his autocratic power. Revolutionary fervor dissipated as rival groups jostled for political influence. The tsar, with his army still loyal, refused to carry out many of the promised reforms. Tsarist autocracy remained intact, but so too did the causes of the discontent that had led to the revolution. Russia lacked an authentic national community, as Nicholas would discover during the First World War, when a new revolution would destroy the Russian imperial state.

### The Irish Identity Conflict

In France, competing notions of "Frenchness" erupted into the Dreyfus Affair. In Russia, the lack of a widespread sense of Russian national identity increased the vulnerability of the tsarist state to revolutionary challenges. In Ireland, two very different forms of national identity took root during this era and led to the brink of civil war.

Theoretically, Ireland was not an imperial or conquered territory, but rather (since 1801) part of the United Kingdom, comprising England, Wales, Scotland, and Ireland. In reality, as we saw in Chapter 20, a chasm yawned between the first three overwhelmingly Protestant and industrialized nations, and the Roman Catholic, economically backward, peasant culture of Ireland. While the English, Scottish, and Welsh economies flourished under the impact of industrialization, the Irish economy stagnated. Peasant desperation fueled revolutionary Irish nationalism, as the economic grievances of Irish Catholics fused with their sense of political and religious repression, and convinced many of the need for independence from Britain. In the 1860s, the Irish Republican Brotherhood, or Fenian movement, endeavored to overthrow British rule by force. The Fenian "Rising" of 1867 failed dismally, but it planted a seed that took deep root in Irish soil—the belief that the British constituted an occupying force that must be violently resisted.

Faced with growing Irish Catholic nationalism, the British resorted to military rule, accompanied by attempts to alleviate peasant grievances through land reform. Such reform measures were always too little, too late. In 1898 Irish nationalists organized themselves as Sinn Fein (pronounced "shin fane"—Gaelic for "Ourselves Alone"), a political movement devoted to complete independence for Ireland by any means necessary. Sinn Fein grew rapidly, and by 1914 could call to arms a paramilitary force of 180,000 fighters. The success of Sinn Fein demonstrated that Irish Catholics had developed their own sense of nationhood, which refused to be subordinate to or absorbed by Britain.

But the refusal of Irish *Catholics* to accept British national identity was matched by the refusal of Irish *Protestants* to consider themselves as anything but British. The descendants of English and Scottish settlers in Ireland, these Protestants constituted a minority of the Irish population as a whole, but made up the majority in the northernmost province of Ulster. Frightened by the idea of belonging to a Catholic state, the Ulster Protestants opposed the British Liberal government's plans to grant Ireland "Home Rule," or limited autonomy, by 1914. The Ulstermen, or "Unionists," made it clear that they would fight to the death to preserve the union of Ireland with Britain. By 1914, they too were smuggling in arms and setting up clandestine paramilitary organizations. Only the outbreak of war in Europe postponed the coming civil war in Ireland.

# Broadening the Political Nation

■ **What forms did mass politics assume during this time of industrial expansion and the spread of modern nationalist ideology?**

Through nation making, liberal and conservative political leaders sought both to strengthen their states and to ensure the loyalty of new political participants—industrial workers, peasants, the petty bourgeoisie. But in this era, mass support for socialist and racist-nationalist political parties challenged the political authority of traditional elites.

## The Politics of the Working Class

The rise of working-class socialist political parties and the emergence of new, more radical forms of trade unionism reflected an escalation of class hostilities. Workers often rejected the political vision offered by their bosses and landlords, and instead fought hard to broaden the political nation on their own terms.

### The Workers' City

In the decades after 1870, the combined impact of agricultural crisis and industrial expansion created large working-class communities in the rapidly growing industrial cities. These working-class communities tended to be increasingly isolated from the middle and upper class. Technological developments such as electrified tram lines, together with the expansion of the railway system, enabled Europe's middle classes to retreat from overcrowded, dirty, disease-ridden city centers to new and burgeoning suburbs. Workers knew members of the middle class only within the limited context of the "boss-employee" relationship—a relationship that was growing more hostile as economic depression drove middle-class employers to try to limit wages and raise productivity.

Within the sprawling industrial cities, industrial workers created a vibrant community life. They developed what sociologists call "urban villages," closely knit neighborhoods in which each family had a clear and publicly acknowledged

**Urban Villages**

Packed into slums, European workers developed a separate working-class culture. This painting by the Belgian painter Léon Frédérick (1856–1940) gives a sense of the crowded, tumultuous, community-oriented world of the urban worker. Painted in 1895, *The Stages of a Worker's Life* also illustrates the gender divisions in working-class culture: The left panel of the triptych shows the man's work world, while the right panel features the nurturing role of women as they care for their children in front of the market stalls where they buy their families' food. In the center panel workers of all ages commingle, with the funeral coach in the background reminding them of their inevitable end.

place. Sharply defined gender roles played an important part in ordering this world. The home became the woman's domain (although many working-class women continued to work outside the home as well). In many regions, the wife controlled the family income and made most of the decisions about family life. Men built up their own cultural and leisure institutions, free from middle-class (and from female) participation and control—the corner pub, the music hall, the football club, the choral society, the brass band. These institutions provided an escape from the physical and emotional confines of work and home; they also secured the bonds of male working-class identity, one that rested on a sharp distinction between "Us"—the ordinary men, the workers, the neighbors—and "Them," the bosses, the owners, the landlords, the people with privilege and power.

## Working-Class Socialism and the Revolutionary Problem

This heightened class identity and hostility were embodied in the emergence of working-class socialist political parties. In the decades after 1870, socialism established itself as a powerful force in European parliamentary politics, the means by which workers sought to claim a place in the political nation. By 1914, socialist parties had been formed in twenty European countries.

Why socialism? As we saw in Chapter 21, by 1870 Karl Marx had published a series of books outlining his economic and political theory of revolutionary socialism. Not many workers had the time, education, or energy necessary for the study of Marx's complex ideas. But Marx's basic points, presented to workers by socialist party activists and organizers, resonated with many workers. Quite simply, most workers had already identified their boss as the enemy, and Marx assured them that they were right. His insistence that class conflict was inherent within the industrial system accorded with their own experience of social segregation and economic exploitation. In addition, the onset of economic depression in the 1870s appeared to confirm Marx's prediction that capitalism would produce ever more serious economic crises, until finally it collapsed under its own weight.

The most dramatic socialist success story was in Germany. Even after it was outlawed in 1878, the German Social Democratic Party (SPD) continued to attract supporters. In 1890, the SPD emerged from the underground as the largest political party in Germany. By 1914, it held 40 percent of the seats in the German Reichstag and served as the model for socialist parties founded in the Netherlands, Belgium, Austria, and Switzerland. Even more important, German socialists constructed a set of institutions that provided

**DOCUMENT**

Socialism: The Gotha Program

German workers with an alternative community. If they chose, they could send their children to socialist day care centers and bury their parents in socialist cemeteries. They could spend their leisure time in socialist bicycling clubs and gymnastic groups and choral societies and chess teams. They could read socialist newspapers, sing socialist songs, save their money in socialist savings banks, and shop at socialist co-operatives.

By the 1890s, the rapid growth of socialist parties such as the SPD persuaded many socialists that working-class revolution was just around the corner. In 1885 SPD leader August Bebel (1840–1913) told Marx's colleague Friedrich Engels, "Every night I go to sleep with the thought that the last hour of bourgeois society strikes soon."[5] Six years later in a speech before the SPD congress, Bebel told the gathered crowd, "I am convinced that the fulfillment of our aims is so close, that there are few in this hall who will not live to see the day."[6]

By the time Bebel made this promise, however, unexpected economic and political developments were creating serious problems for Marxist theory and practice. In 1890, the new German emperor, William II, fired Bismarck. Bismarck's antisocialist legislation was not renewed and the now-legal SPD faced a time of new opportunity, but also new challenges. To improve workers' wages and working conditions, the SPD worked in close connection with the rapidly growing German trade union movement—from 300,000 members in 1890 to 2.5 million in 1913. Such activity raised the fundamental question, what was the role of a socialist party within a nonsocialist state? To continue to attract voters, the SPD needed to push through legislation that would appeal to workers; yet the passage of such legislation, by improving workers' lives within a nonsocialist system, made the possibility of socialist revolution ever more remote. Why should workers resort to violent revolution when participation in parliamentary politics was clearly paying off?

The SPD's dilemma was shared by socialist parties across western Europe. According to Marx, capitalism would generate its own destruction—the growing misery of workers would fuel a social and political revolution. But in western European industrial nations in the last decades of the nineteenth century, working-class living standards were generally rising rather than deteriorating. In addition, the expansion of the franchise seemed to indicate that workers could gain political power without violent revolution. As socialist political parties grew in strength, then, they faced crucial and often divisive questions: Should they work for gradual reforms that would make life better for the worker—and risk making capitalism more acceptable? Could socialists participate in coalition governments with nonsocialists— and so lend legitimacy to parliamentary systems they condemned as oppressive and unequal?

The quest for answers to these questions led some socialists to socialist revisionism°, a set of political ideas most

## DOCUMENT

# The Socialist Culture

*Songs played a vital role in the socialist culture developed in Germany at the end of the nineteenth century. Workers organized singing societies, which competed in local, regional, and national competitions. Rejecting the nationalist and religious songs of the middle-class choral society repertoire, workers often expressed their political ideals in their music. These overly didactic lyrics reveal not only the rage against economic injustice that fueled the socialist movement, but also its fundamental faith in human rationality and in parliamentary politics as an avenue of change.*

### "You Men, All of You" by Ernst Klaar

Already on all sides and throughout the world
The proletariat rises up together—
The fate of the poor is to be changed,
And to be changed through the state.
O, if we stand together firmly,
Who will be able to refuse us our right?
Upward, upward, you new generation,
Defiant let your banner wave!
  Put in the eight-hour day!
  Reduce the misery of toil!
  To our victorious march
  The drum now beats.
  Eight hours are enough!

Source: From "You Men, All of You" by Ernst Klaar, translated by Vernon L. Lidtke in *The Alternative Culture*, 1985. Reprinted by permission.

closely associated with the German socialist theorist Eduard Bernstein (1850–1932). Bernstein rejected the Marxist faith in inevitable violent revolution and argued instead for the gradual and peaceful evolution of socialism through parliamentary politics. Questioning Marx's insistence on the centrality of class struggle in modern politics, Bernstein called for German socialists to abandon their commitment to revolution, to form alliances with liberals, and to carry out immediate social and economic reforms.

In 1899, the German socialist party congress condemned Bernstein's revisionism and reaffirmed its faith in the inevitability of capitalism's collapse and working-class revolution. Bernstein had lost the battle—but he won the war. For regardless of what the congress affirmed as socialist theory, in practice the SPD acted like any other parliamentary party. It focused on improving the lot of its constituency through immediate and incremental legislative change. In the words of one socialist intellectual, the SPD was "a party which, while revolutionary, does not make a revolution."[7]

Its effect, although not its aim, was thus to make the existing political system more responsive to the needs of working-class constituents. Despite the almost hysterical fears of many middle- and upper-class Europeans, the successes of socialist political parties probably worked less to foment revolution than to strengthen parliamentary political systems.

## Radical Trade Unions and the Anarchist Threat

To many at the end of the nineteenth century, however, revolution appeared a genuine possibility. The Great Depression, which shattered middle-class confidence and shrank capitalists' profit margins, led businesses to look for ways to cut costs. As management sought to reduce the number of laborers, to increase the rate of production, and to decrease wages, workers began to organize themselves in new and threatening ways.

The expansion and radicalization of trade unions highlighted growing working-class militancy. For example, in Britain between 1882 and 1913, union membership increased from 750,000 to 4,000,000. While size alone set apart the new unions from their midcentury predecessors, two additional differences marked them as much more subversive. First, the new unions were much more willing to resort to large-scale strikes and to violence. Second, the unions sought to better the lives of a wide range of workers, not just an elite of the highly skilled. In contrast to the unions of the 1850s and 1860s, which had tended to be small, craft-based groupings of skilled workers, the new unions aimed to organize all the male workers in an entire industry—for example, all male textile workers, rather than just the skilled weavers. (Unionists, fighting for higher pay, often resisted the unionization of female workers both because women earned much less than did men and because a central union aim was the "family wage"—a pay rate high enough for a man to support a family without his wife's second income.)

Political leaders reacted ferociously to the unionist challenge. In the coastal port of Hull in Britain, striking dockworkers in 1893 confronted Royal Navy gunboats. A little more than a decade later, the British government responded to a transport workers' strike in Liverpool by quartering 14,000 soldiers in the city and stationing two warships off the coast. Increasingly, "class war" seemed an appropriate label for interactions between workers and their middle-class employers. Even the simple act of getting a shave could prove dangerous for a member of the bourgeoisie: Unionized workers in barbershops were encouraged to "inflict nonfatal cuts on the clients of their capitalist masters."[8]

In the first decade of the twentieth century, the European labor movement became further radicalized by its encounter with the new ideology of syndicalism°. Syndicalists worked to overturn the existing social and political order by marshaling the economic might of the

**The Unions' Challenge**

In 1911 the British government deployed troops in the city of Liverpool to put down working-class labor unrest. In one confrontation, two people were killed.

laboring classes. They focused on the general strike as a means of change. In the syndicalist vision, if every worker in a nation went on strike, the resulting disruption of the capitalist economy would lead to working-class revolution. Thus they placed their revolutionary faith in economic rather than political action—in unions rather than parties, in the strike rather than the vote, and in compulsion rather than compromise. According to the French syndicalist theorist Georges Sorel (1847–1922), workers had to embrace violence to destroy the capitalist state. Sorel did not actually believe that a general strike was possible, but he believed that the idea of the general strike was crucial. In Sorel's view, the general strike served as an essential myth, an inspirational idea that would give workers the motivation and self-confidence they needed to overthrow the state.

In their rejection of parliamentary politics and in their willingness to utilize violent means to achieve their revolutionary ends, syndicalists were heavily influenced by anarchism°. In contrast to socialists who formed political parties to claim for workers a place in the political nation, anarchists shunned parliamentary politics. Opting for direct and violent action such as street fighting and assassination, anarchists aimed to destroy rather than control the state. The Russian anarchist Mikhail Bakunin (1814–1876) insisted that the great obstacle to achieving a just and egalitarian society was the state itself, not capitalism or the industrial middle class.

The combined impact of both syndicalism and anarchism created a climate of social unrest and political turmoil in much of Europe before 1914. In France, where a strong non-Marxist revolutionary tradition already existed, both syndicalism and anarchism possessed significant appeal. Impatient with parliamentary politics, anarchists resorted in the 1890s to a terrorist campaign in Paris, which began with a series of bombings and culminated in the fatal stabbing of President Sadi Carnot in 1894. Other prominent victims of assassination included Empress Elisabeth of Austria-Hungary in 1898, King Humbert of Italy in 1900, and U.S. president William McKinley in 1901.

## The Politics of Race and Nation

The rise of socialist political parties and the spread of revolutionary ideologies such as anarchism and syndicalism fostered middle- and upper-class fears of a worker revolution. But the emergence of mass politics was not limited to left-wing ideologies. In the age of the masses, the right-wing ideas offered by nationalist, racist, and anti-Semitic parties also answered the demands of many ordinary people for a political voice. These parties possessed a special appeal in areas that industrialized late and so still contained a large peasant class profoundly threatened by the economic changes wrought by the continuing Industrial Revolution. Socialist politics also possessed little appeal for members of the petty bourgeoisie, who regarded the vision of working-class rule as a frightening nightmare. Instead, they turned to the new mass politics of nationalism.

Unlike the men who had dominated politics in the past, most newly enfranchised voters possessed only a basic education; they had little time for reading or sustained intellectual work; they worked long hours and therefore needed to be entertained. They needed a new style of politics—one based more on visual imagery and symbolism than on the written word, one that relied on emotional appeals rather than on intellectual debate. Nationalist politics fit the bill perfectly. Unlike socialists, who placed great faith in education and in rational persuasion, nationalist politicians did not recruit supporters with reasoned arguments. Instead, by waving flags, parading in historical costumes or military uniforms, and singing folk songs, they tapped into powerful personal and community memories to persuade voters of their common identity, one based not on shared political ideas or economic interests but rather on ethnic, religious, or linguistic ties. This

was as much a politics of exclusion as of inclusion—it defined the nation by identifying who was "not in" as well as who belonged.

## Nationalism in the Ottoman Empire and Austria-Hungary: The Politics of Division

Nationalist mass politics proved very powerful in eastern Europe, particularly in the multiethnic, industrially underdeveloped Ottoman and Austrian-Hungarian Empires. These regions lacked a large, politically conscious urban working class. What they possessed was an abundant diversity of ethnic, linguistic and religious groups. Modern nationalist ideology taught these groups to identify themselves as nations, and to demand political statehood.

By the 1870s, nationalism had already diminished the Ottoman Empire's European territories. As we saw in Chapter 21, in 1833 Greece won its independence from the Ottomans. In the same period, the Ottomans granted autonomy, although not complete independence, to Serbia and the provinces that became Romania. Determined to hold on to what remained of his European empire, the Ottoman sultan in 1875 and 1876 suppressed nationalist uprisings in Bosnia-Herzegovina and Bulgaria with great ferocity. This repression backfired, however; it gave Russia the excuse it needed to declare war on the Ottoman Empire on behalf of its Slavic "little brothers" in the Balkans. In the aftermath of the Russo-Turkish War (1877–1878), Montenegro, Serbia, and Romania became independent states and Austria-Hungary received oversight of Bosnia-Herzegovina (see Map 22.2). Bulgaria received limited autonomy, which the Bulgars widened into full independence in 1908. The Ottomans had lost the bulk of their territory west of Istanbul.

Ottoman weakness appeared to make Austria-Hungary stronger. The Habsburg Empire not only gained territory—granted the administration of Bosnia-Herzegovina in 1878, Austria-Hungary annexed it outright in 1908—but it also benefited from the weakening of its once-formidable rival. The appearance of strength, however, was deceptive. Straining under the social and economic pressures of late industrialization, Austria-Hungary contained numerous ethnic and linguistic groups competing for power and privileges (see Map 21.4, page 704).

This competition intensified as the franchise was gradually widened in the 1880s and 1890s. (The Austrian half of the empire achieved universal manhood suffrage in 1907.) Various parties emerged that appealed to voters on the basis of ethnic identity and linguistic practice rather than economic interest. Language became a key battleground in this political competition. In a multilingual empire, which language would be taught in the schools? Which language would be required in official communications? Which language would guarantee career advancement? Not surprisingly, politicians tended to agitate for

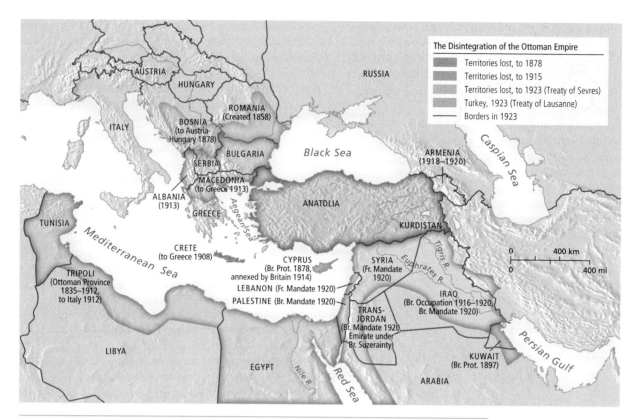

**Map 22.2 The Disintegration of the Ottoman Empire**

As Map 22.2 shows, the disintegration of the Ottoman Empire was a slow process that began at the end of the seventeenth century. By 1870, the Ottoman regime had already lost territory and political control over much of its once-mighty empire to both nationalist independence movements and to rival European powers. From the 1870s on, mass nationalism accelerated Ottoman disintegration. The Ottoman Empire would finally disappear as a consequence of the peace settlement of World War I.

the primacy of their own native language, and to jostle for the political power needed to ensure that primacy.

In Hungary, the ruling Magyar-speaking Hungarian landlords redrew constituency boundaries to give maximum influence to Magyar speakers and to undercut the power of other ethnic and linguistic groups. This policy of "Magyarization" in governmental offices and in the schools bred widespread resentment among non-Hungarians and fostered their own nationalist ambitions and their own political parties.

At the same time in the Austrian half of the empire, Czechs succeeded in gaining greater political power and official support for the Czech language. In response, German nationalist parties within Austria grew more aggressive in asserting German primacy. They called for closer ties with Germany and even a complete break of the link with Hungary. By 1900 the struggle over language laws in the Czech portion of the Austrian Empire had become so intense that no party could establish a majority in the

Reichsrat (the legislative assembly), and Emperor Francis Joseph (r. 1848–1916) resorted to ruling by decree.

In this context of nationalist divisions, anti-Semitic politics proved extremely powerful, particularly in the capital city of Vienna. In the last two decades of the nineteenth century, Vienna's Jewish population swelled, as Austrian Jews from the surrounding countryside came in search of jobs and Russian Jews fled the tsar's anti-Semitic regime.

The growing Jewish presence provided the opportunity for Karl Lueger (1844–1910), a lawyer, self-made man, and power-hungry politician. Lueger's Christian Social party demonstrates how hate-based politics could overcome social and economic divisions among members of a single ethnic or religious community. Lueger used both anti-Semitism and promises of social reform to unite artisans and workers with conservative aristocrats in a German nationalist party. His proposals to exclude Jews from political and economic life proved so popular that he was elected mayor of Vienna in 1897, despite the opposition of

Emperor Francis Joseph. Lueger was still the mayor in 1908, when 18-year-old Adolf Hitler, hoping to attend art school, moved to Vienna. Hitler's application to study art was denied, but he remained in Vienna for several years, soaking in the anti-Semitic political culture.

## Anti-Semitism in Mass Politics

Anti-Semitism played a central role not only in Vienna but across Europe in the new nationalist mass politics. Across Europe, explicitly anti-Semitic parties emerged, while established conservative parties adopted anti-Semitic rhetoric to attract voters. In Germany, the widespread belief that Jews had conspired to cause the Great Depression fueled anti-Semitic politics; by the 1890s anti-Semitic parties had won seats in the Reichstag. In France, nationalists linked Jewish prosperity to French national decline and grew increasingly anti-Semitic in their ideology and rhetoric, until finally the Dreyfus Affair made explicit the connections between hatred of Jews and extremist French nationalism. Many of Dreyfus's opponents saw "Jewishness" and "Frenchness" as incompatible and regarded Dreyfus himself as part of a vast Jewish conspiracy to undermine France's religious, military, and national strength.

To explain the heightened anti-Semitism of this period, we need to understand three developments: the increased emphasis on racial identity, the upsurge in the numbers of Jewish immigrants into Western cities, and Jewish success in the new industrial economy. First, the triumph of nationalism meant a new concern with group boundaries and a greater focus on racial identity. Nationalism raised the question, "Who does *not* belong?" For many Europeans and Americans, race provided the answer. The new nationalism

meant new perceptions of common "racial roots." Ideas about "the English race" or of the shared racial heritage of the French had no scientific basis, but these perceptions of racial links nonetheless proved extremely powerful. In this new nationalistic climate, then, "Jewishness" was increasingly defined not only as a matter of religious belief but also as a racial identity. As a racial marker, Jewishness was not a matter of choice but of blood—something that could not be changed. A Jew who no longer ascribed to the Jewish faith or even a Jew who converted to Christianity remained a Jew. This shift to a more racial definition of Jewishness is one of the factors behind the upsurge in anti-Semitic actions and attitudes at the end of the nineteenth century. If national identity grew from supposedly racial roots, then in the eyes of many Europeans, Jews were a foreign plant. They were non-English, or non-French, or non-German—essentially outsiders whose very presence threatened national unity.

This perception of Jews as outsiders was also exacerbated by the growth in immigrant Jewish urban populations in the 1880s and 1890s. The Russian tsar Alexander III believed that a Jewish conspiracy was responsible for his father's assassination in 1881. He responded by reimposing restrictions on Jewish economic and social life with the May Laws of 1882. Pogroms—mass attacks on Jewish homes and businesses, sometimes organized by local government officials—also escalated. Fleeing this persecution, Jews from the Russian Empire settled in Paris, London, Vienna, and other European cities.

The encounter between these immigrant Jewish communities and their hosts was often hostile. Extremely poor, the immigrants spoke Yiddish rather than the language of their new home, dressed in distinctive clothing,

**The Results of Anti-Semitism**
In this 1905 painting by Samuel Hirszenberg, Hasidic Jews in Russian-governed Poland bury the victim of a pogrom. Hirszenberg called his painting *The Black Banner* in reference to both "The Black Hundreds," armed thugs who belonged to the anti-Semitic "Union of the Russian People," and *The Russian Banner,* the Union's newspaper that was partially funded by the tsar.

and sometimes practiced an ardently emotional style of Judaism that resisted assimilation. As the numbers of Jews escalated in Europe's cities, these new, impoverished, clearly identifiable immigrants received the blame for unemployment, the spread of disease, soaring crime rates, and any other difficulty for which desperate people sought easy explanations.

Many anti-Semites, however, associated Jews not with poverty but with wealth and power. A few Jewish families, such as the internationally connected Rothschild banking dynasty, did possess spectacular fortunes and corresponding political clout, but far more important in explaining the outburst of anti-Semitism in this era is what one historian has labeled the "rise of the Jews,"[9] or Jewish prominence in modern European societies. At the start of the nineteenth century, Jews were barred from political participation in most of Europe and often confined to certain economic roles and even certain territories or city districts. Jews in Russia, for example, could not live outside the area defined as the "Pale of Settlement." In the second half of the century, Jews throughout much of Europe gained civil and political rights. No longer barred from certain sectors of the economy, no longer required to live in certain territories, many Jews moved into new regions and into new economic and political roles. As newcomers, they often took up positions in the newest sectors of the industrial economy. They became department store owners or newspaper editors rather than farmers. At the same time, many Jews assimilated into European societies: They dropped distinctive dress styles and abandoned or modernized their practice of Judaism. They secularized the traditional Jewish emphasis on studying the Torah into an emphasis on education.

As a result of these developments, Jewish communities quickly assumed a significant presence in European economic and political life. In Budapest in 1900, for example, Jews formed 25 percent of the population, yet they accounted for 45 percent of the city's lawyers, more than 40 percent of its journalists, and more than 60 percent of its doctors. In Germany, almost all the large department stores were owned by Jewish businessmen, and in the cities of Frankfurt, Berlin, and Hamburg all the large daily newspapers were in the hands of Jewish proprietors.

The "rise of the Jews" meant that many Europeans linked Jewishness to economic modernity. For independent shopowners and traditional artisans with a great deal to lose from economic modernization, Jews became targets. Fearing the power of corporate capitalism as well as the revolutionary threat of socialism, they perceived both as somehow Jewish. Like Tsar Nicholas II, who blamed the Russian Revolution of 1905 on Jewish conspirators, ordinary men and women reacted to their own personal reversals of fortune by seeking a scapegoat. Jews became the embodiment of threatening change to many newly enfranchised European voters.

## Zionism: Jewish Mass Politics

The heightened anti-Semitism of the last quarter of the nineteenth century convinced some Jews that the Jewish communities of Europe would be safe only when they gained a political state of their own. The ideology of Jewish nationalism was called Zionism°, as Jewish nationalists called for a return to Zion, the biblical land of Palestine. Most Jews in western nations such as France and Britain viewed Zionism with skepticism, but it had a potent appeal in eastern Europe, home to more than 70 percent of the world's Jewish community—and to the most vicious forms of anti-Semitism.

Zionism became a mass movement under the guidance of Theodor Herzl (1860–1904). An Austrian Jew born in Budapest, Herzl was living in Vienna when Karl Lueger was elected mayor. Confronted with the appeal of anti-Semitism to the mass electorate, Herzl began to doubt whether Jews could ever be fully accepted as Austrian citizens. His experience as a journalist reporting on the Dreyfus Affair from Paris confirmed these doubts. The vicious display of anti-Jewish hatred in a prosperous, industrialized, western European state convinced Herzl that Jews would always be outsiders within the existing European nations. In 1896, he published *The Jewish State,* a call for Jews to build a nation-state in Palestine. Herzl gained the financial support of wealthy Jewish businessmen such as Baron Edmund James de Rothschild, but he recognized that for Zionism to succeed, it must capture the imagination and loyalties of ordinary Jews. Through newspapers, popular publications, large rallies, and his own enthusiasm, Herzl made Zionism into an international mass movement.

As a mass movement, Zionism faced strong opposition. Many Jewish leaders argued that Zionism played into the hands of anti-Semites by insisting that Jews did not belong in Europe. In addition, by marking out Palestine as the Jewish "homeland," Zionists ran into a huge political obstacle: Arab nationalism. By the 1890s, Arab leaders had begun to dream of an Arab state, one that would be independent of the Ottoman Empire and that would include Palestine, home to 700,000 Arabs. Nevertheless, by 1914 some 90,000 Jews had settled in Palestine, where they hoped to build a Jewish state.

# Outside the Political Nation? The Experience of Women

■ In what ways did the emergence of feminism in this period demonstrate the potential as well as the limits of political change?

Extending the suffrage to men outside the middle and upper classes also called attention to gender differences, as middle-class women demanded that they, too,

DOCUMENT

John Stuart Mill
on
Enfranchisement
of Women
(1869)

be made part of the political nation. The campaign for women's suffrage, however, was only part of a multifaceted international middle-class feminist movement° that, by the 1870s, demanded a reconsideration of women's roles. To the feminist movement, the vote was not an end in itself, but a means to an end, a way of achieving a radical alteration in cultural values and expectations. At the core of nineteenth-century feminism stood a rejection of the liberal ideology of separate spheres—the insistence that both God and biology destined middle-class men for the public sphere of paid economic employment and political participation, and women for the private sphere of the home. In seeking a place in the political nation, feminists sought not just to enter the public, masculine sphere, but in fact to obliterate many of the distinctions between the public and private spheres altogether and so to reconfigure political and social life.

During this period the feminist movement remained largely middle class in its membership and its concerns. Working-class and peasant women were occupied by the struggle for survival; obtaining the vote seemed fairly irrelevant to a woman listening to her children cry from hunger. Politically active working-class women tended to agree with Karl Marx that class, not gender, constituted the real dividing line in society. For help in bettering their lives, they turned to labor unions and to working-class political parties rather than middle-class feminist organizations. The British working-class feminist Selina Cooper (1868–1946), for example, fought hard for women's rights, but within the context of the British Labour movement. Cooper, who was sent to work in a textile mill at age 10, viewed the widening of women's opportunities and the achievement of working-class political power as two sides of the same coin. Similarly, in Germany, the SDP activist Clara Zetkin (1857–1933) argued that the fight against class oppression was inextricably linked to the fight against women's oppression.

## Changes in the Position of Middle-Class Women

The middle-class women's movement operated within changing economic and social conditions that were pushing middle-class women into more public positions in European society. Married women moved into a new public role as consumers during this period. It was the woman who was the principal target of the new advertising industry, the woman whom the new department stores sought to entice with their lavish window displays and courteous shop clerks, the woman who rode the new tram lines and subways to take advantage of sale days.

The largest change for married middle-class women was much more basic, however. In the last third of the nineteenth century, middle-class men and women began to limit the size of their families. In Britain in the 1890s, the average middle-class family had 2.8 children, a sharp reduction in family size from the middle of the century, when the typical middle-class family had 6 children. This enormous change, characteristic of all the advanced industrial nations, reflected both economic and social developments. As the Great Depression cut into business profits and made economic ventures ever more precarious, middle-class families looked for ways to cut expenses and yet maintain a middle-class lifestyle. At the same time, the growing tendency to keep both boys and girls in school longer meant added financial obligations for the middle-class family. Limiting births, through the use of already well-known methods such as abstinence, withdrawal, and abortion, provided the answer. In working-class families, in which children left school by age 11 or 12 and so began to contribute to the family income much earlier, family size continued to remain large, but in the middle class, married women no longer spent much of their adult life pregnant or nursing, and were thus free for other activities and interests, including feminist activism.

The expectations of unmarried middle-class women were also transformed during this period. In 1850, the unmarried middle-class woman who had to support herself had little choice but to become a governess or a paid companion to an elderly widow. By 1900 her options had widened. As we shall see, the women's movement played a crucial role in this expansion of opportunity, but so also did two more general economic and political developments: the expansion of the state and the Second Industrial Revolution.

The expansion of state responsibilities in this period significantly widened opportunities for women. By the final decade of the nineteenth century, local governments took over many tasks traditionally assigned to church volunteers and especially women charity workers, such as training the poor in proper hygiene and nutrition. Middle-class women quickly claimed both paying and elected positions in the new local bureaucracies, on the argument that women possessed an expertise in managing households and raising children that could be directly translated into managing poorhouses and running schools. Women served on school and welfare boards, staffed government inspectorates, voted in local elections, and were elected to local office. For example, in Britain between 1870 and 1914, approximately 3,000 women were elected to county and municipal governing bodies. In Germany, 18,000 women worked as local welfare officials by 1910. But the largest employers of middle-class women before 1914 were the new state-funded elementary schools. The implementation of compulsory mass education created a voracious demand for teachers and thus a new career path for unmarried women from the middle class as well as from the upper ranks of the working class.

The emergence of new technologies and the retail revolution also created new jobs for women, positions that did

# Men in Black

Within a span of about fifty years, upper- and middle-class European and American men transformed the way they presented their bodies to the world. Before the late eighteenth century, social rank outweighed gender in determining clothing styles. Thus an aristocratic man dressed more like an aristocratic woman than like a male laborer. Aristocrats, both men and women, decorated themselves with expensive jewels, shaped their bodies with corsets and pads, powdered their faces and hair, sported huge hats decorated with ribbons, carried lacy fans, wore high heels, and dressed in brightly colored and elaborately ruffled silks and taffetas. By the middle of the nineteenth century, however, the man had lost his plumage, and decoration had become a distinctly female attribute. The aristocratic man of the 1850s looked like his middle-class counterpart. He dressed in darkly colored, loose-fitting trousers and jackets; wore sensible shoes; and put on a top hat when he went outside. Cosmetics, perfume, ruffles and lace, elaborate jewelry, hats, and fans all retreated to the woman's sphere.

Whether he was engaged actively in business or lived a life of leisure, the new man in black now presented a sharp contrast to his female companions. His clothing associated him with the world of practicality and production; her costume, however, was designed to reinforce the prevailing notions about women's incapacity for public or economic roles. Middle- and upper-class women's clothing not only remained brightly colored, decorative, and luxurious, it also became increasingly constrictive. The full crinolines and hoop skirts of the 1850s and 1860s, for example, made the simple task of sitting down a tricky endeavor, while tight corseting placed strenuous physical activity beyond reach of fashionable women.

Changes in clothing reflect new ideas about the relationships between a man's and a woman's identities and their physical bodies. After 1850 men's clothing styles de-emphasized their bodies. Whereas eighteenth-century aristocrats wore attention-grabbing colors, silk stockings that outlined their legs, short jackets that emphasized their waist, and tight-fitting breeches that highlighted the sexual aspects of the male body, the long loose jackets and trousers of the later nineteenth-century man masked rather than highlighted their wearer's physical characteristics. In contrast, women's fashions increasingly accentuated female sexuality. By shrinking the waist, tightly laced corsets made the bust and hips appear fuller. In the 1880s, the addition of the bustle emphasized the woman's bottom. Such clothing styles fortified the view that a woman's body in many ways determined her destiny, that women were designed to be wives and mothers.

Economic developments led to important changes in women's fashions in the 1890s. As middle-class women began to enter the workforce in large numbers, fashions adapted to fit their new roles. Dresses became more streamlined: Skirts moved slightly above the ankles and shrank in width, and bustles disappeared. But it took the demands of the First World War, when women assumed previously all-male positions in industry, agriculture, and transportation, to effect radical alterations in the way women presented their bodies and themselves to the world.

## For Discussion

Changes in women's employment patterns clearly had an impact on women's dress styles. What other economic developments during this period may help explain changes in fashion?

**Men in Black**
Painting by James Tissot, *Cercle de la Rue Royale,* detail (1868). Although most are barons, marquises, or counts, the men whose portraits Tissot captured in this high-society painting dress like bankers or stockbrokers.

Loose-fitting jackets and trousers hide, rather than highlight, physical characteristics, and are more practical for a day of business.

Dark colors have replaced the bright colors of earlier times; lace, ribbons, and jewelry have disappeared.

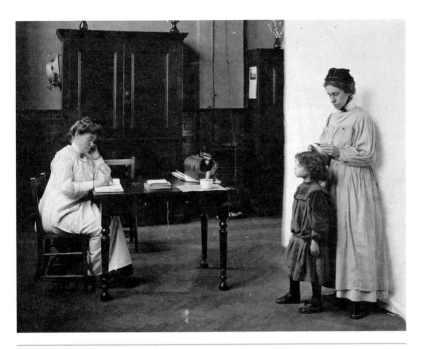

**Women at Work**

The expansion of local and central government interference in daily life created many opportunities for women's paid employment. Here government health inspectors check a schoolgirl for head lice.

## Women and the Law

European legal systems strongly reinforced the liberal ideology of separate spheres for men and women. Law codes often classified women with children, criminals, and the insane. Article 231 of the Napoleonic Code, the legal system of France and the basis of the legal codes of much of western and central Europe, declared that the wife was the dependent of the husband; hence, "the husband owes protection to his wife; the wife owes obedience to her husband." The Russian legal code agreed: "The woman must obey her husband, reside with him in love, respect, and unlimited obedience, and offer him every pleasantness and affection as the ruler of the household." In Russia a woman could not travel without her father's or husband's permission. The husband was also the legal guardian of all children; he alone had the authority to pick their schools, determine their punishments, and approve their marriage partners. Similarly, in Prussia the law declared that only the husband could decide when his baby should stop breastfeeding. English common law,

not involve manual labor and so did not mean a descent into the working class. Middle-class women moved into the work world as typists, telephone and telegraph operators, sales clerks, and bank tellers. During the 1860s in England, the number of women working as commercial clerks and accountants increased tenfold.

Middle-class women thus found new ways to make a living; they did not, however, find the same opportunities as their male counterparts. A woman earned an average of between one-third and two-thirds less than a man working in the same job. The entry of large numbers of women into any job was certain to result in a recasting of that position as unskilled and low-paying. Unlike men, women lost their jobs when they married and found most supervisory positions closed to them.

By the 1880s, an international women's movement had emerged to challenge the legal, political, and economic disabilities facing European and American women. Consisting of a vast web of interconnected organizations, publications, and correspondence networks, the middle-class women's movement sought to challenge the ideology of separate spheres and to establish a new basis for both private and public relations. Its multifaceted campaigns focused on four fronts: the legal impediments facing married women, employment opportunities and higher education for girls and women, the double standard of sexual conduct enshrined in European laws, and national women's suffrage.

based on tradition and precedent rather than on a single, systematized code, proclaimed much the same idea. As Sir William Blackstone explained in his famous *Commentaries on the Laws of England* (1765–1769), "the husband and wife are one person in law," and that person was the husband. A married woman simply disappeared in the eyes of the British common law. Most property brought into a marriage, or given to her or earned by her while married, became the property of her husband.

From the middle of the nineteenth century on, women's groups fought to improve the legal rights of married women. By the end of the 1880s, English married women had won rights to own their own property, control their own income, and keep their children. Two decades later, French women could claim similar rights. In contrast, the German women's movement suffered a sharp defeat with the promulgation of the Civil Code in 1900. The Civil Code, which formulated a single uniform legal system for Germany, proclaimed that "the husband takes the decisions in all matters affecting married life." It granted all parental authority to the husband—over his stepchildren as well as his own children. By German law, "if the parents disagree, the father's opinion takes precedence." While it allowed married women to keep money they earned while married, it declared that all property owned by the wife before marriage or given to her after marriage became the husband's.

# Finding a Place: Employment and Education

In addition to their legal campaigns, feminists also worked to widen women's educational and employment opportunities as part of their effort to enter the public sphere. At the core of this aspect of the women's movement was a simple demographic reality—women outnumbered men in almost every region in Europe. In England by 1900, the higher rates of male emigration and infant mortality meant that there were 1,064 females for every 1,000 males. Clearly, not all women could marry. Thus, providing respectable jobs for middle-class single women was a high priority for early European and American feminists.

The problem of women's jobs quickly proved to be inseparable from the issue of women's education. Even girls from privileged families rarely received rigorous educations before 1850. The minority of girls who did go to school spent their time learning ladylike occupations such as fancy embroidery, flower arranging, and piano playing. Proper posture was more important than any literary or scientific attainments. Widening the world of women's education, then, became a crucial feminist aim and proved to be an area in which they achieved considerable, but still limited, success.

Feminists' educational campaigns in the second half of the nineteenth century had two main emphases: first, improving the quality as well as expanding the number of girls' secondary schools, and second, opening universities to women. The fight to upgrade the quality of girls' secondary education was often difficult. Many parents opposed an academic curriculum for girls, a position reinforced by

medical professionals who argued that girls' brains simply could not withstand the strain of an intellectual education. Dorothea Beale (1831–1906), a pioneer in girls' education in England, established one of the first academically oriented high schools for girls in London in the 1850s, but she faced an uphill battle in persuading reluctant parents to allow her to teach their daughters mathematics. In France, feminists achieved their goal of a state-funded and state-run system of secondary schools for girls in the 1880s. They lost the battle for a university-preparatory curriculum, however, which made it difficult for girls to pass the exams necessary to enter the French university system.

Not surprisingly, the number of women in French universities remained very small throughout this period. Opportunities for university education for women varied enormously. In the United States, women accounted for one-third of all students in higher education as early as 1880, while in Germany, women were not admitted to full-time university study until 1901. In Russia, the development of women's higher education was particularly sporadic. Full-time university study became available to women in Moscow in 1872, and by 1880, women in Russia had some of the best opportunities for higher education in all of Europe. But the involvement of Sofiia Perovskaia—an educated woman—in the assassination of Tsar Alexander II in 1881 convinced the authorities that revolutionary politics and advanced female education went hand in hand. Most educational avenues for Russian women were blocked for more than two decades after the assassination.

Despite such limitations and reverses, the range of jobs open to women did broaden during this period. In 1900, French women won the right to practice law, and in 1903

**On the Way to School**
By the 1880s, the sight of middle-class girls in secondary and university education was not yet commonplace, but no longer rare.

in the French city of Toulouse, a woman lawyer presented a case in a European court for the first time. In 1906, the physicist and Nobel Prize winner Marie Curie became the first woman to hold a university faculty position in France. By the opening decades of the twentieth century, women doctors, although still unusual, were not unheard of. In Russia, women accounted for 10 percent of all physicians by 1914.

## No More Angels

The campaigns for women's legal rights and an expansion of employment and educational opportunities helped women move out of the private and into the public sphere. But the third goal of feminist activity—to eradicate the double standard of sexual conduct—posed a more radical challenge to nineteenth-century middle-class culture and its ideology of separate spheres. By arguing that the same moral standards should apply to both men and women, feminists questioned whether two separate spheres should exist at all.

The ideology of separate spheres glorified women's moral purity and held that the more aggressive, more animal-like natures of men naturally resulted in such male pastimes as heavy drinking and sexual adventurism. The laws as well as the wider culture reflected these assumptions. For example, in France, a woman with an illegitimate child could not institute a paternity suit against the father: Premarital sex was a crime for the woman, but not for the man. Similarly, the English divorce legislation of 1857 declared that a woman's adultery was all that was necessary for a husband to sue for divorce, but a man's adultery was not a sufficient reason to end a marriage. For a wife to divorce her husband, she had to prove that he had committed additional crimes such as bigamy, incest, or bestiality.

To feminists, applying different moral standards to men and women degraded men and blocked women's efforts to better their own lives and society as a whole. As the French feminist leader Maria Desraismes explained, "To say that woman is an angel is to impose on her, in a sentimental and admiring fashion, all duties, and to reserve for oneself all rights. . . . I decline the honor of being an angel."[10]

In their effort to erase the moral distinctions between men and women, feminists fought on a variety of fronts. One key area of struggle was the regulation of prostitution. By the 1870s, many European countries, as well as the United States, had established procedures that made it safer for men to hire prostitutes, while still treating the women involved as criminals. In England, the Contagious Diseases Act, passed in 1870 to address the problem of venereal disease, declared that any woman suspected of being a prostitute could be stopped by the police and required to undergo a genital exam. Men, however, were subject to no such indignities. Feminists such as Josephine Butler (1857–1942)

contended that such legislation made it easier for men to indulge their sexual appetites, while punishing the impoverished women who were forced to sell their bodies to feed themselves and their children. For almost twenty years Butler led a concerted campaign both to repeal the legislation that regulated prostitution and to focus public attention on the lack of employment opportunities for women.

Abuse of alcohol was another key battleground for the women's movement. Arguing that the socially accepted practice of heavy male drinking had devastating consequences for women, in the form of both family poverty and domestic violence, feminist activists backed the temperance or prohibitionist cause. The movement triumphed in the United States in 1919 when decades of agitation from groups such as the Women's Christian Temperance Union led to the passage of the Eighteenth Amendment prohibiting the manufacture and sale of alcoholic beverages. "Prohibition," however, did little to transform gender relations; instead, it simply created new ways for organized crime syndicates to make money. The American prohibition experiment ended in 1933 with the repeal of the Eighteenth Amendment.

In general, feminist moral reform campaigns achieved only limited success. The regulation of prostitution did end in England in 1886 and in the United States, France, and the Scandinavian countries by 1914, but remained in effect in Germany. By 1884 in France, a husband's adultery, like a wife's, could end a marriage, but in England, the grounds for divorce remained differentiated by gender until 1923. In all European countries and in the United States, the sexual double standard remained embedded in both middle- and working-class culture far into the twentieth century.

## The Fight for Women's Suffrage

The slow pace and uneven progress on both the legal and moral fronts convinced many feminists that they would achieve their goals only if they possessed the political clout of the *national* suffrage. In 1867 the National Society for Women's Suffrage was founded in Britain; over the next three decades suffrage societies emerged on the Continent. The French suffragist Hubertine Auclert (1848–1914) described the vote as "the keystone that will give [women] all other rights." As the editor of *La Citoyenne* ("The Citizeness"), Auclert agitated for full citizenship rights for adult women. In an imaginative move, she refused to pay taxes, on the grounds of "no taxation without representation." Auclert was also the first woman to describe herself as a "feminist," a word that entered the English language from the French around 1890.

Auclert and other American and European suffragists had little success. Only in Finland (1906) and Norway (1913) did women gain the national franchise in this period. (By 1913, women also possessed the vote in twelve American

**DOCUMENT**

## In Favor of the Vote for Women

*Many supporters of women's suffrage believed that education, reason, and persuasion would achieve the vote. If suffragists made their case in logical, reasonable terms, they would be able to convince a majority of male voters of the rightness of their cause. This excerpt from a French suffragist pamphlet, published in 1913, is very typical both in its effort to persuade its reader through a careful marshaling of factual evidence and in its belief that the women's vote would transform political life. French women did not win the vote for another thirty years.*

We are going to try to prove that the vote for women is a just, possible and desirable reform. . . .

A woman has responsibility in the family; she ought to be consulted about the laws establishing her rights and duties with respect to her husband, her children, her parents.

Women work—and in ever greater numbers; a statistic of 1896 established that . . . the number of women workers was 35 per cent of the total number of workers, both male and female.

If she is in business, she, like any businessman, has interests to protect. . . .

If a woman is a worker or a domestic, she ought to participate as a man does in voting on unionization laws, laws covering workers' retirement, social security, the limitation and regulation of work hours, weekly days off, labor contracts, etc.

. . .

Finally, her special characteristics of order, economy, patience and resourcefulness will be as useful to society as the characteristics of man and will favor the establishment of laws too often overlooked until now.

The woman's vote will assure the establishment of important social laws.

All women will want:

To fight against alcoholism, from which they suffer much more than men;

To establish laws of health and welfare;

To obtain the regulation of female and child labor;

To defend young women against prostitution;

Finally, to prevent wars and to submit conflicts among nations to courts of arbitration.

Source: From a report presented to Besancon Municipal Council by the Franc-Comtois Group of the Union Française pour le Suffrage des Femmes. Besancon, March 1913, pp. 6–9.

states.) The social upheaval of World War I brought women the vote in Russia (1917), Britain (1918), Germany (1919), Austria (1919), the Netherlands (1919), and the United States (1920). Women in Italy had to wait until 1945; French women did not gain the vote until 1946, Greek women not until 1949. Women in Switzerland did not vote until 1971.

Feminists faced a number of significant obstacles in their battle for the national franchise. In Catholic countries such as France and Italy, the women's suffrage movement failed to become a political force not only because the Church remained fiercely opposed to the women's vote, but also because in Catholicism—in its veneration of the Virgin Mary and other female saints, in its exaltation of family life, in the opportunity for religious vocation as a nun—women found a great many avenues for emotional expression and intellectual satisfaction. Feminism had a much harder time taking root in these countries.

In central and eastern Europe the obstacles were even greater. In much of this region, economic development was far behind that of the western areas of Europe, and thus middle-class culture—the social base of feminism—was also underdeveloped. In the Russian Empire, the middle class was small and any political organization independent of the tsar was seen as a form of treason. No women's suffrage movement existed there until the Revolution of 1905 dramatically changed the political equation. After the revolution won the vote for men but failed to extend it to

women, an organized and vocal women's suffrage campaign emerged.

In contrast to Russia, in England the middle class was both large and politically powerful, and the political structure had shown itself capable of adaptation and evolution. Yet even in England, the site of the first and the strongest European female suffrage movement, women failed to win the vote in the nineteenth century. As a result, a small group of activists resorted to more radical tactics. Led by the imposing mother-and-daughters team of Emmeline (1858–1928), Christabel (1880–1958), and Sylvia Pankhurst (1882–1960), the suffragettes° formed a breakaway women's suffrage group in 1903. Convinced that the mainstream suffragists' tactics such as signing petitions, publishing reasoned arguments, and lobbying politicians would never win the vote, the suffragettes threw respectability to the winds. They adopted as their motto the slogan "Deeds, Not Words," and declared that women would never earn the vote through rational persuasion. Instead, they had to grab it by force. The suffragettes broke up political meetings with the cry "Votes for Women!," chained themselves to the steps of the Houses of Parliament, shattered shop windows, burned churches, destroyed mailboxes, and even, in a direct attack on a cherished citadel of male middle-class culture, vandalized golf courses.

In opting for violence, the suffragettes staged a full frontal assault on a central fortification of middle-class culture—the ideal of the passive, homebound woman. The fortress they were attacking proved well-defended, however. Their opponents reacted with fury. Police broke up suffragette rallies with sexually focused brutality: They dragged suffragettes by their hair, stomped on their crotches, punched their breasts, and tore off their blouses. Once in jail, hunger-striking suffragettes endured the horror of forced feedings. Several jailers pinned the woman to her bed while the doctor thrust a plastic tube down her throat, often lacerating her larynx in the process, and pumped in food until she gagged.

# Conclusion

## The West in an Age of Mass Politics

The clash between the suffragettes and their jailers was only one of a multitude of encounters, many of them violent, among those seeking access to political power and those seeking to limit that access, in the era from 1870 to the start of World War I in 1914. At the same time, changing patterns of industrialization and accelerated urbanization gave rise to other sorts of encounters—between the manager seeking to cut production costs and the employee aiming to protect his wages, for example, or among the newly arrived immigrants in the city, struggling to survive in an unfamiliar culture, and the long-established residents who spoke a different language.

Out of such encounters emerged key questions about the definition of "the West." Where, for example, did the West end? Did it include Russia? "Yes," replied the small revolutionary groups who embraced Karl Marx's socialist theories and argued that Russia would follow Western patterns of economic and political development. Other Russian revolutionaries, however, rejected Western models and sought a revolutionary path unique to Russia. The expansion of the franchise and the processes of making nations raised even more fundamental questions. Was the West defined by democracy? Should it be? Was it synonymous with white, western European men or could people with olive-colored or black skin—or women of any color—participate fully in Western culture and politics? Was "the West" defined by its rationality? In the eighteenth century, Enlightenment thinkers had praised the power of human rationality and looked to reason as the path to social improvement. The rise of a new style of politics, based on emotional appeal and often irrational racist hatred, challenged this faith in reason. But at the same time, developments in industrial organization and technologies, which helped expand European national incomes, seemed to point to the benefits of rational processes.

As we will see in the next chapter, the expansion of Western control over vast areas of Asia and Africa in this

period led an increasing number of Europeans and Americans to highlight economic prosperity and technological superiority as the defining characteristics of the West. Confidence, however, was accompanied by anxiety as these years also witnessed a far-reaching cultural and intellectual crisis. Closely connected to the development of mass politics and changes in social and gender relations, this crisis slowly eroded many of the pillars of middle- and upper-class society and raised searching questions about Western assumptions and values.

## Suggestions for Further Reading

For a comprehensive listing of suggested readings, please go to www.ablongman.com/levack2e/chapter22

Evans, Richard. *The Feminists: Women's Emancipation Movements in Europe, America, and Australasia, 1840–1920.* 1977. A helpful comparative overview.

Kern, Stephen. *The Culture of Time and Space, 1880–1918.* 1983. An innovative work that explores the cultural impact of technological change.

Lidtke, Vernon. *The Alternative Culture: Socialist Labor in Imperial Germany.* 1985. Looks beyond the world of parliamentary politics to assess the meaning and impact of working-class socialism.

Lindemann, Albert. *Esau's Tears: Modern Anti-Semitism and the Rise of the Jews.* 1997. A comprehensive and detailed survey that challenges many assumptions about the roots and nature of modern anti-Semitism.

Mayer, Arno. *The Persistence of the Old Regime: Europe to the Great War.* 1981. Argues that landed elites maintained a considerable amount of economic and political power throughout the nineteenth century.

Milward, A. S., and S. B. Saul. *The Development of the Economies of Continental Europe, 1850–1914.* 1977. A helpful survey.

Moch, Leslie. *Moving Europeans: Migration in Western Europe Since 1650.* 1992. Filled with maps and packed with information, Moch's work explodes many easy assumptions about the movement of Europeans in the nineteenth century.

Nord, Philip. *The Republican Moment: Struggles for Democracy in Nineteenth-Century France.* 1996. Illuminates the struggle to define and redefine France.

Pilbeam, Pamela. *The Middle Classes in Europe, 1789–1914: France, Germany, Italy, and Russia.* 1990. A comparative approach that helps clarify the patterns of social change.

Richards, Thomas. *The Commodity Culture of Victorian England: Advertising and Spectacle, 1851–1914.* 1990. Fascinating study of the manufacturing of desire.

Stearns, Peter N. *Lives of Labor: Work in a Maturing Industrial Society.* 1975. Explores changing economic and social patterns.

Steenson, Gary P. *After Marx, Before Lenin: Marxism and Socialist Working-Class Parties in Europe, 1884–1914.* 1991. Examines both ideology and political practice within Europe's socialist parties.

Weber, Eugen. *Peasants into Frenchmen: The Modernization of Rural France, 1870–1914.* 1976. A very important work that helped shape the way historians think about "nation making."

## Notes

1. Leslie Moch, *Moving Europeans: Migration in Western Europe Since 1650* (1992), 147.

2. Quoted in Eugen Weber, *Peasants into Frenchmen: The Modernization of Rural France, 1870–1914* (1976), 332–333.

3. Norman Kleeblatt, *The Dreyfus Affair: Art, Truth, and Justice* (1987), 96.

4. Quoted in Eric Cahm, *The Dreyfus Affair in French Society and Politics* (1994), 167.

5. Quoted in Robert Gildea, *Barricades and Borders: Europe, 1800–1914* (1987), 317.

6. Quoted in Leslie Derfler, *Socialism Since Marx: A Century of the European Left* (1973), 58.

7. Karl Kautsky, quoted in Eric Hobsbawm, *The Age of Empire, 1875–1914* (1987), 133.

8. Eugen Weber, *France, Fin-de-Siècle* (1986), 126.

9. Albert Lindemann, *Esau's Tears: Modern Anti-Semitism and the Rise of the Jews* (1997).

10. Maria Desraismes, "La Femme et Le Droit," *Eve dans l'humanite* (1891), 16–17.

# The West and the World: Cultural Crisis and the New Imperialism, 1870–1914

# 23

IN THE AUTUMN OF 1898, BRITISH TROOPS MOVED INTO THE SUDAN IN NORTHeast Africa to claim the region for the British Empire. On September 2, the British Camel Corps faced an army of 40,000 fighters. The Sudanese soldiers, Islamic believers known as dervishes who possessed a reputation for military fierceness, were fighting on their home ground against an invading force. Nevertheless, after only five hours of fighting, 11,000 dervishes lay dead. Their opponents lost just forty men. While the dervishes, armed with swords and spears, surged forward in a full-scale frontal assault, the British troops sat safely behind fortified defenses, and, using repeating rifles and Maxim guns (a type of early machine gun), simply mowed down their attackers. According to one participant on the British side, the future prime minister Winston Churchill, the biggest danger to the British soldiers during the battle of Omdurman was boredom: "The mere physical act [of loading, firing, and reloading] became tedious." The dervishes had little chance of boredom. Churchill recalled, "And all the time out on the plain on the other side bullets were shearing through flesh, smashing and splintering bone; blood spouted from terrible wounds; valiant men were struggling through a hell of whistling metal, exploding shells, and spurting dust—suffering, despairing, dying."[1]

The slaughter of 11,000 Sudanese in just over five hours formed but one episode in what many historians call the age of new imperialism, a period that witnessed both the culmination of, and a new phase in, Europe's conquest of the globe. This often-violent encounter between Europe and the regions that Europeans emphatically defined as non-Western was closely connected to the political and economic upheavals examined in Chapter 22. An understanding of the new imperialism, however, demands a close look not

---

**Paul Gauguin, *Matamoe* ("Peacocks in the Country"), 1892** The Fauvist painter Paul Gauguin fled Europe for Tahiti in an effort to restore to his art the strong colors and emotions that he believed characterized non-Western cultures. The sights, sensibilities, and symbolism of Tahitian society profoundly affected his painting—and helped shape modernist art.

only at political rivalries and economic structures, but also at scientific, intellectual, and cultural developments in the last third of the nineteenth century. At the same time that European and American adventurers risked life and limb to chart Africa's rivers, exploit its resources, and subjugate its peoples, Western artists and scientists embarked on explorations into worlds of thought and perception far deeper than the surface reality accessible to the senses, and in so doing challenged the social order and even the meaning of reality itself. The final decades of the nineteenth century and the opening years of the twentieth thus comprised an era of internal fragmentation and external expansion.

This chapter examines the scientific, artistic, and physical explorations that characterized the period between 1870 and 1914 to answer a key question: In what ways did these explorations redefine the West and its relationship with the rest of the world? Three more specific questions guide this examination:

■ How did scientific developments during this period lead to not only greater intellectual and cultural optimism but also deepened anxiety?
■ What factors led many Europeans in this period to believe they were living in a time of cultural crisis?
■ What were the causes and consequences of the new imperialist ideology for both the West and non-Western societies?

# Scientific Transformations

■ How did scientific developments during this period lead to not only greater intellectual and cultural optimism but also deepened anxiety?

During the final third of the nineteenth century, Europeans encountered in new ways both the human body and the wider physical universe. Forced by urbanization to cram more bodies into limited space, men and women grew increasingly aware of the human body, and of the way it interacted with other bodies, both human and microscopic. At the same time, the work of geologists and biologists highlighted the way the body itself had evolved to meet the challenges of survival, while the experiments of chemists and physicists revealed the inadequacies of accepted models for understanding the physical world.

These developments affirmed a central assumption of the dominant middle-class worldview—that human reason and endeavor can guarantee social, intellectual, and moral progress. Scientific advances in the final third of the nineteenth century helped improve the health and hygiene of the Western world. Yet these changes in scientific understandings of both the body and the cosmos also threatened

to destabilize Western society and therefore deepened the cultural anxiety of Europeans and Americans in this period.

## Medicine and Microbes

In the second half of the nineteenth century, and particularly after 1870, a series of developments transformed the practice of Western medicine. Before this time, Western physicians assumed that illness was caused by bad blood and so relied on practices such as leeching (attaching leeches to the skin) and bloodletting (slicing open a vein). These procedures drained large amounts of blood, further weakening already ill patients. Admission into a hospital was sometimes a death sentence. Ignorant of the existence of bacteria and viruses, doctors commonly attended one patient after another without bothering to wash their hands or surgical instruments. The only anesthetic available was alcohol; pain was regarded as inevitable, something to be endured rather than eased.

Urbanization posed a fundamental challenge to such traditional medical practice and helped transform Western medicine. Expanding urban populations served as fertile seedbeds for contagious diseases. Cholera outbreaks, such as the epidemics that ravaged British cities in 1831 and 1848, forced doctors and public officials to pay attention to the relationship between overcrowding, polluted water, and epidemic disease. Hamburg was one of the first cities to undertake the construction of a modern water and sewer system in 1842; in 1848 the London cholera epidemic persuaded public officials to build a vast sewer system (most of which is still in use today).

It was not until the 1860s, however, that germ theory was developed. By exploring the transmission of disease among plants and animals in the French agricultural industry, the chemist Louis Pasteur (1822–1895) discovered the source of contagion to be microscopic living organisms—bacteria. Astonishingly productive, Pasteur developed vaccines against anthrax, hog fever, sheep pox, various poultry and cattle diseases, and rabies. (His process of purifying milk and fermented products is still known as pasteurization.) Following Pasteur, Robert Koch (1843–1910), professor of public health in Berlin, isolated the tuberculosis bacillus in 1882 and the bacteria that cause cholera in 1883.

The work of Pasteur, Koch, and other scientists in tracing the transmission of disease was crucial in improving Western medical practice. Between 1872 and 1900, the number of European deaths from infectious diseases dropped by 60 percent. Once physicians and surgeons accepted that microscopic organisms caused disease, they began to develop techniques to control their spread. The development of antiseptic surgery in the later 1860s improved the patient's odds of surviving the operating table.

The increasing use of anesthetics in the second half of the nineteenth century also improved those odds. In 1847 a

Scottish physician performed the first delivery of a baby using chloroform to dull the mother's pain. Although condemned by many Christian theologians (who regarded pain as both ennobling and a necessary part of sinful human existence), the use of anesthetics spread fairly quickly. Britain's Queen Victoria, who gave birth to nine children, probably articulated the feelings of many patients when she greeted the use of anesthetics in the delivery room with unfettered delight: "Oh blessed chloroform!"

Medical advances such as anesthetic techniques and an understanding of how diseases are spread gave Europeans genuine confidence that the conquest of nature through science would create a healthier environment. But the widespread awareness of germs also heightened anxiety. Isolation of the bacilli that caused an illness did not immediately translate into its cure, and viral infections remained often lethal. Measles, for example, continued to kill at least 7,000 people per year in Britain throughout the nineteenth century. After the 1870s, Europeans were aware that they lived in a world populated by potentially deadly but invisible organisms, carried on the bodies of their servants, their employees, their neighbors, and their family members. Those who could afford to isolate themselves from the danger often did so. As a result, this era witnessed striking growth in the number of seaside resorts as middle- and upper-class Europeans fled from urban centers of contagion.

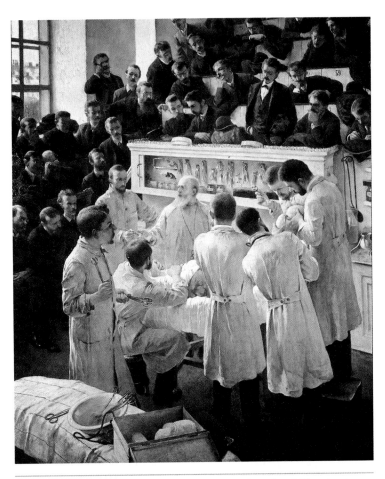

**Adelbert Seligmann, *German Surgeon Theodor Billroth at Work in Vienna* (1890)**
Modern surgery in the making: The patient has been anesthetized, but the modern operating room does not yet exist, nor are the doctors wearing gloves or masks. Billroth, the director of the Second Surgical Clinic in Vienna, pioneered surgical techniques for gastrointestinal illnesses and cancer.

## The Triumph of Evolutionary Science

Developments in geology and biology also led to both confidence and anxiety. Evolutionary science provided a scientific framework in which educated Europeans could understand and justify their own superior social and economic positions. It also, however, challenged basic religious assumptions and depicted the natural world in new and unsettling ways.

Traditionally, Europeans had relied on the opening chapters of the Bible to understand the origins of both nature and humanity. By the 1830s, however, the work of geologists challenged the biblical account. Although a literal reading of the Bible dated the Earth at only 6,000 years old, geologists such as Charles Lyell (1797–1875) argued on the basis of the fossil record and existing geological formations that the Earth had formed over millions of years. Lyell's most famous work was the *Principles of Geology,* first published in 1830 and a nineteenth-century best-seller that

went through eleven editions. In three volumes of very readable prose, packed with illustrative examples, Lyell gently but rigorously refuted the orthodox Christian position that geological change and the extinction of species could be explained by the biblical account of the flood or other such supernatural interventions. Instead, he and others argued that the material world must be seen as the product of natural forces still at work, still observable today.

But how could one explain the tremendous variety of plant and animal species in the world on the basis of natural processes? In 1859, the British scientist Charles Darwin (1809–1882) answered this question in a way that proved quite satisfying to large numbers of educated Europeans—and quite horrifying to others. Darwin had spent two decades thinking about the data he collected during a five-year expedition to the South Pacific in the 1830s. Serving as an unpaid naturalist on the H.M.S. *Beagle* between 1831

**Darwin's Disturbing Mirror**
Simplified and often ridiculous versions of Darwin's ideas almost immediately entered popular culture. Here a monkey version of Darwin holds up a mirror to his fellow creature, who seems surprised by his reflection.

Darwin concluded that life is a struggle for survival, and that even quite small biological variations might help an individual member of a species win out in this struggle. From this understanding came the Darwinian theory° of the evolution of species.

Darwin's evolutionary hypothesis rested on two basic ideas: *variation* and *natural selection.* Variation refers to the small but crucial biological advantages that assist in the struggle for survival: A bird with a slightly longer beak, for example, might gain easier access to scarce food supplies. Over generations, the individuals more adapted for survival displace those without the positive variation. Variation, then, provides the means of natural selection, the process by which new species evolve.

Darwin provided a persuasive explanation for evolutionary change, but the fact that the laws of genetic heredity were not yet understood resulted in two key weaknesses in his formulation—first, its extreme gradualness, in that the process of variation required many, many generations; and second, the lack of a precise explanation of how variations first emerge and how they are inherited. Answers to both problems lay embedded in the research of an Austrian monk, Gregor Mendel (1822–1884). Experimenting in his vegetable garden with what we now call selective breeding, Mendel developed the laws of genetic heredity. Mendel's work was ignored almost completely until the end of the century, when the Dutch botanist Hugo DeVries (1848–1935) used his data to hypothesize that evolution occurred through radical mutations in the reproductive cells of an organism. These mutations are passed on to offspring at the moment of reproduction and, if they offer an advantage in the struggle for existence, enable the offspring to survive and to produce more mutant offspring. Thus evolution can proceed by leaps, rather than gradually over a very long period of time.

Long before these genetic underpinnings of evolution were understood, however, Darwin's theories proved extraordinarily influential. Published in 1859, *The Origin of Species* aroused immediate interest and controversy. This controversy intensified when, in 1871, Darwin published *The Descent of Man,* in which he firmly placed humanity itself within the evolutionary process. Many Christians reacted with horror to a theory that they believed challenged the biblical narrative of Creation and denied a special place for humankind within the physical universe. But the most troubling aspect of Darwin's theory was its view of nature. According to orthodox Christian theology, nature, like the Bible, reveals God to the believer. In the Darwinian universe, however, nature was not a harmonious, well-ordered system that revealed the hand of God. Instead, it was the arena of brutal and bloody competition for survival—"nature red in tooth and claw," as the British poet Alfred Lord Tennyson put it. In such a universe, ideas of purpose and

**DOCUMENT**

On Darwin (1860s)

and 1836, Darwin observed that certain species of animal and plant life, isolated on islands, had developed differently from related species on the coast. After returning to Britain, Darwin read the population theory of Thomas Malthus (1766–1834). Malthus argued that population growth would outstrip food supply, and that in all species, more offspring are produced than can actually survive. Putting together Malthus's theory with his own observations,

## DOCUMENT

### *The Descent of Man*

*First published in 1871,* The Descent of Man *continued and completed Charles Darwin's theory of the evolution of species first introduced in his* Origin of Species *(1859). Darwin's work in many ways affirmed central prejudices and assumptions of his middle-class readers, as the following excerpts demonstrate.*

We have now seen that man is variable in body and mind; and that the variations are induced, either directly or indirectly, by the same general causes, and obey the same general laws, as with the lower animals. Man has spread widely over the face of the earth, and must have been exposed, during his incessant migration, to the most diversified conditions.... The early progenitors of man must also have tended, like all other animals, to have increased beyond their means of subsistence; they must, therefore, occasionally have been exposed to a struggle for existence, and consequently, to the rigid law of natural selection. Beneficial variations of all kinds will thus, either occasionally or habitually, have been preserved and injurious ones eliminated....

Man in the rudest state in which he now exists is the most dominant animal that has ever appeared on this earth. He has spread more widely than any other highly organised form, and all others have yielded before him. He manifestly owes this immense superiority to his intellectual faculties, to his social habits, which lead him to aid and defend his fellows, and to his corporeal structure....

The belief that there exists in man some close relation between the size of the brain and the development of the intellectual faculties is supported by the comparison of the skulls of savage and civilized races, of ancient and modern people, and by the analogy of the whole vertebrate series ... the mean internal capacity of the skull in Europeans is 92.3 cubic inches; in Americans 87.5; in Asiatics 87.1; and in Australians only 81.9 inches.... Nevertheless, it must be admitted that some skulls of very high antiquity, such as the famous one of the Neanderthal, are well developed and capacious.

Source: From *The Descent of Man,* 2nd edition, by Charles Darwin, 1874.

meaning seemed to disappear. Faced with this disturbing vision, many Christians opposed Darwinian science.

Many other Christians, however, welcomed Darwin's evolutionary theory. They argued that evolution did not banish divine purpose from the universe but instead showed God's hand at work in the gradual development of more perfect species. Enthusiastically applying the idea of evolution to the ethical universe, they contended that the history of humanity showed that the morally fittest proved victorious in the ethical sphere, just as the strongest triumphed in the natural world.

By 1870, three-quarters of British scientists surveyed accepted evolutionary theory. More important, many middle-class Europeans and Americans welcomed Darwin's ideas as providing a coherent explanation of change that accorded with their worldview. They saw Darwin's work as a scientific confirmation of their faith in the virtues of competition and in the inevitability of progress. As Darwin himself wrote in *The Origin of Species,* because "natural selection works solely by and for the good of each being, all corporeal [bodily] and mental development will tend to progress toward perfection."

## Social Darwinism and Racial Hierarchies

Darwin's explanation of evolution contributed to a new understanding of biological relationships and of the connections between humanity and the natural world. In the last quarter of the nineteenth century, however, a growing number of writers and social theorists insisted that evolutionary theory could and should be applied more broadly. One of the most influential of this group was the British writer Herbert Spencer (1820–1902). Trained as a civil engineer, Spencer became convinced that evolution held the key to engineering a better human society. A self-confident, eminently practical thinker, Spencer coined the phrase "the survival of the fittest" to describe what he viewed as the most basic explanation of development in both nature and human society. He believed that human societies evolve like plant and animal species. Only the fittest, those able to adapt to changing conditions, survive. A great champion of *laissez-faire* economics (see Chapter 21), Spencer contended that government interference in economic and social affairs interfered with the natural evolutionary process and so hindered rather than assured progress.

Spencer's essentially biological vision of society proved influential in shaping the theories of Social Darwinism°. Arguing that racial hierarchy was the product of natural evolution, the Social Darwinists applied Spencer's ideas about the importance of individual competition and the survival of the fittest to entire races. In their view, the non-white races in Africa and Asia had lost the game. Their so-called backward way of life showed they had failed to compete successfully with white Europeans and thus displayed their biological inferiority. The very popular British novelist Rider Haggard, in his best-selling thriller *She* (1887), summed up the Social Darwinist worldview: "Those who are weak must perish; the earth is to the strong . . . We run to place and power over the dead bodies of those who fail and fall; ay, we win the food we eat from out the mouths of starving babes. It is the scheme of things."

In their effort to construct a scientifically based racial hierarchy, Social Darwinists made use not only of Darwin's idea of natural selection but also of the theory of "recapitulation," first proposed by the German zoologist Ernst Haeckel (1834–1919). According to Haeckel, as an individual matures, he or she moves through the same stages as did the human race during the course of its evolution. For example, the gill slits of a human embryo "recapitulate" the fish stage through which the human race had evolved. The idea of recapitulation enabled scientists to fill in the gaps left by the fossil record. By observing the development of children into adults, they argued, we can witness the evolutionary maturation of the human race.

Social Darwinists used the theory of recapitulation to argue that only white European males had reached the pinnacle of evolutionary development. They contended that nonwhite men, as well as all women, embodied the more primitive stages of evolution through which the white European male had already passed. In other words, the nonwhite races and white women were suffering from arrested development. Their bodies and brains bore witness to their low-ranking position on the evolutionary ladder. Such ideas permeated much of Western culture in the late nineteenth century. Sigmund Freud, for example, argued that "the female genitalia are more primitive than those of the male," while Gustave LeBon compared the average female brain to that of a gorilla. G. A. Henty, a best-selling British novelist, insisted that the "intelligence of the average negro is about equal to that of a European [male] child of ten years old."[2]

Firmly convinced that the inferiority of women and nonwhites was a biological fact, nineteenth-century scientists and large sections of the European public welcomed evolutionary theory as scientific proof of deeply embedded cultural assumptions, such as the benefits of competition, the rightness of white rule and male dominance, and the superiority of Western civilization. Yet evolutionary science also worked to undermine European confidence because with the idea of evolution came the possibility of regression: Was the traffic on the evolutionary ladder all one-way, or could species descend to a lower evolutionary level? Could humanity regress to its animal origins?

The concept of the "inheritance of acquired characteristics," associated with the work of the French scientist Jean-Baptiste Lamarck (1744–1829), played a crucial role in fostering these fears of regression. More than fifty years before Darwin published his *Origin of Species,* Lamarck theorized that acquired characteristics—traits that an individual develops in response to experience or the environment, such as

the stooped back of a miner, the poor vision of a lace maker, or the deep tan of an agricultural laborer—could be passed on to the individual's offspring. Because the process of genetic reproduction was not understood until the twentieth century, Lamarck's theories remained very influential throughout the nineteenth century and possessed deeply disturbing implications. Middle-class Europeans began to speculate that the conditions of urban industrial life were producing undesirable characteristics among urban workers. In their view, characteristics such as physical weakness, sexual promiscuity, and violent criminality were being passed from one generation to the next and were threatening to reverse the evolutionary ascent of Western civilization.

## The Revolution in Physics

Darwin's work revolutionized the field of biology. Between 1880 and 1910 a revolution in physics occurred as well. Although the most dramatic consequences of this revolution—atomic weapons and nuclear energy—would not be realized for another half century, this transformation in scientific understanding contributed to both the exhilaration and the uncertainty that characterized the intellectual and cultural history of Europe in the decades before World War I.

At the core of the revolution in physics lay the question, "What is matter?" For most of the nineteenth century, the answer was simple: Matter was what close observation and measurement, as well as common sense, showed it to be. Material bodies, made up of the building blocks called atoms, rested and moved against a fixed backdrop of space and time. Matter was three-dimensional, defined by height, width, and depth. Accessible to reason, observation, and common sense, the material world could be understood and controlled. The triumph of the theories of Isaac Newton had ensured that for 200 years, educated Westerners regarded the natural world as a precise and predictable machine (see Chapter 16).

As the new century opened, this picture of the universe began to crumble. A series of discoveries and experiments challenged this commonsense view of the universe and offered in its place a much more mysterious and unsettling vista. The discovery of the X-ray in 1895 had already disrupted prevailing assumptions about the solidity and predictability of matter. They were shaken even further in 1898 when the Polish-French chemist Marie Curie (1867–1934) discovered a new element, radium, which did not behave the way matter was supposed to behave. Because it continually emitted subatomic particles, radium did not possess a constant atomic weight. Two years later, the German scientist Max Planck (1858–1947) theorized that a heated body radiates energy not in the continuous, steady, predictable stream most scientists envisaged, but rather in irregular clumps, which he called *quanta.* Although at first dismissed by most scientists as contrary to common sense, Planck's quantum theory accorded with the emerging picture of a changeable universe.

These scientific discoveries provide the context for the work of Albert Einstein (1879–1955), certainly the most famous and readily recognizable scientist of the twentieth century. Bored by his job as a patent clerk, Einstein passed the time speculating on the nature of the cosmos. In 1905, he rang the death knell for the Newtonian universe by publishing an article that introduced to the world the theory of relativity. Einstein rejected the nineteenth-century assumption of the absolute nature of time and space. Instead, he argued, time and space shift relative to the position of the observer. Similarly, matter itself shifts. Mass depends on motion, and thus time, space, and matter intermingle in a universe of relative flux. The result of Einstein's vision was a revolution in perspective. The universe is not three- but four-dimensional: To height, width, and depth, Einstein added *time*.

This new understanding was much harder to grasp than that offered by Newtonian science. With the revolution in physics, much of science became incomprehensible to ordinary men and women, even educated ones. The new science also challenged the basic assumptions that governed nineteenth-century thought by offering a vision of the universe in which what you see is *not* what you get, in which objective reality might well be the product of subjective perception.

## Social Thought: The Revolt Against Positivism

Just as the revolution in physics presented a new and more disturbing picture of the physical universe, so social thinkers in the last third of the nineteenth century began to formulate troubling theories about the nature of human society. As Chapter 21 explained, the mainstream of nineteenth-century thought was positivist: It placed great faith in human reason and therefore in the validity of applying methods drawn from the natural sciences to the study of human affairs. Positivism viewed the world as eminently knowable and progress as ultimately guaranteed, given the capacity of rational human beings to understand and therefore control both physical and human nature. This faith in human reason, however, came under attack in the last decades of the century. In this era, social thinkers (writers and scientists whose work would lay the foundations for new academic disciplines such as sociology, psychology, and anthropology) began to emphasize the role of nonrational forces in determining human conduct.

Social thinkers confronted the power of the nonrational first in the new mass politics of this era. The rise of racist and nationalist political parties demonstrated that individuals were often swayed more by emotion than by rational argument. In an effort to understand and therefore to manipulate political demonstrations, the French theorist Gustave LeBon (1841–1931) developed the discipline of crowd or collective psychology. He showed how appeals to emotion, particularly in the form of symbols and myths, can influence crowd behavior. In LeBon's view, democracy relinquished political control to the easily swayed masses and so would lead only to disaster.

Unlike LeBon, the German social theorist Max Weber (1864–1920) believed in democracy, but he, too, recognized the role of the nonrational in influencing the mass electorate. Weber was both fascinated and frightened by the development of modern industrial society. His studies focused on the "bureaucratization" of modern life—the tendency of both political and economic institutions to become increasingly standardized and to grow ever larger and more impersonal. Weber judged the triumph of bureaucracy as the victory of reason and science over individual prejudice and interest-group politics, and so as a generally progressive force. But at the same time he recognized that because growing bureaucracies could crush both ideals and individuals, they posed a real threat to personal and political freedom. Troubled by the vision of individuals trapped within "the iron cage of modern life," Weber in 1898 suffered a nervous breakdown. After four years Weber was able to free himself from the grip of debilitating depression, but he remained profoundly pessimistic about the future, which he described as "a polar night of icy darkness and hardness."[3]

According to his wife, when Weber fell into depression, "an evil something out of the subterranean unconscious . . . grasped him by its claws."[4] This view of the individual as a captive of the unconscious was central to the revolt against positivism and reached its fullest development in the highly influential work of the Viennese scientist and physician Sigmund Freud (1856–1939). Freud argued that the conscious mind plays only a very limited role in shaping the actions of each individual. His effort to treat patients suffering from nervous disorders led him to hypnosis and dream analysis, and to the conviction that behind the conscious exterior existed a deeper, far more significant reality—the unconscious. In *The Interpretation of Dreams* (1900), Freud argued that beneath the rational surface of each human being surge all kinds of hidden desires, including such irrational drives as the longing for death and destruction.

Freud thought of himself as a scientist. He believed that he could understand human behavior (and treat mental illness) by diving below the rational surface and exploring the submerged terrain of unconscious desire. Yet the emergence of Freudian psychology convinced many educated Western individuals not that the irrational could be uncovered and controlled, but rather that the irrational was *in* control.

# Cultural Crisis:
# The Fin-de-Siècle and the
# Birth of Modernism

■ What factors led many Europeans in this period to believe they were living in a time of cultural crisis?

The growing recognition of the power of irrational forces in shaping human society contributed to a growing cultural crisis. The sense of crisis, and more specifically the fear that Western civilization was declining, that degeneration and decay characterized the contemporary experience, was summed up in a single French phrase: fin-de-siècle°. Literally translated as "end of the century," fin-de-siècle served as a shorthand term for the mood of cultural uneasiness, and even despair, that characterized much of European society in the final decades of the nineteenth century and the opening years of the twentieth. Uncertainty colored many aspects of European thought and culture. Fast-moving economic and social change, coupled with the new scientific ideas, convinced many Europeans that old solutions were no longer sufficient. The quest for new answers fostered the birth of what would become known as *modernism,* a broad label for a series of unsettling developments in thought, literature, and art. Many Europeans celebrated modernism as a release from the restraints imposed by middle-class cultural codes. Others, however, responded fearfully. Both exhilaration and anxiety, then, characterize this time of cultural crisis.

**Edgar Degas, *Absinthe* (1876–1877)**
Parisian café-goers often indulged in absinthe, a strong alcoholic drink flavored with anise. Degas's portrait of one such absinthe drinker is a picture of deterioration: This woman's lined face and weary posture, as well as her sense of isolation, provide an evocative image of the fin-de-siècle.

## The Fin-de-Siècle

A series of social problems common to increasingly urbanized nations reinforced Europeans' fear of degeneration. As cities spread, so too did the perception of a rising crime rate. This perception of a more criminal society went hand-in-hand with the reality of increasing drug and alcohol use. Diners in high society finished their sumptuous meals with a dessert course consisting of strawberries soaked in ether; respectable bourgeois men offered each other cocaine as a quick "pick-me-up" at the end of the working day; middle-class mothers fed restless babies opium-laced syrups; workers bought enough opium-derived laudanum on Saturday afternoon to render them unconscious until work on Monday morning. Using Lamarck's theory of the inheritance of acquired characteristics, scientists contended that addictions could be passed on from generation to generation, thus contributing to national decline and a culture of decadence.

Popular novels of the fin-de-siècle also contributed to the fear of degeneration by depicting Western culture as diseased or barbaric. In a twenty-volume work, the French novelist Émile Zola (1840–1902) traced the decline of a once-proud family to symbolize the decay of all of France. As alcoholism and sexual promiscuity pollute succeeding generations, the family disintegrates. In *Nana* (1880), Zola used the title character, a prostitute, to embody his country. Watching as French soldiers march off to defeat in the Franco-Prussian War, Nana is dying of smallpox, her face "a charnel-house, a heap of pus and blood, a shovelful of putrid flesh."[5] Novels such as *Dr. Jekyll and Mr. Hyde* (1886) and *Dracula* (1897) showed that beneath the cultured exterior of a civilized man lurked a primitive, bloodthirsty beast and so revealed a deep sense of anxiety.

The most influential advocate of the idea that Western culture had degenerated was the German philosopher and poet Friedrich Nietzsche (1844–1900). In Nietzsche's view, most people were little more than sheep, penned in by outdated customs and conventions. Bourgeois morality, rooted in Christianity, helped sap Western culture of its vitality. "Christianity has taken the side of everything weak," Nietzsche claimed. He traced the weakness of Western culture beyond Christianity, however, and back to ancient Greece, to Socrates' exaltation of rationality. In Nietzsche's view, an overemphasis on rational thought had deprived Western culture of the power of more primal urges, such as the irrational, emotional, and instinctive aspects of human nature.

Even more fundamentally, Nietzsche argued that the belief that human reason has direct access to scientific fact is an illusion. Trained as a classical philologist, Nietzsche's study of language convinced him that everything we know must be filtered through a symbolic system—through language or some other means of artistic or mathematic representation. We can know only the representation, not the thing itself. Not even science can uncover "reality." Even the style of Nietzsche's publications worked to expose the limits of reason. Rather than write carefully constructed essays that proceeded in a logical, linear fashion from fact to fact, Nietzsche adopted an elusive, poetic style characterized by disconnected fragments, more accessible to intuitive understanding than to rational analysis.

Nietzsche's writings attracted little attention until the 1890s, when his ideas first exploded in Germany and Austria, and then spread throughout Europe. Nietzsche's call to "become what you are" attracted young enthusiasts, who embraced his conviction that the confining assumptions and aspirations of bourgeois society held back the individual from personal liberation. "God is dead," Nietzsche proclaimed, "and we have killed him." If God is dead, then "there is nobody who commands, nobody who obeys, nobody who trespasses."

## Tightening Gender Boundaries

The fear of degeneration evident throughout European culture and society in the last decades of the nineteenth century also expressed itself in a multifaceted effort to draw more tightly the boundaries around accepted definitions of "maleness" and "femaleness." Both the feminist and the homosexual joined the alcoholic, the drug addict, the prostitute, and the criminal in the list of dangerous and degenerate beings.

As discussed in Chapter 22, the years after 1850 and particularly after 1880 witnessed the birth of modern feminism. The emergence of legal, educational, and political reform campaigns challenged nineteenth-century middle-class domestic ideology. Antifeminists viewed these campaigns with alarm. They insisted that a woman's physiology demanded that she remain in the home. In the view of antifeminists, a woman who chose political activism or paid employment not only risked her own physical and mental

breakdown, she also tended to produce physically and morally degenerate children.

Like feminists, homosexuals were also singled out as threats to the social order. Before 1869, *homosexual* was not a word: Coined by a Hungarian scientist seeking a new label for a new concept, it entered the English language in 1890. Traditionally, Europeans and Americans had viewed same-sex sexual practice as a form of immoral behavior, indulged in by morally lax—but otherwise normal—men. (Few considered the possibility of female homosexual behavior.) In the last third of the nineteenth century, however, the emphasis shifted from *actions* to *identity,* from condemning a specific type of sexual behavior to denouncing a certain group of people now considered abnormal and dangerous. Scientists argued that "the homosexual" was diseased—and that he could communicate this disease to others.

These ideas gained in force as homosexual subcultures increased in number in European and American cities. The anonymity and mobility of urban life offered homosexuals the possibility of creating a space for themselves in which a new, more confident and assertive homosexual identity could be expressed. But these subcultures soon encountered fierce repression as the moral and medical condemnation of male homosexuality became enshrined in legislation. The Penal Code of the new Germany stipulated severe punishment for homosexuality, while the British government in 1885 made illegal all homosexual acts, even those between consenting adults in the privacy of their own home.

The new concern about homosexuality was nurtured by a wider anxiety about the man's role in society, an anxiety provoked not only by the challenge of feminism, but also by the economic changes associated with the rise of corporate capitalism (see Chapter 22). Required by liberal ideology to be aggressive, independent, self-reliant initiators, middle-class males increasingly found themselves bound to desks, demoted from being those who delivered orders to those who received them. No longer masters of their own fates, they were now bit players in the drama of corporate capitalism. Thus the fear of both feminism and homosexuality arose in part from the compelling need to shore up masculine identity.

The new science of sexuality also heightened this concern about the definition of the "normal" man and woman. During the final decades of the nineteenth century, scientists invaded the most intimate areas of human behavior and made important breakthroughs in the understanding of human reproduction and sexual physiology. In 1875, for example, a German physiologist discovered the basic process of fertilization—the union of male and female sex cells. Four years later, scientists for the first time witnessed, with the aid of the microscope, a sperm cell penetrating an egg. In the following decade, scientific research uncovered the link between hormonal secretions and sexual potency, affirmed the existence of erogenous zones, and began to explore the role of chromosomes in reproduction.

# The Trial of Oscar Wilde

In March 1895 the Marquis of Queensberry left a message with the porter of a gentleman's club in London. The message, written on Queensberry's calling card, read "To Oscar Wilde, posing as a *somdomite*." What Queensberry meant to write was *sodomite,* a common term for a man who engaged in sexual relations with other men. By handing the card to the porter, Queensberry openly accused Wilde, a celebrated novelist and playwright, of homosexual—and therefore criminal—activity. Ten years earlier the British Parliament had declared illegal all homosexual activity, even consensual relations between adults in a private home. Queensberry's accusation, then, was extremely serious. Oscar Wilde responded by suing Queensberry for libel—and set in motion a legal process that led to Wilde's imprisonment, and indirectly, to his early death.

Wilde made a reckless mistake when he chose to sue for libel, for in fact Queensberry had not libeled him. Wilde was a homosexual, and he and Queensberry's son, Lord Alfred Douglas, were lovers. Why, then, did Wilde dare to challenge Queensberry? Perhaps the fact that he was married, with two children, seemed to provide a certain shield against the charge of homosexuality. Or perhaps Wilde's successes as a novelist and playwright gave him a misguided sense of invulnerability. With

two of his plays currently appearing on the London stage to favorable reviews, Wilde stood at the pinnacle of his career in the spring of 1895.

Wilde had built that career on a deliberate flouting of middle-class codes of morality. He saw himself as an artist, and insisted that art should be freed from social convention and moral restraint. His "High Society" comedies about privileged elites living scandalous lives and exchanging witty epigrams were far from the morally uplifting drama expected by middle-class audiences.

He also used his public persona to attack the conventional, the respectable, and the orthodox. Widely recognized for his outrageous clothing and conversation, Wilde had consciously adopted the mannerisms of what nineteenth-

century Britons called a "dandy"— a well-dressed, irreverent, artistic, leisured, and most of all, effeminate man. Before the Oscar Wilde trial, such effeminacy did not serve as a sign of, or a code for, homosexual inclinations, but it did signal to many observers a lavish—and loose—lifestyle. Oscar Wilde, then, was a man many British men and women loved to hate.

Even so, when his trial opened Wilde appeared to be in a strong position, the prosecutor rather than the defendant. Because Wilde had Queensberry's card with the "sodomite" charge written right on it, Queensberry faced certain conviction unless he could show that Wilde had engaged in homosexual activity. Wilde knew, of course, that Queensberry would not risk bringing the legal spotlight to bear on his own son's homosexuality.

At first, Queensberry's attorney, Edward Carson, focused on Wilde's published works, trying to use Wilde's own words against him. It proved an ineffective strategy. On the witness stand, Wilde reveled in the attention and ran circles around Carson.

On the second day of the libel trial, however, Wilde's witticisms proved insufficient as Carson began to question him about

**Oscar Wilde and Lord Alfred Douglas**
Although the British government pursued its case against Wilde, it made no effort to put together a case against Douglas.

**Justice in History**

his frequent visits to a male brothel and his associations with a number of young, working-class men who worked as male prostitutes. Suddenly the issue was no longer the literary merit or moral worth of Wilde's published writings, but rather his sexual exploitation of working-class boys. At this point, Wilde withdrew his libel charge against Queensberry, and the court declared the marquis not guilty.

If Queensberry was not guilty of libel in calling Wilde a sodomite, then by clear implication, Wilde was guilty of homosexual activity and therefore a criminal. Within days he was charged with "gross indecency" with another male. The jury in that case failed to reach a verdict, but the state was determined to obtain a conviction and brought the charges again. Wilde was refused bail, and on May 20 he was back in court.

On May 25, 1895—just three months after Queensberry had left his misspelled message with the club porter—Wilde's promising literary career ended. He was found guilty of seven counts of gross indecency with other men. The presiding judge, Sir Alfred Wills, characterized the trial as "the worst case I have ever tried," and declared, "I shall under the circumstances be expected to pass the severest sentence the law allows. In my judgment it is totally inadequate for such a case." He sentenced Wilde to two years at hard labor. The physical punishment took its toll. Wilde died in 1900 at age 46.

In sentencing Wilde, Wills described him as "the centre of a circle of extensive corruption of the most hideous kind." How do we account for the intensity of Wills's language, as well as the severity of Wilde's sentence? Homosexual activity had long been condemned on religious grounds, but this condemnation grew much more fierce in the closing decades of the nineteenth century. In a time of rapid and threatening change, the marking of gender boundaries became a way to create and enforce social order. Wilde crossed those boundaries, and so had to be punished.

Moreover, by the end of the nineteenth century, the state had assumed new responsibilities. Desperate to enhance national strength in a period of heightened international competition, governments intervened in areas previously considered to be the domain of the private citizen. By the turn of the century, western European governments were compelling working-class parents to send their children to school, regulating the hours adults could work, supervising the sale of food and drugs, providing limited forms of old-age pensions and medical insurance—and policing sexual boundaries.

The policing of sexual boundaries became easier after the Wilde trial because it provided a homosexual personality profile, a "Wanted" poster to hang on the walls of Western culture. For many observers of his very well-publicized trial, Wilde became the embodiment of "the homosexual," a particular and peculiar type of person, and a menace to cultural stability. The Wilde trial linked "dandyism" to the new image of the homosexual. Outward stylistic choices such as effeminacy, artistic sensibilities, and flamboyant clothing and conversation became, for many observers, the telltale signs of substantial inner corruption. Thus the Wilde case marked an important turning point in the construction, as well as the condemnation, of a homosexual identity.

## Questions of Justice

1. How does this trial illustrate the role of medical, legal, and cultural assumptions in shaping sexual identity in the late nineteenth century?
2. Did the trial of Oscar Wilde achieve justice? If so, of what kind and for whom?

## Taking It Further

*An Ideal Husband.* 1999. A film adaptation of Oscar Wilde's very funny play, which exemplifies his lighthearted but devastating critique of conventional manners and morals.

Ellman, Richard. *Oscar Wilde.* 1988. An important biography of Wilde.

Hyde, H. Montgomery. *The Trials of Oscar Wilde.* 1962. Includes extensive quotations from the trial transcripts as well as photographs of some of the documentary evidence.

McLaren, Angus. *The Trials of Masculinity: Policing Sexual Boundaries, 1870–1930.* 1997. Places the Wilde trial within a wider cultural context.

This greater understanding of sexual *physiology* went hand in hand with the effort to apply the scientific method to sexual *practice*. With data drawn from biology, anthropology, and human physiology, scientists in Europe and the United States sought to define "normal" sexual behavior. In seven weighty volumes, the British scientist Havelock Ellis (1859–1939) explored the range of child and adult sexuality. Ellis used his data to argue for sex education, legalization of contraception and nudism, and tolerance of homosexuality. Other sex researchers, however, turned to science to buttress middle-class moral codes. The German scientist Richard von Krafft-Ebing labeled homosexuality a pathology in 1886, while many publications condemned masturbation and frequent sexual intercourse. Other works offered support for antifeminism by arguing that female physiology incapacitated women for public life.

Heightened concern about gender boundaries also pervaded the visual art of late-nineteenth-century Europe. Women often appeared as elemental forces, creatures of nature rather than civilization, who threatened to trap, emasculate, engulf, suffocate, or destroy the unwary man. In *Medicine*, by the Austrian painter Gustav Klimt (1862–1918), the liquid portraits of women flow between and into images of sex and death in a disturbing and powerful painting. Such images recur even more graphically in the work of Klimt's student, Egon Schiele (1890–1918). In his very short life Schiele created more than 3,000 works on paper and 300 paintings, many of these depictions of the dangerous female. In works such as *Black-Haired Girl with Raised Skirt* (1911), harsh colors and brazen postures present an unsettling vision of female sexuality. A series of Schiele's paintings with titles such as *Dead Mother* place children in the arms of dead or expressionless women—a direct challenge to the middle-class glorification of motherhood.

## The Birth of Modernism

Schiele's disturbing paintings exemplify the new modernist movement. Although the term modernism° was not commonly used until the 1920s, the main developments it embraced were well underway by 1914. It is a difficult term to define, in part because it refers to a variety of artistic, literary, and intellectual styles. Despite this variety, however, modernist art and literature expressed a set of common attitudes and assumptions that centered on a rejection of established authority. In the final decades of the nineteenth century, many artists tossed aside accepted standards and rules and embarked on a series of bold experiments. Oscar Wilde (1854–1900), the British playwright whose dramas mocked Victorian conventions and outraged middle-class sensibilities, wrote, "It is enough that our fathers believed. They have exhausted the faith-faculty of the species. Their legacy to us is the skepticism of which they were afraid."[6]

**Gustav Klimt, *Medicine* (1901)**
Klimt was commissioned by the University of Vienna to create a work that would celebrate medicine's great achievements. Not surprisingly, the painting he produced provoked great controversy. The woman in the forefront is Hygeia, the Greek goddess of health, but behind her swim images of female sexuality and death. Klimt's paintings often featured women as alluring but engulfing elemental forces.

At the core of modernism was a questioning of all accepted standards and truths, particularly those that shaped the middle-class liberal worldview.

In that liberal worldview, the arts served a useful purpose and were a vital part of civilized society. Going to art galleries, for example, was a popular activity, rather like going to the movies today. Respectable workers and middle-class men and women crowded into exhibitions where they viewed paintings that told an entertaining story and had a clear moral message. Modernism shattered this community between artist and audience. It rejected the idea of art as an instrument of moral or emotional uplift. Modernists argued that art is autonomous—it stands alone, of value in and of itself rather than for any impact it may have on society. Modernist painters, for example, did not seek to tell a story or to preach a sermon, but rather to experiment with line, color, and composition.

In addition to rejecting the idea that art must be useful, modernists also challenged middle-class liberalism by insisting that history is irrelevant. Nineteenth-century culture was "historicist." Fascinated with the process of change over time—with the evolution not only of species but also of ideas and societies—the middle-class mindset viewed history as the orderly forward march of progress. In contrast, modernists argued that fast-moving industrial and technological change had shattered the lines connecting history and modernity. Painters such as the Futurists in Italy and the Vorticists in Britain (two of the many artistic movements that clustered under the modernist umbrella) reveled in the new machine age, a world cut off from anything that had gone before. In their paintings they depicted human beings as machines in motion, moving too fast to be tied down to history.

New musical styles emerging in both popular and high culture in these decades also demonstrated the modernist sense of discontinuity. Ragtime, for example, combined syncopation with unexpected rhythms and sudden stops, while jazz, which developed around the turn of the century in black urban neighborhoods in the United States, created a musical universe of constant change. At the same time, symphonic musicians such as Russian composer Igor Stravinsky (1882–1971) and his Austrian counterpart Arnold Schoenberg (1874–1951) shocked their audiences by tossing aside the convention that a piece should state a central theme, which is then repeated in a sequence of variations. In Stravinsky's ballet *The Rite of Spring* (1913), the meter changes no fewer than twenty-eight times in the final thirty-four bars of the central dance. Similarly, Schoenberg eliminated repetition from his works and used rapid tempo changes.

Modernism also rejected the dominant nineteenth-century faith in the power of human reason and observation, and instead emphasized the role of individual emotion and experience in shaping human understanding. In Paris, for example, a group of artists centered on the Spaniard Pablo Picasso (1881–1973) dared to juxtapose different perspectives and points of view on a single canvas. They called themselves Cubists°. Just as Albert Einstein revolutionized physics by arguing that time and space shift as the position of the observer changes, so Cubism transformed Western visual culture by revealing the incompleteness and even incoherence of individual perception. In one cultural historian's apt description, "Cubists cracked the mirror of art."[7] Their fragmented, jagged, energetic works no longer reflected the world "out there," but instead revealed the artist's fluid and contradictory vision (see page 762).

**Léon Bakst, *Nijinsky in The Afternoon of a Faun* (1912)**
The Russian dancer Vaslav Nijinksy (1890–1950) brought modernism to the ballet, with startling, awkward poses and sudden, jerky moves. In this painting, however, the Russian artist Bakst uses the flowing lines of the Art Nouveau style to evoke Nijinsky in movement.

This emphasis on art as a form of personal expression is also seen in the Expressionist° movement, centered not in France as was Cubism, but in central and eastern Europe. Expressionists such as Egon Schiele argued that art should express the artist's interior vision, not the exterior world. In nude self-portraits, Schiele depicted himself as ugly and emaciated, a graphic expression of his tormented internal universe. His fellow Expressionist, the Russian painter Wassily Kandinsky (1866–1944), went even further in shattering artistic boundaries and splashing his emotions all over the canvas. Kandinsky sought to remove all form from his painting, to create a universe of pure color that would express a fundamental spiritual

## DOCUMENT

# Cubist Painters

*Born in 1880, the Frenchman Guillaume Apollinaire became part of the modernist circle of artists and poets that dominated Parisian cultural life at the turn of the century. His* Cubist Painters, *written in 1911 and published two years later, is both a study and an example of modernism. In its fragmentary style it resembles a Cubist painting; it rejects a point-by-point reasoned narrative for the use of juxtaposition, contrast, and poetic analogies.*

The rainbow is bent, the seasons quiver, the crowds push on to death, science undoes and remakes what already exists, whole worlds disappear forever from our understanding, our mobile images repeat themselves, or revive their vagueness, and the colors, the odors, and the sounds to which we are sensitive astonish us, then disappear from nature—all to no purpose.

The monster, beauty, is not eternal . . .

You cannot carry around on your back the corpse of your father. You leave him with the other dead. You remember him, miss him, speak of him with admiration. And if you become a father yourself, you cannot expect one of your children to be willing to split in two for the sake of your corpse.

. . .

Many new painters limit themselves to pictures which have no real subjects. . . . These painters, while they still look at nature, no longer imitate it, and carefully avoid any representation of natural scenes which they may have observed, and then reconstructed from preliminary studies.

Real resemblance no longer has any importance, since everything is sacrificed by the artist to truth, to the necessities of a higher nature, whose existence he assumes, but does not lay bare. The subject has little or no importance any more.

Generally speaking, modern art repudiates most of the techniques of pleasing devised by the great artists of the past.

. . .

Cubism differs from the old schools of painting in that it aims, not at an art of imitation, but an an art of conception, which tends to rise to the height of creation . . . .

I love the art of today because above all else I love the light, for man loves light more than anything; it was he who invented fire.

Source: Guillaume Apollinaire. *The Cubist Painters: Aesthetic Meditations,* trans. Lionel Abel (1913; New York: Wittenborn and Company, 1944), pp. 9, 10–11, 14, 15.

**Wassily Kandinsky,** *Composition VII* **(1913)**
Kandinsky's experiments in color and form led him to pure abstraction.

gious worship had once cemented community life, the increasingly elaborate rituals of spectator sports now forged new bonds of loyalty and identity. At the same time, the delectable array of colorful products displayed in shop windows promised fulfillment and satisfaction in the here and now, an earthly paradise rather than a heavenly reward.

# The New Imperialism

■ What were the causes and consequences of the new imperialist ideology for both the West and non-Western societies?

Many of those items on display behind the new plate-glass shop windows were the products of imperial conquest. After 1870, Europe entered not only a new age of mass consumption but also a new era of imperialist expansion. Imperialism intertwined with many of the economic, scientific, and cultural developments already examined in this chapter. Telegraphs ensured rapid communication from far-flung empires while mass printing technologies guaranteed that illustrated tales of imperial achievement made their way into homes and schools; Social Darwinism supplied a supposedly scientific justification for the conquest of peoples deemed biologically inferior; swift and decisive victories over other lands and societies helped quell anxiety about European degeneration. For many Europeans—particularly the British, who presided over the largest empire in the world—imperialist domination served as reassuring, even incontrovertible, evidence of the superiority of Western civilization.

## Understanding the New Imperialism

Imperialism was not, of course, new to Europe. In the fifteenth century, Europeans had embarked on the first phase of imperialism, with the extension of European control across coastal ports of Africa and India, and into the New World of the Americas. In the second phase, which began in the late seventeenth century, European colonial empires in both Asia and the Western Hemisphere expanded as governments sought to augment their profits from international trade. Trade motivated much of the imperial activity after 1870 as well, with the need to protect existing imperial possessions often impelling further imperialist conquests. The desire to protect India—the "Jewel in the Crown" of the British Empire—explains much of British imperial acquisition throughout the nineteenth century. Britain's annexation of Burma and Kashmir, its establishment of spheres of influence in the Middle East, and its interests along the coast of Africa were all vitally linked to its concerns in India.

Neither defense of existing empires nor commercial considerations, however, fully explain the headlong rush into empire in the later nineteenth century. After 1870 and particularly after 1880, Europe's expansion into non-European territories became so much more aggressive that historians label this third phase the age of new imperialism°. A few figures illustrate the contrast: Between 1800 and 1880, European colonial empires grew by 6,500,000 square miles, but between 1880 and 1910, these empires increased by an astonishing 8,655,000. In just thirty years, European control of the globe's land surface swelled from 65 to 85 percent. In addition, new players joined the expansionist game. Recently formed nation-states such as Germany and Italy jostled for colonial territory in Africa, the United States began to extend its control over the Western Hemisphere, and Japan initiated its imperialist march into China and Korea. What factors lay behind this new imperialism?

### Technology, Economics, and Politics

Part of the answer lies in the economic developments examined in Chapter 22. The new technologies characteristic of the Second Industrial Revolution meant that industrial Europe increasingly depended on raw materials available only in non-Western regions such as Asia, Africa, and South America. Rubber, for example, was essential not only for tires on the new automobiles, but also for insulating the electrical and telegraph wires now encircling the globe. Palm oil from Africa provided the lubricant needed for industrial machinery. Africa's once-plentiful elephant herds were slaughtered to provide the ivory for many of the new consumer goods now displayed prominently in department store windows and middle-class parlors—piano keys, billiard balls, knife handles. Increasingly dependent on these primary resources, European states were quick to respond to perceived threats to their economic interests. The Germans even coined a word to describe this fear of losing access to essential raw materials: *Torschlusspanik,* or "fear of the closing door."

Competition for markets also accelerated imperial acquisition. With the onset of economic depression in 1873 (discussed in Chapter 22), industrialists were faced with declining demand for their products in Europe. Imperial expansion seemed to provide a solution, with annexed territories seen as captive markets. As an editorial in the largest French mass-circulation newspaper explained in 1891, "every gunshot opens another outlet for French industry."[9]

By the mid-1890s, however, the depression had ended in most regions, and Europe embarked on the longest investment boom it had yet experienced. Western European capital spread across the globe, underwriting railway lines, digging mines, and erecting public utilities in the United States, Latin America, Russia, Asia, and Africa. This global investment boom also contributed to new imperialism. With each railroad or coal mine or dam, European interests in non-European regions expanded, and so did the pressure on European governments to assume formal political control should those interests be threatened, whether by the arrival of other European competitors or by local political instability.

Britain provides an important example of the link between empire and economics. By the end of the nineteenth century, the British Empire covered one-quarter of the globe and contained one-quarter of the world's population. This empire reflected Britain's position at the center of the world's economy, as the chief agent of global economic exchange. Despite the emergence of Germany and the United States as industrial powerhouses, Britain remained the world's largest trading nation. Even more important, British stockbrokers, currency traders, and banks managed the global exchange system that emerged in the last third of the nineteenth century. In this era British loans abroad were larger than the combined investments of Britain's five largest competitors—France, Germany, the Netherlands, the United States, and Belgium.

Imperialism was motivated by more than economic concerns. Political pressures also contributed to imperialist acquisition. First, in the age of mass politics, political leaders needed to find issues that would both appeal to new voters and strengthen the status quo. Imperialism was one such issue. It assured ordinary men that they were part of a superior, conquering people. Tales of dangerous explorations and decisive military victories engaged the emotions and prodded the ordinary individual to identify more closely with the national group.

A second political factor motivating new imperialism was nationalist competition. Newly formed nations such as Italy and Germany sought empires outside Europe as a way to gain both power and prestige within Europe. The nineteenth-century German historian Heinrich von Treitschke explained, "All great nations in the fullness of their strength have desired to set their mark on barbarian lands and those who fail to participate in this great rivalry will play a pitiable role in time to come." Similar concerns about status and strategic advantages motivated nations such as Britain and France both to defend and expand their existing empires.

## The Imperial Idea

New imperialism was not simply a policy embraced by elites for economic, political, and strategic advantage. One of its most distinctive features was the way it functioned as a belief system, as an idea that permeated middle-class and mass culture in the decades after 1870. Images of empire proliferated, appearing in boys' adventure stories, glossy ads for soap and chocolates, picture postcards, cookie tins, and cheap commemorative china plates and mugs. In the music halls and theaters, imperialist songs and dramas received popular applause. At exhibitions and world's fairs, both goods and peoples from conquered regions were put on display to educate the crowds of viewers in the "imperial idea."

**Imperialism from the European Perspective**
France here brings the peoples of Morocco the wealth of Western education, technology, and military discipline.

At the center of this idea stood the assumption of the *rightness* of white European dominance over the world. Europeans would not have sought to remake the world in the European image had they not been convinced of the superiority of that image. What led white Europeans to believe they had both the right and the responsibility to take charge of other cultures and continents?

One key factor was the perceived link between Western Christianity and "civilization." Christian missionaries served as a vanguard of Western culture throughout the nineteenth century. The celebrated Scottish explorer David Livingstone (1813–1873), who mapped out much of central and southern Africa, was a Protestant missionary (although not a very successful one—his only convert eventually renounced the Christian faith). Moreover, missionary society publications introduced their readers to exotic territories, while the societies themselves served as powerful political interest groups that often lobbied for Western territorial expansion to promote the spread of Christian missionary activity.

Europeans also pointed to their advanced technologies as evidence of their material and moral superiority, and as a justification for their imperial rule. Before the nineteenth century, the technological gap between European and non-European societies had not loomed large; in some cases, such as China, non-European societies had held the technological advantage. Industrialization, however, gave Europe the technological edge. Thus Mary Kingsley (1862–1900), a British adventurer who was actually unusually admiring of African culture and customs, wrote, "when I come back from a spell in Africa, the thing that makes me proud of being one of the English is . . . a great railway engine . . . [I]t is the manifestation of the superiority of my race."[10]

DOCUMENT

Mary Kingsley and the Bubi of Fernando Po (1890s)

Although many European Christians regarded the West's technological advantages as a sign that God intended Europe to Christianize (that is, westernize) the globe, a growing number of prominent thinkers, writers, and policymakers viewed the force that conferred this civilizing duty upon Europeans as natural rather than supernatural—biology rather than God. Social Darwinism lent a seemingly scientific authority to the imperial idea by supposedly proving the mental and moral superiority of white Europeans over all peoples of color. Thus the British Lord Milner (1854–1925) explained in a speech in South Africa in 1903: "The white man must rule, because he is elevated by many, many steps above the black man; steps which it will take the latter centuries to climb, and which it is quite possible that the vast bulk of the black population may never be able to climb at all."

DOCUMENT

Imperialism and the White Man's Burden (1899)

Often white Europeans presented the idea of a biologically ordained imperial destiny in somber terms. They saw imperial rule as a heavy responsibility that must be shouldered by the civilized. Men and women in the West had a moral duty to bring the benefits of their civilization to the rest of the world. This idea of the burden of imperialism was dramatically expressed by Rudyard Kipling (1865–1936), the preeminent British poet of new imperialism. In 1899, Kipling urged American policymakers to complete their conquest of the Philippines with these words:

> *Take up the White Man's burden—*
> *Send forth the best ye breed—*
> *Go bind your sons to exile,*
> *To serve your captives' need;*
> *To wait in heavy harness*
> *On fluttered folk and wild—*
> *Your new-caught sullen peoples,*
> *Half devil and half child.*

Not all Europeans embraced the idea of the "White Man's burden," and many rejected the imperialist assump-

tion of Western superiority. Some modernist artists, for example, looked to non-Western cultures for artistic inspiration and argued that these societies had much to teach the West. The Fauves ("wild beasts"), a Paris-based circle of artists that included Henri Matisse (1869–1954) and Paul Gauguin (1848–1903), condemned most Western art as overrefined and artificial, and sought in their own brilliantly colored works to rediscover the vitality that they found in non-Western cultures (see page 742).

Critics of empire often focused on its domestic political and economic implications. The British economist J. A. Hobson (1858–1940) charged that overseas empires benefited only wealthy capitalists while distracting public attention from the need for domestic political and economic reform. Hobson argued that unregulated capitalism led almost inevitably to imperialist expansion. While impoverishing the masses, the capitalist system generates huge surpluses in capital for a very small elite, who must then find somewhere to invest these surpluses. Hobson's ideas proved very influential among European socialists, who condemned imperialism along with capitalism.

Many liberals also condemned imperialism. The British prime minister William Gladstone (1809–1898) clung fast to the liberal belief that free trade between independent nations fostered international peace. Gladstone and other liberals were uneasy about the expense of empire and acutely aware of the contradictions between liberal ideals and imperialist practice. It was difficult, for example, to reconcile the liberal commitment to individual freedom with the widespread use of forced labor in colonial Africa.

Yet between 1880 and 1885—while Gladstone was prime minister—the British Empire expanded at the rate of 87,000 square miles per year, with Gladstone himself ordering the bombardment of Alexandria and the military occupation of Egypt. When Gladstone did hold firm to his anti-imperialist ideals and ordered British troops to withdraw from the Sudan in 1885, he outraged the British public. Critics of empire were in the minority, not only in Britain but throughout Europe. The imperial idea permeated European and much of American culture in the final decades of the nineteenth century.

## The Scramble for Africa

New imperialism reached its zenith in Africa. In 1875 European powers controlled only 11 percent of the African continent. By 1905, 90 percent of Africa was under European control. In just thirty years, between 1875 and 1905, Europeans established thirty new colonies and protectorates encompassing ten million square miles of territory and controlling 110 million Africans (see Map 23.1). The conquest of the African continent was so rapid and

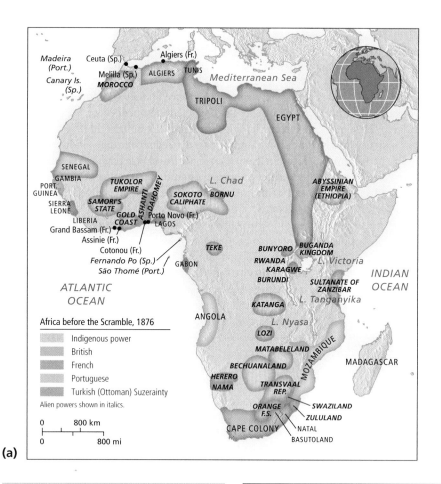

**(a)**

## Map 23.1  (a) Africa Before the Scramble, 1876 and (b) Africa After the Scramble, 1914

A comparison of these two maps reveals the dramatic impact of the new imperialism on African societies. Indigenous empires such as the Sokoto Caliphate in West Africa came under Western rule, as did tribal societies such as the Herero. Even indigenous states ruled by whites of European descent came under European rule, as the examples of the Transvaal and the Orange Free State in South Africa illustrate. Only Ethiopia preserved its independence.

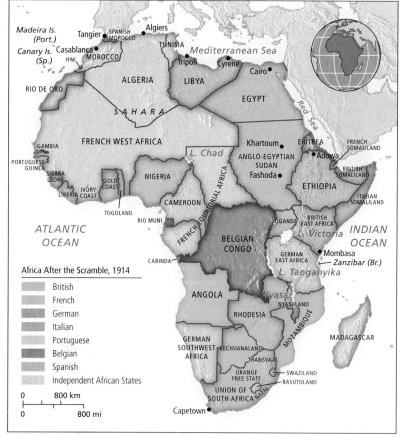

**(b)**

W w        *W w*

W   is   the   Word
Of   an   Englishman   true:
When   given,   it   means
What   he   says,   he   will   do.

W. W.

## A Lesson in the Imperial Idea
As this alphabet reader makes clear, education in imperial ideology began early.

dramatic that as early as 1884 mystified Europeans began to talk about the Scramble for Africa°.

## Overcoming the Obstacles
When the nineteenth century began, Europeans knew little more about the continent of Africa than the ancient Greeks had known. A vast and profitable trading network between European merchants and Africa's coastal regions had developed, centering on the exchange of European goods for African gold and slaves. European efforts to establish settlements in the interior, however, faced three key obstacles—the climate, disease, and African resistance.

Africa was known as "the white man's grave," deservedly so. Seventy-seven percent of the white soldiers sent to West Africa in the early nineteenth century died there, and another 21 percent became invalids. Temperatures of more than 100 degrees Fahrenheit in some regions and constant rainfall in others made travel extremely difficult. The mosquito and the tsetse fly made it deadly. Mosquito bites brought malaria, while the tsetse fly carried trypanosomiasis, or sleeping sickness, an infectious illness that began with a fever and ended in a deadly paralysis. Sleeping sickness also posed a grave danger to livestock and so aggravated the problem of transportation within the African interior. In regions with endemic trypanosomiasis, such as equatorial, southern, and eastern Africa, the use of horses and oxen was impossible. Despite the dangers posed by the climate and disease, Europeans did endeavor to establish inland settlements in Africa but then faced the obstacle of African resistance. In the seventeenth century, for example, the Portuguese set up forts and trading centers in modern Zimbabwe but were driven out by local African populations.

Beginning around 1830, a series of developments altered the relationship between Europe and Africa and prepared the groundwork for European conquest. First, the efforts of European explorers changed the Western vision of Africa. Between 1830 and 1870, adventurers mapped out the chief geographical features of Africa's interior and so illuminated the "Dark Continent" for Europeans. They discovered that central Africa was not the vast, empty desert that Europeans had assumed, but rather a territory with abundant agricultural and mineral resources—and lots of people, all of them potential consumers of European goods.

The shift in the European vision of Africa—from empty desert to potential treasure house—coincided with important changes within Africa itself. In the first half of the nineteenth century, various forces destabilized African political structures and so weakened the African ability to withstand conquest in later decades. Although the precise nature of the destabilizing forces varied by region, one common denominator prevailed—the unsettling impact of early encounters with the West. In the 1830s, for example, Britain and other European powers, pressured by humanitarian and missionary lobby groups, embarked on an effort to stamp out the West African slave trade. They succeeded but only in West Africa. The slave trade shifted to the central and eastern regions of the continent and wreaked havoc with political arrangements there. African slaving nations relied on frequent military raids to obtain their human merchandise. These raids—carried out by Africans against Africans—disrupted agricultural production, shattered trade networks, and undermined the authority of existing political rulers. With political systems in disarray, many African regions were vulnerable to European encroachment.

# Picasso Goes to the Museum

After months of work and more than 800 preparatory sketches, Picasso judged the painting finished at last. But when he showed *Les Demoiselles d'Avignon* to his friend and rival Matisse, the Frenchman thought the work a joke. Another friend and fellow painter, Georges Braques, found it appalling. Picasso did not exhibit the painting for several years; it remained largely unknown until 1939 when it went on display at the Museum of Modern Art in New York City. Today, *Demoiselles* is one of the most well-known modernist works of art in the western world, "the amazing act on which all the art of our century is built."[11] It helped transform the history of Western art and even, perhaps, the history of perception itself.

With its in-your-face sexuality, *Demoiselles* retains its ability to shock. Five naked whores (*demoiselles* means "prostitutes") advertise for trade, twisting their bodies into erotic, even pornographic poses. The painting's eroticism alone, however, does not explain its impact.

The painting as we now know it resulted from a very specific encounter that occurred when Picasso went to a museum in Paris. Some time in 1906 or 1907, when he was already deeply involved in this painting, Picasso viewed African tribal masks on exhibit at the Ethnographic Museum in the Trocadero. This museum visit profoundly excited and upset the Spanish painter. His girlfriend Fernande Olivier reported, "Picasso is going crazy over Negro works and statues."[12] In Picasso's view, these "Negro works and statues" possessed the vitality and authenticity missing from Western art.

Picasso and many modernists believed that Western civilization, with its urbanization and industrialism, its organizations and academies, its codes and regulations, had stifled artistic expression. They saw most modern art as weak and lifeless—the tired-out product of a worn-out society. In contrast, they argued, African art resembled the pictures drawn by children: energetic, playful, creative, colored outside the lines.

This notion of African culture as childlike, of course, reflected the imperialist idea of "backward peoples." Picasso and other modernists rejected the imperialist notion of Western superiority and often sharply criticized Western empires, yet clearly they could not escape imperialist stereotypes. Within the limits of these stereotypes, however, modernists turned the cultural relationship of the West and Africa upside down. Picasso went to African art to learn, not to conquer.

Picasso's encounter with the African masks transformed both this specific painting and modern art itself. After his Trocadero visit, Picasso reconfigured the faces of the two women on the right so that their masklike appearances now clash awkwardly with those of the three other prostitutes. This step destroyed any unity of narrative or composition in the painting: The five figures are no longer part of a single story or share a single point of view. At the same time that Picasso fragmented the painting, he fragmented each of the bodies, flattening them and reducing them to jutting geometric forms. Thus *Demoiselles* pushed Picasso toward Cubism, one of the most influential artistic styles of the twentieth century (see page 755). As the art historian John Golding has written, "In the *Demoiselles* Picasso began to shatter the human figure. . . . He spent the rest of his artistic life dissecting, reassembling, and reinventing it."[13] After Picasso, Western artists spent the rest of the twentieth century dissecting, reassembling, and reinventing the way we see and depict our world.

## For Discussion

Clearly Picasso's encounter with the African sculptures on display at the Trocadero transformed this specific painting. But why is this single work of art so important?

**Pablo Picasso, *Les Demoiselles d'Avignon* (1907)**

*The mask-like features of the prostitutes reflect the influence of African tribal art on Picasso.*

*The edge of the table engages the viewer as a participant in the painting: the viewer's perspective is that of a customer sitting at a table in a brothel.*

Finally, three specific developments shifted the balance of power in the West's favor—the steamship, the "quinine prophylaxis," and the repeating, breech-loading rifle. The steam revolution was inaugurated in 1807 when the *Clermont,* a ship powered by a steam engine invented by the American Robert Fulton, chugged its way along the Hudson River between Albany and New York City. By the 1820s, steamships were widely in use on European lakes and rivers. Steam proved crucial in enabling Western imperialists to overcome the obstacles to traveling through Africa by allowing them to use the continent's extensive but shallow river system.

But until the 1850s and the development of the "quinine prophylaxis," such journeys almost guaranteed death sentences because of the risk of malaria. Steam enabled Westerners to penetrate the African interior; quinine helped them survive once they got there. Produced commercially from 1827 on, quinine was prescribed by doctors for malaria. Death and disability rates from the disease remained high, however, until a series of chance discoveries revealed the importance of taking quinine prophylactically—of saturating the system with quinine before any risk of infection. By the 1860s, Westerners were routinely ingesting quinine in preparation for postings in Africa—and their death rates dropped dramatically.

*African* death rates, however, soared because of the third crucial technology of imperialism—the repeating, breech-loading rifles carried by Europeans from the 1870s on. Before the invention of these rifles, Europeans used muskets or muzzle-loading rifles that had to be loaded one ball or cartridge at a time while standing up, and were prone to foul easily, particularly in damp weather. Such weapons did not provide Europeans with much of a military advantage, even over spears. With the repeating rifle, however, "any European infantryman could now fire lying down, undetected, in any weather, fifteen rounds of ammunition in as many seconds at targets up to half a mile away." As we saw at the beginning of this chapter, in regions such as the Sudan, where armor-clad cavalrymen fought with spears, swords, and arrows like medieval knights, the repeating breech-loader and its descendant the machine gun made the European conquest "more like hunting than war."[14]

### Slicing the Cake: The Conquest of Africa
In the decades after 1870, convinced that the conquest of African territories would guarantee commercial prosperity and strengthen national power, European states moved quickly to beat out their rivals and grab a piece of the continent. As King Leopold II of Belgium (1865–1909) explained in a letter to his ambassador in London in 1876, "I do not want to miss a good chance of getting us a slice of this magnificent African cake."[15]

Leopold's slice proved to be enormous. Presenting himself as a humanitarian whose chief concern was the abolition of the slave trade, he called on the other European

**Congo Atrocities**
Harsh punishments were used by Leopold's forces to subdue the Congolese people and increase his personal profits.

leaders to back his claim to the Congo, a huge region of central Africa comprising territory more than twice as large as central Europe. After a decade of controversy and quarreling, representatives of the European powers met in Berlin in 1884 and agreed to Leopold's demands. At the same time, they used the Berlin Conference to regulate the Scramble for Africa. According to the terms established in Berlin, any state claiming a territory in Africa had to establish "effective occupation" and to plan for the economic development of that region.

But as the history of the Congo Free State demonstrated, colonialism in Africa was far from a humanitarian endeavor. Leopold's personal mercenary army turned the Congo into a hellhole of slavery and death. By claiming all so-called vacant land, Leopold deprived villagers of the grazing, foraging, and hunting grounds they needed to survive. He levied impossibly high rubber quotas for each village, forcing villagers to harvest wild rubber for up to twenty-five days each month while their families starved. Brutal punishments ensured compliance: Soldiers chopped off the hands of villagers who failed to meet their rubber quota. In other cases, babies were chained in sweltering huts until

Belgian King Crushing the Congo Free State—Cartoon

their mothers delivered their quota. At the same time, the Belgians forced black Africans to serve as human mules. This practice spread sleeping sickness from the western coast into the interior. Between 1895 and 1908, an epidemic of sleeping sickness decimated the already weakened population. As an estimated three million people died from the combined effects of forced labor, brutal punishments, starvation, and disease, the enormous profits from the Congo enabled Leopold II to indulge his hobby of building elaborate tourist resorts on the Riviera.

King Leopold's personal brand of imperialism proved so scandalous that in 1908 the Belgian government replaced Leopold's personal rule with state control over the Congo. Yet the king's exploitation of the Congo differed only in degree, not in kind, from the nature of European conquest elsewhere in Africa. Forced labor was common throughout European-controlled areas, as were brutal punishments for any Africans who dared resist. Faced with tribal revolt in Southwest Africa, the German colonial army commander in 1904 ordered that the entire Herero tribe be exterminated. Twenty thousand Africans, including children, were forcibly driven from their villages into the desert to die of thirst.

### African Resistance

As the Herero rebellion demonstrates, Africans frequently resisted the imposition of these often-brutal imperial regimes, but to no avail. The only successful episode of African resistance to European conquest occurred in northern Africa, in the kingdom of Ethiopia (also called Abyssinia). After four centuries of isolation, Ethiopia modernized in the 1850s. By the time of the European Scramble for Africa, Ethiopia had developed not only a modern standing army but also an advanced infrastructure and communications system. These factors enabled the Ethiopian nation, in 1896, to defeat the Italian army at the battle of Adowa.

Adowa, however, was the exception. Most African resistance was doomed by the technological gap that yawned between the indigenous peoples and their European conquerors. A booming arms trade developed between European rifle manufacturers and African states desperate to obtain guns. Frequently, however, the arms shipped to Africa were inferior models—muskets or single-firing muzzle-loaders rather than the up-to-date and deadly efficient repeating rifles and early machine guns possessed by the European invaders.

African military leaders who did obtain advanced weaponry often did not make the strategic leap necessary to adapt their military tactics to new technologies. (As we will see in Chapter 24, European military leaders made similar mistakes in World War I.) In the 1890s, for example, the West African state of Dahomey imported repeating rifles to enable it to resist French annexation. A prosperous, highly centralized state, Dahomey possessed a 4,000-soldier stand-

ing army with a deservedly fierce reputation. Dahomey's military command, however, failed to change the attack drill devised for a musket-based regiment. The troops advanced forward at a run, fired from the hip, and withdrew—a strategy that worked well with muskets because they did not have to be aimed, but that proved disastrous with more advanced weapons. In 1892, French forces, outnumbered six to one, annihilated the Dahomian army. By 1900, Dahomey had become part of the French empire.

Yet even African resistance leaders who did adapt military strategy as well as adopt modern military weapons could not stand for long against the industrial might of Western powers. The most famous African resistance leader, Samori Ture (1830–1900), built a vast West African empire of 115,000 square miles and held off the forces of French imperialism for fifteen years, but he, too, was conquered in the end. Utilizing information obtained by spies sent to infiltrate the French military, Samori trained his massive infantry in modern military maneuvers and armed his elite cavalry troops with 6,000 repeating rifles, used with deadly effect against the French in a series of battles in the 1880s. Even more important, Samori was one of the first military commanders to conceive of the tactics of modern guerilla warfare—hit-and-run attacks, night battles, the crucial advantage of knowing the land. These measures enabled him to elude French capture for more than seven years after the French in 1891 sent a massive force to destroy the Samorian state. Yet 6,000 repeating rifles and guerilla tactics could not hold off the vast weight of French imperialism. Ambushed in 1898, Samori died in exile two years later, with his empire in European control.

The Scramble for Africa provides the most dramatic illustration of new imperialism but certainly not the only one. The same era witnessed the extension of European empires throughout Asia. Moreover, it was in Asia that non-European powers—the United States and Japan—entered the imperial game, and that Russia made its bid for empire.

## Asian Encounters

Unlike most of Africa, many of the diverse states of Asia had already been woven into the web of the Western economy well before 1870. Pacific states such as Java and Malaysia formed a part of the eighteenth-century mercantilist empires established by Dutch, British, Portuguese, and French trading companies. (See Chapter 17.) Throughout the nineteenth century, European governments formalized their control over many of these island states, primarily to protect trade routes or to ensure access to profitable commodities such as rubber, tin, tobacco, and sugar. The Dutch, for example, gradually expanded their East Indies empire, moving from control of the island of Java in 1815 to domination over almost the entire archipelago several decades later. Similarly, Britain steadily expanded its control over India throughout the nineteenth century (see Map 23.2).

A number of factors accelerated the pace of imperialist acquisition in Asia beginning in the 1870s. In the age of steam, the Pacific islands took on strategic significance because European powers and the United States needed coaling stations for their commercial and naval fleets. At the same time, new industrial processes often heightened the economic value of many of these regions. The development of a process for producing dried coconut, for example, made Samoa so valuable that Germany, Britain, and the United States competed for control over the tiny islands.

As in Africa, however, the most important factor in imperialist expansion after 1870 was a phenomenon we can call the *scramble effect:* Imperialist gains by one power led to anxiety and a quicker pace of expansion by its rivals. The steady erosion of Chinese political stability—itself a result of encounters with the West—intensified this Asian scramble. Competition for access to Chinese markets was an important factor in determining the course of Western imperialism throughout much of Asia. The quest for a protected trade route to China, for example, impelled the French to extend their control over neighboring Indochina. By 1893, the Union of French

## Map 23.2   Imperialism in Asia, 1914

The impact of the new imperialism on Asia was not as dramatic as in Africa, but the spread of Western rule is significant nonetheless. This map shows a key development: the entry of non-European powers—Japan and the United States—into the imperialist game. What it does not show is the extent of Western and Japanese influence in China. Profoundly destabilized by foreign intervention, China in 1914 was in the midst of revolution.

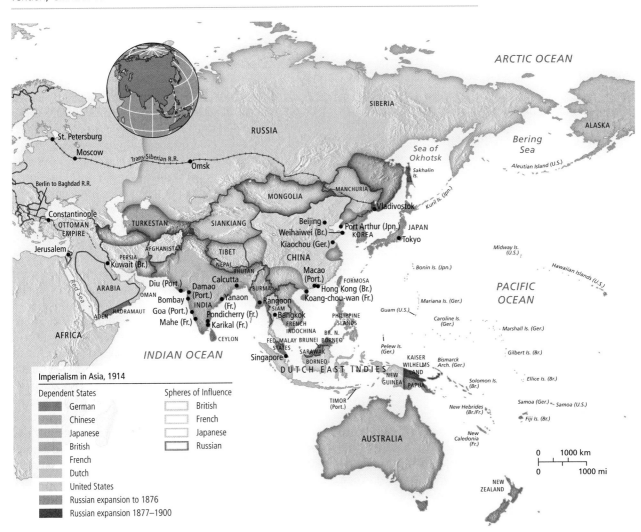

## CHRONOLOGY

## Asia Encounters the West

| | |
|---|---|
| 1840–1842 | The Opium War: Western powers begin to chip away at Chinese territorial sovereignty in China |
| 1853 | Commodore Matthew Perry forces Japan to open its markets to the United States |
| 1868 | The Meiji Restoration in Japan; Japan begins rapid modernization |
| 1885 | Russia establishes control over Central Asia |
| 1893 | Union of French Indochina includes Laos, Cambodia, Tonkin, and Annam |
| 1894–1895 | The Sino-Japanese War: China defeated |
| 1898 | Spanish-American War; United States annexes Puerto Rico, Philippines, Hawaii, and Guam; establishes protectorate over Cuba |
| 1899 | "Open door" policy in China proclaimed by United States |
| 1900–1903 | Boxer Rebellion in China |
| 1901 | Commonwealth of Australia formed |
| 1904–1905 | Russo-Japanese War: Russia defeated |
| 1911 | Revolution in China: overthrow of Manchu Dynasty |

Indochina included the formerly independent states of Laos, Cambodia, Annam, and Tonkin—the latter two better known by their contemporary name of Vietnam.

## Expanding the West: The United States and Australia

In the latter half of the nineteenth century, both the United States and Australia established themselves as extensions of the West. In both of these regions, the nineteenth century was a period of internal consolidation, territorial expansion, and the subjugation of the indigenous populations. Both regions also witnessed a determined effort to create a national identity that explicitly excluded Asian peoples.

For the United States, the acquisition of an empire in Asia followed consolidation of control over much of the North American continent. After emerging victorious from a war with Mexico in 1846, the United States gained the territory of California (which included today's New Mexico and part of Arizona) and so extended its reach to the Pacific. The completion of the transcontinental Union Pacific railroad in 1869 both symbolized this coast-to-coast dominion and accelerated the pace of westward settlement.

The conquest of the continent, however, depended on the defeat of its indigenous peoples. The decades from

1860 through 1890 were punctuated by a series of Indian wars throughout the American West. As in Africa, even those Indians who acquired repeating rifles, such as Crazy Horse's troops who wiped out General George Armstrong Custer (1839–1876) at Little Big Horn in 1876, could not hold out for long against the industrial might of the United States.

With its borders now touching the Pacific Ocean, the United States quickly emerged as an imperialist power in Asia. In 1853, Commodore Matthew Perry used the potent threat of his squadron of four warships to force the opening of Japan to American commerce, and during the 1860s and 1870s the United States participated with the European powers in chipping away at China's national sovereignty to ensure favorable terms of trade there. By the end of the century, the United States had annexed Hawaii and part of Samoa, and as a result of the Spanish-American War had acquired Guam, the Philippines, Cuba, and Puerto Rico.

American acquisition of empire in Asia heightened anti-Asian sentiment within the United States, as many Americans of European descent sought to construct a version of national identity that excluded not only Asians but all peoples of color. The Chinese Exclusion Act, passed in 1882 and renewed in 1902, prohibited Chinese immigration. In 1913, the Alien Land Law, which outlawed land ownership by noncitizens, sought to restrict the property rights of Japanese immigrants. During this same period, legislators in the American South deprived blacks of their right to vote through literacy tests, poll taxes, and violent intimidation, while Jim Crow° or segregation laws defined blacks as second-class citizens, in but not really of the West.

Australia's conquest and consolidation as a Western zone paralleled many of the American developments. Discovered and claimed for the British Crown by Captain James Cook in 1770, Australia was first used by Britain as a dumping ground for convicts. But with the expansion of the wool industry in the decades after 1830, the six British colonies established in Australia became a center of British immigration. In 1901, these colonies joined together in the Commonwealth of Australia, part of the British Empire but a self-governing political entity—and a self-defined "Western" nation, despite its geographical location in the Eastern Hemisphere. Many Australians, including the new nation's first prime minister, Edmund Barton, identified the "West" as "white." Barton, who campaigned on a platform calling for a "White Australia," regarded his country as an outpost of Western civilization.

As in the United States, the process of extending Western civilization demanded the defeat of the indigenous population. At the very start of Britain's occupation of Australia in 1787, King George III had forbidden anyone to "wantonly destroy [the Aboriginal peoples] or give them any unnecessary interruption in the exercise of their several occupations."[16] But the landing of whites intent on building cities, planting farms, and fencing in land for pastures clearly interrupted the nomadic way of life for the estimated 500,000 inhabitants of Australia, living in scattered tribal groupings. In 1795, the first major clash between Aborigines and British settlers occurred. Over the next hundred years, these clashes were frequent—and disastrous for the Aboriginal populations.

The British divided over how to treat the Aborigines. To many British settlers, and as the decades passed, to many in the growing group of Australia-born whites, the Aborigines constituted a clear and violent threat that had to be eradicated. Massacres of Aborigines resulted. Christian and humanitarian groups, as well as the British government in London, opposed this sort of violence and insisted that the Aborigines should be westernized and Christianized. From the 1820s on, mission stations housed and educated Aboriginal children. Forcibly removed from their homes, these children were schooled in British ways and then at age 15 placed in employment as apprentices and domestic servants. Despite these missions, few Aborigines assimilated to the Western way of life. Thus the final decades of the nineteenth century saw a shift in official policy from assimilation to "protection." Aborigines and mixed-race individuals were declared legal wards of the state and required to live on reserves. Aborigines did not receive Australian citizenship until 1967.

White Australians perceived not only the Aborigines but also Asian immigrants as threats to their Western identity. By the 1850s, tens of thousands of Chinese had emigrated to Australia. Arriving as indentured servants, they worked under brutal conditions. Many, for example, labored in the gold mines, where they received one-twelfth of the wages paid to a European. As the numbers of Chinese immigrants grew, so, too, did anti-Chinese sentiment. Most British immigrants and white native Australians, often fiercely divided in their vision of what sort of nation Australia should be, agreed that it should be colored white. One newspaper editor noted, "The Chinese question never fails. At every meeting, somebody in the hall has a word to say in regard to it, and visions of millions of the barbarians swooping upon the colony in a solid body rise in the mental horizons of every man present."[17] In 1888, the Australian government turned back ships containing Chinese immigrants; restrictive immigration legislation soon followed.

## The Continued Expansion of the Russian Empire

As in the United States and Britain, in nineteenth-century Russia, imperial expansion took the form of territorial consolidation across a continent. During this era, Russia continued the colonization of Siberia that had begun in the sixteenth century, when Russian serfs had first fled to Siberia in search of land and freedom. The end of serfdom actually accelerated the Siberian exodus, because peasants now needed to escape the debts imposed on them by the emancipation legislation of 1861 (see Chapter 21). The completion of the trans-Siberian railway in the 1890s made this journey even more appealing. Between 1800 and 1914, seven million Russians settled in or were deported to Siberia.

Just as American expansion westward and the British conquest of Australia dramatically depleted Indian and Aboriginal numbers, so Russian migration into Siberia displaced much of that region's original population. Until 1826 Russians could trade Siberians as slaves; many died because of brutal treatment. Two additional factors were even more devastating to the indigenous Siberians. First, the immigrants brought with them new epidemic diseases. And second, the booming fur trade depleted the animal herds that served as the aborigines' main food source. Disease and famine decimated the Siberian population.

Russia also expanded southward into central Asia, primarily as a preemptive response to the growth of British power in India. Fearing that the British might push northward, the Russians pushed south. By 1885, the Black Sea region, the Caucasus, and Turkestan had all fallen to Russian imperial control, and Muslims now constituted a significant minority of the tsar's subjects. Over the next three decades the oil fields of the Caucasus would become a crucial part of the Russian industrial economy.

By 1914, the Russian Empire stretched from Warsaw in central Europe to Vladivostok on the Sea of Japan—8,660,000 square miles, or one-seventh of the global land surface. Ethnic Russians composed only 45 percent of the population of this vast empire.

As the tsarist regime expanded its Asian empire, it increasingly encroached upon Chinese territory, a move that contributed to the destabilization of China and to growing hostilities between Russia and Japan. By 1860, Russia had gained from China a sizable chunk of land along the Pacific coast and began pressing into Manchuria. Manchuria, however, was a region also coveted by Japanese imperialists. The growing antagonism between Russia and Japan led to the outbreak of the Russo-Japanese War in 1904 and, as we noted in Chapter 22, to a dramatic Japanese victory. Military defeat by a people regarded as racially inferior shocked Russians and led to demands for radical political change. With Tsar Nicholas II's regime clearly weakened and his troops tied up in Manchuria, this domestic discontent exploded in the Russian Revolution of 1905. The return of his soldiers from the Manchurian front enabled Nicholas to withstand this challenge to his authoritarian rule. His regime, however, was fundamentally weakened: Imperialism could be a risky business.

## Japanese Industrial and Imperial Expansion

Japan's victory over Russia in 1905 vividly illustrated its remarkable rise to global power and its emergence as an imperialist player. Until 1853, Japan had remained sealed off from the West, a result of a decision made by the Japanese emperor in the 1630s to close Japanese ports to all foreigners except a small contingent of Dutch and Chinese traders confined to the city of Nagasaki. The Japanese government rebuffed all Western overtures until 1853, when Commodore Perry used warships to force Japan to open two of its ports to American ships. Over the next fifteen tumultuous years, Western powers pushed to expand their economic influence in Japan and Japanese elites fought over the question of how to respond to the West. Anti-Western terrorism became endemic, civil war broke out, and a political revolution ensued.

In 1868, Japan emerged from this turbulent time with a new government. For more than 200 years effective political

**DOCUMENT**

The Meiji Constitution, 1889

control had rested in the hands not of the Japanese emperor, but rather of the "Shogun," the military governor of Japan. When the Shogun adopted pro-Western policies, Japan's warrior nobility tossed him from power and restored the young Emperor Mutsuhito (1867–1912) to effective rule—the Meiji Restoration.

Even more dramatically, these anti-Western elites determined that the only way to resist Western domination was to adopt Western industrial and military technologies and techniques. The next four decades witnessed a thoroughgoing revolution from the top as a modern centralized state, modeled on France, replaced Japan's feudalist political system. Young Japanese men traveled to Europe and the United States to learn Western ways. Western technologies and techniques helped modernize the Japanese economy.

Modernization was not an end in itself, however. The purpose of opening Japan to the West was to build up its

---

**DOCUMENT**

## "A Dream of the Future"

*In 1878, Tachibana Mitsuomi published his "Dream of the Future" in* Hochi Shimbun, *the newspaper that he edited. Tachibana's dream is a nightmare. It reveals the anxiety prevalent in Japan during its time of rapid modernization and increasing contact with Western economies and ideas. In this excerpt, Tachibana projects the consequences of an imaginary decision to lift regulations on the importation of Western capital. In actual fact, no such decision was made. The Japanese government borrowed technology, techniques, and institutions from the West, but restrained the inflow of Western capital, thus retaining control over the Japanese economy.*

*Tachibana's story opens with his bewilderment at suddenly finding himself on a busy street in Tokyo in 1967:*

The houses in the surrounding streets were splendidly built and some of them three, and others five stories high; flags from every merchant's house were waving in the air; all kinds of precious articles were displayed in the shops and carriages and horses were incessantly passing to and fro. Indeed, a most flourishing trade was actually before my eyes. Greatly puzzled at this, I went into a shop and found that the master of the shop was a White man with blue eyes and red hair, wearing handsome clean clothes and sitting in an easy position by a desk; and that those wearing scanty and torn apparel and in the employment of the master of the house, were none but the yellow-coloured and high-cheek-boned brethren of ours. . . . I was informed that . . . all the large houses in the main streets [were] occupied by the Whites. . . .

. . . I then passed into the [side] streets and on looking at the state of the houses, I saw none but immense numbers of my countrymen flocking together like sheep or pigs, in a few poorly-built houses . . . their scanty dress leaving portions of their body uncovered . . . their wives were weeping from the cold, and the children crying from hunger, the husbands being employed by the Western people, and were earning scarcely sufficient wages to fill the mouths of their families. . . .

I, seeing this, could hardly keep from weeping and was sorely puzzled why my countrymen should have fallen to such misery . . . I saw a respectable looking gray-haired old man standing on the bridge . . . I approached him and after bowing to him, I asked, "Is this country Japan? Is this the capital, Tokei [Tokyo]? How is it that the Western people alone are enjoying such great wealth, whilst the Japanese are in such a miserable state? . . . "

*The old man explains to Tochibana that the Japanese "were outdone by the superior strength of capital and intellect" from the West. As a result of lifting regulations on Western investment and ownership within Japan, "those who have control over the wealth of Japan . . . are none but the Western people." Tochibana concludes, "At this, I was very sad and deeply affected, and I was on the point of bursting into tears, when I suddenly awoke and found that it was all a dream."*

Source: From Tachibana Mitsuomi, "A Dream of the Future," *Hochi Shimbun,* October 17, 1878. For the full version and a commentary, refer to Ian Inkster, *Japanese Industrialisation: Historical and Cultural Perspectives* (Routledge: London and New York, 2001), pp. 1–6.

**Japanese Sailors Waiting for Battle Against Russia, 1904**
The Japanese began the war with a surprise attack on Russian ships in Port Arthur. Many in Britain
and the United States admired the Japanese for the audacity of their offensive—rather ironically,
given the moral outrage that greeted a similar surprise attack carried out by the Japanese against
American forces at Pearl Harbor in 1941.

national wealth, and with this wealth, to remake Japan as a global military power. Thus funds poured into building a modern navy, modeled on Britain's, and a powerful conscript-based army, modeled on Germany's. Beginning in the 1890s, Japan used its now formidable military force to push its way into the imperialist game. War with China in 1894 and Russia in 1904 led to the Japanese seizure of Taiwan and Korea, and to expanded Japanese economic influence in Manchuria. One Japanese writer, Tokutomi Soho (1863–1957) proclaimed that Japan's imperial conquests showed that "civilization is not a monopoly of the white man."[18] Certainly imperialist violence was not a white man's monopoly: The Japanese brutally punished Koreans and Taiwanese who dared to protest against their new rulers.

## Scrambling in China

While Japan used its encounter with the West to modernize and militarize its society, China proved far less successful in withstanding Western hegemony. Throughout the nineteenth century, Chinese national sovereignty slowly eroded,

as European powers, soon joined by Russia, the United States, and Japan, jostled for access to China's markets and resources.

We saw in Chapter 20 that Britain's victory over China in the First Opium War in 1842 marked the beginnings of Western encroachment on Chinese territory. During the 1890s, Western influence expanded rapidly. Following China's defeat in the Sino-Japanese War of 1894–1895, Western powers scrambled to claim spheres of influence throughout China. The European powers and the United States did agree in 1899 to back the American "open door" policy, which opposed the formal partitioning of China (as had just occurred in Africa), but this policy increased rather than blocked Western interference in Chinese economic and political affairs.

Chinese opposition to intensified Western encroachment provoked even greater outside interference—and the collapse of the Manchu dynasty that had governed China since the seventeenth century. In 1900, a secret society devoted to purging China of Western influence began attacking foreigners. The Boxer Rebellion (a rough translation of "Harmonious Fists," a name that refers to the society's commitment to the discipline of martial arts) received the covert support of the Chinese government. With more than 200 missionaries and several thousand Chinese Christians killed, and European diplomatic headquarters under attack in Beijing, the West responded in fury. A combined military force, drawing 16,000 soldiers from Russia, Germany, Austria-Hungary, France, Britain, Japan and the United States, crushed the rebellion and sacked Beijing. Required to pay a large indemnity to the West and to grant further trade and territorial concessions to its invaders, the Chinese central government was fatally weakened. In 1911, revolution engulfed China and propelled it into four decades of political and social tumult.

## A Glimpse of Things to Come: The Boer War

Writing at the time of the Opium War (1840–1842), a British journalist in China urged the Chinese to accept what he regarded as the crucial lesson of history: "Ever since the dispersion of man, the richest stream of human blessings has, in the will of Providence, followed a western course." To many Europeans, Australians, and Americans, the rapid expansion of Western imperial control over much of the world after 1870 confirmed this lesson. At the very end of the nineteenth century, however, the British found themselves embroiled in a bloody imperial conflict that challenged this complacent view. The Boer War of 1899–1902 shook British self-confidence and in many ways foreshadowed both the total warfare and the crumbling of empires that

**Concentration Camps**
This illustration, which appeared in the French magazine *Le Petit Journal* in 1901, attempts to depict the anxiety and suffering of both the Boer families and their black servants who were imprisoned in English camps during the Boer War, yet it cannot convey the lack of sanitation that led to rampant disease.

## CHRONOLOGY

### The Struggle for Control in South Africa

| | |
|---|---|
| 1806 | Britain takes control of the Cape Colony from the Dutch |
| 1837 | Boers establish independent republics of Transvaal and Orange Free State |
| 1884 | German annexation of Southwest Africa |
| 1886 | Gold discovered in the Transvaal |
| 1899 | Anglo-Boer War begins |
| 1910 | Self-government granted to South Africa |

would mark the experience of the West in the twentieth century.

The Boer War was the culmination of a century of hostility among British imperialists, Dutch settlers (called Boers, the Dutch word for "farmer"), and indigenous Africans in the southern triangle of Africa. Germany's move into Southwest Africa in 1884 worsened this conflict: The British in the Cape Colony feared that the Boers would work with Germany to limit British expansion in the region. But even more important was the discovery in 1886 of diamonds and gold in the Transvaal, an independent Boer republic. British investors in the profitable diamond and gold mines resented Boer taxation and labor policies, and

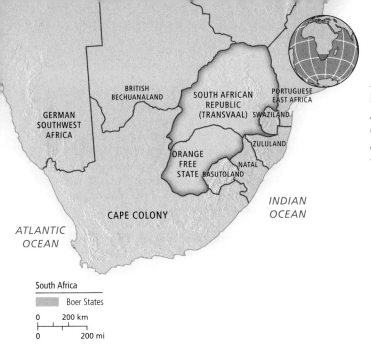

**Map 23.3   South Africa**
After the defeat of the Boer states—the Transvaal and the Orange Free State—in the Boer War, the Union of South Africa comprised the Cape Colony and the two Boer republics.

pressed the British government to use military force to place the Boer republics under British rule.

In 1899, these imperialists got the war they had demanded, but it turned out to be rather different from what they expected. Skilled riflemen who were fighting for their very homes, the Boers proved to be fierce enemies who successfully adopted guerilla tactics against their numerically superior foe. By the spring of 1901, the war had reached a stalemate. The British military command in South Africa then decided to smoke out the Boer fighters through a scorched-earth policy: British troops burned more than 30,000 farms to the ground and confined the Boer women and children, and their black African servants, in poorly provisioned concentration camps. Diseases such as diphtheria and typhus soon took their toll. Almost 20,000 Boer women and children, and at least 14,000 blacks, died in these camps. The British finally defeated the Boers in April 1902, but this victory was limited. The Boer states were brought under British control but the Boers (or Afrikaners, as they were increasingly called) outnumbered other whites in the newly created Union of South Africa (see Map 23.3). After South Africa received self-government in 1910, the Afrikaners dominated the political system and created a nation founded on segregation and racist oppression.

More immediately, Britain emerged from the war with both its military and its humanitarian reputation severely tarnished. The war aroused strong opposition inside Britain and made clear that popular support for imperialism could be rapidly eroded if the costs of imperial conquest proved too high. The conflict between the war's opponents and supporters inside Britain was one that would be repeated within imperialist countries many times over the course of the next several decades as nationalist challenges against imperial rule multiplied and as the imperial idea grew less

IMAGE

The Boer War and Queen Victoria— Dutch Caricature

and less persuasive. More ominously, the sight of noncombatants confined—and dying—in concentration camps would soon become all too familiar. The Boer War thus served as a fitting opening to the twentieth century.

# Conclusion

## Reshaping the West: Expansion and Fragmentation

Africans and Asians who saw their political and social structures topple under the imperialist onslaught would probably have agreed with the Austrian poet Hugo von Hoffmansthal (1874–1929) when he wrote in 1905 that "what other generations believed to be firm is in fact sliding." Hoffmansthal, however, was commenting not on Africa or Asia or any other region of imperialist conquest, but rather on the Western cultural and intellectual landscape, which, like colonial political boundaries, underwent enormous and disturbing change in the period between 1870 and the outbreak of World War I in 1914. In this era, matter itself began to slide, as the Newtonian conception of the world gave way to a new, much more unsettling picture of the physical universe. At the same time, changes in medical practice, the revolt against positivism, and the triumph of Darwin's evolutionary theory helped undermine established assumptions and contributed to the sense that the foundations of Western culture were shifting; so, too, did the birth of modernism as well as broader cultural changes such as the move of middle-class women into the public sphere and the redefinition of sexual boundaries.

In the decades after 1870, then, a series of encounters reshaped the West. Its geographic boundaries expanded as non-European regions such as the United States emerged as significant economic and imperial powers. With Australians claiming Western identity, "the West" even spilled over into the Eastern Hemisphere. Yet fragmentation as well as expansion characterized the Western experience after 1870. At the same time that some social thinkers were proclaiming white cultural superiority, European artists such as Gauguin and Picasso were embracing the visual forms of non-European, nonwhite societies in an effort to push open the boundaries of Western culture. While scientific and technological achievements convinced many Europeans and Americans that the West was destined to conquer the globe, others regarded these scientific and technological changes with profound uneasiness.

The next chapter will show that the sense that old certainties were slipping led some Europeans to welcome the outbreak of war in 1914 as a way to restore heroic values and clear purpose to Western society. The trenches of World War I, however, provided little solidity. Many nineteenth-century political, economic, and cultural structures slid into ruin under the impact of total war.

## Suggestions for Further Reading

For a comprehensive listing of suggested readings, please go to www.ablongman.com/levack2e/chapter23

Adas, Michael. *Machines as the Measure of Men: Science, Technology, and Ideologies of Western Dominance.* 1989. A superb study of the way in which the ideology of empire was inextricably connected with cultural and intellectual developments within the West.

Betts, Raymond F. *The False Dawn: European Imperialism in the Nineteenth Century.* 1975. A general survey that looks at the ideas that underlay imperialism as well as the events that shaped it.

Bowler, Peter. *Evolution: The History of an Idea.* 1989. Looks at the development of evolutionary theory both before and after Darwin.

Butler, Christopher. *Early Modernism: Literature, Music, and Painting in Europe, 1900–1916.* 1994. Wide-ranging and nicely illustrated.

Dijkstra, Bram. *Idols of Perversity: Fantasies of Feminine Evil in Fin-de-Siècle Culture.* 1986. This richly illustrated work shows how anxiety over the changing role of women permeated artistic production at the end of the nineteenth century.

Dodge, Ernest. *Islands and Empires: The Western Impact on the Pacific and East Asia.* 1976. A useful study of Asian imperialism.

Ellis, John. *The Social History of the Machine Gun.* 1975. Lively, nicely illustrated, and informative.

Gould, Stephen Jay. *The Mismeasure of Man.* 1996. A compelling look at the manipulation of scientific data and statistics to provide "proof" for racist and elitist assumptions.

Headrick, Daniel R. *The Tools of Empire: Technology and European Imperialism in the Nineteenth Century.* 1981. Highlights the important role played by technology in determining both the timing and success of Western imperialism.

Hochschild, Adam. *King Leopold's Ghost.* 1998. Blistering account of Leopold's imperialist rule in the Congo.

Pick, Daniel. *Faces of Degeneration: A European Disorder, c. 1848–1918.* 1993. Argues that concern over degeneration formed a central theme in European culture in the second half of the nineteenth century.

Showalter, Elaine. *Sexual Anarchy: Gender and Culture at the Fin de Siècle.* 1990. An illuminating look at the turbulence that characterized gender relations in the fin de siècle.

Sperber, Jonathan. *Popular Catholicism in Nineteenth-Century Germany.* 1984. A look at the religious dimensions of popular culture.

Thornton, A. P. *The Imperial Idea and Its Enemies: A Study in British Power.* 1959; reprinted 1985. An older but still-important look at imperialist ideology and opposition.

Vandervort, Bruce. *Wars of Imperial Conquest in Africa, 1830–1914.* 1998. An up-to-date study by a military historian.

Wesseling, H. L. *Divide and Rule: The Partition of Africa, 1880–1914.* 1996. A solid survey of complex developments.

## Notes

1. Winston Churchill, *The River War: An Account of the Re-Conquest of the Sudan* (1933); quoted in Daniel Headrick, *The Tools of Empire: Technology and European Imperialism in the Nineteenth Century* (1981), 118.

2. Quoted in Anne McClintock, *Imperial Leather: Race, Gender, and Sexuality in the Colonial Contest* (1995), 50.

3. Quoted in H. Stuart Hughes, *Consciousness and Society: The Reorientation of European Social Thought, 1890–1930* (1958), 332.

4. Quoted in Hughes, *Consciousness and Society,* 296.

5. Quoted in Shearer West, *Fin de Siècle* (1993), 24.

6. Quoted in Christopher Butler, *Early Modernism: Literature, Music, and Painting in Europe, 1900–1916* (1994), 2.

7. Stephen Kern, *The Culture of Time and Space, 1880–1918* (1983), 195.

8. From *Elementary Forms.* Quoted in Hughes, *Consciousness and Society,* 284–285.

9. Quoted in William Schneider, *An Empire for the Masses: The French Popular Image of Africa, 1870–1900* (1982), 72.

10. Mary Kingsley, in *West African Studies* (1901), 329–330.

11. Yve-Alain Bois, "Painting as Trauma," in Christopher Green, *Picasso's* Les Demoiselles d'Avignon (2001), 49.

12. Brassaï, *Conversations with Picasso,* trans. Jane Marie Todd (1999), 32.

13. John Golding, "*Les Demoiselles D'Avignon* and the Exhibition of 1988," in Green, *Picasso's* Les Demoiselles, 29.

14. Headrick, *The Tools of Empire,* 101. Headrick is the historian who identified the crucial role of the steamship, the quinine prophylaxis, and the breech-loading, repeating rifle in the conquest of Africa.

15. Quoted in Thomas Pakenham, *The Scramble for Africa, 1876–1912* (1991), 22.

16. Quoted in F. K. Crowley (ed.), *A New History of Australia* (1974), 6.

17. Ibid., 207.

18. Quoted in W. G. Beasley, *Japanese Imperialism, 1894–1945* (1987), 31–33.

# The First World War

# 24

O N THE MORNING OF JULY 1, 1916, IN THE FIELDS OF NORTHERN France near the Somme River, tens of thousands of young British soldiers crawled out of ditches and began to walk across a muddy expanse filled with shards of metal and decomposing human bodies. Encumbered with backpacks weighing more than sixty pounds, the men trudged forward. For the past week their heavy artillery had pummeled the Germans who lay on the other side of the mud. Thus they expected little opposition. In less than sixty seconds, expectations and reality horribly diverged. The German troops, who had waited out the bombardment in the safety of "dugouts"—fortified bunkers scooped from the earth beneath the trenches—raced to their gunnery positions and raked the evenly spaced lines of British soldiers with machine-gun fire. The slowly walking men made easy targets. Those who were lucky enough to make it to the enemy lines found their way blocked by barbed-wire fences—still intact, despite the bombardment. Standing in front of the wire, they were quickly mown down. More than 20,000 British soldiers died that day, thousands within the first minutes of the attack. Another 40,000 were wounded. Yet the attack went on. Between July 1 and November 18, 1916, when the Battle of the Somme finally ended, almost 420,000 British soldiers were killed or wounded. Their French allies lost 200,000 men to death or injury. German casualties are estimated at 450,000.

Such carnage became commonplace during the First World War. At the Battle of Verdun, which began before the Somme conflict and continued after, the French and Germans suffered total casualties of at least 750,000, while in the disastrous Gallipoli offensive of 1915, ANZAC (Australia and New Zealand) troops experienced a casualty rate of 65 percent. Between 1914 and 1918, European commanders sent more than eight million men to their deaths in a series of often futile attacks. The total number of casualties—killed, wounded, and missing—reached more than 37 million.

**Death on the Western Front** This movie still comes from *The Battle of the Somme,* a documentary filmed during the battle and the first "war movie" shown in Britain.

These casualty figures were in part the products of the Industrial Revolution. Between 1914 and 1918 the nations of the West used their factories to churn out ever more efficient tools of killing. The need for machine guns, artillery shells, poison gas canisters, and other implements of modern warfare meant that World War I was the first total war°, a war that demanded that combatant nations mobilize their industrial economies as well as their armies, and thus a war that erased the distinction between civilian and soldier. In total war, victory depended on the woman in the munitions factory as well as the man on the front lines.

The First World War helped redefine the West. By shattering the authoritarian empires of eastern and central Europe and integrating the United States more fully in European affairs, the war ensured that commitment to democratic values became central to one dominant twentieth-century definition of "the West." But the war also strengthened antidemocratic forces: It catapulted into power a communist regime in Russia, intensified eastern Europe's ethnic and nationalist conflicts, and undermined many of the economic structures on which Western stability and prosperity rested. The years after the war, then, would see an acceleration of the fragmentation of Western cultural and social life already underway in the prewar period.

How did the encounter with total war transform Western cultures? Four questions inform this chapter's examination of the origins and experience of the First World War:

- **What factors led Europe into war in 1914?**
- **When, where, and how did the Allies defeat the Central Powers?**

- **How did total war structure the home fronts?**
- **What were the consequences of this war for the European and the global political and international order?**

# The Origins of the First World War

- **What factors led Europe into war in 1914?**

On June 28, 1914, the heir to the throne of the Austrian-Hungarian Empire, Archduke Franz Ferdinand (1863–1914), was assassinated by ethnic Serbian terrorists. Austrian officials accused the Serbian government of involvement with the assassination. One month after the archduke's death, Austria declared war on Serbia. One week later, Europe was at war. Germany entered the war on Austria's side. These two Central Powers°, as they were known, squared off against not only small Serbia but also the colossal weight of Russia, France, and Britain, called the Allies°. By the time the war ended in late 1918, the conflict had embraced not only most of Europe, but also nations from around the globe.

Why did the murder of one man on the streets of a Balkan city lead to the deaths of millions in theaters of war ranging from muddy ditches in northern France to beaches along the Mediterranean, from the mountains of Italy to the deserts of northern Africa and the depths of the Atlantic? To understand the war's origins, we need to exam-

### Arrest of Gavrilo Princip
Princip was only 18 years old when he assassinated Archduke Franz Ferdinand and set into motion the sequence of events that led to the First World War. Because of his young age, he did not receive the death penalty but instead was sentenced to twenty years in prison. He did not serve out his term; he died at age 22 of tuberculosis.

ine four interlocking factors: first, eastern European nationalism; second, the creation of rival alliance systems; third, the requirements of an industrialized military; and finally, the "will to war," the conviction among both policymakers and ordinary people that war would provide a resolution to social and cultural crisis.

## Nationalism in Eastern Europe: Austria-Hungary and the Problem of Serbia

The roots of the First World War extend deep into the soil of nationalist conflict in eastern Europe. Western European national identities coalesced in accordance with existing political boundaries; in eastern Europe, however, the "nation" was defined by ethnic, religious, or linguistic identities rather than political citizenship. More than 27 million subjects of the Habsburg monarchy, for example, did not identify themselves with the Austrian-Hungarian Empire's dominant German or Magyar (Hungarian) peoples.[1] For the Czechs or Slovenians or Serbs, translating national into political identity—creating a "nation-state"—demanded the breakup of empires and a radical redrawing of political boundaries. Unlike in much of western Europe, then, in the East nationalism served as an explosive rather than a unifying force.

The divisive impact of nationalism explains why officials within the vast Austrian-Hungarian Empire regarded the small state of Serbia as a major threat. As a multiethnic, multilinguistic empire, Austria-Hungary's very survival depended on damping down the fires of nationalism wherever they flamed up. Yet much of Serbian politics centered on fanning the nationalist flame. In 1903, a group of Serbian army officers had shot Serbia's despised king and queen, chopped their bodies into little bits, and threw the pieces out the window. The new king, a member of a rival Serbian royal dynasty, recognized that his position on the throne was precarious, to say the least. To remain in power he catered to the demands of radical nationalists, who sought the unification of all Serbs into a Greater Serbian state. Given the fact that more than seven million Serbs lived not in Serbia but in Austria-Hungary, it is not surprising that the Austrian monarchy regarded the call for Serbian unification as a direct threat to its existence.

The hostile relations between Serbia and Austria-Hungary led directly to the outbreak of World War I. In 1908 Austria annexed Bosnia, a region with a large Serbian population. The Serbian government, which viewed Bosnia as an integral part of what it hoped would become Greater Serbia, responded to the Austrian annexation by encouraging Bosnian Serb separatist and terrorist groups. After one such group, the Black Hand, succeeded in assassinating Archduke Franz Ferdinand in the summer of 1914, Austrian officials decided to crush Serbia once and

for all. On July 23 a representative of the Austrian-Hungarian Empire presented the Serbs with an ultimatum, a set of demands that would have given Austria-Hungary the right to an unprecedented degree of involvement in Serbian internal affairs. Austrian diplomats informed the Serbian government that anything short of unconditional acceptance of the impossible ultimatum within just forty-eight hours would be taken as a declaration of war. Serbian officials agreed to comply with every demand except one. On July 28 Austria-Hungary declared war on Serbia.

DOCUMENT

Borijove Jevtic: The Murder of Archduke Franz Ferdinand

## International Competition and Rival Alliance Systems

But why did war between Austria-Hungary and Serbia mean war across Europe? To understand what transformed this Austro-Serbian conflict into a continental war, we need to look beyond the unsettling impact of nationalism in eastern Europe to the heightened international competition that divided Europe into rival alliance systems. Concerned with protecting and enhancing the economic and military might of their states in an increasingly unsettled international climate, diplomats wove a web of alliances across Europe. As we will see, these alliances helped escalate a regional conflict into a European and then a global war.

One crucial factor in the growing intensity of international competition in the prewar years was Germany's unification as a state in 1871. By creating a military and economic powerhouse in the middle of Europe, the unification of the German states upset the balance of power on the Continent. Until 1890, however, the diplomatic maneuvers of Otto von Bismarck (1815–1898), the chancellor of the new nation, ensured a certain degree of stability. Bismarck recognized that Germany's position in the center of Europe made it vulnerable to encirclement by hostile powers. To avoid such an encirclement, Bismarck patched up relations with Austria in the aftermath of the Austrian-Prussian War, an effort that resulted in the signing of the Dual Alliance between Germany and the Austrian Empire in 1879. In 1882, the Dual Alliance became the Triple Alliance° when Italy joined the two Central Powers in a defensive treaty. At the same time, Bismarck was careful to maintain an alliance with Russia. By the terms of the Reinsurance Treaty of 1887, Russia and Germany agreed to remain neutral if either was attacked. Bismarck thus ensured that if Germany were to go to war against its old enemy, France, it would not face battle on two fronts.

But in 1888, a new emperor, Kaiser William II (r. 1888–1918), ascended the German throne. William, an ambitious and impatient young man, dismissed Bismarck in 1890 and launched Germany down a more dangerous path. The new kaiser made a fatal break with Bismarck's policies in two areas. First, William let the Reinsurance Treaty with Russia lapse, thus allowing fiercely anti-German France to form a partnership with Russia, formalized as the Franco-Russian Alliance of 1894. Germany now faced exactly the sort of encirclement by hostile powers, and the resulting threat of a two-front war, that Bismarck had sought to avoid.

Second, William favored a new "world policy" (*Weltpolitik*) for Germany that pushed Britain toward allying with Russia and France. Whereas Bismarck had insisted that Germany's interests were confined to Europe, William

and many prominent Germans wanted to see Germany claim its "place in the sun" as a global imperial and naval power. In 1898 Germany passed a naval law mandating the construction of nineteen battleships; a second law passed in 1900 doubled the number of ships. At the same time Germany adopted a more aggressive stance in Africa.

Such policies were guaranteed to aggravate and alienate Britain. As an island nation with a vast overseas empire, Britain based its military defense system on its naval su-

## Map 24.1   Europe, August 1914

In August 1914 each of the Central Powers faced the challenge of war on two fronts, but the entry of the Ottoman Empire into the war on the side of the Central Powers in November 1914 blocked Allied supply lines to Russia through the Mediterranean.

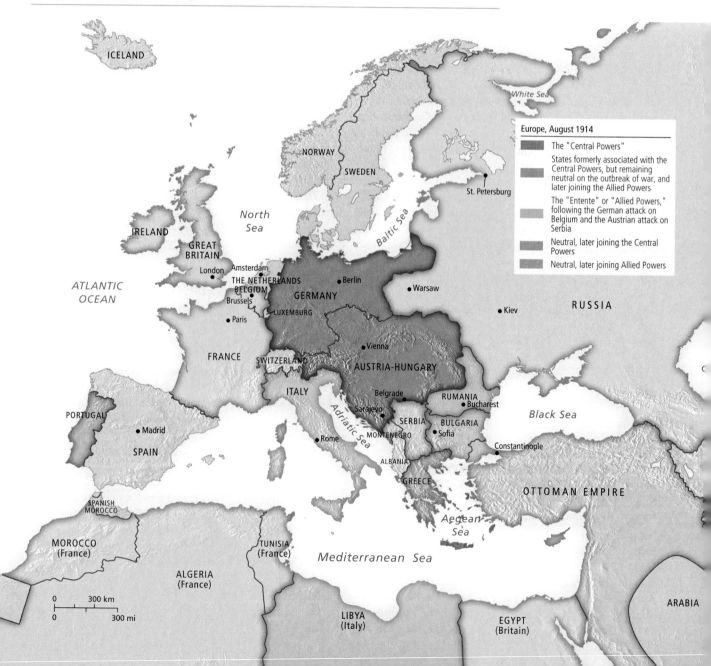

premacy. From the British point of view, a strong German navy was nothing less than a direct challenge to British national security, just as an expanding German empire was bound to conflict with British imperial interests.

Hostility toward German ambitions overcame Britain's long tradition of "splendid isolation" from continental entanglements. In the first decade of the twentieth century, a series of military, imperial, and economic arrangements formed ever-tighter links between Britain and both Russia and France. These arrangements cleared the way for the formation of the Triple Entente° among France, Russia, and Britain. An informal association rather than a formal alliance, the Triple Entente did not *require* Britain to join in a war against Germany. There is no doubt, however, that British officials increasingly viewed Germany as the major threat to British interests.

By the first decade of the twentieth century, then, Europe had split into two opposing camps: the Triple Alliance versus the Triple Entente. To German policymakers, it appeared that Germany stood surrounded by hostile powers. With Italy regarded as unreliable, Germany's alliance with Austria-Hungary took on greater and greater importance. Strengthening this crucial ally became paramount.

These considerations guided German policymaking in July 1914. When Austrian officials debated their response to the assassination of Franz Ferdinand, Kaiser William and his chancellor Theobold von Bethmann-Hollweg (1856–1921) urged a quick and decisive blow against Serbia. According to the Austrian ambassador, the kaiser told him "he would regret if we did not make use of the present moment, which is all in our favour."[2] In what some historians have described as an act akin to issuing a "blank check," the kaiser assured the ambassador that Germany would stand by Austria, even at the risk of a war with Russia.

Why would an Austrian move against Serbia heighten the risk of a wider war with Russia? The basic answer is that such a move threatened Russian interests. Eager to expand its influence in the Balkan region (and so gain access to the Mediterranean Sea), the Russian Empire had for decades positioned itself as the champion of Slavic nationalism in the Balkans and as the protector of small independent Slavic states such as Serbia. Thus both German and Austrian policymakers recognized that if Austria attacked Serbia, Russia might well mobilize against Austria and its ally, Germany (see Map 24.1).

German officials gambled, however, that Russia was not strong enough to wage war on Serbia's behalf. After all, in 1905, Russia had exposed its military shortcomings to the world with its loss in the Russo-Japanese War of 1905 (discussed in Chapter 23). And if they were wrong and Russia did mobilize for war? Then, as Bethmann-Hollweg explained, Germany's chances of winning were "better now than in one or two years' time."[3] German officials were well aware that the tsarist government, in response to its humiliating defeat in 1905, had implemented a military reform

and rearmament program. Given a few more years, the Russian Empire would constitute a formidable foe.

## Mobilization Plans and the Industrialized Military

Germany's alliance with Austria emboldened Austrian policymakers to embark on an aggressive attack on Serbia. In addition, the links between Serbia and Russia made it very likely that this attack against Serbia would pull in the Russian Empire, which of course did not stand alone but was allied with France. Alliances alone do not explain the transformation of the Austro-Serbian conflict into a European war, however. Consider the case of Italy. Although a member of the Triple Alliance, Italy did not join Germany and Austria in August 1914. In fact, when Italy did enter the war in 1915, it did so on the opposing side. Even more significantly, no alliance *required* either Russia or Britain to enter the fray. We need to look at a third factor in the origins of World War I—the widening gap between the expectations of traditional diplomacy and the requirements of an increasingly industrialized military. This growing gap ensured that when preparations for war were underway in the summer of 1914, control of the situation slipped out of the hands of the diplomats and their political superiors and into the grasp of the generals. The generals had planned for a European war. Once set in motion, their plans began to dictate events.

In the decades before 1914 military planning was dominated by a new reality, the railroad. The criss-crossing of the European continent with train tracks gave military planners a new and powerful weapon: the ability to move large numbers of men quickly to precise locations. The speed with which nations could now throw armies into battle almost obliterated the distinction between mobilization and actual war. *Mobilization* refers to the transformation of a standing army into a fighting force—calling up reserves, requisitioning supplies, enlisting volunteers or draftees, moving troops to battle stations. Traditionally, mobilization meant preparation for a possible fight, a process that took months and could be halted if the diplomats succeeded in avoiding war. But the railroads accelerated the mobilization process and thereby changed the very nature of military plans. Aware that the enemy could also mobilize quickly, military planners stressed the importance of preventive attacks, of striking before being struck. Once a nation mobilized, the momentum toward war became almost irresistible.

These factors help explain the origins and impact of the Schlieffen Plan°, the military blueprint that structured German actions—and Allied reactions—in the summer of 1914. The Franco-Russian Alliance, signed in 1894, meant that German military planners had to prepare for the possibility of a two-front war. They devised the Schlieffen Plan for just that eventuality. The plan called for a quick knockout blow against France, which would then allow the German army to concentrate on defeating the much larger force of Russia. The key assumption here was that Russia's mobilization would take time: The vastness of its territory and its underdeveloped industrial infrastructure would slow its military mobilization and so guarantee that Russian troops would not pose an immediate threat to German borders. According to the Schlieffen Plan, the smaller Austrian army would hold off the slowly mobilizing Russians while the German army moved with lightning speed against France (see Map 24.2).

The need for speed dictated the next step in the plan— an attack against France via Belgium. German planners knew that the French expected any German attack to come from the northeast, through Alsace and Lorraine (the provinces taken from France by the victorious Germans after the Franco-Prussian War in 1870). The Schlieffen Plan called for the bulk of the German army to avoid France's heavily fortified northeastern border and instead swing to the west. Moving rapidly in a wide arc, the German army would flood into France through Belgium, encircle Paris, and scoop up the French forces before their generals knew

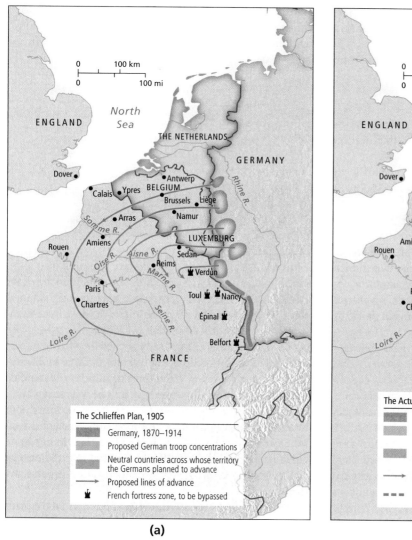

**(a)**

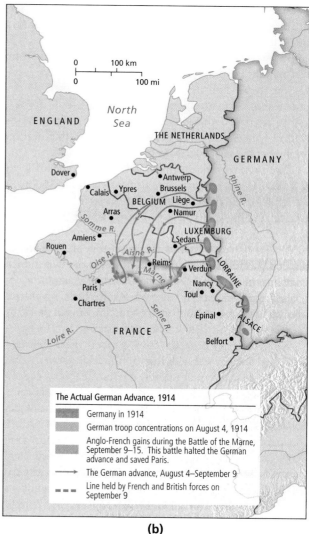

**(b)**

## Map 24.2 The Schlieffen Plan, 1905 (a) and The Actual German Advance, 1914 (b)

Count Alfred von Schlieffen's original plan of 1905 called for the sleeves of the German soldiers on the right flank to brush the English Channel—in a daring move, the German army would sweep in a huge arching movement west. In the fall of 1914 Helmut von Moltke modified Schlieffen's plan: The crucial right flank was only three times as strong as the left, rather than eight times as strong as Schlieffen stipulated, and Moltke moved his troops north and east of Paris instead of south and west. Military historians today still argue over whether Schlieffen's original plan could have succeeded.

what had hit them. With France out of the fight, the German troops would then board trains and speed back to the Eastern Front to join their Austrian allies in defeating the Russians.

The need for speed—the key factor in the Schlieffen Plan—placed enormous pressure on German politicians to treat a Russian declaration of mobilization as a declaration of war itself. And that is what happened. Only two days elapsed between Russia's order of mobilization and the German declaration of war. As soon as Russia began to mobilize, German military leaders pressured their political counterparts to break off diplomatic negotiations so that the troop-laden trains could set off.

Moreover, the plan for a speedy thrust into France meant that Germany went ahead with its invasion of Belgium—a decision that brought Britain into the war. Belgium was a neutral nation, with its neutrality protected by Britain under a long-standing treaty. German policymakers gambled that Britain would stay out of the conflict, but their gamble failed. Germany's unprovoked and brutal invasion of Belgium provided the British government with the public-pleasing moral justification it needed to enter the war with mass support. Thus, just six weeks after a Bosnian terrorist shot an Austrian archduke in Sarajevo, British and German soldiers were killing each other in the mud of northern France.

Bravo, Belgium-British Cartoon, WWI

## The Will to War

The events that pushed those soldiers into that mud were dictated not by diplomatic maneuvers but by the needs of an industrialized military. Unable to rein in the new forces of industrial warfare, diplomats also faced new pressures from public opinion. This public pressure, or the "will to war," constitutes the fourth factor that helps explain the outbreak of World War I in 1914.

Still drawn largely from the aristocracy, diplomats moved from elaborate hall to exclusive dinner, secure in their belief that with their secret agreements and coded dispatches they could manipulate international affairs. Mired in traditional protocol, they also remained enmeshed in traditional assumptions. Prominent among these assumptions was the notion of balancing power among the principal European states. But they sought to maintain a balance of power in a world increasingly unbalanced by the forces of nationalism, mass politics, and industrial change. To these men, the traditions of secret diplomacy made perfect sense. They believed that only a small elite possessed the education, temperament, and background to understand and control international affairs. Increasingly, however, foreign affairs interested and excited the mass public, whose assumptions about the course of international events clashed strongly with those of the career diplomats.

**CHRONOLOGY**

### The Outbreak of the First World War, 1914

| | |
|---|---|
| **June 28** | Assassination of Archduke Franz Ferdinand |
| **July 28** | Austrian-Hungarian declaration of war against Serbia |
| **July 30** | Russian mobilization |
| **July 31** | French, Austrian, and German mobilization |
| **August 1** | German declaration of war on Russia |
| **August 3** | German declaration of war on France |
| **August 4** | German invasion of Belgium; British declaration of war against Germany |

A number of developments accounted for this mass interest in foreign affairs. First, new technologies such as the telegraph, telephone, and camera collapsed distances and made international news much more immediate and accessible. Second, the rise of the popular press—cheap newspapers marketed to a semiliterate public—changed the coverage of foreign affairs. The competition to attract readers increased the pressure on editors and reporters to simplify and color their coverage, to make the often dull, dense, gray complexities of foreign relations into a compelling drama of Good Guys versus Bad Guys. Finally, the emergence of mass nationalism played an important role in shaping public opinion. Well-schooled in national identity, the European masses by 1914 viewed international relations as a vast nationalistic competition. They wanted evidence that "we" were ahead of "them."

Public opinion, therefore, constituted a new ingredient in international affairs in the years before the outbreak of World War I. Public opinion also constituted a real although impossible-to-measure factor in the war's outbreak. In the last weeks of July, pro-war crowds gathered in large cities. In Berlin, for example, a crowd of 30,000 young men and women paraded through the streets on the evening of July 25, singing patriotic songs and massing around statues of German heroes. Not all Europeans greeted the prospect of war with enthusiasm. Middle-class men and women, particularly students, predominated in the cheering crowds. In the countryside, farmers and villagers were more fearful, while in working-class neighborhoods anti-war demonstrations received solid support in July. The declaration of war, however, silenced these demonstrations. Opposition to the war was very much a minority movement after August 1914, even among working-class socialists. The German Social Democratic Party (SPD), for example, sponsored anti-war parades in July, but when war was declared in August, voted overwhelmingly to approve war appropriations. Socialist parties throughout Europe did likewise; national loyalties proved far stronger than class solidarity. In Britain, a total of 2.5 million men

## DOCUMENT

### War as a Unifying Force

*Many Europeans welcomed the outbreak of war because it offered a chance to step aside from peacetime quarrels and factions. This excerpt from* The Diary of a French Army Chaplain, *first published in 1915, illustrates the way political party competition was forgotten as French society mobilized for war. The author, Felix Klein, contrasts the prewar political infighting of the French legislature with the spirit of unity expressed in the declaration of war on August 4, 1914.*

Where, but a few weeks ago, could be found a more grievous spectacle than the first sittings of the new Chamber? And where, even in turning over the annals of many Parliaments, could be found a more admirable scene than that it offered on the 4th August. . . . And in this hot-bed of dissensions, quarrels, selfish desires, boundless ambitions, what trace remained of groups, of rivalries, of hates? Unanimous the respect with which the Presidential message was received; unanimous the adhesion to the Chief of the Government and his noble declaration: "It is the liberties of Europe that are being attacked of which France and her allies and friends are proud to be the defenders. . . . " And without debate, with no dissentient voice, all the laws of national defense, with the heavy sacrifices they imply, are at once voted. . . .

The fact is that we know ourselves no longer; barriers are falling on every side which, both in public and private life, divided us into hostile clans. . . . The relations between citizens are transformed. In the squares, in the streets, in the trains, outside the stations, on the thresholds of houses, each accosts the other, talks, gives news, exchanges impressions; each feels the same anxiety, the same hopes, the same wish to be useful, the same acceptance of the hardest sacrifices.

Source: From *Diary of a French Army Chaplain* by Felix Klein. London: Melrose, 1915.

---

volunteered to fight in the war, with 300,000 enlisting in the first month.

What made the idea of war so appealing to so many men and women in 1914? For some Europeans, war constituted a purging force, a powerful cleanser that would scour the impurities and corruptions from European society. As Chapter 23 explained, the years before 1914 witnessed a widespread cultural crisis in Europe, marked by fears of racial degeneration and gender confusion. War seemed to provide an opportunity for men to reassert their virility and their superiority. It also offered them the chance to be part of something bigger than themselves—to move beyond the boundaries of their often-restricted lives and join in what was presented as a great national crusade. As Carl Zuckmayer, a German playwright and novelist and a volunteer in the conflict, explained later, men like him welcomed the war as bringing "liberation . . . from . . . the saturation, the stuffy air, the petrifaction of our world."[4]

For political leaders, war provided the opportunity to mask social conflicts, to displace domestic hostilities onto the battlefield. We saw in Chapter 22 that the decades before 1914 were characterized by the rise of aggressive and often violent trade union movements and the increasing strength of socialist political parties, as well as anarchist-inspired

### The Will to War

In western Europe, much of the public welcomed the news that war had begun. Here the crowds cheer as a French regiment embarks for the front. Enthusiasm for the war was less marked in working-class and peasant communities than in middle-class areas.

assassinations, ethnic terrorism, and feminist protests. To many European elites, their society seemed on the verge of disintegration. But, as the future British prime minister Winston Churchill explained, war united societies with "a higher principle of hatred."

The war for which university students cheered and for which the politicians and generals had planned was not anything like the war that actually happened, however. Most anticipated a short war. Theorists argued that in the new industrial age, the cost of waging war was so high that no nation would be able to sustain a conflict for very long. Everything depended on throwing as many men and as much materiel as possible into the battlefield at the very beginning. The men who marched off in August 1914 expected that they would be home by Christmas. Instead, if they survived, which few of them did, they would spend not only that Christmas, but the next three, in the midst of unspeakable and unprecedented horror.

# The Experience of Total War

■ When, where, and how did the Allies defeat the Central Powers?

Expecting a German attack through Alsace and Lorraine, French military commanders in August 1914 poured their troops into these provinces. Counting on élan, the French military spirit, to see them to victory, the French troops swung into battle sporting bright red pants and flashy blue tunics. At their head rode the cream of the French military education system, the graduates of the elite Saint-Cyr military academy, who charged forward wearing their parade dress of white gloves and plumed hats. All that color and dash made easy targets for the German machine guns. As one military historian has written, "Never have machine-gunners had such a heyday. The French stubble-fields became transformed into gay carpets of red and blue."[5] Those "gay carpets," colored with the blood and broken bodies of young French men, signaled that this would be a war that shattered expectations, a war of revolutionary possibilities and devastating slaughter.

## The Western Front: Stalemate in the Trenches

Implementing a modified version of the Schlieffen Plan (see Map 24.2), the German troops swept into Belgium in August 1914. By the first week of September the German troops had swung into France and seemed poised to take Paris. The Germans had overstretched their supply lines, however, and French and British forces turned back the

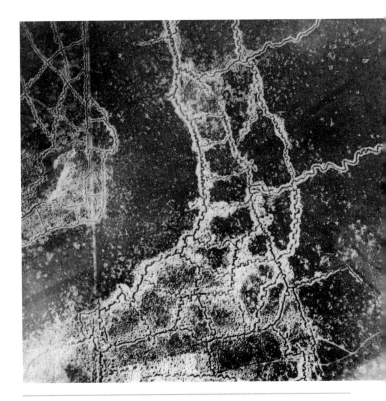

**The Trench System**
In this British reconnaissance photo, we can see the three lines of German trenches on the right, no-man's-land in the center, and the British trenches partly visible on the left. A trench system consisted of three parallel lines: the front or fire trenches, the support trenches, and the reserve trenches, all connected by intersecting communications trenches. If the enemy succeeded in gaining the front trenches, the defending forces could withdraw to the support or even the reserve trenches and still hold the line.

German offensive at the Marne River. In an episode that provided a glimpse of how important the internal combustion engine—and the oil that fueled it—was to become to modern warfare, an ingenious French commander was able to exploit a gap in the German lines by moving troops rapidly from the city of Paris to the front in the only vehicles available: taxicabs. (The army paid the drivers full fare for the trip.)

The taxicabs had saved Paris, but the French and British forces were unable to push the German army out of France. By the middle of October, the German, British, and French forces were huddling in trenches that eventually extended more than 300 miles from the Belgian coast to the borders of Switzerland. There they stayed for the next four years.

## The Troglodyte War
Literary scholar Paul Fussell has used the phrase "the troglodyte war" to sum up what the soldiers experienced on the Western Front.[6] Like prehistoric cavemen, the men on

both sides of the conflict found themselves confined to underground dwellings. As British poet and World War I veteran Siegfried Sassoon explained, "when all is said and done, this war was a matter of holes and ditches."[7]

A Typical British Trench System

From the strategic point of view, these holes and ditches—the trenches—were defensive fortifications, and the long stalemate on the Western Front shows that they worked well. The defensive advantages of the trench system are easy to comprehend. Attacking infantry units faced the dreadful task of walking forward against troops armed with machine guns and sheltered behind wide barbed-wire fences and a thick wall of dirt and sandbags. Despite numerous attempts between the fall of 1914 and the spring of 1918, neither side was able to break through the enemy line.

A discussion of trench strategy, however, conveys nothing of the appalling misery summed up by the term "trench warfare." Imagine standing in a ditch that is about seven or eight feet deep and about three or four feet wide. The walls of the ditches are packed mud, propped up with sandbags. Wooden boards cover the floor, but the mud squelches between them. The top side of the ditch facing the enemy is reinforced with piled sandbags and barbed-wire barricades, thus deepening your sense of being underground. Moreover, the trenches do not run in tidy straight lines. Instead, the trenches zigzag at sharp angles, restricting the range of fire for enemy snipers and limiting the impact of explosives, but also ensuring that everywhere you look you see a wall of mud. Because you are in northern France, it is probably raining. Thus you are standing not on but *in* mud—if you are lucky. In some parts of the line, soldiers stand in muddy water up to a foot deep. On the other side of your sandbag defenses stretches no-man's-land°, the territory dividing the British and French trench systems from the German. Pocked with deep craters from heavy shelling, often a sea of mud churned up by the artillery, no-man's-land is littered with stinking corpses in various states of decomposition—all that is left of the soldiers who died during previous attacks. Your constant companions are lice (the term *lousy* was coined on the Western Front) and rats. For the rats, the war is an endless feast as they grow enormously fat, nibbling their way through the piles of dead.

From 1915 on, the horror of the Western Front escalated with the introduction of a new killing tool—poison gas, first deployed against enemy troops by the Germans in the spring of 1915. The Allies condemned the use of poison gas as inhumane, but within a matter of months the British and French, too, were firing poison gas canisters across the lines. The consequences were appalling: blinded eyes, blistered skin, seared lungs, death by asphyxiation. Gas proved to be an unreliable weapon, however. With a sudden wind shift, artillery units found they had asphyxiated their own troops. By 1916, with the gas mask a standard part of every soldier's uniform, military companies

**Life and Death in the Trenches**
The dead, the dying, and the surviving jostle one another in a French trench.

resembled hordes of insects. And, like insects, they were easily squashed. In the summer of 1915 an average of 300 British men became casualties on the Western Front every day, not because they were wounded in an attack but because they were picked off by snipers, felled by an exploding shell, or wasted by disease brought on by living in the mud amid putrefying corpses.[8]

## The Offensives

The offensives, the attacks launched by both sides on the Western Front, sent the numbers of dead and wounded soaring. None of the elderly commanders—the Germans Helmut von Moltke and Erich von Falkenhayn, the French Joseph Joffre and Ferdinand Foch, and the British Douglas Haig and John French—knew what to make of trench warfare. Schooled to believe that war is about attacking, they sought vainly to move this conflict out of the ditches by throwing vast masses of both artillery and men against the enemy lines. But time and time again these mass attacks were foiled by the machine gun.

## DOCUMENT

# Expectations vs. Reality

*Written by two young upper-middle-class British writers, the following poems illustrate the shift from the initial enthusiasm for the war to later disillusionment and despair. In the first poem, written just as the war began, Rupert Brooke welcomes the war as an ennobling and purifying force that will bring genuine peace. In contrast, Wilfred Owen's later piece flatly describes a soldier asphyxiated by poison gas. Brooke died of blood-poisoning on his way to Gallipoli in 1915; Owen was killed in battle in 1918, just days before the war ended.*

### 1914. *Peace* by Rupert Brooke

Now, God be thanked Who has matched us with His hour,
And caught our youth, and wakened us from sleeping,
With hand made sure, clear eye, and sharpened power,
To turn, as swimmers into cleanness leaping,
Glad from a world grown old and cold and weary
Leave the sick hearts that honor could not move,
And half-men, and their dirty songs and dreary,
And all the little emptiness of love.

### *Dulce et Decorum Est* by Wilfred Owen

Bent double, like old beggars under sacks,
Knock-kneed, coughing like hags,
we cursed through sludge,
Till on the haunting flares we turned our backs
And towards our distant rest began to trudge.
Men marched asleep. Many had lost their boots

But limped on, blood-shod. All went lame; all blind;
Drunk with fatigue; deaf even to the hoots
Of tired, outstripped Five-Nines that dropped behind.
Gas! Gas! Quick, boys!—An ecstasy of fumbling,
Fitting the clumsy helmets just in time;
But someone still was yelling out and stumbling
And flound'ring like a man in fire or lime . . .
Dim, through the misty panes and thick green light,
As under a green sea, I saw him drowning.
In all my dreams, before my helpless sight,
He plunges at me, guttering, choking, drowning.
If in some smothering dreams you too could pace
Behind the wagon that we flung him in,
And watch the white eyes writhing in his face,
His hanging face, like a devil's sick of sin;
If you could hear, at every jolt, the blood
Come gargling from the froth-corrupted lungs,
Obscene as cancer, bitter as the cud
Of vile, incurable sores on innocent tongues,—
My friend, you would not tell with such high zest
To children ardent for some desperate glory,
The old Lie: "Dulce et decorum est
Pro patria mori."*

---

*"It is good and right to die for one's country."

Sources: From "Peace" from "*1914*" *Five Sonnets* by Rupert Brooke. London: Sidgwick & Jackson, 1915; "Dulce et Decorum Est" from *Poems* by Wilfred Owen, with an Introduction by Siegfried Sassoon. London: Chatto and Windus, 1920.

### A New Kind of War

From 1915 on, nerve gas became a part of the soldier's experience. Here tradition meets modernity as horses as well as soldiers are equipped with gas masks.

The Battle of the Somme, described in the opening of this chapter, provides a classic illustration of a failed offensive. The Somme, however, was only one of a number of fruitless attacks launched by both sides on the Western Front. By the end of 1917, the death tolls on the Western Front were astonishing, yet neither side had gained much ground. Soldiers, who enlisted not for a specific term or tour of duty but "for the duration"—until the war ended—became convinced that only the dead escaped from the trenches.

## A Modernist War

To the artists and intellectuals who took up arms and found themselves in the trenches, the war often seemed like a modernist painting that had escaped its frame. The characteristics of modernist art—fragmentation, an emphasis on the isolation and the incommunicability of each individual's perception, surprising juxtaposition—also described the soldier's experience on the Western Front. Confined on all sides by mud walls, he glimpses only a bit of sky. When sent "over the top" in an attack, he knows only his own little part; he is unable to see the battlefield, or comprehend the battle plan, in its entirety. In letters home he finds he cannot communicate to his parents or to his lover the reality in which he is living and expects to die. Yet the front is often close enough to home to receive food packages sent just a few days earlier, so that he might find himself sitting in the mud, a few yards from the skeletal remains of other soldiers, eating a piece of his mother's best lemon tart.

Like modernist artists, soldiers quickly learned to question accepted truths, to mistrust the past, and to doubt the power of human reason. Recruited with promises of glory, they watched rats eat the bodies of their friends. While the generals clung to their history books, which taught that offensives won wars, soldiers died in great numbers. Not surprisingly, the modernist rejection of history resonated in the trenches. The past seemed to offer little of value in this new kind of war. Similarly, the war revealed the absurdity of the nineteenth-century faith in rationality. As the weeks, months, and years wore on, and the death tolls climbed higher and higher, many soldiers were struck by the senselessness, the sheer irrationality, of the conflict. The war often seemed to be governed not by reasoning men but rather by unthinking machines.

The mechanical nature of this war became a dominant theme in soldiers' accounts, just as machines dominated prewar modernist art. Seeking the chance to be heroes, men volunteered to fight and found themselves reduced to interchangeable parts in a colossal war machine. Like mechanical gears, army companies moved in circles: from the firing trenches to the reserve trenches to the support trenches to behind the lines and back to the firing trenches. Thus in works such as *Returning to the Trenches,* British artist Christopher Nevinson (1889–1946) used modernist techniques to represent the reality of mechanized war. In Nevinson's work, the men cease to be individuals. Welded into a single machine, they are propelled into the trenches by a force beyond their control, components of a purely mechanized landscape. French war veteran and writer Georges Duhamel (1884–1966) even likened the front-line ambulances to factory repair shops. The function of the ambulances was to repair the broken-down parts (the soldiers) of the war machine and get them back into production.

We saw in Chapter 23 that in the decades before 1914 members of the press and the general public often condemned modernist styles and idioms as outrageous,

**Returning to the Trenches by Christopher Nevinson (1914–1915)**
Nevinson's work demonstrates the close parallels between wartime reality and modernist representation.

degenerate, and removed from reality. By 1918, however, as Nevinson's painting shows, these forms seemed to offer an accurate, even realistic means of conveying the horror of the war experience. Thus the British cultural historian Samuel Hynes has argued, "modernism had not changed, but reality had."[9]

Yet the realities of this war did change modernism. Horrified by the mass slaughter, many modernist artists abandoned the modernist principle of "art for art's sake," the idea that art has no moral purpose or social responsibility, that it conveys no message. Instead, they used modernist techniques to communicate their outrage. Paul Nash (1889–1940), a British landscape painter and army volunteer, explained in 1918, "I am no longer an artist, interested and curious, I am a messenger who will bring back word from the men who are fighting to those who want the war to go on forever. . . . may it burn their lousy souls."[10] Nash's depiction of the Western Front, *We Are Making a New World* (1918), transformed the landscape genre from an evocation of pastoral tranquility into a cry of pain.

## The War in Eastern Europe

The Western Front was only one in a number of theaters of war. Floundering in the snows of the Italian Alps, the Italian and Austrian armies fought each other along a stationary front for two brutal years after Italy, enticed by the promise of territorial gain, joined the war on the Allies' side. Characterized by futile offensives and essential immobility,

the war in Italy mirrored the conflict on the Western Front. In eastern Europe, however, a different plot unfolded. For three years, massive armies surged back and forth, as the plains and mountains of eastern Europe echoed with the tumult of spectacular advances, headlong retreats, and finally political revolution.

### The Eastern Front: A War of Movement

Much of the movement in eastern Europe consisted of Russians running—running forward in surprising advances, running back in terrifying retreats. When the war began in August 1914, Russia shocked its enemies by fielding a much stronger army much more quickly than German and Austrian military planners had expected. In a two-pronged onslaught, Russian troops headed against the Germans in East Prussia and against the Austrians in Galicia, the northeastern region of the Austrian Empire. Surprised by the speed of the Russian advance, German troops in East Prussia at first fell back, but skillful maneuvering by the German commanders Paul von Hindenburg (1847–1934) and Erich von Ludendorff (1865–1937) turned the Russian tide at the Battle of Tannenberg at the end of August. Within two weeks the Germans had shoved the Russian troops back across the border. In the subsequent months, the Germans advanced steadily into Russian imperial territory. At the same time, a combined German and Austrian assault forced the Russian army to retreat from Austrian Galicia—and more than 300 miles into its own territory. Russian casualties in the offensive stood at 2.5 million.

Over the next two years the pattern of Russian advances and retreats continued. Russian soldiers pushed into Austria-Hungary in June 1916, but could not sustain the attack. The summer of 1917 saw another initially successful Russian advance, but it too soon disintegrated into a retreat (see Map 24.3).

These retreats revealed that Russia's economic and political structures could not withstand the pressures of total war. Russian supply lines were so overextended that the poorly fed and inadequately clothed Russian troops found themselves without ammunition and unable to press ahead. Demoralized by defeat and by the daily grind of life without adequate rations or uniforms or weapons, Russian soldiers began to desert in ever-larger numbers. On the home front Russian workers and peasants grew ever more impatient with wartime deprivations and demands. This disaffection led to revolution. As we will explore in detail later in this chapter, revolution forced the tsar to abdicate in March 1917. In November, the Bolsheviks, a small group of socialist revolutionaries, seized control and moved quickly to pull Russia out of the war.

The Bolshevik military withdrawal finally freed Germany from the burden of waging a two-front war. Signed in March 1918, the Treaty of Brest-Litovsk° ceded to Germany all of Russia's western territories, containing a full one-third of the population of the prewar Russian Empire. Germany now controlled the imperial Russian territories in Poland, the Baltic states, and part of Byelorussia. But because it had to commit large numbers of troops to controlling this new territory, Germany reaped less advantage from this victory than might have been expected.

## Map 24.3   The Eastern and Middle Eastern Fronts, 1915–1918

Unlike the Western Front, the Eastern Front was far from stationary. By 1918, the Central Powers occupied Serbia, Romania, and much of European Russia. The entry of the Ottoman Empire on the side of the Central Powers in November 1914 extended the conflict into the Middle East. In 1915 Ottoman forces not only repelled an initial British advance toward Baghdad but also threatened Egypt. By the end of 1917, however, Arab nationalists helped the British defeat the Central Powers in the Middle East.

## The Forgotten Front: The Balkans

The new Balkan states were no strangers to war by 1914. After shrugging off Ottoman control, Greece, Bulgaria, Romania, and Serbia fought each other in the First and Second Balkan Wars of 1912 and 1913. In southeastern Europe, World War I was thus in many ways the "Third Balkan War," yet another installment in an ongoing competition for territory and power. Bulgaria joined the Central Powers in 1915, hoping to gain back the territory it had lost in the Second Balkan War. To protect its hold on this territory, Romania entered the war on the Allies' side in August 1916 and quickly found itself crushed between invading Bulgarian, German, and Austrian-Hungarian troops.

The Serbian experience was even more bleak. In the first year of the war Austrian and Serbian troops jostled back and forth for control of the country, but in October 1915 Bulgarian, German, and Austrian forces advanced into Serbia from three different directions. By November, the Serbian army had been pushed to the Albanian border. Two hundred thousand Serbian soldiers fled over the snow-swept mountains of Albania to the Adriatic Sea, in a disastrous "Winter March." Austrian troops occupied Serbia and placed the country under military rule. Like most military occupations, this one was brutal. By the war's end, approximately 25 percent of Serbian citizens lay dead.

### The Winter March

Of the 200,000 Serbian soldiers who attempted the "Winter March" in 1915, at least 40,000 died and another 60,000 were wounded.

## The World at War

The imperialist expansion of the later nineteenth century ensured that as soon as the war began, it jumped outside European borders. The British and French Empires supplied the Allies with invaluable military and manpower resources. Australia, New Zealand, Canada, India, South Africa, and Ireland supplied no less than 40 percent of Britain's military manpower during the war. More than 650,000 men from Indochina, Algeria, and French West Africa assisted the French war effort. (One of these men was

### A World at War: Sikh Cavalry Officers

Sikh cavalry officers from India patrol the Western Front. India provided 1.3 million men to assist the British war effort. Indian troops fought—and more than 49,000 Indian soldiers died—in battles in the Middle East, in East Africa, and on the Western Front. Similarly, black Senagalese soldiers fought for France on various fronts; 30,000 Senagalese died during the war.

Ho Chi Minh, who would later lead the Vietnamese struggle against France and then the United States.)

Fighting fronts multiplied around the globe as the major combatants struggled for imperial as well as European supremacy (see Map 24.4). Portugal joined the Allies largely because it hoped to expand its colonial possessions in Africa. Japan, too, entered the war for colonial gain. When the war began in August 1914, Japan seized the opportunity to snatch German colonial possessions in China. In return, Japan contributed to the Allied war effort by using its navy to protect Allied troop and supply ships in both the Pacific and the Mediterranean. By the end of 1914, most of Germany's colonies in the Far East had been occupied by Japanese and ANZAC troops.

The Middle East also became a key theater. When the Ottoman Empire joined the war on the side of Germany and Austria-Hungary in 1914, it posed a serious threat to Britain's economic and military interests in the Mediterranean and Middle East. Britain was desperate to protect Allied access both to the Suez Canal—a vital link to the soldiers and supplies of India, Australia, and New Zealand—and to Persian oil fields, an important source of fuel for the British navy. In a move that would have far-reaching consequences for twentieth-century geopolitics, the British joined forces with Arab nationalists. Led by a British soldier named T. E. Lawrence (1888–1935)—better known as "Lawrence of Arabia"—and inspired by promises of postwar national independence, Arab nationalists used guerilla

## Map 24.4  The World at War

Imperialist relationships and global economics ensured that a European conflict became a world war. In Africa both Portuguese and South African troops fought a bush war against German and native soldiers. Japan, the first non-European power to enter the war, occupied German colonial territories in Asia and the Pacific region. When the United States joined the Allies in April 1917, a number of Latin American countries also declared war on Germany.

warfare to destroy what remained of Ottoman rule in the Middle East. By 1917 the Ottomans had lost control of almost the entire coastal region of the Arabian peninsula bordering the Red Sea, and Lawrence and his Arab allies had captured Jerusalem.

## The War at Sea and the Entry of the United States

Despite the losses of its ally in the Middle East, at the beginning of 1918 Germany looked to be in a winning position. Engulfed in revolution, Russia had dropped out of the war and relieved Germany of the burden of fighting on two fronts. With Serbia and Romania both occupied by their forces, the Central Powers could claim to have won the war in eastern Europe. Yet Germany was far weaker than any map of its eastern conquests in 1917 could indicate. Germany was being strangled from the sea.

While infantrymen rotted in trenches and froze in mountain passes, the German and British navies fought a critical war at sea. German submarines sought to cut Britain's imperial lifeline and starve out its civilian population by sinking ships before they could reach British ports. Almost 14,000 British sailors and civilians died in these submarine attacks. In turn, British destroyers stretched a blockade across all ocean and sea passageways to Germany and its allies.

The Allied blockade proved effective in preventing food and other essential raw materials from reaching Germany, Austria-Hungary, and their associates. Food shortages sparked riots in more than thirty German cities in 1916. When the potato crop that year failed and eliminated one of the only sources of nutrition left, children's rations were limited to *one-tenth* of their actual needs.

Desperate to win the war quickly, German policymakers in 1917 took a huge gamble when they decided to up the tempo of their submarine war against Britain. Suspecting that supposedly neutral American passenger ships were delivering essential war materiel to Britain, they ordered their submarines to sink without warning any ship heading for British shores. The Germans were well aware that this policy of unrestricted submarine warfare would very likely pull the United States into the war. In May 1915, a German submarine had torpedoed the British passenger liner *Lusitania* and killed almost 1,200 people, including 128 Americans. The furious response from the United States had forced Germany to restrict its submarine attacks. By 1917, however, Germany stood on the brink of economic collapse, and German policymakers decided they had no choice but to resume unrestricted attacks on ships heading for British ports. They gambled they could defeat Britain in a last-ditch effort before the addition of the United States to the Allies could make much of a difference. Over

## CHRONOLOGY

### The End of the War, 1917–1918

| 1917 | Stalemate continues on the Western Front |
| --- | --- |
| March | Collapse of the Russian imperial government |
| April | U.S. declaration of war on Germany |
| November | Bolshevik Revolution in Russia |
| December | Bolsheviks sign armistice with Germany; capture of Jerusalem by British troops |
| **1918** | |
| March | Treaty of Brest-Litovsk |
| March–July | German offensive on Western Front, rapid gains |
| July–November | Allied counteroffensive begins |
| September | Bulgaria and Allies sign armistice |
| November 3 | Austria-Hungary sues for peace with Allies |
| November 9 | Kaiser William abdicates |
| November 11 | Fighting ends on Western Front at 11:00 A.M. |

the next eight months German submarines sank 500 British merchant ships.

The United States declared war on Germany in April 1917. Outrage over American deaths at sea served as the most immediate cause of American entry into the war. Four other factors, however, also played a role. First, Franco-British news stories about German atrocities during the invasion of Belgium had persuaded many Americans that right rested on the Allied side. Second, the Russian Revolution of March 1917 removed an important obstacle to American cooperation with the Allies—the tsarist regime. Americans had balked at the idea of allying with the repressive government of Tsar Nicholas II, but the March Revolution, which overthrew Nicholas, reminded many in the United States of the American Revolution and offered American policymakers a more ideologically acceptable wartime partner. Third, by the time President Woodrow Wilson asked the U.S. Congress for a declaration of war, the American economy was thoroughly intertwined with that of the Allies. Trade between the United States and the Allied nations had grown from $825 million in 1914 to more than $3 billion in 1916, and American bankers had loaned more than $2 billion to the Allied governments. Finally, the German government committed a serious blunder in the spring of 1917 when it offered to back Mexico in recovering New Mexico, Arizona, and Texas in exchange for Mexican support should war break out between Germany and the United States. The interception of a telegram sent by the German foreign minister Arthur Zimmermann exposed this offer and inflamed anti-German sentiment in the

United States. The German resumption of unrestricted submarine warfare, then, simply put flame to kindling that was already in place.

The U.S. declaration of war (followed by those of Brazil, Costa Rica, Cuba, Guatemala, Haiti, Honduras, Nicaragua, and Panama) provided an immediate psychological boost for the Allies, but several months passed before American troops arrived on the battlefield in significant numbers. By July 1918, however, the United States was sending 300,000 fresh soldiers to Europe each month. The Allies now had access to an almost unlimited supply of materiel and men. Eventually nearly two million American soldiers were sent to Europe and almost 49,000 American soldiers died in battle.

### Back in Motion:
### The Western Front in 1918

Faced with the prospect of having to fight fresh American forces, German policymakers decided to gamble one more time. On March 2, 1918—before the bulk of the U.S. army had been deployed—the German army launched a massive ground assault against British and French lines. The gamble almost succeeded. In just thirty minutes the German troops broke through the British front line; in seven days, German soldiers advanced forty miles; by April the German army stood just fifty miles from Paris.

What explains this sudden shift on the Western Front from a conflict characterized by stalemate and deadlock to a war of rapid and decisive movement? The answer is that after three and a half years of relentless, pointless slaughter, the German High Command in 1918 finally developed strategies that matched offensive techniques with industrialized killing technology. As we have seen, in the first years of the war commanders remained committed to offensive techniques suited to an age of preindustrial warfare—the mass charge, the cavalry attack. What they failed to realize was that industrial technologies such as the machine gun had transformed the power of defensive war. Certainly Western commanders were well-acquainted with the power of the machine gun. In the imperial conflicts discussed in Chapter 23, the machine gun enabled small European forces to mow down enormous indigenous armies. But on the Western Front, both sides possessed the machine gun. In other words, both sides were good on defense but poor on offense.

In 1918, however, the Germans came up with a new offensive strategy. They did not simply throw masses of men against machine guns. Instead of a frontal assault dictated by commanders sitting well behind the lines, Germany's offensive of 1918 consisted of a series of small group attacks aiming to cut behind British and French positions rather than straight on against them. In addition, the Germans in 1918 scrapped the massive preliminary artillery barrage that signaled when and where an attack was about to begin. In place of the barrage they employed sudden gas and artillery bursts throughout the offensive. The rapid German advance in the spring of 1918 showed that technique had caught up with technology.

In July, however, the Allies stopped the German advance; in August they broke through the German lines and began to push the German army backward. Throughout the summer the push continued. By September the Western Front, which had stood so stationary for so long, was being rolled eastward at a rapid clip.

The final German gamble failed for three reasons: First, the German advance was so rapid that it overstrained German manpower and supply lines; second, the Allies learned from their enemies and adopted the same new offensive strategies; and third, the Allies figured out how to make effective use of a new offensive technology—the tank. Developed in Britain, the tank obliterated the defensive advantages of machine-gun-fortified trenches. A twentieth-century offense met a twentieth-century defense, and the war turned mobile.

1916 Debut of the British Tank

Reinforced with fresh American troops and the promise of more to come, the Allied forces surged forward against the hungry and demoralized Germans. When the Bulgarian, Ottoman, and Austrian armies collapsed in September and October, Germany stood alone. On November 11, 1918, German leaders signed an armistice and the war ended.

# The Home Fronts

■ How did total war structure the home fronts?

The term *home front* was coined during World War I to highlight the fact that this conflict was fought not only by soldiers on the front lines, but also by civilians at home. Created by industrialization, total war demanded the wholehearted mobilization of a combatant nation's productive capacity. Total war recast and in some cases revolutionized not only the economic but also the political, social, and gender relations of the nations involved.

## Industrial War

World War I was the first industrial war. Poison gas, the machine gun, barbed wire, canned foods, mass-produced uniforms and boots, and of course shovels all poured out of Europe's factories and helped shape this war. Even more important, industrialization made it possible for governments to deploy the vast masses of men mobilized in this conflict. Consider this comparison: The Battle of Waterloo, which ended the Napoleonic Wars in 1815, involved 170,000 men; the Battle of Sedan, which ended the Franco-Prussian War in 1870, involved 300,000 soldiers. The first Battle of the Marne, however, fought between the Germans and the

French in September 1914, involved one million combatants. By the war's end, more than 70 million men had been mobilized; in France and Germany, approximately 80 percent of the men of draft age were called up. Only industrialized production could keep these huge armies supplied with weapons, ammunition, and other necessities.

It thus became clear that this war would be won in the factories as much as on the front lines. Those nations that collapsed did so at least in part because they lost the war at home. In Austria-Hungary, factories could not produce enough uniforms to clothe the empire's soldiers. Similarly, Russia's underdeveloped industrial sector and infrastructure meant that its soldiers failed to receive needed supplies. In the end, the Allies (minus Russia) won the war in large part because of their greater economic power.

### The Expansion of the State

At first, no government realized the crucial role that industrial labor would play in this war. Both military and political leaders believed that the war would end quickly, and that success depended on throwing as many men as possible into the front lines. In France, even munitions factories were shut down and their workers sent to the front. Governments practiced "business as usual"—letting the free market decide wages, prices, and supply—with disastrous results. Soaring rates of inflation, the rapid expansion of the black market, growing public resentment over war profiteering (the practice of private businessmen making huge profits off the war), and, most crucially, shortages of essential military supplies, including shells, proved that a total war economy needed total regulation.

Beginning in 1915, both the Allied and Central Powers' governments gradually assumed the power to requisition supplies, dictate wages, limit profits, and forbid workers to change jobs. In Germany, the increasing regulation of the economy was called "war socialism," a misleading term because it was big business rather than ordinary workers who benefited. The German army worked in partnership with large industrial firms to ensure the supply of war materiel to the front lines, while the Auxiliary Service Law of 1916 drafted all men age 17 to 60 for war work. Measures such as these greatly expanded the size and power of the central governments in the combatant states. For example, in 1914 the British office in charge of military purchases employed twenty clerks. By 1918, it had become the Department of Munitions, an enormous bureaucratic empire with 65,000 employees overseeing more than three million men and women working in government-owned and -operated munitions plants.

This expansion of governmental power was one of the most striking aspects of the war experience on the home front. Even in Britain, bastion of liberalism, the demands of total war seriously restricted individual freedom. Flying in the face of tradition, in 1916 Britain's government imposed the draft—a clear example of the requirements of the state overriding the desires of the individual. By the war's end, governments had moved further, not only dictating all aspects of economic life but also controlling many areas of social and intellectual choice. The British government restricted the hours that pubs could be open, as a way of encouraging workers to show up for work sober. It also tampered with time itself, introducing Daylight Saving Time as a means of maximizing war production.

### The Politics of Total War

The war's reliance on industrial production greatly empowered industrial producers—the workers. In 1915 both France and Britain abandoned political party competition and formed coalition governments, which included socialist and working-class representatives. At the same time, political leaders welcomed labor unionists as partners in shaping the wartime economy. In return, French and British union leaders agreed to a ban on labor strikes and the "deskilling" of certain jobs—a measure that allowed unskilled laborers, particularly women, to take the place of skilled workers at much lower rates of pay.

Despite these "no strike" agreements, both Britain and France witnessed a sharp rise in the number of labor strikes in 1916 and in 1917. Faced with the potential of disintegration on the home front, political leaders in Britain and France reacted similarly. Both countries witnessed the emergence of war governments committed to total victory. In Britain, David Lloyd George (1863–1945) became prime minister at the end of 1916. A Welsh artisan's son who had fought hard to reach the top of Britain's class-bound, English-dominated political system, Lloyd George was not a man to settle for a compromise peace. One year later, Georges Clemenceau (1841–1929) became prime minister of France. Nicknamed the "Tiger," Clemenceau demanded victory. When asked to detail his government's program, he replied simply, "*Je fais la guerre!*" ("I make war!").

Making war, however, was not possible without public support, as officials in both France and Britain realized. They cultivated this support in two ways. First, they sought to depict the war as a struggle between democracy and authoritarianism—a crusade not simply for national power or economic gain but for a better world. Second, they recognized that if civilian morale were to be sustained, the basic needs of ordinary citizens had to be met. Both governments intervened regularly in the economy to ensure that workers received higher wages, better working conditions, and a fair distribution of food stocks. In state-owned munitions factories, workers for the first time received benefits such as communal kitchens and day care. Food rationing (although not implemented until quite late in the war) actually improved the diets of many poor families.

The situation in Germany differed significantly. The parliamentary political voice of the German working class, the Social Democratic Party (SPD), was not invited to participate in a coalition government. Instead, until the very last weeks of the war German political leadership remained in the hands of the conservative aristocracy. Increasingly, the aristocratic generals Hindenburg and Ludendorff—the heroes of the Battle of Tannenberg—called the political shots. The army and big industrial firms seized control of German economic life. Given the power to set prices and profit margins, industrialists—not surprisingly—made a killing. Their incomes soared, while ordinary workers were ground down by escalating inflation and chronic food shortages. By 1917, industrial unrest had slowed German war production, and civilian discontent had reached dangerous levels. Unlike the British and the French, the German government proved unable to control the unrest. The success of the Allied blockade meant Germans were starving. In contrast, living standards among employed workers in France and in Britain rose during the war.

## The World Turned Upside Down

By the war's end, changes in the relations among classes and between men and women caused many Europeans to feel as if their world had turned upside down. European workers grew more radical as they realized the possibilities of their own collective power, as well as the potential of the state as an instrument of social change. The fact that by 1917 many of these workers were women also had revolutionary implications. In the work world and in society at large, gender roles, like class relations, underwent a marked shift.

### The War's Impact on Social Relations

In the trenches and on the battlefields, World War I had a leveling effect. For many young middle- and upper-class soldiers, the war provided their first sustained contact with both manual labor and manual laborers. In letters home, they testified to a newfound respect for both, as the horrors of the war experience broke down rigid class barriers.

On the home front, however, social relations grew more rather than less hostile. During the war years, inflation eroded the savings of the middle class and left bourgeois men and women desperately seeking ways to maintain their social and economic status. In Germany and throughout eastern Europe, drastic food shortages and falling real wages produced a revolutionary situation. By contrast, in both Britain and France, a rising standard of living demonstrated to workers the benefits of an active and interventionist state. Yet class hostilities rose in western Europe, too. Workers, having finally tasted the economic pie, fought for a bigger piece, while the middle class fought to defend its shrinking share. Working-class activists demanded that the state continue to regulate the economy in peacetime as it did in waging total war, to improve the standard of living of ordinary workers.

### The War's Impact on Gender Relations

By 1916, labor shortages in key military industries, combined with the need to free up as many men as possible for fighting, meant that governments on both sides actively recruited women for the paid workforce. Women were suddenly everywhere in very visible roles: as bus drivers, eleva-

**Women in the War**
Women often served at the front in extremely dangerous conditions. The two women in this photograph set up a dressing station to treat the wounded just five yards behind the trenches.

tor operators, train conductors, and sales clerks. In eastern Europe, the agricultural labor force came to consist almost entirely of women. In western Europe, women joined labor unions in unprecedented numbers. They took on extremely dangerous positions in munitions factories; they worked just behind the front lines as ambulance drivers and nurses; in 1917 and 1918, they often led the way in walking off the job to demand better conditions.

The impact of the war on women's roles should not be exaggerated, however. Throughout the war, more women continued to work in domestic service—as cooks, maids, nannies—than in any other sector of the economy. The great majority of the women who did move into skilled industrial employment were not new to the world of paid employment. Before 1914 they had worked in different, lower-paying jobs. And they certainly were not treated as men's equals. In government-run factories in Britain, women received as little as 50 percent of men's wages for the same job.

Nevertheless, for many women, the war constituted a profoundly liberating experience. With their husbands away, many wives made decisions on their own for the first time. The average wages of female munitions workers in Britain were three times their prewar earnings. But just as crucially, the war validated women's claims to citizenship. Total war made the female civilian into a combatant. For example, the *Win the War Cookery Book* (1917) urged British housewives to view the preparation of meals in a time of food shortages as part of the war effort: "The British fighting line shifts and extends now *you* are in it. The struggle is not only on land and sea; it is in *your* larder, *your* kitchen and *your* dining room. Every meal you serve is now literally a battle."[11] With "women's work" as central to national survival as men's work, women came to see themselves as an integral part of the national community.

Middle-class women, especially, testified to the freedom the war brought. Before 1914, the position of middle-class women in Europe had undergone important changes, as Chapter 22 detailed. From 1870 on, the numbers of women in higher education and paid employment expanded, women increasingly served in local government, and a European-wide women's suffrage campaign emerged. Despite the rise of these strong challenges to the ideology of separate spheres, however, the predominant idea remained that women were biologically suited for the private confines of home and family and men for the public arena of work and politics. Many middle-class girls continued to live lives marked by immobility and passivity—sheltered within the family home, subject to paternal authority, waiting for a marriage proposal. The war, however, threw women into the public space. The middle-class girl who before 1914 was forbidden to travel without a chaperone might be driving an ambulance, splashing through the mud and blood, or washing the bodies of naked working-class soldiers.

At the same time that the war smashed many of the boundaries to which women had been confined, it sharply narrowed the world of the middle-class male soldier. While women were in charge and on the move—driving buses, flying transport planes, ferrying the wounded—men were stuck in the mud, confined to narrow ditches, waiting for orders. Expecting to be heroes, men of action, they found themselves instead living the sort of immobile, passive lives that had characterized the prewar middle-class women's experience. Ironically, then, at the same time the war gave women new power, it introduced many men, particularly middle-class men, to new levels of powerlessness. In total war, even gender roles turned upside down.

Yet when the war ended, some of these radical changes proved to be very temporary indeed. The much-heralded wartime movement of women into skilled factory jobs and public positions such as bus drivers and train conductors was rapidly reversed. For example, by the terms of the British Restoration of Pre-War Practices Act (1919), women who had taken up skilled factory jobs received two weeks' pay and a train ticket home.

Other changes appeared more permanent. France in 1919 possessed ten times as many female law students and three times as many female medical students as it had in 1914. British women over age 30 received the vote on a limited basis while in the United States, Germany, and most of the new states in eastern Europe, the achievement of female suffrage was more complete. (Women in France, Italy, Switzerland, and Greece remained unenfranchised.) Cultural changes also seemed to signal a gender revolution. Women began to smoke in public; trousers became acceptable female attire; hemlines rose dramatically; the corset and bustle disappeared for good.

## Identifying the Enemy: From Propaganda to Genocide

We have seen that total war demanded an unprecedented expansion of state control over economic affairs. To ensure that their citizens remained committed to the war effort, governments also regulated the production and distribution of ideas. First, they eliminated ideas they viewed as dangerous. Pacifists and war objectors faced prison sentences and even execution. French prime minister Clemenceau adopted a particularly harsh stance toward all dissenting opinion. Journalists and rival politicians—even the former prime minister—who dared suggest that France negotiate with Germany rather than fight on for total victory were thrown in prison.

At the same time, governments worked to create ideas that would encourage a total war mentality. Propaganda now emerged as a crucial political tool. The careful censorship of newspapers and doctoring of photographs ensured that the public received a positive image of the war. In

# Shell Shock: From Woman's Malady to Soldier's Affliction

Broken in mind as well as body, the casualties of World War I forced medical practitioners to think anew about the connections among emotional anguish, physical disabilities, and gender roles. Doctors discovered to their horror and surprise that in the trenches of total war, men's bodies began to act like women's. Pouring into hospital units came thousands of men with the symptoms of a malady that before the war was considered a woman's disease—hysteria.

The word *hysteria* comes from the Greek word *hystera,* for "womb" or "uterus," and for much of Western history doctors believed that women were doomed to suffer from hysteria because of their physical makeup—because they were afflicted with wombs. Physicians long considered the uterus to be an inherently weak and unstable organ, prone even to detach itself from its proper place and wander about the body causing havoc. By the end of the nineteenth century, however, the diagnosis had changed. Doctors continued to regard hysteria as primarily a woman's disease but they were more inclined to view it as a neurosis, a mental and emotional disorder. The symptoms varied enormously but included bouts of shrieking, emotional problems such as depression or breakdown, and physical ailments without any clear physical cause—ranging from abnormal fatigue or insomnia to the inability to walk.

With war came thousands of soldiers with the symptoms of hysteria—men who could not stop shaking, men with healthy limbs who could not move, men certain that rats were nibbling at their bodies. At first, doctors dismissed such symptoms as signs of cowardice: These were men faking illness to avoid doing their duty. But by 1916, with such men accounting for 40 percent of the casualties in British combat zones alone, doctors realized they were dealing with an epidemic of male hysteria.

The war illustrated that hysteria was linked not to the uterus or the weak female nervous system but rather to an environment of immobility and passivity. Neither the length of time a soldier had served nor the intensity or horror of his combat experience were significant in producing breakdowns. Instead, the most important factor was his level of immobility. Men on the Western Front suddenly found themselves in positions of passivity and confinement. Deprived of the ability to make decisions, to determine their future, to act, many men broke down.

Yet the reincarnation of what had been considered a woman's malady as a soldier's affliction did not lead doctors to reexamine their understanding of the woman's body or the woman's role. Instead, they reconfigured the disease. Hysteria became "shell shock." The treatment differed as well. Convinced that female hysteria was a result of the overstimulation of the nervous system, doctors prescribed total rest cures for their female patients. Women found themselves confined to rooms with bare walls and shuttered windows, forbidden to read or to receive visitors. In contrast, doctors ordered male soldiers with shell shock to engage in intense physical and mental activity. Thus, despite the upheaval in gender roles caused by total war, doctors continued to view women's bodies as inherently passive and men's as naturally active. The findings of medical science remained linked to cultural conventions.

**Red Cross Christmas Roll Call Dec. 16-23ʳᵈ**

*The* GREATEST MOTHER *in the* WORLD

**Role Reversal**
In this British Red Cross poster, the soldier is infantilized in the arms of the nurse. Many men found their forced confinement and passivity profoundly unsettling.

## For Discussion

Why does the contrast between the medical treatment of hysteria and that of shell shock indicate that the war had a limited impact on gender roles? What evidence in this chapter points to the opposite conclusion?

**Never Forget!**
This French poster uses the image of a raped woman and her murdered child to arouse anti-German passions. The image recalls the German invasion of neutral Belgium, which soon came to be called "the rape of Belgium." All combatant states produced similar propaganda pieces.

Germany, giant wooden statues of the war hero Hindenburg were paraded to rally war enthusiasm, while in all the combatant nations, poster campaigns used the techniques developed in the new mass advertising industry to arouse patriotic fervor.

Fostering a total war mentality meant not only cultivating love for the Father- or Motherland, but also stirring up hatred for those labeled as the Enemy. In words that were soon set to music and became a popular wartime song, the poet (and army private) Ernst Lissauer (1882–1937) urged Germans to "hate [England] with a lasting hate . . . Hate of seventy millions, choking down."[12] In Britain, anti-German sentiment was so strong that the royal family changed its name from Hanover to Windsor in an effort to erase its German lineage.

In the ethnic cauldron of eastern Europe, this hatred was often directed at minority groups who were perceived as the enemy within: In Austria-Hungary, for example, more than 500 Bosnian Serbs and hundreds of Ukrainians were shot without trial because they were seen as Russian sympathizers.

The most horrific result of the tendency to look for the enemy at home occurred not in Austria-Hungary but in the Ottoman Empire, where suspicion of the Armenian minority resulted in mass murder. Massacres of Armenians under Ottoman rule had punctuated the decades before 1914. The war accentuated the Turkish-Armenian conflict. Recognizing that Armenian loyalty to imperial rule was shaky, to say the least, the Ottoman government decided to eliminate the Armenian population from Turkey. This brutal "solution" to what was described as the "Armenian question" began in April 1915. After arresting Armenian elites (and thus removing potential resistance leaders from Armenian communities) Turkish troops rounded up and killed Armenian men. In some cases, special

**DOCUMENT**
A Turkish Officer Describes the Armenian Massacres

**The Harvest of War**
The Turkish massacre of more than one million Armenians illustrates the destructive consequences of combining nationalist hatred with total war. This criminal horror is often seen as foreshadowing the Jewish Holocaust during World War II.

forces marched the men outside their town or village and then shot them; in other instances, they were pushed into caves and asphyxiated by fires blocking the entrances. The Ottoman government then ordered the women, children, and the elderly deported to Syria. Driven from their homes on short notice, they marched through mountain and desert terrain without food or water. Rapes and executions were commonplace. Between 1915 and 1918, more than one million Armenian men, women, and children died in this attempt at genocide, the murder of an entire people.

# War and Revolution

■ What were the consequences of this war for the European and the global political and international order?

The machinery of total war tore at the social and political fabric of European societies. As seams began to fray and gaping holes appeared, many welcomed what they saw as the opportunity to tear apart the old cloth and create something entirely new. Some of these revolutionaries were Marxists aiming to build a socialist world order. Others were nationalists, determined to assert the rights of their ethnic or linguistic group, or to overthrow their colonial rulers. Not all revolutionaries belonged to underground or terrorist groups. One individual who dared to demand a new world order was the president of the United States, Woodrow Wilson. The peace settlement, however, fell far short of creating a new world. In Europe, many of the conflicts that had caused the war remained unresolved, with disastrous consequences for the next generation. Outside Europe, redesigned imperialist regimes encountered anti-Western forces that emerged from the war stronger than ever before.

## The Russian Revolutions

Tsarist Russia began the war already sharply divided, its 125 million inhabitants splintered into more than one hundred different national groups—from Inuits in the north to Kazakhs in the southeast to Germans in the west. Ethnic hostilities sapped Russia's defenses from the very start. In Poland, for example, many of the four million Jews under Russian imperial rule welcomed the German army as liberators from tsarist violence and repression. In the regions of Latvia and Lithuania, anti-Russian sentiment flared high, and nationalists saw the war as opening the door to national independence.

The war brought political chaos to Russia. Nicholas II (r. 1894–1917), a man of limited intelligence and a remarkable capacity for self-delusion, insisted on going to the front and commanding his army. He left political affairs in the hands of his wife Alexandra (1872–1918) and her spiritual mentor Grigorii Rasputin (1869–1916). Rasputin is one of the more intriguing characters in twentieth-century history. An illiterate, unwashed faith healer from a peasant background, he possessed a well-documented and still-unexplained ability to stop the bleeding of Alexei, the young hemophiliac heir to the throne. To many high-ranking Russians, however, Rasputin was not a miracle worker but a traitor. Because Rasputin opposed the war against Germany, they perceived him as a voice of treason whispering in the German-born tsarina's ear. In 1916 Russian noblemen murdered Rasputin, in hopes of restoring authority and stability to the tsarist government.

## The March Revolution

Rasputin's removal was not enough to stop the forces of revolution stirred up by total war. The political disarray he observed at the highest levels of government dumbfounded the French ambassador, who wrote in January 1917, "I am obliged to report that, at the present moment, the Russian Empire is run by lunatics."[13] The lack of effective political leadership, combined with Russian losses on the battlefield, brought to a boil the simmering disaffection with the tsarist government. Almost two million Russian soldiers had died and many more had been wounded or taken prisoner. Economic and communications networks had broken down, bread prices were rising, and people were hungry. Even members of the tsarist government began to ask not *if* revolution would occur, but *when*.

The answer came on March 8, 1917. A group of women workers in Petrograd staged a demonstration to protest inadequate food supplies. Over the course of the next few days, similar demonstrations flickered across the city; on March 11, they coalesced into a major revolutionary fire when the troops who were ordered to put down the protest joined it instead. Governmental orders lost all authority, and on March 15 Tsar Nicholas was forced to abdicate. The Russian Revolution had begun.

Who now controlled Russia? Two competing centers of power soon emerged: the Provisional Government and the Petrograd Soviet. On March 12, the Duma, or Russian parliament, created a Provisional Government from among its members. Like the Duma, the new Provisional Government was dominated by members of the gentry and middle classes: professionals, businessmen, intellectuals, bureaucrats. These men tended to be liberals who believed that Russia was now moving along the path toward a parliamentary democracy. They quickly enacted important reforms such as universal suffrage, the eight-hour workday, and civic equality for all citizens.

But at the same time that the Provisional Government was struggling to bring order to the chaos of revolutionary Russia, across the empire industrial workers and soldiers formed soviets°, or councils, to articulate their grievances and hopes. As Russian revolutionary socialists in exile

## DOCUMENT

# Revolution in the Front Lines

*At age 25, Maria Botchkareva, a poor Russian woman who had been forced to work as a prostitute, volunteered for service as a soldier. Women served as nurses, ambulance drivers, and transport plane pilots on both sides of the war, but only in Russia did women serve in combat, and even there the presence of a woman on the front lines was quite exceptional. Botchkareva earned a well-deserved reputation as a fierce fighter, and was honored for her bravery. In 1917, she was serving at the front with her company when she heard startling news from the capital.*

The first swallow to warn us of the approaching storm was a soldier from our Company who had returned from a leave of absence at Petrograd: "Oh my! If you but knew, boys, what is going on in the rear! Revolution! Everywhere they talk of overthrowing the Tsar. The capital is aflame with revolution." . . . Finally, the joyous news arrived. The Commander gathered the entire Regiment to read to us the glorious words. . . . The miracle had happened! Tsarism, which enslaved us and thrived on the blood and marrow of the toiler, had fallen. Freedom, Equality and Brotherhood! How sweet were these words to our ears! We were transported. There were tears of joy, embraces, dancing. It all seemed a dream, a wonderful dream. Who ever believed that the hated regime would be destroyed so easily and in our own time?

The Commander read to us the manifesto, which concluded with a fervent appeal to us to hold the line with greater vigilance than ever, now that we were free citizens, to defend our newly won liberty from the attacks of the Kaiser and his slaves. . . . Then came Order No. 1, signed by the Petrograd Soviet of Workmen and Soldiers. Soldiers and officers were now equal, it declared. All the citizens of Free Russia were equal henceforth. . . .

We were dazzled by this shower of brilliant phrases. The men went about as if intoxicated. For four days the festival continued unabated. . . . There were meetings, meetings, and meetings. . . . All duty was abandoned. . . . The front became a veritable insane asylum.

One day, in the first week of the revolution, I ordered a soldier to take up duty at the listening-post. He refused.

Source: From Maria Botchkareva, *Yashka: My Life as Peasant, Officer and Exile* (New York: Frederick A. Stokes Company, 1919), 139–145.

---

across Europe returned to their homeland in the weeks after the March Revolution began, they assumed leading roles in the Petrograd Soviet, which soon became a powerful political rival to the less radical Provisional Government.

The revolution, however, did not originate with nor was it controlled by either the liberals in the Provisional Government or the socialists in the Petrograd Soviet. Nicholas II was overthrown by a popular revolution, and at the core of this popular revolution stood a simply stated demand: "Peace, Land, Bread." Soldiers—and most Russians—wanted an immediate end to a war that had long ceased to make any sense to them. Peasants, as always, wanted land, their guarantee of survival in a chaotic world. And city dwellers wanted bread—food in sufficient quantities and at affordable prices.

The Provisional Government could not satisfy these demands. It did promise the gradual redistribution of royal and monastic lands, but peasants, inspired by the revolution and unconstrained by the liberal regard for law and the rights of private property, wanted land immediately. More important, by the summer of 1917 no Russian government could have provided bread without providing peace. Russia no longer had the resources both to continue its war effort and to reconstruct its economy. The population of the cities began to dwindle as food disappeared from the shops, factories ceased operation because of shortages of raw materials, and currency had little value. Peace appeared impossible, however. Not only did Russia have commitments to its allies, but German armies stood deep within Russian territory. A separate peace with Germany would mean huge territorial losses. And so the war continued.

But so, too, did the revolution. Peasants effected their own land reform by simply seizing the land they wanted. Soldiers declared their own peace by deserting in huge numbers. (Of every 1,000-man troop sent to the front, fewer than 250 men actually made it into combat. The rest deserted.) The Provisional Government grew increasingly unpopular. Not even the appointment of the popular socialist and Petrograd Soviet member Alexander Kerensky (1881–1970) as prime minister could stabilize the government's position.

## The November Revolution

This tumultuous situation created the opportunity for the Bolsheviks°, one of the socialist factions in the Petrograd Soviet, to emerge as a powerful revolutionary force. In April 1917, the Bolshevik leader, Vladimir Lenin (1870–1924), returned from almost twenty years in exile. While still in his teens, Lenin had committed himself to revolution after his older brother was executed for trying to assassinate Tsar Alexander III. Iron-willed and ruthlessly pragmatic, Lenin argued that a committed group of professional revolutionaries could force a working-class revolution on Russia immediately.

**The Revolution's Hero**

In this heroic portrait by Gemalde von A. M. Gerassimow, Lenin pushes the revolution and the Russian people forward.

By the fall of 1917, Bolshevik membership had grown from 10,000 to 250,000, and the party had achieved a majority in the Petrograd Soviet. Lenin now demanded the immediate overthrow of the Provisional Government. "Insurrection is an art," he declared, something to be made, not something that happens spontaneously. By promising "Peace, Land, Bread," Lenin would take control. On November 9, Bolshevik fighters captured the Winter Palace in Petrograd, where the Provisional Government had been sitting.

The *second* Russian Revolution was underway. The Bolsheviks declared a policy of land and peace—land partition with no payment of compensation to estate owners and an immediate peace with Germany, regardless of the cost. (And as we have seen, the cost was high: According to the terms of the Treaty of Brest-Litovsk, signed with Germany in 1918, Russia lost its western territories.) Not everyone in Russia was won over by promises of peace and land, however. Confronted with a diverse array of opponents, the Bolsheviks turned to the methods of terror. After an assassination attempt against Lenin in August 1918, the

Bolshevik secret police received the power to execute without trial. More than 500 individuals were shot in a single day in Petrograd.

During the next two years, the Bolsheviks waged a brutal war against domestic and international opponents of their Communist Revolution. This civil war proved Lenin's promises of "Peace, Land, Bread" to be hollow. Peasant farms were transformed into battlefields as five years of civil war killed off more combatants than had World War I. In the resulting famine, death tolls reached as high as five million. Yet, as the next chapter shows, the Bolsheviks emerged victorious. The Russian Empire was remade as the Soviet Union, a communist state.

## The Spreading Revolution

The victory of the Bolsheviks in Russia inspired socialists across Europe and around the world. In January 1919, communists in Buenos Aires, Argentina, led by Russian immigrants, controlled the city for three days until they were crushed by the Argentine army. British dockworkers struck in support of the Bolshevik Revolution, and in French cities general strikes caused chaos. In Austria, revolutionaries attempted to take control of government buildings in Vienna but were quickly defeated by the Austrian army. In Hungary, Bela Kun, a journalist who had come to admire the Bolsheviks while a prisoner of war in Russia, established a short-lived soviet regime in the spring of 1919.

Revolution also swept through defeated Germany. Disillusion with the kaiser's regime had set in long before Germany had lost the war. Defeat simply accentuated the desire for radical political change. But the first revolutionary step in Germany was a response not to popular desire but to American demands. In October 1918, Germany's military commanders recommended that the German government enter into peace negotiations. U.S. president Woodrow Wilson, however, saw the war as a democratic crusade and so refused to allow the Allies to negotiate with representatives of the kaiser's authoritarian regime. To placate Wilson, the kaiser was forced to overhaul Germany's political system. For the first time, representatives of left-wing and centrist parties—including the SPD, the largest socialist party in Europe—were invited to join the government.

This "revolution from above" coincided with and was challenged by a "revolution from below." Inspired by the success of the Bolshevik Revolution, many German workers rejected the SPD's vision of socialism as too moderate. The members of the SPD believed in working for gradual social reform through parliamentary action and debate. A much more radical alternative was offered by a breakaway socialist faction called the Spartacists (after Spartacus, the gladiator who led a slave revolt against Rome in the first century B.C.E.). Directed by Karl Liebknecht (1871–1919) and Rosa Luxemburg (1870–1919), the Spartacists wanted Germany to follow Russia down the path to communist revolution.

### The Spartacist Revolution in Germany

The effort to establish a soviet government in Berlin took the form of street fighting. This photograph shows one street skirmish that occurred in the city's newspaper district.

In Berlin, thousands rallied behind Liebknecht and Luxemburg. By November 8, communists had declared the establishment of a Soviet republic in the province of Bavaria; the Red Flag—symbol of communism—was flying over eleven German cities; and revolutionaries had seized control of all the main railroad junctions.

On November 9, the head of the SPD, Friedrich Ebert (1871–1925), became chancellor of Germany and the kaiser abdicated. One of Ebert's colleagues in the SPD triumphantly proclaimed from the window of the Reichstag building in Berlin that Germany was now a parliamentary democracy. Almost at that very moment, Karl Liebknecht stood at another window (in the occupied royal palace) and announced that Germany was now a revolutionary communist state. With two opposing versions of revolution on offer, civil war raged until the spring of 1919, when the SPD defeated the communists for control of the new Germany.

## The Failure of Wilson's Revolution

At the beginning of 1919, the representatives of the victorious Allied nations gathered in Paris to draw up the treaties that would wrap up the war. Yet their aims were far higher than simply ending the war; they wished to construct a new Europe and to reconfigure the conduct of international affairs. At the center of this high endeavor was the American college-professor-turned-president Woodrow Wilson. Like the Bolsheviks, Wilson offered a vision of a radical new future. He based *his* version of revolutionary change on the ideal of national self-determination—a world in which "every people should be left free to determine its own polity, its own way of development, unhindered, unthreat-

ened, unafraid, the little along with the great and powerful." The map of Europe would be redrawn, the old empires replaced with independent, ethnically homogenous, democratic nation-states.

These new nation-states would interact differently from the empires of the past. In what he called his Fourteen Points, Wilson demanded a revolution in international affairs. He argued that "Points" such as freedom of the seas, freedom of trade, and open diplomacy (an end to secret treaties) would break down barriers and guarantee peace and prosperity for all peoples. The cornerstone of this new world order would be an international organization, the League of Nations°, which would oversee the implementation of these new measures and would have the power to resolve disputes between nations. Wilson and other planners

---

### CHRONOLOGY

### Revolution in Russia, 1917–1921

**1917**

| | |
|---|---|
| March 8 | St. Petersburg/Petrograd women's protest; revolution begins |
| March 12 | Establishment of Provisional Government |
| March 15 | Abdication of Tsar Nicholas II |
| November 9 | Bolshevik overthrow of the Provisional Government |
| **1918–1921** | Civil war |

# Revolutionary Justice:
# The Nontrial of Nicholas and Alexandra

On July 16, 1918, Bolshevik revolutionaries shot and killed Nicholas II, tsar of Russia; his wife, the tsarina Alexandra; his heir, 14-year-old Alexei; their four daughters—Olga (age 23), Tatiana (age 21), Maria (age 19), and Anastasia (age 17); their three servants; and their physician. When news of the deaths reached other countries, the killings were condemned as murders. The Bolsheviks, however, termed them executions, acts of revolutionary justice.

When Nicholas II abdicated on March 15, 1917, after twenty-three years on the throne, he expected to embark on a life of exile in Britain. Instead, the Provisional Government placed the tsar and his family under house arrest and appointed a Commission of Inquiry to investigate the persistent rumors that the tsar's German-born wife had conspired with Germany to destroy Russia. The commission found no evidence to convict the tsar or his wife of treason, but by the autumn of 1917, its findings were irrelevant. The war with Germany was effectively over, whereas the war against all that the tsar had stood for had just begun.

The civil war that followed the Bolshevik Revolution proved fatal for the royal family. Faced with counterrevolutionary challenges on all sides, the Bolsheviks feared that if Nicholas escaped, he would serve as a symbolic center for these antirevolutionary forces. They decided to move him to a region firmly under Bolshevik control. In April 1918, a special train transported the tsar and his family to Ekaterinburg (about 900 miles east of Moscow), where they were placed in the hands of the Bolshevik-dominated Ural Regional Soviet. Meanwhile, the revolutionary Bolshevik government prepared to try Nicholas publicly for his crimes against the Russian peo-

ple. The charge was no longer secret contacts with Germany—the Bolsheviks themselves had negotiated with Germany and ended Russia's participation in the war—but rather the tsar's both real and symbolic leadership of a politically repressive regime. Leon Trotsky, the head of the Petrograd Soviet, planned to present the case against Nicholas.

But the case was never made. By July, an anti-Bolshevik army was approaching Ekaterinburg from the east. If these troops freed the imperial family, they would score a crucial victory. Told that Ekaterinburg might fall to the enemy within days, the Ural Soviet decided to execute the tsar and his family immediately, most likely with Lenin's approval.

Pavel Medvedev, one of the tsar's guards, later offered a detailed account of the events of the evening of July 16. His interviewer recorded what Medvedev had told him:

> [He said,] The Tsar, the Tsaritsa [Tsarina], the Tsar's four daughters, the doctor, the cook and the lackey came out of their rooms. The Tsar was carrying the heir [Alexei] in his arms. . . . In my presence there were no tears, no sobs and no questions. . . .

Medvedev then testified that he was ordered out of the room. When he returned a few minutes later:

> . . . he saw all the members of the Tsar's family lying on the floor with numerous wounds to their bodies. The blood was gushing. The heir was still alive—and moaning. [The commander] walked over to him and shot him two or three times at point blank range. The heir fell still.[14]

What Medvedev's understated account did not relate were the more gruesome details of the execution. In an effort to preserve

part of the family fortune, the tsar's daughters were wearing corsets into which had been sewn diamonds. When they were shot, the bullets, in the words of one eyewitness, "ricocheted, jumping around the room like hail."[15] Even after several pistols were emptied, one of the girls remained alive. The guards resorted to bayonets.

The killing of not only the tsar but also his wife and children was a startling act, as the Bolsheviks themselves recognized. The Ural Regional Soviet announced the tsar's execution, but said nothing about his family, while the official statement from Moscow reported that "the wife and son of Nicholas Romanov were sent to a safe place."[16]

These omissions and lies reveal the Bolsheviks' own uneasiness with the killings. Why, then, was the entire family shot? The Bolsheviks' determination to win the civil war regardless of the cost provides part of the answer. According to Trotsky, Lenin "believed we shouldn't leave the Whites [the anti-Bolshevik forces] a live banner to rally around."[17] Any of the tsar's children could have served as such a banner. The rapid approach of the White army meant the royal family had to be disposed of quickly. But Trotsky also viewed the killings as an essential and absolute break with the past. In his words, "the execution of the Tsar's family was needed not only to frighten, horrify, and to dishearten the enemy, but also in order to shake up our own ranks, to show them that there was no turning back, that ahead lay either complete victory or complete ruin."[18] For the Bolsheviks, there was no middle ground.

The killing of Tsar Nicholas and his family thus forms part of the pattern of escalating violence that characterized the First World War's

**Tsar Nicholas II and Family**
Tsar Nicholas II, the Tsarina Alexandra, and their family.

revolutionary aftermath. But in the blood of these killings we can also see reflected two ideas that had a powerful impact on postwar political life—first, the subordination of law to the revolutionary state; second, the concept of collective guilt.

The Bolsheviks offered a different idea of justice. As a Bolshevik publication explained in a discussion of the tsar's killing:

> *Many formal aspects of bourgeois justice may have been violated. . . . However, worker-peasant power was manifested in the process, making no exception for the All-Russian murderer, shooting as if he were an ordinary brigand. . . . Nicholas the Bloody is no more.*[19]

In the Bolshevik model, the law was not separate from but rather subordinate to the state. Legal rights and requirements—the "formal aspects of bourgeois justice"—could be suspended in the service of "worker peasant power," as embodied in the revolutionary state.

This concept of the law subordinate to the state helps us understand the tsar's execution without trial; the concept of collective guilt provides a context for the killing of his children. The Bolshevik model of socialism assumed that *class* constituted objective reality. Simply by belonging to a certain social class, an individual could be—and was—designated an enemy of the revolution. The Bolshevik constitution equated citizenship with social class. Workers and peasants received the vote, but seven categories of people, such as those who lived off investment interest,

were disenfranchised. For the next two decades, aristocratic and middle-class origins served as an indelible ink, marking a person permanently as an enemy of the revolutionary state—regardless of that person's own actions or inclinations. Thus, from the Bolshevik perspective, the tsar's children bore the taint of their royal origins. When their continuing existence threatened the revolution, they were shot. Over the next four decades, the concept of collective guilt would result in the deaths of millions in the new Soviet Union.

When World War I ended and representatives of the Allied victors met in Paris in 1919 to build the new postwar world, they sought to establish nationalist-based democracies, in which the rule of law would guarantee the rights of individuals. These two interlinked concepts of law and human rights became for many the defining features of "the West," of democracy, and of civilization itself. The Bolsheviks challenged this definition. They offered instead a definition of democracy based on class and an understand-

ing of the law resting on the demands of continuing revolution.

## Questions of Justice

1. In what ways was the murder of the Russian royal family the by-product of total war rather than the result of any revolutionary ideals?
2. In what ways, if any, were the Bolsheviks correct in arguing that "justice" is never blind, that legal systems always reflect the interests of a society's dominant groups? Is there such a thing as impartial justice?

## Taking It Further

Kozlov, Vladimir, and Vladimir Khrustalëv. *The Last Diary of Tsaritsa Alexandra*. 1997. A translation of the tsarina's diary from 1918.

Rosenberg, William, ed. *Bolshevik Visions: First Phase of the Cultural Revolution in Soviet Russia*. 1990. The section on "Proletarian Legality" explores the Bolsheviks' effort to develop a legal system that embodied their revolutionary ideals.

Steinberg, Mark, and Vladimir Khrustalëv. *The Fall of the Romanovs*. 1999. A detailed account of the last two years of the tsar and his family, based on recently opened archives.

**Wilson and the Peace**
Setting sail for the Paris Peace Conference on December 4, 1918, Wilson believed he was also embarking on a journey in which he would lead Europe into political democracy and international peace.

of the postwar era envisioned the league as a truly revolutionary organization, one that would guarantee that World War I was "the war to end all wars." To replace the system of secret diplomacy and Great Power alliances that had led to the horrors of total war, the league offered an international forum in which all states, big and small, European and non-European, would have a voice and in which negotiations would be conducted openly and democratically. War would become outmoded.

These soaring social and political expectations went largely unrealized. In Paris in 1919 and 1920, the Allies and their defeated enemies signed a series of treaties.* In drawing up these agreements, the treaty writers sought to create a new international order based on three features: a

*These treaties were named after the French palaces in which they were signed—the Treaty of Versailles, with Germany; the Treaty of St. Germain, with Austria; the Treaty of Neuilly, with Bulgaria; the Treaty of Trianon, with Hungary; and the Treaty of Sèvres, with Turkey.

democratic Germany, national self-determination in eastern Europe, and a viable system of international arbitration headed by the League of Nations. They failed in all three.

## The Treaty of Versailles and German Democracy

At the center of the new Europe envisioned by Woodrow Wilson was to be a new democratic Germany. French leader Georges Clemenceau did not share this vision. He had lived through two German invasions of his homeland and wished to ensure that Germany could never again threaten France. Clemenceau proposed the creation of a Rhineland state out of Germany's industrialized western region, both as a neutral buffer zone between France and Germany and as a way to reduce Germany's economic power. The British leader, David Lloyd George, who had just won an election on the campaign slogan "Hang the Kaiser" and who had promised his people that he would squeeze Germany "until the pips squeak," publicly supported Clemenceau's hardline approach to the peace settlement with Germany. In private, however, he expressed fear that such an approach would backfire by feeding the flames of German resentment and undermining the structures of German democracy.

Lloyd George's fears proved well-grounded. The German people bitterly resented the Versailles Treaty°, which they perceived as unjustly punitive. By the terms of the treaty, Germany lost all of its overseas colonies, 13 percent of its European territory, 10 percent of its population, and its ability to wage war. The German army was limited to a defensive force of 100,000 men and allowed no aircraft or tanks. Clemenceau failed in his effort to create a separate Rhineland state, but the Rhineland was demilitarized, emptied of German soldiers and fortifications. In addition, the coalfields of the Saar region were ceded to France for fifteen years (see Map 24.5).

Even more significantly, the Versailles Treaty declared that German aggression had caused the war, and therefore that Germany must recompense the Allies for its cost. In 1921, the Allies presented Germany with a bill for reparations° of 132 billion marks ($31.5 billion). As we will see in the next chapter, this reparations clause helped set up an economic cycle that was to prove devastating for both global prosperity and German democratic politics.

## The Failure of National Self-Determination

The map of Europe drawn by the peace treaties appeared to signal the establishment of a new international order. The old authoritarian empires of eastern and central Europe disappeared, replaced with independent nation-states. In keeping with the principle of national self-determination, Poland once again became an independent nation, with pieces carved out of the German, Austrian, and Russian Empires. One entirely new state was formed out of the rubble of the Austrian-Hungarian Empire—Czechoslovakia. Romania, Greece, and Italy all expanded as a result of serv-

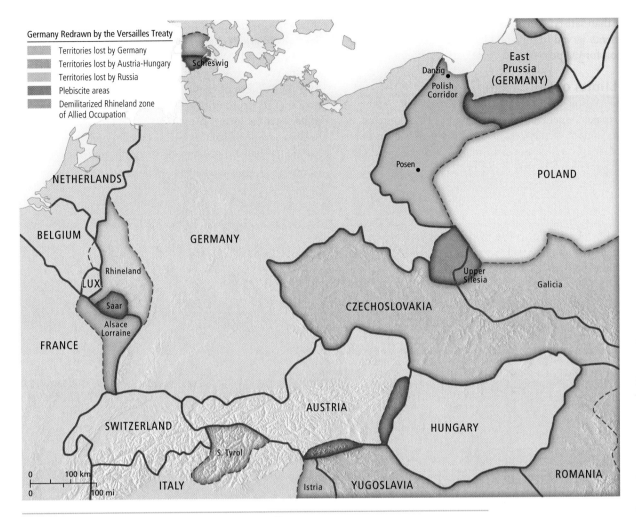

**Map 24.5  Germany Redrawn by the Versailles Treaty**
By the terms of the Versailles Treaty, Germany lost 13 percent of its prewar territory and 10 percent of its prewar population. France regained Alsace and Lorraine; reconstructed Poland was given a corridor to the sea; and the industrialized Rhineland became a demilitarized zone.

ing on the winners' side, while Serbia became the heart of the new Yugoslavia. The defeated nations shrank, some dramatically. Austria, for example, became a mere rump of what had been the mighty Habsburg Empire, while Hungary was reduced to one-third of its prewar size. All that remained of the Ottoman Empire was Turkey.

These changes were heralded as the victory of "national self-determination." But as Woodrow Wilson's own secretary of state, Robert Lansing, complained, "This phrase is simply loaded with dynamite. It will raise hopes which can never be realized." Wilson had called for "every people" to be left free to determine its political destiny—but who constituted "a people"? Did the Macedonians? Should there be an independent Macedonia? Macedonians said yes, but the Paris peace negotiators answered no. Macedonia was enveloped by Yugoslavia and Greece, and in consequence,

throughout the 1920s and 1930s Macedonians waged a terrorist campaign in the Balkans. Wilson's peaceful new world seemed far, far away when in 1923, a Macedonian nationalist group kidnapped the Bulgarian prime minister, chopped off his head, and sliced off his limbs.

The Macedonians were not the only dissatisfied ethnic group in eastern Europe. Even after the peace settlements redrew the map, no fewer than 30 million eastern Europeans remained members of minority groups. Less than 70 percent of Hungarians, for example, lived in Hungary—more than three million were scattered in other states. Over nine million Germans resided outside the borders of Germany. In the newly created Czechoslovakia, one-third of the population was neither Czech nor Slovak. The new state of Yugoslavia contained an uneasy mixture of several ethnic groups, most resentful of the dominant Serbs.

ing nationalist ambitions, then, the peace
to inflame them, thus creating a volatile
ost–World War I world.

**the League**

True to Wilson's vision of a new international order, the
treaty makers included the Covenant of the League of
Nations in each of the treaties. The league, however, never
realized Wilson's high hopes of making war obsolete. One
crucial weakness was that it did not represent every state.

When the league met for the first time in 1920, three significant world powers had no representative present: Germany
and the Soviet Union were excluded, and, in a stunning defeat for President Wilson, the U.S. Senate rejected membership. The failure of these three states to participate in the
league at its beginning stripped the organization of much
of its potential influence.

Two additional factors explain the league's failure. First,
the league had no military power. Although it could levy
economic sanctions against states that flouted its decisions,

## Map 24.6  Europe and the Middle East After World War I

A comparison of this map with Map 24.1 on page 780 illustrates the vital role played by the war in
shaping eastern Europe and the Middle East.

it could do nothing more. And perhaps most important, the will to make the league work was lacking. With Wilson removed from the picture, European leaders were free to pursue their own rather more traditional visions of what the league should be. French politicians, for example, believed that the league's primary reason for existence was to enforce the provisions of the Versailles Treaty—in other words, to punish Germany rather than to restructure international relations.

## The Making of the Modern Middle East

The high hopes that accompanied the end of the war extended beyond the borders of Europe and invigorated nationalist movements throughout Europe's empires. In the Middle East, the war's end meant an entirely new map, but not the end of European dominance. Under terms set by the new League of Nations, the Allies carved Ottoman territory in the Middle East into separate and nominally independent states. These states, however, were judged "not yet able to stand by themselves under the strenuous conditions of the modern world" and so were placed under French or British control (or "Mandate"). Syria and Lebanon fell to the French, while Britain claimed Iraq (Mesopotamia), Palestine, and Transjordan (later called simply Jordan). Britain also continued to exercise its influence over Egypt, Iran (Persia), and what would become Saudi Arabia.

This remaking of the Middle East failed to effect a lasting settlement in the region. First, the new map clashed with promises made to indigenous groups during the war, and so created a long-lasting legacy of mistrust and resentment against the West. Second, the new states imposed on the region were artificial, the creation of the Allied victors rather than a product of historical evolution or of the wishes of the inhabitants themselves. And finally, Western mandatory supervision (which in actual practice differed little from old-fashioned imperial rule) brought with it Western practices and concepts that destabilized regional social and economic structures.

The early history of Iraq exemplifies these three developments. First, the drawing of Iraq, together with Syria, Lebanon, Palestine, and Jordan, betrayed promises made by the British to their Arab allies during the war. In 1915, the British High Commissioner in Egypt, Sir Henry McMahon, wrote to Sharif Husayn (Hussein) ibn Ali, head of the Hashemite dynasty that acted as traditional guardian of Islamic holy sites, and agreed to grant him control over Arab areas liberated from Ottoman rule in exchange for his military support against the Central Powers. This "McMahon-Husayn Correspondence" did not establish precisely the actual boundaries under discussion, but the Hashemites and their supporters believed that they had been promised an independent Arab kingdom centered on Damascus—the same

area that the Allies carved up into the five mandatory states. The British argued they had kept their promise when they placed Husayn's son Faisal on the throne of Iraq and his other son Abdullah on the throne of Jordan, but many Arabs felt betrayed.

The artificiality of Iraq, as well as the other new states, also created a revolutionary situation. In creating Iraq, the Allies glued together three Ottoman provinces—Basra, Baghdad, and Mosul—that had never been treated as a single political or economic unit by the Ottomans, nor regarded as in any way united by the inhabitants themselves. The population of this new state consisted of a volatile mixture of both ethnicities (including Arab, Kurd, and Assyrian) and religions (including not only the majority Shia Muslim community but also Sunni Muslims, Christians, Jews, and Zorastrians). None of these diverse groups identified themselves as "Iraqi." Many of the inhabitants of the new state also lacked a sense of allegiance to their new ruler; they regarded Faisal (along with his brother Abdullah in Jordan) as an imperialist puppet, jumping as British "advisers" pulled the strings.

Finally, the British inadvertently destabilized Iraq's social structures when they set out to make the new state into a friendly regime that would protect British access to both air bases and oil resources. The introduction of British legal and economic concepts destroyed indigenous traditions. For example, by applying the concept of private land ownership to Iraqi customary relations, the British transformed the traditional tie between tribal sheikh and tribesmen into an economic arrangement between landowner and tenants—an arrangement that tended to enrich the landowner while impoverishing the tenants.

Iraq erupted into full-scale rebellion in 1920, a revolt the British quelled with mustard gas bombs. Similar rebellions—and similar use of brutal force, often airborne, to crush such rebellions—occurred throughout much of the Middle East immediately after World War I.

The settlement of the region labeled Palestine destabilized the region even further. As we noted, the Hashemites and their supporters believed that the British had promised that Palestine would be included in an independent Arab kingdom after the war ended. Yet at the same time, British officials pledged support for a Jewish state in Palestine. In making this pledge, British policymakers were influenced by the anti-Semitic myth of a powerful Jewish elite wielding influence over world affairs: More specifically, they believed that Jewish influence could determine whether the U.S. would enter and Russia would remain in the war. Desperate to ensure both, the British government in 1917 issued the Balfour Declaration°. This declaration announced that Britain favored the Zionist goal of a Jewish national homeland in Palestine (the biblical land of Israel).

Palestine in 1920 passed into British hands in the form of a United Nations mandate formally committed to the Balfour Declaration. Ninety percent of the inhabitants of

Palestine in 1920 were Arabs (both Christians and Muslims) who viewed the Zionist dream of a Jewish Palestine as a form of European imperialism that threatened to dispossess them of their land. But as Arthur Balfour (the Conservative politician who gave the Balfour Declaration its name) explained, "in Palestine we do not propose even to go through the form of consulting the wishes of the present inhabitants of the country."[20] Arab protests and riots in Palestine erupted and by 1922, the British government decided to slow the pace of Jewish immigration into the region to alleviate Arab fears. This decision was only a stopgap solution, however; over the next two decades the British faced continuous pressure from both Arab and Jewish nationalist forces. Like the remaking of eastern Europe, the remaking of the Middle East ushered in decades of political turmoil and violence.

# Conclusion

## The War and the West

Sparked by nationalist fervor, international competition, and a widespread will to believe that in war lay the solution to political divisions and cultural fears, World War I quickly slipped out of the control of both the diplomats and the generals. Industrialization changed the face of combat. Total war smashed the boundaries of the battlefield, eroded the distinction between soldier and civilian, and demanded an overhaul of each combatant nation's political, economic, and social structures.

The idea of "the West" also changed as a result of the impact of this war. The entry of American forces in the final year of the war signaled that in the twentieth century, the United States would have to be factored into any definition of "Western culture" or "Western civilization." At the same time, the spread of the war to the Middle East and Africa and the significant role played by soldiers from imperial territories such as Tunisia, India, and Australia demonstrated the global framework that complicated and constrained Western affairs. The war's revolutionary aftermath also had profound consequences for formulations of "Western identity." With the triumph of the Bolshevik Revolution, two versions of modernity now presented themselves—one associated with the United States and capitalism, and the other represented by the new Soviet Union and its communist ideology. Soviet communism's intellectual roots lay in Marxism, a quintessentially Western ideology, one shaped by Western ideals of evolutionary progress and the triumph of human reason. But after the Russian Revolution, communism was increasingly viewed in the West as something foreign, essentially Eastern, the Other against which the West identified itself.

The carnage of World War I also challenged the faith of many Europeans that through industrial development the West was progressing morally as well as materially. In the final decades of the nineteenth century, European and American soldiers had used repeating rifles and machine guns to conquer huge sections of the globe in the name of Western civilization. In 1914, European and American soldiers turned their machine guns on each other. The world the war had created was one of unprecedented destruction. Millions lay dead, with millions more maimed for life. Vast sections of northern France and eastern Europe had been turned into giant cemeteries filled with rotting men and rusting metal. Across central and eastern Europe, starvation continued to claim thousands of victims, while a worldwide influenza epidemic, spread in part by the marching armies, ratcheted up the death tolls even higher. In the new world shaped by relentless conflicts such as the Battle of the Somme, the pessimism and sense of despair that had already invaded much of the arts in the decade before the war became more characteristic of the wider culture. For many Europeans, the optimism and confidence of nineteenth-century liberalism died in the trenches.

Yet, paradoxically, the war also fostered high hopes. Wilson declared that this had been the war to end all wars. The fires of revolution burned high and many in the West believed that on top of the ashes of empire they would now build a better world. The task of reconstruction, however, proved immense; as we shall see in Chapter 25, in many areas, retrenchment replaced revolution. Seeking stability in an increasingly unsettled world, many Europeans and Americans did their best to return to prewar patterns. The failure of the peace settlement ensured that the "war to end all wars" set the stage for the next, far more destructive total war.

## Suggestions for Further Reading

For a comprehensive listing of suggested readings, please go to www.ablongman.com/levack2e/chapter24

Cork, Richard. *A Bitter Truth: Avant-Garde Art and the Great War.* 1994. A beautifully illustrated work that looks at the cultural impact of the war.

Eksteins, Modris. *Rites of Spring: The Great War and the Birth of the Modern Age.* 1989. Explores the links among modernism, the war experience, and modernity.

Ferguson, Niall. *The Pity of War.* 1999. A bold reconsideration of many accepted interpretations of the origins and experience of the war.

Fitzpatrick, Sheila. *The Russian Revolution, 1917–1932.* 1994. As the title indicates, Fitzpatrick sees the revolutions of 1917 as the opening battle in a more than ten-year struggle to shape the new Russia.

Gilbert, Martin. *The First World War: A Complete History.* 1994. A comprehensive account, packed with illuminating detail.

Gilbert, Martin. *The Routledge Atlas of the First World War*. 1994. Much more than a set of maps, Gilbert's atlas provides a very clear and useful survey of both the causes and results of the war.

Higonnet, Margaret. *Lines of Fire: Women's Visions of World War I*. 1998. An important study of women's experiences.

Joll, James. *The Origins of the First World War*. 1984. One of the best and most carefully balanced studies of this complicated question.

Read, Christopher. *From Tsar to Soviets: The Russian People and Their Revolution, 1917–1921*. 1996. An up-to-date study of the popular revolution and its fate.

Winter, J. M. *The Experience of World War I*. 1989. Despite the title, this richly illustrated work not only covers the war itself but also explores the factors that led to its outbreak and outlines its chief consequences.

Winter, J. M., and R. M. Wall, eds. *The Upheaval of War: Family, Work and Welfare in Europe, 1914–1918*. 1988. A series of essays examining the home front experiences.

## Notes

1. Figures from Alan Sharp, "The Genie That Would Not Go Back into the Bottle: National Self-Determination and the Legacy of the First World War and the Peace Settlement," in Seamus Dunn and T. G. Fraser, eds., *Europe and Ethnicity*, (1996), 10.

2. Quotation from Karl Kautsky et al., eds., *The Outbreak of the World War: German Documents* (1924), 76.

3. Quoted in Niall Ferguson, *The Pity of War* (1999), 152.

4. Quoted in Eric Leeds, *No Man's Land: Combat and Identity in World War I* (1979), 17.

5. Allister Horne, *The Price of Glory: Verdun, 1916* (1967), 27.

6. Paul Fussell, *The Great War and Modern Memory* (1975), ch. 2.

7. Siegfried Sassoon, *Memoirs of an Infantry Officer* (1937), 228.

8. Figure from Tony Ashworth, *Trench Warfare, 1914–1918* (1980), 15–16.

9. Samuel Hynes, *A War Imagined: The First World War and English Culture* (1991), 195.

10. Quoted in Richard Cork, *A Bitter Truth* (1994), 198.

11. Quoted in Sheila Rowbotham, *A Century of Women* (1997), 72.

12. Ernst Lessauer, "Hymn of Hate" (1914), in *Jugend* (1914). Translated by Barbara Henderson, *New York Times*, October 15, 1914.

13. Quoted in W. Bruce Lincoln, *Red Victory: A History of the Russian Civil War* (1989), 32.

14. Quoted in Edvard Radzinsky, *The Last Tsar*, trans. Marian Schwartz (1993), 336.

15. From the written account of Yakov Yurovsky, quoted in Radzinsky, *The Last Tsar*, 355.

16. Quoted in William Henry Chamberlin, *The Russian Revolution, 1917–1921*, Vol. 2: *From the Civil War to the Consolidation of Power* (1987), 91.

17. Quoted in Lincoln, *Red Victory*, 151.

18. Ibid., 155.

19. Quoted in Radzinsky, *The Last Tsar*, 326.

20. Quoted in Walid Khalidi (ed.), *From Haven to Conquest: Readings in Zionism and the Palestine Problem Until 1948* (1987), 208.

# Reconstruction, Reaction, and Continuing Revolution: The 1920s and 1930s

# 25

ON SEPTEMBER 14, 1927, AN OPEN CAR ACCELERATED DOWN A STREET in Nice in southern France. In its passenger seat sat a woman, who let her long silk shawl whip in the wind. This woman in free-flowing clothing, speeding down the streets in a convertible, provides a fitting image for Western culture in the decade after World War I. Entranced by the automobile, Americans and Europeans embraced its promise of mobility and freedom. They perceived themselves as moving ahead, breaking through traditional barriers and heading off into new directions. Even more fitting was the identity of that female passenger: Isadora Duncan, by 1927 one of the most famous artists in Europe. In the years before World War I, the American-born Duncan had rejected classical ballet as an artificial form that restricted and deformed the female body. She cast aside ballet's confining toe shoes and tutus, and opted for bare feet and simple tunics. For Duncan, dance was not a force imposed on the body from outside; instead, dance flowed from the body itself. In her break with the highly regulated system of classical ballet, her quest for more natural forms, and her desire to liberate women, both physically and artistically, Duncan serves as an apt symbol for modernity. Moreover, as an American, Duncan appeared to personify the new culture that for many Europeans represented the world of the future. Even her clothing—loose tunics, free-flowing scarves, fluid shawls—symbolized a love of freedom and movement.

Yet freedom is sometimes dangerous and movement can be violent. On that autumn day in 1927 Duncan's long scarf became entangled in the wheel of her car and strangled the dancer. Gruesome as it is, the image of Duncan's sudden death serves as an appropriate introduction to the history of the West in the 1920s and 1930s, the turbulent interlude between two tragic

**"The World Will Soon Be Yours"** This Soviet propaganda poster promises workers around the world a global communist revolution. In *The Communist Manifesto,* Karl Marx had addressed the working classes in these famous words: "Workers of the world, unite! You have nothing to lose but your chains!" Adapting this call, the poster's banner declares, "You have nothing to lose but your chains, but the world will soon be yours."

world wars. The American president Woodrow Wilson had hailed World War I as the "final war for human liberty." Many Europeans agreed; they thought that the war would propel their society down a new road, yet in much of Europe the drive toward freedom ended quickly. The interwar period saw the strangulation of democracy in eastern and southern Europe and the rise of political and cultural ideologies that viewed human liberty as an illusion and mass murder as a tool of the state.

These developments had profound implications for the idea of the West. In the Wilsonian vision, "the West" stood as a culture that promoted individual freedom through democratic politics and capitalist economics. But the success of antidemocratic and anticapitalist ideologies in capturing the hopes and allegiances of large numbers of Europeans illustrated that Wilson's definition of the West was only one among many.

Why was the link between "Western" and "democratic" so fragile? To answer this question, we will look closely at diverse responses to the revolutionary aftermath of World War I. Five more specific questions will guide our examination:

■ **What was the impact of the war on European cultural life?**

■ **In what ways did reconstruction rather than revolution characterize the postwar period?**

■ **What circumstances explain the emergence of the Radical Right?**

■ **What factors led to the polarization of European politics in the 1930s?**

■ **How did the interaction between the West and the world outside change after World War I?**

# Cultural Despair and Desire

■ **What was the impact of the war on European cultural life?**

To many Europeans in the 1920s and 1930s, World War I seemed to have torn a huge and irreparable gash in the fabric of culture and society. It appeared as the sudden and horrifying end to an age of science and progress, an era of technological improvement and social optimism. Yet this perception of a radical cultural break masked fundamental continuities. As we observed in Chapter 23, beginning in the 1870s, anxiety intermingled with optimism in European culture, and widespread fear of degeneration and decay marked Western society. Well before World War I, modernist painters, musicians, and poets pushed beyond the limits of nineteenth-century art and articulated disturbing visions of a world in purposeless flux. The real

change in the years after the war was that modernism's fragmented canvases and dissonant choruses no longer seemed alien; they echoed the sensibilities of societies shattered by total war. But the war had also injected art with an often passionate political intensity. Excitement as well as anxiety thus marked the art and the age. The interwar era was a time of contradictions, one in which many Europeans despaired at the future of their society but many others dreamed of building a new and better world.

## The Waste Land

Within just a few years of the war's end, war memorials were erected in cities, towns, and villages throughout France and Britain. Significantly, these memorials rarely celebrated the Allies' victory; instead, they focused on dead soldiers. Slaughter, not success, was the dominant theme. At Verdun, for example, the memorial was an ossuary, a gigantic receptacle for the skulls and bones of 130,000 men. In some ways, European culture after the war took on the form of an ossuary, as intellectuals and artists looked at the death tolls from the war and concluded that the end product of human reason and scientific endeavor was mass destruction.

In the English-speaking world, the American expatriate poet T. S. Eliot (1888–1965) supplied the most evocative portrait of postwar disillusion. In 1922, Eliot published a lengthy poem called "The Waste Land," which became a metaphor used by many Europeans to express their own sense of the waste wrought by the war. Arising out of Eliot's own personal anguish, "The Waste Land" contains no straightforward narrative. Instead, like a Cubist collage painting, it comprises fragments of conversation, literary allusions, disjointed quotations, mythological references, all clashing and combining in a modernist cry of despair.

The heightened anxiety and loss of certainty that characterized much of Western literature after the war is also clear in the realms of theology and philosophy. In the nineteenth century, theologians emphasized the harmony of religion and science. Their argument that God is present in the world, guiding its rational and progressive evolution, was difficult to sustain in a society that had experienced the absurd slaughter of World War I. In his postwar writings, the Swiss theologian Karl Barth (1886–1968) emphasized human sinfulness and argued that an immense gulf separated humanity from God. Neither scientific analysis nor historical inquiry could bridge the gap. Reaching God demanded a radical leap of faith.

Barth's German colleague Rudolf Bultmann (1884–1976) made the leap of faith even more radical. Bultmann argued that the Jesus Christ depicted in the New Testament—the foundation of Christianity—was largely fictional. In Bultmann's view, the Gospels were something like Eliot's "Waste Land" poem, a collection of fragments originating from myth and folk tale, layered on one another and capable of multiple interpretations. Rational inquiry and scientific methods cannot deliver a certain image of the historical Jesus, who remains essentially unknowable, obscured by the myths built up over centuries. Yet Bultmann, a Lutheran pastor, did not discard his Christian beliefs. Instead, he argued that within and through the Christian mythology rests ultimate spiritual—although not scientific or historical—truth.

Bultmann's form of Christianity is often called Christian existentialism° because Bultmann put a Christian twist on the existentialist philosophy taught by his friend, the philosopher Martin Heidegger (1889–1976). At the core of existentialism was a profound despair. The human condition is one of anxiety and alienation, even *Nausea,* as Heidegger's student Jean-Paul Sartre (1905–1980) entitled one of his most famous works. For Barth and Bultmann, the way out from this anxiety was through submission to God. As an atheist, Heidegger found this route blocked. Instead, he taught that the individual must struggle to rise above mere existence to a consciousness of the genuine and authentic. Sartre's version of existentialism was more pessimistic. At a time when, as we will see, dictatorships were rising across Europe, Sartre insisted that the fundamental fact of human existence is that "man is condemned to be free" in a universe devoid of meaning or reason. Yet Sartre, too, offered a way out from this prison of freedom: Individuals must recognize that they are free to make choices, and then must do so. During World War II, Sartre's own heroic acts in the French Resistance against the Nazis exemplified his insistence on the necessity of making moral choices in an absurd world.

A sense of absurdity and waste dominates much of the visual art of the period. War veteran Otto Dix (1891–1969) filled his canvases with crippled ex-soldiers. The vivid colors and distorted figures of the Expressionist style enabled Dix to articulate his outrage at the world he saw about him. In *Flanders,* painted in 1934, Dix depicted a nightmare of trench soldiers, rotting like blasted trees. Here there is no heroism, only horror.

## Building Something Better

Stuck in the mud, the soldiers in Dix's *Flanders* provide a haunting image of European culture in the interwar years. A very different image takes shape when we examine the work of Dix's contemporaries in the *Bauhaus.* Established in Berlin in 1919 as a school for architects, craftsmen, and designers, the Bauhaus epitomized not the despair but rather the near-utopianism of much of European society after the war. The Bauhaus sought to eliminate the barriers between "art" (what we put on our walls or see in museums) and "craft" (what we actually use in daily life: furniture, textiles, dishes, and the like), and so to enhance daily

## DOCUMENT

## The Waste Land

*T. S. Eliot's "The Waste Land" comprises 434 lines; the excerpt given here is thus just one small piece of a much larger and complex poetic work that provides an evocative portrait of a despairing age. One of its central images, drawn from the English legends of King Arthur, is of an impotent and sickly king, reigning over a dried-up land.*

April is the cruellest month, breeding
Lilacs out of the dead land, mixing
Memory and desire, stirring
Dull roots with spring rain.
Winter kept us warm, covering
Earth in forgetful snow, feeding
A little life with dried tubers.
. . .
But at my back in a cold blast I hear
The rattle of the bones, and chuckle spread from ear to ear.
A rat crept softly through the vegetation
Dragging its slimy belly on the bank
While I was fishing in the dull canal
On a winter evening round behind the gashouse
Musing upon the king my brother's wreck
And on the king my father's death before him.
White bodies naked on the low damp ground
And bones cast in a little low dry garret,
Rattled by the rat's foot only, year to year.

Source: From "The Waste Land" by T. S. Eliot. First published in 1922. Reprinted by permission of Faber and Faber Ltd.

living by making it more effective, efficient, and beautiful. Its founder, Walter Gropius (1883–1969), hoped his students would become nothing less than "the architects of a new civilization."[1]

Gropius's belief that the arts could serve a social purpose was commonly shared in the interwar years. As the British poet W. H. Auden (1907–1973) explained, although good poetry is "not concerned with telling people what to do," it should "[lead] us to the point where it is possible for us to make a rational and moral choice."[2] Many artists abandoned the prewar modernist ideal of "art for art's sake" and produced work steeped in political passion and a desire for a better world.

### Machinery and Movement

Much of the near-utopianism of European culture focused on the transforming power of technology. The "machine aesthetic" triumphed most completely in the Soviet Union, where the Bolsheviks encouraged artistic experiment and

**Otto Dix, *Flanders*
(1934–1935)**

In this painting, the Flanders
landscape is literally shaped by
the bodies of soldiers. Like these
soldiers—and much of postwar
European culture—Dix could not
escape the war. His paintings
reveal a man permanently
wounded.

innovation as part of their revolution. The engineer became the image of a communist hero, and industrial motifs permeated Soviet culture in the 1920s. In the revolutionary theater of Vsevelod Meyerhold, mechanical gestures replaced naturalistic expressions and sets consisted of scaffolding. Similarly, a factory whistle opens the chorus of Dmitri Shostakovich's *Second Symphony* (1927), written to praise industrial labor.

Postwar architecture in the West also provides a vivid illustration of this mechanical faith. A house, explained the Swiss architect Le Corbusier (1887–1965), was "a machine for living in." Le Corbusier and his fellow modernist architects stripped their buildings of all ornament and frequently exposed the essential machinery—the supporting beams, the heating ducts, the elevator shafts. Concrete, steel, and glass became the building materials of choice as modernist skyscrapers—glittering rectangles—transformed urban skylines and testified to the triumph of the human-made.

Closely related to the worship of the machine in the interwar period was a celebration of movement and speed. The automobile evolved from a rich man's toy to a middle-class necessity, made possible by the assembly-line techniques developed in Henry Ford's Detroit factories. The assembly line, which reduced the entire industrial workforce of a factory to a single efficient machine, was imported from the United States into Europe in the later 1920s. The airline industry also took off in this era. In 1919 the first air passenger service between London and Paris began; the next decade saw Europe's major cities linked by air net-

works. The car and the plane became potent symbols of a new age of possibility and opportunity. In 1927, when the American Charles Lindbergh (1902–1974) became the first person to fly across the Atlantic alone, he was hailed not only as a national but as an international hero, an icon of human resourcefulness and technological mastery.

The idea that Western society was moving rapidly and that anything was possible in a world of change shaped much of the culture of the interwar era. Take the popular dance craze of the 1920s—the Charleston. Arms outstretched and legs firing like pistons, the entire body becomes a fast-moving machine. Another American import, Hollywood's "moving pictures," even more clearly represented and stimulated the ideal of a society in motion. The Italians and the French had dominated the movie industry before 1914, but during the war film production in Europe halted. American filmmakers quickly filled the void. After the war, moviegoing became a truly popular pastime—and most of the movies on the screen were made in America. Hollywood presented European audiences with an appealing, if unrealistic, picture of the United States as a land of fabulous wealth, technological modernity, and unlimited mobility.

## Scientific Possibilities

While the United States dominated the fantasy land of popular films in the interwar years, Germany and Britain still clung to their leadership positions in the ongoing scientific revolution. At its most basic level, this revolution overthrew

**Building Something Better**
Built between 1929 and 1930, the Villa Savoye exemplified Le Corbusier's goal to build "a machine for living (in)." The villa's ribbon windows echo industrial architecture but provide openness and light. True to modernist principles, the house has no historical or traditional ornamentation and uses ramps, spiral staircases, and built-in furniture to create a sense of fluidity.

the mechanistic explanation of the universe that had held sway since the first scientific revolution in the seventeenth century. From the 1890s on, scientists began to replace Isaac Newton's now-discredited universe with a new, more complicated model based on Albert Einstein's theory of relativity. As Chapter 23 explained, Einstein's model replaced Newton's static universe with a world in which space, time, matter, and energy are all interchangeable.

In the 1920s and 1930s, this effort to construct an entirely new understanding of the cosmos electrified the discipline of physics and attracted some of the most brilliant young thinkers of the twentieth century. Students from all over the world traveled to Germany and Britain in pursuit of the best teachers and in hopes of joining research teams in both university and state-funded laboratories.

Much of the excitement in physics stemmed from Einstein's concept of matter as "frozen energy." In theory, if the energy could be "thawed out," then this energy could be released. But could this theory become reality? In 1936, the distinguished British scientist Ernest Rutherford (1871–1937), head of one of the most important research laboratories in the Western world, answered that question with a resounding "no." He dismissed the idea of unlocking the atom to release energy as "moonshine." Yet four years earlier, a scientist working in Rutherford's own laboratory had in fact found the key to unlocking the atom. In 1932, James Chadwick (1891–1974) discovered that atoms contain not only positively charged protons and negatively charged electrons, but also neutrons. Because neutrons pos-

sess no electrical charge, they are not repelled by either an atom's protons or its electrons. In theory, then, a bombardment of heavy neutrons could split open an atom's nucleus—a process called nuclear fission. The split nucleus would itself emit neutrons, which would then burst open other atoms, which in turn would emit further neutrons . . . and on and on in a nuclear chain reaction. The result: a colossal burst of energy, energy so abundant that it could perhaps satisfy industrial society's insatiable appetite for energy resources—or produce an atom bomb.

Such possibilities remained purely theoretical—pure "moonshine," in Rutherford's words—until 1938, when two scientists working in Berlin proved Rutherford wrong. Otto Hahn (1879–1968) and Fritz Strassmann (1902–1980) bombarded uranium with a stream of neutrons and broke open the uranium atom. Matter had been unlocked. Within a year, more than 100 articles on the implications of this discovery were published in scientific journals around the world. As one historian has noted, "Physicists viewed the discovery of nuclear fission like the finding of a lost treasure map."[3]

# Out of the Trenches: Reconstructing National and Gender Politics in the 1920s

■ In what ways did reconstruction rather than revolution characterize the postwar period?

As we saw at the end of Chapter 24, in the years immediately following World War I Europe stood on the brink of revolutionary change. The war toppled empires and redrew the map of eastern and central Europe. Gender roles turned upside down, imperial patterns shattered, and social expectations were raised. The American president Woodrow Wilson promised a radically new world of peace and democracy. In Russia, the Bolshevik revolution offered an even more radical vision of communist free-

dom. Despite these expectations and fears, however, retrenchment rather than revolution characterized much of the immediate postwar period. In many areas, World War I was the turning point that failed to turn, as Europeans sought to reconstruct the structures toppled by total war.

## The Reconstruction of Russia: From Tsar to Commissar

Even in the newly formed Soviet Union, the nation that epitomized revolution, important aspects of prewar society reemerged in the postwar period. By 1922 and against all odds, the Bolsheviks had won the civil war and established their authority over most of the regions of the old tsarist empire. The Bolsheviks also reestablished many features of the tsarist regime: authoritarian rule built on violent coer-

**Map 25.1 Europe in the 1920s and 1930s**

The map shows the consequences of not only World War I but also such successor conflicts as 1. the Irish-English struggles, which resulted in the partition of Ireland: Northern Ireland remained a part of Britain while the rest of the island became the independent nation-state of Eire (see p. 840); 2. the war between Bolshevik Russia and its enemies, which widened the western frontiers of the Soviet state (see p. 819); and 3. the Turkish uprising, which kept Turkey intact and independent (see pp. 842–843).

cion, a highly centralized state, a large bureaucratic elite living in conditions of privilege that cut it off from ordinary people, and a peasant economy.

How do we explain the continuity of authoritarian rule in Russia? The first crucial factor was the impact of civil and international war. Across Russia in 1919 the Bolsheviks faced fierce opposition from rival bands of socialists, middle-class liberals, and aristocratic supporters of the tsar. These opponents of the Bolshevik revolution—called the "Whites" to distinguish them from the "Red" Bolsheviks— were supported by foreign troops. Fearing the spread of communist revolution, fourteen different countries (including the United States, Britain, France, and Japan) sent more than 100,000 soldiers to fight in Russia. In addition to these forces, the new Bolshevik state confronted numerous attempts by non-Russian nationalists to throw off the yoke of Russian rule. This was warfare at its most savage. When Ukrainian peasants resisted Russian control, the Bolsheviks resorted to methods of mass reprisal. Entire villages were burned, the men executed, the women and children sent to slower deaths in prison camps. The Bolsheviks did not have a monopoly on murder, however. White forces in the Ukraine massacred more than 100,000 Jews.

As the scale of savagery escalated, so too did Russia's economic disintegration. In the cities, residents faced anarchic conditions. Transportation systems shut down, the water supply ceased to run, and furniture became the only source of fuel. When the furniture ran out, entire families froze to death inside apartment blocks. The urban areas emptied as their inhabitants fled to the countryside. By 1921, Moscow had lost half its residents and Petrograd (formerly St. Petersburg) had lost two-thirds. Yet conditions in the countryside were also brutal. To feed the cities,

the Bolsheviks adopted the policy of "War Communism": requisitioning (stealing) food and seed stores from the peasants. The peasants resisted, both actively, in violent revolt, and passively, by reducing the amount they planted. Food shortages and other war-related hardships increased the population's vulnerability to epidemic disease. Between 1918 and 1921, the number of deaths from the combined impact of the civil war, starvation, and typhus surpassed the number of those who died in World War I.

The need to impose order on this chaotic situation led the Bolsheviks to adopt increasingly authoritarian measures. Like the Jacobins in 1792 during the French Revolutionary Wars, the Bolsheviks turned to terror to defeat their enemies, both domestic and foreign. In the first six years of Bolshevik rule, the Cheka (Lenin's secret police force) executed at least 200,000 people. In contrast, in the fifty years before the Bolsheviks came to power, 14,000 Russians had died at the hands of the tsarist secret police.

But the antidemocratic nature of the Bolshevik regime was not solely a response to the pressures of war. Ideology also helps explain the continuity of authoritarian rule in post-tsarist Russia. Faced with the task of building a communist state in an isolated, economically backward, peasant society, the Bolshevik leader Vladimir Lenin modified Marxist theory. In a peasant society, Lenin argued, the agent of revolutionary change could not be the working class alone: There simply were not enough industrial workers in Russia. Instead, the Bolshevik or Communist Party, an elite of highly disciplined, politically aware and committed individuals, would be the "vanguard" of revolution. Because the masses could not be trusted to make their own decisions, government officials, strictly controlled by the party, would make these decisions for them. The number of

## The High Costs of Civil War

Civil War raged in Russia between 1918 and 1922 as the Bolsheviks fought not only tsarist supporters but also other revolutionary groups and ethnic nationalists. The chaos in the countryside, exacerbated by the Bolshevik policy of seizing peasant produce, resulted in famine.

bureaucrats multiplied and by 1925 had become a privileged elite, with access to the best jobs, food, clothing, and apartments. The rule of the tsar had been replaced not with democracy but with the rule of the commissar, the Communist Party functionary.

In the economic sphere, as in the political system, important continuities shaped the Russian experience. Famine and widespread peasant unrest forced Lenin to revise his program. In 1921 Lenin announced a New Economic Policy (NEP)°. Under NEP, peasants were allowed to sell their produce for profit. Although the state continued to control heavy industry, transport, and banking, NEP encouraged the proliferation of small private businesses and farms— just as the tsar's economic policymakers had done before the war.

# The Reconstruction of National Politics in Eastern and Central Europe

U.S. president Woodrow Wilson's vision of a new international order based on democratic politics offered the war-torn states of Europe a sharp alternative to Bolshevik one-party rule. But in the new states of eastern Europe, democracy proved to be fragile, and in most cases short-lived. Much of old Europe survived the war intact.

## The Defeat of Democracy in Eastern Europe

After the peace negotiations concluded in 1922, postwar eastern Europe certainly looked markedly different from its prewar counterpart (see Map 25.1). The Russian, Austrian-

## CHRONOLOGY

### The Return of Authoritarian Rule to Eastern Europe

1923 Boris III establishes a royalist dictatorship in Bulgaria

1926 Marshal Josef Pilsudski establishes a military dictatorship in Poland

1928 A new constitution gives King Zog in Albania almost unlimited powers

1929 Alexander I establishes a royal dictatorship in Yugoslavia

1932 Fascist leader Gyula Gombos appointed prime minister in Hungary

1938 King Carol establishes a royal dictatorship in Romania

Hungarian, and Ottoman Empires had all disappeared, replaced by a jigsaw puzzle of small independent nations. But lines on the map did not change key political and economic realities. Three important threads tied these new states to their prewar past: ethnic disputes, economic underdevelopment, and antidemocratic politics.

As we saw at the end of Chapter 24, the Allies paid lip service to the ideal of national self-determination but found it impossible to create ethnically homogenous nation-states in eastern Europe. As a result, nationalist-ethnic divisions continued to haunt postwar political structures. In the new Yugoslavia, for example, Croats and Slovenes had expected a federalist system that would grant them local autonomy. Instead, they found themselves in a centralized state under Serbian control. As a result, Croat representatives refused even to sit in the new parliament, and ethnic struggles dominated Yugoslav politics.

Economic difficulties also threatened eastern European stability. In many regions, eastern Europe remained a world of peasants and aristocratic landlords. In Romania, Poland, and Hungary, at least 60 percent of the population worked the land; in Bulgaria and Yugoslavia the figure was 80 percent—versus 20 percent in industrialized Britain. With little industrial growth in these regions and few cities to absorb labor, unemployment rates and land hunger were both high.

Thus ethnic divisions and economic underdevelopment helped destabilize eastern Europe's new democratic political systems. The result was the collapse of democracy across eastern Europe. As the chronology (left) shows, with the exception of Czechoslovakia, every eastern European nation returned to authoritarian politics during the 1920s or early 1930s. In Poland, for example, democracy crumbled in 1926 when the World War I hero Marshal Josef Pilsudski (1867–1935) seized power in a military coup, after parliamentary representatives proved unable to overcome class and ethnic divisions. Pilsudski told the squabbling legislators, "The time has come to treat you like children, because you behave like children."[4] In Yugoslavia, the death of democracy was even more dramatic. Years of escalating ethnic violence peaked in 1928 when a popular Croatian political leader was shot to death on the floor of the legislature. The ensuing ethnic unrest gave King Alexander (a Serb) the excuse he needed to abolish the constitution and replace parliamentary democracy with a royal dictatorship. A brutal repression of Alexander's opponents followed. In Bulgaria, Albania, Hungary, and Romania, too, continuing ethnic conflicts and economic underdevelopment ensured the destruction of democracy.

## The Weakness of the Weimar Republic

In Germany, as in the new states of eastern Europe, the appearance of radical change masked crucial continuities between the pre- and postwar eras. The kaiser's empire gave way to the Weimar Republic°, led by a democratically elected parliamentary government. This democratic political structure, however, sat uneasily atop fundamentally antidemocratic social and political foundations.

The survival of authoritarian attitudes and institutions resulted in part from the civil war that raged throughout Germany in the fall of 1918 and the first months of 1919. In this struggle, communists, inspired by the Bolshevik revolution, fought their one-time colleagues in the more moderate socialist party (the SPD) for control of the new Germany. Anxious to impose order on a potentially anarchic situation, the SPD leaders who now controlled the German government chose not to replace the existing state bureaucracy—the elite corps of aristocratic civil servants that had served the kaiser—but to work with it. To put down the communist threat, they also abandoned their longstanding loathing of the German military and deployed both regular army units and the "Free Corps" (volunteer paramilitary units, often comprising demobilized soldiers addicted to violence). By the spring of 1919, this strange alliance of moderate socialists, traditional aristocrats, soldiers, and thugs had triumphed. In January 1919, Free Corps officers murdered the communist leaders Karl Liebknecht and Rosa Luxemburg in Berlin. Three months later, an equally savage repression crushed the communist soviet in Munich, with the Free Corps killing more than 600 people.

The SPD had won. Yet it lost. By allying with the aristocratic civil service, the army, and the Free Corps, the SPD crushed more than the communist revolution; it also crushed its own chances of achieving significant social change. The officers in the army and the bureaucrats in the civil service were representatives of the old Germany, vehemently opposed to not only communism but also parliamentary democracy. Continuing in positions of authority and influence, they constituted a formidable antidemocratic force at the very heart of the new Germany. The approximately 400,000 men who made up the Free Corps also regarded democratic ideals and the new German republic with contempt—"an attempt of the slime to govern."[5] The attitude of the Free Corps men is summed up in their slogan: "Everything would still have been all right if we had shot more people."[6]

The antidemocratic nature of the Free Corps became clear in 1920, after the Allies imposed restrictions on the size of Germany's military force and most Free Corps units were officially dissolved. Disaffected corpsmen joined the right-wing politician Wolfgang Kapp (1858–1922) and the World War I hero Erich von Ludendorff in an effort to overthrow the Weimar regime. This "Kapp Putsch" quickly fizzled out, defeated by both divisions in the ranks of the rebels and a general strike, but the threat posed by the Free Corps did not disappear. Disguising themselves as athletic societies, haulage companies, and even circuses,

many corps units continued their violent anti-Weimar activities. In 1923, some of these corpsmen tried once again to overthrow the Weimar government by force, with another "putsch," this time originating in a beer hall in Munich and led by a former army corporal named Adolf Hitler. Like the Kapp Putsch, Hitler's "Beer Hall Putsch°" did not succeed. The laughably light sentences imposed on its participants, however, made clear the strength of antirepublican sentiments not only among disgruntled Free Corps men but also far up the ranks of the Weimar judicial system.

Antidemocratic forces in the Weimar Republic fed on the widespread resentment among Germans aroused by the severity of the Versailles Treaty. Many Germans could not separate the birth of the republic from the national humiliation imposed by Versailles. They blamed the moderate socialist government that signed the treaty for this humiliation. Army officers encouraged the idea that Germany could have kept on fighting had it not been "stabbed in the back" by the socialists. This "stab-in-the-back" legend helped undermine support not only for the SPD's moderate socialism but even for democracy itself.

The shaky foundations of democracy in Weimar Germany were eroded further by the dramatic events of 1923. In that year, the German mark collapsed completely and paper money ceased to have any value. This hyperinflation was the unintended by-product of the Weimar government's effort to force the Allies to reconsider reparations. In 1922, the Weimar government halted payments and demanded a new economic settlement. The French retaliated by sending troops into Germany's Ruhr Valley to seize coal as a form of reparations payment. German laborers in the Ruhr Valley resisted the invasion by going on strike. Already relying on a policy of inflationary spending to meet its budget deficit, the German government began printing money with abandon to pay the striking Ruhr workers. The inflation rate surged upward. By January 1923, the mark, which in 1914 could be traded for the American dollar at a rate of 4:1, had plummeted to an exchange rate of 22,400:1. By October, the exchange rate from mark to dollar was at 440,000,000:1. Families who had scrimped for years found they had only enough savings to buy a loaf of bread.

France Demands War Reparations from Germany— *L. A. Times* Cartoon

As a result of this disaster, the French army pulled out of the Ruhr Valley and in 1924 Allied and German representatives drew up the Dawes Plan, which renegotiated reparations. By the end of 1924, the German economy had stabilized; the later 1920s were years of relative prosperity. Yet for many Germans, the memory of hyperinflation tainted the Weimar Republic. Many Germans concluded that democracy meant disorder and degradation. They looked with longing back to the prewar period, an era of supposed social stability and national power.

# The Trial of Adolf Hitler

On February 24, 1924, Adolf Hitler appeared in court in Munich to confront a charge of high treason following his pathetic attempt three months earlier to overthrow the Weimar government by armed rebellion. The trial marked a crucial point in Hitler's career. It gave him a national platform and, even more important, convinced him of the futility of an armed offensive against the state. From 1925 on, Hitler would work through the parliamentary system in order to destroy it. But the trial of Adolf Hitler is also significant in what it reveals about the power of antidemocratic forces in the new Germany. The trial made clear that many in positions of authority and responsibility in the Weimar Republic shared Hitler's contempt for the democratic state. By treating Hitler not as a traitorous thug but rather as an honorable patriot, his prosecutors helped weaken the already fragile structures of German democracy.

Hitler's attempt to overthrow the Weimar Republic by force occurred at the height of hyper-inflation and the ensuing political chaos. By November 8, 1923, when Hitler took up arms, the German mark was worth only one-trillionth of its prewar value. As its currency eroded, the Weimar Republic saw its political legitimacy seeping away as well. Separatist movements in several states threatened the sovereignty of the central government in Berlin. Separatist politics attracted the support of many men from aristocratic backgrounds, members of the traditional conservative elite who viewed Weimar democracy as a foreign and unwelcome import.

Hitler had little interest in the separatist movement, but he believed he could channel its antidemocratic sentiments into a national revolution. He attracted a number of supporters, including one of the most important men in Germany, the World War I hero General Erich von Ludendorff. Seeking to avoid the blame for Germany's defeat in 1918, Ludendorff insisted that his army could have won the war had it not been stabbed in the back by the Social Democratic politicians who now ran the government. Like many German conservatives—and like Hitler—he viewed the Weimar Republic as illegitimate.

On November 8 Hitler made his move. His men surrounded a Munich beer hall where 2,000 supporters of Bavarian separatism had gathered. Hitler declared that both the Bavarian and the national governments had been overthrown and that he was now the head of a new German state, with Ludendorff as his commander-in-chief. Around noon the next day, Hitler, Ludendorff, and several thousand of their followers marched toward the regional government buildings located on one of Munich's main squares. Armed police blocked their passage. In the ensuing fire-fight, seventeen men were killed. Despite the bullets whizzing through the air, Ludendorff marched through the police cordon and stood in the square awaiting arrest. Hitler ran away. Police found him two days later, cowering in a supporter's country house about thirty-five miles outside Munich.

The Beer Hall Putsch had clearly, utterly, completely failed. In jail awaiting trial, Hitler contemplated suicide. Yet later he described his defeat as "perhaps the greatest stroke of luck in my life." The defeat meant a trial; the trial meant a national audience—and an opportunity for Hitler to present his case against the Weimar Republic. He admitted that he had conspired to overthrow the democratically elected Republican government, but he insisted he was not therefore guilty of treason. The real treason had occurred in November 1918, when the Social Democratic government had surrendered to the Allies: "I confess to the deed, but I do not confess to the crime of high treason. There can be no question of treason in an action which aims to undo the betrayal of this country in 1918. . . . I consider myself not a traitor but a German." He argued that he was not aiming for personal power: "In what small terms small minds think! . . . What I had in mind from the very first day was a thousand times more important than becoming a [Cabinet] minister. I wanted to become the destroyer of Marxism." Thus Hitler depicted himself as a patriot, a nationalist motivated by love of Germany and hatred of communists and socialists. "The eternal court of history," according to Hitler, would judge him and his fellow defendants "as Germans who wanted the best for their people and their Fatherland, who were willing to fight and to die."[7]

Despite Hitler's own admission of conspiring against the government, the presiding judge could persuade the three lay judges (who took the place of a jury) to render a guilty verdict only by arguing that Hitler would most likely be pardoned soon. The reluctance of the judges to convict Hitler highlights the extraordinary sympathy shown to him and his political ideas throughout the trial and during his imprisonment. The chief prosecutor offered a rather surprising description of an accused traitor: "Hitler is a highly gifted man, who has risen from humble beginnings to achieve a respected position in public life, the result of much hard work and dedication. . . . As a soldier he did his duty to the utmost. He cannot

**Hitler in Landsberg Prison, 1924**
This photo of Hitler during his short imprisonment was made into a postcard, to be purchased by his supporters.

be accused of having used the position he created for himself in any self-serving way." In delivering the verdict, the judge emphasized Hitler's "pure patriotic motives and honorable intentions." Rather than being deported as a foreign national convicted of a serious crime (Hitler was still an Austrian citizen), Hitler was given a slight sentence of five years, which made him eligible for parole in just six months. In prison he was treated like a visiting dignitary—exempted from work and exercise requirements, provided with prisoners to clean his rooms, even given a special table decorated with a swastika banner in the dining hall. When he was released in September, his parole report described him favorably as "a man of order."[8]

Hitler's gentle treatment reveals the precarious state of democratic institutions in Germany after World War I. Many high-ranking Germans in positions of power and influence (such as judges and prosecutors) viewed parliamentary democracy with loathing. The trial also reveals the willingness of conservative aristocrats to ally with Radical Right groups such as the Nazis. Still not very strong, the Nazis in 1923 were easily reined in. A decade later, however, the conservatives who thought they could ride Hitler to power suddenly found that they were no longer in control.

## Questions of Justice

1. Imagine you are a German war veteran reading about this case in the newspaper in 1924. Why might you be attracted to the party of Adolf Hitler?
2. Hitler appealed to the "eternal court of history." What do you think he meant? How would Hitler have defined "justice"?

## Taking It Further

Gordon, Harold, Jr. *Hitler and the Beer Hall Putsch.* 1972. This lengthy study (more than 600 pages) provides a detailed account of the putsch and its aftermath.

*The Hitler Trial Before the People's Court in Munich,* trans. H. Francis Freniece, Lucie Karcic, and Philip Fandek (3 vols.). 1976. An English translation of the court transcripts.

**George Grosz, "The Pillars of Society" (1926)**
The Expressionist artist George Grosz was, like Otto Dix (see page 816), a World War I veteran and a sharp critic of Weimar Germany. In Grosz's scathing critique, the Weimar state had failed to carry out essential social reforms and thus the old order still survived. In this painting, a drunken military chaplain continues to preach while soldiers slaughter behind his back. In the foreground sits a lawyer, supposedly a modern professional, but out of his head bursts a cavalry officer bent on destruction. To the lawyer's right, a press baron, his limited intelligence indicated by the chamber pot on his head, clutches the newspapers that guarantee his fortune and that delude the masses. To the lawyer's left totters an SPD politician. Both his pudgy, drink-reddened cheeks and the pamphlet he presses to his chest (headlined "Socialism is Work") indicate Grosz's contempt for the gradual reformism of the SPD.

## The Reconstruction of Gender

Many of the patterns that shaped interwar national politics also characterized the politics of gender in these years. World War I wrought a profound upheaval in gender roles in European society. The demands of total war had meant that women moved into economic areas previously designated as "men only." The war, therefore, seemed an important turning point in the history of women in the West. But here again the turning point failed to turn. Important changes in women's expectations did occur, but nineteenth-century gender roles were quickly reconstructed after the war.

### The New Woman

At first sight, the postwar period seems an era of profound change in the roles of women. In the films, magazines, novels, and popular music of the 1920s, the "New Woman" took center stage. Living, working, and traveling on her own, sexually active, she stepped out of the confines of home and family. Women's dress reinforced this idea of a new woman. Whereas nineteenth-century women's clothing had accentuated the womanly body while restricting the woman's movement, the clothing of the 1920s ignored a woman's curves and became much less confining. Complementing this revolution in clothing came a revolution in hairstyle. Women chopped off the long locks regarded for generations as a sign of femaleness and sported fashionable new bobs.

This perception of the New Woman rested on important changes in women's political and economic expectations. By 1920 women in the United States and many European countries had received the right to vote in na-

tional elections and to hold national office. In all the industrialized countries, the expansion of both the health care and service sectors meant new jobs for women as nurses, social workers, secretaries, telephone exchange operators, and clerks. Women's higher-education opportunities also widened in this period.

The biggest change affecting the lives of ordinary women was the spreading practice of limiting family size. We saw in Chapter 22 that by the 1870s middle-class women in Western nations were practicing forms of birth control. In the 1920s and 1930s, an increasing number of working-class women began to do so as well. In Britain, for example, between 1911 and 1931 the average number of

**The "New Woman"**

Almost every aspect of the "New Woman" captured in this 1928 French photograph offended traditionalists: short skirts and bobbed hair, smoking in public, the association with a car and therefore with mobility and illicit sex—all crossing the border into masculine terrain.

## DOCUMENT

# The Threat of the New Woman

*The perceived movement of women into less traditional roles was profoundly upsetting to many Europeans after the war. Much of this distress focused on a clearly visible target: the dramatically different dress and hairstyles sported by fashionable women, as is evident in this description of the New Woman by a French law student in 1925:*

Can one define *la jeune fille moderne* [the young modern woman]? No, no more than the waist on the dresses she wears. Young girls of today are difficult to locate precisely. If you want to be true to French tradition, it would be barbaric, in my opinion, to call our pretty young *parisiennes* young girls.

These beings—without breasts, without hips, without "underwear," who smoke, work, argue, and fight exactly like boys, and who, during the night at the Bois de Boulogne, with their heads swimming under several cocktails, seek out savory and acrobatic pleasures on the plush seats of 5 horsepower Citroens—these aren't young girls!

There aren't any more young girls! No more women either!

Source: Quoted in Mary Louise Roberts, *Civilization Without Sexes: Reconstructing Gender in Postwar France, 1917–1927* (1994), p. 20.

children per family fell from 3.4 to 2.2, with most of this decrease resulting from changes in working-class family size. Fewer pregnancies and fewer mouths to feed meant a significant improvement in women's health and living standards.

## The Reconstruction of Traditional Roles

Despite these important changes, however, women's roles actually altered little in the two decades after World War I. These years witnessed a strong reaction against the wartime gender upheaval and a concerted effort to reconstruct nineteenth-century masculine and feminine ideals.

Both the war's lengthy casualty lists and the drop in the average family size provoked widespread fear about declining populations—and thus declining national strength. Governments, religious leaders, and commercial entrepreneurs joined together to convince women that their destiny lay in motherhood. Sale and purchase of birth control devices became illegal during the 1920s in France, Belgium, Italy, and Spain. France outlawed abortions in 1920. In

Britain after 1929, a woman who had an abortion could be sentenced to life imprisonment.

To encourage population growth, governments also turned to more positive incentives ranging from the symbolic to the economic. Mother's Day, an American invention, crossed into Europe during the 1920s. In France from 1920 on, women who gave birth to at least five children received a bronze medal; those who bore seven or more children earned the silver; and mothers who produced ten offspring brought home the gold. German women had an easier time: They needed only seven children to get the gold. Of more lasting importance was the expansion of welfare services—family allowances, subsidized or state-provided housing, school lunches, health insurance, prenatal and well-baby clinics—with the express aim of strengthening the family, encouraging women to stay at home, and raising the birth rate. Eugenics played an important role in this legislation. National leaders wanted to increase not only the quantity but the quality of the population. On the positive side, this meant improving the health of babies and mothers. More ominously, much of the rhetoric focused on separating the "fit" from the "unfit," with both class and race among the factors that determined who was "fit" to produce children for the nation.

Despite the calls for women to remain at home, many women had to work in paid employment. In the work world, just as in the family, traditional roles were strengthened after World War I. Most working women returned to jobs in domestic service or to factory positions labeled unskilled and therefore low-paying. Women tended to be barred from management positions, assigned to the most repetitive tasks, and paid by piecework, with the result that the wage gap between male and female laborers remained wide. In both Germany and Britain, unemployment benefits were frequently denied to married women workers, even though they had regularly paid into the insurance system while they were working. The numbers of women employed in the clerical and service sectors did rise in this era, but the movement of women into these positions meant such jobs were reclassified as "women's work," a guarantee of low pay and little power.

## Women and the Bolshevik Revolution

In sharp contrast to these efforts to buttress the traditional family structures, in Russia the Bolsheviks promised to revolutionize gender roles. Lenin believed that the family was a middle-class institution doomed to "wither away." In the ideal communist society, marriage would be a mutually beneficial—and in many cases temporary—arrangement between two equally educated and equally waged partners, and both housework and child care would move from the private domestic household into the public sphere of paid employment. To create such a society, the Bolsheviks turned to legislation. One month after seizing power, they legalized divorce and civil marriages. In October 1918, a new family legal code declared women and men equal under the law, made divorce readily available, and abolished the distinction between legitimate and illegitimate children. To free women from housework—described by Lenin as "barbarously unproductive, petty, nervewracking, and stultifying drudgery"[9]—the Bolsheviks established communal child care centers, laundries, and dining rooms. In 1920, just as other nations were outlawing abortion, the practice became legal in Bolshevik Russia.

By 1922, however, the newly created Soviet Union seemed about to self-destruct, and as we have already seen, Lenin retreated from rigorous communist economic ideology to institute the New Economic Policy. NEP also meant significant reversals in the gender revolution. By 1923, the dining halls had been closed and more than half of the day care centers had shut down. The decade of the 1920s was a time of high unemployment for Soviet women. Those who did find jobs received wages that averaged only 65 percent that of men's. An increasing number turned to prostitution. In addition, the traditional patriarchal peasant household—with women in a clearly subordinate role—remained firmly intact. Even in revolutionary Russia, therefore, certain continuities linked the pre- and postwar experience of women.

# The Rise of the Radical Right

■ What circumstances explain the emergence of the Radical Right?

As the revolution in gender roles was reversed, as Lenin's communist revolution shifted into a lower gear, and as Wilson's democratic revolution ran out of gas, a very different sort of revolution was occurring in Italy, a region long on the periphery of European power. The fascist revolution introduced Europe to a new sort of politics, the politics of the Radical Right. Like conservatism, the new Radical Right ideologies—fascism° and its younger cousin, Nazism—dismissed equality as a socialist myth and emphasized the importance of authority. But neither fascism nor Nazism was conservative. These radical political systems sought to use the new technologies of the mass media to mobilize their societies for a program of violent nationalism.

## The Fascist Alternative

Conceived in the coupling of wartime exhilaration and postwar despair, fascism offered an alternative to the existing political ideologies. Fascism was more than a set of political ideas, however. As presented by its creator, Benito Mussolini (1883–1945), fascism was an ongoing performance, a spectacular sound-and-lights show with a cast of millions.

### Mussolini's Rise to Power

Fascism originated in Italy. In 1915 after a fierce internal debate that widened the already huge gaps in Italian society, Italy entered the war on the side of the Allies. Many pro-war Italians viewed the war as a cleansing force, a powerful disinfectant that would leave Italian society stronger and more powerful. Mussolini, a socialist journalist, shared these views. Because the Socialist Party opposed Italy's entry into the war, Mussolini broke with the socialists, joined the army in 1915, and fought until he was wounded in 1917. When the war ended, he sought to create a new form of politics that would translate the military camaraderie and the exhilaration of violent action that he had experienced during the war. The result was fascism.

In March 1919, Mussolini and a little more than 100 men and some women gathered in Milan and declared themselves the fascist movement. Like Mussolini, many of these "fascists of the first hour" were war veterans; a number had served in the *arditi*, elite commando units that fought behind enemy lines. The arditi uniform, a severe black shirt, became the fascist badge of identity. The arditi slogan, "*me ne frego*" ("I don't give a damn") became the blackshirts' creed, a fitting summary of their willingness to throw aside conventional standards and politics.

**The March on Rome, October 28, 1922**
The fascist march on Rome was a carefully orchestrated show of power, not an armed rebellion. Mussolini had already been offered the premiership of Italy, as is clear from his clothing: He has changed his black shirt for a proper suit.

Just three and a half years after the first fascist meeting in Milan, Mussolini became prime minister of Italy. His astonishing rise to power occurred against a backdrop of social turmoil. In 1919 and 1920, more than one million workers were on strike, factory occupations became commonplace, and a wave of land seizures spread across the countryside. Increasingly frightened that revolution would engulf Italy just as it had destroyed tsarist Russia, large landowners and industrialists, as well as the professional and commercial middle classes, looked to Mussolini's fascists for help. Fascist squads disrupted Socialist Party meetings, vandalized the offices of socialist newspapers, broke up strikes, beat up trade unionists, and protected aristocratic estates from attack. By 1922, the fascists were a formidable political force and Mussolini was engaged in negotiations aimed at bringing the fascists into a coalition government. In October 1922, King Victor Emmanuel III (r. 1900–1946) asked Mussolini to become not only a member of the government but its prime minister. Mussolini agreed. In a carefully orchestrated display of muscle, fascists from all over Italy converged in the "March on Rome," a piece of street theater designed to demonstrate Mussolini's mass support, as well as the disciplined might of his followers.

## The Fascist Revolution in Italy

Over the next four years Mussolini used both legal and illegal methods, including murder, to eliminate his political rivals and remake Italy as a one-party state. By 1926, he had succeeded. Party politics, an independent press, and the trade union movement ceased to exist. Victor Emmanuel

## CHRONOLOGY

### Mussolini's Rise to Power

| | |
|---|---|
| 1915–1917 | Serves in the Italian army |
| 1919 | Participates in the creation of the fascist movement |
| 1921 | Fascist Party wins thirty-five seats in parliament |
| 1922 | Becomes prime minister |
| 1925–1926 | Abolishes party politics and establishes himself as dictator |
| 1929 | Signs Lateran Accords with the Roman Catholic Church |

remained on the throne, the official head of state, but power lay in Mussolini's hands. The restored death penalty and a strong police apparatus stood ready to enforce Mussolini's will and to remake Italy into a fascist society.

But what was fascism? Mussolini conceived of fascism as the politics of modernity. He condemned the existing political ideologies as outdated. Socialism exalted the working class; liberalism viewed the individual as the core of society; conservatism clung to social hierarchy. Fascism, however, identified the *nation* as the dominant social reality. With a strong leader at the wheel, with violent action as its fuel, the fascist nation would crash through social and economic barriers and transport its people into a new and more powerful age.

Yet Mussolini's supposedly radical revolution reinforced traditional elite interests. Early fascist promises of land redistribution were quickly forgotten, and the end of democracy meant that the control of local government rested not with elected officials but rather with Mussolini's appointees—usually drawn from the ranks of the traditional agrarian elite. Fascist economic theory, such as it was, promised to replace capitalist competition and the profit motive with corporatism: Committees (or "corporations") made up of representatives of workers, employers, and the state were to direct the economy for the good of the nation. In actuality, workers' rights disappeared while industrialists' profits remained untouched.

Mussolini's revolution, then, was not about leveling society. Mussolini had no intention of giving *actual* political power to ordinary people; he did, however, recognize the importance of giving them the *illusion* of power. The fascist revolution offered individuals a sense of power by making them feel a part of the nation. A series of "after-work" occupational and recreational groups served as a channel for fascist propaganda and connected ordinary people more closely to the fascist state, while at the same time occupying their leisure hours. By 1939, four million Italians were participating in fascist sporting clubs, holiday camps, and cultural outings.

The "Cult of the Duce" also provided an important means of fostering a sense of participation in the life of the nation. Mussolini insisted, "I am Fascism." Carefully choreographed public appearances gave ordinary Italians the chance to see, hear, and adore their Duce ("Leader"), and through contact with his person, to feel a part of the new Italy. To stimulate public adoration of himself, Mussolini paid careful attention to his public image. He ordered that the press ignore his birthdays and the births of his grandchildren: The Duce could not be seen to age. Instead, in photograph after photograph, Mussolini appeared as a man of action. Depicted in planes, in trains, and in racing cars, he was always on the move, always pressing forward.

At the same time, Mussolini combined up-to-date advertising and the latest mass media technologies with age-old rituals inspired largely by the Catholic Church.

Huge public rallies set in massive arenas, carefully staged with lighting and music, inspired his followers. A popular fascist slogan summed up the leadership cult: "Believe, Obey, Fight." Italians were not to think or question; they were to *believe.* What were they to believe? Another slogan provides the answer: "Mussolini is always right."

## The Great Depression and the Spread of Fascism After 1929

The simple certainty offered by a slogan such as Mussolini's proved highly appealing throughout much of Europe after 1929. During the 1930s, fascist movements emerged in almost every European state. The key factor in the spread of fascism was the Great Depression°. On October 24, 1929, the American stock market collapsed. Over the next two years, the American economic crisis evolved into a global depression. Banks closed, businesses collapsed, and unemployment rates rose to devastating levels. Even by the end of the 1930s, the production rates of many nations remained low. Desperate people looked for desperate answers. Fascism provided some of these.

Why did the Depression spread so quickly and last so long? The explanation lies with the changing role of the United States in Europe. World War I accelerated the shift of the world's economic center away from Europe and toward America. New York's stock market emerged to rival London's, and U.S. businesses increasingly displaced European competitors as the chief suppliers of industrial goods to regions such as Latin America. While European nations sold off their domestic and foreign assets and borrowed heavily to pay for the war, the United States moved from the position of debtor to creditor nation. By the end of 1918 Allied nations owed the United States more than $9 billion—and American officials made it clear that they expected this money to be repaid in full, with interest.

The problem of wartime indebtedness quickly became entangled with the issue of German reparations. Britain, France, and Italy could pay off their debts to the United States only if Germany paid reparations to them. Hyperinflation and the near-collapse of the German economy in 1923, however, forced the revision of the reparations schedule established by the Versailles Treaty. In 1924 and again in 1928 American and European financial representatives met to reconfigure (and in 1928 to reduce) the payments. American credit became the fuel that kept the European economy burning. From 1925 on, American investors loaned money to Germany, which used the money to pay reparations to the Allies, which in turn used the money to pay back the United States. The system worked for a short time. Fueled by loans, the German economy kicked into gear. Currencies stabilized, production rose, and American money flowed not only into Germany but into all of Europe. If these loans dried up, however, Europe faced disaster.

In 1929 that disaster struck. With the collapse of the U.S. stock market, savings portfolios lost between 60 and 75 percent of their value almost overnight. Scrambling to scrape up any assets, American creditors liquidated their European investments, and European economies tumbled. Germany, the country whose economy was most directly linked to the United States, saw its industrial output fall by 46 percent, while its number of jobless grew to more than six million.

The political and social disarray that accompanied the Great Depression enhanced the appeal of fascist promises of stability, order, and national strength. In the 1930s, fascist movements emerged across Europe. Few succeeded in seizing the reins of government, but existing authoritarian regimes adopted many fascist trappings in order to stay in power. For example, Romania's King Carol II (r. 1930–1940) faced a strong challenge to his rule from the Iron Guard, the first mass fascist movement in the Balkans. To compete with the guard, Carol embraced its language of national renewal, as well as typically fascist features such as uniformed paramilitaries, a youth group, and mass rallies. In 1938 he abolished all political parties, placed the judicial system under military control, and declared himself a royal dictator. He then dissolved the Iron Guard and garroted its leader.

## The Nazi Revolution

In Germany, the Nazi Party offered a different version of Radical Right ideology. Just as the emergence of fascism was inextricably linked to the career of one man, Benito Mussolini, so Nazism° cannot be separated from Adolf Hitler (1889–1945). To understand the Nazi revolution in Germany, we need first to explore Hitler's rise to power and then to examine the impact of Nazi rule on ordinary people.

### Hitler's Rise to Power

Hitler, an ardent German nationalist, was not a citizen of Germany for most of his life. Born in Austria, Hitler came of age in Vienna, where he made a meager living as a painter while absorbing the anti-Semitic German nationalism that permeated the capital city of the Habsburg Empire. When World War I broke out, Hitler grabbed at the chance to fight the war in a German rather than an Austrian uniform. He regarded army life as "the greatest of all experiences." Hitler served as a German soldier for almost the entire length of the war until he was temporarily blinded by poison gas in 1918. After the war he settled in Munich, home to large bands of unemployed war veterans and a breeding ground for nationalist and racist groups.

The Nazi Party began as one of these small fringe groups, with Hitler quickly emerging as its leader. *Nazi* is shorthand for *National Socialist German Workers' Party,* but this title, like all of Nazi ideology, was a lie. Nazism fiercely opposed socialism, communism, trade unionism, and any political analysis that emphasized class conflict or workers'

## Hitler's Rise to Power

| | |
|---|---|
| **1914–1918** | Serves in the German army |
| **1919–1923** | Establishes himself as a right-wing activist in Munich |
| **1923** | Fails to overthrow the government with the Beer Hall Putsch |
| **1929** | Collapse of the U.S. stock market; onset of Great Depression |
| **1930** | Nazis win 107 seats in German parliament |
| **1932** | Nazis win 230 seats; become largest party in German parliament |
| **1933** | |
| January | Becomes chancellor |
| February | Uses Reichstag fire as pretext to gain emergency powers |
| March | Uses the Enabling Act to destroy democracy in Germany |

rights. For the Nazis, race, not class, constituted the key social reality. To Hitler, all history was the history of racial struggle, and in that racial struggle, the Jews were always the principal enemy. Hitler regarded Jewishness as a biological rather than a religious identity, as a sort of toxic infection that could be passed on to future generations and that posed a threat to the racially pure "Aryans"—white northern Europeans.*

Like Mussolini, Hitler exalted the nation. He believed Germany was destined to become a powerful empire controlling central and eastern Europe. This new age would dawn, however, only after a mighty battle between the racially superior Germans and their numerically superior enemy: the forces of "Judeo-Bolshevism." In Hitler's distorted vision, Jewishness and communism formed two parts of the same evil whole. He saw the Bolshevik victory in Russia and the call for communist world revolution as part of a much larger struggle for Jewish world domination.

In its early days Nazism appealed to men like Hitler, individuals without much power or, apparently, much chance of getting it—demobilized and now unemployed soldiers, small shopkeepers wiped out by postwar inflation, lower-middle-class office clerks anxious to preserve their shaky social status, and workers who had lost their jobs. Nazism

*Aryan *is actually a linguistic term referring to the Indo-Aryan or Indo-European language groups. Anti-Semites such as Hitler misapplied the term to racial groups to lend a supposedly scientific authority to their racism.*

offered a simple explanation of history, a promise of future glory, and a clear and identifiable scapegoat for both personal and national woes. By the time of the Beer Hall Putsch in November 1923, party membership stood at about 55,000.

As we saw earlier in the discussion of postwar Germany, the Beer Hall Putsch failed in its aim to overthrow the Weimar Republic, but it did bring Hitler a national audience. Both his speeches during the ensuing trial for treason and *Mein Kampf* ("My Struggle"), the book he wrote while in prison, publicized his racialized view of German political history. After Hitler emerged from prison, he concentrated on transforming the Nazis into a persuasive political force. To infiltrate German society at all levels, Nazis formed university and professional groups, labor unions, and agrarian organizations, while the Nazi paramilitary organization, the SA (*Sturmabteilung*), terrorized opponents. The party held meetings and rallies incessantly, not just during election periods, and so ensured that Germany was saturated with its message. Even so, in the elections of 1928, Nazi candidates won only 2.6 percent of the vote.

It was the Great Depression that gave the Nazis their chance at power. After 1929, unemployment rates skyrocketed and the Weimar political system began to collapse. No German political leader could put together a viable governing coalition. Parliamentary power dwindled; in all of 1932 the federal parliament met for only thirteen days. As the mechanisms of parliamentary democracy faltered, the German chancellor Heinrich Bruning increasingly relied on a stopgap measure in the German constitution—the presidential emergency decree. The constitution declared that in emergency situations, decrees signed by the German president could become law without parliamentary consent. But this practice meant that power shifted from the parliament to the president, the World War I hero General Paul von Hindenburg. Already in his eighties, Hindenburg was a weak man easily manipulated by a small circle of aristocratic advisors and cronies.

In this unstable climate, political polarization accelerated as Germans looked for extreme solutions to extreme problems. By July 1932, the Nazis had become the largest party in the parliament, winning the support of 37 percent of the German voters. Support for their communist rivals also continued to grow.

Terrified of the threat posed by communism and convinced that Hitler could be easily controlled, a small group of conservative politicians persuaded Hindenburg to offer Hitler the position of chancellor in January 1933. One of the group, Baron Franz von Papen, reassured a friend that Hitler posed "no danger at all. We have hired him for our act. In two months' time we'll have pushed Hitler so far into the corner, he'll be squeaking."[10] But von Papen was wrong.

Within six months Hitler had destroyed what remained of democracy in Germany and established a Nazi dictator-

ship. Almost as soon as he took office he persuaded Hindenburg to pass an emergency decree mandating the seizure of all Communist Party presses and buildings. Then in February a fire destroyed the German parliament building. Declaring (wrongly) that the fire was part of a communist plot against the state, Hitler demanded the power to imprison without warrant or trial. Mass arrests of more than 25,000 of his political opponents followed—not only communists but also social democrats and anyone who dared oppose him openly. At the end of March, German politicians, cowed by Nazi threats of imprisonment, passed the Enabling Act. This key act gave Hitler the power to suspend the constitution and pass legislation without a parliamentary majority. By the summer of 1933, parliamentary political life had ceased to exist in Germany and a dictatorship had destroyed democracy.

Often presented as a model of authoritarian efficiency, the Nazi dictatorship was actually a confusing mass of overlapping bureaucracies, in which ambitious officials competed with each other for power and influence. This planned chaos ensured that none of Hitler's deputies acquired too much authority. It also enhanced the mystery of the state. The individual citizen attempting to make a complaint or resolve a problem would soon feel as if he were engaged in a battle with a multilimbed monster.

This multilimbed monster, however, had only one head: Adolf Hitler. The entire system was designed to make clear that there was only one man in charge, one leader—the *Führer*. Like Mussolini, Hitler realized the importance of personalizing his rule. During election campaigns before 1933 and in the early years of power after, Hitler was constantly on the move, using cars and planes to hit city after city, to deliver speech after speech, to touch person after person. In 1932 and 1933, he conducted election campaigns from the sky, often visiting four or five cities in a single night. He always arrived late, so that his plane could fly above the packed stadium, the focus of every upturned face. Leaders of the Hitler Youth were required to take this oath: "Adolf Hitler is Germany and Germany is Adolf Hitler. He who pledges himself to Hitler pledges himself to Germany."[11]

## National Recovery

Jews, communists, socialists, and other groups defined as enemies of the state faced the constant threat of persecution and imprisonment under the Nazi regime during the 1930s. But for many Germans not in these groups, life got better. Nazi rule brought full employment, restoration of national pride, and a cultural revolution that linked the power of nostalgia to the dynamism of modernity.

Economic depression gave the Nazis the chance at power; economic prosperity (or the appearance of it) enabled them to hold on to this power. Because Hitler perceived himself as a revolutionary, bound by no existing rules, he was able to intensify and accelerate unorthodox economic programs put in place by the preceding government. The rules of economic orthodoxy dictated that in times of depression, a government should cut spending and maintain a balanced budget. Struggling to cope with the broken economy, Hitler's predecessors had set aside the rules and instead began devising a program of deficit spending on things such as a national network of highways (the *Autobahnen*). Hitler took up these plans and ran with them. He made the autobahn a reality, invested heavily in other public works, and after 1936 poured marks into rearmament. These programs created thousands of jobs. By 1938, unemployment in Germany had been defeated, dropping from 44 percent in 1932 to 14.1 percent in 1934 to less than 1 percent in 1938. In contrast, double-digit unemployment rates persisted in much of western Europe.

Germans and non-Germans alike hailed Nazi Germany as an economic success. In many ways, they were wrong. Under Nazi rule, real wages fell and the concentration on rearmament led to shortages in food supplies and in consumer goods. In 1938, meat consumption remained below the level of 1929. Yet many Germans *believed* themselves to be much better off. The expansion of social welfare assistance (for those considered "Aryan") helps explain this perception, as does the establishment of the "Strength through Joy" program (directly inspired by Mussolini's "after-work" organizations), which provided workers with cheap vacations, theater and concert tickets, and weekend outings. But most important, under the Nazis, Germans were working. The abundance of jobs—despite the low wages, despite the disappearance of workers' rights, despite the food shortages—made Hitler an economic savior to many Germans.

Many also viewed him as a national savior, a leader who restored Germany's pride and power. Payment of war reparations, demanded by the humiliating Versailles Treaty, halted in 1930 because of the global economic crisis. Hitler never resumed payment. He also ignored the treaty's military restrictions and rebuilt Germany's armed forces. By 1938, parades featuring row after row of smartly uniformed troops, impressive displays of tanks, and flybys of military aircraft all signaled the revitalization of German military might.

For many ordinary Germans, traumatized and shamed by the sequence of national disasters—military defeat, loss of territory, hyperinflation, political and fiscal crises, unemployment—the sight of troops goose-stepping under the German flag meant a personal as well as a na-

German Painting Idolizing Hitler

**"Heil (Hail) Hitler!"**
An enthusiastic crowd salutes Hitler at a Nazi party rally. The women in the traditional costumes illustrate a key aspect of the Nazis' appeal: their promise to restore women to their traditional domestic roles. The men in military uniform indicate a second source of Nazi popularity: the restoration of military strength and national pride.

tional renaissance. As one Nazi song proclaimed, "And now the me is part of the great We."[12]

To create the "great We," Hitler utilized modern techniques and technology. The Nazis published a glossy illustrated magazine, produced their own films, and littered cities with propaganda posters. Impressed by Mussolini's use of the radio to popularize fascism, Hitler subsidized the production of radios in Germany so that by the end of the 1930s most Germans had access to a radio—and to Hitler's radio talks. He also recognized the power of the cinema, and hired the brilliant filmmaker Leni Riefenstahl (1902–2003) to film Nazi rallies. These still-astonishing films show an overwhelming mass spectacle in which an entire nation appears to be marching in step behind Hitler.

But Hitler also perceived the power of nostalgia for many Germans, and so used modern techniques and technologies to establish the Nazis as bulwarks of tradition. In speeches, posters, and films, the Nazis painted a picture of a mythic Germany, an idyllic community peopled by sturdy blond peasants, small shopkeepers, and independent craftsmen. The Nazis promised that under their leadership, individual Germans would regain meaning and purpose as part of a single national community. Nazi ideology condemned international corporations, large department stores, and supermarket chains as elements of a vast Jewish-controlled conspiracy to deprive ordinary people of their livelihoods.

## Campaigns of Repression and Terror

Part of the appeal of the "great We" that Hitler was creating relied on the demonization and violent repression of the "not Us," those defined as outside or opposed to the nation. Hitler used the existing German police force as well as his own paramilitary troops—the brownshirted SA and the blackshirted SS (*Schutzstaffeln*)—to terrorize those he defined as enemies of the nation. The Nazis first targeted political opponents. By 1934 half of the 300,000 German Communist Party members were in prison or dead; most of the rest had fled the country. The Nazis also persecuted specific religious groups on the basis of their actual or presumed opposition to the Nazi state. Roman Catholics could no longer work in the civil service and faced constant harassment, and about half of Germany's 20,000 Jehovah's Witnesses were sent to concentration camps.

The groups that the Nazis deemed biologically inferior suffered most severely. Beginning in 1933, the Nazi regime forced the sterilization of the Roma (Gypsies), the mentally and physically handicapped, and mixed-race children (in most cases, the offspring of German women and black African soldiers serving in the French occupation force in the Rhineland). By 1939, 370,000 men and women had been sterilized.

The Jewish community—less than 1 percent of the German population—bore the brunt of Nazi racial attacks. To Nazi anti-Semites, Hitler's accession to the German chancellorship was like the opening of hunting season. They beat up Jews in the streets, vandalized Jewish shops and homes, threatened German Christians who associated with Jews, and violently enforced boycotts of Jewish businesses. Anti-Jewish legislation piled up in an effort to convince Germans of the separateness, the "non-Germanness," of Jewish cultural and racial identity. In 1933, "non-Aryans" (Jews) were dismissed from the civil service and the legal profession, and the number of Jewish students in high schools and universities was restricted. Every organization in Germany—youth clubs, sports teams, labor unions, charitable societies—underwent "Nazification," which meant the dismissal of all Jewish members and the appointment of Nazis to leadership roles. In 1935, the "Nuremberg Laws" labeled as Jewish anyone with three or more Jewish grandparents. Marriage or sexual relations between German Jews and non-Jews now became a serious crime.

## Women and the Radical Right

Much of the appeal of both fascism and Nazism lay in the promise to restore order to societies on the verge of disintegration. Restoration of order meant, among other things, the return of women to their proper place. According to Nazi propaganda, "the soil provides the food, the woman supplies the population, and the men make the action."[13] Hitler proclaimed, "the Nazi Revolution will be an entirely male event." Mussolini agreed: "Woman must obey. . . . In our State, she must not count."[14]

In Nazi Germany, the restoration of order translated into a series of financial and cultural incentives to encourage women to stay at home and produce babies. These measures ranged from marriage loans (available only if the wife quit her job) and income tax deductions for families to the establishment of discussion, welfare, and leisure groups for housewives. Not surprisingly, the Nazis also used disincentives. One of the first actions of the new Nazi government was to dismiss women from the civil service and to rule that female physicians could work only in their husbands' practices. By 1937, both women physicians and women Ph.D.s had lost the right to be addressed as "Doctor" or "Professor." Women could no longer work as school principals. Coeducational schools were abolished. Birth control became illegal and penalties for abortion increased while prosecutions doubled.

In fascist Italy, Mussolini's government focused its legislation on both men and women. Unmarried men over age 30 had to pay double income tax (priests were exempt), homosexual relations between men were outlawed, and fatherhood became a prerequisite for men in high-ranking public office. A wide-ranging social welfare program that included family allowances, maternity leaves, and marriage loans sought to strengthen the traditional family. Quotas limited the number of women employed in both the civil service and in private business, while women found themselves excluded entirely from jobs defined as "virile," a varied list that included boat captains, diplomats, high school principals, and history teachers.

# The Polarization of Politics in the 1930s

■ **What factors led to the polarization of European politics in the 1930s?**

The apparent successes of fascist Italy and Nazi Germany appealed to many Europeans and Americans disenchanted with democracy in the era of the Great Depression. During this period, the Soviet Union also seemed a success story. While the capitalist nations struggled with high unemployment rates and falling industrial output, the Soviet Union appeared to be performing economic miracles. Politics in the West thus became polarized between communism on the radical left and fascism and Nazism on the radical right. In both the United States and Europe, however, politicians and policymakers sought to maintain the middle ground, to retain democratic values in a time of extremist ideologies.

## The Soviet Union Under Stalin: Revolution Reconstructed, Terror Extended

Many Europeans looked with envy at the Soviet Union in the 1930s. Unemployment had disappeared; huge industrial cities transformed the landscape; the development of new industries such as chemicals and automobiles, together with a full-scale exploitation of the Soviet Union's massive natural resources, sent production indices soaring. But this economic transformation rested on dead bodies, millions of dead bodies. During the 1930s, mass murder became an integral part of the Soviet regime under Joseph Stalin (1879–1953).

### Stalin's Rise to Power

By 1928, Stalin was the uncontested head of the party. At the time of Lenin's death in 1924, however, few observers would have predicted Stalin's success. Although a stalwart Bolshevik, he stood in the shadow of more charismatic, intellectually able colleagues. How, then, did Stalin seize control of the Communist Party and the Soviet state?

One key factor in Stalin's rise to power was the changing nature of the Communist Party. The party that made the revolution in 1917 comprised only 24,000 members. Following a massive recruitment campaign to honor Lenin's memory, party membership in 1929 stood at more than one and a half million—and only 8,000 of these had been members in 1917. In other words, the vast majority of communists in 1929 had not fought in the revolution. For them, communism was not a revolutionary ideology challenging the tsarist political order; it was itself the political order. Party membership was not a revolutionary act; it was a guarantee of privileged status and career opportunities. Moreover, unlike the original Bolshevik revolutionaries, most of the new members were not well educated or well versed in communist ideology. In fact, 25 percent of the party membership was functionally illiterate.

As party secretary from 1922 on, Stalin led the recruitment drive that enlisted many of these new party members. Other party leaders dismissed Stalin as the "card-index Bolshevik"—the paper-pusher, the gray guy with the boring job. But Stalin, an astute politician, recognized that his card index held enormous power. Not only did he determine the fate of party membership applications, he also decided who got promoted to what and where. Thus, throughout the 1920s Stalin slowly built up a broad base of support within the party. Vast numbers of ordinary communists owed their party membership, and in many cases their livelihoods, to Stalin.

While Stalin expanded his support at the grassroots, a fierce ideological struggle at the highest levels of the Communist Party distracted his rivals for the party leadership. By the time of Lenin's death, the New Economic Policy (NEP) had restored economic stability to the Soviet Union. The nation, however, remained far behind its capitalist competitors in both agricultural and industrial productivity. All communists agreed on the need to launch the Soviet economy into industrialization. The problem was, how could this backward nation obtain the capital it needed for industrial development? One faction of the party, led by Leon Trotsky (1879–1940), argued that the answer was to squeeze the necessary capital out of the peasantry through high taxation and even, if necessary, the confiscation of crops. Trotsky wanted to abandon NEP and its encouragement of small private farming initiatives. The opposing faction, led by Nikolai Bukharin (1888–1938), pointed to the lessons taught by western European industrialization. In the West, industrial capital came from agricultural profits. Bukharin insisted on the need for gradualism: Agricultural development must precede industrialization. "Enrich the peasant," Bukharin argued.

Stalin at first backed Bukharin and those who wished to continue on the NEP course, because he perceived the charismatic Trotsky as the more immediate threat to his ambitions. Once Trotsky had been expelled from the party, however, Stalin reversed course and turned on Bukharin. In 1928, Stalin emerged as the sole leader of the party and as a fierce advocate of the abandonment of NEP, the total socialization of the Soviet economy, and a fast march forward into full-scale industrialization.

## The "Revolution from Above": Collectivization and Industrialization, 1928–1934

As party leader, Stalin placed the Soviet Union firmly back on a revolutionary course, with the aim of catapulting the Soviet Union into the ranks of the industrialized nations.

Stalin Demands Rapid Industrialization of the USSR (1931)

The first step in what was called "the revolution from above" was collectivization°, the replacement of private and village farms with large cooperative agricultural enterprises run by communist managers according to directives received from the central government. Collectivization had both economic and political aims. Regarded as more modern and efficient, collective farms were expected to produce an agricultural surplus and thereby raise the capital needed for industrialization. But in addition, collectivization would realize communist ideals by eradicating the profit motive, abolishing private property, and transforming the peasants into modern state employees.

The peasants resisted this transformation, however. They burned their crops and slaughtered their livestock. Famine followed. The numbers of deaths resulting from collectivization and the famine of 1931–1932 remain the subject of intense controversy; the available quantitative evidence points to death figures between five million and seven million. Ukraine and Kazakhstan were hardest hit. Almost 40 percent of the Kazakh population died from starvation or typhus; the number of dead in Ukraine alone may have reached four million.[15] Perhaps as many as ten million peasants were deported in these years; many of these died either on the way to or in forced labor camps.

While class war raged in the countryside, city dwellers embarked on the second stage of the "revolution from above"—industrialization. In 1931 Stalin articulated the task facing the Soviet Union: "We are fifty or a hundred years behind the advanced countries. We must catch up this distance in ten years. Either we do it or we go under."[16] Doing it demanded, first, unprecedented levels of labor output. Despite the massive investment in heavy industry, the Soviet Union throughout the 1930s remained undermechanized. What it lacked in technology, however, it possessed in population. Thus Soviet industry was highly labor intensive. To ensure that workers produced at the levels needed, the Soviet state under Stalin imposed fierce labor discipline. Only productive workers received ration cards. Internal passports restricted workers' freedom of movement. If fired, a worker was automatically evicted from his or her apartment and deprived of a ration card.

Catching up with the West also demanded reducing already low levels of personal consumption. Eighty percent of all investment went into heavy industry, while domestic construction and light industry—clothing, for example, and furniture—were ignored. Scarcity became the norm, long lines and constant shortages part of every urban resident's existence. Economists estimate that Soviet citizens endured a 40 percent fall in their already low standard of living between 1929 and 1932.

While millions starved in the countryside, young communists acclaimed these years of hardship and horror as an era of heroism. They volunteered to organize collective farms, to work in conditions of extreme brutality at construction sites, to labor long hours in factories and mines. Babies born in this decade received names like "Little Five Years" (for girls) and "Plan" (for boys), reflecting their parents' enthusiasm for the series of Five-Year-Plans issued by the central government as outlines for the new world order. Much of this enthusiasm was stirred up by propaganda campaigns aimed at persuading laborers to work ever harder and sacrifice ever more. Ordinary workers who achieved record-breaking feats of production earned medals, special ceremonies, and material gifts. Immense publicity focused on the gargantuan engineering achievements of the era—the cities built atop swampland, the hydroelectric projects with their enormous dams and power plants, the Moscow subway system. Such publicity made party members feel part of a huge and powerful endeavor. A popular song announced, "We were born to make fairy tales come true."[17]

Just as important as the propaganda campaigns was the reality of unprecedented opportunity. The Soviet Union in the 1930s has been called "the quicksand society," one in which traditional structures and relations (and people too) were swallowed up at a breathtaking pace. As these traditional structures disappeared, new ones emerged, bringing tremendous geographic and social mobility to Soviet society. For example, Nikita Khrushchev (1894–1971), who would succeed Stalin as the head of the party and state in the 1950s, was the son of a poor peasant.

No propaganda campaign and no amount of effort from enthusiastic young communists, however, could provide the Soviet Union with the labor it needed to catch up with the West in ten years. Forced labor was crucial. Throughout the 1930s, as many as five million men, women, and children—peasants, political opponents of Stalin, religious dissenters, ethnic minorities—labored in prison camps.[18] By some estimates, forced labor accounted for no less than 25 percent of all construction work in the Soviet Union in the 1930s. Many of the huge engineering triumphs of the decade rested on the backs of prisoners and deportees.

By the end of the 1930s, Stalin's "revolution from above" had achieved its aim. The pouring of resources into heavy industry and the wringing of every ounce of labor out of an exhausted, cold, and hungry populace succeeded in building the foundations of an industrial society. This society would stand the test of total war in the 1940s.

But Stalin's revolution failed to convert Soviet agriculture into a modern, prosperous sector of the economy. Rural regions remained backward. Peasant villages, for example, were not electrified until the later 1950s. Most peasants regarded the collective farm as belonging not to them or to the community but to the state, just another in a long line of harsh landlords. Under Stalin, peasants were second-class citizens, ineligible for internal passports, with little access to the benefits of Soviet industrialization. Like their ancestors under serfdom, peasants at the end of the 1930s found themselves tied to a particular village, saddled with forced labor obligations, and compelled to spend the bulk of their time farming for someone else's profit. Most peasants viewed the communist state as the enemy, to be ignored when possible, tricked if necessary, and endured no matter what.

## Stalin's Consolidation of Power: The Great Purge and Soviet Society, 1934–1939

By the mid-1930s, the worst seemed to be over. Most villages were collectivized and the mass violence had ended. The 17th Party Congress in 1934 was known as the "Congress of Victors," as the party celebrated its industrial successes and the achievement of collectivization. But for many of the men and women at this congress, the worst was yet to come. Within five years, half of the 2,000 delegates had been arrested; of the 149 elected members of the congress's Central Committee, 98 were shot dead. These Congress delegates, and hundreds of thousands of other Soviet citizens, were victims of the "Great Purge°." In the purge, Stalin's effort to eliminate any possible rival to his power converged with widespread paranoia and economic crisis to produce a nationwide witch-hunt and mass executions.

The early victims of the purge tended to be top-ranking Communist Party officials, many of whom had opposed Stalin on various issues during the 1920s. By charging these powerful men with conspiring against the communist state, Stalin reduced the chances that any competitor might oust him. In a series of three spectacular show trials attended by journalists from all over the world, leading Bolsheviks—some of the Soviet Union's most respected men, such as Nikolai Bukharin—pleaded guilty to charges of conspiracy and sabotage, and were immediately executed. Numerous smaller trials replicated the process throughout the Soviet Union. Non-Russians suffered heavily. By the end of the 1930s, for example, 260 of the 300 party secretaries in Georgia had been killed. The purge also swept the armed forces. Those executed included three of the five Soviet marshals, thirteen of fifteen army commanders, and fifty-seven of eighty corps commanders.

The purge quickly spread beyond the top ranks of the party and military. With the show trials indicating that even the highest-level Bolsheviks were not to be trusted, people began to suspect that traitors lurked within every factory

### "Pictures Can't Lie . . . "

Stalin was not Lenin's closest associate, nor did Lenin select him as his successor. To claim and consolidate his position as sole leader of the Communist Party and of the Soviet Union, Stalin had to falsify history and present himself as Lenin's chosen heir. Murder and mass executions could remove competitors from the present, but to erase them from the past, Stalin turned to the airbrush and the scissors rather than the gun. Pictures showing other Bolsheviks standing next to Lenin were cropped, leaving him with Stalin, or if such a pairing could not be achieved, standing alone. Compare these two photos, taken by the same photographer, within five seconds of each other. In the first, Lev Kamenev and Leon Trotsky—leading Bolsheviks and rivals with Stalin for the party leadership after Lenin's death—stand on the steps to Lenin's left. But in the second, Kamenev and Trotsky have been cut out and some steps have been drawn in. Stalin sought to airbrush Trotsky and Kamenev out of Soviet history, just as he eliminated them from Soviet politics. Trotsky was forced into exile in 1929 and murdered in 1940; Kamenev was executed in 1936.

and local party gathering. At the same time the shortcomings of an overly centralized and poorly run economy were multiplying: Subject to an endless stream of ever-changing and often irrational program and policy directives, managers falsified key economic statistics, while poorly trained workers misused machines and cut all available corners.

People were anxious and hungry, and eager to find someone to blame for breakdowns and failures. The purge made it easy to point the finger, to charge this manager with deliberately failing to order tractors or that engineer with implementing the wrong system of crop rotation to sabotage production. Thus the Great Purge quickly spun out of control to embrace low-level party members, managers in state agencies, factory directors, and engineers. Many were killed without trial, others executed after a legal show, and still others deported to slave labor camps to be worked to death on Stalin's vast construction projects. Death estimates vary widely; at least 750,000 people died, with the numbers of those arrested, imprisoned, or deported running into the millions.[19]

The Great Purge consolidated Stalin's hold on the Soviet Union. It not only eliminated all potential competitors, it also tied huge numbers of people more tightly to Stalin and his version of revolution. The shocking thing about the Great Purge was its popularity. The purge hit primarily urban managers. For the most part, ordinary workers and peasants were safe from its onslaught. These ordinary citizens, who had been ordered about, reprimanded, fined, insulted, and assaulted by these self-same managers, tended to believe that the purge's victims got what they deserved. Moreover, the purge can also be seen as a huge job creation program. Individuals who moved into the positions left vacant by the purge's victims had an enormous material as well as psychological stake in viewing the purge as an act of justice.

## Stalin and the Nation

The popularity of the purge was also closely linked with the emergence of a Stalin-centered personality cult. By the time the purge began, the cult was an omnipresent part of Soviet urban life. Huge posters and statues ensured that Stalin's figure remained constantly in front of Soviet citizens. Textbooks rewrote the history of the Bolshevik revolution to highlight Stalin's contribution and linked every scientific, technological, or economic advance in the Soviet Union to the person and power of Stalin. The scores of letters personally addressed to Stalin that poured into central government offices testify to the success of this cult. To many Soviet citizens, Stalin personified the nation.

Increasingly the *nation*—not the worker, not socialism, not the revolution—assumed the central role in Soviet propaganda. Lenin had condemned Russian nationalism as a middle-class ideology to be eradicated along with capitalism. The working class, not the nation, mattered. But Stalin reversed this aspect of Lenin's revolution. In the 1930s, "Russia" and "the motherland/fatherland" both reappeared in political discourse. The tsarist past, which Lenin had condemned or ignored, was resurrected to emphasize Russian greatness. The imperial anthem resounded once again, while films and books praised strong Russian leaders such as Peter the Great. While this resurgence of Russian nationalism was popular in Russia itself, it spelled real difficulties for the 50 percent of the Soviet population who lived outside Russia and who found it necessary to repress their own sense of national identity—or face deportation.

Exalting the motherland went hand in hand with exalting the mother. Just as Stalin resurrected Russian nationalism in the 1930s, so he sought to resurrect the Russian family. He promoted the family as a vital prop of the national order, an institution to be strengthened rather than encouraged to wither away (as Lenin had insisted). In 1936, Stalin's regime outlawed abortion and made divorce more difficult.

**"People's Dreams Have Come True!"**

In this typical example of "Socialist Realism," an older Soviet citizen points proudly to the achievements of Stalinist industrialization while the young boy, in the uniform of the Pioneers, the Stalinist youth organization, listens eagerly.

СБЫЛИСЬ МЕЧТЫ НАРОДНЫЕ!

## DOCUMENT

# The Cult of the Leader

*The personality cult characterized not only the Radical Right ideologies of Italian fascism and German Nazism, but also the ideological system that stood at the opposite end of the political spectrum: Stalinist communism. Searching for a way to mobilize the masses without granting to them actual political power, Mussolini, Hitler, and Stalin erected around themselves leadership cults. Their own images came to embody the nation. As the following set of excerpts shows, the cults of Mussolini, Hitler, and Stalin took on religious dimensions, with all three men adored as secular saviors.*

## I. Description of Mussolini's Visit to Trieste in 1938

Finally we have seen and heard Him! . . . These first reactions, expressed with indescribable joy, eyes moved to tears and an ineffable, agonizing joy. . . . It is not easy to describe the expression on most faces, on those of the little people as on those of the educated, of the mass as a whole. Expressions of wonderful contentment and pride among those who saw Him pass close by—especially among the dockworkers He visited yesterday—and those whose eyes He met, those who caught His eye. "Never such eyes! The way he looks at you is irresistible! He smiled at me . . . I was close, I could almost touch him. . . . When I saw him my legs trembled" . . . and a thousand other similar statements show and confirm the enormous fascination exercised by his person.

## II. Description of an Early Nazi Rally by Louise Solmitz, Schoolteacher

The April sun shone hot like summer and turned everything into a picture of gay expectation. There was immaculate order and discipline . . . the hours passed. . . .

Expectations rose. There stood Hitler in a simple black coat and looked over the crowd. Waiting. A forest of swastika pennants swished up, the jubilation of this moment was given vent in a roaring salute. . . . How many look up to him with a touching faith! As their helper, their savior, their deliverer from unbearable distress—to him who rescues the Prussian prince, the scholar, the clergyman, the farmer, the worker, the unemployed, who leads them from the parties back into the nation.

## III. Speech by a Woman Delegate at a Workers' Conference in the Soviet Union

Thank you comrade Stalin, our leader, our father, for a happy, merry kolkhoz life!

He, our Stalin, put the steering-wheel of the tractor in our hand. . . . He, the great Stalin, carefully listens to all of us in this meeting, loves us with a great Stalinist love (*tumultuous applause*), day and night thinks of our prosperity, of our culture, of our work. . . .

Long live our friend, our teacher, the beloved leader of the world proletariat, comrade Stalin! (*Tumultuous applause, rising to an ovation. Shouts of "Hurrah!"*)

Sources: "I. Description of Mussolini's Visit to Trieste in 1938," reprinted by permission of the publisher from *The Sacralization of Politics in Fascist Italy* by Emilio Gentile, translated by Keith Botsford, p. 147, Cambridge, Mass.: Harvard University Press. Copyright © 1996 by the President and Fellows of Harvard College. "II. Description of an Early Nazi Rally by Louise Solmitz, Schoolteacher," copyright © 1988 by Claudia Koonz. From *Mothers in the Fatherland: Women, the Family, and Nazi Politics* by Claudia Koonz. Reprinted by permission of St. Martin's Press, LLC. "III. Speech by a Woman Delegate at a Worker's Conference in the Soviet Union," from *Stalin's Peasants: Resistance and Survival in the Russian Village After Collectivization* by Sheila Fitzpatrick. Copyright © 1996 by Oxford University Press, Inc. Published by Oxford University Press, Inc.

Like Western leaders, Stalin also sought to increase the national birth rate by granting pregnant women maternity stipends and increasing the number of prenatal health clinics. There was no effort to pull women out of the workforce, however. Of the more than four million new workers entering the labor force between 1932 and 1937, 82 percent were women. The Soviet Union continued to provide women with access to higher education and professional jobs—women worked as doctors, engineers, scientists, and high-ranking public officials. (And women were deported and executed in huge numbers—one could argue that Stalin was an equal-opportunity killer.)

In the arts, too, Stalinism meant a retreat from the radicalism of Lenin's revolution. Whereas Soviet artists under Lenin had been in the vanguard of modernism, under Stalin art came firmly under state control. Artists knew that their literal survival depended on their conforming to the principles of "Socialist Realism": *Partinost* (loyalty to the state), *Ideinost* (correct ideology and content), and *Narodnost* (easy accessibility to ordinary viewers). The abstract experiments of the early Soviet period gave way to pretty pictures of happily collectivized peasants and portraits of Stalin in heroic poses.

## The Response of the Democracies

The apparent economic successes of fascism and Nazism on the right, and Stalinism on the left, polarized European politics. For many Europeans in the 1930s, it seemed that the middle ground was collapsing beneath their feet, that democracy had failed and that they had no choice but to scramble to one extreme or the other. Yet in both western Europe and in the United States, important steps were taken to ensure not only that democracy survived but that it eventually delivered a decent standard of living to the great mass of ordinary people.

## A Third Way? The Social Democratic Alternative

The effort to meet the challenge of the depression without embracing either Nazism or Stalinism accelerated the development of the political model that would dominate western Europe after World War II: social democracy°. In a social democracy, a democratically elected parliamentary government accepts the responsibility of ensuring a decent standard of living for its citizens. To achieve this goal, the government assumes two important functions—first, regulating an economy containing both private enterprise and nationalized or state-controlled corporations; second, overseeing a welfare state, which guarantees the citizen access to unemployment and sickness benefits, pensions, family allowances, and health services. Although social democracy did not triumph in western Europe until after the massive bloodletting of another total war, the interwar years witnessed important steps toward this third path, an alternative to the extremes of both the Radical Right (fascism and Nazism) and the Radical Left (Stalinism).

One of the most striking experiments in changing the relationship between democratic governments and the economy occurred in the United States. Franklin Delano Roosevelt (1882–1945) became president in 1932 at the height of the Great Depression, when unemployment stood at 24 percent (15 million workers were without jobs) and Washington, D.C., witnessed federal troops called out to quell rioting among unemployed veterans. Promising a "New Deal" of "Relief, Recovery, Reform," Roosevelt tackled the depression with an activist governmental policy that included agricultural subsidies, public works programs, and the Social Security Act of 1935, which set the foundations of the U.S. welfare program.

Yet even with this sharp upswing in government activity, unemployment remained high— ten million workers were without jobs in 1939—and the gross national product (GNP) did not recover to 1929 levels until 1941. In the view of some economists, Roosevelt failed to solve the problem of unemployment because he remained committed to the ideal of a balanced budget. In contrast, the British economist John Maynard Keynes (1883–1946) insisted that in times of depression, the state should not reduce spending and endeavor to live within its budget, but instead should adopt a program of deficit spending to stimulate economic growth. Only when prosperity returned, Keynes advised, should governments increase taxes and cut expenditures to recover the deficits.

The experience of Sweden appeared to confirm Keynes's theory. The Swedish Social Democratic Party took office in 1932 with the intention of using the powers of central government to revive the depressed economy. The government allowed its budget deficit to climb while it financed a massive public works campaign, as well as an increase in welfare benefits ranging from unemployment insurance to maternity allowances to subsidized housing. By 1937 unemployment was shrinking rapidly as the manufacturing sector boomed.

Throughout most of western Europe, however, governments proved far more reluctant to advocate radically new policies, despite an expansion of the state's role in economic affairs. For example, Britain's limited economic recovery in the later 1930s was based largely on private initiatives such as an expansion in housing construction and the emergence of new industries aimed at domestic consumption (radios and other small electronics, household goods, automobiles). In the areas hardest hit by depression—the heavy export industries such as coal, shipbuilding, textiles, and steel, located primarily in northern Britain—the lack of government intervention meant continuing high unemployment rates and widespread poverty and deprivation throughout the 1930s.

### Taking a Stand

British women demonstrate against legislation that tightened requirements for receiving unemployment benefits and caused widespread suffering.

## The Popular Front in France

The limited success of democratic governments in addressing the problems of the Great Depression meant that many experienced the 1930s as a hard, hungry decade when democracy failed to deliver a decent standard of living. The example of France illustrates both the political polarization occurring in Europe in the 1930s and the sharp limits on governments seeking both to maintain democratic politics and to improve the living conditions of their citizens. France lacked such basic welfare benefits as old-age pensions and unemployment insurance. As the economy plummeted, therefore, social unrest rose, and so, too, did the appeal of the fascist movement. In 1934, fascist riots left 17 dead and more than 2,000 injured.

The increasing strength of fascism, combined with the deepening national emergency, led to the formation of the Popular Front, a coalition comprising the centrist Radical Party, the moderate leftist Socialist Party, and the far-left Stalinist Communist Party. In 1936, the Popular Front won the national elections. The Socialist leader Leon Blum (1872–1950) took office as prime minister in the midst of a general strike involving two million workers. He settled the strike to the workers' benefit by granting them a 15 percent pay raise and the right to collective bargaining. Over the next year, Blum nationalized the key war industries and gave workers further pay increases, paid holidays, and a forty-hour workweek.

Many conservative French voters saw Blum's policies of social reform as the first step on the road to Stalinism. Thus they cried, "Better Hitler than Blum!"—in other words, better the Radical Right than the Stalinist Left. The global business community pulled capital out of France, resulting in a major financial crisis and the devaluation of the French franc. Dependent on foreign loans, Blum's government faced sharp pressure to pull back from its program of social and economic reforms. When it tried to do so, its working-class constituency rose in revolt. In May 1937 the suppression of a left-wing demonstration left 7 dead and 200 injured. Blum resigned the next month. The Popular Front in France quickly disintegrated.

## The Spanish Civil War

Spain became the arena in which the struggle of Europe's polarized political forces turned into outright war. In 1931, a democratically elected republican government replaced the Spanish monarchy and in 1936, a Popular Front government, comprising both socialists and communists, took office. In July, army officers led a right-wing rebellion against this government.

The struggle between the left-wing Republican government and the right-wing rebels quickly became an international issue. Both fascist Italy and Nazi Germany supported the rebellion, enabling General Francisco Franco

**The Spanish Civil War**

The Spanish Civil War mobilized women as well as men. These soldiers, fighting in the uniform of the anarchist militia, are defending the barricades of Barcelona against rebel attack.

(1892–1975) and his crack Moroccan troops to cross into Spain from their station in North Africa and launch an all-out offensive against the republic. The Republican government appealed to the democracies for aid, but the only government that came to its assistance was that of the Soviet Union. Soviet tanks and aircraft enabled the besieged city of Madrid to hold out against Franco's forces but at the same time the Soviet intervention split the Republican movement, with anarchists and socialists resisting Stalinist control. Unnerved by the Soviet involvement, the governments of France, Britain, and the United States remained neutral. Appalled by this official inaction, many citizens of these countries served in the International Brigade, which fought for the cause of democracy in Spain.

The Spanish Civil War raged until March 1939, when the last remnants of the Republican forces finally surrendered to Franco. Four hundred thousand men and women died in the war; in the following four years, another 200,000 were executed. Franco established an authoritarian government that crushed Spanish democracy. Spain became a potent symbol for all of Europe. To both fascists and their democratic opponents, Franco's victory illustrated how easily democracy could be destroyed.

# The West and the World: Imperialism in the Interwar Era

■ **How did the interaction between the West and the world outside change after World War I?**

In the interwar struggle between authoritarian and democratic forms of politics, we can see contrasting definitions of "the West" competing for dominance. In this same period, the clash between advocates and enemies of Western imperialism revealed multiple notions of "Western culture" as well. The Allies claimed to have fought during World War I for national self-determination, but they had no intention of allowing their overseas empires the right to determine their own national selves. Britain and France emerged from the war with not only their imperialist ideologies intact but their empires greatly expanded. They divided up Germany's overseas colonies in Africa and Asia, and as we saw in Chapter 24, became the dominant powers in the Middle East.

During the 1920s and 1930s, popular imperialism reached its zenith in Europe. Filmmakers and novelists found that imperial settings formed the perfect backdrop for stirring tales of individual heroism and limitless adventure. Governments also played a role in strengthening the culture of empire. In both Britain and France, imperial history became a required part of school curricula. British children learned to identify the pink-colored sections of the world map as "ours," while a series of colonial exhibitions impressed on the British public the importance of the empire to Britain's economic prosperity. In Belgium, the government promoted the Congo as a "model colony." The economic ties between European states and their imperial territories grew tighter. For example, by 1940 more than 45 percent of French overseas investment went to regions within its empire (see Map 25.2).

## The Irish Revolution

This period, however, also witnessed the emergence of important challenges to the imperial idea. The most successful of these occurred in Ireland. Many Irish men, both Catholic and Protestant, fought for Britain during World War I, but a small group of revolutionary nationalists saw the war as an opportunity for revolt. They mounted an armed rebellion on Easter Monday in 1916. Although quickly and brutally suppressed, the "Easter Rising" became for Irish nationalists

a key moment in the fight for an independent Ireland. The executed leaders of the rising became martyrs for the sacred cause of nationhood, while the ease with which the British crushed the revolt convinced Irish nationalist leaders of the necessity of employing guerilla tactics rather than open military assault to defeat their much more powerful foe.

In 1921, ground down by more than two years of guerilla warfare waged with consummate skill by the Irish Republican Army (IRA), the British government offered Ireland independence. The offer, however, came with strings attached. The new state would remain within the British Empire and Ireland itself would be partitioned. Its six northern counties, dominated by Protestants who opposed Irish independence, were to remain part of Britain. A delegation led by the charismatic IRA chief Michael Collins (the "Big Fella") accepted this offer. It took two years of civil war—a war that cost Collins his life—to persuade many Irish nationalists to do the same. Ireland continued as an uneasy member of the British Empire until the end of the 1930s, when it cut all constitutional ties to Britain. Northern Ireland remains a part of Britain to this day.

## Changing Power Equations: Ideology and Economics

Ireland's revolt against British imperial rule, while unusual in its success, revealed the growing power of anti-imperialist forces across the world. The triumph of communism in Russia helped strengthen these forces. In his publications, Lenin argued that imperialism was the logical consequence of capitalism and its quest for markets, and thus that anti-capitalism and anti-imperialism went hand in hand. Under Lenin, the Soviet Union declared itself the defender of oppressed nationalities everywhere, and provided ideological and material assistance to nationalist independence movements in Indonesia, Indochina, Burma, and most significantly, China, where Soviet advisers helped form the Communist Party in 1921.

Communism alone, however, does not account for the spread of anti-imperialist nationalist movements in the interwar years. Changing economic relationships were crucial. During World War I, the demands of industrial warfare forced Europe's imperial powers to utilize fully their colonial resources, a strategy that brought with it unintended but far-reaching social change. Throughout Europe's empires, wartime economic demands escalated labor migration rates, expanded urban populations, and enveloped once-isolated villages in the global economic web. These changes were not often welcomed by the peoples involved. In Africa, for example, the Allies tailored their colonial economies to meet wartime demands for commodities such as rubber. This policy benefited multinational companies such as Unilever, which pocketed increasing profits, but had a negative impact on local populations: Native merchants

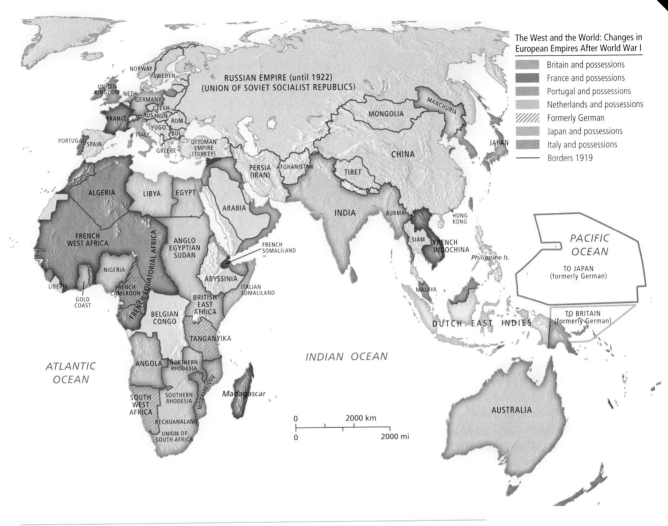

**Map 25.2   The West and the World:
Changes in European Empires After World War I**

Britain, France, and Japan were the principal beneficiaries of Germany's loss of empire after World
War I.

saw their independence and their incomes disappearing;
African peasants lost their land and became waged laborers;
the concentration on cash crops reduced food production at
a time when the population was growing steadily.

In the 1930s, economic conditions grew worse in the
wake of the Great Depression. The sharp fall in the prices of
primary products spelled disaster for regions of the world
that had shifted their agricultural economies to the production of cash crops for export. At the same time, the benefits
of imperial governance diminished. Looking for ways to reduce expenditures, European governments cut funds to
colonial schools, public services, and health care. Direct
taxation rates rose while unemployment rates soared. So,
too, did the numbers attracted to nationalist movements.

## Postwar Nationalism, Westernization, and the Islamic Challenge

These economic and social developments not only helped
subvert the legitimacy of imperialist rule but also fostered
the growth of anti-Western movements, often in religious
form. In Africa, for example, a revival of animist religion
expressed both an explicit rejection of the Christian
teachings brought by European and American missionaries and an implicit refusal of Western cultural and political styles. Throughout many African regions, however,
Islam possessed the most potent appeal. In the growing
cities, immigrants cut off from their village and its religious practices found that Islam provided an alternative

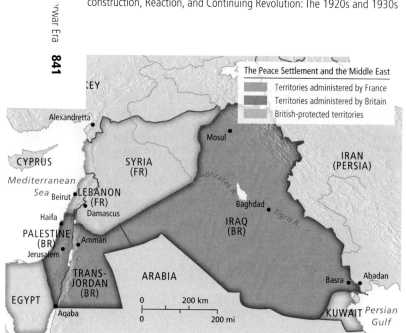

The Peace Settlement and the Middle East
- Territories administered by France
- Territories administered by Britain
- British-protected territories

TURKEY

Alexandretta

CYPRUS

*Mediterranean Sea*
Beirut

LEBANON (FR)
Damascus

Haifa

PALESTINE (BR)
Jerusalem
Amman

TRANS-JORDAN (BR)
Aqaba

EGYPT

SYRIA (FR)

Mosul

*Euphrates R.*

Baghdad

*Tigris R.*

IRAQ (BR)

ARABIA

Basra
Abadan

KUWAIT

IRAN (PERSIA)

*Persian Gulf*

0      200 km
0      200 mi

**Map 25.3  The Peace Settlement and the Middle East**

For many Arab nationalists, the division of the Middle East into Western-controlled "Mandates" was a source of deep discontent. After widespread anti-British riots in Iraq in 1920, the British ceded nominal independence to King Faisal's government. The British, however, retained control over financial, military and diplomatic matters.

cultural identity to that one offered by their European rulers.

The end of World War I marked the beginning of a new era in Islamic history. Feeble though it was by 1914, the Ottoman Empire had nevertheless symbolized a unified Islam: As caliph, the Ottoman sultan claimed religious authority over all Muslims, even those not under Ottoman political rule. The sultan's role as caliph helps explain why the vast majority of Arabs in the Middle East did not join the Hashemites in their alliance with Britain against the Ottomans (see Chapter 24). Most Arabs did not see the Turkish sultan as a foreign oppressor; instead, as Muslims, they regarded him as their rightful leader. For similar reasons, Muslims in British India experienced a profound conflict of loyalties during the war.

The collapse of the Ottoman Empire and the abolition of the Ottoman caliphate in the wake of World War I created a new religious and political environment for Muslims. Many followed Western secular models and turned to ethnic nationalism. Others, however, found both spiritual solace and political identity in Islamic revival movements that sought to unify Muslims under an Islamic ruler and Islamic law once again.

### The Emergence of Pan-Arabism

In the Middle East, pan-Arabism° emerged in the interwar era as a powerful form of nationalism. Just as pan-Slavism promoted the ideal of a single Slavic state, so pan-Arabism insisted that all Arabs—including the minority who were not Muslim—should unite in an Arab state. Three postwar developments nourished pan-Arabism. First, as already noted, the collapse of the Ottoman regime shattered traditional loyalties. But second, the new map of the Middle East drawn by the postwar peace settlement placed Arabs in

states they regarded as artificial, unrelated to dynastic or tribal identities. (See Chapter 24.) Thus nationalist movements centering on these new states—Iraqi nationalism, for example, or Syrian, or Lebanese—possessed little appeal. And finally, as we saw in Chapter 24, the system of "Mandates" created in the wake of the war actually continued imperial rule in a new form (see Map 25.3). As it quickly became clear that Western interests shaped policy in the new Middle Eastern states, resentment grew toward both Western imperialism and toward the state system imposed by the West. These sentiments nourished the pan-Arabist movement.

### State Nationalism on the Western Model

Not all Arab nationalists, however, embraced pan-Arabism. In states such as Egypt, with a national identity not imposed by Western imperialists or the peace settlement, nationalism tended to coalesce around the state itself. Hence in Egypt, the nationalist political party, Wafd, called not for Arabic unity but for Egyptian national freedom. Wafd, whose full name translates as "Egyptian delegation," originated as precisely that, a delegation of Egyptian representatives to the Paris peace conferences after World War I. When the Allies refused to let the delegation participate in the peace process, Wafd organized into a political movement fighting against not only the British but also the British-backed Egyptian monarchy for full Egyptian independence. Although Wafd opposed the monarchical government as too subservient to Western economic and political interests, it sought social and economic reforms that would Westernize and modernize Egypt.

For nationalists such as those in Wafd, the successful nationalist revolution in Turkey provided an important source of inspiration. After World War I, the Allies forced the defeated Ottoman government to sign a humiliating treaty: The Treaty of Sèvres not only dispossessed the Ottoman government of its Middle Eastern empire, it also gave territories in the Anatolian heartland (modern Turkey) to Greece, Italy, an autonomous Kurdistan, and an independent Armenia. In addition, Sèvres stripped the Ottoman government of national sovereignty by ceding to the Allies the right of intervention in economic, military, and foreign affairs. Turkish nationalists, led by Mustafa Kemal Pasha, rejected the Treaty of Sèvres and rose up against the government that dared sign such a document. Kemal's nationalist rebellion overthrew the sultan, defeated a Greek invasion, and forced the Allies to draw up a new settlement. In 1923, the Treaty of Lausanne restored to Turkey much of its territory and its full national sovereignty.

VIDEO
Ataturk
(Mustafa
Kemal)

But while Kemal had no intentions of letting Western powers govern in Turkey, he was not anti-Western. He viewed the West as modern; to modernize Turkey, he believed he had to reconfigure its culture as Western. Thus Kemal declared Turkey a secular republic, outlawed polygamy, granted women civil and legal rights, and required all Turks to take surnames—he became known as Kemal "Ataturk" ("Father of the Turks"). A mass literacy program aimed not only to teach Turks how to read and write, but how to do so using the Latin alphabet. Schoolmasters who dared use Arabic lettering were arrested. Ataturk even condemned the traditional form of Turkish headwear, the fez, as "an emblem of ignorance, negligence, fanaticism, hatred of progress and civilization."[20] To represent Turkey's new Western orientation, Turkish men were ordered to wear bowler hats and Western suits. But while he favored the English bowler hat, Ataturk was less enthusiastic about English political freedom. Despite setting up a parliament elected by universal suffrage, he made full use of emergency executive powers to govern with an iron grip over a one-party state. He also continued the Ottoman policies of repression toward Turkey's Armenian minority.

Kemal Ataturk's secularist, Westernized model of nationalism proved powerful. During the 1920s and 1930s nationalists in the Middle East, Africa, and Asia tended to embrace Western models, even as they rejected Western (or Western-imposed) rulers. They formed parliamentary political parties, advocated Western political ideologies such as liberalism and communism, regarded the state as essentially secular, and saw political independence as a crucial step toward industrial modernization and economic prosperity.

### The Islamic Challenge
Beneath the surface of political life, however, different styles of movements, with very different aims, were coalescing. Throughout the new states of the Middle East, for example, the soaring sales of popular biographies of the Prophet Muhammad and other caliphs, as well as the proliferation

of Islamic leagues and clubs, hinted that many inhabitants of these new states found the secularism of the nationalists as alien as the faces of their Western-imposed rulers or the boundaries on the new European-drawn map.

These sentiments would not harden into explicitly political movements until the 1940s, but both the Wahhabi religious revival in central Arabia during the 1920s and 1930s and the foundation of the Muslim Brotherhood in Egypt in 1928 proved crucial in shaping the relationship of Islam and the West in the later twentieth century.

Founded by Muhammad Abd al-Wahhab (1703–1787) in the eighteenth century, Wahhabism demanded the purification of Islam by ridding it of centuries of heretical accretions such as saint worship and other forms of mysticism, and by returning to a strict interpretation of the *Sharia,* or Islamic law. Over the next century, this militant form of religious revival inspired a number of popular revolts—on the Arabian peninsula (against the Ottomans), in India (against the British), in Algeria (against the French), and in Daghistan (against the Russians). Although all of these revolts were defeated, Wahhabism's call to return to fundamental truths and practices continued to appeal to Muslims, particularly in times of unsettling political change. It is not surprising, then, that Wahhabism revived in the tumultuous period after World War I. The Wahhabi revival in Arabia had a powerful patron: Abd al-Aziz Ibn Saud (ca. 1888–1953), the head of the Saudi dynasty whose conquests on the Arabian peninsula became the basis for the kingdom of Saudi Arabia.

Like Wahhabism, the Islamic Brotherhood (or *Ikhwan*) rejected modernizing interpretations of Islam and sought to reassert the universal jurisdiction of Islamic law. For the Brotherhood, Islam governed not just religious belief but all areas of life. The Brotherhood rejected Western practices and political institutions less because they were foreign than because they were associated with infidels. Working through youth groups, educational institutes, and business enterprises, the Brotherhood spread from its Egyptian base throughout the Middle East during the 1930s.

## Moral Revolution in India

During this same era, a very different sort of anti-Western protest movement took shape in India. In 1916 a British-educated lawyer returned from South Africa, where he had spent twenty years fighting to improve the lot of indentured Indian laborers and developing a revolutionary approach to the fight for national independence. Mohandas Gandhi (1869–1948) called on his followers to fight British rule in India not with armed weapons but with moral force—with nonviolent protest and civil disobedience. As the war ended, Gandhi led a mass protest movement in India against British rule. In this *Satyagraha* ("hold fast to

# From Mohandas to Mahatma: Gandhi's Transformation

In April 1893, a young, well-dressed Indian lawyer purchased a first-class train ticket from Durban to Pretoria (South Africa). The first part of the journey proceeded uneventfully, but then another traveler, a white man, entered the first-class compartment. He turned around and returned with two guards, who demanded that the Indian man sit in third class, with the other "colored" passengers. The young lawyer refused, and so was thrown off the train at the next stop.

Mohandas Gandhi's experience on the train to Pretoria was not unusual. The Indian immigrant community in South Africa had long endured legal discrimination, economic exploitation, and frequent violence; the black African community suffered far worse. But the 24-year-old Gandhi knew little about such things. Growing up as the spoiled youngest son in an upper-caste family in India, he had known privilege rather than prejudice. Even the three years he spent in London studying law did not expose him to racial discrimination. Gandhi, in fact, felt that when he left Britain he was leaving "home." He returned to India in 1891 convinced of the superiority of British law and culture. He banned Indian-style clothing from his household, insisted that his illiterate young wife learn English, and decreed that oat porridge and cocoa be served at breakfast. He saw himself as a successful British lawyer.

But others did not see him that way. When Gandhi asked a British official for a favor for his brother, he was humiliated, actually pushed out the door by a servant. "This shock changed the course of my life," Gandhi later noted.[21] Offered a job in South Africa, he went—and on that train to Pretoria encountered further humiliation. By the time Gandhi finally reached Pretoria, he had decided to fight. He became the leader of the Indian civil rights movement in South Africa.

Gandhi lived in South Africa for 21 years. During these decades, the westernized, Britain-loving lawyer became a Hindu holy man; Mohandas became Mahatma, the "great-souled one." This transformation occurred in part because of Gandhi's sense of betrayal as he encountered the racial discrimination embedded in British imperialism. From his London experience, Gandhi had concluded that Britain epitomized the Western ideals of impartial justice and individual rights. But the British colonial regime he encountered in South Africa violated those ideals. Disillusioned, Gandhi turned back to his Hindu roots.

Western culture also, however, played a positive role in Gandhi's transformation. During his time in South Africa, Gandhi read widely in Christian and Western texts, including Jesus' Sermon on the Mount in the New Testament, and books by nineteenth-century European social and cultural critics that exposed the spiritual and material failures of industrial society. Gandhi's intellectual encounter with these texts helped him formulate the idea of *Satyagraha* ("Truth-Force"). In its most specific sense, Satyagraha is a political tool. Through nonviolent mass civil disobedience, the powerless persuade the powerful to effect political change. But Satyagraha is also a spiritual act, the victory of goodness over violence and evil.

Gandhi's specific encounters with the injustice of imperial rule, first in the home of a British official in India and then on his South African train ride, forced him to embark on a different sort of spiritual and political journey, an exploration of both Western and Hindu thought. This journey transformed Gandhi from Mohandas into Mahatma and led him to Satyagraha—and the transformation of Indian nationalism into a mass movement. By 1948, this movement had made it impossible for the British to govern India.

## For Discussion

Both negative and positive encounters with Western ideas and Western people contributed to Gandhi's transformation "from Mohandas to Mahatma." In what ways have Gandhi's ideas transformed Western culture and politics?

**The Mathatma**
Gandhi drew on both Hindu and Western traditions in formulating his ideal of moral protest.

the truth") campaign, Indians refused to cooperate with the imperial system in any way, including wearing British-made cloth.

Before Gandhi's arrival, the cause of Indian independence belonged to the educated, westernized elite. Gandhi transformed the Indian National Congress into a mass movement by appealing to traditional Indian customs and religious identities. He did not oppose modernization, but he argued that modernization did not necessarily mean westernization, that India could follow its own path. Thus Gandhi rejected Western dress and presented himself in the role of the religious ascetic, a familiar and deeply honored figure in Indian culture. In his insistence that the nationalist struggle be one of "moral force" rather than a physical fight, Gandhi drew on the Hindu tradition of nonviolence. He was careful, however, not to equate "Indian" with "Hindu." He worked hard to incorporate the minority Muslim community into the nationalist movement, and he broke with the traditional Hindu caste system by campaigning for the rights of those deemed "untouchable." Ordinary Indians surged into the movement, calling Gandhi "Mahatma," or "great-souled," a term of great respect.

Unable to decide whether to arrest Gandhi as a dangerous revolutionary or to negotiate with him as a representative of the Indian people, the British did both. In 1931, Gandhi and the viceroy of India (literally the "vice-king," the highest British official in India) met on equal terms for a series of eight meetings. A few months later Gandhi was in prison, along with 66,000 of his nationalist colleagues. Successive British governments did pass a series of measures granting Indians increasing degrees of self-government, but Gandhi and the Indian National Congress demanded full and immediate national independence. The resulting impasse led to escalating unrest and terrorist activity, despite Gandhi's personal commitment to nonviolence. India remained the jewel in Britain's imperial crown, but the glue holding it in place was deteriorating rapidly by the end of the 1930s.

## The Power of the Primitive

When asked what he thought of "Western civilization," Gandhi replied, "I think it would be a very good idea." Just as nationalists outside of the West such as Gandhi began to challenge the equation of the West with civilization, so too did Westerners themselves. For nineteenth-century European culture, "civilization" was what gave the West the right to rule the rest of the world. In the latter decades of the nineteenth century, ideologues had described inhabitants of Asia, Africa, and South America as barbarians who needed the guidance and discipline of the more advanced European white races. But by 1918, in the wake of the war, at least some Europeans were asking, "Who is the barbarian now?"

Developments in psychology further undermined the idea of Western superiority by eroding the boundaries between so-called primitive and modern cultures. In his postwar writings, Sigmund Freud (1856–1939) emphasized that human nature was fundamentally aggressive, even bestial. Freud's three-part theory of personality, developed in the 1920s, argued that within each individual the *id*, the unconscious force of primitive instinct, battles against the controls of the *ego*, or conscious rationality, and the *superego*, the moral values imposed by society. Although Freud taught that the continuity of civilization depended on the repression of the id, many Freudian popularizers insisted that the individual should allow his or her primitive self to run free.

The work of Freud's onetime disciple Carl Jung (1875–1961) also stressed the links between the primitive and the modern. Jung contended that careful study of an individual's dreams will show that they share common images and forms—"archetypes"—with ancient mythologies and world religions. These archetypes point to the existence of the "collective unconscious," shared by all human beings, regardless of when or where they lived. Thus, in Jung's analysis the boundary between "civilized" and "primitive," "West" and "not West," disappeared.

In the work of other thinkers and artists, that boundary remained intact, but Western notions of cultural superiority were turned upside down. The belief that white Western culture was anemic, washed out, and washed up led to a new openness to alternative intellectual and artistic traditions. This era saw a lasting transformation of popular music as the energetic rhythms of African-American jazz worked their way into white musical traditions. Many writers argued that the West needed to look to outside its borders for vibrancy and vitality. The German novelist Herman Hesse (1877–1962) condemned modern industrial society as spiritually barren and celebrated Eastern mysticism as a source of power and wisdom.

Similarly, the *Négritude* movement stressed the history and intrinsic value of black African culture. Founded in Paris in 1935 by French colonial students from Africa and the West Indies, Négritude condemned European culture as weak and corrupted and called for blacks to recreate a separate cultural and political identity. The movement's leading figures, such as Leopold Senghor (1906–2001), who later became the first president of independent Senegal, vehemently opposed the continuation of European empires and demanded African self-rule. Drawing together Africans, Afro-Caribbeans, and black Americans, Négritude assumed the existence of a common black culture that transcended national and colonial boundaries. The movement stole the white racists' stereotype of the "happy dancing savage" and refigured it as positive: Black culture fostered the emotion, creativity, and human connections that white Western industrial society destroyed.

### The Power of the Primitive

When the American dancer Josephine Baker first hit the stage in Paris in 1925, her audience embraced her as the image of African savagery, even though Baker was a city kid from Philadelphia. A Parisian sensation from the moment she arrived, Baker's frenetic and passionate style of dancing, as well as her willingness to appear on stage wearing nothing but a belt of bananas, seemed to epitomize for many Europeans the essential freedom they believed their urbanized culture had lost, and that both the United States and Africa retained. As Baker's belt of bananas, designed by her white French employer, makes clear, much of this idealization of the primitive was deeply embedded in racist stereotypes. But it is also clear that both Baker's blackness and her Americanness represented a positive image of liberation to many Parisians.

# Conclusion

## The Kingdom of Corpses

In 1921, the Goncourt Prize, the most prestigious award in French literature, was awarded not to a native French writer but to a colonial: René Maran, born in the French colony of Martinique. Even more striking than Maran's receiving the prize was the content of the novel for which he was honored. In *Batouala*, Maran mounted a fierce onslaught against Western culture: "Civilization, civilization, pride of the Europeans and charnel house of innocents. . . . You build your kingdom on corpses."[22]

For many in the West, Maran's description of Europe as a kingdom of corpses seemed apt in the aftermath of total war. The 1920s and 1930s witnessed a dramatic reevaluation of Western cultural and political assumptions. Both Soviet communism on the left and Nazism and fascism on the right rejected such key Western ideals as individual rights and the rule of law. Such extremist ideologies seemed persuasive in the climate of despair produced not only by the war, but by the postwar failure of democracy in eastern Europe and the collapse of the global economy after 1929. As a result, the kingdom of corpses grew: in Nazi Germany, in Spain, and most dramatically in the Soviet Union. The kingdom of corpses was, however, a particularly expansionist domain. As the 1930s ended, the West and the world stood on the brink of another total war, one in which the numbers of dead would spiral to nearly incomprehensible levels.

## Suggestions for Further Reading

For a comprehensive listing of suggested readings, please go to www.ablongman.com/levack2e/chapter25

Bookbinder, Paul. *Weimar Germany: The Republic of the Reasonable.* 1996. An innovative interpretation.

Brendon, Piers. *The Dark Valley: A Panorama of the 1930s.* 2000. Fast-paced but carefully researched and comprehensive overview of the histories of the United States, Germany, Italy, France, Britain, Japan, Russia, and Spain.

Carrère D'Encausse, Hélène. *Stalin: Order Through Terror*, Vol. 2: *A History of the Soviet Union, 1917–1953.* 1981. A brief but convincing account of the way Stalin seized and held power in the Soviet Union.

Fischer, Conan. *The Rise of the Nazis.* 1995. Summarizes recent research and includes a section of primary documents.

Fitzpatrick, Sheila. *Everyday Stalinism. Ordinary Life in Extraordinary Times: Soviet Russia in the 1930s.* 1999. Explores the daily life of the ordinary urban worker in Stalinist Russia.

Fitzpatrick, Sheila. *Stalin's Peasants: Resistance and Survival in the Russian Village After Collectivization.* 1995. A superb history from the bottom up.

Getty, J. Arch, and Oleg V. Naumov. *The Road to Terror: Stalin and the Self-Destruction of the Bolsheviks, 1932–1939.* 1999. Interweaves recently discovered documents with an up-to-date interpretation of the Great Purge.

Gilbert, Bentley Brinkerhoff. *Britain 1914–1945: The Aftermath of Power.* 1996. Short, readable overview, designed for beginning students.

Jackson, Julian. *The Popular Front in France: Defending Democracy, 1934–1938.* 1988. A political and cultural history.

Kershaw, Ian. *Hitler.* 1991. A highly acclaimed recent biography.

Kitchen, Martin. *Nazi Germany: A Critical Introduction.* 2004. Short, clearly written, up-to-date. An excellent introduction and overview.

Lewis, Bernard. *The Shaping of the Modern Middle East.* 1994. Concise but comprehensive analysis.

Mack Smith, Denis. *Mussolini: A Biography.* 1983. An engaging read.

Pedersen, Susan. *Family, Dependence, and the Origins of the Welfare State: Britain and France, 1914–1945.* 1993. Shows how welfare policy was inextricably linked to demographic and eugenic concerns.

Rothschild, Joseph. *East Central Europe Between the Wars.* 1974. An older source, but still one of the best accounts of this tumultuous region in this tumultuous time.

Thomas, Hugh. *The Spanish Civil War.* 1977. An authoritative account.

Whittam, John. *Fascist Italy.* 1995. A short synthesis of recent research. Includes a section of primary documents and an excellent bibliographic essay.

Wolpert, Stanley. *Gandhi's Passion: The Life and Legacy of Mahatma Gandhi.* 2001. An intellectual and spiritual biography by one of the foremost historians of modern India.

## Notes

1. Quoted in Peter Gay, *Weimar Culture* (1970), 99.
2. Quoted in T. W. Heyck, *The Peoples of the British Isles from 1870 to the Present* (1992), 200.
3. Martin J. Sherwin, *A World Destroyed: Hiroshima and the Origins of the Arms Race* (1987), 17.
4. Quoted in Martin Gilbert, *A History of the Twentieth Century, Vol. I* (1997), 700.
5. Quoted in Michael Burleigh, *The Third Reich: A New History* (2000), 36.
6. Quoted in Burleigh, *The Third Reich,* 52.
7. Quoted in Joachim Fest, *Hitler* (1973), 190–193.
8. Ibid., 192, 218.
9. Quoted in Wendy Goldman, *Women, the State, and Revolution: Soviet Family Policy and Social Life, 1917–1936* (1993), 5.
10. Quoted in Claudia Koonz, *Mothers in the Fatherland* (1987), 130.
11. Quoted in Fest, *Hitler,* 445.
12. Quoted in Koonz, *Mothers in the Fatherland,* 194.
13. Ibid., 178.
14. Ibid., 56; Victoria DeGrazia, *How Fascism Ruled Women: Italy, 1922–1945* (1992), 234.
15. See J. Arch Getty and Roberta Manning, *Stalinist Terror: New Perspectives* (1993), 11, 265, 268, 280, 290.
16. Quoted in Mark Mazower, *Dark Continent: Europe's Twentieth Century* (1998), 123.
17. Quoted in Sheila Fitzpatrick, *Everyday Stalinism* (1999), 68.
18. See Stephen G. Wheatcroft, "More Light on the Scale of Repression and Excess Mortality in the Soviet Union in the 1930s," in Getty and Manning, *Stalinist Terror,* 275–290.
19. "Appendix 1: Numbers of Victims of the Terror," in J. Arch Getty and Oleg V. Naumov, *The Road to Terror: Stalin and the Self-Destruction of the Bolsheviks, 1932–1939* (1999), 587–594.
20. Quoted in Felix Gilbert, *The End of the European Era* (1991), 162.
21. Mohandas K. Gandhi, *An Autobiography: The Story of My Experiments with Truth* (1957), 120.
22. Quoted in Tyler Stovall, *Paris Noir: African Americans in the City of Light* (1996), 32.

# World War II

I N THE WEEKS IMMEDIATELY PRECEDING THE END OF THE SECOND WORLD WAR in Europe, many Allied soldiers faced their most difficult assignment yet. Hardened combat veterans, accustomed to scenes of slaughter and destruction, broke down and wept as they encountered a landscape of horror beyond their wildest nightmares: the world of the Nazi concentration and death camps. As one American war correspondent put it, "we had penetrated at last to the center of the black heart, to the very crawling inside of the vicious heart."[1] The American soldiers who opened the gates of the camp in Mauthausen, Austria, never forgot their first sight of the prisoners there: "By the thousands they came streaming . . . Hollow, pallid ghosts from graves and tombs, terrifying, rot-colored figures of misery marked by disease, deeply ingrained filth, inner decay. . . . squat skeletons in rags and crazy grins."[2]

Similarly, the British troops who liberated Bergen-Belsen in Germany were marked indelibly by what they encountered within the camp's walls. Bergen-Belsen had become the dumping ground for tens of thousands of prisoners evacuated from camps in eastern Europe, as the Nazi SS desperately retreated in front of the advancing Soviet army. Already sick and starving, these prisoners were jammed, 1,200 at a time, into barracks built to accommodate a few hundred. By March 1945, both drinking water and food had disappeared, human excrement dripped from bunk beds until it coated the floors of the barracks, and dead bodies piled up everywhere. In these conditions, the only living beings to flourish were the microorganisms that cause typhus. Floundering in this sea of human want, British soldiers, doctors, and nurses did what they could; even so, 28,000 of Bergen-Belsen's 60,000 inmates died in the weeks following liberation.

In Mauthausen and Bergen-Belsen, in the piles of putrefying bodies and among the crowds of skeletal survivors, American and British soldiers encountered the results of Adolf Hitler's effort to redefine the West. In Hitler's vision, Western civilization comprised ranks of white, northern Europeans, led by Germans, marching in step to a cadence dictated by the antidemocratic

## CHAPTER OUTLINE

- The Coming of War

- Europe at War, 1939–1941

- The World at War, 1941–1945

- The War Against the Jews

- The Home Front: The Other Wars

---

**Wilhelm Becker, *Bombing Raid in Berlin* (1943)** The intentional and intensive bombing of civilian centers was one of the defining characteristics of the Second World War.

state. To realize this vision, he turned to total war and to mass murder. This quest to reconfigure the West as a race-based German empire also led Hitler to join hands with an ally outside the West: Japan. The German-Japanese alliance between transformed a European war into a global conflict. Thus, understanding World War II demands that we look not only at the results of Nazi racial ideology but also at global power relations and patterns of economic dependency. Like Hitler, Japan's governing elites longed for empire—in their case, an Asian empire to ensure both Japanese access to the resources and Japanese domination over the peoples of the Pacific region. With such access and such domination, they hoped to insulate Japan's economic and political structures from Western influence or control. The Pacific war thus constituted the most brutal in a long series of encounters between Japanese elites and the West. As we examine both the European and the Pacific theaters of war, we will need, then, to ask how competing definitions of "the West" helped shape this conflict. We will also confront the question of results: How did the cataclysm known as World War II re-define the West?

To organize its exploration of the many facets of World War II, this chapter focuses on five questions:

- What were the expectations concerning war in the 1920s and 1930s, and how did these hopes and fears lead to armed conflict in both Europe and Asia?
- How did Nazi Germany conquer the continent of Europe by 1941?
- Why did the Allies win in 1945?
- How and why did the war against the Jews take place, and what were its consequences?
- What did total war mean on the home front?

# The Coming of War

- What were the expectations concerning war in the 1920s and 1930s, and how did these hopes and fears lead to armed conflict in both Europe and Asia?

The 1914–1918 war had been proclaimed the "war to end all wars." Instead, a little more than twenty years later, total war once again engulfed Europe and then the world. Adolf Hitler's ambitions for a German empire in eastern Europe account for the immediate outbreak of war in September 1939. But other, longer-term factors also contributed and help explain the origins of World War II. During the 1930s, the uneasy peace was broken by a series of military conflicts. These confrontations underlined the fragility of the post–World War I international settlement and foreshadowed the horrors to come in World War II.

## An Uneasy Peace

The origins of the Second World War are closely tied to the settlement of the First. Rather than ending war for all time, the treaties negotiated after 1918 created an uneasy peace, one that could not be sustained. As we have already seen, much of Hitler's appeal to his German followers lay in his openly displayed contempt for the economic and military terms of the Versailles Treaty. But the peace settlement of World War I led to World War II in other, less direct ways as well. First, the redrawing of the map of eastern and central Europe fostered political instability in these regions. The mapmakers failed to fulfill the nationalist ambitions of many groups—the Macedonians, the Croats, the Ukrainians, and a host of others—and created as many territorial resentments as they resolved. For example, Germans could not forget that parts of Silesia now belonged to Poland, and Hungarians mourned the loss of traditionally Hungarian lands to Czechoslovakia, Romania, and Yugoslavia. Demands for boundary revisions, as well as ethnic hostilities and economic weaknesses, debilitated the new central and eastern European states carved out of the prewar Austrian-Hungarian, Russian, and German Empires.

Second, the League of Nations, created to replace the competitive alliance systems that many blamed for starting World War I, could not realize the high hopes of its planners. Poorly organized, lacking military power, boycotted by the United States and at various times excluding the key nations of Germany and the Soviet Union, the league proved too weak to serve as the basis of a new international order. Instead, alliances, such as that between the French and Polish governments or the "Little Entente" of Czechoslovakia, Yugoslavia, and Romania, formed the framework of a more traditional and very precarious international system.

Finally, the peace settlements created resentments among the war's winners as well as its losers. Italian nationalists argued that their nation's contribution to the Allies' victory should have been more fully compensated and looked longingly at territories granted to Yugoslavia, Austria, and Albania. Japanese nationalists, too, felt betrayed by the peace. Japan had cooperated fully with Britain and the United States during the First World War and expected this cooperation to be rewarded in the postwar era. Instead, many Japanese contended that the peace settlement disregarded Japan's economic needs and international ambitions. The results of the postwar Washington Conference particularly enraged Japanese nationalists. The conference, convened in Washington, D.C., in 1921, assembled representatives of the war's nine victorious powers—Britain, France, Italy, the United States, Belgium, the Netherlands, Portugal, China, and Japan—who pledged themselves to uphold China's territorial integrity and political independence as a means of restoring stability to the region. European and especially American capital poured into China during the

1920s while Western advisers assisted in the reform of the Chinese tax and currency systems. Japanese nationalists, however, viewed a united, Western-oriented China not as a guarantor of regional stability but rather as a threat to Japanese political power and economic development.

## The 1930s: Prelude to World War II

The onset of the Great Depression in 1929 heightened international instability. Throughout Europe economic nationalism intensified as nations responded to economic collapse by throwing up tariff walls in an effort to protect their own industries. In addition, leaders sought escape from economic difficulties through territorial expansion. In Japan, the collapse of export markets for Japanese raw silk and cotton cloth made it difficult for the Japanese to pay for their vital imports of oil and other industrial resources. Anti-Western Japanese nationalists contended that Western capitalism was terminally ill and that the time had come for Japan to embark on a course of aggressive imperialist expansion to ensure its access to vital resources. In 1931, Japanese forces seized Manchuria.

Similarly, Mussolini proclaimed empire as the answer to Italy's economic woes, as well as a way to recreate the glories of ancient Rome. Seeking

### CHRONOLOGY

## On the Road to World War II

| | |
|---|---|
| **1919** | Versailles Treaty |
| **1921–1922** | Washington Conference |
| **1929** | Onset of the Great Depression |
| **1931** | Japan invades Manchuria |
| **1933** | Hitler becomes chancellor of Germany |
| **1935** | Hitler announces a German air force and military conscription; Italy invades Ethiopia |
| **1936** | German troops occupy the Rhineland; civil war breaks out in Spain; Hitler and Mussolini form the Rome-Berlin Axis |
| **1937** | Japan advances against China; Rape of Nanking |
| **1938** | |
| March | Germany annexes Austria (the *Anschluss*) |
| September | Munich Conference: Germany occupies the Sudetenland |
| **1939** | |
| March 15 | Germany invades Czechoslovakia |
| August 23 | German-Soviet Non-Aggression Pact |
| September 1 | Germany invades Poland |
| September 3 | Great Britain and France declare war on Germany |

### The Prelude to World War II
The Japanese resumption of their war in China in 1937 added to the horrors of the 1930s. Here a photographer captured the agony of a baby separated from its parents in the railway station in Shanghai.

to expand Italy's North African empire and to avenge Italy's humiliating defeat at the Battle of Adowa in 1896, when Ethiopian troops had beaten back an Italian invasion, Mussolini ordered his army into Ethiopia in 1935. The Italian forces inflicted on the Ethiopian people many of the horrors soon to come to the European continent, including the saturation bombing of civilians, the use of poison gas, and the establishment of concentration camps. At the end of June 1936, Ethiopia's now-exiled Emperor Haile Selassie (1892–1975) addressed the Assembly of the League of Nations and warned, "It is us today. It will be you tomorrow."[3]

One year after Italian troops invaded Ethiopia, civil war broke out in Spain. As Chapter 25 explained, the war between the elected republican government and General Franco's rebels quickly became an international conflict. Hitler and Mussolini sent troops and equipment to assist Franco, and Stalin responded by sending aid to communists fighting on the republican side. Reluctant to ally with Stalin, the governments of France, Britain, and the United States remained neutral, and seemed, therefore, to signal that aggressors could act with impunity.

While the Spanish Civil War raged, the Japanese resumed their advance in China. The Japanese conquest was brutal. In what became known as the Rape of Nanking (Nanjing), soldiers used babies for bayonet practice, gang-raped as many as 20,000 young girls and women, and left the bodies of the dead to rot in the street. The League of Nations had condemned Japan's seizure of Manchuria in 1931 but could do little else.

## Map 26.1   The Expansion of Germany in the 1930s

Beginning with the remilitarization of the Rhineland in 1936, Hitler embarked on a program of German territorial expansion. This map also indicates the expansion of the Soviet Union into Poland as a result of the secret terms of the German-Soviet Non-Aggression Pact.

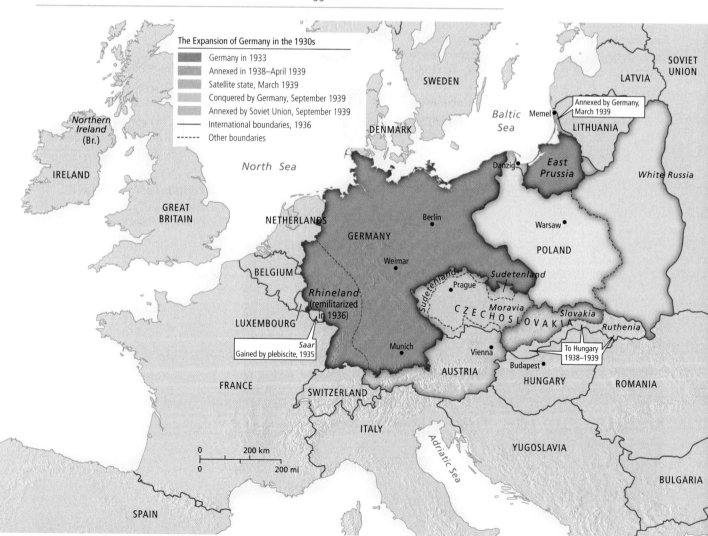

Against this backdrop of military aggression and the democracies' inaction, Hitler made his first moves to establish a German empire in Europe (see Map 26.1). In 1933, he withdrew Germany from the League of Nations and two years later announced the creation of a German air force and the return of mass conscription—in deliberate violation of the terms of the Versailles Treaty. In 1936, Hitler allied with Mussolini in the Rome-Berlin Axis° and again violated his treaty obligations when he sent German troops into the Rhineland, the industrially rich region on Germany's western border. Yet France and Britain did not respond. Two years later, in March 1938, Germany broke the Versailles Treaty once more by annexing Austria after an intense Austrian Nazi propaganda campaign punctuated by violence.

After the successful *Anschluss* ("joining") of Germany and Austria, Hitler demanded that the Sudetenland, the western portion of Czechoslovakia inhabited by a German-speaking majority, be joined to Germany as well. He seemed finally to have gone too far. France and the Soviet Union had pledged to protect the territorial integrity of Czechoslovakia. In September 1938, Europe stood on the brink of war. The urgency of the situation impelled Britain's prime minister Neville Chamberlain (1869–1940) to board an airplane for the first time in his life and fly to Munich to negotiate with Hitler. After intense negotiations that excluded the Czech government, Chamberlain and French prime minister Edouard Daladier agreed to grant Hitler the right to occupy the Sudetenland immediately. Assured by Hitler that this "Munich Agreement" satisfied all his territorial demands, Chamberlain flew home to a rapturous welcome. Crowds cheered and church bells rang when he claimed to have achieved "peace in our time."

"Peace in our time" lasted for six months. In March 1939, German troops occupied the rest of Czechoslovakia

and Hitler's promises proved to be worthless. On August 23, Hitler took out an insurance policy against fighting a two-front war by persuading Stalin to sign the German-Soviet Non-Aggression Pact°. The pact publicly pledged the two powers not to attack each other; it also secretly divided Poland between them and promised Stalin substantial territorial gains—much of eastern Poland and the Baltic regions of Latvia, Estonia, and parts of Lithuania. On September 1, 1939, German troops invaded Poland. The British and French declared war against Germany on September 3. Two weeks after German troops crossed Poland's borders in the west, the Soviets pushed in from the east and imposed a regime of murderous brutality. The Second World War had begun.

## Evaluating Appeasement

Could Hitler have been stopped before he catapulted Europe into World War II? The debate over this question has centered on British policy during the 1930s. France advocated an aggressive policy toward Germany in the 1920s, even to the point of sending troops into the Rhineland in 1923 to seize reparations. But during the 1930s, debilitating economic and political crises left France too weak to respond strongly to Hitler. With the United States remaining aloof from European affairs and the now-communist Soviet Union regarded as a pariah state, Britain assumed the initiative in responding to Hitler's rise to power and his increasingly aggressive actions.

After World War II broke out, one term came to be equated with passivity and cowardice in the face of aggression. That term was appeasement°—the policy of conciliation and negotiation that British policymakers,

**"Peace in Our Time"**
In September 1938, British prime minister Neville Chamberlain announced his diplomatic triumph: With the German annexation of the Sudetenland, Hitler declared himself satisfied and Chamberlain announced "peace in our time."

particularly Neville Chamberlain, pursued in their dealings with Hitler in the 1930s. Chamberlain, however, was not a coward and was far from passive. Convinced he had a mission to save Europe from war, he actively sought to accommodate Hitler. Chamberlain thought like the businessmen who voted for him. He believed that through negotiation a suitable agreement—the "best price"—can always be found. His fundamental failure was not passivity or cowardice but rather his insistence that Hitler was a man like himself. Chamberlain could not believe that Hitler would find a war worth the price Germany would need to pay.

For Chamberlain, and many other Europeans, the alternative to appeasement was a total war that would surely destroy Western civilization. They remembered the last war with horror and agreed that the next war would be even worse, for it would be an air war. The years after 1918 saw the aviation industry come into its own in Europe and the United States, and both military experts and ordinary people recognized the disastrous potential of airborne bombs. Stanley Baldwin (1867–1947), Chamberlain's predecessor as prime minister, told the British public that there was no defense against a bomber force: "The bomber will always get through." The horrendous civilian casualties inflicted by the Italian air force in Ethiopia and by the bombing of Spanish cities in the Spanish Civil War convinced many Europeans that Baldwin was right, and that war was completely unacceptable. Just two years after the British Peace Pledge Union was founded in 1934, it had 100,000 supporters pledged not to fight in a war.

Motivated by the desire to avoid another horrible war, appeasement also rested on two additional pillars—first, the assumption that many of Germany's grievances were legitimate; second, the belief that only a strong Germany could neutralize the threat posed by Soviet communism. During the 1920s, many historians, political scientists, and policymakers studied the diplomatic records concerning the outbreak of World War I and concluded that the treaty makers at Versailles were wrong in blaming Germany for starting the war. During the 1920s, then, British leaders sought to renegotiate reparations, to press the French into softening their anti-German policies, and to draw Germany back into the network of international diplomatic relations. Hitler's rise to power gave added impetus to a policy already in place. British leaders argued that they could rob Hitler of much of his appeal by rectifying legitimate German grievances.

British policymakers' fear of communism reinforced their desire to stabilize Germany. Many politicians applauded Hitler's moves against German communists and welcomed the military resurgence of Germany as a strong bulwark against the threat posed by Soviet Russia. The startling announcement of the German-Soviet Non-Aggression Pact in the summer of 1939 revealed the hollowness of this bulwark, just as the German invasion of

Czechoslovakia in March had exposed Hitler's promises of peace as worthless.

# Europe at War, 1939–1941

■ How did Nazi Germany conquer the continent of Europe by 1941?

German soldiers crossed the Polish border on September 1, 1939; just two years later, Hitler appeared to have achieved his goal of establishing a Nazi empire in Europe. By the autumn of 1941, almost all of continental Europe was either allied to or occupied by Nazi Germany.

## A New Kind of Warfare

During these two years, the German army moved from triumph to triumph as a result of its mastery of the new technology of offensive warfare. Executing a strategy of attack that fully utilized the products of modern industry, the German military demonstrated the power of a mobile, mechanized offensive force. Germany's only defeat during these years came in the Battle of Britain, when Germany confronted a mobile, mechanized defense. Like Germany's victories, this defeat highlighted the central role of industrial production in modern warfare.

## The Conquest of Poland

In its attack on Poland, the German army made use of a new kind of warfare. As Chapter 24 explained, in World War I a full frontal infantry assault proved no match for a deeply entrenched defensive force armed with machine guns. In the 1920s and 1930s, military strategists theorized that the way to avoid the stalemate of trench warfare was to use both the airplane and the tank to construct an "armored fist" strong and swift enough to break through even the most well-fortified enemy defenses. The bomber plane provided a mobile bombardment, one that shattered enemy defenses, broke vital communication links, and clogged key transport routes. Simultaneously, motorized infantry and tank formations punched through enemy lines.

Germany's swift conquest of Poland provided the world with a stunning demonstration of this new offensive strategy. Most of the German army, like all of the Polish, moved on foot or by horseback, as soldiers had done for centuries. Fast-moving motorized divisions, however, bludgeoned through the Polish defenses, penetrated deep into enemy territory, and secured key positions. While these units wreaked havoc on the ground, the Luftwaffe—the German air force—rained ruin from the air. Thirteen hundred planes shrieked across the Polish skies and in just one day destroyed the far smaller, less modern Polish air force, most of whose planes never left the ground. Warsaw surrendered after just ten days.

## Blitzkrieg in Western Europe

Western newspaper reporters christened this new style of warfare blitzkrieg°—lightning war. Western Europeans experienced blitzkrieg firsthand in the spring of 1940. The German army invaded Denmark and Norway in early April, routed the French and British troops sent to aid the Norwegians, and moved into western Europe in May. The Netherlands fell in just four days; Belgium, supported by French and British units as in World War I, held out for two weeks.

On May 27, 1940, the British army and several divisions of the French force found themselves trapped in a small pocket on the northern French coast called Dunkirk. Their destruction seemed certain. But over the next week, the

### Blitzkrieg

In blitzkrieg, the tank and bomber plane worked together to punch openings in the enemy's defenses. Motorized infantry divisions then poured through the holes.

### CHRONOLOGY

## Europe at War

**1939**

| | |
|---|---|
| September | German-Soviet conquest of Poland |

**1940**

| | |
|---|---|
| April 9 | German blitzkrieg against Denmark and Norway begins |
| May 10 | Germans attack western Europe |
| June 22 | Fall of France |
| July 10 | Battle of Britain begins |
| September 7 | London Blitz begins |
| September 17 | Hitler cancels plans for invasion of Britain |

**1941**

| | |
|---|---|
| March | U.S. Congress passes Lend-Lease Act |
| April | German invasion of the Soviet Union postponed; German offensives in Yugoslavia, Greece, and North Africa |
| June 22 | German invasion of the Soviet Union begins |
| September | German siege of Leningrad begins |
| December | German advance halted outside Moscow |

only Allied success in the campaign unfolded. The British Royal Air Force (RAF) succeeded in holding off the Luftwaffe and enabling the British navy and a flotilla of fishing and recreational boats manned by British civilians to evacuate these troops. By June 4, 110,000 French and almost 240,000 British soldiers had been brought safely back to Britain. But, as the newly appointed British prime minister Winston Churchill (1874–1965) reminded his cheering people, "wars are not won by evacuation."

Over the next two weeks the Germans steadily advanced through northern France, and on June 14, German soldiers marched into Paris. The French Assembly voted to disband and to hand over power to the World War I war hero Marshal Philippe Pétain (1856–1951), who established an authoritarian government. On June 22 this new Vichy regime° (named after the city Pétain chose for his capital) signed an armistice with Germany that pledged French collaboration with the Nazi regime. Theoretically, Pétain's authority extended over all of France, but in actuality the Vichy regime was confined to the south, with Germany occupying France's western and northern regions, including Paris, as well as the Atlantic seaboard. One million French soldiers became prisoners of war. Germany, with its allies and satellites, held most of the continent.

## The Battle of Britain

After the fall of France, Hitler hoped that Britain would accept Germany's domination of the continent and agree to a negotiated peace. But his hopes went unrealized. Military disaster in Norway had thoroughly discredited Prime Minister Chamberlain and his halfhearted approach to war making. A member of Chamberlain's own party, Leo Amery, spoke for the nation when he shouted at Chamberlain, "In the name of God, go!" Chamberlain went. Party politics were suspended for the duration of the war, and the British government passed to an all-party coalition headed by Winston Churchill, a vocal critic of Britain's appeasement policy since 1933. Never a humble man, Churchill wrote that when he accepted the position of prime minister, "I felt as if I were walking with Destiny, and that all my past life had been but a preparation for this hour and this trial . . . I was sure I should not fail." In his first speech as prime minister, Churchill promised, "Victory—victory at all costs."

Faced with the British refusal to negotiate, Hitler ordered his General Staff to prepare for a land invasion of Britain. But placing German troops in the English Channel while Britain's Royal Air Force still flew the skies would be a certain military disaster. Thus, a precondition of invasion was the destruction of the RAF. On July 10, German bomber raids on English southern coastal cities opened the Battle of Britain, a battle waged in the air—and in the factories. Fortunately for Britain, from 1935 on the government's defense policy had accorded priority to the RAF. In the summer of 1940, British factories each month produced twice the number of fighter aircraft coming out of German plants in the same period. Preparing for air attack, the British had constructed a shield comprising fighter planes, anti-aircraft gun installations, and a chain of radar stations. These preparations, its higher production rates of aircraft, and the fact that RAF pilots were fighting in the skies above their homes gave the British the advantage. On September 17, 1940, Hitler announced that the invasion of Britain was postponed indefinitely.

## The Invasion of the Soviet Union

War against Britain had never been one of Hitler's central goals, however. His dreams of the "Third Reich," a renewed Germanic European empire that was to last a thousand years, centered on conquest of the Soviet Union. Hitler believed that the rich agricultural and industrial resources of the vast Russian empire rightly belonged to the superior German race. He also believed that Soviet communism was an evil force and a potential threat to German stability and prosperity. Moreover, one of Hitler's aims in invading the Soviet Union was to realize his dream of a new racial order

## DOCUMENT

# In the Tanks

*If World War I was the war of the trenches, then World War II was the war of the tanks. In the Battle of Kursk on the eastern front, for example, the Russians and Germans sent a thousand tanks into combat on a single day (July 12, 1943). In the first two years of the war, just the sight of these armored monsters crashing through barriers could demoralize an entire infantry regiment. By 1942, however, both sides had developed effective antitank defensive systems. For the men in the tanks, the experience of combat was harrowing.*

### Alan Gilmour, 48th Royal Tank Regiment (Britain), Tunisia, 1943

In the low padded compartment . . . we crouch, the two of us shapeless figures engulfed in a miasma of smoke and dust through which the facia lights barely penetrate. Behind us in the turret the crew are choking with the fumes of cordite which the fans are powerless to dissipate. Cut off from visible contact with the outside world, the wireless operator, wedged in his seat, cannot possibly know in which direction the vehicle is moving. To all five of us, the intercom, our lifeline, relays a bedlam of orders, distortions, and cries from another world.

### Nat Frankel, American Private, France, 1944

It takes twenty minutes for a medium tank to incinerate; and the flames burn slowly, so figure it takes ten minutes for a hearty man within to perish. You wouldn't even be able to struggle for chances are both exits would be sheeted with flame and smoke. You would sit, read *Good Housekeeping*, and die like a dog. Steel coffins indeed!

### Anonymous British Tank Company Commander, Italian Front, 1944

We were ordered to make the attack in the face of an antitank screen firing down the line of advance. We knew that we should not get far. . . . armour-piercing shot seemed to come from all directions. . . . the tanks were knocked out one by one. Most of them burst into flames immediately. A few were disabled, the turrets jammed or the tank made immobile. As the survivors jumped out, some of them made a dash across the open. . . . but they were almost all mown down by German machine gun fire.

Sources: From Bryan Perrett, *Through Mud and Blood: Infantry*. Published by Robert Hale, 1975. Reprinted by permission of Watson, Little, Ltd., licensing agents; from Nat Frankel and Larry Smith, *Patton's Best: An Informal History of the 4th Armored Division*. Hawthorne Books, New York, 1978; and from Douglas Orgill, *The Gothic Line*, Heinemann, 1967. Reprinted by permission of John Johnson Limited.

in Europe. This dream demanded a war against the Jews, the majority of whom lived in Poland and the Soviet Union.

## A Crucial Postponement

In July 1940, at the very start of the Battle of Britain, Hitler ordered his military advisers to begin planning a Soviet invasion. By December the plan was set: German troops were to invade the Soviet Union in April 1941. But they did not. Hitler postponed the invasion for two crucial months because the ambitions of an incompetent ally—Mussolini—threatened to undermine the economic base of the Nazi war machine.

Italy was ill-equipped to fight a broad-based war. Its military budget was only one-tenth the size of Germany's, its tanks and aircraft were outdated, it had no aircraft carriers or anti-aircraft defenses, and most crucially, it lacked an adequate industrial base. Yet in 1940 Mussolini's hopes of rebuilding the Roman Empire drove him to launch just such a war. In July 1940, Italian troops invaded British imperial territories in North Africa, and in October Mussolini's soldiers marched into Greece. By the spring of 1941, the Italian advance was in trouble. The British army in North Africa pushed the Italians back into Libya while the Greeks mounted a fierce resistance against the invaders.

Hitler feared the consolidation of British power in Africa and was even more terrified that Mussolini's adventurism would pull the British into eastern Europe. If Britain were able to build air bases in Greece, the Balkans

## Map 26.2    The Nazi Empire in 1942

By 1942, Nazi Germany occupied or was allied to not only most European countries but also much of North Africa and the Middle East. Spain, Portugal, Ireland, Iceland, Sweden, and Switzerland remained neutral. Great Britain and the Soviet Union east of Moscow remained unconquered.

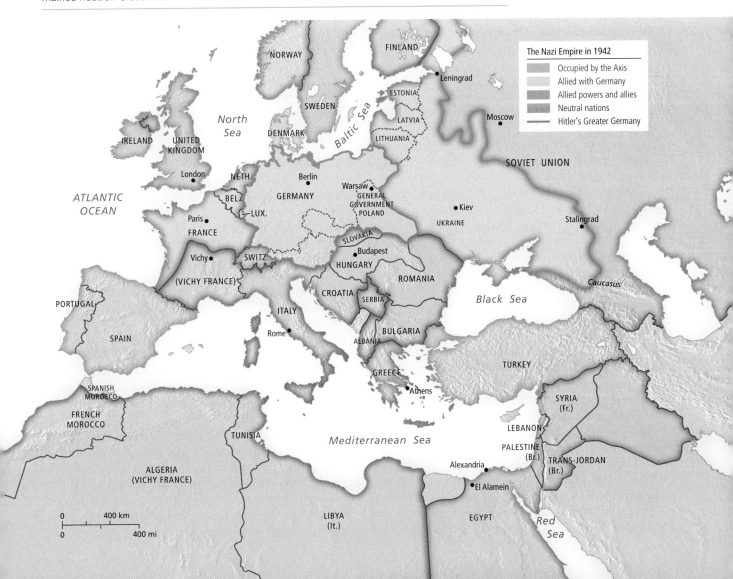

would lie open to British bombing runs. The British could then cripple the German war effort. Germany received 50 percent of its cereal and livestock from the Balkan region, 45 percent of its aluminum ore from Greece, and 90 percent of its tin from Yugoslavia. Most crucially, the oil fields of Romania constituted Germany's chief source of this vital war-making resource. Without oil, there would be no *blitz* in *blitzkrieg*.

These economic considerations led Hitler to delay the invasion of the Soviet Union while the German army mopped up Mussolini's mess in the Balkans and North Africa. In April 1941, German armored units punched through Yugoslavian defenses and encircled the hapless Yugoslav army. Greece came next. The British sent troops as well as state-of-the-art tanks and airplanes to aid the Greeks, but by the end of April Greece was in German hands. Meanwhile, in North Africa German field marshal Erwin Rommel's (1891–1944) Afrika Korps recaptured all the territory taken by the British the previous year.

In the summer of 1941, then, Germany stood triumphant, with dramatic victories in North Africa and the Balkans (see Map 26.2). But these victories came at a high price. They had postponed the German invasion of the Soviet Union. By the winter of 1941, the delay in beginning the Soviet invasion would imperil the German army.

### Early Success
On June 22, 1941, the largest invading force the world had yet seen began to cross the Soviet borders. Three million German soldiers, equipped with 2,770 modern aircraft and 3,350 tanks, went into battle. In a matter of days, most of the Soviet air force was destroyed. By October 1941, only four months after the invasion began, German tanks were within eighty miles of Moscow, Kiev had fallen, and Leningrad was besieged. An astonishing 45 percent of the Soviet population was under German occupation, and the Germans controlled access to much of the Soviet Union's natural and industrial resources, including more than 45 percent of its grain and 65 percent of its coal, iron, and steel.

The early German victories in the Soviet campaign illustrated the power of blitzkrieg. Although the bulk of the German army traveled on foot or horseback (the Germans went into the Soviet Union with 700,000 horses), its spearhead force consisted of tank and motorized infantry divisions. This force shattered the Soviet defensive line and then moved quickly to seize key targets. Two additional factors contributed to the initial German success. First, Stalin's stubborn refusal to believe that Hitler would violate the Non-Aggression Pact and attack the Soviet Union weakened Russian resistance. Soviet intelligence sources sent in more than eighty warnings of an imminent German attack; all, however, were classified as "doubtful" and a number of the messengers were punished, some even executed. Even as German troops poured over the border and German bombs fell on Soviet cities, Stalin distrusted

the news of a German invasion and ignored his generals' pleas for a counterassault.

A second factor that contributed to the early German victories was the popularity of the invasion among many of the peoples being invaded. The initial German advance occurred in territories where Stalin's rule had brought enormous suffering. In areas that had come under Soviet rule in the previous two years—eastern Poland and the Baltic states—anti-Soviet sentiment was especially high. Ceded to the Soviets by the German-Soviet Non-Aggression Pact, these regions were still bleeding from the imposition of Stalinist terror after 1939. Over two million ethnic Poles had been thrown into cattle cars and sent to Siberian labor camps. Thousands had been shot, including 10,000 Polish army officers who were marched to the Katyn forest and gunned down in front of mass graves. To many in these regions, then, the Germans at first seemed like liberators.

### The Fatal Winter
On October 10, Hitler's spokesman announced to the foreign press corps that the destruction of the Soviet Union was assured. German newspapers proclaimed, "CAMPAIGN IN THE EAST DECIDED!"[4] But within just a few months, the German advance had stalled. Leningrad resisted its besiegers and Moscow remained beyond the Germans' reach.

Three obstacles halted the German invasion: stiffening Soviet resistance, the difficulty of supplying the Germans' overstretched lines, and the Russian weather. German troops rapidly squandered the huge reserves of anti-Stalinist sentiment in occupied Soviet territory by treating the local populations with fierce cruelty. Both SS and German army units moved through Soviet territories like a plague of locusts, stripping the regions of livestock, grain, and fuel. The Nazi governor of Ukraine insisted, "I will pump every last thing out of this country."[5] By 1941, both Ukraine and Galicia were devastated by human-made famine. German atrocities in the occupied territories strengthened the will to resist among the Soviets still in the Germans' path. Anti-German partisan units worked behind the German lines, sabotaging their transportation routes, hijacking their supplies, and murdering their patrols. They found the Germans especially vulnerable to this sort of attack because of their overstretched supply lines. Ironically, the Germans had succeeded too well: Since June they had advanced so far so fast that they overstrained their supply and communication lines.

The weather worsened these logistical problems. An early October snowfall, which then melted, turned Russia's dirt roads to impassable mud. By the time the ground froze several weeks later, the German forces, like Napoleon's army 130 years earlier, found themselves fighting the Russian winter. Subzero temperatures wreaked havoc with transportation lines. Horses froze to death, and machinery refused to start. Men fared just as badly. Dressed in light-weight spring uniforms and forced to camp out in the cold, German soldiers fell victim to frostbite. By the end of the winter, the casualty list numbered more than 30 percent of the German East Army.

At the close of the winter of 1941–1942, the German army still occupied huge sections of the Soviet Union and controlled the vast majority of its agricultural and industrial resources. More than three million Soviet soldiers had been killed and another three million captured. But the failure to deal the Soviets a quick death blow in 1941 gave Stalin and his military high command a crucial advantage—*time.* In the zones soon to be occupied by the German army, Soviet laborers dismantled entire factories and shipped them eastward to areas out of German bombing range. Between August and October 1941, 80 percent of the Soviet war industry was in pieces, scattered among railway cars, heading to safety in Siberia. With time, these factories could be rebuilt and the colossal productive power of the Soviet Union geared for the war effort. And that is what happened. By 1943, Russia was outproducing Germany: 24,000 tanks versus 17,000; 130,000 artillery pieces versus 27,000; 35,000 combat aircraft versus 25,000. In a total war, in which victory occurs on the assembly line as well as on the front line, these were ominous statistics for Hitler and his dreams of a German empire.

# The World at War, 1941–1945

■ Why did the Allies win in 1945?

In December 1941, as the German advance slowed in the Soviet Union, Japanese expansionism in the Pacific fused with the war in Europe and drew the United States into the conflict. Neither Japan nor Germany could compete with the United States on the factory floor. Over the next four years, as millions of soldiers, sailors, and civilians lost their lives in a gargantuan and complicated conflict, industrial production continued to supply a crucial advantage to the Allies.

## The Globalization of the War

Even before 1941, Europe's imperialist legacy ensured that World War II was not confined to Europe. As we have seen, Mussolini's desire to expand his North African empire pushed the fighting almost immediately outside European borders. In addition, Britain would never have been able to stand alone against the German-occupied continent without access to the manpower and materials of its colonies and Commonwealth. German efforts to block British access to these resources spread the war into the Atlantic, where British merchant marines battled desperately against German submarines to keep open the sea lanes into Britain.

Britain also drew heavily on the resources of the United States. Throughout 1941 the United States maintained a precarious balance between neutrality and support for the British war effort, as American naval escorts accompanied supply ships loaded with goods for Britain across the Atlantic. In March, the U.S. Congress passed the Lend-Lease Act°, which guaranteed to supply Britain all needed military supplies, with payment postponed until after the war ended. The passage of Lend-Lease was one of the most important decisions in all of World War II. It gave first Britain and then the Soviets access to the incredible might of American industry.

At the same time that the United States was drawing closer to Britain, its relations with Japan were growing increasingly hostile. In 1941 the Japanese occupied Indochina, and the United States responded by placing an embargo on trade in oil with Japan. Threatened with the loss of a key resource, Japanese policymakers viewed this boycott as tantamount to an act of war. Japan's imperial ambitions demanded that it move decisively before its oil ran out. The South Pacific, a treasure house of mineral and other resources, beckoned.

Between December 7 and 10, 1941, Japanese forces attacked American, British, and Dutch territories in the Pacific—Hong Kong, Wake and Guam Islands, the Philippines, Malaya, Molucca in the Dutch East Indies, and most dramatically, the U.S. Pacific fleet base at Pearl Harbor. After an attack that lasted only a few hours, the American Pacific fleet in Hawaii lay gutted. Guam fell immediately; Wake held out until December 23; Hong Kong surrendered on Christmas Day; by February, Malaya had been defeated. On February 15, 1942, the garrison of 130,000 British, Indian, Australian, and local troops surrendered Singapore to a Japanese force less than half its size. By May, this astounding success had been cemented with the conquest of Indonesia, Burma, and the Philippines. In just a few months, the Japanese had established themselves as imperial overlords of the South Pacific, with its wealth of raw materials (see Map 26.3).

The audacity of the Japanese attack impressed Hitler. Although he had long feared American industrial power, he declared war on the United States on December 11, 1941. In Europe Germany now faced the alliance of Britain, the Soviet Union, and the United States. Even against such an alliance, Germany appeared to occupy a strong position. By January a spectacular offensive in North Africa had brought Rommel's forces within two hundred miles of the strategically vital Suez Canal. And in June the German army resumed its advance in the Soviet Union. Within a few months German troops stood at the borders of Russia's oil fields in the southern Caucasus. With Germany on the offensive in the east and Japan controlling the Pacific, the Allies looked poised to lose the war.

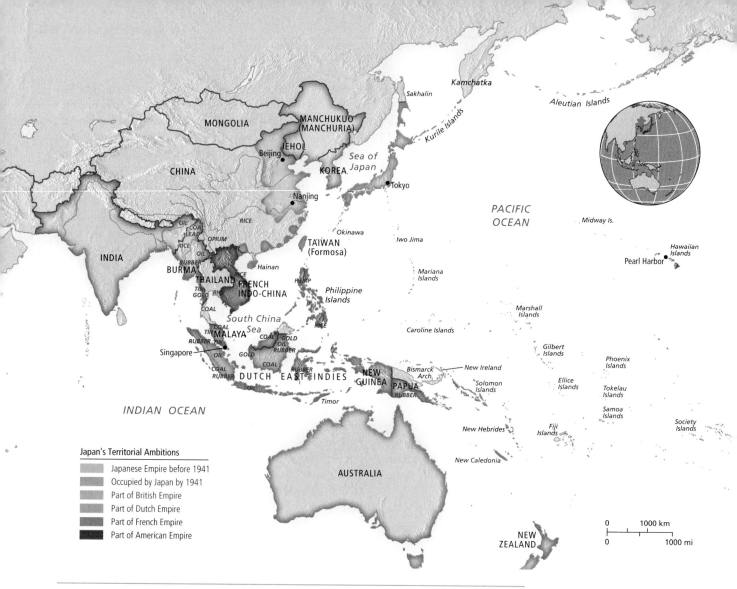

**Map 26.3   Japan's Territorial Ambitions**
Lacking its own supply of natural resources, Japan embarked on imperial conquest.

**Japan's Territorial Ambitions**

- Japanese Empire before 1941
- Occupied by Japan by 1941
- Part of British Empire
- Part of Dutch Empire
- Part of French Empire
- Part of American Empire

# From Allied Defeat to Allied Victory

Twelve months later the situation had changed, and the Allies were on the road to eventual victory. This road, however, proved long and arduous. The period from 1943 through 1945 was marked by horrendous human suffering, unprecedented attacks on civilians, and cataclysmic military battles. Yet in the end American and Soviet industrial supremacy, allied with a superior military strategy, pushed the balance in the Allies' favor.

VIDEO
FDR on Winning the War

## The Turning Point: Midway, El Alamein, and Stalingrad

The second half of 1942 proved the turning point as three very different battles helped transform the course of the war. In the Pacific, victory at the Battle of Midway gave the

U.S. forces a decisive advantage. In North Africa, British forces experienced their first battlefield victory at El Alamein. And in Europe, the Battle of Stalingrad dealt Germany a blow from which it never recovered.

The Battle of Midway resulted from the Japanese effort to ensure its air supremacy by drawing the U.S. Pacific fleet's aircraft carriers into battle. To do so, the Japanese attacked Midway Island, a U.S. outpost, on June 4, 1942. By midmorning the Japanese had shot down two-thirds of the American planes. But then an American dive-bomber group, which had gotten lost, suddenly found itself above the main Japanese carriers. Caught in the act of refueling and rearming the strike force, their decks cluttered with gas lines and bombs, the carriers made remarkably combustible targets. In five minutes, three of Japan's four carriers were destroyed; the fourth was sunk later in the day. Japan's First

**The Surrender of Singapore**

In one of the most humiliating moments in British military history, General Arthur Percival surrenders the Union Jack, and Singapore, to the Japanese in February 1942. More than 130,000 troops were taken prisoner by a Japanese force containing half that number. The Japanese had captured the island's water reservoirs and so had placed Percival in a helpless situation.

Air Fleet was decimated. The destruction of the Japanese fleet dealt Japan a blow from which it could not recover. The United States possessed the industrial resources to rebuild its lost ships and airplanes. Japan did not. In five explosive minutes at Midway the course of the Pacific war changed.

In contrast, the battle of El Alamein marked the culmination of over two years of fighting in North Africa. In September 1940, Mussolini had ordered his troops to advance from Libya (an Italian colony) into Egypt, as part of his effort to establish an Italian empire in the Mediterranean. That winter British and Australian troops not only pushed the Italians back but drove far into Libya itself. The stakes were too high for Hitler to let his Italian ally lose: Control over North Africa and the Middle East meant control over both the strategically and economically vital Suez Canal and the southern shipping lanes of the Mediterranean, as well as access to key oil fields. The Germans entered the conflict and by June 1941, the German Afrika Korps, led by Field Marshal Erwin Rommel, had muscled the British back into Egypt. For more than a year the two armies pushed each other back and forth across the desert. But finally British field marshal Bernard Montgomery, an abrasive, arrogant man whose meticulous battle strategy included the leaking of false plans, caught the Germans by surprise at El Alamein in October 1942. One month later combined British and American forces landed in Morocco and Algeria, and over the next six months

## CHRONOLOGY

### 1942: The Turning Point

**1941**

| | |
|---|---|
| December 7 | Japan bombs Pearl Harbor |
| December 11 | Germany declares war on United States |

**1942**

| | |
|---|---|
| January 21 | Rommel's Second Offensive begins in North Africa |
| February 15 | Surrender of British forces to Japan at Singapore |
| April 22 | British retreat from Burma |
| May 6 | Japan completes conquest of the Philippines |
| June 4 | Battle of Midway |
| August 7 | First U.S. Marine landing on Guadalcanal |
| August 23 | German Sixth Army reaches Stalingrad |
| October 23 | Battle of El Alamein begins |
| November 8 | Anglo-American landing in North Africa begins |
| November 23 | German Sixth Army cut off at Stalingrad |

pushed Germany out of North Africa. The following year North Africa served as the Allies' jumping-off point for their invasion of southern Italy in July 1943. El Alamein thus marked a crucial turning point in the war. Churchill said of it, "It is not the beginning of the end, but it may be the end of the beginning."[6]

Churchill's apt description fits the third turning point of 1942, the battle of Stalingrad, as well. In July the German army was sweeping southward toward the oil-rich Caucasus. Hitler ordered the southern offensive split into two, with one arm reaching up to conquer Stalingrad on the Volga River. The conquest of Stalingrad would give the Germans control over the main waterway for the transport of oil and food from the Caucasus to the rest of the Soviet Union: The Soviet lifeline would be cut. But by dividing his offensive, Hitler widened his front from 500 to 2,500 miles. By the time the German Sixth Army reached Stalingrad on August 23, German resources were fatally overstretched.

Recognizing Germany's vulnerability, Stalin's generals assured him they could attack the exposed German lines and then encircle the German Sixth Army—but only if Stalingrad's defenders could hold on for almost two months while they assembled the necessary men and machinery. An epic urban battle ensued, with the Russian and German soldiers fighting street by street, house by house, room by room. By November, the Russians had surrounded the Germans. When the German commander, General Friedrich von Paulus (d. 1953), requested permission to surrender, Hitler replied, "The army will hold its position to the last soldier and the last cartridge."[7] Paulus finally disobeyed orders and surrendered on January 30, 1943, but by then his army had almost ceased to exist. The Germans

were never able to make up the losses in manpower, material, or morale they suffered at Stalingrad.

## The Allies on the Offensive

The Allies were now on the offensive. In 1942 British bomber command ordered the intensive bombing of German civilian centers. Soon joined by the American air force, the RAF bombers brought the war home to the German people.

The Allies followed their victory in North Africa with an invasion of Italy. This campaign was a response, first, to Stalin's pleas that his Allies open a "Second Front" in Europe and so relieve the pressure on Russian troops and, second, to Churchill's desire to protect British economic and imperial interests in the Mediterranean. The Italian offensive began on July 10, 1943, when Anglo-American forces landed in Sicily, prepared to push up into what Churchill called the "soft underbelly" of German-controlled Europe. Within just fifteen days, Mussolini had been overthrown in a high-level coup and his successor opened peace negotiations with the Allies. But then German muscle hardened the "soft underbelly": The German army occupied Italy. British and American soldiers faced a long, brutal, slow-moving push up the peninsula. Ridged with mountains and laced with rivers, Italy formed a natural defensive fortress. In an eight-month period, the Allied forces advanced only seventy miles.

The European war was decided, then, not in the mountains of Italy but on the eastern front. Beginning in the summer of 1943, the Russians steadily pushed back the Germans. By the spring of 1944 the Red Army had reached the borders of Poland. In August Soviet troops turned south into Romania and Hungary. By February 1945 they were within 100 miles of Berlin (see Map 26.4).

Two interconnected factors proved vital in the Soviet victory over the Germans in the east. The first was the evolution of Soviet military strategy. By 1943, the Red Army had learned important lessons from being on the receiving end of blitzkrieg. It had not only increased its tank units, but it had concentrated these into armies in which motorized infantry regiments accompanied massive numbers of tanks, antitank battalions, and mobile anti-aircraft artillery. In addition, a vast expansion in the number of radios and field telephones overcame the organizational chaos that had greeted the German invasion in 1941.

These changes in technique and technology were closely connected to achievements in industrial production, the second key factor in the Soviet victory. Mobile armored forces depended on factories churning out steel, rubber, oil, and all the various machine parts needed by a modern army. Access to the industrial wealth of the United States pro-

**Stalingrad: Turning Point on the Eastern Front**
The battle for Stalingrad proved to be not only the turning point in the European war, but also a conflict that tested human endurance to the utmost. German and Russian soldiers fought street by street, house by house, room by room in the bitter Russian winter.

vided the Soviet Union with assistance in this task. By 1943, Lend-Lease deliveries of aircraft and tanks were pouring into Soviet ports. Lend-Lease supplied the Soviet Union with the basics needed to keep its army moving: rails and locomotives, jeeps, trucks and gasoline, and 15 million pairs of boots. Yet the Soviets did not rely only on imports. The Soviet industrial effort was enormous. In 1943, Russia manufactured four times as many tanks as it imported, and Soviet production of tanks and antitank guns was double that of Germany.

## The Fall of Germany

As the Red Army closed in on Germany from the east, the British and Americans pushed in from the west. On June 6, 1944, the Allies carried out the largest amphibious operation the world had ever seen. Five seaborne divisions (two American, two British, and one Canadian) and three airborne divisions (two American and one British) crossed the English Channel and landed on a sixty-mile stretch of coastline in northern France. The "D-Day" landings illustrated the Allied advantage in manpower and material. Against the Allies' eight divisions, the Germans had four; against the Allies' 5,000 fighter planes, the Germans could send up 169.

Yet the strength of the German resistance—particularly on Omaha Beach, where the U.S. landing encountered more than 4,000 casualties—signaled that the road to Berlin would not be easy. The Allies faced the formidable task of uprooting the Germans from territory where they had planted themselves five years earlier. For ten long months, the British, American, Canadian, and imperial troops fought a series of hard-won battles. By March 1945, as the Russian army approached Berlin from the east, the British and American armies reached Germany's Rhine border and by mid-April stood within fifty miles of Berlin.

The Allies agreed, however, to leave the conquest of Berlin to the Soviet Army. In this climactic battle of the European war, 320,000 Germans, many of them young

## Map 26.4   Allied Victory in Europe, 1942–1945
Beginning in late 1942, Allied forces moved onto the offensive.

# The GI

On January 26, 1942, the first soldiers from the United States arrived in Britain to prepare for the invasion of Nazi-controlled Europe. By the spring of 1944, Britain was host to a million and a half American soldiers, sailors, and airmen, awaiting the opening of the Second Front in Europe. The coming of the "Yanks" to war-weary, bomb-blasted Britain was an event of more than military significance. For the majority of individuals on both sides, it was their first prolonged encounter with another culture, another way of life. Cultural clashes were commonplace. Forgetting that most essential items were strictly rationed, the GIs (slang that comes from the military label "government issue") at times infuriated their hosts with insensitive complaints about cold rooms, inadequate food, and the shabby style of British dress. The British found the Americans naive, supremely self-confident, alarmingly friendly, and most of all, BIG.

The bigness of the GI is a constant theme in British descriptions and recollections. One British man, urging greater toleration for the GIs, explained to his countrymen, "An American is like a large dog trying to be friendly with everyone in the room, whilst wrecking everything with its tail wagging." A Lancashire nurse recalled her first sight of GIs: "They all seemed to be handsome six-footers with friendly grins and toothpaste advert teeth." But we know that not every GI stationed in Britain was tall and husky; the average height of American servicemen in this era was 5'10". How do we explain this focus on the bigness of the GI body?

A number of factors helped shape British perceptions. First, the bigness of America in general was a constant obsession of both the GIs and their British hosts. *Meet the U.S. Army,* a publication distributed in British schools, told the children, "In the USA, you can get in a car— a high-powered car at that—and drive for a week or more in a comparatively straight line without running into the sea." Second, the Americans *looked better.* The GI's uniform was of a higher-quality fabric and a closer fit than that of the average British soldier's: American privates often found that their flashy uniforms led not only British civilians but even British soldiers to mistake them for officers. Third, compared to the British, the Americans were big eaters and big spenders. An American private earned five times as much as his British counterpart—and spent it with abandon. British pubgoers were sometimes dismayed to find that American soldiers had already consumed the pub's entire stock of beer. Undisciplined by rationing, American appetites seemed huge to the British. One soldier enjoyed his dinner in a British home: "Only afterwards did I discover that I had eaten the family's special rations for a *month.*" GIs also had access to items such as chocolate and canned fruit that had long been unobtainable in Britain. And finally, different cultural norms magnified the impact of the GI's presence. Americans spoke more loudly. They used exaggerated expressions that struck the more understated British as boastful. They tended to lounge, to slouch, to lean against walls, to throw their bodies around in ways that startled many British, schooled in more restrained patterns of public behavior. All of these factors combined to ensure that the GI made an indelible impression on British culture.

Embraced with enthusiasm by many British citizens (particularly women), derided by others (particularly men) as "overfed, overpaid, oversexed, and over here," the GI's body became a symbol, a shorthand reference to American power, influence, and plenty. As World War II ended and the Cold War began, and as the United States took on a new role as the undisputed leader of the "West," the American soldier became a familiar figure throughout western Europe, the visible reminder of the reconfiguration of military and economic dominance.[8]

## For Discussion

What other bodies became symbols or shorthand references during World War II? What did these bodies symbolize?

**Wartime Encounters**
British women entertain GIs headed for the front in France.

**The Human Body in History**

boys, fought three million Soviet troops. Even so, it took eleven days before the city's commander surrendered on May 2. Two days earlier, Hitler had taken a cyanide capsule and then shot himself with his service pistol. On May 7, 1945, General Alfred Jodl (1890–1946) signed the unconditional surrender of German forces.

## The Air War, the Atom Bomb, and the Fall of Japan

When Germany surrendered, the war in the Pacific was still raging. After the Midway battle of 1942, the United States steadily, but slowly, agonizingly, pushed the Japanese back island by island. Japanese industry could not make up for the weapons and ammunition expended in these brutal battles. In contrast, American factories were just gearing up. Whereas in 1940 American assembly lines produced only a little more than 2,000 aircraft, by 1944 they had manufactured over 96,000 bombers and fighters. American productivity per worker hour was five times that of Japan.

While U.S. troops moved closer to the Japanese mainland, British and Indian troops rebuffed a Japanese attempt to invade India and pushed the Japanese out of Burma. Australian forces, with American assistance, held the line at New Guinea and forestalled a Japanese invasion of Australia. By February 1945, then, when U.S. Marines landed on the small island of Iwo Jima, just 380 miles from

### CHRONOLOGY
### The Long March Toward Allied Victory

**1943**

| | |
|---|---|
| February | German surrender at Stalingrad; Red Army goes on the offensive; Allied round-the-clock bombing of Germany begins; Japanese surrender at Guadalcanal |
| May | German surrender in North Africa |
| July 10 | Allied invasion of Italy begins |

**1944**

| | |
|---|---|
| January | Lifting of the siege of Leningrad |
| June 4 | Allies liberate Rome |
| June 6 | D-Day landings; Allied offensive in France begins |
| August 24–26 | Allied liberation of Paris |
| September | Allies liberate the Netherlands, Belgium, and Luxembourg |
| October | U.S. invasion of Philippines |

Japan's home islands, the Japanese war effort was in tatters and an Allied victory was ensured.

Obtaining this final victory, however, proved far from easy. In the month of fighting for the island of Iwo Jima, one-third of the American landing force died or suffered injury. The April conquest of Okinawa was even more hard-won. Outnumbered two to one, the Japanese endured

**The Battle for Berlin**
On April 20, 1945, Hitler celebrated his fifty-sixth birthday and made a rare visit out of his Berlin bunker to visit with the troops defending his city. As this photograph shows, these "soldiers" were just children. Ten days later, Hitler committed suicide.

unbelievable losses—110,000 of the 120,000 soldiers on the island died. Yet they still inflicted serious damage on the attacking force, killing or wounding 50,000 Americans before the fight was over. (Nobody bothered to count how many Okinawans died in a battle they had done nothing to provoke; estimates range as high as 160,000.)

## The Air War

Despite the high price exacted to win them, the battles of Iwo Jima and Okinawa were significant victories: The United States now had the bases it needed to bomb Japanese cities. This air war utilized tactics and technologies developed over the previous five years in Europe. For many European civilians, World War II was the war of the bomber. In Britain, until late 1941, civilian deaths outnumbered military, and most civilians died in bombing raids. During autumn 1940, Londoners endured the "Blitz"—seventy-six consecutive nights of mass bombing. By May 1941, almost every main industrial city in Britain had been bombed, and 43,000 noncombatants lay dead. British bombers, joined in 1943 by the American air force, retaliated in kind, and as the war wore on, developed new techniques of airborne destruction. In May 1942, British planes destroyed Cologne with the world's first 1,000-bomber raid, and one year later, introduced the world to the horror of the firestorm with the bombing of Hamburg. In this human-made catastrophe, fires caused by incendiary bombs combine with winds to suck the oxygen out of the air and raise temperatures to combustible levels. As one survivor recalled, "The smallest children lay like fried eels on the pavement."[9] In a single night, 45,000 of Hamburg's residents were killed. In total, more than 500,000 German civilians died in bombing attacks. Twenty percent of the dead were children.

In 1945 the conquests of Iwo Jima and Okinawa enabled the U.S. air command to adopt the British tactics perfected in the skies over Germany as a key strategy to defeat Japan. On one March evening, American bombs and the ensuing firestorm killed 85,000 residents of Tokyo. Over the next five months, American bombers hit sixty-six Japanese cities, burned 180 square miles, and killed approximately 330,000 Japanese. At the same time, a U.S. naval blockade cut Japan off from its supply lines.

## The Manhattan Project

While American bombers pulverized Japanese cities during the spring and summer of 1945, a multinational group of scientists fought a very different sort of battle in a secret military installation in New Mexico. The Manhattan Project°, the code name for the joint British-American-Canadian effort to construct an atom bomb, was an extraordinary endeavor, the biggest and most expensive weapons research and development project up to that point in history. Comprising thirty-seven installations in nineteen

---

## DOCUMENT

# Living Under the Bombs

*During the 1930s, European statesmen and politicians condemned the aerial bombing of civilian populations as an act of barbarity and criminality. Once World War II began, the targeting of civilians in order to break home front morale and impede industrial production became commonplace. Analysts disagree about the military effectiveness of urban bombing, but no one can dispute the human horror.*

*In this first excerpt, an elderly air warden from Hull, one of Britain's northern port cities, is speaking. One night, when he returned from his post, he found that his street:*

Was as flat as this 'ere wharfside—there was just my 'ouse like—well, part of my 'ouse. My missus were just making me a cup of tea for when I come 'ome. She were in the passage between the kitchen and the wash'ouse, where it blowed 'er. She were burnt right up to 'er waist. 'Er legs were just two cinders. And 'er face— The only thing I could recognize 'er by was one of 'er boots—I'd 'ave lost fifteen 'omes if I could 'ave kept my missus. We used to read together. I can't read mesen [myself]. She used to read to me like. We'd 'ave our armchairs on either side o' the fire, and she read me bits out o' the paper. We 'ad a paper every evening. Every evening.

*In the following excerpt, a German woman, 19 years old on July 28, 1943, recalls the bombing of Hamburg and the firestorm it induced:*

We came to a door which was burning just like a ring in a circus through which a lion has to jump. . . . I struggled to run against the wind in the middle of the street but could only reach a house on the corner. . . . We got to the Loschplatz [park] all right but I couldn't go across the Eiffestrasse [street] because the asphalt had melted. There were people on the roadway, some already dead, some still lying alive but stuck in the asphalt. They must have rushed on to the roadway without thinking. Their feet had got stuck and then they put out their hands to try to get out again. They were on their hands and knees screaming.

Sources: Excerpt from a Mass-Observation typescript report, filed at Mass-Observations offices, no. 844, August 23, 1941. Copyright © by the Trustees of the Mass-Observation Archive. Reprinted by permission; and from Martin Middlebrook, *The Battle of Hamburg*, Allen Lane, 1980. Reprinted by permission of the author.

American states and in Canada, it employed 120,000 individuals. Yet this gargantuan effort was top-secret, unknown even to American vice president Harry Truman, who first learned of the project only after President Roosevelt died.

The Manhattan Project originated as part of the war against Germany, not Japan. When the European war began, a number of scientists—many of them eastern and central European émigrés who had fled the Nazis, many of them Jewish—feared that Germany, with its stellar tradition of scientific research and state-of-the-art laboratories, possessed the potential for developing an atom bomb. They pressured the British and American governments to build the Bomb before Hitler did so. Britain took the initial lead by creating a committee to oversee atomic research in spring 1940. By the following summer, British research had persuaded the Americans that an atom bomb could be constructed. In October 1941—two months before Japan bombed Pearl Harbor—Roosevelt and Churchill agreed to create an atomic partnership.

For three years the Manhattan Project scientists labored to unlock the atom's power. They finally succeeded on July 16, 1945, when the world's first atomic explosion—the Trinity test—detonated over the desert of New Mexico. The date of the Trinity test is crucial because by the time of the test, Nazi Germany had already fallen to the Allies, and Japan was staggering under the combined effects of the American naval blockade and nightly bombing raids (see Map 26.5). Given this situation, the decision to use atom bombs against Japan generated controversy from the very start. Many of the scientists on the Manhattan Project opposed the decision, as did important American military officials such as General Dwight Eisenhower (1890–1969), supreme commander of the Allied forces in Europe; General Douglas MacArthur (1880–1964), supreme commander of the Allied forces in the Pacific; and Admiral William Leahy (1875–1959), chairman of the U.S. Joint Chiefs of Staff.

Advocates of dropping the atom bomb on Japan argued that the fierce Japanese resistance encountered by Americans at Iwo Jima and Okinawa and by the British in Burma signaled that an invasion of Japan's home islands would result in horrifying casualties. Leahy noted to Truman that if casualty rates were as high as those on Okinawa, then the numbers of Americans killed in the first phase of the invasion could reach 50,000.

An invasion of Japan was, however, not a foregone conclusion in the spring and summer of 1945. Leahy and others argued that the naval blockade would end the war *without* an invasion, and in 1946, the U.S. Strategic Bombing Survey concluded that "in all probability prior to 1 November 1945, Japan would have surrendered . . . even if no invasion had been planned or contemplated." Survey officials, of course, had the benefit of hindsight, an advantage denied to Truman and his advisers in the summer of 1945. But more important, from Truman's perspective, continuing to blockade and to drop conventional bombs on Japan

**The Mushroom Cloud**
The detonation of the atomic bomb over Hiroshima on August 6, 1945, produced what would become one of the most familiar images of the post–World War II age.

meant continuing to put American soldiers in harm's way, a cost he was unwilling to pay. The atom bomb's appeal was not in its potential to kill tens of thousands in a single night; conventional bombs were already doing that, and doing it rather effectively. But the idea of massive casualties, caused by a single atomic bomb, dropped by a single plane, promised to have an enormous psychological impact on the Japanese, and so to end the war more quickly and to bring Allied servicemen home.

## A Light Brighter Than a Thousand Suns

As a result, at 8:15 A.M. on August 6, 1945, an American plane named the *Enola Gay* (after the pilot's mother) dropped an atom bomb above the city of Hiroshima. A

DOCUMENT

An Eyewitness to Hiroshima (1945)

**Map 26.5 Japan in 1945**

By the summer of 1945, American bombing raids had decimated many Japanese cities, including Tokyo. Hiroshima escaped unscathed until August 6, 1945. Nagasaki received the second atom bomb on August 9 only because clouds obscured the primary target of Kokura.

## CHRONOLOGY

### The End of World War II

**1945**

| | |
|---|---|
| March 16 | American victory on Iwo Jima |
| April | Berlin encircled by Red Army |
| April 11 | American troops reach Elbe River in Germany |
| April 30 | Hitler commits suicide |
| May 7 | Official German surrender |
| June 22 | American victory at Okinawa |
| August 6 | U.S. drops atomic bomb on Hiroshima |
| August 8 | Soviet Union enters war against Japan |
| August 9 | United States drops atomic bomb on Nagasaki |
| September 2 | Official Japanese surrender |

light "brighter than a thousand suns" flashed in the sky. Temperatures at the site of the atomic explosion reached 5,400 degrees Fahrenheit. All those exposed within two miles of the center suffered primary thermal burns—their blood literally boiled and their skin peeled off in strips. Scientists calculated that the atom bomb produced casualties 6,500 times more efficiently than an ordinary bomb. Of Hiroshima's wartime population of 400,000, 140,000 died by the end of 1945, with another 60,000 dying in the next five years.

The Japanese reacted to the atomic bombing of Hiroshima with incomprehension and confusion. They literally did not know what had hit them. Within the high levels of the Japanese government, gradual realization of the atomic bomb's power strengthened the position of those officials who recognized that Japan must now give up. A hardline faction of the military, however, wished to fight on.

Then, on August 8, the Soviet Union declared war on Japan. The next day American forces dropped an atom bomb on the city of Nagasaki and killed 70,000 outright, with another 70,000 dying over the next five years. On August 10, Emperor Hirohito (1901–1989) told his military leaders to surrender. Viewed in the West as an implacable warlord, Hirohito was actually a man with fairly limited political power who had been pressing for peace since June. Negotiations between the Allies and the Japanese continued until August 15, when the war officially ended.

In Hiroshima and Nagasaki, however, another war was raging, this time against an unseen and at first unrecognized enemy—radiation. The lingering horror of radiation sickness, accounts of which were at first dismissed by many Americans as Japanese propaganda, signaled that the atom bomb was not just a bigger weapon, not simply more bang for the buck. In the months after the war's end, Europeans and Americans came to recognize that the revolutionary new force of atomic power had introduced the world to new possibilities—and new horrors.

## The War Against the Jews

■ How and why did the war against the Jews take place, and what were its consequences?

In the months following the war's end, the world also confronted a very different sort of horror, as people began to piece together the story of Hitler's war against the Jews. For European Jews, World War II brought unprecedented terror and, for millions, death. Chapter 25 explained that hatred of the Jewish people stood at the heart of Hitler's world view and Nazi ideology. Yet anti-Semitism alone cannot explain the mass murder that we now call the

Holocaust°, nor was the Holocaust the product of a detailed plan carefully plotted by Hitler long before he came to power. The decision to murder Europe's Jews evolved over time, in the context of total war.

## From Emigration to Extermination: The Evolution of Genocide

During the 1930s, Nazi policies focused on forcing German Jews to emigrate. By 1938, these policies had driven out about 25 percent of Germany's Jewish population. At the same time, however, the unification of Germany and Austria, followed by the seizure first of the Sudetenland and then all of Czechoslovakia, meant 300,000 more Jews in the expanded Germany. These numbers skyrocketed with the outbreak of the war. The invasion of Poland brought almost two million more Jews under German control. Pushing Jews to emigrate no longer seemed a workable solution to what the Nazis defined as the "Jewish Problem." But even more important, the fact of war itself made a radicalization of policy and a turn toward murderous violence much more acceptable.

**The Holocaust Underway in Lithuania, July 1941**
Nazi soldiers adopt a supervisory role while citizens in the Lithuanian city of Kovno murder their Jewish neighbors.

The German occupation of Poland marked the first step toward the Nazi construction of a new racial order in Europe. Hitler intended the Slavic populations, defined in his racist hierarchy as biologically inferior, to serve as a vast labor pool for their German superiors. To reduce the Polish people to slaves, the Nazis embarked on a wholesale destruction of Polish society and culture. They seized businesses and bank accounts, replaced Polish place names with German, closed universities and high schools, and murdered Polish intellectuals and professionals. By the time the war ended in 1945, more than 20 percent of Poland's population had died.

Within the context of their larger plan of racial reordering, Nazi officials talked about "eliminating" Jews from Poland. At this point, however, "elimination" did not yet mean total extermination but instead referred to vaguely articulated plans for mass deportations. German policy toward the Jews in Poland initially focused on "ghettoization." The Nazis forcibly expelled Jews from their homes and confined them in ghettos sealed off from their non-Jewish neighbors. Packed into overcrowded apartments, with inadequate food rations and appalling sanitary conditions, the ghetto populations lived in a nightmare of disease, starvation, and death.

In the almost two-year period between the invasion of Poland and the invasion of the Soviet Union, an estimated 30,000 Jews died, killed outright by German soldiers or dying a more lingering death from starvation and disease as a result of deportation and ghettoization. Yet the suffering had only begun. In the summer or fall of 1941, the Nazis decided on what they termed the Final Solution° to the "Jewish problem": genocide.

The German invasion of the Soviet Union helped shape the "Final Solution." Marching with the forces of the regular army were special mobile units of the SS called Einsatzgruppen° ("strike forces"). With the army providing logistical support, these small motorized units (about 3,000 men in all) took on the task of liquidating those designated as enemies of the Nazi Reich—which meant killing communists and Jews.

Most of these murders followed the same general pattern: SS soldiers rounded up all of the Jewish men, women, and children in a town or village and marched them in batches to a field or woods. They ordered the first batch to dig a large ditch. They then stripped their victims of their clothing, lined them up on the edge of the ditch, and shot them at point-blank range. Subsequent batches were lined up and shot as well, so that by the end of a day's worth of killing, dead and dying bodies filled the ditch. A thin layer of soil was then thrown on top, transforming the ditch into a mass grave. Estimates of the final death count of the Einsatzgruppen actions range from 1.5 to 2 million.

In their war against the Jews, the Einsatzgruppen found ready allies among large sectors of the occupied population. Recall that the earliest stages of the German invasion of the

**Einsatzgruppen Action**
A soldier shoots the last remaining Jew in a Ukrainian village.

**Map 26.6 Poland and the Death Camps**
The Nazis set up a vast network of concentration and labor camps across Europe, but built death camps only in Poland.

Soviet Union took place in the territories that had been seized by the Soviets in 1939 as a result of the German-Soviet Non-Aggression Pact. Hence the local populations often welcomed the German troops as liberators and aided the SS in hunting down and killing Jews. In Lvov in eastern Galicia, for example, anti-Soviet Ukrainian fighters turned on the large Jewish community and in two days of violence killed at least 7,000 Jews—*before* the Einsatzgruppen had even arrived.

## The Death Camps: Murder by Assembly Line

On January 20, 1942, senior German officials met in a villa in Wannsee, outside Berlin, to finalize plans for killing every Jew in Europe. SS lieutenant colonel Adolf Eichmann

(1906–1962) listed the number of Jews in every country; even the Jewish populations in neutral countries such as Sweden and Ireland showed up on the target list. The Wannsee Conference marked the beginning of a more systematic approach to murdering European Jews, one that built on the experience gained by the Einsatzgruppen in the Soviet war.

To accomplish mass murder, the Einsatzgruppen had become killing machines. By trial and error, they discovered the most efficient ways of identifying and rounding up Jews, shooting them quickly, and burying the bodies. But the Einsatzgruppen actions also revealed the limits of conventional methods of killing. Shooting took time, used up valuable ammunition, and required large numbers of men. Moreover, even the best-trained and carefully indoctrinated soldiers eventually cracked under the strain of shooting unarmed women and children at close range. A systematic approach was needed, one that would utilize advanced killing technology and provide a comfortable distance between the killers and the killed. This perceived need resulted in a key Nazi innovation: the death camp.

The death camp was a specialized form of a concentration camp. From 1933 on, Hitler's government had sentenced communists, Jehovah's Witnesses, the Roma, and anyone else defined as an enemy of the regime to forced labor in concentration camps. After the war began, the concentration camp system expanded dramatically. Scattered throughout Nazi-controlled Europe, concentration camps became an essential part of the Nazi war economy. Some firms, such as the huge chemical conglomerate I. G. Farben,

IMAGE

Emaciated Woman at Bergen-Belsen

established factories inside or right next to camps, which provided vital supplies of forced labor. All across Europe during the war, concentration camp inmates died in huge numbers from the brutal physical labor, torture, and diseases brought on by malnutrition and inadequate housing and sanitary facilities. But it was only in Poland that the Nazis constructed death camps, specialized concentration camps with only one purpose—murder, primarily the murder of Jews (see Map 26.6).

The death camps marked the final stage in a vast assembly line of murder. In early 1942 the trains conveying Jewish victims to the death camps began to rumble across Europe. Jewish ghettos across Nazi-occupied Europe emptied as their inhabitants moved in batches to their deaths. Individuals selected for extermination followed orders to gather at the railway station for deportation to "work camps" farther east. They were then packed into cattle cars, more than 100 people per car, all standing up for the entire journey. Deprived of food and water, with hardly any air, and no sanitary facilities, often for several days, many Jews died en route. The survivors stumbled off the trains into a nightmare world. At some camps, SS guards culled stronger Jews from each transport to be worked to death as slave laborers. Most, however, walked straight from the transport trains into a reception room, where they were told to undress, and then herded into a "shower room"—actually a gas chamber. Carbon monoxide gas or a pesticide called Zyklon-B killed the victims. After the poison had done its work, Jewish slaves emptied the chamber and burned the bodies in vast crematoria, modeled after industrial bake ovens.

DOCUMENT

The Holocaust: Memoirs from the Commandant of Auschwitz (1940s)

The Nazis thus constructed a vast machine of death. In this machine, slave laborers constituted key components, each with identification numbers tattooed onto their

## DOCUMENT

## The "Jager Report"

*Karl Jager was a German businessman who joined the SS in 1932. In 1941 he was appointed Commander of Einsatzkommando 3 of Einsatzgruppe A, which was given the task of ridding Lithuania of Jews. The following is an excerpt from his nine-page report on his squad's activities in the summer and fall of 1941. The first six pages contain a day-by-day tally of the number of "executions" (murders) carried out. The final total: 137,346 Jews killed. Jager became a farm laborer after the war, but in 1959 he was arrested; he hanged himself before he could be tried for war crimes.*

Kauen [Kaunas], 1 December 1941. Secret Reich Business!
. . .
Today I can confirm that our objective, to solve the Jewish problem for Lithuania, has been achieved by EK 3. In Lithuania there are no more Jews. . . . It was only possible to achieve our objective . . . by forming a raiding squad consisting of specially selected men led by SS-Obersturmfuhrer Hamann, who grasped my aims completely and understood the importance of ensuring cooperation with the Lithuanian partisans and the relevant civilian authorities.

The execution of such actions is first and foremost a matter of organization. The decision to clear each district of Jews systematically required a thorough preparation of each individual action and a reconnaissance of the prevailing conditions in the district concerned. The Jews had to be assembled at one or several places. Depending on the number of Jews a place for the graves had to be found and then the graves dug. . . .

In Rokiskis 3,208 people had to be transported $4^1/_2$ km before they could be liquidated. In order to get this work done within 24 hours, over sixty of the eighty available Lithuanian partisans had to be detailed for cordon duty. The rest, who had to be relieved constantly, carried out the work together with my men. . . . It was only through the efficient use of time that it was possible to carry out up to five actions of week, while still coping with any work that arose in Kauen, so that no backlog was allowed to build up.

The actions in Kauen itself, where there was an adequate number of reasonably well-trained partisans available, were like parade-ground shootings in comparison with the often enormous difficulties which had to be faced elsewhere.

All the officers and men in my Kommando took an active part in the major actions in Kauen. . . . I consider the Jewish action more or less terminated as far as Einsatzkommando 3 is concerned.

*Source: "The Good Old Days": The Holocaust as Seen by Its Perpetrators and Bystanders. Eds. Ernst Klee et al. (1991), pp. 46–58.*

forearms, a type of human "bar coding." Along a murderous assembly line the human raw material moved from arrival through selection to the undressing rooms to the gas chamber to the crematoria. Approximately three million Jews died in these factories of death. The death camp victims joined the millions who starved or died of disease in the ghettoes, suffocated in the cattle cars, were shot in mass graves, or worked to death in the labor camps. Children were especially vulnerable. Of the Jewish children living in 1939 in the regions already or soon to be under German control, only 11 percent survived.

In total, the Holocaust claimed the lives of approximately six million Jews. The numbers of Roma victims remains unclear. Somewhere between 200,000 and 600,000 died in what the Roma call the *Porajmos*—the Devouring. Jews and Gypsies were the only groups singled out for total extermination based on their supposed biological identity. But Hitler's drive to create his new Germany claimed three to five million other victims as well. Five to fifteen thousand homosexuals perished. So, too, did at least three million Polish Christians.

## The Allies' Response

Allied leaders had access to surprisingly accurate information about the Holocaust from very early on. British code breakers translated German military radio transmissions throughout the summer of 1941 so that as the German army—and the Einsatzgruppen—moved into the Soviet Union, British officials confronted intercepted messages such as this one from August 27: "Regiment South shot 914 Jews; the special action staff with police battalion 320 shot 4,200 Jews." By June 1942, Allied leaders knew that death camps existed.

Such information quickly became accessible to ordinary people. British and American newspaper readers and radio listeners received numerous reports about Jewish massacres; after 1942, these reports told about the death camps. But this information had to compete with other war news and many of these articles were written in a skeptical tone, as both reporters and editors had a difficult time believing that such atrocities could be taking place. Pressure from Jewish and non-Jewish public-interest groups did succeed in pushing the British and American governments to issue an inter-Allied declaration in December 1942 that in no uncertain terms announced and condemned Hitler's effort to exterminate European Jewry. This declaration was broadcast all over the world.

Despite this official acknowledgment of the mass murder of Jews, the Allies did not act directly to stop the killings. Should the Allies then be considered bystanders in the crime of the Holocaust? Some historians contend that anti-Semitism in both British and American society structured the Allies' military priorities and prevented leaders from exploring strategies such as sending in commando units, bombing the rail lines into the death camps, or even bombing the camps themselves. Other historians argue these alternatives were not militarily feasible, and that the Allies did the only thing they could do on the Jews' behalf—win the war as quickly as possible.

In the months after the war ended, Allied leaders struggled to bring Nazi leaders to trial to account for their crimes. What one participant called "the greatest trial in history" opened on November 14, 1945. For eleven months, a tribunal of four judges—American, British, French, and Soviet—sat in a courtroom in the German city of Nuremberg to judge nineteen prominent German military, political, and industrial leaders. The Nuremberg trials°, broadcast by the crowds of journalists packed into the courtroom, offered the world its first encounter with the Holocaust. The trials highlighted the Nazi onslaught against European Jewry as one of the most horrendous of the Nazis' many "crimes against humanity," a category first introduced into international law at Nuremberg.

Liberating the Concentration Camps

# The Home Front: The Other Wars

■ **What did total war mean on the home front?**

As the Holocaust made vividly clear, for many Europeans during World War II the home front was not a place of safety or normalcy but a place where other wars were fought. The spreading resistance against the Nazi regime, as well as bombing raids and forced labor obligations, obliterated the distinction between combatant and noncombatant, blurred gender roles, and provoked calls for radical social change.

## The Limits of Resistance

Throughout the war individuals and groups in occupied Europe performed heroically, hiding Jews and others on the run, sabotaging equipment, disrupting transportation systems, and relaying secret information to the Allies. In the Soviet Union and in mountainous regions of Yugoslavia, Italy, and southern France, where the terrain offered shelter for guerillas, anti-Nazi fighters formed partisan groups that attacked German army units. In one of the best-known cases of resistance, the Jews in the Warsaw ghetto rose up in the spring of 1943. Armed with only one or two submachine guns and a scattering of pistols, rifles, hand grenades, and gasoline bombs, Jewish fighters held off the far superior German military force for more than a month. In the

### Mass Grave at Bergen-Belsen

British soldiers liberated the camp of Bergen-Belsen on April 15, 1945. For many prisoners, however, death provided their only "liberation." The Allies forced German civilians living in the regions around camps such as these to view the mass graves, in an effort to compel them to face up to their passive participation in the Holocaust. Few Germans accepted responsibility.

end, however, the ghetto was leveled, and all its survivors deported to Nazi death camps.

Both men and women participated in the Resistance, the struggle against Nazi rule. In Yugoslavia, 100,000 women fought as soldiers in the partisan ranks: 25,000 were killed and 40,000 injured. Most women in the Resistance were not in combat units. Instead, they played gender stereotypes to great advantage: They hid bombs in baby carriages, tucked vital messages under their shopping, disarmed Germans with feminine charm. One Italian partisan used to catch rides on German trucks to deliver her illegal communications: "What was there to fear? You only had to give them a few smiles."[10] With men at risk of being rounded up for forced labor in Germany, women often shouldered the burden of distributing clandestine publications, delivering supplies and arms, and finding safe houses.

But only a minority of Europeans, men or women, fought in the Resistance. As the Dutch historian Louis de Jong has noted of European actions and attitudes under Nazi occupation, "Unwilling adjustment was the rule, intentional resistance the exception."[11] Why did so few Europeans join the Resistance? Important factors include the Germans' military might, their success at infiltrating Resistance organizations, and their willingness to use brutal force to crush any threat. The German network of concentration camps throughout occupied Europe possessed enormous deterrent value. Concerned for their own and their families' safety, most Europeans hoped simply to keep their heads down and survive the war.

The German practice of exacting collective retribution for Resistance actions particularly undercut mass support for anti-German efforts. In 1942, for example, British intelligence forces parachuted Czech agents into German-held Czechoslovakia. The agents assassinated the chief SS official in the region, Reinhard Heydrich (1904–1942), but they were immediately betrayed by one of their own. In retaliation, the Germans massacred the entire population of the village of Lidice. Similarly, an assassination attempt against Hitler in 1944 led to mass arrests and the executions of an estimated 5,000 Germans.

In Germany itself and in countries allied to rather than conquered by the Germans, potential resisters had to convince themselves that patriotism demanded working against their own government. In France until 1943, resistance meant opposing the lawfully instituted but collaborationist Vichy government of Marshal Pétain. As a World War I hero, Pétain had an almost godlike reputation in France and was popular even with those who did not share his authoritarian conservatism. As a result, in the early years of the war many French men and women viewed the members of the Resistance as traitors against France, rather than as heroes fighting against the Nazis. By 1943, however, an alternative focus of national loyalty had emerged: the Free French headed by General Charles De Gaulle (1890–1970), a career military man who had gone into exile rather than accept the armistice with Nazi Germany. After the Anglo-American landing in North Africa in November 1942, De Gaulle claimed Algeria as a power base and declared himself

# The Trial of Adolf Eichmann

On May 23, 1960, David Ben-Gurion (1886–1973), the prime minister of Israel, made a spectacular announcement: Israeli secret service agents had kidnapped Adolf Eichmann, a wanted Nazi war criminal, and smuggled him into Israel to await trial. Eichmann, the head of the Gestapo's Jewish Affairs unit, had implemented Nazi policies on Jewish emigration and deportation. His office sorted through the complicated bureaucratic procedures to ensure that the trains laden with Jews kept to their schedules and delivered their human cargo to the gas chambers on time. It was to Eichmann that Jewish leaders came to plead for emigration visas and for work permits. It was with Eichmann that Jewish leaders negotiated about the timing, size, and composition of deportations. For many Jews, then, Eichmann represented German power and came to personify Nazi evil. He had disappeared in the chaotic final days of World War II and eventually made his way to Argentina, where, as "Ricardo Klement," he lived a quiet, respectable life with his wife and children—until 1960.

From the moment of Ben-Gurion's sensational announcement, the Eichmann case occupied the attention of the world. Six hundred foreign correspondents attended the trial, which was one of the first to be filmed by television cameras. More than 1,500 documents were submitted and 120 witnesses testified in the 114 sessions held between April 11 and August 14, 1961. Three judges, each of whom had been born in Germany and had emigrated to Palestine in 1933, heard the evidence. On December 15, they sentenced Eichmann to death. He died by hanging on May 31, 1962, the first execution in Israel, which had abolished capital punishment for all crimes except genocide.

The Eichmann trial told the story of Jewish suffering during World War II to the widest possible audience. Both Ben-Gurion and the chief prosecutor, Gideon Hausner, stated publicly that the trial aimed to construct "a living record of a gigantic human and national disaster," and so educate both young Israelis and the entire world in the causes and consequences of the Holocaust.[12] As Hausner explained in his emotional opening statement, he saw himself as the spokesman for "six million accusers . . . [whose] ashes were piled up in the hills of Auschwitz and in the fields of Treblinka, or washed away by the rivers of Poland."[13] Hausner (who, like many Israelis, had lost most of his relatives in the Nazi death camps) called more than 100 witnesses, many of them death camp survivors. Their testimony, published or broadcast throughout the world, painted an unforgettable and detailed picture of the horror of genocide.

By the time the prosecution rested its case, no one could doubt that Eichmann was a guilty man, one who had played an essential role in the murder of millions. Yet the Eichmann trial attracted an enormous amount of criticism and continues to arouse great controversy. Critics charged that to achieve moral justice for Holocaust victims and survivors, the Israeli court committed a legal injustice against Eichmann. The trial was not only made possible by a violation of international law (Eichmann's kidnapping), it also was filled with irregularities, including the introduction of testimony that did not pertain to the specific crimes charged. Critics also disputed Israel's legal right to try Eichmann: The crimes had not occurred in Israeli territory, nor were Eichmann's victims Israeli citizens. (Israel did not exist until 1948.)

In reply to these critics, Hausner and other supporters of the prosecution insisted that justice demanded that Eichmann be brought to trial, and that the Israeli government had pursued the only course of action open to it. In the Eichmann trial, then, we confront a case in which what was legal on the one hand and what was just on the other appeared very much at odds. There is no doubt that Eichmann was guilty of horrendous crimes; there is also no doubt that the Israeli government stepped beyond the boundaries of international law in kidnapping Eichmann.

The Eichmann trial also raised important questions about the nature of the Holocaust. Was it a crime perpetrated by a few very evil men, or did the evil penetrate deep into German, and European, society? The prosecution's case sought to depict Eichmann as a monster, a brilliant and demonic mastermind responsible for the deaths of millions of Jews. As Hausner contended, "it was [Eichmann's] word that put gas chambers into action; he lifted the telephone, and railway trains left for the extermination centers; his signature it was that sealed the doom of tens of thousands."[14] Such a depiction provided a comforting explanation for the Holocaust—it was perpetrated not by ordinary human beings but by monstrous devils.

Yet many trial observers and subsequent historians argued that such a depiction was simply wrong. This argument appeared in forceful terms in the most well-known critique of the prosecution—Hannah Arendt's *Eichmann in Jerusalem: A Report on the Banality of Evil,* published in 1963. Arendt (1906–1975), a Jewish philosopher who had fled Nazi Europe in 1941, argued that the evidence provided in the trial

*Eichmann sits on the left in a cage of bulletproof glass.*

*The three judges hear the case from the high table on the right.*

**Eichmann on Trial**

showed Eichmann to be a fairly commonplace man, motivated by ambition as much as by ideology, a rather plodding bureaucrat obsessed with trivial details—in other words, an ordinary man, capable of extraordinary evil.

Must ordinary men be held responsible for following evil orders? This is the final question raised by the Eichmann trial. Defense attorney Robert Servatius insisted that the Holocaust was an "act of state," a crime carried out by a political regime, for which no civil servant could bear the blame. Eichmann only followed orders. Servatius concluded his arguments by asking Eichmann how he viewed "this question of guilt." Eichmann replied,

*Where there is no responsibility, there can be no guilt. . . .*

*The questions of responsibility and conscience are for the leadership of the state. . . . I condemn and regret the act of extermination of the Jews which the leadership of the German state ordered. But I myself could not jump over my own shadow. I was a tool in the hands of superior powers and authorities.[15]*

Eichmann's judges disagreed. In declaring Eichmann guilty of genocide, they argued,

*We reject absolutely the accused's version that he was nothing more than a "small cog" in the extermination machine. . . . He was not a puppet in the hands of others. His place was among those who pulled the strings.[16]*

## Questions of Justice

1. Even if Eichmann's assertion that he was simply "a tool in the hands of superior powers and authorities" could be proven correct, to what degree was he culpable for his actions?
2. In the Eichmann case, the letter of the law and justice appeared to be at odds. In what situations—if any—must the law be broken to ensure that justice prevails? Who has the authority to make such a judgment?

## Taking It Further

Laqueur, Walter. "Hannah Arendt in Jerusalem: The Controversy Revisited," in Lyman H. Legters, ed., *Western Society After the Holocaust.* 1983. Examines the impact of Arendt's critique of the trial.

*The Trial of Adolf Eichmann: Record of Proceedings in the District Court of Jerusalem.* Vols. 1–9. 1993–1995. The basic primary source.

the head of a Free French provisional government. French patriots could declare themselves loyal to this alternative government and fight in the Resistance against both Nazi rule and Vichy collaboration.

In many areas—for example, much of Italy after the German army occupied the country in 1943—a genuine spirit of unity characterized the Resistance struggle, with socialists, communists, and Catholics working together not only to defeat the Nazis but also to create the foundations of a better society. In other areas, divisions within the Resistance limited its impact. Conservative army officers fighting to preserve the prewar status quo clashed with guerilla groups that espoused radical political goals. Fighting among Resistance factions shaded into civil war. In Ukraine, nationalists fought against communist partisans as well as the Germans. In Greece, the communist-dominated National Liberation Front battled not only the Nazis but also a rival Resistance group, the royalist National Greek Democratic Union.

## Civil War in Yugoslavia

The fiercest struggle occurred in Yugoslavia, where political and ethnic divisions split both the country and the Resistance. Wartime Yugoslavia experienced a bloodletting unmatched anywhere in Europe except in the German-occupied regions of Poland and the Soviet Union. Parts of the country such as Slovenia and Macedonia were occupied by German or German-allied armies and endured brutal repression. The scale of violence peaked in the fascist state of Croatia, created after the German invasion of 1941. This Nazi-sponsored regime immediately embarked on a savage program of ethnic homogenization, with a ferocious campaign of terror against Jews, Bosnian Muslims, and Serbs.

In Yugoslavia, therefore, the Resistance was not simply or even primarily aimed at the Germans. Guerilla bands of Serbian soldiers called *Chetniks* supported the now-exiled Yugoslav monarchy and regarded the Croatian regime as their main enemy, although, like the Croatian fascists, the Chetniks also slaughtered both Muslims and Jews. In the midst of this bloody free-for-all, a second Resistance group emerged, one based not on ethnicity but on political ideology. Led by communist Josip Broz (1892–1980), alias "Tito," these partisans saw the war as a chance for social revolution and promised equality for all in a reunited Yugoslavia. Tito's partisans focused on fighting Germans (diverting ten German divisions from the eastern front), but they also fought their fellow Yugoslavs, with the royalist Chetniks fiercely opposing Tito's aim of a communist state.

Tito's partisans won the civil war. In 1944 they fought alongside the Soviet army and liberated Yugoslavia from German control. With 90 percent of the vote in the first postwar election, Tito assumed control of the new communist state of Yugoslavia, a position he held for the next thirty-five years. Beneath the uniform surface created by communist ideology, however, the jagged edges of ethnic division remained sharp.

## Under Occupation

In occupied Europe, Nazi racial ideology shaped the experience of both soldiers and civilians. The Nazis drew a sharp line between the peoples of western Europe—the Dutch, Norwegian, Danes, and Flemish, all considered of racially superior "Germanic stock"—and the Slavs of eastern Europe. The ferocity of Nazi brutality increased exponentially in the eastern occupied regions.

The German treatment of prisoners of war (POWs) illustrates the contrast between the western and eastern European experience during World War II. By the end of 1941, 2.5 million Soviet soldiers had been captured. By February 1942, two million of these had died, both from starvation and from epidemic diseases nurtured by the poor conditions in the camps. In contrast, of the more than one million French soldiers captured by the Germans in 1940, nineteen out of twenty returned home at the end of the war. When dealing with western European POWs, the Germans abided by international rules; in eastern Europe, World War II was a game without rules and without limits.

The German occupation of western Europe was less heavy-handed than in the east, particularly during the first half of the war. The Nazis believed that "Germanic" peoples such as the Dutch could be taught to become good Nazis and therefore spared them the extreme violence and mindless brutality that characterized the German occupation in the east. Moreover, in western Europe the Germans sought to work with rather than to annihilate political and economic elites. For example, in both Belgium and the Netherlands civil servants continued to do their prewar jobs. Nonetheless, the German occupation in the west, even in the first two years of the war, was far from lenient. The Nazis forced occupied countries to pay exorbitant sums to cover the costs of their own occupation. In addition, they were required to sell both manufactured products and raw materials to Germany at artificially low prices. Anyone who spoke out against the Nazis faced imprisonment or death. The occupation grew even more harsh after 1943 as German military losses piled up, stocks of food and essential supplies dwindled, and German demands for civilian labor increased.

For millions of European men and women, the war meant forced labor in Germany. With the need to free up German men for the front lines, the Nazis faced crucial labor shortages in almost every sector of the economy. Placing the economy on an all-out war footing would have meant imposing unpopular measures such as the conscrip-

**The *Hongerwinter***

By the fall of 1944, the southern provinces of the Netherlands were liberated, but the north remained under German occupation. After Dutch railway employees refused to transport any more German troops, the Germans retaliated by blocking all food shipments to the north. Twenty thousand Dutch civilians died in the resulting "Hunger Winter."

tion of women for industrial labor, lengthening working hours, and prohibiting holidays. The Nazis chose instead to recruit labor from conquered territories. Within days of the invasion of Poland, Polish POWs were working in German fields. By August 1944, German farmers and factory owners employed over 5.7 million foreign civilian laborers (one-third of whom were women) and almost two million POWs. These foreign workers accounted for more than half the labor in German agriculture and in German munitions plants and one-third of the labor force in key war industries such as mining, chemicals, and metals.

Hostile, hungry, and often untrained for the jobs in which they were placed, foreign workers proved to be less productive than German laborers. Nevertheless, foreign labor played a crucial role in wartime Germany, not only in fueling the German war machine but also in maintaining German civilian morale. Foreign labor cushioned German civilians from the impact of total war and reassured them that they belonged to a superior race. Many German factory owners were relieved to find they now had a labor force with few political rights. The director of one aircraft manufacturing firm explained, "The great advantage of employing foreigners . . . is that we only have to give orders. There

is no refusal, no need to negotiate."[17] The labor of foreigners also benefited the German working class. Nazi regulations stipulated that German workers were to regard themselves as the masters of the foreign laborers working alongside them. Thus ordinary Germans held positions of privilege and power. Some families even found themselves able to afford new luxuries. Beginning in 1942, the Nazi regime brought Russian women into Germany to serve as maids in German households. As a result, according to a report in January 1943, "even those households with many children, whose financial situation previously did not permit them to hire domestic help, can now afford to maintain a worker."[18]

## The Women's War

As we have seen, women joined the ranks of the Resistance and were forced to labor in German industries. Women also tended to bear the brunt of home front deprivation, as they were the ones who had to get a meal on the table and clothe their children in the face of severe rationing. Basic household goods such as frying pans, toothbrushes, bicycle tires,

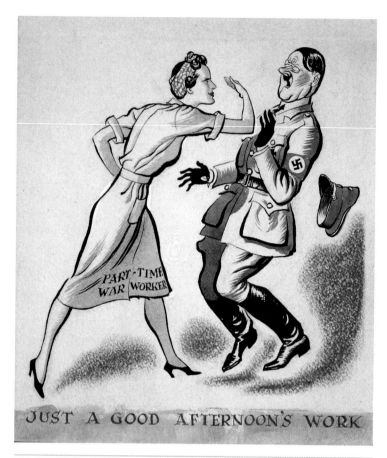

**Some Women's War**
British women did not have to endure the hell of Nazi occupation or forced labor. They did, however, participate fully in the war effort. Only the Soviet Union mobilized its women more completely.

Russian women also served in combat. By 1944, 246,000 women were in front-line units. For all Soviet citizens, male and female, life on the home front meant endless labor, inadequate food supplies, and constant surveillance under martial law. Stalin demanded an all-out war against not only the German invaders but also anyone at home who undermined the war effort in any way. The Soviet government established a compulsory sixty-hour workweek and issued ration cards only to those who worked.

Until 1943, the German home front contrasted sharply with that of Britain and the Soviet Union. The Nazi policy toward female employment rested on Hitler's conviction that Germany had lost World War I in part because of the collapse of morale on the home front. As a result, Hitler placed a high priority on maintaining civilian morale. Generous allowances for soldiers meant that their wives, unlike in Britain, did not have to work to feed their families. In the first years of the war, the Nazi government rationed clothing and food supplies but did not dramatically cut consumption levels. Moreover, Hitler hesitated to conscript middle-class German women for industrial labor. For Hitler, ideology came before economics. He believed that the future of the "German race" depended on middle-class women being protected from the strains of paid labor so that they could bear healthy Aryan babies.

In Germany the use of foreign labor took the place of the full-scale mobilization of women. Top-ranking Nazis explicitly linked the use of foreign workers to gender considerations. At the end of 1941, for example, Hermann Göring (1893–1946) announced that Soviet workers would be brought into Germany to guarantee "that in future, the German women should not be so much in evidence in the work process."[19] The number of women in the German workforce actually fell by 500,000 between 1939 and 1941. German women who did work were prohibited from working long hours or at night, and from performing heavy physical labor. Instead, eastern European workers (many of them women) were given the tough jobs and the poor hours. At the Krupp metalworks factory, for example, German women worked for six hours at light jobs during the day; Russian women did the heavy labor during the twelve-hour night shift.

Military necessity eventually undercut Nazi gender ideology. The fall of Stalingrad marked a turning point in Nazi policy toward German women at work. With losses on the eastern front averaging 150,000 men per month, the German army desperately needed more men. At the same time, the German war economy demanded more workers. In response, Hitler's deputy Joseph Goebbels (1897–1945)

baby bottles, and batteries almost disappeared; food was in short supply; clothing had to be recycled. It was Europe's women who became experts at "make do and mend," as British government pamphlets advised.

British women were fully mobilized. They did not serve in combat, but they were drafted for service in civilian defense, war-related industry, or the armed forces. Women accounted for 25 percent of the civilians who worked in Britain's Air Raid Protection services as wardens, rescuers, and telephone operators. All citizens—male or female—working less than 55 hours per week had to perform compulsory fire-watching duties from 1941 on. The numbers of women employed in male-dominated industries such as metals and chemicals rose dramatically.

Only the Soviet Union mobilized women more fully than Britain. Soviet women constituted 80 percent of the agricultural and 50 percent of the industrial labor force. All Soviet adult men and women under age 45 who were not engaged in essential war work were required to work eleven hours a day constructing defenses. Unlike in Britain, declared that Germany must fight a total war, which meant total mobilization of the home front. The final, desperate year of the war saw a concentrated use of female labor in Nazi Germany.

Of all the combatant states, the United States stands out as unique with regard to the home front. The United States never fully mobilized its economy, and more than 70 percent of its adult women remained outside the paid workforce. Rationing was comparatively minimal and consumption levels in the United States high. In fact, for many families, the war years brought prosperity after years of economic depression. But most important, American cities were never bombed, and thus the United States was able to maintain a clear distinction between soldier and civilian, man and woman—a distinction that was blurred in other combatant nations.

## What Are We Fighting For?

To mobilize their populations for total war, governments had to convince their citizens of the importance of the war effort. Maintaining morale and motivating both civilians and soldiers to endure deprivation and danger demanded that leaders supply a persuasive answer to the question: What are we fighting for?

### Myth Making and Morale Building

All nations—democratic or authoritarian—rely on myths, on stories of national origins and identity, to unify disparate individuals, classes, and groups. In times of total war, such myths become crucial. During World War II, the process of myth making was institutionalized by government agencies responsible for propaganda. In Britain, the newly formed Ministry of Information (democracies tend to shy away from using the word *propaganda*) took on the task of propping up civilian morale. Staffed by upper-class men, the MOI's efforts often betrayed its class composition: Many of its posters and leaflets adopted a hectoring tone, subjecting ordinary citizens to a barrage of do's and don'ts. Far more effective were the speeches of Prime Minister Winston Churchill, whose romantic vision of Britain as a still-great power destined to triumph was exactly the myth that the beleaguered British needed. In Germany, strict censorship had already subordinated the arts and entertainment industries to the demands of the state. The war heightened this control as censorship tightened even further, paper shortages limited the production of books and periodicals, and the threat of being drafted for the eastern front kept artists in line.

In all the combatant nations, governments enlisted artists, entertainers, and the technologies of the mass media for myth making and morale building. The British artist Henry Moore's (1898–1986) drawings of ordinary people in air raid shelters (completed under an official commission) evoke the survival of civilized values in the midst of unspeakable degradation. Perhaps the most famous musical work from the war is Dmitri Shostakovich's (1906–1975) *Seventh Symphony*—now universally known as the *Leningrad Symphony* and a symbol of human resilience. Shostakovich composed the early drafts of this work in Leningrad while German shells were falling, and it was actually performed in Leningrad in August 1942, while the city was still under siege.

During the war, film came into its own as an artistic form capable of creating important myths of national unity. Laurence Olivier's version of Shakespeare's *Henry V* (1944) comforted British moviegoers with its classic story of a stirring English military victory against huge odds. In Italy, a group of filmmakers known as the Neo-Realists created a set of films that dramatized the Resistance spirit of national unity. Shot on location, with amateur actors and realistic sets, films such as Roberto Rossellini's *Open City* (1945) depicted lower-class life with honesty and respect and called for the creation of a better society from the rubble of the old.

### Planning for Reconstruction

Rossellini's call for the creation of a new society was echoed throughout Europe during the war. Across Europe a consensus emerged on the need for *social democracy,* a society in which the state intervenes in economic life to ensure both public welfare and social justice. As early as December 1942, a government committee set out a radical plan for a new Britain. In rather unusual language for an official document, the committee's report identified "five giants on the road to reconstruction": Want, Disease, Ignorance, Squalor, and Idleness. To slay these giants, the committee recommended that the state assume responsibility for ensuring full employment and a minimum standard of living for all through the provision of family allowances, social welfare programs, and a national health service. The Beveridge Report (named after the committee's chairman) became a bestseller in Britain and the basis for a number of postwar European social welfare plans. Churchill, however, reacted lukewarmly to its proposals—a major reason for his defeat in the election of June 1945. The Labour Party, which enthusiastically endorsed the Beveridge Report and campaigned with slogans such as "Fair Shares for All," won by a landslide. Similarly, Charles De Gaulle found that in order for his Free French Committee to be recognized as the provisional government of France, he had to display a commitment to democracy and radical social reform. Thus he espoused women's suffrage, and his government promised not only free medical services and expanded family allowances, but also the nationalization of key industries and economic planning.

Four factors explain this radical reorientation of European politics. First, and most important, as the war dragged on and the death tolls mounted, European men

## Wartime Gains

British children began enjoying free school milk during the war, as part of the state's efforts both to ensure equitable distribution of resources and to shore up the health of the population. Popular sentiment demanded that such communal efforts be continued in peacetime as well.

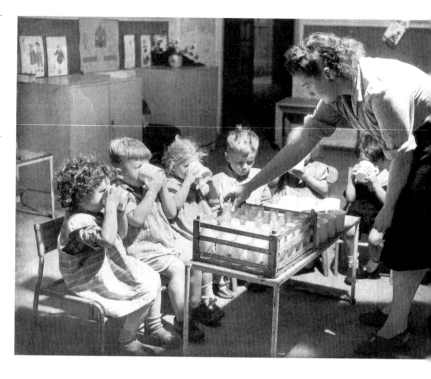

and women demanded that their suffering be worthwhile. They wanted to know that they were fighting not to rebuild the depressed and divided societies of the 1930s, but to construct a new Europe. Second, the war (and the ongoing revelations of Nazi atrocities) completely discredited the politics of the far right. This sort of politics, whether fascist, Nazi, or conservative-authoritarian, disappeared from legitimate political discussion. But in Europe (although not in the United States) the liberal ideal of the free and self-interested individual competing in an unregulated economy also lay in ruins, the victim of the prewar Great Depression. The new Europe, then, had to be built along different lines. The third factor that explains the radical reorientation of European politics was the combatant nations' success in mobilizing their economies for total war. If governments could regulate economies to fight wars, why could they not regulate economies for peacetime prosperity? Finally, the important role of socialists and communists in the Resistance enhanced the respectability of radical political ideas. Out of the Resistance came a determination to break the mold of prewar politics and create a new Europe. In France, for example, the Resistance Charter of 1944 demanded the construction of a "more just social order" through the nationalization of key industries, the establishment of a comprehensive social security system, and the recognition of the rights of workers to participate in management.

More generally, the Resistance raised key questions about the role of the individual in modern society. In the 1930s, many Europeans had been persuaded by Hitler,

Mussolini, and other far-right theorists that the individual was not important, that only the state mattered. But what the Resistance revealed is the power of human choice and the need for individual action in a world run amok. Despite—even because of—the horrors of the war, Europeans such as the French writer Albert Camus (1913–1960) emerged convinced of the power of human action: "A pessimist with respect to the human condition, I am an optimist with respect to man." Thus democracy reclaimed the activist state from fascism and Nazism on the one hand, and Stalinism on the other. Europeans saw that the power of the state could be used to improve the well-being of its citizens without at the same time trampling on the rights of the individual.

# Conclusion

### The New West: After Auschwitz and the Atom Bomb

The wartime encounter with the Nazi vision of the West as a race-based authoritarian order was crucial; from it emerged a sharpened commitment within the West to the processes and values of democracy. But to present the Second World War as a conflict between democracy and Nazism is to oversimplify. To defeat Nazi Germany, the democracies of Britain and the United States allied with Stalin's Soviet Union, a dictatorial regime that matched Hitler's Germany in its contempt for democratic values and human rights and that surpassed it in state-sanctioned mass murder.

The Soviet Union emerged from the war as the dominant power in eastern Europe; as we will see in the next chapter, the presence of the Red Army obliterated any chance to establish democratic governments in this region. The tensions inherent in the Anglo-American alliance with the Soviets led directly to the Cold War, the ideological and political conflict that dominated the post-World War II world and that once again forced a redefinition of the West. From 1949 until 1989, it was easy to draw the West on any map: One simply shaded in the United States and the countries allied to it—and against the Soviet Union. At the same time, however, a new division emerged. World War II marked the beginning of the end of European imperial control over the non-European world. The postwar era would thus see growing tensions between "North" and "South"—between the industrially developed nations and the underdeveloped regions seeking to shrug off their colonial past.

Much of the impetus for imperial control over non-European regions had come from the conviction of Western supremacy. During World War II, however, Japanese victories had exposed the illusion of Western military invincibility. And after the war, the gradual realization of the full horror of the Holocaust demolished any lingering claim to Western cultural superiority. What sort of superior position could be claimed by a culture in which educated, supposedly civilized men sent children into gas chambers disguised as showers? The atomic bombings of Hiroshima and Nagasaki added more questions to the ongoing debate about the meaning of the West. With the best of intentions, some of the greatest minds in the Western world had produced weapons designed to kill and maim tens of thousands of civilians within seconds. Had Western technology outdistanced Western ethics? And what about the implications of such technologies in a democratic society? For example, would the need to control such weapons lead to measures that eroded individual freedoms? Thus the assembly-line techniques of mass murder developed by the Nazis and, in very different ways, the sheer efficiency of the atom bomb in obliterating urban populations forced both individuals and their political leaders to confront the destructive potential of Western industrialism. For centuries, the use of the methods of scientific inquiry to uncover truth and achieve both material and moral progress had supported Westerners' self-identification and their sense of cultural superiority. But World War II demonstrated that the best of science could produce the worst of weapons, that technology and technique could combine in the death factory. The task of accepting this knowledge, and facing up to its implications, helped shape Western culture after 1945.

## Suggestions for Further Reading

For a comprehensive listing of suggested readings, please go to www.ablongman.com/levack2e/chapter26

Alperovitz, Gar. *Atomic Diplomacy: Hiroshima and Potsdam. The Use of the Atomic Bomb and the American Confrontation with Soviet Power.* 1994. The first edition of this book, published in 1965, sparked an ongoing scholarly debate about the role of Cold War concerns in shaping U.S. decision making at the end of World War II.

Browning, Christopher. *Ordinary Men: Reserve Police Battalion 101 and the Final Solution in Poland.* 1992. A powerful account of the participation of a group of "ordinary men" in mass murder.

Calder, Angus. *The People's War: Britain, 1939–1945.* 1969. Lengthy—but worth the effort for students wishing to explore the war's impact on British society. (Those who want a shorter account can turn to Robert Mackay, *The Test of War: Inside Britain 1939–45* [1999].)

Frayn, Michael. *Copenhagen.* 1998. A remarkable play in which Frayn dramatizes a meeting (that actually did occur) between the German atomic physicist Werner Heisenberg and his Danish anti-Nazi colleague Niels Bohr. Contains both extremely clear explanations of the workings of atomic physics and a provocative exploration of the moral issues involved in the making of the atom bomb.

Friedlander, Saul. *Nazi Germany and the Jews, 1933–1939.* 1998. An important study of the evolution of Nazi anti-Semitic policy before the war.

Hilberg, Raul. *Perpetrators, Victims, Bystanders: The Jewish Catastrophe, 1933–1945.* 1992. As his title indicates, Hilberg looks at the three principal sets of participants in the Holocaust.

Iriye, Akira. *The Origins of the Second World War in Asia and the Pacific.* 1987. Part of Longman's "Origins of Modern Wars" series aimed at university students, this short and readable study highlights the major issues and events.

Keegan, John. *The Second World War.* 1989. Provides clear explanations of military technologies and techniques; packed with useful maps and vivid illustrations.

Kitchen, Martin. *Nazi Germany at War.* 1995. A short and nicely organized survey of the German home front.

Marrus, Michael R. *The Holocaust in History.* 1987. A clearly written, concise account of historians' efforts to understand the Holocaust. Highly recommended.

Moore, Bob, ed. *Resistance in Western Europe.* 2000. A collection of essays that explores recent research on this controversial topic.

Overy, Richard. *Russia's War: A History of the Soviet War Effort, 1941–1945.* 1997. A compelling account, written to accompany the television documentary *Russia's War.*

Paxton, Robert. *Vichy France: Old Guard and New Order, 1940–1944.* 1972. A now-classic study of the aims and evolution of France's collaborationist government.

Rhodes, Richard. *The Making of the Atomic Bomb.* 1986. A lengthy but very readable account; very good at explaining the complicated science involved.

Rhodes, Richard. *Masters of Death: The SS-Einsatzgruppen and the Invention of the Holocaust.* 2002. Compelling account of the Einsatzgruppen actions during the German invasion of the Soviet Union.

Rock, William R. *British Appeasement in the 1930s.* 1977. A balanced and concise appraisal.

Weinberg, Gerhard. *A World at Arms: A Global History of World War II.* 1994. Places the war within a global rather than simply a European context.

## Notes

1. Quoted in Robert H. Abzug, *Inside the Vicious Heart: Americans and the Liberation of Nazi Concentration Camps* (1985), 19.

2. Quoted in Gordon Horwitz, *In the Shadow of Death: Living Outside the Gates of Mauthausen* (1991), 167.

3. Quoted in Piers Brendon, *The Dark Valley: A Panorama of the 1930s* (2000), 282.

4. Quoted in Richard Overy, *Russia's War* (1998), 95.

5. Quoted in Mark Mazower, *Dark Continent: Europe's Twentieth Century* (1999), 157.

6. Quoted in Peter Clarke, *Hope and Glory: Britain, 1900–1990* (1996), 204.

7. Quoted in Joachim Fest, *Hitler* (1973), 665.

8. Quotations from Juliet Gardiner, *"Over Here"—The GIs in Wartime Britain* (1992), 62, 53, 132.

9. Quoted in Richard Rhodes, *The Making of the Atomic Bomb* (1988), 474.

10. Quoted in Jane Slaughter, *Women in the Italian Resistance 1943–1945* (1997), 63.

11. Quoted in Bob Moore, ed., *Resistance in Western Europe* (2000), 210.

12. Gideon Hausner, *Justice in Jerusalem* (1966), 291.

13. Ibid., 323–324.

14. From Hausner's opening statement; quoted in Moshe Pearlman, *The Capture and Trial of Adolf Eichmann* (1963), 149.

15. Ibid., 463–465.

16. Ibid., 603; Hausner, *Justice in Jerusalem,* 422.

17. Quoted in Ulrich Herbert, *Hitler's Foreign Workers* (1997), 306.

18. Ibid., 149, 189.

19. Ibid., 149.

# Redefining the West After World War II

# 27

O N ONE APPARENTLY ORDINARY DAY IN AUGUST 1961, WESTERN European television viewers witnessed an extraordinary sight. While the news cameras rolled, policemen from East Berlin—the section of Berlin controlled by East Germany's communist government—played tug-of-war with firemen from West Berlin, the half of the city that belonged to the democratic state of West Germany. Between them was not a length of rope, but rather a middle-aged German woman. This horrifying contest had been set in motion by the construction of the Berlin Wall. Appalled by the growing numbers of East German citizens who were fleeing communist rule through the gateway of West Berlin, the East German and Soviet authorities decided to shut the gate. In the early morning hours of August 13, East German workers erected a barbed-wire fence along Berlin's east-west dividing line. In some cases, this line ran right through apartment buildings. For the next few weeks, these apartments provided literal "windows to the west." West Berlin firemen waited with blankets ready to catch anyone willing to jump out of a window—and out of communist eastern Europe. The woman caught on camera was one of a number of Berliners who sought to jump out a window in search of freedom.

These windows closed quickly. The communist authorities bricked them up; later they leveled entire apartment buildings to create a moat in front of what was now the armed fortress of East Berlin. The barbed-wire fence became a concrete wall buttressed by gun towers, lit by searchlights, and patrolled by armed guards with "shoot to kill" orders.

The unidentified woman literally caught between West and East serves as an appropriate symbol for Europe during the 1950s and 1960s. In these decades, the Cold War between the United States and the Soviet Union influenced European politics, culture, and society. European governments and their populations found their freedom of maneuver checked by Cold War constraints. The woman's desperation to reach the West reminds us that American influence in western Europe should not be equated with Soviet

**No!** The fear of nuclear war colored the post–World War II decades, as this 1958 poster from the Soviet Union attests.

**Tug-of-War at the Berlin Wall**
Caught by the television cameras, this woman sought to escape through her window into West Berlin. She succeeded.

Significantly, the Cold War turned "hot" not in Europe but in places such as Korea, Cuba, and Vietnam. The developing world served as the site of crucial Cold War conflicts in this era. The postwar years witnessed the widening of the economic gap between "North" and "South"—between the industrialized nations, largely located in the Northern Hemisphere, and the economically underdeveloped regions (many but certainly not all of which were situated south of the equator), now shrugging off colonial rule and seeking both political independence and economic prosperity. Thus, as Europeans encountered each other across the Cold War divide, they also encountered non-Europeans across a huge economic gulf. Two very different contests—North versus South and West versus East—quickly became entangled with each other as the Cold War moved beyond Europe's borders to the developing regions.

To explore the impact of these encounters on the postwar West, this chapter addresses four questions:

- Why and how did the world step from World War II to the Cold War?
- What was the impact of decolonization and the Cold War on the global balance of power?
- What patterns characterized the history of the Soviet Union and eastern Europe after the death of Stalin?
- What patterns characterized the history of western Europe in the 1950s and 1960s?

# A Dubious Peace, 1945–1949

- Why and how did the world step from World War II to the Cold War?

World War II ended in the spring of 1945, but the killing did not. Postwar purges and deportations ensured that the death totals continued to mount, while in many regions, world war gave way to civil war. Most significantly, as the "hot" war waned, the Cold War between the Soviet Union and the countries it controlled, and the United States and its Western allies, began.

## Devastation, Death, and Continuing War

If there was peace in Europe and Asia in 1945, it was the "peace of a graveyard," with an estimated 55 million people dead. In the immediate postwar period, the death statistics continued to rise as the victors turned with vengeful fury against the vanquished. In Czechoslovakia, purges killed 30,000 collaborators between 1945 and 1948. In Yugoslavia, Tito ordered the massacre of anticommunists. No one

control of eastern Europe: Cultural and economic dominance are not the same as political tyranny. Nevertheless, many Europeans in the West as well as the East felt that they no longer controlled their own societies.

The Cold War was in part an encounter of two clashing ideologies, as much a battle of ideas and values as weapons and warriors. Both sides laid claim to universal cultures—to have achieved a way of life that would benefit *all* human societies. This ideological encounter forced a redefinition of "the West." Previous chapters have described the way in which this cultural construct shifted over time. By the late nineteenth century, Christianity, although still important, played a less central role in defining "the West" than did a mix of other factors, including the possession of industrial technology, the illusion of white superiority based on pseudoscientific racist theorizing, and faith in both capitalist economics and liberal political values. The Cold War added an anti-Soviet stance and a fear of communist ideology to the mix. These additions at times eroded the Western commitment to democracy, particularly within the developing world.

knows how many died; some estimates range as high as 60,000.

Those left alive faced the overwhelming task of reconstruction. Throughout Europe, the bombers had rendered most highways, rail tracks, and waterways unusable. With laborers, seed, fertilizer, and basic equipment all in short supply, agricultural production in 1945 stood below 50 percent of prewar levels. Less visible, but just as devastating, was the destruction of the financial system. Few European currencies were worth much. In occupied Germany, cigarettes replaced marks as the unit of exchange.

One of the most serious problems facing Europe was that of the refugees or displaced persons (DPs). The war, and Hitler's attempt at racial reordering, had uprooted millions from their homes. The DP problem grew even larger as a result of the peace settlement. The Soviet Union kept the Polish territories it had claimed in 1939 and Poland received a large chunk of what had been prewar Germany. The new Polish government then expelled the German inhabitants from this region. In Czechoslovakia, Romania, Yugoslavia, and Hungary, too, ethnic Germans were forced out. More than 11 million Germans suffered from these

## Map 27.1  Europe in the Cold War

As this map shows, during the Cold War the "West" was defined culturally and politically, rather than in geographic terms. Greece and Turkey stand far to the east in Europe, yet their membership in NATO placed both within the "West."

deportations. As many as two million died en route to Germany. In addition, between 1945 and 1948, eastern European governments forcibly transferred seven million non-German refugees, in a brutal solution to the ethnic divisions that had destabilized prewar political structures.

Forced deportation can be understood as a continuation of war—a war carried out by governments against groups marked as dangerous because of their ethnic makeup. Other forms of war also continued after 1945. Ukrainian nationalists kept up a guerilla war against the Soviets until the early 1950s. In Greece civil war between communist and anticommunist forces raged until 1949, while in Trieste (along the Italian-Yugoslav border) civil war continued until 1954. In the forests and marshes of Poland, anticommunist guerilla groups fought against the new communist regime until 1956.

## From Hot to Cold War

The Cold War
Military
Stand-off

The conflict that aroused the most alarm and posed the greatest threat to the dubious peace after 1945 was the Cold War°, the struggle for global supremacy between the United States and the Soviet Union.

Within just a few years of the defeat of Germany and Japan, the allies became enemies, and what Winston Churchill called an "Iron Curtain" dropped between eastern and western Europe. The divisions of the Cold War were rooted in World War II, nurtured by the fears and hopes it aroused.

### Fraying Seams, 1943–1945

Each of the Allied leaders had different aims and interests. To ensure his own and the Soviet Union's security, Stalin demanded communist-controlled governments along the Soviet borders. In contrast, U.S. president Franklin D. Roosevelt believed that global international security and economic prosperity depended on the establishment of European democracies, committed to capitalist economic principles and practices. British prime minister Winston Churchill possessed a third set of aims. Concerned about the postwar balance of power in Europe and the maintenance of the British Empire, Churchill recognized that once Germany was defeated, a power vacuum would exist in central and eastern Europe. He feared that the Soviets might prove too eager to fill that vacuum. A permanent Soviet presence in the Balkans particularly threatened British military and economic interests throughout the Mediterranean. The "Big Three°," then, came to the negotiating table with

**The Big Three I (Yalta, February 1945)**
From 1941 until April 1945, the Big Three meant Churchill, Roosevelt, and Stalin. At the very end of the war, however, the composition of the Big Three suddenly changed, as Harry Truman replaced Roosevelt and Clement Attlee replaced Churchill.

clashing interests and aims; even before the war ended, the fabric of the alliance was under strain.

Reluctant to place too much pressure on the alliance's fraying seams, Roosevelt opted for postponing the hard decisions. He was not seeking simply to sidestep controversy. Rather, he hoped that the controversial questions would be settled after the war by a new international body, the United Nations (UN). In Roosevelt's vision, such a body could succeed where the now-discredited League of Nations had failed: It could guarantee that conciliation and negotiation would replace armed conflict in settling disputes between countries. Roosevelt recognized that if the Soviet Union refused to participate in the United Nations, the UN, like the league, would be a failure. Therefore he sought to avoid confrontations that might give Stalin a reason to block Soviet membership in the UN.

Roosevelt also hoped that new international economic structures would provide a framework for settling the disputes that divided the Allies. In 1944 leading American and European economists gathered in New Hampshire to construct a system for postwar economic revival. Well aware of the economic chaos that had followed World War I, and desperate to avoid a repeat of the Great Depression of the 1930s, they drew up the Bretton Woods Agreement°, which became the basic framework for the Western postwar economic order. To keep the global economy running smoothly, Bretton Woods established the American dollar as the world's reserve currency and fixed the currency exchange rates of its forty-four participating nations. It also established two new international economic institutions—the International Monetary Fund (IMF), to maintain the stability of member currencies, and the World Bank, to encourage global economic development.

Through the establishment of such international organizations as the IMF and the UN, Roosevelt sought "the end of the system of unilateral action, the exclusive alliances, the spheres of influence, the balances of power, and all the expedients that have been tried for centuries and have always failed." Yet neither Stalin nor Churchill shared Roosevelt's vision. Standing on opposite ends of the political spectrum, the Russian communist and the English aristocrat both continued to believe in precisely those "spheres of influence, the balances of power" that Roosevelt proclaimed outmoded. In the worldview of both Stalin and Churchill, armed force, not a new international organization, would determine the shape of the postwar world. As Stalin pointed out to Tito, the Yugoslav communist leader, "Everyone imposes his own system as far as his armies can reach. It cannot be otherwise."

By 1945, Stalin's army had a long reach. When the Big Three met in Yalta in February 1945, the communist partisans controlled Yugoslavia, and the Soviet Army had occupied Romania, Bulgaria, Hungary, and much of Czechoslovakia. This situation was in part the result of earlier Big Three negotiations. Throughout 1942 and 1943,

Stalin had pressed his Allies to open a Second Front in Europe and so relieve the pressure on Soviet forces. Churchill, concerned about the prospect of Soviet armies moving into eastern Europe, wanted to push into German-dominated Europe through the Balkans—and thus ensure that British and American forces were on the ground in eastern Europe when the war ended. But at the first Big Three summit in Tehran in 1943, Stalin and Roosevelt overruled Churchill and agreed that the Anglo-American invasion would be a single, concentrated attack across the English Channel into France (the D-Day invasion of June 1944). This decision left eastern Europe open to the Red Army.

The presence of the Red Army in eastern Europe weakened the negotiating positions of Churchill and Roosevelt at Yalta. Roosevelt's desire to obtain Stalin's commitment to enter the war against Japan also reduced his bargaining power. A series of problematic compromises resulted. Stalin signed a declaration promising free elections in eastern Europe; at the same time, Roosevelt and Churchill agreed that such freely elected governments should be pro-Soviet. Germany's future remained undecided although the Big Three agreed to share the postwar occupation by dividing Germany, as well as the symbolically and strategically vital city of Berlin, into occupation zones controlled by the United States, the Soviet Union, France, and Britain.

The final Big Three summit in the German city of Potsdam in July 1945 did not bridge the gap between the Soviet Union and its allies. At this summit, Stalin faced two unfamiliar negotiating partners. The new U.S. president Harry Truman (1884–1972) replaced Roosevelt, who had died in April, and midway through the summit, the new British prime minister, Labour Party leader Clement Attlee, arrived to take Churchill's place. The change of personnel made little difference, however. Stalin was determined to maintain control over the territories occupied by his armies, while the British and Americans increasingly saw Stalin's demands as a threat to both democratic ideals and the European balance of power. Moreover, during the summit Truman received a telegraph informing him of the successful Trinity test of the atomic bomb in New Mexico (see Chapter 26). This news meant that the war against Japan would soon be over—and that the Americans and British no longer needed or wanted Stalin to join the war in the Pacific. With Western incentives for placating Stalin now removed, the tone of the negotiations became more hostile.

Yet the wartime alliance had not yet completely torn apart. Throughout the rest of 1945 and 1946 Truman hoped to resolve the allies' differences and resisted the idea of a permanent American military presence in Europe. Stalin, too, was unwilling to push too far. He not only feared American military might, but also wished to retain access to Western economic assistance and expertise. In addition, to get his economy moving again, Stalin needed to scale back military expenditures. Thus he proceeded with rapid demilitarization: Soviet army strength went from 12 million men in 1945 to 3 million by 1948. He also adopted a policy of passivity for communist parties operating in regions that he viewed as part of the Western sphere of influence. He refused to assist Greek communists seeking to overthrow the British-backed monarchical regime, and he ordered communist parties in western Europe to participate with non-communists in coalition governments.

During this period, however, the British pushed Truman to adopt a hard line toward Stalin and his demands. British foreign policy was in the hands of the foreign secretary, Ernest Bevin (1881–1951). A labor leader with a history of fighting against communist efforts to control British unions, Bevin was a fierce anti-Stalinist. He was also an ardent British nationalist who regarded the maintenance of the British Empire, particularly in the Mediterranean and the Middle East, as crucial to preserving Britain's Great Power status in the postwar world. Bevin thus urged the United States to stand tough when the Soviets demanded a stake in what had been Italy's North African empire and he urged a strong response when Stalin delayed pulling Russian troops out of Iran. (Soviet and British troops had occupied Iran during the war to keep its oil supplies out of German hands.)

### Torn in Two, 1946–1949

Within just a few years of the war's end, clashing aims and interests had shredded the wartime alliance. Three key developments—the breakdown of cooperation over Germany, the Truman Doctrine°, and the Marshall Plan°—tore apart the former allies.

Allied cooperation in the occupation of defeated Germany quickly broke down over economic issues. At Potsdam, Truman and Attlee had agreed to Stalin's demand for German reparations. By 1946, however, British and American authorities became convinced that Germany faced mass starvation. To feed the Germans in the British zone, Attlee's government imposed bread rationing on the British public—a drastic step never taken during the war itself. The British and Americans decided that the immediate priority must be German economic recovery. To stabilize Germany's economy, they combined their zones into a single economic unit and, much to Stalin's fury, stopped reparations deliveries to Soviet territory.

The announcement of the Truman Doctrine the following year intensified the hostilities between Stalin and the West. In February 1947 Attlee's government informed Truman's administration that it could not afford to continue its fight against communist rebels in Greece. The United States immediately assumed Britain's role in Greece, but more importantly, Truman used this development to issue the Truman Doctrine, which committed the U.S. to the policy of containment°, resisting communist expansion wherever in the world it occurred.

President Harry Truman: The Truman Doctrine (1947)

## Curtains and Camps

*The Cold War gave rise to a new set of metaphors, as politicians, diplomats, and journalists struggled to find ways to explain the new world order. Two of the most compelling metaphors arose very early: the "Iron Curtain," coined by Winston Churchill in 1946, and "the two camps," used in a speech by Stalin's spokesman Andrei Zhdanov in 1947.*

*In 1946, Churchill was still the leader of Britain's Conservative Party but was no longer prime minister. On a visit to the United States, he gave a pivotal speech that warned of a divided Europe.*

From Stettin in the Baltic to Trieste in the Adriatic, an iron curtain has descended across the Continent. Behind that line lie all the capitals of the ancient states of Central and Eastern Europe. Warsaw, Berlin, Prague, Vienna, Budapest, Belgrade, Bucharest and Sofia, all these famous cities and the populations around them lie in what I must call the Soviet sphere, and all are subject in one form or another, not only to Soviet influence but to a very high and, in many cases, increasing measure of control from Moscow. . . .

*At the founding meeting of the Cominform in September 1947, Zhdanov delivered a speech that clearly articulated the postwar division of the world into two hostile blocs.*

In the post-war period sharp changes have taken place in the international situation. . . . Two opposite political lines took shape: at one pole, the policy of the USSR and the democratic countries, aimed at undermining imperialism and strengthening democracy; at the other pole the policy of the USA and Britain, aimed at strengthening imperialism and strangling democracy. . . .

Thus two camps have come into being. . . .

The Truman-Marshall Plan is only one component part . . . of a general plan of worldwide expansionist policy that is being carried out by the USA in all parts of the world. . . . Yesterday's aggressors, the capitalist magnates of Germany and Japan, are being groomed by America for a new role, that of serving as an instrument of the USA's imperialist policy in Europe and Asia. . . . Under these conditions it is essential for the anti-imperialist and democratic camp to close ranks, work out a common programme of actions and develop its own tactics against the main forces of the imperialist camp. . . .

Sources: From a speech by Winston Churchill, delivered to Westminster College, Fulton, Missouri, March 5, 1946; and from G. Procacci (ed.), *The Cominform: Minutes of the Three Conferences 1947, 1948, 1949*, Milan, 1994.

## A War of Words

The poster on the left demonstrates the official Soviet view of NATO: an American device to dominate Europe. The poster on the right warns Italian voters that if they vote for the Italian Communist Party, the Soviet Union will be their boss.

The Marshall Plan further divided Europe into two hostile camps. In 1947, U.S. secretary of state General George Marshall (1880–1959) toured Europe and grew alarmed at the devastation and despair that he witnessed across the Continent. Fearing that hungry Europeans might turn to communism, Marshall proposed that the United States underwrite Europe's economic recovery. Initially, Marshall's proposal received little attention in the United States, but in Britain, Foreign Secretary Ernest Bevin heard a report of it on the radio. Believing that British interests demanded a firm American commitment to Europe, Bevin perceived the Marshall Plan as the first step toward establishing this ongoing U.S. presence. He called the plan "a lifeline to sinking men." Bevin's French counterpart, Foreign Minister Georges Bidault (1899–1983), shared his enthusiasm, and together they helped make the Marshall Plan a reality. With representatives from twelve other European states, Bevin and Bidault drew up a list of European resources and requirements and devised a four-year plan for European economic reconstruction. In 1948, the first food shipments from the United States reached European ports. Eventually $17 billion in aid poured into Europe, while a new international body, the Organization for European Economic Cooperation (OEEC), worked to coordinate aid, eliminate trade barriers, and stabilize currencies.

The Marshall Plan helped integrate the economies of western Europe and accelerated Europe's leap into postwar prosperity. Stalin's response to the plan, however, cemented the division of East and West. The United States offered aid to any country that chose to accept it, including the Soviet Union and the states of eastern Europe, but required participating governments to join the OEEC. Stalin viewed the OEEC as an instrument of American economic domination and so refused to allow eastern European governments to accept Marshall aid. When the Czechs tried to do so, he engineered a communist coup that destroyed what remained of democracy in Czechoslovakia.

## The Outbreak of the Cold War

**1943**

| | |
|---|---|
| November | Tehran Conference |

**1944**

| | |
|---|---|
| August | Soviet Army advances into Balkans |
| October | Soviets link up with Tito's partisans in Yugoslavia |

**1945**

| | |
|---|---|
| January | Soviet Army advances into Poland |
| February | Yalta Conference |
| July | Potsdam Conference |
| August | United States drops atomic bombs on Hiroshima and Nagasaki |

**1946**

| | |
|---|---|
| March | Churchill gives his "Iron Curtain" speech in Missouri |

**1947**

| | |
|---|---|
| February | Truman Doctrine announced |
| June | Marshall Plan announced |
| **1948** | Stalinist terror in eastern Europe underway |

**1949**

| | |
|---|---|
| April | Formation of North Atlantic Treaty Organization (NATO) |
| May | Official formation of West Germany (Federal Republic of Germany) |
| August | Soviet atomic bomb test |

In 1949, the basic Cold War pattern that would hold for forty years took shape. The British and American zones of occupied Germany, joined with the French zone, became the Western-allied state of West Germany. The Soviet zone became communist East Germany. In April 1949 nine western European nations[1] allied with the United States and Canada in the North Atlantic Treaty Organization (NATO)°, a military alliance specifically aimed at repelling a Soviet invasion of western Europe. Months later, on August 29, 1949, the Soviet Union tested its own atomic bomb. Over the next few years, Stalin forced his eastern European satellites into an anti-Western military alliance (finalized as the Warsaw Pact° in 1955) and both the United States and the Soviet Union developed hydrogen

bombs. Europe stood divided into two hostile military blocs, each dominated by a superpower in possession of a nuclear arsenal.

# The West and the World: Decolonization and the Cold War

■ **What was the impact of decolonization and the Cold War on the global balance of power?**

While the conflict between East and West dominated much of the postwar period, it soon blended with a very different struggle, that between the peoples of the developing nations and European imperialism. By the end of the 1960s, the age of the vast European overseas empires had finally ended. As decolonization became entangled with Cold War rivalries, superpower influence replaced European imperial control in many areas of the world. The Soviet Union and the United States used economic and military aid, as well as covert action, to cajole and coerce newly independent nations into choosing sides in the global Cold War conflict. The superpowers served as magnetic poles, drawing competing nationalist forces toward themselves and so entangling Cold War concerns with nationalist independence struggles throughout the world.

## The End to the Age of European Empires

In the economic hard times following World War II, European governments regarded their empires as more crucial than ever. Faced with the reality of superpower domination in Europe, nations such as Britain and France looked to their imperial possessions to give them international power and prestige. The war, however, had aroused nationalists' demands for independence from European rule to a fever pitch. They pointed to the inherent contradiction between the Allies' claim to be fighting for democracy and the fact that many Allied states denied democratic rights to their imperial subjects. In the Pacific region, many colonial nationalists had sided with the Japanese against the British, Dutch, and French, whom they regarded not as defenders of democracy but as imperial overlords. The Japanese internment of the Dutch population in Indonesia in 1942 allowed nationalists to assume positions in the country's government. In Burma, the student-based nationalist movement, led by Aung San (1915–1947), supported the Japanese invasion. Similarly, the Indian nationalist Subhas Chandra Bose

(1897–1945) formed a National Army that fought alongside the Japanese and against the British. Of the 45,000 Indian troops captured by the Japanese in the conquests of Malaya and Singapore, 40,000 chose to join Bose's army.

When the war ended, these nationalists resisted European efforts to reimpose imperial rule, and a series of bloody colonial conflicts resulted. In Indonesia, for example, war raged from 1945 to 1949, as the Dutch fought bitterly to keep hold of a region they viewed as vital to their economic survival. They lost the fight, however, and in 1949 the nationalist Ahmed Sukarno led his country into independence.

Like the Dutch, the British found their empire in revolt in the postwar period. Throughout the war Churchill had placed a high priority on preserving the British Empire, but the economic and military demands of total war significantly weakened Britain's ability to control its far-flung possessions. Clement Attlee, who succeeded Churchill as prime minister in July 1945, sought to retain Britain's hold on its essential imperial interests by jettisoning those that Britain no longer needed—or could no longer afford.

## CHRONOLOGY

### The End to European Empire

**1946** French colonial war in Indochina begins

**1947** India, Pakistan, and Burma achieve independence

**1948** State of Israel established; apartheid regime in South Africa comes into power

**1949** Indonesia achieves independence from Dutch rule

**1954** Defeat of French forces in Indochina; partition Vietnam; beginning of Franco-Algerian War

**1955** Bandung Conference: the "Third World" is born

**1957** Kwame Nkrumah becomes first prime minister of Ghana

**1960** Congo, Nigeria, and most French colonies in Africa become independent

**1962** Algeria achieves independence from French rule

**1963** Jomo Kenyatta becomes first prime minister of Kenya

**1965** U.S. bombing of North Vietnam begins

**1967** Suharto ousts Sukarno as leader of Indonesia

## Map 27.2   After Empire: Independent Asia

Dates of national formation often give no indication of the continuing political upheaval and violence that afflicted the countries of Asia in the postwar period. The formation of the nations of Vietnam, Laos, and Cambodia in 1953–1954, for example, did not mean an end to warfare in Indochina.

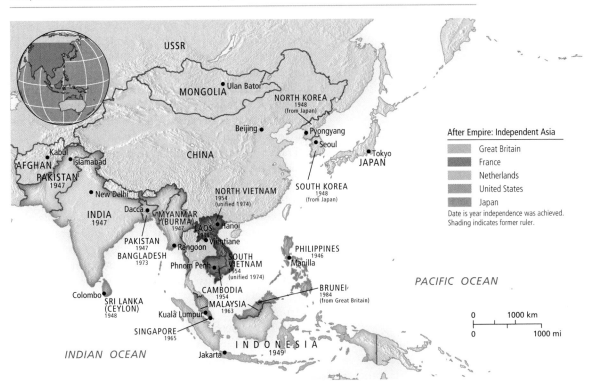

The British first jettisoned the Indian subcontinent. During World War II, the refusal of Indian nationalists to cooperate with the war effort made clear that Britain could no longer rule India. After the war, therefore, Attlee's government opened negotiations with nationalist leaders. Muslim nationalists led by Muhammad Ali Jinnah (1876–1948) refused to accept citizenship in an independent state dominated by Hindus, and won from the British the creation of a separate Muslim state—Pakistan. India and Pakistan, as well as Burma, received independence in August 1947 (see Map 27.2). The partition of the Indian subcontinent sparked widespread devastation, just as the redrawing of boundary lines in eastern Europe had resulted in brutal deportations and mass death. More than ten million people fled their homes and became refugees—Muslims fearing Hindu rule, Hindus fearing Muslim rule, Sikhs fear-

The Tandon Family at Partition (1947)

ing both. Mahatma Gandhi traveled from village to village in some of the most afflicted areas and begged for an end to the killing, but the death tolls reached 250,000—and included Gandhi himself, who was shot by an assassin just six months after India achieved independence.

In Palestine, too, British retreat led to bloodshed. After the war in Europe ended, European Jewish refugees, persuaded by Hitler that a Jew could be safe only in a Jewish state, poured into British-controlled Palestine. Many soon found themselves waging guerilla warfare against the British, who sought to maintain regional political stability by limiting Jewish immigration. Faced with mounting violence as well as growing international pressure to grant Jewish demands for statehood, the British turned the problem over to the new United Nations. At the end of 1947, the UN adopted a plan calling for the partition of Palestine into a Jewish and Arab state. Arab leaders rejected the plan, however, and the British pulled out their troops in May 1948 without transferring authority to either party. Jewish leaders immediately proclaimed the new state of Israel, and the region erupted into all-out war. After nine months of fighting, an uneasy peace descended, based on a partition of Palestine among Israel, Jordan, and Egypt (see Map 27.3). Approximately 750,000 Palestinian Arabs became stateless refugees.

By withdrawing from hot spots such as India and Palestine, the British hoped to preserve and stabilize what remained of the British Empire. During the 1950s, successive British governments sought to diminish the force of nationalism throughout their colonial territories by diverting it down channels of constitutional reform and systems of power sharing—and then fiercely stomping down on nationalists who broke out of these channels. Many African leaders, such as Kwame Nkrumah (1957–1966) in Ghana and Jomo Kenyatta (1963–1978) in Kenya, moved from British prison cells to prime ministerial or presidential offices. Neither compromise nor coercion could stem the tide of nationalism, and by the end of the 1960s, the British Empire had been reduced to an assortment of island territories.

France, too, saw its empire disintegrate in the postwar decades despite efforts to resist nationalist movements. In Indochina, the nationalist leader Ho Chi Minh (1890–1969) adopted the U.S. Declaration of Independence for his model when he proclaimed independence in September 1945. The stirring rhetoric, however, failed to convince the French, who fought for almost a decade to retain their hold in southeast Asia. But in 1954, the French army suffered a decisive defeat at Dien Bien Phu in Vietnam, and French rule in Indochina ended.

Humiliated by this defeat, French army officers responded ferociously to the outbreak of a nationalist revolt in Algeria that same year. Many prominent politicians and ordinary men and women shared the army's view that France had been pushed too far and must now stand fast.

## Map 27.3 Israel and Its Neighbors, 1949

The map inset outlines the United Nations' plan to partition Palestine into Jewish and Arab states, with Jerusalem as an international zone. This plan was not implemented.

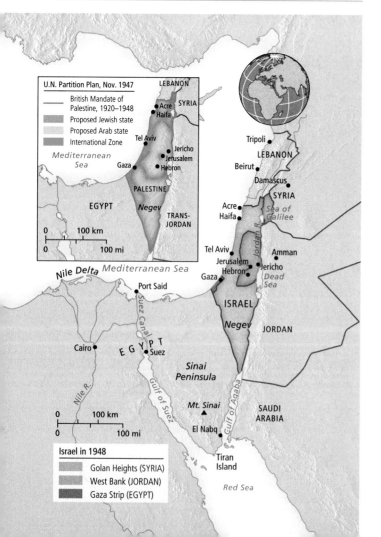

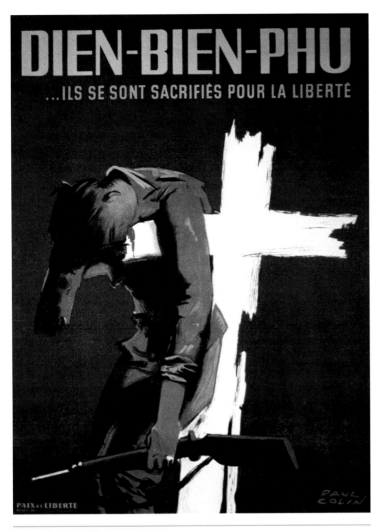

# DIEN-BIEN-PHU
## ...ILS SE SONT SACRIFIÉS POUR LA LIBERTÉ

PAIX et LIBERTÉ

PAUL COLIN

**Imperial Sacrifice**

This poster reminds French men and women of the sacrifice made by their army at the Battle of Dien Bien Phu in Vietnam: "They sacrificed themselves for your liberty." The memory of the army's defeat at Dien Bien Phu helped strengthen French determination to hold on to Algeria.

France teetered on the brink of civil war, with French army officers preparing for an assault on Paris. The World War II hero Charles De Gaulle forced through a new constitution, which sharply tilted the balance of power in French domestic politics toward the president (conveniently De Gaulle himself).

## The Imperialist Legacy

As the Algerian crisis showed, decolonization was not something that just happened "out there" in the world beyond the West; rather it had an often profound impact on Western politics. In the United States, for example, the burgeoning African-American civil rights movement directly linked its struggle to the colonial independence movements happening at the same time. As the civil rights leader Martin Luther King Jr. (1929–1968) asserted, "the determination of Negro Americans to win freedom from all forms of oppression springs from the same deep longing that motivates oppressed peoples all over the world."[2] Organizations such as the National Association for the Advancement of Colored People (NAACP), founded in 1910, had long fought against racial discrimination in the United States, but in the 1950s, in part inspired by nationalists' battles around the globe, the civil-rights struggle became a mass movement with an innovative program of "freedom rides," lunch counter sit-ins, boycotts, and voter registration campaigns.

The legacy of imperialist rule lingered long, particularly in areas with large white European settlements such as Rhodesia and South Africa. Despite UN sanctions and a violent black nationalist movement, white settlers in Rhodesia (present-day Zimbabwe) retained a lock on political and economic power until 1980. In South Africa, the white supremacist Afrikaner Nationalist Party assumed control in 1948 and implemented the policies of apartheid°, the rigid segregation of communities based on race. To break down any chance of resistance, the apartheid regime deliberately accentuated tribal divisions among black South Africans and denied them basic human rights. The "No Trial Act" of 1963, for example, gave the government the right to detain anyone, without charge or trial, for as long as it chose.

Imperialism also left a long-lasting economic legacy. European states lost their monopoly on the raw materials and markets of their one-time colonies, yet in the postcolonial era, African states grew more economically dependent than ever on the West, a development that anti-Western

VIDEO

Creating Apartheid in South Africa

The result was the Franco-Algerian War, a brutal fight that raged from 1954 until the early 1960s. By the time Algeria claimed independence in 1962 (see Map 27.4), approximately 200,000 Algerian nationalist fighters had been killed or imprisoned. Fifteen thousand French soldiers and auxiliary forces were dead, as were almost 23,000 civilians in both France and Algeria.

The Franco-Algerian War seriously divided French society, called into question the meaning of French democracy, and transformed France's political structure. Supporters of the French army in Algeria saw it as a force fighting on behalf of Western civilization against barbarism (both Muslim and communist). Critics, pointing to the evidence that the French army used torture against its enemies, argued that the war threatened to corrupt French society. By 1958

# Rejecting the West

*Born in Martinique, Frantz Fanon became a champion of Algerian independence. He died of leukemia in 1961, shortly before an independent Algeria came into being. His writings, published posthumously, articulated clearly the discontent of the colonized. Riveting dissections of the relations of power in Western capitalism, they also helped inspire the protests of 1968.*

"The last shall be first and the first last."* Decolonization is the putting into practice of this sentence. . . . The naked truth of decolonization evokes for us the searing bullets and bloodstained knives which emanate from it. For if the last shall be first, this will only come to pass after a murderous and decisive struggle between the two protagonists.

. . . As soon as the native begins to pull on his moorings, and to cause anxiety to the settler, he is handed over to well-meaning souls who in cultural congresses point out to him the specificity and wealth of Western values. But . . . it so happens that when the native hears a speech about Western culture he pulls out his knife—or at least he makes sure it is within reach. The violence with which the supremacy of white values is affirmed and the aggressiveness which has permeated the victory of these values over the ways of life and thought of the native mean that, in revenge, the native laughs in mockery when Western values are mentioned in front of him.

. . . For centuries the capitalists have behaved in the under-developed world like nothing more than war criminals. Deportations, massacres, forced labour and slavery have been the main methods used by capitalism to increase its wealth, its gold or diamond reserves, and to establish its power. . . . So when we hear the head of a European state declare with his hand on his heart that he must come to the help of the poor under-developed peoples, we do not tremble with gratitude. Quite the contrary; we say to ourselves: "It's a just reparation which will be paid to us."

---

\* *Fanon is quoting Jesus' words in Matthew 19:30. But as the rest of the excerpt makes clear, Fanon's interpretation of this verse contrasts with the usual Christian emphasis on submission.*

Source: From Frantz Fanon, *The Wretched of the Earth*, translated by Constance Farrington. Copyright © 1963 by Présence Africaine. Used by permission.

---

African nationalists labeled "neo-colonialism." Desperate for cash, newly independent African governments increased production of cash crops for export—cotton, coffee, nuts, sugar—and also expanded their mining industries, producing uranium, lithium, copper, tin, gold, diamonds, and zinc for Western markets. Such exports were extremely vulnerable to fluctuations in demand and prices. At the same time, African nations became ever more dependent on importing manufactured goods from the industrialized West, with aid from Western nations often contingent on trading deals requiring such imports.

For many of the newly independent nations of Africa and Asia, political stability proved as elusive as economic prosperity. To be solid, democratic political structures must rest on a foundation of popular participation, yet almost a century of imperialist rule made such participation very problematic. For example, when the Congo became independent in 1960, it possessed only sixteen university graduates out of a population of 13 million—the result of the Belgian policy of restricting Congolese children to a basic education. In Africa as a whole, 80 percent of the African people could not read or write. Not surprisingly, then, by 1966 military regimes had replaced elected governments in the former colonial territories of Nigeria, Congo Brazzaville, Burkina Faso, Algeria, the Benin Republic, and the Central African Republic. In many newly independent states, competition between rival groups for power led to civil war. Nigeria, which gained independence from Britain in 1960, was overcome by political corruption and regional secession. In its civil war, which began in 1966, at least one million people died, either in battle or from starvation. The Congo stepped directly from Belgian rule in 1960 into a protracted civil war.

## The Globalization of the Cold War

The process of decolonization often became entangled with Cold War rivalries, and in many regions, superpower influence replaced imperial control. In the Congo, for example, both overt and covert superpower involvement prolonged the civil war and destabilized the post-independence political structure. Despite fears of World War III and a Europe devastated by nuclear weapons, the Cold War actually turned hot only in places like the Congo—in the developing nations, at the intersection of superpower rivalries and nationalist conflicts.

### The Korean War, 1950–1953

The first such intersection occurred in Korea. Once part of the Japanese Empire, Korea, like Germany, was divided after World War II. A Soviet-linked communist regime as-

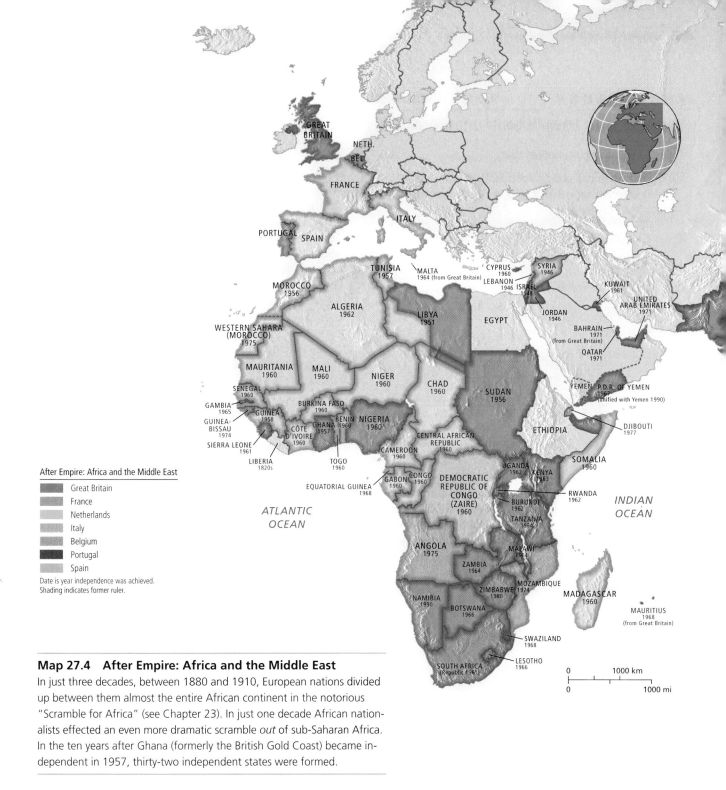

**Map 27.4   After Empire: Africa and the Middle East**

In just three decades, between 1880 and 1910, European nations divided up between them almost the entire African continent in the notorious "Scramble for Africa" (see Chapter 23). In just one decade African nationalists effected an even more dramatic scramble *out* of sub-Saharan Africa. In the ten years after Ghana (formerly the British Gold Coast) became independent in 1957, thirty-two independent states were formed.

sumed power in North Korea, and an anticommunist state propped up by the United States controlled the south. In 1950, North Korean troops invaded South Korea in an attempt to unite the country under communist rule. This civil war, a struggle between rival groups of Korean nationalists, was quickly swallowed up by the Cold War. A UN-sponsored, largely American army fought alongside South Korean troops, while the Soviet Union supplied

arms and Communist China provided soldiers to support North Korea.

The Korean War accelerated the globalization of the Cold War. As a result of the Korean conflict, the French government was able to persuade Truman's administration to support its struggle against Ho Chi Minh and the communist nationalists in Indochina, thus drawing the United States onto the path that would lead to its war in Vietnam.

The conflict in Korea also welded Japan firmly into the Western alliance. As the U.S. army turned to the Japanese for vital military supplies, more than $3.5 billion poured into and rejuvenated the Japanese economy. (American military orders for trucks guaranteed the success of a struggling new Japanese firm called Toyota.) Transformed from an occupied enemy to a staunch ally and an economic powerhouse, Japan became the dam holding back "the red tide that threatens to engulf the world."[3] Thus, in a curious way, Japan—geographically as far "East" as one can get—became a part of the "West."

The Korean War also solidified the Cold War and U.S. interests within Europe. Fearing that the war's outbreak signaled a more aggressive Soviet policy in Europe as well as Asia, western European leaders pushed for the transformation of NATO from a loose defensive alliance to a coordinated fighting force. This transformation, however, came at a price. As the U.S. military budget exploded from $13.5 billion to $50 billion per year, Truman's administration demanded that its European allies strengthen their own military forces and permit the rearmament of West Germany. With the trauma of German conquest and occupation so recently behind them, many Europeans were horrified by the prospect. Britain's prime minister Clement Attlee warned, "The policy of using Satan to defeat Sin is very dangerous." Even within West Germany the proposal aroused strong opposition, although Konrad Adenauer (1876–1967), the new state's first chancellor, argued that only a rearmed West Germany could prevent the forcible reunification of Germany on Soviet terms. After four years of controversy and a failed effort to create a western European army (the European Defense Community, or EDC), West Germany rearmed, as the United States had initially demanded, under the NATO umbrella.

## Changing Temperatures in the Cold War, 1953–1960

In 1953, both sides in the Cold War changed leaders. Stalin died in March, just a few months after a new Republican administration headed by President Dwight Eisenhower (1890–1969) took office in the United States. This change of leadership heralded a new phase in the Cold War. When Eisenhower took office, he condemned Truman's policy of *containing* communism as defeatist, a "negative, futile and immoral policy . . . which abandons countless human beings to a despotism and Godless terrorism."[4] Instead, he committed the United States to *roll back* communism and insisted that communist aggression would be met with massive nuclear retaliation. This newly aggressive American stance was matched on the other side of the Cold War divide. After a period of uncertainty following Stalin's death in 1953, Nikita Khrushchev (1955–1964) emerged in 1955 as the new Soviet leader. Loud and boisterous, given to off-the-cuff remarks and spontaneous displays of emotion, Khrushchev contrasted sharply with the disciplined, reserved Stalin. (It is hard to imagine Stalin taking off his shoe and beating it on a table, as Khrushchev did in front of the television cameras at an assembly of the United Nations.) Khrushchev played a dangerous game of nuclear bluff, in which he persistently and often quite successfully convinced allies and foes alike that the Soviet Union possessed a far stronger nuclear force than it actually did.

Both Khrushchev and Eisenhower recognized, however, that nuclear weapons made total war unwinnable and both sought ways to break out of the positions into which they were frozen by Cold War hostilities. Thus the period from 1953 until 1964 was characterized by thawing superpower relations followed by the icy blasts of renewed hostilities. In 1955, for example, representatives of Britain, France, the United States, and the Soviet Union met in Geneva for the first summit of the Cold War. This initial thaw ended one year later when Khrushchev sent tanks into Hungary to crush a nationalist rebellion—a clear demonstration that he would permit no challenge to Soviet authority in eastern Europe.

The Soviets' successful launch of the first human-made satellite, *Sputnik,* in 1957 was even more chilling. Khrushchev claimed—falsely—that the Soviets possessed an advanced intercontinental ballistic missile (ICBM) force and that Soviet factories were producing rockets "like sausages from a machine."[5] To western Europeans, *Sputnik* had especially ominous implications. The development of ICBMs meant that American cities were now vulnerable to a Soviet nuclear strike. Europeans began to ask themselves whether the United States would actually risk Chicago to save Paris: If the Soviets invaded western Europe with conventional forces, would the Americans respond with nuclear weapons and so open their own cities to nuclear retaliation?

Yet in the late 1950s, the Cold War ice seemed to be breaking once again. In 1958 the Soviet Union announced a voluntary suspension on nuclear testing. The United States and Britain followed suit and nuclear test ban talks opened in Geneva. The next year Khrushchev spent twelve days touring the United States—much to his regret, security concerns kept him from visiting Disneyland. The communist leader impressed Americans as a down-to-earth, ordinary sort of guy, a man rather than a monster. Khrushchev ended his U.S. visit with the promise of another four-power summit in 1960.

## On the Brink: The Berlin Wall and the Cuban Missile Crisis

These warming relations, however, turned frosty in 1960 after the Soviet Union announced it had shot down an American spy plane and captured its pilot. This announcement aborted the planned summit and initiated one of the most dangerous periods in the post–World War II era, during which the construction of Berlin Wall° provided a concrete symbol of the Cold War divide. As we saw at the beginning of this chapter, the continuing outflow of East Germans to the West through Berlin led the East German communist leader Walter Ulbricht (1893–1973) and Khrushchev to take dramatic action in 1961. Two weeks after the wall went up, the Soviet Union ended a three-year moratorium on nuclear testing. The new American president John F. Kennedy (1961–1963) increased military spending and called for an expanded civil defense program to prepare for nuclear war. Across Europe men and women feared that their countries would become a nuclear wasteland.

Such a war was narrowly avoided in the fall of 1962 as once again the Cold War intersected with a nationalist struggle. In 1959, a nationalist revolutionary movement led by Fidel Castro (b. 1926) toppled Cuba's pro-U.S. dictator. Castro quickly aligned Cuba with the Soviet Union. In 1962, Kennedy learned that the Soviets were building nuclear missile bases in Cuba. What Kennedy did not know was that the Soviet forces in Cuba were armed with nuclear weapons—and with the discretionary power to use these weapons if U.S. forces attacked. Some of Kennedy's advisers urged just such an attack, but instead the president used secret diplomatic channels to broker a compromise. Khrushchev removed the missiles and in exchange, Kennedy withdrew NATO's nuclear missiles from Turkey and guaranteed that the United States would not invade Cuba.

In the aftermath of the crisis, both the United States and the Soviet Union backed off from brinkmanship. In 1963, the superpowers agreed to stop aboveground nuclear testing with the Nuclear Test Ban treaty and set up between

them the "hotline," a direct communications link (at first not a telephone but a system of telegraph lines and teleprinters) to encourage immediate personal consultation in the event of a future crisis.

## Cold War Arenas: Vietnam and the Middle East

Yet relations between the superpowers remained tense throughout the 1960s, and the globalization of the Cold War accelerated. In both Southeast Asia and the Middle East, as the superpowers replaced European empires as regional powerbrokers, nationalist conflicts and regional power struggles escalated.

The transformation of the Vietnam War from a nationalist struggle against European imperial rule into a Cold War conflict illustrates this process clearly. After the defeat of French imperial forces at Dien Bien Phu in 1954, rival Vietnamese nationalists fought to control the Indochinese peninsula. Ho Chi Minh and his communist regime in North Vietnam relied on the Soviet Union and China for support, while American military and economic aid propped up an anticommunist government in South Vietnam. Under the Kennedy presidency (1961–1963), the number of military advisers in Vietnam expanded rapidly, as did American involvement in South Vietnamese politics.

When Kennedy's successor, Lyndon Johnson (1908–1973), took office, he issued a clear order, "Win the war!" In 1964, the American Congress granted Johnson the authority to take "all necessary measures" to do so. By 1968, more than 500,000 American soldiers were fighting in Vietnam. Fifty-eight thousand GIs died during the war—as did well over one million Vietnamese.

Like Vietnam, the Middle East also became a Cold War arena as the superpowers replaced the French and British in the region. During the 1950s, Gamel Abdel Nasser, a vehemently anti-Western Arab nationalist who took control of Egypt after the overthrow of the monarchy in 1952, proved adept at playing the superpowers against each other. When the United States withdrew its promised funding for the Aswan High Dam power plant, a massive project intended to harness the energy of the Nile River to fuel Egypt's economic development, Nasser simply turned to the Soviet Union for military and economic assistance.

The Six-Day War of June 1967 escalated the tendency of Middle Eastern states to pick sides in the Cold War. After a decade of heightened Arab nationalist rhetoric calling for the destruction of Israel, the Israeli government moved in a preemptive strike. Facing a surprise attack on three fronts, Arab forces quickly crumbled. In just six days of fighting, Israel gained possession of the Sinai peninsula from Egypt, the West Bank from Jordan, the Golan Heights from Syria—and one million stateless Palestinian refugees. (See Map 27.5.) In the wake of the war, U.S. foreign policy shifted to decisive support for Israel. In turn, Egypt, Syria, Iraq, Sudan, and Libya aligned with the Soviet Union.

## The Third World

Many newly independent nations sought to resist being pulled into the orbit of either superpower. In 1955, Ahmed Sukarno (1949–1966), the nationalist leader who had led Indonesia out from under Dutch rule six years before, hosted the Bandung Conference of "nonaligned" nations. Bandung signaled the desire of many national leaders to find a place for their nations between or apart from the United States or the Soviet Union. French jour-

nalists at the conference gave these nations a collective label—neither the first (Western, capitalist) nor the second (Eastern, communist) but rather the Third World°. Few of these nonaligned nations had much power on their own, but the General Assembly of the United Nations provided them with an important forum for making their voice heard. As the pace of decolonization accelerated, the number of independent nations voting in the UN grew.

## Map 27.5 The Results of the Six-Day War

A comparison of this map with Map 27.3 ("Israel and Its Neighbors, 1949," p. 894) reveals the startling results of the war of 1967. Israel's conquest of the Sinai peninsula, the Golan Heights, and the Gaza Strip vastly increased its territorial holdings—and the resentment of Palestinians. Israel withdrew from western Sinai in 1975 and from the whole of the peninsula in 1981. The West Bank and the Gaza Strip were placed under Palestinian self-rule in 1994.

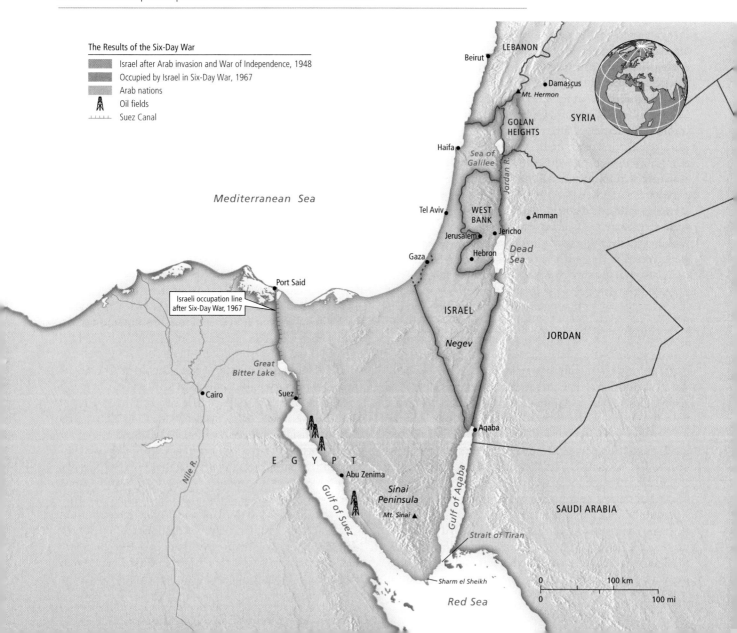

Genuine independence, however, proved difficult to retain as even Sukarno, the nonaligned movement's founder, discovered. Sukarno's quest for material and military assistance led him into the Soviet sphere of influence by the mid-1960s. In 1967, General Mohamed Suharto (b. 1921) overthrew Sukarno in a bloody coup. With his country's rivers clogged with the headless corpses of 100,000 victims, Suharto aligned Indonesia with the West.

# The Soviet Union and Eastern Europe in the 1950s and 1960s

■ **What patterns characterized the history of the Soviet Union and eastern Europe after the death of Stalin?**

Divided by the Cold War, the peoples of western and eastern Europe in the 1950s and 1960s followed separate paths. For the citizens of eastern Europe and the Soviet Union, the end of World War II brought renewed terror. Stalin's death in 1953 inaugurated a period of political reform and the seeming promise of prosperity, but by the end of the 1960s, economic stagnation and political discontent characterized life in the Soviet bloc.

## From Stalinist Terror to De-Stalinization

As the Red Army slowly pushed the Germans out of Soviet territory and then back through eastern Europe in the final years of World War II, many of the inhabitants of these regions found that liberation from German occupation did not mean freedom, and that the end of the war did not mean peace. Stalin accused entire ethnic groups, such as the Chechens, of collaborating with the Germans. Soviet soldiers loaded hundreds of thousands of men, women, and children onto freezing freight cars without adequate supplies of food, water, or warm clothing, and shipped them eastward. An estimated 25 percent of these people died on the journey or in the first few years of barren existence in their new homes. These deportations continued into the early 1950s.

Terror also marked the daily lives of eastern Europeans in the late 1940s and early 1950s, as Stalin imposed his control over the Soviet satellite states. Developments in Yugoslavia played a crucial role in shaping the terror in eastern Europe. In 1948, Yugoslavia's communist leader, Tito, broke with Stalin and refused to let the Soviets dictate Yugoslavia's foreign and domestic policies. Alarmed by his loss of control over Yugoslavia, Stalin strove frantically to tighten his grip on the rest of eastern Europe by eliminating

## CHRONOLOGY

### The Soviet Bloc in the Postwar Era

**1948**  Yugoslav leader Tito breaks with Stalin; terror underway in Eastern Europe

**1953**  Death of Stalin; relaxation of terror in eastern Europe and Soviet Union

**1955**  Khrushchev emerges as new Soviet leader

**1956**  Khrushchev's "Secret Speech," de-Stalinization accelerates; unrest in Poland results in new regime under Gomułka; Hungarian Revolution crushed by Soviet forces

**1964**  Khrushchev ousted; Brezhnev era begins

**1968**  Prague Spring crushed

any potential Tito imitators from these societies. The Cold War provided Stalin with additional incentives to battle against any possible threat to his personal power. Stalin insisted that a Western conspiracy to divide and conquer the Soviet bloc could be defeated only by a thoroughgoing purge of communist ranks.

The citizens of eastern Europe thus experienced a replay of the Soviet terror of the 1930s. Labor and prison camps soon dotted eastern European maps. Between 1948 and 1953, many more communists were killed by their own party members than had died at the hands of the Nazis during World War II. Arrested, charged with sabotage or espionage, and savagely tortured, prominent communists were convicted in public show trials at which they recited the confessions that had been prepared for them. As in the Soviet Union a decade earlier, the terror quickly spread beyond the communist ranks. Factory supervisors were assigned quotas; they knew if they did not come up with a required number of names of "criminals," they would be imprisoned. In Budapest, frightened citizens watched the police vans that slid through the street every Monday, Wednesday, and Friday night at two A.M., picking up the next allotment of victims. The security forces targeted anyone remotely connected to "the West," including veterans of the Spanish Civil War and members of international organizations such as the Boy Scouts. Jews, considered "cosmopolitan" and therefore potentially pro-Western, were particularly suspect. Only Stalin's death in 1953 caused the wave of persecution to recede.

Soviet leaders jostled for power after Stalin's death but by 1955 Nikita Khrushchev had triumphed over his rivals and claimed control. A true communist success story, Khrushchev was born to illiterate peasants, began work as a coal miner at age 14, and rose to the top of the Soviet system.

# Show Time:
# The Trial of Rudolf Slánský

On the night of July 31, 1951, Rudolf Slánský—general secretary of the Communist Party of Czechoslovakia (CPC) and the second most powerful man in Prague—left his 50th birthday party and headed home, a frightened man. Outwardly, nothing was wrong. The CPC had celebrated the day in style. The communist president, Klement Gottwald, presented to Slánský the medal of the Order of Socialism, the highest honor awarded in Czechoslovakia. Telegrams of congratulations poured in from all over the country. But the huge stack of congratulatory telegrams contained no greeting from Stalin. Slánský knew he was in trouble.

At another place and in another time, Slánský's fear could be dismissed as mere paranoia. But in the upper ranks of the Communist Party in Czechoslovakia in 1951, signs of Stalin's approval or disapproval were literally a matter of life or death. The Stalinist purge of eastern Europe was well underway, with thousands arrested, tortured, imprisoned, or killed.

Slánský knew he was vulnerable on three counts. First, he held a rank high enough to ensure a spectacular show trial. As the Soviet Great Purge of the 1930s had demonstrated, trials and executions of leading communists worked both to terrorize Stalin's potential rivals and, by rousing ordinary citizens to perpetual vigilance, to cement mass loyalty to the regime. But for a trial to be a genuine show, the defendant had to be worth showing. Slánský, as the CPC general secretary, was the perfect defendant.

Slánský was a target for Stalin's purge, second, because he was a Czech, and Stalin viewed his Czech colleagues with particular suspicion. Czechoslovakia was the only state in eastern Europe with a history of successful democracy and without Soviet troops in occupation after 1945. Moreover, the CPC had participated with noncommunists in a coalition government longer than any other eastern European communist party.

Such differences linked the CPC to the ideology of "national communism," which taught that the Soviet path to communism was not the only one, that each nation must find its own route. "National communism" became a heresy in Stalin's eyes after his break with the Yugoslav communist leader Tito in 1948. Tito had dared to lead Yugoslavia down a different path and had dared to defy Stalin's leadership. Determined to prevent any additional defections from his eastern European empire, Stalin embarked on a quest for real or potential "titoists." To save his own skin, CPC leader Klement Gottwald needed to demonstrate his willingness to uproot titoism from his party and his government. Slánský became that demonstration.

Finally, Slánský was vulnerable because he was a Jew. When the purges in eastern Europe began in 1948, anti-Semitism played no prominent role, but by 1950 the intersection of Middle Eastern power plays, Cold War hostilities, Stalin's paranoia, and the still-powerful tradition of Jew-hating in eastern European culture made Jewish communists particularly suspect. Aiming to establish a Soviet presence in the Middle East after the war, Stalin had tried to persuade the new state of Israel to align with the Soviet Union by offering the new Israeli government diplomatic recognition and arms deals. But Stalin's efforts failed. By 1950, Israel had become an ally of the United States. Stalin responded with fury. All Jews came under suspicion of "Zionist" (that is, pro-Israel and therefore pro-Western) tendencies.

Stalin's failure to send Slánský a birthday telegram signaled that Slánský was now on the list of suspects. Over the following months Soviet advisers and home-grown Czech torturers pressured prisoners already caught in the net of the purge to confess that they were part of a Slánský-led conspiracy to overthrow the communist government and to turn Czechoslovakia against the Soviet Union. These torture-induced confessions were then used to prepare a flimsy case against Slánský and thirteen other men (eleven of them Jews).

Shortly before midnight on November 24, 1951, security agents arrested Slánský at his home. A lifelong atheist, Slánský could say nothing except "Jesus Maria." He knew what was coming. Instrumental in initiating the Stalinist purge in Czechoslovakia, Slánský had approved the arrests and torture of many of his colleagues. Ironically, he had drafted the telegram asking Stalin to send Soviet advisers to assist in the Czech purge—the very same advisers who decided to target Slánský.

For the next year, Slánský endured mental and physical torture, directed by these advisers. Common torture tactics included beatings and kickings; prolonged periods without sleep, food, or water; all-night interrogation sessions; and being forced to stand in one place or march in circles for days on end. One interrogator recalled, "Instead of getting evidence, we were told that they were villains and that we had to break them."[6] Breaking Slánský took six months; the remaining months were spent defining and refining the details of his imaginary crimes against the communist regime, and rehearsing for the all-important show trial.

Slánský's trial, which began on November 20, 1952, was in every sense a show. Before the trial began, party officials had already determined the verdict and the sentences. Prosecutors, defense attorneys, judges, and the accused spoke the lines of a script written by security agents. Thus, one year after his arrest, Slánský stood up in court and pleaded guilty to the crimes of high treason, espionage, and sabotage. A founding member of the CPC, he said he had conspired to overthrow the communist government. A resistance fighter during World War II, he confessed to working with the Nazis against the communists. A zealous Stalinist, he announced that he was a titoist-Zionist who had plotted to hand Czechoslovakia to the Americans.

Why did Slánský make such a ludicrous confession? Fear of further torture is clearly one motive, but other factors also came into play. Communists such as Slánský believed that the interests of the party always came first, ahead of individual rights, ahead of abstractions such as "truth." Slánský may have believed that his confession, false though it was, served the party. As one experienced interrogator noted about a different defendant, "He'll confess; he's got a good attitude toward the party."[7] In addition, Slánský may have been promised, as were other show trial defendants, that his life would be spared and his family protected if he confessed.

In his closing statement Slánský said, "I deserve no other end to my criminal life than that proposed by the state prosecutor."[8] The prosecutor demanded the death penalty. Slánský was executed on December 3, 1952. Ten of his co-accused also hanged. Their families were stripped of their party memberships and privileges, deported with only the barest essentials to designated districts, and assigned to manual labor.

## Questions of Justice

1. In what ways did Cold War concerns shape Slánský's trial?
2. What sort of justice was served in the trial of Rudolf Slánský?

## Taking It Further

Lukes, Igor. "The Rudolf Slánský Affair: New Evidence." *Slavic Review* 58, 1 (Spring 1999): 160–187. Illuminating study of the role of Cold War intrigue in determining Slánský's fate.

Kaplan, Karel. *Report on the Murder of the General Secretary.* 1990. Kaplan emigrated from Czechoslovakia to West Germany in the late 1970s, with a stack of hidden documents, and wrote this report.

**Rudolf Slánský on Trial**
Slánský, already a broken man, bows his head as he hears his death sentence on November 27, 1952.

Recognized as a man with talent by the Communist Party, he trained as an engineer and helped build the Moscow subway system. Khrushchev owed everything to the Communist Party, and he never forgot it. Confident in the moral and material superiority of communism, Khrushchev believed that the Soviet Union would win the Cold War on the economic battlefield. But this ultimate victory would take place only if Soviet living standards substantially improved, and only if the Stalinist systems of terror and rigid centralized control were dismantled.

Nikita Khrushchev Challenges the West to Disarm

Khrushchev's determination to set communism on a new course became clear in February 1956 when, in a lengthy speech before the Twentieth Congress of the Communist Party, he shocked his listeners by detailing and condemning Stalin's crimes. This "Secret Speech" marked the beginning of de-Stalinization, a time of greater openness in the Communist bloc as governments dismantled many of the controls on speech and publication, and for the first time in years dissent and debate reappeared in public life.

The most dramatic sign of de-Stalinization was the release of at least four and a half million prisoners from slave labor camps. As one Soviet citizen recalled, their return was disturbing: "in railway trains and stations, there appeared survivors of the camps, with leaden grey hair, sunken eyes, and a faded look; they choked and dragged their feet like old men."[9] These survivors often returned to find their spouses remarried, their children embarrassed by their presence, their world destroyed. Some, such as Alexander Solzhenitsyn, wrote horrifying accounts of their experiences. Solzhenitsyn's books narrated the daily degradation of prison life and provided a detailed map of the network of slave labor camps that he christened "The Gulag Archipelago."

De-Stalinization certainly did not mean an end to all cultural controls in the Soviet Union, as artists discovered in the early 1960s. At first, Khrushchev's ascendancy seemed to promise that Soviet artists could finally break out of the prison of Socialist Realism to which Stalinist doctrine had confined them (see Chapter 25). In 1956, works by Picasso that had lain unseen in state museums for decades were finally put on exhibit. Inspired by what was to them truly revolutionary work, Soviet artists turned to producing their own nonfigurative, abstract art. But the display of some of this work in Moscow in 1962 made clear the limits of de-Stalinization. Khrushchev thundered, "What's hung here is simply anti-Soviet. It's immoral."[10] Within days, the artists who had dared to experiment found themselves censured, expelled, and unemployed.

De-Stalinization also did not mean an end to all political and religious repression. In 1959 the Gulag still held at least a million prisoners. As part of his effort to revitalize communist culture, Khrushchev embarked on a massive offensive against religious practice, which included the razing of churches, the arrest of clergy, the closure of seminaries and monasteries, and even in some cases the forcible removal of children from Christian homes. At the same time, anti-Semitism continued to mark communist policy and practice, with Soviet Jews targeted for harassment and repression.

Most ominously for the future of the Soviet Union itself, de-Stalinization failed to remedy long-term economic weaknesses. In 1962, per capita consumption of consumer goods stood at only 40 to 60 percent that of France, West Germany, and Britain. In agriculture, the economic sector where the Soviet Union lagged the furthest behind the West, Khrushchev embarked on an ambitious reform program, which included rapid mechanization, a massive chemical fertilizer program, and the plowing of virgin lands. He refused to retreat from collectivization, however. As a result, the fundamental productivity problem remained unsolved—and in fact worsened in the long term as immense ecological damage was inflicted on the Soviet countryside. Soil erosion increased exponentially, nitrogen runoff from fertilized fields contaminated water supplies, and over-irrigation led to salinization and a decline in soil fertility. The full force of these problems would not be felt until the 1980s, but as early as 1963 the Soviet Union had to import Western grain, a humiliating admission of failure for Khrushchev's regime.

## Re-Stalinization and Stagnation: The Brezhnev Era

Khrushchev's reforms unsettled many high-ranking communists; as a result, he was forced out of office in 1964. After a short period of collective leadership, Leonid Brezhnev (1906–1982) emerged as the new Soviet leader, a position he held until his death in 1982. A polite man with no interest in literature, art, or original ideas, Brezhnev was far more reassuring to Soviet bureaucrats than the flamboyant Khrushchev, whose boisterous embrace of new ideas and ambitious schemes had proven so destabilizing. Fifty-eight years old and already physically ailing when he assumed the party leadership, the increasingly decrepit Brezhnev matched his era.

Under Brezhnev the Soviet economy stagnated. Growth rates in both industrial production and labor productivity slowed during the second half of the 1960s. In the 1970s, growth virtually ceased. This economic stagnation was, however, masked by improving living standards. Brezhnev continued Khrushchev's policies of free higher education and rising wages, while accelerating the expansion of consumer goods. State subsidies ensured that the cost of utilities, public transport, and rents remained far lower than in the West (although apartments were in short supply), and an extensive welfare system eased pressures on ordinary people.

By the middle of the 1960s, the Soviet Union appeared to have achieved a sort of stability. It was, however, a stability built on repression as well as stagnation. Judging de-Stalinization to be a risky business, Brezhnev and his colleagues embarked on a rehabilitation of Stalin's reputation. As statues of the dictator began to reappear, the limited cultural and intellectual freedoms introduced under Khrushchev vanished. Never subtle, state officials took to bulldozing outdoor art shows as rigid censorship and repression once again characterized Soviet society. Those who expressed dissident views soon found themselves denied employment and educational opportunities, imprisoned, sent to the Gulag, or confined indefinitely in a psychiatric ward.

Yet dissent did not disappear. Soviet society may have resembled a stagnant pond by the 1970s, but beneath the surface churned dangerous currents that, in the late 1980s, would engulf the entire communist system. Reviving a practice employed by reformers under the tsarist regime, dissidents evaded the censors by *samizdat* or "self-publishing." Novels, plays, poetry, political treatises, and historical studies were circulated privately, copied by hand or duplicated on treasured (and often confiscated) typewriters and photocopiers and distributed more widely. Nonconformist artists, banned from official exhibitions, used private apartments to show their work.

Nationalism among the non-Russian populations served as the source of much discontent within the Soviet Union during this era. As the Soviet economy grew, Russian managers and technicians were sent to places such as oil-rich Kazakhstan. Russian immigration to the Baltic states was particularly dramatic: In 1970, native Latvians made up only 59 percent of the Latvian population. Resentment of these Russian immigrants, perceived as the privileged representatives of a colonialist power, escalated. By the mid-1960s, clandestine nationalist political organizations had emerged in almost every non-Russian republic of the Soviet Union.

## Diversity and Dissent in Eastern Europe

Despite the uniformity imposed by Soviet-style communist systems during these decades, the nations of eastern Europe developed in different ways. De-Stalinization contributed to this diversification. In his "Secret Speech" of 1956, Khrushchev declared, "it is ridiculous to think that revolu-

### De-Stalinization

On October 31, 1956, Hungarian demonstrators pulled down a huge statue of Joseph Stalin and then dragged it two miles through the city center. Stalin's head still sits at an intersection in Budapest.

tions are made to order"[11] and so indicated that communist nations could follow paths diverging from the road traveled by the Soviet Union.

### 1956 and After

But just how far from the Soviet road could those paths go? The contrasting fates of Poland and Hungary in 1956 provide the answer. In Poland, popular protests against rigid Stalinist controls proved strong enough in 1956 to bring back into power Władisław Gomułka (1905–1982). An influential Polish communist who had been purged in the Stalinist terror of 1951, Gomułka succeeded in establishing a uniquely Polish brand of communism, one that abandoned collective farming and efforts to control Polish Catholicism and yet remained loyal to the Warsaw Pact.

During these same years, Hungary also pursued a de-Stalinizing "New Course" under the leadership of a reformist communist. Unlike Gomułka, however, Imre Nagy (1896–1958) proved unable to resist demands for a break with the Soviet Union. On October 31, Hungary withdrew from the Warsaw Pact—or tried to. Four days later, Khrushchev sent in the tanks. As many as 20,000 Hungarians may have died as the Red Army crushed all resistance.[12] Nagy was executed in 1958.

The repression of the Hungarian revolt defined the limits of de-Stalinization in eastern Europe: The Soviet

Union's satellite states could not follow paths that led out of the Warsaw Pact. Within the confines of this structure and of the one-party state, however, the governments of eastern Europe continued to pursue different courses. East Germany became the most industrially advanced and urbanized country in eastern Europe, while Poland's countryside was dotted with family farms. Perhaps most surprisingly, post-1956 Hungary became the most liberal country in the Eastern bloc under Nagy's successor, János Kádár (1912–1989), a reformist communist who, like Gomułka, had survived torture and imprisonment during the Stalinist terror of the early 1950s. Kádár encouraged debate within the Communist Party, loosened censorship on film studios and publishers, and permitted private business ventures. In sharp contrast, Romanians endured the reign of the "mini-Stalins." Gheorghe Gheorghiu-Dej (1901–1965) and Nicolai Ceauşescu (1918–1989) imposed not only one-party but one-man control over the country through Stalinist methods of terror.

Within the diverse experiences of eastern Europeans, certain commonalities characterized the post-1956 era. Except in Romania and even more oppressive Albania, living standards improved. Educational opportunities expanded, the supply of consumer goods increased, and political repression became less overt. Even so, overcentralization, bureaucratic mismanagement, and political corruption ensured that living standards remained below those of the West. Moreover, the very consumer goods that were supposed to persuade eastern European citizens of the superiority of the communist system instead demonstrated its deficiencies. With a radio, a Hungarian teenager could tune into Radio Free Europe and hear of a livelier, more abundant society in the West. In East Germany, television watchers could view West German networks and catch a glimpse of Western prosperity.

## The Prague Spring

Discontent and dissent simmered throughout the eastern bloc during the 1960s and then, in 1968, boiled over in Czechoslovakia. During the 1960s, a reform movement emerged in the ranks of the Czechoslovakian Communist Party. It included both Slovaks, who believed that the regime's highly centralized policies favored Czechs, and the new elite of highly educated technocrats who resented the power of poorly educated party superiors. At the beginning of 1968, this resentment fueled an intraparty revolution which brought to power the reformist Communist (and Slovak) Alexander Dubček (1921–1992). Dubček embarked on a program of radical reform, aimed at achieving "socialism with a human face." This more humane socialism included freedom of speech, press, assembly, and travel; the removal of Communist Party controls from social and cultural life; and decentralization of the economy.

Dubček's effort to reform the system from the top quickly merged with a wider popular protest movement that had arisen among intellectuals, artists, students, and workers. The result was the "Prague Spring"°—the blossoming of political and social freedoms throughout Czechoslovakia, but especially in the capital city of Prague.

Well aware of the fate of Hungary in 1956, Dubček reassured Brezhnev and the other Soviet leaders that these reforms would not lead Czechoslovakia out of the Warsaw Pact. But by the summer of 1968, many of the ideas of the Prague activists were filtering through to other eastern European countries and to the Soviet Union itself. In Ukraine, nationalist protesters looked to Prague for inspiration, while in Poland, student riots, which broke out in all the major cities, featured placards reading "Poland is awaiting its own Dubček." Frightened communist leaders throughout the eastern bloc demanded that Brezhnev act to stifle the Prague Spring.

On the night of August 20–21, 80,000 troops—drawn from not only the Soviet Union but also Poland, Hungary, and East Germany—crossed the Czech border. They were immediately confused: Czechs had removed road signs and painted over street numbers in order to confound the invaders. Thirty Czechs died on the first day of the invasion, and hundreds more were injured. The resistance spread. Workers went on strike, 20,000 Czechs marched in Prague to protest the invasion, and children ran in front of the tanks, shaking their fists. But over the next several weeks, the Prague Spring was crushed. The scientists, artists, and intellectuals who had supported the movement found themselves either in prison or unemployed. As one Communist Party journal explained, the new regime "will not permit all flowers to blossom. We will cultivate, water, and protect only one flower, the red rose of Marxism."

But that rose needed an army to hold it up. In the fall of 1968, Brezhnev acknowledged that Soviet domination in eastern Europe rested on force alone when he articulated what came to be known as the "Brezhnev Doctrine." Formally a commitment to support global socialism, the Brezhnev Doctrine was essentially a promise to use the Red Army to stomp on any eastern European effort to achieve fundamental change.

Even more important, after 1968 eastern Europeans recognized the futility of attempting to reform a system that had now been revealed as beyond reform. Many, perhaps most, eastern Europeans retreated to private worlds of friendship and family life (or to the easy escape provided by alcohol). Others, however, refused to give up or to give in to a system they now viewed as utterly corrupt. They sought, in the words of the Czech playwright and dissident Václav Havel (b. 1936), to "live in truth" in the midst of a society based on lies. As the Polish author Konstanty Gebert explained, living in truth raised "a small, portable barricade between me and silence, submission, humiliation, shame. Impregnable for tanks, uncircumventable. As long as I man it, there is, around me, a small area of freedom."

# The West: Consensus, Consumption, and Culture

■ What patterns characterized the history of western Europe in the 1950s and 1960s?

As in eastern Europe, in western Europe both the experience of total war and Cold War concerns helped shape postwar societies. The desire to make the suffering of the war years worthwhile, as well as fear of communism, furthered the integration of Europe's economies and helped define the political centrism characteristic of western Europe in the 1950s and 1960s. The dominant fact of the postwar years was, however, material prosperity as western European economies embarked on two decades of dramatic economic growth and consumer spending.

## The Triumph of Democracy

In sharp contrast to the interwar years, the parties in power in western Europe in the 1950s and 1960s, and the voters who put them there, agreed on the viability and virtues of parliamentary democracy. The new constitutions of France, West Germany, and Italy guaranteed the protection of individual rights, and French and Italian women achieved suffrage. The democratic ideal of the universal franchise had finally been realized in most of western Europe.

Citizenship, though, meant more than the right to vote after 1945. As the social democratic vision triumphed in western Europe after World War II, the meaning of citizenship broadened to include the right to a decent standard of living. Through the nationalization of key industries, the establishment of public agencies to oversee and encourage investment and trade, and the manipulation of interest rates and currency supplies, governments assumed the task of ensuring full employment and material well-being for their citizens. A slogan of the German Social Democratic Party—"as much competition as possible, as much planning as necessary"—sums up an approach common to much of western Europe at this time.

This commitment, however, embraced a variety of national styles. The British stressed the nationalization of heavy industry, while the French emphasized the role of centralized planning. Led by the pragmatic visionary Jean Monnet (1888–1979), France's postwar Planning Commission set economic targets and directed investment. In contrast, in West Germany, where centralized direction of the economy was linked to Nazism, politicians chose a more free-market path to industrial success.

Yet even in West Germany, citizens had access to an extensive welfare system. With the construction of comprehensive welfare states, postwar governments undertook to guarantee their citizens adequate incomes and medical care. By the end of the 1950s, the average western European working-class family received 63 percent of its income from wages. The substantial remaining income came from welfare benefits such as family allowances, national health services, sickness and disability insurance, and old-age pensions. In addition, state-run vaccination and inoculation programs, stricter sanitation regulation, and the development of policies to control communicable diseases all meant an improvement in the health of Europe's populations.

As we saw in Chapter 26, this triumph of social democracy was rooted in the suffering of World War II, when Europeans grew determined to create a better world out of the rubble of total war. This determination remained, but much of the radicalism of the wartime spirit quickly receded as the Cold War constricted the parameters of political debate. The mainstream political parties—Christian Democrats or Conservatives on the right, Social Democrats or Socialists on the left—agreed in refusing to allow Communist Party members to participate in governing coalitions. In France and Italy, communist parties consistently drew 20 to 30 percent of the vote but were effectively marginalized by their exclusion from office after 1948.

With the communists isolated, and with the ideologies of the extremist Right such as fascism and Nazism discredited by the horrors of the war, western European politics took on a new and marked stability during the 1950s and early 1960s. Christian Democratic° parties—which have no American or British counterpart—flourished on the Continent during the postwar era. Drawing on a Roman Catholic base for their support and espousing a largely conservative social ideology combined with a progressive commitment to the welfare state, Christian Democratic parties dominated much of European politics in the 1950s and 1960s. Christian Democrats played significant roles in the political life of France and Belgium, governed West Germany between 1949 and 1969, and provided every prime minister except two in Italy between 1945 and 1993.

Three factors account for Christian Democracy's success. First, as anticommunists and advocates of the free market, Christian Democrats benefited from Cold War anxieties and more directly from American aid and support. Second, because they were based on religion (Roman Catholicism) rather than class, Christian Democratic parties were able to appeal to both middle-class and working-class voters, and particularly to women, who tended to be more religious and to vote more conservatively than men. But finally and most important, the triumph of Christian Democracy rested on its dramatic transformation from a right-wing to a centrist political movement. In the interwar period, Christian Democracy, rooted in a religious and political tradition based on hierarchy and authoritarianism, had veered close to fascism. But during World War II, many Catholics served in the resistance movement, where they absorbed progressive political ideas. This war-inspired desire to use the power of the state to improve the lives of ordinary people blended with more traditional Catholic paternalism. After the war the Christian Democrats not only jettisoned their authoritarianism and embraced democracy, they also supported the construction of comprehensive welfare states.

## Prosperity in the West

These political developments unfolded against an economic backdrop of increasing prosperity. In the first half of the 1950s, Europeans moved rapidly from the austerity of the immediate postwar years to an age of unprecedented affluence.

### Economic Integration

One important factor in this new prosperity was the greater coordination of western European economies. World War II provided the impetus for this economic integration. Fighting in conditions of unprecedented horror, Europeans looked for ways to guarantee a lasting peace. In 1943, Jean Monnet (1888–1979), who would oversee French economic planning in the postwar era, declared, "there will be no peace in Europe, if the states are reconstituted on the basis of national sovereignty." In July 1944, Resistance leaders from France, Italy, the Netherlands, and a number of other countries met in Geneva to embrace Monnet's vision and declare their support for a federal, democratic Europe.

No such radical restructuring of Europe occurred, but the push toward greater European union moved forward in the years after 1945, impelled by Cold War concerns. Opposition to Stalin helped western Europeans see themselves as part of a single region with common interests. At the same time, American postwar planners—anxious to restore economic prosperity to Europe in order to lessen the appeal of communism—urged their European colleagues to dismantle trade barriers and coordinate national economic plans, and required recipients of Marshall aid to develop transnational economic institutions. Looking back on this early stage of European integration, the Belgian prime minister (and ardent proponent of European union) Paul-Henri Spaak (1899–1972) wrote in the later 1960s, "Europeans, let us be modest. It is the fear of Stalin and the daring views of Marshall which led us into the right path."[13]

Spaak was a socialist, but many Christian Democrats also promoted European economic union, including Konrad Adenauer, the first chancellor of West Germany; Alcide de Gaspari, the postwar prime minister of Italy; and the French foreign minister Robert Schuman (1886–1963). Schuman's upbringing opened him to an internationalist

**DOCUMENT**

A Common Market and European Integration (1960)

perspective: Reared in Alsace under both German and French rule, Schuman had served as a German army officer before he entered French politics.

Desperate to break down the nationalist and economic rivalries that had led to World War II, Schuman in 1950 proposed the merger of the German and French coal and steel industries. The resulting European Coal and Steel Community (ECSC), established in 1952, comprised not only Germany and France, but also Italy, Belgium, the Netherlands, and Luxembourg. It proved to be an economic success, stimulating economic growth throughout the member economies.

Heartened by the success of the ECSC, the six member nations in 1957 formed the European Economic Community° (EEC) or Common Market°. The EEC sought not only to establish an enormous free trade zone across member boundaries, but also to coordinate policies on wages, prices, immigration, and social security. Between 1958 and 1970, trade among its six member states increased fivefold. The rapid movement of goods, services, and even workers ensured that the economies of member states flourished. In contrast, Britain, which had chosen to remain outside the EEC in order to preserve its preferential trading relationships with its former and current colonies, struggled to compete, with growth rates below those of its continental competitors.

### The Age of Affluence

If a European living in 1930 had been transported by a time machine to the Europe of 1965, he or she would probably have been most astonished, however, not by European economic integration but by the cornucopia of consumer goods spilling over the lives of ordinary Europeans. After years of wartime rationing, Europeans went on a spending spree and did not stop. A swift and unprecedented climb in real wages—by 80 percent in England, for example, between 1950 and 1970—helps explain why. So too does the construction of the welfare state. With full employment and comprehensive welfare services offering unprecedented financial security, Europeans shrugged off habits of thrift.

This spending spree transformed both the interiors of European homes and their exterior environment. The postwar period witnessed a boom in housing construction. The annual volume of construction rose by 80 percent between 1950 and 1957. With new houses came new household goods. Items such as refrigerators and washing machines, once unaffordable luxuries, now became increasingly common in ordinary homes. In France, for example, the stock of home appliances rose by 400 percent between 1949 and 1957.

At the same time, the automobile revolutionized much of both the rural and urban landscape. Highways, few and far between in 1950, cut across the countryside, and parking meters, unknown in Europe before 1959, dotted city streets. In 1964, the archbishop of Florence presided over a

DOCUMENT

## The Age of Affluence

*Full employment and rising real wages meant that the European working class joined the mass consumer society in the postwar era. In Alan Sillitoe's novel* Saturday Night and Sunday Morning, *20-year-old Arthur Seaton seethes with unarticulated anger over continuing class divisions and his own powerlessness, yet he is well aware of the stark material contrast between the 1930s and the 1950s. Seaton credits the war, not the welfare state, with the material improvements he observes around him. He confronts his father on Monday morning before heading to work:*

"You'll go blind one day, dad," he said, for nothing, taking the words out of the air for sport, ready to play with the consequences of whatever he might cause.

Seaton turned to him uncomprehendingly, his older head still fuddled. It took ten cups of tea and as many Woodbines [cigarettes] to set his temper right after the weekend. "What do you mean?" he demanded, intractable at any time before ten in the morning.

"Sittin' in front of the TV. You stick to it like glue from six to eleven every night. It can't be good for yer. You'll go blind one day. You're bound to. I read it in the *Post* last week that a lad from the Medders went blind . . . "

"Ye're barmy," Seaton said. "Go an tell yer stories somewhere else . . . "

The subject was dropped. His father cut several slices of bread and made sandwiches with cold meat left from Sunday dinner. Arthur teased him a lot, but in a way he was glad to see the TV standing in a corner of the living-room, a glossy panelled box looking, he thought, like something plundered from a spaceship. The old man was happy at last, anyway, and he deserved to be happy, after all the years before the war on the dole [on unemployment benefit], five kids and the miserying that went with no money and no way of getting any. And now he had a sit-down job at the factory, all the Woodbines he could smoke, money for a pint [of beer] if he wanted one, though he didn't as a rule drink, a holiday somewhere, a jaunt on the firm's trip to Blackpool [a seaside resort], and a television-set to look into at home. The difference between before the war and after the war didn't bear thinking about. War was a marvellous thing in many ways, when you thought about how happy it had made so many people in England.

. . . Once out of doors they were aware of the factory rumbling a hundred yards away. . . . The thousands that worked there took home good wages. . . . With the wages you got you could save up for a motor-bike or even an old car, or you could go on a ten-day binge and get rid of all you'd saved. Because it was no use saving your money year after year. A mug's game, since the value of it got less and less and in any case you never knew when the Yanks were going to do something daft like dropping the H-bomb on Moscow.

Source: From *Saturday Night and Sunday Morning* by Alan Sillitoe, copyright © 1958 by Alan Sillitoe. Used by permission of Alfred A. Knopf, a division of Random House, Inc.

thanksgiving service in a gas station to celebrate the completion of a highway linking Milan and Naples. Out-of-town shopping centers, geared to the convenience of car owners, proliferated while city centers decayed.

Spending begot more spending. Credit buying (what the British called "buying on the never-never") became commonplace and made possible even more consumption. Television commercials (first seen in the mid-1950s), the Yellow Pages (first distributed in Europe in the early 1960s), and color advertising supplements in the Sunday newspapers (an innovation, again, of the early 1960s) all encouraged a culture of consumption.

## Western Culture and Thought in the Age of Consumption

Cultural developments in Western society highlight the shift from an era structured by the memories of World War II to a period shaped by prosperity. Existentialism and modernism retained their dominant cultural position in the later 1940s and 1950s. By the beginning of the 1960s, however, artists began to retreat from engagement with the horrors of World War II and the overwhelming challenges of the Cold War. Instead, they produced works that reflected, commented on, and reveled in the cascade of consumer abundance that was transforming Western culture.

## Finding Meaning in the Age of Auschwitz and the Atom Bomb

Forged in the despair of the 1930s (see Chapter 25), existentialism remained a powerful cultural force in the early postwar era. Jean-Paul Sartre's conviction that existence has no intrinsic meaning, and yet that the individual retains the freedom to act and therefore make meaning, resounded loudly in a world that had experienced both the Holocaust and the Resistance. The existentialist emphasis on individual action as the source of meaning could lead to a life of political activism—Sartre, for example, worked with the French Resistance and became a prominent participant in left-wing political causes in the 1950s and 1960s. On the other hand, existentialism also justified political disengagement. In the Irish-French playwright Samuel Beckett's (1906–1989) existentialist masterpiece *Waiting for Godot* (1952), two tramps sit in an empty universe, waiting for someone who never comes. In this absurd void, politics has no relevance or resonance.

Existentialist themes echo throughout the visual arts in the 1950s. The sculptures of the Swiss artist Alberto Giacometti (1901–1966) are the embodiments of existentialist anguish—fragile, insubstantial, they appear ready to

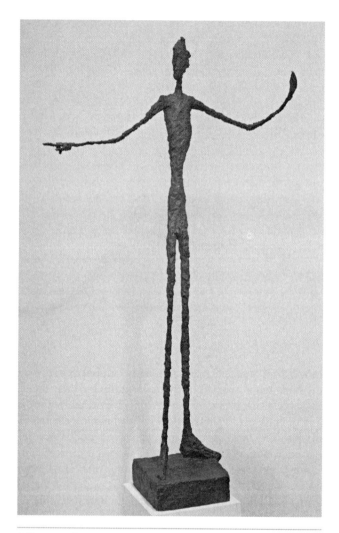

**Alberto Giacometti, *Man Pointing* (1947)**
Giacometti's sculptures embodied existentialist anguish. His account of this piece's creation seems to be lifted from a Samuel Beckett play or one of Jean-Paul Sartre's novels: "Wanting to create from memory [the figures] I had seen, to my terror the sculptures became smaller and smaller, they had a likeness only when they were small, yet their dimensions revolted me, and tirelessly I began again, only to end several months later at the same point."

crack under the strain of being. While Giacometti's sculptures embody existentialist terror, the works of the preeminent British painter of the 1950s, Francis Bacon (1909–1992), evoke outright nausea. Bacon's disturbing canvases are case studies in the power of the subconscious. He painted the people he saw around him, but his perceptions were of a society disfigured by slaughter. Slabs of meat, dripping in blood, figure prominently. Bacon explained, "When you go into a butcher's shop . . . you can think of the whole horror of life, of one thing living off another."[14] By the end of the decade, solitary figures, secluded in claustrophobic settings and embodying Sartre's description of human existence as essentially isolated, recurred frequently in Bacon's work.

In this period, the terrors of the nuclear age also helped shape cultural consciousness. Because figurative painting seemed utterly incapable of capturing the power and terror of the atomic age, the Bomb reinforced the hold of abstract art over the avant-garde. But abstract art itself changed. Formal geometric abstractions had characterized much of prewar art; after the war, a new modernist movement, Abstract Expressionism, displayed more spontaneous styles. The Abstract Expressionist Jackson Pollock

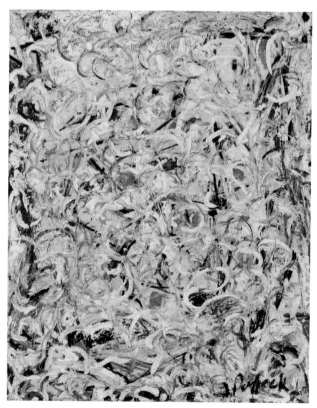

**Jackson Pollock, *Shimmering Substance* (1946)**
Many of Pollock's postwar works—huge paintings that pulse with power—show an obsession with heat and light, surely no coincidence in the dawn of the nuclear age.

(1912–1956), for example, invented an entirely new way of painting. Placing the canvas on the ground, he moved around and in it, dripping or pouring paint. In Pollock's works, the canvas has no clear center, no focal point. Instead, it disintegrates, like matter itself. As Pollock explained, "New needs need new techniques . . . The modern painter cannot express his age, the airplane, the atom bomb . . . in the old forms."[15]

Most people confronted their nuclear fears not in art galleries, but rather in movie theaters and popular fiction. In the movies, various nuclear-spawned horrors, including giant spiders, ants, and turtles, wreaked weekly havoc on the Western world. Fittingly enough, many of these films were produced in Japan. Throughout the 1950s, nuclear war and the postnuclear struggle for survival also filled the pages of popular fiction. Probably the most important "nuclear" novel, however, confined mention of atomic bombs to a single sentence. In *Lord of the Flies* (1954), British author William Golding (1911–1993) told the simple but brutal story of a group of schoolboys stranded on an island after they flee atomic attack. Their moral deterioration poses basic questions about the meaning of civilization, a question brought to the forefront of Western society by its use of advanced science and technology to obliterate civilian populations during World War II.

## Culture and Ideas in the World of Plenty

By the early 1960s, however, artists began to turn away from such big questions and to focus instead on the material stuff of everyday existence. In works such as the British artist Richard Hamilton's *Just What Is It That Makes Today's Homes So Different, So Appealing?* (1956), artists satirized and yet celebrated postwar materialism and revealed their fascination with the plethora of material objects pouring off assembly lines. Hamilton was a leading force in the Independent Group, a loose association of British artists, designers, and architects that sought in their work to embody the "aesthetics of plenty"—the idea that consumer affluence had smashed the barriers between fine art and popular culture. The Independent Group, along with other movements such as "New Realism" in France and "Capitalist Realism" in West Germany, helped shape what became known as pop art°.

Pop artists dismissed the anguish of Bacon and Giacometti as the concerns of an older generation still mired in World War II. Pop art looked outward rather than inward, and focused on the material rather than the spiritual. Pop artists spoke in the vocabulary of mass material culture, and even relied on mass production and mass marketing.

By doing so, they challenged accepted ideas about the role of both art and the artist in Western society. When Gerhard Richter (b. 1932) placed himself in the furniture display of a West German department store and called the resulting "piece" *Living with Pop* (1963) he turned the artist, as well as art, into a commodity, something to be bought and sold just like anything else. In the age of consumption, pop advocates declared, the individual artist's intentions were unimportant, and concepts such as artistic genius were irrelevant.

Similar themes also characterized developments in social thought. Existentialism had elevated the individual as the only source of meaning in an absurd universe. In the late 1950s, however, a new social theory, structuralism°, pushed the individual off center stage. Structuralism, which French anthropologist Claude Levi-Strauss (b. 1908) first introduced to a wide audience, transformed a number of

**Richard Hamilton, *Just What Is It That Makes Today's Homes So Different, So Appealing?* (1956)**
British artist Richard Hamilton was one of the leading figures in the pop art of the 1950s.

academic disciplines, including literary criticism, political theory, sociology, and even history. Levi-Strauss argued that the myths told in all cultures, whether that of Brazilian Indian tribes still using Stone Age tools or medieval French peasants or contemporary Londoners, shared certain "deep structures," repeated patterns such as pairings and oppositions that help give order to the cultural world. The actual stories are unimportant. To use a newspaper metaphor offered by the intellectual historian Roland Stromberg, the structuralist is interested not in the content of the articles but in the layout of the page—the arrangement of articles, the juxtaposition of images, the shape of headlines. By analyzing the "layout" of cultures, the structuralist can uncover the basic structures of human thought. In structuralism, then, as in pop art, the individual matters little. Human beings exist within a ready-built structure that shapes and dictates the way they perceive the world.

## Science and Religion in an Age of Mass Consumption

At the same time that structuralists depicted the individual as stuck within a cultural and linguistic web, his or her choices firmly constrained by the sticky fibers of that web, radical breakthroughs in the biological sciences posited that perhaps the web lay inside the individual, its fibers comprising chemicals and chromosomes that determined individual capabilities. In 1953, the British biologist Francis Crick (1916–2004) and his American colleague James Watson (b. 1928) discovered the structure of DNA, the basic building block of genetic material. Crick and Watson's model of the "double helix," the intertwined spirals of chemical units that, in a sense, issue the instructions for an individual's development, caught the attention of the world. As biologists and geneticists furthered their investigations into human genetic inheritance, they raised exciting yet potentially disturbing possibilities, such as the cloning of living organisms and genetic manipulation, and added a new dimension to the perennial debate about individual freedom.

Other scientific developments assured human beings more freedom from their physical environment than ever

before. Motivated by the Cold War, the space race launched humanity beyond the confines of Earth, culminating in 1969 with the American astronaut Neil Armstrong's moon walk. Medical breakthroughs in this era seemed to promise that infectious diseases could be eradicated. Large-scale production of penicillin transformed ordinary medical care, as did rapid development of vaccines against many childhood killers such as measles. In 1953, the American Jonas Salk announced the first successful clinical trial of a polio vaccine. In this era, blood transfusions become more commonplace, along with the development of organ transplants, following the first successful kidney transplant in Chicago in 1950. Like washing machines and television sets, a long and healthy life suddenly appeared accessible to many people in the West.

While scientists were claiming more control over the physical environment, the organized churches continued to offer spiritual authority and sustenance. Church attendance, which had declined in most Western countries in the interwar period, rose during the 1950s. In the United States between 1942 and 1960, church membership per capita grew faster than at any time since the 1890s. No European nation shared this dramatic religious upsurge; nevertheless, except in Scandinavia, western Europe experienced a gentle religious revival. In Britain during the 1950s, church membership, Sunday school enrollment, and the numbers of baptisms and religious marriages all increased. In West Germany, the rate of churchgoing rose among Protestants from 1952 until 1967. Throughout Catholic Europe, the vibrancy of Christian Democratic politics reflected the vital position of the Catholic Church in society.

In the 1960s, however, the situation changed dramatically. Europeans abandoned the church sanctuary in favor of the department store, the sports stadium, and the sofa in front of the television set. Declining rates of church attendance, a growing number of civil rather than religious marriage ceremonies, and an increased reluctance to obey Church teaching on issues such as premarital sexual relations all pointed to the secularization of European society. By the 1970s, churchgoing rates in both Protestant and Catholic countries were in freefall. In what had once been called "Christendom," the fastest-growing religious community was Islam.

The churches did not remain stagnant during this time of change. A number of Protestant theologians argued that Christianity could maintain its relevance in this more secular society only by adapting the biblical message to a modern context. The British theologian (and Anglican bishop) John Robinson achieved great notoriety in 1963 when he proclaimed the "death of God." Most of those who jeered at or cheered for Robinson's statement missed his point: The language in which Christians articulate their faith must be updated to make sense in the modern world.

The biggest change occurred in Roman Catholicism. In 1963 the Second Vatican Council—widely known as Vatican II°—convened in Rome, the first catholic council to

## CHRONOLOGY

## Medical Breakthroughs

**1950**  First kidney transplant

**1952**  First sex-change operation

**1952**  Polio vaccine first produced

**1953**  Discovery of DNA

**1957**  CAT scan developed

**1967**  First heart transplant

meet since 1870. In calling the council, Pope John XXIII (r. 1958–1963) sought to modernize and rejuvenate the Church, a process that, he recognized, would demand "a change in mentalities, ways of thinking and prejudices, all of which have a long history."[16] John did not live to see this change in mentalities take place, but his successor Paul VI (r. 1963–1978) presided over a quiet revolution.

The Church emerged from Vatican II less hierarchical and more open, with local and regional councils sharing more power with the papacy. For ordinary Catholics, the most striking changes occurred in the worship service, where a number of reforms narrowed the gap between priest and people. The priest moved from in front of to behind the altar, so that he could face the congregation; he spoke in the vernacular rather than in Latin; and all worshipers, not only the priest, received the wine at communion.

Vatican II was less revolutionary in its approach to sexual issues and gender roles. The council said nothing about homosexuality, reaffirmed the traditional doctrine of clerical celibacy, and insisted that only men could be ordained as priests. The council left open the question of birth control but three years later, the pope declared contraceptive use to be contrary to Church teaching. The issues of clerical celibacy, women's ordination, and contraceptive use would bedevil the Church for the rest of the century.

**McDonald's on the Champs-Elysées in Paris**
In the postwar era, the United States functioned as a symbol of modernity. The McDonald's hamburger franchise represented the United States to many Europeans because it typified modernity's standardization and mass consumerism. Assembly-line production lowered costs and made dining out affordable to the masses.

# Social Encounters in the Age of Affluence

With the unprecedented prosperity of the postwar years came a series of encounters between different cultural and social groups. As trade and production increased in Europe, so, too, did the volume and variety of goods imported from elsewhere. The demand for laborers rose as well, bringing with it a rising tide of immigration and of women's employment. Affluence also permitted more young people than ever before to attend colleges and universities. The encounters that resulted from these developments both shaped and were shaped by western Europeans' efforts to make sense of the new material world.

## Americanization, Coca-Colonization, and the Gaullist Protest

For many Europeans, this new world seemed overwhelmingly American, as U.S.-based corporations scattered branch offices throughout western Europe, and U.S.-produced goods filled the shelves of European shops. The U.S. presence in science and technology was also formidable. The United States invested more in scientific research and development, produced more graduates in the sciences and engineering than all other Western countries combined, and came out on top in terms of numbers of papers published and patents registered.

American domination of popular culture was even more striking. Immediately after World War II, the U.S. government forced European states to dismantle quotas on American film imports by threatening to withhold much-needed loans. By 1951, American productions accounted for more than 60 percent of film showings in western Europe. American television, too, quickly established a central position in European mass culture. In the mid-1950s, few European households had a television, while the average American family was watching more than five hours of programming every day. In the second half of the decade, then, as the number of television owners in Europe began to expand rapidly (more than doubling between 1955 and 1956), American television networks were well-situated to take advantage of this new market. By 1960, CBS, ABC, and NBC were selling their programs to the world. The popular *Lone Ranger* series, for example, appeared in twenty-four countries. Language itself seemed subject to American takeover. Words such as *babysitter* and *comics* entered directly into German, while French children coveted *les jeans* and *le chewing-gum*.

Europeans differed in their response to the new American presence. Many enthusiastically embraced American culture, equating it with greater openness and freedom. Others, however, feared that American products such as Coca-Cola would not only conquer European markets but degrade European tastes. Europeans spoke with alarm about the "brain drain" as scientists and academics headed across the Atlantic to the richer universities of the United States. They argued that even as Europe was losing its colonial possessions, it was itself undergoing colonization, or at least "coca-colonization."[17]

One of the most powerful voices protesting "coca-colonization" belonged to Charles De Gaulle, France's president throughout the 1960s. De Gaulle is usually classified as politically conservative, but the politics of "Gaullism"° are not easy to place on any simple left-right political spectrum. De Gaulle combined a fierce anticommunism and an ardent defense of traditional social values with a firm commitment to a strong state and centralized direction of the economy. Perhaps most centrally, Gaullism championed France and Frenchness. In De Gaulle's imagination, France was "like the princess in the fairy stories or the Madonna in the frescoes, as dedicated to an exalted and exceptional destiny . . . France cannot be France without greatness."[18]

De Gaulle did not sympathize in any way with the Soviet Union, but he believed that the more immediate threat to the French way of life came from American culture. Taken in 1960 to view a new highway in California, De Gaulle gazed somberly at the sight of cars weaving in and out on a traffic cloverleaf and commented, "I have the impression that all this will end very badly."[19] To reduce American influence in Europe, and thus to restore France to its rightful position of grandeur and glory, De Gaulle pursued independent foreign and military policies. He extended diplomatic recognition to China, made a state visit to Moscow, and withdrew French forces from NATO command (although France remained formally a part of the NATO alliance). In 1960 France exploded its own atomic bomb.

Like De Gaulle, Europeans across the political spectrum feared their countries' becoming secondhand versions of the United States, yet the cultural history of this era was one of reciprocal encounters rather than one-way Americanization. Europeans consumed American products with great gusto, but in the process they adapted these products to suit their own needs. In the late 1950s, for example, four young working-class men from the northern British seaport of Liverpool latched on to the new American rock and roll, mixed in their own regional musical styles, and transformed popular music not only in Europe but also in the United States. The impact of the Beatles testified to the power of European culture to remake American cultural products. Even McDonald's, when it arrived in European cities in the 1960s, made subtle changes to the composition of its fast food to appeal to the differing tastes of the new markets.

## Immigration and Ethnic Diversity

A second set of encounters that transformed European societies during this era resulted from the presence of rising numbers of immigrants, who brought with them new and in many cases non-Western cultural traditions. Immigration was the by-product of both decolonization and economic prosperity. As European imperial control collapsed, white settlers retreated to their country of origin, and colonial "losers"—indigenous groups that had allied with the now-defeated colonial powers—fled because they feared discrimination, retribution, or perhaps simply a loss of status. In France, for example, Algerian independence led to the influx not only of Algeria's white French population but also of 80,000 Algerian Harkis whose loyalty to the

**Immigrants Arriving in Britain, 1956**

Many immigrants from regions within the British Empire had been taught that Britain was the "mother country" or "home." They were shocked to discover that once in Britain, they were regarded as foreign and as inferior.

colonial administration jeopardized their place in the new Algeria.

At the same time, as northern and western European states experienced both soaring economic growth figures and a slowing rate of population increase, governments undertook to recruit foreign labor. Beginning in 1955, the West German government negotiated a series of immigration contracts with Italy, Greece, Turkey, Yugoslavia, and the North African states. In Britain, both public and private agencies turned for workers to the West Indies, India, and Pakistan. France recruited workers from Spain and Italy, as well as its colonial territories such as Algeria, Morocco, Tunisia, Senegal, Mali, and Guadeloupe. By the beginning of the 1970s, the nations of northern and western Europe were home to approximately nine million immigrants, half of these from the less prosperous Mediterranean states of Portugal, Spain, Italy, and Greece. The other half came from Turkey, Yugoslavia, and countries in Asia, Africa, and the Caribbean.

These workers did the dirtiest, most dangerous, least desirable jobs. They worked the night shifts, emptied the bedpans, dug the ditches, and cleaned the toilets. They lived in substandard housing, often confined to isolated dormitories or inner-city slums, and accepted low, often illegally low, pay rates. The reason they did so is starkly presented in the table below. Despite racial discrimination and economic exploitation, western Europe offered greater economic opportunities than were available in the immigrants' homelands.

The majority of the early immigrants were single men. They tended to see themselves, and were seen by their host countries, as "guestworkers," temporary laborers who would earn money and then return home to their native lands. By the mid-1960s, however, families were beginning to join these men, and a second generation of "immigrants" was being born. This generation changed the face of Europe. By the 1980s European societies had become multiethnic.

**The Appeal of Immigration—Annual Per Capita Gross National Product in the Mid-1960s**

| | |
|---|---|
| Pakistan | $125 |
| Turkey | $353 |
| Jamaica | $520 |
| Spain | $822 |
| Italy | $1,272 |
| Britain | $1,977 |
| France | $2,324 |

Source: Leslie Page Moch, *Moving Europeans: Migration in Western Europe Since 1650* (1992), 177.

The emergence of urban ethnic subcultures immeasurably enlivened European cultures and economies (and diets); it also complicated domestic politics and raised challenging questions about the relationship between national and ethnic identity. Racism became more overt as the white settler groups who returned "home" in the wake of decolonization often brought with them hardened racist attitudes, and the presence of nonwhite minority groups, clustered in certain cities, sparked resentment in societies unused to cultural diversity.

## The Second Sex?

In 1949, the French writer Simone de Beauvoir (1908–1986) published *The Second Sex*. In this influential critique of gender divisions in Western industrial society, de Beauvoir argued that women remained the "second sex"— that despite changes in their political and legal status, women were still defined by their relationship to men rather than by their own actions or achievements. Over the next two decades, the new prosperity pushed women into higher education and the labor force and so, in the long run, worked to undermine the traditional gender roles that de Beauvoir described. In the short run, however, affluence accentuated women's domestic identity.

A number of changes both reflected and reinforced postwar domesticity. The most important were demographic. Marriage rates rose and the marriage age dropped in the postwar years. In the United States between 1940 and 1957, the fertility rate rose by 50 percent. Europe experienced a baby "boomlet" rather than a baby boom. European birth rates rose in the late 1940s but dropped again in the 1950s (whereas U.S. fertility rates remained high into the 1960s). Nevertheless, although family sizes were small, a higher percentage of western European women than ever before had children.

By exalting women's maternal identity, both religion and popular culture provided a potent ideology for these demographic changes. The Roman Catholic Church of the 1950s placed renewed emphasis on Mary, the paragon of motherhood. Pope Pius XII (r. 1939–1958) particularly encouraged the growth of devotion to Mary. He proclaimed in 1950 that Mary had ascended bodily into heaven (the Doctrine of the Assumption) and designated 1954 as the Year of Mary. This Marian devotion encouraged women to regard motherhood as a holy calling, the very core of female identity. Popular culture reinforced this religious message, with its glossy images of what families should look like and how they should interact. In television programs and in the articles and advertisements of women's magazines, the woman stayed at home, presiding over an expanding array of household machines that, in theory, reduced her housework burden and freed her to focus on the satisfactions of motherhood.

At the same time, a number of cultural, economic, and technological changes transformed the Western home into a much more private place. Because of the boom in house

### The Kitchen Debate

The kitchen—stocked with an abundance of attractively packaged foods and a glittering array of time-saving appliances—symbolized not only material plenty but also moral stability. In the Western domestic ideal, the kitchen represented the center of family life and the woman's proper domain. When Vice President Richard Nixon traveled to Moscow in 1959 to open an American exhibition, he pointed to the display model of a suburban kitchen as evidence of Western superiority. Khrushchev refused to be impressed. Nixon and Khrushchev's argument became known as the "Kitchen Debate."

building, by the mid-1950s couples forced by wartime deprivation to live with their parents could now move into their own apartment or house. Accelerated suburbanization, made possible by the expansion of private car ownership and the spread of highway networks, meant that relatives now lived farther apart. "Family" increasingly meant the nuclear family.

Prosperity accentuated the family's isolation. Economic growth translated into a rapid drop in the number of domestic servants as workers turned to better-paying jobs and household appliances took their place. Because the new houses and apartment buildings possessed modern conveniences such as indoor plumbing, communal baths, toilets, and washhouses gradually disappeared. Television moved the social center away from cinemas, cafés, and pubs to the family living room.

Cold War concerns also accentuated the Western woman's domestic role in two very different ways. First, anticommunist propaganda hailed domesticity as a sign of Western superiority, by contrasting the favorable lot of Western women to their Soviet counterparts, who led lives of almost endless labor. The vast majority of Soviet women combined their domestic duties with full-time outside employment, often in jobs involving heavy manual labor, and they spent a substantial portion of each day lining up to purchase scarce goods. Second, the nuclear age made the nuclear family seem all the more important. Feeling increasingly helpless in a superpower-dominated world on the brink of nuclear annihilation, Europeans tended to withdraw for shelter to family life.

For some women, this shelter was more like a prison. In *The Captive Wife*, published in 1966, the British sociologist Hannah Gavron (b. 1944) asked, "Have all the great changes

in the position of women in the last one hundred and fifty years come to nothing?" In *The Feminine Mystique* (1963), the American journalist Betty Friedan (b. 1921) identified what she called "the problem that had no name," a crisis of identity and purpose among middle-class, educated women confined in the role of housewife and mother.

Whether a nightmare or a dream, the domestic ideal remained removed from the reality of many women's lives in the postwar era. In the poorer social classes, women by necessity continued to work outside the home, as they always had. At the same time, the new culture of consumption demanded that many women, clinging precariously to the middle rungs of the social ladder, take on paid employment to pay for the ever-expanding list of household necessities.

A new pattern of employment emerged that reconciled the new domesticity with the needs of expanding economies. Increasingly, single women, including those in the middle class, worked until they married. Many continued to do so until the first child arrived and resumed paid employment after the last child had left home or at least started school. This work was regarded, however, as secondary to their main job—the making of a home and the rearing of children. Part-time employment, with lower wages and few or no benefits, expanded accordingly. Everywhere pay rates remained unequal.

Inequalities in legal status continued as well. Until 1964 and the passage of the Matrimonial Act, for example, a married French woman could not open her own bank account, run a shop, or apply for a passport without her husband's permission. Traditional gender roles remained firmly intact, despite the material and political changes of the postwar era.

## DOCUMENT

# Rock and Revolution

*In 1967, the Beatles, already global superstars, released* Sgt. Pepper's Lonely Hearts Club Band. *Called the "most influential rock album ever produced,"* Sgt. Pepper's *revolutionized rock music. The complexity of its compositions impressed serious music critics, who for the first time acknowledged that rock music was worth listening to. The album's lyrics, too, received unprecedented praise, with one reviewer comparing the last song on the album ("A Day in the Life") to T. S. Eliot's modernist masterpiece, "The Waste Land" (see Chapter 24). Although not overtly political,* Sgt. Pepper's *illustrates many of the themes of the protests that marked the era in which it was produced. Infused with a sense of playfulness and celebration, the album called its listeners to burst out of the confines of order, authority, and rationality, and embrace instead the values of human community and emotional liberation.*

### She's Leaving Home

Wednesday morning at five o'clock as the day begins
Silently closing her bedroom door
Leaving the note that she hoped would say more
She goes downstairs to the kitchen clutching her
    handkerchief
Quietly turning the backdoor key
Stepping outside she is free.
She (We gave her most of our lives)
is leaving (Sacrificed most of our lives)
home (We gave her everything money could buy)

She's leaving home after living alone
For so many years. Bye, bye
Father snores as his wife gets into her dressing gown
Picks up the letter that's lying there
Standing alone at the top of the stairs
She breaks down and cries to her husband
Daddy our baby's gone.
Why would she treat us so thoughtlessly
How could she do this to me.
She (We never thought of ourselves)
is leaving (Never a thought for ourselves)
home (We struggled hard all our lives to get by)
She's leaving home after living alone
For so many years. Bye, bye
Friday morning at nine o'clock she is far away
Waiting to keep the appointment she made
Meeting a man from the motor trade.
She (What did we do that was wrong)
is having (We didn't know it was wrong) fun
Fun is the one thing that money can't buy
Something inside that was always denied
For so many years. Bye, bye
She's leaving home bye bye

Source: "She's Leaving Home" by John Lennon and Paul McCartney. Copyright © 1967 (Renewed) Sony/ATV Tunes LLC. All rights administered by Sony/ATV Music Publishing, 8 Music Square West, Nashville, TN 37203. All rights reserved. Used by permission.

## The Protest Era

The unprecedented prosperity of the West in this era permitted a dramatic expansion of higher-education systems. By the later 1960s, the expanding university campuses became the center of powerful protests as political demonstrations exploded in almost every Western country and in the developing nations well. In France, a student demonstration blossomed into a full-scale social revolt. Within a few days, eight million French men and women were on strike. "Paris '68" came to symbolize the political and social discontent of many in the West, particularly the youth, during these years.

Much of this discontent focused on the New Left° argument that ordinary people, even in democratic societies, possessed little power. Appalled by the excesses of Stalinism and concerned about the growth of large corporations and of the state itself in the West, New Left thinkers such as the German philosopher Herbert

### The Protests of 1968
French students battle police in Paris during the tumultuous spring of 1968.

# The Pill: Controlling the Female Body

In the postwar period, all sorts of pills appeared on the shelves of American and European pharmacies. Offered in a myriad of colors and sizes, they promised all sorts of remedies for all sorts of ailments. But only one earned the designation "*the* Pill"—the oral contraceptive, first marketed in the United States in 1960. In 1993, the *Economist* (a respected British weekly news magazine) listed the Pill as one of the seven wonders of the modern world. A revolutionary contraceptive, the Pill helped alter the place of the female body in Western culture.

The Pill's entry into the mass market coincided with two other developments. First, sexual practices and attitudes changed significantly among some sectors of the population—particularly middle-class men and women with university educations. Second, the birth rate slowed throughout the United States and western Europe. Thus it is often assumed that the Pill caused both a sexual and demographic revolution.

This assumption is incorrect. Although by 1965 the Pill was the most popular form of birth control in the United States (used by 80 percent of white, non-Catholic, college graduates between ages 20 and 24), in Europe it became a part of women's lives much more slowly. Introduced to Britain in 1961, the Pill was not mass-marketed there until the late 1960s. In France and Czechoslovakia, withdrawal remained the most popular form of birth control until well into the 1970s, when the Pill began to be distributed widely. In Italy, contraceptives of all types, including the Pill, were illegal until 1971. In Ireland, they remain illegal for unmarried men and women. In the Soviet Union, the Pill was never widely accessible. Most Soviet women relied on withdrawal, rhythm, and abortion—on the average, four to six abortions during the childbearing years. Moreover, throughout Europe and the United States, the Pill always remained more popular with the wealthier sectors of society. Because women who wanted to use it were required to visit their doctor every six months, many poor women viewed the Pill as prohibitively expensive (and many single women simply could not obtain a prescription).

The Pill, then, did not cause the sexual revolution. It did, however, have a radical impact. The Pill offered a new, yet ambivalent way of viewing the female body. Other methods of birth control dealt with the consequences of sexual intercourse (the barrier methods, withdrawal, and abortion) or sought to limit its practice (rhythm). The Pill, however, was not an external object to be inserted or applied or fitted. By manipulating the female reproductive cycle, it actually altered the body itself, permitting women to experience what had been defined as an exclusively male prerogative—the detachment of sexual intercourse from pregnancy. At the same time, the Pill allowed women to distance themselves from their bodies. One of the problems with other forms of female contraceptives was that they required women to touch their genitals, a requirement that many European and American women found distasteful.

The Pill also raised important questions about controlling the female body. During the course of the twentieth century, childbirth had altered radically in the Western world. No longer occurring at home and presided over by women, childbirth now occurred in the hospital, where doctors—usually male—were in charge. It had become "medicalized": The birthing woman had become a patient, a medical problem, in need of drugs and other scientific devices. The Pill fit with this process. Although many women hailed it as a liberator that allowed them to control their own bodies, the Pill was initially marketed to doctors very differently. In its advertising, the Searle pharmaceutical company assured doctors that the Pill would allow them to supervise and regulate their patients' birth control practices. The Pill, then, offered the promise of controlling the female body; the question was, who was in charge?

## For Discussion

Why has the Pill become a powerful symbol of changes in women's roles in the contemporary era?

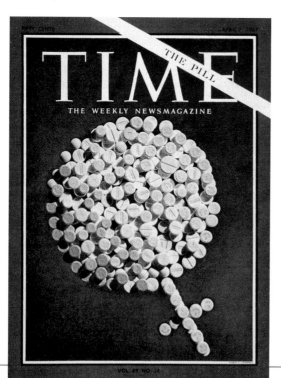

**One Little Pill**
In 1967, *Time* magazine's cover story on the Pill was titled "Freedom from Fear."

Marcuse (1898–1979) warned that expanding corporate and state power threatened the individuality and independence of the ordinary citizen. They argued that debate might seem open, but that experts and elites, not ordinary people, made the actual choices. Hence the protesters demanded "participatory" rather than parliamentary democracy, the revitalization of citizenship through active participation in decision making.

Discarding orthodox political solutions went hand in hand with overturning traditional social rules. In their demand for "liberation," the students focused as much on cultural as on economic and political issues. Commentators began to talk about a sexual revolution as practices became commonplace that in the 1950s were labeled immoral or bohemian—couples living together before marriage or individuals engaging in sexual relationships with a variety of partners.

The protests of the later 1960s were also linked to the wider context of decolonization and the Cold War. Protesters identified their struggle for a more open politics with colonial independence movements. Rejecting both Soviet-style communism and free-market capitalism, they turned for inspiration to the newly emerging nations of Latin America and Asia. Seeking to break free from the confines of the Cold War, they fiercely criticized American involvement in Vietnam, in which they believed the United States served not as "the leader of the free world" but rather as an imperialist oppressor.

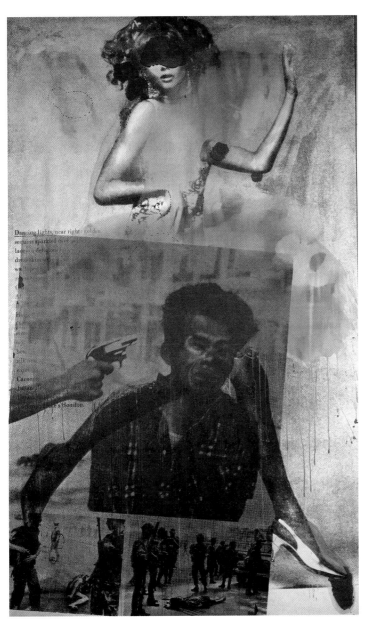

### Wolf Vostell, *Miss America, 1968*

By juxtaposing Miss America, a symbol of American luxury and even decadence, with one of the most notorious photographs to come out of the Vietnam War, the German artist Wolf Vostell articulated a powerful protest. Associated Press photographer Eddie Adams won the Pulitzer Prize for the photograph of General Nguyen Ngoc Loan, the chief of the U.S.-backed South Vietnamese National Police, caught in the act of executing a Vietcong suspect (a supporter of the communist North Vietnam) on the streets of Saigon in 1968. Broadcast to 20 million viewers on the American television network channel NBC, this photograph was reproduced in countless newspapers, magazines, and books published across the world. For many, it became a symbol of a war gone wrong.

# Conclusion

## New Definitions, New Divisions

The Cold War was in part an ideological encounter, with both sides laying claim to the title "democratic." When Soviet tanks rolled through the streets of Budapest in 1956, they flattened not only the Hungarian Revolution but also any illusions about the democratic nature of Soviet-style communism. Yet the hope that the communist system could be reformed, that Marx's original concern for social justice and political equality could be reclaimed, remained—until twelve years later when the tanks rolled again in an eastern European city. The crushing of the Prague Spring destroyed any hope of a democratic eastern Europe within the confines of the Cold War.

In contrast, democracy took firm root in western Europe during the postwar era, even in nations with antidemocratic cultural traditions such as West Germany and Italy. Yet in 1968, protesters in Paris and in cities throughout the world challenged the easy linkage of "the West" with democracy. They pointed out that the increasing scale and complexity of industrial society deprived ordinary people of opportunities for genuine participation in political decision making. And they pointed to the way that Cold War divisions superseded democratic commitments. Despite its abandonment of democratic practices to reinforce racial apartheid, for example, South Africa considered itself, and was considered by other powers, as part of "the West." Within the Cold War context, "the West" sometimes seemed to mean simply "anti-Soviet."

By the early 1970s, the sharp bipolarities of West versus East had begun to break down. Over the next three decades, economic crisis, combined with revolutionary changes in eastern European and Soviet affairs, would reshape the contemporary world. By the early 1990s, the Cold War was over and nationalist conflicts, often fueled by vicious ethnic and religious hatreds, once again played front and center, after twenty years of being upstaged by superpower hostilities.

## Suggestions for Further Reading

For a comprehensive listing of suggested readings, please go to www.ablongman.com/levack2e/chapter27

Ansprenger, Franz. *The Dissolution of Colonial Empires.* 1989. A clear and comprehensive account (that unfortunately includes no maps).

Castles, Stephen, et al. *Here for Good: Western Europe's New Ethnic Minorities.* 1984. A useful exploration of the impact of postwar immigration, despite the rather rigid Marxist analysis.

Crampton, R. J. *Eastern Europe in the Twentieth Century—And After.* 1997. Detailed chapters on the 1950s and 1960s, including a substantial discussion of the Prague Spring.

Cronin, James. *The World the Cold War Made: Order, Chaos, and the Return of History.* 1996. An intelligent and thought-provoking overview of the impact of the Cold War.

Fineberg, Jonathan. *Art Since 1940: Strategies of Being.* 1995. A big, bold, lavishly illustrated volume that makes the unfashionable argument that individuals matter.

Fink, Carole, et al. *1968: The World Transformed.* 1998. A collection of essays that explores both the international and the domestic political context for the turmoil of 1968.

Gaddis, John Lewis. *The Cold War: A New History.* 2005. A comprehensive overview by a prominent Cold war historian.

Gross, Jan T., ed. *The Politics of Retribution in Europe: World War II and Its Aftermath.* 2000. This series of essays makes clear that war did not end in Europe in May 1945.

Isaacs, Jeremy, and Taylor Downing. *Cold War: An Illustrated History.* 1998. The companion book to the CNN television series. Filled with memorable photographs.

Judge, Edward, and John Langdon. *A Hard and Bitter Peace: A Global History of the Cold War.* 1999. An extremely useful survey for students. Excellent maps.

Keep, John. *Last of the Empires: A History of the Soviet Union, 1945–1991.* 1995. Looks beyond the Kremlin to explore social, cultural, and economic developments.

Mazrui, Ali, and Michael Tidy. *Nationalism and New States in Africa.* 1984. Offers a thematic rather than chronological account of African state building.

Poiger, Uta. *Jazz, Rock, and Rebels: Cold War Politics and American Culture in a Divided Germany.* 2000. Explores the interplay among youth culture, Americanization, and political protest.

de Senarclens, P. *From Yalta to the Iron Curtain: The Great Powers and the Origins of the Cold War.* 1995. A look at the diplomatic, political and military concerns that created the Cold War.

Stromberg, Roland. *After Everything: Western Intellectual History Since 1945.* 1975. A swiftly moving tour through the major intellectual developments.

Urwin, Derek. *A Political History of Western Europe Since 1945.* 1997. Readable, reasonably up-to-date, and comprehensive.

Wyman, Mark. *DPs: Europe's Displaced Persons, 1945–1951.* 1989. An important study of an often-neglected topic.

Zubok, Vladislav, and Constantine Pleshakov. *Inside the Kremlin's Cold War: From Stalin to Khrushchev.* 1996. A close examination of the Cold War on the Soviet side.

## Notes

1. The original signatories of the NATO treaty were Iceland, Norway, Great Britain, Belgium, the Netherlands, Luxembourg, France, Italy, and Portugal. Greece and Turkey joined the alliance in 1951, West Germany in 1954, and Spain in 1982. Sweden, Finland, Switzerland, Austria, Yugoslavia, and Albania remained nonaligned with either the United States or the Soviet Union.

2. Quoted in Donald W. White, *The American Century* (1996), 328.

3. Quotation from *Time* magazine, 1950; quoted in Martin Walker, *The Cold War and the Making of the Modern World* (1993), 66–67.

4. Quoted in Walker, *The Cold War,* 83.

5. Quoted in White, *The American Century,* 286.

6. Quoted in Karel Kaplan, *Report on the Murder of the General Secretary* (1990), 159.

7. Ibid., 242.

8. Ibid., 231.

9. Quoted in John L. H. Keep, *Last of the Empires: A History of the Soviet Union, 1945–1991* (1995), 79.

10. Quoted in Michael Scammell, *From Gulag to Glasnost: Nonconformist Art in the Soviet Union,* eds. Alla Rosenfeld and Norton T. Dodge (1995), 61.

11. Quoted in Walker, *The Cold War,* 105.

12. Official Hungarian statistics reported 3,000 dead. John Lewis Gaddis places the number at 20,000 in *We Now Know: Rethinking Cold War Evidence* (1997).

13. Quoted in Robert Paxton, *Europe in the Twentieth Century* (1997), 578.

14. Quoted in Jonathan Fineberg, *Art Since 1940: Strategies of Being* (1995), 144.

15. Ibid., 89.

16. Quoted in Adrian Hastings, *Modern Catholicism: Vatican II and After* (1991), 29.

17. Reinhold Wagnleitner, *Coca-Colonization and the Cold War: The Cultural Mission of the United States in Austria After the Second World War* (1994).

18. Quoted in Felix Gilbert, *The End of the European Era, 1890 to the Present* (1991), 429.

19. Quoted in Richard Kuisel, *Seducing the French: The Dilemma of Americanization* (1993), 147.

# The West in the Contemporary Era: New Encounters and Transformations

# 28

O N THE EVENING OF NOVEMBER 9, 1989, EAST GERMAN BORDER guards stationed at the wall that divided East and West Berlin gazed out nervously at an unprecedented sight. Thousands of their fellow citizens had gathered in front of the gates and were demanding to be let through into the western half of the city. This demand was extraordinary; in the twenty-eight years that the Berlin Wall had stood, more than 200 people had been shot trying to cross it. But the autumn of 1989 was no ordinary time. A radically reformist regime had emerged in the Soviet Union and publicly proclaimed that its eastern European allies could no longer rely on the Soviet army to assist them in putting down domestic dissent. Poland and Hungary were in the process of replacing communist governments with pluralist parliamentary systems. And in East Germany, 200,000 disaffected citizens had taken advantage of relaxed border controls in Hungary and Czechoslovakia to flee to the West in just a few weeks, while more than one million had joined illegal protest demonstrations.

On November 9, in response to overwhelming public pressure, the East German government announced that it would drastically relax the requirements for obtaining an exit visa to visit or emigrate to the West. In a press conference to announce the upcoming changes, the East Berlin Communist Party boss Gunter Schabowski gave a carelessly worded reply to a reporter's question about the new travel policy—and sparked a revolution. Schabowski indicated, wrongly, that as of the next morning, anyone who wanted to head to the West could obtain an automatic exit visa at the border. The news spread quickly, and huge crowds gathered at the checkpoints that dotted the Berlin Wall. The nervous border guards had no idea what to do. Neither did their superiors, who refused to issue the guards any clear instructions. As the crowds pressed forward, the guards gave in and

**And the Wall Came Tumbling Down** Berliners celebrate the fall of the Berlin Wall in November 1989.

opened the gates. While television cameras broadcast the scene to an astonished world, tens of thousands of East Germans walked, ran, and danced across the border that had for so long literally and symbolically divided West from East. Elated with their new freedom and energized with a sense of power and possibility, they then turned on the wall itself. Jumping on top of it, they transformed it from an instrument of coercion and division into a platform for partying. Caught, the East German government saw no way to close the gates. Within a few days, and again without any official approval, ordinary Germans, equipped with hammers and chisels, began to dismantle the wall that the politicians had erected almost three decades earlier.

As extraordinary as the fall of the wall was, the events that followed over the next two years proved even more dramatic—the collapse of communist regimes throughout eastern Europe, the end of the Cold War, the disintegration of the Soviet Union, and the onset of civil war in Yugoslavia and in many formerly Soviet regions. Over the next two decades, both governments and ordinary people—not only throughout Europe but across the globe—struggled to build new structures to suit the vastly changed geopolitical landscape.

How did the meaning of "the West" change with the collapse of communism and the sundering of the Iron Curtain that had once divided Europe? This chapter will look at four key questions as it seeks to understand the causes and consequences of these dramatic developments and their implications for Western identity:

- How did economic and political developments in the 1970s and 1980s undermine the international structures of the postwar era?
- What factors explain not only the outbreak but also the success of the revolutions of 1989–1991?
- What were the consequences of these revolutions for the societies of eastern Europe?
- What were the implications of these developments for the meaning of "the West" itself?

# Economic Stagnation and Political Change: The 1970s and 1980s

- How did economic and political developments in the 1970s and 1980s undermine international structures of the postwar era?

As the 1960s drew to a close, the risk of nuclear war seemed to recede with the onset of detente°, the effort to stabilize superpower relations through negotiations and arms control. But stability remained elusive.

Economic crisis heightened political and social polarization, while the renewal of the Cold War at the end of the 1970s destabilized both international and domestic relations.

## The 1970s: A More Uncertain Era

In the early 1970s, the United States and Europe—both East and West—entered a new era. Detente signaled a relaxing of the Cold War tensions that had structured so much of international relations since the end of World War II. But at the same time, economic developments warned that the easy affluence of the postwar era had ended.

### The Era of Detente

Changes in the Cold War climate were first felt in West Germany. In 1969 the West Berlin mayor and Social Democratic Party (SPD) leader Willy Brandt (1913–1992) became chancellor. For the first time in its history, West Germany had a government that was not led by a Christian Democrat. Brandt proceeded to implement a new *Ostpolitik* or "Eastern policy"—the opening of diplomatic and economic relations between West Germany and the Soviet Union and its satellite states. In the triumphant climax of Ostpolitik, East and West Germany recognized the legitimacy of each other's existence in 1972 and in the next year, both Germanys entered the United Nations.

During this era, the leaders of the superpowers also acted to break down the bipolarities of the Cold War. By the end of the 1960s, both the Soviet Union and the United States faced stagnating economies, and both were spending $50 million per day on nuclear weapons. These economic pressures led Soviet and American leaders to embrace detente. In November 1969 Soviet and American negotiators began the Strategic Arms Limitation Talks (SALT). Signed in 1972, the agreement froze the existing weapons balance. With both superpowers possessing sufficient nuclear weaponry to destroy the globe several times over, SALT may seem to have been inconsequential, but it helped arrest the armaments spiral and, more important, revealed a shift in Cold War power relations.

Important changes within the communist world also contributed to detente. Throughout the 1930s and 1940s, the Chinese communist leader Mao Zedong was an obedient disciple of Stalin. In the 1950s, however, relations cooled when Mao challenged Khrushchev's aim of "peaceful coexistence" with the West. Khrushchev, in turn, opposed Mao's "Great Leap Forward." This effort to transform a peasant society into an industrial powerhouse in one single year led to the deaths of an estimated 30 million Chinese, victims of starvation and Mao's fantasies. Horrified, Khrushchev suspended economic aid to China in 1960. By the time the first Chinese atomic bomb exploded in 1964, the split between China and the Soviet Union was open and irrevocable. U.S. president Richard

Nixon (1913–1994) and his national security adviser Henry Kissinger (b. 1923) decided to take advantage of this Sino-Soviet split. In 1971, Nixon announced the lifting of travel and trade restrictions with China and then sent shock waves through the world by visiting China himself. Nixon's reconciliation with communist China was a turning point: In the 1950s and 1960s, "East versus West" had formed a basic building block of international relations. In the 1970s, the shape of international politics looked much less clear.

## Economic Crisis in the West

The economic outlook also blurred in this era as the 1970s brought an unprecedented combination of high inflation and high unemployment rates. Commentators labeled this new reality stagflation°—the escalating prices of a boom economy combined with the joblessness of an economy going bust. Between 1974 and 1976 the average annual growth rate within western European nations dropped to zero.

War and oil played important roles in creating this economic crisis. In October 1973, Egyptian and Syrian armies attacked Israel. When Soviet forces began airlifting supplies to the invading troops, Israel appealed to the U.S. for military aid. In retaliation for American assistance to Israel, the oil-producing states, or OPEC (Organization of Petroleum Exporting Countries), imposed an embargo on sales to the U.S. and more than quintupled the price of a barrel of oil. In 1979 political revolution in Iran doubled the price again. These price increases vastly accelerated the inflationary spiral.

### Inflation and Economic Performance in the West

| | France | Great Britain | Italy | United States | West Germany |
|---|---|---|---|---|---|
| Inflation over Previous Year (percent) | | | | | |
| 1970 | 5.2% | 6.4% | 5.0% | 5.9% | 3.4% |
| 1975 | 11.8 | 24.2 | 17.0 | 9.1 | 6.0 |
| 1979 | 9.1 | 13.4 | 14.8 | 11.3 | 4.1 |
| Gross Domestic Product (Percentage Growth/Decline over Previous Year) | | | | | |
| 1970 | +5.7% | +2.3% | +5.3% | −0.3% | +5.1% |
| 1975 | +0.2 | −20.6 | −23.6 | −0.1 | −1.6 |
| 1979 | +3.3 | +2.4 | +2.7 | +2.4 | +4.2 |

Source: Martin Walker, *Cold War: A History* (1993), 234.

Yet rising oil prices were not the sole cause of the economic crisis of the 1970s and 1980s. Two other factors also contributed. First, in 1973 U.S. president Richard Nixon took drastic action to defend the weakening dollar. He decided to let the dollar "float," to let market forces rather than fixed currency exchange rates determine the dollar's value against other currencies. This decision gutted the Bretton Woods Agreement, which had governed international economic affairs since World War II (see Chapter 27), and introduced a more volatile economic era. Whereas the Bretton Woods system had worked to direct the flow of capital to countries in need of investment, the new unregulated system allowed capital to surge into markets in which investors could reap immediate gains. National economies lay vulnerable to speculative attacks. No fewer than sixty-nine countries experienced serious banking crises, and the annual economic growth rates of the developed nations fell by one-third in the decades that followed the collapse of Bretton Woods.

A second factor in the economic crisis of the 1970s was international competition. Both western Europe and the United States struggled to compete with the emerging Asian and South/Latin American economies. Western societies possessed a politicized workforce that demanded relatively high wages and extensive social services. Increasingly, manufacturing concerns moved south and east, to take advantage of the lack of labor regulation and protection in the developing world.

## Consequences of the Crisis

The economic crisis had stark social consequences. As the economic pie grew smaller, competition for slices grew fierce. The 1970s saw a resurgence of industrial unrest in western Europe. In Britain, conflict with the unions brought down three successive governments in a decade. In both Italy and West Germany, workers became increasingly militant and succeeded in winning large wage increases. These industrial settlements only worsened the problem of inflation. Workers demanded large pay increases to meet the rising cost of living, but employers, faced with having to pay higher wages, raised the prices of their goods and services. And so the cost of living continued to climb.

The new economic climate of austerity also led to heightened racial conflict throughout much of western Europe. We saw in Chapter 27 that postwar governments struggling to cope with labor shortages had encouraged immigration, both from the poorer countries of southern and eastern Europe and from colonial or former colonial regions such as Algeria, India, and Jamaica. By 1971, nine million immigrants were living in northern and western Europe.

With the onset of economic crisis, these immigrant communities soon found themselves under attack. European governments reacted to rising unemployment rates by halting labor immigration. By 1975 West Germany, France, the Netherlands, Britain, Belgium, Sweden, and Switzerland had all banned further immigration. Because it explicitly (although incorrectly) linked the presence of immigrants to unemployment, anti-immigration legislation helped solidify racist attitudes among many sectors of the European population. Violence against immigrants began to escalate.

Ironically, anti-immigration legislation actually increased the size of immigrant communities. West Germany saw its number of foreign residents rise by 13 percent between 1974 and 1982; in the same period, France witnessed a 33 percent increase. Foreign workers scrambled to get into western Europe before the doors shut, and once they were in, were reluctant to leave because of the well-grounded fear that they would not be able to return. Family members came too—only Switzerland banned the entry of dependents.

In the 1980s, then, what sociologists call "migration streams" solidified into ethnic minority communities—not "guestworkers," but rather a permanent part of western European societies. By 1991, 25 percent of the inhabitants of France were either immigrants or the children or grandchildren of immigrants. For both economic and social reasons, minority groups clustered in certain areas in certain cities. In West Germany in the early 1980s, ethnic minorities constituted 6 percent of the population as a whole, but 24 percent of the population of Frankfurt—and in the city's central district, 80 percent.

The resulting encounters among peoples of different religious and ethnic traditions reshaped European culture. In Britain, for example, Afro-Caribbean styles of dress and music had a profound influence on white working-class youth culture. These encounters also posed a potent challenge to ideas of national identity. By the 1980s, British journalists were writing about "third-generation immigrants," as if someone born in Britain to British citizenship were somehow less British than other British citizens. Such terminology indicated a deep reluctance to classify individuals with brown or black skin as British, an inability to conceive of national identity as anything but white. In France, the highly centralized education system became the site of hostile encounters, as Islamic parents fought for the rights of their daughters to attend school in traditional Muslim headdress, a practice resisted by some French authorities who feared that "Frenchness" would be diluted if immigrants failed to accept the traditions of the host society.

In both France and Britain, immigrants could become or already were legal citizens. In West Germany, Switzerland, and the Scandinavian countries, however, foreign workers remained foreign, with no chance of obtaining citizenship. Thus by the 1980s, a dangerous situation had emerged in these countries, with the children of foreign workers growing up in a society in which they had no political rights.

DOCUMENT

## "Young, British, and White"

*During the 1980s, racist violence increased in Britain, as throughout much of Europe. Overtly racist political parties such as the National Front capitalized on anti-immigrant sentiment to recruit new members for their movements. In this document, the American journalist Bill Buford describes a birthday party held in a pub for one young member of the National Front. The excerpt begins with a dangerous moment: football (soccer) rivalries are threatening to divide the partygoers.*

On the far side, some of the new members had started in on their football chants, just as Neil had feared. These appeared to be West Ham supporters. They were then answered, from the other side of the room, by Chelsea supporters.\* A contrapuntal chorus of West Ham and Chelsea songs followed, one that sent Neil scurrying through his record collection. It was time to change the music. . . . It was time to play the White Power music.

None of the songs was played on any of the established radio stations or sold in any of the conventional shops. It was a mail-order or cash-in-hand music trade, and from the titles you could see why: "Young, British, and White"; "England Belongs to Me"; "Shove the Dove"; "England" and "British Justice." These were the lyrics of "The Voice of Britain":

Our old people cannot walk the streets alone.
They fought for this nation and this is what they get back.
They risked their lives for Britain, and now Britain belongs
   to aliens.
It's about time Britain went and took it back.

This is the voice of Britain.
You'd better believe it.
This is the voice of Britain
C'mon and fly the flag now.
. . .

The music was delivered with the same numbing, crushing percussion that had characterized everything else that had been played that evening. . . . There was one refrain I could follow, and that was because it was played repeatedly, and because, each time, everyone joined in. It seemed to be the theme song.

Two pints of lager[†] and a packet of crisps.[‡]
Wogs[§] out! White power!
Wogs out! White power!
Wogs out! White power!

It was interesting to contemplate that the high-point of the evening was organized around this simple declaration of needs: a lad needed his lager; a lad needed his packet of crisps; a lad needed his wog.

---

\* *West Ham and Chelsea = rival English soccer teams.*
[†] *"Lager" = beer.*
[‡] *"Packet of crisps" = bag of potato chips.*
[§] *"Wog" = racially derogatory term for Southeast Asians.*

Source: From *Among the Thugs: The Experience, and the Seduction, of Crowd Violence* by Bill Buford. Copyright © 1991, 1990 by William Buford. Used by permission of W. W. Norton & Company, Inc. and The Random House Group Limited.

---

These "foreigners" experienced widespread discrimination in education, housing, and employment. In West Germany in the late 1970s, more than 40 percent of "foreign" workers lived in housing without a bath or shower. (Only 6 percent of German citizens did so.) Forced to live in such substandard accommodation by poverty, immigrants were often then stereotyped as dirty and uncivilized.

Explicitly racist political parties capitalized on the new anti-immigration sentiment. In France, for example, Jean-Marie Le Pen (b. 1928), a veteran of the Algerian war, created the *Front National* in 1974 as an anti-immigration party. In Le Pen's view, "Everything comes from immigration. Everything goes back to immigration." Unemployment, rising crime rates, an increase in illegitimate births, crowded schools, AIDS—Le Pen blamed it all on nonwhite immigrants. Appealing particularly to young, male working-class voters, Le Pen's party remained a threatening political presence for the next three decades.

## The 1980s: The End of Political Consensus in the West

The economic crisis of the 1970s called into question the social democratic assumptions that had governed political life since World War II. Western Europeans had emerged from the horror of total war in 1945 determined to build better societies. Rejecting the extremes of communism on the left and fascism on the right, they took the centrist social democratic path. Two features characterized social democracies—first, mixed economies that combined nationalization of key industries with private enterprise, and second, an interventionist state that took responsibility for maintaining full employment and providing extensive welfare services. The stagflation of the 1970s, however, seemed to indicate that these social democratic solutions no longer worked. Discontented voters looked for radically new answers. In Spain, Portugal, and Greece, they turned to socialist parties. Throughout most of western Europe and in the United States, however, New Conservatism° dominated political society.

## The New Conservatives

Three leaders epitomized the New Conservatism: the Republican Ronald Reagan in the United States (1911–2004), the Christian Democrat Helmut Kohl in West Germany (b. 1930), and the Conservative Margaret Thatcher in Britain (b. 1925). On the most fundamental level, the New Conservatives rejected the postwar emphasis on social improvement in favor of policies intended to create more opportunities for individual achievement. Thatcher even insisted, "There is no such thing as society." In the New Conservative worldview, there was instead the individual, freely competing in a world governed by market forces rather than governmental regulations or state planning. As Kohl demanded during his 1983 campaign, "Less state, more market; fewer collective burdens, more personal performance; fewer encrusted structures, more mobility, self-initiative, and competition." Privatization of nationalized or state-owned industries constituted a key part of the New Conservative agenda—removing the state from the economy and allowing private enterprises to compete. In Britain under Thatcher, the coal industry, transport, and utilities were all shifted to private ownership.

New Conservatives also mounted an attack on the welfare state, insisting that rising social expenditures, funded by rising taxes, lay at the heart of the economic crisis that had afflicted the West since the early 1970s. They pointed to the fact that the years between 1960 and 1981 had seen a dramatic rise in social spending (for programs such as health, disability, and unemployment insurance; pensions; and family allowances). Minimizing the successes of these social programs in reducing poverty, New Conservatives instead linked rising social expenditures to surging inflation and declining economic growth rates.

Yet New Conservative fiscal policies did not actually break sharply from their social democratic predecessors. Reagan, for example, used deficit spending to finance skyrocketing military budgets (up by 40 percent during his administration). The real break lay in the New Conservatives' willingness to tolerate high unemployment rates. By imposing high interest rates on their economies, Thatcher and Reagan brought inflation under control. High interest rates, however, overvalued the British pound and the American dollar. As a result, manufacturers found it hard to sell their products abroad and many went under. In Britain, 13 percent of the workforce was unemployed by 1984. In West Germany, too, Kohl's policies of holding down taxes and government expenditures were accompanied by unemployment rates of more than 9 percent in the mid-1980s.

By the end of the 1980s, as a result of falling global oil prices and the Reagan military spending spree that primed the pump of the global economy, Western economies re-

**Spending on Social Services as a Percentage of the Gross Domestic Product**

|      | France | West Germany | Sweden | United Kingdom |
|------|--------|--------------|--------|----------------|
| 1960 | 13.2   | 15.5         | 11.0   | 10.8           |
| 1965 | 15.6   | 16.5         | 13.8   | 11.8           |
| 1970 | 15.1   | 17.1         | 18.6   | 13.1           |
| 1975 | 23.9   | 23.7         | 25.0   | 17.1           |
| 1980 | 26.3   | 24.0         | 31.9   | 18.1           |
| 1985 | 28.7   | 23.8         | 30.7   | 20.3           |

Source: Susan Pedersen, *Family, Dependence, and the Origins of the Welfare State: Britain and France, 1914–1945*, 1993, p. 416. Reprinted with the permission of Cambridge University Press.

turned to growth. But the average late-1980s growth rates of 2 to 3 percent per year were lower than those of 5 to 6 percent that had characterized Western economies in the 1950s and 1960s. At the same time, unemployment rates tended to hover between 5 and 7 percent—levels that would have been regarded as unacceptably high in the earlier period. A new political culture, based on lowered expectations, had come into being.

Even Europe's leftist parties had to adapt to this new political culture. Socialist and social democratic governments in Sweden, Italy, Greece, Spain, and France followed New Conservatives along the path of reduced health and social security expenditures, as well as wage cuts. The most dramatic example of this adaptation of the left occurred in France. In 1981, French voters elected Socialist Party leader François Mitterrand (1916–1996) to the presidency. In his first year in office, Mitterrand implemented a series of radical social democratic measures, including a rise in the minimum wage, a reduction in the workweek, expanded social welfare, and higher taxes for the wealthy. But in 1982, Mitterrand was forced by a series of economic catastrophes—falling exports, rising trade and budget deficits, soaring inflation rates—to cut social spending and to let unemployment rates rise.

## New Challenges and New Identities: New Feminism

The triumph of New Conservatism demonstrated that economic crisis had shattered the post–World War II social democratic consensus. The protests of the 1960s also helped break apart this consensus, and in the 1970s, two offshoots of these protests—new feminism and environmentalism—offered new cultural and political alternatives. New feminism° emerged directly out of the student protest movement of the 1960s. Female activists grew frustrated at being

## The Greenham Common Protests

In the spring of 1983, protesters formed a fourteen-mile human chain across Greenham Common in England to protest against NATO's deployment of cruise missiles. The protest was part of a much wider movement in western Europe and the United States, which articulated wide-spread public discontent with the renewal of the Cold War. It also played a pivotal role in British feminism, as female activists established a women-only camp at the Greenham Common military base.

denied a voice in the movement—"we cook while the men talk of revolution."[1] At the same time, they were increasingly eager to connect analyses of political subordination to experiences of sexual repression. Their efforts to liberate women from political and cultural limits and expectations gave birth to what was, by the 1980s, an international feminist movement.

Economic and demographic changes buttressed the new feminism. The numbers of women working outside the home rose in these decades—up by 50 percent in Italy between 1970 and 1985, for example. By the late 1970s, women in France accounted for more than 34 percent of the labor force; in Britain, 31 percent; in West Germany, 37 percent. During the same decade, the age at which men and women first married began to climb and birth rates continued to fall.

Western politics gradually responded to the changes in women's roles. By the mid-1980s, women averaged about one-third of the members of parliament in Sweden, and women members accounted for approximately half of Norway's cabinets. In the British general elections of 1992, twice as many women stood as parliamentary candidates compared to 1979.

The movement, however, refused to confine its focus to the world of party politics, arguing instead that "the personal is political." Much of the new feminist critique fo-

cused on the female body—its image, its oppression, its control. Feminists challenged feminine stereotypes through attacks on beauty pageants and critiques of the fashion industry and sought the reform of legal codes to outlaw spousal rape and to legalize abortion. Legalization of abortion occurred first in northern Europe: in Britain in 1967, in Denmark in 1970. Catholic Europe followed: In Italy abortions became legally available in 1978, in France in 1979.

In the economic and educational spheres, feminists demanded equal pay for equal work and greater access to educational and professional opportunities. They pressed for more generous parental leave policies, family allowances, and child care provisions. In addition, with women accounting for approximately half of the university students in many Western countries, feminists began to alter the content of the curriculum. Challenging the male biases that had regarded women's contributions as irrelevant and women's lives as insignificant, for example, feminist historians brought to light the "hidden history" of women.

## New Challenges and New Identities: Environmentalism

**DOCUMENT**

Chico Mendes on the Rain Forest

Environmentalists added their voice to the political cacophony of the 1970s and 1980s. They challenged the fundamental structures of industrial economies (whether capitalist or communist), particularly their inherent emphasis on "more, bigger, faster, now." The movement embraced the ideas of unorthodox economists such as Britain's E. F. Schumacher (1911–1977), who insisted that quantitative measures of economic growth (such as the GNP) failed to factor in environmental destruction and social dislocation, and that in many contexts, "small is beautiful." At the heart of radical environmentalism was the concept of natural limits, of "Spaceship Earth"—the vision of the planet as a "single spaceship, without unlimited reservoirs of anything."[2]

New media-savvy organizations such as Greenpeace publicized the environmentalist cause with colorful protests, such as sailing in small rubber dinghies to challenge whaling fleets. The most popular of radical environmentalist targets was nuclear power. From the mid-1970s on, protests against the construction of nuclear power plants in western Europe drew tens of thousands of supporters. The movement's slogan, "Nuclear Power? No Thanks," was translated into more than forty languages.

The environmental movement helped create a new sort of political party. Green politics° drew its ideas not only from environmentalism but also from feminism. The Greens contended that the degradation of the natural environment stemmed from the same root as discrimination against women—an obsession with physical power and an unwillingness to tear down hierarchical structures. By the late 1980s Green Parties had sprouted in fifteen western European countries. The Greens were the most successful in West Germany, where they sat in the legislature from 1983 and formed an important voting bloc.

## From Detente to Renewed Cold War

At the same time that economic crisis, feminist protest, and the new environmental awareness undermined political consensus, rising superpower tensions put an end to the era of detente and caused greater rifts within western European societies. In the first half of the 1970s, detente had appeared to be flourishing. In 1975 representatives of 32 European states, Canada, the United States, and the Soviet Union signed the Helsinki Accords. They declared their acceptance of all existing European borders, agreed to a policy of joint notification of all major military exercises (thus reducing the chances of accidental nuclear war), and promised to safeguard the human rights of their citizens.

Yet the Helsinki Accords marked not only the culmination but also the beginning of the end of the detente era. First, eastern European and Soviet dissidents used the Helsinki human rights clauses to publicize the human rights abuses committed by their governments and to

demand fundamental reforms. Second, U.S. president Jimmy Carter, who took office in 1976, chose to place human rights at the center of his foreign policy. Carter's approach infuriated Soviet leaders, who resented what they regarded as his meddling in their internal affairs. As detente crumbled, the arms race accelerated, with both the Warsaw Pact and NATO increasing their defense budgets and deploying intermediate-range nuclear missiles. Detente finally died in December 1979, when Soviet troops invaded Afghanistan. Calling the invasion "the most serious threat to peace since the Second World War," Carter warned that if the Soviets moved toward the Middle East, he would not hesitate to use nuclear weapons.

With the election of New Conservatives such as Thatcher in 1979 and Reagan in 1980, the renewal of the Cold War took on a greater intensity. Reagan labeled the Soviet Union the "Evil Empire"—a reference to the popular *Star Wars* film series that was first released in the 1970s—and revived the anticommunist attitudes and rhetoric of the 1950s. Thatcher strongly supported Reagan's decision to accelerate the arms buildup begun by Carter. Her hard-line anticommunism won her the nickname "Iron Lady" from Soviet policymakers.

The renewal of the Cold War, like the end of economic prosperity, opened up large rifts within western European societies. NATO's decision to deploy its new generation of nuclear missiles drew hundreds of thousands of protesters into the streets of London, Bonn, Amsterdam, and other cities. Many of these protesters demanded not only the cancellation of the cruise missiles but also a withdrawal from NATO's nuclear umbrella.

### War in Afghanistan

The Soviet invasion of Afghanistan in 1979 helped end the era of detente. It also catapulted the Soviet army into a winless war, one that many commentators labeled "the Soviet Vietnam."

# Revolution in the East

■ **What factors explain not only the outbreak but also the success of the revolutions of 1989–1991?**

Between 1989 and 1991, revolution engulfed eastern Europe and the Soviet Union. The appointment of Mikhail Gorbachev (1985–1991) as Soviet Communist Party secretary in 1985 proved pivotal. Gorbachev's efforts to reform the Soviet system led to a series of breathtaking changes: Soviet control over eastern Europe ended, the Cold War came to an abrupt halt, the Soviet Union itself ceased to exist. Ironically, Gorbachev set in motion the first two of these developments precisely to avoid the third.

## The Crisis of Legitimacy in the East

While Western countries in the 1970s struggled with stagflation and disappearing economic growth rates, the Soviet Union posted record-breaking production figures. By 1984, for example, the Soviet Union was producing 80 percent more steel and six times as much iron ore than the United States. But Soviet prosperity was an illusion. Published growth and productivity statistics had little to do with actual economic performance. The Soviet economy continued to be hampered by overcentralization. The state planning commission, GOSPLAN, had the impossible task of coordinating the production of over four million different products in at least 50,000 factories. "Success" in Soviet industry meant fulfilling arbitrary quotas, regardless of the quality of goods produced, the actual demand for the product, or the cost of producing it.

The Soviet command economy also proved far too rigid to keep pace with global economic change. While triumphantly proclaiming its fulfillment of the heavy industrial expansion planned by Khrushchev in the early 1960s, Soviet leaders in the 1970s failed to recognize that increasingly, microchips counted for far more than iron ore—that fiber optics, not steel, would buttress the new modernity. When the first Soviet home computer reached the market in the 1980s, it cost ten times as much as the comparable Western model.

By the 1980s, the only growth sectors in the Soviet economy were oil and vodka—and then the bottom dropped out of the oil market. After peaking at $35 per barrel in 1981, oil prices began a steady decade-long fall. For the Soviet economy, the results were catastrophic.

The Soviet leadership proved incapable of responding to the economic crisis. Throughout the 1970s, Soviet leader Leonid Brezhnev's increasing physical frailty mirrored that of the country at large. Like many of his colleagues, Brezhnev had been a child at the time of the Russian Revolution; he knew only Soviet rule and had risen into major office very young because of the employment opportunities created by Stalin's Great Purge. In 1982, the average age of members of the Politburo was 68. These men had a vested interest in maintaining the status quo, not in carrying out fundamental reform.

The Soviet Union's satellite states in eastern Europe also lurched from apparent prosperity into economic crisis during this period. During the 1970s, the Soviets provided oil to their eastern European allies at prices far below the market value and so shielded these economies from some of the tensions afflicting their western European rivals. At the same time, eastern European governments borrowed heavily from Western banks. Western loans did not, however, solve fundamental problems such as overcentralization and the divorce of prices from production costs.

In the 1980s, the debt-laden economic structures of eastern Europe began to collapse. Governments found that they had to borrow simply to service their existing debt. And, as oil prices fell, the Soviet Union responded by charging market value for oil sales to their satellites, thus depriving these economies of a crucial support. Ordinary people soon felt the impact of this economic crisis, as governments restricted the flow of consumer goods and imposed higher prices.

## The Moment of Solidarity, the Moment of Punk

Events in Poland at the end of the decade illustrated how economic discontent and political dissent could create a revolutionary situation. Faced with negative economic growth rates, the Polish government announced price increases for meat and other essentials in July 1980. Poles hit the streets in angry protest. This protest gave birth to Solidarity°. Led by a charismatic and politically savvy electrician named Lech Wałęsa (b. 1943), Solidarity was both a trade union and a political movement. It demanded not only the right to unionize and strike, but also the liberation of political prisoners, an end to censorship, and a rollback of the state's power. Within just a few months, ten million Poles had joined Solidarity's ranks.

Fearing Soviet military intervention, the Polish communist government cracked down. In December 1981 Prime Minister Wojciech Jaruzelski declared martial law and arrested more than 10,000 Solidarity members (including Wałęsa). Like the Hungarian Revolution in 1956 and the Prague Spring of 1968, Solidarity seemed to be one more futile and defeated protest in eastern Europe.

But Solidarity refused to be defeated. Both in prison and out, its members resolved to act as if they were free. They met in small groups, published newspapers and ran a radio station, and organized election boycotts. Solidarity remained a political presence and a moral force in Polish society throughout the 1980s, and in 1989 it emerged to lead Poland into democracy.

Before 1989 no other eastern European country experienced a protest movement as dramatic as Solidarity, yet

# Rock and the Velvet Revolution

In September 1968, less than one month after the armies of the Soviet Union and its satellite states had crushed the Prague Spring, a Czech bass player named Milan Hlavsa formed a rock band. The military invasion and the subsequent political crackdown throughout Czechoslovakia appalled Hlavsa, but it never occurred to him that he could do anything to change the harsh reality of life in the communist bloc. He certainly did not see forming a rock band as a political act; he and the other members of the band liked Western rock music (particularly the "psychedelic" music of Frank Zappa, the Velvet Underground, and the Doors), and they wanted to play in a rock band. Yet the encounter between the communist state and the anarchic energy of psychedelic rock helped undermine communist rule and so contributed to the transformation of eastern Europe.

Hlavsa and his friends called their band "The Plastic People of the Universe" (PPU), after a Frank Zappa song, and PPU quickly became the most popular psychedelic group in Prague. But almost as quickly the band ran into trouble. As part of the post-1968 crackdown, the communist government insisted that rock bands conform to a set of official guidelines governing how, what, and where they performed. PPU refused and, in

January 1970, lost its professional license. In the communist system, the state not only controlled broadcasting and recording, but even owned the distribution of musical instruments and electrical equipment. Without a license, PPU lost access to rehearsal and recording space, and their instruments as well. But the band played on by repairing cast-off instruments and constructing homemade amplifiers from old transistor radios. Banned in 1972 from performing in Prague, PPU moved to the countryside and when it was banned in 1974 from playing anywhere, it dove underground. Fans alerted other fans when the band would be playing at some remote farm or within some woods, while recordings made in houses and garages circulated illegally. During this period PPU became more than just a rock band; it became the center of what artistic director and manager Ivan Jirous labeled the "Second Culture." An alternative to the official communist "First Culture," the "Second Culture" comprised musicians, fans, artists, writers, and anyone else who sought to carve out a space of individuality and integrity in a society based on conformity and lies.

On March 17, 1976, the Secret Police arrested twenty-seven musicians, including every member of PPU. Six months later rock music went on trial. In response to inter-

national protests, the Czech government released most of the twenty-seven rockers. But Jirous and the band's saxophonist, Vratislav Brabenec, as well as two musicians from other groups, were found guilty of "organized disturbance of the peace" and sentenced to between eight and eighteen months in prison.

In the courtroom the day of the sentencing sat Václav Havel, an ardent Frank Zappa fan as well as a playwright who used his art to mount veiled attacks on the communist system. The imprisonment of Jirous and Brabenec infuriated Havel. For the next several years, he opened his farmhouse to PPU for illegal concerts and recording sessions. More important, Havel walked out of the courtroom convinced that the time had come to challenge communism openly. On January 1, 1977, Havel and other artists and intellectuals announced the formation of "Charter 77" to publicize human rights abuses under communism. Over the next decade many Charter members, including Havel, spent time in prison. Yet, calling the state to account for its crimes, Charter 77 helped weaken the communist regime. When revolution came in 1989, that regime toppled with astounding ease. PPU had split up two years before and so did not sing in the new era, but fittingly, one of the first individuals that President Václav Havel invited to the new free Czechoslovakia was an aging psychedelic rocker named Frank Zappa.

## For Discussion

Imagine that the post-1968 Communist government in Czechoslovakia simply ignored the PPU. Would events have unfolded any differently? Why or why not?

**Rocking the Bloc**
In 1977, the Plastic People of the Universe play an illegal concert in Václav Havel's farmhouse.

**The Moment of Solidarity**

Lech Wałęsa addresses workers in the Gdansk shipyard in 1980. Note the pictures of the pope and the Virgin Mary—Roman Catholicism served as a vital source of national unity and identity, one opposed to communism.

throughout the region economic hardship fed widespread political alienation and a deepening longing for radical change. One sign of the widening gap between the communist authorities and the people they governed was the emergence of punk music as a cultural force among eastern European youth.

Punk had first appeared in Britain in the mid-1970s, the product of economic decline and social division. Dressed in clothes that deliberately mocked the consumerism and respectability of mainstream middle-class society—ripped trousers held together with safety pins, dog collars, spiked and outrageously colored hair—punks promoted a do-it-yourself style of rock music that also spat on middle-class standards. Punk rockers rarely had any musical training or expertise; even talent was not actually necessary. All that was needed was rage, which was readily available.

The nihilistic message of bands such as Britain's Sex Pistols—"no future for you, no future for me"—resonated in eastern Europe. With names like Doom, Crisis, Shortage, Paralysis, Sewage, and Dead Organism, Eastern punk bands, like their Western models, often expressed utter despair: "No goal, no future, no hope, no joy!" But this nihilism butted against explicit political protest. At punk concerts in Poland, bands and their audiences stood in silent homage to Solidarity. In Hungary, the members of one punk group received prison sentences for a performance in which they mocked their government as a "rotten, stinking communist gang" while tearing up a live chicken.[3]

## Nature and the Nation

The dissatisfaction expressed by punk bands permeated eastern European society, and increasingly took political form. Just as the emergence of radical environmentalism demonstrated a strong current of dissatisfaction with the political order in the West, so similar movements in the East pushed for radical change.

For decades, the conquest of nature had been a key part of Soviet ideology: "We cannot wait for favors from nature; our task is to take from her."[4] Beginning in the 1930s, Soviet engineers sought to fill what they regarded as nature's "empty spaces" with exotic plant and animal life, thus wreaking havoc with the ecological balance of much of the Soviet environment. In the early 1960s, Khrushchev's "Virgin Lands" scheme introduced intensive chemical fertilization and irrigation across huge swathes of Soviet territory, resulting in the fall of lake water levels, the destruction of wetlands, and the salinization of extensive stretches of land.

The situation worsened in the 1970s. The rapid expansion of heavy industry focused on churning out products, not on human safety or environmental sustainability. Communist governments throughout the Soviet bloc ignored the most basic environmental precautions, dumping both untreated sewage and nuclear waste directly into lakes and rivers. By 1977, Soviet scientists concluded that Lake Baikal—the most voluminous and deepest freshwater lake in the world, home to more than 800 plant and 1,500 animal species—had experienced irreversible environmental degradation.

As a result of this wholesale destruction, environmentalist protest groups emerged in the Soviet Union and throughout eastern Europe. Because Soviet officials regarded the environment as insignificant, they tended to view environmentalist protest as unimportant, as a "safe" outlet for popular frustration. Thus environmentalism became one of the few areas in communist society that permitted ordinary people free expression and in which public opinion was allowed a voice. Environmental activism worked like a termite infestation, nibbling away from within at the structures of Soviet communism.

Environmentalism also proved crucial in underlining nationalist identity and fueling nationalist protest. The various national and ethnic groups within the vast Soviet empire watched their forests disappear, their lakes dry up, and their ancient cities bulldozed, as a result of decisions made in faraway Moscow by men they regarded as foreigners—as *Russians* rather than as *comrades.* By the 1980s, schools in Latvia issued gas masks as a routine safety precaution because of the dangers of chemical spills. Many Latvians concluded that they would be better off independent of Soviet control.

# Gorbachev and Radical Reform

In 1982, the decrepit Leonid Brezhnev died—and so, in rapid succession, did his two successors, Yuri Andropov (1982–1984) and Konstantin Chernenko (1984–1985). The time had come for a generational change. When Mikhail Gorbachev succeeded Chernenko, he was 54 years old. Compared to his elderly colleagues on the Politburo, he looked like a teenager.

Gorbachev's biography encompassed the drama of Soviet history. He was born, in 1931, into the turmoil of collectivization. One-third of the inhabitants of his native village in Stavropol were executed or imprisoned or died from famine or disease in the upheavals of the early 1930s. Both of his grandfathers were arrested on trumped-up charges. Yet Gorbachev's family continued to believe in the Communist dream. During World War II his father served in the Red Army (and was twice wounded), and in 1948 Gorbachev and his father together won the Order of Red Banner of Labor for harvesting almost six times the average crop. Because of this award and his academic abilities, Gorbachev won entry to Moscow University. After earning degrees in economics and law, he rose through the ranks of the provincial Communist Party. In 1978, at age 47, he became the youngest member of the Communist Party Central Committee, the key leadership body in the Soviet Union.

## Glasnost and Perestroika

Gorbachev came to power in 1985, convinced that the Soviet system was ailing, and that the only way to restore it to health was through radical surgery. What he did not anticipate was that such surgery would in fact kill the patient. His surgical tools were glasnost and perestroika, two Russian terms without direct English equivalents.

Glasnost°, sometimes translated as "openness," "publicity," or "transparency," meant abandoning the deception and censorship that had always characterized the Soviet system, for a policy based on open admission of failures and problems. To Gorbachev, "Broad, timely, and frank information is testimony of faith in people . . . and for their capacity to work things out themselves."[5]

Not surprisingly, Soviet citizens remained wary of Gorbachev's talk of glasnost—until April 1986 and the Chernobyl nuclear power plant disaster. Operator error at the Ukrainian power plant led to the most serious nuclear accident in history. In the days following the accident, thirty-five plant workers died; over the next five years the cleanup effort would claim at least 7,000 lives. The accident placed more than four million inhabitants of Ukraine and Belarus at risk from excess radiation and spread a radioactive cloud that extended all the way to Scotland. When news of the accident first reached Moscow, party officials acted as they had always done: They denied that anything had happened. But monitors in Western countries quickly

**Glasnost**

Mikhail Gorbachev meets with workers in Moscow in 1985.

picked up on the excess radiation spewing into the atmosphere. Gorbachev initiated an about-face and insisted that accurate information about the disaster be released to the public. Chernobyl became the first Soviet media event. In 1986, 93 percent of the Soviet population had access to a television set and what they saw on their screens convinced them that glasnost was real. A powerful change had occurred in Soviet political culture.

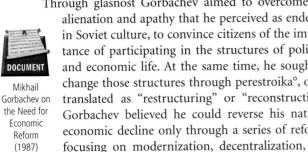

**DOCUMENT**

Mikhail Gorbachev on the Need for Economic Reform (1987)

Through glasnost Gorbachev aimed to overcome the alienation and apathy that he perceived as endemic in Soviet culture, to convince citizens of the importance of participating in the structures of political and economic life. At the same time, he sought to change those structures through perestroika°, often translated as "restructuring" or "reconstruction." Gorbachev believed he could reverse his nation's economic decline only through a series of reforms focusing on modernization, decentralization, and the introduction of a limited market.

Gorbachev knew, however, that even limited economic reforms threatened the vested interests of communist bureaucrats. Thus the success of economic perestroika depended on political perestroika. The culmination of political restructuring came in May 1989, when Soviet voters entered the voting booths to elect the Congress of People's Deputies, and for the first time in Soviet history they had a choice of candidates. True, all of these candidates were members of the Communist Party, but just one year later, Gorbachev ended the Communist Party's monopoly on parliamentary power, and the Soviet Union entered the brave new world of multiparty politics.

### Ending the Cold War

Restructuring Soviet economics and politics led almost inevitably to restructuring international relations—and to ending the Cold War. By the 1980s, at least 18 percent of the Soviet GNP was absorbed by the arms race; Gorbachev concluded that the Soviet Union simply could not afford the Cold War. As soon as Gorbachev took office, he signaled to the West his desire to resume arms control negotiations. The results of these negotiations were startling. In December 1987, Gorbachev and U.S. president Ronald Reagan signed the INF (Intermediate Nuclear Forces) Treaty, agreeing to the total elimination of land-based intermediate-range nuclear missiles. In 1991, the Soviets and Americans signed the Strategic Arms Reduction Treaty (START I), pledging themselves to a mutual reduction of intercontinental ballistic missiles (ICBMs). The nuclear arms race had ended.

At the same time, Gorbachev signaled an end to Soviet global intervention by reducing Soviet military commitments abroad. In 1989, he brought the Red Army home from both Afghanistan and Mongolia and removed Soviet-sponsored Cuban forces from Angola.

## The Revolutions of 1989 in Eastern Europe

Even more remarkably, by the end of 1990, the Red Army had pulled out of every state in eastern Europe except East Germany and Poland (and would soon withdraw from these countries as well). The Soviet Union could not afford to wage the Cold War, nor could it afford to maintain the eastern European empire that was both a cause and a consequence of that conflict.

In his first informal meetings with eastern European communist leaders in 1985, Gorbachev told them they should no longer expect Soviet tanks to enforce their will on rebellious populations. By the time Gorbachev addressed the UN General Assembly at the end of 1988 and declared that the nations of eastern Europe were free to choose their own paths, dramatic changes were already underway.

Hungary and Poland were the first to jettison communist rule. Even before Gorbachev took power, economic crisis had driven both of these states to embrace fundamental reforms. In the early 1980s Hungary moved toward a Western-oriented, market-driven economy by joining the World Bank and the International Monetary Fund (IMF) and establishing a stock market. Political reforms accompanied these economic changes. In 1983, Hungarian voters

### CHRONOLOGY

#### Revolution in Eastern Europe

**1989**

| | |
|---|---|
| January | Noncommunist parties and unions legalized in Hungary |
| February | Roundtable talks between Polish government and Solidarity |
| June | Free elections in Poland |
| September | Solidarity forms government in Poland |
| November | Fall of Berlin Wall; reformist communists overthrow Zhivkov in Bulgaria |
| December | Collapse of communist government in Czechoslovakia and East Germany; execution of Ceauşescu in Romania |

**1990**

| | |
|---|---|
| March | Free elections in East Germany and Hungary |
| October | Reunification of Germany |
| December | Wałęsa elected president of Poland |

for the first time had a choice of candidates (all still Communist Party members); eighteen months later, independent candidates were allowed to run—and many were elected. In Poland, Jaruzelski's government also experimented with restoring some measures of a market economy and with political liberalization. Once martial law ended in 1983, censorship loosened considerably. Newspapers published criticisms of governmental policy that would never have been permitted before 1980.

With Gorbachev in power, the pace of reform in both Poland and Hungary accelerated rapidly. In January 1989, Hungary took the leap into political pluralism by legalizing noncommunist political parties and trade unions. In February, Solidarity and Polish communist officials began "roundtable talks" aimed at restructuring Poland's political system. In June, Poland held the first free elections in the Soviet bloc. Solidarity swept the contest and formed the first noncommunist government in eastern Europe since 1948.

A bewildered world waited to see if Gorbachev would send in the tanks. Only one day before the Polish elections, the Chinese communist government, oblivious to the television cameras that broadcast the horrible scenes around the globe, had used brutal force to crush a student pro-democracy uprising centered in Beijing's Tiananmen Square. Hundreds died. Horrified by the carnage, Gorbachev insisted that "the very possibility of the use or threat of force [in Poland] . . . is totally unacceptable."[6]

With the prop of the Red Army removed, the communist states of eastern Europe toppled easily. In November

VIDEO

Escaping the
Berlin Wall

1989, the Berlin Wall fell. The collapse of the wall echoed to the sound of communist governments crashing throughout eastern Europe. In December, after a year of ever-widening protest demonstrations, the communist government in Czechoslovakia resigned. Alexander Dubček, the hero of the Prague Spring of 1968, returned in triumph to assume the leadership of parliament, and the playwright and leading dissident Václav Havel (b. 1936) became the Czech president. In March 1990, the Christian Democrats took over the government from the communists in East Germany; seven months later the states of East and West Germany ceased to exist, and a single Germany was reborn. At the end of the year, reform-minded Communist Party members in Bulgaria overthrew the government of Todor Zhivkov, who had been in power for thirty-five years.

All of these revolutions occurred with very little bloodshed. The pace of change in Czechoslovakia was so smooth, in fact, that the events earned the nickname "the Velvet Revolution." But in Romania, the revolutionary cloth came soaked in blood. In December 1989, Romania's dictator Nikolai Ceauşescu ordered the army to fire on a peaceful protest; hundreds died. In a matter of days, however, the soldiers turned against Ceauşescu. Fighting spread across the nation as the dictator's security forces battled with both the demonstrators and the army. Ceauşescu and his wife

**"Comrades, It's Over!"**
This Hungarian political poster sums up the revolutions of 1989.

went into hiding, but on Christmas Day they were caught and executed by a firing squad. The televised pictures of their dead bodies were broadcast around the world. A new government was formed under Ion Iliescu (b. 1930), a reformist communist who had attended Moscow University with Gorbachev.

## The Disintegration of the Soviet Union

By 1990, Gorbachev was one of the best-known leaders in the Western world. Both Western political leaders and ordinary people praised Gorbachev for ending the Cold War and loosening the Soviet hold on eastern Europe. But for Gorbachev, these changes in the international structure were means to an end—freeing the Soviet economy for prosperity and thereby saving the communist system. But prosperity eluded his grasp, and the system he sought to save disintegrated.

Between 1985 and 1991, Gorbachev's administration started and stopped twelve different national economic plans, in ever-more-desperate attempts to prop up the Soviet economy. These reforms seemed only to worsen the economic crisis. By 1990, food and other essential goods were scarce, prices had risen by 20 percent since the year before, and both productivity figures and incomes were falling. Dramatic increases in the number of prostitutes (accompanied by a tripling of the rate of venereal disease in Moscow), abandoned babies, and the homeless population all signaled a society in the midst of economic breakdown.

By the early 1990s Gorbachev faced fierce opposition not only from hard-line communists who opposed his reforms, but also from more liberal reformers who viewed the communist system as utterly broken, and who wanted to accelerate the shift to a capitalist economy. These reformers found a spokesman in Boris Yeltsin (b. 1931), a charismatic, boisterous politician who became the president of Russia (as distinct from the Soviet Union) in 1991. As Gorbachev increasingly began to tack toward the right,

Yeltsin emerged as the leader who would keep the revolution on course. When communist hard-liners attempted to overthrow Gorbachev in August 1991, it was Yeltsin who led the popular resistance movement that defeated the coup attempt.

Gorbachev was finally ousted not by a political coup but by the power of nationalism. Glasnost had allowed separatist nationalist movements within the Soviet Union to surface from the underground, but Gorbachev, despite his commitment to freedom of choice for eastern Europe, firmly opposed the breakup of the Soviet Union. In 1990, he deployed troops to quell nationalist rioting in both Azerbaijan and Georgia and to counter independence movements in the Baltic states of Latvia, Estonia, and Lithuania. Short of an all-out civil war, however, there was little Gorbachev could do to hold the union together. By December 1991, the Soviet Union had broken apart (see Map 28.1). On December 25, Gorbachev resigned his office as president of a state that no longer existed.

**IMAGE**

Statue of Lenin Toppled During the Soviet Collapse

---

**Map 28.1   The Former Soviet Union**

In December 1991, the Soviet empire disintegrated. In its place stood fifteen independent and very diverse republics, ranging from tiny and impoverished Moldova to relatively affluent and European-ized Latvia to Russia itself, still the dominant power in the region but economically stagnant.

### The Disintegration of the Soviet Union

Gorbachev attempted to halt the disintegration of the Soviet Union by sending in crack Soviet troops to wrest back control of public buildings in Vilnius, Lithuania. Fourteen protesters died, and Lithuania asserted its independence.

# In the Wake of Revolution

■ **What were the consequences of these revolutions for the societies of eastern Europe?**

With the Cold War over and the long struggle between communism and capitalism clearly won by the latter, one best-selling author talked of the "end of history," by which he meant the end of the ideological struggles that had so defined the last two centuries of historical development.[7] But such talk was premature. "History" returned with a vengeance in the 1990s. As nationalism replaced the capitalist-communist struggle, many of the divisive issues that had led to world war in 1914 and 1939 moved back to center stage. The former Soviet Union and all the former Soviet satellite states in eastern Europe experienced high inflation rates, high unemployment, and economic instability in the wake of the revolution. Many faced nationalist hostilities from minority groups; some confronted the ultimate challenge of civil war.

## Crisis Throughout the Former Soviet Union

For many ordinary Russians, the ending of the Soviet regime meant freedom of the worst kind—freedom to be hungry, freedom to be homeless, freedom to be afraid. In January 1992, Yeltsin applied "shock therapy" to the ailing Russian economy. He lifted price controls, abolished subsidies, and privatized state industries. By mid-1994, the state sector of the Russian economy had shrunk to under 40 percent. But the economy did not prosper. Prices climbed dra-

matically and the closure of unproductive businesses sent unemployment rates upward, while at the same time cuts in government spending severed welfare lifelines. By 1995, 80 percent of Russians were no longer earning a living wage. Food consumption fell to the same level as the early 1950s, with meat almost disappearing from the diets of many.

The economic situation worsened in 1998, when Russia effectively went bankrupt. The value of the ruble collapsed and the state defaulted on its loans. Even Russians with jobs found it difficult to make ends meet. Workers at the Moscow McDonald's, for example, had regarded themselves as privileged: They were paid regularly and well. But overnight in 1998, the value of their paycheck dropped by 70 percent. Workers in state jobs simply were not paid at all.

For many Russians, capitalism meant lawlessness. Managers of state industries were often able to manipulate privatization for their own private enrichment, so they grew fabulously wealthy, while ordinary employees experienced sharp pay cuts or the loss of their jobs. By the mid-1990s, a new force had appeared in Russian life—the "Russian Mafia," crime syndicates with international links that used extortion and intimidation to seize control of large sectors of the economy.

In the non-Russian republics, often the situation was even worse. The end of the Soviet Union meant the end of Soviet subsidies for these impoverished regions. Tajikistan, for example, had depended on Soviet financial aid to prop up the extensive irrigation system that allowed its farmers to grow cotton for export. The collapse of the Soviet Union meant the collapse of the Tajikistan economy. By the end of the 1990s, almost half of Tajikistan's 6.2 million inhabitants were struggling to survive in the face of severe food shortages. In Moldova, the economy shrank by 60 percent between 1991 and 2001, while life expectancy rates fell by five years. One Moldovan elementary school principal admitted she was "hungry for Soviet days," which she recalled as a time when salaries were steady and health care universally available.[8] In the post-Soviet era, Moldovans resorted to marketing their body organs to Western entrepreneurs for $3,000 each.

The economic and social collapse that followed the end of the Soviet Union fostered a climate of desperation in which extremist nationalism flourished. Independence did not mean stability in the republics of Georgia, Armenia, and Azerbaijan, all of which experienced civil war in the 1990s. In Russia itself, Yeltsin faced strong opposition from nationalist groups who viewed the breakup of the Soviet Union as a humiliation for Mother Russia.

The sharpest nationalist challenge to Yeltsin came from Chechnya, one of twenty-one autonomous republics within the larger Russian Federation. When the Soviet Union broke up, Chechnya became part of independent Russia. But the Chechens demanded their own state, and in 1991 declared Chechnya independent. The Chechen-Russian dispute simmered until 1994 when Yeltsin committed 30,000 troops to forcing Chechnya back within Russia's embrace. In the ensuing twenty-month conflict, 80,000 died and 240,000 were wounded—80 percent of these Chechen civilians. Yeltsin negotiated a truce in the summer of 1996, but four years later his successor, Vladimir Putin (b. 1952), renewed the war.

While Putin continued Yeltsin's battle against Chechen independence, his assumption of the presidency signaled a change in Russia's direction—but just where Russia was heading was not very clear. On the one hand, the well-manicured, tightly controlled, even austere Putin promised a more competent, stable style of government than Russia had experienced under the hard-drinking, jovial, often erratic Yeltsin. Yet Putin soon displayed authoritarian instincts. He moved quickly to centralize power under his own control and ran roughshod over such key democratic touchstones as freedom of the press and the right to a fair trial. Western governments struggled with the question of how to encourage Russia's economic stabilization without sacrificing its still fledgling democracy.

## Eastern Europe: Stumbling Toward Democracy

Like the former Soviet Union, the states of Eastern Europe found the path from communist rule to democracy far from easy. The dissolution of the Soviet bloc meant that economic networks established over the last four decades suddenly disintegrated. In addition, Western advisers and the International Monetary Fund, which controlled access to much-needed loans, insisted that the new governments follow programs of "austerity" aimed at cutting government spending and curbing inflation. The result was economic hardship far beyond what any Western electorate would have endured. In Poland, for example, the new Solidarity-led government instituted the "Big Bang" on New Year's Day 1990. Controls disappeared and prices jumped between 30 and 600 percent overnight. The inflation rate for 1990 in Poland was a remarkable 550 percent. Even in 1995, when the economy had stabilized, inflation remained at 20 percent, while joblessness stood at 15 percent.

But by the second half of the 1990s, it was clear that Poland was succeeding in moving from communism to capitalism. With some measures of market reform already in place before 1988, both Poland and Hungary were the best prepared for the transition from a command to a capitalist economy. The Czech Republic and the Baltic nations also moved fairly rapidly through the most difficult stages of this transition. In countries such as Romania, Bulgaria, and Albania, economic instability continued, with the majority of their populations experiencing severe poverty.

Political stability was also hard-won during this decade. The revolutionary coalitions that had led the charge against communist rule in 1989–1990 quickly fragmented as their members moved from the heady idealism of challenging authoritarianism to the nitty-gritty of parliamentary politics. In addition, voters who were fed up with economic hardship turned to the people who represented a more stable past. Between 1993 and 1995, ex-communists returned to power in Lithuania, Hungary, Bulgaria, and Poland. In Romania, they had never left. Yet the revolutions of 1989 were not reversed. Ex-communists continued with the economic liberalization programs of their opponents, although in many cases opting for a more gradual transition. No former communist regime returned to authoritarian rule or a centralized state-run economy.

A far greater threat to eastern European democracy was posed by the revival of pre–World War II political ideas and styles. For example, the claim of Josef Antall, Hungary's prime minister in the early 1990s, to be the leader of "all Hungarians" (two million of whom lived in Romania and another 600,000 in Slovakia) recalled the vehement Hungarian nationalism of the 1920s and 1930s. Much of eastern Europe witnessed a resurgence of ethnic hostilities in the 1990s. In Czechoslovakia, Hável's government could not bridge the regional-ethnic divide that opened up between the Czech half of the country and Slovakia. In 1993, Czechoslovakia ceased to exist, replaced by the separate nations of the Czech Republic and Slovakia. The breakup of Czechoslovakia occurred peacefully, but ethnic divisions turned violent in much of eastern Europe. In Romania escalating discrimination against the Hungarian and Roma minority populations stirred up memories of interwar racist violence. Throughout eastern Europe, anti-Semitic rhetoric returned to political discourse. In 1990, Lech Wałęsa's election campaign was tainted by anti-Jewish references; graffiti appeared on the walls of Warsaw buildings: "Jews to the ovens."

## The "German Problem"?

The problems that engulfed Germany after its eastern and western halves reunited in October 1990 illustrated the difficulties faced by eastern Europeans as they struggled to adjust to a post–Cold War, post-Soviet world. Almost half the population of East Germany crossed the border into West Germany in the first week after the fall of the Berlin Wall. They returned home dazzled by the consumer delights they saw in store windows and eager for a chance to grab a piece of the capitalist pie. West German chancellor Helmut Kohl recognized the power of these desires, and skillfully forced the pace of reunification. When the two Germanys united at the end of 1990, Kohl became the first chancellor of the new German state.

Kohl trusted that West Germany's economy was strong enough to pull its bankrupt new partner into prosperity, but he proved overly optimistic. The residents of the former East Germany soon found their factories closing and their livelihoods gone. These economic troubles quickly leached over into the western regions of Germany. By 1997, unemployment in Germany stood at 12.8 percent—the highest since World War II. In the eastern regions, over 20 percent of the population was out of work.

For the women of the former East Germany, life in the new Germany meant an especially intense culture clash. The concept of the male breadwinner/head of household was enshrined in the West German legal code until the end of the 1970s and prominent in West German culture for a long time after. Many women from the former East Germany found this concept alien. In East Germany, women had expected to work full time and to have access to state-provided day care, abortion, and contraceptives. In the new united Germany, which adhered to West German legal and cultural traditions, more conventional gender roles and conceptions of sexual morality dominated. For at least some East German women, then, the end of communist rule was not unambiguously liberating.

At the same time, economic despair throughout much of the former East Germany resulted in racial violence. Looking for scapegoats, eastern German youths targeted the foreign workers in their cities. Violent attacks against Turkish workers escalated in the 1990s, as did support for neo-Nazi organizations.

In 1998, these economic and social problems led German voters to reject Kohl and the Christian Democrats. The Social Democrats, out of office since 1982, took charge under the leadership of Gerhard Schroeder (b. 1944). Schroeder, however, was unable to reverse the economic slide. By 2001, the German economy was standing still, with a GDP growth rate of little more than zero. The gap between the former West and East Germanys remained wide, with easterners enduring the worst of the German economic crisis. In a hugely controversial effort to resolve the crisis, Schroeder in 2004 forced through legislation that scaled back German welfare benefits. Many Germans, however, saw this move as a repudiation of the social democratic promise of guaranteeing a decent standard of living to all Germans. In September 2005, Shroeder's Social Democrats lost their majority in the German parliament. The Christian Democrats, however, also failed to gain a majority. The inconclusive results of the election revealed a worrying lack of consensus among voters about Germany's direction in the twenty-first century.

## The Breakup of Yugoslavia

In Yugoslavia the "return of history" proved most marked and, given the nature of that history, most horrific. When the communist guerilla leader Tito seized control of the Yugoslav state after World War II, he sought to free Yugoslavia from the divisive and bloody battles of its recent past. But in the 1980s and 1990s, the revival of nationalist hostilities within Yugoslavia led to civil war and

### DOCUMENT

### "How's the Family?"

*The conflict in Yugoslavia was a civil war, which meant that frequently the fighters knew their enemy personally. Victims of ethnic cleansing testified that it was their neighbors, colleagues, or schoolmates who had thrust them out of their homes, killed their fathers and brothers, and raped their mothers and sisters. The men at the top also knew each other. In this excerpt, a transcript of a telephone conversation made in Croatia in 1991, the Serb military commander Ratko Mladic is speaking to his Croat counterpart:*

"Is that you, Mladic?"

"Yes it is, you old devil, what do you want?"

"Three of my boys went missing near . . . and I want to find out what happened to them."

"I think they're all dead."

"I've got one of their parents on to me about it, so I can tell them for certain that they're gone?"

"Yep, certain. You have my word. By the way, how's the family?"

"Oh not so bad, thanks. How about yours?"

"They're doing just fine, we're managing pretty well."

"Glad to hear it. By the way, now I've got you on the line, we've got about twenty bodies of yours near the front and they've been stripped bare. We slung them into a mass grave and they're now stinking to high heaven. Any chance of you coming to pick them up because they really are becoming unbearable. . . ?"

Source: From Misha Glenny, *The Fall of Yugoslavia* (1994), p. 28.

state-sanctioned mass murder, to scenes of carnage and to mass atrocities not seen in Europe since the 1940s.

Although Yugoslavia had appeared on European maps since the end of World War I, one could argue it did not really exist until after World War II. During the 1920s and 1930s, the subjects of the Serbian monarchy did not regard themselves as "Yugoslavs"; they were Serbs or Croats, Muslims or Montenegrins, Albanians or Slovenians. And during World War II, as we saw in Chapter 26, Serbs and Croats fought each other with a savage intensity—a bitter reminder of the lack of a single national Yugoslav identity.

To construct a united nation out of Yugoslavia's diverse and often hostile cultures, Tito utilized two tools—federalism and communism. A federal political structure consisting of six equal republics prevented Serbia, or any other of the republics, from dominating Yugoslavia. Communism served as a unifying ideology, a cluster of ideas that transcended the divisions of race, religion, and language. Ethnic identities and rivalries were declared unacceptable, part of the bourgeois past that had supposedly been left behind.

Yugoslavs often said, however, that their nation consisted of "six nationalities, five languages, four religions, . . . and one Tito." According to this folk wisdom, Tito—not communism, not federalism—was the glue that held together this diverse state. In 1980, Tito died. Ominously, the year after his death saw the outbreak of riots between ethnic Albanians and Serbs in the province of Kosovo. Even more ominously, Tito's death coincided with the onset of serious economic crisis. The drastic rise in oil prices in 1979 undercut the Yugoslav economy, as did its rising debt load. Between 1979 and 1985 real wages fell in Yugoslavia by almost 25 percent. By 1987, inflation was raging at 200 percent per year; two years later it had burst through into hyperinflation—200 percent *per month.*

Under pressure from this economic crisis, the federal structure built by Tito began to collapse, as the wealthier Yugoslav republics such as Croatia sought to loosen the ties that bound them to the poorer republics such as Serbia. Then, in 1989, the revolutions that swept through the Soviet satellite states shattered the hold of communism on Yugoslavia as well. Ethnic nationalism, long simmering under the surface of Yugoslavian political life, poured into the resulting ideological void. New leaders emerged with new agendas.

In Serbia, the former communist functionary Slobodan Milošević (b. 1941) transformed himself into a popular spokesman for aggressive Serbian nationalism. Milošević used rallies and the mass media, which he controlled, to

## CHRONOLOGY

### The Shattering of Yugoslavia

| | |
|---|---|
| **1989** | Slobodan Milošević becomes president of Yugoslavian Republic of Serbia |
| **1991** | |
| July | Civil war in Croatia begins |
| **1992** | |
| April | Civil war in Bosnia begins |
| **1994** | |
| April | NATO air strikes against Bosnian Serb positions begin |
| **1995** | |
| December | Dayton Accords |
| **1998** | Large-scale fighting in Kosovo between Albanians and Serbs |
| **1999** | |
| March | NATO air strikes against Serbia |
| June | Cease-fire in Kosovo |
| **2000** | |
| October | Milošević defeated in Serbian elections |
| **2001** | |
| June | Milošević extradited to the Hague to be tried for genocide |

convince Serbs that their culture was under attack and to paint himself as the defender of that culture. To enhance Serbia's power—and his own—Milošević fiercely opposed any talk of destroying the Yugoslav federation. Moreover, Milošević possessed a powerful weapon to enforce his will: the Yugoslav army, the fourth-largest fighting force in Europe, dominated by Serbs.

Thus, when Croatia declared independence in June 1991, the result was civil war. Milošević mobilized the Yugoslav army against the Croatian separatists. In 1992 the war spread to Bosnia-Herzegovina after its government, too, declared independence. The war quickly degenerated into an ethnic bloodbath, with memories of World War II shaping the conflict. Serbs viewed Croats as the direct heirs of the murderous Nazi-backed Croatian fascists, responsible for the mass slaughter of Serbs (and Jews) in World War II. In turn, Croats called all Serbs "Chetniks," linking them to the anti-Croat Serbian guerilla bands of the war years. (See Chapter 26.) The presence of paramilitary forces also heightened the brutality of the war. With no military discipline and often possessing criminal records, the

## Map 28.2   The Former Yugoslavia

The breakup of Yugoslavia began in June 1991 with the Slovenian and Croatian declarations of independence. Bosnia and Macedonia soon followed.

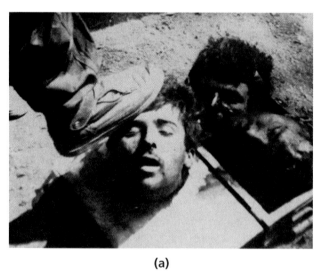

(a)

(b)

## Bosnian War Atrocities

(a) Serbian heads, found after Serb fighters raided a Muslim base in northern Bosnia in 1993. (b) A mass grave of Muslim civilians in Pilica, northwest of Srebrenica, in the spring of 1996. Twelve thousand of the men and boys of Srebrenica tried to flee to safety—about half made it; many of those that didn't were forced by Serb fighters to dig their own graves and then shot in front of them. The citizens of Srebenica who did not flee were told by Bosnian Serbian general Ratko Mladic, "No one will harm you." Mladic then ordered his soldiers to shoot all Muslim men between ages 17 and 60. Reviewing the evidence against Mladic, the UN tribunal noted, "These are truly scenes from hell, written on the darkest pages of human history."

volunteers in these units plunged into a fury of plunder, murder, and rape.

This war introduced the world to the horrors of ethnic cleansing° and rape camps. By 1994, all sides within the Bosnian war were practicing ethnic cleansing, although it is clear that Serbs initiated the practice and used it most extensively. To create all-Serb zones within Croatia and Bosnia, Serb paramilitary units embarked on a campaign of terror designed to force Muslims and Croats to abandon their homes and villages. They burned mosques, closed schools, and vandalized houses. Most villagers fled; the paramilitaries tortured and often killed those who stayed. Women were sometimes rounded up and placed in special camps where they were subjected to regular, systematic rape. An estimated 20,000 women, most of them Muslim, endured this vicious effort to subjugate and humiliate a people.

With Serbia assisting the Bosnian Serbs and Croatia assisting the Bosnian Croats, the Muslim community within Bosnia suffered the most intensely, and begged western governments to abandon their positions of neutrality and to stop the atrocities. Finally, in 1994, NATO planes began bombing Serb positions, the first time in its history that NATO had gone into combat. One year later, the Dayton Accords, signed in Dayton, Ohio, brought an uneasy peace to Bosnia (see Map 28.2).

Peace eluded Serbia during this period, however. The sort of vicious nationalism embodied by Milošević demanded a constant supply of enemies and a continuous cycle of violence. In 1998, large-scale fighting between Serbs and Albanians erupted in the province of Kosovo. Ethnic cleansing, mass rape, and a huge exodus of refugees began once again. After a NATO bombing campaign in Serbia, NATO and Russian troops moved into Kosovo, and in 2001, a police helicopter transported Milošević to the Netherlands to be tried for genocide before the International War Crimes Tribunal.

# Rethinking the West

■ What were the implications of these developments for the meaning of "the West" itself?

At the start of the 1990s, a sense of triumphalism characterized much of Western culture—at its simplest, expressed as "we won the Cold War." But who was "we"? For forty years, the Cold War had provided a clear enemy and thus a clear identity: The West was anticommunist, anti-Soviet, anti–Warsaw Pact. Communism's loss of credibility, the disintegration of the Soviet Union, and the dismantling of the Warsaw Pact all demanded that the West revise itself. But so, too, did other important so-

cial, political, and cultural changes that occurred in the wake of the tumultuous events of the later 1960s and the economic downturn of the 1970s.

## The European Union

With the ending of the Cold War, the nations of western Europe, united under the umbrella of the European Union° (EU), moved to take on a much more important role in global affairs. We saw in Chapter 27 that the EU began in the 1950s as the Common Market or EEC (European Economic Community), an economic free-trade organization of six western European nations. By the end of the millennium, this organization had become a powerful entity possessing not only economic but also political clout, a potential counterweight to the United States.

During the 1970s and 1980s, the EEC widened both its membership and its areas of cooperation. Britain, Denmark, and Ireland joined in 1973, Greece in 1981, Spain and Portugal in 1986. (Austria, Finland, and Sweden joined in the 1990s.) In 1979, a European Parliament chosen directly by European voters met for the first time. Throughout these decades, the European Court of Justice gradually began to assert the primacy of the European Community over national law, thus pushing western Europe down the road toward political integration. The EEC—the European Economic Community—became the EC, or the European Community, a political and cultural as well as economic organization.

The pace of change accelerated in the 1980s and 1990s as the Single European Act of 1985 and the Maastricht Agreements of 1991 replaced the European *Community* (EC) with the European *Union* (EU), defined by France's President Mitterrand as "one currency, one culture, one social area, one environment." The establishment of the EU meant visible changes for ordinary Europeans. They saw their national passports replaced by a common EU document, and border controls eliminated. The creation of a single EU currency—the euro, which replaced national currencies in 2002—tore down one of the most significant economic barriers between European countries. At the same time, the powers of the European Parliament expanded and member states moved toward establishing common social policies (such as labor rights).

European Union Flag

While these developments occurred, Europeans also faced the unexpected challenge posed by the ending of the Cold War. Should the European Union (often called simply "Europe") now include East as well as West? Attracted by the undoubted prosperity of the EU, the nations of the former Soviet bloc answered that question with a resounding "yes." The leaders of western Europe, however, looked with trepidation at the prospect of joining their countries to eastern Europe's shattered economies and divided societies and drew up a list of rigorous qualifications for applicant nations. To be recognized as belonging to "Europe," nations applying for EU membership had to meet a set of complex financial requirements that demonstrated both the essential stability of their economies and their commitment to market capitalism. Thus "Europe" was defined, first of all, as capitalist. But a set of political requirements made clear that "Europe" also meant a commitment to democratic politics. Applicants' voting processes, treatment of minority groups, policing methods, and judicial systems were all scrutinized, as the EU used its considerable economic clout to nurture fledgling democratic structures in eastern Europe. In 2004, Estonia, Latvia, Lithuania, Poland, the Czech Republic, Slovakia, Slovenia, and Hungary, as well as Cyprus and Malta, all joined the EU (see Map 28.3).

Many Europeans greeted both the launch of the euro in 2002 and the dramatic expansion of the EU in 2004 as signs that the dream of a united Europe was being realized. Other Europeans, however, perceived this dream as a nightmare. "Euro-skeptics" questioned the economic value of unification. They pointed out that throughout the 1990s, the U.S. economy continued to outperform that of the EU, and European unemployment rates were often high. Britain, Denmark, and Sweden all refused to join the conversion to the euro, fearing that their economies would be dragged down by their slower-performing EU partners. Small traders and independent producers opposed the seemingly endless stream of orders and regulations issued by EU bureaucrats and the way in which economic integration privileged large, international firms over small, local shops. Many Europeans feared the growing political power of the EU and saw it as a threat to national sovereignty. Still others predicted that the expansion of the EU would mean the loss of jobs as western European firms moved eastward to take advantage of the lower wage rates and lax standard of work-

### Map 28.3 Contemporary Europe

The revolutions of 1989 and their aftermath mark a clear turning point in European history, as a comparison of this map and that of "Europe in the Cold War" (p. 887) will show. Significant changes include the breakup of the Soviet Union and Yugoslavia, the replacement of Czechoslovakia by the Czech Republic and Slovakia, and the unification of Germany.

Contemporary Europe

- Member nations of European Union
- Acceding nations to join EU on January 1, 2007
- Candidate for admission

ers' protections in eastern Europe. All of these fears came into the open in the spring of 2005 when voters in both France and the Netherlands rejected a proposed EU constitution. These "no" votes from traditionally pro-EU states forced the shelving of the constitution and raised serious doubts about both the process and the pace of Europe's political and economic unification.

## Islam, Terrorism, and European Identity

Significantly, the expansion of the EU in 2004 did not include Turkey. A member of NATO since 1952, Turkey first applied for associate membership in the EU (then the EEC) in 1959 but did not succeed in becoming an associate until 1991. In 2004 EU officials announced that talks on Turkey's entry as a full member would begin in 2005, but denied to the Turkish government any guarantees. A number of issues had frustrated Turkey's efforts to join the EU, including its refusal to recognize the independence of Cyprus, the clash between Turkey's repressive penal system and EU human rights legislation, and its poverty. If Turkey joined the EU, it would immediately become the most populous and the poorest member of the union. Opponents to Turkey's bid for membership feared that the European economy could not absorb the expected massive influx of impoverished Turkish migrant workers. They also, however, opposed full membership in "Europe" for Turkey because most Turks are Muslim, and for many Europeans, "European" and "Islamic" described clashing cultures.

### Muslim Communities in Europe

The struggle over Turkish membership in the EU was just one of many controversies in contemporary Europe resulting from an ongoing battle to reconcile European identity with a growing Islamic cultural and political presence. By 2004, the number of European Muslims stood at 20 million—5 percent of the EU's population. Because the European Muslim birth rate is three times the non-Muslim birth rate, the percentage of Muslims within Europe is likely to continue to expand.

There is, of course, no single "Muslim Europe." In eastern European countries such as Bulgaria, Albania, and Bosnia, Muslims were part of the indigenous nation, the descendants of those who converted to Islam centuries earlier during the era of Ottoman rule. In western Europe, by contrast, most Muslims were immigrants or the children or grandchildren of immigrants, drawn to the West by greater economic and educational opportunities.

Even in western Europe, the Muslim experience varied. The majority of Britain's two million Muslims had roots in India or Pakistan, and thus received citizenship because of their Commonwealth inheritance; in contrast, until the passage of new citizenship laws in 2004, few of the three

million Muslims living in Germany—most of them Turks or of Turkish descent—could claim the rights of citizenship. Many Muslims were highly educated and prosperous, but overall, the Muslim standard of living throughout Europe lagged behind that of non-Muslims: Muslims were far more likely to be unemployed; to work in low-paying, dead-end jobs; to live in substandard housing; and to possess fewer educational qualifications than their non-Muslim neighbors. Many of these "neighbors," however, lived far away, as Muslims, responding both to poverty and discrimination as well as their own desire to retain their distinct communities, tended to cluster in certain areas and cities, part of a subculture largely separate from and, in some cases, increasingly hostile to the majority culture. As minarets began to rival church steeples in the skylines of European cities, an increasing number of non-Muslim Europeans argued that Western culture itself was under threat. The decision of Iran's Ayatollah Khomeini to issue a death sentence against the British writer Salman Rushdie in 1989 forced many of these tensions and hostilities into the open but provided no easy answers to questions about Islamic, European, and Western identity.

### Terrorism, the West, and the Middle East

Terrorism both deepened hostilities between Muslims and non-Muslims in the West and made the resolution of these hostilities even more urgent. This textbook has traced the way in which "the West" changed meaning, often in response to places and peoples defined as "not West." With the ending of the Cold War, the West lost its main enemy, but a replacement stood readily at hand. In 1996, the American president Bill Clinton (b. 1946) identified terrorism as "the enemy of our generation." In the post–Cold War world, terrorism in many ways replaced communism as the new foe against which the West defined itself. Many Europeans and Americans, however, not only viewed terrorism as "not West," they also linked "terrorism" with "Islam."

Terrorism directly opposes what many now regard as the bedrock of Western culture—a commitment to democracy and the rule of the law. Because terrorists seek to achieve political ends through violence and intimidation, terrorism short-circuits the democratic process: Decision-making shifts from the ballot box to the bomb. Yet the equation of the West with law and democracy conveniently ignores the history of the West and of terrorism itself. Together with fascism and Nazism, terrorism is one of the less savory products of Western political culture. Terrorism grew out of late nineteenth-century anarchism, which advocated violence as a means of political change (see Chapter 22). Like the assassins who killed Tsar Alexander II in 1881, contemporary terrorists belonged to groups lacking access to political power. Unable to achieve their goals through political persuasion (lobbying, campaigning, winning votes), they endeavored to destabilize the societies they opposed through acts of terror. In the twentieth century, thwarted

# The Sentencing of Salman Rushdie

In February 1989, the Ayatollah Khomeini, political leader of Iran and spiritual head of the Shi'a Muslim community, issued a death sentence against the novelist Salman Rushdie and offered an award of $2.5 million to any faithful Muslim who killed him. Rushdie, a British citizen who had never been tried in any Iranian or Islamic court, immediately went into hiding, where he remained for several years. His death sentence ignited the "Satanic Verses Affair," a tumultuous international crisis caused by a resounding clash of cultural assumptions and expectations.

The crisis centered on a book. In the early autumn of 1988 Viking Penguin published Rushdie's *The Satanic Verses,* a difficult novel about the complexities and contradictions of the modern immigrant experience. Born in India and raised in an Islamic home, Rushdie wrote *The Satanic Verses* to describe "migration, metamorphosis, divided selves, love, death, London, and Bombay."[9] The novel received immediate critical acclaim, with reviewers praising it as an astonishing work of postmodernist fiction.

Other readers judged it differently. Many Muslims around the world regarded the book as a direct attack on the foundations of their religious faith. One scene in the novel particularly horrified devout Muslims. In this episode, the central character has a psychotic breakdown and falls into a dream: Muhammad appears as a corrupt businessman, and prostitutes in a brothel take on the names of the Prophet's wives.

The novel aroused intense controversy from the moment of its publication. The government of India banned it almost immediately; within a matter of weeks, several other states followed suit. Anti-Rushdie demonstrations in both India and Pakistan turned violent, resulting in fifteen deaths. Bookstores selling the novel received bombing and death threats. In western Europe, hostilities between Muslims and non-Muslims intensified. Then, on February 14, 1989, an announcer on Radio Tehran read aloud the text of a *fatwa,* or decree, issued by the Ayatollah Khomeini:

> *I would like to inform all the intrepid Muslims of the world that the author of the book entitled* The Satanic Verses, *which has been compiled, printed and published in opposition to Islam, the Prophet and the Koran, as well as those publishers who were aware of its contents, have been sentenced to death. I call on all zealous Muslims to execute them quickly, wherever they find them. . . . Whoever is killed on this path will be regarded as a martyr, God willing.*

Western governments reacted quickly against Khomeini's call for Rushdie's death. The twelve nations of the European Community, the United States, Sweden, Norway, Canada, Australia, and Brazil all condemned Khomeini's judgment, recalled their ambassadors from Tehran, and cancelled high-level diplomatic contacts with Iran. British prime minister Margaret Thatcher provided police protection for Rushdie and dismissed British Muslim demands to ban the book: "It is an essential part of our democratic system that people who act within the law should be able to express their opinions freely."[10]

Large numbers of Muslims, including many who spoke out against Rushdie's book, also condemned Khomeini's fatwa. Some Muslim scholars contended that the Ayatollah's fatwa was a scholarly opinion, not a legally binding judgment; others argued that Rushdie could not be condemned without a trial, or that because Rushdie lived in a society without an Islamic government, he was not bound by Islamic law.

But many ordinary Muslims ignored these high-level theological and legal disputes and greeted the Ayatollah's fatwa with delight. The news of the Ayatollah's fatwa brought crowds of cheering Muslims into the city streets. In Manchester and Bradford, young British Muslim men insisted they would kill Rushdie if given the chance. In Paris, demonstrators marched to cries of "We are all Khomeinists!"

Why did Khomeini's fatwa arouse such popular enthusiasm within Western Muslim communities? A partial answer to this question is that many Muslims were frustrated with what they regarded as the unequal application of the laws of censorship. Faced with what they saw as a hate-filled, pornographic caricature of Islam, they demanded that Western governments use the laws censoring pornography and banning hate crimes to block the publication of Rushdie's book. In Britain, Muslims were particularly outraged that the existing law against blasphemy protected only Christianity, the official state religion.

But the controversy was not simply a dispute about censorship. For some Muslims, Rushdie's *Satanic Verses* epitomized Western secular society, with its scant regard for tradition or religious values. As Dr. Kalim Siddiqui of the pro-Iranian Muslim Institute in Britain proclaimed, "western civilization is fundamentally an immoral civilization. Its 'values' are free of moral constraints."[11] From this perspective, Khomeini's fatwa condemned not just one book or one author, but an entire culture that seemed inherently opposed to Islam. Khomeini had already proven himself a forceful leader in the Iranian hostage crisis of 1979–1980, when he successfully thumbed his nose at American power. Now once again he seemed willing to take on the West to defend Islam.

The anti-Western stance of some radical Muslims was mirrored by the anti-Islam position soon occupied by some Rushdie supporters. In one of the most ironic twists in the entire Satanic Verses Affair, Rushdie's books, which condemned the endemic racism in British society and exposed the falsehood of Western claims to cultural superiority, were championed by individuals who articulated precisely the sort of Western cultural chauvinism against which Rushdie had written so passionately. For example, Robert Maxwell, a multimillionaire communications tycoon, offered $10 million to any individual

"who will, not kill, but civilise the barbarian Ayatollah" by forcing him to recite publicly the Ten Commandments.[12] Many western Europeans agreed with the conclusion drawn in this letter to a British daily newspaper: "The lesson of the Rushdie affair is that it was unwise to let Muslim communities establish themselves in our midst."[13] The lines were drawn, with Islam standing for irrationalism, barbarity, intolerance, and ignorance, while the "West" was linked to democracy, reason, freedom, and civilization. At precisely the moment when the crumbling of communism and the ending of the Cold War deprived the West of one of its defining attributes, the Satanic Verses Affair offered up a new Other against which the West could define itself.

## Questions of Justice

1. On what grounds are publications censored in secular, Western societies? Given the existence of this censorship, should Rushdie's book have been banned?
2. In what ways does the Satanic Verses Affair illuminate the tensions within many European societies from the 1970s on, as communities struggled to adapt to the challenges of ethnic and religious diversity?

## Taking It Further

Bowen, David G., ed. *The Satanic Verses: Bradford Responds*. 1996. This collection of essays and documents helps explains why many British Muslims viewed the British government's failure to censor Rushdie's book as an act of injustice.

**A Clash of Cultures?**
In London, a policeman chases a demonstrator during a protest against the publication of *The Satanic Verses*.

nationalism provided especially fertile soil for the growth of terrorism. In Northern Ireland, assassinations and bombings became commonplace after the Irish Republican Army (IRA) turned to terror to pressure the British government to relinquish its control over the province. In Spain, the Basque separatist group Eta has for three decades waged a campaign of terror to achieve its aim of an independent Basque state. Terrorism is thus one of the negative aspects of "Western civilization." Yet by the 1990s, terrorism was often perceived as the antithesis of the West, as an outside threat, usually bearing an Arabic face and carrying a copy of the Qur'an.

Terrorist activity sparked by the Palestinian-Israeli conflict helped create this perception. Frustrated by the failure of the United Nations to implement its 1947 resolution promising a Palestinian state, Palestinian nationalists (most but not all of whom were Muslim) in 1964 formed the Palestine Liberation Organization (PLO). Like the IRA in Northern Ireland or Eta in Spain, the PLO saw violence as the only means to its nationalist ends. The PLO's commitment to terrorism deepened after the Six-Day War of 1967, which (as we saw in Chapter 27) led to Israel occupying East Jerusalem, the West Bank, and the Golan Heights. During subsequent decades the PLO took its campaign of terror around the world, bombing airports, targeting tourists, and persuading many in the West that "Arab," "Muslim," and "terrorist" were interchangeable terms.

At the same time, U.S. support for Israel convinced many Muslims that "the West" (often equated simply with the United States) was an enemy. Between 1949 and 1998, Israel received more American aid than any other country. As Israel went on the offensive against not only Palestinian terrorism but also popular Palestinian uprisings in the 1980s and 1990s (the first and second "intifadahs"), Palestinians and their supporters argued that the United States was bankrolling a repressive regime, and that Israel was a Western colonialist outpost (see Map 28.4).

## Islamism and the West

Western perceptions of a link between Islam and terrorism were further strengthened by the development of Islamism°. Also called Islamic fundamentalism or *jihadism* (after the Islamic idea of "jihad," or holy war), Islamism is explicitly anti-Western—and is rejected by most Muslims as a corruption or negation of Islamic values. Islamism views Western culture as a threat to Islamic identity; regards the United States as the standard-bearer of the West and thus as a particular enemy of Muslim interests; and accepts violence, including the murder of civilians, as an acceptable means to its ends.

A confluence of developments helped swell the Islamist tide. Modernity itself created in its wake a fundamentalist surge, not only within Islam but within other religious traditions such as Christianity and Hinduism. In times of often confusing change and growing secularization, men and

women sought clear answers and the guarantee of order through rigid religious systems. This guarantee of order particularly appealed to the children of Muslim immigrants in western Europe. Many in this generation, young men in particular, felt betrayed by the cultures in which they lived. Their ongoing struggle against poverty, discrimination, and disempowerment turned many European Muslims toward Islamism.

A series of international developments also nourished Islamism. First, the West's willingness during the Cold War to prop up unpopular and corrupt governments turned the Western promise of democracy into a sham for many Muslims. In Iran, for example, the United States supported the autocratic regime of the Shah. In 1979 a popular revolution vaulted into power the Ayatollah Khomeini (1901–1989), who rapidly reversed the westernizing and modernizing policies of the Shah and decried the United States as the "Great Satan."

DOCUMENT

Ayatollah Khomeini's Vision of Islamic Government

The Gulf War of 1991 sharpened these hostilities. In this conflict American and British forces led a twenty-eight-country coalition in a military intervention to drive invading Iraqi forces out of tiny but oil-rich Kuwait. The war itself could not be construed as "the West versus Islam" or "the West versus the East": One Arab and Islamic country had invaded another. But in the aftermath of the war, U.S. forces remained in American-controlled bases in Saudi Arabia, home of some of the most holy sites in Islam. For Islamists, the presence of the United States in this region both sullied Islamic purity and insulted Arabic political independence.

Finally, the wars in both Bosnia and Chechnya fed Islamist hatred of the West. The initial passivity of both western Europe and the United States while Muslim men and boys were slaughtered and Muslim women and girls raped during the Bosnian war of 1992–1995 convinced many European Muslims that Western governments had an anti-Muslim agenda. This perception grew stronger when western states refused to back the Chechens (who are Muslim) in what many view as the Chechen war of independence against Russian oppression, ongoing from 1994.

Significantly, many Islamists viewed Russia as part of the West against which they were fighting. The predominantly Muslim states of the Caucasus had a long history of fighting against Russian rule, and Soviet communism had been no more tolerant of Islam than it had been of Judaism or Christianity. Most important, however, was yet another recent war: the Soviet-Afghan War of 1979–1989. To Islamists, the Afghan guerillas fighting both the pro-Soviet Afghan regime and the Soviet army came to represent the wider struggle to free Islam from Western control and purify it from Western corruption. More practically, many Islamists received military training in this conflict.

Ironically, many of these Islamist rebels in Afghanistan were supported by the United States. Soviet troops withdrew from Afghanistan in defeat in 1989. The pro-Soviet Afghan government collapsed, and after a period of turmoil, the Taliban, a revolutionary Islamist group, seized control.

Events in Afghanistan seemed a long way away from Europe and the United States—until September 11, 2001, when Islamists declared open war on the West in one of the most deadly episodes of terrorism yet seen. Three jets hijacked by Islamist terrorists (most of them Saudi) smashed into the World Trade Center in New York City and the Pentagon (the U.S. military headquarters in Washington, D.C.), while a fourth crashed in Pennsylvania. Almost 3,000 people died. U.S. and European intelligence officers quickly linked the suicide pilots to Al Qaeda, an Islamist terrorist organization run by Osama bin Laden, a wealthy Saudi exile. Evidence of ideological and financial links between bin Laden and the Taliban led the United States to begin air attacks against Afghanistan in October 2001. The Taliban regime fell within weeks, but bin Laden remained at large and the "war against terror" continued.

In March 2003, this widely ranging war took a new turn when U.S. and British forces attacked Iraq. No direct connection linked Osama bin Laden to Iraq's government,

## Map 28.4  The Middle East in the Contemporary Era

Although placed under Palestinian self-rule in 1994, the West Bank and Gaza Strip remain contested areas, sites of frequent confrontations between Palestinians and Israelis.

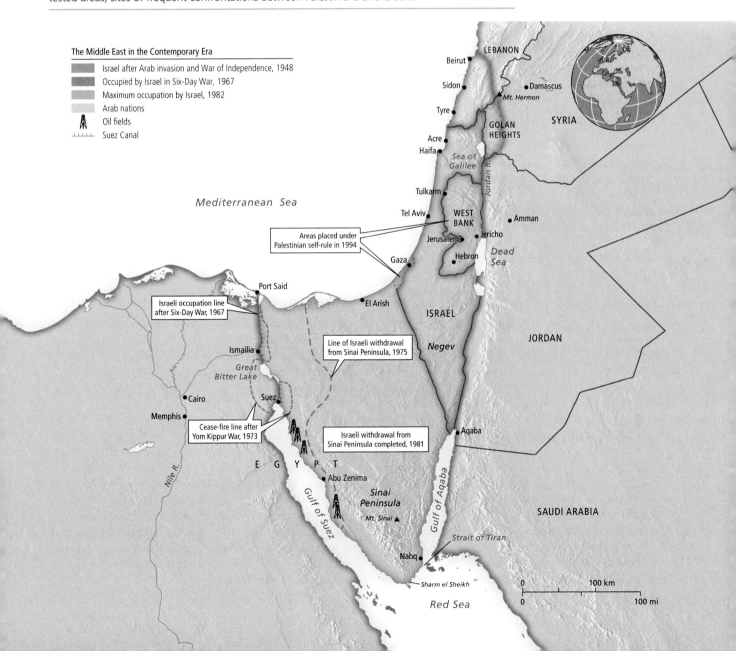

which was firmly controlled by Saddam Hussein, a secular dictator with a long history of torturing and killing Islamists like bin Laden who threatened his personal power. But in the world after "9/11," Saddam Hussein's refusal to allow UN inspections of his weapons factories convinced both the American and British governments that Iraq possessed the ability to launch a terrorist strike, in the form of biological or chemical weapons, against Western targets. The result was the first preemptive war ever waged by U.S. forces and, after a three-week conflict involving both air strikes and land battles, the toppling of Saddam Hussein's dictatorial regime. Many Iraqis cheered the dictator's overthrow, but other Iraqis—and many Arabs in the surrounding states—condemned the Anglo-American intervention as yet another episode in a long history of Western imperial intrusions on Arab territory.

The war in Iraq proved controversial, especially after Al Qaeda demonstrated its continuing ability to carry out lethal terrorist attacks. On the third anniversary of "9/11"—September 11, 2004—almost 200 people died after four bombs exploded on commuter trains during the rush hour in Madrid. Al Qaeda linked the bombing to Spain's support of the Iraq war.

## Euro-Islam

Almost one year later, on July 7, 2005, a similar spate of bombings during the morning rush hour in London killed over 50 people and injured more than 700. Significantly, the men involved in this attack were not only linked to Al Qaeda, they were also British. The London bombings revealed the power of Islamism within the West itself. Thus, in the wake of 9/11 and the attacks that followed, the question of Western identity was more troublesome than ever. European and American Muslims found their loyalties questioned, their religious beliefs regarded as grounds for suspicion. The long, complex history of Islam in the West was often ignored, replaced by a simplistic "Them" versus "Us" mentality.

Yet the encounter between Islam and Europe was far from wholly negative. The majority of European Muslims rejected Islamism. Many, particularly those of the second and third generations of immigrant families, endeavored to create a new identity: Euro-Islam°. Regarding themselves as fully Muslim and fully European, these individuals insisted that no contradiction existed between Islam and what many Westerners view as the core values of the West—democratic politics, respect for individual differences, and civil liberties guaranteed by law to all, regardless of race and gender.

Euro-Islam has produced significant theological innovations within the Islamic community. Traditional Islamic theology cuts the world into two: *dar al-Islam,* or "house of Islam," and *dar al-harb,* or "house of war." In *dar-al-Islam,*

**The Terrorist Age: Madrid, March 11, 2004**
On March 11, 2004, a series of bombs ripped through four commuter trains in the Spanish capital city. Al Qaeda claimed responsibility for the attack, which killed 191 people and injured more than 1,500.

Islamic law prevails. In *dar-al-harb* (most of the contemporary world), Muslims cannot properly practice Islam and so live in a state of constant spiritual war. But Euro-Islamic proponents such as the Swiss scholar Tariq Ramadan argue there is a third "house": *dar ash-shahada,* or "house of testimony," regions—such as western Europe or the United States—where Muslims can profess and live their faith in community with non-Muslims.

European Muslim women have also played an important role in shaping Euro-Islam. Muslim women such as the members of the French group *Ni Putes Ni Soumises* (Neither Whores Nor Submissives) have been at the forefront of campaigns to eradicate such traditional practices as female circumcision and the forced marriage of young girls to men from their parents' or grandparents' homelands and to claim an equal place for women within the context of both Europe and of Islam.

**An Identity Struggle**

In the wake of 9/11, European Muslims fought to assert their Western identity. Symbols became particularly important; this teacher won her battle in German courts to wear her Islamic head scarf in the classroom of a state school. In France, however, Islamic girls in head scarves were not permitted in schoolrooms.

## Into the Postmodern Era

The end of the Cold War, the formation of the European Union, and the growth of significant Muslim communities within western Europe all demanded a reevaluation and re-definition of West. So, too, did a number of intellectual, artistic, and technological developments that together helped created the postmodern era. A grab-bag term covering a huge array of styles and stances, postmodernism° at its core constitutes the rejection of Western cultural supremacy and, more particularly, a challenge to the idea that Western science and rationality had constructed a single, universally applicable form of "modernity."

## The Making of the Postmodern

Postmodernism resulted from the joining of three specific intellectual and cultural streams: postmodernist architecture, postmodernist art, and the literary theories of poststructuralism.

Postmodernism first clearly took form in architecture, perhaps because the failures of modernist architecture were so obvious by the early 1970s. Motivated by an intense faith in both human rationality and modern technology, modernist architects had sought to build new forms of housing that they believed would enable people to live better, more beautiful lives. But the concrete high-rises they constructed failed to connect with the needs and emotions of their inhabitants, and many became derelict, crime-ridden, graffiti-scarred tenements.

Faced with this sense of failure, a new generation—the postmodernists—insisted that architects needed to start communicating with ordinary people. The American architect Charles Jencks (b. 1939) argued that because people tend to rely on the familiar to make sense of their world, modernism was wrong to reject traditional forms. For example, most Europeans and Americans connect domestic housing with gabled roofs (ask a child to draw a picture of a house and see if he or she draws a flat roof). Was it surprising, Jencks asked, that the concrete rectangles used by modernists for housing proved profoundly alienating to many people? Postmodernist *anti-elitism* thus led to *eclecticism*, to re-creating and combining forms and styles from past eras (such as gabled roofs), and to efforts to revive local and regional styles. Why should the streets of Tokyo look like the center of London or downtown Chicago? Instead, postmodernists embraced an architecture rooted in the specifics of time and place. In addition to being anti-elitist and eclectic, then, postmodernist architecture was also *anti-universalist:* It condemned modernism for its assumption that the same modern (and Western) ideals and forms fit all individuals and all societies.

The same sorts of criticism of modernism surfaced in the art world, as the wider political context of the late 1960s and early 1970s transformed the visual arts in three ways. First, in the wake of the protests of 1968, artists—many coming out of left-wing activist environments—rejected ideologies based on hierarchy and authority. This rejection led to an attack on the modernist idea of the "avant-garde," a small elite of artistic geniuses fighting to advance the frontiers of aesthetic excellence. Even more than their modernist predecessors, postmodernist artists celebrated the possibilities of the mass media and condemned distinctions between "high" and popular culture. Second, the experience of political protest led many artists to reject the modernist ideal of "art for art's sake," insisting instead that art had to say something to the world around it. To communicate with a wider public, they plundered both the past and popular culture for familiar forms and material. As the art critic

## Postmodernism at Play

Designed by the American architect Frank Gehry and his Czech collaborator Vlado Mulunić, the "Dancing Building" fills a bomb site left vacant in central Prague since World War II. Also called "Fred and Ginger" (after the famous Hollywood dancing duo Fred Astaire and Ginger Rogers), this postmodernist piece both delighted and enraged the people of Prague.

Edit DeAk explained, postmodernist art relied on "the shock of recognition instead of the shock of the new."[14] Finally, feminism proved crucial in shaping the new art. Women began to challenge the dominance of men in the art world not only by highlighting the systematic exclusion of women from gallery and museum exhibitions, but also by questioning the aesthetic hierarchy that relegated to the lower status of "craft" traditionally female art forms such as weaving.

By the end of the 1970s, postmodernist practices in art and architecture both were reinforced by and in turn strengthened a growing body of literary and cultural theory often called *poststructuralism*. The theory of poststructuralism centered on the work of an assorted group of French thinkers whose ideas were taken up in American universities and then filtered back into European intellectual circles. These thinkers included Jacques Derrida (1930–2004) and Roland Barthes (1915–1980) in literary studies, Michel Foucault (1926–1984) in history, and Jacques Lacan (1901–1981) in psychoanalytic theory.

Like postmodernist theories in architecture and art, poststructuralism began as an exploration into the problems of communication. Jacques Derrida argued that the world we see and experience is a world structured by language—we cannot even understand or express our very selves apart from language. But because there is no inherent match between a word (what Derrida called a "signifier") and the thing or idea to which that word refers (the "signified"), communication is never straightforward. An endless variety of meanings and interpretations results, and thus, Derrida argued, we must abandon the idea of a fixed or single truth, of ultimate or universal meaning. In a related argument, Roland Barthes declared the "Death of the Author," by which he meant that the purpose of literary study is not to ask, "What does the author mean?" but instead to explore the way in which the reader creates his or her own meanings.

This effort to challenge any center of authority (sometimes called "decentering") linked the poststructuralist concern with communication to its analysis of power. Michel Foucault and Jacques Lacan dissected hierarchies of authority (not only in the political sphere but also in academic disciplines, for example, or in the medical world), and the way these authorities created and manipulated seemingly objective bodies of knowledge to retain their hold on power.

Postmodernism in its most general form emerged by the later 1980s out of the blending of these poststructuralist theories of communication and power with the critique of modernism already flourishing in architecture and the arts. Thinkers, writers, and artists argued that Western elites had shaped global culture and had ignored or distorted the cultures of non-Western and minority groups. This view of culture as bound up in a global contest for power disturbed many more traditional thinkers (with "modernist" now increasingly perceived as traditional) who continued to insist that criteria of aesthetic excellence ("Beauty") and objective standards of knowledge ("Truth") did exist. These critics warned that cultural "decentering" would destroy the social cohesion and political stability of the West.

## Postmodern Cultures and Postindustrial Technologies

In many ways popular culture confirmed postmodern theories. In Britain, for example, the "Big Beat" songs that dominated the club scene in the late 1990s were produced not by vocalists or instrumentalists but by disc jockeys who lifted snatches from old records, played them at different speeds, and combined them with contrasting styles. Like postmodernist paintings, Big Beat contained chunks of the past, recycled in startling new ways. More generally, a series of technological developments meant that popular culture was clearly "decentered," that at the very least a multitude of popular cultures coexisted and that the individual consumer of culture, like Barthes's reader, was free to make meaning as he or she chose. The videocassette recorder (VCR), first marketed in 1975, not only transported film viewing from the public to the private sphere, it also provided the film viewer with the possibility to tailor the film to his or her own preferences—to adjust the volume or choose another soundtrack entirely, to omit or fast-forward through certain scenes, to replay others endlessly. Similarly, the proliferation of cable and satellite television stations during the 1980s and 1990s fragmented the viewing audience and made it impossible to speak of popular culture in the singular.

Postmodernist concerns with communication and codes, with the way in which interpretations can be endlessly modified, and with the abolition of a single center of authority certainly seemed appropriate for an era that many called "the Information Age" and others called the postindustrial society°. The industrial phase of economic development had been characterized by an emphasis on production. But in the postindustrial phase, the *making* of things becomes less important than the *marketing* of them. A postindustrial society, in fact, is characterized less by *things* in general than by *images, ideas, and information.*

If the factory symbolized industrial society, then the epitome of the postindustrial era is the home computer, with its capacity to disperse information, market products, and endlessly duplicate yet constantly alter visual and verbal images. By the end of the 1990s, relatively inexpensively priced home computers gave their users access to libraries, art galleries, and retail outlets from across the world, and provided, for entrepreneurs, the opportunity to make (and lose) enormous fortunes by exploiting this new image-oriented means of marketing products and information—all without any central regulating authority. Governments scrambled desperately to impose control on the proliferating technologies of the postindustrial age, but in true postmodern fashion the centers of authority broke down. Existing laws that regulated pornography, for example, proved difficult to apply to the Internet, the vast global communications web.

Similarly, developments in medical technologies raised important questions about authority and ownership. In 1978, Louise Brown was born in Britain, the world's first "test-tube baby." Over the next twenty years, assisted fertility treatment resulted in the births of more than a million babies. As the technology grew more sophisticated, so too did the ethical and political questions. Societies strug-

## CHRONOLOGY

### Medical Challenges and Achievements

**1977** First diagnosed case of AIDS

**1978** First test-tube baby

**1980** Worldwide eradication of smallpox

**1982** First use of genetic engineering (insulin manufactured from bacteria)

**1983** First artificially created chromosome

**1984** HIV identified

**1985** First use of laser surgery to clear blocked arteries

**1997** Successful cloning of sheep

**2001** Human genome decoded

gled to determine the legality of practices such as commercial surrogate motherhood, in which a woman rents her womb to a couple, and postmenopausal motherhood, in which a woman past childbearing age is implanted with a fertilized egg.

Genetic research provoked even more debate about which authorities or what principles should guide scientific research. In 1997, British scientists introduced the world to Dolly the sheep, the first mammal cloned from an adult. Many scientists declared that the cloning of human beings, long part of science fiction and horror stories, was inevitable, even if declared immoral by religious leaders and illegal by political authorities. The announcement in February 2001 that the human genome had been decoded—that scientists had mapped the sequencing of the human genome, or set of instructions in every cell in the human body—immediately raised such questions as, Who owns this information? Who has the authority to decide how it is to be used?

### Postmodern Patterns in Religious Life

Postmodern patterns—the fragmentation of cultures, the collapse of centers of authority, the supremacy of image—also characterized Western religious faith and practice after the 1970s. Christianity no longer served as a common cultural bond. In a time of increasing immigration and cultural diversity, Islam was the fastest-growing religious community in western Europe. In Britain, Muslims outnumbered Methodists by two to one. By the end of the twentieth century, established Protestant churches in western Europe faced a serious crisis, with regular churchgoers now a small minority of the population—less than 5 percent in most countries. The decline of the mainline churches in the United States was also dramatic, although a greater percentage of Americans—25 to 30 percent—attended church regularly. Religious faith became a private matter, the mark of subcultures (often defined by an "Us versus Them" mentality), rather than a bond tying together individuals and groups into a cohesive national culture.

At the same time, however, the long-reigning Pope John Paul II (r. 1978–2005) experienced unprecedented popularity. The most well-traveled and populist-oriented of twentieth-century popes, John Paul II became a media star, met with the same sort of cheering crowds and tee-shirt vendors that accompanied famous rock bands. Much of his popularity rested on his intimate connection with Poland's Solidarity, and therefore with an image of liberation. Born Karol Wojtyla, John Paul was the first non-Italian pope since 1523 and the first-ever Polish pope. Twelve million people—one-third of the Polish population—greeted him in Warsaw in 1979 when he made the first visit by any pope to a communist country. Many Solidarity members testified to the importance of this visit in empowering them to challenge the political order fourteen months later. But the pope's support for Solidarity did not mean he supported other forms of rebellion against authority. Opposing the promise of continuing change inherent in Vatican II (see Chapter 27), John Paul II adopted a thoroughly authoritarian approach to church government and took an uncompromising stand against birth control, married clergy, and the ordination of women. Confronted with the postmodernist message that authority had fragmented and that no universal truth existed, many Christians found the pope's uncompromising stand a source of great comfort.

Yet the papacy of John Paul II confirmed as well as contradicted postmodernist ideas; much of the pope's popularity was based on image rather than authority. Despite censoring liberal Catholic theologians, the pope was unable to bring into line an increasingly rebellious flock throughout Europe and the United States. In the United States, millions turned out to cheer the pope waving from an open car (the "popemobile"), yet the percentage of American Catholics using birth control—in direct violation of papal teachings—mirrored that of the population at large. By the 1980s, Catholic Italy boasted the second-lowest birth rate in the world (after China), with the one-child family becoming the norm. It was hard to avoid the conclusion that in much of Western Roman Catholicism, as in much of postmodern society, image ruled while authority dissipated.

# The Global Challenge

At the same time that postmodern artists and theorists were questioning the validity of Western cultural forms, economic and environmental developments called into doubt other key assumptions of Western societies. Both the globalization of market capitalism and a worldwide environmental crisis crashed down national borders, limited the scope of action open to individual governments, and raised significant questions about the ecological sustainability of Western habits of consumption.

## The Global Economy

In the 1990s, a number of technological and economic developments helped make national borders even more permeable and accelerated the globalization of economic production. Personal computers, fax machines, and wireless telephones all ensured that "the office" could be anywhere. Fiber-optic cables that transmitted signals 4,000 times faster than their copper predecessors made instant communication across national boundaries a reality.

Technological innovations demanded organizational change. In the postindustrial economy, firms had to be more flexible, able to respond immediately to rapidly changing markets and technologies. They did not want too much capital investment in one way of doing things, in one kind of machinery, in one labor force, in one stock of supplies. Rather than economies of scale, they looked for other economies, such as subcontracting, outsourcing, and downsizing. The worker became more vulnerable. Concepts such as "a job for life" or "loyalty to the firm" had little relevance as companies merged and fragmented, shedding large number of workers in the endless pursuit of efficiency and the competitive edge. In this global economy, multinational corporations, with quick access to cheap Third World labor and raw materials, possessed significant economic power. In 2000, corporations such as ExxonMobil and DaimlerChrysler had annual revenues that exceeded the GDP of Norway or Singapore.

Increasingly, however, it was the far more nebulous "markets" that dictated the course of economic and political affairs across the world. In the 1990s, the volatility that had characterized the global economy since the collapse of the Bretton Woods Agreement in 1973 (see Chapter 27) became even more intense as currency speculators moved their money in and out of currency markets with astonishing rapidity, and with often devastating consequences for the countries involved. In 1997, for example, Thailand was forced to devalue its currency, and the economic catastrophe of collapsing currencies and stock markets quickly spread to Indonesia, Malaysia, the Philippines, and South Korea. By 1998, the Japanese economy had slid into serious recession.

As the Asian economic crisis of the later 1990s revealed, "the markets," rather than elected leaders, played an increasingly important role in determining a country's path. So, too, did the dictates of the World Bank and the IMF, the institutions that directed the flow of aid and loans throughout much of the world. The IMF, for example, insisted that governments receiving loans follow the orthodoxy of "austerity"—cutting government spending on social and welfare programs and restricting the flow of money supply to reduce inflation. Thus economists in offices far away, not

## DOCUMENT

# The West and the Rest

*In 1998, economic historian David Landes published* The Wealth and Poverty of Nations: Why Some Are So Rich and Some So Poor. *Landes, a professor at Harvard University, had been writing on the history of industrial and technological change since the 1950s. Now he turned his attention to the present and endeavored to answer one of the most pressing problems of the contemporary era. His introduction laid out the key issues.*

The old division of the world into two power blocs, East and West, has subsided. Now the big challenge and threat is the gap in wealth and health that separates the rich and poor. These are often styled North and South, because the division is geographic; but a more accurate signifier would be the West and the Rest, because the division is also historic. Here is the greatest single problem and danger facing the world of the Third Millennium. The only other worry that comes close is environmental deterioration, and the two are intimately connected, indeed are one. They are one because wealth entails not only consumption but also waste, not only production but also destruction. It is this waste and destruction, which has increased enormously with output and income, that threatens the space we live and move in.

How big is the gap between rich and poor and what is happening to it? Very roughly and briefly: the difference in income per head between the richest industrial nation, say Switzerland, and the poorest nonindustrial country, Mozambique, is about 400 to 1. Two hundred and fifty years ago, this gap between richest and poorest was perhaps 5 to 1, and the difference between Europe and, say, East or South Asia (China or India) was around 1.5 or 2 to 1.

. . . Our task (the rich countries), in our own interest as well as theirs, is to help the poor become healthier and wealthier. If we do not, they will seek to take what they cannot make; and if they cannot earn by exporting commodities, they will export people. In short, wealth is an irresistible magnet; and poverty is a potentially raging contaminant: it cannot be segregated, and our peace and prosperity depend in the long run on the well-being of others.

. . . the best way to understand a problem is to ask: How and why did we get where we are? How did the rich countries get so rich? Why are the poor countries so poor? Why did Europe ("the West") take the lead in changing the world?

A historical approach does not ensure an answer. Others have thought about these matters and come up with diverse explanations. Most of these fall into two schools. Some see Western wealth and dominion as the triumph of good over bad. The Europeans, they say, were smarter, better organized, harder working; the others were ignorant, arrogant, lazy, backward, superstitious. Others invert the categories. The Europeans, they say, were aggressive, ruthless, greedy, unscrupulous, hypocritical; their victims were happy, innocent, weak—waiting victims and hence thoroughly victimized. . . . both of these manichean visions have elements of truth, as well as of ideological fantasy. Things are always more complicated than we would have them.

Source: From *The Wealth and Poverty of Nations: Why Some Are So Rich and Some So Poor* by David S. Landes. Copyright © 1998 by David S. Landes. Used by permission of W. W. Norton & Company, Inc.

elected leaders, called the shots. Moreover, both the World Bank and the IMF embodied the characteristic Western confidence of the postwar era. Local traditions and leaders were ignored, replaced instead by outside economists and agronomists who believed that an infusion of Western economic and technological expertise would set the rest of the world on the path to economic growth.

By the 1990s, the widening gap between "North" and "South," the rich and poor nations of the world, called into question these easy assumptions. Meetings of the World Bank, the IMF, and the "G8" (Japan, the United States, Britain, Canada, France, Germany, Italy, and Russia) were disrupted by "antiglobalization" campaigners who highlighted the social costs of global capitalism, particularly the devastation wrought by what was called the "debt crisis." More than fifty of the world's poorest countries (thirty-six in Africa) were paying off their debts to Western banks and governments by withdrawing money from sanitation,

health, and education programs. Relief organizations estimated that as many as seven million children died each year during the 1990s because of the debt crisis.

## The Environmental Crisis

The urgency of the environmental crisis also revealed the limitations of Western expertise. By 1985, 257 multilateral treaties mandated some form of environmental protection—restrictions on trade in endangered species, wetlands preservation, forest conservation, regulation of industrial emissions. Almost half of these had been signed since 1970. Yet the degradation of the planet proceeded apace. At the end of the millennium, half of the world's rivers were polluted or running dry, and the number of people displaced by water crises stood at 25 million (versus 21 million war-related refugees). In the 1980s, almost half of the world's tropical forests were cleared, posing a serious threat to the planet's biodiversity.

The destruction of the rain forests contributed to what is perhaps the largest threat facing not only Western but global civilization at the beginning of the third millennium—global warming. Global warming is linked to industrial development. The burning of fossil fuels such as oil and coal (which releases carbon dioxide into the atmosphere) and deforestation (which reduces the "natural sinks" that absorb the gas) together produce the "greenhouse effect"—the trapping of solar radiation in the Earth's atmosphere, with rising temperatures as a result. Faced with predictions of widespread climate change (and resulting economic devastation on a colossal scale), representatives from 160 countries met in Kyoto in 1997 and agreed to cut "greenhouse gas emissions" by 10 percent. In 2001, however, U.S. president George W. Bush rejected the Kyoto Agreements. Without the cooperation of the world's largest producer of greenhouse gases, the Kyoto Agreements' impact would be minimal.

Europeans, both political leaders and ordinary citizens, reacted with fury to the American withdrawal from the Kyoto Agreements. They condemned the unilateral American action as that of a superpower out of control, no longer constrained by the Cold War to march in step with its allies. This perception of the United States as a bullying "hyperpower" was strengthened in 2003 by the Anglo-American invasion of Iraq. Across Europe, anti-war rallies drew huge crowds as Europeans protested against what they perceived to be an unwarranted use of American military force. As new divisions and alliances emerged both within and outside Europe, the meaning of "the West" remained a subject of intense debate.

**North versus South**

An Ethiopian farmer wages a losing war against drought and famine.

would Melbourne—or Budapest or Warsaw. Nevertheless, the economic and social trauma that afflicted Russia and the poorer nations of the former Soviet bloc such as Romania and Bulgaria in the 1990s and after demonstrates that the "West" retains its distinct identity, for clearly the gap between it and the "East" remains wide. The admittedly hesitant, still incomplete spread of the Western ideal of democracy has thrown a fragile bridge across that gap. But perhaps the real divide for the twenty-first century stretches between "North" and "South"—the huge and growing difference between the global Haves and the Have-Nots. Whether any bridge can stretch across that span remains to be seen.

# Conclusion

## Where Is the West Now?

In England, the most popular fast food is not fish and chips, long the quintessential English national supper, nor is it the Big Mac, as opponents of economic globalization might predict. Instead it is curry, the gift of the minority South Asian immigrant community. In the new millennium, "the West" may no longer serve as an important conceptual border marker. By many of the criteria explored in this textbook—economic, technological, political, and cultural—Tokyo would be defined as a Western city. So, too,

## Suggestions for Further Reading

For a comprehensive listing of suggested readings, please go to
www.ablongman.com/levack2e/chapter28

Ardagh, John. *Germany and the Germans: The United Germany in the Mid-1990s.* 1996. A snapshot of a society in the midst of social and economic change.

Hughes, H. Stuart. *Sophisticated Rebels: The Political Culture of European Dissent, 1968–1987.* 1988. A perceptive and imaginative exploration of "dissenters," ranging from Solidarity and Soviet dissidents to German Greens, Welsh nationalists, and an assortment of novelists and philosophers.

Kavanagh, Dennis. *Thatcherism and British Politics: The End of Consensus?* 1987. Kavanagh answers the question posed in his title with a convincing "yes."

Lewis, Jane, ed. *Women and Social Policies in Europe: Work, Family and the State.* 1993. A series of essays exploring the position of women in western Europe. Packed with statistics and useful tables.

McNeill, John. *Something New Under the Sun: An Environmental History of the Twentieth Century.* 2000. Argues that twentieth-century human economic activity has transformed the ecology of the globe—an ongoing experiment with a potentially devastating outcome.

Ost, David. *Solidarity and the Politics of Anti-Politics: Opposition and Reform in Poland Since 1968.* 1990. Although the bulk of this account was written before the Revolution of 1989, it provides a compelling study of Solidarity's emergence, impact, and ideology.

Rogel, Carole. *The Breakup of Yugoslavia and the War in Bosnia.* 1998. Designed for undergraduates, this work includes a short but detailed historical narrative, biographies of the main personalities, and a set of primary documents.

Rosenberg, Tina. *The Haunted Land: Facing Europe's Ghosts After Communism.* 1995. Winner of the Pulitzer Prize, this disturbing account focuses on the fundamental moral issues facing postcommunist political cultures.

Sandler, Irving. *Art of the Postmodern Era: From the Late 1960s to the Early 1980s.* 1996. Much more broad-ranging than the title suggests, this well-written, blessedly jargon-free work sets both contemporary art and the theories of the postmodern within the wider historical context.

Stokes, Gale. *The Walls Came Tumbling Down: The Collapse of Communism in Eastern Europe.* 1993. A superb account, firmly embedded in history.

Young, John W. *Cold War Europe, 1945–1991: A Political History.* 1996. A solid survey.

See also the works by Crampton, Cronin, Gaddis, Isaacs and Downing, Judge and Langdon, Keep, and Urwin listed at the end of Chapter 27.

## Notes

1. Quoted in Robert Paxton, *Europe in the Twentieth Century* (1997), 613.

2. Kenneth Boulding, "The Economics of the Coming Spaceship Earth," first published in 1966, reprinted in *Toward a Steady-State Economy,* ed. Herman Daly (1973).

3. Quotations from Timothy W. Ryback, *Rock Around the Bloc: A History of Rock Music in Eastern Europe and the Soviet Union* (1990), 184–185, 176.

4. Quoted in D. J. Peterson, *Troubled Lands: The Legacy of Soviet Environmental Destruction* (1993), 12.

5. Quoted in Archie Brown, *The Gorbachev Factor* (1996), 125.

6. Quoted in R. J. Crampton, *Eastern Europe in the Twentieth Century—And After* (1997), 408.

7. Francis Fukuyama, *The End of History and the Last Man* (1992).

8. Quoted in *The Observer* (London), (April 8, 2001), 20.

9. Salman Rushdie, "Please, Read *Satanic Verses* Before Condemning It," *Illustrated Weekly of India* (October 1988). Reprinted in M. M. Ahsan and A. R. Kidwai, *Sacrilege Versus Civility: Muslim Perspectives on The Satanic Verses Affair* (1991), 63.

10. Quoted in Malise Ruthven, *A Satanic Affair: Salman Rushdie and the Wrath of Islam* (1991). 562.

11. Quoted in Ruthven, *A Satanic Affair,* 100.

12. *Bookseller,* London (February 24, 1989). Quoted in Lisa Appignanesi and Sara Maitland, *The Rushdie File* (1990), 103–104.

13. *The Sunday Telegraph* (June 24, 1990). Quoted in Ahsan and Kidwai, *Sacrilege Versus Civility,* 80.

14. Quoted in Irving Sandler, *Art of the Postmodern Era* (1996), 4.

# Glossary

**absolutism** (p. 478) A form of government in the seventeenth and eighteenth centuries in which the ruler possessed complete and unrivalled power.

**alchemy** (p. 518) A form of learned magic that was intended to turn base metals into precious ones.

**Allies** (p. 778) During World War I, the states allied against the Central Powers of Germany and Austria-Hungary. During World War II, the states allied against the regimes of Nazi Germany, fascist Italy and imperial Japan.

**anarchism** (p. 728) Ideology that views the state as unnecessary and repressive, and rejects participation in parliamentary politics in favor of direct, usually violent, action.

**anticlericalism** (p. 758) Opposition to the political influence of the Roman Catholic Church.

**apartheid** (p. 895) System of racial segregation and discrimination put into place in South Africa in 1948.

**appeasement** (p. 853) British diplomatic and financial efforts to stabilize Germany in the 1920s and 1930s and so avoid a second world war.

**aristocracy** (p. 576) A term that originally applied to those who were considered the most fit to rule and later identified the wealthiest members of society, especially those who owned land.

**Auschwitz** (p. 869) Technically Auschwitz-Birkenau; death camp in Poland that has become the symbol of the Holocaust.

***auto-da-fé*** (p. 451) Meaning literally a "theater of faith," an *auto* was practiced by the Catholic Church in early modern Spain and Portugal as an extended public ritual of penance designed to cause physical pain among the sinful and promote fear of God's judgment among those who witnessed it.

**balance of power** (p. 487) An arrangement in which various countries form alliances to prevent any one state from dominating the others.

**Balfour Declaration** (p. 809) Declaration of 1917 that affirmed British support of a Jewish state in Palestine.

**baroque** (p. 483) A dynamic style in art, architecture, and music intended to elicit an emotional response. It was closely associated with royal absolutism in the seventeenth century.

**Beer Hall Putsch** (p. 821) Failed Nazi effort to overthrow the German government by force in 1923.

**Berlin Wall** (p. 899) Constructed by the East German government, the wall physically cut the city of Berlin in two and prevented East German citizens from access to West Germany; stood from 1961 to 1989.

**Big Three** (p. 888) Term applied to the British, Soviet, and U.S. leaders during World War II: until 1945, Churchill, Stalin, and Roosevelt; by the summer of 1945, Attlee, Stalin, and Truman.

**blitzkrieg** (p. 855) "Lightning war;" offensive military tactic making use of airplanes, tanks, and motorized infantry to punch through enemy defenses and secure key territory. First demonstrated by the German army in World War II.

**boers** (p. 548) Dutch farmers in the colony established by the Dutch Republic in South Africa.

**Bolsheviks** (p. 801) Minority group of Russian socialists, headed by Lenin, who espoused an immediate transition to a socialist state. It became the Communist Party in the Soviet Union.

**bourgeoisie** (p. 583) A social group, technically consisting of those who were burghers in the towns, that included prosperous merchants and financiers, members of the professions, and some skilled craftsmen known as "petty bourgeoisie."

**Bretton Woods Agreement** (p. 889) Agreement signed in 1944 that established the post-World War II economic framework in which the U.S. dollar served as the world's reserve currency.

**brinkmanship** (p. 899) Style of Cold War confrontation in which each superpower endeavored to convince the other that it was willing to wage nuclear war.

**capital** (p. 652) All the physical assets used in production, including fixed capital, such as machinery, and circulating capital, such as raw materials; more generally the cost of these physical assets.

**Carnival** (p. 455) The most popular annual festival in much of Europe before modern times. Also known as Mardi Gras, the festival took place for several days or even weeks before the beginning of Lent and included all kinds of fun and games.

**Central Powers** (p. 778) Germany and Austria-Hungary in World War I.

***chinoiserie*** (p. 564) A French word for an eighteenth-century decorative art that combined Chinese and European motifs.

**Christian Democracy, Christian Democratic parties** (p. 907) Conservative and confessionally based (Roman Catholic) political parties that dominated much of western European politics after World War II.

**class** (p. 578) A large and often cohesive social group that was conscious of its shared economic and political interests.

**classicism** (p. 580) A style in art, architecture, music, and literature that emphasizes proportion, adherence to traditional forms, and a rejection of emotion and enthusiasm.

**Cold War** (p. 888) Struggle for global supremacy between the United States and the Soviet Union, waged from the end of World War II until 1990.

**collectivization** (p. 834) The replacement of private and village farms with large cooperative agricultural enterprises run by state-employed managers. Collectivization was a key part of Joseph Stalin's plans for modernizing the Soviet economy and destroying peasant opposition to communist rule.

**colons** (p. 568) White planters in the French Caribbean colony of Saint Domingue (Haiti).

**Common Market** (p. 908) Originally comprising West Germany, France, Italy, Belgium, Luxembourg, and the Netherlands, the Common Market was formed in 1957 to integrate its members' economic structures and so foster both economic prosperity and international peace. Also called the European Economic Community (EEC). Evolved into the European Union (EU).

**communism** (p. 680) The revolutionary form of socialism developed by Karl Marx and Friedrich Engels that promoted the overthrow of bourgeois or capitalist institutions and the establishment of a dictatorship of the proletariat.

**Concert of Europe** (p. 678) The joint efforts made by Austria, Prussia, Russia, Britain, and France during the years following the Congress of Vienna to suppress liberal and nationalist movements throughout Europe.

**Confessions** (p. 450) The formal sixteenth-century statements of religious doctrine: the Confession of Augsburg for Lutherans, the Helvetic Confessions for Calvinists, the Thirty-Nine Articles for Anglicans, and the decrees of the Council of Trent for Catholics.

**Congress of Vienna** (p. 638) A conference of the major powers of Europe in 1814–1815 to establish a new balance of power at the end of the Napoleonic Wars.

**conservatism** (p. 678) A nineteenth-century ideology intended to prevent a recurrence of the revolutionary changes of the 1790s and the implementation of liberal policies.

**containment** (p. 890) Cold War policy of blocking communist expansion; inaugurated by the Truman Doctrine in 1947.

**cosmology** (p. 514) A theory concerning the structure and nature of the universe such as those proposed by Aristotle in the fourth century B.C.E. and Copernicus in the sixteenth century.

**creoles** (p. 548) People of Spanish descent who had been born in Spanish America.

**Cubism** (p. 755) Modernist artistic movement of the early twentieth century that emphasized the fragmentation of human perception through visual experiments with geometric forms.

**Darwinian theory of evolution** (p. 746) Scientific theory associated with nineteenth-century scientist Charles Darwin that highlights the role of variation and natural selection in the evolution of species.

**Decembrists** (p. 687) Russian liberals who staged a revolt against Tsar Nicholas I on the first day of his reign in December 1825.

**de-Christianization** (p. 625) A program inaugurated in France in 1793 by the radical Jacobin and former priest Joseph Fouché that closed churches, eliminated religious symbols, and attempted to establish a purely civic religion.

**deduction** (p. 521) The logical process by which ideas and laws are derived from basic truths or principles.

**deists** (p. 529) Seventeenth- and eighteenth-century thinkers who believed that God created the universe and established immutable laws of nature but did not subsequently intervene in the operation of nature or in human affairs.

**demand** (p. 653) The desire of consumers to acquire goods and the need of producers to acquire raw materials and machinery.

**demonic magic** (p. 531) The invocation of evil spirits with the goal of utilizing their supernatural powers to change the course of nature or to alter human behavior.

**de-Stalinization** (p. 904) Khrushchev's effort to decentralize political and economic control in the Soviet Union after 1956.

**detente** (p. 924) During the 1970s, a period of lessened Cold War hostilities and greater reliance on negotiation and compromise.

**dialectic** (p. 680) The theory that history advanced in stages as the result of the conflict between different ideas or social groups.

**dialectical materialism** (p. 680) The socialist philosophy of Karl Marx according to which history advanced as the result of material or economic forces and would lead to the creation of a classless society.

**division of labor** (p. 649) The assignment of one stage of production to a single worker or group of workers to increase efficiency and productive output.

**Dreyfus Affair** (p. 721) The trials of Captain Alfred Dreyfus on treason charges dominated French political life in the decade after 1894 and revealed fundamental divisions in French society.

**dualistic** (p. 522) A term used to describe a philosophy, such as that of René Descartes, in which a rigid distinction is made between body and mind or between the material and the immaterial world.

**Dutch Revolt** (p. 466) The rebellion against Spanish rule of the seven northern provinces of the Netherlands between 1579 and 1648, which resulted in the independence of the Republic of the United Provinces.

**Edict of Nantes** (p. 463) Promulgated by King Henry IV in 1598, the edict allowed the Huguenots to build a quasi-independent state within the kingdom of France, giving them the right to have their own troops, church organization, and political autonomy within their walled towns, but banning them from the royal court and the city of Paris. King Louis XIV revoked the edict in 1685.

**Einsatzgruppen** (p. 869) Loosely translated as strike force or task force; SS units given the task of murdering Jews and Communist Party members in the areas of the Soviet Union occupied by Germany during World War II.

**empires** (p. 542) Large political formations consisting of different kingdoms or territories outside the boundaries of the states that control them.

**enclosure** (p. 652) The consolidation of scattered agricultural holdings into large, compact fields which were then closed off by hedges, bushes, or walls, giving farmers complete control over the uses of their land.

**enlightened despots** (p. 600) The term assigned to absolute monarchs who initiated a series of legal and political reforms in an effort to realize the goals of the Enlightenment.

**Enlightenment** (p. 585) An international intellectual movement of the eighteenth century that emphasized the use of reason and the application of the laws of nature to human society.

**ethnic cleansing** (p. 943) A term introduced during the wars in Yugoslavia in the 1990s; the systematic use of murder, rape, and violence by one ethnic group against members of other ethnic groups in order to establish control over a territory.

**Euro-Islam** (p. 950) The identity and belief system being forged by European Muslims who argue that Islam does not contradict or reject European values.

**European Economic Community (EEC)** (p. 908) Originally comprising West Germany, France, Italy, Belgium, Luxembourg, and the Netherlands, the EEC was formed in 1957 to integrate its members' economic structures and so foster both economic prosperity and international peace. Also called the Common Market.

**European Union (EU)** (p. 943) A successor organization to the EEC; the effort to integrate European political, economic, cultural, and military structures and policies.

**existentialism** (p. 815) Twentieth-century philosophy that emerged in the interwar era and influenced many thinkers and artists after World War II. Existentialism emphasizes individual freedom in a world devoid of meaning or coherence.

**Expressionism** (p. 755) Modernist artistic movement of the early twentieth century that used bold colors and experimental forms to express emotional realities.

**factories** (p. 544) Trading posts established by European powers in foreign lands.

**fanatic** (p. 460) Originally referring to someone possessed by a demon, a fanatic came during the sixteenth century to mean a person who expressed immoderate enthusiasm in religious matters or who pursued a supposedly divine mission, often to violent ends.

**fascism** (p. 826) Twentieth-century political ideology that rejected the existing alternatives of conservatism, communism, socialism, and liberalism. Fascists stressed the authoritarian power of the state, the efficacy of violent action, the need to build a national community, and the use of new technologies of influence and control.

**federalists** (p. 617) The name assigned by radical Jacobins to provincial rebels who opposed the centralization of the state during the French Revolution.

**feminism, feminist movement** (p. 733) International movement that emerged in the second half of the nineteenth century and demanded broader political, legal, and economic rights for women.

**Final Solution** (p. 869) Nazi term for the effort to murder every Jew in Europe during World War II.

*fin-de-siecle* (p. 750) French term for the "turn of the century"; used to refer to the cultural crisis of the late nineteenth century.

**franchise** (p. 602) The right to vote; also called suffrage.

**freemasons** (p. 598) Members of secret societies of men and women that flourished during the Enlightenment, dedicated to the creation of a society based on reason and virtue and committed to the principles of liberty and equality.

**French Wars of Religion** (p. 461) A series of political assassinations, massacres, and military engagements between French Catholics and Calvinists from 1560 to 1598.

**Gaullism** (p. 914) The political ideology associated with twentieth-century French political leader Charles DeGaulle. Gaullism combined the advocacy of a strong, centralized state with social conservatism.

**German-Soviet Non-Aggression Pact** (p. 853) Signed by Stalin and Hitler in 1939, the agreement publicly pledged Germany and the Soviet Union not to attack each other, and secretly divided up Poland and the Baltic states between the two powers.

**Girondins** (p. 616) The more conservative members of the Jacobin party who favored greater economic freedom and opposed further centralization of state power during the French Revolution.

**glasnost** (p. 943) Loosely translated as openness or honesty; Gorbachev's effort after 1985 to break with the secrecy that had characterized Soviet political life.

**Great Depression in Trade and Agriculture** (p. 712) Downturn in prices and profits, particularly in the agricultural sector, in Europe from 1873 through the 1880s.

**Great Depression** (p. 828) Calamitous drop in prices, reduction in trade, and rise in unemployment that devastated the global economy in 1929.

**Great Purge** (p. 835) Period of mass arrests and executions particularly aimed at Communist Party members. Lasting from 1934 to 1939, the Great Purge enabled Stalin to consolidate his one-man rule over the Soviet Union.

**Green movement, Green politics** (p. 930) A new style of politics and set of political ideas resulting from the confluence of environmentalism, feminism, and anti-nuclear protests of the 1970s.

**Holocaust** (p. 869) Adolf Hitler's effort to murder all the Jews in Europe during World War II.

**Huguenots** (p. 461) The term for French Calvinists, who constituted some 10 percent of the population by 1560.

**hyperinflation** (p. 821) Catastrophic price increases and currency devaluation, such as that which occurred in Germany in 1923.

**ideologies** (p. 676) Theories of society and government that form the basis of political programs.

**Ideologues** (p. 631) A group of liberal writers and philosophers in France who objected to Napoleon's religious policy on the grounds that it would inaugurate a return of religious superstition.

**induction** (p. 521) The mental process by which theories are established only after the systematic accumulation of large amounts of data.

**industrial capitalism** (p. 662) A form of capitalism characterized by the ownership of factories by private individuals and the employment of wage labor.

**intendants** (p. 481) French royal officials who became the main agents of French provincial administration in the seventeenth century.

**Islamism** (p. 948) Islamic radicalism or *jihadism*. The ideology that insists that Islam demands a rejection of Western values and that violence in this struggle against the West is justified.

**Jacobins** (p. 614) A French political party supporting a democratic republic that found support in political clubs throughout the country and dominated the National Convention from 1792 until 1794.

**Jim Crow** (p. 768) Series of laws mandating racial segregation throughout the American South.

**Junkers** (p. 493) The traditional nobility of Prussia.

*laissez-faire* (p. 676) The principle that governments should not regulate or otherwise intervene in the economy unless it is necessary to protect property rights and public order.

**League of Nations** (p. 803) Association of states set up after World War I to resolve international conflicts through open and peaceful negotiation.

**Lend-Lease Act** (p. 859) Passed in March 1941, the act gave Britain access to American industrial products during World War II, with payment postponed for the duration of the war.

**liberalism** (p. 676) An ideology based on the conviction that individual freedom is of supreme importance and the main responsibility of government is to protect that freedom.

**Mafia** (p. 700) Organizations of armed men who took control of local politics and the economy in late nineteenth-century Sicily.

**magic** (p. 457) Learned opinion described two kinds of magic: natural magic, which involved the manipulation of occult forces believed to exist in nature, and demonic magic, which called upon evil spirits to gain access to power. Widely accepted as a reality until the middle of the seventeenth century.

**Manhattan Project** (p. 866) Code name given to the secret Anglo-American project that resulted in the construction of the atom bomb during World War II.

**Marshall Plan** (p. 890) The use of U.S. economic aid to restore stability to Europe after World War II and so undercut the appeal of communist ideology.

**mechanical philosophy** (p. 522) The seventeenth-century philosophy of nature, championed by René Descartes, holding that nature operated in a mechanical way, just like a machine made by a human being.

**mercantilism** (p. 484) The theory that the wealth of a state depended on its ability to import fewer commodities than it exported and thus acquire the largest possible share of the world's monetary supply. The theory encouraged state intervention in the economy and the regulation of trade.

**mesmerism** (p. 599) A pseudoscience developed by Franz Anton Mesmer in the eighteenth century that treated sickness by massaging or hypnotizing the patient to produce a crisis that restored health.

**metropolis** (p. 542) The parent country of a colony or imperial possession.

**modernism** (p. 754) Term applied to artistic and literary movements from the late nineteenth century through the 1950s. Modernists sought to create new aesthetic forms and values.

**Montagnards** (p. 616) Members of the radical faction within the Jacobin party who advocated the centralization of state power during the French Revolution and instituted the Reign of Terror.

**nabobs** (p. 564) Members of the British East India Company who made fortunes in India and returned to Britain, flaunting their wealth.

**Napoleonic Code** (p. 631) The name given to the Civil Code of 1804, promulgated by Napoleon, which gave France a uniform and authoritative code of law.

**nation** (p. 681) A large community of people who possess a sense of unity based on a belief that they have a common homeland and share a similar culture.

**nationalism** (p. 681) The belief that the people who form a nation should have their own political institutions and that the interests of the nation should be defended and promoted at all costs.

**national self-determination** (p. 681) The doctrine advanced by nationalists that any group that considers itself a nation has the right to be ruled only by the members of their own nation and to have all members of the nation included in that state.

**nation-state** (p. 681) A political structure sought by nationalists in which the boundaries of the state and the nation are identical, so that all the members of a nation are governed by the same political authorities.

**NATO (North Atlantic Treaty Organization)** (p. 892) Defensive anti-Soviet alliance of the United States, Canada, and the nations of western Europe established in 1949.

**natural magic** (p. 525) The use of magical words and drawings to manipulate the occult forces that exist in nature without calling on supernatural beings for assistance.

**nawabs** (p. 561) Native provincial governors in eighteenth-century India.

**Nazism** (p. 829) Twentieth-century political ideology associated with Adolf Hitler that adopted many fascist ideas but with a central focus on racism and particularly anti-Semitism.

**neoclassicism** (p. 580) The revival of the classical art and architecture of ancient Greece and Rome in the eighteenth century.

**Neoplatonism** (p 522) A philosophy based on the teachings of Plato and his successors that flourished in Late Antiquity, especially in the teachings of Plotinus. Neoplatonism influenced Christianity in Late Antiquity. During the Renaissance Neoplatonism was linked to the belief that the natural world was charged with occult forces that could be used in the practice of magic.

**NEP (New Economic Policy)** (p. 820) Lenin's economic turnaround in 1921 that allowed and even encouraged small private businesses and farms in the Soviet Union.

**New Conservatism** (p. 928) Political ideology that emerged at the end of the 1970s combining the free market approach of nineteenth-century liberalism with social conservatism.

**new feminism** (p. 928) Re-emergence of the feminist movement in the 1970s.

**new imperialism** (p. 759) The third phase of modern European imperialism, that occurred in the late nineteenth and early twentieth centuries and extended Western control over almost all of Africa and much of Asia.

**New Left** (p. 917) Leftwing political and cultural movement that emerged in the late 1950s and early 1960s; sought to develop a form of socialism that rejected the over-centralization, authoritarianism, and inhumanity of Stalinism.

**nobility** (p. 570) Members of the aristocracy who received official recognition of their hereditary status, including their titles of honor and legal privileges.

**no-man's-land** (p. 786) The area between the combatants' trenches on the Western Front during World War I.

**North Atlantic Treaty Organization (NATO)** (p. 892) Defensive anti-Soviet alliance of the United States, Canada, and the nations of western Europe established in 1949.

**Nuremberg trials** (p. 872) Post-World War II trials of members of the Nazi Party and German military; conducted by an international tribunal.

**Old Regime** (p. 600) The political order of eighteenth-century France, dominated by an absolute monarch and a privileged nobility and clergy.

**pan-Arabism** (p. 842) Nationalist ideology that called for the political unification of all Arabs, regardless of religious affiliation.

**paradigm** (p. 525) A conceptual model or intellectual framework within which scientists conduct their research and experimentation.

**parlements** (p. 481) The highest provincial courts in France, the most important of which was the Parlement of Paris.

**perestroika** (p. 935) Loosely translated as "restructuring;" Gorbachev's effort to decentralize, reform, and thereby strengthen Soviet economic and political structures.

**personal rule** (p. 500) The period from 1629 to 1640 in England when King Charles I ruled without Parliament.

**philosophes** (p. 581) The writers and thinkers of the Enlightenment, especially in France.

**pop art** (p. 911) Effort by artists in the 1950s and 1960s both to utilize and to critique the material plenty of post-World War II popular culture.

**popular sovereignty** (p. 625) The claim that political power came from the people and that the people constituted the highest political power in the state.

**positivism** (p. 682) The philosophy developed by August Comte in the nineteenth century according to which human society passed through a series of stages, leading to the final positive stage in which the accumulation of scientific data would enable thinkers to discover the laws of human behavior and bring about the improvement of society.

**postindustrialism, postindustrial society** (p. 953) A service-rather than manufacturing-based economy characterized by an emphasis on marketing and information and by a proliferation of communications technologies.

**postmodernism** (p. 951) Umbrella term covering a variety of artistic styles and intellectual theories and practices; in general, a rejection of a single, universal, Western style of modernity.

**Prague Spring** (p. 906) Short-lived popular effort in 1968 to reform Czechoslovakia's political structures; associated with the phrase "socialism with a human face."

**prerogative** (p. 499) The set of powers exercised by the English monarch alone, rather than in conjunction with Parliament.

**Price Revolution** (p. 448) After a long period of falling or stable prices that stretched back to the fourteenth century, Europe experienced sustained price increases between about 1540 and 1640, causing widespread social and economic turmoil.

**proletariat** (p. 680) The word used by Karl Marx and Friedrich Engels to identify the class of workers who received their income from wages.

**protectionism** (p. 550) The policy of shielding domestic industries from foreign competition through a policy of levying tariffs on imported goods.

**Reign of Terror** (p. 620) A purging of alleged enemies of the French state between 1793 and 1794, superintended by the Committee of Public Safety, that resulted in the execution of 17,000 people.

**reparations** (p. 806) Payments imposed upon Germany after World War I by the Versailles Treaty to cover the costs of the war.

**revisionism, socialist revisionism** (p. 727) The belief that an equal society can be built through participation in parliamentary politics rather than through violent revolution.

**romanticism** (p. 683) An artistic and literary movement of the late eighteenth and nineteenth centuries that involved a protest against classicism, appealed to the passions rather than the intellect, and emphasized the beauty and power of nature.

**Rome-Berlin Axis** (p. 853) Alliance between Mussolini's Italy and Hitler's Germany formed in 1936.

**Schlieffen Plan** (p. 781) German military plan devised in 1905 that called for a sweeping attack on France through Belgium and the Netherlands.

**Scramble for Africa** (p. 763) The frenzied imposition of European control over most of Africa that occurred between 1870 and 1914.

**Second Industrial Revolution** (p. 713) A new phase in the industrialization of the processes of production and consumption, underway in Europe in the 1870s.

**seigneur** (p. 582) The lord of a French estate who received payments from the peasants who lived on his land.

**separate spheres** (p. 595) The theory that men and women should conduct their lives in different social and political environments, confining women to the domestic sphere and excluding them from the public sphere of political involvement.

**sepoys** (p. 562) Indian troops serving in the armed forces of the British East India Company.

**Social Darwinism** (p. 747) The later-nineteenth-century application of the theory of evolution to entire human societies.

**social democracy** (p. 838) Political system in which a democratically elected parliamentary government endeavors to ensure a decent standard of living for its citizens through both economic regulation and the maintenance of a welfare state.

**Solidarity** (p. 931) Trade union and political party in Poland that led an unsuccessful effort to reform the Polish communist state in 1981; survived to lead Poland's first non-communist government since World War II in 1989.

**soviets** (p. 800) Workers' and soldiers' councils formed in Russia during the Revolution of 1917.

**Spanish Armada** (p. 465) A fleet of 132 ships, which sailed from Portugal to rendezvous with the Spanish army stationed in the Netherlands and launch an invasion of England in 1588. The English defeated the Armada as it passed through the English Channel.

**spiritualists** (p. 428) A tendency within Protestantism, especially Lutheranism, to emphasize the power of personal spiritual illumination, called the "inner Word," a living form of the Scriptures written directly on the believer's soul by the hand of God.

**stagflation** (p. 925) Term coined in the 1970s to describe an economy troubled by both high inflation and high unemployment rates.

**states** (p. 542) Consolidated territorial areas that have their own political institutions and recognize no higher political authority.

**structuralism** (p. 911) Influential post-World War II social theory that explored the common structures of language and thought.

**suffragettes** (p. 738) Feminist movement that emerged in Britain in the early twentieth century. Unlike the suffragists, who sought to achieve the vote for women through rational persuasion, the suffragettes adopted the tactics of violent protest.

**supply** (p. 653) The amounts of capital, labor, and food that are needed to produce goods for the market as well as the quantities of those goods themselves.

**syndicalism** (p. 728) Ideology of the late nineteenth and early twentieth century that sought to achieve a working-class revolution through economic action, particularly through mass labor strikes.

**Third World** (p. 900) Term coined in 1955 to describe nations that did not align with either the Soviet Union or the United States; commonly used to describe the industrially underdeveloped nations.

**Time of Troubles** (p. 474) The period from 1604 to 1613 when Russia fell into chaos, which ended when the national assembly elected Tsar Michael Romanov, whose descendants ruled Russia until they were deposed in 1917.

**total war** (p. 778) A war that demands extensive state regulation of economic production, distribution, and consumption; and that blurs (or erases entirely) the distinction between civilian and soldier.

**Treaty of Brest-Litovsk** (p. 790) Treaty between Germany and Bolshevik-controlled Russia, signed in March, 1918, that ceded to Germany all of Russia's western territories.

**Triple Alliance** (p. 779) Defensive alliance of Germany, Austria-Hungary, and Italy, signed in 1882.

**Triple Entente** (p. 781) Informal defensive agreement linking France, Great Britain, and Russia before World War I.

**Truman Doctrine** (p. 890) Named after U.S. president Harry Truman, the doctrine that in 1947 inaugurated the Cold War policy of resisting the expansion of communist control.

**universal law of gravitation** (p. 518) A law of nature established by Isaac Newton in 1687 holding that any two bodies attract each other with a force that is directly proportional to the product of their masses and indirectly proportional to the square of the distance between them. The law was presented in mathematical terms.

**universal male suffrage** (p. 615) The granting of the right to vote to all adult males.

**Utilitarians** (p. 678) Nineteenth-century British liberals who promoted social and economic policies that in their view would provide the greatest good for the greatest number of people.

**Vatican II** (p. 912) Popular term for the Second Vatican Council that convened in 1963 and introduced a series of changes within the Roman Catholic Church.

**Versailles Treaty** (p. 806) Treaty between Germany and the victorious Allies after World War I.

**Vichy, Vichy regime, Vichy government** (p. 855) Authoritarian state established in France after defeat by the German army in 1940.

**Warsaw Pact** (p. 892) Military alliance of the Soviet Union and its eastern European satellite states in the Cold War era.

**Weimar Republic** (p. 821) The democratic German state constructed after defeat in World War I and destroyed by the Nazis in 1933.

**witch-hunt** (p. 457) Refers to the dramatic increase in the judicial prosecution of alleged witches in either church or secular courts from the middle of the sixteenth to the middle of the seventeenth centuries.

**Zionism** (p. 732) Nationalist movement that emerged in the late nineteenth century and sought to establish a Jewish political state in Palestine (the Biblical Zion).

# Credits

Unless otherwise acknowledged, all photographs are the property of Pearson Education, Inc.
Page abbreviations are as follows: (**T**) Top, (**B**) Bottom, (**L**) Left, (**R**) Right, (**C**) Center.

## What Is the West?
**2** Canali Photobank **4** European Space Agency/Photo Researchers, Inc. **5** Courtesy of Adler Planetarium & Astronomy Museum, Chicago, Illinois (W-264). **8** American Museum of Natural History Library (AMNH#314372)

## Chapter 14
**442** Erich Lessing/Art Resource, NY **446** Scala/Art Resource, NY **453** akg-images **454** Erich Lessing/Art Resource, NY **455** Erich Lessing/Art Resource, NY **456** Erich Lessing/Art Resource, NY **459** Erich Lessing/Art Resource, NY **459** Time Life Pictures/Getty Images **463** Musée de Beaux Arts Lausanne/Dagli Orti/The Art Archive **465** Snark/Art Resource, NY **469** By kind permission of His Grace the Duke of Bedford and the Trustees of the Bedford Estates **471** Erich Lessing/Art Resource, NY **474** Art Resource, NY

## Chapter 15
**476** Réunion des Musées Nationaux/Art Resource, NY **482** Philippe de Champaigne, 1602–1674. Triple Portrait of Cardinal Richelieu, oil on canvas, 58.4 × 72.4 cm. © The National Gallery, London (NG798) **483** Réunion des Musées Nationaux/Art Resource, NY **490** Museo del Prado/Art Resource, NY **491** Scala/Art Resource, NY **492** Bildarchiv Prüßischer Kulturbesitz/Art Resource, NY **498** Stapleton Collection, UK/Bridgeman Art Library **500** Museum of London, UK/Bridgeman Art Library **503** This item is reproduced by permission of the Huntington Library, San Marina, California **507** Museum Boijmans van Beuningen, Rotterdam **508** Rijksmuseum Foundation, Amsterdam

## Chapter 16
**512** Archivo Iconografico, S.A./Corbis **515** (**R**) From *The Cosmographical Glass*, 1559 **515** (**L**) © 1982 Instructional Resources Corporation **516** (**T**) By permission of the British Library (Neg No. 2204) **516** (**B**) The Library of Congress (LC USZ62-95165) **518** Giraudon/Art Resource, NY **519** Ashmolean Museum, Oxford University (BI313) **520** Wellcome Library, London **522** Erich Lessing/Art Resource, NY **529** Herzog August Bibliothek, Wolfenbuttel, Germany/Bridgeman Art Library **533** Erich Lessing/Art Resource, NY **536** Réunion des Musées Nationaux/Art Resource, NY **538** Corbis

## Chapter 17
**540** Victoria & Albert Museum, London/Art Resource, NY **546** Private Collection Pairs/Dagli Orti/The Art Archive **547** British Museum/Art Resource, NY **556** Museum of London **559** Joseph Mallord William Turner, English, 1775–1851. *Slave Ship (Slavers Throwing Overboard the Dead and Dying, Typhoon Coming On)*, 1840. Oil on canvas. 90.8 × 122.6 cm (35¾ × 48¼ in.). Museum of Fine Arts, Boston. Henry Lillie Pierce Fund. 99.22. Photograph © 2006 Museum of Fine Arts Boston

**560** Benson Latin American Collection, University of Texas-Austin **562** Museo de Arte, Sao Paulo, Brazil/Giraudon/Bridgeman Art Library **565** Private Collection/The Stapleton Collection/Bridgeman Art Library **566** The Library of Congress **567** Réunion des Musées Nationaux/Art Resource, NY **571** Museo Bolivar Caracas/Dagli Orti/The Art Archive

## Chapter 18
**574** Erich Lessing/Art Resource, NY **579** National Gallery, London **581** akg-images **583** By courtesy of the Trustees of the Goodwood Collection **584** Erich Lessing/Art Resource, NY **587** Scottish National Portrait Gallery (PG1057) **588** *Engravings by Hogarth*, plate 95 **592** akg-images/Archives CDA/St-Genés **594** Bibliothèque Nationale de France, Paris (50C 5452) **598** Corbis **601** From *Constituto Criminalis Theresiana*, 1769 **602** Art Resource, NY

## Chapter 19
**606** Giraudon/Art Resource, NY **608** Erich Lessing/Art Resource, NY **614** (**R**) akg-images **614** (**L**) akg-images **615** Bibliothèque Nationale de France, Paris (80C 103369) **616** Bibliothèque Nationale de France, Paris (45B M89) **619** Giraudon/Art Resource, NY **622** Erich Lessing/Art Resource, NY **624** Annenberg Rare Book & Manuscript Library, University of Pennsylvania (Revolutions de Paris No. 161: Aug 4–11, 1792) **626** Photothèque des Musées de las Ville de Paris/Cliché: Andreani **627** Giraudon/Art Resource, NY **629** Réunion des Musées Nationaux/Art Resource, NY **634** Réunion des Musées Nationaux/Art Resource, NY **636** Erich Lessing/Art Resource, NY

## Chapter 20
**642** Guildhall Library, Corporation of London/Bridgeman Art Library **644** From *The White Slaves of England*, 1853 **645** Royal Commission on the Ancient and Historical Monuments of Scotland; SC679552 **647** Science Museum, London/Science and Society Picture Library **649** From *History of the Cotton Manufacture in Great Britain*, 1836 **650** Lewis Carroll's Album. The Gernsheim Collection, Harry Ransom Research Center, University of Texas-Austin **657** Deutsche Bahn Museum, Nürnberg **658** akg-images **664** Rickitt Collection of Slides/The Slide Center **666** *Punch*, 1847 **667** Attributed to Frederick Calvert, *South-West Prospect of Birmingham*, 1829 Birmingham Museums & Art Gallery. **668** Manchester Art Gallery, UK/Bridgeman Art Library **669** National Gallery, London

## Chapter 21
**674** Réunion des Musées Nationaux/Art Resource, NY **679** The Granger Collection, New York **683** Genève, Bibliothèque publique et universitaire **684** Bridgeman Art Library **687** Réunion des Musées Nationaux/Art Resource, NY **689** Giraudon/Art Resource, NY **691** The Royal Archives © 2003 Her Majesty Queen Elizabeth II. **695** Gemälde von Anton von Werner, 1885. Friedrichsruh, Bismarck-Museum, Bildarchiv

# Index

X ray, 748

Yalta meeting (1945): Big Three at, 888
(illus.), 889
Year of Mary (1954), 915
Yeltsin, Boris, 937, 939
Yiddish language, 731–732
Yorktown: British surrender at, 567, 567
(illus.)
"You Men, All of You" (Klaar), 727
Youth movement: in 1960s, 917–919, 917
(illus.)
Yugoslavia: ethnic groups in, 807; after First
World War, 807, 820; Nazis and, 858;

Second World War resistance in, 872,
873; civil war in, 876; after Second
World War, 886, 889, 901; breakup of,
940–943
Yugoslavia (former), 942 (map); atrocities
in, 942 (illus.)

Zarathustra. *See* Zoroaster and
Zoroastrianism
Zealand: province of, 466
Zetkin, Clara, 733
Zhdanov, Andrei, 890
Zhivkov, Todor, 936
Zimbabwe, 895

Zimmermann, Arthur, 793
Zimmermann telegram, 793
Zionism, 732; Balfour Declaration and, 809;
Palestine and, 810; Stalin's persecution
of Jews and, 902–903. *See also* Jews
and Judaism
Zoë (Russia), 473
Zola, Émile, 722, 750
*Zollverein* (customs union), 655, 656
(map), 693, 701
Zones: in Germany, 890, 891
*Zong* (slave ship), 558, 559 (illus.)
Zoroaster and Zoroastrianism: in Iraq, 809
Zuckmayer, Carl, 784

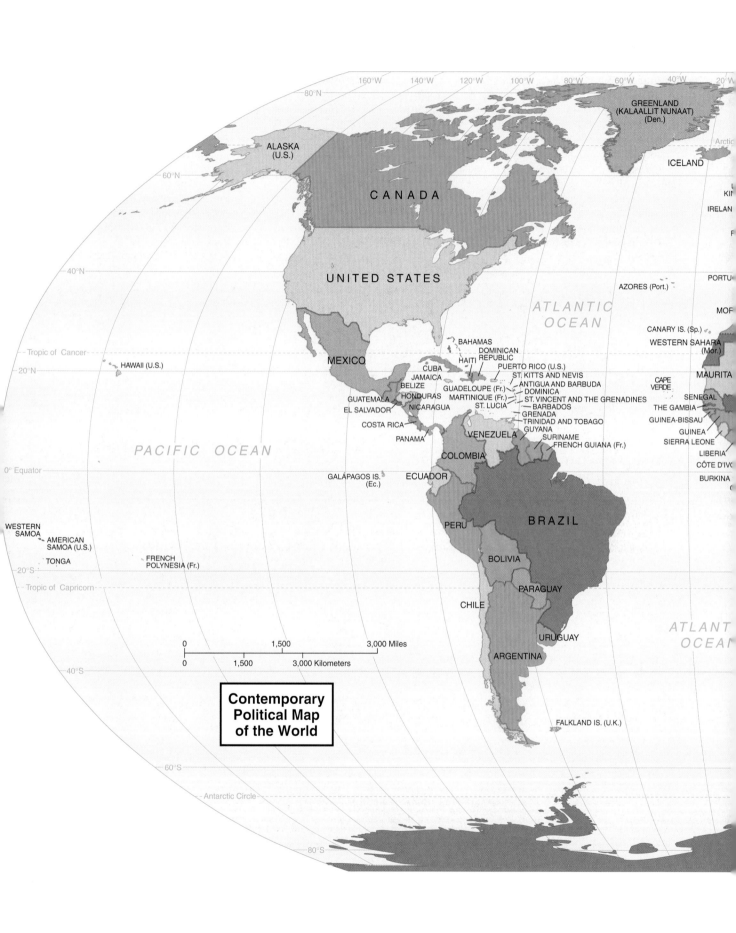

160°W  140°W  120°W  100°W  80°W  60°W  40°W  20°W

80°N

GREENLAND
(KALAALLIT NUNAAT)
(Den.)

Arctic

ALASKA
(U.S.)

60°N

ICELAND

U.
KIN

C A N A D A

IRELAND

40°N

UNITED STATES

PORTU

ATLANTIC
OCEAN

AZORES (Port.)

MOR

CANARY IS. (Sp.)

Tropic of Cancer

WESTERN SAHARA
(Mor.)

HAWAII (U.S.)

20°N

BAHAMAS

MEXICO

DOMINICAN
REPUBLIC

HAITI

CUBA

PUERTO RICO (U.S.)

MAURITA

JAMAICA

ST. KITTS AND NEVIS

CAPE
VERDE

BELIZE

GUADELOUPE (Fr.)

ANTIGUA AND BARBUDA

DOMINICA

SENEGAL

GUATEMALA

HONDURAS

MARTINIQUE (Fr.)

ST. VINCENT AND THE GRENADINES

THE GAMBIA

EL SALVADOR

NICARAGUA

ST. LUCIA

BARBADOS

GUINEA-BISSAU

COSTA RICA

GRENADA

TRINIDAD AND TOBAGO

GUINEA

PANAMA

VENEZUELA

GUYANA

SIERRA LEONE

SURINAME

LIBERIA

COLOMBIA

FRENCH GUIANA (Fr.)

CÔTE D'IVO

PACIFIC OCEAN

0° Equator

GALÁPAGOS IS.
(Ec.)

ECUADOR

BURKINA

WESTERN
SAMOA

AMERICAN
SAMOA (U.S.)

PERU

BRAZIL

TONGA

FRENCH
POLYNESIA (Fr.)

BOLIVIA

20°S

Tropic of Capricorn

PARAGUAY

CHILE

ATLANT
OCEAN

URUGUAY

0        1,500       3,000 Miles

0      1,500    3,000 Kilometers

ARGENTINA

40°S

**Contemporary
Political Map
of the World**

FALKLAND IS. (U.K.)

60°S

Antarctic Circle

80°S

# Atlas

# HOW TO READ A MAP AND WHY IT MATTERS

Maps are one of the many tools that historians use to help them understand what is happening in space and time. There is a wide array of information that maps can convey. Some provide information about political boundaries past and present; others, topographic and physical maps, show geographical features such as rivers, mountains, deserts, and other land or water formations; while still others represent historical data, such as population growth or specialized thematic topics. Maps communicate this information, allowing the viewer to analyze, interpret, and make conclusions about the subject matter. Since maps are depictions of what places look like, they help to put history in a physical context, providing a type of visual imagery to go along with the historic narrative. They can also show change over time by demonstrating growth or decline through map symbols.

It is important to recognize that maps, like other sources, come with their own point of view and that the way in which they are drawn, or the "projection" used, affects what the viewer sees. The Mercator projection, for example, originally a valuable map for sailors since it showed true direction, actually distorts what it is showing by making areas further from the equator larger than they actually are. It could be argued that this displays a Eurocentric bias since it makes it appear that Europe and the United States are larger than they are in reality. Polar projections, in which the map centers on either the north or south pole, are used for maps of the northern and southern hemispheres and are useful when discussing subjects focused on these areas, such as air traffic patterns or Cold War arsenals (missiles were aimed over the North Pole, as it represented the shortest distance between Moscow and Washington, DC). Cartograms are special maps where the size of a country is drawn relative to one its characteristics, such as the size of its population, showing an altered view of the physical world in order to make a specific point.

In history, being able to read and interpret maps matters for three main reasons: (1) knowing where places are; (2) being able to visualize the movement of peoples, ideas, and commodities; and (3) understanding the difference location can make in human endeavors.

### MAPS SHOW WHERE PLACES ARE

Maps are key to understanding the absolute and relative location of places. They provide the precise location where cities and empires have been located, where battles have taken place, and where religions, ideas, and inventions have originated. Knowing the location of places is the first step in answering some of the more interesting questions of "Why there?" "Why then?" Maps also show where a place is in relation to other places or geographic features. Whether societies evolved near rivers and coasts or are land-locked is an important consideration in historical thinking. The geo-political importance of control over nearby straits, access to trading networks, or being part of a disease exchange all factor into the importance of knowing relative location.

### MAPS SHOW MOVEMENT

Maps also show movement: the voluntary and forced migration of peoples, the spread of ideas, including religion, and the trade of commodities. Maps can help provide information as to directional flows as well as volume, changes over time, and patterns of movement. One cannot discuss the Atlantic slave trade without fully comprehending that most of the enslaved people were transported from West Africa to Brazil and the Caribbean, not to the American South. A map that shows the direction and volume of the slave trade provides a visual reminder of this important fact. In a similar vein, seeing on a map how vulnerable Russia and the Soviet Union were to western and eastern invasion by first the Mongols, then Napoleon, and then Hitler, helps one better understand the rationale behind Soviet expansion into Eastern Europe.

### MAPS SHOW THE IMPORTANCE OF LOCATION ON HUMAN ENDEAVORS

Maps can also help us appreciate that *where* something happens can affect *what* happens in economic, physical, and human terms. Looking at a physical map of Europe, one can appreciate how port cities along the Mediterranean as well as along rivers such as the Danube, the Rhine, and the Thames were able to become great trading centers, bringing in goods from throughout the region, as well as other regions, depending on the time and place. Maps can also show climate, population data, religious composition, and natural resources, which can help us understand such questions as why cities and societies grow and diminish and how they interact in peace and at war.

### HOW TO READ A MAP

To analyze maps, it helps to recognize their central parts: the title, orientation, date, author, legend (or key), and scale (TODALS). When looking at a map, first read the *title*. It will indicate the main topic of the map: political units, physical features, or a theme. Reading the title first will help you focus your attention. The *orientation,* or the direction in which the map is "pointed," will be shown on a compass rose, a design that shows direction. Most maps today have north "at the top." However, this was not always the case: Medieval maps ("T" maps) had Jerusalem in the center and the east at the top. The *date* a map is made is also important, as our understanding changes over time, and older maps may no longer be accurate. If the *author* of a map is included, this can help you establish its credibility and whether it might represent any bias. The *legend,* or key, of a map shows what the colors, symbols, or markings on the map represent and is essential to understanding the map's story. Maps will also often include a *scale,* which tells you the relationship between distance on the map and actual distance on the earth (for example, one inch on the map represents 10 miles). Understanding the scale on a map helps viewers understand how large (and near or far apart) places actually are. In addition to these central parts, many maps include a caption. Reading the caption before examining the map can help you direct your attention and gain further insight into what the map is intended to portray and its significance in a larger context. All of these elements are tools at your disposal to help you get the most out of a map.

All maps can be "read," as one would read a document or an image, for further insights into history. The 1994 Geography for Life National Standards affirm, "Students must appreciate that viewing the past from both spatial and chronological points of view can lead to a greater awareness and depth of understanding of physical and human events, and is an essential ingredient in the interpretation of the world today." Without maps, history would be missing an important conceptual and analytical tool.

## MAP 14.1
### Russian Under Peter the Great

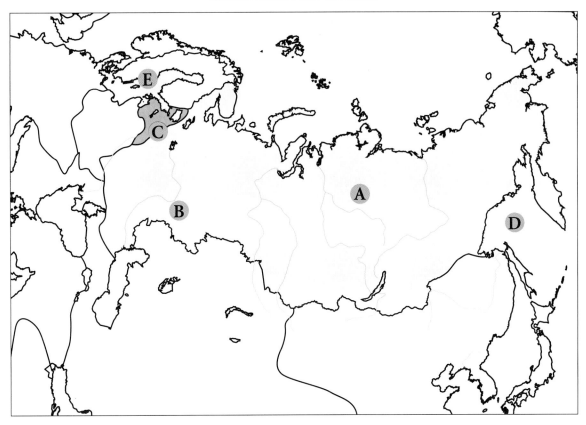

MAP ANALYSIS

1. Which letter on this map identifies the Baltic Sea?

_____

2. Which letter on this map identifies the Volga River?

_____

3. Which letter on this map identifies the Sea of Okhotsk?

_____

4. Which letter on the map identifies St. Petersburg?

_____

5. Which letter(s) on this map identify the Russian empire in 1696?

_____

# MAP 14.2
## European Population Density, ca. 1600

## MAP ANALYSIS

1. What countries had a population density of 60 people per square mile or less?

_____

_____

_____

2. What countries had areas where the population density exceeded 60 people per square mile?

_____

_____

_____

3. What major cities are located in areas where the population density exceeded 60 people per square mile?

_____

_____

_____

4. What major cities are located in areas where the population density did not reach 60 people per square mile, and at what density are they located?

_____

_____

_____

MAP 15.1
Europe After the Peace of Westphalia

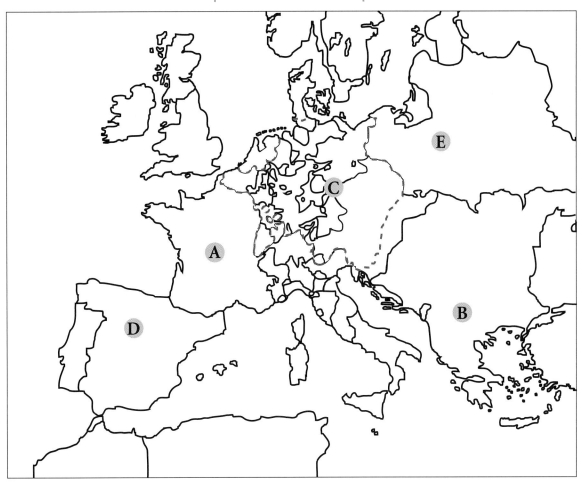

MAP ANALYSIS

1. Which letter on this map identifies France?

_____

2. Which letter on this map identifies Poland?

_____

3. Which letter on this map identifies Spain?

_____

4. Which letter on this map identifies the Holy Roman Empire?

_____

5. Which letter on this map identifies the Ottoman Empire?

_____

# MAP 15.2
## Europe Under Absolute Monarchy, 1715

MAP 15.2
Europe Under Absolute Monarchy, 1715

**MAP ANALYSIS**

1. What states were under Bourbon control in 1715?

_____

_____

_____

2. According to the map on page 486 in the textbook, what territory was France attempting to acquire between 1679 and 1714 and was France successful in acquiring those territories?

_____

_____

_____

3. According to the map on page 493 in the textbook, what territories given to Spain by the Treaty of Westphalia were under Habsburg control in 1715?

_____

_____

_____

4. According to this map, what other states were under Habsburg control in 1715?

_____

_____

_____

## MAP 16.1
World Boundaries, ca. 1453

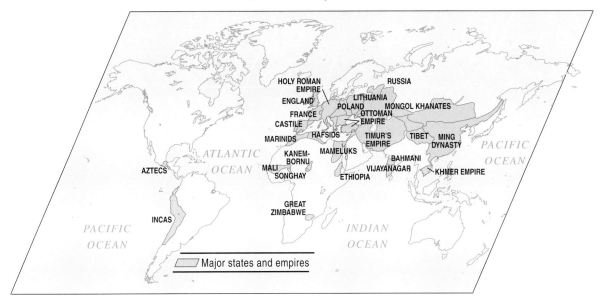

MAP ANALYSIS

1. What major European states were established by 1453?

_____

_____

_____

2. What major states were established in the Middle East, South Asia, and East Asia by 1453?

_____

_____

_____

3. What major states were established in Africa by 1453?

_____

_____

_____

4. What major states were established in the Americas by 1453?

_____

_____

_____

5. What continents had no major states or empires in 1453?

_____

_____

_____

MAP 16.2
The Growth of Brandenburg-Prussia, 1618-1786

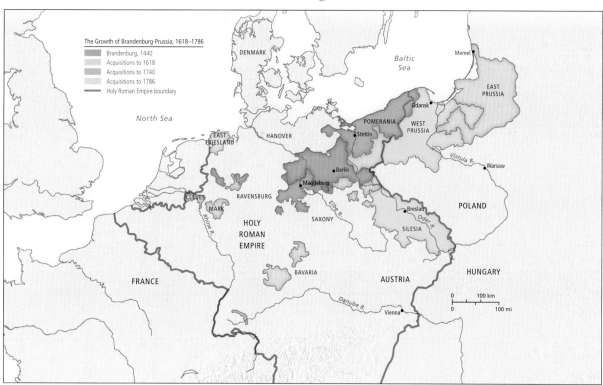

The Growth of Brandenburg-Prussia, 1618–1786

- Brandenburg, 1440
- Acquisitions to 1618
- Acquisitions to 1740
- Acquisitions to 1786
- Holy Roman Empire boundary

MAP ANALYSIS

1. What territories and cities were part of Brandenburg-Prussia by 1618?

_____

_____

_____

2. What territory was acquired by 1740?

_____

_____

_____

3. What territories were acquired by 1786?

_____

_____

_____

4. What parts of Brandenburg-Prussia were included in the Holy Roman Empire?

_____

_____

_____

MAP 17.1
British India

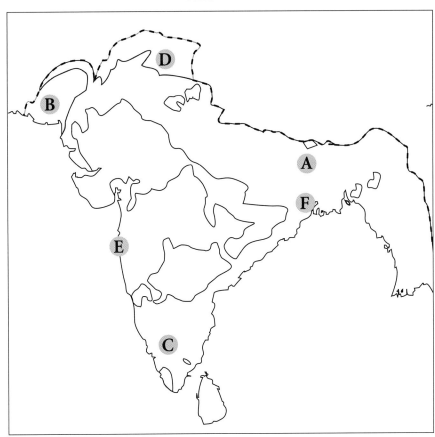

MAP ANALYSIS

1. Which letter on this map identifies Bombay?

_____

2. Which letter on this map identifies Calcutta?

_____

3. Which letter on this map identifies Mysore?

_____

4. Which letter on this map identifies Bengal?

_____

5. Which letter on this map identifies Baluchistan?

_____

6. Which letter on this map identifies Kashmir?

_____

MAP 17.2
The Beginnings of Colonial Rule in Africa

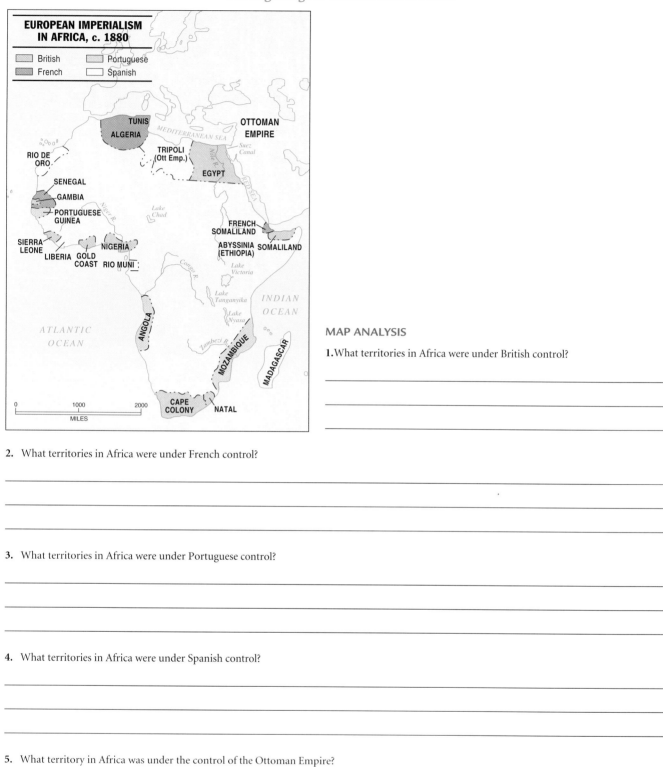

**EUROPEAN IMPERIALISM IN AFRICA, c. 1880**

- British
- French
- Portuguese
- Spanish

**MAP ANALYSIS**

1. What territories in Africa were under British control?

_____

_____

_____

2. What territories in Africa were under French control?

_____

_____

_____

3. What territories in Africa were under Portuguese control?

_____

_____

_____

4. What territories in Africa were under Spanish control?

_____

_____

_____

5. What territory in Africa was under the control of the Ottoman Empire?

_____

6. What territories were unclaimed by foreign powers?

_____

_____

_____

MAP 18.1
European Empires in 1763

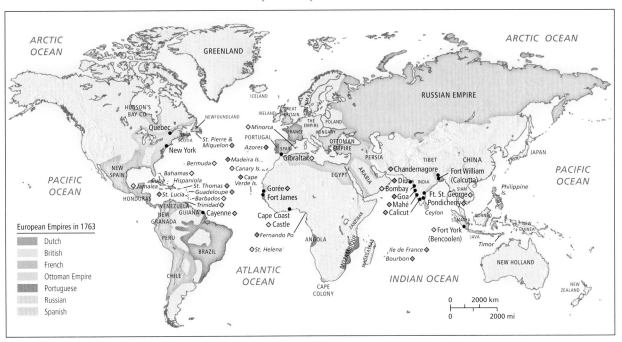

MAP ANALYSIS

1.  What parts of the globe were under Dutch control by 1763?

   _____

   _____

   _____

2.  What parts of the globe were under British control by 1763?

   _____

   _____

   _____

3.  What parts of the globe were under French control by 1763?

   _____

   _____

   _____

4.  What parts of the globe were under the control of the Ottoman Empire by 1763?

   _____

   _____

   _____

5.  What parts of the globe were under Portuguese control by 1763?

   _____

   _____

   _____

(continued)

**6.** What parts of the globe were under Russian control by 1763?

_____

_____

_____

**7.** What parts of the globe were under Spain control by 1763?

_____

_____

_____

MAP 18.2
World Boundaries, ca. 1700

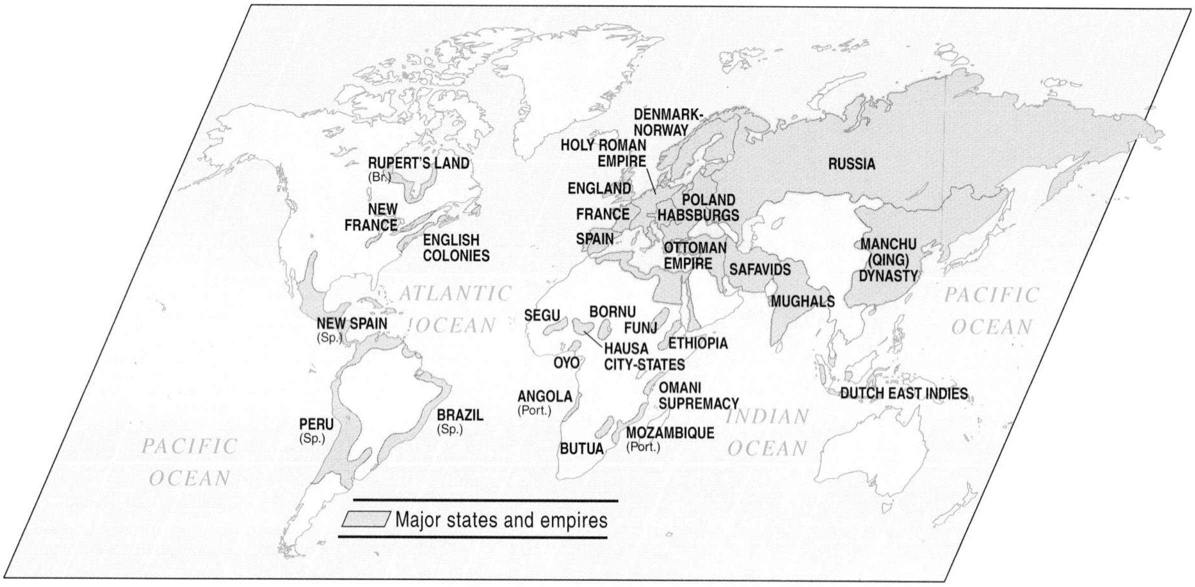

MAP ANALYSIS

**1.** What major European states were established by 1700?

_____

_____

_____

**2.** What major states were established in the Middle East, South Asia, and East Asia by 1700?

_____

_____

_____

**3.** What major states were established in Africa by 1700?

_____

_____

_____

**4.** What major states were established in the Americas by 1700?

_____

_____

_____

MAP 19.1
Napoleonic Europe

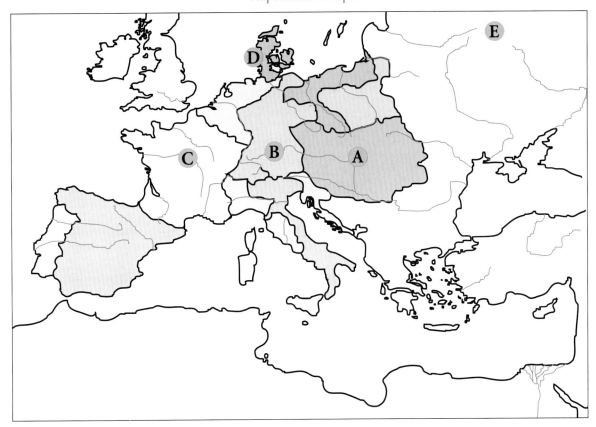

MAP ANALYSIS

1. Which letter on this map identifies the origin of Napoleon's empire?

_____

2. Which letter(s) on this map identify allies of Napoleonic France?

_____

3. Which letter(s) on this map identify dependent states of Napoleon's empire?

_____

4. Which letter on this map identifies the site of Napoleon's final defeat?

_____

MAP 19.2
Europe After the Congress of Vienna, 1815

## MAP ANALYSIS

1. What states were included in the German Confederation after the Congress of Vienna in 1815?

_____

_____

_____

2. What remaining states constituted the Austrian Empire?

_____

_____

3. What other lands, formerly under Napoleon's control, were made independent by the Congress of Vienna?

_____

_____

_____

4. Compare this map to the one found on page 635 in the textbook. What happened to the Duchy of Warsaw after the Congress of Vienna?

_____

_____

_____

MAP 20.1
The Industrialization of Europe, 1850

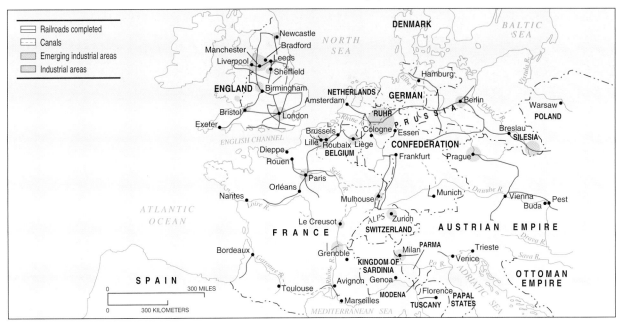

## MAP ANALYSIS

1. What country had established industrial areas by 1850?

   _____

2. What industrial cities were located in this country?

   _____

   _____

   _____

3. What other cities/regions were emerging in 1850 as industrial areas?

   _____

   _____

   _____

4. What states had completed a system of railroads by 1850?

   _____

   _____

   _____

5. What is the importance of railroads and canals to industry?

   _____

   _____

   _____

6. What might stop a state from building or completing railroad and canal systems?

   _____

   _____

   _____

# MAP 20.2
## The Concentration of Industry in Great Britain, 1750-1820

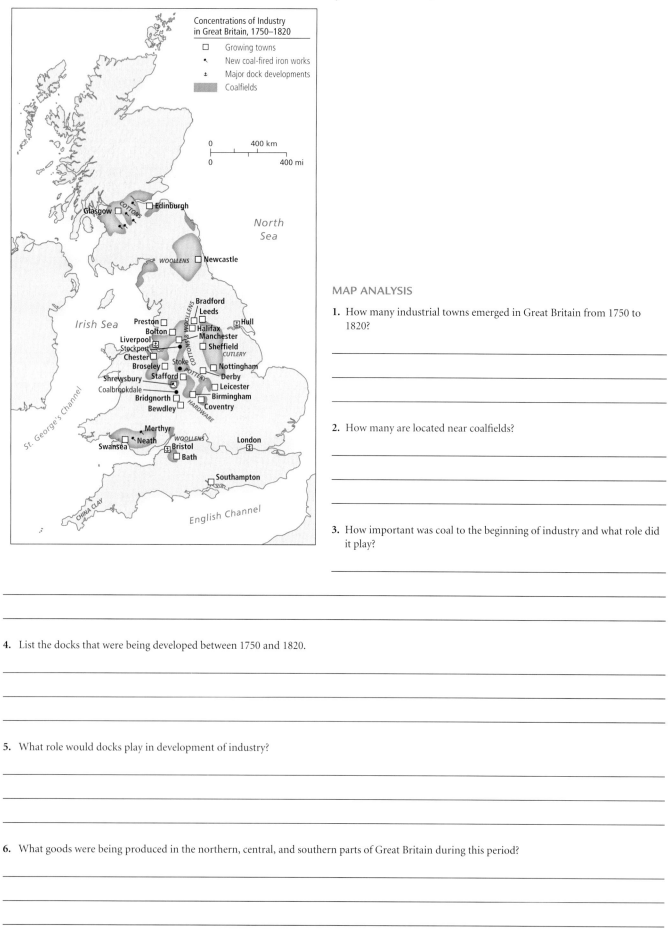

**Concentrations of Industry in Great Britain, 1750–1820**

☐ Growing towns
↖ New coal-fired iron works
⬘ Major dock developments
▓ Coalfields

0   400 km
0   400 mi

North Sea

Irish Sea

St. George's Channel

English Channel

Glasgow   COTTONS   Edinburgh
WOOLLENS   Newcastle
Bradford
Leeds
Preston   Hull
Bolton   Halifax
WOOLLENS
Liverpool   Manchester
Stockport   Sheffield
Chester   CUTLERY
COTTONS
Broseley   Stoke   Nottingham
POTTERY
Shrewsbury   Stafford   Derby
Coalbrookdale   Leicester
Bridgnorth   Birmingham
Bewdley   Coventry
HARDWARE

Merthyr
Neath   WOOLLENS   London
Swansea   Bristol
Bath

Southampton

CHINA CLAY

## MAP ANALYSIS

**1.** How many industrial towns emerged in Great Britain from 1750 to 1820?

_____

_____

_____

**2.** How many are located near coalfields?

_____

_____

_____

**3.** How important was coal to the beginning of industry and what role did it play?

_____

_____

_____

**4.** List the docks that were being developed between 1750 and 1820.

_____

_____

_____

**5.** What role would docks play in development of industry?

_____

_____

_____

**6.** What goods were being produced in the northern, central, and southern parts of Great Britain during this period?

_____

_____

_____

MAP 21.1
The Unification of Italy

Kingdom of Sardinia,
to 1859

Acquisitions by Sardinia,
1859

Annexed by Sardinia, 1860;
established Kingdom of Italy

To Kingdom of Italy,
1866

To Kingdom of Italy,
1870

0 _____ 200 Miles

0 _____ 200 Kilometers

**MAP ANALYSIS**

1. According to this map, what state is responsible for initiating the unification of Italy?

_____

_____

_____

2. What territory was acquired by Sardinia in 1859?

_____

_____

_____

3. What happened in the following year?

_____

_____

_____

4. What was the first territory annexed by the Kingdom of Italy and in what year did this take place?

_____

_____

_____

5. What was the last territory added to the Kingdom of Italy?

_____

_____

_____

## MAP 21.2
### Nationalities Within the Habsburg Empire

Nationalities Within the Habsburg Empire

| | |
|---|---|
| Germans | Slovenes |
| Czechs | Croats and Serbs |
| Slovaks | Romanians |
| Italians | Ruthenians (Ukrainians) |
| Poles | Magyars (Hungarians) |

0        200 km

0        200 mi

## MAP ANALYSIS

1. How many separate nationalities existed within the Habsburg Empire?

_____

_____

_____

2. What nationalities were located along military frontiers?

_____

_____

_____

3. What major cities are included in the Habsburg Empire?

_____

_____

_____

4. What internal setbacks might arise in trying to unify such a diverse empire?

_____

_____

_____

## MAP 22.1
### The Decline of the Ottoman Empire

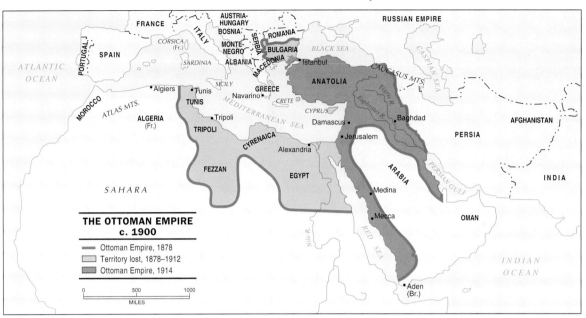

MAP ANALYSIS

1. What territories did the Ottoman Empire consist of in 1878?

_____

_____

_____

2. According to the map on page 730 in the textbook, what territories were lost prior to 1878?

_____

_____

_____

3. List the territories lost by the Ottoman Empire prior to 1915.

_____

_____

_____

4. According to this map, what major cities did the Ottoman Empire still control in 1914?

_____

_____

_____

5. According to the map on page 730 in the textbook, what territories were lost by 1923?

_____

_____

_____

MAP 22.2
The Persian Gulf Region, ca. 1900

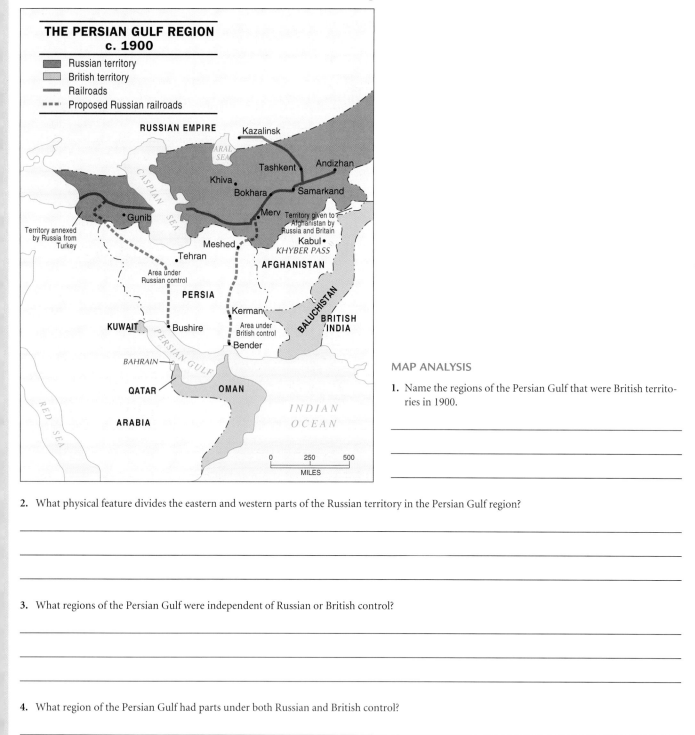

THE PERSIAN GULF REGION
c. 1900

- Russian territory
- British territory
- Railroads
- Proposed Russian railroads

RUSSIAN EMPIRE

Kazalinsk

ARAL SEA

Tashkent    Andizhan

Khiva

Bokhara    Samarkand

CASPIAN SEA

Gunib

Merv    Territory given to
Afghanistan by
Russia and Britain

Territory annexed
by Russia from
Turkey

Meshed    Kabul

KHYBER PASS

Tehran

AFGHANISTAN

Area under
Russian control

PERSIA

Kerman

BALUCHISTAN

KUWAIT    Bushire    Area under
British control

BRITISH
INDIA

Bender

BAHRAIN    PERSIAN GULF

QATAR    OMAN

INDIAN
OCEAN

RED SEA

ARABIA

0    250    500
MILES

**MAP ANALYSIS**

1. Name the regions of the Persian Gulf that were British territories in 1900.

_____

_____

_____

2. What physical feature divides the eastern and western parts of the Russian territory in the Persian Gulf region?

_____

_____

_____

3. What regions of the Persian Gulf were independent of Russian or British control?

_____

_____

_____

4. What region of the Persian Gulf had parts under both Russian and British control?

_____

_____

_____

5. Why might Russia propose the construction of railroads through Persia?

_____

_____

_____

MAP 23.1
Imperialism in Southeast Asia, ca. 1914

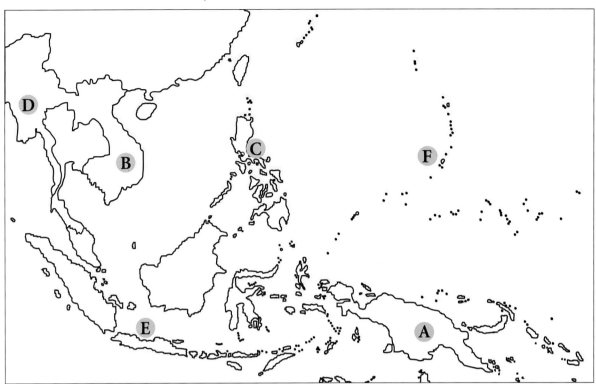

MAP ANALYSIS

1. Which letter on this map identifies the Philippines?

_____

2. Which letter on this map identifies Burma?

_____

3. Which letter on this map identifies Guam?

_____

4. Which letter on this map identifies Papua?

_____

5. Which letter on this map identifies Java?

_____

6. Which letter on this map identifies Indochina?

_____

MAP 23.2
The Partition of Africa Between 1870 and 1914

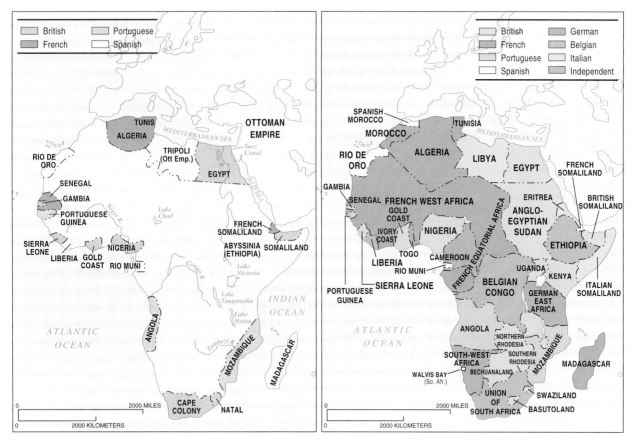

## MAP ANALYSIS

1. How many African states did the British control in 1914 as opposed to 1870?

_____

2. How many African states did the French control in 1914 as opposed to 1870?

_____

3. How many African states did the Portuguese control in 1914 as opposed to 1870?

_____

4. How many African states did the Spanish control in 1914 as opposed to 1870?

_____

5. How many states come under German, Belgian, and Italian control by 1914?

_____

6. What African states gained their independence by 1914?

_____

_____

_____

MAP 24.1
Europe After the Great War

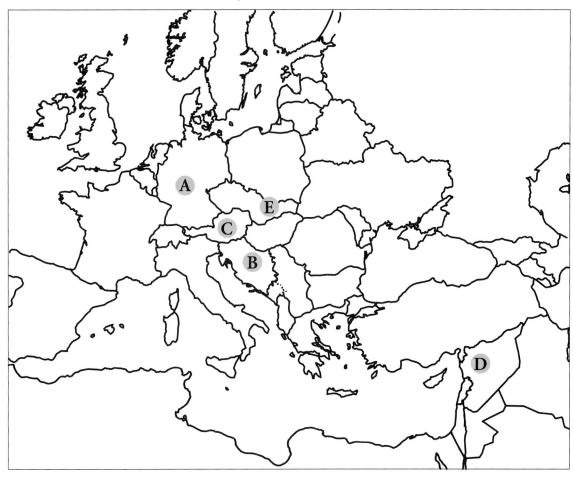

MAP ANALYSIS

1. Which letter on this map identifies Austria?

_____

2. Which letter on this map identifies Czechoslovakia?

_____

3. Which letter on this map identifies Germany?

_____

4. Which letter on this map identifies Syria?

_____

5. Which letter on this map identifies Yugoslavia?

_____

# MAP 24.2
## The Eastern Front, 1915–1918

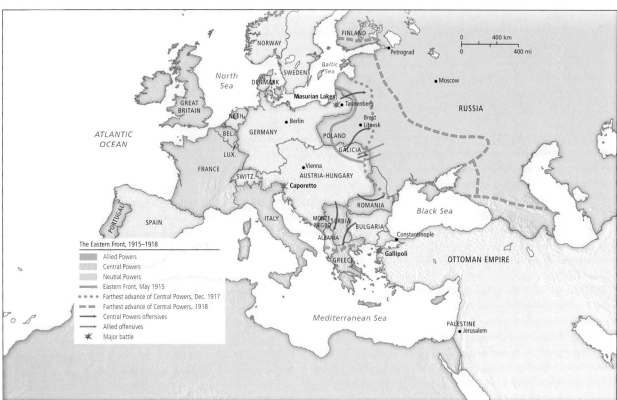

The Eastern Front, 1915–1918

- Allied Powers
- Central Powers
- Neutral Powers
- —— Eastern Front, May 1915
- •••• Farthest advance of Central Powers, Dec. 1917
- ---- Farthest advance of Central Powers, 1918
- —→ Central Powers offensives
- ⇉ Allied offensives
- ✳ Major battle

## MAP ANALYSIS

1. What nations made up the Allied Powers in World War I?

_____

_____

_____

2. What nations made up the Central Powers in World War I?

_____

_____

_____

3. What nations remained neutral throughout the conflict?

_____

_____

_____

4. What advances were made by the Central Powers in 1917 and 1918, and what might this reveal about their plan towards the end of the war?

_____

_____

_____

5. How might the defeat of the Central Powers affect nations located outside of Western Europe, such as the Ottoman Empire?

_____

_____

_____

MAP 25.1
The Middle East in the 1920s

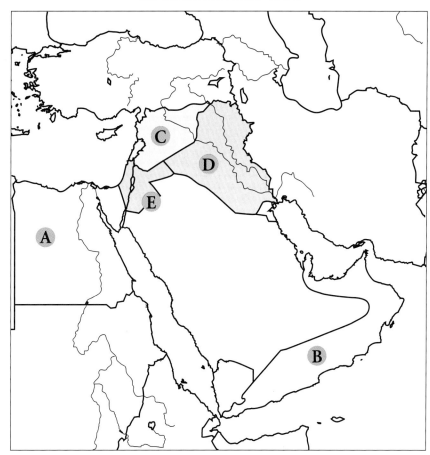

MAP ANALYSIS

1. Which letter on this map identifies Iraq?

_____

2. Which letter on this map identifies Palestine and the Transjordan?

_____

3. Which letter on this map identifies Syria and Lebanon?

_____

4. Which letter on this map identifies Egypt?

_____

# MAP 25.2
## Eastern Europe and the Soviet Union, 1919–1939

## MAP ANALYSIS

1. How did the borders of Poland and Romania change between 1914 and 1919?

_____

_____

_____

2. What happened to Austria-Hungary after World War I?

_____

_____

_____

3. What cities were within the borders drawn for Russia by the Treaty of Brest-Litovsk?

_____

_____

_____

4. What cities did Russia reclaim by 1920?

_____

_____

_____

5. What new countries existed in Eastern Europe after 1920?

_____

_____

_____

MAP 26.1
Europe in World War II

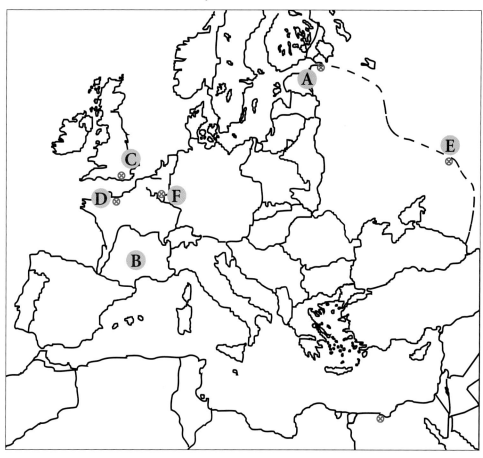

MAP ANALYSIS

1. Which letter on this map identifies the Battle of Britain?

_____

2. Which letter on this map identifies Vichy France?

_____

3. Which letter on this map identifies the Battle of Stalingrad?

_____

4. Which letter on this map identifies the Battle of Leningrad?

_____

5. Which letter on this map identifies the Battle of the Bulge?

_____

6. Which letter on this map identifies Normandy?

_____

# MAP 26.2
## China in the Era of Revolution and Civil War

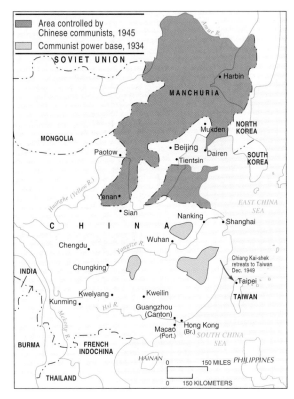

## MAP ANALYSIS

**1.** What major cities were included in Guomandang China between 1928 and 1937?

_____

_____

_____

**2.** Where were the warlords situated in China who posed threats to the Guomandang regime?

_____

_____

_____

**3.** Where in China were communist power bases located in 1934?

_____

_____

_____

**4.** Where did the Long March begin in China, what areas did it go through, and where did it end?

_____

_____

_____

**5.** Where did Chinese nationalists, like Chiang Kai-Shek, retreat to in 1949?

_____

_____

_____

## MAP 27.1
### The Cold War Military Standoff

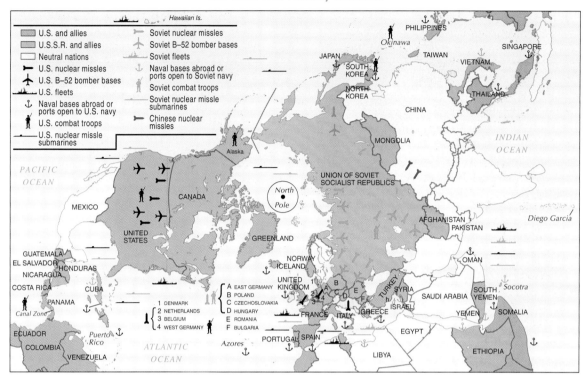

## MAP ANALYSIS

**1.** List the allies of the United States during the Cold War.

_____

_____

_____

**2.** List the allies of the U.S.S.R. during the Cold War.

_____

_____

_____

**3.** What nations remained neutral during the Cold War?

_____

_____

_____

**4.** What international ports were open to the U.S. navy during the Cold War?

_____

_____

_____

**5.** What international ports were open to the Soviet navy during the Cold War?

_____

_____

_____ (continued)

**6.** Where were U.S. combat troop posted during the Cold War?

_____

_____

_____

**7.** Where were Soviet combat troops posted during the Cold War?

_____

_____

_____

MAP 27.2

The Partition of South Asia: The Formation of India, Pakistan, Bangladesh, and Sri Lanka

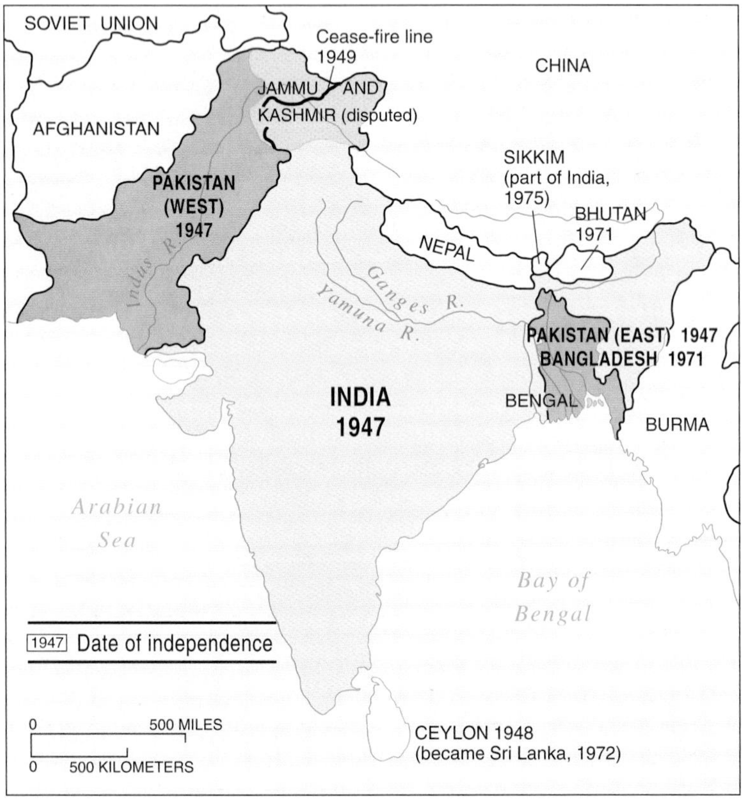

**MAP ANALYSIS**

**1.** What were the first South Asian states granted independence, and when did they become independent?

_____

_____

_____

**2.** What was eastern Pakistan called in 1971?

_____

**3.** In what year did Sri Lanka gain its independence, and by what name was it formerly known?

_____

**4.** What territories were located on the eastern border of Western Pakistan?

_____

_____

_____

**5.** What other countries bordered Pakistan and India?

_____

_____

_____

## MAP 28.1
### The Contemporary Middle East

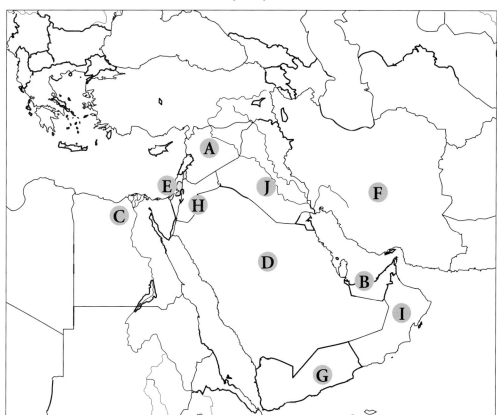

MAP ANALYSIS

1. Which letter on this map identifies the United Arab Emirates?

_____

2. Which letter on this map identifies Yemen?

_____

3. Which letter on this map identifies Jordan?

_____

4. Which letter on this map identifies Oman?

_____

5. Which letter on this map identifies Saudi Arabia?

_____

6. Which letter on this map identifies Israel?

_____

7. Which letter on this map identifies Iraq?

_____

8. Which letter on this map identifies Iran?

_____

MAP 28.2
The European Union in the Europe of 2003

## MAP ANALYSIS

1. What nations were members of the European Union in 2003?

_____

_____

2. What nations were prospective members of the European Union in 2003?

_____

_____

3. According to Chapter 28 in the textbook, what are the benefits of joining the European Union?

_____

_____

4. What problems might arise for nations who are not members of the European Union?

_____

_____

5. Why might nations like Switzerland and Norway choose not to join the European Union?

_____

_____